SEVENTH EDITION

FINANCIAL MANAGEMENT

THEORY AND PRACTICE

EUGENE F. BRIGHAM
UNIVERSITY OF FLORIDA

LOUIS C. GAPENSKI
UNIVERSITY OF FLORIDA

THE DRYDEN PRESS
HARCOURT BRACE COLLEGE PUBLISHERS

Fort Worth · Philadelphia · San Diego · New York
Orlando · Austin · San Antonio
Toronto · Montreal · London · Sydney · Tokyo

Publisher Liz Widdicombe
Acquisitions Editor Rick Hammonds
Developmental Editor Barbara J. C. Rosenberg and Shana Lum

Project Management Elm Street Publishing Services, Inc.
Compositor The Clarinda Company
Text Type 10/12 ITC Garamond Book

Cover Image FPG International/Telegraph Colour Library

Address for Editorial Correspondence
The Dryden Press, 301 Commerce Street, Suite 3700, Fort Worth, TX 76102

Address for Orders
The Dryden Press, 6277 Sea Harbor Drive, Orlando, FL 32887
1-800-782-4479, or 1-800-433-0001 (in Florida)

ISBN: 0-03-098066-6
Library of Congress Catalogue Number: 93-19110

Printed in the United States of America
  4 5 6 7 8 9 0 1 2 032 9 8 7 6 5 4 3

The Dryden Press
Harcourt Brace College Publishers

THE DRYDEN PRESS
SERIES IN FINANCE

GITMAN AND JOEHNK
PERSONAL FINANCIAL PLANNING
Sixth Edition

GREENBAUM AND THAKOR
CONTEMPORARY FINANCIAL INTERMEDIATION

HARRINGTON AND EADES
CASE STUDIES IN FINANCIAL DECISION MAKING
Third Edition

HAYES AND MEERSCHWAM
FINANCIAL INSTITUTIONS: CONTEMPORARY CASES IN THE FINANCIAL SERVICES INDUSTRY

JOHNSON
ISSUES AND READINGS IN MANAGERIAL FINANCE
Third Edition

KIDWELL, PETERSON, AND BLACKWELL
FINANCIAL INSTITUTIONS, MARKETS, AND MONEY
Fifth Edition

KOCH
BANK MANAGEMENT
Second Edition

KOHN
MONEY, BANKING, AND FINANCIAL MARKETS
Second Edition

LEE AND FINNERTY
CORPORATE FINANCE: THEORY, METHOD, AND APPLICATION

MAISEL
REAL ESTATE FINANCE
Second Edition

MARTIN, COX, AND MACMINN
THE THEORY OF FINANCE: EVIDENCE AND APPLICATIONS

MAYO
FINANCE: AN INTRODUCTION
Fourth Edition

MAYO
INVESTMENTS: AN INTRODUCTION
Fourth Edition

PETTIJOHN
PROFIT+

REILLY
INVESTMENT ANALYSIS AND PORTFOLIO MANAGEMENT
Fourth Edition

REILLY
INVESTMENTS
Third Edition

SEARS AND TRENNEPOHL
INVESTMENT MANAGEMENT

SEITZ
CAPITAL BUDGETING AND LONG-TERM FINANCING DECISIONS

SEIGEL AND SIEGEL
FUTURES MARKETS

SMITH AND SPUDECK
INTEREST RATES: PRINCIPLES AND APPLICATIONS

STICKNEY
FINANCIAL STATEMENT ANALYSIS: A STRATEGIC PERSPECTIVE
Second Edition

TURNBULL
OPTION VALUATION

WESTON AND BRIGHAM
ESSENTIALS OF MANAGERIAL FINANCE
Tenth Edition

WESTON AND COPELAND
MANAGERIAL FINANCE
Ninth Edition

WOOD AND WOOD
FINANCIAL MARKETS

THE HARCOURT BRACE COLLEGE OUTLINE SERIES

BAKER
FINANCIAL MANAGEMENT

PREFACE

Our original goal in writing *Financial Management* was to create a text (1) that is sufficiently current and complete to give students an operational knowledge of finance, (2) that combines theory and applications, and (3) that is sufficiently self-contained for use both in follow-on case courses and, upon graduation, on the job. Further, we wanted a text that students find "user friendly," meaning one that they enjoy reading and can learn from on their own.

The book begins with basic concepts, focusing on the economic environment (including financial markets), risk, and the valuation process, and it then shows how specific techniques and decision rules can be used to help maximize the value of the firm. This structure has three important advantages:

1. Explaining early in the book how financial markets operate, and how security prices are determined within these markets, lays the groundwork for explaining how financial management can affect the value of the firm. Also, this organization gives students an early exposure to methods of risk analysis, to discounted cash flow techniques, and to valuation concepts, which in turn permits us to use and reinforce these key concepts throughout the book.

2. Structuring the book around markets and valuation concepts provides a unifying theme. Some texts develop a series of topics in modular form and then attempt to integrate them in later chapters. The organization of *Financial Management* gives students a better and more comprehensive understanding of how the topics interact with one another.

3. Students—even those who do not plan to major in finance—generally enjoy working with stock and bond valuation models, rates of return, and the like. By opening with a discussion of security markets and prices, the very organization of *Financial Management* enhances student motivation and performance.

INTENDED MARKET AND USE

Financial Management is designed primarily for use as an introductory MBA text. However, it can be used as an undergraduate introductory text either with exceptionally good students or in institutions in which the introductory course is taught over two terms.

There is too much material in the text to cover everything thoroughly in one term, and it is certainly not possible to go over all the material in class. However, most students, and especially MBA students, can read on their own and understand reasonably well all but the most technical sections, so classroom coverage of all topics is not necessary. In our introductory MBA course, we have taken two somewhat different approaches. At times, we have covered only the material in Chapters 1 through 18. At other times, we have gone through the entire text. Obviously, we cover things in greater depth when we assign less material. In both situations, however, we expect students to learn much of the assigned material by reading the book, and we concentrate on the more difficult concepts in our lectures.

We have made a special effort to make the text useful as a reference book, both for corporate finance case courses and for on-the-job applications after graduation. We put into the book those materials that students are most likely to need when dealing with real-world financial decisions.

MAJOR CHANGES IN THE SEVENTH EDITION

The financial management environment has changed significantly since 1990, when we last updated the book: Academic researchers have been busy developing new theory, business practitioners have made increasing use of financial theory, and feedback from the real world has led to modifications and improvements in existing theory. We have made a concerted effort to incorporate these changes in the seventh edition. Additionally, we received many comments from users who liked the book but felt that we should alter the order of topic presentation to ease the transition from accounting to finance. After careful consideration, we implemented the following changes in the seventh edition.

1. General update. The entire book has been reviewed for completeness, ease of exposition, and currency. Hundreds of small changes have been made to keep the text up-to-date. Particular emphasis has been placed on (1) including the Clinton administration's latest tax law changes, (2) updating the real-world examples, and (3) including the latest changes in the financial environment and in financial theory.

2. Chapter organization. The organization of the text has been changed to reflect reviewers' suggestions. Note, though, that the chapters are generally self-contained and modular, so topic ordering can be altered to fit different instructors' situations.

   a. Financial statement analysis has been moved forward in the text from Chapter 22 to Chapter 2. This move provided three major advantages:

(1) The early discussion of financial statements allows instructors to use this topic as a bridge from accounting to financial management. Thus, students can "ease into" financial management from familiar ground.

(2) Covering financial statement analysis early gives instructors a vehicle for introducing students to the effects of financial management on the firm's future profitability. For example, one can discuss briefly how excessive inventories would affect the profitability ratios or how capital structure might affect the riskiness of debt and equity and, hence, the cost of capital. Thus, students obtain an early overview of financial management, and this helps them recognize that the various decisions to be discussed during the course are interrelated and must be considered in an integrated manner as one plans for the firm's future.

(3) If instructors plan to emphasize spreadsheets in the course, financial statement analysis is an excellent starting point to illustrate the usefulness of spreadsheets.

b. A new part—Part V, "Planning and Budgeting"—was added. First, these topics are simply too important to "bury" in the back of the text, as we had done in the past. Second, the addition facilitates the transition from long-term strategic decisions (capital budgeting, capital structure, and dividend policy) to short-term operating decisions. Finally, the book is now neatly divided into two halves, the first dealing with background information and long-term strategic decisions and the second with short-term operating decisions made within the framework of the firm's strategic plan.

c. The material on capital structure has been reorganized. In the sixth edition, we had one chapter which focused on capital structure theory and a second chapter which focused on finding the target structure in practice. Although this organization was satisfactory, it was not pedagogically optimal. For example, capital structure theory was discussed before such fundamental matters as business versus financial risk. Thus, students had to grapple with theory before they had a good feel for the impact of financial leverage on accounting returns. Now, capital structure theory and practice are presented in a manner which allows us to relate one to the other rather than treating them as independent topics. The new organization begins with accounting relationships, then presents capital structure theory, and finally concludes with a section on how firms determine their capital structures in practice.

3. **Alternative time value solutions.** Chapter 6, "Discounted Cash Flow Analysis," has been completely rewritten. We now begin each major section with a verbal description of a specific time value issue, then we present a time line to show graphically the cash flows that are involved, then we give the equation which must be solved, and finally we present three methods for solving the equation: (1) a numerical solution, (2) a tabular solution, and (3) a financial calculator solution. The time lines help students visualize the problem at hand, the equations help them understand the mathematics of the solution, and the three-pronged solution approach helps them understand alternative solution techniques. Each student can focus on the solution technique that he or she will actually use, which

increasingly is the financial calculator. With this approach to time value, financial calculators are no longer seen as "black boxes" but rather as efficient ways to solve time value equations.

4. New chapters.   The changing financial environment motivated us to add the following two chapters:

a.   A multinational financial management chapter has replaced end-of-chapter sections because it seemed more useful to focus on multinational issues in a chapter devoted to the subject. Of course, we continue to use multinational examples when pertinent throughout the text.

b.   We have added a chapter on bankruptcy, reorganization, and liquidation. In the sixth edition, we treated this topic in an appendix to the debt chapter, but with the added strain placed on companies by weak economic conditions, this topic warrants a separate chapter.

5. Spreadsheet analysis.   To reinforce our view that spreadsheet analysis is now an integral part of financial management, we have taken the following actions:

a.   We have included a diskette containing *Lotus 1-2-3* models for selected end-of-chapter problems in the book itself, rather than making the models available to instructors for further distribution to students. These models permit instructors to incorporate *Lotus 1-2-3* into the course without requiring students to construct models. If instructors want to go further with spreadsheet analysis and have students actually construct or modify models, our *Lotus* book and *Casebook,* which are discussed later in the Preface, would be useful.

b.   A new ancillary, which is called the *Technology Supplement* and which contains calculator and spreadsheet tutorials, is now available. Students with limited or no spreadsheet or financial calculator experience can use this supplement to learn both the basics of spreadsheet modeling and how to use the financial functions on certain leading calculators. Although the spreadsheet tutorial is based on *Lotus 1-2-3,* the command structure of most spreadsheet software packages is sufficiently similar to permit the tutorial to be used with whatever software is available to students. The tutorial, along with the diskette and models, provides students with an excellent introduction to spreadsheet modeling and its use in financial decision making. Thus, students can learn on their own the skills necessary to create and/or use spreadsheet models. The *Technology Supplement* can be copied locally and given (or sold at cost) to students.

6. Blueprints.   A new ancillary, called *Blueprints,* has been created for the seventh edition. Students often have trouble getting good notes in class because they have to choose between writing things down and listening to what is being said. *Blueprints,* which provides a more efficient way for students to take notes, can be reproduced locally and purchased (at cost) by students. This supplement contains much of the material that would be presented in class by instructors who use the Mini Cases at the end of each chapter for their lectures. (Both acetate and electronic transparencies, and complete lecture solutions to the Mini Cases, are available to instructors.) Since most of the lecture material is already in *Blueprints,*

students can spend more time listening and digesting, and taking notes only as necessary to amplify the preprinted material.

7.   Lecture Presentation Software.   Previously we have used the Mini Cases and transparencies as a complete lecture system with good results. But just as new computer and communication technologies alter the world of finance, so do these advances influence the ways in which we now learn and teach. Dr. Larry Wolken of Texas A&M University brought to our attention the advantages of lecture software and shared his computerized "slide show" with us. He found this mode of presentation particularly helpful for his large sections (although it is also useful for small classes), allowing him to conduct his lecture and discussion from anywhere in the classroom and still control the visual presentation.

Originally we thought of simply formatting the existing transparencies into the slide show, but then we realized that we would not be creating the optimal computerized lecture package. We reasoned that an instructor lecturing from the slide show would not want to go back and forth from the projection screen and a darkened room to the blackboard with all lights on. Thus, we decided that to take full advantage of the technology available to us and to provide the most useful lecture vehicle, we would have to broaden the scope of the *Lecture Presentation Software*.

As it now exists, the *Lecture Presentation Software* covers each chapter in its entirety and can serve as the backbone of the lecture. Of course, the Mini Cases and *Blueprints* still tie in with the slide show, but not exclusively.

Lecture Presentation Software furnishes complete verbal as well as graphic support for a lecture, with notes that can appear just on the computer screen or on a printout of the slides. The graphs, figures, and lists are broken down into steps, which are highlighted by different colors, so that instructors can discuss and explain the processes instead of having to manipulate and annotate the actual transparencies. Also, the software has the capability of showing a completed image, without the stages separated, so that the amount of emphasis and time devoted to particular topics can be adjusted.

Lecture Presentation Software can be used with either Macintosh or DOS-based computer systems and a computer screen projector. The *Lecture Presentation Software* is available upon adoption to instructors.

8.   Test Bank.   The *Test Bank* has been completely revised. First, the new *Test Bank* has a much more challenging set of conceptual questions, which will test the knowledge of even the brightest MBA students. Second, the *WordPerfect* version of the *Test Bank* has the solutions in endnote format; this automatically generates a key (with fully explained answers) to every test and also makes it extremely easy to reorder the test into multiple versions.

LECTURE MATERIALS

The seventh edition contains a complete "lecture support system" that instructors can use to increase the efficiency and effectiveness of their lectures. To begin, the text contains Mini Cases at the end of each chapter (except Chapter 1) which can

form the basis for the lecture on that chapter. When Mini Cases are used for lectures, students see the context in which various tools are used, which improves their motivation and understanding.

The *Instructor's Manual* contains very detailed solutions to the Mini Cases set up in a lecture note format. Furthermore, transparencies based on the Mini Cases provide instructors both with a lecture "script" and with a quick, easy-to-read way of conveying the material to students. Since *Blueprints* is based on the Mini Cases, students who use *Blueprints* will have what amounts to a hard copy of the transparencies, which greatly helps their note taking. Taken together, the Mini Cases, *Instructor's Manual* solutions, acetate transparencies, a computer graphics "slide show" version of the transparencies, and *Blueprints* provide a coherent lecture package that many experienced, and most novice, instructors can use to improve their classroom presentations.

For our own classes, we develop a Course Pack, which contains (1) our syllabus, (2) some of our old exams to give the students a good idea of how we plan to test them, (3) the *Blueprints* chapters as taken directly from the *Blueprints* supplement, and (4) several "exam-type" questions and problems, which we place immediately following each *Blueprints* chapter. Since we use the Mini Cases as the basis for our lectures, we ask students to read the chapter and scan the Mini Case. Then we lecture on the chapter by going through the case. We use the electronic slide show version of the transparencies to save time (writing on the blackboard can be very time consuming), and our students use *Blueprints* so that they can listen to the lecture and still end up with coherent notes. We encourage questions and discussion, and the Mini Case format stimulates both. Generally, it takes about two hours to lecture on one of the Mini Cases, so we allocate that much time to each of them. If we have extra time, we go into the exam-type problems at the end of the *Blueprints* chapter in the students' Course Packs. (We try to schedule pre-exam reviews, and if we do, we use these questions for the review.) Finally, we copy the Mini Case solution from the *Instructor's Manual* and place it in the library so students who missed the class can still see what we covered.

ANCILLARY MATERIALS

The following materials are available to adopters free of charge:

1. Instructor's Manual. This comprehensive, 700-page manual contains (1) a suggested course outline, (2) expanded solutions to the Mini Cases, and (3) answers to all end-of-chapter questions and problems.

2. Transparencies and Masters. A set of over 240 transparency acetates with masters, designed to accompany the Mini Cases for use as lecture illustrations, is available from The Dryden Press. Note that the transparency masters can be modified. Thus, new transparencies can be created from the modified masters, so instructors can tailor lectures to meet their unique requirements.

3. Technology Supplement. The *Technology Supplement* contains tutorials for the most commonly used financial calculators and the most popular spread-

sheet program, *Lotus 1-2-3*. This supplement (or parts of it) can be copied locally and purchased by students.

4. Blueprints. *Blueprints* contains printouts of the transparencies plus other related materials, and it provides students with an efficient system for note taking when the Mini Cases are used as the basis for class lectures. Like the *Technology Supplement, Blueprints* can be copied locally and purchased by students.

5. Lecture Presentation Software. This software, available for both Macintosh and DOS-based systems, is a computerized lecture slide show, covering all the essential issues presented in the textbook. The separate concepts and stages of a particular graph, figure, or list have been separated and appear as individual "slides" so that the instructor can focus on specific steps and issues.

6. Test Bank. A revised and enlarged *Test Bank* with more than 1,000 class-tested multiple-choice questions and problems is available both in book form and on diskettes. The diskettes may be obtained in either a computerized test bank format or in *WordPerfect,* which facilitates editing, adding your own questions, and the like. The questions are arranged, within each chapter, by type (true/false, multiple-choice questions, and multiple-choice problems), by topic, and by degree of difficulty. Some of these problems can be extracted and used in a Course Pack, as discussed previously.

7. Supplemental Problems. In addition to the end-of-chapter problems, the Mini Cases, and the *Test Bank* problems, a set of supplemental problems, organized by topic and level of difficulty, is also be available.

Several additional items are available for purchase by students through bookstores:

1. Study Guide. This supplement outlines the key sections of each chapter and provides students with a set of questions and solutions similar to those in the text and in the *Test Bank*.

2. Casebooks. Two new casebooks, *Cases in Financial Management, Directed Versions,* and *Cases in Financial Management, Nondirected Versions,* by Eugene F. Brigham and Louis C. Gapenski, contain cases which illustrate applications of the concepts and methodologies developed in *Financial Management.* The directed casebook contains 41 cases with end-of-case questions which, in essence, direct students toward a reasonable resolution to each case. The nondirected casebook contains 20 cases selected from the directed casebook, but with a guidance paragraph in place of the questions. Thus, the nondirected version requires students to develop their own solution strategy for each case. Most of the cases (both directed and nondirected) have accompanying *Lotus* models. *Lotus* is not essential for working the cases, but it does reduce number crunching and thus leaves more time for students to consider conceptual issues.

In addition to the two casebooks, The Dryden Press has developed the *By Request* case system, which allows instructors to create their own casebooks by combining any set of cases selected from the directed and nondirected casebooks. This system gives instructors the flexibility to mix and match cases to best meet the needs of each particular class and section. We usually assign a few directed

cases in the introductory MBA finance course, but when we are using *Financial Management* in the second corporate finance course, we use about 12 nondirected cases.

3. **Readers.**   A readings book, *Issues and Readings in Managerial Finance* edited by Ramon E. Johnson, provides an excellent mix of theoretical and practical articles which can be used to supplement the text. Another supplemental reader is *Advances in Business Financial Management: A Collection of Readings* edited by Philip L. Cooley, which provides a broader selection of articles from which to choose.

4. **Lotus Book.**   Eugene F. Brigham, Dana A. Aberwald, and Louis C. Gapenski have written a supplemental book, *Finance with Lotus 1-2-3: Text and Models,* designed to teach students how to use *1-2-3* for financial modeling. This book takes students from formatting and copying diskettes to the development of macros and other complex procedures, and it provides students with substantially more information about spreadsheet modeling than does the *Technology Supplement.* The book was written to be used in a self-taught mode, and our students go through it on their own.

ACKNOWLEDGMENTS

This book reflects the efforts of a great many people over a number of years. First, we would like to thank the following professors, who reviewed this edition in detail and provided many useful comments and suggestions:

Robert Button	Sally Hamilton
Anand Desai	Linda Klein
Richard Fendler	Coleen Pantalone

Also, earlier versions of individual chapters or entire sections were sent to professors and professionals doing research on specific topics. We are grateful for the insights provided by

▶ Edward I. Altman of New York University on "Bankruptcy, Reorganization, and Liquidation"

▶ William Beranek of the University of Georgia on Part VI, "Working Capital Management and Financing"

▶ Ben S. Branch of the Bank of New England and the University of Massachusetts on "Bankruptcy, Reorganization, and Liquidation"

▶ David T. Brown of the University of Florida on "Bankruptcy, Reorganization, and Liquidation"

▶ Myron Gordon of the University of Toronto on "Capital Structure Decisions: Parts 1 and 2" and "Dividend Policy"

▶ Robert Kieschnick of George Mason University on "Mergers, LBOs, Divestitures, and Holding Companies"

▶ James Schallheim of the University of Utah on "Lease Financing"

▶ Robert Strong of the University of Maine at Orono on "Valuation Models"

▶ Robert Taggart of Boston College on "The Cost of Capital," "The Basics of Capital Budgeting," and "Project Cash Flow Analysis"

▶ Jonathan Tiemann of Wells Fargo Nikko Investment Advisors on "Common Stock, Preferrred Stock, and the Investment Banking Process"

▶ Sheridan Titman of the University of California, Los Angeles, on "Risk and Return: Parts 1 and 2"

▶ Alan L. Tucker of Temple University on "Multinational Financial Management"

▶ David Ziebart of the University of Illinois at Urbana on "Analysis of Financial Statements"

In addition, we would like to thank the following people, whose reviews and comments on prior editions and companion books have contributed to this edition: Mike Adler, Syed Ahmad, Ed Altman, Bruce Anderson, Ron Anderson, Bob Angell, Vince Apilado, Henry Arnold, Bob Aubey, Gil Babcock, Peter Bacon, Kent Baker, Tom Bankston, Les Barenbaum, Charles Barngrover, Bill Beedles, Moshe Ben-Horim, Bill Beranek, Tom Berry, Bill Bertin, Tom Berry, Roger Bey, Dalton Bigbee, John Bildersee, Russ Boisjoly, Keith Boles, Geof Booth, Kenneth Boudreaux, Helen Bowers, Oswald Bowlin, Don Boyd, G. Michael Boyd, Pat Boyer, Joe Brandt, Elizabeth Brannigan, Greg Brauer, Mary Broske, Dave Brown, Kate Brown, Bill Brueggeman, Kirt Butler, Bill Campsey, Bob Carleson, Severin Carlson, David Cary, Steve Celec, Don Chance, Antony Chang, Susan Chaplinsky, Jay Choi, S. K. Choudhury, Lal Chugh, Maclyn Clouse, Margaret Considine, Phil Cooley, Joe Copeland, David Cordell, John Cotner, Charles Cox, David Crary, John Crockett, Roy Crum, Brent Dalrymple, Bill Damon, Joel Dauten, Steve Dawson, Sankar De, Miles Delano, Fred Dellva, Bernard Dill, Greg Dimkoff, Les Dlabay, Mark Dorfman, Gene Drycimski, Dean Dudley, David Durst, Ed Dyl, Dick Edelman, Charles Edwards, John Ellis, Dave Ewert, John Ezzell, Michael Ferri, Jim Filkins, John Finnerty, Susan Fischer, Steven Flint, Russ Fogler, Dan French, Michael Garlington, Jim Garvin, Adam Gehr, Jim Gentry, Philip Glasgo, Rudyard Goode, Walt Goulet, Bernie Grablowsky, Theoharry Grammatikos, Ed Grossnickle, John Groth, Alan Grunewald, Manak Gupta, Sam Hadaway, Don Hakala, Gerald Hamsmith, William Hardin, John Harris, Paul Hastings, Bob Haugen, Steve Hawke, Del Hawley, Robert Hehre, George Hettenhouse, Hans Heymann, Kendall Hill, Tom Hindelang, Linda Hittle, Ralph Hocking, J. Ronald Hoffmeister, Jim Horrigan, John Houston, John Howe, Keith Howe, Steve Isberg, Jim Jackson, Kose John, Craig Johnson, Keith Johnson, Ramon Johnson, Ray Jones, Manuel Jose, Gus Kalogeras, Mike Keenan, Bill Kennedy, Joe Kiernan, Rick Kish, Don Knight, Dorothy Koehl, Jaroslaw Komarynsky, Duncan Kretovich, Harold Krogh, Charles Kroncke, Joan Lamm, P. Lange, Howard Lanser, Martin Laurence, Ed Lawrence, Wayne Lee, Jim LePage, Jules Levine, John Lewis, Chuck Linke, Bill Lloyd, Susan Long, Judy Maese, Bob Magee, Ileen Malitz, Phil Malone, Terry Maness, Chris Manning, Terry Martell, D. J. Masson, John Mathys, John McAlhany, Andy McCollough, Bill McDaniel, Robin McLaughlin, Tom McCue, Jamshid Mehran, Larry Merville, Rick Meyer, Jim Millar, Ed Miller, John Mitchell, Carol Moerdyk, Bob Moore, Barry Morris, Gene Morris, Fred Morrissey,

Chris Muscarella, David Nachman, Tim Nantell, Don Nast, Bill Nelson, Bob Nelson, Bob Niendorf, Tom O'Brien, Dennis O'Connor, John O'Donnell, Jim Olsen, Robert Olsen, Jim Pappas, Stephen Parrish, Glenn Petry, Jim Pettijohn, Rich Pettit, Dick Pettway, Hugo Phillips, John Pinkerton, Gerald Pogue, R. Potter, Franklin Potts, R. Powell, Chris Prestopino, Jerry Prock, Howard Puckett, Herbert Quigley, George Racette, Rob Radcliffe, Bill Rentz, Ken Riener, Charles Rini, John Ritchie, Pietra Rivoli, Antonio Rodriguez, E. M. Roussakis, Dexter Rowell, Jim Sachlis, Abdul Sadik, Thomas Scampini, Kevin Scanlon, Frederick Schadler, Mary Jane Scheuer, Carl Schweser, John Settle, Alan Severn, Sol Shalit, Frederic Shipley, Dilip Shome, Ron Shrieves, Neil Sicherman, J. B. Silvers, Clay Singleton, Joe Sinkey, Stacy Sirmans, Jaye Smith, Steve Smith, Don Sorenson, David Speairs, Ken Stanly, Ed Stendardi, Alan Stephens, Don Stevens, Jerry Stevens, Glen Strasburg, Philip Swensen, Ernie Swift, Paul Swink, Gary Tallman, Dennis Tanner, Russ Taussig, Richard Teweles, Ted Teweles, Andrew Thompson, George Trivoli, George Tsetsekos, Mel Tysseland, David Upton, Howard Van Auken, Pretorious Van den Dool, Pieter Vanderburg, Paul Vanderheiden, Jim Verbrugge, Patrick Vincent, Steve Vinson, Susan Visscher, John Wachowicz, Mike Walker, Sam Weaver, Kuo Chiang Wei, Bill Welch, Fred Weston, Norm Williams, Tony Wingler, Ed Wolfe, Don Woods, Michael Yonan, Dennis Zocco, and Kent Zumwalt.

Special thanks are due to Fred Weston, Myron Gordon, Merton Miller, and Franco Modigliani, who have done much to help develop the field of financial management and who provided us with instruction and inspiration; to Roy Crum, who coauthored the multinational finance chapter; to Art Herrmann, who coauthored the bankruptcy chapter; to Larry Wolken, who offered his hard work and advice for the development of the *Lecture Presentation Software;* to Susan Ball, Mary Alice Hanebury, and Kay Mangan, who helped us develop the *Lotus 1-2-3* models; to Steve Bouchard, who helped with the *Test Bank;* to Eileen Barak, who helped with the electronic transparencies; to Dana Aberwald, who helped on the ancillaries; and to Carol Stanton and Bob Karp, who provided both word processing and editorial support.

Both our colleagues and our students at the University of Florida gave us many useful suggestions, and The Dryden Press and Elm Street Publishing Services staffs—especially Rick Hammonds, Karen Hill, Lisé Johnson, Shana Lum, Barbara Rosenberg, and Liz Widdicombe—helped greatly with all phases of text development, production, and marketing.

ERRORS IN THE TEXT

At this point, authors generally say something like this: "We appreciate all the help we received from the people listed above, but any remaining errors are, of course, our own responsibility." And in many books, there are plenty of remaining errors. Having experienced difficulties with errors ourselves, both as students and as instructors, we resolved to avoid this problem in *Financial Management.* As a result of our error-detection procedures, we are convinced that the book is relatively free of mistakes.

Partly because of our confidence that few errors remain, but primarily because we want very much to detect any errors that may have slipped by so we can correct them in subsequent printings, we decided to offer a reward of $10 per error (conceptual error, misspelled word, arithmetic mistake, and the like) to the first person who reports it to us. (Any error that has follow-through effects is counted as two errors only.) Two accounting students have set up a foolproof audit system to make sure we pay off. Accounting students tend to be skeptics!

CONCLUSION

Finance is, in a real sense, the cornerstone of the free enterprise system. Good financial management is therefore vitally important to the economic health of business firms, and hence to the nation and the world. Because of its importance, financial management should be thoroughly understood, but this is easier said than done. The field is relatively complex, and it is undergoing constant change in response to shifts in economic conditions. All of this makes financial management stimulating and exciting but also challenging and sometimes perplexing. We sincerely hope that the seventh edition of *Financial Management* will help you understand the financial problems faced by businesses today, as well as the best ways to solve those problems.

Eugene F. Brigham
College of Business Administration

Louis C. Gapenski
College of Business Administration
College of Health Related Professions

P.O. Box 117160
University of Florida
Gainesville, Florida 32611-7160
September 1993

CONTENTS IN BRIEF

CONTENTS

P A R T   I

INTRODUCTION TO FINANCIAL MANAGEMENT

AN OVERVIEW OF FINANCIAL MANAGEMENT

he first week of November 1992 witnessed the replacement of two world-renowned leaders: Bill Clinton replaced George Bush as president of the United States, and John L. "Jack" Smith replaced Robert Stempel as chief executive officer (CEO) of General Motors.

The change at GM, that bastion of old-line industrial America, was a real shock. The major difference between the Clinton and Smith victories is that it is not unusual for voters to elect a new president, but until recently it was rare indeed for a corporate board of directors to oust a reigning chief in favor of new blood.

GM's problems began years ago, when foreign automakers, particularly the Japanese, started to gain U.S. market share at the expense of the domestic manufacturers. In spite of the increased competition, U.S. manufacturers failed to respond with quality products that met consumers' needs. In the early to mid-1980s, Ford and Chrysler did embark on cost-cutting and product-development programs that turned their fortunes around, but GM never got back on track.

At GM, CEO Roger Smith, who led the company from 1981 to 1990, ruled the board of directors with an iron hand. He withheld key financial data and budget-allocation proposals from the board until the day before meetings, and he sometimes even distributed them as the meeting convened. The monthly sessions were rigidly structured, and Smith adjourned them promptly at five minutes to noon, leaving little time for discussion. Smith could deal with the board in this way because few members had the ability or desire to take him on. As late as 1989, for example, 3 of the 15 board members were GM executives who owed Smith their jobs. Another four were what one critic called "we, the people" members: generally minorities, women, or retired statesmen. Of the other eight

directors, two were retired businessmen and a third ran GM's primary Detroit bank. For their service on the board, directors received $45,000 annually and a new GM car for personal use four times a year.

By 1987, evidence of GM's mismanagement had become so apparent that the directors could no longer ignore it. Smith then tried to pack the board with three more insiders, but the directors rebelled. Soon thereafter, American Express CEO James Robinson quit the board, apparently in frustration with Smith's intransigence and his own lack of clout. Nevertheless, since Smith was due to retire in 1990, the majority of the board chose to do nothing, hoping they would get better results from Smith's successor.

When it was time to pick Smith's successor, the board settled on Robert Stempel, the in-house favorite, for CEO, but they questioned Stempel's choice of his long-time friend, Lloyd Reuss, as president. When Stempel persisted, the board withheld from Reuss the title of chief operating officer. Stempel took office August 1, 1990, and several outside directors soon realized they had made a mistake. Out of loyalty to old friends and old ways, Stempel was slow to make changes. He concentrated on the engineering and manufacturing functions but seemed oblivious to organizational, cost, and marketing issues. It seemed obvious to everyone that GM needed to drastically and quickly cut capacity to reduce costs, but such actions were slow to materialize. Stempel's repeated admonitions to stockholders for patience quickly wore thin, and the board became increasingly alarmed at mounting losses and hints from credit-rating agencies that GM's once impeccable financial position was becoming shaky.

As the situation deteriorated, a new and revitalized board emerged, composed of many CEOs who had braved corporate crises of their own, often doing what GM should have done—downsizing and cutting costs—to ensure their firms' ability to survive in a global marketplace. The directors fired their first public shot in April 1992, when they removed Reuss as president and put in Jack Smith, the successful head of GM's international operations. Along with Reuss, two other old-line managers were demoted and removed from the board. The board also revived its inactive executive committee and replaced Stempel as chairman with outside director John Smale, the retired CEO of Procter & Gamble. By ordering Stempel to report to Smale, the board had, in effect, demoted the chairman and CEO. Some directors thought the demotion would encourage Stempel to quit, but he hung on. By mid-October, newspaper stories indicating that the outside directors were preparing to remove Stempel began to appear. Detroit reporters started a career deathwatch, pursuing Stempel in public, at one point even chasing him through a hotel kitchen. Finally, on October 26, Stempel announced his resignation, and on November 3, the board announced a new management team.

The episode at GM raises many important financial management issues concerning forms of business organization and corporate control. What is a corporation, and how do its owners—the stockholders—exercise control? What re-

sponsibilities do directors have to the firm's stockholders? Do directors owe any allegiance to the firm's managers? Finally, whose interests should managers consider most important: their own, the firm's employees, or its stockholders? These issues, along with many others, are discussed in this chapter.

The purpose of this chapter is to give you an overview of financial management. After you finish the chapter, you should have a reasonably good idea of what finance majors might do after graduation. You should also have a better understanding of (1) some of the forces that will affect financial management in the future; (2) the way businesses are organized; (3) the place finance has in a firm's organization; (4) the relationships financial managers have with their counterparts in the accounting, marketing, production, and personnel departments; and (5) the goals of a firm and the way financial managers can contribute to their attainment.

CAREER OPPORTUNITIES IN FINANCE

Finance consists of three interrelated areas: (1) *money and capital markets,* which deals with securities markets and financial institutions; (2) *investments,* which focuses on the decisions of individuals and financial and other institutions as they choose securities for their investment portfolios; and (3) *financial management,* or "business finance," which involves the actual management of nonfinancial firms. The career opportunities within each field are many and varied, but financial managers must have a knowledge of all three areas if they are to do their jobs well.

MONEY AND CAPITAL MARKETS

Many finance majors go to work for financial institutions, including banks, insurance companies, investment companies, savings and loans, and credit unions. For success here one needs a knowledge of the factors that cause interest rates to rise and fall, the regulations to which financial institutions are subject, and the various types of financial instruments (mortgages, auto loans, certificates of deposit, and so on). One also needs a general knowledge of all aspects of business administration, because the management of a financial institution involves accounting, marketing, personnel, and computer systems, as well as financial management. An ability to communicate, both orally and in writing, is important, and "people skills," or the ability to get others to do their jobs well, are critical.

The most common initial job in this area is a bank officer trainee, where you go into bank operations and learn about the business, from tellers' work, to cash management, to making loans. You could expect to spend a year or so being ro-

tated among these different areas, after which you would settle into a department, often as an assistant manager in a branch. Alternatively, you might become a specialist in some area such as real estate, and be authorized to make loans going into millions of dollars, or in the management of trusts, estates, and pension funds. Similar career paths are available with insurance companies, investment companies, credit unions, and consumer loan companies.

INVESTMENTS

Finance graduates who go into investments generally work for a brokerage house such as Merrill Lynch, either in sales or as a security analyst. Others work for a bank, a mutual fund, or an insurance company in the management of their investment portfolios, for a financial consulting firm which advises individual investors or pension funds on how to invest their funds, or for an investment banker whose primary function is to help businesses raise new capital. The three main functions in the investments area are (1) sales, (2) the analysis of individual securities, and (3) determining the optimal mix of securities for a given investor.

FINANCIAL MANAGEMENT

Financial management is the broadest of the three areas, and the one with the greatest number of job opportunities. Financial management is important in all types of businesses, including banks and other financial institutions, as well as industrial and retail firms. Financial management is also important in governmental operations, from schools to hospitals to highway departments. The types of jobs one encounters in financial management range from decisions regarding plant expansions to choosing what types of securities to issue to finance expansion. Financial managers also have the responsibility for deciding the credit terms under which customers may buy, how much inventory the firm should carry, how much cash to keep on hand, whether to acquire other firms (merger analysis), and how much of the firm's earnings to plow back into the business versus pay out as dividends.

Regardless of which area you go into, you will need a knowledge of all three areas. For example, a banker lending to businesses cannot do his or her job well without a good understanding of financial management, because he or she must be able to judge how well a business is operated. The same thing holds true for one of Merrill Lynch's security analysts, and even stockbrokers must have an understanding of general financial principles if they are to give intelligent advice to their customers. At the same time, corporate financial managers need to know what their bankers are thinking about and how investors are likely to judge their corporations' performances, thus determining their stock prices. So, if you decide to make finance your career, you will need to know something about all three areas.

SELF-TEST QUESTIONS

What are the three main areas of finance?

If you have definite plans to go into one area, why is it necessary that you know something about the other areas?

FINANCIAL MANAGEMENT IN THE 1990s

When financial management emerged as a separate field of study in the early 1900s, the emphasis was on the legal aspects of mergers, the formation of new firms, and the various types of securities that firms could issue to raise capital. During the Depression of the 1930s, the emphasis shifted to bankruptcy and reorganization, to corporate liquidity, and to the regulation of security markets. During the 1940s and early 1950s, finance continued to be taught as a descriptive, institutional subject, viewed more from the standpoint of an outsider rather than from that of management. However, a movement toward theoretical analysis began during the late 1950s, and the focus of financial management shifted to managerial decisions regarding the choice of assets and liabilities so as to maximize the value of the firm. The focus on valuation continued into the 1990s, but the analysis was expanded to include (1) *inflation* and its effects on business decisions; (2) *deregulation* of financial institutions and the resulting trend toward large, broadly diversified financial services companies; (3) the dramatic increase in both the use of *computers* for analysis and the electronic transfer of information; and (4) the increased importance of *global* markets and business operations. The two most important future trends are likely to be the continued globalization of business and a further increase in the use of computer technology.

THE GLOBALIZATION OF BUSINESS

Four factors have made the trend toward globalization mandatory for many businesses: (1) Improvements in transportation and communications have lowered shipping costs and made international trade more feasible. (2) The political clout of consumers, who desire low-cost, high-quality products, has helped lower trade barriers designed to protect inefficient, high-cost domestic manufacturers. (3) As technology has become more advanced, the cost of developing new products has increased, and, as development costs rise, so must unit sales if the firm is to be competitive. The world market is obviously larger than any national market. (4) In a world populated with multinational firms able to shift production to wherever costs are lowest, a firm whose manufacturing operations are restricted to one country cannot compete unless costs in its home country happen to be low, a condition that does not necessarily exist for many U.S. corporations. As a result of these four factors, survival requires that most manufacturers produce and sell globally.

Service companies, including banks, advertising agencies, and accounting firms, are also being forced to "go global," because such firms can better serve their

multinational clients if they have worldwide operations. There will, of course, always be some purely domestic companies, but you should keep in mind that the most dynamic growth, and the best employment opportunities, are often with companies that operate worldwide.

COMPUTER TECHNOLOGY

The remainder of the 1990s will see continued advances in computer and communications technology, and this technology will revolutionize the way financial decisions are made. Companies will have networks of personal computers linked to one another, to the firms' own mainframe computers, and to their customers' and suppliers' computers. Thus, financial managers will be able to share information and to have "face-to-face" meetings with distant colleagues through video teleconferencing. The ability to access and analyze data on a real-time basis will also mean that quantitative analyses will be used routinely to "test out" alternative courses of action. As a result, the next generation of financial managers will need stronger computer and quantitative skills than were required in the past.

SELF-TEST QUESTIONS

How has financial management changed from the early 1900s to the 1990s?

How might a person become better prepared for a career in financial management?

INCREASING IMPORTANCE OF FINANCIAL MANAGEMENT

The historical trends discussed in the previous section have greatly increased the importance of financial management. In earlier times, the marketing manager would project sales, the engineering and production staffs would determine the assets necessary to meet those demands, and the financial manager's job was simply to raise the money needed to purchase the required plant, equipment, and inventories. That situation no longer exists—decisions are now made in a much more coordinated manner, and the financial manager generally has direct responsibility for the control process.

Eastern and Delta Airlines can be used to illustrate both the importance of financial management and the effects of financial decisions. In the 1960s, Eastern's stock sold for more than $60 per share while Delta's sold for $10. By the early 1990s, Delta had become one of the world's strongest airlines, and its stock was selling for more than $50 per share. Eastern, on the other hand, had gone bankrupt and was no longer in existence. Although many factors combined to produce these divergent results, financial decisions exerted a major influence. Because Eastern had traditionally used a great deal of debt while Delta had not, Eastern's costs increased significantly, and its profits were lowered, when interest rates rose dur-

ing the 1980s. Rising rates had only a minor effect on Delta. Further, when fuel price increases made it imperative for the airlines to buy new, fuel-efficient planes, Delta was able to do so, but Eastern was not. Finally, when the airlines were deregulated, Delta was strong enough to expand into developing markets, to buy assets from failing airlines, and to cut prices as necessary to attract business, but Eastern was not.

The Delta-Eastern story, and others like it, are now well known, so all companies today are greatly concerned with financial planning, and this has increased the importance of corporate financial staffs. Indeed, the value of financial management is reflected in the fact that more chief executive officers (CEOs) in the top 1,000 U.S. companies started their careers in finance than in any other functional area.

It is also becoming increasingly important for people in marketing, accounting, production, personnel, and other areas to understand finance in order to do a good job in their own fields. Marketing people, for instance, must understand how marketing decisions affect and are affected by funds availability, by inventory levels, by excess plant capacity, and so on. Similarly, accountants must understand how accounting data are used in corporate planning and are viewed by investors.

Thus, there are financial implications in virtually all business decisions, and nonfinancial executives simply must know enough finance to work these implications into their own specialized analyses.[1] Because of this, every student of business, regardless of his or her major, should be concerned with financial management.

SELF-TEST QUESTIONS

Explain why financial planning is important to today's chief executives.

Why do marketing people need to know something about financial management?

THE FINANCIAL MANAGER'S RESPONSIBILITIES

The financial manager's task is to acquire and use funds so as to maximize the value of the firm. Here are some specific activities which are involved:

1. Forecasting and planning. The financial manager must interact with other executives as they look ahead and lay the plans which will shape the firm's future.

2. Major investment and financing decisions. A successful firm usually has rapid growth in sales, which requires investments in plant, equipment, and inventory. The financial manager must help determine the optimal sales growth rate, and he or she must help decide on the specific assets to acquire and the best way

---

[1]It is an interesting fact that the course "Financial Management for Nonfinancial Executives" has the highest enrollment in most executive development programs.

to finance those assets. For example, should the firm finance with debt, equity, or some combination of the two, and, if debt is used, how much of it should be long term and how much should be short term?

3. Coordination and control. The financial manager must interact with other executives to insure that the firm is operated as efficiently as possible. All business decisions have financial implications, and all managers—financial and otherwise— need to take this into account. For example, marketing decisions affect sales growth, which in turn influences investment requirements. Thus, marketing decision makers must take account of how their actions affect (and are affected by) such factors as the availability of funds, inventory policies, and plant capacity utilization.

4. Dealing with the financial markets. The financial manager must deal with the money and capital markets. As we shall see in Chapter 3, each firm affects and is affected by the general financial markets where funds are raised, where the firm's securities are traded, and where its investors either make or lose money.

In summary, financial managers make decisions regarding which assets their firms should acquire, how those assets should be financed, and how the firm should manage its existing resources. If these responsibilities are performed optimally, financial managers will help to maximize the values of their firms, and this will also maximize the long-run welfare of consumers and employees.

SELF-TEST QUESTION

What are four specific activities with which financial managers are involved?

ALTERNATIVE FORMS OF BUSINESS ORGANIZATION

There are three main forms of business organization: (1) sole proprietorships, (2) partnerships, and (3) corporations. In terms of numbers, about 80 percent of businesses are operated as sole proprietorships, while the remainder are divided equally between partnerships and corporations. Based on dollar value of sales, however, about 80 percent of all business is conducted by corporations, about 13 percent by sole proprietorships, and about 7 percent by partnerships. Because most business is conducted by corporations, we will concentrate on them in this book. However, it is important to understand the differences among the three forms.

SOLE PROPRIETORSHIP

A *sole proprietorship* is an unincorporated business owned by one individual. Going into business as a sole proprietor is easy—one merely begins business operations. However, even the smallest establishments must be licensed by a governmental unit.

The proprietorship has three important advantages: (1) It is easily and inexpensively formed, (2) it is subject to few government regulations, and (3) the business pays no corporate income taxes.

The proprietorship also has three important limitations: (1) It is difficult for a proprietorship to obtain large sums of capital; (2) the proprietor has unlimited personal liability for business debts, which can result in losses that exceed the money he or she invested in the company; and (3) the life of a business organized as a proprietorship is limited to the life of the individual who created it. For these three reasons, sole proprietorships are restricted primarily to small-business operations. However, businesses are frequently started as proprietorships and then converted to corporations when their growth causes the disadvantages of being a proprietorship to outweigh the advantages.

PARTNERSHIP

A *partnership* exists whenever two or more persons associate to conduct a noncorporate business. Partnerships may operate under different degrees of formality, ranging from informal, oral understandings to formal agreements filed with the secretary of the state in which the partnership was formed. The major advantage of a partnership is its low cost and ease of formation. The disadvantages are similar to those associated with proprietorships: (1) unlimited liability, (2) limited life of the organization, (3) difficulty of transferring ownership, and (4) difficulty of raising large amounts of capital. The tax treatment of a partnership is similar to that for proprietorships, which is often an advantage, as we demonstrate in Chapter 3.

Regarding liability, the partners can potentially lose all of their personal assets, even those assets not invested in the business, because, under partnership law, each partner is liable for the business's debts. Therefore, if any partner is unable to meet his or her pro rata claim in the event the partnership goes bankrupt, the remaining partners must make good on the unsatisfied claims, drawing on their personal assets if necessary. The partners of the national accounting firm Laventhol and Horwath, a huge partnership which recently went bankrupt as a result of suits filed by investors who relied on faulty audit statements, are learning all about the perils of doing business as a partnership. Thus, a Texas partner who audits a savings and loan which goes under can bring ruin to a millionaire New York partner who never went near the S&L.[2]

The first three disadvantages — unlimited liability, impermanence of the organization, and difficulty of transferring ownership — lead to the fourth, the difficulty partnerships have in attracting substantial amounts of capital. This is no particular problem for a slow-growing business, but if a business's products or services really

---

[2]However, it is possible to limit the liabilities of some of the partners by establishing a *limited partnership,* wherein one partner is designated the *general partner* and others *limited partners.* Limited partnerships are quite common in real estate investment, but they do not work well with most types of businesses, including accounting firms, because one partner (the general partner) is rarely willing to assume all of the business's risk, and the other partners (the limited partners) are unwilling to relinquish control.

catch on, and if it needs to raise large amounts of capital in order to capitalize on its opportunities, the difficulty in attracting capital becomes a real drawback. Thus, growth companies such as Hewlett-Packard and Apple Computer generally begin life as a proprietorship or partnership, but at some point they find it necessary to convert to a corporation.

CORPORATION

A *corporation* is a legal entity created by a state. It is separate and distinct from its owners and managers. This separateness gives the corporation three major advantages: (1) *Unlimited life* — A corporation can continue after its original owners and managers are deceased. (2) *Easy transferability of ownership interest* — Ownership interests can be divided into shares of stock, which in turn can be transferred far more easily than can proprietorship or partnership interests. (3) *Limited liability* — To illustrate the concept of limited liability, suppose you invested $10,000 in a partnership which then went bankrupt owing $1 million. Because the owners are liable for the debts of a partnership, you could be assessed for a share of the company's debt, and you could be held liable for the entire $1 million if your partners could not pay their shares. Thus, an investor in a partnership is exposed to unlimited liability. On the other hand, if you invested $10,000 in the stock of a corporation which then went bankrupt, your potential loss on the investment would be limited to your $10,000 investment.[3] These three factors — unlimited life, easy transferability of ownership interest, and limited liability — make it much easier for corporations than for proprietorships or partnerships to raise money in the general capital markets.

The corporate form offers significant advantages over proprietorships and partnerships, but it does have two primary disadvantages: (1) Corporate earnings are subject to double taxation — the earnings of the corporation are taxed at the corporate level, and then any earnings paid out as dividends are taxed again as income to the stockholders. (2) Setting up a corporation, and filing required state and federal reports, is more complex and time-consuming than for a proprietorship or a partnership.

A proprietorship or a partnership can commence operations without much paperwork, but setting up a corporation requires that the incorporators prepare a charter and a set of bylaws. Although personal computer software that creates charters and bylaws is now available, a lawyer is required if the fledgling corporation has any nonstandard features. The *charter* includes the following information: (1) name of the proposed corporation, (2) types of activities it will pursue, (3) amount of capital stock, (4) number of directors, and (5) names and addresses of directors. The charter is filed with the secretary of the state in which the firm will be incorporated, and, when it is approved, the corporation is officially in exis-

---

[3]In the case of small corporations, the limited liability feature is often a fiction, because bankers and other lenders frequently require personal guarantees from the stockholders of small, weak businesses.

tence.[4] Then, after the corporation is in operation, quarterly and annual financial and tax reports must be filed with state and federal authorities.

The *bylaws* are a set of rules drawn up by the founders of the corporation to aid in governing the internal management of the company. Included are such points as (1) how directors are to be elected (all elected each year, or perhaps one-third each year for three-year terms); (2) whether the existing stockholders will have the first right to buy any new shares the firm issues; and (3) procedures for changing the bylaws themselves, should conditions require it.

The value of any business other than a very small one will probably be maximized if it is organized as a corporation for these three reasons:

1. Limited liability reduces the risks borne by investors, and, other things held constant, *the lower the firm's risk, the higher its value*.

2. A firm's value is dependent on its *growth opportunities*, which, in turn, are dependent on the firm's ability to attract capital. Since corporations can attract capital more easily than can unincorporated businesses, they are better able to take advantage of growth opportunities.

3. The value of an asset also depends on its *liquidity*, which means the ease of selling the asset and converting it to cash at a "fair market value." Since an investment in the stock of a corporation is much more liquid than a similar investment in a proprietorship or partnership, this too means that the corporate form of organization can enhance the value of a business.

As we will see later in the chapter, most firms are managed with value maximization in mind, and this, in turn, has caused most large businesses to be organized as corporations.

SELF-TEST QUESTIONS

What are the key differences between sole proprietorships, partnerships, and corporations?

Explain why the value of any business other than a very small one will probably be maximized if it is organized as a corporation.

FINANCE IN THE ORGANIZATIONAL STRUCTURE OF THE FIRM

Organizational structures vary from firm to firm, but Figure 1-1 presents a fairly typical picture of the role of finance within a corporation. The chief financial officer—who often has the title of vice-president: finance—reports to the president. The financial vice-president's key subordinates are the treasurer and the controller. In most firms the treasurer has direct responsibility for managing the firm's

---

[4]Note that more than 60 percent of major U.S. corporations are chartered in Delaware, which has, over the years, provided a favorable legal environment for corporations. It is not necessary for a firm to be headquartered, or even to conduct operations, in its state of incorporation.

normal, that is, close to the average for all firms, and just sufficient to attract capital. If one company attempts to exercise social responsibility, it will have to raise prices to cover the added costs. If the other businesses in its industry do not follow suit, their costs and prices will be lower. The socially responsible firm will not be able to compete, and it will be forced to abandon its efforts. Thus, any voluntary socially responsible acts that raise costs will be difficult, if not impossible, in industries that are subject to keen competition.

What about oligopolistic firms with profits above normal levels — cannot such firms devote resources to social projects? Undoubtedly they can, and many large, successful firms do engage in community projects, employee benefit programs, and the like to a greater degree than would appear to be called for by pure profit or wealth maximization goals.[5] Furthermore, many such firms contribute large sums to charities. Still, publicly owned firms are constrained in such actions by capital market factors. To illustrate, suppose a saver who has funds to invest is considering two alternative firms. One firm devotes a substantial part of its resources to social actions, while the other concentrates on profits and stock prices. Most investors are likely to shun the socially oriented firm, thus putting it at a disadvantage in the capital market. After all, why should the stockholders of one corporation subsidize society to a greater extent than those of other businesses? For this reason, even highly profitable firms (unless they are closely held rather than publicly owned) are generally constrained against taking unilateral cost-increasing social actions.

Does all this mean that firms should not exercise social responsibility? Not at all, but it does mean that most significant cost-increasing actions will have to be put on a *mandatory* rather than a voluntary basis, at least initially, to insure that the burden falls uniformly on all businesses. Thus, such social benefit programs as fair hiring practices, minority training, product safety, pollution abatement, and antitrust actions are most likely to be effective if realistic rules are established initially and then enforced by government agencies. Of course, it is critical that industry and government cooperate in establishing the rules of corporate behavior, that the costs as well as the benefits of such actions be accurately estimated and taken into account, and that firms follow the spirit as well as the letter of the law in their actions.

In spite of the fact that many socially responsible actions must be mandated by government, in recent years numerous firms have been voluntarily taking actions, especially in the area of environmental protection, because these actions help sales. For example, many detergent manufacturers now use recycled paper for their containers, and food companies are packaging more and more products in materials that consumers can recycle or that are biodegradable. To illustrate, McDonald's has replaced its styrofoam boxes, which take years to break down in landfills, with paper wrappers that are less bulky and decompose more rapidly. Some companies, such as the Body Shop and Ben & Jerry's Ice Cream, go to great lengths to be socially responsible. According to the president of the Body Shop,

---

[5]Even firms like these often find it necessary to justify such projects at stockholder meetings by stating that these programs will contribute to long-run profit maximization.

the role of business is to promote the public good, not just the good of the firm's shareholders. Furthermore, she believes that it is impossible to separate business from social responsibility. For some firms, socially responsible actions may not even be very costly, because the companies often heavily advertise such actions, and many consumers prefer to buy from socially responsible companies rather than from companies that shun social responsibility.

STOCK PRICE MAXIMIZATION AND SOCIAL WELFARE

If a firm attempts to maximize its stock price, is this good or bad for society? In general, it is good. Aside from such illegal actions as attempting to form monopolies, violating safety codes, and failing to meet pollution control requirements, *the same actions that maximize stock prices also benefit society.* First, note that stock price maximization requires efficient, low-cost plants that produce high-quality goods and services at the lowest possible cost. Second, stock price maximization requires the development of products that consumers want and need, so the profit motive leads to new technology, to new products, and to new jobs. Finally, stock price maximization necessitates efficient and courteous service, adequate stocks of merchandise, and well-located business establishments—factors that are all necessary to make sales, and sales are necessary for profits. Therefore, actions which help a firm increase the price of its stock are also beneficial to society at large. This is why profit-motivated, free-enterprise economies have been so much more successful than socialistic and communistic economic systems. Since financial management plays a crucial role in the operation of successful firms, and since successful firms are absolutely necessary for a healthy, productive economy, it is easy to see why finance is important from a social standpoint.[6]

SELF-TEST QUESTIONS

What is management's primary goal?

What actions could be taken to remove management if it departs from the goal of maximizing shareholder wealth?

What would happen if one firm attempted to exercise costly social responsibility, while its competitors did *not* exercise social responsibility?

How does the goal of stock price maximization benefit society at large?

---

[6]People sometimes argue that firms, in their efforts to raise profits and stock prices, increase product prices and gouge the public. In a reasonably competitive economy, which we have, prices are constrained by competition and consumer resistance. If a firm raises its prices beyond reasonable levels, it will simply lose its market share. Even giant firms like General Motors lose business to the Japanese and Germans, as well as to Ford and Chrysler, if they set prices above levels necessary to cover production costs plus a "normal" profit. Of course, firms *want* to earn more, and they constantly try to cut costs, to develop new products, and so on, and thereby to earn above-normal profits. Note, though, that if they are indeed successful and do earn above-normal profits, those very profits will attract competition which will eventually drive prices down, so again the main long-term beneficiary is the consumer.

BUSINESS ETHICS

The word *ethics* is defined in Webster's dictionary as "standards of conduct or moral behavior." Business ethics can be thought of as a company's attitude and conduct toward its employees, customers, community, and stockholders. High standards of ethical behavior demand that a firm treat each party that it deals with in a fair and honest manner. A firm's commitment to business ethics can be measured by the tendency of the firm and its employees to adhere to laws and regulations relating to such factors as product safety and quality, fair employment practices, fair marketing and selling practices, the use of confidential information for personal gain, community involvement, bribery, and illegal payments to foreign governments to obtain business.

There are many instances of firms engaging in unethical behavior. For example, in recent years the employees of several prominent Wall Street investment banking houses have been sentenced to prison for illegally using insider information on proposed mergers for their own personal gain, and E. F. Hutton, a large brokerage firm, lost its independence through a forced merger after it was convicted of cheating its banks out of millions of dollars in a check kiting scheme. Drexel Burnham Lambert, one of the largest investment banking firms, went bankrupt, and its "junk bond king," Michael Milken, who had earned $550 million in just one year, was sentenced to 10 years in prison plus charged a huge fine for securities-law violations. Recently, Salomon Brothers was implicated in a Treasury-auction bidding scandal which resulted in the removal of key officers and a significant reorganization of the firm.

In spite of all this, the results of a recent study indicate that the executives of most major firms in the United States believe that their firms should, and do, try to maintain high ethical standards in all of their business dealings. Furthermore, most executives believe that there is a positive correlation between ethics and long-run profitability. For example, Chemical Bank suggested that ethical behavior has increased its profitability because such behavior (1) avoids fines and legal expenses, (2) builds public trust, (3) attracts business from customers who appreciate and support its policies, (4) attracts and keeps employees of the highest caliber, and (5) supports the economic viability of the communities in which it operates.

Most firms today have in place strong codes of ethical behavior, and about half of all large firms conduct training programs designed to ensure that all employees understand the correct behavior in different business situations. However, it is imperative that top management — the chairman, president, and vice-presidents — be openly committed to ethical behavior, and that they communicate this commitment through their own personal actions as well as through company policies, directives, and punishment/reward systems.

SELF-TEST QUESTIONS

How would you define "business ethics"?

Is "being ethical" good for profits in the long run? In the short run?

AGENCY RELATIONSHIPS

It has been recognized for a long time that firms' managers may have personal goals that compete with shareholder wealth maximization. The fact that managers are empowered by the owners of the firm—the shareholders—to make decisions creates a potential conflict of interest that falls under a general concept called *agency.*

An *agency relationship* arises whenever one or more individuals, called *principals,* hire one or more other individuals, called *agents,* to perform some service and then delegate decision-making authority to the agents. Within the financial management context, the primary agency relationships are those (1) between stockholders and managers and (2) between debtholders and stockholders.[7]

AGENCY CONFLICTS

A potential agency conflict arises whenever the manager of a firm owns less than 100 percent of the firm's common stock. If a firm is a proprietorship managed by the owner, the owner-manager will take actions to maximize his or her own welfare or, in economic terms, utility. The owner-manager will probably measure utility primarily by personal wealth, but other factors, such as leisure time and perquisites, will be traded off against personal wealth in the utility maximizing process.[8] Thus, not only will the owner-manager derive all of the benefits from actions that maximize the business's value, but he or she will also bear all of the costs of leisure time and perquisite consumption. However, if the owner-manager relinquishes a portion of his or her ownership by selling some of the firm's stock to outside investors, a potential conflict of interest, called an *agency conflict,* arises. For example, the owner-manager may now decide to lead a more relaxed life-style and not work as strenuously to maximize shareholder wealth, because less of this wealth will now accrue to the owner-manager. Also, the owner-manager may decide to consume more perquisites, because some of the cost of perquisite consumption will now be borne by the outside shareholders. In essence, the fact that the owner-manager will not gain all the benefits of the wealth created by his or her efforts increases the incentive to take actions that are not in the best interests of all shareholders.

In most large corporations, potential agency conflicts are quite important, because large firms' managers generally own only a small percentage of the stock. In this situation, shareholder wealth maximization could take a back seat to any number of possible managerial goals. For example, many people have argued that agent/

---

[7]The classic work on the application of agency theory to financial management is Michael C. Jensen and William H. Meckling, "Theory of the Firm, Managerial Behavior, Agency Costs, and Ownership Structure," *Journal of Financial Economics,* October 1976, 305–360.

[8]*Perquisites* are executive fringe benefits such as luxurious offices, executive assistants, expense accounts, limousines, corporate jets, generous retirement plans, and the like.

managers' primary goal is to maximize the size of the firm.[9] By creating a large, rapidly growing firm, managers (1) increase their job security because a hostile takeover is less likely; (2) increase their own power, status, and salaries; and (3) create more opportunities for their lower- and middle-level managers. Furthermore, since the managers of most large firms own only an infinitesimal percentage of the stock, it has been argued that they have a voracious appetite for salaries and perquisites and that they generously contribute corporate dollars to their favorite charities because outside stockholders bear most of the cost.

AGENCY COSTS

Obviously, managers can be encouraged to act in the stockholders' best interests through incentives, constraints, and punishments. But these tools are effective only if shareholders can observe all of the actions taken by managers. A *moral hazard* problem, wherein agents take unobserved actions in their own interests, arises because it is virtually impossible for shareholders to monitor all managerial actions. In general, to reduce agency conflicts and the moral hazard problem, stockholders must incur *agency costs,* which include all costs borne by shareholders to encourage managers to maximize shareholder wealth rather than act in their own self-interests. There are three major categories of agency costs: (1) expenditures to monitor managerial actions, such as audit costs; (2) expenditures to structure the organization in a way that will limit undesirable managerial behavior, such as appointing outside investors to the board of directors; and (3) opportunity costs which are incurred when shareholder-imposed restrictions, such as requirements for stockholder votes on certain issues, limit the ability of managers to take actions that contribute to shareholder wealth.

   In the absence of any shareholder efforts to affect managerial behavior, and hence with zero agency costs, there will almost certainly be some loss of shareholder wealth due to improper managerial actions. Conversely, agency costs would be very high if shareholders attempted to ensure that every managerial action coincided exactly with shareholder interests. Thus, the optimal amount of agency costs to be borne by shareholders should be viewed like any other investment decision—agency costs should be increased as long as each dollar spent returns more than a dollar in shareholder wealth.

MANAGERIAL INCENTIVES

There are two extreme positions regarding how to deal with shareholder–manager agency conflicts. At one extreme, if a firm's managers were compensated solely on the basis of stock price changes, agency costs would be low because managers would have a great deal of incentive to maximize shareholder wealth. However, it

---

[9]See J. R. Wildsmith, *Managerial Theories of the Firm* (New York: Dunellen, 1974).

would be difficult, if not impossible, to hire competent managers under these terms, because the firm's earnings stream would be affected by economic events that were not under managerial control. At the other extreme, stockholders could monitor every managerial action, but this would be very costly and inefficient. The optimal solution lies somewhere between the extremes, where executive compensation is tied to performance but some monitoring is also done. In addition to monitoring, the following mechanisms encourage managers to act in shareholders' interests: (1) performance-based incentive plans, (2) direct intervention by shareholders, (3) the threat of firing, and (4) the threat of takeover.

Performance-Based Incentive Plans.   Firms are increasingly tying managers' compensation to the company's performance by instituting performance-based incentive plans. In the 1950s and 1960s, most of these plans involved *executive stock options,* which allow managers to purchase stock at some time in the future at a given price. Here the options have value only if the market price of the stock rises above the exercise price of the option. These plans relied on the assumption that allowing managers to purchase stock at a fixed price would provide an incentive for them to take actions that would increase the stock's price. This type of plan lost favor in the 1970s, however, because the options generally did not pay off; the stock market declined during the 1970s because of rising interest rates, so stock prices did not necessarily reflect managerial performance. Further, it was recognized that if interest rates fall in the economy, stock prices will tend to rise, even for poorly managed firms. This situation existed during the 1980s. Since incentive plans should be based on factors over which managers have control, and since managers cannot control broad market movements, stock option plans proved to be poor incentive devices.

Because of concerns over stock option plans, there has been a trend away from the exclusive use of such plans as managerial incentives. Whereas 61 of the 100 largest U.S. firms used stock options as their sole incentive compensation device in 1970, not one of the largest 100 companies relied exclusively on such a plan in 1993. Rather, almost all firms are now using some form of performance shares. *Performance shares* are shares of stock given to executives on the basis of performance as defined by objective measures such as earnings per share, return on assets, return on equity, and so forth. For example, Honeywell uses growth in earnings per share as its primary performance measure. The firm has two overlapping four-year periods, beginning two years apart. At the start of each period, participating executives are allocated a certain number of performance shares, say, 10,000 shares for the president down to 1,000 shares for a lower-level manager. If the company achieves, say, a targeted 13 percent average annual growth in earnings per share, the managers will earn 100 percent of their shares. If corporate performance is above the target, Honeywell's managers can earn even more shares, up to a maximum of 130 percent, which requires a 16 percent growth rate. However, if growth is below 13 percent, they get less than 100 percent of the shares, and below a 9 percent growth rate they get none. Executives must remain with the firm through the entire performance period (four years) to qualify for the performance shares.

Performance shares will have value even when the company's stock price remains flat or decreases because of poor stock market conditions, whereas stock options have no value under similar conditions, even though managers may have been successful in boosting per-share earnings. Of course, the value of the performance shares received depends on market performance, because 1,000 shares of Honeywell stock are a lot more valuable if the stock sells for $60 than if it sells for only $40.

All incentive-based compensation plans—executive stock options, performance shares, profit-based bonuses, and so forth—are supposed to accomplish two goals. First, they offer executives an incentive to take actions that will contribute to shareholder wealth maximization. Second, incentive compensation plans help companies attract and retain managers with the confidence to stake their financial future on their own abilities and motivation, and such individuals make the best top-level executives. Well-designed plans can accomplish both goals.

Direct Intervention by Shareholders.   Although a great deal of stock is owned by individuals, an increasing percentage is owned by institutional investors such as insurance companies, pension funds, and mutual funds. Indeed, in 1993 more than half of all stock was owned by institutions, and the institutional money managers have the clout, if they choose to use it, to exercise considerable influence over a firm's operations. In fact, the ownership of some firms is dominated by institutional investors; for example, Lotus Development has 82 percent institutional ownership, and Reynolds Metals has 77 percent. Institutional investors can influence a firm's managers in two ways. First, they can talk with a firm's management and make suggestions regarding how the business should be run. In effect, institutional investors can act as lobbyists for the body of stockholders. Second, any shareholder who owns at least $1,000 of a company's stock for one year can sponsor a proposal which must be voted on at the annual stockholders' meeting, even if the proposal is opposed by management. Although shareholder-sponsored proposals are nonbinding and are limited to issues outside day-to-day operations, the voting results of these proposals are clearly heard by top management.

To illustrate the increasingly active role played by institutional shareholders, consider what happened recently at Lockheed, a major defense contractor. When a new CEO, Daniel Tellep, took over the company, he instituted a restructuring plan that was supposed to yield excellent returns to shareholders, but things did not work out, and the stock price dropped from $55 to $36. Lockheed's institutional investors, who owned 46 percent of the firm's stock, launched a series of shareholder proposals that (1) would remove the company's poison pill, (2) would require confidential proxy voting so management would not know who was voting for or against any management or shareholder proposals, and (3) would eliminate certain antitakeover provisions by amending the company's charter.[10] Clearly,

---

[10]A *poison pill* is an action by managers that makes the firm effectively worthless to potential acquirers who might otherwise be willing to buy the firm at a large premium over the current market price. In general, poison pills are thought to offer more protection to managers than to stockholders. Also,

these proposals would make Lockheed a more likely takeover target, and Tellep and the board opposed them all. Separately, raider Harold Simmons had bought 19 percent of Lockheed's stock and was asking for 6 seats on the 15-person board. Management said no, so Simmons announced his own slate of candidates for the board. The institutional investors then told both Tellep and Simmons that they could only support a board that would agree to the shareholder proposals, so both Tellep and Simmons agreed to support them. When the votes were counted, Tellep's board candidates won, but all three proposals passed. Seeing the power of the institutions, Tellep offered them three seats on an expanded board. In spite of this, shareholder pressure on Tellep remains. A major institutional investor said, "We see that Simmons hasn't sold his stock, we haven't, and the other large holders haven't. . . . But if things don't improve," he added, "next year the vote might be different."

Why are institutions suddenly taking such an interest in the management of companies they own? The primary reason is that they no longer have an easy exit from the market. Their portfolios are so big that if they decided to dump a stock in a hurry, the stock's price would take a free-fall. Rather than throwing up their hands and selling the stock, many institutional investors have decided to stay and work with management. Also, there has been considerable pressure on pension fund managers from the Department of Labor, which supervises pension fund investment practices under the Employee Retirement Income Security Act (ERISA). Under ERISA, pension fund managers are required to vote in the best interests of the funds' beneficiaries, which often means voting against corporate management. Finally, the Securities and Exchange Commission (SEC) has been expanding the number of issues that shareholders can address in shareholder-sponsored proposals. In its latest move, the SEC ruled that executive compensation is a legal topic for proposals. In the past, executive compensation was classified as a matter of "ordinary business" and hence not addressable in shareholder proposals. Similarly, the SEC recently forced several companies to allow shareholders to vote on "golden parachute" executive retirement packages.[11]

The most fundamental change that institutional investors support is a more independent board of directors—institutional investors see a management-controlled board as the weak link in the chain of managerial accountability to shareholders. Too often, according to most experts on corporate control, the directors are in management's hip pocket, and that is why institutional investors are pressing for truly independent boards. In fact, many institutional investors would like to see

---

confidential proxy voting is important because corporate executives have been known to threaten to move pension fund assets from fund managers who vote against management. Because the executives of one company often serve on other companies' boards, a "club" attitude prevails, and the CEO of Company A might take action against his or her pension fund manager if that manager voted against the management of Company B. Company B's management, of course, would be expected to protect Company A's management in return. Because of this situation, public pension fund managers, such as the managers of the California Public Employees' Retirement System (CALPERS), have thus far taken the lead in exercising their voting power.

[11]A *golden parachute* is a contract provision that gives a corporate executive a large severance payment if the company is taken over by another company and the executive loses his or her job.

an outside director installed as chairman of the board, as was done in our GM example, because they do not trust an inside chairman to serve the shareholders first and his or her management's interests second.

The Threat of Firing. Until recently, the probability of a large firm's management being ousted by its stockholders was so remote that it posed little threat. This situation existed because the ownership of most firms was so widely distributed, and management's control over the voting mechanism so strong, that it was almost impossible for dissident stockholders to get the votes needed to overthrow the managers. However, as noted previously, that situation is changing.

Consider the case of Baltimore Bancorp. Recently, its chairman, Harry L. Robinson, spurned a friendly $17-per-share takeover offer from rival First Maryland Bancorp. Dismayed stockholders saw the stock price drop to $5 a share, and, led by a Baltimore businessman, they revolted. A slate of dissident directors was nominated, and they lined up the support of T. Rowe Price, a Baltimore mutual fund management company which held about 9 percent of the bank's stock. At Baltimore Bancorp's next annual meeting, shareholders elected the dissident directors, who won all 6 of the board seats that were up for election. Subsequently, the board ousted Robinson, and a new management team was put in place.

For every obvious case of shareholders' exercising their ownership rights and ousting current management, such as at Baltimore Bancorp, there have been many more less obvious occurrences. In recent years, the CEOs or other top executives at American Express, Goodyear, General Motors, and IBM have all resigned amid speculation that their departures were connected to their companies' poor performance. More and more, the reasons for executive departures are shifting from "poor health" and "personal reasons" to "at the request of the board."

The Threat of Takeover. *Hostile takeovers* (when management does not want the firm to be taken over) are most likely to occur when a firm's stock is undervalued relative to its potential because of poor management. In a hostile takeover, the managers of the acquired firm are generally fired, and any who are able to stay on lose the autonomy they had prior to the acquisition. Thus, managers have a strong incentive to take actions which maximize stock prices. In the words of one company president, "If you want to keep control, don't let your company's stock sell at a bargain price."

ANOTHER AGENCY CONFLICT: STOCKHOLDERS VERSUS CREDITORS

In addition to the agency conflict between stockholders and managers, a second agency conflict also merits discussion — that between creditors and stockholders. Creditors have a claim on part of the firm's earnings stream (the interest and principal payments on the debt) as well as a claim on the firm's assets in the event of bankruptcy. However, the stockholders have control — through the firm's managers — of the decisions that affect the profitability and risk of the firm. Creditors lend funds to a firm at rates that are based, among other factors, (1) on the riskiness of the firm's existing assets, (2) on expectations concerning the riskiness

of future asset additions, (3) on the firm's existing capital structure (that is, the amount of debt financing used), and (4) on expectations concerning future capital structure decisions. These are the primary determinants of the riskiness of a firm's cash flows, and hence the safety of its debt issues, so creditors base their required rates of return on these factors.

Now suppose the stockholders, acting through management, cause the firm to take on a large new project that has a greater risk than was anticipated by the firm's creditors. This increased risk will cause the required rate of return on the firm's debt to increase, which in turn will cause the value of the outstanding debt to fall. If the risky capital investment is successful, all of the benefits will go to the firm's stockholders, because creditors' returns are fixed at the old, low-risk rate. However, if the project is unsuccessful, the bondholders will have to share in the losses. From the stockholders' point of view, the capital investment game has a payoff of "heads I win, tails you lose," which is obviously not a good game for the creditors. Similarly, suppose managers increase the firm's level of debt, without changing its assets, in an effort to leverage up stockholders' return on equity. If the old debt does not have seniority over the new debt, its value will decrease, because an increased number of creditors will have claims against the firm's cash flows and assets. In both the riskier asset and the increased leverage situations, the firm's stockholders would gain at the expense of the firm's creditors.

It should be noted that in most situations, actions that maximize a firm's total value (the market value of its debt and equity) will also maximize its stock price. However, a situation could arise in which a firm's total value falls but its stock price rises. This situation can occur if the value of the firm's outstanding debt falls by more than the increase in the value of the firm's equity. In this case, the overall value of the firm can decrease even as the stock price increases. It is easy to see that problems can arise when managers favor one group, the stockholders, over another, the bondholders.

Can and should stockholders, through their managers/agents, try to expropriate wealth from the firm's creditors? In general, the answer is no. First, such behavior is unethical, and there is no room for unethical behavior in the business world. Second, if such attempts are made, creditors will protect themselves against stockholders by placing restrictive covenants in future debt agreements. Finally, if creditors perceive that a firm's managers are trying to take advantage of them, they will either refuse to deal further with the firm or else will charge a higher than normal interest rate to compensate for the risk of possible exploitation. Thus, firms which deal unfairly with creditors either lose access to the debt markets or are saddled with high interest rates and restrictive covenants, all of which are detrimental to shareholders.

In view of these constraints, it follows that to best serve their shareholders, managers must also play fairly with creditors, which means abiding by both the letter and the spirit of credit agreements. Managers, as agents of both shareholders and creditors, must act in a manner that is fairly balanced between the interests of the two classes of security holders. Similarly, because of other constraints and sanctions, management actions which would expropriate wealth from any of the firm's other *stakeholders,* including its employees, customers, suppliers, and com-

munity, will ultimately be to the detriment of its shareholders. We conclude that in our society, acting in the best interests of shareholders requires the fair treatment of all parties whose economic position is affected by managerial decisions.

SELF-TEST QUESTIONS

What are agency conflicts? Within corporate finance, what are the two major agency conflicts?

What are agency costs, and who bears them?

What are some mechanisms that encourage managers to act in the best interests of stockholders? In the best interests of bondholders?

Why should managers not take actions that are clearly unfair to any of the firm's stakeholders?

MANAGERIAL ACTIONS TO MAXIMIZE SHAREHOLDER WEALTH

To maximize the price of a firm's stock, what types of actions should its management take? First, consider the question of stock prices versus profits: Will *profit maximization* also result in stock price maximization? In answering this question, we must consider the matter of total corporate profits versus *earnings per share (EPS)*.

For example, suppose Xerox had 100 million shares outstanding and earned $400 million, or $4 per share. If you owned 100 shares of the stock, your share of the total profits would be $400. Now suppose Xerox sold another 100 million shares and invested the funds received in assets which produced $100 million of income. Total income would rise to $500 million, but earnings per share would decline from $4 to $500/200 = $2.50. Now your share of the firm's earnings would be only $250, down from $400. You (and other current stockholders) would have suffered an earnings dilution, even though total corporate profits had risen. Therefore, other things held constant, *if management is interested in the well-being of its current stockholders, it should concentrate on earnings per share rather than on total corporate profits.*

Will maximization of expected earnings per share always maximize stockholder welfare, or should other factors be considered? Think about the *timing of the earnings*. Suppose Xerox had one project that would cause earnings per share to rise by $0.20 per year for 5 years, or $1 in total, while another project would have no effect on earnings for 4 years but would increase earnings by $1.25 in the fifth year. Which project is better? In other words, is $0.20 per year for 5 years better or worse than $1.25 in Year 5? The answer depends on which project adds the most to the value of the stock, which in turn depends on the time value of money to investors. Thus, timing is an important reason to concentrate on wealth as measured by the price of the stock rather than on earnings alone.

Another issue relates to *risk*. Suppose one project is expected to increase earnings per share by $1, while another is expected to raise earnings by $1.20 per

share. The first project is not very risky; if it is undertaken, earnings will almost certainly rise by about $1 per share. However, the other project is quite risky, so, although our best guess is that earnings will rise by $1.20 per share, we must recognize the possibility that there may be no increase whatsoever, or even a loss. Depending on how averse stockholders are to risk, the first project might be preferable to the second.

The riskiness inherent in projected earnings per share (EPS) also depends on *how the firm is financed.* As we shall see, many firms go bankrupt every year, and the greater the use of debt, the greater the threat of bankruptcy. *Consequently, while the use of debt financing may increase projected EPS, debt also increases the riskiness of projected future earnings.*

Another issue is the matter of paying dividends to stockholders versus retaining earnings and reinvesting them in the firm, thereby causing the earnings stream to grow over time. Stockholders like cash dividends, but they also like the growth in EPS that results from plowing earnings back into the business. The financial manager must decide exactly how much of the current earnings to pay out as dividends rather than to retain and reinvest—this is called the *dividend policy decision.* The optimal dividend policy is the one that maximizes the firm's stock price.

We see, then, that the firm's stock price is dependent on the following factors:

1. Projected earnings per share
2. Timing of the earnings stream
3. Riskiness of the projected earnings
4. Use of debt
5. Dividend policy

Every significant corporate decision should be analyzed in terms of its effect on these factors and, hence, on the price of the firm's stock. For example, suppose Occidental Petroleum's coal division is considering opening a new mine. If this is done, can it be expected to increase EPS? Is there a chance that costs will exceed estimates, that prices and output will fall below projections, and that EPS will be reduced because the new mine was opened? How long will it take for the new mine to show a profit? How should the capital required to open the mine be raised? If debt is used, by how much will this increase Occidental's riskiness? Should Occidental reduce its current dividends and use the cash thus saved to finance the project, or should it maintain its dividends and finance the mine with external capital? Financial management is designed to help answer questions like these, plus many more.

SELF-TEST QUESTIONS

Will profit maximization always result in stock price maximization?

Identify five factors which affect the firm's stock price, and explain the effects of each of them.

THE EXTERNAL ENVIRONMENT

Although managerial actions affect the value of a firm's stock, external factors also influence stock prices. Included among these factors are legal constraints, the general level of economic activity, tax laws, and conditions in the stock market. Figure 1-2 diagrams these general relationships. Working within the set of external constraints shown in the box at the extreme left, management makes a set of long-run strategic policy decisions which chart a future course for the firm. These policy decisions, along with the general level of economic activity and the level of corporate income taxes, influence the firm's expected profitability, the timing of its cash flows, their eventual transfer to stockholders in the form of dividends, and the degree of risk inherent in projected earnings and dividends. Profitability, timing, and risk all affect the price of the firm's stock, but so does another factor, conditions in the stock market as a whole, because all stock prices tend to move up and down together to some extent.

SELF-TEST QUESTION

Identify some factors beyond a firm's control which influence its stock price.

ORGANIZATION OF THE BOOK

The primary goal of management is to help maximize the value of the firm. To achieve this goal, managers must have a general understanding of how businesses are organized, how financial markets operate, how interest rates are determined,

FIGURE 1-2 SUMMARY OF MAJOR FACTORS AFFECTING STOCK PRICES

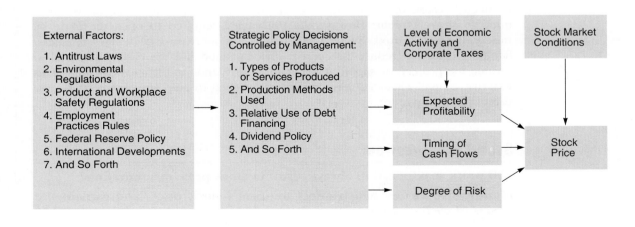

how the tax system operates, and how accounting data are used to evaluate a business's performance. In addition, they must have a good understanding of some fundamental concepts, including discounted cash flow analysis, risk analysis, asset valuation, and evaluation of investment opportunities. This background information is essential for anyone involved with making the kinds of decisions that affect the value of a firm's securities.

The organization of this book reflects these considerations, so we begin, in Part I, with some background information on financial markets, institutions, taxes, and interest rates, plus a discussion of how accounting data are used to evaluate the firm's past performance and present condition.

Part II covers the fundamental concepts upon which financial management is built — risk analysis, the relationship between risk and return, discounted cash flow analysis, and the formal models used to evaluate securities and other assets. The concepts discussed in Parts I and II are used throughout the remainder of the book.

Part III covers *capital budgeting,* a key financial management decision area which involves investments in fixed assets. In a sense, firms make two types of decisions: *strategic decisions* and *operating decisions.* Every successful firm of any size has a business plan, which is a guide to future operations, and specific decisions are made within the framework of the plan. For example, if General Motors plans to revamp its North American operations to increase its share of the U.S. auto market, then it will have to make investments in equipment to automate some of its plants. Specific investment decisions will be made within the framework of the corporate plan, using the capital budgeting analysis techniques discussed in Part III.

If GM or any other company is to acquire new assets, those assets will have to be financed, and Part IV deals with alternative financing strategies. As you will see, the primary financing decision relates to the use of debt versus equity, or the *capital structure decision.* There are advantages and disadvantages to using debt, and capital structure decisions can have a profound effect on a firm's risk, profitability, and stock price. A related decision, the *dividend policy decision,* involves how much of its earnings the firm should retain in the business to support growth versus paying them out as dividends to the stockholders. Stockholders like the growth that reinvested earnings provides, but they also like cash dividends, so management must decide how to allocate earnings between retentions and dividends.

Parts I through IV deal to a large extent with theory and with strategic planning. These are important topics, but the execution of strategic plans is equally important in determining a firm's success. In the remainder of the book, we show how theory is applied to operating decisions. We begin Part V with a discussion of long- and short-run financial planning. Most well-run businesses use computer models as an integral part of their planning process, because such models are ideally suited for showing what can be expected under different financial policies and under different economic conditions. For example, General Motors has a long-term model that forecasts the company's financial requirements, its key financial ratios, and its earnings per share under different financial plans. The projected outcomes vary significantly depending on both financial decisions and the state of the

economy — some plans will produce better results if the economy is strong, but other plans work better if the economy is weak. These models can be used to estimate the effects of different capital budgeting decisions, capital structure policies, dividend policies, and working capital decisions, and they can be applied either to the company as a whole or to specific operating units. We describe the key elements of computer models, which will help you understand how financing and investment decisions affect one another and the firm.

Part VI builds on the planning/forecasting framework developed in Part V, with an emphasis on current assets and current liabilities, or *working capital management.* Working capital management involves both policy and implementation. For example, companies make policy decisions regarding the optimal amounts of inventory, accounts receivable, and cash to hold, and about the optimal types and amounts of short-term credit to use. However, these policy decisions always recognize that the optimal levels of current assets and types of short-term credit are directly related to the level of sales, that sales levels can change quickly, and, hence, that working capital decisions must be made continuously and in "real time." Some people regard short-term decisions as being "less glamorous" than long-term decisions, but (1) most corporate failures result from a failure at the operating level, not at the strategic level, (2) 90 percent of all business students will spend 90 percent of their time dealing with current assets and liabilities, and (3) success in short-term operations is a requirement for promotion to the strategic arena, where long-term decisions are made.

Part VII focuses on the institutional details of long-term financing. Here we discuss the key features of stocks and bonds, the characteristics of warrants, convertibles, and lease financing, and procedures for issuing securities.

Finally, in Part VIII, we take up several special topics, including bankruptcy, mergers, and multinational financial operations, which can best be handled after you have covered the basics presented in the earlier chapters.

It is worth noting that there is no perfect organization for a book such as this one. Therefore, some instructors may choose to cover the chapters in a sequence different from the order in the book. Accordingly, we wrote the chapters in a modular, self-contained format, which will make reordering relatively easy.

SUMMARY

This chapter has provided an overview of financial management. The key concepts covered are listed below.

▶ Finance consists of three interrelated areas: (1) *money and capital markets,* (2) *investments,* and (3) *financial management.*

▶ Financial management has undergone significant changes over time, but four issues have received the most emphasis in recent years: (1) *inflation* and its effects on interest rates, (2) *deregulation of financial institutions,* (3) a dramatic increase in the *use of telecommunications* for transmitting information *and of computers* for analyzing the effects of alternative financial decisions,

and (4) the increased importance of *global financial markets and business operations.*

▶ *Financial managers* are responsible for *obtaining and using funds* in a way that will *maximize the value of their firms.*

▶ The three main forms of business organization are the *sole proprietorship,* the *partnership,* and the *corporation.*

▶ Although each form of organization offers some advantages and disadvantages, *most business is conducted by corporations because this organizational form maximizes most firms' values.*

▶ The primary goal of management should be to *maximize stockholders' wealth,* and this means *maximizing the price of the firm's stock.* Furthermore, actions which maximize stock prices also increase social welfare.

▶ An *agency relationship* arises whenever one or more individuals (principals) hire one or more other individuals (agents) to perform some service and then delegate decision-making authority to the agents. The primary agency relationships within financial management are those between stockholders and managers and those between debtholders and stockholders.

▶ A *moral hazard* problem, wherein agents take unobserved actions that are in their own best interests, can arise, because it is virtually impossible for shareholders to monitor all managerial actions.

▶ To reduce potential agency conflicts and moral hazard problems, stockholders must incur *agency costs.* There are three major categories of agency costs: (1) expenditures to monitor managerial actions, (2) expenditures to structure the organization in a way that will limit undesirable managerial behavior, and (3) opportunity costs which are incurred when shareholder-imposed restrictions limit managers' ability to take actions that contribute to shareholder wealth.

▶ In addition to *monitoring,* there are a number of ways to encourage managers to act in the best interests of stockholders, including (1) *performance-based incentive plans,* (2) *direct intervention by shareholders,* (3) *the threat of firing,* and (4) *the threat of takeover.*

▶ The *price of the firm's stock* depends on the firm's *projected earnings per share,* the *timing of its earnings,* the *riskiness of the projected earnings,* its *use of debt,* and its *dividend policy.*

QUESTIONS

1-1 Define each of the following terms:

a. Proprietorship; partnership; corporation

b. Stockholder wealth maximization

c. Social responsibility; business ethics

d. Normal profits; normal rate of return

e. Agency relationships; agency costs

f. Leveraged buyout (LBO)

g. Poison pill; golden parachute

h. Performance shares; executive stock options

i. Profit maximization

j. Earnings per share

k. Dividend policy

1-2 What are the three principal forms of business organization? What are the advantages and disadvantages of each?

1-3 Would the "normal" rate of return on investment be the same in all industries? Would "normal" rates of return change over time? Explain.

1-4 Would the role of the financial manager be likely to increase or decrease in importance relative to other executives if the rate of inflation increased? Explain.

1-5 Should stockholder wealth maximization be thought of as a long-term or a short-term goal —for example, if one action would probably increase the firm's stock price from a current level of $40 to $50 in 6 months and then to $60 in 5 years, but another action would probably keep the stock at $40 for several years but then increase it to $80 in 5 years, which action would be better? Can you think of some specific corporate actions which might have these general tendencies?

1-6 Drawing on your background in accounting, can you think of any accounting procedure differences that might make it difficult to compare the relative performance of different firms?

1-7 Would the management of a firm in an oligopolistic or in a competitive industry be more likely to engage in what might be called "socially conscious" practices? Explain your reasoning.

1-8 What is the difference between stock price maximization and profit maximization? Under what conditions might profit maximization not lead to stock price maximization?

1-9 If you were the president of a large, publicly owned corporation, would you make decisions to maximize stockholders' welfare or your own personal interests? What are some actions stockholders could take to insure that management's interests and those of stockholders coincided? What are some other factors that might influence management's actions?

1-10 The president of International Microchips Inc. (IMI) made this statement in the company's annual report: "IMI's primary goal is to increase the value of the common stockholders' equity over time." Later on in the report, the following announcements were made:

a. The company contributed $2 million to the symphony orchestra in Seattle, its headquarters city.

b. The company is spending $600 million to open a new plant in Venezuela. No revenues will be produced by the plant for 4 years, so earnings will be depressed during this period versus what they would have been had the decision not been made to open the new plant.

c. The company is increasing its relative use of debt. Whereas assets were formerly financed with 30 percent debt and 70 percent equity, henceforth the financing mix will be 45/55.

d. The company uses a great deal of electricity in its manufacturing operations, and it generates most of this power itself. Plans are to utilize nuclear fuel rather than coal to produce electricity in the future.

e. The company has been paying out half of its earnings as dividends and retaining the other half. Henceforth, it will pay out only 40 percent as dividends.

Discuss how each of these actions would be reacted to by IMI's stockholders, customers, and labor force, and then how each action might affect IMI's stock price.

SELECTED ADDITIONAL REFERENCES

For alternative views on firms' goals and objectives, see the following articles:

Cornell, Bradford, and Alan C. Shapiro, "Corporate Stakeholders and Corporate Finance," *Financial Management,* Spring 1987, 5–14.

Donaldson, Gordon, "Financial Goals: Management versus Stockholders," *Harvard Business Review,* May-June 1963, 116–129.

Meckling, William H., and Michael C. Jensen, "Reflections on the Corporation as a Social Invention," *Midland Corporate Finance Journal,* Fall 1983, 6–15.

Seitz, Neil, "Shareholder Goals, Firm Goals and Firm Financing Decisions," *Financial Management,* Autumn 1982, 20–26.

Treynor, Jack L., "The Financial Objective of the Widely Held Corporation," *Financial Analysts Journal,* March-April 1981, 68–71.

The following articles extend our discussion of agency relationships:

Barnea, Amir, Robert A. Haugen, and Lemma W. Senbet, "Market Imperfections, Agency Problems, and Capital Structure: A Review," *Financial Management,* Summer 1981, 7–22.

Hand, John H., William P. Lloyd, and Robert B. Rogow, "Agency Relationships in the Close Corporation," *Financial Management,* Spring 1982, 25–30.

For a general review of academic finance, together with an extensive bibliography of key research articles, see

Cooley, Philip L., and J. Louis Heck, "Significant Contributions to Finance Literature," *Financial Management,* Tenth Anniversary Issue 1981, 23–33.

Weston, J. Fred, "Developments in Finance Theory," *Financial Management,* Tenth Anniversary Issue 1981, 5–22.

For more information on managerial compensation, see

Cooley, Philip L., and Charles E. Edwards, "Ownership Effects on Managerial Salaries in Small Business," *Financial Management,* Winter 1982, 5–9.

Hudson, Carl D., John S. Jahera, Jr., and William P. Lloyd, "Further Evidence on the Relationship between Ownership and Performance," *Financial Review,* May 1992, 227–239.

Lambert, Richard A., and David F. Larker, "Executive Compensation, Corporate Decision-Making and Shareholder Wealth: A Review of the Evidence," *Midland Corporate Finance Journal,* Winter 1985, 6–22. The Winter 1985 issue of the *Midland Corporate Finance Journal* contains several other articles pertaining to executive compensation.

Long, Michael S., "The Incentives Behind the Adoption of Executive Stock Option Plans in U.S. Corporations," *Financial Mangement,* Autumn 1992, 12–21.

"Stern Stewart Roundtable on Management Incentive Compensation and Shareholder Value," *Journal of Applied Corporate Finance,* Summer 1992, 110–130.

For more information on the role of corporate directors, see

"Corporate Governance: The Role of Boards of Directors in Takeover Bids and Defenses," *Journal of Applied Corporate Finance,* Summer 1989, 6–35.

ANALYSIS OF FINANCIAL STATEMENTS

O*f all the documents that large companies publish, none receives as much attention as the annual report to shareholders. At some companies, top executives begin work on the report as much as six months before its publication, and most hire professional designers and writers to ensure that the final product looks sharp and reads well.*

Obviously, so much fuss would hardly be necessary if the only goal of an annual report were to inform shareholders about financial results. But, in fact, most big companies have turned their annual reports into flashy management showcases. In slick magazine format, using four-color photos, feature stories, and elaborate graphics, each firm tells the story its chairman would like to see told. Indeed, to get the desired results, most annual reports are now produced by the director of public relations instead of the chief financial officer.

Because of their puffery, annual reports have lost credibility with serious seekers of financial information. Instead, Wall Street analysts and other sophisticated investors prefer more straightforward financial disclosure documents, such as 10-Ks, which contain more detailed and unadorned information and which must by law be filed with the Securities and Exchange Commission.

Of course, a company's philosophy and personality do count, and few other documents can offer better insights into these intangibles than an annual report. Most financial analysts believe, however, that companies owe it to their investors to distinguish between the fanfare and the facts. They want to see annual reports that realistically examine the firm's business affairs and that factually discuss projects which will affect corporate performance. Indeed, they would like to see

annual reports become the equivalent of management report cards, detailing strengths and weaknesses and plans for improvement. Given such information, shareholders would be better equipped to make intelligent investment decisions.

One chief executive who agrees with the financial analysts is Warren Buffett, legendary chairman of Berkshire Hathaway and former chairman of Salomon Brothers Inc. Describing his attitude toward his readers, Buffett says, "I assume I have a very intelligent partner who has been away for a year and needs to be filled in on all that's happened." Consequently, in his chairman's letter, which begins the annual report, Buffet often admits mistakes and emphasizes the negative. For example, in one recent report he wrote, "We continue to look for ways to expand our insurance operation, but your reaction to this intent should not be unrestrained joy. Some of our expansion efforts—largely initiated by your chairman—have been lackluster, while others have been expensive failures."

Buffett also uses his letters to educate his shareholders and to help them interpret the data presented in the rest of the report. In one letter he lamented the complexities of accounting and observed, "The Yānomamö Indians employ only three numbers: one, two, and more than two. Maybe their time will come."

Buffett's letters, although probably a bit too subjective for financial reporting purists, represent a giant step in the desired direction. In fact, Berkshire Hathaway's annual reports contain no photographs, colored ink, bar charts, or graphs, freeing readers to focus on the company's financial statements and Buffett's interpretation of them. Some CEOs might contend that such a barebones approach is too dull for the average stockholder and, further, that some readers may actually be intimidated by the information overload. But Buffett would no doubt counter that, whatever its shortcomings, his approach shows much greater respect for shareholders' intelligence and capacity to understand than does the average annual report.

As you read this chapter, think about the kinds of information that corporations provide their stockholders. Do the basic financial statements provide adequate data for investment decisions? What other information might be helpful? Also, consider the pros and cons of Chairman Buffett's decision to include long, frank, and frequently self-critical letters in his company's annual reports. Would you suggest that other companies follow suit?

If management is to maximize shareholder value, it must take advantage of the firm's strengths and correct its weaknesses. Financial statement analysis involves a comparison of the firm's performance with that of other firms in the same industry. This helps management identify deficiencies and then take actions to improve performance. In this chapter, we discuss how financial managers (and investors) eval-

uate the firm's current position. Then, in later chapters, we will examine the types of actions that a financial manager can take to improve his or her company's position in the future, thus increasing the price of its stock.

The chapter should, for the most part, be a review of concepts you learned in accounting. However, accounting focuses on how financial statements are *made,* whereas our focus is on how they are *used* by management to improve the firm's performance and by investors to set a value on the firm's stock.

FINANCIAL STATEMENTS AND REPORTS

Of the various reports corporations issue to their stockholders, the *annual report* is probably the most important. Two types of information are given in this report. First, there is a verbal section, often presented as a letter from the chairman, that describes the firm's operating results during the past year and then discusses new developments that will affect future operations. Second, the annual report presents four basic financial statements—the *income statement,* the *balance sheet,* the *statement of retained earnings,* and the *statement of cash flows.* Taken together, these statements give an accounting picture of the firm's operations and financial position. Detailed data are provided for the two most recent years, along with historical summaries of key operating statistics for the past five or ten years.[1]

The quantitative and verbal information are equally important. The financial statements report *what has actually happened* to assets, earnings, and dividends over the past few years, whereas the verbal statements attempt to explain why things turned out the way they did. For example, the earnings of MicroDrive Inc., a producer of disk drives for microcomputers, dropped in 1993, to $113.5 million versus $118 million in 1992. Management reported that the drop resulted from a 3-month strike that kept the firm from fully utilizing new plant and equipment that had been financed mostly with new debt. However, management then went on to paint a more optimistic picture for the future, stating that full operations had been resumed, that several new products had been introduced, and that 1994 profits were expected to rise sharply. Of course, an increase in profitability may not occur, and analysts should compare management's past statements with subsequent results. In any event, *the information contained in an annual report is used by investors to form expectations about future earnings and dividends.* Therefore, the annual report is obviously of great interest to investors.

For illustrative purposes, we shall use data taken from MicroDrive's financial statements throughout this chapter. Formed in 1965, MicroDrive has grown stead-

---

[1]Firms also provide quarterly reports, but these are much less comprehensive than the annual reports. In addition, larger firms file even more detailed statements, giving breakdowns for each major division or subsidiary, with the Securities and Exchange Commission (SEC). These reports, called *10-K reports,* are made available to stockholders upon request to a company's corporate secretary. Finally, many larger firms also publish *statistical supplements,* which give financial statement data and key ratios going back 10 to 20 years.

TABLE 2-1		1993	1992
MICRODRIVE INC.:	Net sales	$3,000.0	$2,850
INCOME STATEMENTS	Costs excluding depreciation	$2,616.2	$2,497
FOR YEARS ENDING	Depreciation	100.0	90
DECEMBER 31	Total operating costs	$2,716.2	$2,587
(MILLIONS OF	Earnings before interest and taxes (EBIT)	$ 283.8	$ 263
DOLLARS, EXCEPT	Less interest	88.0	60
FOR PER-SHARE	Earnings before taxes (EBT)	$ 195.8	$ 203
DATA)	Taxes (40%)	78.3	81
	Net income before preferred dividends	$ 117.5	$ 122
	Preferred dividends	4.0	4
	Net income available to common stockholders	$ 113.5	$ 118
	Common dividends	$ 57.5	$ 53
	Addition to retained earnings	$ 56.0	$ 65
	Per-share data:		
	Common stock price	$23.00	$24.00
	Earnings per share (EPS)[a]	$ 2.27	$ 2.36
	Dividends per share (DPS)[a]	$ 1.15	$ 1.06

[a]There are 50,000,000 shares of common stock outstanding. Note that EPS is based on earnings after preferred dividends—that is, on net income available to common stockholders. Calculations of EPS and DPS for 1993 are as follows:

$$\text{EPS} = \frac{\text{Net income}}{\text{Common shares outstanding}} = \frac{\$113,500,000}{50,000,000} = \$2.27.$$

$$\text{DPS} = \frac{\text{Dividends paid to common stockholders}}{\text{Common shares outstanding}} = \frac{\$57,500,000}{50,000,000} = \$1.15.$$

ily and has earned a reputation for being one of the best firms in the microcomputer components industry.

THE INCOME STATEMENT

Table 2-1 gives the 1993 and 1992 *income statements* for MicroDrive. Net sales are shown at the top of each statement, after which various costs, including income taxes, are subtracted to obtain the net income available to common stockholders. A report on earnings and dividends per share is given at the bottom of the statement. In financial management, earnings per share (EPS) is called "the bottom line," denoting that of all the items on the income statement, EPS is the most important. MicroDrive earned $2.27 per share in 1993, down from $2.36 in 1992, but it still raised the dividend from $1.06 to $1.15.

THE BALANCE SHEET

The left-hand side of MicroDrive's year-end 1993 and 1992 *balance sheets,* which are given in Table 2-2, shows the firm's assets, while the right-hand side shows the

TABLE 2-2   MicroDrive Inc.: December 31 Balance Sheets (Millions of Dollars)

Assets	1993	1992	Liabilities and Equity	1993	1992
Cash	$ 10	$ 15	Accounts payable	$ 60	$ 30
Marketable securities	0	65	Notes payable	110	60
Accounts receivable	375	315	Accruals	140	130
Inventories	615	415	Total current liabilities	$ 310	$ 220
Total current assets	$1,000	$ 810	Long-term bonds	754	580
Net plant and equipment	1,000	870	Total debt	$1,064	$ 800
			Preferred stock (400,000 shares)	$ 40	$ 40
			Common stock (50,000,000 shares)	$ 50	$ 50
			Paid-in capital	80	80
			Retained earnings	766	710
			Common equity	$ 896	$ 840
Total assets	$2,000	$1,680	Total liabilities and equity	$2,000	$1,680

Note: The bonds have a sinking fund requirement of $20 million a year. Sinking funds are discussed in Chapter 20, but in brief, a sinking fund simply involves the periodic repayment of long-term debt. Thus, MicroDrive was required to pay off $20 million of its mortgage bonds during 1992. The current portion of the long-term debt is included in notes payable here, although in a more detailed balance sheet it would be shown as a separate item under current liabilities.

liabilities and equity, or the claims against these assets. The assets are listed in order of their "liquidity," or the length of time it typically takes to convert them to cash. The claims are listed in the order in which they must be paid: Accounts payable must generally be paid within 30 days, notes are payable within 90 days, and so on, down to the stockholders' equity accounts, which represent ownership and need never be "paid off."

Some additional points about the balance sheet are worth noting:

1. Cash versus other assets. Although the assets are all stated in terms of dollars, only cash represents actual money. Marketable securities are highly liquid investments which can be converted to cash quickly; receivables are bills others owe MicroDrive; inventories show the dollars the company has invested in raw materials, work-in-process, and finished goods available for sale; and net plant and equipment reflect the amount of money MicroDrive paid for its fixed assets when it acquired those assets at some time in the past, less accumulated depreciation. MicroDrive can write checks at present for a total of $10 million (versus current liabilities of $310 million due within a year). The noncash assets should produce cash over time, but they do not represent cash in hand, and the amount of cash they would bring if they were sold today could be higher or lower than the values at which they are carried on the books.

2. Liabilities versus stockholders' equity. The claims against assets are of two types—liabilities (or money the company owes) and the stockholders' own-

ership position.[2] The *common equity,* or *net worth,* is a residual. For example, for 1993,

$$\text{Assets} \quad - \quad \text{Liabilities} \quad - \text{ Preferred stock } = \text{ Common equity.}$$
$$\$2,000,000,000 - \$1,064,000,000 - \quad \$40,000,000 \quad = \quad \$896,000,000.$$

Suppose assets decline in value—for example, suppose some of the accounts receivable are written off as bad debts. Liabilities and preferred stock remain constant, so the value of the common equity must decline. Therefore, the risk of asset value fluctuations is borne by the common stockholders. Note, however, that if asset values rise (perhaps because of inflation), these benefits will accrue exclusively to the common stockholders.

3.   Preferred versus common stock.   As we will see in Chapter 19, preferred stock is a hybrid, or a cross between common stock and debt. In the event of bankruptcy, preferred stock ranks below debt but above common stock. Also, the preferred dividend is fixed, so preferred stockholders do not benefit if the company's earnings grow. Finally, many firms do not use any preferred stock, and those that do generally do not use very much of it. Therefore, when the term "equity" is used in finance, we generally mean "common equity" unless the word "total" is included.

4.   Breakdown of the common equity account.   A detailed discussion of the common equity accounts is given in Chapter 19, but a brief preview of that discussion is useful here. First, note that the common equity section is divided into three accounts—common stock, paid-in capital, and retained earnings. The *retained earnings* account is built up over time as the firm "saves" a part of its earnings rather than paying all earnings out as dividends. The other two common equity accounts arise from the issuance of stock to raise capital.

The breakdown of the common equity accounts is important for some purposes but not for others. For example, a potential stockholder would want to know whether the company actually earned the funds reported in its equity accounts or whether the funds came mainly from selling stock. A potential creditor, on the other hand, would be more interested in the total amount of money the owners put up than in the breakdown of accounts. In the remainder of this chapter, we generally aggregate the three common equity accounts and call this sum *common equity* or *net worth.*

5.   Depreciation methods.   Companies often use the most accelerated method permissible to calculate depreciation for tax purposes but use straight line, which

---

[2]One could divide liabilities into (1) debts owed to someone and (2) other items, such as deferred taxes, reserves, and so on. Because we do not make this distinction, the terms *debt* and *liabilities* are used synonymously. It should be noted that firms occasionally set up reserves for certain contingencies, such as the potential costs involved in a lawsuit currently in the courts. These reserves represent an accounting transfer from retained earnings to the reserve account. If the company wins the suit, retained earnings will be credited, and the reserve will be eliminated. If it loses, a loss will be recorded, cash will be reduced, and the reserve will be eliminated.

TABLE 2-3

MICRODRIVE INC.:
STATEMENT OF
RETAINED EARNINGS
FOR YEAR ENDING
DECEMBER 31,
1993 (MILLIONS OF
DOLLARS)

Balance of retained earnings, December 31, 1992	$710.0
Net income, 1993	113.5
Dividends to common stockholders	(57.5)[a]
Balance of retained earnings, December 31, 1993	$766.0

[a]Here, and throughout the book, parentheses are used to denote negative numbers.

results in a lower depreciation charge, for stockholder reporting. However, MicroDrive has elected to use rapid depreciation for both stockholder reporting and tax purposes. Had MicroDrive elected to use straight line depreciation for stockholder reporting, its 1993 depreciation expense would have been almost $25 million less, so its net income would have been higher, as would its EPS. The $1 billion shown for "net plant" on its balance sheet, and hence its retained earnings, would also have been approximately $25 million higher.

6. The time dimension.   The balance sheet may be thought of as a snapshot of the firm's financial position *at a point in time*—for example, on December 31, 1992. Thus, on December 31, 1992, MicroDrive had $65 million of marketable securities, but this account had been reduced to zero by the end of 1993. The income statement, on the other hand, reports on operations *over a period of time*—for example, during calendar year 1993, which is also the company's fiscal year, MicroDrive had sales of $3 billion, and its net income available to common stockholders was $113.5 million. The balance sheet changes every day as inventories are increased or decreased, as fixed assets are added or retired, as bank loans are increased or decreased, and so on. Companies whose businesses are seasonal have especially large changes in their balance sheets. Therefore, firms' balance sheets will change over the year, depending on the date on which the statement is constructed.

STATEMENT OF RETAINED EARNINGS

Changes in the common equity accounts between balance sheet dates are reported in the *statement of retained earnings.* MicroDrive's statement is shown in Table 2-3. The company earned $113.5 million during 1993, paid out $57.5 million in common dividends, and plowed $56 million back into the business. Thus, the balance sheet item "retained earnings" increased from $710 million at the end of 1992 to $766 million at the end of 1993.

Note that the balance sheet account "retained earnings" represents a *claim against assets,* not assets per se. Further, firms retain earnings primarily to expand the business, and this means investing in plant and equipment, in inventories, and

so on, *not* in a bank account. Increases in retained earnings represent the recognition that income generated by the firm during the accounting period has been invested in assets. In other words, increases in retained earnings result because common stockholders allow the firm to reinvest in its own operations funds that otherwise could be distributed as dividends. *Thus, retained earnings as reported on the balance sheet do not represent cash and are not "available" for the payment of dividends or anything else.*[3]

ACCOUNTING INCOME VERSUS CASH FLOW

When you studied income statements in accounting, the emphasis was probably on determining the net income of the firm. In finance, however, we focus on *cash flows*. The value of an asset (or a whole firm) is determined by the cash flows it generates. The firm's net income is important, but cash flows are even more important, because dividends must be paid in cash and because cash is necessary to purchase the assets required to sustain operations.

As we discussed in Chapter 1, the goal of the firm should be to maximize the price of its stock. Since the value of any asset, including a share of stock, depends on the cash flows produced by the asset, managers should strive to maximize cash flows available to investors over the long run. A business's cash flows are generally equal to cash from sales, minus cash operating costs, minus interest charges, and minus taxes. Before we go any further, though, we need to discuss depreciation, which is an operating cost.

Recall from your accounting course that depreciation is an annual charge against income which reflects the estimated dollar cost of the capital equipment used up in the production process. For example, suppose a machine with a life of 5 years which has a zero expected salvage value was purchased in 1992 for $100,000 and placed into service in 1993. This $100,000 cost is not expensed in the purchase year; rather, it is charged against production over the machine's 5-year depreciable life. If the depreciation expense were not taken, profits would be overstated, and taxes would be too high. The annual depreciation charge is deducted from sales revenues, along with such other costs as labor and raw materials, to determine income. However, because the $100,000 was expended back in 1992, the depreciation charged against income in 1993 through 1997 is not a cash outlay, as are labor or raw materials charges. *Depreciation is a noncash charge, so it must be added back to net income to obtain an estimate of the cash flow from operations.*

---

[3]The amount reported in the retained earnings account is *not* an indication of the amount of cash the firm has. Cash (as of the balance sheet date) is found in the cash account — an asset account. A positive number in the retained earnings account indicates only that in the past, according to generally accepted accounting principles, the firm has earned an income, but its dividends have been less than its reported income. Even though a company reports record earnings and shows an increase in the retained earnings account, it still may be short of cash.

The same situation holds for individuals. You might own a new BMW (no loan), lots of clothes, and an expensive stereo, and, hence, have a high net worth, but if you had only 23 cents in your pocket plus $5 in your checking account, you would still be short of cash.

To see how depreciation affects cash flows, consider the following simplified income statement (Column 1) and cash flow statement (Column 2). Here we assume that all sales revenues were received in cash during the year and that all costs except depreciation were paid in cash during the year. Cash flow is seen to equal net income plus depreciation:

	Income Statement (1)	Cash Flow Statement (2)	
Sales revenues	$1,500	$1,500	
Costs except depreciation	1,050	1,050	
Depreciation (DEP)	150	—	
Total costs	$1,200	$1,050	(Cash costs)
Earnings before taxes	$ 300	$ 450	(Pre-tax cash flow)
Taxes (40%)	120	120	(From Column 1)
Net income (NI)	$ 180		
Add back depreciation	150		
Net cash flow = NI + DEP	$ 330	$ 330	

As we shall see in Chapter 7, a stock's value is based on the *present value of the cash flows* which investors expect it to provide in the future. Although any individual investor could sell the stock and receive cash for it, the *cash flow* provided by the stock itself is the expected future dividend stream, and that expected dividend stream provides the fundamental basis for the stock's value.

Because dividends are paid in cash, a company's ability to pay dividends depends on its cash flows. Cash flow is generally related to *accounting profit,* which is simply net income as reported on the income statement. Although companies with relatively high accounting profits generally have relatively high cash flows, the relationship is not precise. Therefore, investors are concerned about cash flow projections as well as profit projections.

Firms can be thought of as having two separate but related bases of value: *existing assets,* which provide profits and cash flows, and *growth opportunities,* which represent opportunities to make new investments that will increase future profits and cash flows. The ability to take advantage of growth opportunities often depends on the availability of the cash needed to buy new assets, and the cash flows from existing assets are often the primary source of the funds used to make profitable new investments. This is another reason why both investors and managers are concerned with cash flows as well as profits.

For our purposes, it is useful to divide cash flows into two classes: (1) operating cash flows and (2) other cash flows. *Operating cash flows* are those that arise from normal operations, and they are, in essence, the difference between sales revenues and cash expenses, including taxes paid. *Other cash flows* arise from the issuance of stock, from borrowing, or from the sale of fixed assets. Our focus here is on operating cash flows.

Operating cash flows can differ from accounting profits (or net income) for three primary reasons:

1. All the taxes reported on the income statement may not have to be paid during the current year, or, under certain circumstances, the actual cash payments for

taxes may exceed the tax figure deducted from sales to calculate net income. The reasons for these tax cash flow differentials are discussed in detail in accounting courses.

2.   Sales may be on credit; hence, they do not represent cash.

3.   Some of the expenses (or costs) deducted from sales to determine profits may not be cash costs. Most important, depreciation is not a cash cost.

Thus, operating cash flows could be larger or smaller than accounting profits during any given year.

As a company like MicroDrive goes about its business, it makes sales, which lead (1) to a reduction of inventories, (2) to an increase in cash, and, (3) if the amount collected exceeds the cost of the item sold, to a profit. These transactions cause the balance sheet to change, and they are also reflected in the income statement. It is critical that you understand (1) that businesses deal with *physical* units like autos, computer components, or aluminum, (2) that physical transactions are translated into dollar terms through the accounting system, and (3) that the purpose of financial analysis is to examine the accounting numbers in order to determine how efficiently the firm is making and selling physical goods and services.

Several factors make financial analysis difficult. One of them is the variations that exist in accounting methods among firms. For example, different depreciaton methods can lead to differences in reported profits for otherwise identical firms, and a good financial analyst must be able to adjust for these differences if he or she is to make valid comparisons among companies. Another factor involves timing—an action is taken at one point in time, but its full effects cannot be accurately measured until some later period.

To understand how timing influences the financial statements, one must understand the *cash flow cycle.* The cash (and marketable securities) account is the focal point of the cycle. Certain events, such as collecting accounts receivable or borrowing money from the bank, will cause the cash account to increase, while other events such as the payment of taxes, interest, dividends, and accounts payable will cause it to decline. Similar comments could be made about all the balance sheet accounts—their balances rise, fall, or remain constant depending on events that occur during the period under study, which for MicroDrive is January 1, 1993, through December 31, 1993.

Projected increases in sales may require the firm to raise cash by borrowing from its bank or by selling new stock. For example, if MicroDrive anticipates an increase in sales, it will (1) expend cash to buy or build fixed assets through the capital budgeting process; (2) step up purchases of raw materials, thereby increasing both raw materials inventories and accounts payable; (3) increase production, which will lead to an increase in both accrued wages and work-in-process; and (4) eventually build up its finished goods inventory. Some cash will have been expended and hence been removed from the cash account, and the firm will have obligated itself to expend still more cash within a few weeks to pay off its accounts payable and its accrued wages. These cash-using events will have occurred *before* any new cash has been generated from sales. Even when the expected sales do occur, there will still be a lag in the generation of cash until receivables are

collected—because MicroDrive grants credit for 30 days, it will have to wait 30 days after a sale is made before cash comes in. Depending on how much cash the firm had at the beginning of the build-up, on the length of its production-sales-collection cycle, and on how long it can delay payment of its own payables and accrued wages, MicroDrive may have to obtain substantial amounts of additional cash by selling stock or bonds, or by borrowing from the bank.

If the firm is profitable, its sales revenues will exceed its costs, and its cash inflows will eventually exceed its cash outlays. However, even a profitable business can experience a cash shortage if it is growing rapidly. It may have to pay for plant, materials, and labor before cash from the expanded sales starts flowing in. For this reason, rapidly growing firms generally require large bank loans or capital from other sources.

An unprofitable firm such as Eastern Airlines before its bankruptcy will have larger cash outlays than inflows. This, in turn, will lower the cash account and also cause a slowdown in the payment of accrued wages and accounts payable, and it may also lead to heavy borrowings. Accordingly, liabilities rise to excessive levels in unprofitable firms. Similarly, an overly ambitious expansion plan will result in excessive inventories and fixed assets, while too lenient a credit/collection policy will result in high accounts receivable, which eventually will result in bad debts and reduced profits.

If a firm runs out of cash and cannot obtain enough to meet its obligations, then it cannot operate, and it will have to declare bankruptcy. In fact, Eastern Airlines and thousands of other companies have been forced to do just that. Therefore, an accurate cash flow forecast is a critical element in financial management. Financial analysts are well aware of all this, and they use the analytical techniques discussed in the remainder of this chapter to help discover cash flow problems before they become serious.

STATEMENT OF CASH FLOWS

The cash flow cycle is converted into numerical form and reported in annual reports as the *statement of cash flows*. This statement is designed to show how the firm's operations have affected its cash position and to help answer questions such as these: Is the firm generating the cash needed to purchase additional fixed assets for growth? Is growth so rapid that external financing is required both to maintain operations and for investment in new fixed assets? Does the firm have excess cash flows that can be used to repay debt or to invest in new products? This information is useful for both financial managers and investors, so the statement of cash flows is an important part of the annual report. Table 2-4 is MicroDrive's statement of cash flows as it would appear in the company's annual report.

The top part of Table 2-4 shows cash flows generated by and used in operations—for MicroDrive, operations provided net cash flows of *minus* $2.5 million. The operating cash flows are generated principally from the day-to-day operations of the firm, and this amount can be determined by adjusting the net income figure to account for other cash flows related to operations plus noncash

LIQUIDITY RATIOS

A *liquid asset* is one that can be easily converted to cash at a "fair market value," and a firm's "liquidity position" deals with this question: Will the firm be able to meet its current obligations? MicroDrive has debts totaling $310 million that must be paid off within the coming year. Will it have trouble satisfying those obligations? A full liquidity analysis requires the use of cash budgets (described in Chapter 16), but by relating the amount of cash and other current assets to the firm's current obligations, ratio analysis provides a quick, easy-to-use measure of liquidity. Two commonly used *liquidity ratios* are discussed in this section.

Current Ratio.   The *current ratio* is calculated by dividing current assets by current liabilities:

$$\text{Current ratio} = \frac{\text{Current assets}}{\text{Current liabilities}}$$

$$= \frac{\$1,000}{\$310} = 3.2 \text{ times.}$$

$$\text{Industry average} = 4.2 \text{ times.}$$

Current assets normally include cash, marketable securities, accounts receivable, and inventories. Current liabilities consist of accounts payable, short-term notes payable, current maturities of long-term debt, accrued income taxes, and other accrued expenses (principally wages and taxes).

If a company is getting into financial difficulty, it begins paying its bills (accounts payable) more slowly, borrowing from its bank, and so on. If current liabilities are rising faster than current assets, the current ratio will fall, and this could spell trouble. Because the current ratio provides an indicator of the extent to which the claims of short-term creditors are covered by assets that are expected to be converted to cash fairly quickly, it is a commonly used measure of liquidity.

MicroDrive's current ratio is well below the average for its industry, 4.2, so its liquidity position is relatively weak. Still, since current assets are scheduled to be converted to cash in the near future, it is highly probable that they could be liquidated at close to their stated value. With a current ratio of 3.2, MicroDrive could liquidate current assets at only 31 percent of book value and still pay off current creditors in full.[4]

Although industry average figures are discussed later in some detail, it should be noted at this point that an industry average is not a magic number that all firms should strive to maintain—in fact, some very well-managed firms will be above the average while other good firms will be below it. However, if a firm's ratios are far removed from the average for its industry, an analyst should be concerned

---

[4]$1/3.2 = 0.31$, or 31 percent. Note that $0.31(\$1,000) = \$310$, the amount of current liabilities.

about why this variance occurs. Thus, a deviation from the industry average should signal the analyst (or management) to check further.

Quick, or Acid Test, Ratio. The *quick, or acid test, ratio* is calculated by deducting inventories from current assets and then dividing the remainder by current liabilities:

$$\text{Quick, or acid test, ratio} = \frac{\text{Current assets} - \text{Inventories}}{\text{Current liabilities}}$$

$$= \frac{\$385}{\$310} = 1.2 \text{ times.}$$

$$\text{Industry average} = 2.1 \text{ times.}$$

Inventories are typically the least liquid of a firm's current assets, so they are the assets on which losses are most likely to occur in the event of liquidation. Therefore, a measure of the firm's ability to pay off short-term obligations without relying on the sale of inventories is important.

The industry average quick ratio is 2.1, so MicroDrive's 1.2 ratio is low in comparison with the ratios of other firms in its industry. Still, if the accounts receivable can be collected, the company can pay off its current liabilities even without having to liquidate its inventory.

ASSET MANAGEMENT RATIOS

The second group of ratios, the *asset management ratios,* measures how effectively the firm is managing its assets. These ratios are designed to answer this question: Does the total amount of each type of asset as reported on the balance sheet seem reasonable, too high, or too low in view of current and projected sales levels? MicroDrive and other companies must borrow or obtain capital from other sources to acquire assets. If they have too many assets, their interest expenses will be too high, and hence their profits will be depressed. On the other hand, if assets are too low, profitable sales may be lost.

Inventory Turnover. The *inventory turnover ratio* is defined as sales divided by inventories:

$$\text{Inventory turnover ratio} = \frac{\text{Sales}}{\text{Inventories}}$$

$$= \frac{\$3,000}{\$615} = 4.9 \text{ times.}$$

$$\text{Industry average} = 9.0 \text{ times.}$$

As a rough approximation, each dollar of MicroDrive's inventory value is sold out and restocked, or "turned over," 4.9 times per year.[5]

MicroDrive's turnover of 4.9 times is much lower than the industry average of 9 times. This suggests that MicroDrive is holding excessive stocks of inventory; excess stocks are, of course, unproductive and represent an investment with a low or zero rate of return. MicroDrive's low inventory turnover ratio makes us question the current ratio. With such a low turnover, we must wonder whether the firm is holding damaged or obsolete goods not actually worth their stated value.

Two problems arise in calculating and analyzing the inventory turnover ratio. First, sales are stated at market prices, so if inventories are carried at cost, as they generally are, the calculated turnover overstates the true turnover ratio. Therefore, it would be more appropriate to use cost of goods sold in place of sales in the numerator of the formula. However, established compilers of financial ratio statistics, such as Dun & Bradstreet, use the ratio of sales to inventories carried at cost. To develop a figure that can be compared with those published by Dun & Bradstreet and similar organizations, it is necessary to measure inventory turnover with sales in the numerator, as we do here.

The second problem lies in the fact that sales occur over the entire year, whereas the inventory figure is for one point in time. For this reason, it is better to use an average inventory measure.[6] If the firm's business is highly seasonal, or if there has been a strong upward or downward sales trend during the year, it is essential to make some such adjustment. To maintain comparability with industry averages, however, we did not use the average inventory figure.

Days Sales Outstanding. *Days sales outstanding (DSO),* also called the *average collection period (ACP),* is used to appraise accounts receivable, and it is calculated by dividing average daily sales into accounts receivable to find the number of days' sales that are tied up in receivables. Thus, the DSO represents the average length of time that the firm must wait after making a sale before receiving cash. MicroDrive has 45 days' sales outstanding, well above the 36-day industry average.[7]

---

[5]"Turnover" is a term that originated many years ago with the old Yankee peddler, who would load up his wagon with goods, then go off on his route to peddle his wares. The merchandise was his "working capital," because it was what he actually sold, or "turned over," to produce his profits, whereas his "turnover" was the number of trips he took each year. Annual sales divided by inventory equaled turnover, or trips per year. If he made 10 trips per year, stocked 100 pans, and made a gross profit of $5 per pan, his annual gross profit would be $(100)($5)(10) = $5,000$. If he went faster and made 20 trips per year, his gross profit would double, other things held constant.

[6]Preferably, the average inventory value should be calculated by summing the monthly figures during the year and dividing by 12. If monthly data are not available, one can add the beginning and ending figures and divide by 2; this will adjust for growth but not for seasonal effects.

[7]Because information on credit sales is generally unavailable, total sales must be used. Since all firms do not have the same percentage of credit sales, there is a chance that the days sales outstanding will be somewhat in error. Also, note that by convention the financial community generally uses 360 rather than 365 as the number of days in the year for purposes such as this. Finally, it would be better to use *average* receivables, either an average of the monthly figures or (Beginning receivables + Ending receivables)/2 = ($315 + $375)/2 = $345 in the formula. Had the annual average receivables been used, MicroDrive's DSO would have been $345.00/$8.333 = 41 days. The 41-day figure is the more accurate one, but because the industry average was based on year-end receivables, we used 45 days for our comparison. The DSO is discussed further in Chapter 18.

$$\text{DSO} = \begin{array}{c}\text{Days}\\\text{sales}\\\text{outstanding}\end{array} = \frac{\text{Receivables}}{\text{Average sales per day}} = \frac{\text{Receivables}}{\text{Annual sales}/360}$$

$$\frac{\$375}{\$3,000/360} = \frac{\$375}{\$8.333} = 45 \text{ days.}$$

$$\text{Industry average} = 36 \text{ days.}$$

The DSO can also be evaluated by comparison with the terms on which the firm sells its goods. For example, MicroDrive's sales terms call for payment within 30 days, so the fact that 45 days' sales, not 30 days', are outstanding indicates that customers, on the average, are not paying their bills on time. If the trend in DSO over the past few years has been rising, but the credit policy has not been changed, this would be even stronger evidence that steps should be taken to expedite the collection of accounts receivable.

Fixed Assets Turnover. The *fixed assets turnover ratio* measures how effectively the firm uses its plant and equipment. It is the ratio of sales to net fixed assets:

$$\text{Fixed assets turnover ratio} = \frac{\text{Sales}}{\text{Net fixed assets}}$$

$$= \frac{\$3,000}{\$1,000} = 3.0 \text{ times.}$$

$$\text{Industry average} = 3.0 \text{ times.}$$

MicroDrive's ratio of 3.0 times is equal to the industry average, indicating that the firm is using its fixed assets about as intensively as are the other firms in the industry. MicroDrive seems to have neither too much nor too few fixed assets in relation to other firms.

A major potential problem can exist when the fixed assets turnover ratio is used to compare different firms. Recall from accounting that all assets except cash and accounts receivable reflect the historical costs of the assets. Inflation has caused the value of many assets that were purchased in the past to be seriously understated. Furthermore, older assets have been depreciated by a greater amount, regardless of the actual impact of age on value. Therefore, if we were comparing an old firm which had acquired many of its fixed assets years ago at low prices with a new company which had acquired its fixed assets only recently, we probably would find that the old firm had a higher fixed assets turnover. However, this would be more reflective of the inability of accountants to deal with fixed asset values than of any inefficiency on the part of the new firm. The accounting profes-

sion is trying to devise ways of making financial statements reflect current values rather than historical values. If balance sheets were actually stated on a current value basis, this would eliminate the problem of comparisons, but at the moment, the problem still exists. Since financial analysts typically do not have the data necessary to make adjustments, they must simply recognize that a problem exists and deal with it judgmentally. In MicroDrive's case, the issue is not a serious one because all firms in the industry have been expanding at about the same rate; thus, the balance sheets of the comparison firms are indeed comparable.[8]

Total Assets Turnover.   The final asset management ratio, the *total assets turnover ratio*, measures the turnover of all of the firm's assets; it is calculated by dividing sales by total assets:

$$\text{Total assets turnover ratio} = \frac{\text{Sales}}{\text{Total assets}}$$

$$= \frac{\$3,000}{\$2,000} = 1.5 \text{ times.}$$

$$\text{Industry average} = 1.8 \text{ times.}$$

MicroDrive's ratio is somewhat below the industry average, indicating that the company is not generating a sufficient volume of business given its total asset investment. Sales should be increased, some assets should be disposed of, or a combination of these steps should be taken.

Note that MicroDrive's 1993 fixed assets turnover is in line with the industry average, but its total assets turnover is weak. Together, these ratios indicate that the problem lies with MicroDrive's level of current assets. Examination of the firm's current assets turnover ratio would confirm this observation.

DEBT MANAGEMENT RATIOS

The extent to which a firm uses debt financing, or *financial leverage,* has three important implications: (1) By raising funds through debt, stockholders can maintain control of a firm with a limited investment. (2) Creditors look to the equity, or owner-supplied funds, to provide a margin of safety; if the stockholders have provided only a small proportion of the total financing, the risks of the enterprise are borne mainly by its creditors. (3) If the firm earns more on investments financed with borrowed funds than it pays in interest, the return on the owners' capital is magnified, or "leveraged."

---

[8]See FASB Statement 33, *Financial Reporting and Changing Prices,* September 1979, for a discussion of the effects of inflation on financial statements and what the accounting profession is trying to do to provide better and more useful balance sheets and income statements.

To understand better how the use of debt, or financial leverage, affects risk and return, consider Table 2-5. Here we are analyzing two companies that are identical except for the way they are financed. Firm U (for "unleveraged") has no debt, whereas Firm L (for "leveraged") is financed half with equity and half with debt that bears an interest rate of 15 percent. Both companies have $100 of assets and $100 of sales. Their expected ratio of operating income (also called earnings before interest and taxes, or EBIT) to assets, or the *basic earning power (BEP) ratio,* is EBIT/Total assets = $30/$100 = 0.30 = 30%. Thus, both firms expect to earn 30 percent, before taxes, on their assets. Of course, things could turn out poorly, in which case the basic earning power ratio would be lower; in the table, we show the earning power ratio declining from 30 percent to 2.5 percent under poor conditions.

TABLE 2-5

EFFECTS OF FINANCIAL
LEVERAGE ON
STOCKHOLDERS'
RETURNS

Firm U (Unleveraged)

Current assets	$ 50	Debt	$ 0
Fixed assets	50	Common equity	100
Total assets	$100	Total liabilities and equity	$100

	Expected Conditions (1)	Poor Conditions (2)
Sales	$100.00	$82.50
Operating costs	70.00	80.00
Operating income (EBIT)	$ 30.00	$ 2.50
Interest	0.00	0.00
Earnings before taxes (EBT)	$ 30.00	$ 2.50
Taxes (40%)	12.00	1.00
Net income (NI)	$ 18.00	$ 1.50
ROE_U = NI/Common equity = NI/$100 =	18.00%	1.50%

Firm L (Leveraged)

Current assets	$ 50	Debt (interest = 15%)	$ 50
Fixed assets	50	Common equity	50
Total assets	$100	Total liabilities and equity	$100

	Expected Conditions (1)	Poor Conditions (2)
Sales	$100.00	$82.50
Operating costs	70.00	80.00
Operating income (EBIT)	$ 30.00	$ 2.50
Interest	7.50	7.50
Earnings before taxes (EBT)	$ 22.50	($ 5.00)
Taxes (40%)	9.00	(2.00)
Net income (NI)	$ 13.50	($ 3.00)
ROE_L = NI/Common equity = NI/$50 =	27.00%	(6.00%)

Even though both companies' assets have the same expected earning power, under normal conditions Firm L should provide its stockholders with a return on equity of 27 percent versus only 18 percent for Firm U. However, financial leverage can cut both ways. As we show in Column 2 of the income statements, if sales are lower and costs are higher than were expected, the return on assets will be lower than was expected. Under these conditions, the leveraged firm's return on equity falls especially sharply, and losses occur. For example, under the "poor conditions" in Table 2-5, the unleveraged firm still shows a profit, but the firm which uses debt shows a loss, and a negative return on equity. This occurs because Firm L needs cash to service its debt, while Firm U does not. Firm U, because of its strong balance sheet, could ride out the recession and be ready for the next boom. Firm L, on the other hand, must pay interest of $7.50 regardless of its level of sales. Consequently, when day-to-day operations do not generate sufficient operating income to provide cash to meet the interest payments, cash would be depleted and the firm probably would need to raise additional funds. This situation is evident for Firm L when poor economic conditions exist, because only $2.50 in operating income is generated, but the interest payment for debt is three times this amount. Because it would be running a loss, Firm L would have a hard time selling stock to raise capital, and the losses would cause lenders to raise the interest rate, increasing L's problems still further. As a final result, Firm L just might not survive to enjoy the next boom.

We see, then, that firms with relatively high debt ratios have higher expected returns when the economy is normal, but they are exposed to risk of loss when the economy is in a recession. Firms with low debt ratios are less risky, but they also forgo the opportunity to leverage up their return on equity. The prospects of high returns are desirable, but investors are averse to risk. Therefore, decisions about the use of debt require firms to balance higher expected returns against increased risk. Determining the optimal amount of debt for a given firm is a complicated process, and we defer a discussion of this topic until Chapters 12 and 13. For now we will simply look at two procedures analysts use to examine the firm's debt in a financial statement analysis: (1) They check balance sheet ratios to determine the extent to which borrowed funds have been used to finance assets *(capitalization ratios)*, and (2) they review income statement ratios to determine the number of times fixed charges are covered by operating profits *(coverage ratios)*. These two sets of ratios are complementary, so analysts use both types.

Total Debt to Total Assets.   The ratio of total debt to total assets, generally called the *debt ratio*, measures the percentage of funds provided by creditors:

$$\text{Debt ratio} = \frac{\text{Total debt}}{\text{Total assets}}$$

$$= \frac{\$310 + \$754}{\$2,000} = \frac{\$1,064}{\$2,000} = 53.2\%.$$

$$\text{Industry average} = 40.0\%.$$

Total debt includes both current liabilities and long-term debt. Creditors prefer low debt ratios, because the lower the ratio, the greater the cushion against creditors' losses in the event of liquidation. Stockholders, on the other hand, can benefit from leverage because it magnifies earnings.

MicroDrive's debt ratio is 53.2 percent; this means that its creditors have supplied more than half the firm's total financing. Since the average debt ratio for this industry — and for manufacturers generally — is about 40 percent, MicroDrive would find it difficult to borrow additional funds without first raising more equity capital. Creditors would be reluctant to lend the firm more money, and management would probably be subjecting the firm to the risk of bankruptcy if it sought to increase the debt ratio any further by borrowing additional funds.[9]

Times Interest Earned. The *times-interest-earned (TIE) ratio* is determined by dividing earnings before interest and taxes (EBIT in Table 2-1) by the interest charges:

$$\text{Times-interest-earned (TIE) ratio} = \frac{\text{EBIT}}{\text{Interest charges}}$$

$$= \frac{\$283.8}{\$88} = 3.2 \text{ times.}$$

$$\text{Industry average} = 6.0 \text{ times.}$$

The TIE ratio measures the extent to which operating income can decline before the firm is unable to meet its annual interest costs. Failure to meet this obligation can bring legal action by the firm's creditors, possibly resulting in bankruptcy. Note that earnings before interest and taxes, rather than net income, is used in the numerator. Because interest is paid with pre-tax dollars, the firm's ability to pay current interest is not affected by taxes.

MicroDrive's interest is covered 3.2 times. Thus, the firm generates $3.20 in operating income per dollar of interest expense. Since the industry average is

---

[9]The ratio of debt to equity is also used in financial analysis. The debt-to-assets (D/A) and debt-to-equity (D/E) ratios are simply transformations of each other:

$$D/E = \frac{D/A}{1 - D/A}, \text{ and } D/A = \frac{D/E}{1 + D/E}.$$

MicroDrive's debt-to-equity ratio is

$$\frac{0.532}{1 - 0.532} = \frac{0.532}{0.468} \approx 1.14.$$

Thus, for each dollar of capital supplied by stockholders (including preferred), creditors have supplied $1.14.

6 times, MicroDrive is covering its interest charges by a relatively low margin of safety, so the TIE ratio reinforces our conclusion based on the debt ratio that MicroDrive would face difficulties if it attempted to borrow additional funds.

Fixed Charge Coverage.   The *fixed charge coverage ratio* is similar to the times-interest-earned ratio, but it is more inclusive because it recognizes that many firms use long-term leases and also must make sinking fund payments.[10] Leasing has become widespread in certain industries in recent years, making this ratio preferable to the times-interest-earned ratio for many purposes. MicroDrive's annual long-term lease payments are $28 million, and it must make an annual $20 million sinking fund payment to help retire its debt. Because sinking fund payments must be paid with after-tax dollars, whereas interest and lease payments are paid with pre-tax dollars, the sinking fund payment must be divided by $(1 - \text{Tax rate})$ to find the before-tax income required to pay taxes and still have enough left to make the sinking fund payment.

Fixed charges include interest, annual long-term lease obligations, and sinking fund payments, and the fixed charge coverage ratio is defined as follows:[11]

$$\text{Fixed charge coverage ratio} = \frac{\text{EBIT} + \text{Lease payments}}{\text{Interest charges} + \text{Lease payments} + \dfrac{\text{Sinking fund payments}}{(1 - \text{Tax rate})}}$$

$$= \frac{\$283.8 + \$28}{\$88 + \$28 + \dfrac{\$20}{0.6}} = 2.1 \text{ times.}$$

$$\text{Industry average} = 5.5 \text{ times.}$$

MicroDrive's fixed charges are covered only 2.1 times, as opposed to an industry average of 5.5 times. Again, this indicates that the firm is weaker than average, and

---

[10]Generally, a long-term lease is defined as one that extends for more than 1 year. Thus, rent incurred under a 6-month lease would not be included in the fixed charge coverage ratio, but rental payments under a 1-year or longer lease would be defined as a fixed charge and would be included. A sinking fund is a required annual payment designed to reduce the balance of a debt or preferred stock issue. Sinking funds are discussed in Chapter 20.

[11]Note that $20/0.6 = $33.33. Therefore, if the company had pre-tax income of $33.33, it could pay taxes at a 40 percent rate and have exactly $20 left with which to make the sinking fund payment. Thus, a $20 sinking fund payment requires $20/0.6 = $33.33 of pre-tax income. Dividing by $(1 - T)$ is called "grossing up" an after-tax value to find the corresponding pre-tax value. Also note that the fixed charge coverage ratio can be defined in several different ways, depending on what management regards as "fixed" charges. For example, the grossed up preferred stock dividend could be added to the denominator if management was totally committed to maintaining the preferred dividend.

this points out the difficulties MicroDrive would probably encounter if it attempted to increase its debt.

PROFITABILITY RATIOS

Profitability is the net result of a number of policies and decisions. The ratios examined thus far provide some information about the way the firm is operating, but the *profitability ratios* show the combined effects of liquidity, asset management, and debt management on operating results.

Profit Margin on Sales.   The *profit margin on sales,* often just called the *profit margin,* is calculated by dividing net income by sales, and it gives the profit per dollar of sales:

$$\text{Profit margin on sales} = \frac{\text{Net income available to common stockholders}}{\text{Sales}}$$

$$= \frac{\$113.5}{\$3,000} = 3.8\%.$$

Industry average = 5.0%.

MicroDrive's profit margin is below the industry average of 5 percent, indicating that its sales are too low, its costs are too high, or both.

Basic Earning Power (BEP).   The *basic earning power (BEP) ratio,* which we discussed earlier, is calculated by dividing earnings before interest and taxes (EBIT) by total assets:

$$\text{Basic earning power ratio} = \text{BEP} = \frac{\text{EBIT}}{\text{Total assets}}$$

$$= \frac{\$283.8}{\$2,000} = 14.2\%.$$

Industry average = 17.2%.

This ratio shows the raw earning power of the firm's assets, before the influence of taxes and leverage, and it is useful for comparing firms with different tax situations and different degrees of financial leverage. Because of its low turnover ratios

and low profit margin on sales, MicroDrive is not getting as high a return on its assets as is the average computer component company.[12]

Return on Total Assets.   The ratio of net income to total assets measures the *return on total assets (ROA)* after interest and taxes:

$$
\begin{array}{c}
\text{Return on} \\
\text{total assets} \\
\text{(ROA)}
\end{array}
=
\dfrac{\text{Net income available to common stockholders}}{\text{Total assets}}
$$

$$
= \dfrac{\$113.5}{\$2,000} = 5.7\%.
$$

Industry average = 9.0%.

MicroDrive's 5.7 percent return is well below the 9 percent average for the industry. This low return results from the company's low basic earning power plus its above-average use of debt, both of which cause its net income to be relatively low. Note that this ratio is often just called *return on assets.*

Return on Common Equity.   The ratio of net income to common equity measures the *return on common equity (ROE),* or the *rate of return on stockholders' investment:*

$$
\begin{array}{c}
\text{Return on} \\
\text{common equity} \\
\text{(ROE)}
\end{array}
=
\dfrac{\text{Net income available to common stockholders}}{\text{Common equity}}
$$

$$
= \dfrac{\$113.5}{\$896} = 12.7\%.
$$

Industry average = 15.0%.

MicroDrive's 12.7 percent return is below the 15 percent industry average, but it is not as far below as the return on total assets. This somewhat better result is due

---

[12]Notice that EBIT is earned throughout the year, whereas the total assets figure is an end-of-the-year number. Therefore, it would be conceptually better to calculate this ratio as EBIT/Average assets = EBIT/[(Beginning assets + Ending assets)/2]. We have not made this adjustment because the published ratios used for comparative purposes do not include it, but when we construct our own comparative ratios, we do make the adjustment. Incidentally, the same adjustment would also be appropriate for the next two ratios, ROA and ROE.

to the company's greater use of debt, a point that is analyzed in detail later in the chapter. Note that this ratio is generally just called *return on equity.*

MARKET VALUE RATIOS

A final group of ratios, the *market value ratios,* relates the firm's stock price to its earnings and book value per share. These ratios give management an indication of what equity investors think of the company's past performance and future prospects. If the firm's liquidity, asset management, debt management, and profitability ratios are all good, then its market value ratios will be high, and its stock price will probably be as high as can be expected.

Price/Earnings Ratio.   The *price/earnings (P/E) ratio* shows how much investors are willing to pay per dollar of reported profits. MicroDrive's stock sells for $23, so with an EPS of $2.27, its P/E ratio is 10.1:

$$\text{Price/earnings (P/E) ratio} = \frac{\text{Price per share}}{\text{Earnings per share}}$$

$$= \frac{\$23.00}{\$2.27} = 10.1 \text{ times.}$$

$$\text{Industry average} = 12.5 \text{ times.}$$

P/E ratios are higher for firms with higher growth prospects, other things held constant, but they are lower for riskier firms. Since MicroDrive's P/E ratio is below those of other computer components companies, this suggests that the company is regarded as being somewhat riskier than most, as having poorer growth prospects, or both.

Market/Book Ratio.   The ratio of a stock's market price to its book value gives another indication of how equity investors regard the company. Companies with relatively high rates of return on equity generally sell at higher multiples of book value than those with low returns. First, we find MicroDrive's book value per share:

$$\text{Book value per share} = \frac{\text{Common equity}}{\text{Shares outstanding}}$$

$$= \frac{\$896}{50} = \$17.92.$$

TABLE 2-6   MicroDrive Inc.: Summary of Financial Ratios

Ratio	Formula for Calculation	1992	1993	1993 Industry Average	Comment
Liquidity					
Current	$\dfrac{\text{Current assets}}{\text{Current liabilities}}$	3.7×	3.2×	4.2×	Poor
Quick, or acid, test	$\dfrac{\text{Current assets} - \text{Inventories}}{\text{Current liabilities}}$	1.8×	1.2×	2.1×	Poor
Asset Management					
Inventory turnover	$\dfrac{\text{Sales}}{\text{Inventories}}$	6.9×	4.9×	9.0×	Poor
Days sales outstanding (DSO)	$\dfrac{\text{Receivables}}{\text{Annual sales}/360}$	40 days	45 days	36 days	Poor
Fixed assets turnover	$\dfrac{\text{Sales}}{\text{Net fixed assets}}$	3.3×	3.0×	3.0×	OK
Total assets turnover	$\dfrac{\text{Sales}}{\text{Total assets}}$	1.7×	1.5×	1.8×	Somewhat low
Debt Management					
Total debt to total assets	$\dfrac{\text{Total debt}}{\text{Total assets}}$	47.6%	53.2%	40.0%	High (risky)
Times-interest-earned (TIE)	$\dfrac{\text{Earnings before interest and taxes (EBIT)}}{\text{Interest charges}}$	3.4×	3.2×	6.0×	Low (risky)
Fixed charge coverage	$\dfrac{\text{Earnings before interest and taxes} + \text{Lease payments}}{\text{Interest charges} + \text{Lease payments} + \dfrac{\text{SF payments}}{(1 - T)}}$	2.4×	2.1×	5.5×	Low (risky)
Profitability					
Profit margin on sales	$\dfrac{\text{Net income available to common stockholders}}{\text{Sales}}$	4.1%	3.8%	5.0%	Poor
Basic earning power	$\dfrac{\text{Earnings before interest and taxes (EBIT)}}{\text{Total assets}}$	12.1%	14.2%	17.2%	Poor
Return on total assets (ROA)	$\dfrac{\text{Net income available to common stockholders}}{\text{Total assets}}$	7.0%	5.7%	9.0%	Poor
Return on common equity (ROE)	$\dfrac{\text{Net income available to common stockholders}}{\text{Common equity}}$	14.0%	12.7%	15.0%	Poor
Market Value					
Price/earnings (P/E)	$\dfrac{\text{Price per share}}{\text{Earnings per share}}$	10.2×	10.1×	12.5×	Low
Market/book	$\dfrac{\text{Market price per share}}{\text{Book value per share}}$	1.4×	1.3×	1.7×	Low

Now we divide the market price per share by the book value to get a *market/book (M/B) ratio* of 1.3 times:

$$\text{Market/book ratio} = \frac{\text{Market price per share}}{\text{Book value per share}}$$

$$= \frac{\$23.00}{\$17.92} = 1.3 \text{ times.}$$

Industry average = 1.7 times.

Investors are willing to pay less for MicroDrive's book value than for that of an average computer components company.

The typical railroad, which has a very low rate of return on assets, has a market/book value ratio of less than 0.5. On the other hand, very successful firms such as Microsoft (which makes the operating system for virtually all PCs) achieve high rates of return on their assets, and their market values are well in excess of their book values. At the beginning of 1993, Microsoft's book value per share was $7.95 versus a market price of $93, so its market/book ratio was $93/$7.95 = 11.7 times.

COMPARATIVE AND TREND ANALYSES

In our discussion of MicroDrive's ratios, we focused on *comparative analysis;* that is, we compared MicroDrive's ratios with the average ratios for its industry. Another useful ratio analysis tool is *trend analysis,* where we analyze the trend of a single ratio over time. Trend analysis gives clues whether a firm's financial situation is improving, holding constant, or deteriorating. Table 2-6 summarizes MicroDrive's comparative and trend analyses for the past two years.

It is easy to combine comparative and trend analyses in a single graph such as the one shown in Figure 2-1. Here we plotted MicroDrive's ROE and the industry average ROE over the past five years. The graph shows that MicroDrive's ROE has been declining since 1990 even though the industry average has been relatively stable. Other ratios could be analyzed similarly.

DU PONT ANALYSIS

Ratio analysis provides a detailed examination of a firm's liquidity, asset management, debt management, and profitability, as well as an indication of how equity investors regard the firm. However, ratio analysis does not tie these factors together well, nor does it provide an overview of the firm's financial condition. The financial managers at the Du Pont Company identified a relationship among four key ratios which allows analysts to easily summarize a firm's financial condition. The relationship is called the *Du Pont equation.*

To begin our discussion of Du Pont analysis, note that the profit margin times the total assets turnover gives the rate of return on assets (ROA):

items and, working with engineers, purchasing agents, and other operating personnel, seek ways of holding down costs. Total asset turnover measures asset utilization, and MicroDrive's financial analysts, working with both production and marketing people, can investigate ways of minimizing the investment in various types of assets. At the same time, the treasury staff can analyze the effects of alternative financing strategies on the equity multiplier, seeking to hold down interest expense and the risks brought on by using debt while still using leverage to increase the rate of return on equity.

Equation 2-3 provides a useful comparison between a firm's performance as measured by ROE and the performance of an average firm in the industry:

$$\text{MicroDrive: ROE} = (3.8\%)(1.5)(2.23) \approx 12.7\%.$$

$$\text{Industry: ROE} = (5.0\%)(1.8)(1.67) \approx 15.0\%.$$

We see (1) that the average computer components company has a significantly higher profit margin, and thus better control over expenses; (2) that the average firm has a higher total asset turnover, and thus is using its assets more productively; but (3) that MicroDrive has offset some of these advantages with its higher financial leverage, although this increased use of leverage increases MicroDrive's risk. We have only performed a comparative analysis here, but the Du Pont equation could be developed for several years and used in a trend analysis.

The Du Pont equation is especially useful for summarizing a firm's financial condition because it decomposes stockholder profitability into three important determinants: (1) expense control, (2) asset utilization, and (3) debt utilization. Thus, analysts often use it to get a "quick and dirty" feel for a firm's financial condition. With the Du Pont equation information at hand, analysts can focus their attention on those aspects of the firm's performance that appear to be sub par.

As a result of such an analysis, Al Jackson, MicroDrive's president, recently announced a series of moves designed to cut operating costs by more than 20 percent per year. Jackson also announced that the company intended to concentrate its capital in markets where profit margins are reasonably high, and that if competition increases in certain of its product markets (such as the low-price end of the disk drive market), MicroDrive will withdraw from those markets. MicroDrive is seeking a high return on equity, and Jackson recognizes that if competition drives profit margins too low in a particular market, it then becomes impossible to earn high returns on the capital invested to serve that market. Therefore, if it is to achieve a high ROE, MicroDrive may have to develop additional new products and shift capital into new areas. The company's future depends on this type of analysis, and if it succeeds in the future, then the Du Pont analysis will have helped it achieve that success.

SELF-TEST QUESTIONS

Identify two ratios that are used to analyze a firm's liquidity position, and write out their equations.

Identify four ratios that are used to measure how effectively a firm is managing its assets, and write out their equations.

Identify three ratios that are used to measure the extent to which a firm uses debt financing, and write out their equations.

Identify four ratios that show the combined effects of liquidity, asset management, and debt management on profitability, and write out their equations.

Identify two ratios that relate a firm's stock price to its earnings and book value per share, and write out their equations.

Explain how the Du Pont equation combines several ratios to reveal the basic determinants of ROE.

How can comparative and trend analyses be used to help interpret ratio results?

COMMON SIZE ANALYSIS

In a *common size analysis*, all income statement items are divided by sales, and all balance sheet items are divided by total assets. Thus, a common size income statement shows each item as a percentage of sales, and a common size balance sheet shows each item as a percentage of total assets. The significant advantage of common size statements is that they facilitate comparisons of balance sheets and income statements over time and across companies.

Table 2-7 contains MicroDrive's common size income statements, along with the composite statement for the industry. (Note: Rounding may cause addition/subtraction differences in Tables 2-7 and 2-8.) MicroDrive's costs are somewhat

TABLE 2-7
MICRODRIVE INC.:
COMMON SIZE
INCOME STATEMENTS

	1992	1993	1993 Industry Average
Net sales	100.0%	100.0%	100.0%
Costs excluding depreciation	87.6	87.2	86.7
Depreciation	3.2	3.3	2.8
Total operating costs	90.8%	90.5%	89.5%
Earnings before interest and taxes (EBIT)	9.2%	9.5%	10.5%
Less interest	2.1	2.9	1.7
Earnings before taxes (EBT)	7.1%	6.5%	8.8%
Taxes (40%)	2.8	2.6	3.8
Net income before preferred dividends	4.3%	3.9%	5.0%
Preferred dividends	0.1	0.1	0.0
Net income available to common stockholders (profit margin)	4.1%	3.8%	5.0%

TABLE 2-8

MICRODRIVE INC.:

COMMON SIZE

BALANCE SHEETS

	1992	1993	1993 Industry Average
Assets			
Cash and marketable securities	4.8%	0.5%	3.2%
Accounts receivable	18.8	18.8	15.3
Inventories	24.7	30.8	22.7
Total current assets	48.2%	50.0%	41.2%
Net plant and equipment	51.8	50.0	58.8
Total assets	100.0%	100.0%	100.0%
Liabilities and Equity			
Accounts payable	1.8%	3.0%	2.6%
Notes payable	3.6	5.5	3.2
Accruals	7.7	7.0	7.3
Total current liabilities	13.1%	15.5%	13.1%
Long-term bonds	34.5	37.7	26.9
Total debt	47.6%	53.2%	40.0%
Preferred equity	2.4	2.0	0.0
Common equity	50.0	44.8	60.0
Total liabilities and equity	100.0%	100.0%	100.0%

above average, as is its depreciation. Note also that MicroDrive's interest expenses are relatively high, but its taxes are relatively low because of its low EBIT. The net effect of all these forces is a relatively low profit margin.

Table 2-8 contains MicroDrive's common size balance sheets, along with the industry average. Three striking differences are revealed: (1) MicroDrive's accounts receivable are significantly higher than the industry average, (2) its inventories are significantly higher, and (3) MicroDrive uses far more fixed charge capital (debt and preferred) than the average firm.

The conclusions reached in a common size analysis generally parallel those derived from ratio analysis. However, occasionally a serious deficiency is highlighted only by one of the two analytical techniques. Thus, a thorough financial statement analysis will include both ratio and common size analyses, as well as a Du Pont analysis.

SELF-TEST QUESTIONS

How are common size statements created?

What advantage do common size statements have over regular statements?

Is it useful to include in a financial statement analysis both ratio analysis and common size analysis? Explain.

SOURCES OF INDUSTRY DATA

The preceding analysis pointed out the need to compare the company in question with other firms in its industry. In this section, we describe some of the sources of industry data.

EXTERNAL SOURCES

One useful set of comparative data is Dun & Bradstreet (D&B), which, in its *Key Business Ratios,* provides 14 ratios for a large number of industries. Useful ratios can also be found in the *Annual Statement Studies* published by Robert Morris Associates, which is the national association of bank loan officers. The Federal Trade Commission's *Quarterly Financial Report* gives a set of ratios for manufacturing firms by industry group and size of firm. Trade associations also compile industry average financial ratios.

Each of the listed organizations uses a somewhat different set of ratios, designed for its own purposes. For example, D&B deals mainly with small firms, many of which are proprietorships, and it is concerned largely with the creditors' viewpoint. Accordingly, D&B's ratios emphasize current assets and liabilities, and it provides no market value ratios whatever. Therefore, when you select a comparative data source, be sure that your emphasis is similar to that of the organization whose data you use, or else recognize the limitations of its ratios for your purposes. Additionally, there are often minor definitional differences in the ratios presented by different sources — for example, one may report ROE as net income divided by year-end common equity (Value Line does this), while another may divide by average common equity (Salomon Brothers does this). Therefore, before mixing ratios from different sources, be sure to verify the exact definitions of the ratios used. From this discussion, it is apparent that the structure of a financial ratio analysis is dictated to a large degree by the extent and type of industry data available.

INTERNAL SOURCES

Larger firms will generally create their own comparative data using a computerized data base supplied by a financial services firm. For example, Standard and Poor's Compustat Services markets CDs which cover several thousand industrial and non-industrial companies.

To illustrate, the *Compustat* primary industry file consists of data on approximately 900 companies. For most companies, annual data are available for the past 20 years, and quarterly data for the last 20 quarters. The data, which are picked up from reports filed with the SEC, are in the form of annual report statements, and the records are updated on a weekly basis to reflect new data as companies report them. Firms which subscribe to the *Compustat* service can use this data base to create up-to-date, tailor-made statistics that best serve their individual needs.

SELF-TEST QUESTIONS

What are some external sources of comparative industry data?

Explain how a firm could create its own comparative industry financial data base.

PROBLEMS IN FINANCIAL STATEMENT ANALYSIS

In our earlier discussion of the ratios, we mentioned some of the problems one encounters in financial statement analysis. In this section, we discuss some additional problems and limitations.

DEVELOPING AND USING COMPARATIVE DATA

Many large firms operate a number of different divisions in quite different industries, and in such cases, it is difficult to develop meaningful industry averages. This tends to make financial statement analysis more useful for small firms with single product lines than for large, multiproduct companies.

Additionally, most firms want to be better than average (although half will be above and half below the median), so merely attaining average performance is not necessarily good. As a target for high-level performance, it is preferable to look at the industry leaders' ratios. Compilers of ratios such as D&B and Robert Morris Associates generally report industry ratios in quartiles. For example, D&B might report that 25 percent of the firms in the aluminum industry have a current ratio above 4.8, that the median is 2.5, and that 25 percent are below 1.6. This gives the analyst an idea of the distribution of ratios within an industry, and he or she can make better judgments about how the firm in question compares with the top firms in its industry.

DISTORTION OF COMPARATIVE DATA

Inflation has badly distorted firms' balance sheets. Further, reported profits are affected because past inflation affects both depreciation charges and the cost of inventory included in the cost of goods sold. Thus, a financial statement analysis for one firm over time, or a comparative analysis of firms of different ages or which use different accounting methods, must be interpreted with caution and judgment. Inflation's effects are discussed in detail in a later section.

Seasonal factors can also distort ratio analysis. For example, the inventory turnover ratio for a food processor will be radically different if the balance sheet figure used for inventory is the one just before versus just after the close of the canning season. Receivables, and also current liabilities, are often similarly affected. These problems can be minimized by using 12-month average figures for balance sheet items.

NOTES TO FINANCIAL STATEMENTS

Information which can significantly affect a firm's financial condition is often contained in the notes to its financial statements. These notes contain information on the firm's pension plan, on its noncapitalized lease agreements, on its recent acquisitions and divestitures, on its accounting policies, and so forth. For example, the notes to MicroDrive's financial statements contain the following information:

1. Inventories are valued at the lower of cost or market, with costs determined by the last-in, first-out (LIFO) method.

2. Receivables were reduced by $51.3 million in 1993 and by $42.7 million in 1992 to allow for doubtful accounts.

3. Noncancellable operating lease commitments are $26.8 million for 1994, $23.3 million for 1995, and $21.1 million for 1996.

4. As of December 31, 1993, the firm had a $968.2 million actuarial present value of vested pension benefits and $881.6 million in pension fund assets, so its unfunded pension liability was $86.6 million.

Clearly, this information has a bearing on MicroDrive's financial position, and it should be considered, either directly or indirectly, by the financial analyst. The decreasing lease commitment means that, other factors held constant, MicroDrive's fixed charge coverage ratio will improve in the future unless it signs new lease contracts. The unfunded pension liability means that the book value of the equity is in a sense overstated, so the general creditors' position is weaker than it would appear at first glance. Other potential problems might be revealed in a more detailed analysis. Indeed, professional analysts occasionally use the footnote information to recast financial statements on a common basis before they even begin to develop and compare ratios, and to these analysts the notes are especially vital.

INTERPRETATION OF RESULTS

It is difficult to generalize about whether a particular ratio is "good" or "bad." For example, a high quick ratio may show a strong liquidity position, which is good, or an excessive amount of cash, which is bad, because cash is a nonearning asset. Similarly, a high asset turnover ratio may denote either a firm that uses its assets efficiently or one that is undercapitalized and simply cannot afford to buy enough assets. Also, firms often have some ratios which look "good" and others which look "bad," making it difficult to tell whether the firm is, on balance, in a strong or a weak position. For this reason, ratio analysis is normally used as an input to judgmental decisions.[15]

---

[15]There are several quantitative approaches to summarizing the information obtained from a ratio analysis. For one example, see Chapter 23, where we discuss multiple discriminant analysis.

DIFFERENCES IN ACCOUNTING TREATMENT

Different accounting practices can distort ratio comparisons. For example, there are four commonly used inventory valuation methods: (1) specific identification, (2) first-in, first-out (FIFO), (3) last-in, first-out (LIFO), and (4) weighted average. During inflationary periods, LIFO produces a higher cost of goods sold and a lower end-of-period inventory valuation than do the other methods.

Of course, no problem would occur if firms being compared used the same accounting policies. Fortunately, most firms in a given industry normally do use similar procedures.

Other accounting practices can also create distortions. For example, if one firm uses short-term, noncapitalized leases to obtain a substantial amount of its productive equipment, then its reported assets may be low relative to its sales. At the same time, if the lease liability is not shown as a debt, then leasing may artificially improve the debt and turnover ratios. Again, this problem has been reduced but not eliminated by the accountants' requirement that firms capitalize most large nonoperating leases.

WINDOW DRESSING

Firms sometimes employ *window dressing* to make their financial statements look better to analysts. To illustrate, a Chicago builder borrowed on a 2-year note on December 29, 1993, held the proceeds of the loan as cash for a few days, and then paid off the loan ahead of time on January 4, 1994. This improved his current and quick ratios, and made his year-end 1993 balance sheet look good. However, the improvement was strictly temporary; a week later, the balance sheet was back at the old level.

On an even larger scale, E. F. Hutton and several other brokerage houses followed the practice of recording checks they had written, but which had not yet been cleared through the banking system, as current liabilities rather than simply deducting them from reported cash balances. Hutton had been systematically overdrawing its bank accounts, and the question was raised, during investigations into this practice, why its negative cash balances did not alert its bankers that something was amiss. It turned out that, presumably to avoid having to report negative cash, Hutton recorded checks received as cash, but it recorded checks written as current liabilities rather than as deductions from cash.

EFFECTS OF INFLATION

The high inflation rates of the late 1970s and early 1980s drew increased attention to the need to assess both the impact of inflation on business and the success of management in coping with it. Numerous reporting methods have been proposed to adjust accounting statements for inflation, but no consensus has been reached either on how to do this or even on the practical usefulness of the resulting data. Nevertheless, the Financial Accounting Standards Board issued Statements 33, 82, and 89, which encourage but do not require businesses to disclose supplementary data to reflect the effects of general inflation.

Financial Statement Effects.   Traditionally, financial statements have been prepared on the basis of historical costs, that is, the actual number of dollars paid for each asset purchased. However, inflation has caused the purchasing power of dollars to change over time, and as a result, financial statements can be badly distorted. To illustrate, a $100,000 expenditure on industrial land in 1993 would, in general, purchase far less acreage than a $100,000 expenditure in 1953, so adding 1993 dollars and 1953 dollars is much like adding apples and oranges. Nevertheless, this is done when the typical balance sheet is constructed. To help eliminate this disparity, the assets acquired in different years may be restated in *constant* dollars, each of which has equal purchasing power.

To reflect the effects of inflation, and thus to express operating results in dollars of comparable purchasing power, FASB encourages companies to show in annual reports what it characterizes as "income from continuing operations" calculated as if all its depreciable assets had been purchased with current-year dollars, and consequently its depreciation were based on higher-valued assets. Such an adjustment comes closer to showing what profits might be in the long run, when the old, undervalued assets have been replaced with new, inflated-value assets, and depreciation is correspondingly higher.

FASB also encourages firms to present a supplementary 5-year comparison of selected financial data in current dollars. Operating revenues, net income, and cash dividends per common share are typically restated in constant dollars. This allows investors to see what portion of growth stems from inflation effects as opposed to true economic growth.

Effects of Inflation on Ratio Analysis.   If a ratio analysis is based on "regular" financial statements, unadjusted for inflation, then distortions can creep in. Obviously, there will be a tendency for the value of the fixed assets to be understated, and inventories will also be understated if the firm uses LIFO accounting. At the same time, increasing rates of inflation will lead to increases in interest rates, which in turn will cause the value of the outstanding long-term debt to decline. Further, profits will vary from year to year as the inflation rate changes, and these variations will be especially severe if inventory is charged to cost of goods sold based on the FIFO method.

These factors tend to make ratio comparisons over time for a given company, and across companies at any point in time, less reliable than would be the case in the absence of inflation. This is especially true if a company changes its accounting procedures (say, from straight line to accelerated depreciation, or from FIFO to LIFO), or if various companies in a given industry use different accounting methods. Analysts can attempt to restate financial statements to put everything on a common basis, but, at best, this can only reduce the problem, not eliminate it. Indeed, with the present state of the art, financial analysts cannot do much more than base their financial statement analysis of a firm on its existing accounting data. However, analysts ought to recognize that there are weaknesses in this approach, and they should apply judgment in interpreting the data.

Financial statement analysis is useful, but analysts should be aware of the problems discussed in this section and then must make adjustments as necessary. Finan-

cial statement analysis conducted in a mechanical, unthinking manner is dangerous; however, used intelligently and with good judgment, it can provide useful
insights into a firm's operations.

SELF-TEST QUESTIONS

**Explain how each of the following factors could present problems to an
analyst conducting a financial statement analysis:**
   (1) Development of comparative data
   (2) Seasonal/cyclical data distortions
   (3) Differences in accounting treatment
   (4) Window dressing
   (5) Inflation

**Should analysts consider the information contained in the notes to the
financial statements when analyzing a firm's financial condition? Explain.**

SUMMARY

The primary purposes of this chapter were (1) to describe the basic financial statements and (2) to discuss techniques used by investors and managers to analyze
the statements. The key concepts covered are listed below.

▶ The four basic statements contained in the annual report are the *balance
   sheet,* the *income statement,* the *statement of retained earnings,* and the
   statement of cash flows. Investors use the information provided in these statements to form expectations about the future levels of earnings and dividends,
   and about the firm's riskiness.

▶ *Operating cash flows* differ from reported *accounting income.* Investors
   should be more interested in a firm's projected cash flows than in reported
   earnings, because it is cash, not paper profits, that is paid out as dividends and
   plowed back into the business to produce growth.

▶ *Financial statement analysis* generally begins with the calculation of a set of
   financial ratios designed to reveal the relative strengths and weaknesses of a
   company as compared to other companies in the same industry, and to show
   whether the firm's position has been improving or deteriorating over time.

▶ *Liquidity ratios* show the relationship of a firm's current assets to its current
   liabilities, and thus indicate the firm's ability to meet its maturing debts.

▶ *Asset management ratios* measure how effectively a firm is managing its assets.

▶ *Debt management ratios* reveal (1) the extent to which the firm is financed
   with debt and (2) its likelihood of defaulting on its debt obligations.

▶ *Profitability ratios* show the combined effects of liquidity, asset management,
   and debt management policies on operating results.

▶ *Market value ratios* relate the firm's stock price to its earnings and book value
   per share.

▶ *Trend analysis* reveals whether the firm's ratios are improving or deteriorating over time, while *comparative analysis* indicates how the firm compares with other firms or with industry averages.

▶ *Du Pont analysis* is designed to show how the profit margin on sales, the total assets turnover ratio, and the use of debt interact to determine the rate of return on equity.

▶ In a *common size analysis,* a firm's income statement and balance sheet are expressed in percentages. This facilitates comparisons among firms of different sizes and for a single firm over time.

Financial statement analysis has limitations, but used with care and judgment, it can be very helpful.

QUESTIONS

2-1   Define each of the following terms:

a.   Annual report; income statement; balance sheet

b.   Equity, or net worth; paid-in capital; retained earnings

c.   Cash flow cycle

d.   Statement of retained earnings; statement of cash flows

e.   Depreciation; inventory valuation methods

f.   Liquidity ratios: current ratio; quick, or acid test, ratio

g.   Asset management ratios: inventory turnover ratio; days sales outstanding (DSO); fixed assets turnover ratio; total assets turnover ratio

h.   Financial leverage: debt ratio; times-interest-earned (TIE) ratio; fixed charge coverage ratio

i.   Profitability ratios: profit margin on sales; basic earning power (BEP) ratio; return on total assets (ROA); return on common equity (ROE)

j.   Market value ratios: price/earnings (P/E) ratio; market/book (M/B) ratio

k.   Trend analysis; comparative analysis

l.   Du Pont equation

m.   "Window dressing"; seasonal effects on ratios

n.   Common size statements

2-2   What four statements are contained in most annual reports?

2-3   If a "typical" firm reports $10 million of retained earnings on its balance sheet, could its directors declare a $10 million cash dividend without any qualms whatsoever?

2-4   Financial ratio analysis is conducted by four groups of analysts: managers, equity investors, long-term creditors, and short-term creditors. What is the primary emphasis of each of these groups in evaluating ratios?

2-5   Why would the inventory turnover ratio be more important when analyzing a grocery chain than an insurance company?

2-6   Profit margins and turnover ratios vary from one industry to another. What differences would you expect to find between a grocery chain and a steel company? Think particularly about the turnover ratios and the profit margin, and think about the Du Pont equation.

2-7 How does inflation distort ratio analysis comparisons, both for one company over time (trend analysis) and when different companies are compared? Are only balance sheet items or both balance sheet and income statement items affected?

2-8 If a firm's ROE is low and management wants to improve it, explain how using more debt might help.

2-9 How might (a) seasonal factors and (b) different growth rates distort a comparative ratio analysis? Give some examples. How might these problems be alleviated?

2-10 Indicate the effects of the transactions listed in the following table on total current assets, current ratio, and net income. Use (+) to indicate an increase, (−) to indicate a decrease, and (0) to indicate either no effect or an indeterminate effect. Be prepared to state any necessary assumptions, and assume an initial current ratio of more than 1.0. (Note: A good accounting background is necessary to answer some of these questions; if yours is not strong, just answer the questions you can handle.)

	Total Current Assets	Current Ratio	Effect on Net Income
a. Cash is acquired through issuance of additional common stock.	___	___	___
b. Merchandise is sold for cash.	___	___	___
c. Federal income tax due for the previous year is paid.	___	___	___
d. A fixed asset is sold for less than book value.	___	___	___
e. A fixed asset is sold for more than book value.	___	___	___
f. Merchandise is sold on credit.	___	___	___
g. Payment is made to trade creditors for previous purchases.	___	___	___
h. A cash dividend is declared and paid.	___	___	___
i. Cash is obtained through short-term bank loans.	___	___	___
j. Short-term notes receivable are sold at a discount.	___	___	___
k. Marketable securities are sold below cost.	___	___	___
l. Advances are made to employees.	___	___	___
m. Current operating expenses are paid.	___	___	___
n. Short-term promissory notes are issued to trade creditors in exchange for past due accounts payable.	___	___	___
o. Ten-year notes are issued to pay off accounts payable.	___	___	___
p. A fully depreciated asset is retired.	___	___	___
q. Accounts receivable are collected.	___	___	___
r. Equipment is purchased with short-term notes.	___	___	___
s. Merchandise is purchased on credit.	___	___	___
t. The estimated taxes payable are increased.	___	___	___

SELF-TEST PROBLEMS (SOLUTIONS APPEAR IN APPENDIX C)

ST-1 (Debt ratio) K. Billingsworth & Co. had earnings per share of $4 last year, and it paid a $2 dividend. Total retained earnings increased by $12 million during the year, while book value per share at year end was $40. Billingsworth has no preferred stock, and no new common stock was issued during the year. If Billingsworth's year-end debt (which equals its total liabilities) was $120 million, what was the company's year-end debt/assets ratio?

ST-2 **(Ratio analysis)** The following data apply to A.L. Kaiser & Company (millions of dollars):

Cash and marketable securities	$100.00
Fixed assets	$283.50
Sales	$1,000.00
Net income	$50.00
Quick ratio	2.0×
Current ratio	3.0×
DSO	40 days
ROE	12%

Kaiser has no preferred stock—only common equity, current liabilities, and long-term debt.

a. Find Kaiser's (1) accounts receivable, (2) current liabilities, (3) current assets, (4) total assets, (5) ROA, (6) common equity, and (7) long-term debt.

b. In Part a, you should have found Kaiser's accounts receivable = $111.1 million. If Kaiser could reduce its DSO from 40 days to 30 days while holding other things constant, how much cash would it generate? If this cash were used to buy back common stock (at book value) and thus reduced the amount of common equity, how would this affect (1) the ROE, (2) the ROA, and (3) the total debt/total assets ratio?

PROBLEMS

2-1 **(Ratio analysis)** Data for Bowlin Beverages Company and its industry averages follow.

a. Calculate the indicated ratios for Bowlin.

b. Construct the Du Pont equation for both Bowlin and the industry.

c. Outline Bowlin's strengths and weaknesses as revealed by your analysis.

d. Suppose Bowlin had doubled its sales as well as its inventories, accounts receivable, and common equity during 1993. How would that information affect the validity of your ratio analysis? (Hint: Think about averages and the effects of rapid growth on ratios if averages are not used. No calculations are needed.)

Bowlin Beverages Company: Balance Sheet as of December 31, 1993

Cash	$ 77,500	Accounts payable	$ 129,000
Receivables	336,000	Notes payable	84,000
Inventories	241,500	Other current liabilities	117,000
Total current assets	$ 655,000	Total current liabilities	$ 330,000
Net fixed assets	292,500	Long-term debt	256,500
		Common equity	361,000
Total assets	$ 947,500	Total liabilities and equity	$ 947,500

**Bowlin Beverages Company: Income Statement
for Year Ended December 31, 1993**

Sales		$1,607,500
Cost of goods sold:		
Materials	$717,000	
Labor	453,000	
Heat, light, and power	68,000	
Indirect labor	113,000	
Depreciation	41,500	1,392,500
Gross profit		$ 215,000
Selling expenses		115,000
General and administrative expenses		30,000
Earnings before interest and taxes (EBIT)		$ 70,000
Interest expense		24,500
Earnings before taxes (EBT)		$ 45,500
Federal and state income taxes (40%)		18,200
Net income		$ 27,300

Ratio	Bowlin	Industry Average
Current assets/current liabilities	_____	2.0×
Days sales outstanding	_____	35 days
Sales/inventories	_____	6.7×
Sales/total assets	_____	3.0×
Net income/sales	_____	1.2%
Net income/total assets	_____	3.6%
Net income/equity	_____	9.0%
Total debt/total assets	_____	60.0%

2-2 **(Balance sheet analysis)** Complete the balance sheet and sales information in the table that follows for Visscher Industries using the following financial data:

Debt ratio: 50%
Quick ratio: 0.80×
Total assets turnover: 1.5×
Days sales outstanding: 36 days
Gross profit margin on sales: (Sales − Cost of goods sold)/Sales = 25%
Inventory turnover ratio: 5×

Balance Sheet

Cash	_____		Accounts payable	_____
Accounts receivable	_____		Long-term debt	60,000
Inventories	_____		Common stock	
Fixed assets	_____		Retained earnings	97,500
Total assets	$300,000		Total liabilities and equity	=====
Sales	_____		Cost of goods sold	_____

2-3 **(Du Pont analysis)** The Lanser Lighting Company, a manufacturer and wholesaler of high-quality light fixtures, has been experiencing low profitability in recent years. As a result, the board of directors has replaced the president of the firm with a new president, Joan Lamm, who has asked you to make an analysis of the firm's financial position using the Du Pont equation. The most recent industry average ratios and Lanser's financial statements are as follows:

Industry Average Ratios

Current ratio	2×	Sales/fixed assets	6×
Debt/total assets	30%	Sales/total assets	3×
Times-interest-earned	7×	Profit margin on sales	3%
Sales/inventory	10×	Return on total assets	9%
Days sales outstanding	24 days	Return on common equity	12.9%

Lanser Lighting Company: Balance Sheet as of December 31, 1993 (Millions of Dollars)

Cash	$ 45	Accounts payable	$ 45
Marketable securities	33	Notes payable	45
Net receivables	66	Other current liabilities	21
Inventories	159	Total current liabilities	$111
Total current assets	$303	Long-term debt	24
Gross fixed assets	$225	Total liabilities	$135
Less depreciation	78	Common stock	$114
Net fixed assets	$147	Retained earnings	201
		Total stockholders' equity	$315
Total assets	$450	Total liabilities and equity	$450

Lanser Lighting Company: Income Statement for Year Ended December 31, 1993 (Millions of Dollars)

Net sales	$795.0
Cost of goods sold	660.0
Gross profit	$135.0
Selling expenses	73.5
Depreciation expense	12.0
Earnings before interest and taxes	$ 49.5
Interest expense	4.5
Earnings before taxes (EBT)	45.0
Taxes (40%)	18.0
Net income	$ 27.0

a. Calculate those ratios that you think would be useful in this analysis.

b. Construct the Du Pont equation for Lanser, and compare the company's ratios to the industry average ratios.

c. Do the balance sheet accounts or the income statement figures seem to be primarily responsible for the low profits?

d. Which specific accounts seem to be most out of line in relation to other firms in the industry?

e. If Lanser had a pronounced seasonal sales pattern, or if it grew rapidly during the year, how might that affect the validity of your ratio analysis? How might you correct for such potential problems?

2-4 **(Ratio analysis)** Horrigan's Accessories Inc. forecasted 1994 financial statements follow, along with some industry average ratios.

a. Calculate Horrigan's 1994 forecasted ratios, compare them with the industry average data, and comment briefly on Horrigan's projected strengths and weaknesses.

b. What do you think would happen to Horrigan's ratios if the company initiated cost-cutting measures that allowed it to hold lower levels of inventory and substantially decreased the cost of goods sold? No calculations are necessary. Think about which ratios would be affected by changes in these two accounts.

Horrigan's Accessories Inc.: Forecasted Balance Sheet as of December 31, 1994

Cash	$ 72,000
Accounts receivable	439,000
Inventories	894,000
Total current assets	$1,405,000
Land and building	238,000
Machinery	132,000
Other fixed assets	61,000
Total assets	$1,836,000
Accounts and notes payable	$ 432,000
Accruals	170,000
Total current liabilities	$ 602,000
Long-term debt	404,290
Common stock	575,000
Retained earnings	254,710
Total liabilities and equity	$1,836,000

Horrigan's Accessories Inc.: Forecasted Income Statement for 1994

Sales	$4,290,000
Cost of goods sold	3,580,000
Gross operating profit	$ 710,000
General administrative and selling expenses	236,320
Depreciation	159,000
Miscellaneous	134,000
Earnings before taxes (EBT)	$ 180,680
Taxes (40%)	72,272
Net income	$ 108,408
Number of shares outstanding	23,000

Per-Share Data

EPS	$4.71
Cash dividends	$0.95
P/E ratio	5×
Market price (average)	$23.57

Industry Financial Ratios (1994)[a]

Quick ratio	$1.0\times$
Current ratio	$2.7\times$
Inventory turnover[b]	$7.0\times$
Days sales outstanding	32 days
Fixed assets turnover[b]	$13.0\times$
Total assets turnover[b]	$2.6\times$
Return on assets	9.1%
Return on equity	18.2%
Debt ratio	50.0%
Profit margin on sales	3.5%
P/E ratio	$6.0\times$

[a]Industry average ratios have been constant for the past four years.

[b]Based on year-end balance sheet figures.

Work the following parts only if you are using the computer problem diskette.

c. Suppose Horrigan's Accessories Inc. is considering installing a new computer system which would provide tighter control of inventories, accounts receivable, and accounts payable. If the new system is installed, the following data are projected (rather than the data given earlier) for the indicated balance sheet and income statement accounts:

Accounts receivable	$ 395,000
Inventories	700,000
Other fixed assets	150,000
Accounts and notes payable	275,000
Accruals	120,000
Cost of goods sold	3,450,000
Administrative and selling expenses	248,775
P/E ratio	$6\times$

How do these changes affect the projected ratios and the comparison with the industry averages? (Note that any changes to the income statement will change the amount of retained earnings; therefore, the model is set up to calculate 1994 retained earnings as 1993 retained earnings plus net income minus dividends paid. The model also adjusts the cash balance so that the balance sheet balances.)

d. If the new computer were even more efficient than Horrigan's management had estimated, and thus caused the cost of goods sold to decrease by $125,000 from the projections in Part c, what effect would that have on the company's financial position?

e. If the new computer were less efficient than Horrigan's management had estimated, and caused the cost of goods sold to increase by $125,000 from the projections in Part c, what effect would that have on the company's financial position?

f. Change, one by one, the other items in Part c to see how each change affects the ratio analysis. Then think about, and write a paragraph describing, how computer models like this one can be used to help make better decisions about the purchase of such things as a new computer system.

2-5 **(Ratio calculation)**   Assume you are given the following relationships for Delano Designs Inc.:

Sales/total assets	$1.5 \times$
Return on assets (ROA)	3%
Return on equity (ROE)	5%

Calculate Delano's profit margin and debt ratio.

2-6 **(Liquidity ratios)**   The Ezzell's Apparel Company has $1,312,500 in current assets and $525,000 in current liabilities. Its initial inventory level is $375,000, and it will raise funds as additional notes payable and use them to increase inventory. How much can Ezzell's short-term debt (notes payable) increase without pushing its current ratio below 2.0? What will be the firm's quick ratio after Ezzell has raised the maximum amount of short-term funds?

2-7 **(Ratio calculations)**   The Ferri Furniture Company had a quick ratio of 1.4, a current ratio of 3.0, an inventory turnover of 6 times, total current assets of $810,000, and cash and marketable securities of $120,000 in 1993. What were Ferri's annual sales and its DSO for that year?

2-8 **(Times-interest-earned ratio)**   Swensen Associates has $500,000 of debt outstanding, and it pays an interest rate of 10 percent annually. Swensen's annual sales are $2 million; its average tax rate is 20 percent; and its net profit margin on sales is 5 percent. If the company does not maintain a TIE ratio of at least 5 times, its bank will refuse to renew the loan, and bankruptcy will result. What is Swensen's TIE ratio?

2-9 **(Return on equity)**   Powell Manufacturing's ROE last year was only 3 percent, but its management has developed a new operating plan designed to improve things. The new plan calls for a total debt ratio of 60 percent, which will result in interest charges of $300 per year. Management projects an EBIT of $1,000 on sales of $10,000, and it expects to have a total assets turnover ratio of 2.0. Under these conditions, the average tax rate will be 30 percent. If the changes are made, what return on equity will Powell earn?

2-10 **(Return on equity)**   The Martell Auto Parts Company, which is just being formed, needs $1 million of assets, and it expects to have a basic earning power ratio of 20 percent. Martell will own no securities, so all of its income will be operating income. If it chooses to, Martell can finance up to 50 percent of its assets with debt, which will have an 8 percent interest rate. Assuming a 40 percent tax rate on all taxable income, what is the *difference* between its expected ROE if Martell finances with 50 percent debt versus its expected ROE if it finances entirely with common stock?

2-11 **(Conceptual: Return on equity)**   Which of the following statements is most correct? (Hint: Work Problem 2-10 before answering 2-11, and consider the solution setup for Problem 2-10 as you think about Problem 2-11.)

   a. If a firm's expected basic earning power (BEP) is constant for all of its assets and exceeds the interest rate on its debt, then adding assets and financing them with debt will raise the firm's expected rate of return on common equity (ROE).

   b. The higher its tax rate, the lower a firm's BEP ratio will be, other things held constant.

   c. The higher the interest rate on its debt, the lower a firm's BEP ratio will be, other things held constant.

   d. The higher its debt ratio, the lower a firm's BEP ratio will be, other things held constant.

   e. Statement a is false, but b, c, and d are all true.

2-12 (Return on equity) The Quigley Company has sales of $200,000, a net income of $15,000, and the following balance sheet:

Cash	$ 10,000	Accounts payable	$ 30,000
Receivables	50,000	Other current liabilities	20,000
Inventories	150,000	Long-term debt	50,000
Net fixed assets	90,000	Common equity	200,000
Total assets	$300,000	Total liabilities and equity	$300,000

a. The company's new owner thinks that inventories are excessive and can be lowered to the point where the current ratio is equal to the industry average, 2.5×, without affecting either sales or net income. If inventories are sold off and not replaced so as to reduce the current ratio to 2.5×, if the funds generated are used to reduce common equity (stock can be repurchased at book value), and if no other changes occur, by how much will the ROE change?

b. Now suppose we wanted to take this problem and modify it for use on an exam, that is, to create a new problem which you have not seen to test your knowledge of this type of problem. How would your answer change if (1) We doubled all the dollar amounts? (2) We stated that the target current ratio was 3.0×? (3) We stated that the target was to achieve an inventory turnover ratio of 2× rather than a current ratio of 2.5×? (Hint: Compare the ROE obtained with an inventory turnover ratio of 2× to the original ROE obtained before any changes are considered.) (4) We said that the company had 10,000 shares of stock outstanding, and we asked how much the change in Part a would increase EPS? (5) What would your answer to (4) be if we changed the original problem to state that the stock was selling for twice book value, so common equity would not be reduced on a dollar-for-dollar basis?

c. Now explain how we could have set the problem up to have you focus on changing accounts receivable, or fixed assets, or using the funds generated to retire debt (we would give you the interest rate on outstanding debt), or how the original problem could have stated that the company needed *more* inventories and it would finance them with new common equity or with new debt.

MINI CASE

Donna Jamison was recently hired as a financial analyst by Computron Industries, a manufacturer of electronic calculators. Her first task was to conduct a financial analysis of the firm covering the last two years. To begin, she gathered the following financial statements and other data.

BALANCE SHEETS	1993	1992
Assets:		
Cash	$ 52,000	$ 57,600
Accounts receivable	402,000	351,200
Inventories	836,000	715,200
Total current assets	$1,290,000	$1,124,000
Gross fixed assets	$ 527,000	$ 491,000
Less accumulated depreciation	166,200	146,200
Net fixed assets	$ 360,800	$ 344,800
Total assets	$1,650,800	$1,468,800

j. Although financial statement analysis can provide useful information about a company's operations and its financial condition, this type of analysis does have some potential problems and limitations, and it must be used with care and judgment. What are some problems and limitations?

SELECTED ADDITIONAL REFERENCES AND CASES

The effects of alternative accounting policies on both financial statements and ratios based on these statements are discussed in the investment textbooks referenced in Chapter 4, and also in the many excellent texts on financial statement analysis. For example, see

Gibson, Charles H., and Patricia A. Frishkoff, *Financial Statement Analysis* (Boston: Kent, 1986).

Hawkins, David F., *Corporate Financial Reporting and Analysis* (Homewood, Ill.: Irwin, 1986).

For further information on the relative usefulness of various financial ratios, see

Chen, Kung H., and Thomas A. Shimerda, "An Empirical Analysis of Useful Financial Ratios," *Financial Management,* Spring 1981, 51–60.

Considerable work has been done to establish the relationship between bond ratings and financial ratios. For one example, see

Belkaoui, Ahmed, *Industrial Bonds and the Rating Process* (London: Quorum Books, 1983).

For sources of ratios and common size statements, see the following:

Dun & Bradstreet, *Key Business Ratios* (New York: Updated annually).

Financial Research Associates, *Financial Studies of the Small Business* (Arlington, Va.: Updated annually).

Robert Morris Associates, *Annual Statement Studies* (Philadelphia: Updated annually).

The following Brigham-Gapenski cases focus on financial analysis:

Case 35, "Mark X Company (A)," which illustrates the use of ratio analysis in the evaluation of a firm's existing and potential financial positions.

Case 36, "Garden State Container Corporation," which is similar in content to Case 35.

THE FINANCIAL ENVIRONMENT: MARKETS, INSTITUTIONS, INTEREST RATES, AND TAXES

I
n December 1991, after 17 months of recession, Chairman Alan Greenspan of the Federal Reserve Board took two drastic actions in an attempt to halt the recession: He announced that the Fed (1) was cutting the discount rate that it charges on loans to banks from 4.5 percent to 3.5 percent, its lowest level in 27 years, and (2) was lowering the federal funds rate (the interest rate charged on overnight loans between banks) from 4.5 percent to 4 percent. The announcement came as a surprise—this was the biggest interest-rate cut in a decade. Previous Fed actions had been small, cautious quarter-point reductions which had been announced with minimum fanfare to keep the financial markets convinced of the Fed's commitment to fight inflation.

Greenspan's announcement came in response to growing criticism from the White House, Congress, and private economists, who accused the Fed of worrying too much about bond-market psychology and too little about the rapidly deteriorating confidence of both consumers and business executives. In addition, new forecasts by the Fed's economists (who had earlier been confident that the economy was recovering) showed an economy "dead in the water." Finally, a survey of manufacturers revealed that manufacturing activity had fallen to its lowest level of the year.

The financial system responded immediately to Greenspan's announcement. Morgan Guaranty Trust Co. cut its prime lending rate from 7.5 percent to 6.5

bonds of the largest U.S. corporations are traded, is a prime example of a capital market.

4. *Mortgage markets* deal with loans on residential, commercial, and industrial real estate, and on farmland, while *consumer credit markets* involve loans on autos and appliances, as well as loans for education, vacations, and so on.

5. *World, national, regional,* and *local markets* also exist. Thus, depending on an organization's size and scope of operations, it may be able to borrow all around the world, or it may be confined to a strictly local, even neighborhood, market.

6. *Primary markets* are the markets in which corporations raise new capital. If GE were to sell a new issue of common stock to raise capital, this would be a primary market transaction. The corporation selling the newly created stock receives the proceeds from the sale in a primary market transaction. *Secondary markets* are markets in which existing, already outstanding, securities are traded among investors. Thus, if Margaret White decided to buy 1,000 shares of IBM stock, the purchase would occur in the secondary market. The New York Stock Exchange is a secondary market, since it deals in outstanding as opposed to newly issued stocks and bonds. Secondary markets also exist for mortgages, various other types of loans, and other financial assets. The corporation whose securities are being traded is not involved in a secondary market transaction and, thus, does not receive any funds from such a sale.

Other classifications could be made, but this breakdown is sufficient to show that there are many types of financial markets.

A healthy economy is dependent on efficient transfers of funds from people who are net savers to firms and individuals who need capital. Without efficient transfers, the economy simply could not function: Carolina Power & Light could not raise capital, so Raleigh's citizens would have no electricity; the Johnson family would not have adequate housing; and Kathy Hanks would have no place to invest her savings. Obviously, the level of employment and productivity, hence our standard of living, would be much lower. Therefore, it is absolutely essential that our financial markets function efficiently—not only quickly, but also at a low cost.[1]

Table 3-1 gives a listing of the most important instruments traded in the various financial markets. The instruments are arranged from top to bottom in ascending order of typical length of maturity. As we go through the book, we will look in much more detail at many of these instruments. For example, we will see that there are actually many varieties of corporate bonds, ranging from "plain vanilla flavored" bonds, to bonds that are convertible into common stocks, and to bonds whose interest payments vary depending on the rate of inflation. Still, the table gives an idea of the characteristics and costs of the instruments traded in the major financial markets.

---

[1] As the Commonwealth of Independent States (the former Soviet Union) and the Eastern European nations move toward capitalism, just as much attention must be paid to the establishment of cost-efficient financial markets as to electrical power, transportation, communications, and other infrastructure systems. Economic efficiency is simply impossible without a good system for allocating capital within the economy.

TABLE 3-1 SUMMARY OF MAJOR MARKET INSTRUMENTS, MARKET PARTICIPANTS, AND SECURITY CHARACTERISTICS

Instrument	Market	Major Participants	Security Characteristics		
			Riskiness	Original Maturity	Interest Rate on 5/5/93[a]
U.S. Treasury bills	Money	Sold by U.S. Treasury to finance federal expenditures	Default-free	91 days to 1 year	3.2%
Banker's acceptances	Money	Firm's promise to pay, guaranteed by bank	Low degree of risk if guaranteed by a strong bank	Up to 180 days	3.3%
Commercial paper	Money	Issued by financially secure firms to large investors	Low default risk	Up to 270 days	3.4%
Negotiable certificates of deposit (CDs)	Money	Issued by major money-center commercial banks to large investors	Riskier than Treasury bills	Up to 1 year	3.3%
Money market mutual funds	Money	Invest in Treasury bills, CDs, and commercial paper; held by individuals and businesses	Low degree of risk	No specific maturity (instant liquidity)	3.5%
Eurodollar market time deposits	Money	Issued by banks outside U.S.	Default risk is a function of issuing bank	Up to 1 year	3.4%
Consumer credit loans	Money	Issued by banks/ credit unions/ finance companies to individuals	Risk is variable	Variable	Variable
U.S. Treasury notes and bonds	Capital	Issued by U.S. government	No default risk, but price can decline if interest rates rise	2 to 30 years	6.9%
Mortgages	Capital	Borrowings from commercial banks and S&Ls by individuals and businesses	Risk is variable	Up to 30 years	7.2%
State and local government bonds	Capital	Issued by state and local governments to individuals and institutional investors	Riskier than U.S. government securities, but exempt from most taxes	Up to 30 years	6.0%

(continued)

[a]Interest rates are for longest maturity securities of the type and for the strongest securities of a given type. Thus, the 6.0% interest rate shown for state and local government bonds reflects the rate on 30-year, Aaa bonds. Lower-rated bonds had higher interest rates.

SELF-TEST QUESTIONS

Distinguish between physical asset markets and financial asset markets.

What is the difference between spot and futures markets?

Distinguish between money and capital markets.

TABLE 3-1   *continued*

Instrument	Market	Major Participants	Security Characteristics		
			Riskiness	Original Maturity	Interest Rate on 5/5/93[a]
Corporate bonds	Capital	Issued by corporations to individuals and institutional investors	Riskier than U.S. government securities, but less risky than preferred and common stocks; varying degree of risk within bonds depending on strength of issuer	Up to 50 years	7.4%
Leases	Capital	Similar to debt in that firms can lease assets rather than borrow and then buy the assets	Risk similar to corporate bonds	Generally 3 to 20 years	Similar to bond yields
Preferred stocks	Capital	Issued by corporations to individuals and institutional investors	Riskier than corporate bonds, but less risky than common stock	Unlimited	6 to 8%
Common stocks	Capital	Issued by corporations to individuals and institutional investors	Risky	Unlimited	10 to 15%

[a]Common stocks are expected to provide a "return" in the form of dividends and capital gains rather than interest. Of course, if you buy a stock, while you may *expect* to earn 10 percent on your money, the stock's price may decline and cause you to experience a 100 percent loss. Also, tax considerations tend to lower the interest (dividends) paid on preferred stock.

What is the difference between primary and secondary markets?

Why are financial markets essential for a healthy economy?

FINANCIAL INSTITUTIONS

Transfers of capital between savers and those who need capital take place in the three different ways diagrammed in Figure 3-1:

1. *Direct transfers* of money and securities, as shown in the top section, occur when a business sells its stocks or bonds directly to savers, without going through any type of financial institution. The business delivers its securities to savers, who in turn give the firm the money it needs.

2. As shown in the middle section, transfers may also go through an *investment banking house* such as Morgan Stanley, which serves as a middleman and facili-

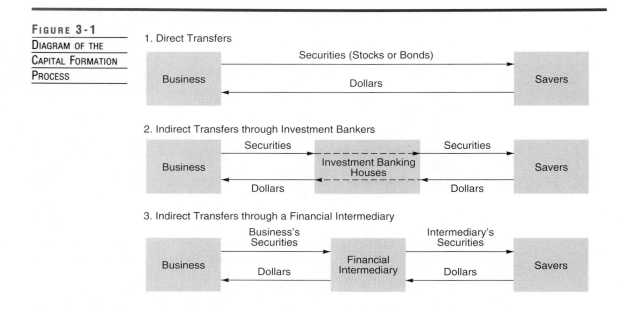

Figure 3-1

Diagram of the Capital Formation Process

tates the issuance of securities. The company sells its stocks or bonds to the investment bank, which in turn sells these same securities to savers. The businesses' securities and the savers' money merely "pass through" the investment banking house. However, the investment bank does buy and hold the securities for a period of time, so it is taking a chance — it may not be able to resell them to savers for as much as it paid. Because new securities are involved and the corporation receives money from the sale, this is a primary market transaction.

3. Transfers can also be made through a *financial intermediary* such as a bank or mutual fund. Here the intermediary obtains funds from savers, issuing its own securities in exchange, and it then uses the money to purchase and then hold a business's securities. For example, a saver might give dollars to a bank, receiving from it a certificate of deposit, and then the bank might lend the money to a small business in the form of a mortgage loan. Thus, intermediaries literally create new forms of capital — in this case, certificates of deposit, which are both safer and more liquid than mortgages and thus are better securities for most savers to hold. The existence of intermediaries greatly increases the efficiency of money and capital markets.

For simplicity, we assumed that the entity which needs capital is a business, specifically a corporation, but it is easy to visualize the demander of capital as a home purchaser, a government unit, and so on.

Direct transfers of funds from savers to businesses are possible and do occur on occasion, but it is generally more efficient for a business to enlist the services of an *investment banking house.* Merrill Lynch, Salomon Brothers, Dean Witter,

and Goldman Sachs are examples of financial service corporations which offer investment banking services. Such organizations (1) help corporations design securities with the features that are currently most attractive to investors, (2) buy these securities from the corporation, and (3) then resell them to savers. Although the securities are sold twice, this process is really one primary market transaction, with the investment banker acting as a middleman to facilitate the transfer of capital from savers to businesses.

The *financial intermediaries* shown in the third section of Figure 3-1 do more than simply transfer money and securities between firms and savers—they literally create new financial products. Since the intermediaries are generally large, they gain economies of scale in analyzing the creditworthiness of potential borrowers, in processing and collecting loans, and in pooling risks and thus helping individual savers diversify, hence "not put all their financial eggs in one basket." Further, a system of specialized intermediaries can enable savings to do more than just draw interest. For example, individuals can put money into banks and get both interest income and a convenient way of making payments (checking), or put money into life insurance companies and get both interest income and protection for their beneficiaries.

In the United States and other developed nations, a large set of specialized, highly efficient financial intermediaries has evolved. The situation is changing rapidly, however, and different types of institutions are performing services that were formerly reserved for others, causing institutional distinctions to become blurred. Still, there is a degree of institutional identity, and here are the major classes of intermediaries:

1. *Commercial banks,* which are the traditional "department stores of finance," serve a wide variety of savers and those with needs for funds. Historically, the commercial banks were the major institutions which handled checking accounts and through which the Federal Reserve System expanded or contracted the money supply. Today, however, several other institutions also provide checking services and significantly influence the effective money supply. Conversely, commercial banks are providing an ever-widening range of services, including stock brokerage services and insurance.

Note that commercial banks are quite different from investment banks. Commercial banks lend money, whereas investment banks help companies raise capital from other parties. Prior to 1933, commercial banks offered investment banking services, but the Glass-Steagall Act, which was passed in that year, prohibited commercial banks from engaging in investment banking. Thus, the Morgan Bank was broken up into two separate organizations, one of which is now the Morgan Guaranty Trust Company, a commercial bank, while the other is Morgan Stanley, a major investment banking house. Note also that Japanese and European banks can offer both commercial and investment banking services. This severely hinders U.S. banks in global competition, so efforts are being made by many commercial bankers to get Glass-Steagall repealed.

2. *Savings and loan associations (S&Ls),* which have traditionally served individual savers and residential and commercial mortgage borrowers, take the funds

of many small savers and then lend this money to home buyers and other types of borrowers. Because the savers obtain a degree of liquidity that would be absent if they bought the mortgages or other securities directly, perhaps the most significant economic function of the S&Ls is to "create liquidity" which would otherwise be lacking. Also, the S&Ls have more expertise in analyzing credit, setting up loans, and making collections than individual savers, so they reduce the cost and increase the availability of real estate loans. Finally, the S&Ls hold large, diversified portfolios of loans and other assets and thus spread risks in a manner that would be impossible if small savers were directly making mortgage loans. Because of these factors, savers benefit by being able to invest their savings in more liquid, better managed, and less risky accounts, whereas borrowers benefit by being able to obtain more capital, and at lower costs, than would otherwise be possible. In the 1980s, the S&L industry experienced severe problems when (1) short-term interest rates on savings accounts rose well above the returns being earned on mortgages and (2) commercial real estate suffered a severe slump resulting in high mortgage default rates. Together, these events forced many S&Ls to either merge with stronger institutions or close their doors. Today, the S&L industry is smaller and more focused, with companies either playing the traditional S&L role discussed above or acting as mortgage originators and collection agents, wherein the mortgages originated are immediately sold to a governmental agency such as the Government National Mortgage Association.

3. *Mutual savings banks,* which are similar to S&Ls, operate primarily in the northeastern states, accept savings primarily from individuals, and lend mainly on a long-term basis to home buyers and consumers.

4. *Credit unions* are cooperative associations whose members have a common bond, such as being employees of the same firm. Members' savings are loaned only to other members, generally for auto purchases, home improvements, and even home mortgages. Credit unions often are the cheapest source of funds available to individual borrowers.

5. *Pension funds* are retirement plans funded by corporations or government agencies for their workers and administered primarily by the trust departments of commercial banks or by life insurance companies. Pension funds invest primarily in bonds, stocks, mortgages, and real estate.

6. *Life insurance companies* take savings in the form of annual premiums, then invest these funds in stocks, bonds, real estate, and mortgages, and finally make payments to the beneficiaries of the insured parties. In recent years, life insurance companies have also offered a variety of tax-deferred savings plans designed to provide benefits to the participants when they retire.

7. *Mutual funds* are corporations which accept money from savers and then use these funds to buy stocks, long-term bonds, or short-term debt instruments issued by businesses or government units. These organizations pool funds and thus reduce risks by diversification. They also achieve economies of scale, which lower the costs of analyzing securities, managing portfolios, and buying and selling securities. Different funds are designed to meet the objectives of different types of

savers. Hence, there are bond funds for those who desire safety, stock funds for savers who are willing to accept significant risks in the hope of higher returns, and still other funds that are used as interest-bearing checking accounts (the *money market funds*). There are literally thousands of different mutual funds with dozens of different goals and purposes.

Financial institutions have historically been heavily regulated, with the primary purpose of this regulation being to insure the safety of the institutions and thus to protect depositors. However, these regulations—which have taken the form of prohibitions on nationwide branch banking, restrictions on the types of assets the institutions can buy, ceilings on the interest rates they can pay, and limitations on the types of services they can provide—have tended to impede the free flow of capital from surplus to deficit areas, and thus have hurt the efficiency of our capital markets. Recognizing this fact, Congress has authorized some major changes, and more will be forthcoming.

The result of the ongoing regulatory changes has been a blurring of the distinctions between the different types of institutions. Indeed, the trend in the United States today is toward huge *financial service corporations,* which own banks, S&Ls, investment banking houses, insurance companies, pension plan operations, and mutual funds, and which have branches across the country and even around the world. Examples of financial service corporations, most of which started in one area and have now diversified to cover most of the financial spectrum, include Transamerica, Merrill Lynch, American Express, Citicorp, Fidelity, and Prudential.

SELF-TEST QUESTIONS

Identify the three different ways capital is transferred between savers and borrowers.

What is the difference between a commercial bank and an investment bank?

List the similarities and differences between investment banking houses and financial intermediaries.

List the major types of intermediaries and briefly describe each's function.

THE STOCK MARKET

As noted earlier, secondary markets are those in which outstanding, previously issued securities are traded. By far the most active secondary market, and the most important one to financial managers, is the *stock market*. It is here that the prices of firms' stocks are established, and, since the primary goal of financial management is to maximize the firm's stock price, a knowledge of this market is essential for anyone involved in managing a business.

THE STOCK EXCHANGES

There are two basic types of stock markets: (1) *organized exchanges,* which include the New York Stock Exchange (NYSE), the American Stock Exchange (AMEX), and several regional exchanges and (2) the less formal *over-the-counter market.* Since the organized exchanges have actual physical market locations and are easier to describe and understand, we shall consider them first.

The *organized security exchanges* are tangible physical entities. Each of the larger ones occupies its own building, has specifically designated members, and has an elected governing body—its board of governors. Members are said to have "seats" on the exchange, although everybody stands up. These seats, which are bought and sold, give the holder the right to trade on the exchange. There are 1,366 seats on the New York Stock Exchange, and in 1993, NYSE seats were selling for about $600,000.

Most of the larger investment banking houses operate *brokerage departments,* which own seats on the exchanges and designate one or more of their officers as members. The exchanges are open on all normal working days, with the members meeting in a large room equipped with telephones and other electronic equipment that enable each member to communicate with his or her firm's offices throughout the country.

Like other markets, security exchanges facilitate communication between buyers and sellers. For example, Merrill Lynch (the largest brokerage firm) might receive an order in its Atlanta office from a customer who wants to buy 100 shares of IBM stock. Simultaneously, Dean Witter's Denver office might receive an order from a customer wishing to sell 100 shares of IBM. Each broker communicates by wire with the firm's representative on the NYSE. Other brokers throughout the country are also communicating with their own exchange members. The exchange members with *sell orders* offer the shares for sale, and they are bid for by the members with *buy orders.* Thus, the exchanges operate as *auction markets.*[2]

---

[2]The NYSE is actually a modified auction market, wherein people (through their brokers) bid for stocks. Originally—about 200 years ago—brokers would literally shout, "I have 100 shares of Apex for sale; how much am I offered?" and then sell to the highest bidder. If a broker had a buy order, he or she would shout, "I want to buy 100 shares of Apex; who'll sell at the best price?" The same general situation still exists, although the exchanges now have members known as *specialists* who facilitate the trading process by keeping an inventory of shares of the stocks in which they specialize. If a buy order comes in at a time when no sell order arrives, the specialist will sell off some inventory. Similarly, if a sell order comes in, the specialist will buy and add to inventory. The specialist sets a *bid price* (the price the specialist will pay for the stock) and an *asked price* (the price at which shares will be sold out of inventory). The bid and asked prices are set at levels designed to keep the inventory in balance. If many buy orders start coming in because of favorable developments or sell orders come in because of unfavorable events, the specialist will raise or lower prices to keep supply and demand in balance. Bid prices are somewhat lower than asked prices, with the difference, or *spread,* representing the specialist's profit margin.

Special facilities are available to help institutional investors such as mutual funds or pension funds sell large blocks of stock without depressing their prices. In essence, brokerage houses which cater to institutional clients will purchase blocks (defined as 10,000 or more shares) and then resell the stock to other institutions or individuals. Also, when a firm has a major announcement which is likely to cause its stock price to change sharply, it will ask the exchanges to halt trading in its stock until the announcement has been made and digested by investors. Thus, when Texaco announced that it planned to acquire Getty Oil, trading was halted for one day in both Texaco and Getty stocks.

THE OVER-THE-COUNTER MARKET

In contrast to the organized security exchanges, the *over-the-counter market* is a nebulous, intangible organization. An explanation of the term "over-the-counter" will help clarify exactly what this market is. The exchanges operate as auction markets — buy and sell orders come in more or less simultaneously, and exchange members match these orders. If a stock is traded less frequently, perhaps because it is the stock of a new or a small firm, few buy and sell orders come in, and matching them within a reasonable length of time would be difficult. To avoid this problem, some brokerage firms maintain an inventory of such stocks — they buy when individual investors want to sell and sell when investors want to buy. At one time the inventory of securities was kept in a safe, and the stocks, when bought and sold, were literally passed over the counter.

Today, the over-the-counter market is defined to include all facilities that are needed to conduct security transactions not conducted on the organized exchanges. These facilities consist of (1) the relatively few *dealers* who hold inventories of over-the-counter securities and who are said to "make a market" in these securities, (2) the thousands of brokers who act as *agents* in bringing these dealers together with investors, and (3) the computers, terminals, and electronic networks that provide a communications link between dealers and brokers. The dealers who make a market in a particular stock continuously quote a price at which they are willing to buy the stock (the *bid price*) and a price at which they will sell shares (the *asked price*). Each dealer's prices, which are adjusted as supply and demand conditions change, can be read off computer screens all across the country. The spread between bid and asked prices represents the dealer's markup, or profit.

Brokers and dealers who make up the over-the-counter market are members of a self-regulating body known as the *National Association of Securities Dealers (NASD)*, which licenses brokers and oversees trading practices. The computerized trading network used by NASD is known as the NASD Automated Quotation System (NASDAQ), and *The Wall Street Journal* and other newspapers provide information on NASDAQ transactions.

In terms of numbers of issues, the majority of stocks are traded over-the-counter. However, because the stocks of most large companies are listed on the exchanges, about two-thirds of the dollar volume of stock trading takes place on the exchanges. In recent years, many large companies, including Microsoft, Intel, MCI, and Apple, have elected to remain NASDAQ stocks, so the over-the-counter market is growing faster than the exchanges.

SOME TRENDS IN SECURITY TRADING PROCEDURES

From the NYSE's inception in 1792 until the 1970s, the vast majority of all stock trading occurred on the Exchange and was conducted by member firms. The NYSE established a set of minimum brokerage commission rates, and no member firm could charge a commission lower than the set rate. This was a monopoly, pure and simple. However, on May 1, 1975, the Securities and Exchange Commission (SEC), with strong prodding from the Antitrust Division of the Justice Department,

forced the NYSE to abandon its fixed commissions. Commission rates declined dramatically, falling in some cases as much as 90 percent from former levels.

These changes were a boon to the investing public, but not to the brokerage industry. A number of "full-service" brokerage houses went bankrupt, and others were forced to merge with stronger firms. The number of brokerage houses has declined from literally thousands in the 1960s to a much smaller number of large, strong, nationwide companies, many of which are units of diversified financial service corporations. Deregulation has also spawned a number of "discount brokers," some of which are affiliated with commercial banks or mutual fund investment companies.[3]

SELF-TEST QUESTIONS

What are the two basic types of stock markets, and how do they differ?

How has deregulation changed security trading procedures?

THE COST OF MONEY

Capital in a free economy is allocated through the price system. *The interest rate is the price paid to borrow debt capital, whereas in the case of equity capital, investors expect to receive dividends and capital gains.* The factors which affect the supply of and the demand for investment capital, and hence the cost of money, are discussed in this section.

The four most fundamental factors affecting the cost of money are (1) *production opportunities,* (2) *time preferences for consumption,* (3) *risk,* and (4) *inflation.* To see how these factors operate, visualize an isolated island community where the people live on fish. They have a stock of fishing gear which permits them to survive reasonably well, but they would like to have more fish. Now suppose Mr. Crusoe had a bright idea for a new type of fishnet that would enable him to double his daily catch. However, it would take him a year to perfect his design, to build his net, and to learn how to use it efficiently, and Mr. Crusoe would probably starve before he could put his new net into operation. Therefore, he might suggest to Ms. Robinson, Mr. Friday, and several others that if they would give him one fish each day for a year, he would return two fish a day during all of the next year. If someone accepted the offer, then the fish which Ms. Robinson or one of the others gave to Mr. Crusoe would constitute *savings;* these savings

---

[3]Full-service brokers give investors information on different stocks and make recommendations as to which stocks to buy. Discount brokers generally do not give advice—they merely execute orders, although there has been a growing trend toward providing limited investment advice in recent years. Some brokerage houses (institutional houses) cater primarily to institutional investors such as pension funds and insurance companies, while others cater to individual investors and are called "retail houses." Large firms such as Merrill Lynch generally have both retail and institutional brokerage operations.

in existence. The going interest rate, which can be designated as either k or i, but for purposes of the discussion here is designated as k, is initially 10 percent for the low-risk securities in Market A.[5] Borrowers whose credit is strong enough to qualify for this market can obtain funds at a cost of 10 percent, and investors who want to put their money to work without much risk can obtain a 10 percent return. Riskier borrowers must obtain higher-cost funds in Market B. Investors who are more willing to take risks invest in Market B expecting to earn a 12 percent return but also realizing that they might actually receive much less.

If the demand for funds declines, as it typically does during business recessions, the demand curve will shift to the left, as shown in Curve D_2 in Market A. The market-clearing, or equilibrium, interest rate in this example declines to 8 percent. Similarly, you should be able to visualize what would happen if the Federal Reserve tightened credit: The supply curve, S_1, would shift to the left, and this would raise interest rates and lower the level of borrowing in the economy.

Capital markets are interdependent. For example, if Markets A and B were in equilibrium before the demand shift to D_2 in Market A, this means that investors were willing to accept the higher risk in Market B in exchange for a *risk premium* of 12% − 10% = 2%. After the shift to D_2, the risk premium would initially increase to 12% − 8% = 4%. In all likelihood, this much larger premium would induce some of the lenders in Market A to shift to Market B; this, in turn, would cause the supply curve in Market A to shift to the left (or up) and that in Market B to shift to the right. The transfer of capital between markets would raise the interest rate in Market A and lower it in Market B, thus bringing the risk premium back closer to the original level, 2 percent.

There are many capital markets in the United States. U.S. firms also invest and raise capital throughout the world, and foreigners both borrow and lend capital in the United States. There are markets in the United States for home loans; farm loans; business loans; federal, state, and local government loans; and consumer loans. Within each category, there are regional markets as well as different types of submarkets. For example, in real estate there are separate markets for first and second mortgages and for loans on single-family homes, apartments, office buildings, shopping centers, vacant land, and so on. Within the business sector, there are dozens of types of debt and also several different markets for common stocks.

There is a price for each type of capital, and these prices change over time as shifts occur in supply and demand conditions. Figure 3-3 shows how long- and short-term interest rates to business borrowers have varied since the 1950s. Notice that short-term interest rates are especially prone to rise during booms and then fall during recessions. (The shaded areas of the chart indicate recessions.) When the economy is expanding, firms need capital, and this demand for capital pushes rates up. Also, inflationary pressures are strongest during business booms, and that also exerts upward pressure on rates. Conditions are reversed during recessions such as the one in 1991 and 1992. Slack business reduces the demand for credit,

---

[5]The letter k is the traditional symbol for interest rates, but i is being used frequently today because this term corresponds to the interest rate key on most financial calculators.

FIGURE 3-3   LONG- AND SHORT-TERM INTEREST RATES, 1955–1992

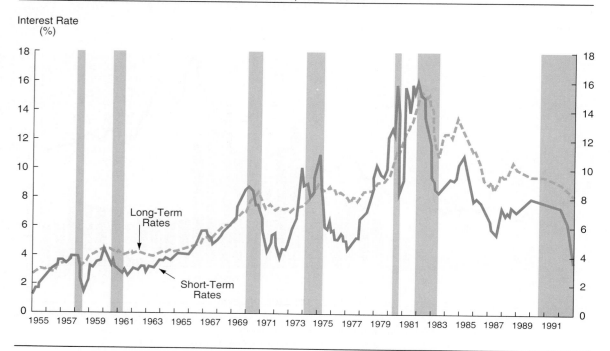

Notes:

a. The shaded areas designate business recessions.

b. Short-term rates are measured by four- to six-month loans to very large, strong corporations, and long-term rates are measured by AAA corporate bonds.

Source: *Federal Reserve Bulletin.*

the rate of inflation falls, and the result is a drop in interest rates. Furthermore, the Federal Reserve often lowers short-term rates during recessions to help stimulate the economy.

These tendencies do not hold exactly—the period after 1984 is a case in point. The price of oil fell dramatically in 1985 and 1986, reducing inflationary pressures on other prices and easing fears of serious long-term inflation. Earlier, these fears had pushed interest rates to record levels. The economy from 1984 to 1987 was fairly strong, but the declining fears about inflation more than offset the normal tendency of interest rates to rise during good economic times, and the net result was lower interest rates.[6]

---

[6]Short-term rates are responsive to current economic conditions, whereas long-term rates primarily reflect long-run expectations for inflation. As a result, short-term rates are sometimes above and sometimes below long-term rates. The relationship between long-term and short-term rates is called the *term structure of interest rates.* This topic is discussed later in the chapter.

FIGURE 3-4   RELATIONSHIP BETWEEN ANNUAL INFLATION RATES AND LONG-TERM INTEREST RATES, 1955–1992

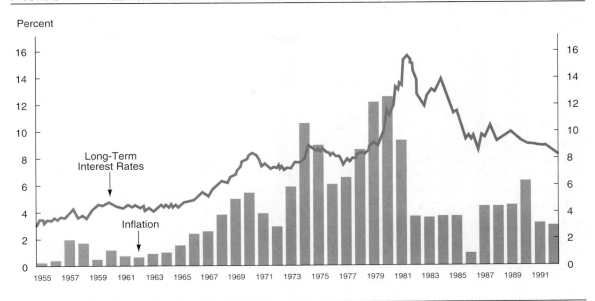

Notes:

a. Interest rates are those on AAA long-term corporate bonds.

b. Inflation is measured as the annual rate of change in the Consumer Price Index (CPI).

Source: *Federal Reserve Bulletin.*

The relationship between inflation and long-term interest rates is highlighted in Figure 3-4, which plots rates of inflation along with long-term interest rates. Prior to 1965, when the average rate of inflation was about 1 percent, interest rates on AAA-rated bonds generally ranged from 4 to 5 percent. As the war in Vietnam accelerated in the late 1960s, the rate of inflation increased, and interest rates began to rise. The rate of inflation dropped after 1970 and so did long-term interest rates. However, the 1973 Arab oil embargo was followed by a quadrupling of oil prices in 1974, which caused a spurt in inflation, which in turn drove interest rates to new record highs in 1974 and 1975. Inflationary pressures eased in late 1975 and 1976 but then rose again after 1976. In 1980, inflation rates hit the highest level on record, and fears of continued double-digit inflation pushed interest rates up to historic highs. From 1981 through 1986, the inflation rate dropped sharply, and in 1986 inflation was only 1.1 percent, the lowest level in 25 years. Currently (in May 1993), inflation is about 3 percent, and long-term interest rates to strong corporations have declined to about 7.4 percent.

SELF-TEST QUESTIONS

How are interest rates used to allocate capital among firms?

What happens to market-clearing, or equilibrium, interest rates in a capital market when the demand for funds declines? What happens when inflation increases or decreases?

Why does the price of capital change during booms and recessions?

How does risk affect interest rates?

THE DETERMINANTS OF MARKET INTEREST RATES

In general, the quoted (or nominal) interest rate on a debt security, k, is composed of a real risk-free rate of interest, k*, plus several premiums that reflect inflation, the riskiness of the security, and the security's marketability (or liquidity). This relationship can be expressed as follows:

$$\text{Quoted interest rate} = k = k^* + IP + DRP + LP + MRP. \qquad \text{(3-1)}$$

Here

k = the quoted, or nominal, or market, rate of interest on a given security.[7] There are many different securities, hence many different quoted interest rates.

k* = the real risk-free rate of interest; k* is pronounced "k-star," and it is the rate that would exist on a riskless security if zero inflation were expected.

IP = inflation premium. IP is equal to the average expected inflation rate over the life of the security.

DRP = default risk premium. This premium reflects the possibility that the issuer will not pay interest or principal on a security at the stated time and in the stated amount. DRP is zero for U.S. Treasury securities, but it rises as the riskiness of issuers increases.

LP = liquidity, or marketability, premium. This is a premium charged by lenders to reflect the fact that some securities cannot be converted to cash on

---

[7]The term *nominal* as it is used here means the *stated* rate as opposed to the *real* rate, which is adjusted to remove the effects of inflation. If you bought a 10-year Treasury bond in January 1993, the quoted, or nominal, rate would be about 6.7 percent, but if inflation averages 4 percent over the next 10 years, the real rate would be about 6.7% − 4% = 2.7%. In Chapter 6 we will use the term nominal in yet another way: to distinguish between quoted rates and effective annual rates when compounding occurs more frequently than once a year.

short notice at a "reasonable" price. LP is very low for Treasury securities, but it is relatively high on securities issued by very small firms.

MRP = maturity risk premium. As we will explain later, longer-term bonds are exposed to a significant risk of price declines, and a maturity risk premium is charged by lenders to reflect this risk.

If we combine k* + IP and let this sum equal k_{RF}, then we have this expression:

$$k = k_{RF} + DRP + LP + MRP. \qquad (3\text{-}2)$$

Here,

k_{RF} = the quoted, or market, risk-free rate of interest. This is the quoted interest rate on a security such as a U.S. Treasury bill, which is very liquid and free of most risks. Note that k_{RF} does include a premium for expected inflation, as $k_{RF} = k* + IP$.

We discuss the components whose sum makes up the quoted, or nominal, rate on a given security in the following sections.

THE REAL RISK-FREE RATE OF INTEREST, k*

The *real risk-free rate of interest, k*,* is defined as the interest rate that would exist on a riskless security if no inflation were expected, and it may be thought of as the rate of interest that would exist on short-term U.S. Treasury securities in an inflation-free world. The real risk-free rate is not static—it changes over time depending on economic conditions, especially (1) on the rate of return corporations and other borrowers can expect to earn on productive assets and (2) on people's time preferences for current versus future consumption. Borrowers' expected returns on real asset investments set an upper limit on how much they can afford to pay for borrowed funds, while savers' time preferences for consumption establish how much consumption they are willing to defer, and hence the amount of funds they will lend at different levels of interest. It is difficult to measure the real risk-free rate precisely, but most experts think that in the United States k* has fluctuated in the range of 1 to 4 percent in recent years.

THE NOMINAL, OR QUOTED, RISK-FREE RATE OF INTEREST, k_{RF}

The *nominal,* or *quoted, risk-free rate, k_{RF},* is the real risk-free rate plus a premium for expected inflation: $k_{RF} = k* + IP$. To be strictly correct, the risk-free rate should mean the interest rate on a totally risk-free security—one that has no risk of default, no maturity risk, no liquidity risk, and no risk of loss if inflation

increases. There is no such security, hence there is no observable truly risk-free rate. However, there is one security that is free of most risks—a U.S. Treasury bill (T-bill), which is a short-term security issued by the U.S. government. Treasury bonds (T-bonds), which are longer-term government securities, are free of default and liquidity risks, but T-bonds are exposed to some risk due to changes in the general level of interest rates.

If the term "risk-free rate" is used without either the modifier "real" or the modifier "nominal," people generally mean the quoted (nominal) rate, and we will follow that convention in this book. Therefore, when we use the term "risk-free rate" or the symbol "k_{RF}," we mean the nominal risk-free rate, which includes an inflation premium equal to the average expected inflation rate over the life of the security. In general, we use the T-bill rate to approximate the short-term risk-free rate, and the T-bond rate to approximate the long-term risk-free rate. So, whenever you see the term "risk-free rate," assume that we are referring either to the quoted U.S. T-bill rate or to the quoted T-bond rate.

INFLATION PREMIUM (IP)

Inflation has a major impact on interest rates because it erodes the purchasing power of the dollar and lowers the real rate of return on investments. To illustrate, suppose you saved $1,000 and invested it in a Treasury bill that matures in 1 year and will pay 5 percent interest. At the end of the year you will receive $1,050—your original $1,000 plus $50 of interest. Now suppose the inflation rate during the year is 10 percent, and it affects all items equally. If beer had cost $1 per bottle at the beginning of the year, it would cost $1.10 at the end of the year. Therefore, your $1,000 would have bought $1,000/$1 = 1,000 bottles at the beginning of the year but only $1,050/$1.10 = 955 bottles at the end. Thus, in *real terms,* you would be worse off—you would receive $50 of interest, but it would not be sufficient to offset inflation. You would thus be better off buying 1,000 bottles of beer (or some other storable asset such as land, timber, apartment buildings, wheat, or gold) than buying the Treasury bill.

Investors are well aware of all this, so when they lend money, they build in an *inflation premium (IP)* equal to the expected inflation rate over the life of the security. As discussed previously, for a short-term, default-free U.S. Treasury bill, the actual interest rate charged, $k_{T\text{-bill}}$, would be the real risk-free rate, k^*, plus the inflation premium (IP):

$$k_{T\text{-bill}} = k_{RF} = k^* + IP.$$

Therefore, if the real risk-free rate of interest were $k^* = 3\%$, and if inflation were expected to be 4 percent (and hence IP = 4%) during the next year, then the quoted rate of interest on 1-year T-bills would be 7 percent. In January 1993, the expected 1-year inflation rate was about 3 percent, and the yield on 1-year T-bills was about 3.7 percent. This implies that the real risk-free rate on short-term securities at that time was about 0.7 percent.

It is important to note that the rate of inflation built into interest rates is the *rate of inflation expected in the future,* not the rate experienced in the past. Thus, the latest reported figures might show an annual inflation rate of 3 percent, but that is for a past period. If people on the average expect a 6 percent inflation rate in the future, then 6 percent would be built into the current rate of interest. Note also that the inflation rate reflected in the quoted interest rate on any security is the *average rate of inflation expected over the security's life.* Thus, the inflation rate built into a 1-year bond is the expected inflation rate for the next year, but the inflation rate built into a 30-year bond is the average rate of inflation expected over the next 30 years.[8]

Expectations for future inflation are closely, but not perfectly, correlated with rates experienced in the recent past. Therefore, if the inflation rate reported for last month increased, people would tend to raise their expectations for future inflation, and this change in expectations would cause an increase in interest rates.

DEFAULT RISK PREMIUM (DRP)

The risk that a borrower will *default* on a loan, which means not to pay the interest or the principal, also affects the market interest rate on a security: The greater the default risk, the higher the interest rate lenders charge. Treasury securities have no default risk; thus, they carry the lowest interest rates on taxable securities in the United States. For corporate bonds, the higher the bond's rating, the lower its default risk, and, consequently, the lower its interest rate.[9] Here are some representative interest rates on long-term bonds during January 1993:

	Rate	**DRP**
U.S. Treasury	7.4%	—
AAA	8.1	0.7%
AA	8.4	1.0
A	8.7	1.3

The difference between the quoted interest rate on a T-bond and that on a corporate bond with similar maturity, liquidity, and other features is the *default risk premium (DRP).* Therefore, if the bonds listed above were otherwise similar, the default risk premium would be DRP = 8.1% − 7.4% = 0.7 percentage points

---

[8]To be theoretically precise, we should use a *geometric average.* Also, because millions of investors are active in the market, it is impossible to determine exactly the consensus expected inflation rate. Survey data are available, however, which give us a reasonably good idea of what investors expect over the next few years. For example, in 1980 the University of Michigan's Survey Research Center reported that people expected inflation during the next year to be 11.9 percent and that the average rate of inflation expected over the next 5 to 10 years was 10.5 percent. Those expectations led to record-high interest rates. However, the economy cooled in 1981 and 1982, and, as Figure 3-4 showed, actual inflation dropped sharply after 1980. This led to gradual reductions in the *expected future* inflation rate. In 1993, as we write this, the expected future inflation rate is about 3 percent. As inflationary expectations dropped, so did quoted market rates of interest.

[9]Bond ratings, and bonds' riskiness in general, will be discussed in detail in Chapter 20. For now, merely note that bonds rated AAA are judged to have less default risk than bonds rated AA, AA bonds are less risky than A bonds, and so on. Ratings are designated AAA or Aaa, AA or Aa, and so forth, depending on the rating agency. In this book, the designations are used interchangeably.

for AAA corporate bonds, $8.4\% - 7.4\% = 1.0$ percentage point for AA, and $8.7\% - 7.4\% = 1.3$ percentage points for A corporate bonds. Default risk premiums vary somewhat over time, but the January 1993 figures are representative of levels in recent years.

LIQUIDITY PREMIUM (LP)

Liquidity is generally defined as the ability to convert an asset to cash quickly at a "fair market value." Assets have varying degrees of liquidity, depending on the characteristics of the market in which they are traded. For instance, there exist very active and easily accessible secondary markets for financial assets such as government notes and bonds, and for the stocks and bonds of large corporations, but the markets for real estate are illiquid because it takes time to ascertain the value of a piece of property and to locate a suitable buyer. Therefore, most financial assets are considered more liquid than real assets. Of course, the most liquid asset of all is cash, and the more easily an asset can be converted to cash at a "fair market value," the more liquid it is considered. Consequently, short-term financial assets generally are more liquid than long-term financial assets. Because liquidity is important, investors evaluate liquidity and include *liquidity premiums (LPs)* when market rates of securities are established. Although it is very difficult to accurately measure liquidity premiums, a differential of at least two and probably four or five percentage points exists between the least liquid and the most liquid financial assets of similar default risk and maturity.

MATURITY RISK PREMIUM (MRP)

U.S. Treasury securities are free of default risk in the sense that one can be virtually certain that the federal government will pay interest on its bonds and will also pay them off when they mature. Therefore, the default risk premium on Treasury securities is essentially zero. Further, active markets exist for Treasury securities, so their liquidity premiums are also close to zero. Thus, as a first approximation, the rate of interest on a Treasury bond should be the risk-free rate, k_{RF}, which is equal to the real risk-free rate, k^*, plus an inflation premium, IP. However, an adjustment is needed for long-term Treasury bonds. The prices of long-term bonds decline sharply whenever interest rates rise, and since interest rates can and do rise, all long-term bonds, even Treasury bonds, have an element of risk called *interest rate risk*. As a general rule, the bonds of any organization, from the U.S. government to Continental Airlines, have more interest rate risk the longer the maturity of the bond.[10] Therefore, a *maturity risk premium (MRP)*, which is higher the longer the years to maturity, must be included in the required interest rate.

---

[10]For example, if someone had bought a 30-year Treasury bond for $1,000 in 1972, when the long-term interest rate was 7 percent, and held it until 1981, when long-term T-bond rates were about 14.5 percent, the value of the bond would have declined to about $514. That would represent a loss of almost half the investment, and it demonstrates that long-term bonds, even U.S. Treasury bonds, are not riskless. However, had the investor purchased short-term T-bills in 1972 and subsequently reinvested the principal each time the bills matured, he or she would still have had $1,000. This point will be discussed in detail in Chapter 7.

The effect of maturity risk premiums is to raise interest rates on long-term bonds relative to those on short-term bonds. This premium, like the others, is extremely difficult to measure, but (1) it seems to vary over time, rising when interest rates are more volatile and uncertain, then falling when interest rates are more stable, and (2) in recent years, the maturity risk premium on 30-year T-bonds appears to have generally been in the range of one or two percentage points.[11]

We should mention that although long-term bonds are heavily exposed to interest rate risk, short-term bills are heavily exposed to *reinvestment rate risk.* When short-term bills mature and the funds are reinvested, or "rolled over," a decline in interest rates would necessitate reinvestment at a lower rate, and hence would lead to a decline in interest income. To illustrate, suppose you had $100,000 invested in 1-year T-bills, and you lived on the income. In 1981, short-term rates were about 15 percent, so your income would have been about $15,000. However, your income would have declined to about $9,000 by 1983, and to under $4,000 by 1993. Had you invested your money in long-term T-bonds, your income (but not the value of the principal) would have been stable.[12] Thus, although "investing short" preserves one's principal, the interest income provided by short-term T-bills varies from year to year, depending on reinvestment rates.

SELF-TEST QUESTIONS

Write out an equation for the nominal interest rate on any debt security.

Distinguish between the *real* risk-free rate of interest, k*, and the *nominal,* or *quoted,* or *market,* risk-free rate of interest, k$_{RF}$.

How is inflation considered when interest rates are determined by investors in the financial markets? Explain.

Does the interest rate on a T-bond include a default risk premium? Explain.

Distinguish between liquid and illiquid assets, and identify some assets that are liquid and some that are illiquid.

Briefly explain the following statement: "Although long-term bonds are heavily exposed to interest rate risk, short-term bills are heavily exposed to reinvestment rate risk."

---

[11]The MRP has averaged 1.4 percentage points over the last 66 years. See *Stocks, Bonds, Bills, and Inflation: 1993 Yearbook* (Chicago: Ibbotson Associates, 1993).

[12]Long-term bonds also have some reinvestment rate risk. To actually earn the quoted rate on a long-term bond, the interest payments must be reinvested at the quoted rate. However, if interest rates fall, the interest payments must be reinvested at a lower rate; thus, the realized return would be less than the quoted rate. Note, though, that the reinvestment rate risk is lower on a long-term bond than on a short-term bond because only the interest payments (rather than interest plus principal) on the long-term bond are exposed to reinvestment rate risk. Only zero coupon bonds, discussed in Chapters 7 and 20, are completely free of reinvestment rate risk.

THE TERM STRUCTURE OF INTEREST RATES

A study of Figure 3-3 reveals that at certain times, such as in 1992, short-term interest rates are lower than long-term rates, whereas at other times, such as in 1980 and 1981, short-term rates are higher than long-term rates. The relationship between long- and short-term rates, which is known as the *term structure of interest rates,* is important to corporate treasurers, who must decide whether to borrow by issuing long- or short-term debt, and to investors, who must decide whether to buy long- or short-term bonds. Thus, it is important to understand (1) how long- and short-term rates are related to each other and (2) what causes shifts in their relative positions.

To begin, we can look up in a source such as *The Wall Street Journal* or the *Federal Reserve Bulletin* the interest rates on Treasury bonds of various maturities at a given point in time. For example, the tabular section of Figure 3-5 presents

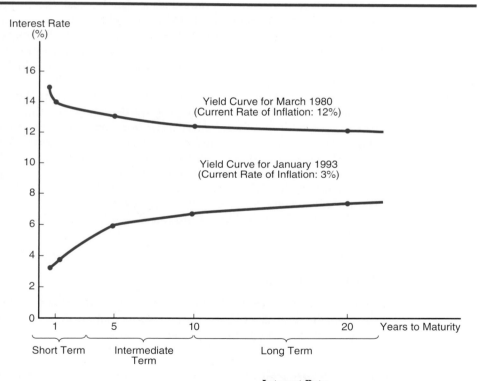

FIGURE 3-5
U.S. TREASURY BOND INTEREST RATES ON DIFFERENT DATES

		Interest Rate	
Term to Maturity		**March 1980**	**January 1993**
6 months		15.0%	3.5%
1 year		14.0	3.7
5 years		13.5	6.2
10 years		12.8	6.7
20 years		12.5	7.4

interest rates for different maturities on two dates. The set of data for a given date, when plotted on a graph such as that in Figure 3-5, is called the *yield curve* for that date. The yield curve changes both in position and in slope over time. In March of 1980, all rates were relatively high, and short-term rates were higher than long-term rates, so the yield curve on that date was *downward sloping.* However, in January of 1993, all rates had fallen, and short-term rates were lower than long-term rates, so the yield curve at that time was *upward sloping.* Had we drawn the yield curve during January of 1982, it would have been essentially horizontal, for long-term and short-term bonds on that date had about the same rate of interest. (See Figure 3-3.)

Figure 3-5 shows yield curves for U.S. Treasury securities, but we could have constructed them for corporate bonds; for example, we could have developed yield curves for BellSouth, General Motors, Chrysler, or any other company that borrows money over a range of maturities. Had we constructed such curves and plotted them on Figure 3-5, the corporate yield curves would have been above those for Treasury securities on the same date because the corporate yields would include default risk premiums, but they would have had the same general shape as the Treasury curves. Also, the riskier the corporation, the higher its yield curve; thus, Chrysler, which is in a relatively weak financial position, would have had a yield curve substantially higher than that of BellSouth, which is rated an AAA company.

Historically, in most years long-term rates have been above short-term rates, so usually the yield curve has been upward sloping. For this reason, people often call an upward-sloping yield curve a *"normal" yield curve* and a yield curve which slopes downward an *inverted,* or *"abnormal," yield curve.* Thus, in Figure 3-5 the yield curve for March 1980 was inverted, but the one for January 1993 was normal. We explain in the next section why an upward slope is the normal situation, but, briefly, the reason has to do with maturity risk premiums — short-term securities are less risky than longer-term securities, hence short-term rates are normally lower than long-term rates.

TERM STRUCTURE THEORIES

Several theories have been proposed to explain the shape of the yield curve. The three major ones are (1) the market segmentation theory, (2) the liquidity preference theory, and (3) the expectations theory.

Market Segmentation Theory.   Briefly, the *market segmentation theory* states that each lender and each borrower has a preferred maturity. For example, a person borrowing to buy a long-term asset like a house, or an electric utility borrowing to build a power plant, would want a long-term loan. However, a retailer borrowing in September to build its inventories for Christmas would prefer a short-term loan. Similar differences exist among savers — for example, a person saving up to take a vacation next summer would want to lend in the short-term

market, but someone saving for retirement 20 years hence would probably buy long-term securities.

The thrust of the market segmentation theory is that the slope of the yield curve depends on supply/demand conditions in the long-term and short-term markets. Thus, according to this theory, the yield curve could at any given time be either flat, upward sloping, or downward sloping. An upward-sloping yield curve would occur when there was a large supply of short-term funds relative to demand, but a shortage of long-term funds. Similarly, a downward-sloping curve would indicate relatively strong demand in the short-term market compared to that in the long-term market. A flat curve would indicate balance between the two markets.

Liquidity Preference Theory.   The *liquidity preference theory* states that long-term bonds normally yield more than short-term bonds for two reasons: (1) Investors generally prefer to hold short-term securities, because such securities are more liquid in the sense that they can be converted to cash with little danger of loss of principal. Investors will, therefore, generally accept lower yields on short-term securities, and this leads to relatively low short-term rates. (2) Borrowers, on the other hand, generally prefer long-term debt, because short-term debt exposes them to the risk of having to repay the debt under adverse conditions. Accordingly, borrowers are willing to pay a higher rate, other things held constant, for long-term funds than for short-term funds, and this also leads to relatively low short-term rates. Thus, lender and borrower preferences both operate to cause short-term rates to be lower than long-term rates. Taken together, these two sets of preferences — and hence the liquidity preference theory — imply that under normal conditions, a positive maturity risk premium (MRP) exists, and the MRP increases with years to maturity, causing the yield curve to be upward sloping.

Expectations Theory.   The *expectations theory* states that the yield curve depends on expectations about future inflation rates. Specifically, k_t, the nominal interest rate on a U.S. Treasury bond that matures in t years, is found as follows under the expectations theory:

$$k_t = k^* + IP_t.$$

Here k^* is the real risk-free interest rate, and IP_t is an inflation premium which is equal to the average expected rate of inflation over the t years until the bond matures. Under the pure expectations theory, the maturity risk premium (MRP) is assumed to be zero, and, for Treasury securities, the default risk premium (DRP) and liquidity premium (LP) are also zero.

To illustrate, suppose that in late December of 1993 the real risk-free rate of interest was k* = 3% and expected inflation rates for the next 3 years were as follows:[13]

	Expected Annual (1-Year) Inflation Rate	Expected Average Inflation Rate from 1993 to Indicated Year
1994	4%	4%/1 = 4.0%
1995	6%	(4% + 6%)/2 = 5.0%
1996	8%	(4% + 6% + 8%)/3 = 6.0%

Given these expectations, the following pattern of interest rates should exist:

	Real Risk-free Rate (k*)		Inflation Premium, Which Is Equal to the Average Expected Inflation Rate (IP_t)		Nominal Treasury Bond Rate for Each Maturity (k_{T-bond})
1-year bond	3%	+	4.0%	=	7.0%
2-year bond	3%	+	5.0%	=	8.0%
3-year bond	3%	+	6.0%	=	9.0%

Had the pattern of expected inflation rates been reversed, with inflation expected to fall from 8 percent to 6 percent and then to 4 percent, the following situation would have existed:

	Real Risk-free Rate		Average Expected Inflation Rate		Treasury Bond Rate for Each Maturity
1-year bond	3%	+	8.0%	=	11.0%
2-year bond	3%	+	7.0%	=	10.0%
3-year bond	3%	+	6.0%	=	9.0%

---

[13]Technically, we should be using geometric averages, rather than arithmetic averages, but the differences are not material in this example. To illustrate, if the expected inflation rate is 4 percent in 1994 and 6 percent in 1995, the geometric average 2-year inflation rate is

$$[(1.04)(1.06)]^{1/2} - 1.0 = 0.04995 = 4.995\%,$$

compared with a 5.0 percent arithmetic average. Over 1994–1996, the geometric average 3-year inflation rate is

$$[(1.04)(1.06)(1.08)]^{1/3} - 1.0 = 0.05987 = 5.987\%,$$

while the arithmetic average is 6.0 percent. Note, however, that the differences between arithmetic and geometric averages are more significant when inflation rates run in double digits.

In general, the geometric average inflation rate is found as

$$[(1 + I_1)(1 + I_2) \ldots (1 + I_t) \ldots (1 + I_n)]^{1/n} - 1.0,$$

where I_t is the expected inflation rate in Year t and n is the number of years in the geometric average. For a discussion of this point, see Robert C. Radcliffe, *Investment: Concepts, Analysis, and Strategy*, 4th ed. (Glenview, Ill.: Scott, Foresman, 1993), Chapter 6.

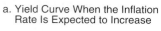

FIGURE 3-6

HYPOTHETICAL

EXAMPLE OF THE

TERM STRUCTURE OF

INTEREST RATES

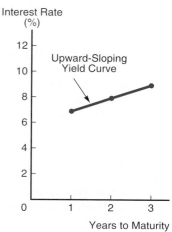

a. Yield Curve When the Inflation
   Rate Is Expected to Increase

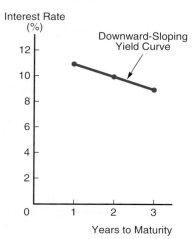

b. Yield Curve When the Inflation
   Rate Is Expected to Decline

These hypothetical data are plotted in Figure 3-6. According to the expectations theory, whenever the annual rate of inflation is expected to decline, the yield curve must be downward sloping, whereas it must be upward sloping if inflation is expected to increase.

Various tests of the theories have been conducted, and these tests indicate that all three theories have some validity. Thus, the shape of the yield curve at any given time is affected (1) by supply/demand conditions in long- and short-term markets, (2) by liquidity preferences, and (3) by expectations about future inflation. One factor may dominate at one time, another at a different time, but all three affect the term structure of interest rates.

SELF-TEST QUESTIONS

What is a yield curve, and what information would you need to draw this curve?

Discuss each of the following theories: (1) market segmentation theory, (2) liquidity preference theory, and (3) expectations theory.

Distinguish between the shapes of a "normal" yield curve and an "abnormal" yield curve, and explain when each might exist.

FACTORS THAT INFLUENCE SUPPLY/DEMAND CONDITIONS

As stated earlier, supply/demand conditions are a primary determinant of the yield curve. The four most important factors that influence the supply and demand for

money are (1) Federal Reserve policy, (2) the level of the federal budget deficit, (3) the foreign trade balance, and (4) the level of business activity.

FEDERAL RESERVE POLICY

As you probably learned in your economics courses, (1) the money supply has a major effect on both the level of economic activity and the rate of inflation, and (2) in the United States, the Federal Reserve Board controls the money supply. If the Fed wants to stimulate the economy, as it did in 1991 and 1992, it increases growth in the money supply. The initial effect of such an action is to cause interest rates to decline. However, a larger money supply may also lead to an increase in the expected rate of inflation, which in turn could push interest rates up. The reverse holds if the Fed tightens the money supply.

To illustrate, in 1981 inflation was quite high, so the Fed tightened up the money supply. The Fed deals primarily in the short-term end of the market, so this tightening had the direct effect of pushing short-term interest rates up sharply. At the same time, the very fact that the Fed was taking strong action to reduce inflation led to a decline in expectations for long-run inflation, which led to a drop in long-term bond yields. Short-term rates decreased shortly thereafter.

In 1991, the situation was just the reverse. To combat the recession, the Fed took steps to reduce interest rates. Short-term rates first fell, and later long-term rates also dropped, but not as sharply. These lower rates will benefit heavily indebted businesses and individual borrowers, and home mortgage refinancings will put additional billions of dollars into consumers' pockets. Savers will, of course, lose out, but the net effect will benefit the economy. In time, lower rates will encourage businesses to borrow for investment, give new life to the housing market, and bring down the value of the dollar relative to other currencies, which will help U.S. exporters and lower the trade deficit.

During periods when the Fed is actively intervening in the markets, the yield curve will be distorted. Short-term rates will be temporarily "too low" if the Fed is easing credit, and "too high" if it is tightening credit. Long-term rates are not affected as much by Fed intervention.

FEDERAL DEFICITS

If the federal government spends more than it takes in from tax revenues, it runs a deficit, and that deficit must be covered either by borrowing or by printing money (increasing the money supply). If the government borrows, this added demand for funds pushes up interest rates. If it prints money, this increases expectations for future inflation, which also drives up interest rates. Thus, the larger the federal deficit, other things held constant, the higher the level of interest rates. Whether long- or short-term rates are more affected depends on how the deficit is financed, so we cannot state, in general, how deficits will affect the slope of the yield curve.

FOREIGN TRADE BALANCE

Businesses and individuals in the United States buy from and sell to people and firms in other countries. If we buy more than we sell (that is, if we import more than we export), we are said to be running a *foreign trade deficit*. When trade deficits occur, they must be financed, and the main source of financing is debt. In other words, if we import $200 billion of goods but export only $100 billion, we run a trade deficit of $100 billion, and we must borrow the $100 billion.[14] Therefore, the larger our trade deficit, the more we must borrow, and as we increase our borrowing, this drives up interest rates. Also, foreigners are willing to hold U.S. debt if and only if the interest rate on this debt is competitive with interest rates in other countries. Therefore, if the Federal Reserve attempts to lower interest rates in the United States, causing our rates to fall below rates abroad, then foreigners will sell U.S. bonds, those sales will depress bond prices, and the result will be higher U.S. rates. Thus, the existence of a deficit trade balance hinders the Fed's ability to combat a recession by lowering interest rates.

The United States has been running annual trade deficits since the mid-1970s, and the cumulative effect of these deficits is that the United States is by far the largest debtor nation of all time. As a result, our interest rates are very much influenced by interest rate trends in other countries around the world (higher rates abroad lead to higher U.S. rates). Because of all this, U.S. corporate treasurers—and anyone else who is affected by interest rates—must keep up with developments in the world economy.

BUSINESS ACTIVITY

Figure 3-3, presented earlier, can be examined to see how business conditions influence interest rates. Here are the key points revealed by the graph:

1. Because inflation increased from 1955 to 1981, the general tendency during this period was toward higher interest rates. However, since the 1981 peak, the trend has generally been downward.

2. Until 1966, short-term rates were almost always below long-term rates. Thus, in those years the yield curve was almost always "normal" in the sense that it was upward sloping.

3. The shaded areas in the graph represent recessions, during which both the demand for money and the rate of inflation tend to fall, and, at the same time, the Federal Reserve tends to increase the money supply in an effort to stimulate the economy. As a result, there is a tendency for interest rates to decline during recessions. Currently, in early 1993, we are in a slow-growth recovery. The Fed's actions

---

[14]The deficit could also be financed by selling assets, including gold, corporate stocks, entire companies, and real estate. The United States has financed its massive trade deficits by all of these means in recent years, but the primary method has been by borrowing.

to keep interest rates low are intended to stimulate the economy. Low interest rates should stimulate business investment and consumer spending and, consequently, bring an end to the economic doldrums.

4. During recessions, short-term rates decline more sharply than long-term rates. This occurs because (1) the Fed operates mainly in the short-term sector, so its intervention has the strongest effect here, and (2) long-term rates reflect the average expected inflation rate over the next 20 to 30 years, and this expectation generally does not change much, even when the current rate of inflation is low because of a recession.

SELF-TEST QUESTIONS

Name four factors which influence supply/demand conditions, and hence interest rates, and explain their effects.

How does the Fed stimulate the economy? How does the Fed affect interest rates?

INTEREST RATE LEVELS AND STOCK PRICES

Interest rates have two effects on corporate profits: (1) First, because interest is a cost, the higher the rate of interest, the lower a firm's profits, other things held constant. (2) Second, interest rates affect the level of economic activity, and economic activity affects corporate profits. Interest rates obviously affect stock prices because of their effects on profits, but, perhaps even more important, they have an effect due to competition in the marketplace between stocks and bonds. If interest rates rise sharply, investors can get higher returns in the bond market, which induces them to sell stocks and to transfer funds from the stock market to the bond market. Stock sales in response to rising interest rates obviously depress stock prices. Of course, the reverse occurs if interest rates decline. Indeed, the bull market of December 1991, when the Dow Jones Industrial Index rose 10 percent in less than a month, was caused almost entirely by a sharp drop in long-term interest rates.

The experience of Kansas City Power, the electric utility serving western Missouri and eastern Kansas, can be used to illustrate the effects of interest rates on stock prices. In 1983 the firm's stock sold for $9.50 per share, and, since the firm paid a $1.17 dividend, the dividend yield was $1.17/$9.50 = 12.3%. Kansas City Power's bonds at the time yielded about the same amount. Thus, if someone had saved $100,000 and invested it in either the stock or the bonds, his or her annual income would have been about $12,300. (The investor might also have expected the stock price to grow over time, providing some capital gains, but that point is not relevant to this example.)

By 1993, interest rates were lower, and Kansas City Power's bonds were yielding only 8 percent. If the stock still yielded 12.3 percent, investors would be much

more inclined to invest in the stock than in the bonds. Thus, investment money would flow into the stock rather than the bonds, and the stock price would be bid up. Indeed, this is exactly what happened, and Kansas City Power's stock sold for $22 in early 1993. In all, the stock price rose 132 percent over the period, while the firm's dividend increased from $1.17 to $1.46, or by 25 percent. Thus, the major factor in the stock price rise was not the growth in dividends but rather the fact that interest rates had fallen. The $22 stock price produced a dividend yield of $1.46/$22 = 6.6%, which was in line with the firm's current bond yield and, hence, with interest rates in general.

SELF-TEST QUESTION

In what two ways do changes in interest rates affect stock prices?

INTEREST RATES AND BUSINESS DECISIONS

The yield curve for January 1993, shown earlier in Figure 3-5, indicates how much the U.S. government had to pay in early 1993 to borrow money for 1 year, 5 years, 10 years, and so on. A business borrower would have had to pay somewhat more, but assume for the moment that we are back in 1993 and that the yield curve for that year also applies to your company. Now suppose your company has decided (1) to build a new plant with a 20-year life which will cost $1 million and (2) to raise the $1 million by selling an issue of debt (or borrowing) rather than by selling stock. If you borrowed in 1993 on a short-term basis—say, for one year—your interest cost for that year would be only 3.5 percent, or $35,000, whereas if you used long-term (20-year) financing, your cost would be 7.4 percent, or $74,000. Therefore, at first glance, it would seem that you should use short-term debt.

However, this could prove to be a horrible mistake. If you use short-term debt, you will have to renew your loan every year, and the rate charged on each new loan will reflect the then-current short-term rate. Interest rates could return to their March 1980 levels, so by 1994 you could be paying 14 percent, or $140,000, per year. These high interest payments would cut into and perhaps eliminate your profits. Your reduced profitability could easily increase your firm's risk to the point where its bond rating would be lowered, causing lenders to increase the risk premium built into the interest rates they charge, which in turn would force you to pay even higher rates. These very high interest rates would further reduce your profitability, worrying lenders even more, and making them reluctant to renew your loan. If your lenders refused to renew the loan and demanded payment, as they have every right to do, you might have trouble raising the cash. If you had to make price cuts to convert physical assets to cash, you might incur heavy operating losses, or even bankruptcy.

On the other hand, if you used long-term financing in 1993, your interest costs would remain constant at $74,000 per year, so an increase in interest rates in the

economy would not hurt you. You might even be able to buy up some of your bankrupt competitors at bargain prices—bankruptcies increase dramatically when interest rates rise, primarily because many firms do use short-term debt.

Does all this suggest that firms should always avoid short-term debt? Not necessarily. If inflation falls in the next few years, so will interest rates. If you had borrowed on a long-term basis for 7.4 percent in January 1993, your company would be at a major disadvantage if its debt were locked in at 7.4 percent while its competitors (who used short-term debt in 1993 and thus rode interest rates down in subsequent years) had a borrowing cost of only 3 or 4 percent. On the other hand, large federal deficits and President Clinton's fiscal package might drive inflation and interest rates up to new record levels. In that case, you would wish you had borrowed on a long-term basis in 1993.

Financing decisions would be easy if we could develop accurate forecasts of future interest rates. Unfortunately, predicting future interest rates with consistent accuracy is somewhere between difficult and impossible—people who make a living by selling interest rate forecasts say it is difficult, but many others say it is impossible.

Even if it is difficult to predict future interest rate *levels,* it is easy to predict that interest rates will *fluctuate*—they always have, and they always will. This being the case, sound financial policy calls for using a mix of long- and short-term debt, as well as equity, in such a manner that the firm can survive in most interest rate environments. Further, the optimal financial policy depends in an important way on the nature of the firm's assets—the easier it is to sell off assets and thus to pay off debts, the more feasible it is to use large amounts of short-term debt. This makes it more feasible to finance current assets than fixed assets with short-term debt. We will return to this issue later in the book, when we discuss working capital policy.

SELF-TEST QUESTIONS

If short-term interest rates are lower than long-term rates, why might a firm still choose to finance with long-term debt?

Explain the following statement: "The optimal financial policy depends in an important way on the nature of the firm's assets."

THE FEDERAL INCOME TAX SYSTEM

The value of any financial asset, including stocks, bonds, and mortgages, as well as the values of most real assets such as plants or even entire firms, depends on the stream of cash flows produced by the asset. Cash flows from an asset consist of *usable* income plus depreciation, and usable income means income *after taxes.*

Our tax laws can be changed by Congress, and in recent years changes have occurred almost every year. Indeed, a major change has occurred, on average, every 3 to 4 years since 1913, when our federal income tax system began. Further,

certain parts of our tax system are tied to the rate of inflation, so changes occur automatically each year, depending on the rate of inflation during the previous year. Therefore, although this chapter will give you a good background on the basic nature of our tax system, you should consult current rate schedules and other data published by the Internal Revenue Service (available in U.S. post offices) before you file your personal or business tax return.

Currently (1993), federal income tax rates for individuals go up to almost 35 percent, and, when state and city income taxes are included, the marginal tax rate on an individual's income can exceed 40 percent. Business income is also taxed heavily. The income from partnerships and proprietorships is reported by the individual owners as personal income and, consequently, is taxed at rates going up to 40 percent or more. Corporate profits are subject to federal income tax rates of up to 39 percent, in addition to state income taxes. Because of the magnitude of the tax bite, taxes play an important role in most financial decisions.

As we write this, Congress and the new Clinton administration are debating the merits of different changes in the tax laws (which we discuss in detail in a later section). Even in the unlikely event that Congress does not change the tax laws, changes will still occur because certain aspects of the tax calculation are tied to the rate of inflation. Thus, by the time you read this section, tax rates and/or other factors will be different from those we provide. Still, if you understand the discussion here, you will also understand the basics of our tax system, and you will know how to operate under any revised tax code.

Taxes are so complicated that university law schools offer master's degrees in taxation to practicing lawyers, many of whom also have CPA certifications. In a field complicated enough to warrant such detailed study, we can cover only the highlights. This is really enough, though, because business managers and investors should and do rely on tax specialists rather than trusting their own limited knowledge. Still, it is important to know the basic elements of the tax system as a starting point for discussions with tax experts.

INDIVIDUAL INCOME TAXES

Individuals pay taxes on wages and salaries, on investment income (dividends, interest, and profits from the sale of securities), and on the profits of proprietorships and partnerships. Our tax rates are *progressive*—that is, the higher one's income, the larger the percentage paid in taxes. Table 3-2 gives the 1993 tax rates for single individuals and married couples filing joint returns under the rate schedules in effect in May 1993.

1. *Taxable income* is defined as gross income less a set of exemptions and deductions which are spelled out in the instructions to the tax forms individuals must file. When filing a tax return in 1994 for the tax year 1993, each taxpayer will receive an exemption of $2,350 for each dependent, including the taxpayer, which reduces taxable income. However, this exemption is indexed to rise with inflation, and the exemption is phased out for high-income taxpayers. Also, certain expenses, such as mortgage interest paid, state and local income taxes paid, and charitable

TABLE 3-2   INDIVIDUAL TAX RATES FOR 1993 (AS OF MAY 1993)

Single Individuals

If Your Taxable Income Is	You Pay This Amount on the Base of the Bracket	Plus This Percentage on the Excess over the Base	Average Tax Rate at Top of Bracket
Up to $22,100	$ 0	15%	15.0%
$22,100–$53,500	3,315	28	22.6
Over $53,500	12,107	31	31.0

Married Couples Filing Joint Returns

If Your Taxable Income Is	You Pay This Amount on the Base of the Bracket	Plus This Percentage on the Excess over the Base	Average Tax Rate at Top of Bracket
Up to $36,900	$ 0	15%	15.0%
$36,900–$89,150	5,535	28	22.6
Over $89,150	20,165	31	31.0

Notes:

a. The incomes at which the 28 and 31 percent rates take effect, as well as the ranges for the additional taxes discussed below, are indexed with inflation each year, so they will change from those shown in the table in future years, even if the tax laws are unchanged.

b. A *personal exemption* of $2,350 in 1993 per person or dependent can be deducted from gross income to determine taxable income. Thus, a husband and wife, with two children, would have a 1993 exemption of 4 × $2,350 = $9,400. The amount of the exemption is scheduled to increase with inflation. However, if the gross income exceeds certain limits (generally, $162,700 for joint returns and $108,450 for single individuals), the exemption is phased out, and this has the effect of raising the effective tax rate on incomes over the specified limit by about 0.5 percent per family member, or 2.0 percent for a family of four. In addition, taxpayers can claim *itemized deductions* for charitable contributions and certain other items, but these deductions are reduced if the gross income exceeds $108,450, and this has the effect of raising the effective tax rate on most high-income taxpayers by about 0.93 percent. The combined effect of the loss of exemptions and reduction of itemized deductions is thus about 3 percent, so the marginal tax rate for high-income individuals goes up to about 34 percent.

In addition, high-income taxpayers who have "earned income" (as opposed to income from capital such as dividends) are hit with an additional 2.9 percent tax that goes into the Medicare fund, thus increasing their marginal tax rate to over 35 percent. Also, there is the social security tax, which, for a self-employed person, amounts to about 12.4 percent of income up to $57,600. Finally, high-income older taxpayers who are eligible for social security payments lose those payments; this amounts to yet another tax. All of this can push the effective marginal tax rate up close to 50 percent.

The Tax Code is extremely complex with respect to the items covered in this note, so we make no attempt to be specific and exact.

contributions, can be deducted and thus be used to reduce taxable income, but again, high-income taxpayers lose some of this benefit.

2. The *marginal tax rate* is defined as the tax on the last unit of income. Marginal rates begin at 15 percent, rise to 28 and then to 31 percent. Note, though, that when consideration is given to the phase-out of exemptions and deductions, plus social security, the marginal tax rate actually goes up to well over 35 percent.

3. One can calculate *average tax rates* from the data in Table 3-2. For example, if Jill Smith, a single individual, had taxable income of $35,000, her tax bill would be $3,315 + ($35,000 − $22,100)(0.28) = $3,315 + $3,612 = $6,927. Her *average tax rate* would be $6,927/$35,000 = 19.8% versus a *marginal rate* of 28

percent. If Jill received a raise of $1,000, bringing her income to $36,000, she would have to pay $280 of it as taxes, so her after-tax raise would be $720. In addition, her social security taxes would also increase.

4. As indicated in the notes to the table, current legislation provides for tax brackets to be indexed to inflation to avoid the *bracket creep* that occurred during the 1970s and that in reality raised tax rates substantially.[15]

Taxes on Dividend and Interest Income. Dividend and interest income received by individuals from corporate securities is added to other income and thus is taxed at rates going up to about 35 percent. Since corporations pay dividends out of earnings that have already been taxed, there is *double taxation* of corporate income.

It should be noted that under U.S. tax laws, interest on most state and local government bonds, called *municipals* or *"munis,"* is not subject to federal income taxes (or state taxes in the state of issue). Thus, investors get to keep all of the interest received from most municipal bonds but only a fraction of the interest received from bonds issued by corporations or by the U.S. government. This means that a lower-yielding muni can provide the same after-tax return as a higher-yielding corporate bond. For example, a taxpayer in the 31 percent marginal tax bracket who could buy a muni that yielded 10 percent would have to receive a before-tax yield of 14.49 percent on a corporate or U.S. Treasury bond to have the same after-tax income:

$$\frac{\text{Equivalent pre-tax yield}}{\text{on taxable bond}} = \frac{\text{Yield on muni}}{1 - \text{Marginal tax rate}}$$

$$= \frac{10\%}{1 - 0.31} = 14.49\%.$$

[15]For example, if you were single and had a taxable income of $22,100, your tax bill would be $3,315. Now suppose inflation caused prices to double and your income, being tied to a cost-of-living index, rose to $44,200. Because our tax rates are progressive, if tax brackets were not indexed, your taxes would jump to $9,503. Your after-tax income would thus increase from $18,785 to $34,697, but, because prices have doubled, your real income would *decline* from $18,785 to $17,348.50 (calculated as one-half of $34,697). You would be in a higher tax bracket, so you would be paying a higher percentage of your real income in taxes. If this happened to everyone, and if Congress failed to change tax rates sufficiently, real disposable incomes would decline because the federal government would be taking a larger share of the national product. This is called the federal government's "inflation dividend." However, since tax brackets are now indexed, if your income doubled due to inflation, your tax bill would double, but your after-tax real income would remain constant at $18,785. Bracket creep was a real problem during the 1970s and early 1980s, but indexing—if it stays in the law—will put an end to it.

If we know the yield on the taxable bond, we can use the following equation to find the equivalent yield on a muni:

$$\text{Yield on muni} = \begin{pmatrix} \text{Pre-tax yield} \\ \text{on taxable} \\ \text{bond} \end{pmatrix} (1 - \text{Marginal tax rate})$$

$$= 14.49\% \ (1 - 0.31) = 14.49\%(0.69) = 10.0\%.$$

The exemption from federal taxes stems from the separation of federal and state powers, and its primary effect is to help state and local governments borrow at lower rates than would otherwise be available to them.

Capital Gains versus Ordinary Income.   Assets such as stocks, bonds, and real estate are defined as *capital assets.* If you buy a capital asset and later sell it for more than your purchase price, the profit is called a *capital gain;* if you suffer a loss, it is called a *capital loss.* An asset sold within one year of the time it was purchased produces a *short-term gain or loss,* whereas one held for more than one year produces a *long-term gain or loss.* Thus, if you buy 100 shares of Disney stock for $127 per share and sell them for $137 per share, you make a capital gain of 100 × $10, or $1,000. However, if you sell the stock for $117 per share, you will have a $1,000 capital loss. If you hold the stock for more than one year, the gain or loss is long-term; otherwise, it is short-term. If you sell the stock for exactly $127 per share, you make neither a gain nor a loss; you simply get your $12,700 back, and no tax is due.

From 1921 through 1986, long-term capital gains were taxed at substantially lower rates than ordinary income. For example, in 1986 long-term capital gains were taxed at only 40 percent of the tax rate on ordinary income. The tax law changes which took effect in 1987 eliminated this differential, and from 1987 through 1990 all capital gains income (both long-term and short-term) was taxed as if it were ordinary income. However, beginning in 1991, the maximum tax rate on long-term capital gains was capped at 28 percent.

There has been a great deal of controversy over the proper tax rate for capital gains. It has been argued that lower tax rates on capital gains (1) stimulate the flow of venture capital to new, start-up businesses (which generally provide capital gains as opposed to dividend income) and (2) cause companies to retain and reinvest a high percentage of their earnings in order to provide their stockholders with lightly taxed capital gains as opposed to highly taxed dividend income. Thus, it was argued that elimination of the favorable rates on capital gains retarded investment and economic growth. The proponents of preferential capital gains tax rates lost the argument in 1986, but in 1990 they did succeed in getting the rate capped at 28 percent versus the top marginal rate of about 35 percent. You should not be surprised if the capital gains differential is changed again in the future, as a capital gains cut is favored by many members of the U.S. House and Senate. Even if a

capital gains cut is not passed by Congress, any raising of individual tax rates would increase the capital gains differential, assuming that the current 28 percent cap is maintained.

Since capital gains are taxed at lower rates, this has implications for dividend policy — it favors lower payouts, hence higher earnings retention. Favorable treatment of capital gains also favors stock investments over bond investments, because part of the income from stock normally comes from capital gains. We will discuss this issue in more detail in later chapters.

CORPORATE INCOME TAXES

The corporate tax structure, shown in Table 3-3 as of May 1993, is relatively simple. To illustrate, if a firm had $75,000 of taxable income, its tax bill would be

$$\text{Taxes} = \$7,500 + 0.25(\$25,000)$$
$$= \$7,500 + \$6,250 = \$13,750,$$

and its average tax rate would be $13,750/$75,000 = 18.3%. Note that for all income over $335,000, one can simply calculate the corporate tax as 34 percent of all taxable income. Thus, the corporate tax is progressive up to $335,000 of income, but it is constant thereafter.[16]

Interest and Dividend Income Received by a Corporation. Interest income received by a corporation is taxed as ordinary income at regular corporate tax rates. However, 70 percent of the dividends received by one corporation from another is excluded from taxable income, while the remaining 30 percent is taxed at the ordinary tax rate.[17] Thus, a corporation earning more than $335,000 and

---

[16]Prior to 1987, many large, profitable corporations such as General Electric and Boeing paid no income taxes. The reasons for this were as follows: (1) expenses, especially depreciation, were defined differently for calculating taxable income than for reporting earnings to stockholders, so some companies reported positive profits to stockholders but losses — hence no taxes — to the Internal Revenue Service; and (2) some companies which did have tax liabilities used various tax credits to offset taxes that would otherwise have been payable. This situation was effectively eliminated in 1987.

The principal method used to eliminate this situation is the Alternative Minimum Tax (AMT). Under the AMT, both corporate and individual taxpayers must figure their taxes in two ways, the "regular" way and the AMT way, and then pay the higher of the two. The AMT is calculated as follows: (1) Figure your regular taxes. (2) Take your taxable income under the regular method and then add back certain items, especially income on certain municipal bonds, depreciation in excess of straight line depreciation, certain research and drilling costs, itemized or standard deductions (for individuals), and a number of other items. (3) The income determined in (2) is defined as AMT income, and it must then be multiplied by the AMT tax rate (24% in 1993) to determine the tax due under the AMT system. An individual or corporation must then pay the higher of the regular tax or the AMT tax.

[17]The size of the dividend exclusion actually depends on the degree of ownership. Corporations that own less than 20 percent of the stock of the dividend-paying company can exclude 70 percent of the dividends received; firms that own more than 20 percent but less than 80 percent can exclude 80 percent of the dividends; and firms that own more than 80 percent can exclude the entire dividend payment. Since most companies own less than 20 percent of other companies, we will, in general, assume a 70 percent dividend exclusion.

TABLE 3-3 CORPORATE TAX RATES FOR 1993 (AS OF MAY 1993) If a Corporation's Taxable Income Is	It Pays This Amount on the Base of the Bracket	Plus This Percentage on the Excess over the Base	Average Tax Rate at Top of Bracket
Up to $50,000	$ 0	15%	15.0%
$50,000 to $75,000	7,500	25	18.3
$75,000 to $100,000	13,750	34	22.3
$100,000 to $335,000	22,250	39	34.0
Over $335,000	113,900	34	34.0

Note:

For income in the range of $100,000 to $335,000, a surtax of 5% is added to the base rate of 34%. This surtax, which eliminates the effects of the lower rates on income below $75,000, results in a marginal tax rate of 39% for income in the $100,000 to $335,000 range.

paying a 34 percent marginal tax rate would pay only $(0.30)(0.34) = 0.102 = 10.2\%$ of its dividend income as taxes, so its effective tax rate on intercorporate dividends would be 10.2 percent. If this firm had $10,000 in pre-tax dividend income, its after-tax dividend income would be $8,980:

$$
\begin{aligned}
\text{After-tax income} &= \text{Before-tax income} - \text{Taxes} \\
&= \text{Before-tax income} - (\text{Before-tax income})(\text{Effective tax rate}) \\
&= \text{Before-tax income}(1 - \text{Effective tax rate}) \\
&= \$10,000\,[1 - (0.30)(0.34)] \\
&= \$10,000(1 - 0.102) = \$10,000(0.898) = \$8,980.
\end{aligned}
$$

If the corporation pays its own after-tax income out to its stockholders as dividends, the income is ultimately subjected to *triple taxation:* (1) the original corporation is first taxed, (2) the second corporation is then taxed on the dividends it received, and (3) the individuals who receive the final dividends are taxed again. This is the reason for the 70 percent exclusion on intercorporate dividends, which at least reduces the impact of triple taxation.

If a corporation has surplus funds that can be invested in marketable securities, the tax factor favors investment in stocks, which pay dividends, rather than in bonds, which pay interest. For example, suppose GE had $100,000 to invest, and it could buy either bonds that paid interest of $8,000 per year or preferred stock that paid dividends of $7,000. GE is in the 34 percent tax bracket; therefore, its tax on the interest, if it bought bonds, would be $0.34(\$8,000) = \$2,720$, and its after-tax income would be $5,280. If it bought preferred stock, its tax would be $0.34[(0.30)(\$7,000)] = \$714$, and its after-tax income would be $6,286. Other

TABLE 3-4		Use Bonds (1)	Use Stock (2)
CASH FLOWS TO			
INVESTORS UNDER	Earnings before interest and taxes (EBIT)	$1,500,000	$1,500,000
BOND AND STOCK	Interest	1,500,000	0
FINANCING	Taxable income	$ 0	$1,500,000
	Federal-plus-state taxes (40%)	0	600,000
	After-tax income	$ 0	$ 900,000
	Income to investors	$1,500,000	$ 900,000
	Advantage to bond financing	$ 600,000	

factors might lead GE to invest in bonds, but the tax factor certainly favors stock investments when the investor is a corporation.[18]

Interest and Dividends Paid by a Corporation.   A firm's operations can be financed with either debt or equity capital. If it uses debt, it must pay interest on this debt, whereas if it uses equity, it will pay dividends to the equity investors (stockholders). The interest paid by a corporation is deducted from its operating income to obtain its taxable income, but dividends paid are not deductible. Therefore, a firm needs $1 of pre-tax income to pay $1 of interest, but if it is in the 40 percent federal-plus-state tax bracket, it needs $1.67 of pre-tax income to pay $1 of dividends:

$$\frac{\text{Pre-tax income needed}}{\text{to pay \$1 of dividends}} = \frac{\$1}{1 - \text{Tax rate}} = \frac{\$1}{0.60} = \$1.67.$$

To illustrate, Table 3-4 shows the situation for a firm with $1.5 million of earnings before interest and taxes (EBIT). As shown in Column 1, if the firm were financed entirely by bonds, and if it made interest payments of $1.5 million, its taxable income would be zero, taxes would be zero, and its investors would receive the entire $1.5 million of EBIT. (The term *investors* includes both stockholders and bondholders.) As shown in Column 2, if the firm had no debt and was therefore financed only by stock, all of the $1.5 million of EBIT would be taxable

---

[18]This illustration demonstrates why corporations favor investing in lower-yielding preferred stocks over higher-yielding bonds. When tax consequences are considered, the yield on the preferred stock, $[1 - 0.34(0.30)](7.0\%) = 6.286\%$, is higher than the yield on the bond, $(1 - 0.34)(8.0\%) = 5.280\%$. Also, note that corporations are restricted in their use of borrowed funds to purchase other firms' preferred or common stocks. Without such restrictions, firms could engage in *tax arbitrage,* whereby the interest on borrowed funds reduces taxable income on a dollar-for-dollar basis, but taxable income is increased by only $0.30 per dollar of dividend income. Thus, current tax laws reduce the 70 percent dividend exclusion in proportion to the amount of borrowed funds used to purchase the stock.

income to the corporation, the tax would be $1,500,000(0.40) = $600,000$, and investors would receive only $0.9 million versus $1.5 million under debt financing.

Of course, it is generally not possible to finance exclusively with debt capital, and the risk of doing so would offset the benefits of the higher expected income. *Still, the fact that interest is a deductible expense has a profound effect on the way businesses are financed—our tax system favors debt financing over equity financing.* This point is discussed in more detail in Chapters 12 and 13.

Corporate Capital Gains.   Before 1987, corporate long-term capital gains were taxed at lower rates than ordinary income, as is true for individuals. Under current law, however, corporations' capital gains are taxed at the same rates as their operating income.

Corporate Loss Carry-Back and Carry-Forward.   Ordinary corporate operating losses can be carried back *(carry-back)* to each of the preceding 3 years and forward *(carry-forward)* for the next 15 years in the future to offset taxable income in those years. For example, an operating loss in 1994 could be carried back and used to reduce taxable income in 1991, 1992, and 1993, and forward, if necessary, and used in 1995, 1996, and so on, to the year 2009. The loss is typically applied first to the earliest year, then to the next earliest year, and so on, until losses have been used up or the 15-year carry-forward limit has been reached.

To illustrate, suppose Apex Corporation, with a 40 percent tax rate, had a $2 million *pre-tax* profit (taxable income) in 1991, 1992, and 1993, and then, in 1994, Apex lost $12 million as shown in Table 3-5. The company would use the carry-back feature to recompute its taxes for 1991, using $2 million of the 1994 operating losses to reduce the 1991 pre-tax profit to zero. This would permit it to recover the amount of taxes paid in 1991. Therefore, in 1995 Apex would receive a refund of its 1991 taxes because of the loss experienced in 1994. Because $10 million of the unrecovered losses would still be available, Apex would repeat this

TABLE 3-5		1991	1992	1993
APEX CORPORATION:	Original taxable income	$2,000,000	$2,000,000	$2,000,000
CALCULATION OF	Carry-back credit	− 2,000,000	− 2,000,000	− 2,000,000
LOSS CARRY-BACK	Adjusted income	$ 0	$ 0	$ 0
AND CARRY-FORWARD	Taxes on adjusted income	0	0	0
USING A $12	Taxes previously paid (40%)	800,000	800,000	800,000
MILLION 1994 LOSS	Difference = Tax refund	$ 800,000	$ 800,000	$ 800,000

Total refund check received in 1995 as a result of 1994 loss: $800,000 + $800,000 + $800,000 = $2,400,000.

Amount of loss carry-forward available for use in 1995–2009:

1994 loss	$12,000,000
Carry-back losses used	6,000,000
Carry-forward losses still available	$ 6,000,000

procedure for 1992 and 1993. Thus, in 1995 the company would pay zero taxes for 1994 and also would receive a refund for taxes paid from 1991 through 1993. Apex would still have $6 million of unrecovered losses to carry forward, subject to the 15-year limit, until the entire $12 million loss had been used to offset taxable income. The purpose of permitting this loss treatment is, of course, to avoid penalizing corporations whose incomes fluctuate substantially from year to year.

Improper Accumulation to Avoid Payment of Dividends.   Corporations could refrain from paying dividends to permit their stockholders to avoid personal income taxes on dividends. To prevent this, the Tax Code contains an *improper accumulation* provision which states that earnings accumulated by a corporation are subject to penalty rates *if the purpose of the accumulation is to enable stockholders to avoid personal income taxes.* A cumulative total of $250,000 (the balance sheet item "retained earnings") is by law exempted from the improper accumulation tax for most corporations. This is a benefit primarily to small corporations.

The improper accumulation penalty applies only if the retained earnings in excess of $250,000 are *shown to be unnecessary to meet the reasonable needs of the business.* A great many companies do indeed have legitimate reasons for retaining more than $250,000 of earnings. For example, earnings may be retained and used to pay off debt, to finance growth, or to provide the corporation with a cushion against possible cash drains caused by losses. How much a firm should properly accumulate for uncertain contingencies is a matter of judgment. We shall consider this matter again in Chapter 14, which deals with corporate dividend policy.

Consolidated Corporate Tax Returns.   If a corporation owns 80 percent or more of another corporation's stock, it can aggregate income and file one consolidated tax return; thus, the losses of one company can be used to offset the profits of another. (Similarly, one division's losses can be used to offset another division's profits.) No business ever wants to incur losses (you can go broke losing $1 to save 34¢ in taxes), but tax offsets do make it more feasible for large, multidivisional corporations to undertake risky new ventures or ventures that will suffer losses during a developmental period.

TAXATION OF SMALL BUSINESSES: S CORPORATIONS

The Internal Revenue Code provides that small businesses which meet certain restrictions as spelled out in the code may be set up as corporations and thus receive the benefits of the corporate form of organization—especially limited liability—yet still be taxed as proprietorships or partnerships rather than as corporations. These corporations are called *S corporations.* For a corporation that elects S corporation status for tax purposes, all of the income of the business is reported as personal income by the owners, and it is taxed at the rates that apply to individuals. This would be preferred by owners of small corporations in which

all or most of the income earned each year is distributed as dividends because the income would be taxed only once at the individual level. If the business were taxed as a "regular" corporation, the income first would be taxed at the corporate level, and then the dividends paid out would be subject to personal taxes.

THE CLINTON TAX PROPOSAL

As we finish this chapter in June 1993, the Clinton administration has proposed a comprehensive tax package that, for the most part, would raise income tax rates for both individuals and corporations. At this point in time, it is impossible to say whether Congress will adopt the entire package or when it will take effect. Thus, it is impossible to incorporate the Clinton proposal into the tax tables presented earlier. However, because there is a good chance that much, if not all, of the proposal eventually will be adopted, it is important to understand its key features.

Individual Taxes. The proposal would add a 36 percent tax bracket to individual tax rates. The new, higher bracket would take effect at $140,000 of taxable income for married couples filing joint returns and at $115,000 for single individuals. In addition, a 10 percent surtax would be added on all taxable income over $250,000. The joint effect of these changes would be a top marginal tax rate of $36\% + 0.10(36\%) = 39.6\% \approx 40$ percent for families and individuals with taxable incomes over $250,000. At the same time, the proposal holds the tax rate on capital gains at 28 percent, so, if enacted, the proposal would broaden the differential between the highest rate on ordinary income and that on capital gains, which would provide a further incentive for high-income investors to shift taxable interest and dividend income to tax-exempt interest (muni) income and long-term capital gains.

In addition to raising regular tax rates, the proposal would also raise the alternative minimum tax rate from 24 percent to 26 or 28 percent, depending on the amount of alternative minimum tax income (AMTI). Finally, the proposal would extend the 2.9 percent Medicare tax to include all earned income (wages and self-employment income), whereas current law places a $135,000 income cap on Medicare taxes. Employees pay half (1.45 percent) of the Medicare tax, while employers pay the other half. Self-employed individuals, however, pay the entire 2.9 percent. Therefore, the marginal tax rate for a self-employed individual earning over $250,000 would be $39.6\% + 2.9\% = 42.5\%$. In addition, there would be a social security tax of 12.4 percent on the first $57,600 of income earned during 1993, and, lurking in the wings, is an as-yet unspecified tax to help cover Hillary Rodham Clinton's health care reform plan.

Corporate Taxes. The major corporate tax feature of the Clinton proposal is the addition of a 35 or 36 percent tax bracket for corporate taxable income above $10 million. In addition, the benefit of the 34 percent bracket would be phased out beginning at $15 million of corporate income. Therefore, large corporations would be subject to a 35 or 36 percent marginal and average tax rate.

SELF-TEST QUESTIONS

**Explain what is meant by the statement: "Our tax rates are progressive."
Are tax rates progressive for all income ranges?**

Explain the difference between marginal tax rates and average tax rates.

What is "bracket creep," and how did the government avoid it in the late 1980s?

What are capital gains and losses, and how are they differentiated from ordinary income?

How does the federal income tax system treat corporate dividends received by a corporation versus those received by an individual? Why is this distinction made?

What is the difference in tax implications between interest and dividends paid by a corporation? Do tax laws favor debt or equity financing?

DEPRECIATION

Depreciation plays an important role in income tax calculations. Congress specifies, in the tax code, the life over which assets can be depreciated for tax purposes and the methods of depreciation which can be used. Since these factors have a major influence on the amount of depreciation a firm can take in a given year, and thus on the firm's taxable income, depreciation has an important effect on taxes paid and cash flows from operations. We will discuss in detail how depreciation is calculated, and how it affects income and cash flows, when we take up project cash flow analysis in Chapter 10.

SUMMARY

In this chapter we discussed the nature of financial markets, the types of institutions that operate in these markets, how interest rates are determined, some of the ways in which interest rates affect business decisions, and the Federal income tax system. The key concepts covered are listed below.

▶ There are many different types of *financial markets.* Each market serves a different region or deals with a different type of security.

▶ Transfers of capital between borrowers and savers take place (1) by *direct transfers* of money and securities; (2) by transfers through *investment banking houses,* which act as middlemen; and (3) by transfers through *financial intermediaries,* which create new securities.

▶ The *stock market* is an especially important market because this is where stock prices (which are used to "grade" managers' performances) are established.

▶ There are two basic types of stock markets—the *organized exchanges* and the *over-the-counter market.*

▶ Capital is allocated through the price system—a price must be paid to "rent" money. Lenders charge *interest* on funds they lend, while equity investors receive dividends and capital gains in return for letting firms use their money.

▶ Four fundamental factors affect the cost of money: (1) *production opportunities*, (2) *time preferences for consumption*, (3) *risk*, and (4) *inflation.*

▶ The *risk-free rate of interest, k_{RF},* is defined as the real risk-free rate, k*, plus an inflation premium (IP): $k_{RF} = k^* + IP$.

▶ The *nominal* (or *quoted*) *interest rate* on a debt security, *k,* is composed of the real risk-free rate, k*, plus premiums that reflect inflation (IP), default risk (DRP), liquidity (LP), and maturity risk (MRP):

$$k = k^* + IP + DRP + LP + MRP.$$

▶ If the *real risk-free rate of interest and the various premiums were constant over time,* interest rates in the economy would be stable. However, both the real rate and the premiums—especially the premium for expected inflation—*do change over time, causing market interest rates to change.* Also, Federal Reserve intervention to increase or decrease the money supply, as well as international currency flows, lead to fluctuations in interest rates.

▶ The relationship between the yields on securities and the securities' maturities is known as the *term structure of interest rates,* and the *yield curve* is a graph of this relationship.

▶ The yield curve is normally *upward sloping*—this is called a *normal yield curve*—but the curve can slope downward (an *inverted yield curve*) if the demand for short-term funds is relatively strong or if the rate of inflation is expected to decline.

▶ *Interest rate levels have a profound effect on stock prices.* Higher interest rates (1) slow down the economy, (2) increase interest expenses and thus lower corporate profits, and (3) cause investors to sell stocks and transfer funds to the bond market. Each of these factors tends to depress stock prices.

▶ Interest rate levels have a significant influence on *corporate financial policy.* Because interest rate levels are difficult if not impossible to predict, sound financial policy calls for using a mix of short- and long-term debt, and also for positioning the firm to survive in any future interest rate environment.

▶ The value of any asset depends on the stream of *after-tax cash flows* it produces. Tax rates and other aspects of our tax system are changed by Congress every year or so.

▶ In the United States, income tax rates are *progressive*—the higher one's income, the larger the percentage paid in taxes, up to a point.

▶ Assets such as stocks, bonds, and real estate are defined as *capital assets.* If a capital asset is sold for more than the purchase price, the profit is called a *capital gain.* If the capital asset is sold for a loss, it is called a *capital loss.*

▶ Operating income paid out as dividends is subject to *double taxation:* the income is first taxed at the corporate level, and then shareholders must pay personal taxes on their dividends.

▶ *Interest income* received by a corporation is taxed as *ordinary income;* however, 70 percent of the dividends received by one corporation from another are excluded from *taxable income.* The reason for this exclusion is that corporate dividend income is ultimately subjected to *triple taxation.*

▶ Because interest paid by a corporation is a *deductible* expense while dividends are not, our tax system favors debt financing over equity financing.

▶ Ordinary corporate operating losses can be *carried back* to each of the preceding 3 years and *carried forward* for the next 15 years to offset taxable income in those years.

▶ *S corporations* are small businesses which have the limited-liability benefits of the corporate form of organization yet obtain the benefits of being taxed as a partnership or a proprietorship.

QUESTIONS

3-1 Define each of the following terms:

a. Money market; capital market

b. Primary market; secondary market

c. Investment banker; financial service corporation

d. Financial intermediary

e. Mutual fund; money market fund

f. Organized security exchanges; over-the-counter market

g. Production opportunities; time preferences for consumption

h. Real risk-free rate of interest, k^*; nominal risk-free rate of interest, k_{RF}

i. Inflation premium (IP)

j. Default risk premium (DRP)

k. Liquidity; liquidity premium (LP)

l. Interest rate risk; maturity risk premium (MRP)

m. Reinvestment rate risk

n. Term structure of interest rates; yield curve

o. "Normal" yield curve; inverted ("abnormal") yield curve

p. Market segmentation theory; liquidity preference theory

q. Expectations theory

r. Progressive tax

s. Marginal and average tax rates

t. Bracket creep

u. Capital gain or loss

v. Tax loss carry-back and carry-forward

w. Improper accumulation

x. S corporation

3-2 What are financial intermediaries, and what economic functions do they perform?

3-3 Suppose interest rates on residential mortgages of equal risk were 7 percent in California and 9 percent in New York. Could this differential persist? What forces might tend to equalize rates? Would differentials in borrowing costs for businesses of equal risk located in California and New York be more or less likely to exist than differentials in residential mortgage rates? Would differentials in the cost of money for New York and California firms be more likely to exist if the firms being compared were very large or if they were very small? What are the implications of all this for the pressure now being put on Congress to permit banks to engage in nationwide branching?

3-4 What would happen to the standard of living in the United States if people lost faith in the safety of our financial institutions? Why?

3-5 How does a cost-efficient capital market help to reduce the prices of goods and services?

3-6 Which fluctuate more, long-term or short-term interest rates? Why?

3-7 Suppose you believe that the economy is just entering a recession. Your firm must raise capital immediately, and debt will be used. Should you borrow on a long-term or a short-term basis? Why?

3-8 Suppose the population of Area Y is relatively young while that of Area O is relatively old, but everything else about the two areas is equal.

a. Would interest rates likely be the same or different in the two areas? Explain.

b. Would a trend toward nationwide branching by banks and savings and loans, and the development of nationwide diversified financial corporations, affect your answer to Part a?

3-9 Suppose a new process was developed which could be used to make oil out of seawater. The equipment required is quite expensive but it would, in time, lead to very low prices for gasoline, electricity, and other types of energy. What effect would this have on interest rates?

3-10 Suppose a new and much more liberal Congress and administration were elected, and their first order of business was to take away the independence of the Federal Reserve System and to force the Fed to greatly expand the money supply. What effect would this have

a. On the level and slope of the yield curve immediately after the announcement?

b. On the level and slope of the yield curve that would exist two or three years in the future?

3-11 It is a fact that the federal government (1) encouraged the development of the savings and loan industry; (2) virtually forced the industry to make long-term, fixed-interest-rate mortgages; and (3) forced the savings and loans to obtain most of their capital as deposits that were withdrawable on demand.

a. Would the savings and loans be better off in a world with a normal or an inverted yield curve?

b. Would the savings and loan industry be better off if the individual institutions sold their mortgages to federal agencies and then collected servicing fees or if the institutions held the mortgages that they originated?

3-12 Suppose interest rates on Treasury bonds rose from 7 to 14 percent as a result of increased government borrowing. What effect would this have on the price of an average company's common stock?

3-13 Suppose you owned 100 shares of Ford Motor stock, and the company earned $3 per share during the last reporting period. Suppose further that Ford could either pay all its earnings out as dividends (in which case you would receive $300) or retain the earnings in the business, buy more assets, and cause the price of the stock to go up by $3 per share (in which case the value of your stock would rise by $300).

 a. How would the tax laws influence what you, as a typical stockholder, would want the company to do?

 b. Would your choice be influenced by how much other income you had? Why might the desires of a 45-year-old doctor differ with respect to corporate dividend policy from those of a pension fund manager or a retiree living on a small income?

 c. How might the corporation's decision with regard to dividend policy influence the price of its stock?

3-14 What does *double taxation of corporate income* mean?

3-15 If you were starting a business, what tax considerations might cause you to prefer to set it up as a proprietorship or a partnership rather than as a corporation?

3-16 Explain how the federal income tax structure affects the choice of financing (use of debt versus equity) of U.S. business firms.

3-17 For someone planning to start a new business, is the average or the marginal tax rate more relevant?

SELF-TEST PROBLEMS (SOLUTIONS APPEAR IN APPENDIX C)

ST-1 (Inflation rates) Assume that it is now January 1, 1994, and the rate of inflation is expected to be 6 percent throughout 1994. However, increased government deficits and renewed vigor in the economy are then expected to push inflation rates higher. Investors expect the inflation rate to be 7 percent in 1995, 8 percent in 1996, and 9 percent in 1997. The real risk-free rate, k*, is currently 3 percent. Assume that no maturity risk premiums are required on bonds with 5 years or less to maturity. The current interest rate on 5-year T-bonds is 11 percent.

 a. What is the average expected inflation rate over the next 4 years?

 b. What should be the prevailing interest rate on 4-year T-bonds?

 c. What is the implied expected inflation rate in 1998, or Year 5, given that bonds which mature in that year yield 11 percent?

ST-2 (Effect of form of organization on taxes) John Thompson is planning to start a new business, JT Enterprises, and he must decide whether to incorporate or to do business as a sole proprietorship. Under either form, Thompson will initially own 100 percent of the firm, and tax considerations are important to him. He plans to finance the firm's expected growth by drawing a salary just sufficient for his family living expenses, which he estimates will be about $40,000, and by retaining all other income in the business. Assume that as a married man with one child, Thompson has income tax exemptions of 3 × $2,350 = $7,050, and he estimates that his itemized deductions for each of the three years will be $8,750. He expects JT Enterprises to grow and to earn income of $60,000 in 1994, $90,000 in 1995, and $110,000 in 1996. Which form of business organization will allow Thompson to pay the lowest taxes (and retain the most income) during the period from 1994 to 1996? Assume that the tax rates given in the chapter are applicable for all future years. (Social Security taxes would also have to be paid, but ignore them.)

PROBLEMS

(Note: By the time this book is published, Congress may have changed rates and/or other provisions of current tax law—as noted in the chapter, such changes occur fairly often. Work all problems on the assumption that the tax tables in the chapter are still current.)

3-1   (Yield curves) Suppose you and most other investors expect the rate of inflation to be 7 percent next year, to fall to 5 percent during the following year, and then to remain at a rate of 3 percent thereafter. Assume that the real risk-free rate, k*, is 2 percent and that maturity risk premiums on Treasury securities rise from zero on very short-term bonds (those that mature in a few days) by 0.2 percentage points for each year to maturity, up to a limit of 1.0 percentage point on 5-year or longer-term T-bonds.

   a. Calculate the interest rate on 1-, 2-, 3-, 4-, 5-, 10-, and 20-year Treasury securities, and plot the yield curve.

   b. Now suppose Exxon, an AAA-rated company, had bonds with the same maturities as the Treasury bonds. As an approximation, plot an Exxon yield curve on the same graph with the Treasury bond yield curve. (Hint: Think about the default risk premium on Exxon's long-term versus its short-term bonds.)

   c. Now plot the approximate yield curve of Long Island Lighting Company, a risky nuclear utility.

3-2   (Yield curves) The following yields on U.S. Treasury securities were taken from a recent issue *The Wall Street Journal:*

Term	Rate
6 months	3.9%
1 year	4.3
2 years	5.0
3 years	5.6
4 years	6.2
5 years	6.5
10 years	7.1
20 years	7.5
30 years	7.6

Plot a yield curve based on these data. (Note: If you looked the data up in the *Journal*, you would find that some of the bonds—for example, the 3 percent issue which matures in February 1995—will show very low yields. These are "flower bonds," which are generally owned by older people and are associated with funerals because they can be turned in and used at par value to pay estate taxes. Thus, flower bonds always sell at close to par and have a yield which is close to the coupon yield, irrespective of the "going rate of interest." "Flower" bonds no longer are issued; the last one was issued in 1971 with a coupon of 3.5 percent and a maturity of 1998. Also, the yields quoted in the *Journal* are not for the same point in time for all bonds, so random variations will appear. An interest rate series that is purged of flower bonds and random variations, and hence provides a better picture of the true yield curve, is known as the "constant maturity series"; this series can be obtained from the *Federal Reserve Bulletin.*)

3-3   (Inflation and interest rates) In late 1980 the U.S. Commerce Department released new figures which showed that inflation was running at an annual rate of close to 15 percent. However, many investors expected the new Reagan administration to be more effective in controlling inflation than the Carter administration had been. At the time, the prime rate of interest was 21 percent, a record high. However, many observers believed that the ex-

tremely high interest rates and generally tight credit, which resulted from the Federal Reserve System's attempts to curb the inflation rate, would shortly bring about a recession, which in turn would lead to a decline in the inflation rate and also in the rate of interest. Assume that at the beginning of 1981 the expected rate of inflation for 1981 was 13 percent; for 1982, 9 percent; for 1983, 7 percent; and for 1984 and thereafter, 6 percent.

a. What was the average expected inflation rate over the 5-year period 1981–1985? (Use the arithmetic average.)

b. What average *nominal* interest rate would, over the 5-year period, be expected to produce a 2 percent real risk-free rate of return on 5-year Treasury securities?

c. Assuming a real risk-free rate of 2 percent and a maturity risk premium which starts at 0.1 percent and increases by 0.1 percent each year, estimate the interest rate in January 1981 on bonds that mature in 1, 2, 5, 10, and 20 years, and draw a yield curve based on these data.

d. Describe the general economic conditions that could be expected to produce an upward-sloping yield curve.

e. If the consensus among investors in early 1981 had been that the expected rate of inflation for every future year was 10 percent (that is, $I_t = I_{t+1} = 10\%$ for $t = 1$ to ∞), what do you think the yield curve would have looked like? Consider all the factors that are likely to affect the curve. Does your answer here make you question the yield curve you drew in Part c?

3-4 **(Loss carry-back, carry-forward)** The Keenan Company has made $150,000 before taxes during each of the last 15 years, and it expects to make $150,000 a year before taxes in the future. However, in 1993 the firm incurred a loss of $650,000. The firm will claim a tax credit at the time it files its 1993 income tax return, and it will receive a check from the U.S. Treasury. Show how it calculates this credit, and then indicate the firm's tax liability for each of the next 5 years. Assume a 30 percent tax rate on *all* income to ease the calculations.

3-5 **(Loss carry-back, carry-forward)** The projected taxable income of the Kalogeras Corporation, formed in 1993, is indicated in the table below. (Losses are shown in parentheses.) What is the corporate tax liability for each year? Use tax rates as shown in the text.

Year	Taxable Income
1993	($ 95,000)
1994	70,000
1995	55,000
1996	80,000
1997	(150,000)

3-6 **(Form of organization)** Carol Moerdyk has operated her small repair shop as a sole proprietorship for several years, but projected changes in her business's income have led her to consider incorporating.

Moerdyk is married and has two children. Her family's only income, an annual salary of $45,000, is from operating the business. (The business actually earns more than $45,000, but Carol reinvests the additional earnings in the business.) She itemizes deductions, and she is able to deduct $6,000. These deductions, combined with her four personal exemptions for 4 × $2,350 = $9,400, give her a taxable income of $45,000 − $6,000 − $9,400. (Assume the personal exemption remains at $2,350.) Of course, her actual taxable income, if she does not incorporate, would be higher by the amount of reinvested income. Moerdyk

estimates that her business earnings before salary and taxes for the period 1993 to 1995 will be:

Year	Earnings before Salary and Taxes
1993	$65,000
1994	85,000
1995	95,000

a. What would her total taxes (corporate plus personal) be in each year under
(1) A non-S corporate form of organization? (1993 tax = $7,440.)
(2) A proprietorship? (1993 tax = $9,091.)

b. Should Moerdyk incorporate? Discuss.

Work the following parts only if you are using the computer problem diskette.

c. Suppose Moerdyk decides to pay out (1) 50 percent or (2) 100 percent of the after-salary corporate income in each year as dividends. Would such dividend policy changes affect her decision about whether or not to incorporate?

d. Suppose business improves, and actual earnings before salary and taxes in each year are twice the original estimate. Assume that if Moerdyk chooses to incorporate she will continue to receive a salary of $45,000 and to reinvest additional earnings in the business. (No dividends would be paid.) What would be the effect of this increase in business income on Moerdyk's decision to incorporate or not incorporate?

3-7 **(Personal taxes)** Mary Jane Scheuer has this situation for the year 1993: salary of $60,000; dividend income of $10,000; interest on McDonnell Douglas bonds of $5,000; interest on state of Florida municipal bonds of $10,000; proceeds of $22,000 from the sale of Microsoft stock purchased in 1984 at a cost of $9,000; and proceeds of $22,000 from the November 1993 sale of Microsoft stock purchased in October 1993 at a cost of $21,000. Mary Jane gets one exemption ($2,350), and she has allowable itemized deductions of $5,000; these amounts will be deducted from her gross income to determine her taxable income.

a. What is Mary Jane's federal tax liability for 1993?

b. What are her marginal and average tax rates?

c. If she had some money to invest and was offered a choice of either state of Florida bonds with a yield of 9 percent or more McDonnell Douglas bonds with a yield of 11 percent, which should she choose, and why?

d. At what marginal tax rate would Mary Jane be indifferent in her choice between the Florida and McDonnell Douglas bonds?

3-8 **(Expected rate of interest)** Suppose the annual yield on a 2-year Treasury bond is 11.5 percent, while that on a 1-year bond is 10 percent. k* is 3 percent, and the maturity risk premium is zero.

a. Using the expectations theory, forecast the interest rate on a 1-year bond during the second year. (Hint: Under the expectations theory, the yield on a 2-year bond is equal to the average yield on 1-year bonds in Years 1 and 2.)

b. What is the expected inflation rate in Year 1? Year 2?

3-9 **(Expected rate of interest)** Assume that the real risk-free rate is 4 percent and that the maturity risk premium is zero. If the nominal rate of interest on 1-year bonds is 11 percent and that on comparable-risk 2-year bonds is 13 percent, what is the 1-year interest rate that

is expected for Year 2? What inflation rate is expected during Year 2? Comment on why the average interest rate during the 2-year period differs from the 1-year interest rate expected for Year 2.

3-10 (Corporate tax liability) The Tanner Corporation had a 1993 taxable income of $365,000 from operations after all operating costs but before (1) interest charges of $50,000, (2) dividends received of $15,000, (3) dividends paid of $25,000, and (4) income taxes. What is the firm's income tax liability and its after-tax income? What are the company's marginal and average tax rates on taxable income?

3-11 (Corporate tax liability) The Apilado Corporation had $200,000 of taxable income from operations in 1993.

   a. What is the company's federal income tax bill for the year?

   b. Assume the firm receives an additional $40,000 of interest income from some bonds it owns. What is the tax on this interest income?

   c. Now assume that Apilado does not receive the interest income but does receive an additional $40,000 as dividends on some stock it owns. What is the tax on this dividend income?

3-12 (Maturity risk premium) Assume that the real risk-free rate, k^*, is 3 percent and that inflation is expected to be 8 percent in Year 1, 5 percent in Year 2, and 4 percent thereafter. Assume also that all Treasury bonds are highly liquid and free of default risk. If 2-year and 5-year Treasury bonds both yield 10 percent, what is the difference in the maturity risk premiums (MRPs) on the two bonds, that is, what is MRP_5 minus MRP_2?

3-13 (After-tax yield) The Cotner Corporation has $10,000 which it plans to invest in marketable securities. It is choosing between AT&T bonds, which yield 11 percent, state of Florida muni bonds, which yield 8 percent, and AT&T preferred stock, with a dividend yield of 9 percent. Cotner's corporate tax rate is 20 percent, and 70 percent of the dividends received are tax exempt. Assuming that the investments are equally risky and that Cotner chooses strictly on the basis of after-tax returns, which security should be selected? What is the after-tax rate of return on the highest-yielding security?

3-14 (Interest rates) Due to the recession, the rate of inflation expected for the coming year is only 3 percent. However, the rate of inflation in Year 2 and thereafter is expected to be constant at some level above 3 percent. Assume that the real risk-free rate, k^*, is 2 percent for all maturities and that the expectations theory fully explains the yield curve, so there are no maturity premiums. If 3-year Treasury bonds yield 2 percentage points more than 1-year bonds, what rate of inflation is expected after Year 1?

**M I N I
C A S E**

Assume that you recently graduated with a degree in finance and have just reported to work as an investment advisor at the firm of Balik and Kiefer Inc. Your first assignment is to explain the nature of the U.S. financial markets and institutions to Michelle DelaTorre, a professional tennis player who has just come to the United States from Chile. DelaTorre is a highly ranked tennis player who expects to invest substantial amounts of money through Balik and Kiefer. She is also very bright, and, therefore, she would like to understand in general terms what will happen to her money. Your boss has developed the following set of questions, which you must ask and answer to explain the U.S. financial system to Dela-Torre.

a.   What is a financial market? How are financial markets differentiated from markets for physical assets?

b.   Differentiate between money markets and capital markets.

c.   Differentiate between a primary market and a secondary market. If Apple Computer decided to issue additional common stock, and DelaTorre purchased 100 shares of this stock from Merrill Lynch, the underwriter, would this transaction be a primary market transaction or a secondary market transaction? Would it make a difference if DelaTorre purchased previously outstanding Apple stock in the over-the-counter market?

d.   Describe the three primary ways in which capital is transferred between savers and borrowers.

e.   Securities can be traded on organized exchanges or in the over-the-counter market. Define each of these markets, and describe how stocks are traded in each of them.

f.   What do we call the price that a borrower must pay for debt capital? What is the price of equity capital? What are the four most fundamental factors that affect the cost of money, or the general level of interest rates, in the economy?

g.   What is the real risk-free rate of interest (k^*) and the nominal risk-free rate (k_{RF})? How are these two rates measured?

h.   Define the terms inflation premium (IP), default risk premium (DRP), liquidity premium (LP), and maturity risk premium (MRP). Which of these premiums is included when determining the interest rate on (1) short-term U.S. Treasury securities, (2) long-term U.S. Treasury securities, (3) short-term corporate securities, and (4) long-term corporate securities? Explain how the premiums would vary over time and among the different securities listed above.

i.   What is the term structure of interest rates? What is a yield curve? At any given time, how would the yield curve facing a given company such as AT&T or Chrysler (whose bonds are classified as "junk bonds") compare with the yield curve for U.S. Treasury securities? Draw a graph to illustrate your answer.

j.   Several theories have been advanced to explain the shape of the yield curve. The three major ones are (1) the market segmentation theory, (2) the liquidity preference theory, and (3) the expectations theory. Briefly describe each of these theories. Do economists regard one as being "true"?

k.   Suppose most investors expect the rate of inflation to be 5 percent next year, 6 percent the following year, and 8 percent thereafter. The real risk-free rate is 3 percent. The maturity risk premium is zero for bonds that mature in 1 year or less, 0.1 percent for 2-year bonds, and the MRP increases by 0.1 percent per year thereafter for 20 years, after which it is stable. What is the interest rate on 1-year, 10-year, and 20-year Treasury bonds? Draw a yield curve with these data. Is your yield curve consistent with the three term structure theories?

l.   Working with DelaTorre has required you to put in a lot of overtime, so you have had very little time to spend on your private finances. It's now April 1, and you have only two weeks left to file your income tax return. You have managed to get all the information together that you will need to complete your return. Balik and Kiefer Inc. paid you a salary of $45,000, and you received $3,000 in dividends from common stock that you own. You are single, so your personal exemption is $2,350, and your itemized deductions are $4,650.
   (1)   On the basis of the information above and the 1993 individual tax rate schedule, what is your tax liability?
   (2)   What are your marginal and average tax rates?

m. Assume that a corporation has $100,000 of taxable income from operations, $5,000 of interest income, and $10,000 of dividend income. What is the company's tax liability?

n. Assume that after paying your personal income tax, as calculated in Part l, you have $5,000 to invest. You have narrowed your investment choice down to California bonds with a yield of 7 percent or IBM bonds with a yield of 10 percent. Which one should you choose, and why? At what marginal tax rate would you be indifferent to the choice between California and IBM bonds, assuming equal risk?

SELECTED ADDITIONAL REFERENCES

Recent textbooks which focus on interest rates and financial markets include

Fabozzi, Frank J., *Bond Markets: Analysis and Strategies* (Englewood Cliffs, N.J.: Prentice-Hall, 1992).

Johnson, Hazel J., *Financial Institutions and Markets: A Global Perspective* (New York: McGraw-Hill, 1993).

Kidwell, David S., Richard Peterson, and David Blackwell, *Financial Institutions, Markets, and Money* (Fort Worth, Tex.: Dryden Press, 1993).

Kohn, Mier, *Money, Banking, and Financial Markets* (Fort Worth, Tex.: Dryden Press, 1993).

Livingston, Miles, *Money and Capital Markets* (Miami: Kolb, 1992).

Smith, Stephen D., and Raymond E. Spudeck, *Interest Rates: Theory and Application* (Fort Worth, Tex.: Dryden Press, 1993).

For current empirical data and a forecast of monetary conditions, see the most recent edition of this annual publication:

Salomon Brothers, *Supply and Demand for Credit* (New York).

The classic works on term structure theories include the following:

Culbertson, John M., "The Term Structure of Interest Rates," *Quarterly Journal of Economics,* November 1957, 489–504.

Fisher, Irving, "Appreciation and Interest," *Publications of the American Economic Association,* August 1896, 23–29 and 91–92.

Hicks, J. R., *Value and Capital* (London: Oxford University Press, 1946).

Lutz, F. A., "The Structure of Interest Rates," *Quarterly Journal of Economics,* November 1940, 36–63.

Modigliani, Franco, and Richard Sutch, "Innovations in Interest Rate Policy," *American Economic Review,* May 1966, 178–197.

For additional information on financial institutions, see

Campbell, Tim S., *Financial Institutions, Markets, and Economic Activity* (New York: McGraw-Hill, 1982).

Gup, Benton E., *The Management of Financial Institutions* (Boston: Houghton Mifflin, 1984).

Kaufman, George G., *The U.S. Financial System: Money, Markets, and Institutions* (Englewood Cliffs, N.J.: Prentice-Hall, 1983).

Mishkin, Frederic S., *Money, Banking, and Financial Markets* (Boston: Little, Brown, 1986).

Wilcox, James A., *Current Readings on Money, Banking, and Financial Markets: 1989–1990 Edition* (Glenview, Ill.: Scott, Foresman/Little, Brown, 1989).

Williamson, J. Peter, *The Investment Banking Handbook* (New York: John Wiley & Sons, 1988).

The following articles provide additional information on the effect of corporate taxes on business behavior:

Angell, Robert J., and Tony Wingler, "A Note on Expensing versus Depreciating under the Accelerated Cost Recovery System," *Financial Management,* Winter 1982, 34–35.

Comiskey, Eugene E., and James R. Hasselback, "Analyzing the Profit and Tax Relationship," *Financial Management,* Winter 1973, 57–62.

McCarty, Daniel E., and William R. McDaniel, "A Note on Expensing versus Depreciating under the Accelerated Cost Recovery System: Comment," *Financial Management,* Summer 1983, 37–39.

For a good reference guide to tax issues, see

Federal Tax Course (Englewood Cliffs, N.J.: Prentice-Hall, published annually).

VALUATION CONCEPTS

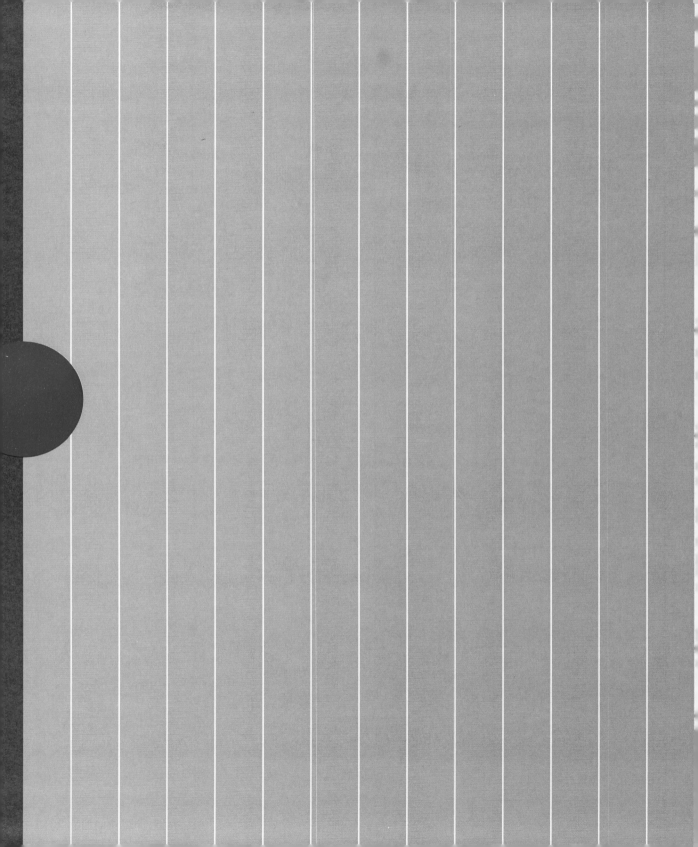

RISK AND RETURN: PART 1

I*n its "Investing in 1993" issue,* Business Week *presented its ideas of where the U.S. economy was heading and also listed the asset mix recommendations of eight well-known investment strategists. The magazine predicted that Bill Clinton would be taking over the reins of government with an economic team of moderates in tow. Thus, he would probably take a moderate approach to helping the U.S. economy, which would most likely expand in 1993 at a moderate rate of 3 percent or so. This would be enough to produce moderate corporate profits, so stocks should, on average, make only modest gains. At the same time, interest rates should hold a steady course, neither climbing nor falling very much.*

In light of Business Week's *forecast for a year of moderation, what were the eight investment strategists recommending for their clients' investment portfolios? Here are their recommendations:*

Strategist	Firm	Portfolio Mix		
		Stocks	Bonds	Cash
Steven Einhorn	Goldman Sachs	70%	25%	5%
Edward Kerschner	Paine Webber	65	35	0
Rao Chalasani	Kemper Securities	60	35	5
Charles Clough	Merrill Lynch	60	30	10
Michael Sherman	Shearson Lehman Brothers	55	30	15
Eric Miller	Donaldson Lufkin Jenrette	50	40	10
David Shulman	Salomon Brothers	50	35	15
A. Rama Krishna	First Boston	40	30	30

A "normal" asset mix consists of 50 to 60 percent stocks, 30 to 40 percent bonds, and the remainder, if any, in cash. (In this context, "cash" really means

short-term, very liquid securities such as T-bills or money market mutual funds.)
Thus, the majority of the recommendations are clustered in the middle. Only
Steven Einhorn and Edward Kerschner are very bullish on stocks, with 70 percent
and 65 percent allocations, respectively. Even the most bearish on stocks,
A. Rama Krishna, is not completely pessimistic. He says that he expects a stock
market decline early in 1993, at which point he will increase his recommended
stock percentage.

The real point of interest in the strategists' recommendations is not that they
vary in their recommended allocations but that none of them recommends hold-
ing a single asset class. In fact, seven of the eight recommend holding stocks,
bonds, and cash. If we pressed the strategists for more detail, there is little doubt
that most would recommend that the stock portfolio contain both high-dividend
and high-growth stocks, both domestic and foreign stocks, and stocks from a
number of different industries. Further, the bond portfolio would contain issues
of several different maturities, along with some high-rated issues such as govern-
ment bonds and some low-rated issues ("junk" bonds).

Why do the top investment strategists recommend that investors hold a mix
of security types rather than invest exclusively in the type that is expected to
provide the highest returns? The answers are simple. First, do not put all of your
financial eggs in one basket — by diversifying across asset types, investors can
reduce some of their risk. Second, higher expected returns can be obtained only
by bearing more risk — to increase expected returns, investors must invest in
higher-risk securities such as high-growth stocks and junk bonds. These two con-
cepts are the cornerstones of investing. In this chapter, we present a formal dis-
cussion of why the old "eggs in one basket" adage holds true, and in Chapter 5
we discuss the relationship between risk and return. Keep the points presented
here in mind as you read through the next two chapters. At the end, you should
be able to make some judgments of your own regarding the advice offered by
the eight investment strategists.

Since risk analysis is critically important to investment decisions, it is essential
that one understand how risk is defined and analyzed. We will see in Chapter 4
that risk can be defined in two ways: (1) as *total risk,* which focuses on a single
asset and which involves the dispersion of outcomes around the expected return
on that asset, and (2) as *market risk,* which focuses on a portfolio of assets and
which measures each asset's contribution to the riskiness of the portfolio.

Measuring risk is only one part of the task. We must be able to relate risk to
expected returns and to answer this question: How much return is required to
compensate for a given degree of risk? As we shall see in Chapter 5, the Capital
Asset Pricing Model (CAPM) provides one neat, precise answer to this question.

state of the economy. Thus, T-bills have zero risk.[1] However, the actual, or realized,

However, the CAPM has not been and cannot be confirmed empirically—it may or may not represent the way investors behave, so a CAPM-based analysis may or may not lead to a decision that will maximize the firm's value. This fact does not invalidate the CAPM, but it does raise a flag, forcing us to consider alternatives for specifying how risk should be measured and how the expected return required to compensate for a given degree of risk should be established.

DEFINING AND MEASURING RISK

Risk is defined in *Webster's* as "a hazard; a peril; exposure to loss or injury." Thus, risk refers to the chance that some unfavorable event will occur. If you engage in skydiving, you are taking a chance with your life—skydiving is risky. If you bet on the horses, you are risking your money. If you invest in speculative stocks (or, really, *any* stock), you are taking a risk in the hope of making an appreciable return.

To illustrate the riskiness of financial assets, suppose an investor buys $100,000 of short-term government bonds that yield 10 percent. In this case, the rate of return on the investment, 10 percent, can be estimated quite precisely, and the investment is defined as being essentially risk-free. However, if the $100,000 were invested in the stock of a company just being organized to do research that might lead to a cure for AIDS, then the investment's return could not be precisely estimated. One might analyze the situation and conclude that the *expected* rate of return, in a statistical sense, is 20 percent, but it should also be recognized that the *actual* rate of return could range from, say, +1,000 percent to −100 percent, and, because there is a significant danger of actually earning a return considerably less than the expected return, the stock investment would be described as being relatively risky.

Investment risk, then, is related to the probability of earning a return less than the expected return—the greater the chance of low or negative returns, the riskier the investment. However, it is useful to define risk more precisely, and we will do so in later sections.

SELF-TEST QUESTION

Explain the concept of investment risk.

PROBABILITY DISTRIBUTIONS AND EXPECTED RATES OF RETURN

Since risk refers to the probability of earning a return less than the expected return, probability distributions provide the foundation for risk measurement. To illustrate, suppose you are the financial manager of a firm which has $100,000 to

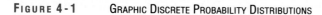

FIGURE 4-1   GRAPHIC DISCRETE PROBABILITY DISTRIBUTIONS

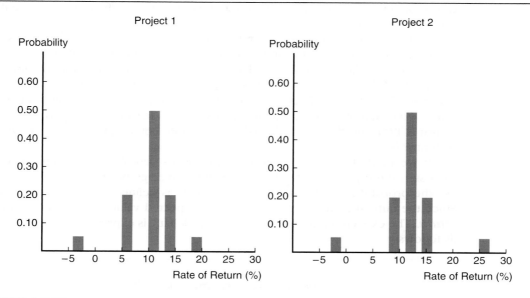

The expected rates of return on the other three investment alternatives were calculated similarly and are shown in Table 4-1.

Discrete probability distributions can be expressed in graphic as well as tabular form. Figure 4-1 shows bar graphs (or histograms) for Projects 1 and 2. The range of possible rates of return for Project 1 is from −3.0 to +19.0 percent, and the range for Project 2 is from −2.0 to +26.0 percent. Note that the height of each bar represents the probability of occurrence, and that the sum of the probabilities for each alternative equals 1.00. Also, note that the distribution of rates of return for Project 2 is symmetric, whereas the distribution for Project 1 is skewed to the left. Similar graphs for the T-bills and the corporate bonds would show the returns on the T-bills represented by a single spike, while the returns on the corporate bonds would have a graph that is skewed to the right.

SELF-TEST QUESTIONS

What is a probability distribution?

Define the term "expected rate of return."

TOTAL RISK VERSUS MARKET RISK

The remainder of Chapter 4 and all of Chapter 5 are devoted to defining risk, measuring risk, and discussing relationships between risk and required rates of

probability of occurrence attached to each outcome. Thus, Table 1-1 contains four probability distributions, one for each of the four investment alternatives. The T-bills' rate of return is known with certainty — it is 8 percent irrespective of the

return. However, before we get into the details, it is useful to look forward to see where we are headed.

There are many ways that risk can be defined and measured; in Chapters 4 and 5 we concentrate on two types of risk: (1) *total risk,* which is the riskiness of an asset held in isolation, and (2) *market risk,* which is an asset's relevant, or effective, risk if it is held as one of a large number of assets in a well-diversified portfolio of securities. To illustrate total risk, suppose an investor holds a single risky asset, say, a stock. In this case, the stock's risk is measured by the dispersion of returns about its expected return. The greater this dispersion, the higher the probability that the return will fall far below the expected return, and hence the greater the risk of the stock. However, when an investor holds a large number of stocks in a portfolio, say, 40 or more, the important issue becomes the overall, or aggregate, risk of the portfolio of stocks, because losses on one stock may be offset by extraordinary gains on another stock. In this situation, the relevant risk of each stock is its market risk, which measures the stock's contribution to the overall riskiness of the portfolio. The greater the impact of a stock on the overall riskiness of a portfolio (the more it increases the portfolio's risk), the higher the market risk of the stock. As we will see in Chapter 5, a stock's market risk is affected by its total risk, but it is also influenced by the correlation of its returns with the returns on a portfolio of stocks.

Combining stocks into portfolios reduces risk, because those stocks that experience less-than-expected returns will be offset to some degree by stocks whose returns are greater than expected. Thus, rational investors will hold portfolios of stocks rather than single stocks. Further, since most investors are rational, a stock's risk, and hence its price, will generally be based on its market risk and not on its total risk. The concepts of total and market risk are applicable to all risky assets: securities such as stocks and bonds, real estate, precious metals, corporate capital investments, and so on. Our discussion in Chapters 4 and 5 will focus on securities, but in Chapter 11 we will extend total and market risk concepts to corporate project analysis.

SELF-TEST QUESTIONS

Differentiate between total risk and market risk.

Are these concepts applicable only to securities? Explain.

TOTAL RISK ANALYSIS: ASSETS HELD IN ISOLATION

We can use the concepts of probability distributions and expected values to help measure risk. We know that risk is present when the estimated distribution has more than one possible outcome, but how should risk be measured and quantified? To answer this question, we first focus our attention on *total risk,* which is the relevant risk for assets held in isolation.

TABLE 4-2

RETURN AND RISK
MEASURES FOR THE
TABLE 4-1
INVESTMENT
ALTERNATIVES

Expected Rate of Return or Risk Measure	Investment Alternatives			
	T-Bills	Corporate Bonds	Project 1	Project 2
1. Expected return ($\hat{k}$)	8.00%	9.20%	10.30%	12.00%
2. Variance (Var or σ^2)	0.00	0.71	19.31	23.20
3. Standard deviation (SD or σ)	0.00%	0.84%	4.39%	4.82%
4. Coefficient of variation (CV)	0.00	0.09	0.43	0.40

percent standard deviation, while Project Y has a 10 percent expected rate of return and a 5 percent standard deviation. However, if the projects' returns are approximately normal, then Project X would have a very small probability of a negative return in spite of its 10 percent standard deviation, while Project Y, even with a standard deviation only half as large, would have a much higher probability of a loss. Therefore, to use the standard deviation as a measure of the *relative* risk for investments when expected returns differ, we should standardize the standard deviation and calculate the risk per unit of return. This is accomplished by using the *coefficient of variation (CV)*, which is defined as the standard deviation divided by the expected value:

$$\text{Coefficient of variation} = CV = \frac{\sigma}{\hat{k}}. \qquad (4\text{-}4)$$

$$\text{Project X: } CV_X = 10\%/30\% = 0.33.$$
$$\text{Project Y: } CV_Y = 5\%/10\% = 0.50.$$

Thus, we see that Project Y actually has more risk per unit of expected return than Project X. Therefore, one could argue that Y is riskier than X in spite of the fact that X's standard deviation is larger.

Row 4 of Table 4-2 contains the coefficients of variation of the four original investment alternatives. We see that the rankings using coefficient of variation to measure risk are different than the rankings based on standard deviation: Project 2 is riskier than Project 1 using standard deviation, but the opposite is true when we correct for return differences and measure risk by coefficient of variation.

SUBJECTIVE VERSUS OBJECTIVE PROBABILITY DISTRIBUTIONS

Thus far we have used subjectively estimated probability distributions in all of our examples of future, or *ex ante,* risk and return. We could apply the same techniques to historical, or *ex post,* data to obtain *objective* as opposed to *subjective*

risk measures, provided historical data are available. For example, suppose investments similar to Project 2 have been made in each of the last 10 years. In this case, we would have 10 historical, or realized, rates of return ($\bar{k}$, pronounced "k-bar") for the project. We could use these returns to determine Project 2's historical average, or *mean,* rate of return, variance, and standard deviation. We would have ten values, and we could use the following procedures to evaluate them:

1. Average historical return = $\bar{k}_{Avg} = \dfrac{\sum\limits_{t=1}^{n} \bar{k}_t}{n}$.

2. Variance = $\sigma^2 = \dfrac{\sum\limits_{t=1}^{n} (\bar{k}_t - \bar{k}_{Avg})^2}{n-1}$.

3. Standard deviation = $\sigma = \sqrt{\dfrac{\sum\limits_{t=1}^{n} (\bar{k}_t - \bar{k}_{Avg})^2}{n-1}}$.

These equations are used to analyze sample data, and here we are treating the ten years of data as if they were drawn from a larger universe of data. Of course, to use historical data to forecast future results, we must have reason to believe that conditions in the future will be similar to conditions in the past. If we do, then we could use the historical, or ex post, distribution as a proxy for the future, or ex ante, distribution, and the calculated average rate of return, variance, standard deviation, and coefficient of variation could be used to evaluate Project 2. Of course, this type of analysis cannot be used for entirely new ventures—if historical data are not available, we must rely on subjective probability estimates.

This discussion of subjective versus objective probability distributions illustrates an important point—in financial analysis, we generally face *two* sources of risk: (1) the risk associated with uncertain outcomes, given a known probability distribution, and (2) the additional risk that arises because our assumed distribution may itself be incorrect. Risk analysis may appear to be quite precise, but in fact, a great deal of judgment is normally involved.

SELF-TEST QUESTIONS

What are some measures of total risk?

Is one of the risk measures better than the others?

Differentiate between subjective and objective probability distributions.

MARKET RISK ANALYSIS: ASSETS HELD IN PORTFOLIOS

Thus far, we have considered the riskiness of the four investment alternatives on the assumption that each is held in isolation. Now we analyze the riskiness of assets

held in *portfolios,* or combinations of assets. As we shall see, an asset held as part of a portfolio is generally less risky than the same asset held in isolation. Indeed, an asset that would be quite risky if held in isolation may not be risky at all if it is held in a well-diversified portfolio. Thus, considering risk in a portfolio context could completely change our conclusions based on a total risk analysis.

Expected Return on a Portfolio

The expected rate of return on a portfolio is simply the weighted average of the expected returns of the individual securities in the portfolio:

$$\text{Expected return on a portfolio} = \hat{k}_p = \sum_{i=1}^{n} x_i \hat{k}_i. \qquad (4\text{-}5)$$

Here $\hat{k}_p$ is the expected rate of return on the portfolio; x_i is the fraction of the portfolio invested in the ith asset; $\hat{k}_i$ is the expected rate of return on the ith asset; and n is the number of assets in the portfolio. For example, suppose Stock A has an expected return of $\hat{k}_A = 10\%$, Stock B has $\hat{k}_B = 15\%$, and you plan to invest your money in these two stocks. If you put all your money in A, your one-stock portfolio would have an expected return of $\hat{k}_p = \hat{k}_A = 10\%$. If you invest only in B, your expected return would be $\hat{k}_p = \hat{k}_B = 15\%$. If you put half your money in each stock, then your expected portfolio return would be $\hat{k}_p = 0.5(10\%) + 0.5(15\%) = 12.5\%$, a weighted average of the two stocks' returns. Of course, after the fact and a year later, the realized rates of return on Stocks A and B, the $\bar{k}_i$ values, would probably be different from their expected values, so $\bar{k}_p$ would be somewhat different from $\hat{k}_p = 12.5\%$.[5]

Portfolio Risk

As we just saw, the expected return on a portfolio is a weighted average of the expected returns on the individual stocks in the portfolio, and each stock's contribution to the expected portfolio return is $x_i \hat{k}_i$. However, unlike the situation with returns, the standard deviation of a portfolio, σ_p, is generally *not* a weighted aver-

---

[5]The realized rate of return on a portfolio, $\bar{k}_p$, is

$$\text{Realized return on a portfolio} = \bar{k}_p = \sum_{i=1}^{n} x_i \bar{k}_i,$$

where $\bar{k}_i$ is the realized rate of return on the ith asset.

age of the standard deviations of the individual securities in the portfolio, and each stock's contribution to the portfolio's standard deviation is *not* $x_i\sigma_i$. Indeed, it is theoretically possible to combine two stocks which are, individually, quite risky as measured by their standard deviations, and to form from these risky assets a portfolio which is completely riskless, with $\sigma_p = 0\%$. To illustrate, consider the situation in Figure 4-2, which shows realized rates of return for Stocks W and M and for a portfolio invested 50 percent in each stock. (These stocks are called W and M because their returns graphs in Figure 4-2 resemble a W and an M.) Panel a shows realized returns in a time series format, while Panel b shows ex ante probability distributions of returns, assuming the distributions are approximately normal. The two stocks, each with $\sigma_i = 22.6\%$, would be quite risky if they were held in isolation, but when they are combined to form Portfolio WM, with $\sigma_p = 0.0\%$, they are not risky at all.

The reason Stocks W and M can be combined to form a riskless portfolio is that their returns move countercyclically to one another—when W's returns fall, those of M rise, and vice versa. In statistical terms, we say that the returns on Stocks W and M are *perfectly negatively correlated,* with r = correlation coefficient = -1.0.[6]

The opposite of perfect negative correlation, where r = -1.0, is perfect positive correlation, where r = $+1.0$. Returns on two perfectly positively correlated stocks would move up and down together, and a portfolio consisting of two such stocks would be just as risky as the individual stocks. This point is illustrated in Figure 4-3, where we combine Stocks M and M′, which are perfectly positively correlated. We see that the portfolio's standard deviation is equal to that of the individual stocks, indicating that diversification does nothing to reduce risk if the portfolio consists of perfectly positively correlated stocks.

Figures 4-2 and 4-3 demonstrate that (1) when two stocks are perfectly negatively correlated (r = -1.0), all risk can be diversified away, but (2) when two stocks are perfectly positively correlated (r = $+1.0$), diversification does no good whatever. In reality, most stocks are positively correlated, but not perfectly so. For New York Stock Exchange stocks, the correlation coefficient for the returns on two randomly selected stocks is about $+0.6$, and for most pairs of stocks, r lies in the range of $+0.5$ to $+0.7$. *Under such conditions, combining stocks into portfolios reduces risk but does not eliminate it completely.* Figure 4-4 illustrates this point with two stocks whose correlation coefficient is r = $+0.65$. The portfolio's average realized return is 15.0 percent, which is exactly the same as the average return for each of the two stocks. However, the portfolio's standard deviation is 20.6 percent, which is less than the standard deviation of either stock. Thus, the

---

[6]*Correlation* is defined as the tendency of two variables to move together. The *correlation coefficient, r,* measures this tendency, and it can range from $+1.0$, denoting that the two variables move up and down in perfect synchronization, to -1.0, denoting that the variables always move in exactly opposite directions. A correlation coefficient of zero suggests that the two variables are not related to one another; that is, changes in one variable are *independent* of changes in the other. We will discuss correlation in more detail in a later section.

FIGURE 4-2 RATE OF RETURN DISTRIBUTIONS FOR TWO PERFECTLY NEGATIVELY CORRELATED
STOCKS (r = −1.0) AND FOR PORTFOLIO WM

a. Rates of Return

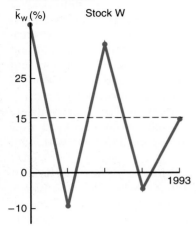
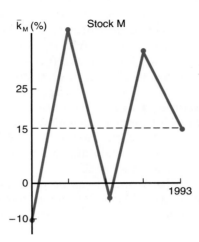
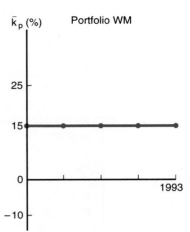

b. Probability Distribution of Returns

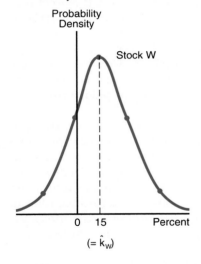
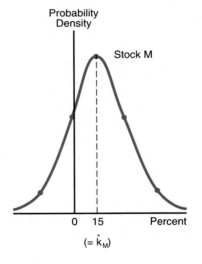
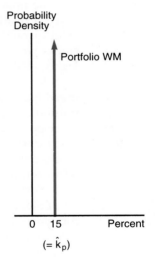

Year	Stock W $\hat{k}_W$	Stock M $\hat{k}_M$	Portfolio WM $\hat{k}_P$
1989	40%	(10%)	15%
1990	(10)	40	15
1991	35	(5)	15
1992	(5)	35	15
1993	15	15	15
Average return =	15%	15%	15%
Standard deviation =	22.6%	22.6%	0.0%

FIGURE 4-3

RATE OF RETURN DISTRIBUTIONS FOR TWO PERFECTLY POSITIVELY CORRELATED
STOCKS (r = +1.0) AND FOR PORTFOLIO MM'

a. Rates of Return

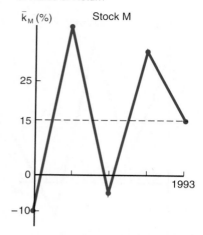

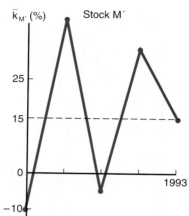

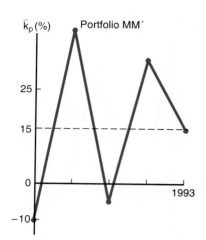

b. Probability Distribution of Returns

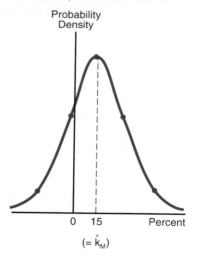

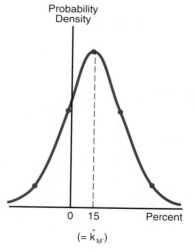

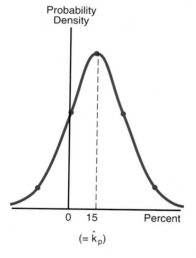

Year	Stock M k_M	Stock M' $k_{M'}$	Portfolio MM' k_P
1989	(10%)	(10%)	(10%)
1990	40	40	40
1991	(5)	(5)	(5)
1992	35	35	35
1993	15	15	15
Average return =	15%	15%	15%
Standard deviation =	22.6%	22.6%	22.6%

a. Rates of Return

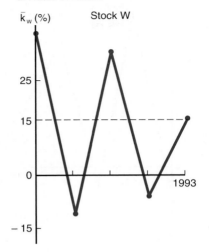
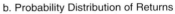
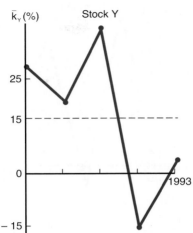
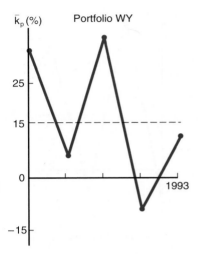

b. Probability Distribution of Returns

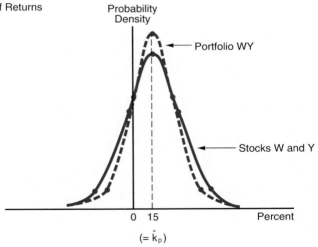

Year	Stock W k_W	Stock Y k_Y	Portfolio WY k_P
1989	40%	28%	34%
1990	(10)	20	5
1991	35	41	38
1992	(5)	(17)	(11)
1993	15	3	9
Average return =	15%	15%	15%
Standard deviation =	22.6%	22.6%	20.6%

portfolio's risk is *not* an average of the risks of its component stocks—diversification has reduced, but not eliminated, risk.[7]

From these examples we see that in one extreme case (r = −1.0), risk can be completely eliminated, while in the other extreme case (r = +1.0), diversification does no good whatever. In between these extremes, combining two stocks into a portfolio reduces but does not eliminate the riskiness inherent in the individual stocks.[8]

MEASURING PORTFOLIO RISK

In the preceding section, we examined portfolio risk at an intuitive level. We now describe how portfolio risk is actually measured and dealt with in practice. First, the riskiness of a portfolio is measured by the standard deviation of its return distribution, and Equation 4-6 is used to calculate this standard deviation:[9]

$$\text{Portfolio standard deviation} = \sigma_p = \sqrt{\sum_{i=1}^{n} (k_{pi} - \hat{k}_p)^2 P_i}. \qquad (4\text{-}6)$$

Here σ_p is the portfolio's standard deviation; k_{pi} is the return on the portfolio under the ith state of the economy; $\hat{k}_p$ is the expected rate of return on the portfolio; P_i is the probability of occurrence of the ith state of the economy; and there are n economic states. This equation is exactly the same as Equation 4-3, for the standard deviation of a single asset, except that here the asset is a portfolio of assets (for example, a mutual fund).

Covariance and the Correlation Coefficient.   Two key concepts in portfolio analysis are (1) *covariance* and (2) the *correlation coefficient*. Covariance is a measure which combines the variance (or volatility) of a stock's returns with the tendency of those returns to move up or down at the same time other stocks move up or down. For example, the covariance between Stocks A and B tells us whether

---

[7]To be precise, a portfolio of two stocks will have less risk than the lower-risk stock only if the correlation coefficient between the stocks is less than the ratio of the stocks' standard deviations, where the ratio is constructed with the lower standard deviation in the numerator. Thus, for Portfolio AB to have less risk than Stock A, $r_{AB} < \sigma_A/\sigma_B$.

[8]For ease of illustration, our examples showed stocks which had the same average realized return and standard deviation. The implications would be the same if we had used stocks with differing returns and standard deviations.

[9]Alternative risk measures, such as the coefficient of variation or semivariance, could also be used to measure the risk of a portfolio, but since portfolio returns (1) are approximately normally distributed and (2) have reasonably similar expected values, these refinements are generally not necessary and hence are not used.

the returns of the two stocks tend to rise and fall together, and how large those movements tend to be. Equation 4-7 defines the covariance (Cov) between Stocks A and B:

$$\text{Covariance} = \text{Cov(AB)} = \sum_{i=1}^{n} (k_{Ai} - \hat{k}_A)(k_{Bi} - \hat{k}_B) P_i. \qquad (4\text{-}7)$$

The first term in parentheses after the Σ is the deviation of Stock A's return from its expected value under the ith state of the economy; the second term is Stock B's deviation under the same state; and P_i is the probability of the ith state occurring. Before going through an example, note these points:

1. If the returns on A and B tend to move together, the terms in parentheses will both be positive or both be negative for each state of the economy; that is, if k_{Ai} is above its expected value, $\hat{k}_A$, then k_{Bi} generally will be above $\hat{k}_B$, and vice versa. Therefore, if the returns move together, the terms in parentheses will both be positive or both be negative, hence the product $(k_{Ai} - \hat{k}_A)(k_{Bi} - \hat{k}_B)$ will be positive, while if the returns move counter to one another, the products will tend to be negative. However, if the two stocks' returns fluctuate randomly, then the products will sometimes be positive and sometimes be negative, and the sum of the products will be close to zero because the positives and negatives will tend to cancel out. Therefore, if Stocks A and B tend to move together, their covariance, Cov(AB), will be positive, while if they tend to move counter to one another, Cov(AB) will be negative. If they fluctuate randomly, Cov(AB) could be either positive or negative, but, in either event, it will be close to zero.

2. If the return on either A or B is highly uncertain, then it will have a high standard deviation, its parentheses' terms will tend to be large, the products will tend to be large, and the absolute size of Cov(AB) also will tend to be large. However, Cov(AB) will be small, even if σ_A and/or σ_B is large, if A and B move randomly, because the plus and minus terms will cancel out.

3. If either stock has a zero standard deviation, and hence is riskless, then all of its deviations $(k_i - \hat{k})$ will be zero, and Cov(AB) also will be zero. Similarly, if one asset is not completely riskless, but it does have a relatively low risk, then its deviations will tend to be small, and this, too, will hold down the size of Cov(AB).

4. Therefore, Cov(AB) will be large and positive if two assets have large standard deviations and tend to move together; it will be large and negative for two high σ assets which move counter to one another; and it will be small if the two assets' returns move randomly, rather than up or down with one another, or if either of the assets has a small standard deviation.

To illustrate the calculation process, first look at Table 4-3, which presents the probability distributions of the rates of return on four stocks, and at Figure 4-5, which plots scatter diagrams between returns on several pairs of the stocks.

TABLE 4-3

PROBABILITY DISTRIBUTIONS OF STOCKS E, F, G, AND H

Probability of Occurrence	Rate of Return Distribution			
	E	**F**	**G**	**H**
0.1	10.0%	6.0%	14.0%	2.0%
0.2	10.0	8.0	12.0	6.0
0.4	10.0	10.0	10.0	9.0
0.2	10.0	12.0	8.0	15.0
0.1	10.0	14.0	6.0	20.0
$\hat{k} =$	10.0%	10.0%	10.0%	10.0%
$\sigma =$	0.0%	2.2%	2.2%	5.0%

FIGURE 4-5

SCATTER DIAGRAMS

a. Returns on E and F (r = 0)

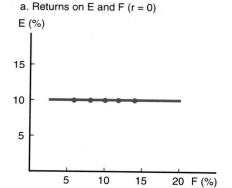

b. Returns on F and G (r = − 1.0)

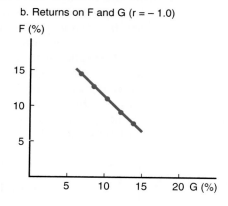

c. Returns on F and H (r ≈ 0.9)

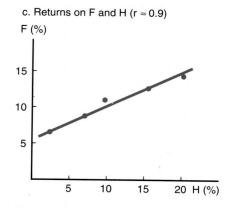

d. Returns on G and H (r ≈ − 0.9)

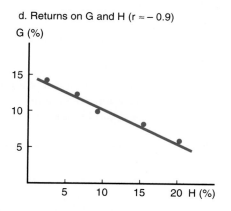

Notes:

a. The lines shown in each graph are called *regression lines;* they will be discussed in detail in Chapter 5.

b. These graphs are drawn as if each point had an equal probability of occurrence.

We can use Equation 4-7 to calculate the covariance between Stocks F and G as follows:

$$\text{Cov(FG)} = \sum_{i=1}^{5} (k_{Fi} - \hat{k}_F)(k_{Gi} - \hat{k}_G)P_i$$

$$= (6 - 10)(14 - 10)(0.1) + (8 - 10)(12 - 10)(0.2)$$
$$+ (10 - 10)(10 - 10)(0.4) + (12 - 10)(8 - 10)(0.2)$$
$$+ (14 - 10)(6 - 10)(0.1)$$

$$= -4.8.$$

The negative sign indicates that the rates of return tend to move in opposite directions, which is consistent with the pattern shown in Panel b of Figure 4-5.

If we calculated the covariance between Stocks F and H, we would find $\text{Cov(FH)} = +10.8$, indicating that these assets tend to move together, as indicated by the positive slope in Panel c. A zero covariance, as between Stocks E and F, indicates that there is no relationship between the variables; that is, the variables are independent. (E's return is always 10 percent; therefore, $\sigma_E = 0\%$, so the covariance of E with any other asset must be zero.)

It is difficult to interpret the magnitude of the covariance term, so a related statistic, the correlation coefficient, is often used to measure the degree of comovement between two variables. The correlation coefficient standardizes the covariance by dividing by a product term; this facilitates comparisons by putting things on a similar scale. The correlation coefficient, r, is calculated as follows for variables A and B:

$$\text{Correlation coefficient(AB)} = r_{AB} = \frac{\text{Cov(AB)}}{\sigma_A \sigma_B}. \qquad (4\text{-}8)$$

The sign of the correlation coefficient is the same as the sign of the covariance, so a positive sign means that the variables move together, a negative sign indicates that they move in opposite directions, and, if r is close to zero, they move independently of one another. Moreover, the standardization process confines the correlation coefficient to values between -1.0 and $+1.0$. Finally, note that Equation 4-8 can be solved to find the covariance:

$$\text{Cov(AB)} = r_{AB}\sigma_A\sigma_B. \qquad (4\text{-}8a)$$

Using Equation 4-8, we find the correlation coefficient between Stocks F and G to be -1.0 (except for a rounding error):

$$r_{FG} = \frac{-4.8}{(2.2)(2.2)} \approx -1.0.$$

These two stocks are said to be perfectly negatively correlated. As Panel b of Figure 4-5 shows, the regression line for these two assets' rates of return is negatively sloped, and all points lie exactly on the line. Whenever the points are all on the regression line, r must be equal to 1.0 if the line slopes up and to -1.0 if the line slopes down.

The correlation coefficient between Stocks F and H is $+0.9$. Thus, there is a strong positive relationship—their regression line is upward sloping, but all points are not exactly on the line. Except in the case where one of the assets has zero variance, the closer the points are to the regression line, the higher the absolute value of the correlation coefficient.

The Two-Asset Case.   Under the assumption that the distributions of returns on the individual securities are normal, a complicated looking but operationally simple equation can be used to determine the riskiness of a two-asset portfolio:[10]

$$\text{Portfolio SD} = \sigma_p = \sqrt{x^2\sigma_A^2 + (1-x)^2\sigma_B^2 + 2x(1-x)r_{AB}\sigma_A\sigma_B}. \quad \textbf{(4-9)}$$

Here x is the fraction of the portfolio invested in Security A, so $(1-x)$ is the fraction invested in Security B.

SELF-TEST QUESTIONS

What is a portfolio of assets?

How is the riskiness of a portfolio measured?

What does the correlation coefficient measure?

EFFICIENT PORTFOLIOS

One important use of the statistical relationships we have discussed thus far is to select *efficient portfolios*—defined as those portfolios which provide the highest expected return for any degree of risk, or the lowest degree of risk for any expected return. To illustrate the concept, assume that two investment securities, A and B, are available, and we can allocate our funds between the securities in any proportion. Suppose Security A has an expected rate of return of $\hat{k}_A = 5\%$ and a

---

[10]Equation 4-9 is derived from Equation 4-6 in standard statistics books. Notice that if $x = 1$, all of the portfolio is invested in Security A, and Equation 4-9 reduces to σ_A:

$$\sigma_p = \sqrt{\sigma_A^2} = \sigma_A.$$

The portfolio contains but a single asset, so the risk of the portfolio and that of the asset are identical. Equation 4-9 could be expanded to include any number of assets by adding additional terms, but we shall not do so here.

standard deviation of returns $\sigma_A = 4\%$, while $\hat{k}_B = 8\%$ and $\sigma_B = 10\%$. Our first task is to determine the set of *attainable* portfolios, and then from this attainable set to select the *efficient* subset.

To construct the attainable set, we need data on the degree of correlation between the two securities' expected returns, r_{AB}. Let us work with three different assumed degrees of correlation, $r_{AB} = +1.0$, $r_{AB} = 0$, and $r_{AB} = -1.0$, and, using them, develop the portfolios' expected returns, $\hat{k}_p$, and standard deviations, σ_p. (Of course, only one correlation can exist; our example simply shows three alternative situations that might exist.)

To calculate $\hat{k}_p$, we use Equation 4-5, substituting the given values for $\hat{k}_A$ and $\hat{k}_B$, and then solving for $\hat{k}_p$ at different values of x. For example, when x equals 0.75, then $\hat{k}_p = 5.75\%$:

$$\hat{k}_p = x_A\hat{k}_A + x_B\hat{k}_B$$

$$= 0.75(5\%) + 0.25(8\%) = 5.75\%.$$

Other values of $\hat{k}_p$ were found similarly, and they are shown in Table 4-4.

Next, we use Equation 4-9 to find σ_p. Substitute the given values for σ_A, σ_B, and r_{AB}, and then solve Equation 4-9 for σ_p at different values of x. For example, in the case where $r_{AB} = 0$ and $x = 0.75$, then $\sigma_P = 3.9\%$:

$$\sigma_p = \sqrt{x^2\sigma_A^2 + (1 - x)^2\sigma_B^2 + 2x(1 - x)r_{AB}\sigma_A\sigma_B}$$

$$= \sqrt{(0.5625)(16) + (0.0625)(100) + 2(0.75)(0.25)(0)(4)(10)}$$

$$= \sqrt{9.00 + 6.25} = \sqrt{15.25} = 3.9\%.$$

Table 4-4 gives $\hat{k}_p$ and σ_p values for $x = 1.00, 0.75, 0.50, 0.25$, and 0.00, and Figure 4-6 gives plots of $\hat{k}_p$, σ_p, and the attainable set of portfolios, for each correlation. In both the table and the graphs, note the following points:

1. The three graphs across the top row of Figure 4-6 designate Case I, where the two assets are perfectly positively correlated, that is, $r_{AB} = +1.0$. The three graphs

TABLE 4-4 $\hat{k}_p$ AND σ_p UNDER VARIOUS ASSUMPTIONS	Proportion of Portfolio in Security A (Value of x)	Proportion of Portfolio in Security B (Value of 1 − x)	Case I ($r_{AB} = +1.0$)		Case II ($r_{AB} = 0$)		Case III ($r_{AB} = -1.0$)	
			$\hat{k}_p$	σ_p	$\hat{k}_p$	σ_p	$\hat{k}_p$	σ_p
	1.00	0.00	5.00%	4.0%	5.00%	4.0%	5.00%	4.0%
	0.75	0.25	5.75	5.5	5.75	3.9	5.75	0.5
	0.50	0.50	6.50	7.0	6.50	5.4	6.50	3.0
	0.25	0.75	7.25	8.5	7.25	7.6	7.25	6.5
	0.00	1.00	8.00	10.0	8.00	10.0	8.00	10.0

FIGURE 4-6   ILLUSTRATIONS OF PORTFOLIO RETURNS, RISK, AND THE ATTAINABLE SET OF PORTFOLIOS

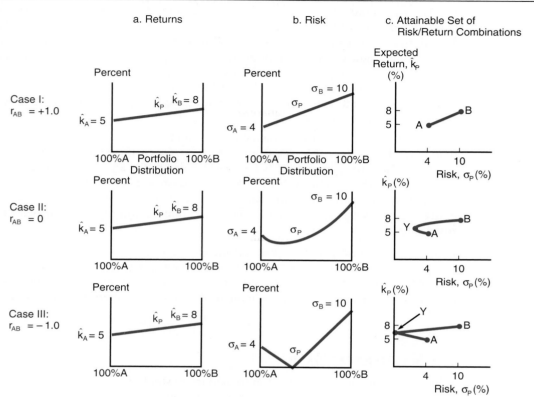

in the middle row of Figure 4-6 are for the zero correlation case, and the three in the bottom row are for perfect negative correlation.

2. All three cases are theoretical in the sense that we would rarely encounter $r_{AB} = -1.0$, 0.0, or $+1.0$. Generally, in the real world, r_{AB} would be in the range of $+0.5$ to $+0.7$ for most stocks. Case II (zero correlation) produces graphs which, pictorially, most closely resemble real-world examples.

3. The left column of graphs shows how the expected portfolio returns vary with different combinations of A and B. We see that these graphs are identical in each of the three cases: The portfolio return, $\hat{k}_p$, is a linear function of x, and it does not depend on the correlation of the assets in the portfolio. This is also seen from the $\hat{k}_p$ columns in Table 4-4.

4. The middle column of graphs shows how risk is affected by the portfolio mix. Starting from the top, we see that portfolio risk, σ_p, is linear in Case I, where $r_{AB} = +1.0$; it is nonlinear in Case II; and Case III shows that risk can be com-

pletely diversified away if $r_{AB} = -1.0$. Thus, σ_p, unlike $\hat{k}_p$, does depend on correlation.

5. The right column of graphs shows the *attainable,* or *feasible,* set of portfolios constructed with different mixes of Securities A and B. Each of the three graphs was plotted from pairs of $\hat{k}_p$ and σ_p as shown in Table 4-4. For example, Point A in the upper right graph is the point $\hat{k}_p = 5\%$, $\sigma_p = 4\%$ from the Case I data in Table 4-4. All other points on the curves were plotted similarly. With only two securities, the attainable set is a curve or line, and we can achieve each risk/return combination on the relevant curve by allocating our investment funds between Securities A and B.

6. Are all portfolios on the attainable set equally good? The answer is no: Only that part of the attainable set from Y to B in Cases II and III is defined to be *efficient.* The part from A to Y is inefficient because for any degree of risk on the line segment AY, a higher return can be found on segment YB. Thus, no rational investor would hold a portfolio that lay on segment AY. In Case I, however, the entire feasible set is also efficient—here no combination of the securities can be ruled out.

From these examples we see that in one extreme case $(r = -1.0)$, risk can be completely eliminated, while in the other extreme case $(r = +1.0)$, diversification does no good whatever. In between these extremes, combining two stocks into a portfolio reduces but does not eliminate the riskiness inherent in the individual stocks.[11]

THE MULTI-ASSET CASE

What would happen if we added more and more stocks to the portfolio? In general, the riskiness of a portfolio will decline as the number of stocks held increases. If we added enough stocks, could we completely eliminate risk? In general, the answer is no, but the extent to which adding stocks to a portfolio reduces the portfolio's risk depends on the degree of correlation among the stocks: The smaller the correlation coefficient, the lower the remaining risk in a large portfolio. Indeed, if we could find enough stocks whose correlation coefficients were zero (or negative), all risk could be eliminated. However, in the typical case, where the correlations among the individual stocks are positive but less than $+1.0$, some but not all risk can be eliminated.

---

[11]If we differentiate Equation 4-9, set the derivative equal to zero, and then solve for x, we obtain the fraction of the portfolio that should be invested in Security A if we wish to form the least-risky portfolio. Here is the equation:

$$\text{Minimum risk portfolio: } x = \frac{\sigma_B(\sigma_B - r_{AB}\sigma_A)}{\sigma_A^2 + \sigma_B^2 - 2r_{AB}\sigma_A\sigma_B}.$$

As a rule, we limit x to the range 0 to $+1.0$; that is, if the solution value is x > 1.0, set x = 1.0, and if x is negative, set x = 0. A negative x would imply short sales, and x > 1.0 would imply borrowing.

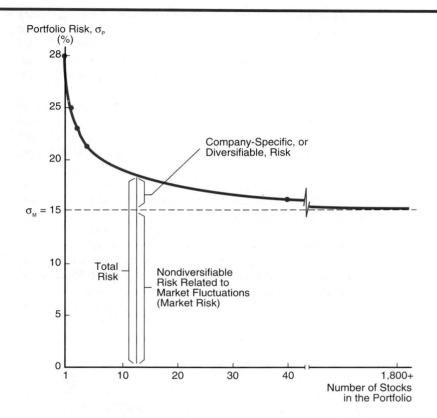

FIGURE 4-7

EFFECT OF PORTFOLIO
SIZE ON PORTFOLIO
RISK

As noted previously, it is very difficult, if not impossible, to find stocks whose expected returns are negatively correlated—most stocks tend to do well when the national economy is strong and poorly when it is weak.[12] Thus, even very large portfolios end up with a certain degree of risk. Consider, for example, Figure 4-7, which shows how portfolio risk is affected by forming larger and larger portfolios of New York Stock Exchange (NYSE) stocks. Standard deviations are plotted for an average one-stock portfolio, an average two-stock portfolio, and so on, up to a portfolio consisting of all 1,800 + common stocks listed on the Exchange. The graph shows that the riskiness of a portfolio consisting of NYSE stocks tends to decline and to approach a limit asymptotically as the size of the portfolio increases.

---

[12]It is not too hard to find a few stocks that happened to decline because of a particular set of circumstances in the past while most other stocks were advancing; it is much harder to find stocks that could logically be *expected* to decline in the future when other stocks are rising.

According to data accumulated in recent years, σ_1, the standard deviation of returns of an average one-stock portfolio (or an average stock), is approximately 28 percent, whereas a portfolio consisting of all stocks, which is called the *market portfolio,* would have a standard deviation of about 15 percent. The market portfolio's standard deviation is given the symbol σ_M, so $\sigma_M = 15\%$, as shown in Figure 4-7.

Since an average stock held in isolation would have a riskiness of $\sigma_i \approx 28\%$, and a very large portfolio would have $\sigma_M = 15\%$, almost half of the riskiness inherent in an average stock can be eliminated by holding it in a portfolio. Further, it is not necessary to hold all stocks—a portfolio consisting of about 40 randomly selected stocks will have σ_p close to σ_M.

SELF-TEST QUESTIONS

Define the term "efficient portfolio."

Explain what happens to the riskiness of the portfolio when more and more randomly selected stocks are added to an average, one-stock portfolio.

COMPONENTS OF A STOCK'S TOTAL RISK

That part of a stock's risk which can be eliminated by holding a well-diversified portfolio is called *diversifiable,* or *company-specific, risk.* Diversifiable risk is caused by such company-specific events as lawsuits, strikes, successful and unsuccessful marketing programs, and winning and losing major contracts. Since occurrences that are unique to a particular firm (or to its industry) are random, their effects on a portfolio can be eliminated by diversification—bad events in one firm will be offset by good events in another. *Nondiversifiable,* or *market, risk,* on the other hand, stems from such external events as war, inflation, recession, and high interest rates, which have an impact on all firms, and hence cannot be eliminated by diversification. Market risk is also known as *systematic risk,* because it shows the degree to which a stock moves systematically with other stocks, and diversifiable risk is sometimes called *unsystematic risk.*

We know that investors demand a premium for bearing risk; that is, the higher the riskiness of a security, the higher its expected return must be to induce investors to buy (or hold) the security. However, if investors are primarily concerned with *portfolio risk* rather than the risk of the individual securities in the portfolio, how should the riskiness of individual stocks be measured? The answer is this: *The relevant riskiness of an individual stock is its contribution to the riskiness of a well-diversified portfolio.* In other words, the riskiness of Stock X to a doctor who has a portfolio of 40 stocks, or to a trust officer managing a 150-stock portfolio, is the effect that Stock X has on the portfolio's riskiness. The stock might be quite

risky if held in isolation, but if much of its risk can be eliminated by diversification, the stock's *relevant risk,* which is its contribution to the portfolio's risk, might be small.

SELF-TEST QUESTIONS

Explain the difference between company-specific and market risk. Which one is "relevant," and why?

CHOOSING THE OPTIMAL PORTFOLIO

With only two assets, the feasible set of portfolios is a line or curve as shown in the third column of graphs back in Figure 4-6. However, if we were to increase the number of assets, we would obtain an area such as the shaded area in Figure 4-8. The points A, H, G, and E represent single securities (or portfolios containing only one security). All the other points in the shaded area, including its boundaries, represent portfolios of two or more securities. The shaded area is called the *feasible,* or *attainable, region.* Each point in this area represents a particular portfolio with a risk of σ_p and an expected return of $\hat{k}_p$. For example, point X represents one such portfolio's risk and expected return, as do B, C, and D.

Given the full set of potential portfolios that could be constructed from the available assets, which portfolio should actually be held? This choice involves two separate decisions: (1) determining the *efficient* set of portfolios and (2) choosing from the efficient set the single portfolio that is best for the individual investor.

FIGURE 4-8

THE EFFICIENT SET OF INVESTMENTS

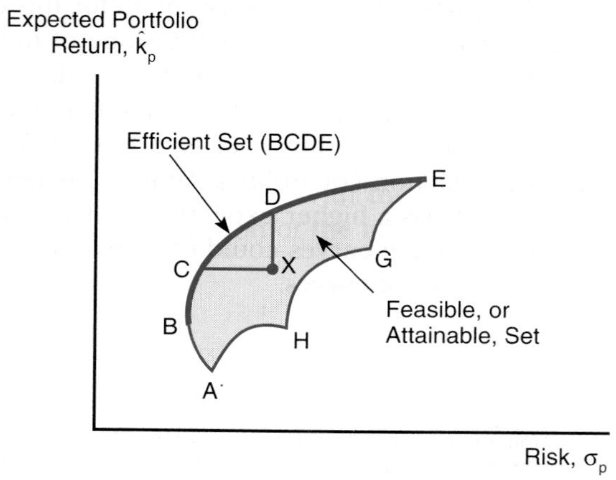

Expected Portfolio Return, $\hat{k}_p$

Efficient Set (BCDE)

Feasible, or Attainable, Set

Risk, σ_p

FIGURE 4-10

SELECTING THE
OPTIMAL PORTFOLIO
OF RISKY ASSETS

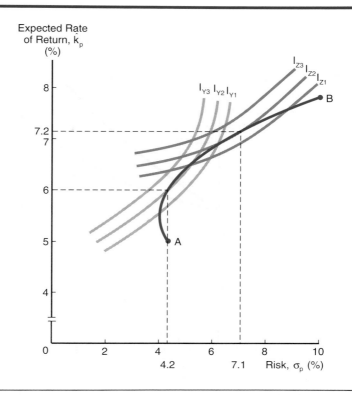

SELF-TEST QUESTIONS

What is the efficient frontier?

What are indifference curves?

Conceptually, how does an investor choose his or her optimal portfolio?

SUMMARY

The primary goals of this chapter were (1) to show how risk is measured for assets held in isolation and (2) to explain how an asset's risk is affected when the asset is held as part of a portfolio of assets. The key concepts covered are listed below:

▶ In general, *risk* can be defined as the probability that some unfavorable event will occur.

▶ *Investment risk* is related to the probability of earning a return less than the expected return — the greater the chance of low or negative returns, the riskier the investment.

▶ The *expected return* on an investment is the expected value of the probability distribution of its possible returns.

▶ Rational investors hold *portfolios* of risky assets, and they are more concerned with the riskiness of the portfolio than with the riskiness of individual assets.

▶ *Total risk,* which is measured by the dispersion of returns about the mean, is relevant for an asset only if the asset is held in isolation.

▶ When assets are combined into portfolios, the relevant risk is an asset's *market risk,* which is the contribution of the asset to the riskiness of the portfolio.

▶ An asset's total risk can be measured by its *variance* of returns, σ^2, its *standard deviation* of returns, σ, or its *coefficient of variation* of returns, *CV*. For comparing assets' total risks, CV is generally the preferred measure.

▶ The *expected rate of return on a portfolio, $\hat{k}_p$,* is the weighted average return of the component assets, but the *standard deviation of a portfolio, σ_p,* is not the weighted average of the component assets' standard deviations.

▶ Since most assets are not perfectly positively *correlated,* combining assets into portfolios generally reduces risk.

▶ An asset's total risk consists of *company-specific (diversifiable) risk,* which can be eliminated by diversification, and *market risk,* which cannot be eliminated by diversification.

▶ The *feasible set* of portfolios represents all portfolios that can be constructed from a given set of assets.

▶ An *efficient portfolio* is one that offers the most return for a given amount of risk or the least risk for a given amount of return.

▶ The *optimal portfolio* for an investor is defined by the tangency point between the *efficient set* of portfolios and the investor's highest *indifference curve.*

In the next chapter, we will continue the discussion of risk and return by (1) adding a risk-free asset and showing how it affects investors' choices, (2) defining a statistic which can be used to measure market risk (the "beta coefficient"), and (3) examining the relationship between risk and expected rates of return.

QUESTIONS

4-1 Define the following terms, using graphs or equations to illustrate your answers wherever possible:

a. Risk; probability distribution

b. Expected rate of return, $\hat{k}$

c. Standard deviation, σ; variance, σ^2; coefficient of variation (CV)

d. Total risk

e. Market risk

f. Portfolio

    g. Expected return on a portfolio, $\hat{k}_p$

    h. Correlation coefficient, r

    i. Company-specific risk

    j. Feasible set

    k. Efficient portfolio

    l. Efficient frontier

    m. Indifference curve

    n. Optimal portfolio

4-2 The continuous probability distribution of a less risky expected return is more peaked than that of a risky return. What shape would the continuous probability distribution have for (a) completely certain returns and (b) completely uncertain returns?

4-3 Suppose you owned a portfolio consisting of $500,000 worth of long-term U.S. government bonds.

    a. Would your portfolio be riskless?

    b. Now suppose you hold a portfolio consisting of $500,000 worth of 30-day Treasury bills. Every 30 days your bills mature and you reinvest the principal ($500,000) in a new batch of bills. Assume that you live on the investment income from your portfolio and that you want to maintain a constant standard of living. Is your portfolio truly riskless?

    c. You should have concluded that both long-term and short-term portfolios of government securities have some element of risk. Can you think of any asset that would be completely riskless?

4-4 A life insurance policy is a financial asset. The premiums paid represent the investment's cost.

    a. How would you calculate the expected return on a life insurance policy?

    b. Suppose the owner of the life insurance policy has no other financial assets—the person's only other asset is "human capital," or lifetime earnings capacity. What is the correlation coefficient between returns on the insurance policy and returns on the policyholder's human capital?

    c. Life insurance companies have to pay administrative costs and sales representatives' commissions; hence, the expected rate of return on insurance premiums is generally low or even negative. Use the portfolio concept to explain why people buy life insurance in spite of negative expected returns.

SELF-TEST PROBLEM   (SOLUTION APPEARS IN APPENDIX C)

ST-1 (Portfolio risk)   Stocks A and B have the following historical dividend and price data:

Year	Stock A Dividend	Stock A Year-End Price	Stock B Dividend	Stock B Year-End Price
1988	—	$12.25	—	$22.00
1989	$1.00	9.75	$2.40	18.50
1990	1.05	11.00	2.60	19.50
1991	1.15	13.75	2.85	25.25
1992	1.30	13.25	3.05	22.50
1993	1.50	15.50	3.25	24.00

a. Calculate the realized rate of return (or holding period return) for each stock in each year. Then assume that someone had held a portfolio consisting of 50 percent of A and 50 percent of B. (The portfolio is rebalanced every year so as to maintain these percentages.) What would the realized rate of return on the portfolio have been in each year from 1989 through 1993? What would the average returns have been for each stock and for the portfolio? [Hint: The realized rate of return in any Period, t, is $\bar{k}_t = (D_t + P_t - P_{t-1})/P_{t-1}$.]

b. Now calculate the standard deviation of returns for each stock and for the portfolio.

c. On the basis of the extent to which the portfolio has a lower risk than the stocks held individually, would you guess that the correlation coefficient between returns on the two stocks is closer to $+0.9$ or to -0.9?

d. If you added more stocks at random to the portfolio, what is the most accurate statement of what would happen to σ_p?

(1) σ_p would remain constant.

(2) σ_p would decline to somewhere in the vicinity of 15 percent.

(3) σ_p would decline to zero if enough stocks were included.

PROBLEMS

4-1 (Expected returns) Stocks A and B have the following probability distributions of expected future returns:

Probability	A	B
0.1	(25%)	(40%)
0.2	5	0
0.4	15	16
0.2	30	40
0.1	45	66

a. Calculate the expected rate of return, $\hat{k}$, for Stock B. ($\hat{k}_A = 15\%$.)

b. Calculate the standard deviation and coefficient of variation of expected returns for Stock A. (Those for Stock B are 27.0 percent and 1.59.) Is it possible that most investors might regard Stock B as being *less* risky than Stock A? Explain.

4-2 (Expected returns) Suppose you were offered (1) $1 million or (2) a gamble where you would get $2 million if a head were flipped but zero if a tail came up.

a. What is the expected value of the gamble?

b. Would you take the sure $1 million or the gamble?

c. If you choose the sure $1 million, are you a risk averter or a risk seeker?

d. Suppose you actually take the sure $1 million. You can invest it in either a U.S. Treasury bond that will return $1,075,000 at the end of a year or a common stock that has a 50-50 chance of being either worthless or worth $2,300,000 at the end of the year.

(1) What is the expected dollar profit on the stock investment? (The expected profit on the T-bond investment is $75,000.)

(2) What is the expected rate of return on the stock investment? (The expected rate of return on the T-bond investment is 7.5 percent.)

(3) Would you invest in the bond or the stock?

(4) Just how large would the expected profit (or the expected rate of return) have to be on the stock investment to make *you* invest in the stock?

(5) How might your decision be affected if, rather than buying one stock for $1 million, you could construct a portfolio consisting of 100 stocks with $10,000 in each? Each of these stocks has the same return characteristics as the one stock, that is, a 50-50 chance of being worth either zero or $23,000 at year end. Would the correlation between returns on these stocks matter?

4-3   **(Total risk analysis)**   The Groth Corporation is considering three possible capital projects for next year. Each project has a 1-year life, and project returns depend on next year's state of the economy. The estimated rates of return are shown in the table:

State of the Economy	Probability of Each State Occurring	Rates of Return If State Occurs		
		A	B	C
Recession	0.25	10%	9%	14%
Average	0.50	14	13	12
Boom	0.25	16	18	10

a. Find each project's expected rate of return, variance, standard deviation, and coefficient of variation.

b. Rank the alternatives on the basis of (1) expected return and (2) risk. Which alternative would you choose?

4-4   **(Portfolio effects and market risk analysis)**   Refer to the three alternative projects contained in Problem 4-3. Assume that the Groth Corporation is going to invest one-third of its available funds in each project. That is, Groth will create a portfolio of three equally weighted projects.

a. What is the expected rate of return on the portfolio?

b. What are the variance and standard deviation of the portfolio?

c. What are the covariance and correlation coefficient between Projects A and B? Between Projects A and C?

4-5   **(Realized rates of return)**   Stocks A and B have the following historical dividend and price data:

	Stock A		Stock B	
Year	Dividend	Year-End Price	Dividend	Year-End Price
1988	—	$22.50	—	$43.75
1989	$2.00	16.00	$3.40	35.50
1990	2.20	17.00	3.65	38.75
1991	2.40	20.25	3.90	51.75
1992	2.60	17.25	4.05	44.50
1993	2.95	18.75	4.25	45.25

a. Calculate the realized rate of return (or holding period return) for each stock in each year. Then assume that someone had held a portfolio consisting of 50 percent of A and 50 percent of B (the portfolio was rebalanced at the end of each year). What would the realized rate of return on the portfolio have been in each year from 1989 through 1993? What would the average returns have been for each stock and for the portfolio? [Hint: The realized rate of return in any Period, t, is $\bar{k}_t = (D_t + P_t - P_{t-1})/P_{t-1}$.]

b. Now calculate the standard deviation of returns for each stock and for the portfolio.

(Work Parts c through e only if you are using the computer problem diskette.)

c. Add Stock C to the portfolio; C has the following historical dividend and price data:

Stock C

Year	Dividend	Year-End Price
1988	—	$23.40
1989	$1.85	23.90
1990	1.95	31.50
1991	2.05	27.20
1992	2.15	32.25
1993	2.25	26.00

Assume that the portfolio contains 33⅓ percent of A, 33⅓ percent of B, and 33⅓ percent of C. How does this affect the portfolio return and standard deviation?

d. Make some other changes in the portfolio percentages, making sure the percentages sum to 100 percent. For example, put 100 percent in A; 25 percent in A, 25 percent in B, and 50 percent in C; and so forth. Explain why $\bar{k}_p$ and σ_p change.

e. Would you rather have a portfolio consisting of one-third of each stock or a portfolio with 50 percent A and 50 percent B? Explain.

M I N I
C A S E

Barbara Orban's first assignment at Southern Commerce Bank is to invest $1 million from an estate for which the bank is trustee. Because the estate is expected to be distributed to the heirs in about one year, Orban has been instructed to plan for a 1-year holding period. Further, her boss has restricted her to the following investment alternatives:

State of the Economy	Probability	Estimated Rate of Return				
		T-Bills	Paragon	Luster	Apex	Market Portfolio
Recession	0.05	8.0%	(22.0%)	28.0%	10.0%	(13.0%)
Below average	0.20	8.0	(2.0)	14.7	(10.0)	1.0
Average	0.50	8.0	20.0	0.0	7.0	15.0
Above average	0.20	8.0	35.0	(10.0)	45.0	29.0
Boom	0.05	8.0	50.0	(20.0)	30.0	43.0
	1.00					

The bank's economic and forecasting staff developed probability estimates for the state of the economy, and the trust department has a sophisticated computer program which estimated the rate of return on each alternative under each state of the economy. Paragon Inc. is an electronics firm; Luster Corporation owns gold mines in the United States and Canada; and Apex Company manufactures tires and various other rubber and plastics products. The bank also maintains an "index fund" which owns a market-weighted fraction of all publicly traded stocks, and Orban can invest in that fund and thus obtain average stock market results. Place yourself in Orban's position, and answer the following questions:

a. Define the term "investment risk."

b. Why is the T-bill return independent of the state of the economy? Do T-bills promise a completely risk-free return? Why are Paragon's returns expected to move with the economy, whereas Luster's are expected to move counter to the economy?

c. Calculate the expected rate of return on each alternative. Based solely on expected returns, which alternative should Orban choose?

d. Briefly explain the concepts of total risk and market risk.

e. Orban recognizes that basing a decision solely on expected returns is appropriate only for risk-neutral individuals. Since the trust's beneficiaries, like virtually everyone, are risk averse, the riskiness of each alternative is an important aspect of the decision. One possible measure of risk is the standard deviation of returns. Calculate this value for each alternative. What type of risk is measured by the standard deviation?

f. Orban just remembered that the coefficient of variation (CV) is generally regarded as being a better measure of total risk than the standard deviation when the alternatives being considered have widely differing expected returns. Calculate the CVs for the different securities. Does the CV produce the same risk ranking as the standard deviation?

g. Orban wondered what would happen if she created a two-stock portfolio by investing $500,000 in Paragon and $500,000 in Luster. What are the expected return and the standard deviation for this portfolio? How does the riskiness of the portfolio compare with the riskiness of the two individual stocks if they were held in isolation?

h. What would happen to the riskiness of the portfolio if more and more randomly selected stocks were added to an average, one-stock portfolio?

i. Should portfolio effects influence the way investors think about the riskiness of individual stocks? If you chose to hold a one-stock portfolio and consequently were exposed to more risk than diversified investors, could you expect to be compensated for all of your risk; that is, could you earn a risk premium on that part of your risk that could have been eliminated by diversifying?

j. Construct a reasonable, but hypothetical, graph which shows risk, as measured by portfolio standard deviation, on the X axis and expected rate of return on the Y axis. Now add an illustrative feasible (or attainable) set of portfolios, and show what portion of the feasible set is efficient. What makes a particular portfolio efficient? Don't worry about specific values when constructing the graph—merely illustrate how things look with "reasonable" data.

k. Now add a set of indifference curves to the graph created for Part j. What do these curves represent? What is the optimal portfolio for this investor? Finally, add a second set of indifference curves which leads to the selection of a different optimal portfolio. Why do the two investors choose different portfolios?

SELECTED ADDITIONAL REFERENCES AND CASES

Probably the best sources of additional information on probability distributions and single-asset risk measures are statistics textbooks. For example, see

Kohler, Heinz, *Statistics for Business and Economics* (Glenview, Ill.: Scott, Foresman, 1988).

Mendenhall, William, Richard L. Schaeffer, and Dennis D. Wackerly, *Mathematical Statistics with Applications* (Boston: Duxbury, 1981).

Probably the best place to find an extension of portfolio theory concepts is one of the investments textbooks. These are some good ones:

Francis, Jack C., *Investments: Analysis and Management* (New York: McGraw-Hill, 1980).

Radcliffe, Robert C., *Investment: Concepts, Analysis, and Strategy* (Glenview, Ill.: Scott, Foresman, 1993).

Reilly, Frank K., *Investment Analysis and Portfolio Management* (Hinsdale, Ill.: Dryden Press, 1989).

Sharpe, William F., *Investments* (Englewood Cliffs, N.J.: Prentice-Hall, 1985).

Those who want to start at the beginning in studying portfolio theory should see
Markowitz, Harry M., "Portfolio Selection," *Journal of Finance,* March 1952, 77–91.
———, "Foundations of Portfolio Theory," *Journal of Finance,* June 1991, 469–477.

The following case covers many of the concepts discussed in this chapter as well as concepts to be covered in Chapter 5:
Case 2, "Peachtree Securities, Inc. (A)," in Brigham, Eugene F., and Louis C. Gapenski, *Cases in Financial Management* (Fort Worth, Tex.: Dryden Press, 1994).

CONTINUOUS PROBABILITY DISTRIBUTIONS

APPENDIX 4A

In Chapter 4, we illustrated risk/return concepts using discrete distributions, and we assumed that only five states of the economy could exist. In reality, however, the state of the economy can range from a deep recession to a fantastic boom, and there are an infinite number of possibilities in between. It is inconvenient to work with a large number of outcomes using discrete distributions, but it is relatively easy to deal with such situations with *continuous distributions,* since they can be completely specified by only two or three summary statistics such as the mean (or expected value), standard deviation, and a measure of skewness. In the past, financial managers did not have the tools necessary to use continuous distributions in practical risk analyses. Now, however, firms have access to computers and powerful software packages, such as the *Interactive Financial Planning System (IFPS)* and *@ RISK,* an add-in for *Lotus 1-2-3,* which can process continuous distributions. Thus, if financial risk analysis is computerized, as is increasingly the case, it is often preferable to use continuous distributions to express the distribution of outcomes.[1]

UNIFORM DISTRIBUTION

One continuous distribution that is often used in financial models is the *uniform distribution,* in which each possible outcome has the same probability of occurrence as any other outcome; hence, there is no clustering of values. Figure 4A-1 shows two uniform distributions.

Distribution A of Figure 4A-1 has a range of −5 to +15 percent. Therefore, the absolute size of the range is 20 units. Since the entire area under the density function must equal 1.00, the height of the distribution, h, must be 0.05: 20h = 1.0, so h = 1/20 = 0.05. We can use this information to find the probability of different outcomes. For example, suppose we want to find the probability that the rate of return will be less than zero. The

---

[1]Computerized risk analysis techniques are discussed in detail in Chapter 11.

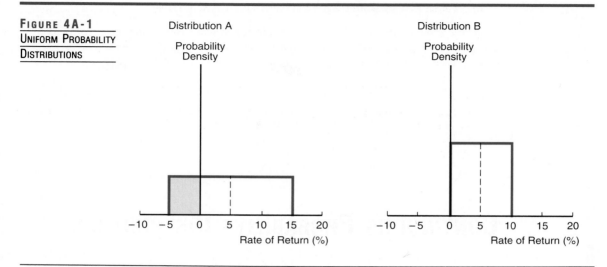

FIGURE 4A-1
UNIFORM PROBABILITY
DISTRIBUTIONS

Distribution A

Distribution B

Note: The expected rate of return for both distributions is $\hat{k} = 5\%$.

probability is the area under the density function from -5 to 0 percent; that is, the shaded area:

$$Area = [\text{Right point} - \text{Left point}][\text{Height of distribution}]$$
$$= [0 - (-5)][0.05] = 0.25 = 25\%.$$

Similarly, the probability of a rate of return between 5 and 15 is 50 percent:

$$Probability = Area = [15 - 5][0.05] = 0.50 = 50\%.$$

The expected rate of return is the midpoint of the range, or 5 percent, for both distributions in Figure 4A-1. Since there is a smaller probability of the actual return falling very far below the expected return in Distribution B, Distribution B depicts a less risky situation in the total risk sense.

TRIANGULAR DISTRIBUTION

Another useful continuous distribution is the *triangular distribution*. This type of distribution, which is illustrated in Figure 4A-2, has a clustering of values around the most likely outcome, and the probability of occurrence declines in each direction from the most likely outcome. Distribution C has a range of -5 to $+15$ percent and a most likely return of $+10$ percent. Distribution D has a most likely return of 5 percent, but its range is only from 0 to $+10$ percent. Note that Distribution C is skewed to the left, while Distribution D is symmetric. The expected rate of return for Distribution C is 6.67 percent, whereas that

FIGURE 4A-2

TRIANGULAR

PROBABILITY

DISTRIBUTIONS

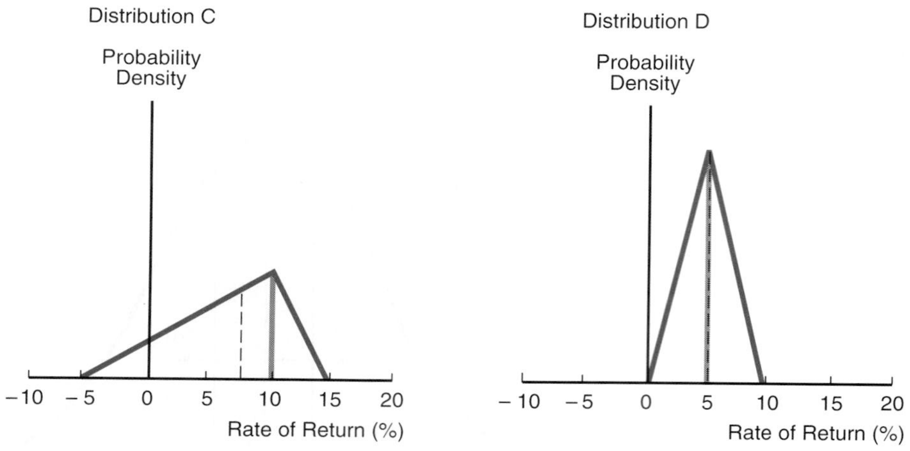

Distribution C

Probability
Density

Rate of Return (%)

Distribution D

Probability
Density

Rate of Return (%)

Note: The most likely rate of return is 10 percent for Distribution C and 5 percent for Distribution D; the expected rates of return are $\hat{k}_C = 6.67\%$ and $\hat{k}_D = 5\%$.

of D is only 5 percent.[2] However, it is obvious by inspection that Distribution C is riskier; its dispersion about the mean is greater than that for Distribution D, and it has a significant chance of actual losses, whereas losses are not possible in Distribution D.

NORMAL DISTRIBUTION

Because it is discussed so much in statistics courses, is so easy to use, and conforms well to so many real-world situations, the most commonly used continuous distribution is the *normal distribution*. It is symmetric about the expected value, and its tails extend out to plus and minus infinity. Figure 4A-3 is a normal distribution with an expected, or mean (μ, pronounced "mu"), rate of return of 10 percent and a standard deviation (σ, or sigma) of 5 percent. Approximately 68.3 percent of the area under any normal curve lies within $\pm 1\sigma$ of its mean, 95.5 percent lies within $\pm 2\sigma$, and 99.7 percent lies within $\pm 3\sigma$. Therefore, the probability of actually achieving a rate of return within the range of 5 to 15 percent ($\mu \pm 1\sigma$) is 68.3 percent, and so forth. Obviously, the smaller the standard deviation, the smaller the probability of the actual outcome deviating very much from the expected value, and hence the smaller the total risk of the investment.

---

[2]Note that the most likely outcome equals the expected outcome only when the distribution is symmetric. If the distribution is skewed to the left, the expected outcome falls to the left of the most likely outcome, and vice versa. Also, note that the expected outcome of a triangular distribution is found by using this equation:

(Lower limit + Most likely outcome + Upper limit)/3.

Thus, the expected rate of return for Distribution C is $(-5\% + 10\% + 15\%)/3 = 6.67\%$.

ager might be asked to supply this information for sales of a given product, or an engineer might be asked to estimate the construction costs of a capital project.

2. A financial analyst could then use these input data to help evaluate the riskiness of a given decision. For example, the analyst might conclude that the probability is 50 percent that the actual rate of return on a project will be between 5 and 10 percent, that the probability of a loss (negative rate of return) on the project is 15 percent, or that the probability of a return greater than 10 percent is 25 percent. Generally, such an analysis would be done by using a computer program. We shall return to this topic in Chapter 11.

In theory, we should use the specific distribution that best represents the true situation. Sometimes the true distribution is known, but with most financial data, it is not known. For example, we might think that interest rates could range from 8 to 15 percent next year, with a most likely value of 10 percent. This suggests a triangular distribution. Or we might think that interest rates next year can best be represented by a normal distribution, with a mean of 10 percent and a standard deviation of 2.5 percent. The point is, there is simply no type of distribution that is always "best"; you need to be familiar with different types of distributions and their properties, and then you must select the best distribution for the problem at hand.

RISK AND RETURN: PART 2

O ne of the most useful references for individuals working in investments and portfolio management is Stocks, Bonds, Bills, and Inflation, *published annually by Ibbotson Associates. The latest Ibbotson report presents a history of the total returns realized
from 1926 through 1992 in the following six U.S. capital*
markets:

*1. Small-company stocks, as represented by the smallest 20 percent of
stocks (by market value) listed on the New York Stock Exchange.*

*2. Common stocks, as represented by the Standard and Poor's 500 Stock
Composite Index (S&P 500).*

*3. Long-term corporate bonds, as represented by the Salomon Brothers long-
term, high-grade corporate bond total return index.*

*4. Long-term government bonds, as represented by a U.S. Treasury bond with a
20-year maturity.*

*5. Intermediate-term government bonds, as represented by a U.S. Treasury bond
with a five-year maturity.*

*6. U.S. Treasury bills, as represented by a U.S. Treasury bill with a maturity of
approximately 30 days.*

*A long-term perspective of capital market history reveals the general rela-
tionship between risk and return across different asset classes, as well as the
relationship between nominal and real (inflation-adjusted) returns. By studying
the past, one can make inferences about what is likely to happen in the future.
Although most of the events that occurred from 1926 through 1992 will not be*

185

repeated, similar events, such as economic recessions and booms, will undoubtedly recur, and such events will probably affect future investment returns in much the same way as they did in the past.

The Ibbotson report presents historical data in many different formats, but perhaps the most widely used is the annual return data. For example, the 1993 *Yearbook, which contains data for 67 years (1926 through 1992), provides the following total return information, along with inflation data:*

Investment	Average Annual Return	Highest Annual Return	Lowest Annual Return
Small-company stocks	17.6%	142.9%	− 58.0%
Common stocks	12.4	54.0	− 43.3
Long-term corporate bonds	5.8	43.8	− 8.1
Long-term government bonds	5.2	40.4	− 9.2
Intermediate-term government bonds	5.3	29.1	− 2.3
U.S. Treasury bills	3.8	14.7	0.0
Inflation	3.2	18.2	− 10.3

The most striking feature of the historical data is the significant difference in risk and return characteristics among the investments. Although small-company stocks averaged a 17.5 percent annual return, the return on T-bills averaged only 3.8 percent. In fact, the return on T-bills barely kept pace with inflation, earning on average only 60 basis points (0.6 percentage points) above inflation. When taxes are considered, the real average return on T-bills was negative. For example, an investor who paid on average only 20 percent in taxes would have an after-tax average return on T-bills of only 0.8(3.8%) ≈ 3.0%, which means a real loss of about 20 basis points per year.

Why do the historical returns vary so widely among the investments? The answer is simple: risk. To see this more clearly, note that an investor in small-company stocks would have lost 58 percent of the value of his or her portfolio in one of the past 67 years (to be precise, in 1937), while the worst pre-tax experience for an investor holding T-bills was a breakeven year. In general, we see that a strong relationship exists between risk and return—the higher the risk, the higher the return. Although we have not quantified the riskiness of the listed investments, a numerical analysis would lead to the same conclusion—namely, to obtain higher returns, investors must accept greater risk.

In this chapter we will formalize the risk/return relationship in a manner that will permit you to specify how much return is required for a given amount of risk. You will see that greater risk must be compensated for with higher returns. This is a fundamental principle of finance that has significant implications for virtually all finance decisions.

We began our discussion of risk and return in Chapter 4. There we saw that some of the total risk inherent in an asset can be eliminated by diversification; thus, investors should hold portfolios of assets. Further, each investor should choose between alternative portfolios based on his or her degree of risk aversion as reflected by indifference curves. In this chapter, we continue the discussion of risk and return by adding a risk-free asset to the set of investment opportunities. As we will see, this leads all investors (in theory) to hold the same diversified portfolio of risky assets, and then to account for differing degrees of risk aversion by combining the risky portfolio in different proportions with the risk-free asset. However, this basic question remains to be answered: How much return is required to compensate for a given amount of risk? The Capital Asset Pricing Model (CAPM) provides one neat, precise answer. However, the CAPM has not been, and indeed cannot be, confirmed empirically — it may or may not represent the way investors actually behave. Thus, other risk/return models have been proposed, and we close this chapter with a discussion of the CAPM's most prominent competitor, the Arbitrage Pricing Theory (APT).

THE CAPITAL ASSET PRICING MODEL

As we saw in the preceding chapter, the riskiness of a portfolio as measured by its standard deviation of returns is generally less than the average risk of the individual assets in the portfolio. This phenomenon, in turn, has important implications for the required rate of return on any given security. Investors should (and generally do) hold portfolios of securities, not just one security, so it is reasonable to consider the riskiness of any security in terms of its contribution to the riskiness of a portfolio rather than in terms of its riskiness if held in isolation. The *Capital Asset Pricing Model (CAPM)* specifies the relationship between risk and required rates of return on assets when they are held in well-diversified portfolios.

BASIC ASSUMPTIONS OF THE CAPM

As in all financial theories, a number of assumptions were made in the development of the CAPM; they are summarized in the following list:[1]

1. All investors are single-period expected utility of terminal wealth maximizers who choose among alternative portfolios on the basis of each portfolio's expected return and standard deviation.

---

[1]The CAPM was originated by William F. Sharpe in his article "Capital Asset Prices: A Theory of Market Equilibrium under Conditions of Risk," which appeared in the September 1964 issue of the *Journal of Finance.* Note that Professor Sharpe won the Nobel Prize in economics for his capital asset pricing work. The assumptions inherent in Sharpe's model were spelled out by Michael C. Jensen in "Capital Markets: Theory and Evidence," *Bell Journal of Economics and Management Science,* Autumn 1972, 357–398.

2. All investors can borrow or lend an unlimited amount at a given risk-free rate of interest, k_{RF}, and there are no restrictions on short sales of any asset.[2]

3. All investors have identical estimates of the expected values, variances, and covariances of returns among all assets; that is, investors have homogeneous expectations.

4. All assets are perfectly divisible and perfectly liquid (that is, marketable at the going price).

5. There are no transactions costs.

6. There are no taxes.

7. All investors are price takers (that is, all investors assume that their own buying and selling activity will not affect stock prices).

8. The quantities of all assets are given and fixed.

Theoretical extensions in the literature have relaxed many of the basic CAPM assumptions, and in general these extensions have yielded results that are reasonably consistent with the basic theory. However, even the extensions contain assumptions which are both strong and unrealistic. Therefore, the validity of the model can only be established through empirical tests. More will be said later in this chapter about the empirical validity of the CAPM, but first we must discuss its basic properties and conclusions.

SELF-TEST QUESTIONS

What are the assumptions inherent in the CAPM?

In what sense are these assumptions unrealistic? Explain.

THE CAPITAL MARKET LINE

Figure 4-10 in Chapter 4 showed the set of portfolio opportunities for the two-asset case, and it illustrated how indifference curves can be used to select the optimal portfolio from the feasible set. In Figure 5-1, we have constructed a similar diagram for the multi-asset case, but here we also include a risk-free asset with a return k_{RF}. The riskless asset by definition has zero risk, and hence $\sigma = 0\%$, so it is plotted on the vertical axis.

Figure 5-1 shows both the feasible set of portfolios of risky assets (the shaded area) and a set of indifference curves (I_1, I_2, I_3), which represent the trade-off

---

[2]In a short sale, one borrows a stock and then sells it, expecting to buy it back later (at a lower price) in order to repay the person from whom the stock was borrowed. If you sell short and the stock price rises, you lose; you gain if the stock price falls after you go short.

between risk and expected return for a particular investor. Point N, where indifference curve I_1 is tangent to the efficient set, represents a possible portfolio choice; it is the point on the efficient set of risky portfolios where the investor obtains the highest possible return for a given amount of risk, σ_p, and the smallest degree of risk for a given expected return, $\hat{k}_p$.

However, the investor can do better than Portfolio N; he or she can reach a higher indifference curve. In addition to the feasible set of risky portfolios, we now have a risk-free asset that provides a riskless return, k_{RF}. Given the possibility of investing in the risk-free asset, investors can create new portfolios that combine the risk-free asset with a portfolio of risky assets. This enables them to achieve any combination of risk and return on the straight line connecting k_{RF} with M, the point of tangency between that straight line and the efficient frontier of risky asset portfolios.[3] Some portfolio on the line $k_{RF}MZ$ will be preferred to each risky portfolio on the efficient frontier BNME, so the points on the line $k_{RF}MZ$ now represent the best attainable combinations of risk and return.

Given the new opportunity set $k_{RF}MZ$, our investor will move from Point N to Point R, which is on his or her highest attainable risk/return indifference curve. Note that any point on the old efficient frontier BNME (except the point of tangency M) is dominated by some point along the line $k_{RF}MZ$. In general, since investors can include both the risk-free security and a fraction of the risky portfolio, M, in a portfolio, it will be possible to move to a point such as R. In addition, if the investor can borrow as well as lend (lending is equivalent to buying risk-free debt securities) at the riskless rate, k_{RF}, it is possible to move out on the line

---

[3]The risk/return combinations between a risk-free asset and a risky asset (a single stock or a portfolio of stocks) will always be linear. To see this, consider the following equations, which were developed in Chapter 4, for return, $\hat{k}_p$, and risk, σ_p, for any combination x and $(1 - x)$:

$$\hat{k}_p = xk_{RF} + (1 - x)\hat{k}_M, \qquad \text{(4-5a)}$$

and

$$\sigma_p = \sqrt{x^2\sigma_{RF}^2 + (1 - x)^2\sigma_M^2 + 2x(1 - x)r_{RF/M}\sigma_{RF}\sigma_M}. \qquad \text{(4-9a)}$$

Equation 4-5a is linear. For Equation 4-9a, we know that k_{RF} is the risk-free asset, so $\sigma_{RF} = 0$; hence, σ_{RF}^2 is also zero. Using this information, we can simplify Equation 4-9a as follows:

$$\sigma_p = \sqrt{(1 - x)^2\sigma_M^2} = (1 - x)\sigma_M.$$

Thus, σ_p is also linear when a riskless asset is combined with a portfolio of risky assets.

If expected returns as measured by $\hat{k}_p$ and risk as measured by σ_p are both linear functions of x, then the relationship between $\hat{k}_p$ and σ_p, when graphed as in Figure 5-1, must also be linear. For example, if 100 percent of the portfolio is invested in k_{RF} with a return of 8 percent, the portfolio return will be 8 percent and σ_p will be 0. If 100 percent is invested in M, with $k_M = 12\%$ and $\sigma_M = 10\%$, then $\sigma_p = 1.0(10\%) = 10\%$, and $\hat{k}_p = 0(8\%) + 1.0(12\%) = 12\%$. If 50 percent of the portfolio is invested in M and 50 percent in the risk-free asset, then $\sigma_p = 0.5(10\%) = 5\%$, and $\hat{k}_p = 0.5(8\%) + 0.5(12\%) = 10\%$. Plotting these points will reveal the linear relationship given as $k_{RF}MZ$ in Figure 5-1.

FIGURE 5-1

INVESTOR
EQUILIBRIUM:
COMBINING THE RISK-
FREE ASSET WITH THE
MARKET PORTFOLIO

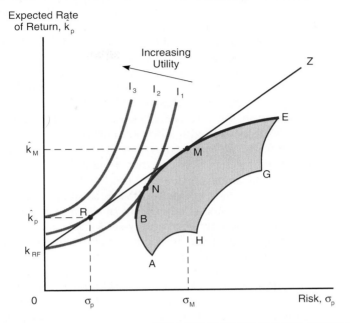

segment MZ, and one would do so if his or her indifference curve were tangent to $k_{RF}MZ$ to the right of Point M.[4]

All investors should hold portfolios lying on the line $k_{RF}MZ$ under the conditions assumed in the CAPM. This implies that they should hold portfolios that are combinations of the risk-free security and the risky portfolio M. Thus, the addition of the risk-free asset totally changes the efficient set: The efficient set now lies along line $k_{RF}MZ$ rather than along the curve BNME. Also, note that if the capital market is to be in equilibrium, M must be a portfolio that contains every risky asset in exact proportion to that asset's fraction of the total market value of all assets; that is, if Security i is x percent of the total market value of all securities, x percent of the market portfolio M must consist of Security i. (In other words, M is the market-value-weighted portfolio of *all* risky assets in the economy.) Thus, all

---

[4]An investor who is highly averse to risk will have a steep indifference curve and will end up at a point such as R, holding some of the risky market portfolio and some of the riskless asset. An investor only slightly averse to risk will have a relatively flat indifference curve, which will cause him or her to move out beyond M toward Z, borrowing to do so. This investor might buy stocks on margin, which means borrowing and using the stocks as collateral. If individuals' borrowing rates are higher than k_{RF}, then the line $k_{RF}MZ$ will tilt down (that is, be less steep) beyond M. This condition would invalidate the basic CAPM, or at least require it to be modified. Therefore, the assumption of equal lending and borrowing rates is crucial to CAPM theory.

investors should hold portfolios which lie on the line $k_{RF}MZ$, with the particular location of a given individual's portfolio being determined by the point at which his or her indifference curve is tangent to the line.

The line $k_{RF}MZ$ in Figure 5-1 is called the *Capital Market Line (CML)*. It has an intercept of k_{RF} and a slope of $(\hat{k}_M - k_{RF})/\sigma_M$.[5] Therefore, the equation for the Capital Market Line may be expressed as follows:

$$\text{CML:} \quad \hat{k}_p = k_{RF} + \left(\frac{\hat{k}_M - k_{RF}}{\sigma_M}\right)\sigma_p. \qquad (5\text{-}1)$$

Equation 5-1 tells us that the expected rate of return on any efficient portfolio (that is, any portfolio on the CML) is equal to the riskless rate plus a risk premium, and the risk premium is equal to $(\hat{k}_M - k_{RF})/\sigma_M$ multiplied by the portfolio's standard deviation, σ_p. Thus, the CML specifies a linear relationship between expected return and risk, with the slope of the CML being equal to the expected return on the market portfolio of risky stocks, $\hat{k}_M$, minus the risk-free rate, k_{RF}, which is called the *market risk premium,* all divided by the standard deviation of returns on the market portfolio, σ_M:

$$\text{Slope of the CML} = (\hat{k}_M - k_{RF})/\sigma_M.$$

For example, suppose $k_{RF} = 10\%$, $\hat{k}_M = 15\%$, and $\sigma_M = 15\%$. Then, the slope of the CML would be $(15\% - 10\%)/15\% = 0.33$, and if a particular portfolio had $\sigma_p = 10\%$, then its $\hat{k}_p$ would be

$$\hat{k}_p = 10\% + 0.33(10\%) = 13.3\%.$$

A riskier portfolio with $\sigma_p = 20\%$ would have $\hat{k}_p = 10\% + 0.33(20\%) = 16.6\%$.

Equation 5-1 states that the expected return on an efficient portfolio in equilibrium is equal to a risk-free return plus a risk premium which is equal to the slope of the CML multiplied by the standard deviation of the portfolio's returns. This relationship is graphed in Figure 5-2. The CML is drawn as a straight line with an intercept at k_{RF}, the risk-free return, and a slope equal to the market risk premium ($\hat{k}_M - k_{RF}$) divided by σ_M. The slope of the CML reflects the aggregate attitude of investors toward risk.

---

[5]Recall that the slope of any line is measured as $\Delta Y/\Delta X$, or the change in height associated with a given change in horizontal distance. k_{RF} is at 0 on the horizontal axis, so $\Delta X = \sigma_M - 0 = \sigma_M$. The vertical axis difference associated with a change from k_{RF} to $\hat{k}_M$ is $\hat{k}_M - k_{RF}$. Therefore, slope $= \Delta Y/\Delta X = (\hat{k}_M - k_{RF})/\sigma_M$.

FIGURE 5-2
THE CAPITAL MARKET
LINE (CML)

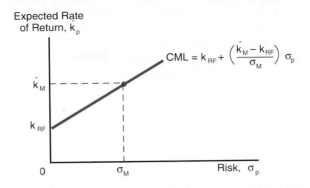

Note: We did not draw it in, but you can visualize the shaded space shown in Figure 5-1 in this graph, and the CML as the line formed by connecting k_{RF} with the tangent to the shaded space.

SELF-TEST QUESTIONS

Draw the feasible set of risky assets, the efficient frontier, the risk-free asset, and the CML on one risk/return graph.

Write out the equation for the CML and explain its meaning.

THE SECURITY MARKET LINE

The next step in the development of the CAPM takes us from risk and returns on efficient portfolios to risk and returns on individual securities. Under the CAPM theory, the riskiness of a security is measured by its beta coefficient ("b," discussed in detail in a later section). In short, beta measures the volatility of a stock's returns relative to the returns on the market portfolio. By definition, an average stock has a beta of 1.0, a stock that is more volatile than the market has a beta greater than 1.0, and a stock that is less volatile than the market has a beta less than 1.0. The equation relating a security's risk as measured by beta and its return is known as the *Security Market Line (SML):*

$$\text{SML: } k_i = k_{RF} + (k_M - k_{RF})b_i. \qquad (5\text{-}2)$$

Here

k_i = the required rate of return on the *i*th stock. (We earlier defined $\hat{k}_i$ to be the expected rate of return. In equilibrium, $k_i = \hat{k}_i$.)

k_{RF} = the riskless rate of return, generally measured by the rate of return on U.S. Treasury securities.

k_M = the required rate of return on a portfolio consisting of all stocks, or the market portfolio. In equilibrium, required returns must equal expected returns, so $k_M = \hat{k}_M$. Note that k_A = the required rate of return on an average stock in the market portfolio.[6] Thus, $k_A = k_M$.

$(k_M - k_{RF})$ = RP_M = the market risk premium, or the price of risk for an average stock. It is the additional return over the riskless rate required to compensate investors for assuming an "average" amount of risk.

b_i = the beta coefficient of the *i*th stock. Betas are discussed in a later section.

$(k_M - k_{RF})b_i$ = RP_i = the risk premium on the *i*th stock. A stock's risk premium is less than, equal to, or greater than the premium on an average stock depending on whether its beta is less than, equal to, or greater than 1.0.

Thus, if $k_{RF} = 9\%$, $k_M = 13\%$, and $b_i = 0.5$, then by Equation 5-2, $k_i = 11\%$:

$$k_i = 9\% + (13\% - 9\%)0.5$$
$$= 9\% + (4\%)0.5$$
$$= 9\% + 2\% = 11\%.$$

Figure 5-3 shows the SML when $k_{RF} = 9\%$ and $k_M = 13\%$. Several features of the graph are worth noting:

1. Required rates of return are shown on the vertical axis, and risk as measured by beta is shown on the horizontal axis.

2. Riskless securities have $b_i = 0$; therefore, k_{RF} appears as the vertical axis intercept.

3. The slope of the SML [$\Delta Y/\Delta X = (k_M - k_{RF})/(1.0 - 0.0) = (k_M - k_{RF}) = 13\% - 9\% = 4$ percentage points in our example] reflects the degree of risk aversion in the economy—the greater the average investor's aversion to risk, then (1) the steeper the slope of the SML, (2) the greater the risk premium for any risky asset, and (3) the higher the required rate of return on risky assets in general. Note that beta is *not* the slope of the SML; the slope of the line in Figure 5-3 is

---

[6]The term "average stock" is a bit like "average U.S. family." The average family might have 2.73 members, its head might be 34.6 years old, its annual income might be $28,362, and so on. No one family actually conforms to average, but each family can be compared with the statistical average. Similarly, the "average stock" is a statistical concept measured in terms of its expected rate of return, standard deviation of returns, and covariance with other stocks.

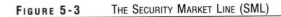

FIGURE 5-3   THE SECURITY MARKET LINE (SML)

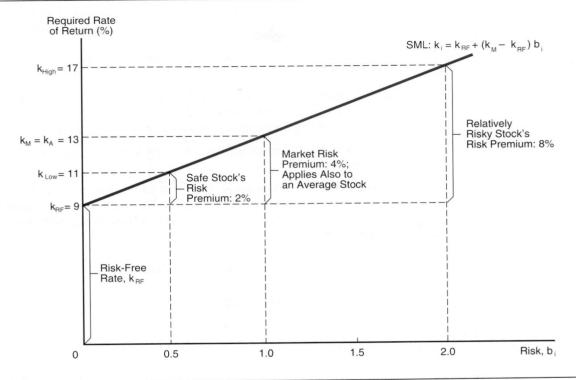

the market risk premium, a constant 4 percentage points for each one-unit increase in beta, while beta itself is calculated as described in a later section.

4. Required rates of return and risk premiums are shown for stocks with $b_i = 0.5$, $b_i = 1.0$, and $b_i = 2.0$.

As we can see from the SML, required rates of return depend not only on market risk as measured by beta, but also on the risk-free rate and the market risk premium. Since these variables change, the SML is not stable over time.

THE IMPACT OF INFLATION

The risk-free rate as measured by the rate on U.S. Treasury securities is a *nominal rate,* and it consists of two elements: (1) a *real inflation-free rate of return, k*,* and (2) an *inflation premium, IP,* equal to the anticipated rate of inflation.[7] Thus,

---

[7]Long-term Treasury bonds also contain a maturity risk premium, MRP. Here we include the MRP in k* to simplify the discussion.

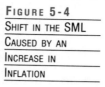

FIGURE 5-4
SHIFT IN THE SML
CAUSED BY AN
INCREASE IN
INFLATION

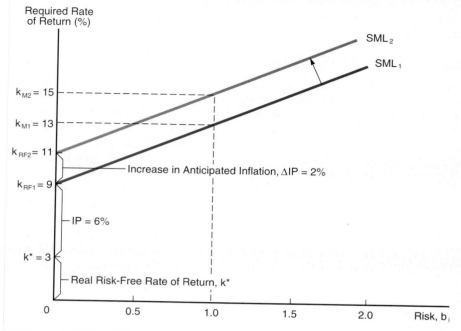

$k_{RF} = k^* + IP$. The real rate on long-term Treasury bonds has historically ranged from 2 to 4 percent, with a mean of about 3 percent. Therefore, if no inflation were expected, long-term Treasury bonds would yield about 3 percent. However, when inflation is present, a premium must be added to the real risk-free rate of return to compensate investors for the loss of purchasing power that results from inflation. Therefore, the 9 percent k_{RF} shown in Figure 5-3 might be thought of as consisting of a 3 percent real risk-free rate of return plus a 6 percent inflation premium: $k_{RF} = k^* + IP = 3\% + 6\% = 9\%$.

If the expected rate of inflation rose to 8 percent, this would cause k_{RF} to rise to 11 percent. Such a change is shown in Figure 5-4. Notice that under the CAPM, the increase in k_{RF} also causes an *equal* increase in the rate of return on all risky assets, because the inflation premium is built into the required rate of return of both riskless and risky assets.[8] For example, the rate of return on an average stock,

---

[8]Recall that the inflation premium for any asset is equal to the average expected rate of inflation over the life of the asset. Thus, in this analysis we must assume either that all securities plotted on the SML graph have the same life or else that the expected rate of future inflation is constant.

It should also be noted that k_{RF} in a CAPM analysis can be proxied by either a long-term rate (the T-bond rate) or a short-term rate (the T-bill rate). Traditionally, the T-bill rate was used, but in recent years there has been a movement toward use of the T-bond rate because there is a closer relationship between T-bond yields and stock returns than between T-bill yields and stock returns. We will discuss this in more detail in Chapter 8.

k_M, increases from 13 to 15 percent. Other risky securities' returns also rise by 2 percentage points.

CHANGES IN RISK AVERSION

The slope of the Security Market Line reflects the extent to which investors are averse to risk—the steeper the slope of the line, the greater the marginal investor's risk aversion. If investors were indifferent to risk, and if k_{RF} were 9 percent, then risky assets would also provide an expected return of 9 percent. If there were no risk aversion, there would be no risk premium, so the SML would be horizontal. As risk aversion increases, so does the risk premium and, thus, the slope of the SML.

Figure 5-5 illustrates an increase in risk aversion. The market risk premium rises from 4 to 6 percent, and k_M rises from 13 to 15 percent. The returns on other risky assets also rise, and the effect of this shift in risk aversion is more pronounced on riskier securities. For example, the required return on a low-risk stock with $b_i = 0.5$ increases by only 1 percentage point, from 11 to 12 percent, whereas that on a high-risk stock with $b_i = 1.5$ increases by 3 percentage points, from 15 to 18 percent.

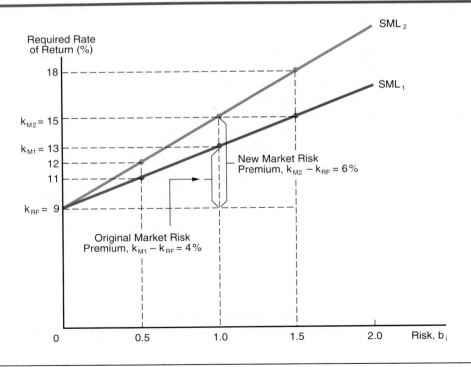

FIGURE 5-5

SHIFT IN THE SML CAUSED BY INCREASED RISK AVERSION

CHANGES IN A STOCK'S BETA COEFFICIENT

As we shall see later in the book, a firm can affect its market risk, and hence its beta, through changes in the composition of its assets as well as through its use of debt financing. A company's beta can also change as a result of external factors, such as increased competition in its industry, the expiration of basic patents, and the like. When such changes occur, the required rate of return also changes, and this will affect the price of the firm's stock. For example, consider Smith Electronics Corporation, with a beta equal to 1.0. Now suppose some action occurred that caused Smith Electronics's beta to increase from 1.0 to 1.5. If the conditions depicted in Figure 5-3 held, Smith's required rate of return would increase from

$$k_1 = k_{RF} + (k_M - k_{RF})b_i$$
$$= 9\% + (13\% - 9\%)1.0$$
$$= 13\%$$

to

$$k_2 = 9\% + (13\% - 9\%)1.5$$
$$= 15\%.$$

Any change which affects the required rate of return on a security, such as a change in its beta coefficient or in expected inflation, will have an impact on the price of the security. We will examine in detail the relationship between a security's required rate of return and its stock price in Chapter 7.

SELF-TEST QUESTIONS

Write out the equation for and graph the SML.

What happens to the SML graph (1) when inflation increases or (2) when inflation decreases?

What happens to the SML graph (1) when risk aversion increases or (2) when risk aversion decreases?

What are the key differences between the CML and the SML?

PHYSICAL ASSETS VERSUS SECURITIES

In a book on the financial management of business firms, why do we spend so much time on the riskiness of security investments? Why not concentrate on the riskiness of such business assets as plant and equipment? *The reason is that, for a management whose goal is stock price maximization, the overriding considera-*

tion is the riskiness of the firm's stock, and the relevant risk of any physical asset must be measured in terms of its effect on the stock's risk. For example, suppose Goodyear Tire Company is considering a major investment in a new product, re-capped tires. Sales of recaps, hence the earnings on the new operation, are highly uncertain, so it would appear that the new venture is quite risky. However, sup-pose returns on the recap business are negatively correlated with Goodyear's reg-ular operations—when times are good and people have plenty of money, they buy new tires, but when times are bad, they tend to buy more recaps. Therefore, re-turns would be high on regular operations and low on the recap division during good times, but the opposite situation would occur during recessions. The result might be a pattern like that shown in Figure 4-2 back in Chapter 4 for Stocks W and M. Thus, what appears to be a risky investment when viewed on a stand-alone basis might not be very risky when viewed within the context of the company as a whole.

This analysis can be extended to the corporation's owners, the stockholders. Because the stock of Goodyear and other companies is owned by stockholders, the real issue each time a company makes a major asset investment is this: How does this investment affect the risk of our stockholders? Again, the stand-alone risk of an individual project might look quite high, but viewed in the context of the project's effect on stockholders' risk, the project might not be very risky. We will address this subject in detail in Chapter 11.

SELF-TEST QUESTION

Explain the following statement: "The stand-alone risk of an individual project might look quite high, but viewed in the context of the project's effect on stockholders' risk, the project might not be very risky."

THE CONCEPT OF BETA

An *average stock*, by definition, must move up and down in step with the general market as measured by some index such as the S&P 500 or the New York Stock Exchange Index. Such a stock will, by definition, have a beta of 1.0, which indicates that if the market moves up or down by 10 percentage points, the stock will also tend to move up or down by 10 percentage points. A portfolio of such $b = 1.0$ stocks will move up and down in synchronization with the broad market averages, and this portfolio will be just as risky as the averages. If a stock has $b = 0.5$, the stock is only half as volatile as the market—it rises and falls only half as much as the market—and a portfolio of such stocks will be only half as risky as a portfolio of $b = 1.0$ stocks. On the other hand, if $b = 2.0$, the stock is twice as volatile as an average stock, so a portfolio of such stocks will be twice as risky as an average portfolio.

Betas are calculated and published by Merrill Lynch, Value Line, and numerous other organizations. The beta coefficients of some well-known companies, as re-

TABLE 5-1	Stock	Beta
ILLUSTRATIVE LIST OF	Harley-Davidson	1.60
BETA COEFFICIENTS	Dell Computer	1.45
	Avon Products	1.30
	Ryan's Family Steak Houses	1.20
	B.F. Goodrich	1.10
	Unocal	1.00
	Harcourt General	0.90
	Bassett Furniture	0.80
	Potomac Electric Power	0.65
	Homestake Mining	0.25

Source: Value Line, April 30, 1993.

ported by Value Line, are shown in Table 5-1.[9] Most stocks have betas in the range of 0.75 to 1.50, and the average for all stocks is 1.0 by definition.

PORTFOLIO BETA COEFFICIENTS

A portfolio consisting of low-beta securities will itself have a low beta, as the beta of any set of securities is the weighted average of the individual securities' betas:

$$\text{Portfolio beta} = b_p = \sum_{i=1}^{n} x_i b_i. \qquad (5\text{-}3)$$

Thus, if a high-beta stock (one whose beta is significantly greater than 1.0) is added to an average-risk portfolio ($b_p = 1.0$), then the beta and consequently the riskiness of the portfolio will increase. Conversely, if a low-beta stock (one whose beta is significantly less than 1.0) is added to an average risk portfolio, the portfolio's beta and risk will decline. *Therefore, since a stock's beta measures its contribution to the riskiness of a portfolio, beta is the appropriate measure of the stock's riskiness.*

To illustrate, if you hold a $100,000 portfolio consisting of $10,000 invested in each of ten stocks, and if each stock has a beta of 0.8, then your portfolio will have $b_p = 0.8$, it will be less risky than the market, and it should experience relatively narrow price swings and hence have relatively small rate of return fluctuations.

[9]These betas are called "historical," or "ex post," betas because they are based strictly on historical, or past, data. Other types of betas, such as adjusted and fundamental betas, are also in wide use today. The different types of betas will be discussed in Chapter 8.

Now suppose you sell one of the existing stocks and replace it with a stock with b = 2.0. This action will increase the riskiness of your portfolio from b_{p1} = 0.8 to b_{p2} = 0.92 as calculated using Equation 5-3:

$$b_{p2} = \sum_{i=1}^{n} x_i b_i = 0.9(0.8) + 0.1(2.0) = 0.92.$$

Had a stock with b = 0.6 been added, your portfolio's beta would have declined from 0.8 to 0.78.

CALCULATING BETA COEFFICIENTS: THE CHARACTERISTIC LINE

When Professor Sharpe developed the CAPM, he noted that the market risk of a given stock can be measured by its tendency to move with the general market. His procedure for determining market risk is illustrated in Figure 5-6, which is explained in the following paragraphs.[10] First, however, familiarize yourself with the definitions of the terms used in Figure 5-6:

$\bar{k}_J$ = historical (realized) rate of return on Stock J. (Recall that $\hat{k}_J$ and k_J are defined as Stock J's expected and required returns, respectively.)

$\bar{k}_M$ = historical (realized) rate of return on the market.

a_J = vertical axis intercept term for Stock J.

b_J = slope, or beta coefficient, for Stock J.

e_J = random error, reflecting the difference between the actual return on Stock J in a given year and the return predicted by the regression line.

The historical returns on Stock J are given in the lower section of Figure 5-6, along with historical returns on the market, $\bar{k}_M$. Notice that when returns on the market are high, returns on Stock J likewise tend to be high, and when the market is down, Stock J's returns are low. This general relationship is expressed more precisely in the regression line shown in Figure 5-6.

Recall what the term *regression equation* means: The equation Y = a + bX + e is the standard form of a simple linear regression. It states that the dependent variable, Y, is equal to a constant, a, plus b times X, where X is the "independent" variable, plus a random error term. Thus, the rate of return on Stock J during a given time period depends on what happens to the general stock market, which is measured by $\bar{k}_M$, plus random events which affect Stock J but do not affect most other stocks.

---

[10]It should be noted that beta analysis in practice is somewhat more difficult than our discussion makes it sound. We will see this in Chapter 8.

FIGURE 5-6
CALCULATING BETA
COEFFICIENTS

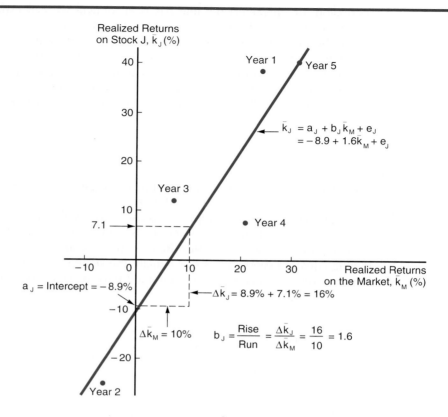

Year	Stock J($\bar{k}_J$)	Market ($\bar{k}_M$)
1	38.6%	23.8%
2	(24.7)	(7.2)
3	12.3	6.6
4	8.2	20.5
5	40.1	30.6
Average $\bar{k}$ =	14.9%	14.9%
$\sigma_{\bar{k}}$ =	26.5%	15.1%

In general, the regression equation is obtained by ordinary least squares regression analysis, using either a calculator with statistical functions or a computer with a regression software package such as *Lotus 1-2-3*'s data regression function. The plot of the regression equation is called the *regression line*. In his 1964 article which developed the CAPM, Sharpe called the regression line the stock's *characteristic line*. Thus, a stock's beta is the slope of its characteristic line.

To illustrate the regression process, assume that we have drawn the regression line in Figure 5-6 "by hand" without the benefit of a statistical package. Once the

6. If the stock market never fluctuated, then stocks would have no market risk. Of course, the market does fluctuate, so market risk is present; even if you hold an extremely well-diversified portfolio, you will still suffer losses if the market falls. In recent years, the standard deviation of annual market returns, σ_M, has been about 15 percent. However, on a single day, October 19, 1987, the Dow Jones Industrial Average, one measure of the market, lost 23 percent of its value.

7. Beta is a measure of relative market risk, but the *actual* market risk of Stock J is $b_J^2\sigma_M^2$. Market risk can also be expressed in standard deviation form, $b_J\sigma_M$, so Stock J's market risk is $b_J\sigma_M = 1.6(15.1\%) = 24.2\%$, while its total risk is $\sigma_J = 26.5\%$. For any given level of market volatility as measured by the market's standard deviation, σ_M, the higher a stock's beta, the higher its market risk. If beta were zero, the stock would have no market risk, while if beta were 1.0, the stock would be exactly as risky as the market—assuming the stock is held in a diversified portfolio—and the stock's market risk would be σ_M.

8. The diversifiable risk can and should be eliminated by diversification, so the *relevant* risk is market risk, not total risk. If Stock J had b = 0.5, then the stock's relevant risk would be $b_J\sigma_M = 0.5(15.1\%) = 7.55\%$. A portfolio of such low-beta stocks would have a standard deviation of expected returns of $\sigma_p = 7.55\%$, or one-half the standard deviation of expected returns on a portfolio of average (b = 1.0) stocks. Had Stock J been a high-beta stock (b = 2.0), then its relevant risk would have been $b_J\sigma_M = 2.0(15.1\%) = 30.2\%$. A portfolio of b = 2.0 stocks would have $\sigma_p = 30.2\%$, so such a portfolio would be twice as risky as a portfolio of average stocks.

9. A stock's risk premium depends only on its market risk, not its total risk: $RP_J = (k_M - k_{RF})b_J$. Mr. S might own only Stock J, and hence be concerned with its total risk and seek a return based on that risk. However, if other investors hold well-diversified portfolios, they would face less risk from Stock J. Therefore, if Stock J offered a return high enough to satisfy Mr. S, it would represent a bargain for other investors, who would then buy it, pushing its price up and its yield down in the process. Since most financial assets are held by diversified investors, and since any given security can have only one price and hence only one rate of return, market action drives each stock's risk premium to the level specified by its relevant, or market, risk.

SELF-TEST QUESTIONS

Explain the meaning and significance of a stock's beta coefficient. Illustrate your explanation by drawing, on one graph, the characteristic lines for stocks with low, average, and high risk. (Hint: Let your three characteristic lines intersect at $\bar{k}_i = \bar{k}_M = 9\%$, the assumed risk-free rate.)

What is the relationship among total risk, market risk, and diversifiable risk?

EMPIRICAL TESTS OF THE **CAPM**

As noted earlier, the CAPM was developed on the basis of a set of unrealistic assumptions. If those assumptions were all true, then the CAPM would also have to be true. However, since the assumptions are not completely correct, the basic SML equation, $k_i = k_{RF} + (k_M - k_{RF})b_i$, might or might not represent an accurate description of how investors behave and of how rates of return are established in the marketplace. For example, if many investors are not fully diversified, and hence have not eliminated all diversifiable risk from their portfolios, then (1) beta would not be an adequate measure of risk and (2) the SML would not explain how required returns are set. Also, if the interest rate that investors must pay to borrow money is greater than the risk-free rate (that is, if the borrowing rate is greater than the lending rate), then the CML would not continue in a straight line beyond Point M as it does in Figure 5-1, and this too would invalidate the SML. And, of course, taxes and brokerage costs do exist, and their presence could distort the CAPM relationships.

For all these reasons, it is entirely possible that the CAPM is not completely valid, in which case the SML will not produce accurate estimates of k_i. Therefore, the CAPM must be tested empirically and validated before it can be used with any real confidence. The literature dealing with empirical tests of the CAPM is quite extensive, so we can give here only a synopsis of some of the key work.

TESTS OF THE STABILITY OF BETA COEFFICIENTS

According to the CAPM, the beta used to estimate a stock's market risk should reflect investors' estimates of the stock's *future* volatility in relation to that of the market. Obviously, we do not know now how a stock will be related to the market in the future, nor do we know how the average investor views this expected future relative volatility. All we have are data on past volatility, which we can use to plot the characteristic line and to calculate *historical betas.* If historical betas are stable over time, then there would seem to be reason for investors to use past betas as estimators of future volatility. For example, if Stock J's beta had been stable in the past, then its historical b_J would probably be a good proxy for its *ex ante,* or expected, b_J. By "stable" we mean that if b_J were calculated by using data from the period of, say, 1988 to 1992, then this same beta (approximately) should be found from 1993 to 1997.

Robert A. Levy, Marshall E. Blume, and others have studied the question of beta stability in depth.[12] Levy calculated betas for individual securities, as well as for portfolios of securities, over a range of time intervals. He concluded (1) that

---

[12]See Robert A. Levy, "On the Short-Term Stationarity of Beta Coefficients," *Financial Analysts Journal,* November-December 1971, 55–62, and Marshall E. Blume, "Betas and Their Regression Tendencies," *Journal of Finance,* June 1975, 785–796.

the betas of individual stocks are unstable, and hence that past betas for *individual securities* are *not* good estimators of their future risk, but (2) that betas of portfolios of ten or more randomly selected stocks are reasonably stable, and hence that past *portfolio* betas are good estimators of future portfolio volatility. In effect, the errors in the estimates of individual securities' betas tend to offset one another in a portfolio. The work of Blume and others supports Levy's position.

The conclusion that follows from the beta stability studies is that the CAPM is a better concept for structuring investment portfolios than it is for purposes of estimating the cost of capital for individual securities. We will return to this issue in Chapter 8, when we discuss cost of capital estimation procedures.

Tests of the CAPM Based on the Slope of the SML

As we have seen, the CAPM states that a linear relationship exists between a security's required rate of return and its beta. Further, when the SML is graphed, the vertical axis intercept should be k_{RF}, and the required rate of return for a stock (or portfolio) with b = 1.0 should be k_M, the required rate of return on the market. Various researchers have attempted to test the validity of the model by calculating betas and realized rates of return, plotting these values in graphs such as that in Figure 5-7, and then observing whether or not (1) the intercept is equal to k_{RF}, (2) the regression line is linear, and (3) the line passes through the point b = 1.0, k_M. Monthly historical rates of return are generally used for stocks, and

Figure 5-7

Tests of the CAPM

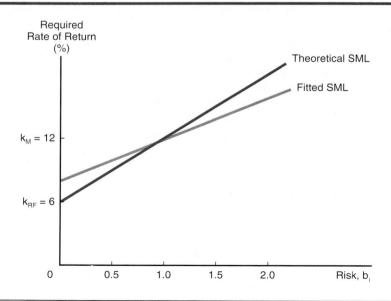

both 30-day Treasury bill rates and long-term Treasury bond rates have been used to estimate the value of k_{RF}. Also, most of the studies actually analyze portfolios rather than individual securities because security betas are so unstable.

Before discussing the results of the tests, it is critical to recognize that although the CAPM is an ex ante, or forward-looking model, the data used to test it are entirely historical. There is no reason to believe that *realized* rates of return over past holding periods are necessarily equal to the *expected* rates of return with which the model should deal. Also, historical betas may or may not reflect either current or expected future risk. This lack of ex ante data makes it extremely difficult to test the true CAPM. Still, for what it is worth, here is a summary of the key results:

1. The evidence generally shows a significant positive relationship between realized returns and systematic risk. However, the slope of the relationship is usually less than that predicted by the CAPM.

2. The relationship between risk and return appears to be linear. Empirical studies give no evidence of significant curvature in the risk/return relationship.

3. Tests that attempt to assess the relative importance of market and company-specific risk do not yield definitive results. The CAPM theory implies that company-specific risk is not relevant, yet both kinds of risk appear to be positively related to security returns; that is, higher returns seem to be required to compensate for diversifiable as well as market risk. However, it may be that the observed relationships are at least partly spurious; that is, they may reflect statistical problems rather than the true nature of capital markets.

4. Richard Roll has questioned whether it is even conceptually possible to test the CAPM.[13] Roll showed that the linear relationship which prior researchers had observed in graphs like that in Figure 5-7 resulted from the mathematical properties of the models being tested, hence that a finding of linearity proved nothing whatsoever about the validity of the CAPM. Roll's work did not disprove the CAPM theory, but he did show that it is virtually impossible to prove that investors behave in accordance with its predictions.

5. If the CAPM were completely valid, it should apply to all financial assets, including bonds. In fact, when bonds are introduced into the analysis, they *do not* plot on the SML. This is worrisome, to say the least.

CURRENT STATUS OF THE CAPM

The CAPM is extremely appealing at an intellectual level: It is logical and rational, and once someone works through and understands the mathematics, his or her

---

[13]See Richard Roll, "A Critique of the Asset Pricing Theory's Tests," *Journal of Financial Economics,* March 1977, 129–176.

reaction is usually to accept it without question. However, doubts begin to arise when one thinks about the assumptions upon which the model is based, and these doubts are as much reinforced as reduced by the empirical tests. Our own views as to the current status of the CAPM are as follows:

1. The CAPM framework, with its focus on market as opposed to total risk, is clearly a useful way to think about the riskiness of assets in general. Thus, as a conceptual model, the CAPM is of truly fundamental importance.

2. Although the CAPM appears to provide neat, precise answers to important questions about risk and required rates of return, the answers are really not clear. The simple truth is that we do not know precisely how to measure any of the inputs required to implement the CAPM. These inputs should all be ex ante, yet only ex post data are available. Further, as we shall see in Chapter 8, historical data on $\bar{k}_M$, k_{RF}, and betas vary greatly depending on the time period studied and the methods used to estimate them. Thus, although the CAPM appears precise, its inputs cannot be estimated with precision, so estimates of k_i found through use of the CAPM are subject to potentially large errors.

3. Because the CAPM is logical in the sense that it represents the way people who want to maximize returns while minimizing risk ought to behave, assuming they can get all the necessary data, the model is a useful conceptual tool. Attempts will, of course, be made to improve it and to make it more operational.

4. A recently published study by Eugene F. Fama and Kenneth R. French of the University of Chicago seriously challenges the CAPM.[14] Fama and French examined the relationships between stock betas and stock returns on thousands of stocks over the past 50 years. According to the CAPM, on average, high-beta stocks should provide higher returns than low-beta stocks. However, their study revealed no relationship between historical betas and historical returns — low-beta stocks provided about the same historical returns as high-beta stocks.

It will take much debate to decide whether the Fama–French study truly invalidates the CAPM. At this point, however, our own feeling is that the CAPM is purely an expectational model, and as such, its logic is sound. The problem, as with most tests, is that we only have historical data, not expectational data, available for testing. So, the fact that no relationship is found between historical betas and historical returns does not convince us that the CAPM concept is wrong, even though it may be difficult, if not impossible, to implement the CAPM numerically because expectational data are unavailable.

5. It is appropriate to think about many financial problems in a CAPM framework. However, it is equally important to recognize the limitations of the CAPM when using it in practice. We will elaborate on this point in Chapters 8 and 11.

---

[14]See Eugene F. Fama and Kenneth R. French, "The Cross-Section of Expected Stock Returns," *Journal of Finance,* June 1992, 427–465.

SELF-TEST QUESTIONS

What are the two major types of tests that have been performed to test the validity of the CAPM? (Hint: Beta stability and slope of the SML.)

Are there any reasons to question the validity of the CAPM? Explain.

ARBITRAGE PRICING THEORY

The CAPM is a single-factor model. That is, it specifies that risk is a function of only one factor, the relationship between a security's return and the market return, or, equivalently, the security's beta coefficient. Perhaps the risk/return relationship is more complex. If so, we might expect a stock's required return to be a function of more than one factor. For example, what if investors, because personal taxes on capital gains are taxed at a lower rate, value capital gains income more highly than dividend income? Then, for two stocks with the same market risk, the stock paying the higher dividend would have a higher required rate of return. In that case, required returns would be a function of both market risk and dividend yield, or two factors.

Further, what if many factors were required to specify the equilibrium risk/return relationship rather than just one or two? Stephen Ross has proposed an approach called the *Arbitrage Pricing Theory (APT)*.[15] The APT can include any number of risk factors, so the required return could be a function of two, three, four, or even more factors. We should note at the outset that the APT is based on complex mathematical and statistical theory which goes far beyond the scope of this text. Although the APT model is widely discussed in the current academic literature, practical usage to date has been limited. However, usage may increase, so students of finance should at least have an intuitive idea of what the APT is all about.

The CAPM states that each stock's required return is equal to the risk-free rate, plus the market risk premium times the stock's beta coefficient:

$$k_i = k_{RF} + (k_M - k_{RF})b_i. \qquad (5\text{-}5)$$

The realized return, $\bar{k}_i$, will actually turn out to be

$$\bar{k}_i = \hat{k}_i + (\bar{k}_M - \hat{k}_M)b_i + e_i; \qquad (5\text{-}6)$$

---

[15]See Stephen A. Ross, "The Arbitrage Theory of Capital Asset Pricing," *Journal of Economic Theory,* December 1976, 341–360.

that is, the realized return, $\bar{k}_i$, will be equal to the expected return, $\hat{k}_i$, plus an increment or decrement, $(\bar{k}_M - \hat{k}_M)b_i$, whose magnitude depends jointly on the stock's sensitivity to market returns, b_i, and the realized excess or shortfall in the market return, plus a random error term, e_i.

The market return, $\bar{k}_M$, is in turn determined by a number of factors, including domestic economic activity as measured by gross domestic product (GDP), the strength of the world economy, the level of inflation, changes in tax laws, and so forth. Further, different groups of stocks are affected in different ways by these fundamental factors. Thus, rather than specifying a stock's returns as a function of one factor (returns on the market), one could specify required and realized returns on individual stocks as a function of various fundamental economic factors. If this were done, we would transform Equation 5-6 into 5-7:

$$\bar{k}_i = \hat{k}_i + (\bar{F}_1 - \hat{F}_1)b_{i1} + \cdots + (\bar{F}_j - \hat{F}_j)b_{ij} + e_i, \qquad (5\text{-}7)$$

where

$\bar{k}_i$ = realized rate of return on Stock i.

$\hat{k}_i$ = expected rate of return on Stock i.

$\bar{F}_j$ = realized value of economic Factor j.

$\hat{F}_j$ = expected value of Factor j.

b_{ij} = sensitivity of Stock i to economic Factor j.

e_i = effect of unique events on the realized return of Stock i.

Equation 5-7 shows that the realized return on any stock is equal to the stock's expected return plus increments or decrements which depend on (1) unexpected changes in fundamental economic factors, (2) the sensitivity of the stock to these changes, plus (3) a random term which reflects changes in those factors unique to the firm or industry.

Certain stocks or groups of stocks are most sensitive to Factor 1, others to Factor 2, and so forth, and every portfolio's returns would depend on what happened to the different fundamental factors. Theoretically, one could construct a portfolio such that (1) the portfolio was riskless and (2) the net investment in it was zero (some stocks would be sold short, with the proceeds from the short sales being used to buy the stocks held long). Such a zero investment portfolio must have a zero expected return, or else arbitrage operations would occur, which in turn would cause the prices of the underlying assets to change until the portfolio's expected return was zero. Using some complex mathematics and a brief list of

assumptions including the short sales assumption, the APT equivalent of the CAPM's Security Market Line can be developed from Equation 5-7:[16]

$$k_i = k_{RF} + (\lambda_1 - k_{RF})b_{i1} + \cdots + (\lambda_j - k_{RF})b_{ij}. \qquad (5\text{-}8)$$

Here λ_j is the required rate of return on a portfolio with unit sensitivity to the *j*th economic factor ($b_j = 1.0$) and zero sensitivity to all other factors. Thus, for example, $(\lambda_2 - k_{RF})$ is the risk premium on a portfolio with $b_2 = 1.0$ and all other $b_j = 0.0$. Note that Equation 5-8 is identical in form to the SML, but it permits a stock's required return to be a function of multiple factors.

To illustrate the APT concept, assume that all stocks' returns depend on only three risk factors: inflation, industrial production, and the aggregate degree of risk aversion (the cost of bearing risk, which we assume is reflected in the spread between the yields on Treasury and low-grade bonds). Further, suppose (1) the risk-free rate is 8.0 percent; (2) the required rate of return is 13 percent on a portfolio with unit sensitivity ($b = 1.0$) to inflation and zero sensitivities ($b = 0.0$) to industrial production and degree of risk aversion; (3) the required return is 10 percent on a portfolio with unit sensitivity to industrial production and zero sensitivities to inflation and degree of risk aversion is 10.0 percent; and (4) the required return is 6 percent on a portfolio (the risk-bearing portfolio) with unit sensitivity to the degree of risk aversion and zero sensitivities to inflation and industrial production. Finally, assume that Stock i has factor sensitivities (betas) of 0.9 to the inflation portfolio, 1.2 to the industrial production portfolio, and -0.7 to the risk-bearing portfolio. Stock i's required rate of return, according to the APT, would be 16.3 percent:

$$k_i = 8\% + (13\% - 8\%)0.9 + (10\% - 8\%)1.2 + (6\% - 8\%)(-0.7)$$
$$= 16.3\%.$$

Note that if the required rate of return on the market was 15.0 percent and Stock i had a CAPM beta of 1.1, then its required rate of return, according to the CAPM, would be 15.7 percent:

$$k_i = 8\% + (15\% - 8\%)1.1 = 15.7\%.$$

The primary theoretical advantage of the APT is that it permits several economic factors to influence individual stock returns, whereas the CAPM assumes that the impact of all factors, except those unique to the firm, can be captured in

---

[16]See Thomas E. Copeland and J. Fred Weston, *Financial Theory and Corporate Policy* (Reading, Mass.: Addison-Wesley, 1988).

a single measure, the volatility of the stock with respect to the market portfolio. Also, the APT requires fewer assumptions than the CAPM and hence is a more general theory. Most importantly, the APT does not assume that all investors hold the market portfolio, a CAPM requirement that clearly is not met in practice. However, the APT faces several major hurdles in implementation, of which the most severe is that the APT does not identify the relevant factors beforehand. Thus, APT does not tell us what factors influence returns, nor does it even indicate how many factors should appear in the model. There is some empirical evidence that only three or four factors are relevant: perhaps inflation, industrial production, the spread between low- and high-grade bonds, and the term structure of interest rates, but no one knows for sure.

The APT's proponents note that it is not actually necessary to identify the relevant factors. Researchers use a complex statistical procedure called *factor analysis* to develop the APT parameters. Basically, they start with hundreds, or even thousands, of stocks and then create several different portfolios, where the returns on each portfolio are not highly correlated with returns on the other portfolios. Thus, each portfolio is apparently more heavily affected by one of the unknown factors than are the other portfolios. Then, the required rate of return on each portfolio becomes the λ for that unknown economic factor, and the sensitivities of each individual stock's returns to the returns on that portfolio are the factor sensitivities (betas). Unfortunately, the results of factor analysis are not easily interpreted, hence it does not provide significant insights into the underlying economic determinants of risk.

The APT is in an early stage of development, and there are still many unanswered questions. Nevertheless, the basic premise of the APT—that returns can be a function of several factors rather than just one—has considerable intuitive appeal. If the factors can be identified, and if the theory can be satisfactorily explained to practitioners, then the APT might replace the CAPM as the primary model describing the relationship between risk and return.

SELF-TEST QUESTIONS

What is the primary difference between the APT and the CAPM?

What are some disadvantages of the APT?

SUMMARY

Chapter 5 completes our discussion of risk and return. The primary goals of this chapter were (1) to show how the addition of the risk-free asset affects individual investment decisions and (2) to explain how risk affects rates of return. The key concepts covered are listed below:

▶ The *Capital Asset Pricing Model (CAPM)* describes the relationship between market risk and required rates of return.

▶ The CAPM is based on an extensive set of *assumptions.*

▶ The *Capital Market Line (CML)* describes the risk/return relationship for efficient portfolios; that is, for portfolios that consist of a mix of the market portfolio and a riskless asset.

▶ The *Security Market Line (SML)* describes the risk/return relationship for individual assets. The required rate of return for any Stock i is equal to the *risk-free rate* plus the *market risk premium* times the stock's *beta coefficient:* $k_i = k_{RF} + (k_M - k_{RF})b_i$.

▶ Stock i's *beta coefficient, b_i,* is a measure of the stock's *market risk.* Beta measures the *volatility* of returns on a security *relative to returns on the market,* which is the portfolio of all risky assets.

▶ The beta coefficient is measured by the slope of the stock's *characteristic line,* which is found by regressing historical returns on the stock versus the historical returns on the market.

▶ A *high-beta stock* is more volatile than an average stock, while a *low-beta stock* is less volatile than average. An *average-beta stock* has b = 1.0, by definition.

▶ The *beta of a portfolio* is a weighted average of the betas of the individual securities in the portfolio.

▶ Even though the expected rate of return on a stock is generally equal to the stock's required return, a number of things can happen to cause the required rate of return to change: (1) the *risk-free rate* can change because of changes in anticipated inflation, (2) the *beta coefficient* can change, and (3) *investors' aversion to risk* can change.

▶ Although the CAPM provides a convenient framework for thinking about risk and return issues, it *cannot be proven empirically,* and its parameters are very difficult to estimate. Thus, the CAPM should be used with caution in practice.

▶ Deficiencies in the CAPM have motivated theorists to seek other risk/return equilibrium models; the *Arbitrage Pricing Theory (APT)* is one important new model.

In the next two chapters, we will see how a security's required rate of return affects its value. Then, in most of the remainder of the book, we will examine the ways in which a firm's management can influence a stock's riskiness and hence its price.

QUESTIONS

5-1 Define the following terms, using graphs or equations to illustrate your answers wherever feasible:

a. Capital Asset Pricing Model (CAPM)

b. Capital Market Line (CML)

c. Market risk; company-specific risk; relevant risk

d. Beta coefficient, b; average stock's beta, $b_A = b_M$

    e.   Security Market Line (SML); SML equation

    f.   Market risk premium

    g.   Average stock

    h.   Characteristic line

    i.   Arbitrage Pricing Theory (APT)

5-2   Security A has an expected rate of return of 6 percent, a standard deviation of expected returns of 30 percent, a correlation coefficient with the market of −0.25, and a beta coefficient of −0.5. Security B has an expected return of 11 percent, a standard deviation of returns of 10 percent, a correlation with the market of 0.75, and a beta coefficient of 0.5. Which security is more risky? Why?

5-3   If investors' aversion to risk increased, would the risk premium on a high-beta stock increase more or less than that on a low-beta stock? Explain.

SELF-TEST PROBLEM (SOLUTION APPEARS IN APPENDIX C)

ST-1 (Security Market Line)   Dalton Bigbee is a major department store chain. Its stock has a beta of 0.8, the risk-free rate is 8.0 percent, and the required rate of return on the market is 13.0 percent.

    a.   What is the market risk premium?

    b.   What is the required rate of return on Bigbee's stock?

    c.   Graph the Security Market Line (SML) and indicate Bigbee's required rate of return on the graph.

    d.   What would Bigbee's required rate of return be if inflation expectations increased by 2 percentage points? (Assume no change in risk aversion.)

    e.   Return to the 8 percent risk-free rate. What would Bigbee's required rate of return be if investors' risk aversion increased, and the market risk premium rose to 7 percentage points?

    f.   Return to the 5 percentage point market risk premium. What would the firm's required rate of return be if Bigbee's beta increased to 1.2?

PROBLEMS

5-1 (Market risk analysis)   The Grunewald Company has developed the following data regarding the rates of return available on a potential project and the market:

State of the Economy	Probability of Each State Occurring	Rates of Return If State Occurs	
		Market	**Project**
Deep recession	0.05	(20%)	(30%)
Mild recession	0.25	10	5
Average	0.35	15	20
Mild boom	0.20	20	25
Strong boom	0.15	25	30

Further, Grunewald's financial analysts estimate the risk-free rate at 8 percent.

a. What are the expected rates of return on the market and the project?

b. What is the market's beta? The project's?

c. What is the required rate of return on the project according to the CAPM?

d. Should the project be accepted?

5-2 **(Market versus total risk)** Your eccentric uncle died and left you $100,000. However, the will stipulated that the entire amount must be invested in common stocks. Specifically, $50,000 must be invested in a single stock (one-stock portfolio) and the other $50,000 must be invested in a 100-stock portfolio. You are very risk averse, so you want to minimize the riskiness of each $50,000 investment.

a. How would you choose your single-stock portfolio?

b. How would you choose the stocks in your 100-stock portfolio?

c. Should you view the riskiness of your one-stock portfolio in isolation, or should you consider the fact that you really own 101 stocks?

5-3 **(Security Market Line)** Suppose $k_{RF} = 10\%$, $k_M = 14\%$, and $b_A = 1.4$.

a. What is k_A, the required rate of return on Stock A?

b. Now suppose k_{RF} (1) increases to 11 percent or (2) decreases to 9 percent. The slope of the SML remains constant. How will this affect k_M and k_A?

c. Now assume k_{RF} remains at 10 percent, but k_M (1) increases to 15 percent or (2) falls to 12 percent. The slope of the SML does *not* remain constant. How will this affect k_A?

d. Now assume that k_{RF} remains at 10 percent and k_M at 14 percent, but beta (1) rises to 1.6 or (2) falls to 0.75. How will this affect k_A?

5-4 **(Portfolio beta and Security Market Line)** The Guardian Investment Fund has a total investment of $400 million in five stocks:

Stock	Investment	Stock's Beta Coefficient
A	$120 million	0.5
B	100 million	2.0
C	60 million	4.0
D	80 million	1.0
E	40 million	3.0

The beta coefficient for a fund such as this can be found as a weighted average of the betas of the fund's investments. The current risk-free rate is 7 percent, and the market return has the following estimated probability distribution for the next year:

Probability	Market Return
0.1	8%
0.2	10
0.4	12
0.2	14
0.1	16

a. What is the estimated equation for the Security Market Line (SML)?

b. Compute the required rate of return on the Guardian Investment Fund.

c. Suppose management receives a proposal to buy a new stock. The investment needed to take a position in the stock is $50 million; it will have an expected return of 16 percent; and its estimated beta coefficient is 2.5. Should the new stock be purchased? At what expected rate of return would management be indifferent to purchasing the stock?

5-5 **(Characteristic line and Security Market Line)**   You are given the following set of data:

Historical Rates of Return

Year	NYSE	Stock X
1	(26.5%)	(14.0%)
2	37.2	23.0
3	23.8	17.5
4	(7.2)	2.0
5	6.6	8.1
6	20.5	19.4
7	30.6	18.2

a.   Use a calculator with a linear regression function (or the spreadsheet model) to determine Stock X's beta coefficient, or plot these data points on a scatter diagram, draw in the regression line, and then estimate the value of the beta coefficient.

b.   Determine the arithmetic average rates of return for Stock X and the NYSE over the period given. Calculate the standard deviations of returns for both Stock X and the NYSE.

c.   Assuming (1) that the situation during Years 1 to 7 is expected to hold true in the future (that is, $\hat{k}_X = \bar{k}_X$; $\hat{k}_M = \bar{k}_M$; and both σ_X and b_X in the future will equal their past values), and (2) that Stock X is in equilibrium (that is, it plots on the Security Market Line), what is the risk-free rate?

d.   Plot the Security Market Line.

e.   Suppose you hold a large, well-diversified portfolio and are considering adding to the portfolio either Stock X or another stock, Stock Y, that has the same beta as Stock X but a higher standard deviation of returns. Stocks X and Y have the same expected returns; that is, $\hat{k}_X = \hat{k}_Y = 10.6\%$. Which stock should you choose?

5-6 **(Characteristic line)**   You are given the following set of data:

Historical Rates of Return

Year	NYSE	Stock Y
1	4.0%	3.0%
2	14.3	18.2
3	19.0	9.1
4	(14.7)	(6.0)
5	(26.5)	(15.3)
6	37.2	33.1
7	23.8	6.1
8	(7.2)	3.2
9	6.6	14.8
10	20.5	24.1
11	30.6	18.0
Mean =	9.8%	9.8%
σ =	19.6%	13.8%

a.   Construct a scatter diagram showing the relationship between returns on Stock Y and the market, and then draw a freehand approximation of the regression line. What is the approximate value of the beta coefficient? If you have a calculator with a linear regression function or the spreadsheet model, check the approximate value of beta obtained from the graph.

b.   Give a verbal interpretation of what the regression line and the beta coefficient show about Stock Y's volatility and relative riskiness as compared with those of other stocks.

c. Suppose the scatter of points had been more spread out, but the regression line was exactly where your present graph shows it. How would this affect (1) the firm's risk if the stock is held in a one-asset portfolio and (2) the actual risk premium on the stock if the CAPM holds exactly?

d. Suppose the regression line had been downward-sloping and the beta coefficient had been negative. What would this imply about (1) Stock Y's relative riskiness, (2) its correlation with the market, and (3) its probable risk premium?

e. Construct an illustrative probability distribution graph of returns on portfolios consisting of (1) only Stock Y, (2) 1 percent each of 100 stocks with beta coefficients similar to that of Stock Y, and (3) all stocks (that is, the distribution of returns on the market). Use as the expected rate of return the arithmetic mean as given previously for both Stock Y and the market and assume that the distributions are normal. Are the expected returns "reasonable"; that is, is it reasonable that $\hat{k}_Y = \hat{k}_M = 9.8\%$?

5-7 **(SML and CML comparison)** The beta coefficient of an asset can be expressed as a function of the asset's correlation with the market as follows:

$$b_i = \frac{r_{iM}\sigma_i}{\sigma_M}.$$

a. Substitute this expression for beta into the Security Market Line (SML), Equation 5-2. This results in an alternative form of the SML.

b. Compare your answer to Part a with the Capital Market Line (CML), Equation 5-1. What similarities are observed? What conclusions can be drawn?

MINI CASE

In the Chapter 4 Mini Case, Barbara Orban, an analyst at Southern Commerce Bank, was instructed to evaluate some investment opportunities. The analysis was begun in Chapter 4, but not completed. Again place yourself in Orban's position, and complete the analysis by answering the following questions:

a. What is the Capital Asset Pricing Model (CAPM)? What are the assumptions that underlie the model?

b. Review your answers to Parts j and k of the Chapter 4 Mini Case. Then create a risk/return (σ, k) graph which shows the efficient frontier of portfolios. Now add the risk-free asset. What impact does this have on the efficient frontier?

c. Write out the equation for the Capital Market Line (CML) and draw it on the graph. Interpret the CML. Now add a set of indifference curves, and illustrate how an investor's optimal portfolio is some combination of the risky portfolio and the risk-free asset. What is the composition of the risky portfolio?

d. The expected rates of return and the beta coefficients of each alternative as supplied by the bank's computer program are as follows:

Security	Expected Return ($\hat{k}$)	Risk (Beta)
Paragon	18.0%	1.29
Market	15.0	1.00
Apex	12.5	0.68
T-bills	8.0	0.00
Luster	1.3	(0.86)

What is a beta coefficient, and what does it measure?

e. Construct the Security Market Line (SML) and use it to calculate the required rate of return on each alternative. How do the expected rates of return compare with the required rates of return? Does the fact that Luster has a required rate of return that is less than the risk-free rate make any sense? What are the market risk and the required return of a 50-50 portfolio of Paragon and Luster? Of Paragon and Apex?

f. Suppose investors raised their inflation expectations by 3 percentage points over current estimates as reflected in the 8 percent T-bill rate. What effect would this have on the SML and on the returns of high- and low-risk securities? Suppose instead that investors' risk aversion increased enough to cause the market risk premium to increase by 3 percentage points. What effect would this have on the SML and on returns of high- and low-risk securities?

g. What is a characteristic line? How is this line used to estimate a stock's beta coefficient? Write out and explain the formula that relates total risk, market risk, and diversifiable risk.

h. What are two potential tests that can be conducted to verify the CAPM? What are the results of such tests? What is Roll's critique of CAPM tests?

i. Briefly explain the difference between the CAPM and the Arbitrage Pricing Theory (APT).

SELECTED ADDITIONAL REFERENCES AND CASES

Probably the best place to find more information on CAPM and APT concepts is one of the investments textbooks. These are some good recent ones:

Francis, Jack C., *Investments: Analysis and Management* (New York: McGraw-Hill, 1980).

Radcliffe, Robert C., *Investment: Concepts, Analysis, and Strategy* (Glenview, Ill.: Scott, Foresman, 1993).

Reilly, Frank K., *Investment Analysis and Portfolio Management* (Hinsdale, Ill.: Dryden Press, 1989).

Sharpe, William F., *Investments* (Englewood Cliffs, N.J.: Prentice-Hall, 1985).

For a thorough discussion of beta stability, see

Kolb, Robert W., and Ricardo J. Rodriguez, "The Regression Tendencies of Betas: A Reappraisal," *The Financial Review,* May 1989, 319–334.

———, "Is the Distribution of Betas Stationary?" *Journal of Financial Research,* Winter 1990, 279–283.

Those who want to start at the beginning in studying portfolio theory and the CAPM should see

Lintner, John, "Security Prices, Risk, and Maximal Gains from Diversification," *Journal of Finance,* December 1965, 587–616.

Markowitz, Harry M., "Portfolio Selection," *Journal of Finance,* March 1952, 77–91.

Mossin, Jan, "Security Pricing and Investment Criteria in Competitive Markets," *American Economic Review,* December 1969, 749–756.

Sharpe, William F., "Capital Asset Prices: A Theory of Market Equilibrium under Conditions of Risk," *Journal of Finance,* September 1964, 425–442.

———, "Capital Asset Prices with and without Negative Holdings," *Journal of Finance,* June 1991, 489–509.

Literally thousands of articles providing theoretical extensions and tests of the CAPM theory have appeared in finance journals. Some of the more important earlier papers are contained in a book compiled by Jensen:

Jensen, Michael C., ed., *Studies in the Theory of Capital Markets* (New York: Praeger, 1972).

For one challenge to the CAPM, see

Wallace, Anise, "Is Beta Dead?" *Institutional Investor,* July 1980, 23–30.

For a recent article supporting a positive link between market risk and return, see

Marston, Felicia, and Robert S. Hanes, "Risk and Return: A Revisit Using Expected Returns," *Financial Review,* February 1993, 117–137.

For additional discussion of Arbitrage Pricing Theory, see

Bower, Dorothy H., Richard S. Bower, and Dennis E. Logue, "A Primer on Arbitrage Pricing Theory," *Midland Corporate Finance Journal,* Fall 1984, 31–40.

Bubnys, Edward L., "Simulating and Forecasting Utility Stock Returns: Arbitrage Pricing Theory vs. Capital Asset Pricing Model," *The Financial Review,* February 1990, 1–23.

Goldenberg, David H., and Ashok J. Robin, "The Arbitrage Pricing Theory and Cost-of-Capital Estimation: The Case of Electric Utilities," *Journal of Financial Research,* Fall 1991, 181–196.

Robin, Ashok, and Ravi Shukla, "The Magnitude of Pricing Errors in the Arbitrage Pricing Theory," *Journal of Financial Research,* Spring 1991, 65–82.

Additional references concerning the use of the CAPM are given in Chapter 8.

The following case covers many of the concepts discussed in this chapter:

Case 2, "Peachtree Securities, Inc. (A)," in Brigham, Eugene F., and Louis C. Gapenski, *Cases in Financial Management* (Forth Worth, Tex.: Dryden Press, 1993).

DISCOUNTED CASH FLOW ANALYSIS

T   *he cover story in a recent issue of* Fortune *was entitled, "Will You Be Able to Retire?" Although you may laugh when we say the article should be of interest to you, the fact is it should be. The article began with some well-known facts: (1) The savings rate in the United States is the lowest of any major industrial nation. (2) The ratio of workers to retirees, which was 17 to 1 in 1950 and is currently down to 3 to 1, will decline to less than 2 to 1 after the Year 2000. (3) Because of points 1 and 2, the Social Security system is in serious trouble. The article then went on to present some figures on how much money the "Baby Boom" generation (people born in the post–World War II period from 1946 through 1968) will need when they retire, given projected trends in inflation. Next, it presented statistics on the amount of money members of that generation are saving, and the rates of return savers are getting on their investments. Finally, the article concluded that even relatively affluent Baby Boomers (those with current incomes of about $85,000) will have trouble maintaining a reasonable standard of living when they retire, and that the children of the Boomers (some of you) will probably end up having to support their parents.*

What does the retirement plight of the Baby Boomers (and their children) have to do with discounted cash flow analysis? Actually, a great deal. The concepts covered in this chapter are exactly the ones Fortune *used to forecast the Boomers' retirement needs, their probable wealth at retirement, and the resulting shortfall.*

Financial managers also deal with discounted cash flow (DCF) concepts every day. For example, these concepts are used (1) when new projects are being

evaluated, (2) when firms are analyzing whether it is less expensive to purchase or to lease an asset, and (3) when firms are deciding whether it makes sense to refund a bond issue (sell a new bond and use the proceeds to retire an existing issue). In each of these situations, DCF analysis is used to find the present, or current, value of future cash flows, which is a vital step in the decision process. As you study this chapter, think about how the concepts discussed might be used in real-world financial analyses. Then, as you progress through the remainder of the text, you will understand why discounted cash flow analysis is often called "the cornerstone of finance."

In Chapter 1 we saw that the primary goal of financial management is to maximize the value of the firm's stock. We also saw that stock values depend in part on the timing of the cash flows investors expect to receive from an investment—a dollar expected soon is worth more than a dollar expected in the distant future. Therefore, it is essential that financial managers have a clear understanding of discounted cash flow analysis and its impact on the value of the firm. These concepts are discussed in this chapter, where we show how the timing of cash flows affects asset values and rates of return.

The principles of discounted cash flow analysis as developed here have many applications, ranging from setting up schedules for paying off loans to decisions about whether to acquire new equipment. *In fact, of all the concepts used in finance, none is more important than discounted cash flow (DCF) analysis, which is often called time value of money analysis.* Since this concept is used throughout the remainder of the book, it is vital that you understand the material in this chapter before you move on to other topics.[1]

TIME LINES

One of the most important tools in time value of money analysis is the *time line,* which is used to help us visualize what is happening in a particular problem and then to help us set up the problem for solution. To illustrate the time line concept, consider the following diagram:

---

[1]This chapter, and indeed the entire book, is written on the assumption that students have financial calculators. As a result, procedures for obtaining financial calculator solutions are set forth in each of the major sections, along with procedures for obtaining solutions by using regular calculators or tables. It is highly desirable for each student to obtain a financial calculator and to learn how to use it, for financial calculators and computers—and not clumsy, rounded, and incomplete tables—are used exclusively in businesses.

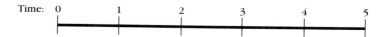

Time 0 is today; Time 1 is one period from today, or the end of Period 1; Time 2 is two periods from today, or the end of Period 2; and so on. Thus, the numbers on top of the tick marks represent end-of-period values. Often the periods are years, but other time intervals such as semiannual periods, quarters, months, or even days are also used. If each period on the time line represents a year, the interval from the tick mark corresponding to 0 to the tick mark corresponding to 1 would be Year 1, the interval from the tick mark corresponding to 1 to the tick mark corresponding to 2 would be Year 2, and so on. Note that each tick mark corresponds to the end of one period as well as the beginning of the next period. In other words, the tick mark at Time 1 represents the *end* of Year 1, and it also represents the *beginning* of Year 2 because Year 1 has just passed.

Cash flows are placed directly below the tick marks, and interest rates are shown directly above the time line. Unknown cash flows, which you are trying to find in the analysis, are indicated by question marks. Now consider the following time line:

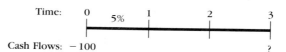

Here the interest rate for each of the three periods is 5 percent; a single amount (or lump sum) cash *outflow* is made at Time 0; and the Time 3 value is an unknown *inflow*. Since the initial $100 is an outflow (an investment), it has a minus sign. Since the Period 3 amount is an inflow, it does not have a minus sign. Note that no cash flows occur at Times 1 and 2. Note also that we generally do not show dollar signs on time lines to reduce clutter.

Now consider the following situation, where a $100 cash outflow is made today, and we will receive an unknown amount at the end of Time 2:

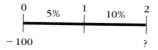

Here the interest rate is 5 percent during the first period, but it rises to 10 percent during the second period. If the interest rate is constant in all periods, we show it only in the first period, but if it changes, we show all the relevant rates on the time line.

Time lines are essential when you are first learning discounted cash flow concepts, but even experts use time lines to analyze complex problems. We will be using time lines throughout the book, and you should get into the habit of using them when you work problems.

"works," so 5 is the number of years it takes for $78.35 to grow to $100 if the interest rate is 5 percent.

2. **Tabular Solution:**

$$FV_n = PV(1 + i)^n = PV(FVIF_{i,n})$$

$$\$100 = \$78.35(FVIF_{5\%,n})$$

$$FVIF_{5\%,n} = \$100/\$78.35 = 1.2763.$$

Now look down the 5% column in Table A-3 until you find FVIF = 1.2763. This value is in Row 5, which indicates that it takes 5 years for $78.35 to grow to $100 at a 5 percent interest rate.[6]

3. **Financial Calculator Solution:**

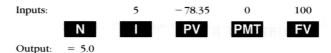

Inputs: 5   −78.35   0   100
                         N   I   PV   PMT   FV
Output: = 5.0

Enter I = 5, PV = −78.35, PMT = 0, and FV = 100, and then press N to get N = 5.

SELF-TEST QUESTIONS

Assuming that you are given PV, FV, and the interest rate, i, write out an equation that can be used to determine the time period, n.

Assuming that you are given PV, FV, and the time period, n, write out an equation that can be used to determine the interest rate, i.

Explain how financial calculators can be used to solve for i and n.

FUTURE VALUE OF AN ANNUITY

An *annuity* is a series of equal payments made at fixed intervals for a specified number of periods. For example, $100 at the end of each of the next three years is a 3-year annuity, and $50 at the beginning of each of the next six months is a

---

[6]The problem could also be solved as follows:

$$PV = FV_n(PVIF_{i,n})$$

$$\$78.35 = \$100(PVIF_{5\%,n})$$

$$PVIF_{5\%,n} = \$78.35/\$100 = 0.7835.$$

This value corresponds to n = 5 years in Table A-1.

6-month annuity. The payments are given the symbol PMT, and they can occur at either the beginning or the end of each period. If the payments occur at the *end* of each period, as they typically do, the annuity is called an *ordinary, or deferred, annuity.* If payments are made at the *beginning* of each period, the annuity is an *annuity due.* Since ordinary annuities are more common in finance, when the term "annuity" is used in this book, you should assume that the payments occur at the end of each period unless otherwise noted.

ORDINARY ANNUITIES

An ordinary, or deferred, annuity consists of a series of equal payments made at the *end* of each period. If you deposit $100 at the end of each year for 3 years in a savings account that pays 5 percent interest per year, how much will you have at the end of 3 years? To answer this question, we must find the future value of the annuity, FVA_n. Each payment is compounded out to the end of Period n, and the sum of the compounded payments is the future value of the annuity, FVA_n.

Time Line:

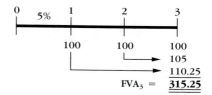

Here we show the regular time line as the top portion of the diagram, but we also show how each cash flow is compounded to produce the value FVA_n in the lower portion of the diagram.

Equation:

$$FVA_n = PMT(1 + i)^0 + PMT(1 + i)^1 + PMT(1 + i)^2 + \ldots + PMT(1 + i)^{n-1}$$

$$= PMT \sum_{t=1}^{n} (1 + i)^{n-t}. \qquad (6\text{-}3)$$

Notice that the first line of Equation 6-3 presents the annuity payments in reverse order of payment, and the superscript in each term indicates the number of periods of interest each payment receives. In other words, because the first annuity payment was made at the end of Period 1, interest would be earned in Period 2 through Period n only; thus, compounding would be for n − 1 periods rather than n periods, compounding for the second annuity payment would be for Period 3 through Period n, or n − 2 periods, and so on. The last annuity payment is made

at the same time the computation is made, so there is no time for interest to be earned; thus, the superscript 0 represents the fact that no interest is earned. Simplifying the first line produces the last line of Equation 6-3.

1. Numerical Solution:

The lower section of the time line shows the numerical solution. The future value of each cash flow is found, and those FVs are summed to find the FV of the annuity. This is a tedious process for long annuities.

2. Tabular Solution:

The summation term in Equation 6-3 is called the *Future Value Interest Factor for an Annuity (FVIFA$_{i,n}$)*:[7]

$$FVIFA_{i,n} = \sum_{t=1}^{n} (1 + i)^{n-t} = \frac{(1 + i)^n - 1}{i}. \qquad (6\text{-}3a)$$

FVIFAs have been calculated for various combinations of i and n; Table A-4 in Appendix A contains a set of FVIFA factors. To find the answer to the 3-year, $100 annuity problem, first refer to Table A-4 and look down the 5% column to the third period; the FVIFA is 3.1525. Thus, the future value of the $100 annuity is $315.25:

$$FVA_n = PMT(FVIFA_{i,n})$$

$$FVA_3 = \$100(FVIFA_{5\%,3}) = \$100(3.1525) = \$315.25.$$

3. Financial Calculator Solution:

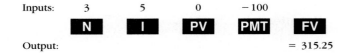

Inputs: 3   5   0   −100

| N | I | PV | PMT | FV |

Output: = 315.25

Note that in annuity problems, the PMT key is used in conjunction with the N and I keys, plus either the PV or the FV key, depending on whether you are trying to find the PV or the FV of the annuity. In our example, you want the FV, so press the FV key to get the answer, $315.25. Since there is no initial payment, we input PV = 0.

---

[7]The third term in Equation 6-3a is found by applying the algebra of geometric progressions. This equation is useful in situations where the required values of i and n are not in the tables and no financial calculator is available.

ANNUITIES DUE

Had the three $100 payments in the previous example been made at the *beginning* of each year, the annuity would have been an *annuity due*. On the time line, each payment would be shifted to the left one year; therefore, each payment would be compounded for one extra year.

1. Time Line and Numerical Solution:

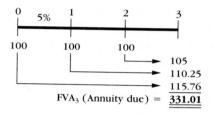

Again, the regular time line is shown at the top of the diagram, and the values as calculated with a regular calculator are shown in the right column.

2. Tabular Solution:

In an annuity due, each payment is compounded for one additional period, so the future value of the entire annuity is equal to the future value of an ordinary annuity compounded for one additional period. Here is the tabular solution:

$$\text{FVA}_n \text{ (Annuity due)} = \text{PMT}(\text{FVIFA}_{i,n})(1 + i) \qquad \text{(6-3b)}$$

$$= \$100(3.1525)(1.05) = \$331.01.$$

The payments occur earlier, so more interest is earned. Therefore, the future value of the annuity due is larger, $331.01 versus $315.25 for the ordinary annuity.

3. Financial Calculator Solution:

Most financial calculators have a switch, or key, marked "DUE" or "BEG" that permits you to switch from end-of-period payments (ordinary annuity) to beginning-of-period payments (annuity due). When the beginning mode is activated, the display will normally show the word "BEGIN." Thus, to deal with annuities due, switch your calculator to "BEGIN" and proceed as before:

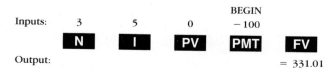

Enter N = 3, I = 5, PV = 0, PMT = −100, and then press FV to get the answer, $331.01. *Since most problems specify end-of-period cash flows, you should always switch your calculator back to "END" mode after you work an annuity due problem.*

SELF-TEST QUESTIONS

What is the difference between an ordinary annuity and an annuity due?

How do you modify the equation for determining the value of an ordinary annuity in order to determine the value of an annuity due?

Which annuity has the greater *future* value: an ordinary annuity or an annuity due? Why?

Explain how financial calculators can be used to solve future value of annuity problems.

PRESENT VALUE OF AN ANNUITY

Suppose you were offered the following alternatives: (1) a 3-year annuity with payments of $100 at the end of each year or (2) a lump sum payment today. You have no need for the money during the next three years, so if you accept the annuity, you would simply deposit the payments in a savings account that pays 5 percent interest per year. Similarly, the lump sum payment would be deposited into the same account. How large must the lump sum payment today be to make it equivalent to the annuity? Here is the setup:

Time Line:

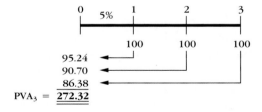

The regular time line is shown at the top of the diagram, and the numerical solution values are shown in the left column. The PV of the annuity, PVA_n, is $272.32.

Equation:

The general equation used to find the PV of an ordinary annuity is shown on the next page.[8]

---

[8]The summation term is called the *PVIFA*, and, using the geometric progression solution process, its value is found to be

$$PVA_n = PMT\left(\frac{1}{1+i}\right)^1 + PMT\left(\frac{1}{1+i}\right)^2 + \ldots + PMT\left(\frac{1}{1+i}\right)^n$$

$$= PMT\sum_{t=1}^{n}\left(\frac{1}{1+i}\right)^t. \qquad\qquad (6\text{-}4)$$

1. Numerical Solution:

The present value of each cash flow is found and then summed to find the PV of the annuity. This procedure is shown in the lower section of the time line diagram, where we see that the PV of the annuity is $272.32.

2. Tabular Solution:

The summation term in Equation 6-4 is called the *Present Value Interest Factor for an Annuity (PVIFA$_{i,n}$),* and values for the term at different values of i and n are shown in Table A-2 at the back of the book. Thus,

$$PVA_n = PMT(PVIFA_{i,n}). \qquad\qquad (6\text{-}4a)$$

To find the answer to the 3-year, $100 annuity problem, simply refer to Table A-2 and look down the 5% column to the third period. The PVIFA is 2.7232, so the present value of the $100 annuity is $272.32:

$$PVA_n = PMT(PVIFA_{i,n})$$

$$PVA_3 = \$100(PVIFA_{5\%,3}) = \$100(2.7232) = \$272.32.$$

3. Financial Calculator Solution:

Inputs: 3   5   −100   0

N	I	PV	PMT	FV

Output: = 272.32

Enter N = 3, I = 5, PMT = −100, and FV = 0, and then press the PV key to find the PV, $272.32.

$$\sum_{t=1}^{n}\left(\frac{1}{1+i}\right)^t = \frac{1-\dfrac{1}{(1+i)^n}}{i} = \frac{1}{i} - \frac{1}{i(1+i)^n}.$$

This form of the equation is useful for dealing with annuities when the values for i and n are not in the tables and no financial calculator is available.

One especially important application of the annuity concept relates to loans with constant payments, such as mortgages and auto loans. With such loans, called *amortized loans,* the amount borrowed is the present value of an ordinary annuity, and the payments constitute the annuity stream. We will examine constant payment loans in more depth in a later section of this chapter.

ANNUITIES DUE

Had the three $100 payments in our earlier example been made at the beginning of each year, the annuity would have been an *annuity due.* Each payment would be shifted to the left one year, so each payment would be discounted for one less year. Here is the time line setup:

1. Time Line and Numerical Solution:

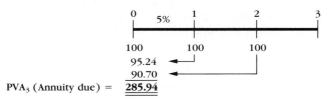

Again, we find the PV of each cash flow and then sum these PVs to find the PV of the annuity due. This procedure is illustrated in the lower section of the time line diagram. Since the cash flows occur sooner, the PV of the annuity due exceeds that of the ordinary annuity, $285.94 versus $272.32.

2. Tabular Solution:

In an annuity due, each payment is discounted for one less period. Since its payments come in faster, an annuity due is more valuable than an ordinary annuity, and this higher value is found by multiplying the PV of an ordinary annuity by $(1 + i)$:

$$\text{PVA}_n \text{ (Annuity due)} = \text{PMT}(\text{PVIFA}_{i,n})(1 + i) \qquad \text{(6-4b)}$$

$$= \$100(2.7232)(1.05) = \$285.94.$$

3. Financial Calculator Solution:

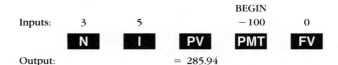

Switch to the beginning-of-period mode, and then enter N = 3, I = 5, PMT = −100, and FV = 0, and then press PV to get the answer, $285.94. *Again, since most problems deal with end-of-period cash flows, don't forget to switch your calculator back to the "END" mode.*

SELF-TEST QUESTIONS

Which annuity has the greater present value: an ordinary annuity or an annuity due? Why?

Explain how financial calculators can be used to find present values of annuities.

PERPETUITIES

Most annuities call for payments to be made over some finite period of time—for example, $100 per year for three years. However, some annuities go on indefinitely, or perpetually, and these annuities are called *perpetuities.* The present value of a perpetuity is found by applying Equation 6-5.[9]

$$ PV \text{ (Perpetuity)} = \frac{\text{Payment}}{\text{Interest rate}} = \frac{PMT}{i}. \tag{6-5} $$

Perpetuities can be illustrated by some British securities issued after the Napoleonic Wars. In 1815, the British government sold a huge bond issue and used the proceeds to pay off many smaller issues that had been floated in prior years to pay for the wars. Since the purpose of the bonds was to consolidate past debts, the bonds were called *consols.* Suppose each consol promised to pay $100 per year in perpetuity. (Actually, interest was stated in pounds.) What would each bond be worth if the opportunity cost rate, or discount rate, was 5 percent? The answer is $2,000:

$$ PV \text{ (Perpetuity)} = \frac{\$100}{0.05} = \$2,000 \text{ if } i = 5\%. $$

Suppose the interest rate rose to 10 percent; what would happen to the consol's value? The value would drop to $1,000:

$$ PV \text{ (Perpetuity)} = \frac{\$100}{0.10} = \$1,000 \text{ at } i = 10\%. $$

---

[9]The derivation of Equation 6-5 is given in Appendix 4A of Eugene F. Brigham and Louis C. Gapenski, *Intermediate Financial Management,* 4th ed. (Forth Worth, Tex.: Dryden Press, 1993).

We see that the value of a perpetuity changes dramatically when interest rates change. Perpetuities are discussed further in Chapter 7, where procedures for finding the value of various types of securities are discussed.

SELF-TEST QUESTIONS

What happens to the value of a perpetuity when interest rates increase? What happens when interest rates decrease? Why do these changes occur?

UNEVEN CASH FLOW STREAMS

The definition of an annuity includes the words *constant payment*—in other words, annuities involve payments that are equal in every period. Although many financial decisions do involve constant payments, other important decisions involve uneven, or nonconstant, cash flows; for example, common stocks typically pay an increasing stream of dividends over time, and fixed asset investments such as new equipment normally do not generate constant cash flows. Consequently, it is necessary to extend our time value discussion to include *uneven cash flow streams.*

Throughout the book, we will follow convention and reserve the term *payment (PMT)* for annuity situations where the dollar amounts are constant, and we will use the term *cash flow (CF)* to denote uneven dollar amounts. Financial calculators are set up to follow this convention, so if you are using one and dealing with uneven cash flows, you will need to use the cash flow register.

PRESENT VALUE OF AN UNEVEN CASH FLOW STREAM

The PV of an uneven cash flow stream is found as the sum of the PVs of the individual cash flows of the stream. For example, suppose we must find the PV of the following cash flow stream, discounted at 6 percent:

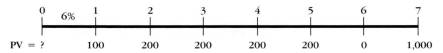

	0	6%	1	2	3	4	5	6	7
PV = ?			100	200	200	200	200	0	1,000

The PV will be found by applying this general present value equation:

$$PV = CF_1\left(\frac{1}{1+i}\right)^1 + CF_2\left(\frac{1}{1+i}\right)^2 + \ldots + CF_n\left(\frac{1}{1+i}\right)^n$$

$$= \sum_{t=1}^{n} CF_t\left(\frac{1}{1+i}\right)^t = \sum_{t=1}^{n} CF_t(PVIF_{i,t}). \tag{6-6}$$

We could find the PV of each individual cash flow using the numerical, tabular, or financial calculator methods, and then sum these values to find the present value of the stream. Here is what the process would look like:

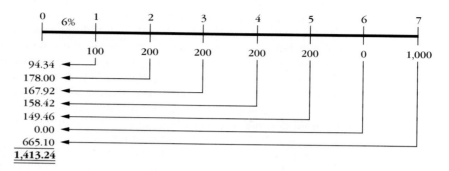

All we did was to apply Equation 6-6, show the individual PVs in the left column of the diagram, and then sum these individual PVs to find the PV of the entire stream.

The present value of a cash flow stream can always be found by summing the present values of the individual cash flows as shown above. However, cash flow regularities within the stream may allow the use of shortcuts. For example, notice that Cash Flows 2 through 5 represent an annuity. We can use that fact to solve the problem in a slightly different manner:

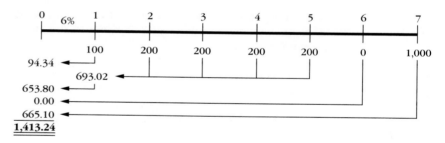

The Year 2−5 cash flows represent an ordinary annuity, so we find its PV at Year 1 (one period before the first payment). This PV ($693.02) must then be discounted back one more period to get its Year 0 value.

Problems involving uneven cash flows can be solved in one step with most financial calculators. First, you input the individual cash flows, in chronological order, into the cash flow register. Cash flows are usually designated CF_0, CF_1, CF_2, CF_3, and so on. Next, you enter the interest rate. At this point, you have substituted in all the known values of Equation 6-6, so you only need to press the NPV key to find the present value of the stream. The calculator has been programmed to find the PV of each cash flow and then to sum these values to find the PV of the entire stream. To input the cash flows for this problem, enter 0 (because $CF_0 = 0$), 100, 200, 200, 200, 200, 0, 1000 in that order into the cash flow register, enter I = 6,

and then press NPV to obtain the answer, $1,413.19, which differs slightly from the long-form solution because of rounding differences.

Two points should be noted. First, when dealing with the cash flow register, the calculator uses the term "NPV" rather than "PV." The N stands for "net," so NPV is the abbreviation for "Net Present Value," which is simply the net present value of a series of positive and negative cash flows. Our example has no negative cash flows, but if it did, we would simply input them with negative signs.

The second point to note is that annuities can be entered into the cash flow register more efficiently by using the N_j key. (On some calculators, you are prompted to enter the number of times the cash flow occurs, and on still other calculators the procedures for inputting data, as we discuss next, may be different. You should consult your calculator manual to determine the appropriate steps for your specific calculator.) In this illustration, you would enter $CF_0 = 0$, $CF_1 = 100$, $CF_2 = 200$, $N_j = 4$ (which tells the calculator that the 200 occurs 4 times), $CF_6 = 0$, and $CF_7 = 1000$. Then enter $I = 6$ and press the NPV key, and 1,413.19 will appear in the display. Also, note that amounts entered into the cash flow register remain in the register until they are cleared. Thus, if you had previously worked a problem with eight cash flows and then moved to a problem with only four cash flows, the calculator would assume that the cash flows from the first problem belonged to the second problem. Therefore, you must be sure to clear the cash flow register before starting a new problem.

FUTURE VALUE OF AN UNEVEN CASH FLOW STREAM

The future value of an uneven cash flow stream (sometimes called the *terminal value*) is found by compounding each payment to the end of the stream and then summing the future values:

$$FV_n = CF_1(1 + i)^{n-1} + CF_2(1 + i)^{n-2} + \ldots + CF_n(1 + i)^{n-t}$$

$$= \sum_{t=1}^{n} CF_t(1 + i)^{n-t} = \sum_{t=1}^{n} CF_t(FVIF_{i,n-t}). \qquad (6\text{-}7)$$

The future value of our illustrative uneven cash flow stream is $2,124.92:

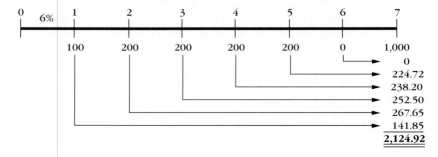

Some financial calculators have a net future value (NFV) key which, after the cash flows and interest rate have been entered into the calculator, can be used to obtain the future value of an uneven cash flow stream. In any event, it is easy enough to compound the individual cash flows to the terminal year and then to sum them to find the FV of the stream. Also, we are generally more interested in the present value of an asset's cash flow stream than in the future value because the present value represents today's value, which we can compare to the price of the asset. Finally, note that the net present value can be used to find the net future value: $NFV = NPV(1 + i)^n$. Thus, in this example, and using the calculator NPV, $NFV = \$1,413.19(1.06)^7 = \$2,124.92$, which equals the NFV shown on the time line on the previous page.

SOLVING FOR i WITH UNEVEN CASH FLOW STREAMS

It is relatively easy to solve for i numerically or with the tables when the cash flows are lump sums or annuities. However, it is *extremely difficult* to solve for i if the cash flows are uneven, as you will have to go through many tedious trial-and-error calculations. With a financial calculator, though, it is easy to find the value of i. Simply input the CF values into the cash flow register and then press the IRR key. IRR stands for "internal rate of return," which is the percentage return on an investment. We will defer further discussion of this calculation for now, but we will take it up later in our discussion of capital budgeting methods in Chapter 9.[10]

SELF-TEST QUESTIONS

Give two examples of financial decisions that would typically involve uneven flows of cash.

What is meant by the term "terminal value"?

SEMIANNUAL AND OTHER COMPOUNDING PERIODS

In all of our examples thus far, we have assumed that interest is compounded once a year, or annually. This is called *annual compounding*. Suppose, however, that you put \$100 into a bank which states that it pays a 6 percent annual interest rate but that interest is credited each six months. This is called *semiannual com-*

---

[10]To obtain a solution, at least one of the cash flows must have a negative sign, indicating that it is an investment. Since none of the CFs in our example were negative, the cash flow stream has no IRR. However, had we input a cost for CF_0, we could have obtained an IRR, which would be the rate of return earned on the CF_0 investment. For example, an investment of $CF_0 = -\$1,000$ results in an IRR of 13.96 percent.

pounding. How much would you accumulate at the end of one year, two years, or some other period under semiannual compounding?

To illustrate semiannual compounding, assume that $100 is placed into an account at an interest rate of 6 percent and left there for 3 years. First, consider again what happens under annual compounding:

1. **Time Line, Equation, and Numerical Solution:**

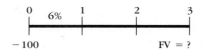

$$FV_n = PV(1 + i)^n = \$100(1.06)^3$$
$$= \$119.10.$$

2. **Tabular Solution:**

$$FV_3 = \$100(FVIF_{6\%,3}) = \$100(1.1910) = \$119.10.$$

3. **Financial Calculator Solution:**

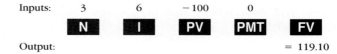

Now consider what happens under semiannual compounding. Here we have n = 2 × 3 = 6 semiannual periods, and you will earn i = 6%/2 = 3% every six months. Note that on most types of contracts, interest is quoted as an annual rate, and if compounding occurs more frequently than once a year, that fact is stated, along with the rate. In our example, the quoted rate is "6 percent, compounded semiannually." Here is how we find the FV after 3 years at 6 percent with semiannual compounding:

Time Line:

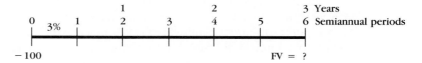

1. **Equation and Numerical Solution:**

$$FV_n = PV(1 + i)^n = \$100(1.03)^6$$
$$= \$100(1.1941) = \$119.41.$$

Here i_{Nom} is the nominal, or quoted, rate, m is the number of times compounding occurs per year, and n is the number of years. For example, when banks pay daily interest, the value of m is set at 365 and Equation 6-9 is applied.[14]

To illustrate further the effects of compounding more frequently than annually, consider the interest rate charged on credit cards. Many banks charge 1.5 percent per month, and, in their advertising, they state that the *Annual Percentage Rate (APR)* is 18.0 percent. However, the true rate is the effective annual rate of 19.6 percent:[15]

$$\left(\quad 0.18 \right)^{12}$$

Here i = rate per period = annual rate/compounding periods per year = 6%/2 = 3%, and n = the total number of periods = years × periods per year = 3 × 2 = 6.

2. **Tabular Solution:**

$$FV_6 = \$100(FVIF_{3\%,6}) = \$100(1.1941) = \$119.41.$$

Look up FVIF for 3%, 6 periods in Table A-3 and complete the arithmetic.

3. **Financial Calculator Solution:**

Inputs:	6	3	− 100	0	
	N	**I**	**PV**	**PMT**	**FV**
Output:					= 119.41

Enter N = years × periods per year = 3 × 2 = 6, I = annual rate/periods per year = 6/2 = 3, PV = − 100, and PMT = 0, and then press FV to find the answer, $119.41 versus $119.10 under annual compounding. The FV is larger under semi-annual compounding because interest on interest is being earned more frequently.

Throughout the world economy, different compounding periods are used for different types of investments. For example, bank accounts generally pay interest daily; most bonds pay interest semiannually; and stocks generally pay dividends quarterly.[11] If we are to properly compare securities with different compounding periods, we need to put them on a common basis. This requires us to distinguish between *nominal,* or *quoted, interest rates* and *effective annual rates.*[12]

The nominal, or quoted, interest rate in our example is 6 percent. *The effective annual rate (EAR) is defined as that rate which would produce the same ending (future) value if annual compounding had been used.* In our example, the effective annual rate is the rate which would produce an FV of $119.41 at the end of Year 3.

We can determine the effective annual rate, given the nominal rate and the number of compounding periods per year, by solving this equation:

$$\text{Effective annual rate} = \text{EAR} = \left(1 + \frac{i_{Nom}}{m} \right)^{m} - 1.0. \qquad \text{(6-8)}$$

---

[11]Some banks and savings and loans even pay interest compounded *continuously.* Continuous compounding is discussed in Appendix 6A.

[12]The term *nominal rate* as it is used here has a different meaning than the way it was used in Chapter 3. There, nominal interest rates referred to stated market rates as opposed to real (zero inflation) rates. In this chapter, the term *nominal rate* means the stated, or quoted, annual rate as opposed to the effective annual rate. In both cases, though, *nominal* means *stated,* or *quoted,* as opposed to some adjusted rate.

2. **Tabular Solution:**

$$PVA_n = PMT(PVIFA_{i,n})$$

$$= \$100(PVIFA_{8\%,3}) = \$100(2.5771) = \$257.71.$$

3. **Financial Calculator Solution:**

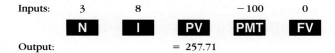

Inputs: 3   8   −100   0

N   I   PV   PMT   FV

Output: = 257.71

Now let's change the situation. For example, suppose the annuity calls for payments of $50 each 6 months rather than for $100 per year, and the interest rate is 8 percent, compounded semiannually. Here is the time line:

Time Line:

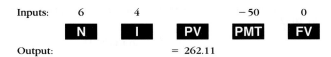

	1	2	3 Years
0	2	4	6 Semiannual periods

0 4% 1   2   3   4   5   6 Semiannual periods

PV = ?   −50 −50 −50 −50 −50 −50

1. **Numerical Solution:**
Find the PV of each cash flow by discounting at 4 percent. Treat each tick mark on the time line as a period, so there would be 6 periods. The PV of the annuity is $262.11 versus $257.71 under annual compounding.

2. **Tabular Solution:**

$$PVA_n = PMT(PVIFA_{i,n})$$

$$= \$50(PVIFA_{4\%,6}) = \$50(5.2421) = \$262.11.$$

3. **Financial Calculator Solution:**

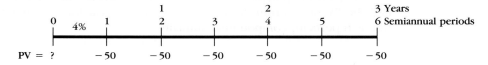

Inputs: 6   4   −50   0

N   I   PV   PMT   FV

Output: = 262.11

The semiannual payments come in sooner, so the $50 semiannual annuity is more valuable than the $100 annual annuity.

SELF-TEST QUESTIONS

What changes must you make in your calculations to determine the future value of an amount that is being compounded at 8 percent semiannually versus one being compounded annually at 8 percent?

More frequent compounding: $FV_n = PV\left(1 + \dfrac{i_{Nom}}{m}\right)^{mn}.$ (6-9)

---

[13]Most financial calculators are programmed to find the EAR or, given the EAR, to find the nominal rate. This is called "interest rate conversion," and you simply enter the nominal rate and the number of compounding periods per year and then press the EFF% key to find the EAR.

Why is semiannual compounding better than annual compounding from a saver's standpoint?

What are meant by the terms "annual percentage rate," "effective annual rate," and "nominal interest rate"?

How does the term "nominal rate" used in this chapter differ from the term as it was used in Chapter 3?

FRACTIONAL TIME PERIODS

In all of the examples used thus far in the chapter, we have assumed that payments occur at either the beginning or the end of periods but not at some date *within* a period. However, we often encounter situations that require compounding or discounting over fractional periods. For example, suppose you deposited $100 in a bank that pays 10 percent interest, compounded annually. If you leave your money in the bank for 9 months, or 0.75 of the year, how much would you have in your account?

Time Line and Equation:

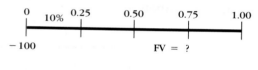

$$FV_n = PV(1 + i)^n.$$

1. Numerical Solution:

$$FV_n = \$100(1.10)^{0.75} = \$100(1.0741) = \$107.41.$$

2. Financial Calculator Solution:

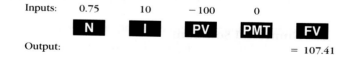

Present values, annuities, and problems where you must find interest rates or numbers of periods can all be handled with ease. Note, though, that financial calculators are essential for many fractional year problems—the tables are useless.[16]

---

[16]An alternative (different) way to deal with this problem is to divide the interest rate expressed as a decimal by 360 (or 365), multiply by the number of days (0.75 × 360 or 365), and then multiply the result by the beginning amount to find the interest earned, $7.50 in this case. Banks typically use this calculation to determine the interest on *loans* but not on deposits.

COMPARISON OF DIFFERENT TYPES OF INTEREST RATES

Before closing this chapter, it is useful to review the three types of interest rates and the way each is used in discounted cash flow analysis.

NOMINAL, OR QUOTED, RATE, i_{Nom}

This is the rate that is quoted by borrowers and lenders. Practitioners in the stock, bond, mortgage, commercial loan, consumer loan, banking, and other markets express all financial contracts in terms of nominal rates. So, if you talk with a banker, broker, mortgage lender, auto finance company, or student loan officer about rates, the nominal rate is the one he or she will normally quote you. However, to be meaningful, the quoted nominal rate must also include the number of compounding periods per year. For example, a bank might offer 8.5 percent, compounded quarterly, on CDs, or a mutual fund might offer 8 percent, compounded monthly, on its money market account.

Nominal rates can be compared with one another, *but only if the instruments being compared use the same number of compounding periods per year.* Thus, to compare an 8.5 percent, annual payment CD with an 8 percent, daily payment money market fund, we would need to put both instruments on an *effective annual rate (EAR)* basis.

Note also that the nominal rate is never shown on a time line, and it is never used as an input in a financial calculator, unless compounding occurs only once a year (in which case i_{Nom} = periodic rate = EAR). If more frequent compounding occurs, you must use either the periodic rate or the effective annual rate as discussed below.[18]

PERIODIC RATE, i_{Per}

This is the rate charged by a lender or paid by a borrower each period. It can be a rate per year, per 6-month period, per quarter, per month, per day, or per any other time interval (usually one year or less). For example, a bank might charge 1 percent per month on its credit card loans, or a finance company might charge 3 percent per quarter on consumer loans. We find the periodic rate as follows:

$$\text{Periodic rate, } i_{Per} = i_{Nom}/m, \qquad (6\text{-}10)$$

---

[18]Some calculators have a switch which permits you to specify the number of payments per year. We find it less confusing to set this switch to 1 and then leave it there. We prefer to work with "periods" when more than one payment occurs each year because this maintains a consistency between number of periods and the periodic interest rate.

which implies that

$$i_{Nom} = (\text{Periodic rate})(m) = \text{APR}. \qquad (6\text{-}11)$$

Here i_{Nom} is the nominal annual rate, m is the number of compounding periods per year, and APR is the annual percentage rate. *The APR is never shown on a time line or used in actual calculations; it is simply reported to borrowers.*

To illustrate, consider a finance company loan at 3 percent per quarter:

$$\text{Nominal annual rate} = i_{Nom} = (\text{Periodic rate})(m) = (3\%)(4) = 12\% = \text{APR},$$

and

$$\text{Periodic rate} = i_{Nom}/m = 12\%/4 = 3\% \text{ per quarter.}$$

If there is one payment per year, or if interest is added only once a year, then m = 1 and the periodic rate is equal to the nominal rate. *But, in all cases where interest is added or payments are made more frequently than annually, the periodic rate is less than the nominal rate.*

Note that in most of the examples we have used thus far, the interest compounding period is the same as the payment period. *The periodic rate can be used directly in calculations, but only if the number of payments per year is consistent with the number of interest compounding periods.*

To illustrate use of the periodic rate, suppose you make the following eight quarterly payments of $100 each into an account which pays 12 percent, compounded quarterly. How much would you have after two years?

Time Line and Equation:

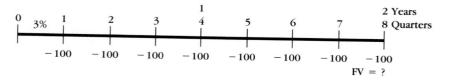

$$FVA_n = \sum_{t=1}^{n} PMT(1 + i)^{n-t} = \sum_{t=1}^{8} \$100(1.03)^{8-t}.$$

1. Numerical Solution:

Compound each $100 payment at $12/4 = 3$ percent for the appropriate number of periods, and then sum these individual FVs to find the FV of the payment stream, $889.23.

2. Tabular Solution:

Look up FVIFA for 3%, 8 periods, in Table A-4, and complete the arithmetic:

$$FVA_n = PMT(FVIFA_{i,n})$$
$$= \$100(FVIFA_{3\%,8}) = \$100(8.8923) = \$889.23.$$

3. Financial Calculator Solution:

Inputs: 8   3   0   −100

| N | I | PV | PMT | FV |

Output: = 889.23

Input N = 2 × 4 = 8, I = 12/4 = 3, PV = 0, and PMT = −100, and then press the FV key to get FV = $889.23.

Effective Annual Rate (EAR)

This is the rate which, under annual compounding (m = 1), would produce the same result as if we had used a given periodic rate with m compounding periods per year. The EAR is found as follows:

$$EAR = \left(1 + \frac{i_{Nom}}{m}\right)^m - 1.0, \tag{6-8}$$

or with the interest conversion feature of a financial calculator.

In the EAR equation, i_{Nom}/m is the periodic rate and m is the number of periods per year. For example, suppose you could borrow using either a credit card which charges 1 percent per month or a bank loan with a 12 percent quoted nominal interest rate that is compounded quarterly. Which should you choose? To answer this question, the cost rate of each alternative must be expressed as an EAR:

$$\text{Credit card loan: EAR} = (1 + 0.01)^{12} - 1.0 = (1.01)^{12} - 1.0$$
$$= 1.126825 - 1.0 = 0.126825 = 12.6825\%.$$

$$\text{Bank loan: EAR} = (1 + 0.03)^4 - 1.0 = (1.03)^4 - 1.0$$
$$= 1.125509 - 1.0 = 0.125509 = 12.5509\%.$$

Thus, the credit card loan is slightly more costly than the bank loan. This result should have been intuitive to you — both loans have the same 12 percent nominal rate, yet you would have to make monthly payments on the credit card versus quarterly payments under the bank loan.

SELF-TEST QUESTIONS

Define the nominal (or quoted) rate, the periodic rate, and the effective annual rate.

How are the nominal rate, the periodic rate, and the effective annual rate related? Can you think of a situation where all three of these rates will be the same?

SUMMARY

Financial decisions often involve situations in which someone pays money at one point in time and receives money at some later time. Dollars that are paid or received at two different points in time are different, and this difference is recognized and accounted for by *discounted cash flow (DCF) analysis.* We summarize below the types of DCF analysis and the key concepts covered in this chapter, using the data shown in Figure 6-3 to illustrate the various points. Refer to the figure constantly, and try to find in it an example of the points covered as you go through this summary.

▸ *Compounding* is the process of determining the *future value (FV)* of a cash flow or a series of cash flows. The compounded amount, or future value, is equal to the beginning amount plus the interest earned.

▸ Future value: $FV_n = PV(1 + i)^n = PV(FVIF_{i,n})$.
(single payment)

Example: $961.50 compounded for 1 year at 4 percent:

$$FV_1 = \$961.50(1.04)^1 = \$1,000.$$

▸ *Discounting* is the process of finding the *present value (PV)* of a future cash flow or a series of cash flows; discounting is the reciprocal of compounding.

▸ Present value: $\quad PV = \dfrac{FV_n}{(1 + i)^n} = FV_n\left(\dfrac{1}{1 + i}\right)^n = FV_n(PVIF_{i,n})$.
(single payment)

FIGURE 6-3

ILLUSTRATION FOR
CHAPTER SUMMARY
($i = 4\%$)

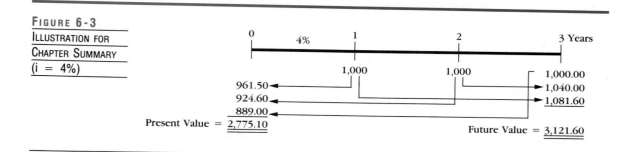

Example: $1,000 discounted back for 2 years at 4 percent:

$$PV = \frac{\$1,000}{(1.04)^2} = \$1,000\left(\frac{1}{1.04}\right)^2 = \$1,000(0.9246) = \$924.60.$$

▶ An *annuity* is defined as a series of equal periodic payments (PMT) for a specified number of periods.

▶ Future value (annuity)

$$FVA_n = PMT(1+i)^0 + PMT(1+i)^1 + PMT(1+i)^2 + \ldots + PMT(1+i)^{n-1}$$

$$= PMT \sum_{t=1}^{n} (1+i)^{n-t} = PMT(FVIFA_{i,n}).$$

Example: FVA of 3 payments of $1,000 when i = 4%:

$$FVA_3 = \$1,000(3.1216) = \$3,121.60.$$

▶ Present value: (annuity)

$$PVA_n = \frac{PMT}{(1+i)^1} + \frac{PMT}{(1+i)^2} + \ldots + \frac{PMT}{(1+i)^n}$$

$$= PMT \sum_{t=1}^{n} \left[\frac{1}{1+i}\right]^t = PMT(PVIFA_{i,n}).$$

Example: PVA of 3 payments of $1,000 when i = 4%:

$$PVA_3 = \$1,000(2.7751) = \$2,775.10.$$

▶ An annuity whose payments occur at the *end* of each period is called an *ordinary annuity.* The formulas above are for ordinary annuities.

▶ If each payment occurs at the beginning of the period rather than at the end, then we have an *annuity due.* In Figure 6-3, the payments would be shown at Years 0, 1, and 2 rather than at Years 1, 2, and 3. The PV of each payment would be larger, because each payment would be discounted back one year less, and hence the PV of the annuity would also be larger. Similarly, the FV of the annuity due would also be larger because each payment would be compounded for an extra year. The following formulas can be used to convert the PV and FV of an ordinary annuity to an annuity due:

$$PVA(\text{annuity due}) = PVA \text{ of an ordinary annuity} \times (1+i).$$

Example: PVA of 3 beginning-of-year payments of $1,000 when i = 4%:
$$PVA(\text{annuity due}) = \$1,000(2.7751)(1.04) = \$2,886.10.$$

$$FVA(\text{annuity due}) = FVA \text{ of an ordinary annuity} \times (1+i).$$

Example: FVA of 3 beginning-of-year payments of $1,000 when i = 4%:
FVA (annuity due) = $1,000(3.1216)(1.04) = $3,246.46.

▶ If the time line in Figure 6-3 were extended out forever so that the $1,000 payments went on forever, we would have a *perpetuity* whose value could be found as follows:

$$\text{Value of perpetuity} = \frac{\text{PMT}}{i} = \frac{\$1,000}{0.04} = \$25,000.$$

▶ If the cash flows in Figure 6-3 were unequal, we could not use the annuity formulas. To find the PV or FV of an uneven series, find the PV or FV of each individual cash flow and then sum them. However, if some of the cash flows constitute an annuity, then the annuity formula can be used to calculate the present value of that part of the cash flow stream.

▶ *Financial calculators* have built-in programs which perform all of the operations discussed in this chapter. It would be useful for you to buy such a calculator and to learn how to use it. Even if you do, though, it is essential that you understand the logical processes involved.

▶ DCF calculations generally involve equations which have four variables, so if you know three of the values, you (or your calculator) can solve for the fourth.

▶ If you know the cash flows and the PV (or FV) of a cash flow stream, you can *determine the interest rate.* For example, in the Figure 6-3 illustration, if you were given the information that a loan called for 3 payments of $1,000 each, and that the loan had a value today of PV = $2,775.10, then you could find the interest rate that caused the sum of the PVs of the payments to equal $2,775.10. Since we are dealing with an annuity, we could proceed as follows:
a. Recognize that PVA_n = $2,775.10 = $1,000($PVIFA_{i,3}$).
b. Solve for $PVIFA_{i,3}$:

$$PVIFA_{i,3} = \$2,775.10/\$1,000 = 2.7751.$$

c. Look up 2.7751 in Table A-2, on the third row. It is in the 4% column, so the interest rate must be 4 percent. If the factor did not appear in the table, this would indicate that the interest rate was not a whole number. In this case, you could not use this procedure to find the exact rate. In practice, though, this is not a problem, because most people use financial calculators to find interest rates.

▶ Thus far in the summary we have assumed that payments are made, and interest is earned, at the end of each year, or annually. However, many contracts call for more frequent payments; for example, mortgage and auto loans call for monthly payments, and most bonds pay interest semiannually. Similarly, most

c. Suppose you deposited the $1,000 in 4 payments of $250 each on January 1 of 1995, 1996, 1997, and 1998. How much would you have in your account on January 1, 1998, based on 8 percent annual compounding?

d. Suppose you deposited 4 equal payments in your account on January 1 of 1995, 1996, 1997, and 1998. Assuming an 8 percent interest rate, how large would each of your payments have to be for you to obtain the same ending balance as you calculated in Part a?

ST-2 **(Time value of money)**   Assume that it is now January 1, 1994, and you will need $1,000 on January 1, 1998. Your bank compounds interest at an 8 percent annual rate.

a. How much must you deposit on January 1, 1995, to have a balance of $1,000 on January 1, 1998?

b. If you want to make equal payments on each January 1 from 1995 through 1998 to accumulate the $1,000, how large must each of the 4 payments be?

c. If your father were to offer either to make the payments calculated in Part b ($221.92) or to give you a lump sum of $750 on January 1, 1995, which would you choose?

d. If you have only $750 on January 1, 1995, what interest rate, compounded annually, would you have to earn to have the necessary $1,000 on January 1, 1998?

e. Suppose you can deposit only $186.29 each January 1 from 1995 through 1998, but you still need $1,000 on January 1, 1998. What interest rate, with annual compounding, must you seek out to achieve your goal?

f. To help you reach your $1,000 goal, your father offers to give you $400 on January 1, 1995. You will get a part-time job and make 6 additional payments of equal amounts each 6 months thereafter. If all of this money is deposited in a bank which pays 8 percent, compounded semiannually, how large must each of the 6 payments be?

g. What is the effective annual rate being paid by the bank in Part f?

h. *Reinvestment rate risk* was defined in Chapter 3 as being the risk that maturing securities (and coupon payments on bonds) will have to be reinvested at a lower rate of interest than they were previously earning. Is there a reinvestment rate risk involved in the preceding analysis? If so, how might this risk be eliminated?

ST-3 **(Effective annual rates)**   Bank A pays 8 percent interest, compounded quarterly, on its money market account. The managers of Bank B want its money market account to equal Bank A's effective annual rate, but interest is to be compounded on a monthly basis. What nominal, or quoted, rate must Bank B set?

Problems

6-1 **(Present and future values for different periods)**   Find the following values, *using the equations,* and then work the problems using a financial calculator or the tables to check your answers. Disregard rounding differences. (Hint: If you are using a financial calculator, you can enter the known values and then press the appropriate key to find the unknown variable. Then, without clearing the TVM register, you can "override" the variable which changes by simply entering a new value for it and then pressing the key for the unknown variable to obtain the second answer. This procedure can be used in Parts b and d, and in many other situations, to see how changes in input variables affect the output variable.)

a. An initial $500 compounded for 1 year at 6 percent.

b. An initial $500 compounded for 2 years at 6 percent.

    c.   The present value of $500 due in 1 year at a discount rate of 6 percent.

    d.   The present value of $500 due in 2 years at a discount rate of 6 percent.

6-2   **(Present and future values for different interest rates)** Use the tables or a financial calculator to find the following values. See the hint for Problem 6-1.

    a.   An initial $500 compounded for 10 years at 6 percent.

    b.   An initial $500 compounded for 10 years at 12 percent.

    c.   The present value of $500 due in 10 years at a 6 percent discount rate.

    d.   The present value of $1,552.90 due in 10 years at a 12 percent discount rate and at a 6 percent rate. Give a verbal definition of the term *present value,* and illustrate it using a time line with data from this problem. As a part of your answer, explain why present values are dependent upon interest rates.

6-3   **(Time for a lump sum to double)** To the closest year, how long will it take $200 to double if it is deposited and earns the following rates? [Notes: (1) See the hint for Problem 6-1. (2) This problem cannot be solved exactly with some financial calculators. For example, if you enter PV = − 200, PMT = 0, FV = 400, and I = 7 in an HP-12C, and then press the N key, you will get 11 years for Part a. The correct answer is 10.2448 years, which rounds to 10, but the calculator rounds up. However, the HP-10B and HP-17B give the correct answer. You should look up FVIF = 400/200 = 2 in the tables for Parts a, b, and c, but figure out Part d.]

    a.   7 percent.

    b.   10 percent.

    c.   18 percent.

    d.   100 percent.

6-4   **(Future value of an annuity)** Find the *future value* of the following annuities. The first payment in these annuities is made at the *end* of Year 1; that is, they are *ordinary annuities.* (Note: See the hint to Problem 6-1. Also, note that you can leave values in the TVM register, switch to "BEG," press FV, and find the FV of the annuity due.)

    a. $400 per year for 10 years at 10 percent.

    b. $200 per year for 5 years at 5 percent.

    c. $400 per year for 5 years at 0 percent.

    d.   Now rework Parts a, b, and c assuming that payments are made at the *beginning* of each year; that is, they are *annuities due.*

6-5   **(Present value of an annuity)** Find the *present value* of the following *ordinary annuities* (see note to Problem 6-4.):

    a. $400 per year for 10 years at 10 percent.

    b. $200 per year for 5 years at 5 percent.

    c. $400 per year for 5 years at 0 percent.

    d.   Now rework Parts a, b, and c assuming that payments are made at the *beginning* of each year; that is, they are *annuities due.*

6-6   **(Uneven cash flow stream)**

    a.   Find the present values of the following cash flow streams. The appropriate interest rate is 8 percent. (Hint: It is fairly easy to work this problem dealing with the individual cash flows. However, if you have a financial calculator, read the section of the manual which describes how to enter cash flows such as the ones in this problem. This will

take a little time, but the investment will pay huge dividends throughout the course. Note, if you do work with the cash flow register, then you must enter $CF_0 = 0$.)

Year	Cash Stream A	Cash Stream B
1	$100	$300
2	400	400
3	400	400
4	400	400
5	300	100

   b. What is the value of each cash flow stream at a 0 percent interest rate?

6-7 **(Effective rate of interest)** Find the interest rates, or rates of return, on each of the following:

   a. You *borrow* $700 and promise to pay back $749 at the end of 1 year.

   b. You *lend* $700 and receive a promise to be paid $749 at the end of 1 year.

   c. You borrow $85,000 and promise to pay back $201,229 at the end of 10 years.

   d. You borrow $9,000 and promise to make payments of $2,684.80 per year for 5 years.

6-8 **(Future value for various compounding periods)** Find the amount to which $500 will grow under each of the following conditions:

   a. 12 percent compounded annually for 5 years.

   b. 12 percent compounded semiannually for 5 years.

   c. 12 percent compounded quarterly for 5 years.

   d. 12 percent compounded monthly for 5 years.

6-9 **(Present value for various compounding periods)** Find the present value of $500 due in the future under each of the following conditions:

   a. 12 percent nominal rate, semiannual compounding, discounted back 5 years.

   b. 12 percent nominal rate, quarterly compounding, discounted back 5 years.

   c. 12 percent nominal rate, monthly compounding, discounted back 1 year.

6-10 **(Future value of an annuity for various compounding periods)** Find the future values of the following ordinary annuities:

   a. FV of $400 each 6 months for 5 years at a nominal rate of 12 percent, compounded semiannually.

   b. FV of $200 each 3 months for 5 years at a nominal rate of 12 percent, compounded quarterly.

   c. The annuities described in Parts a and b have the same amount of money paid into them during the 5-year period and both earn interest at the same nominal rate, yet the annuity in Part b earns $101.60 more than the one in Part a over the 5 years. Why does this occur?

6-11 **(Effective versus nominal interest rates)** Universal Bank pays 7 percent interest, compounded annually, on time deposits. Regional Bank pays 6 percent interest, compounded quarterly.

   a. Based on effective interest rates, in which bank would you prefer to deposit your money?

   b. Could your choice of banks be influenced by the fact that you might want to withdraw your funds during the year as opposed to at the end of the year? In answering this question, assume that funds must be left on deposit during the entire compounding period in order for you to receive any interest.

6-12 (Amortization schedule)

a. Set up an amortization schedule for a $25,000 loan to be repaid in equal installments at the end of each of the next 5 years. The interest rate is 10 percent.

b. How large must each annual payment be if the loan is for $50,000? Assume that the interest rate remains at 10 percent and that the loan is paid off over 5 years.

c. How large must each payment be if the loan is for $50,000, the interest rate is 10 percent, and the loan is paid off in equal installments at the end of each of the next 10 years? This loan is for the same amount as the loan in Part b, but the payments are spread out over twice as many periods. Why are these payments not half as large as the payments on the loan in Part b?

6-13 (Effective rates of return) Assume that AT&T's pension fund managers are considering two alternative securities as investments: (1) Security Z (for zero intermediate-year cash flows), which costs $422.41 today, pays nothing during its 10-year life, and then pays $1,000 after 10 years or (2) Security B, which has a cost today of $1,000 and which pays $80 at the end of each of the next 9 years and then $1,080 at the end of Year 10.

a. What is the rate of return on each security?

b. Assume that the interest rate AT&T's pension fund managers can earn on the fund's money falls to 6 percent immediately after the securities are purchased and is expected to remain at that level for the next 10 years. What would the price of each security change to, what would the fund's profit be on each security, and what would be the percentage profit (profit divided by cost) for each security?

c. Assuming that the cash flows for each security had to be reinvested at the new 6 percent market interest rate, (1) what would be the value attributable to each security at the end of 10 years and (2) what "actual, after-the-fact" rate of return would the fund have earned on each security? (Hint: The "actual" rate of return is found as the interest rate which causes the PV of the compounded Year 10 amount to equal the original cost of the security.)

d. Now assume all the facts as given in Parts b and c except assume that the interest rate *rose* to 12 percent rather than fell to 6 percent. What would happen to the profit figures as developed in Part b and to the "actual" rates of return as determined in Part c? Explain your results.

6-14 (Required annuity payments) A father is planning a savings program to put his daughter through college. His daughter is now 13 years old. She plans to enroll at the university in 5 years, and it should take her 4 years to complete her education. Currently, the cost per year (for everything—food, clothing, tuition, books, transportation, and so forth) is $12,500, but a 5 percent inflation rate in these costs is forecasted. The daughter recently received $7,500 from her grandfather's estate; this money, which is invested in a bank account paying 8 percent interest compounded annually, will be used to help meet the costs of the daughter's education. The rest of the costs will be met by money the father will deposit in the savings account. He will make 6 equal deposits in the account in each year from now until his daughter starts college. These deposits will begin today and will also earn 8 percent interest.

a. What will be the present value of the cost of four years of education at the time the daughter becomes 18? [Hint: Calculate the future value of the cost (at 5%) for each year of her education, then discount three of these costs back (at 8%) to the year in which she turns 18, then sum the four costs.]

b. What will be the value of the $7,500 which the daughter received from her grandfather's estate when she starts college at age 18? (Hint: Compound for 5 years at 8%.)

c. If the father is planning to make the first of 6 deposits today, how large must each deposit be for him to be able to put his daughter through college?

6-15 (Present value comparison) Which amount is worth more at 14 percent: $1,000 in hand today or $2,000 due in 6 years?

6-16 (Growth rates) Hanebury Corporation's 1993 sales were $12 million. Sales were $6 million 5 years earlier (in 1988).

    a. To the nearest percentage point, at what rate have sales been growing?

    b. Suppose someone calculated the sales growth for Hanebury Corporation in Part a as follows: "Sales doubled in 5 years. This represents a growth of 100 percent in 5 years, so, dividing 100 percent by 5, we find the growth rate to be 20 percent per year." Explain what is wrong with this calculation.

6-17 (Expected rate of return) Washington-Pacific invests $4 million to clear a tract of land and to set out some young pine trees. The trees will mature in 10 years, at which time Washington-Pacific plans to sell the forest at an expected price of $8 million. What is Washington-Pacific's expected rate of return?

6-18 (Effective rate of interest) Your broker offers to sell you a note for $13,250 that will pay $2,345.05 per year for 10 years. If you buy the note, what rate of interest (to the closest percent) will you be earning?

6-19 (Effective rate of interest) A mortgage company offers to lend you $85,000; the loan calls for payments of $8,273.59 per year for 30 years. What interest rate is the mortgage company charging you?

6-20 (Required lump sum payment) To complete your last year in business school and then go through law school, you will need $10,000 per year for 4 years, starting next year (that is, you will need to withdraw the first $10,000 one year from today). Your rich uncle offers to put you through school, and he will deposit in a bank paying 7 percent interest a sum of money that is sufficient to provide the four payments of $10,000 each. His deposit will be made today.

    a. How large must the deposit be?

    b. How much will be in the account immediately after you make the first withdrawal? After the last withdrawal?

6-21 (Repaying a loan) While Mary Corens was a student at the University of Florida, she borrowed $12,000 in student loans at an annual interest rate of 9 percent. If Mary repays $1,500 per year, how long, to the nearest year, will it take her to repay the loan?

6-22 (Reaching a financial goal) You need to accumulate $10,000. To do so, you plan to make deposits of $1,250 per year, with the first payment being made a year from today, in a bank account which pays 12 percent annual interest. Your last deposit will be less than $1,250 if less is needed to round out to $10,000. How many years will it take you to reach your $10,000 goal, and how large will the last deposit be?

6-23 (Present value of a perpetuity) What is the present value of a perpetuity of $100 per year if the appropriate discount rate is 7 percent? If interest rates in general were to double and the appropriate discount rate rose to 14 percent, what would happen to the present value of the perpetuity?

6-24 (PV and effective annual rate) Assume that you inherited some money. A friend of yours is working as an unpaid intern at a local brokerage firm, and her boss is selling some securities which call for four payments, $50 at the end of each of the next 3 years, plus a payment of $1,050 at the end of Year 4. Your friend says she can get you some of these

securities at a cost of $900 each. Your money is now invested in a bank that pays an 8 percent nominal (quoted) interest rate but with quarterly compounding. You regard the securities as being just as safe, and as liquid, as your bank deposit, so your required effective annual rate of return on the securities is the same as that on your bank deposit. You must calculate the value of the securities to decide whether they are a good investment. What is their present value to you?

6-25 (Loan amortization) Assume that your aunt sold her house on December 31 and that she took a mortgage in the amount of $10,000 as part of the payment. The mortgage has a quoted (or nominal) interest rate of 10 percent, but it calls for payments every 6 months, beginning on June 30, and the mortgage is to be amortized over 10 years. Now, one year later, your aunt must file a Form 1099 with the IRS and with the person who bought the house, informing them of the interest that was included in the two payments made during the year. (This interest will be income to your aunt and a deduction to the buyer of the house.) To the closest dollar, what is the total amount of interest that was paid during the first year?

6-26 (Loan amortization) Your company is planning to borrow $1,000,000 on a 5-year, 15%, annual payment, fully amortized term loan. What fraction of the payment made at the end of the second year will represent repayment of principal?

6-27 (Nonannual compounding)

a. It is now January 1, 1994. You plan to make 5 deposits of $100 each, one every 6 months, with the first payment being made *today*. If the bank pays a nominal interest rate of 12 percent but uses semiannual compounding, how much will be in your account after 10 years?

b. You must make a payment of $1,432.02 ten years from today. To prepare for this payment, you will make 5 equal deposits, beginning today and for the next 4 quarters, in a bank that pays a nominal interest rate of 12 percent, quarterly compounding. How large must each of the 5 payments be?

6-28 (Nominal rate of return) Anne Lockwood, manager of Oaks Mall Jewelry, wants to sell on credit, giving customers 3 months in which to pay. However, Anne will have to borrow from her bank to carry the accounts payable. The bank will charge a nominal 15 percent, but with monthly compounding. Anne wants to quote a nominal rate to her customers (all of whom are expected to pay on time) which will exactly cover her financing costs. What nominal annual rate should she quote to her credit customers?

6-29 (Required annuity payments) Assume that your father is now 50 years old, that he plans to retire in 10 years, and that he expects to live for 25 years after he retires, that is, until he is 85. He wants a fixed retirement income that has the same purchasing power at the time he retires as $40,000 has today (he realizes that the real value of his retirement income will decline year by year after he retires). His retirement income will begin the day he retires, 10 years from today, and he will then get 24 additional annual payments. Inflation is expected to be 5 percent per year from today forward; he currently has $100,000 saved up; and he expects to earn a return on his savings of 8 percent per year, annual compounding. To the nearest dollar, how much must he save during each of the next 10 years (with deposits being made at the end of each year) to meet his retirement goal?

6-30 (Amortization schedule) Set up an amortization schedule for a $30,000 loan to be repaid in equal installments at the end of each of the next 20 years at an interest rate of 10 percent.

a. What is the annual payment?

Work parts b and c only if you are using the computerized problem diskette.

b. Set up an amortization schedule for a $60,000 loan to be repaid in 20 equal annual installments at an interest rate of 10 percent. What is the annual payment?

c. Set up an amortization schedule for a $60,000 loan to be repaid in 20 equal annual installments at an interest rate of 20 percent. What is the annual payment?

M I N I
C A S E

Assume that you are nearing graduation and that you have applied for a job with a local bank. As part of the bank's evaluation process, you have been asked to take an examination which covers several financial analysis techniques. The first section of the test addresses discounted cash flow analysis. See how you would do by answering the following questions.

a. Draw time lines for (a) a $100 lump sum cash flow at the end of Year 2, (b) an ordinary annuity of $100 per year for 3 years, and (c) an uneven cash flow stream of − $50, $100, $75, and $50 at the end of Years 0 through 3.

b. (1) What is the future value of an initial $100 after 3 years if it is invested in an account paying 10 percent annual interest?
(2) What is the present value of $100 to be received in 3 years if the appropriate interest rate is 10 percent?

c. We sometimes need to find how long it will take a sum of money (or anything else) to grow to some specified amount. For example, if a company's sales are growing at a rate of 20 percent per year, how long will it take sales to double?

d. What is the difference between an ordinary annuity and an annuity due? What type of annuity is shown below? How would you change it to the other type of annuity?

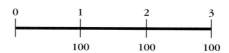

e. (1) What is the future value of a 3-year ordinary annuity of $100 if the appropriate interest rate is 10 percent?
(2) What is the present value of the annuity?
(3) What would the future and present values be if the annuity were an annuity due?

f. What is the present value of the following uneven cash flow stream? The appropriate interest rate is 10 percent, compounded annually.

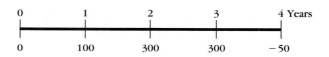

g. What annual interest rate will cause $100 to grow to $125.97 in 3 years?

h. (1) Will the future value be larger or smaller if we compound an initial amount more often than annually, for example, every 6 months, or *semiannually*, holding the stated interest rate constant? Why?

(2) Define (a) the stated, or quoted, or nominal rate (i_{Nom}), (b) the periodic rate (i_{Per}), and (c) the effective annual rate (EAR).

(3) What is the effective annual rate for a nominal rate of 10 percent, compounded semiannually? Compounded quarterly? Compounded daily?

(4) What is the future value of $100 after 3 years under 10 percent semiannual compounding? Quarterly compounding?

i. Will the effective annual rate ever be equal to the nominal (quoted) rate?

j. (1) What is the value at the end of Year 3 of the following cash flow stream if the quoted interest rate is 10 percent, compounded semiannually?

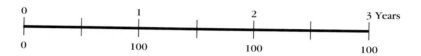

(2) What is the PV of the same stream?

(3) Is the stream an annuity?

(4) An important rule is that you should *never* show a nominal rate on a time line or use it in calculations unless what condition holds? (Hint: Think of annual compounding, when i_{Nom} = EAR = i_{Per}.) What would be wrong with your answer to questions j (1) and j (2) if you used the nominal rate 10% rather than the periodic rate $i_{Nom}/2$ = 10%/2 = 5%?

k. (1) Construct an amortization schedule for a $1,000, 10 percent annual rate loan with 3 equal installments.

(2) What is the annual interest expense for the borrower, and the annual interest income for the lender, during Year 2?

l. Suppose on January 1, 1994, you deposit $100 in an account that pays a nominal, or quoted, interest rate of 11.33463 percent, with interest added (compounded) daily. How much will you have in your account on October 1, or after 9 months?

m. Now suppose you leave your money in the bank for 21 months. Thus, on January 1, 1994, you deposit $100 in an account that pays a 12 percent effective annual interest rate. How much will be in your account on October 1, 1995?

n. Suppose someone offered to sell you a note calling for the payment of $1,000 fifteen months from today. They offer to sell it to you for $850. You have $850 in a bank time deposit which pays a 6.76649 percent nominal rate with daily compounding, which is a 7 percent effective annual interest rate, and you plan to leave the money in the bank unless you buy the note. The note is not risky—you are sure it will be paid on schedule. Should you buy the note? Check the decision in three ways: (1) by comparing your future value if you buy the note versus leaving your money in the bank, (2) by comparing the PV of the note with your current bank account, and (3) by comparing the EAR on the note versus that of the bank account.

o. Suppose the note discussed in Part n had a cost of $850, but called for 5 quarterly payments of $190 each, with the first payment due in 3 months rather than $1,000 at the end of 15 months. Would it be a good investment for you?

easy to ascertain what dividend IBM paid last year and the dividend it is currently paying, but those figures are not the basis for the value of the stock today. Rather, the relevant dividends are those that will be paid in the future. Will IBM's board cut the dividend again, or might it increase the dividend in the near future? Furthermore, was the January 1993 cut a response to temporary difficulties, or was it a signal of long-term problems that will permanently depress the firm's ability to increase its dividend over time? The answers to these and similar questions, which will not be known for years, are needed to estimate the dividend stream which provides the basis for IBM's stock value.

In this chapter, we will discuss how assets are valued. As you read the chapter, think about Jacobson's problem of whether to sell his IBM stock. Could he have used the techniques covered in the chapter to reach the decision to sell his stock some time ago and thus have avoided the large losses he incurred? Of course, for him and many other investors, that is water over the dam. As Jacobson said, the catastrophe that wasted his nest egg "really hurts a great deal, and I think about it daily." Perhaps you can avoid a similar disaster.

In Chapter 1 we noted that the goal of financial management is to maximize the values of firms. Then, in Chapter 5, we saw how investors determine the rates of return they require on securities, and in Chapter 6 we examined discounted cash flow (DCF) analysis. Now, in this chapter, we use DCF concepts to explain how investors establish the values of stocks and bonds. The material covered in the chapter is obviously important to investors, and it is equally important to financial managers. *Indeed, since all important corporate decisions should be analyzed in terms of how they will affect the price of the firm's stock, it is essential that managers know how stock prices are determined.*

GENERAL VALUATION MODEL

Since the values of most assets stem from streams of expected cash flows, all such assets are valued in essentially the same way: (1) The cash flow stream must be estimated, which involves finding both the expected cash flow for each period and the riskiness of that cash flow. (2) The required rate of return for each cash flow is established on the basis of its riskiness and the returns available on other investments; these rates could be constant over time, or different rates might be required for each cash flow. (3) Each cash flow is then discounted by its required rate of return. (4) Finally, these present values are summed to find the value of the asset. Equation 7-1 formalizes this process.[1]

---

[1]Equation 7-1 is presented in *risk-adjusted discount rate* format. Later, in Chapter 11, we will see that assets can also be valued by the *certainty equivalent* method.

$$V = \frac{CF_1}{(1 + k_1)^1} + \frac{CF_2}{(1 + k_2)^2} + \cdots + \frac{CF_t}{(1 + k_t)^t} + \cdots + \frac{CF_n}{(1 + k_n)^n}$$

$$= \sum_{t=1}^{n} \frac{CF_t}{(1 + k_t)^t}. \tag{7-1}$$

Here V is the current, or present, value of the asset; CF_t is the expected cash flow at Time t; k_t is the required rate of return for each period's cash flow; and n is the number of periods over which cash flows are expected to be generated. If the cash flow stream exhibits certain regularities, and if the required rate of return is constant, then Equation 7-1 can be reduced to a simpler form. We will examine several reduced forms in this chapter.

Note that the basic valuation model can be applied to physical assets as well as to financial assets. *Physical assets* are such assets as land, buildings, equipment, and even whole businesses. *Financial assets,* or *securities,* are pieces of paper which represent claims against physical assets. Moreover, business securities are generally broken down into three primary classes: (1) *debt,* which is a contractual obligation calling for specific payments; (2) *preferred stock,* which is also contractual in nature but which has a claim to income and assets after the firm's debt; and (3) *common stock,* which represents ownership and which has a residual claim to all income and assets after the claims of debtholders and preferred stockholders have been satisfied.

There are also variations within each of the primary types of business securities. For example, there is long-term and short-term debt, and some debt calls for periodic interest payments during its life and then a return of the principal in a lump sum at maturity, whereas other debt calls for amortization of the principal over the life of the debt. Some debt calls for fixed interest payments; other debt calls for variable interest payments, or even for payment in gold, silver, or oil rather than money. Some debt (and preferred stock) is convertible into common stock; some is backed by a mortgage on specific assets; and some is backed only by the firm's general credit strength.

Each of these variations calls for a somewhat different application of Equation 7-1. Indeed, since investment bankers have created an almost limitless variety of securities, with new ones being created every day, one could spend his or her career developing variations of the basic valuation model. However, at this point, we shall deal with models for the three basic business securities—bonds, preferred stock, and common stock. Later in the book, we shall go on to physical asset valuation (capital budgeting) and also to such special cases as option securities, leases, and mergers.

SELF-TEST QUESTIONS

Why is valuation an important concept to financial managers?

Write out the formula for the general valuation model and then describe its meaning in words.

BOND VALUATION

A *bond* is a long-term debt contract issued by a business or governmental unit. For example, on January 2, 1994, Allied Food Products borrowed $50 million by selling 50,000 individual bonds for $1,000 each. Allied received the $50 million, and it promised to pay the bondholders $7.5 million in annual interest and to repay the $50 million on a specified date. The lenders were willing to give Allied $50 million, so the value of the bond issue was $50 million. But how did the investors decide that the issue was worth $50 million? As a first step in explaining how the values of this and other bonds are determined, we need to define some terms:

1. **Par value.**   The *par value* is the stated face value of the bond; it is usually set at $1,000, although multiples of $1,000 (for example, $5,000) are often used. The par value generally represents the amount of money the firm borrows and promises to repay at some future date.

2. **Coupon interest rate.**   The bond requires the issuer to pay a specified number of dollars of interest each year (or, more typically, each six months). When this *coupon payment,* as it is called, is divided by the par value, the result is the *coupon interest rate.* For example, Allied's bonds have a $1,000 par value, and they pay $150 in interest each year. The bond's coupon interest is $150, so its coupon interest rate is $150/$1,000 = 15 percent. The $150 is the yearly "rent" on the $1,000 loan. This payment, which is fixed at the time the bond is issued, remains in force, by contract, during the life of the bond. Incidentally, some time ago, most bonds literally had a number of small (½- by 2-inch) dated coupons attached to them, and on the interest payment date, the owner would clip off the coupon for that date and either cash it at his or her bank or mail it to the company's paying agent, who then mailed back a check for the interest. A 30-year, semi-annual bond would start with 60 coupons, whereas a 5-year, annual payment bond would start with only 5 coupons. Today, most bonds are *registered*—no physical coupons are involved, and interest checks are mailed automatically to the registered owners of the bonds. Even so, people continue to use the terms *coupon* and *coupon interest rate* when discussing registered bonds.

3. **Maturity date.**   Bonds generally have a specified *maturity date* on which the par value must be repaid. Allied's bonds, which were issued on January 2, 1994, will mature on January 1, 2009; thus, they had a 15-year maturity at the time they were issued. Most bonds have *original maturities* (the maturity at the time the bond is issued) of from 10 to 40 years, but any maturity is legally permissible. Of course, the effective maturity of a bond declines each year after it has been issued. Thus, Allied's bonds had a 15-year original maturity, but in 1995 they will have a 14-year maturity, and so on.

4. **Call provisions.**   Most bonds have a provision whereby the issuer may pay them off prior to maturity. This feature is known as a *call provision,* and it is discussed in detail in Chapter 20. If a bond is callable, and if interest rates in the economy decline, then the company can sell a new issue of low-interest-rate bonds and use the proceeds to retire the old, high-interest-rate issue, just as a homeowner can refinance a home mortgage.

5. New issues versus outstanding bonds. As we shall see, a bond's market price is determined primarily by its coupon interest payments — the higher the coupon, other things held constant, the higher the market price of the bond. At the time a bond is issued, the coupon is generally set at a level that will cause the market price of the bond to equal its par value. If a lower coupon were set, investors simply would not be willing to pay $1,000 for the bond, while if a higher coupon were set, investors would clamor for the bond and bid its price up over $1,000. Investment bankers can judge quite precisely the coupon rate that will cause a bond to sell at its $1,000 par value.

A bond that has just been issued is known as a *new issue*. (*The Wall Street Journal* classifies a bond as a new issue for about one month after it has first been issued.) Once the bond has been on the market for a while, it is classified as an *outstanding bond,* also called a *seasoned issue.* Newly issued bonds generally sell very close to par, but the prices of outstanding bonds vary widely from par. Coupon interest payments are constant, so when economic conditions change, a bond with a $150 coupon that sold at par when it was issued will sell for more or less than $1,000 thereafter.

THE BASIC BOND VALUATION MODEL

As we noted previously, the value of any financial asset — a stock, a bond, a lease, and even a physical asset such as an apartment building or a piece of machinery — is based on the present value of the cash flows the asset is expected to produce. In the case of a bond, the cash flows consist of interest payments during the life of the bond plus a return of the principal amount borrowed, generally the par value, when the bond matures. In a time line format, here is the situation:

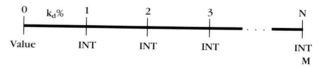

Here

k_d = the appropriate interest rate on the bond = 15%. We used the term "i" or "I" to designate the interest rate in Chapter 6 because those terms are used on financial calculators, but "k," with the subscript "d" to designate the rate on a debt security, is normally used in finance.[2]

N = the number of years before the bond matures = 15. Note that N declines each year after the bond has been issued, so a bond that had a maturity of 15 years when it was issued (original maturity = 15) will have N = 14

---

[2]The appropriate interest rate on debt securities was discussed in Chapter 3. The bond's riskiness, liquidity, and years to maturity, as well as supply and demand conditions in the capital markets, all influence the interest rate on bonds.

Had interest rates risen from 15 to 20 percent during the first year after issue rather than fallen, the value of the bond would have declined to $769.49:

$$V_B = \$150(PVIFA_{20\%,14}) + \$1,000(PVIF_{20\%,14})$$
$$= \$150(4.6106) + \$1,000(0.0779) = \$769.49.$$

In this case, the bond would sell at a *discount* of $230.51 below its par value:

$$Discount = Price - Par\ value = \$769.49 - \$1,000.00$$
$$= -\$230.51.$$

The total expected future yield on the bond would again consist of a current yield and a capital gains yield, but now the capital gains yield would be *positive*. The total yield would be 20 percent. To see this, calculate the price of the bond with 13 years left to maturity, assuming that interest rates remain at 20 percent. With a calculator, enter N = 13, I = 20, PMT = 150, and FV = 1000, and then press PV to obtain the bond's value, $773.37. Using the tables, proceed as follows:

$$V_B = \$150(PVIFA_{20\%,13}) + \$1,000(PVIF_{20\%,13})$$
$$= \$150(4.5327) + \$1,000(0.0935) = \$773.41\ (rounding\ difference).$$

Notice that the capital gain for the year is the difference between the bond's value in Year 13 and the bond's value in Year 14, or $773.41 − $769.49 = $3.92. The interest yield, capital gains yield, and total yield are calculated as follows:

Interest, or current, yield = $150/$769.49 = 0.1949 = 19.49%

Capital gains yield = $3.92/$769.49 = 0.0051 = 0.51%

Total rate of return, or yield = $153.92/$769.49 = 0.2000 = 20.00%

The discount or premium on a bond may also be calculated as the PV of the difference in interest payments, discounted at the new interest rate:

$$\begin{array}{c} Discount \\ or\ premium \end{array} = \left[\begin{array}{c} Interest\ payment \\ on\ the\ old\ bond \end{array} - \begin{array}{c} Interest\ payment \\ on\ the\ new\ bond \end{array} \right] (PVIFA_{k_d,N}).$$

Here N = years to maturity on the old bond and k_d = current rate of interest on a new bond. For example, if interest rates had risen to 20 percent 1 year after the Allied bonds were issued, the discount on them would have been calculated as follows:

$$Discount = (\$150 - \$200)(4.6106) = -\$230.53.$$

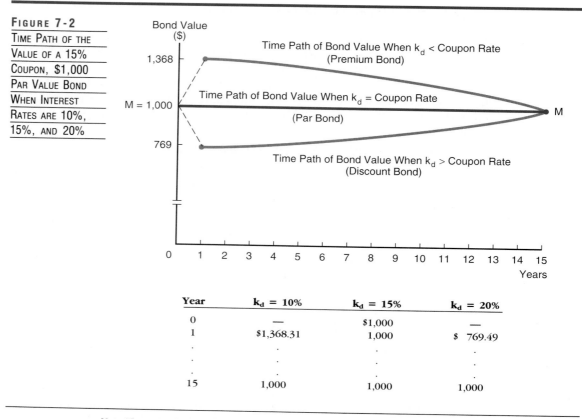

FIGURE 7-2

TIME PATH OF THE VALUE OF A 15% COUPON, $1,000 PAR VALUE BOND WHEN INTEREST RATES ARE 10%, 15%, AND 20%

Year	$k_d = 10\%$	$k_d = 15\%$	$k_d = 20\%$
0	—	$1,000	—
1	$1,368.31	1,000	$ 769.49
.	.	.	.
.	.	.	.
.	.	.	.
15	1,000	1,000	1,000

Note: The curves for 10% and 20% have a slight bow.

(The minus sign indicates discount.) This value agrees, except for rounding, with the − $230.51 value calculated previously. From these calculations, we see that the discount is equal to the present value of the interest payments you would sacrifice if you were to buy a low-coupon old bond rather than a high-coupon new bond. The longer the bond has left to maturity, the greater the sacrifice, hence the greater the discount.

Figure 7-2 graphs the value of the bond over time, assuming that interest rates in the economy (1) remain constant at 15 percent, (2) fall to 10 percent and then remain constant at that level, or (3) rise to 20 percent and remain constant at that level. Of course, if interest rates do *not* remain constant, then the price of the bond will fluctuate. However, regardless of what future interest rates do, the bond's price will approach $1,000 as it nears the maturity date (barring bankruptcy, in which case the bond's value might drop to zero).

Figure 7-2 illustrates the following key points:

1. Whenever the going rate of interest, k_d, is equal to the coupon rate, a bond will sell at its par value. Normally, the coupon rate is set equal to the going interest rate when a bond is issued, so it initially sells at par.

2. Interest rates do change over time, but the coupon rate remains fixed after the bond has been issued. Whenever the going rate of interest is *greater than* the coupon rate, a bond's price will fall *below* its par value. Such a bond is called a *discount bond.*

3. Whenever the going rate of interest is *less than* the coupon rate, a bond's price will rise *above* its par value. Such a bond is called a *premium bond.*

4. Thus, an *increase* in interest rates will cause the price of an outstanding bond to *fall,* whereas a *decrease* in rates will cause it to *rise.*

5. The market value of a bond will always approach its par value as its maturity date approaches, provided the firm does not go bankrupt.

These points are very important, for they show that bondholders may suffer capital losses or make capital gains, depending on whether interest rates rise or fall after the bond was purchased. And, as we saw in Chapter 3, interest rates do indeed change over time.

FINDING THE INTEREST RATE ON A BOND: YIELD TO MATURITY

Suppose you were offered a 14-year, 15 percent coupon, $1,000 par value bond at a price of $1,368.31. What rate of interest would you earn on your investment if you bought the bond and held it to maturity? This rate is called the bond's *yield to maturity (YTM),* and it is the interest rate discussed by bond traders when they talk about rates of return. To find the yield to maturity, you could solve Equation 7-2 or 7-3 for k_d:

$$V_B = \$1,368.31 = \frac{\$150}{(1 + k_d)^1} + \cdots + \frac{\$150}{(1 + k_d)^{14}} + \frac{\$1,000}{(1 + k_d)^{14}}$$

$$= \$150(PVIFA_{k_d,14}) + \$1,000(PVIF_{k_d,14}).$$

Here, you must substitute values for PVIFA and PVIF until you find a pair that "works" and forces this equality:

$$\$1,368.31 = \$150(PVIFA_{k_d,14}) + \$1,000(PVIF_{k_d,14}).$$

What would be a good interest rate to use as a starting point? First, you know that the bond is selling at a premium over its par value ($1,368.31 versus $1,000), so the bond's yield to maturity must be *below* its 15 percent coupon rate. Therefore, you might try a rate of 12 percent. Substituting interest factors for 12 percent, you obtain

$$\$150(6.6282) + \$1,000(0.2046) = \$1,198.83 \neq \$1,368.31.$$

The calculated bond value, $1,198.83, is *below* the actual market price, so the YTM is *not* 12 percent. To raise the calculated value, you must *lower* the interest rate used in the process, because lower interest rates mean higher bond prices. Inserting interest factors for 10 percent, you obtain

$$V_B = \$150(7.3667) + \$1,000(0.2633)\$263.30 = \$1,368.31.$$

This calculated value is equal to the market price of the bond, so 10 percent is the bond's yield to maturity: $k_d = YTM = 10.0\%$.[5]

As you might guess, by far the easiest way to find a bond's YTM is with a financial calculator:

Inputs:	14		-1368.31	150	1000
	N	**I**	**PV**	**PMT**	**FV**
Output:		$= 10$			

Simply enter N = 14, PV = -1368.31 (or 1368.31 on some calculators), PMT = 150, and FV = 1000, and then press the I key. The answer, 10 percent will then appear.

The yield to maturity, which is (approximately) the bond's expected rate of return, is identical to the total rate of return discussed in the preceding section.[6] The YTM for a bond that sells at par consists entirely of an interest yield, but if the bond sells at a price other than its par value, the YTM consists of the interest yield plus a positive or negative capital gains yield. Note also that a bond's yield to maturity changes whenever interest rates in the economy change, and this is almost daily. One who purchases a bond and holds it until it matures will receive the YTM that existed on the purchase date, but the bond's calculated YTM will change frequently between the purchase date and the maturity date.

YIELD TO CALL

If you purchased a bond that was callable and the company called it, you would not have the option of holding it until it matured, so the yield to maturity would not be earned. For example, if Allied's 15 percent coupon bonds were callable,

---

[5]A few years ago, bond traders all had specialized tables called *bond tables* that gave yields on bonds of different maturities selling at different premiums and discounts. Because calculators are so much more efficient (and accurate), bond tables are rarely used anymore.

[6]Actually, a bond's YTM is the *promised rate of return* if it is held to maturity. The YTM is a bond's expected rate of return only if (1) the probability of default is zero, (2) the probability of a call is zero, and (3) interest rates are expected to remain at their current levels over the life of the bond.

and if interest rates fell from 15 percent to 10 percent, then the company could call in the 15 percent bonds, replace them with 10 percent bonds, and save $150 − $100 = $50 interest per bond per year. This would be beneficial to the company, but not to the bondholders.

If current interest rates are well below an outstanding bond's coupon rate, then a callable bond is likely to be called, and investors should estimate the expected rate of return on the bond as the *yield to call (YTC)* rather than as the yield to maturity. To calculate the YTC, solve this equation for k_d:

$$\text{Price of callable bond} = \sum_{t=1}^{N} \frac{\text{INT}}{(1 + k_d)^t} + \frac{\text{Call price}}{(1 + k_d)^N}. \qquad (7\text{-}4)$$

Here N is the number of years until the company can call the bond; call price is the price the company must pay in order to call the bond (it is often set equal to the par value plus one year's interest); and k_d is the YTC.

To illustrate the yield-to-call calculation, suppose Allied's bonds had a provision that the company, if it wanted to, could call the bonds 10 years after the issue date at a price of $1,150. Suppose further that interest rates had fallen, such that one year after issuance, k_d was 10 percent and the price of the bonds was $1,368.31. Here is the setup for finding the bond's YTC with a financial calculator:

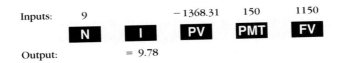

Inputs: 9   − 1368.31   150   1150

      [N]   [I]   [PV]   [PMT]   [FV]

Output: = 9.78

The YTC is 9.78 percent—this is the return you would earn if you bought the bond at a price of $1,368.31 and it was called 9 years from today at a price of $1,150. (The bond could not be called for 10 years after issuance, and 1 year has gone by, so there are 9 years left until the first call date.)

Do you think Allied *will* call the bonds when they become callable? Allied's action will depend on what the going interest rate is when the bonds become callable. If the going rate remains at k_d = 10%, then Allied could save 15% − 10% = 5%, or $50 per bond per year, by calling them and replacing the 15 percent bonds with a new 10 percent issue. There would be costs to the company to refund the issue, but the interest savings would probably be worth the cost, so Allied would probably refund the bonds. Therefore, there is a good chance that you would actually end up earning YTC = 9.78% rather than YTM = 10% if you bought the bonds under the indicated conditions.

The analysis used to decide whether or not to call a bond is covered in detail in Chapter 20 and Appendix 20A. In the balance of this chapter, we assume that bonds are not callable unless otherwise noted, but some of the end-of-chapter problems deal with yield to call.

BOND VALUES WITH SEMIANNUAL COMPOUNDING

Although some bonds pay interest annually, most actually pay interest semi-annually. To evaluate semiannual payment bonds, we must modify the bond valuation models (Equations 7-2 and 7-3) as follows:

1. Divide the annual coupon interest payment by 2 to determine the amount of interest paid each 6 months.

2. Multiply the years to maturity, N, by 2 to determine the number of semiannual periods.

3. Divide the annual interest rate, k_d, by 2 to determine the periodic (semiannual) interest rate.

By making these changes, we obtain the following equations for finding the value of a bond that pays interest semiannually:

$$V_B = \sum_{t=1}^{2N} \frac{INT/2}{(1 + k_d/2)^t} + \frac{M}{(1 + k_d/2)^{2N}} \qquad (7\text{-}2a)$$

$$= \frac{INT}{2}(PVIFA_{k_d/2,2N}) + M(PVIF_{k_d/2,2N}). \qquad (7\text{-}3a)$$

To illustrate, assume now that Allied Food Products' bonds pay $75 interest each 6 months rather than $150 at the end of each year. Thus, each interest payment is only half as large, but there are twice as many of them. If the annual (nominal) required rate of interest on this 15-year semiannual payment bond is 10 percent, its value is found as follows:

$$V_B = \$75(PVIFA_{5\%,30}) + \$1,000(PVIF_{5\%,30})$$
$$= \$75(15.3725) + \$1,000(0.2314) = \$1,384.34.$$

With a financial calculator, enter N = 30, k = I = 5, PMT = 75, FV = 1000, and then press the PV key to obtain the bond's value, $1,384.31 (rounding difference):

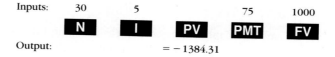

Inputs: 30   5   75   1000

Output: = −1384.31

The value with semiannual interest payments is slightly larger than $1,380.32, the value when interest is paid annually.

Students sometimes want to discount the maturity value at 10 percent over 15 years rather than at 5 percent over 30 six-month periods. This is incorrect. Logically, all cash flows in a given contract must be discounted at the same peri-

odic rate, the 5 percent semiannual rate in this instance. For consistency, bond traders *must* use the same discount rate for all cash flows, including the cash flow at maturity, and they do.

Note that when we changed the coupon payments from annual to semiannual, we obtained the discount rate by dividing the 10 percent nominal required rate of interest by 2, which produced a 5 percent semiannual discount rate. When we apply this rate, we are actually assuming an effective annual rate (EAR) of interest of 10.25 percent:

$$EAR = (1.05)^2 - 1.0 = 1.1025 - 1.0 = 0.1025 = 10.25\%.$$

If we wanted to discount the semiannual bond using a 10 percent effective annual rate, then the semiannual discount rate would be 4.88 percent rather than the 5 percent used in the example:

$$EAR = (1 + \text{Semiannual rate})^2 - 1.0 = 10.0\% = 0.10$$

$$(1 + \text{Semiannual rate})^2 = 1.10$$

$$1 + \text{Semiannual rate} = 1.0488$$

$$\text{Semiannual rate} = 0.0488 = 4.88\%.$$

At a 4.88 percent semiannual discount rate, the bond's value is $1,408.33 versus $1,384.31 at a 5 percent semiannual rate.

In practice, bond professionals work with nominal rates; that is, the required interest rate in our example would be stated as 10 percent, and the actual discount rate applied in the valuation process would be 5 percent per semiannual period. Since bond traders, dealers, and investors all value bonds in this way, we will use this convention throughout the text. Bond professionals tend to deal exclusively in semiannual coupon bonds, so this valuation method usually causes no problems. Note, however, that a 10 percent nominal rate (or a 10 percent yield to maturity) under semiannual compounding implies a 10.25 percent effective annual rate, so when bonds are being compared to securities with compounding other than semiannual, it is best to think in terms of a bond's effective annual rate rather than its nominal rate.

INTEREST RATE RISK ON A BOND

As we saw in Chapter 3, interest rates go up and down over time, and such changes give rise to two types of risk that fall under the general classification of *interest rate risk*. First, an increase in interest rates leads to a decline in the values of outstanding bonds. Since interest rates can rise, bondholders face the risk of losses in the values of their portfolios. This risk is called *price risk*. Second, many bondholders (including such institutional bondholders as pension funds and life insurance companies) buy bonds to build funds for some future use. These bondholders reinvest the cash flows (interest payments plus repayment of principal when the

bonds mature or are called). If interest rates decline, the bondholders will earn a lower rate of return on reinvested cash flows, and this will reduce the future value of their portfolios relative to the values they would have had if interest rates had not fallen. This risk is called *reinvestment rate risk.*

We see, then, that any given change in interest rates has two separate effects on bondholders—it changes the current values of their portfolios (price risk), and it also changes the rates of return at which the cash flows from their portfolios can be reinvested (reinvestment rate risk). Note that these two risks tend to offset one another. For example, an increase in interest rates will lower the current value of a bond portfolio, but since the future cash flows produced by the portfolio will then be reinvested at a higher rate of return, the future value of the portfolio will be increased. In this section we will look at just how these two effects operate to affect bondholders' positions.[7]

Suppose you bought some 15 percent Allied bonds at a price of $1,000, and interest rates subsequently rose to 20 percent. As we saw before, the price of the bonds would fall to $769.49, so you would have a loss of $230.51 per bond.[8] One's exposure to price risk is higher on bonds with long maturities than on those maturing in the near future. This point can be demonstrated by showing how the value of a 1-year bond with a 15 percent coupon fluctuates with changes in k_d and then comparing these changes with those on a 14-year bond as calculated previously. The 1-year bond's values at different interest rates are shown below:

Value at $k_d = 10\%$:

$$V_B = \$150(\text{PVIFA}_{10\%,1}) + \$1,000(\text{PVIF}_{10\%,1})$$
$$= \$150(0.9091) + \$1,000(0.9091) = \$1,045.47.$$

---

[7]Actually, we will stop short of a full examination of the effects of interest rate changes on bondholders' positions, as such an examination would go well beyond the scope of the text. We can note, though, that a concept called *duration* has been developed to help fixed income investors deal with interest rate risk, and, with a properly structured portfolio (one that has the proper duration), most of the risks of changing interest rates can be eliminated because price risk and reinvestment rate risk can be made to offset one another. A bond's duration can be thought of as the "average date" that a holder will receive cash flows (interest and principal repayment) on the bond. For a zero coupon bond, with only one cash inflow, the duration is the same as the maturity. For coupon bonds, the duration is less than the years to maturity. The duration of an annual coupon bond is calculated by use of this formula:

$$\text{Duration} = \sum_{t=1}^{n} \frac{t(\text{PVCF}_t)}{\sum_{t=1}^{n} \text{PVCF}_t} = \sum_{t=1}^{n} \frac{t(\text{PVCF}_t)}{\text{Value}}.$$

Here n is the bond's years to maturity, t is the year each cash flow occurs, and PVCF_t is the present value of the cash flow at Year t discounted at the current rate of interest. Note that the denominator of the equation is merely the current value of the bond.

[8]You would have an *accounting* (and tax) loss only if you sold the bond; if you held it to maturity, you would not have such a loss. However, even if you did not sell, you would still have suffered a *real economic loss in an opportunity cost sense* because you would have lost the opportunity to invest at 20 percent and would be stuck with a 15 percent bond in a 20 percent market. Thus, in an economic sense "paper losses" are just as bad as realized accounting losses.

Value at $k_d = 15\%$:

$$V_B = \$150(0.8696) + \$1,000(0.8696) = \$1,000.04 \approx \$1,000.$$

Value at $k_d = 20\%$:

$$V_B = \$150(0.8333) + \$1,000(0.8333) = \$958.30.$$

You could obtain the first value with a financial calculator by entering $N = 1$, $I = 10$, $PMT = 150$, and $FV = 1000$, and then pressing PV to get $\$1,045.45$. With everything still in your calculator, enter $I = 15$ to override the old $I = 10$, and press PV to find the bond's value at $k_d = I = 15$; it is $\$1,000$. Then enter $I = 20$ and press the PV key to find the last bond value, $\$958.33$. (Rounding differences occur in these calculations.)

The values of the 1-year and 14-year bonds at several current market interest rates are summarized and plotted in Figure 7-3. Notice how much more sensitive the price of the long-term bond is to changes in interest rates. At a 15 percent interest rate, both the long- and the short-term bonds are valued at $\$1,000$. When rates rise to 20 percent, the long-term bond falls to $\$769.47$, but the short-term bond falls only to $\$958.33$.

For bonds with similar coupons, this differential sensitivity to changes in interest rates always holds true—the longer the maturity of the bond, the greater its price changes in response to a given change in interest rates. Thus, even if the risk of default on two bonds is exactly the same, the one with the longer maturity is typically exposed to more price risk from a rise in interest rates.[9]

The logical explanation for this difference in price risk is simple. Suppose you bought a 14-year bond that yielded 15 percent, or $\$150$ a year. Now suppose interest rates on comparable-risk bonds rose to 20 percent. You would be stuck with only $\$150$ of interest for the next 14 years. On the other hand, had you bought a 1-year bond, you would have had a low return for only 1 year. At the end of the year, you would get your $\$1,000$ back, and you could then reinvest it and receive 20 percent, or $\$200$ per year, for the next 13 years. Thus, price risk reflects the length of time one is committed to a given investment.

Although a 1-year bond has less price risk than a 14-year bond, the 1-year bond exposes the buyer to more reinvestment rate risk. Suppose you bought a 1-year bond that yielded 15 percent, and then interest rates on comparable-risk bonds fell to 10 percent. After 1 year, when you got your $\$1,000$ back, you would have to invest it at only 10 percent, so you would lose $\$150 - \$100 = \$50$ in annual interest. Had you bought the 14-year bond, you would have continued to receive $\$150$ in annual interest payments even if rates fell. If you reinvested those coupon

---

[9]If a 10-year bond were plotted in Figure 7-3, its curve would lie between those of the 14-year bond and the 1-year bond. The curve of a 1-month bond would be almost horizontal, indicating that its price would change very little in response to an interest rate change, but a perpetuity would have a very steep slope.

FIGURE 7-3

VALUE OF LONG- AND
SHORT-TERM 15%
ANNUAL COUPON
RATE BONDS AT
DIFFERENT MARKET
INTEREST RATES

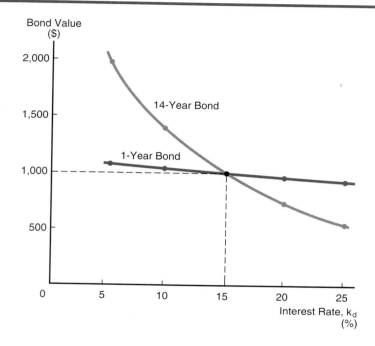

| | **Value of** | |
Current Market Interest Rate, k_d	**1-Year Bond**	**14-Year Bond**
5%	$1,095.24	$1,989.86
10	1,045.45	1,368.33
15	1,000.00	1,000.00
20	958.33	769.47
25	920.00	617.59

Note: Bond values were calculated using a financial calculator.

payments, you would have to accept a lower rate of return, but you would still be much better off than if you had been holding the 1-year bond.

BOND PRICES IN RECENT YEARS

We have just seen that the prices of outstanding bonds rise and fall inversely with changes in interest rates. Figure 7-4 shows what has happened to the price of a typical bond, Alabama Power's 7½ percent, 30-year bond which matures in 2002. When this bond was issued in 1972, it was worth $1,000, but at the interest rate peak from 1981 to 1982, it sold for only $520. However, the ensuing drop in interest rates caused the price of the bond to rise, and by 1993 it was almost back

FIGURE 7-4   ALABAMA POWER 7½%, 30-YEAR BOND: MARKET VALUE AS INTEREST RATES CHANGE

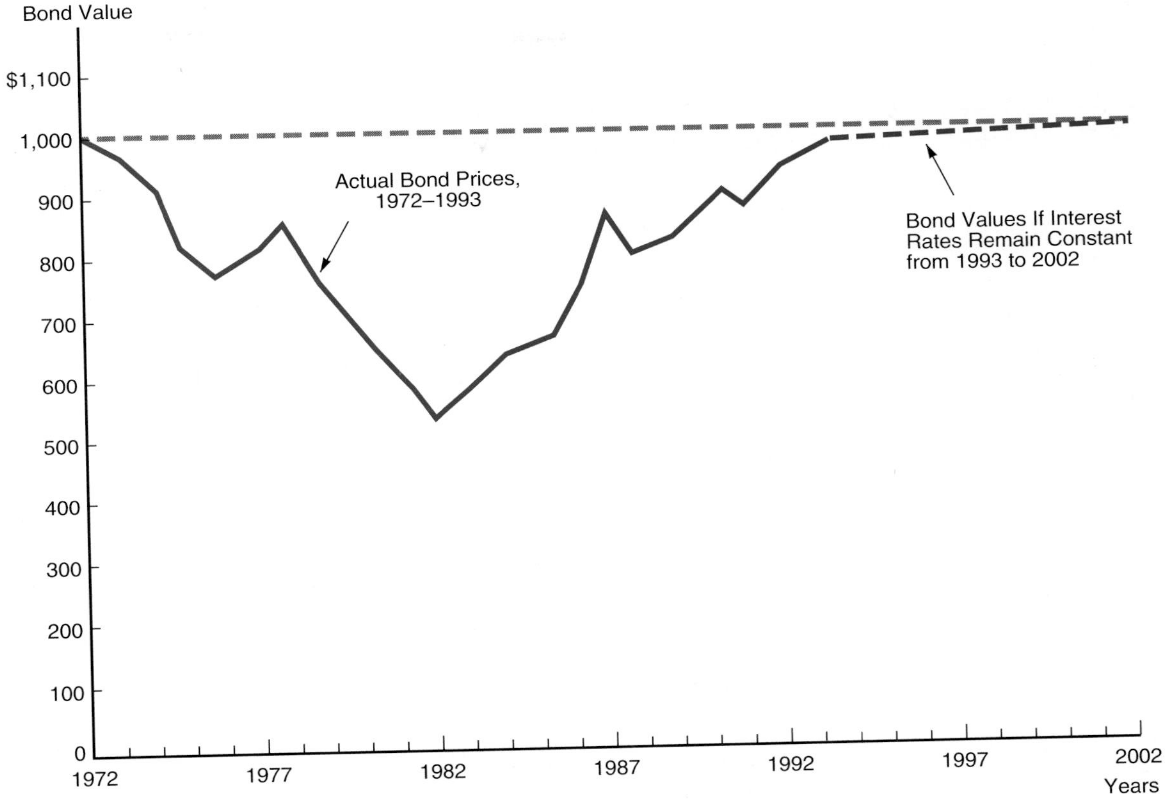

Note: The line from 1993 to 2002 appears linear, but it actually has a slight curve.

to par at $990. The graph also shows that if interest rates remain at the 1993 level, the price of the bond will gradually rise, and it will sell for $1,000 (plus accrued interest) just before it matures in 2002.

BOND MARKETS

Corporate bonds are traded primarily in the over-the-counter market. Most bonds are owned by and traded among the large financial institutions (for example, life insurance companies, mutual funds, and pension funds, all of which deal in very large blocks of securities), and it is relatively easy for the over-the-counter bond

FIGURE 7-5
NYSE BOND MARKET
TRANSACTIONS,
MAY 11, 1993

CORPORATION BONDS
Volume, $43,180,000

Bonds	Cur Yld	Vol	Close	Net Chg.
ATT 4⅜96	4.4	142	99⅝ −	⅛
ATT 5½97	5.5	60	100⅜ +	⅛
ATT 4⅜99	4.7	76	94 −	1
ATT 6s00	6.0	666	100⅛	...
ATT 5⅛01	5.4	44	94½ +	⅜
ATT 8⅝31	7.7	484	111½ −	¼
ATT 7⅛02	6.8	140	105¼ −	¼
ATT 8⅛22	7.6	270	107 +	¼
ATT 8⅛24	7.6	20	107½ +	¼
ATT 4½96	4.5	55	100¼	...

Source: *The Wall Street Journal,* May 12, 1993.

dealers to arrange the transfer of large blocks of bonds among the relatively few holders of the bonds. It would be much more difficult to conduct similar operations in the stock market among the literally millions of large and small stockholders, so a higher percentage of stock trades occur on the exchanges.

Information on bond trades in the over-the-counter market is not published, but a representative group of bonds is listed and traded on the bond division of the NYSE. Figure 7-5 gives a section of the bond market page of *The Wall Street Journal* for trading on May 11, 1993. A total of 454 issues were traded on that date, but we show only the bonds of AT&T. Note that AT&T had 10 different bonds that were traded on May 11; the company actually had 16 bond issues outstanding, but some of them did not trade on that date.

The AT&T and other bonds can have various denominations, but, for convenience, we generally think of each bond as having a par value of $1,000—this is how much the company borrowed per bond and how much it must someday repay. However, since other denominations are possible, for trading and reporting purposes bonds are quoted as percentages of par. Looking at the first bond listed, we see that there is a 4⅜ just after the company's name; this indicates that the bond is of the series which pays 4⅜ percent interest, or 0.04375($1,000) = $43.75 of interest per year. The 4⅜ percent is the bond's *coupon rate.* The 96 which comes next indicates that this bond matures and must be repaid in the year 1996; it is not shown in the figure, but this bond was issued in 1956, so it had a 40-year original maturity. The 4.4 in the second column is the bond's *current yield,* which is defined as the annual interest payment divided by the closing price of the bond: Current yield = $43.75/$996.25 = 4.39%, rounded to 4.4 percent. The 142 in the third column indicates that 142 of these bonds were traded on May 11, 1993. Since the price shown in the fourth column is expressed as a percentage of par, the bond closed at 99⅝ percent, which translates to $996.25, down ⅛ of 1 percent, or $1.25, from the previous day's close.

Coupon rates are generally set at levels which reflect the "going rate of interest" on the day a bond is issued. If the rates were set lower, investors simply would not buy the bonds at the $1,000 par value, so the company could not borrow the

money it needed. Thus, bonds generally sell at their par values on the day they are issued, but bond prices fluctuate thereafter as interest rates change. As seen in Figure 7-5, some of AT&T's bonds sold above par, and some below par, but not one bond sold at par on May 11.

All of the bonds traded on a given day are listed in the newspaper (and hence in Figure 7-5) in alphabetical order by company and in the order of the dates on which they were originally issued, beginning with the earliest bond issued. Thus, the coupon rates shown in Figure 7-5 generally rise as we move down the list, reflecting the fact that interest rates have generally risen over time, except for the past few years.

SELF-TEST QUESTIONS

In what two primary forms do corporations raise capital?

What is meant by the terms "new issue" and "seasoned issue"?

Explain, verbally, the following equation:

$$V_B = \sum_{t=1}^{N} \frac{INT}{(1 + k_d)^t} + \frac{M}{(1 + k_d)^N}.$$

Explain what happens to the price of a bond if (1) interest rates rise above the bond's coupon rate or (2) interest rates fall below the bond's coupon rate.

Write out a formula that can be used to calculate the discount or premium on a bond, and explain it.

Differentiate between price risk and reinvestment rate risk.

How does the calculation of a bond's value differ between a bond that is likely to be called and one that is not?

How is the bond valuation formula shown just above changed to deal with bonds that have semiannual coupons rather than annual coupons?

PREFERRED STOCK VALUATION

Preferred stock is a *hybrid* — it is similar to bonds in some respects and to common stock in other respects. Preferred dividends are similar to interest payments on bonds in that they are fixed in amount and generally must be paid before common stock dividends can be paid. However, like common dividends, preferred dividends can be omitted without bankrupting the firm, and many preferred issues have no specific maturity date.

Most preferred stocks entitle their owners to regular, fixed dividend payments. If the payments last forever, the issue is a perpetuity whose value V_{ps}, is found as follows:

$$V_{ps} = \frac{D_{ps}}{k_{ps}}. \qquad (7\text{-}5)$$

V_{ps} is the value of the preferred stock, D_{ps} is the preferred dividend, and k_{ps} is the required rate of return. Allied Food Products has preferred stock outstanding which pays a dividend of $10 per year. If the required rate of return on this preferred stock is 10 percent, its value is $100, found by solving Equation 7-5 as follows:

$$V_{ps} = \frac{\$10.00}{0.10} = \$100.00.$$

If we know the current price of a perpetual preferred stock and its dividend, we can solve for the current rate being earned, as follows:

$$k_{ps} = \frac{D_{ps}}{V_{ps}}. \qquad (7\text{-}5a)$$

SELF-TEST QUESTION

In what way is preferred stock similar to bonds, and in what respect is it similar to common stock?

COMMON STOCK VALUATION

Common stock represents an ownership interest in a corporation, but to the typical investor, a share of common stock is simply a piece of paper characterized by two features:

1. It entitles its owner to dividends, but only if the company has earnings out of which dividends can be paid and only if management chooses to pay dividends rather than to retain and reinvest all the earnings. Whereas a bond contains a *promise* to pay interest, common stock provides no such promise to pay dividends—if you own a stock, you may *expect* a dividend, but your expectations may not in fact be met. To illustrate, Long Island Lighting Company (LILCO) had paid dividends on its common stock for more than 50 years, and people expected these dividends to continue. However, when the company encountered severe problems a few years ago, it stopped paying dividends. Note, though, that LILCO continued to pay interest on its bonds; if it had not, then it would have been declared bankrupt, and the bondholders could have taken over the company.

2. Stock can be sold at some future date, hopefully at a price greater than the purchase price. If the stock is actually sold at a price above its purchase price, the investor will receive a *capital gain.* Generally, at the time people buy common stocks, they do expect to receive capital gains; otherwise, they would not buy the stocks. However, after the fact, one can end up with capital losses rather than capital gains. LILCO's stock price dropped from $17.50 to $3.75 in one year, so the *expected* capital gains on that stock turned out to be *actual* capital losses.

DEFINITIONS OF TERMS USED IN THE STOCK VALUATION MODELS

Common stocks provide an expected future cash flow stream, and a stock's value is found in the same manner as the values of other financial assets—namely, as the present value of the expected future cash flow stream. The expected cash flows consist of two elements: (1) the dividends expected in each year and (2) the price investors expect to receive when they sell the stock. The expected final stock price includes the return of the original investment plus an expected capital gain.

We saw in Chapter 1 that managers seek to maximize the values of their firms' stocks. A manager's actions affect both the stream of income to investors and the riskiness of that stream. Therefore, the manager needs to know how alternative actions are likely to affect stock prices, so at this point we develop some models to help show how the value of a share of stock is determined. We begin by defining the following terms:

D_t = dividend the stockholder *expects* to receive at the end of Year t. D_0 is the most recent dividend, which has already been paid; D_1 is the first dividend expected, and it will be paid at the end of this year; D_2 is the dividend expected at the end of 2 years; and so forth. D_1 represents the first cash flow a new purchaser of the stock will receive. Note that D_0, the dividend which has just been paid, is known with certainty. However, all future dividends are expected values, so the estimate of D_t may differ among investors.[10]

P_0 = actual *market price* of the stock today.

$\hat{P}_t$ = expected price of the stock at the end of each Year t (pronounced "P hat t"). $\hat{P}_0$ is the *intrinsic,* or *theoretical, value* of the stock today as seen by the particular investor doing the analysis; $\hat{P}_1$ is the price expected at the end of 1 year; and so on. Note that $\hat{P}_0$ is the intrinsic value of the stock today based on a particular investor's estimate of

---

[10]Stocks generally pay dividends quarterly, so theoretically we should evaluate them on a quarterly basis. However, in stock valuation, most analysts work on an annual basis because the data generally are not precise enough to warrant refinement to a quarterly model. For additional information on the quarterly model, see Charles M. Linke and J. Kenton Zumwalt, "Estimation Biases in Discounted Cash Flow Analysis of Equity Capital Cost in Rate Regulation," *Financial Management,* Autumn 1984, 15–21.

the stock's expected dividend stream and the riskiness of that stream. Hence, whereas P_0 is fixed and is identical for all investors, $\hat{P}_0$ could differ among investors depending on how optimistic they are regarding the company. The caret, or "hat," is used to indicate that $\hat{P}_t$ is an estimated value. $\hat{P}_0$, the individual investor's estimate of the intrinsic value today, could be above or below P_0, the current stock price, but an investor would buy the stock only if his or her estimate of $\hat{P}_0$ were equal to or greater than P_0.

Since there are many investors in the market, there can be many values for $\hat{P}_0$. However, we can think of a group of "marginal" investors whose actions actually determine the market price. For these marginal investors, P_0 must equal $\hat{P}_0$; otherwise, a disequilibrium would exist, and buying and selling in the market would change P_0 until $P_0 = \hat{P}_0$ for marginal investors.

g = expected *growth rate* in dividends. (If we assume that dividends are expected to grow at a constant rate, g is also equal to the expected rate of growth in the stock's price.) Different investors may use different g's to evaluate a firm's stock, but the market price, P_0, is set on the basis of the g estimated by marginal investors.

k_s = minimum acceptable, or *required, rate of return* on the stock, considering both its riskiness and the returns available on other investments. The determinants of k_s were discussed in detail in Chapter 5.

$\hat{k}_s$ = *expected rate of return* which an investor who buys the stock actually expects to receive. $\hat{k}_s$ (pronounced "k hat s") could be above or below k_s, but one would buy the stock only if $\hat{k}_s$ were equal to or greater than k_s.

$\bar{k}_s$ = *actual,* or *realized, rate of return* (pronounced "k bar s"). You may *expect* to obtain a return of $\hat{k}_s$ = 15 percent if you buy Exxon stock today, but if the market goes down, you may end up next year with an actual realized return that is much lower, perhaps even negative.

D_1/P_0 = expected *dividend yield* on the stock during the coming year. If the stock is expected to pay a dividend of $1 during the next 12 months, and if its current price is $10, then the expected dividend yield is $1/$10 = 0.10 = 10%.

$\dfrac{\hat{P}_1 - P_0}{P_0}$ = expected *capital gains yield* on the stock during the coming year. If the stock sells for $10 today, and if it is expected to rise to $10.50 at the end of 1 year, then the expected capital gain is $\hat{P}_1 - P_0$ = $10.50 − $10.00 = $0.50, and the expected capital gains yield is $0.50/$10 = 0.05 = 5%.

Expected total return = $\hat{k}_s$ = expected dividend yield (D_1/P_0) plus expected capital gains yield $[(\hat{P}_1 - P_0)/P_0]$. In our example, the *expected total return* = $\hat{k}_s$ = 10% + 5% = 15%.

EXPECTED DIVIDENDS AS THE BASIS FOR STOCK VALUES

Stock prices are determined as the present value of a stream of cash flows, and the basic stock valuation equation is similar to the bond valuation equation. What are the cash flows that corporations provide to their stockholders? First, think of yourself as an investor who buys a stock with the intention of holding it (in your family) forever. In this case, all that you (and your heirs) will receive is a stream of dividends, and the value of the stock today is calculated as the present value of an infinite stream of dividends:

$$
\begin{aligned}
\text{Value of stock} = \hat{P}_0 &= \text{PV of expected future dividends} \\
&= \frac{D_1}{(1 + k_s)^1} + \frac{D_2}{(1 + k_s)^2} + \cdots + \frac{D_\infty}{(1 + k_s)^\infty} \\
&= \sum_{t=1}^{\infty} \frac{D_t}{(1 + k_s)^t}.
\end{aligned}
\tag{7-6}
$$

What about the more typical case, where you expect to hold the stock for a finite period and then sell it—what will be the value of $\hat{P}_0$ in this case? Unless the company is likely to be liquidated and thus to disappear, *the value of the stock is again determined by Equation 7-6.* To see this, recognize that for any individual investor, the expected cash flows consist of expected dividends plus the expected sale price of the stock. However, the sale price the current investor receives will depend on the dividends some future investor expects. Therefore, for all present and future investors in total, expected cash flows depend on expected future dividends. To put it another way, unless a firm is liquidated or sold to another concern, the cash flows it provides to its stockholders will consist only of a stream of dividends; therefore, the value of a share of its stock must be established as the present value of that expected dividend stream.

The general validity of Equation 7-6 can also be confirmed by asking the following question: Suppose I buy a stock and expect to hold it for 1 year. I will receive dividends during the year plus the value $\hat{P}_1$ when I sell out at the end of the year. But what will determine the value of $\hat{P}_1$? The answer is that it will be determined as the present value of the dividends during Year 2 plus the stock price at the end of that year, which in turn will be determined as the present value of another set of future dividends and an even more distant stock price. This process can be continued ad infinitum, and the ultimate result is Equation 7-6.[11]

---

[11]We should note that investors periodically lose sight of the long-run nature of stocks as investments and forget that in order to sell a stock at a profit, one must find a buyer who will pay the higher price. If you analyzed a stock's value in accordance with Equation 7-6, concluded that the stock's market price exceeded a reasonable value, and then bought the stock anyway, then you would be following the "bigger fool" theory of investment—you think that you may be a fool to buy the stock at its excessive price, but you also think that when you get ready to sell it, you can find someone who is an even bigger fool. The bigger fool theory was widely followed in the summer of 1987, just before the stock market lost over one-third of its value in the October 1987 crash.

Equation 7-6 is a generalized stock valuation model in the sense that the time pattern of D_t can be anything: D_t can be rising, falling, or constant, or it can even be fluctuating randomly, and Equation 7-6 will still hold. Often, however, the projected stream of dividends follows a systematic pattern, in which case we can develop a simplified (that is, easier to evaluate) version of the stock valuation model expressed in Equation 7-6. In the following sections we consider the cases of zero growth, constant growth, and nonconstant growth.

STOCK VALUES WITH ZERO GROWTH

Suppose dividends are not expected to grow at all but to remain constant. Here we have a *zero growth stock,* for which the dividends expected in future years are equal to some constant amount — that is, $D_1 = D_2 = D_3$ and so on. Therefore, we can drop the subscripts on D and rewrite Equation 7-6 as follows:

$$\hat{P}_0 = \frac{D}{(1 + k_s)^1} + \frac{D}{(1 + k_s)^2} + \ldots + \frac{D}{(1 + k_s)^\infty}. \qquad (7\text{-}6a)$$

As we noted in Chapter 6 in connection with the British consol bond and also in our discussion of preferred stocks, a security that is expected to pay a constant amount each year forever is called a perpetuity. *Therefore, a zero growth stock is a perpetuity.*

Although a zero growth stock is expected to provide a constant stream of dividends into the indefinite future, each dividend has a smaller present value than the preceding one, and as N gets very large, the present value of the future dividends approaches zero. To illustrate, suppose D = \$1.15 and k_s = 13.4%. We can rewrite Equation 7-6a as follows:

$$\hat{P}_0 = \frac{\$1.15}{(1.134)^1} + \frac{\$1.15}{(1.134)^2} + \frac{\$1.15}{(1.134)^3} + \ldots + \frac{\$1.15}{(1.134)^{50}} + \ldots + \frac{\$1.15}{(1.134)^{100}} + \ldots$$

$$= \quad \$1.01 \quad + \quad \$0.89 \quad + \quad \$0.79 \quad + \ldots + \quad \$0.002 \quad + \ldots + \$0.000004 + \ldots$$

We can also show the perpetuity in graph form, as in Figure 7-6. The horizontal line shows the constant dividend stream, D_t = \$1.15. The descending step function curve shows the present value of each future dividend. If we extended the analysis on out to infinity and then summed the present values of all the future dividends, the sum would be equal to the value of the stock.

As we saw in Chapter 6, the value of any perpetuity is simply the payment divided by the discount rate, so the value of a zero growth stock reduces to this formula:

$$\hat{P}_0 = \frac{D}{k_s}. \qquad (7\text{-}7)$$

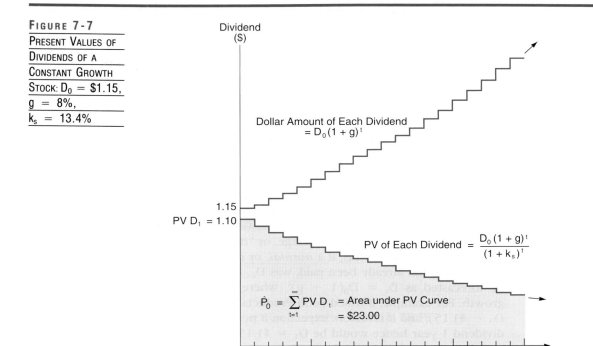

F IGURE 7 - 7

P RESENT V ALUES OF
D IVIDENDS OF A
C ONSTANT G ROWTH
S TOCK: D_0 = \$1.15,
g = 8%,
k_s = 13.4%

Dividend
($)

Dollar Amount of Each Dividend
= $D_0(1 + g)^t$

1.15

PV D_1 = 1.10

PV of Each Dividend = $\dfrac{D_0(1 + g)^t}{(1 + k_s)^t}$

$\hat{P}_0 = \displaystyle\sum_{t=1}^{\infty} PV\, D_t$ = Area under PV Curve
= \$23.00

0   5   10   15   20
Years

Inserting values into Equation 7-9, we find the value of our illustrative stock to be \$23.00:

$$\hat{P}_0 = \frac{\$1.15(1.08)}{0.134 - 0.08} = \frac{\$1.242}{0.054} = \$23.00.$$

The *constant growth model* as set forth in the last term of Equation 7-9 is often called the Gordon Model, after Myron J. Gordon, who did much to develop and popularize it.

Note that Equation 7-9 is sufficiently general to encompass the zero growth case described earlier: If growth is zero, this is simply a special case of constant growth, and Equation 7-9 is equal to Equation 7-7. Note also that a necessary condition for the derivation of the simplified form of Equation 7-9 is that k_s be greater than g. If the equation is used in situations where k_s is not greater than g, the results will be meaningless.

The concept underlying the valuation process for a constant growth stock is graphed in Figure 7-7. Dividends are growing at the rate g = 8%, but because

$k_s > g$, the present value of each future dividend is declining. For example, the dividend in Year 1 is $D_1 = D_0(1 + g)^1 = \$1.15(1.08) = \$1.242$. However, the present value of this dividend, discounted at 13.4 percent, is $PV(D_1) = \$1.242/(1.134)^1 = \$1.095$. The dividend expected in Year 2 grows to $\$1.242(1.08) = \$1.341$, but the present value of this dividend falls to $\$1.04$. Continuing, $D_3 = \$1.449$ and $PV(D_3) = \$0.993$, and so on. Thus, the expected dividends are growing, but the present value of each successive dividend is declining, because the dividend growth rate (8%) is less than the rate used for discounting the dividends to the present (13.4%).

If we summed the present values of each future dividend, this summation would be the value of the stock, $\hat{P}_0$. When g is a constant, this summation is equal to $D_1/(k_s - g)$, as shown in Equation 7-9. Therefore, if we extended the lower step function curve in Figure 7-7 on out to infinity and added up the present values of each future dividend, the summation would be identical to the value given by Equation 7-9, $23.00.

Growth in dividends occurs primarily as a result of growth in *earnings per share (EPS)*. Earnings growth, in turn, results from a number of factors, including (1) inflation, (2) the amount of earnings the company retains and reinvests, and (3) the rate of return the company earns on its equity (ROE). Regarding inflation, if output (in units) is stable and if both sales prices and input costs rise at the inflation rate, then EPS will also grow at the inflation rate. EPS will also grow as a result of the reinvestment, or plowback, of earnings. If the firm's earnings are not all paid out as dividends (that is, if some fraction of earnings is retained), the dollars of investment behind each share will rise over time, which should lead to growth in earnings and dividends.

EXPECTED RATE OF RETURN ON A CONSTANT GROWTH STOCK

We can solve Equation 7-9 for k_s, again using the hat to denote that we are dealing with an expected rate of return:[14]

$$\begin{array}{ccccc} \text{Expected rate} \\ \text{of return} \end{array} = \begin{array}{c} \text{Expected} \\ \text{dividend} \\ \text{yield} \end{array} + \begin{array}{c} \text{Expected growth} \\ \text{rate, or capital} \\ \text{gains yield} \end{array}$$

$$\hat{k}_s = \frac{D_1}{P_0} + g. \qquad (7\text{-}10)$$

---

[14]The k_s value of Equation 7-9 is a *required* rate of return, but when we transform it to obtain Equation 7-10, we are finding an *expected* rate of return. Obviously, the transformation requires that $k_s = \hat{k}_s$. This equality holds if the stock market is in equilibrium, a condition that will be discussed later in the chapter.

Thus, if you buy a stock for a price $P_0 = \$23$, and if you expect the stock to pay a dividend $D_1 = \$1.242$ one year from now and to grow at a constant rate $g = 8\%$ in the future, then your expected rate of return will be 13.4 percent:

$$\hat{k}_s = \frac{\$1.242}{\$23} + 8\% = 5.4\% + 8\% = 13.4\%.$$

In this form, we see that $\hat{k}_s$ is the *expected total return* and that it consists of an *expected dividend yield,* $D_1/P_0 = 5.4\%$, plus an *expected growth rate or capital gains yield,* $g = 8\%$.

Suppose this analysis had been conducted on January 1, 1994, so $P_0 = \$23$ is the January 1, 1994, stock price and $D_1 = \$1.242$ is the dividend expected at the end of 1994. What is the expected stock price at the end of 1994 (or the beginning of 1995)? We would again apply Equation 7-9, but this time we would use the 1995 dividend, $D_2 = D_1(1 + g) = \$1.242(1.08) = \$1.3414$:

$$\hat{P}_{1/1/1995} = \frac{D_{1995}}{k_s - g} = \frac{\$1.3414}{0.134 - 0.08} = \$24.84.$$

Now notice that $24.84 is 8 percent greater than P_0, the $23 price on January 1, 1994:

$$\$23(1.08) = \$24.84.$$

Thus, we would expect to make a capital gain of $24.84 − $23 = $1.84 during 1994, and a capital gains yield of 8 percent:

$$\text{Capital gains yield}_{1994} = \frac{\text{Capital gain}}{\text{Beginning price}} = \frac{\$1.84}{\$23} = 0.08 = 8\%.$$

We could extend the analysis on out, and in each future year the expected capital gains yield would always equal g, the expected dividend growth rate.

Continuing, the dividend yield in 1995 could be estimated as follows:

$$\text{Dividend yield}_{1995} = \frac{D_{1995}}{\hat{P}_{1/1/95}} = \frac{\$1.3414}{\$24.84} = 0.054 = 5.4\%.$$

The dividend yield for 1996 could also be calculated, and again it would be 5.4 percent. Thus, *for a constant growth stock,* the following conditions must hold:

1. The dividend is expected to grow forever at a constant rate, g.
2. The stock price is expected to grow at this same rate.
3. The expected dividend yield is a constant.
4. The expected capital gains yield is also a constant, and it is equal to g.

5. The expected total rate of return, $\hat{k}_s$, is equal to the expected dividend yield plus the expected growth rate: $\hat{k}_s$ = dividend yield + g.

The term *expected* should be clarified—it means expected in a probabilistic sense, as the statistically expected outcome. Thus, if we say the growth rate is expected to remain constant at 8 percent, we mean that the best prediction for the growth rate in any future year is 8 percent, not that we literally expect the growth rate to be exactly equal to 8 percent in each future year. In this sense, the constant growth assumption is a reasonable one for many large, mature companies.

NONCONSTANT GROWTH

Firms typically go through *life cycles.* During the early part of their lives, their growth is much faster than that of the economy as a whole; then they match the economy's growth; and finally their growth is slower than that of the economy.[15] Automobile manufacturers in the 1920s and computer software firms such as Microsoft in the 1990s are examples of firms in the early part of the cycle; these firms are called *supernormal growth* firms. Figure 7-8 illustrates supernormal growth and also compares it with normal growth, zero growth, and negative growth.[16]

In the figure, the dividends of the supernormal growth firm are expected to grow at a 30 percent rate for 3 years, after which the growth rate is expected to fall to 8 percent, the assumed average for the economy. The value of this firm, like any other, is the present value of its expected future dividends as determined by Equation 7-6. In the case in which D_t is growing at a constant rate, we simplified Equation 7-6 to $\hat{P}_0 = D_1/(k_s - g)$. In the supernormal case, however, the expected growth rate is not a constant—it declines at the end of the period of supernormal growth. To find the value of such a stock, or of any nonconstant growth stock when the growth rate will eventually stabilize, we proceed in three steps:

1. Find the PV of the dividends during the period of nonconstant growth.

2. Find the price of the stock at the end of the nonconstant growth period, at which point it has become a constant growth stock, and discount this price back to the present.

[15]The life cycle concept could be broadened to *product cycle,* which would include both small, start-up companies and large companies like IBM, which periodically introduce new products that give sales and earnings a boost. We should also mention *business cycles,* which alternately depress and boost sales and profits. The growth rate just after a major new product has been introduced, or just after a firm emerges from the depths of a recession, is likely to be much higher than the "expected long-run average growth rate," which is the proper number for a DCF constant growth analysis.

[16]A negative growth rate indicates a declining company. A mining company whose profits are falling because of a declining ore body is an example. Someone buying such a company would expect its earnings, and consequently its dividends and stock price, to decline each year, and this would lead to capital losses rather than capital gains. Obviously, a declining company's stock price will be relatively low, and its dividend yield must be high enough to offset the expected capital loss and still produce a competitive total return. Students sometimes argue that they would not be willing to buy a stock whose price was expected to decline. However, if the annual dividends are large enough to *more than offset* the falling stock price, the stock still could provide a good return.

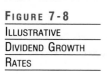

FIGURE 7-8
ILLUSTRATIVE
DIVIDEND GROWTH
RATES

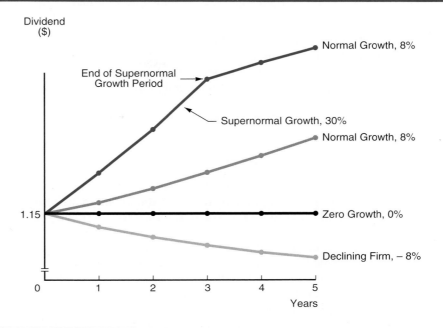

3. Add these two components to find the intrinsic value of the stock, $\hat{P}_0$.

Figure 7-9 can be used to illustrate the process for valuing nonconstant growth stocks, assuming the following five facts exist:

k_s = stockholders' required rate of return = 13.4%. This rate is used to discount the cash flows.

N = years of supernormal growth = 3.

g_s = rate of growth in both earnings and dividends during the supernormal growth period = 30%. (Note: The growth rate during the supernormal growth period could vary from year to year. Also, there could be several different supernormal growth periods, for example, 30% for 3 years, then 20% for 3 years, and then a constant 8%.) This rate is shown directly on the time line.

g_n = rate of normal, constant growth after the supernormal period = 8%. This rate is also shown on the time line, after Year 3.

D_0 = last dividend the company paid = $1.15.

The valuation process as diagrammed in Figure 7-9 is explained in the steps set forth below the time line. The value of the supernormal growth stock is calculated to be $39.21.

FIGURE 7-9

PROCESS FOR
FINDING THE VALUE
OF A SUPERNORMAL
GROWTH STOCK

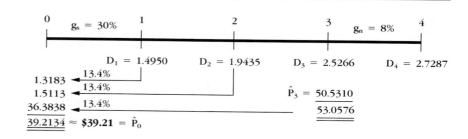

Step 1. Calculate the dividends expected at the end of each year during the supernormal growth period. Calculate the first dividend, $D_1 = D_0(1 + g_s)$ = $1.15(1.30) = \$1.4950$. Here g_s is the growth rate during the 3-year supernormal growth period, 30 percent. Show the \$1.4950 on the time line as the cash flow for Year 1. Now calculate $D_2 = D_1(1 + g_s) = \$1.4950(1.30) = \$1.9435$, and then $D_3 = D_2(1 + g_s) = \$1.9435(1.30) = \$2.5266$. Show these values on the time line as the cash flows for Years 2 and 3.

Step 2. The price of the stock is the PV of dividends from Year 1 to infinity, so in theory we could project each future dividend, with growth at the normal growth rate, $g_n = 8\%$, used to calculate D_4 and other dividends. However, we know that after D_3 has been paid, which is at the end of Year 3, the stock becomes a constant growth stock, so we can use the constant growth formula to find $\hat{P}_3$, which is the PV of the dividends from Year 4 to infinity as evaluated at Year 3.

First, we determine $D_4 = \$2.5266(1.08) = \$2.7287$ for use in the formula, and then we calculate $\hat{P}_3$ as follows:

$$\hat{P}_3 = \frac{D_4}{k_s - g_n} = \frac{\$2.7287}{0.134 - 0.08} = \$50.5310.$$

Now we show this \$50.5310 on the time line as a second cash flow at Year 3. The \$50.5310 is a Year 3 cash flow in the sense that the owner of the stock could sell it for \$50.5310 at Year 3 and also in the sense that \$50.5310 is the present value equivalent of the dividend cash flows from Year 4 to infinity. Note that the *total cash flow* at Year 3 consists of the sum of $D_3 + \hat{P}_3 = \$2.5266 + \$50.5310 = \$53.0576$.

Step 3. Now that the cash flows have been placed on the time line, we can discount each cash flow at the required rate of return, $k_s = 13.4\%$. Since 13.4% is not shown in the tables, it is necessary to discount each flow by dividing by $(1.134)^t$, where $t = 1$ for Year 1, $t = 2$ for Year 2, and $t = 3$ for Year 3. If you do this, you should get the PVs shown to the left below the time line. The sum of the PVs is the value of the supernormal growth stock, \$39.21.

(continued)

FIGURE 7-9
continued

If you have a financial calculator, you can find the PV of the cash flows as shown on the time line by using the cash flow (CFLO) register of your calculator. Here you would enter 0 for CF_0 because you get no cash flow at Time 0, $CF_1 = 1.495$, $CF_2 = 1.9435$, and $CF_3 = 2.5266 + 50.531 = 53.0576$. Then enter I $= 13.4$, and press the NPV key to find the value of the stock, $39.21.

SELF-TEST QUESTIONS

Explain the following statement: "Whereas a bond contains a promise to pay interest, common stock provides an expectation but no promise of dividends."

What are the two elements of a stock's expected returns?

Write out and explain the valuation model for a zero growth stock.

Write out and explain the valuation model for a constant growth stock.

How does one calculate the capital gains yield and the dividend yield of a stock?

Explain how one would find the value of a nonconstant growth stock.

STOCK MARKET EQUILIBRIUM

Recall from Chapter 5 that the required return on Stock X, k_X, can be found using the Security Market Line (SML) equation as it was developed in our discussion of the Capital Asset Pricing Model (CAPM):

$$k_X = k_{RF} + (k_M - k_{RF}) b_X.$$

If the risk-free rate of return is 8 percent, if the market risk premium is 4 percent, and if Stock X has a beta of 2, then the investor will require a return of 16 percent on Stock X, calculated as follows:

$$k_X = 8\% + (12\% - 8\%) 2.0$$

$$= 16\%.$$

This 16 percent required return is shown as a point on the SML in Figure 7-10.

The investor will want to buy Stock X if the expected rate of return is more than 16 percent, will want to sell it if the expected rate of return is less than 16 percent, and will be indifferent, hence will hold but not buy or sell, if the expected rate of return is exactly 16 percent. Now suppose the investor's portfolio contains

FIGURE 7-10

EXPECTED AND
REQUIRED RETURNS
ON STOCK X

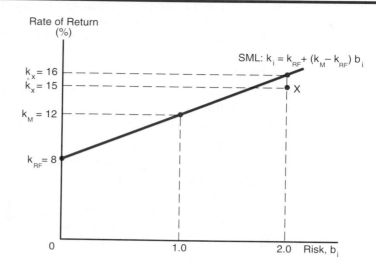

Stock X, and he or she analyzes the stock's prospects and concludes that its earnings, dividends, and price can be expected to grow at a constant rate of 5 percent per year. The last dividend was $D_0 = \$2.8571$, so the next expected dividend is

$$D_1 = \$2.8571(1.05) = \$3.$$

Our investor observes that the present price of the stock, P_0, is $30. Should he or she purchase more of Stock X, sell the present holdings, or maintain the present position?

The investor can calculate Stock X's *expected rate of return* as follows:

$$\hat{k}_X = \frac{D_1}{P_0} + g = \frac{\$3}{\$30} + 5\% = 15\%.$$

This value is plotted on Figure 7-10 as Point X, which is below the SML. Because the expected rate of return is less than the required return, this investor would want to sell the stock, as would other holders. However, few people would want to buy at the $30 price, so the present owners would be unable to find buyers unless they cut the price of the stock. Thus, the price would decline, and this decline would continue until the stock's price reached $27.27, at which point the market for this security would be in *equilibrium*, because the expected rate of return, 16 percent, would be equal to the required rate of return:

$$\hat{k}_X = \frac{\$3}{\$27.27} + 5\% = 11\% + 5\% = 16\% = k_X.$$

Had the stock initially sold for less than $27.27, say at $25, events would have been reversed. Investors would have wanted to buy the stock because its expected rate of return would have exceeded its required rate of return, and buy orders would have driven the stock's price up to $27.27.

To summarize, in equilibrium these two related conditions must hold:

1. The expected rate of return as seen by the marginal investor must equal the required rate of return: $\hat{k}_i = k_i$.

2. The actual market price of the stock must equal its intrinsic value as estimated by the marginal investor: $P_0 = \hat{P}_0$.

Of course, some individual investors may believe that $\hat{k}_i > k$ and $\hat{P}_0 > P_0$, and hence they would invest most of their funds in the stock, while other investors may have an opposite view and would sell all of their shares. However, it is the marginal investor who establishes the actual market price, and for this investor, $\hat{k}_i = k_i$ and $P_0 = \hat{P}_0$, for if these conditions do not hold, trading will occur until they do hold.

CHANGES IN EQUILIBRIUM STOCK PRICES

Stock market prices are not constant—they undergo violent changes at times. For example, on October 19, 1987, the Dow Jones average dropped 508 points, and the average stock lost about 23 percent of its value in just one day. Some stocks lost over half of their value that day. To see how such changes can occur, let us assume that Stock X is in equilibrium, selling at a price of $27.27 per share. If all expectations were exactly met, during the next year the price would gradually rise to $28.63, or by 5 percent. However, many different events could occur to cause a change in the equilibrium price of the stock. To illustrate, consider again the set of inputs used to develop Stock X's price of $27.27, along with a new set of assumed input variables:

	Variable Value	
	Original	New
Risk-free rate, k_{RF}	8%	7%
Market risk premium, $k_M - k_{RF}$	4%	3%
Stock X's beta coefficient, b_X	2.0	1.0
Stock X's expected growth rate, g_X	5%	6%
D_0	$2.8571	$2.8571
Price of Stock X	$27.27	?

Now give yourself a test: How would the change in each variable, by itself, affect the price, and what is your guess as to the new stock price?

Every change, taken alone, would lead to an increase in the price. The first three variables influence k_X, which declines from 16 to 10 percent:

$$\text{Original } k_X = 8\% + 4\%(2.0) = 16\%.$$

$$\text{New } k_X = 7\% + 3\%(1.0) = 10\%.$$

Using these values, together with the new g value, we find that $\hat{P}_0$ rises from $27.27 to $75.71.[17]

$$\text{Original } \hat{P}_0 = \frac{\$2.8571(1.05)}{0.16 - 0.05} = \frac{\$3}{0.11} = \$27.27.$$

$$\text{New } \hat{P}_0 = \frac{\$2.8571(1.06)}{0.10 - 0.06} = \frac{\$3.0285}{0.04} = \$75.71.$$

At the new price, the expected and required rates of return will be equal:[18]

$$\hat{k}_X = \frac{\$3.0285}{\$75.71} + 6\% = 10\% = k_X.$$

Evidence suggests that stocks, especially those of large companies, adjust rapidly to disequilibrium situations. Consequently, equilibrium ordinarily exists for any given stock, and, in general, required and expected returns are equal. Stock prices certainly change, sometimes violently and rapidly, but this simply reflects changing conditions and expectations. There are, of course, times when a stock continues to react for several months to a favorable or unfavorable development, but this does not signify a long adjustment period; rather, it simply illustrates that as more new pieces of information about the situation become available, the market adjusts to them. The ability of the market to adjust to new information is discussed in the next section.

THE EFFICIENT MARKETS HYPOTHESIS

A body of theory called the *Efficient Markets Hypothesis (EMH)* holds (1) that stocks are always in equilibrium and (2) that it is impossible for an investor to consistently "beat the market." Essentially, those who believe in the EMH note that there are 100,000 or so full-time, highly trained, professional analysts and traders operating in the market, while there are fewer than 3,000 major stocks. Therefore, if each analyst followed 30 stocks (which is about right, as analysts tend to specialize in the stocks in a specific industry), there would be 1,000 analysts following each stock. Further, these analysts work for organizations such as Citibank, Merrill Lynch, Prudential Insurance, Fidelity Investments, and the like, which have billions of dollars available with which to take advantage of bargains. As a result of SEC disclosure requirements and electronic information networks, as new information

---

[17]A price change of this magnitude is by no means rare. The prices of *many* stocks double or halve during a year. For example, during 1992 Western Digital, a disk-drive maker, increased in value by 229 percent; on the other hand, Gitano, an apparel maker, fell by 80 percent.

[18]It should be obvious by now that *realized* rates of return are not necessarily equal to expected and required returns. Thus, an investor might have *expected* to receive a return of 15 percent if he or she had bought Western Digital or Gitano stock in early 1992, but, after the fact, the realized return on Western Digital was far above 15 percent, whereas that on Gitano was far below.

about a stock becomes available, these 1,000 analysts all receive and evaluate it at approximately the same time. Therefore, the price of the stock adjusts almost immediately to reflect any new developments.

Financial theorists generally define three forms, or levels, of market efficiency:

1. The *weak form* of the EMH states that all information contained in past price movements is fully reflected in current market prices. Therefore, information about recent trends in stock prices is of no use in selecting stocks—the fact that a stock has risen for the past three days, for example, gives us no useful clues as to what it will do today or tomorrow. People who believe that weak-form efficiency exists also believe that "tape watchers" and "chartists" are wasting their time.[19]

2. The *semistrong form* of the EMH states that current market prices reflect all *publicly available* information. If this is true, no abnormal returns can be earned by analyzing stocks.[20] Thus, if semistrong-form efficiency exists, it does no good to pore over annual reports or other published data because market prices will have adjusted to any good or bad news contained in such reports as soon as they came out. However, insiders (say, the presidents of companies), even under semistrong-form efficiency, can still make abnormal returns on their own companies' stocks.

3. The *strong form* of the EMH states that current market prices reflect all pertinent information, whether publicly available or privately held. If this form holds, even insiders would find it impossible to earn abnormal returns in the stock market.[21]

Many empirical studies have been conducted to test for the three forms of market efficiency. Most of these studies suggest that the stock market is indeed highly efficient in the weak form and reasonably efficient in the semistrong form, at least for the larger and more widely followed stocks. However, the strong-form EMH does not hold, so abnormal profits can be made by those who possess inside information.

What bearing does the EMH have on financial decisions? Since stock prices do seem to reflect public information, most stocks appear to be fairly valued. This does not mean that new developments could not cause a stock's price to soar or to plummet, but it does mean that stocks, in general, are neither overvalued nor undervalued—they are fairly priced and in equilibrium. However, there are certainly cases in which corporate insiders have information not known to outsiders.

---

[19]Tape watchers are people who watch the NYSE tape, while chartists plot past patterns of stock price movements. Both are called "technicians," and both believe that they can see if something is happening to the stock that will cause its price to move up or down in the near future.

[20]An abnormal return is one that exceeds the return justified by the riskiness of the investment; that is, a return that plots above the SML in a graph like Figure 7-10.

[21]Several cases of illegal insider trading have made the news headlines recently. These cases involved employees of several major investment banking houses and even an employee of the SEC. In the most famous case, Ivan Boesky admitted to making $50 million by purchasing the stock of firms he knew were about to merge. He went to jail, and he had to pay a large fine, but he helped disprove the strong-form EMH.

If the EMH is correct, it is a waste of time for most of us to analyze stocks by looking for those that are undervalued. If stock prices already reflect all publicly available information and hence are fairly priced, one can "beat the market" only by luck, and it is difficult, if not impossible, for anyone to consistently outperform the market averages. Empirical tests have shown that the EMH is, in its weak and semistrong forms, valid. However, people such as corporate officers who have inside information can do better than the averages, and individuals and organizations that are especially good at digging out information on small, new companies also seem to do consistently well. Also, some investors may be able to analyze and react more quickly than others to releases of new information, and these investors may have an advantage over others. However, the buy-sell actions of those investors quickly bring market prices into equilibrium. Therefore, it is generally safe to assume that $\hat{k} = k$, that $\hat{P}_0 = P_0$, and that stocks plot on the SML.[22]

ACTUAL STOCK PRICES AND RETURNS

Our discussion thus far has focused on *expected* stock prices and *expected* rates of return. Anyone who has ever invested in the stock market knows that there can be, and there generally are, large differences between *expected* and *realized* prices and returns.

We can use IBM to illustrate this point. In early 1991, IBM's stock price was about $120 per share. Its 1990 dividend, D_0, had been $4.84, but analysts expected the dividend to grow at a constant rate of about 8 percent in the future. Thus, an average investor who bought IBM at a price of $120 would have expected to earn a return of about 12.4 percent:

$$\hat{k}_s = \frac{\text{Expected dividend}}{\text{yield}} + \frac{\text{Expected growth rate, which is also}}{\text{the expected capital gains yield}}$$

$$= \frac{D_0(1 + g)}{P_0} + g = \frac{\$5.23}{\$120} + 8\%$$

$$= 4.4\% + 8.0\% = 12.4\%.$$

In fact, things did not work out as expected. The computer market in 1991 was weaker than had been predicted, so IBM's earnings did not grow as fast as expected, and its dividend remained at $4.84. So, rather than growing, IBM's stock price declined, and it closed on December 31, 1991, at $89, down $31 for the

---

[22]Market efficiency also has important implications for managerial decisions, especially those pertaining to common stock issues, stock repurchases, and tender offers. Stocks appear to be fairly valued, so decisions based on a stock's being undervalued or overvalued must be approached with caution. However, managers do have better information about their own companies than outsiders, and this information can legally be used to the companies' (but not the managers') advantage.

FIGURE 7-11
S&P 500 INDEX,
1967–1992

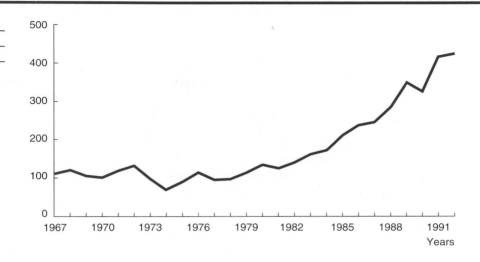

year. Thus, on a beginning-of-the-year investment of $120, the actual return on IBM for 1991 was −21.8 percent:

$$\bar{k}_s = \text{Actual dividend yield} + \text{Actual capital gains yield}$$

$$= \frac{\$4.84}{\$120} + \frac{-\$31}{\$120} = 4.0\% - 25.8\% = -21.8\%.$$

Many other stocks performed similarly to IBM's, or worse, in 1991.

Figure 7-11 shows how the price of an average share of stock has varied in recent years, and Figure 7-12 shows how total realized returns have varied. The market trend has been strongly up, but it has gone up in some years and down in others, and the stocks of individual companies have likewise gone up and down. We know from theory that expected returns as estimated by a marginal investor are always positive, but in some years, as Figure 7-12 shows, negative returns have been realized. Of course, even in bad years some individual companies do well, so the "name of the game" in security analysis is to pick the winners. Financial managers attempt to take actions which will put their companies into the winners' column, but they don't always succeed. In subsequent chapters, we will examine the actions that managers can take to increase the odds of their firms doing relatively well in the marketplace.

STOCK MARKET REPORTING

Figure 7-13, taken from *The Wall Street Journal*, is a section of the stock market page for stocks listed on the NYSE. For each stock, the NYSE report provides specific data on the trading that took place the prior day. Similar information is avail-

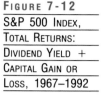

FIGURE 7-12

S&P 500 INDEX,
TOTAL RETURNS:
DIVIDEND YIELD +
CAPITAL GAIN OR
LOSS, 1967–1992

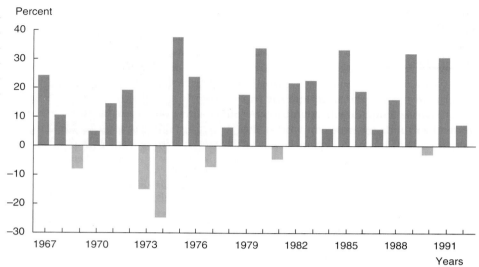

able for stocks listed on the other exchanges as well as for stocks traded over-the-counter.

Stocks are listed alphabetically, from AAR Industries to Zweig; the data in Figure 7-13 were taken from the top portion of the listing. We will examine the data for Abbott Laboratories, (AbbotLab), shown about halfway down the table. The two columns on the left show the highest and lowest prices at which the stocks have sold during the past year; Abbott Labs has traded in the range from $34 to $22⅝ during the preceding 52 weeks. The figure just to the right of the company's symbol is the dividend; Abbott Labs had a current indicated annual dividend rate of $0.68 per share and a dividend yield (which is the dividend divided by the closing stock price) of 2.5 percent. Next comes the ratio of the stock's price to its annual earnings (the P/E ratio), followed by the volume of trading for the day: 986,700 shares of Abbott Labs stock were traded on May 11, 1993. Following the volume come the high and low prices for the day, and then the closing price. On May 11, Abbott Labs traded as high as $27⅝ and as low as $27⅛, while the last trade was at $27½. The last column gives the change from the closing price on the previous day. Abbott Labs was up ⅛, or $0.125, so the previous close must have been $27.50 − $0.125 = $27.375.

There are several other points to note in Figure 7-13. First, the "pf" following the stock name of the ANR listing tells us that this one is a preferred stock rather than a common stock. Second, a "▲" preceding the columns containing a stock's 52-week high and low prices indicates that the price hit a new 52-week high, whereas a "▼" preceding the columns containing a stock's 52-week high and low prices indicates a new 52-week low. ASA hit a new high on May 11, 1993. Third, an "x" preceding the columns containing the 52-week high and low prices and

▶ The *value of a share of stock* is calculated as the *present value of the stream of dividends* it is expected to provide in the future.

▶ The equation used to find the *value of a constant,* or *normal, growth stock* is

$$\hat{P}_0 = \frac{D_1}{(k_s - g)}.$$

▶ The *expected total rate of return* from a stock consists of an *expected dividend yield* plus an *expected capital gains yield.* For a constant growth firm, both the expected dividend yield and the expected capital gains yield are constant.

▶ The equation for the *expected rate of return on a constant growth stock* can be expressed as follows: $\hat{k}_s = D_1/P_0 + g$.

▶ A *zero growth stock* is one whose future dividends are not expected to grow at all, while a *supernormal growth stock* is one whose earnings and dividends are expected to grow much faster than the economy as a whole over some specified time period.

▶ To find the *present value of a supernormal growth stock,* (1) find the dividends expected during the supernormal growth period, (2) find the price of the stock at the end of the supernormal growth period, (3) discount the dividends and the projected price back to the present, and (4) sum these PVs to find the current value of the stock, $\hat{P}_0$. The value of any nonconstant growth stock can be found in this manner.

▶ The *Efficient Markets Hypothesis (EMH)* holds (1) that stocks are always in equilibrium and (2) that it is impossible for an investor to consistently "beat the market." Therefore, according to the EMH, stocks are always fairly valued ($\hat{P}_0 = P_0$), the required return on a stock is equal to its expected return ($k = \hat{k}$), and all stocks' expected returns plot on the SML.

▶ Finally, in this chapter we saw that differences can and do exist between expected and realized returns in the stock and bond markets—only for short-term, risk-free assets are expected and actual (or realized) returns equal.

Questions

7-1 Define each of the following terms:

a. Bond

b. Par value; maturity date; call provision

c. Coupon payment; coupon interest rate

d. Premium bond; discount bond

e. Current yield (on a bond); yield to maturity (YTM); yield to call (YTC)

f. Interest rate risk; price risk; reinvestment rate risk

g. Intrinsic value ($\hat{P}_0$); market price (P_0)

h. Required rate of return, k_s; expected rate of return, $\hat{k}_s$; actual, or realized, rate of return, $\bar{k}_s$

i. Capital gains yield; dividend yield; expected total return

j. Zero growth stock; perpetuity

k. Normal, or constant, growth; supernormal, or nonconstant, growth

l. Equilibrium

m. Efficient Markets Hypothesis (EMH); three forms of EMH

7-2 Two investors are evaluating AT&T's stock for possible purchase. They agree on the expected value of D_1 and also on the expected future dividend growth rate. Further, they agree on the riskiness of the stock. However, one investor normally holds stocks for 2 years, while the other normally holds stocks for 10 years. On the basis of the type of analysis done in this chapter, they should both be willing to pay the same price for AT&T's stock. True or false? Explain.

7-3 A bond that pays interest forever and has no maturity date is a perpetual bond. In what respect is a perpetual bond similar to a no-growth common stock, and to a share of preferred stock?

7-4 Is it true that the following equation can be used to find the value of an N-year bond that pays interest once a year?

$$V_B = \sum_{t=1}^{N} \frac{\text{Annual interest}}{(1 + k_d)^t} + \frac{\text{Par value}}{(1 + k_d)^N}.$$

7-5 "The values of outstanding bonds change whenever the going rate of interest changes. In general, short-term interest rates are more volatile than long-term interest rates. Therefore, short-term bond prices are more sensitive to interest rate changes than are long-term bond prices." Is this statement true or false? Explain.

7-6 The rate of return you would get if you bought a bond and held it to its maturity date is called the bond's yield to maturity. If interest rates in the economy rise after a bond has been issued, what will happen to the bond's price and to its YTM? Does the length of time to maturity affect the extent to which a given change in interest rates will affect the bond's price?

7-7 If you buy a *callable* bond and interest rates decline, will the value of your bond rise by as much as it would have risen if the bond had not been callable? Explain.

7-8 If you bought a share of common stock, you would typically expect to receive dividends plus capital gains. Would you expect the distribution between dividend yield and capital gains to be influenced by the firm's decision to pay more dividends rather than to retain and reinvest more of its earnings?

7-9 Is it true that the following expression can be used to find the value of a constant growth stock?

$$\hat{P}_0 = \frac{D_0}{k_s + g}.$$

SELF-TEST PROBLEMS (SOLUTIONS APPEAR IN APPENDIX C)

ST-1 (Stock growth rates and valuation) You are considering buying the stocks of two companies that operate in the same industry; they have very similar characteristics except for their dividend payout policies. Both companies are expected to earn $6 per share this year. However, Company D (for "dividend") is expected to pay out all of its earnings as dividends, while Company G (for "growth") is expected to pay out only one-third of its earnings, or $2 per share. D's stock price is $40. G and D are equally risky. Which of the following is most likely to be true?

a. Company G will have a faster growth rate than Company D. Therefore, G's stock price should be greater than $40.

b. Although G's growth rate should exceed D's, D's current dividend exceeds that of G, and this should cause D's price to exceed G's.

c. An investor in Stock D will get his or her money back faster because D pays out more of its earnings as dividends. Thus, in a sense, D is like a short-term bond, and G is like a long-term bond. Therefore, if economic shifts cause k_d and k_s to increase, and if the expected streams of dividends from D and G remain constant, Stocks D and G will both decline, but D's price should decline further.

d. D's expected and required rate of return is $\hat{k}_s = k_s = 15\%$. G's expected return will be higher because of its higher expected growth rate.

e. On the basis of the available information, the best estimate of G's growth rate is 10 percent.

ST-2 (Bond valuation) The Pennington Corporation issued a new series of bonds on January 1, 1971. The bonds were sold at par ($1,000), have a 12 percent coupon, and mature in 30 years, on December 31, 2000. Coupon payments are made semiannually (on June 30 and December 31).

a. What was the YTM of Pennington's bonds on January 1, 1971?

b. What was the price of the bond on January 1, 1976, 5 years later, assuming that the level of interest rates had fallen to 10 percent?

c. Find the current yield and capital gains yield on the bond on January 1, 1976, given the price as determined in Part b.

d. On July 1, 1994, Pennington's bonds sold for $916.42. What was the YTM at that date?

e. What were the current yield and capital gains yield on July 1, 1994?

f. Now assume that you purchased an outstanding Pennington bond on March 1, 1994, when the going rate of interest was 15.5 percent. How large a check must you have written to complete the transaction? This is a hard question! (Hint: $PVIFA_{7.75\%,13} = 8.0136$ and $PVIF_{7.75\%,13} = 0.3789$.)

ST-3 (Constant growth stock valuation) Ewald Company's current stock price is $36, and its last dividend was $2.40. In view of Ewald's strong financial position and its consequent low risk, its required rate of return is only 12 percent. If dividends are expected to grow at a constant rate, g, in the future, and if k_s is expected to remain at 12 percent, what is Ewald's expected stock price 5 years from now?

ST-4 (Supernormal growth stock valuation) Snyder Computer Chips Inc. is experiencing a period of rapid growth. Earnings and dividends are expected to grow at a rate of 15 percent during the next 2 years, at 13 percent in the third year, and at a constant rate of 6 percent

thereafter. Snyder's last dividend was $1.15, and the required rate of return on the stock is 12 percent.

a. Calculate the value of the stock today.

b. Calculate $\hat{P}_1$ and $\hat{P}_2$.

c. Calculate the dividend yield and capital gains yield for Years 1, 2, and 3.

PROBLEMS

7-1 **(Bond valuation)** Suppose Ford Motor Company sold an issue of bonds with a 10-year maturity, a $1,000 par value, a 10 percent coupon rate, and semiannual interest payments.

a. Two years after the bonds were issued, the going rate of interest on bonds such as these fell to 6 percent. At what price would the bonds sell?

b. Suppose that, 2 years after the initial offering, the going interest rate had risen to 12 percent. At what price would the bonds sell?

c. Suppose that the conditions in Part a existed — that is, interest rates fell to 6 percent 2 years after the issue date. Suppose further that the interest rate remained at 6 percent for the next 8 years. What would happen to the price of the Ford Motor Company bonds over time?

7-2 **(Perpetual bond valuation)** The bonds of the McCue Corporation are perpetuities with a 10 percent coupon. Bonds of this type currently yield 8 percent, and their par value is $1,000.

a. What is the price of the McCue bonds?

b. Suppose interest rate levels rise to the point where such bonds now yield 12 percent. What would be the price of the McCue bonds?

c. At what price would the McCue bonds sell if the yield on these bonds were 10 percent?

d. How would your answers to Parts a, b, and c change if the bonds were not perpetuities but had a maturity of 20 years?

7-3 **(Constant growth stock valuation)** Your broker offers to sell you some shares of Stanton & Co. common stock that paid a dividend of $2 *yesterday.* You expect the dividend to grow at the rate of 5 percent per year for the next 3 years, and if you buy the stock you plan to hold it for 3 years and then sell it.

a. Find the expected dividend for each of the next 3 years; that is, calculate D_1, D_2, and D_3. Note that $D_0 = \$2$.

b. Given that the appropriate discount rate is 12 percent and that the first of these dividend payments will occur 1 year from now, find the present value of the dividend stream; that is, calculate the PV of D_1, D_2, and D_3, and then sum these PVs.

c. You expect the price of the stock 3 years from now to be $34.73; that is, you expect $\hat{P}_3$ to equal $34.73. Discounted at a 12 percent rate, what is the present value of this expected future stock price? In other words, calculate the PV of $34.73.

d. If you plan to buy the stock, hold it for 3 years, and then sell it for $34.73, what is the most you should pay for it?

e. Use Equation 7-9 to calculate the present value of this stock. Assume that $g = 5\%$, and it is constant.

f. Is the value of this stock dependent upon how long you plan to hold it? In other words, if your planned holding period were 2 years or 5 years rather than 3 years, would this affect the value of the stock today, $\hat{P}_0$?

7-4 **(Return on common stock)** You buy a share of Hoffmeister Corporation stock for $21.40. You expect it to pay dividends of $1.07, $1.1449, and $1.2250 in Years 1, 2, and 3, respectively, and you expect to sell it at a price of $26.22 at the end of 3 years.

a. Calculate the growth rate in dividends.

b. Calculate the expected dividend yield.

c. Assuming that the calculated growth rate is expected to continue, you can add the dividend yield to the expected growth rate to get the expected total rate of return. What is this stock's expected total rate of return?

7-5 **(Constant growth stock valuation)** Investors require a 15 percent rate of return on Shipley Company's stock ($k_s = 15\%$).

a. What will be Shipley's stock value if the previous dividend was $D_0 = \$2$ and if investors expect dividends to grow at a constant compound annual rate of $(1) -5$ percent, (2) 0 percent, (3) 5 percent, and (4) 10 percent?

b. Using data from Part a, what is the Gordon (constant growth) model value for Shipley's stock if the required rate of return is 15 percent and the expected growth rate is (1) 15 percent or (2) 20 percent? Are these reasonable results? Explain.

c. Is it reasonable to expect that a constant growth stock would have $g > k_s$?

7-6 **(Stock and bond reporting)** Look up the prices of Southwestern Bell's stock and bonds in *The Wall Street Journal* (or some other newspaper which provides this information).

a. What was the stock's price range during the last year?

b. What is Southwestern Bell's current dividend? What is its dividend yield?

c. What change occurred in Southwestern Bell's stock price the day the newspaper was published?

d. If Southwestern Bell were to sell a new issue of $1,000 par value long-term bonds, approximately what coupon interest rate would it have to set on the bonds if it wanted to bring them out at par? (Note: Southwestern Bell bonds trade on the AMEX.)

e. If you had $10,000 and wanted to invest it in Southwestern Bell, what return would you expect to get if you bought the bonds and what return if you bought Southwestern Bell's stock? (Hint: Think about capital gains when you answer the latter part of this question.)

7-7 **(Discount bond valuation)** Assume that in February 1967 the Los Angeles Airport authority issued a series of 3.4 percent, 30-year bonds. Interest rates rose substantially in the years following the issue, and as they did, the price of the bonds declined. In February 1980, 13 years later, the price of the bonds had dropped from $1,000 to $650. In answering the following questions, assume that the bond requires annual interest payments.

a. Each bond originally sold at its $1,000 par value. What was the yield to maturity of these bonds when they were issued?

b. Calculate the yield to maturity in February 1980.

c. Assume that interest rates stabilized at the 1980 level and stayed there for the remainder of the life of the bonds. What would have been the bonds' price in February 1993, when they had 4 years remaining to maturity?

d. What will the price of the bonds be the day before they mature in 1997? (Disregard the last interest payment.)

e. In 1980 the Los Angeles Airport bonds were classified as "discount bonds." What happens to the price of a discount bond as it approaches maturity? Is there a "built-in capital gain" on such bonds?

f. The coupon interest payment divided by the market price of a bond is called the bond's *current yield*. Assuming the conditions in Part c, what would have been the current yield of a Los Angeles Airport bond (1) in February 1980 and (2) in February 1993? What would have been its capital gains yields and total yields (total yield equals yield to maturity) on those same two dates?

7-8 **(Supernormal growth stock valuation)** It is now January 1, 1994. Bigbee Electric Inc. has just developed a solar panel capable of generating 200 percent more electricity than any solar panel currently on the market. As a result, Bigbee is expected to experience a 15 percent annual growth rate for the next 5 years. By the end of 5 years, other firms will have developed comparable technology, and Bigbee's growth rate will slow to 5 percent per year indefinitely. Stockholders require a return of 12 percent on Bigbee's stock. The most recent annual dividend (D_0), which was paid yesterday, was $1.75 per share.

a. Calculate Bigbee's expected dividends for 1994, 1995, 1996, 1997, and 1998.

b. Calculate the value of the stock today, $\hat{P}_0$. Proceed by finding the present value of the dividends expected at the end of 1994, 1995, 1996, 1997, and 1998 plus the present value of the stock price which should exist at the end of 1998. The year-end 1998 stock price can be found by using the constant growth equation. Notice that to find the December 31, 1998, price, you use the dividend expected in 1999, which is 5 percent greater than the 1998 dividend.

c. Calculate the expected dividend yield, D_1/P_0, the capital gains yield expected in 1994, and the expected total return (dividend yield plus capital gains yield) for 1994. (Assume that $\hat{P}_0 = P_0$, and recognize that the capital gains yield is equal to the total return minus the dividend yield.) Also calculate these same three yields for 1998.

d. How might an investor's tax situation affect his or her decision to purchase stocks of companies in the early stages of their lives, when they are growing rapidly, versus stocks of older, more mature firms? When does Bigbee's stock become "mature" in this example?

e. Suppose your boss tells you she believes that Bigbee's annual growth rate will be only 12 percent during the next 5 years and that the firm's normal growth rate will be only 4 percent. Without doing any calculations, what general effect would these growth-rate changes have on the price of Bigbee's stock?

f. Suppose your boss also tells you that she regards Bigbee as being quite risky and that she believes the required rate of return should be 14 percent, not 12 percent. Again without doing any calculations, how would the higher required rate of return affect the price of the stock, its capital gains yield, and its dividend yield?

Work the following parts only if you are using the computer problem diskette.

g. Rework Part e, using the computerized model to determine what Bigbee's expected dividends and stock price would be under the conditions given.

h. Suppose your boss tells you that she regards Bigbee as being quite risky and that she believes the required rate of return should be higher than the 12 percent originally specified. Rework the problem under the conditions given in Part e, except change the

required rate of return to (1) 13 percent, (2) 15 percent, and (3) 20 percent to determine the effects of the higher required rates of return on Bigbee's stock price.

7-9   **(Supernormal growth stock valuation)**   Thompson Technologies Corporation (TTC) has been growing at a rate of 20 percent per year in recent years. This same growth rate is expected to last for another 2 years.

a.   If D_0 = $1.60, k = 10%, and g_n = 6%, what is TTC's stock worth today? What are its expected dividend yield and capital gains yield at this time?

b.   Now assume that TTC's period of supernormal growth is to last another 5 years rather than 2 years. How would this affect its price, dividend yield, and capital gains yield? Answer in words only.

c.   What will be TTC's dividend yield and capital gains yield once its period of supernormal growth ends? (Hint: These values will be the same regardless of whether you examine the case of 2 or 5 years of supernormal growth; the calculations are very easy.)

d.   Of what interest to investors is the changing relationship between dividend yield and capital gains yield over time?

7-10   **(Yield to call)**   It is now January 1, 1994, and you are considering the purchase of an outstanding Aikman Corporation bond that was issued on January 1, 1992. The Aikman bond has a 9.5 percent annual coupon and a 30-year original maturity (it matures on December 31, 2021). There is a 5-year call protection (until December 31, 1996), after which time the bond can be called at 109 (that is, at 109 percent of par, or $1,090). Interest rates have declined since the bond was issued, and the bond is now selling at 116.575 percent of par, or $1,165.75. You want to determine both the yield to maturity and the yield to call for this bond. (Note: The yield to call considers the effect of a call provision on the bond's probable yield. In the calculation, we assume that the bond will be outstanding until the call date, at which time it will be called. Thus, the investor will have received interest payments for the call-protected period and then will receive the call price—in this case, $1,090—on the call date.)

a.   What is the yield to maturity in 1994 for the Aikman bond? What is its yield to call?

b.   If you bought this bond, which return do you think you would actually earn? Explain your reasoning.

c.   Suppose the bond had sold at a discount. Would the yield to maturity or the yield to call have been more relevant?

7-11   **(Equilibrium stock price)**   The risk-free rate of return, k_{RF}, is 11 percent; the required rate of return on the market, k_M, is 14 percent; and The Andrews Company's stock has a beta coefficient of 1.5.

a.   If the dividend expected during the coming year, D_1, is $2.25, and if g = a constant 5%, at what price should Andrews's stock sell?

b.   Now suppose the Federal Reserve Board increases the money supply, causing the risk-free rate to drop to 9 percent and k_M to fall to 12 percent. What would this do to the price of the stock?

c.   In addition to the change in Part b, suppose investors' risk aversion declines; this fact, combined with the decline in k_{RF}, causes k_M to fall to 11 percent. At what price would Andrews's stock sell?

d.   Now suppose Andrews has a change in management. The new group institutes policies that increase the expected constant growth rate to 6 percent. Also, the new management stabilizes sales and profits and thus causes the beta coefficient to decline from 1.5

to 1.3. Assume that k_{RF} and k_M are equal to the values in Part c. After all these changes, what is Andrews's new equilibrium price? (Note: D_1 goes to $2.27.)

7-12 (Beta coefficients) Suppose Crum Chemical Company's management conducts a study and concludes that if Crum expanded its consumer products division (which is less risky than its primary business, industrial chemicals), the firm's beta would decline from 1.2 to 0.9. However, consumer products have a somewhat lower profit margin, and this would cause Crum's constant growth rate in earnings and dividends to fall from 7 to 5 percent.

a. Should management make the change? Assume the following: $k_M = 12\%$; $k_{RF} = 9\%$; $D_0 = $2.

b. Assume all the facts as given above except the change in the beta coefficient. How low would the beta have to fall to cause the expansion to be a good one? (Hint: Set $\hat{P}_0$ under the new policy equal to $\hat{P}_0$ under the old one, and find the new beta that will produce this equality.)

7-13 (Bond valuation) The Braver Company has two bond issues outstanding. Both bonds pay $100 annual interest plus $1,000 at maturity. Bond L has a maturity of 15 years and Bond S a maturity of 1 year.

a. What will be the value of each of these bonds when the going rate of interest is (1) 5 percent, (2) 8 percent, and (3) 12 percent? Assume that there is only one more interest payment to be made on Bond S.

b. Why does the longer-term (15-year) bond fluctuate more when interest rates change than does the shorter-term bond (1-year)?

7-14 (Yield to maturity) The Glasgo Company's bonds have 4 years remaining to maturity. Interest is paid annually; the bonds have a $1,000 par value; and the coupon interest rate is 9 percent.

a. What is the yield to maturity at a current market price of (1) $829 or (2) $1,104?

b. Would you pay $829 for one of these bonds if you thought that the appropriate rate of interest was 12 percent—that is, if $k_d = 12\%$? Explain your answer.

7-15 (Perpetual bond rate of return) What will be the rate of return on a perpetual bond with a $1,000 par value, an 8 percent coupon rate, and a current market price of (a) $600, (b) $800, (c) $1,000, and (d) $1,400? Assume interest is paid annually.

7-16 (Declining growth stock valuation) Miller Mining Company's ore reserves are being depleted, so its sales are falling. Also, its pit is getting deeper each year, so its costs are rising. As a result, the company's earnings and dividends are declining at the constant rate of 5 percent per year. If $D_0 = $5 and $k_s = 15\%$, what is the value of Miller Mining's stock?

7-17 (Rates of return and equilibrium) The beta coefficient for Stock C is $b_c = 0.4$, whereas that for Stock D is $b_D = -0.5$. (Stock D's beta is negative, indicating that its rate of return rises whenever returns on most other stocks fall. There are very few negative beta stocks, although collection agency stocks are sometimes cited as an example.)

a. If the risk-free rate is 9 percent and the expected rate of return on an average stock is 13 percent, what are the required rates of return on Stocks C and D?

b. For Stock C, suppose the current price, P_0, is $25; the next expected dividend, D_1, is $1.50; and the stock's expected constant growth rate is 4 percent. Is the stock in equilibrium? Explain, and describe what will happen if the stock is not in equilibrium.

7-18 (Supernormal growth stock valuation) Assume that the average firm in your company's industry is expected to grow at a constant rate of 6 percent, and its dividend yield is 7 percent. Your company is about as risky as the average firm in the industry, but it has just

successfully completed some R&D work which leads you to expect that its earnings and dividends will grow at a rate of 50 percent $[D_1 = D_0(1 + g) = D_0(1.50)]$ this year and 25 percent the following year, after which growth should match the 6 percent industry average rate. The last dividend paid (D_0) was $1. What is the value per share of your firm's stock?

7-19 (Financial calculator needed; Effective annual rate) Assume that as investment manager of Southeastern Electric Company's pension plan (which is exempt from income taxes), you must choose between Wal-Mart bonds and AT&T preferred stock. Assume the bonds have a $1,000 par value, they mature in 20 years, they pay $40 each 6 months, they are callable at Wal-Mart's option at a price of $1,080 after 5 years (ten 6-month periods), and they sell at a price of $897.40 per bond. The preferred stock is a perpetuity; it pays a dividend of $2 each quarter, and it sells for $95 per share. What is the *most likely* effective annual rate of return (EAR) on the *higher*-yielding security?

7-20 (Nominal interest rate) Nodine Corporation's 14 percent coupon rate, semiannual payment, $1,000 par value bonds which mature in 30 years are callable at a price of $1,050 five years from now. The bonds sell at a price of $1,353.54, and the yield curve is flat. Assuming that interest rates in the economy are expected to remain at their current level, what is the best estimate of Nodine's nominal interest rate on new bonds?

7-21 (Supernormal growth stock valuation) Mangan Corporation is expanding rapidly, and it currently needs to retain all of its earnings, hence it does not pay any dividends. However, investors expect Mangan to begin paying dividends, with the first dividend of $1.00 coming 3 years from today. The dividend should grow rapidly—at a rate of 50 percent per year— during Years 4 and 5. After Year 5, the company should grow at a constant rate of 8 percent per year. If the required return on the stock is 15 percent, what is the value of the stock today?

- -

**M I N I
C A S E**

Robert Balik and Carol Kiefer are senior vice presidents of the Mutual of Chicago Insurance Company. They are co-directors of the company's pension fund management division, with Balik having responsibility for fixed income securities (primarily bonds) and Kiefer being responsible for equity investments. A major new client, the California League of Cities, has requested that Mutual of Chicago present an investment seminar to the mayors of the represented cities, and Balik and Kiefer, who will make the actual presentation, have asked you to help them by answering the following questions.

(Section I: Bond valuation)

a. What are the key features of a bond?

b. How is the value of any asset whose value is based on expected future cash flows determined?

c. How is the value of a bond determined? What is the value of a 1-year, $1,000 par value bond with a 10 percent annual coupon if its required rate of return is 10 percent? What is the value of a similar 10-year bond?

d. (1) What would be the value of the bond described in Part c if, just after it had been issued, the expected inflation rate rose by 3 percentage points, causing investors to require a 13 percent return? Would we now have a discount or a premium bond?

   (2) What would happen to the bond's value if inflation fell, and k_d declined to 7 percent? Would we now have a premium or a discount bond?

(3) What would happen to the value of the 10-year bond over time if the required rate of return remained at 13 percent or remained at 7 percent?

e. (1) What is the yield to maturity on a 10-year, 9 percent annual coupon, $1,000 par value bond that sells for $887.00? That sells for $1,134.20? What does the fact that a bond sells at a discount or at a premium tell you about the relationship between k_d and the bond's coupon rate?

(2) What is the current yield, the capital gains yield, and the total return in each case?

f. What is price risk? Which bond in Part c has more price risk, the 1-year bond or the 10-year bond?

g. What is reinvestment rate risk? Which bond in Part c has more reinvestment rate risk, assuming a 10-year investment horizon?

h. Redo Parts c and d, assuming the bonds have semiannual rather than annual coupons.

i. Suppose you could buy, for $1,000, either a 10 percent, 10-year, annual payment bond or a 10 percent, 10-year, semiannual payment bond. They are equally risky. Which would you prefer? If $1,000 is the proper price for the semiannual bond, what is the proper price for the annual payment bond?

j. What is the value of a perpetual bond with an annual coupon of $100 if its required rate of return is 10 percent? 13 percent? 7 percent? Assess the following statement: "Because perpetual bonds match an infinite investment horizon, they have little price risk."

k. Suppose a 10-year, 10 percent, semiannual coupon bond with a par value of $1,000 is currently selling for $1,135.90, producing a yield to maturity of 8 percent. However, the bond can be called after 5 years for a price of $1,050.

(1) What is the bond's yield to call (YTC)?

(2) If you bought this bond, do you think you would be more likely to earn the YTM or the YTC?

(Section II: Stock valuation) To illustrate the common stock valuation process, Balik and Kiefer have asked you to analyze the Bon Temps Company, an employment agency that supplies word processor operators and computer programmers to businesses with temporarily heavy workloads. You are to answer the following questions.

a. (1) Write out a formula that can be used to value any stock, regardless of its dividend pattern.

(2) What is a constant growth stock? How are constant growth stocks valued?

(3) What happens if the constant $g > k_s$? Will many stocks have $g > k_s$?

b. Assume that Bon Temps has a beta coefficient of 1.2, that the risk-free rate (the yield on T-bonds) is 10 percent, and that the required rate of return on the market is 15 percent. What is the required rate of return on the firm's stock?

c. Assume that Bon Temps is a constant growth company whose last dividend (D_0, which was paid yesterday) was $2.00 and whose dividend is expected to grow indefinitely at a 6 percent rate.

(1) What is the firm's expected dividend stream over the next 3 years?

(2) What is the firm's current stock price?

(3) What is the stock's expected value one year from now?

(4) What are the expected dividend yield, the capital gains yield, and the total return during the first year?

d. Now assume that the stock is currently selling at $21.20. What is the expected rate of return on the stock?

e. What would the stock price be if its dividends were expected to have zero growth?

f. Now assume that Bon Temps is expected to experience supernormal growth of 30 percent for the next 3 years, then to return to its long-run constant growth rate of 6 percent. What is the stock's value under these conditions? What is its expected dividend yield and capital gains yield in Year 1? In Year 4?

g. Suppose Bon Temps is expected to experience zero growth during the first 3 years and then to resume its steady-state growth of 6 percent in the fourth year. What is the stock's value now? What is its expected dividend yield and its capital gains yield in Year 1? In Year 4?

h. Finally, assume that Bon Temps's earnings and dividends are expected to decline by a constant 6 percent per year, that is, $g = -6\%$. Why would anyone be willing to buy such a stock, and at what price should it sell? What would be the dividend yield and capital gains yield in each year?

i. What does market equilibrium mean?

j. If equilibrium does not exist, how will it be established?

k. What is the Efficient Markets Hypothesis, what are its three forms, and what are its implications?

SELECTED ADDITIONAL REFERENCES AND CASES

Many investment textbooks cover stock and bond valuation models in depth and detail. Some of the better ones are listed in the Chapter 4 references.

The seminal work on stock valuation models is

Williams, John Burr, *The Theory of Investment Value* (Cambridge, Mass.: Harvard University Press, 1938).

The following classic articles extend J. B. Williams' works:

Durand, David, "Growth Stocks and the Petersburg Paradox," *Journal of Finance,* September 1957, 348–363.

Gordon, Myron J., and Eli Shapiro, "Capital Equipment Analysis: The Required Rate of Profit," *Management Science,* October 1956, 102–110.

For some recent works on valuation, see

Bey, Roger P., and J. Markham Collins, "The Relationship between Before- and After-Tax Yields on Financial Assets," *The Financial Review,* August 1988, 313–343.

Brooks, Robert, and Billy Helms, "An N-Stage, Fractional Period, Quarterly Dividend Discount Model," *Financial Review,* November 1990, 651–657.

Taylor, Richard W., "The Valuation of Semiannual Bonds between Interest Payment Dates," *The Financial Review,* August 1988, 365–368.

Tse, K. S. Maurice, and Mark A. White, "The Valuation of Semiannual Bonds between Interest Payment Dates: A Correction," *Financial Review,* November 1990, 659–662.

The following case in the Brigham-Gapenski casebook covers many of the valuation concepts contained in Chapter 3:

Case 3, "Peachtree Securities, Inc. (B)."

CAPITAL BUDGETING

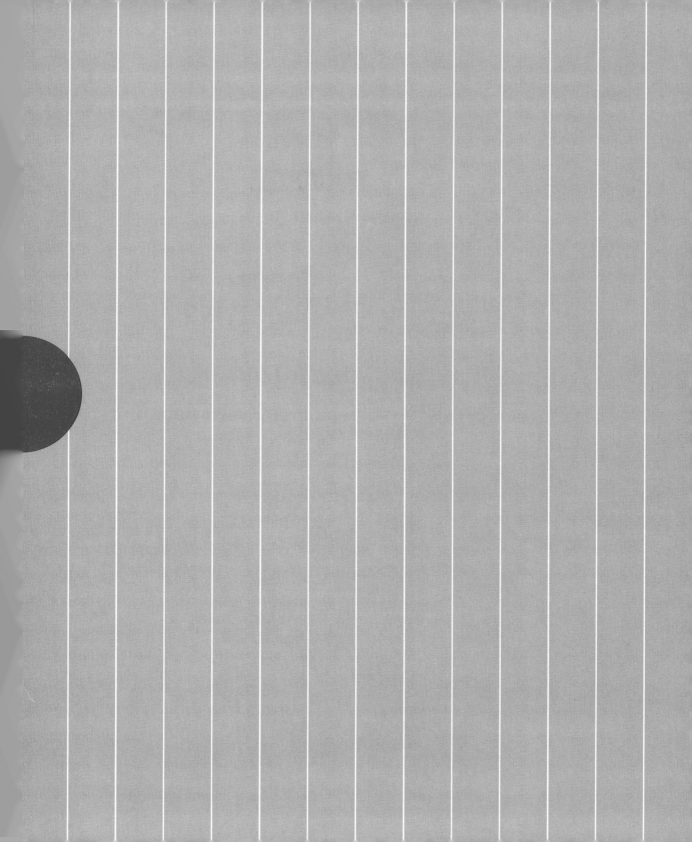

THE COST OF CAPITAL

I n early 1993, word leaked out that Boeing, in a brazen move that shook up the world's aviation industry, was considering teaming up with two members of its archrival, the Airbus Industrie consortium, to pursue the development of a 600-seat jetliner. Seattle-based Boeing and European aircraft industry giants Deutsche Aerospace and British Aerospace were investigating a joint venture that would leave the Airbus consortium very much in the lurch.

Given the costs of developing and marketing a superjumbo jet, Boeing took the position that the more companies involved, the merrier, as long as Boeing was the lead partner. Despite some skepticism about the need for a 600-seat plane, Boeing thought that it must maintain its lead in the high-capacity jet market. For 20 years, its 400-seat 747 has enjoyed a profitable monopoly in the jumbo-jet market. However, Boeing's position had recently been weakened as Airbus's newest planes, the A330 and A340, had eaten into the lower end of the 747 market, and Airbus's development of a superjumbo plane could put a fatal squeeze on Boeing.

Although Boeing had $4.6 billion cash on hand, its management decided that it could not risk the new project alone, as development costs of the superjumbo were estimated at a staggering $10 to $15 billion. Deutsche Aerospace chose to participate because the joint venture would provide it with a degree of independence from the Airbus consortium, which is dominated by a French government—owned company. Since Deutsche Aerospace became fully privatized several years ago, it has bought 51 percent of Fokker, a Dutch plane maker, and a deal with Boeing would be yet another way to flex its muscles and demonstrate its ability to function as an independent company. Meanwhile, British Aerospace

had been experiencing weakness in the corporate-jet market, and it felt a need to expand its presence in new markets.

At this time, the $15-billion question is whether there is a sufficient market for a mammoth jet that will cost $225 to $250 million per plane. British Airways is apparently keen on the idea, and several other airlines, including United, JAL, and Lufthansa, have expressed interest. Clearly, though, the superjumbo would appeal only to airlines having long-distance, high-volume routes.

The first phase of the joint venture, which would take about a year if it materializes, calls for studies of market demand and shared-production schemes. Later phases of the venture, which could take as long as eight years, would involve detailed design and production planning. Given the gargantuan dimensions of any such superjumbo aircraft, new factories would have to be built in every country where it would be coproduced.

A venture of this magnitude would take many years and would require billions of dollars before even one dollar of sales revenue could be collected. Furthermore, the capital supplied by the venture partners would not be costless: (1) each partner's own investors would require some return on the capital they supplied to the firm, and (2) if the partners were not involved in the joint venture, they would be able to use the funds for other purposes. Thus, before making the decision to form the joint venture, each participant will have to consider the cost of the capital tied up in the venture and be confident that its share of the venture's profits will be sufficient to cover its capital costs.

This chapter will help you understand how Boeing and other companies estimate the cost of capital (debt, preferred stock, and common equity) required for ventures such as the superjumbo project. Then, in subsequent chapters, you will see how capital costs affect the go/no-go decision on such projects. An incorrect estimate of the cost of capital can lead to incorrect investment decisions, so cost of capital estimation is an important aspect of financial management.

A firm's cost of capital is critically important for three reasons: (1) Maximizing the value of a firm requires that the costs of all inputs, including capital, be minimized, and to minimize the cost of capital we must be able to estimate it. (2) Capital budgeting decisions require an estimate of the cost of capital. (3) Many other types of decisions, including those related to public utility regulation, leasing, bond refunding, and short-term asset management, require estimates of the cost of capital.

At the 1991 Annual Meeting of the Financial Management Association, a day-long panel discussion focused on cost of capital. Here, financial managers from Hershey Foods and Du Pont, among others, discussed procedures for estimating corporations' cost of capital. All of the panelists agreed that while the task is difficult, it is essential to good decision making, especially in the key capital budgeting area. Further, they agreed that the overall corporate cost-of-capital estimate should be viewed only as the first step in the development of divisional and specific proj-

ect costs of capital. In this chapter, we discuss the actual process of estimating a firm's overall, or weighted average, cost of capital. Then, in Chapter 11, we discuss the adjustment process used to estimate divisional and project costs of capital.

CAPITAL COMPONENTS AND COSTS

In developing the firm's overall cost of capital, we first identify and then determine the cost of each capital component, and we then combine the component costs to form the *weighted average cost of capital (WACC).* Capital, as we use the term, represents the funds used to finance the firm's assets and operations. The sales which produce profits are not possible without the assets that are shown on the left side of the balance sheet, and those assets must be financed from the sources shown on the right side. Thus, capital constitutes the entire right-hand side of the balance sheet, including both short-term and long-term debt, preferred stock, and common equity.

CAPITAL COMPONENTS

Our first task is to decide which capital sources should be included when we estimate the WACC. Since the cost of capital is used primarily in the process of making long-term investment decisions, our discussion will focus on the development of the cost of capital for capital budgeting purposes. First, consider the firm's short-term, non-interest-bearing liabilities: accounts payable, accrued wages, and accrued taxes. All of these items arise from normal operations—if sales increase, then funds are spontaneously (automatically) generated from these sources. In capital budgeting analyses, the dollar amount of the spontaneously generated liabilities associated with a given project is subtracted from the amount that would otherwise be required to finance the project. To illustrate, assume that a potential project has a total cost of $2,000,000, consisting of $1,500,000 of fixed assets and $500,000 of required new current assets, say, inventories. However, if payables and accruals will spontaneously increase by $200,000 if the project is undertaken, then these funds serve to offset the increase in current assets. Thus, the project's required net current assets (or net working capital) would be only $300,000, and the net funds required for the project would be only $1,800,000.

Increase in fixed assets		$1,500,000
Increase in current assets	$500,000	
Less: Increase in spontaneous liabilities	200,000	300,000
Net funds required for project		$1,800,000

It is the cost of this $1,800,000 that concerns us—will the return on the project be high enough to cover the cost of the $1,800,000 of nonspontaneous capital required to undertake it? Since we are concerned only with the cost of the nonspontaneous capital, spontaneously generated current liabilities are not included when the WACC is estimated.

We must also decide how to treat short-term notes payable, often bank loans, which are not generated spontaneously. The answer depends on whether the firm deliberately uses short-term debt to finance long-term investments. If short-term debt is only used as temporary financing to support cyclical or seasonal fluctuations in current assets, it should not be included in the firm's WACC. However, if the firm does use short-term debt as part of its permanent financing, then such debt should be included when the cost of capital is estimated. As we will show in Chapter 16, the use of nonspontaneous short-term debt to finance long-term assets is quite risky, and it is not common among well-managed firms. Therefore, in this chapter, we shall assume that interest-bearing short-term debt is used to support cyclical or seasonal working capital, and since our primary focus is on developing a cost of capital for use in capital budgeting, we shall exclude short-term debt when we estimate the WACC unless otherwise noted. Long-term debt, preferred stock, and common equity (common stock plus retained earnings) are the primary sources of capital for capital expansion, so they are the components included in the WACC estimate.

In summary, the relevant capital components for cost of capital purposes include (1) that portion of short-term interest-bearing debt that is considered to be permanent financing; (2) all long-term debt; (3) all preferred stock; and (4) all common equity. Non-interest-bearing liabilities such as accounts payable and accruals are netted out in the capital budgeting cash flow estimation process and hence are excluded from the cost of capital calculations.

TAXES

In developing the costs for the different capital components, the issue of taxes arises: Should we use a before- or an after-tax cost? In considering this question, remember that stockholders are concerned primarily with the cash flows that are available for their use; namely, those cash flows available to common shareholders after corporate taxes have been paid. Therefore, if management is to maximize stockholder well-being and thereby maximize the price of the stock, all analyses must fully reflect the impact of taxes. Although the tax benefits of debt financing, which arise due to the tax deductibility of interest expense, can be included in either the cash flows or the WACC, the most common approach to capital budgeting is to include the tax benefits in the WACC, so we will express all debt component costs on an after-tax basis.

HISTORICAL VERSUS NEW, OR MARGINAL, COSTS

Another issue is this: Is the historical, or embedded, cost of the capital that was raised in the past relevant, or should we focus on the cost of new, marginal funds? Embedded costs are important for some decisions. For example, the average cost of all the capital raised in the past and still outstanding is relevant to regulators who determine the allowed rate of return for a public utility. However, in financial management, the WACC is used primarily to make capital budgeting decisions, and

these decisions hinge on the cost of new, or marginal, capital. *Thus, for our purposes in this chapter, the relevant costs are not historical costs but, rather, the marginal costs of new funds to be raised during the planning period.*

SELF-TEST QUESTIONS

Which financing sources are typically included, and which are excluded, when a firm estimates its WACC? Explain.

Should the component cost estimates be on a before-tax or after-tax basis? Why?

Should the component cost estimates reflect historical or marginal costs? Why?

COST OF DEBT

As discussed in the previous section, the relevant cost of debt is the after-tax cost of new debt. Although estimating this cost is conceptually straightforward, some problems arise in practice. First, as noted in an earlier section, it is necessary to decide whether or not short-term debt should be included in the WACC. Second, not all long-term debt has a fixed and known payment schedule: Companies use both fixed and floating rate debt, straight and convertible debt, and debt both with and without sinking funds, and each form of debt generally has a somewhat different cost.

It is unlikely that the financial manager will know at the start of a planning period the exact types and amounts of debt that will be used in the future: The type of debt actually used will depend on the specific assets to be financed and on capital market conditions as they develop over time. Even so, the financial manager does know what types of debt are typical for his or her firm. For example, National Computer Corporation (NCC), a full-line computer manufacturer, typically sells commercial paper to raise short-term money to finance cyclical working capital needs, and it uses 30-year bonds to raise long-term debt capital. Thus, for planning purposes, NCC's managers include only long-term debt in their WACC estimate, and they assume that this debt will consist of 30-year bonds.

Assume that it is January 1994, and NCC's financial managers are developing the firm's WACC estimate for the coming year. How should they determine the component cost of debt? Most financial managers would begin by discussing current and prospective interest rates with their firms' investment bankers. Assume that NCC's bankers stated that a new 30-year, noncallable, straight bond issue would require an 11 percent coupon rate with semiannual payments, and that it would be offered to the public at a $1,000 par value. Flotation costs are estimated to be 1 percent of the issue, or $10 for every $1,000 par value bond. Thus, the net proceeds from each bond would be $1,000 minus a $10 flotation cost, or $990. NCC's marginal federal-plus-state tax rate is 40 percent.

With this information, we would estimate the cost of debt in two steps:

1. Find the *before-tax flotation-adjusted cost to the company:*

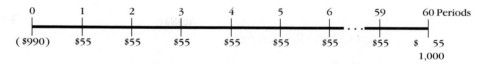

$$\begin{array}{c}\text{Net proceeds}\\ \text{of bond}\end{array} = \sum_{t=1}^{2n} \frac{\text{Semiannual}}{(1 + k_d/2)^t} + \frac{\text{Par value}}{(1 + k_d/2)^{2n}} \qquad \text{(8-1)}$$

$$\$990 = \sum_{t=1}^{60} \frac{\$55}{(1 + k_d/2)^t} + \frac{\$1,000}{(1 + k_d/2)^{60}}.$$

Using a financial calculator, we find $k_d/2 = 5.56\%$, so the flotation-adjusted cost of debt is $k_d = 11.12\%$.

2. Adjust for taxes using this equation:

$$\begin{aligned}\text{After-tax cost of debt} &= \text{Pre-tax cost}(1 - T)\\ &= (\text{Flotation-adjusted } k_d)(1 - T) \qquad \text{(8-2)}\\ &= 11.12\%(0.60) = 6.67\%.\end{aligned}$$

Note that most public offerings of debt have flotation costs of less than one percentage point, and flotation costs are even lower on private placements. Thus, if flotation costs were simply ignored, and the component cost of debt were found as $k_d(1 - T)$, the error would not be very large.[1] In our own example, $k_d(1 - T)$ = 11%(0.60) = 6.60%, hence the error would be only seven basis points.[2]

---

[1]It is sometimes suggested that the effective annual rate cost of debt should be used in the WACC. In our example, the flotation-adjusted effective annual rate is $(1.0556)^2 - 1.0 = 0.1143 = 11.43\%$. That position would be correct only if the cost of common stock were based on a quarterly compounding model and if, in capital budgeting, an attempt were made to determine exactly when, during the year, cash flows would come in rather than assuming end-of-year flows. In view of the uncertainties inherent in cost of equity estimation, and the even greater uncertainties about the cash flows of projects over their operating lives, we (and most people in industry) think it would be pointless to attempt to estimate effective rates and intra-year cash flows; it would even be misleading in that such calculations would imply greater accuracy than exists in the basic data. Further, it would be inconsistent to combine an effective bond yield with a nominal return on equity — the bond's cost would be inflated vis-à-vis that of the equity. Finally, note that the flotation cost can be amortized over the life of the bond (\$10/30 = \$0.33 per year, or \$0.167 per semiannual period). This saves taxes in the amount of \$0.167(T) = \$0.167(0.40) = \$0.067 per period. Theoretically, we should take this tax savings into account, but ignoring it does not introduce a material error.

[2]A basis point is 1/100 of a percentage point. Investment bankers in particular use this term.

Before closing our discussion of the cost of debt, we should note one additional point regarding the tax adjustment. In our example, we used a marginal tax rate of 40 percent. Therefore, we were implicitly assuming that NCC's marginal tax rate over the next 30 years will remain at 40 percent. However, there are three potential problems with this assumption: (1) The value of the tax deduction depends on the taxable income for each year, and a change in taxable income might lead to a change in the marginal tax rate, hence to a change in the after-tax cost of debt. (2) Tax losses can only be carried back for three years; therefore, several years of consecutive losses would mean that the benefits of tax deductibility could not be realized in the year the interest is paid. Instead, this benefit would be delayed until the firm becomes profitable, and this would raise the after-tax cost of debt. (3) Congress could raise or lower corporate tax rates, which would also have an effect on the after-tax cost of debt. For all these reasons, we should recognize that firms cannot be certain of the true effects of tax deductibility, so the true after-tax cost of debt could be higher or lower than the estimated cost.

SELF-TEST QUESTIONS

What impact does flotation cost have on the cost of debt? Is this cost generally material?

How is the before-tax cost of debt converted to an after-tax cost?

How could changes in the tax rate cause the actual after-tax cost of debt to differ from the estimated cost?

COST OF PREFERRED STOCK

A number of firms, including National Computer Corporation, use preferred stock as part of their permanent financing mix. To determine this cost, we first note that preferred dividends are not tax deductible, so the company bears their full cost. *Therefore, no tax adjustment is necessary when calculating the cost of preferred stock.* Second, although preferred was formerly issued without a stated maturity date, much of the preferred issued recently has a call feature, a sinking fund, or both. Finally, although it is not mandatory that preferred dividends be paid, firms generally do have every intention of paying preferred dividends, because if they fail to do so (1) they cannot pay dividends on their common stock, (2) they will find it difficult to raise additional funds in the capital markets, and (3) in some cases preferred stockholders have the right to assume control of the firm.

With these points in mind, assume that NCC's investment bankers indicated that the firm could sell *perpetual* preferred stock with a 10 percent yield. If the stock had a par value of $100, then the annual dividend would be $10. Additionally, the investment bankers stated that flotation costs would amount to 2.5 percent of the par value. Thus, the firm would net $97.50 from each share sold, and

it would have an obligation to pay \$10 of dividends per share per year. We calculate the component cost of perpetual preferred stock as follows:

$$\text{Component cost of perpetual preferred stock} = k_{ps} = \frac{D_{ps}}{P_n}. \tag{8-3}$$

Here D_{ps} is the annual preferred dividend and P_n is the price the firm receives net of flotation costs. Applying Equation 8-3 to our example, we find NCC's cost of preferred stock to be 10.26 percent:[3]

$$k_{ps} = \frac{D_{ps}}{P_n} = \frac{\$10}{\$97.50} = 0.1026 = 10.26\%.$$

SELF-TEST QUESTIONS

Describe how the cost of preferred stock is estimated.

Is a tax adjustment required when estimating the cost of preferred stock? Explain.

COST OF RETAINED EARNINGS

A firm can raise common equity capital in two ways: (1) by retaining earnings and (2) by issuing new common stock. Thus, when we consider NCC's component cost of equity, we must consider the costs of two different types of equity. We first examine the cost of retained earnings.

The costs of debt and preferred stock are based on the return that investors require on these securities, and the cost of equity obtained by retaining earnings can be defined similarly: *It is k_s, the rate of return stockholders require on the firm's common stock.* The firm's net income after taxes and after preferred dividends literally belongs to its common stockholders. Bondholders are compensated

---

[3]Most preferred stocks pay quarterly dividends, so we could calculate an effective return based on quarterly compounding. However, for the same reasons we discussed in Footnote 1 in connection with debt, it would be inappropriate (or at least not worthwhile) to do so. We should also note that firms have begun to issue variable, or floating, rate bonds and preferred stocks. Since future capital market rates are difficult if not impossible to predict, future interest payments and preferred dividends are normally estimated on the basis of current rates, hence the expected costs of floating rate securities are the same as for identical fixed rate securities. However, the realized cost of a floating rate issue can be higher or lower than expected, depending on the actual rates over the life of the security, whereas the realized cost of a fixed rate security is known with relative certainty. Note also that current tax laws do not permit either preferred or common stock flotation costs to be expensed against taxable income. Finally, note that many preferred issues have sinking funds, mandatory call provisions, or both. The costs of nonperpetual preferred stocks are estimated similarly to bonds.

by interest payments; preferred stockholders are compensated by fixed dividend payments; and the firm's remaining income belongs to its common stockholders and serves to "pay the rent" on stockholders' capital. Management may either pay out earnings in the form of dividends or retain earnings for reinvestment in the business. If part of the earnings is retained, an *opportunity cost* is incurred: Stockholders could have received those earnings as dividends and then invested that money in stocks, bonds, real estate, and so on. *Thus, the firm should earn on its retained earnings at least as much as its stockholders themselves could earn on alternative investments of equivalent risk.*

What rate of return can stockholders expect to earn on other investments of equivalent risk? The answer is k_s, because they can earn that return simply by buying the stock of the firm in question or that of a similar firm. Therefore, if our firm cannot invest retained earnings and earn at least k_s, then it should pay those earnings to its stockholders so that they can invest the money themselves in assets that do provide a return of k_s.

Whereas debt and preferred stocks are contractual obligations which have easily determined costs, it is not at all easy to estimate k_s. However, three methods can be used: (1) the Capital Asset Pricing Model (CAPM), (2) the discounted cash flow (DCF) model, and (3) the bond-yield-plus-risk-premium approach. These methods should not be regarded as mutually exclusive — no one dominates the others, and all are subject to error when used in practice. Therefore, when faced with the task of estimating a company's cost of equity, we generally use all three methods and then choose among them on the basis of our confidence in the data used for each in the specific case at hand.

SELF-TEST QUESTIONS

What are the two types of common equity whose costs must be estimated? Explain why there is a cost for retained earnings.

THE CAPM APPROACH

As we saw in Chapter 5, the Capital Asset Pricing Model is based on some unrealistic assumptions, and it cannot be empirically verified. Still, because of its logical appeal, the CAPM is often used in the cost of capital estimation process.

Under the CAPM we assume that the cost of equity is equal to the risk-free rate plus a risk premium that is based on the stock's beta coefficient and the market risk premium as set forth in the Security Market Line (SML) equation:

$$k_s = \text{Risk-free rate} + \text{Risk premium}$$
$$= k_{RF} + (k_M - k_{RF})b_i.$$

Given estimates of (1) the risk-free rate, k_{RF}, (2) the firm's beta, b_i, and (3) the required rate of return on the market, k_M, we can estimate the required rate of

return on the firm's stock, k_s. This required return can then be used as an estimate of the cost of retained earnings.

ESTIMATING THE RISK-FREE RATE

The starting point for the CAPM cost of equity estimate is k_{RF}, the risk-free rate. There is really no such thing as a truly riskless asset in the U.S. economy. Treasury securities are free of default risk, but long-term T-bonds will suffer capital losses if interest rates rise, and a portfolio invested in short-term T-bills will provide a volatile earnings stream because the rate paid on T-bills varies over time.

Since we cannot in practice find a truly riskless rate upon which to base the CAPM, what rate should we use? Our preference — and this preference is shared by most practitioners — is to use the rate on long-term Treasury bonds. Here are our reasons:

1. Capital market rates include a real, riskless rate (generally thought to vary from 2 to 4 percent) plus a premium for inflation which reflects the expected inflation rate over the life of the security, be it 30 days or 30 years. The expected rate of inflation is likely to be relatively high during booms and low during recessions. Therefore, during booms T-bill rates tend to be high to reflect the high current inflation rate, whereas in recessions T-bill rates are generally low. T-bond rates, on the other hand, reflect expected inflation rates over a long period, so they are far less volatile than T-bill rates.

2. Common stocks are long-term securities, and although a particular stockholder may not have a long investment horizon, most stockholders do invest on a long-term basis. Therefore, it is reasonable to think that stock returns embody long-term inflation expectations similar to those embodied in bonds rather than the short-term expectations in bills. Therefore, the cost of equity should be more highly correlated with T-bond rates than with T-bill rates.

3. Treasury bill rates are subject to more random disturbances than are Treasury bond rates. For example, bills are used by the Federal Reserve System to control the money supply, and bills are also used by foreign governments, firms, and individuals as a temporary safe haven for money. Thus, if the Fed decides to stimulate the economy, it drives down the bill rate, and the same thing happens if trouble erupts somewhere in the world and money flows into U.S. dollars seeking safety. T-bond rates are also influenced by Fed actions and by international money flows, but not to the same extent as T-bill rates. This is another reason why T-bill rates are more volatile than T-bond rates and, most experts agree, more volatile than k_s.

4. T-bills are essentially free of price risk, but they are exposed to a relatively high degree of reinvestment rate risk. Long-term investors such as pension funds and life insurance companies are as concerned about reinvestment rate risk as price risk. Therefore, most long-term investors would feel equally exposed to risk if they held bills or bonds.

5. When the CAPM is used to estimate a particular firm's cost of equity over time, bond rates produce more reasonable results. When T-bill rates were low in 1977

and 1978, the CAPM cost of equity estimate was about 11 percent. When T-bill rates shot up in 1979 and 1980, the T-bill-based CAPM estimate more than doubled, to 23 percent. The company's bond yields, meanwhile, only rose from 9 to 14 percent. Neither we nor the company's management believed that the cost of equity rose by 12 full percentage points at a time when the cost of long-term debt was rising by only 5 percentage points. CAPM estimates based on T-bond yields produced much more reasonable results.[4]

In light of the preceding discussion, it is our view that the cost of common equity is more logically related to Treasury bond rates than to T-bill rates. This leads us to favor T-bonds as the base rate, or k_{RF}, in a CAPM cost of equity analysis. T-bond rates can be found in *The Wall Street Journal* or the *Federal Reserve Bulletin*. Generally, we use the yield on a 20-year T-bond as the proxy for the risk-free rate. Assuming that this rate was 8.0 percent in January 1994, we would use this as our estimate for k_{RF} in a January 1994 CAPM cost of equity estimate.

ESTIMATING THE MARKET RISK PREMIUM

The market risk premium, $RP_M = k_M - k_{RF}$, can be estimated on the basis of (1) ex post, or historical, returns or (2) ex ante, or forward-looking, returns.

Ex Post Risk Premiums.   A very complete, accurate, and up-to-date ex post risk premium study is available annually from Ibbotson Associates, who examine market data over long periods of time to find the average annual rates of return on stocks, T-bills, T-bonds, and a set of high-grade corporate bonds.[5] For example, Table 8-1 summarizes some results from their 1993 study, which covers the period 1926–1992.

Note that common stocks provided the highest average return over the 67-year period, while Treasury bills gave the lowest. T-bills barely covered inflation over the period, but common stocks provided a substantial real return. However, the superior returns on stock investments had its cost—stocks were by far the riskiest of the investments listed as judged by the standard deviation, and they

---

[4]All of this can be illustrated by a true but not-very-funny story. A particular state public utility commission hired a professor who used T-bill rates as the base rate in his CAPM analysis to estimate the cost of capital for the state's utilities. Each utility's cost of capital in turn was built into its electric, gas, or telephone rates. Therefore, the lower the cost of capital, the lower the utility service rates, and the lower the service rates, the less political heat the commission faced. This particular commission was very politically sensitive—so much so that one of its staff members admitted privately that the commission had selected its cost of capital expert on the basis of who could produce the lowest number.

The commission hired the professor in 1978, when T-bill rates were very low, as were his CAPM cost of equity estimates based on the T-bill rate. But the rate cases did not come up until 1979, and by then, the bill rate had gone through the roof. As a result, the professor's cost of equity estimates were even higher than the companies were asking permission to earn! At that point, the commission rejected the CAPM approach and sent the professor home.

[5]See *Stocks, Bonds, Bills and Inflation: 1993 Yearbook* (Chicago: Ibbotson Associates, 1993). Also, note that Ibbotson Associates now recommends using the T-bond rate as the proxy for the risk-free rate when using the CAPM. Before 1988, Ibbotson Associates recommended that T-bills be used.

TABLE 8-1		Arithmetic Mean	Standard Deviation
SELECTED IBBOTSON ASSOCIATES DATA, 1926–1992			
	Total Return Data		
	Common stocks	12.4%	20.6%
	Long-term corporate bonds	5.8	8.5
	Long-term government bonds	5.2	8.6
	Treasury bills	3.8	3.3
	Inflation rate	3.2	4.7
	Risk Premium Data		
	Common stocks over T-bills	8.6%	20.9%
	Common stocks over T-bonds	7.1	21.0
	T-bonds over T-bills	1.4	Not available

would also rank as riskiest in a CAPM framework. To further illustrate the risk differentials, the range of annual returns on stocks was from -43.3 to 54.0 percent, while the range on T-bills was only 0.0 to 14.7 percent. The Ibbotson study provides strong empirical support for the premise discussed in earlier chapters — namely, that higher returns can be obtained only by bearing greater risk.

The Ibbotson study also reports the risk premiums, or differences, among the various securities. For example, Ibbotson found the average risk premium of stocks over T-bonds to be 7.1 percentage points.[6] However, these premiums have large standard deviations, so one must use them with caution. For example, the standard deviation of the stocks over T-bonds premium is 21 percent. Also, it should be noted that the choice of the beginning and ending periods can have a major impact on the calculated risk premiums. Ibbotson Associates used the longest period available to them, but had their data begun some years earlier or later, or ended earlier, their results would have been seriously affected. Indeed, over many periods their data would indicate *negative* risk premiums, which would lead to the conclusion that Treasury securities have a higher required return than common stocks, which

---

[6]It is worth noting that Ibbotson Associates calculates average returns on two bases: (1) by taking each of the 67 annual holding period returns and deriving the arithmetic average of these annual returns, and (2) by finding the compound annual rate of return over the whole period, which amounts to a geometric average. The stocks over T-bonds risk premium as measured by arithmetic averages is 1.8 percentage points higher than the geometric mean risk premium. This leads to the question of which average to use. The arithmetic average is most consistent with the standard CAPM; under the CAPM, investors are supposed to be concerned with returns during the next period (say, one year) and to focus on the expected return and the standard deviation of this return.

It has also been argued that the 1926–1992 risk premiums overstate "true" risk premiums, because there was a long-term trend during most of that period toward more inflation, and the rising inflation rate raised long-term interest rates, lowered bond prices, and resulted in realized yields on long-term bonds that were below the ex ante expected yields. If realized bond yields were below expected yields, then the risk premium as measured by $\bar{k}_{Stocks} - \bar{k}_{Bonds} = RP_{Market}$ will overstate the "true" required risk premium. If this is correct, then the 7.1 percentage point market risk premium of stocks over T-bonds reported by Ibbotson Associates is too large for use in the CAPM.

in turn is contrary to both financial theory and common sense. All this suggests that historical risk premiums should be approached with caution. As one business-man muttered after listening to a professor give a lecture on the CAPM, "Beware of academicians bearing gifts!"

Ex Ante Risk Premiums.   The ex post approach to risk premiums used by Ib-botson Associates assumes that investors expect future results, on average, to equal past results. However, as we noted, the estimated risk premium varies greatly de-pending on the period selected, and, in any event, investors today probably expect results in the future to be different from those achieved during the Great Depres-sion of the 1930s, during the World War II years of the 1940s, and during the peaceful boom years of the 1950s, all of which are included (and given equal weight with more recent results) in the Ibbotson Associates data. The questionable assumption that future expectations are equal to past realizations, together with the sometimes nonsensical results obtained in historical risk premium studies, has led to a search for ex ante risk premiums.

The most common approach to ex ante premiums is to use the discounted cash flow (DCF) model to estimate the expected market rate of return, $\hat{k}_M = k_M$, then to calculate RP_M as $k_M - k_{RF}$, and finally to use this estimate of RP_M in the SML. This procedure recognizes that if markets are in equilibrium, the expected rate of return on the market portfolio is also its required rate of return, so when we estimate $\hat{k}_M$, we also estimate k_M:

$$\begin{array}{c} \text{Expected} \\ \text{rate of return} \end{array} = \hat{k}_M = \frac{D_1}{P_0} + g = k_{RF} + RP_M = k_M = \begin{array}{c} \text{Required} \\ \text{rate of return} \end{array}.$$

Since D_1 for the market, say, the S&P 500, can be predicted quite accurately, and since the current market value of the index (used for P_0) is also known, the major task is to estimate g, the average expected long-term growth rate for the market index. Even here, however, the estimation task is simplified, because one can more reasonably assume a constant long-term growth rate for a portfolio of mature stocks such as the S&P 500 than for any one stock.

Financial services companies such as Merrill Lynch publish, on a regular basis, a forecast based on DCF methodology for the expected rate of return on the mar-ket, $\hat{k}_M$. For example, Merrill Lynch puts out such a forecast in its bimonthly pub-lication *Quantitative Analysis.* One can subtract the current T-bond rate from such a market forecast to obtain an estimate of the current market risk premium, RP_M. To illustrate, assume that Merrill Lynch's reported expected return on the market in January 1994 was 14.0 percent. The T-bond rate, as mentioned earlier, is assumed to be 8.0 percent. Thus, Merrill Lynch's implied market risk premium over T-bonds would be 6.0 percentage points.

Two potential problems arise when we attempt to use data from organizations such as Merrill Lynch. First, what we really want is *investors'* expectations, not those of security analysts. However, this is probably not a major problem, since several studies have proved beyond much doubt that investors, on average, form

their own expectations on the basis of professional analysts' forecasts. The second problem is that there are a number of securities firms besides Merrill Lynch, and, at any given time, different analysts' forecasts of future market returns are somewhat different. This suggests that it would be most appropriate to obtain a number of forecasts of $\hat{k}_M$, and then to use the average value to estimate RP_M for use in the SML. A service (Institutional Brokers Estimate System, or IBES) publishes data on the forecasts of essentially all widely followed analysts, so one can use the IBES aggregate growth rate forecast, along with an aggregate dividend yield, to develop a consensus RP_M forecast, and thus avoid potential bias from the use of only one organization's estimate. However, we have followed the forecasts of several of the larger organizations over a period of several years, and we have rarely found their $\hat{k}_M$ estimates to differ by more than ± 0.3 percentage points from one another. Therefore, for present purposes, the assumed Merrill Lynch $\hat{k}_M = k_M = 14.0\%$ and $RP_M = 6.0$ percentage points may be considered to be a "reasonable" proxy for the expectations of the marginal investor. Note, though, that ex ante risk premiums are not stable: they vary over time. Therefore, when using the CAPM to estimate the cost of equity, it is best to use current estimates of the ex ante RP_M.

ESTIMATING BETA

The last parameter needed for a CAPM cost of equity estimate is the beta coefficient. Recall from Chapter 5 that a stock's beta is a measure of its volatility relative to that of an average stock, and that betas are generally estimated from the stock's characteristic line by running a linear regression between past returns on the stock in question and past returns on some market index. We will define betas developed in this manner as *historical betas.*

Note, however, that historical betas show how risky a stock was *in the past,* whereas investors are interested in *future* risk. It may be that a given company appeared to be quite safe in the past, but that things have changed, and its future risk is judged to be higher than its past risk, or vice versa. AT&T is a good example. AT&T was among the bluest of the blue chips when it owned the regional telephone companies, but investors now recognize that AT&T as it exists today faces far more intense competition than it ever faced in the past. Chrysler, on the other hand, was practically bankrupt a few years ago, but it now appears to be reasonably healthy. Therefore, one would think that Chrysler's risk had declined while AT&T's had increased.

Now consider the use of beta as a measure of a company's risk. If we use a historical beta in a CAPM framework to measure the firm's cost of equity, we are implicitly assuming that the company's future risk is the same as its past risk. This would be a troublesome assumption for a company like Chrysler or AT&T today. But what about most companies in most years? As a general rule, is future risk sufficiently similar to past risk to warrant the use of historical betas in a CAPM framework? For individual firms, past risk is often *not* a good predictor of future risk, and historical betas of individual firms are often not very stable.

Since historical betas may not be good predictors of future risk, researchers have sought ways to improve them. This has led to the development of two different types of betas: (1) adjusted betas and (2) fundamental betas. *Adjusted betas* grew largely out of the work of Marshall E. Blume, who showed that true betas tend to move toward 1.0 over time.[7] Therefore, one can begin with a firm's pure historical statistical beta, make an adjustment for the expected future movement toward 1.0, and produce an adjusted beta which will, on average, be a better predictor of the future beta than would the unadjusted historical beta. The adjustment process involves some complex statistics, so we shall not cover it here.

Other researchers have extended the adjustment process to include such fundamental risk variables as financial leverage, sales volatility, and the like. The end product here is a *fundamental beta*.[8] These betas are constantly adjusted to reflect changes in a firm's operations and capital structure, whereas with historical betas (including adjusted ones), such changes might not be reflected until several years after the company's "true" beta had changed.

Adjusted betas are obviously heavily dependent on unadjusted historical betas, and so are fundamental betas as they are actually calculated. Therefore, the plain old historical beta, calculated as the slope of the characteristic line, is important even if one goes on to develop a more exotic version. With this in mind, it should be noted that several different sets of data can be used to calculate historical betas, and the different data sets produce different results. Here are some points to note:

1. Betas can be based on historical periods of different lengths. For example, data for the past one, two, three, and so on, years may be used. Most people who calculate betas today use five years of data, but this choice is arbitrary, and different lengths of time usually alter significantly the calculated beta for a given company.[9]

2. Returns may be calculated on holding periods of different lengths—a day, a week, a month, a quarter, a year, and so on. For example, if it has been decided to analyze data on NYSE stocks over a 5-year period, then we might obtain $52(5) = 260$ weekly returns on each stock and on the market index. We could also use $12(5) = 60$ monthly returns, or $1(5) = 5$ annual returns. The set of returns on each stock, however large it turns out to be, would then be regressed on the corresponding market returns to obtain the stock's beta. In statistical analysis, it is

---

[7] See Marshall E. Blume, "Betas and Their Regression Tendencies," *Journal of Finance,* June 1975, 785–796.

[8] See Barr Rosenberg and James Guy, "Beta and Investment Fundamentals," *Financial Analysts Journal,* May-June 1976, 60–72. Rosenberg, a professor at the University of California at Berkeley, later set up a company which calculates fundamental betas by a proprietary procedure and then sells them to institutional investors.

[9] A commercial provider of betas once told the authors that his firm, and others, did not know what the right period was to use, but they decided to use five years in order to reduce the apparent differences between various services' betas, because large differences reduced everyone's credibility!

TABLE 8-2		Merrill Lynch	Value Line
BETA COEFFICIENTS			
FOR FIVE COMPANIES	Chrysler	1.36	1.30
	Polaroid	1.14	1.10
	IBM	0.89	0.95
	Mobil	0.64	0.75
	Southwestern Public Service	0.51	0.70

generally better to have more rather than fewer observations, because using more observations generally leads to greater statistical confidence. This suggests the use of weekly returns, and, say, five years of data, for a sample size of 260, or even daily returns for a still larger sample size. However, the shorter the holding period, the more likely the data are to exhibit random "noise," and the greater the number of years of data, the more likely it is that the company's basic risk position will have changed (for example, see the preceding comments on Chrysler and AT&T). Thus, the choice of both the number of years of data and the length of the holding period for calculating rates of return involves trade-offs between a desire to have many observations versus a desire to rely on recent and consequently more relevant data.

3. The value used to represent "the market" is also an important consideration, as the index used can have a significant effect on the calculated beta. Most analysts today use the New York Stock Exchange Composite Index (based on about 1,800 common stocks, weighted by the value of each company), but others use the S&P 500 Index or some other group, including one (the Wilshire Index) with more than 5,000 stocks. In theory, the broader the index, the better the beta: Indeed, the index should really include returns on all stocks, bonds, leases, private businesses, real estate, and even "human capital." As a practical matter, however, we cannot get accurate returns data on most other types of assets, so measurement problems largely restrict us to stock indexes.

The bottom line of all this is that one can calculate betas in many different ways and, depending on the method used, different betas, hence different costs of capital, will result. To illustrate this point, consider Table 8-2, which contains the beta coefficients for five well-known companies as reported in May 1993 by Merrill Lynch and Value Line. Merrill Lynch uses the S&P 500 as the market index, while Value Line uses the New York Stock Exchange Composite Index. Further, Value Line betas are adjusted, while the Merrill Lynch betas listed in Table 8-2 are pure historical betas. Merrill Lynch uses five years of monthly returns, or 60 observations; Value Line uses 260 weekly observations.

Where does this leave financial managers regarding the proper beta? They must "pay their money and take their choice." Some managers calculate their own betas, using whichever procedure seems most appropriate under the circum-

Since historical betas may not be good predictors of future risk, researchers have sought ways to improve them. This has led to the development of two different types of betas: (1) adjusted betas and (2) fundamental betas. *Adjusted betas* grew largely out of the work of Marshall E. Blume, who showed that true betas tend to move toward 1.0 over time.[7] Therefore, one can begin with a firm's pure historical statistical beta, make an adjustment for the expected future movement toward 1.0, and produce an adjusted beta which will, on average, be a better predictor of the future beta than would the unadjusted historical beta. The adjustment process involves some complex statistics, so we shall not cover it here.

Other researchers have extended the adjustment process to include such fundamental risk variables as financial leverage, sales volatility, and the like. The end product here is a *fundamental beta*.[8] These betas are constantly adjusted to reflect changes in a firm's operations and capital structure, whereas with historical betas (including adjusted ones), such changes might not be reflected until several years after the company's "true" beta had changed.

Adjusted betas are obviously heavily dependent on unadjusted historical betas, and so are fundamental betas as they are actually calculated. Therefore, the plain old historical beta, calculated as the slope of the characteristic line, is important even if one goes on to develop a more exotic version. With this in mind, it should be noted that several different sets of data can be used to calculate historical betas, and the different data sets produce different results. Here are some points to note:

1. Betas can be based on historical periods of different lengths. For example, data for the past one, two, three, and so on, years may be used. Most people who calculate betas today use five years of data, but this choice is arbitrary, and different lengths of time usually alter significantly the calculated beta for a given company.[9]

2. Returns may be calculated on holding periods of different lengths—a day, a week, a month, a quarter, a year, and so on. For example, if it has been decided to analyze data on NYSE stocks over a 5-year period, then we might obtain 52(5) = 260 weekly returns on each stock and on the market index. We could also use 12(5) = 60 monthly returns, or 1(5) = 5 annual returns. The set of returns on each stock, however large it turns out to be, would then be regressed on the corresponding market returns to obtain the stock's beta. In statistical analysis, it is

---

[7]See Marshall E. Blume, "Betas and Their Regression Tendencies," *Journal of Finance,* June 1975, 785–796.

[8]See Barr Rosenberg and James Guy, "Beta and Investment Fundamentals," *Financial Analysts Journal,* May-June 1976, 60–72. Rosenberg, a professor at the University of California at Berkeley, later set up a company which calculates fundamental betas by a proprietary procedure and then sells them to institutional investors.

[9]A commercial provider of betas once told the authors that his firm, and others, did not know what the right period was to use, but they decided to use five years in order to reduce the apparent differences between various services' betas, because large differences reduced everyone's credibility!

	Merrill Lynch	Value Line
TABLE 8-2		
BETA COEFFICIENTS		
FOR FIVE COMPANIES		
Chrysler	1.36	1.30
Polaroid	1.14	1.10
IBM	0.89	0.95
Mobil	0.64	0.75
Southwestern Public Service	0.51	0.70

generally better to have more rather than fewer observations, because using more observations generally leads to greater statistical confidence. This suggests the use of weekly returns, and, say, five years of data, for a sample size of 260, or even daily returns for a still larger sample size. However, the shorter the holding period, the more likely the data are to exhibit random "noise," and the greater the number of years of data, the more likely it is that the company's basic risk position will have changed (for example, see the preceding comments on Chrysler and AT&T). Thus, the choice of both the number of years of data and the length of the holding period for calculating rates of return involves trade-offs between a desire to have many observations versus a desire to rely on recent and consequently more relevant data.

3. The value used to represent "the market" is also an important consideration, as the index used can have a significant effect on the calculated beta. Most analysts today use the New York Stock Exchange Composite Index (based on about 1,800 common stocks, weighted by the value of each company), but others use the S&P 500 Index or some other group, including one (the Wilshire Index) with more than 5,000 stocks. In theory, the broader the index, the better the beta: Indeed, the index should really include returns on all stocks, bonds, leases, private businesses, real estate, and even "human capital." As a practical matter, however, we cannot get accurate returns data on most other types of assets, so measurement problems largely restrict us to stock indexes.

The bottom line of all this is that one can calculate betas in many different ways and, depending on the method used, different betas, hence different costs of capital, will result. To illustrate this point, consider Table 8-2, which contains the beta coefficients for five well-known companies as reported in May 1993 by Merrill Lynch and Value Line. Merrill Lynch uses the S&P 500 as the market index, while Value Line uses the New York Stock Exchange Composite Index. Further, Value Line betas are adjusted, while the Merrill Lynch betas listed in Table 8-2 are pure historical betas. Merrill Lynch uses five years of monthly returns, or 60 observations; Value Line uses 260 weekly observations.

Where does this leave financial managers regarding the proper beta? They must "pay their money and take their choice." Some managers calculate their own betas, using whichever procedure seems most appropriate under the circum-

stances. Others use betas calculated by organizations such as Merrill Lynch or Value Line, perhaps using one service or perhaps averaging the betas of several services. The choice is a matter of judgment and data availability, for there is no "right" beta. With luck, the betas derived from different sources will, for a given company, be close together. If they are not, then our confidence in the CAPM cost of capital estimate will be diminished.

ILLUSTRATION OF THE CAPM APPROACH

We are now in a position to estimate National Computer's cost of equity from retained earnings by the CAPM method. We use as the risk-free rate the assumed T-bond rate in January 1994, which is 8.0 percent, and Merrill Lynch's assumed estimate of the expected return on the market, $\hat{k}_M = k_M = 14.0\%$. Thus, we can write the SML equation for January 1994 as follows:

$$k_s = k_{RF} + (k_M - k_{RF})b_i$$
$$= 8.0\% + (14.0\% - 8.0\%)b_i = 8.0\% + (6.0\%)b_i.$$

Therefore, if we know a company's beta, we can insert it into the SML equation and estimate the company's cost of retained earnings, k_s. We have two estimates of NCC's beta, an adjusted beta of 1.10 and an unadjusted beta of 1.20. Using the adjusted beta, we obtain $k_{NCC} = 14.6\%$:

$$k_{NCC} = 8.0\% + (6.0\%)1.1 = 14.6\%.$$

Using the unadjusted beta, we obtain an estimate of 15.2 percent. Therefore, on the basis of this CAPM analysis, National Computer Corporation's cost of retained earnings falls in the range of 14.6 to 15.2 percent.

Rather than using single values, we could have developed high and low estimates for the risk-free rate and the market risk premium. Then, by combining all of the low estimators and all of the high estimators, we could have estimated the extreme low and high values of NCC's cost of retained earnings. Obviously, this range would have been greater than 14.6 to 15.2 percent.

SELF-TEST QUESTIONS

What is the best proxy for the risk-free rate when using the CAPM? Why?

Explain the two methods used to estimate the market risk premium.

What are the three types of betas that can be used in the CAPM, and how do they differ?

Should the CAPM estimate of k_s be thought of as a precise point or a range?

THE DCF APPROACH

The second major procedure for estimating the cost of retained earnings is the discounted cash flow (DCF) approach. We know that the intrinsic value of a stock, $\hat{P}_0$, is the present value of its expected dividend stream:

$$\hat{P}_0 = \frac{D_1}{(1 + k_s)^1} + \frac{D_2}{(1 + k_s)^2} + \frac{D_3}{(1 + k_s)^3} + \cdots + \frac{D_\infty}{(1 + k_s)^\infty}.$$

Also, we know that we can recast this equation, given the market price of the stock, P_0, and solve for $\hat{k}_s$, the implied expected return:

$$P_0 = \frac{D_1}{(1 + \hat{k}_s)^1} + \frac{D_2}{(1 + \hat{k}_s)^2} + \frac{D_3}{(1 + \hat{k}_s)^3} + \cdots + \frac{D_\infty}{(1 + \hat{k}_s)^\infty}.$$

Finally, we know that in equilibrium, $\hat{k}_s = k_s$, so if a stock is in equilibrium, as it generally is, then an estimate of the expected rate of return also provides us with an estimate of the required rate of return.

If a stock is expected to grow at a constant rate, we can use the constant growth model to estimate $\hat{k}_s$:

$$\hat{k}_s = \frac{D_1}{P_0} + g.$$

Here P_0 is read from *The Wall Street Journal,* and next year's annual dividend, D_1, can be estimated relatively easily. It is not easy to estimate the growth rate expected by the marginal investor, but three approaches to estimating g are discussed below.

HISTORICAL GROWTH RATES

First, if earnings and dividend growth rates have been relatively stable in the past, and if investors expect these trends to continue, then the past realized growth rate may be used as an estimate of the expected future growth rate. To illustrate, consider Figure 8-1, which gives EPS and DPS data from 1979 to 1993 for NCC, along with a plot of these data on a semilog scale. Note these points:

1. Time period. We show 15 years of data in Figure 8-1, but we could have used 25 years, 5 years, or 10 years. There is no rule as to the appropriate number of years to analyze when calculating historical growth rates. However, the period chosen should reflect, to the extent possible, the conditions expected in the future.

2. Compound growth rate, point-to-point. The easiest historical growth rate to calculate is the compound rate between two dates. For example, EPS grew at an annual rate of 7.5 percent from 1979 to 1993, and DPS grew at a 4.8 percent

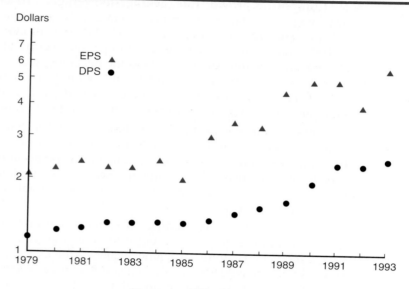

FIGURE 8-1

NATIONAL COMPUTER CORPORATION: SEMILOG PLOT OF EPS AND DPS, 1979–1993

Year	EPS	DPS
1979	$2.08	$1.20
1980	2.23	1.30
1981	2.38	1.33
1982	2.26	1.40
1983	2.21	1.40
1984	2.40	1.40
1985	2.00	1.40
1986	3.02	1.43
1987	3.56	1.54
1988	3.40	1.64
1989	4.65	1.72
1990	5.12	1.95
1991	5.14	2.20
1992	4.05	2.20
1993	5.73	2.30

rate during this same period.[10] Note that the point-to-point growth rate could change radically if we used two different points. For example, if we calculated the 5-year EPS growth rate from 1987 to 1992, we would obtain 2.6 percent, but the 5-year rate one year later, from 1988 to 1993, is 11.0 percent. This radical change occurs because the point-to-point rate is extremely sensitive to the beginning and ending years chosen.

---

[10]To obtain g_{EPS} using a financial calculator, enter 2.08 as PV, 5.73 as FV, 14 as N (because, with 15 data points, we have 14 growth periods: 1993 − 1979 = 14), and then press I to obtain the growth rate, 7.5 percent.

3. Compound growth rate, average-to-average. To alleviate the problem of beginning and ending year sensitivity, some analysts use an average-to-average calculation. For example, to calculate NCC's EPS growth rate over the period 1987 to 1992, Value Line's analysts would (1) get the average EPS over the years 1986 to 1988 and use this value ($3.33) as the beginning year, (2) get the average EPS over the years 1991 to 1993 and use this value ($4.97) as the ending year, and (3) calculate a growth rate of 8.3 percent based on these data. This procedure is superior to the simple point-to-point calculation for purposes of estimating g.

4. Least squares regression. A third way, and in our view the best way, to estimate historical growth rates is by log-linear least squares regression. The regression method gives consideration to all data points in the series; thus, it is the least likely to be biased by a randomly high or low beginning or ending year. The only practical way to estimate a least squares growth rate is with a computer or a financial calculator.[11]

5. Earnings versus dividends. If earnings and dividends are growing at the same rate, there is no problem, but if these two growth rates are unequal, we do have a problem. First, the DCF model calls for the expected *dividend* growth rate. However, if EPS and DPS are growing at different rates, something is going to have to change — these two series cannot indefinitely grow at two different rates. There is no rule for handling differences in historical g_{EPS} and g_{DPS}, and where they differ, this simply demonstrates yet another problem with using historical growth as a proxy for expected future growth. Like many aspects of finance, judgment is required when estimating growth rates.

Table 8-3 summarizes the historical growth rates we have just discussed. It is obvious that one can take a given set of historical data and, depending on the years and the calculation method used, obtain a large number of quite different growth rates. Now recall our purpose in making these calculations: We are seeking the future dividend growth rate that investors expect, and we reasoned that, if past growth rates have been stable, then investors might base future expectations on

---

[11]Log-linear regression is a standard time-series linear regression in which the data points are plotted as natural logarithms. The advantage of a log-linear regression is that the slope of the regression line is the average annual growth rate assuming continuous compounding. In a standard time-series linear regression of EPS or DPS, the slope of the regression line is the average annual dollar change. To find the EPS growth rate with a financial calculator, use the regression routine, entering years as the X variable and ln EPS as the Y variable. Obtain the slope coefficient of the regression, b, which is the annual growth rate assuming continuous compounding. Then find e^b, which produces the value $1 + g$, where g is the effective annual growth rate. For example, using the EPS data in Figure 8-1, we obtain a slope coefficient of b = 0.07607, then find $e^{0.07607} = 1.07903$, so g = 7.903%. The exact regression procedures are calculator specific, but with an HP 17B, one would enter the years and the EPS and DPS data, specify an exponential model (EXP), find the slope coefficient m, go into the math menu and press the exponential key (EXP = e^x) to find $1 + g$, and subtract 1.0 to obtain the growth rate. With an HP 10B, one would enter the EPS or DPS data, convert to natural logs (LN), complete the regression and determine the slope coefficient (m), convert to e^x, and then subtract 1.0 to obtain the growth rate. Other calculators require somewhat different procedures. Also, note that the same procedures can be used with *Lotus 1-2-3* to find the growth rate — get ln EPS, run a regression, then find @EXP(regression coefficient), which is $1 + g$. Finally, note that these procedures can be used to find the growth rate of any variable that changes over time, not just EPS.

TABLE 8-3 NATIONAL COMPUTER CORPORATION: HISTORICAL GROWTH RATES	Method (Period)	EPS	DPS	Average
	Point-to-point (1988–1993)	11.0%	7.0%	9.0%
	Point-to-point (1979–1993)	7.5	4.8	6.2
	Average-to-average (1987–1992)	8.3	7.7	8.0
	Average-to-average (1980–1992)	6.9	4.7	5.8
	Least squares regression (1988–1993)	6.6	7.6	7.1
	Least squares regression (1979–1993)	7.9	4.6	6.3

past trends. This is a reasonable proposition, but, unfortunately, one rarely finds much historical stability. Therefore, the use of historical growth rates in a DCF analysis must be applied with judgment, and also be used (if at all) in conjunction with other growth estimation methods as discussed next.

RETENTION GROWTH MODEL

Another method for estimating the growth rate is to use the *retention growth model:*

$$g = b(r). \tag{8-4}$$

Here r is the expected future return on equity, and b is the fraction of its earnings that a firm is expected to retain.[12] Equation 8-4 produces a constant growth rate, and when we use it we are, by implication, making four important assumptions: (1) We expect the payout rate, and thus the retention rate, b = 1 − Payout, to remain constant; (2) we expect the return on equity on new investment, r, to equal the firm's current ROE, which implies that we expect the return on equity to remain constant; (3) the firm is not expected to issue new common stock, or, if it does, we expect this new stock to be sold at a price equal to its book value; and (4) future projects are expected to have the same degree of risk as the firm's existing assets.

NCC has had an average return on equity of about 15 percent over the past 15 years. The ROE has been relatively steady, but even so it has ranged from a low of 11.0 percent to a high of 17.6 percent during this period. In addition, NCC's dividend payout rate has averaged 0.52 over the past 15 years, so its retention rate,

---

[12]Since there are more terms for which symbols are needed than there are letters in the alphabet, some letters are used to denote several different things. This is one of those instances, and b is standard notation for both the beta coefficient and the retention rate. Note also that the retention rate is the complement of the payout rate, that is, Retention rate = (1 − Payout rate).

b, has averaged $1.0 - 0.52 = 0.48$. Using Equation 8-4, we estimate g to be 7.2 percent:

$$g = 0.48(15\%) = 7.2\%.$$

This figure, together with the historical EPS and DPS growth rates examined earlier, might lead us to conclude that National Computer's expected growth rate is in the range of 6.5 to 7.5 percent. Therefore, if we forecasted NCC's next annual dividend to be $2.40, and if its current stock price is $32, then its dividend yield would be $D_1/P_0 = \$2.40/\$32 = 0.075$ or 7.5%, and its DCF cost of capital would be in the range of 14.0 to 15.0 percent:

$$\text{Lower end: } k_{NCC} = \hat{k}_{NCC} = 7.5\% + 6.5\% = 14.0\%.$$

$$\text{Upper end: } k_{NCC} = \hat{k}_{NCC} = 7.5\% + 7.5\% = 15.0\%.$$

This is reasonably close to the 14.6 to 15.2 percent range found by use of the CAPM method.

ANALYSTS' FORECASTS

A third growth rate estimating technique calls for using security analysts' forecasts. Analysts publish growth rate estimates for most of the larger publicly owned companies. For example, Value Line provides such forecasts on about 1,700 companies, and all of the larger brokerage houses provide similar forecasts. Further, several companies compile analysts' forecasts on a regular basis and provide summary information such as the median and range of forecasts on widely followed companies. These growth rate summaries, such as the one compiled by Lynch, Jones & Ryan in its *Institutional Brokers Estimate System (IBES),* can be ordered for a fee and obtained either in hardcopy format or as on-line computer data.

However, these forecasts often involve nonconstant growth. For example, in January 1994, analysts were forecasting that NCC would have a 10.4 percent annual growth rate in earnings and dividends over the next 5 years, or from 1994 through 1998, and they were forecasting a steady-state growth rate beyond 1998 of 6.5 percent. On the basis of the current $32 market price and a D_1 of $2.40, we can use the nonconstant growth stock valuation approach developed in Chapter 7 to find the expected rate of return. However, obtaining the solution is no trivial matter—we used a *Lotus 1-2-3* model and found $\hat{k}_s = k_s$ to be 15.0 percent.

As an alternative, a nonconstant growth forecast can be used to develop a proxy constant growth rate. Computer simulations indicate that dividends beyond Year 50 contribute very little to the value of any stock—the present value of dividends beyond Year 50 is virtually zero, so for practical purposes, we can ignore anything beyond 50 years. If we consider only a 50-year horizon, we can develop a weighted average growth rate and use it as a constant growth rate for cost of capital purposes. In the NCC case, we assumed a growth rate of 10.4 percent for

5 years followed by a growth rate of 6.5 percent for 45 years, which produces an average growth rate of 0.10(10.4%) + 0.90(6.5%) = 6.9%. This constant growth proxy results in $k_s = \hat{k}_s = 14.4\%$:

$$k_s = \hat{k}_s = \frac{\$2.40}{\$32} + 6.9\%$$

$$= 7.5\% + 6.9\% = 14.4\%.$$

These nonconstant growth DCF calculations suggest a range for k_s of 14.4 to 15.0 percent.

SELF-TEST QUESTIONS

What are the three most commonly used methods for estimating the future dividend growth rate?

Briefly describe the retention growth method for estimating the dividend growth rate. What are its underlying assumptions?

Can the DCF model be used to estimate k_s for a nonconstant growth stock? Explain.

BOND-YIELD-PLUS-RISK-PREMIUM APPROACH

A third method for estimating the required rate of return on retained earnings calls for adding an estimated risk premium to the company's own bond yield:

$$k_s = \text{Company's own bond yield} + \text{Risk premium}.$$

As discussed earlier, a corporate treasurer can easily estimate his or her own firm's bonds' yield to maturity if the bonds are publicly traded, or ask an investment banker for k_d if the bonds are not traded. The real problem occurs when trying to estimate the appropriate risk premium for the firm.

As we saw in Table 8-1, the average historical risk premium of stocks over corporate bonds as reported by Ibbotson Associates is 7.1 percentage points. If risk premiums were stable over time, or if they fluctuated randomly about a stable mean, then the average historical premium could be used with confidence to estimate the current risk premium. However, risk premiums are not stable, so some analysts argue that more reliance should be placed on the current level of the risk premium than on its historical average. Studies suggest that risk premiums are reasonably stable during periods when interest rates are stable, but that they become volatile during periods in which interest rates are volatile.

There are two common methods of estimating current risk premiums: a survey approach and a DCF-based approach similar to the method we discussed earlier in

connection with the market risk premium. One example of the survey approach is the work of Charles Benore, a security analyst with Paine Webber. Benore has for several years surveyed a large number of institutional investors, asking them what premium above the return on the company's bonds would make them indifferent between the stock and the bonds. In one survey, Benore found that most investors required a premium of from 2 to 4 percentage points on stock over the company's bond yield, with a mean value of 3.6 percentage points. This mean could be used as an estimate of the risk premium. Benore's survey analyzes only public utility companies, but the approach is applicable to any company or industry. Note, though, that in some years Benore has reported average risk premiums as high as 6 percent, but in other years he found values closer to 3 percent. The high premiums occurred during periods of low interest rates, and the low premiums in high-rate periods. Thus, Benore's studies confirm that risk premiums are not stable, hence that using old survey data is questionable.

The second method for estimating risk premiums is based on the DCF model. To illustrate, we assumed earlier that in January 1994 Merrill Lynch, using the DCF approach, estimated that the required rate of return on the market, as measured by the S&P 500, was 14.0 percent. At the same time, assume that the *Federal Reserve Bulletin* reported that the yield on an average (A-rated) corporate long-term bond was 10.2 percent. Using these data, we would estimate the risk premium of an average stock over an average bond to be 14.0% − 10.2% = 3.8 percentage points, or 380 basis points. However, one should recognize that the figure of 3.8 percentage points is not precise; we would, ourselves, conclude that the risk premium of an average company's stock over its own bonds, in January 1994, was somewhere between 3.3 and 4.3 percentage points.

We can apply the DCF-based risk premium approach to estimate the required rate of return for NCC. The company has been experiencing some problems from lower-cost foreign producers, and its bonds are rated Baa. Therefore, whereas if the *Federal Reserve Bulletin* reported that an average corporate bond yielded 10.2 percent in January 1994, NCC's relatively risky bonds yielded 11.0 percent, ignoring flotation costs. (Our studies indicate that the average NYSE company's bonds are rated A; NCC's bonds are rated below A.) Assuming that every company's required equity return exceeds its own cost of debt by the same risk premium, we would determine the high and low values of NCC's cost of equity as follows:

$$\text{Low: } k_{NCC} = 11.0\% + 3.3\% = 14.3\%.$$

$$\text{High: } k_{NCC} = 11.0\% + 4.3\% = 15.3\%.$$

Had NCC had a higher bond rating, its cost of debt and consequently its estimated cost of equity would have been lower.[13]

---

[13]Note that if you know a company's bond rating, or can estimate from an analysis of its financial statements what rating it would have if its debt were rated, then you could find its approximate k_d in Moody's or Standard & Poor's bond yield publications. This procedure is useful for outsiders analyzing companies that have no publicly traded debt. The company's own treasurer would always know, or could quickly find out, the value of k_d from the firm's investment bankers.

		Estimate	
Method		**Low**	**High**
CAPM		14.6%	15.2%
DCF (constant growth)		14.0	15.0
DCF (nonconstant growth)		14.4	15.0
Bond yield plus risk premium		14.3	15.3
Average		14.3%	15.1%
Overall average		14.7%	

TABLE 8-4
ESTIMATED REQUIRED
RATES OF RETURN
FOR NATIONAL
COMPUTER
CORPORATION

Note again, however, that risk premiums have not been stable over time, so it may not be appropriate, as a general rule, to add 3.3 to 4.3 percentage points to a company's bond yield to indicate its cost of equity. In recent years, our work suggests that the over-own-debt risk premium has ranged from about 2 to about 5 percentage points. (The low premium occurred when interest rates were quite high and people were reluctant to invest in long-term bonds because of a fear of runaway inflation, further increases in interest rates, and losses on investments in bonds. The high premiums occurred in periods when interest rates were relatively low.) Therefore, we repeat our earlier warning: Use a current risk premium when estimating equity capital costs by the bond-yield-plus-risk-premium method.

SELF-TEST QUESTIONS

Describe the basic concept underlying the bond-yield-plus-risk-premium approach.

How can the risk premium be estimated?

COMPARISON OF THE CAPM, DCF, AND RISK PREMIUM METHODS

We have discussed three methods for estimating the required rate of return on retained earnings—CAPM, DCF, and bond yield plus risk premium. Table 8-4 summarizes the results for National Computer. We see that the estimates range from 14.0 to 15.3 percent, that the average highs and average lows produce a range of 14.3 to 15.1 percent, and that the overall average is 14.7 percent. In our view, there is sufficient consistency in the results to warrant the use of 14.7 percent as our estimate of the cost of retained earnings for National Computer. If the methods produced widely varied estimates, then the financial manager would have to use his or her judgment as to the relative merits of each estimate, and then choose the estimate which seemed most reasonable under the circumstances. In general, this choice would be made on the basis of the financial manager's confidence in the input parameters of each approach.

SELF-TEST QUESTION

How would you choose between widely different estimates of k_s?

COST OF NEWLY ISSUED COMMON EQUITY

The cost of retained earnings as estimated in the preceding section is appropriate when retained earnings are being used to finance expansion. However, if the firm is expanding so rapidly that its retained earnings have been exhausted, then it must raise equity by selling newly issued common stock, and common equity has a higher cost than retained earnings. Specifically, the sale of new common equity, as with the sale of preferred stock and debt, involves flotation costs. These costs lower the net usable dollars produced by new stock issues, and this in turn increases the cost of the funds. We took account of flotation costs in our estimates of the costs of debt and preferred stock, and the same general approach can be used with common equity.

When the firm sells new common stock, it nets $P_0(1 - F)$, where F is the percentage flotation cost expressed in decimal form. Note that F consists of issuance expenses such as printing costs and investment banker commissions, as well as price effects resulting from market pressure and information asymmetries, topics which are discussed in detail in Chapters 13 and 19. To begin, the constant growth DCF model, modified to include flotation costs, is used to estimate $\hat{k}_e$, the cost of equity raised by selling new common stock:

$$\text{Net proceeds} = P_0(1 - F) = \frac{D_1}{\hat{k}_e - g}. \qquad \text{(8-5)}$$

Solving Equation 8-5 for $\hat{k}_e$ produces this expression:

$$\hat{k}_e = \frac{D_1}{P_0(1 - F)} + g. \qquad \text{(8-5a)}$$

This procedure recognizes that the purchaser of a share of newly issued stock will expect the same dividend stream as the holder of an old share, but the company will, because of flotation expenses, receive less money from the sale of the new share, $P_0(1 - F)$, than the value of the old share, P_0. Therefore, the money raised from the sale of new stock will have to "work harder" to produce the earnings needed to provide the dividend stream. As a result, $k_e > k_s$.

Note also that we could rewrite Equation 8-5a as follows:

$$\hat{k}_e = \frac{D_1/P_0}{(1 - F)} + g = \frac{\text{Dividend yield}}{(1 - F)} + g. \qquad \textbf{(8-5b)}$$

Equations 8-5a and 8-5b are equivalent, and either can be used, depending on the form of the available data. Using Equation 8-5a and a growth estimate of 6.5 percent, we obtain NCC's DCF cost of new common equity:

$$\hat{k}_e = \frac{\$2.40}{\$32(1 - 0.15)} + 6.5\%$$

$$= 8.8\% + 6.5\% = 15.3\%.$$

The DCF value for $\hat{k}_e$ is 15.3 percent versus the DCF $\hat{k}_s = 14.0\%$ for retained earnings that we estimated earlier, so the flotation cost adjustment is $+1.3$ percentage points, meaning that new outside equity costs about 1.3 percentage points more than retained earnings according to the DCF method:

$$\text{Flotation cost adjustment} = \text{DCF } \hat{k}_e - \text{DCF } \hat{k}_s$$

$$= 15.3\% - 14.0\%$$

$$= 1.3\%.$$

Notice that only one method (DCF) is commonly used to estimate the flotation cost adjustment, whereas three methods are used to estimate k_s. However, the DCF adjustment factor can also be added to the CAPM and risk premium estimates of the cost of retained earnings to find the cost of new stock as estimated by those methods. For National Computer, our final estimate of the cost of retained earnings was 14.7 percent. Thus, NCC's cost of new equity is estimated to be 16.0 percent:

$$k_e = k_s + \text{Flotation cost adjustment}$$

$$= 14.7\% + 1.3\% = 16.0\%.$$

SELF-TEST QUESTIONS

Explain why the cost of new common stock is higher than the cost of retained earnings.

How is the flotation cost adjustment factor estimated?

Weighted Average Cost of Capital

Thus far, we have discussed how to estimate the component costs of debt, preferred stock, retained earnings, and new common stock. Now we must combine these elements to form a weighted average cost of capital, WACC. Each firm has in mind a target capital structure, defined as that mix of debt, preferred, and common equity which causes its stock price to be maximized. Further, when the firm raises new capital, it generally tries to finance so as to keep the actual capital structure reasonably close to the target over time. Here is the general formula for the weighted average cost of capital:

$$\text{WACC} = w_d k_d (1 - T) + w_{ps} k_{ps} + w_{ce}(k_s \text{ or } k_e). \qquad \text{(8-6)}$$

Here w_d, w_{ps}, and w_{ce} are the target weights for debt, preferred stock, and common equity, respectively. The cost of the debt component of the WACC would itself be an average of several items if the firm uses several types of debt for its permanent financing, while the common equity used in the calculation will be either the cost of retained earnings, k_s, or the cost of new common stock, k_e.

One point should be made immediately: *The WACC is the weighted average cost of each new dollar of capital raised at the margin* — it is not the average cost of all the dollars the firm has raised in the past, nor is it the average cost of all the dollars the firm will raise during the current year. We are primarily interested in obtaining a cost of capital for use in capital budgeting, and for such purposes a *marginal cost* is required.[14] That means, conceptually, that we must estimate the cost of each dollar the firm raises during the year. Each of those dollars will consist of some debt, some preferred, and some common equity, and the equity will be either retained earnings or new common stock.

To illustrate, suppose National Computer has a target capital structure calling for 30 percent debt, 10 percent preferred stock, and 60 percent common equity. As we estimated earlier, the company's before-tax cost of debt, k_d, is 11.0 percent, ignoring flotation costs; its cost of preferred stock, k_{ps}, is 10.3 percent; its cost of common equity from retained earnings, k_s, is 14.7 percent; and its cost of equity from new common stock sales, k_e, is 16.0 percent. Further, the company's marginal tax rate is 40 percent.

Now suppose the firm needs to raise $100. In order to keep its capital structure on target, it must obtain $30 as debt, $10 as preferred, and $60 as common equity. (Common equity can come either from retained earnings or from the sale

---

[14]The only use we can think of for the average cost of all the capital a firm has raised, as opposed to the marginal cost of capital, is in public utility regulation, where utility commissions are supposed to set rates such that customers pay for all costs of service, including the cost of the capital that was used to buy the assets that are used to provide service.

of new stock.) The weighted average cost of the $100, assuming the equity portion is from retained earnings, is calculated as follows, using Equation 8-6:

$$\text{WACC} = w_d k_d (1 - T) + w_{ps} k_{ps} + w_{ce} k_s$$

$$= 0.3(11.0\%)(0.6) + 0.1(10.3\%) + 0.6(14.7\%) \approx 11.8\%.$$

Every dollar of new capital that NCC obtains consists of 30 cents of debt with an after-tax cost of 6.6 percent, 10 cents of preferred with a cost of 10.3 percent, and 60 cents of common equity with a cost of 14.7 percent. The average cost of each new dollar is 11.8 percent.

The weights could be based on the accounting values shown on the firm's balance sheet (book values), or on the market values of the different securities shown on the balance sheet, or on management's estimation of the firm's optimal capital structure, which becomes the firm's target market value weights. The correct weights are the firms' target weights, and the rationale for using the target weights is discussed in detail in Chapters 12 and 13.

THE MARGINAL COST OF CAPITAL (MCC) SCHEDULE

NCC's optimal capital structure calls for 30 percent debt, 10 percent preferred, and 60 percent equity, so each new (or marginal) dollar will be raised as 30 cents of debt, 10 cents of preferred, and 60 cents of common equity. Otherwise, the capital structure would not stay on target. As long as the firm's debt has an after-tax cost of 6.6 percent, its preferred has a cost of 10.3 percent, and its common equity has a cost of 14.7 percent, then its weighted average cost of capital will be 11.8 percent. Thus, each new dollar will be raised as 30 cents of debt, 10 cents of preferred, and 60 cents of equity, and each new (or marginal) dollar will have a weighted average cost of 11.8 percent.

BREAKS, OR JUMPS, IN THE MCC SCHEDULE

Could NCC raise an unlimited amount of new capital at the 11.8 percent cost? The answer is *no*. As companies raise larger and larger sums during a given time period, the costs of both the debt and the equity components begin to rise, and as this occurs, the weighted average cost of new dollars also rises. Thus, just as corporations cannot hire unlimited numbers of workers at a constant wage, neither can they raise unlimited amounts of capital at a constant cost. At some point, the cost of each new dollar will increase above 11.8 percent.

Where will this point occur? As a first step to determining the point of increasing costs, recognize that all of NCC's existing capital was raised in the past, and all of it is invested in assets which are used in operations. Now suppose the capital budget calls for net expenditures of $100 million during 1994. This new (or marginal) capital will presumably be raised so as to maintain the 30/10/60 debt/pre-

ferred/common equity relationship. Therefore, the company will obtain $30 million of debt, $10 million of preferred, and $60 million of common equity.[15] The new common equity could come from two sources: (1) that part of this year's profits which management decides to retain in the business rather than use for dividends (but not from earnings retained in the past, because those dollars will have already been invested) or (2) the sale of new common stock.

The debt will have an interest rate of 11.0 percent, or an after-tax cost of 6.6 percent. The preferred stock will have a cost of 10.3 percent. The cost of common equity will be k_s if the equity is obtained by retained earnings, but it will be k_e if the company must sell new common stock. Consider first the case where the new equity comes from retained earnings. As we have seen, the company's cost of retained earnings is 14.7 percent, and its weighted average cost of capital when using retained earnings as the common equity component is 11.8 percent.

Now consider the case in which the company expands so rapidly that its retained earnings for the year are not sufficient to meet its needs for new equity, forcing it to sell new common stock. Since we previously estimated the cost of new equity, k_e, to be 16.0 percent, the WACC using new common stock is

$$\text{WACC} = w_d k_d (1 - T) + w_{ps} k_{ps} + w_{ce} k_e$$

$$= 0.3(11.0\%)(0.6) + 0.1(10.3\%) + 0.6(16.0\%) \approx 12.6\%.$$

Thus, we see that the WACC is 11.8 percent so long as retained earnings are used, but it jumps to 12.6 percent as soon as the firm exhausts its retained earnings and is forced to sell new common stock.

How much new capital can NCC raise before it exhausts its retained earnings and is forced to sell new common stock? Assume that the company expects to have total earnings of $20 million for the year, and that it has a policy of paying out about 48 percent of its earnings as dividends. Thus, its *payout ratio,* which is the proportion of net income paid out as dividends, is 0.48. The *retention ratio,* which is the proportion of net income retained within the firm, is 1 − Payout ratio = 1 − 0.48 = 0.52. Therefore, the addition to retained earnings will be 0.52($20,000,000) = $10,400,000 during the year. How much *total financing* (debt and preferred plus this $10.4 million of retained earnings) can be done before the retained earnings are exhausted and the firm is forced to sell new common stock? In effect, we are seeking some amount of capital, X, which is defined as a *break point* and which represents the total financing that can be done before NCC is forced to sell new common stock. We know that 60 percent of X will be

---

[15]In reality, the company might raise the entire $100 million by issuing new debt, or perhaps by issuing new common stock. By issuing large blocks of securities, there are savings on flotation costs. However, over the long haul the firm will stick to its target capital structure. Thus, any financing deviation in one year will be offset by opposite financing deviations in future years, so the cost of capital remains a function of the target capital structure regardless of year-to-year financing decisions.

the new retained earnings, while 40 percent will be debt plus preferred. We also know that retained earnings will amount to $10.4 million. Therefore,

$$0.6X = \text{Retained earnings} = \$10,400,000.$$

Solving for X, which is the *retained earnings break point,* we obtain

$$\text{Break point} = X = \frac{\text{Retained earnings}}{\text{Equity fraction}} = \frac{\$10,400,000}{0.6} = \$17,333,333.$$

Thus, the company can raise a total of $17,333,333, consisting of $10,400,000 of retained earnings and $17,333,333 − $10,400,000 = $6,933,333 of new debt and preferred stock supported by these new retained earnings, without altering its capital structure:

New debt supported by retained earnings	$ 5,200,000	30%
Preferred stock supported by retained earnings	1,733,333	10
Retained earnings	10,400,000	60
Total expansion supported by retained earnings (that is, break point for retained earnings)	$17,333,333	100%

The left panel of Figure 8-2 graphs NCC's first approximation marginal cost of capital schedule. Each dollar has a weighted average cost of 11.8 percent until the company has raised a total of $17,333,333. However, if the firm raises $17,333,334 or more, each additional (or marginal) dollar will contain 60 cents of equity *obtained by selling new common equity at a cost of 16.0 percent,* so the WACC rises from 11.8 to 12.6 percent.

THE MCC SCHEDULE BEYOND THE RETAINED EARNINGS BREAK POINT

There is a jump, or break, in NCC's MCC schedule at $17,333,333 of new capital. Could there be other breaks in the schedule? Yes, there could be. The cost of capital could also rise due to increases in the cost of debt or the cost of preferred stock, or as a result of further increases in flotation costs as the firm issues more and more common stock. Some people have argued that the costs of capital components other than common stock should not rise. Their argument is that as long as the capital structure does not change, and presuming that the firm uses new capital to invest in profitable projects with the same degree of risk as its existing projects, investors should be willing to invest unlimited amounts of additional capital at the same rate. However, this argument assumes an infinitely elastic demand for a firm's securities. As we show in Chapter 19, the demand curve of investors for securities is downward sloping, so the more securities sold during a given period, the lower the price received for the securities, and the higher the required rate of return. In this situation, the more new financing required, the higher the firm's WACC.

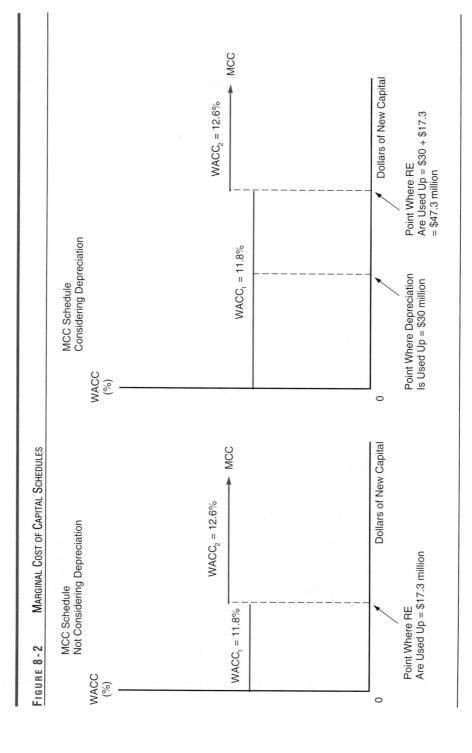

FIGURE 8-2   MARGINAL COST OF CAPITAL SCHEDULES

FIGURE 8-3   MARGINAL COST OF CAPITAL SCHEDULE BEYOND THE RETAINED EARNINGS BREAK POINT

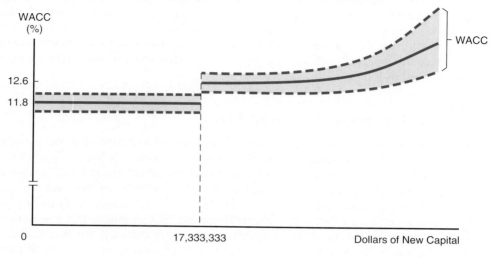

As a result of all this, firms face increasing MCC schedules, such as the one shown in Figure 8-3. Here we have identified a specific retained earnings break point (excluding depreciation), but because of estimation difficulties, we have not attempted to identify precisely any additional break points. However, we have (1) shown the MCC schedule to be upward sloping, reflecting a positive relationship between capital raised and capital costs, and (2) indicated our inability to precisely measure these costs by using a band of costs rather than a single line. Note that this band exists even at the first dollar of capital raised — our component costs are only estimates, these estimates become more uncertain as the firm requires more and more capital, and thus the band widens as the amount of new capital raised increases. In a later section we will show how the MCC schedule is used to help determine a firm's optimal level of new investment. Then, in Chapter 11, we will address this topic in detail.

SELF-TEST QUESTIONS

What is the formula for a firm's WACC?

What weights should be used to estimate a firm's WACC? Why?

What is an MCC schedule?

What is the retained earnings break point?

What happens to the MCC schedule beyond the retained earnings break point?

OTHER ISSUES REGARDING THE COST OF CAPITAL

Before concluding this chapter, we will discuss several items that affect the cost of capital. The purpose here is as much to raise questions as to answer them. Still, the material does have important practical implications, so anyone involved with financial management should be aware of the issues and understand how they affect the practical, rule-of-thumb procedures that financial managers are necessarily forced to follow.

THE EFFECTS OF PERSONAL TAXES

We discussed earlier that whenever a firm retains a portion of its net income rather than paying all earnings out in dividends, there is an *opportunity cost* to the stockholders. National Computer has a required rate of return on equity (retained earnings) of 14.7 percent. This suggests that shareholders could invest retained earnings, if they were paid out in dividends, in the stock market in firms of similar risk and receive a 14.7 percent return. Therefore, NCC should retain and reinvest earnings only if the projects in which the retained earnings are invested yield 14.7 percent or more on the equity invested. The value $k_s = 14.7\%$ is defined as the opportunity cost of retained earnings. However, note that we have implicitly assumed that the stockholders (1) pay no income tax on dividends received and (2) incur no brokerage costs when they reinvest dividends. To the extent that these assumptions are not met, the opportunity cost of retained earnings might be lower than the required rate of return, k_s.

Although taxes and brokerage costs are a fact of life, publicly owned firms can repurchase their own stock in the marketplace and earn a return equal to k_s on the investment. Thus, publicly held firms should not invest retained earnings in capital budgeting projects which have expected returns less than k_s, because firms have the opportunity to earn k_s on stock repurchases. However, personal tax effects are important for closely held firms, and such firms may have a cost of retained earnings that is less than k_s.[16]

COST OF DEPRECIATION-GENERATED FUNDS

The very first increment of internal funds used to finance any year's investments in new assets is depreciation-generated funds. Further, in their statements of cash

---

[16]For closely held firms, this expression can be used to estimate the cost of retained earnings, k_r:

$$k_r = k_s(1 - T_s)(1 - B).$$

Here k_s is the stockholders' required rate of return, T_s is the *stockholders'* marginal tax rate, and B is the percentage brokerage cost expressed in decimal form. To illustrate, if NCC were a closely held firm, and $T_s = 28\%$ and $B = 5\%$, then its cost of retained earnings would be 10.1 percent:

$$k_r = 14.7\%(1 - 0.28)(1 - 0.05) \approx 10.1\%.$$

flows, corporations generally show depreciation to be one of the most important, if not the most important, source of funds.[17] Of course, depreciation is an allowance for the annual reduction in value of a firm's fixed assets. Thus, for an ongoing firm, depreciation-generated funds would be used first to replace worn-out and obsolete assets, and then any remaining funds would be available to purchase new assets or to return to investors.

For capital budgeting purposes, should depreciation be considered "free" capital, should it be ignored completely, or should a charge be assessed against it? *The answer is that a charge should indeed be assessed against depreciation-generated funds, and the cost used should be the weighted average cost of capital before outside equity is used.* The reasoning here is that the firm could, if it so desired, distribute the depreciation-generated funds to its stockholders and creditors, the parties who financed the assets in the first place, so these funds definitely have an opportunity cost. For example, suppose a firm has $10 million of depreciation-generated funds available. Its equity has a cost of $k_s = 15\%$, and its debt has an after-tax cost of $k_d(1 - T) = 12\%(0.66) \approx 7.9\%$. If it has a 50-50 capital structure, and if it uses no preferred stock, then its WACC would be $0.5(7.9\%) + 0.5(15\%) \approx 11.4\%$.

Now suppose the firm has no projects available to it, not even projects which replace worn-out equipment, that return 11.4 percent or more. It obviously should not raise new capital, and it should not even retain any earnings for internal investment, because stockholders would be better off receiving the earnings as dividends and investing the funds themselves at $k_s = 15\%$, or having the company repurchase its stock. Going on, this firm should not even invest its depreciation-generated $10 million. If it did keep and invest this money, it would receive a return of less than 11.4 percent. If it distributed the $10 million to its investors, with $5 million going to stockholders and $5 million to bondholders so as to maintain the target capital structure, then the stockholders could buy the stock of companies with similar risk and earn 15 percent on their money, and bondholders could buy the bonds of companies with similar risk and earn 12 percent. (Such distributions would, under most conditions, be returns of capital, and hence not taxable. If the equity distribution were taxable, then the company could repur-

---

[17]Depreciation is a noncash charge. To illustrate, suppose a company reports the following income statement:

Sales	$100.0
Cash costs	60.0
Depreciation	20.0
Taxable income	$ 20.0
Taxes (34%)	6.8
Net income	$ 13.2

If sales are all collected during the year, and if all costs except depreciation are paid in cash during the year, then the cash flow from operations available for dividends or reinvestment will be $33.2:

Cash flow = Net income + Depreciation = $13.2 + $20 = $33.2.

TABLE 8-5		Tax Books (1)	Stockholder Books (2)
ILLUSTRATION OF XYZ			
COMPANY'S 1993	Sales	$100.0	$100.0
DEFERRED TAXES	Costs except depreciation	60.0	60.0
(MILLIONS OF	Depreciation (noncash charge)	20.0	10.0
DOLLARS)	Operating income	$ 20.0	$ 30.0
	Taxes:		
	Current (34%)	6.8	6.8[a]
	Deferred (noncash charge)	—	3.4[b]
	Net income	$ 13.2	$ 19.8
	Cash flow[c]	$ 33.2	$ 33.2

[a]Taken from tax books.

[b]Deferred taxes represent the difference between taxes actually paid and taxes that would have been paid had straight line depreciation been used for tax purposes:

$$\text{Deferred taxes} = \$30(0.34) - \$6.8 = \$3.4.$$

[c]Cash flow = Net income + Noncash expenses
= Net income + Depreciation + Deferred taxes.

chase its shares rather than make a direct distribution to stockholders.) *The conclusion from all this is that depreciation has a cost which is approximately equal to the weighted average cost of capital before external equity is used.*

Since depreciation-generated funds have the same cost as the firm's WACC when retained earnings are used for the equity component, it is not necessary to consider them when estimating the WACC. However, depreciation does influence the point at which the WACC increases due to flotation costs on new stock sales. As shown in the right panel of Figure 8-2, presented earlier, depreciation-generated funds push the point where the WACC increases out to the right by $30 million, NCC's projected 1994 depreciation expense. This topic will be discussed further in Chapter 11.

COST OF DEFERRED TAXES

Most companies show "deferred taxes" as a liability on their balance sheets. Deferred taxes arise principally from the use of accelerated depreciation for tax purposes along with straight line depreciation for reporting purposes. For example, suppose the XYZ Company uses accelerated depreciation for tax purposes but straight line for book (or stockholder reporting) purposes. Its accelerated depreciation for 1993 might be $20 million versus $10 million had it used straight line. The company's tax and book income statements are given in Table 8-5. As a result of using accelerated depreciation, the company writes off assets for tax purposes over a period which is shorter than the assets' economic lives. Therefore, in the early years of an asset's life, tax depreciation is high, so actual taxes are low. Later on, tax depreciation will be low, so actual taxes will be high relative to the taxes that would have resulted from the use of straight line depreciation. Thus, deferred

taxes represent the taxes that do not have to be paid currently but which will have to be paid at some future date.

Companies keep a "running total" of the accumulated deferred taxes that have accrued over time, and the net balance is reported on the balance sheet as a "reserve for deferred taxes." Thus, XYZ Company would add $3.4 million to the accumulated deferred tax figure reported on its 1992 balance sheet. In later years, when tax depreciation falls below straight line depreciation, the "reserve for deferred taxes" will be drawn down, and a credit will appear on the income statement seen by investors.[18]

Deferred taxes represent a noncash charge, so they constitute a source of funds in a cash flow sense. In effect, deferred taxes represent an interest-free loan from the federal government, so they constitute zero cost capital. However, just like depreciation, deferred taxes have an opportunity cost. The deferred tax cash flow, $3.4 million for XYZ Company in 1993, could be turned over to the firm's investors. Therefore, deferred taxes, like depreciation, have a cost equal to the firm's WACC using retained earnings as the equity component. Indeed, deferred taxes arise solely because a firm records a different depreciation expense on its tax books than on the books used to report income to shareholders. To see this, note in Table 8-5 that the shareholder books show deferred taxes of $3.4 million and a net income that is $19.8 − $13.2 = $6.6 million greater than shown on the tax books. The deferred taxes and incremental net income sum to $10 million, which is the same as the difference in the depreciation expense between the two sets of books. Thus, the tax books show an additional $10 million in depreciation cash flow, while the shareholder books show an extra $10 million of reported net income plus deferred taxes.

Deferred taxes are treated the same way as depreciation cash flows: they are not included when estimating the firm's WACC, but the point at which the WACC increases due to having used up retained earnings should be extended out to the right by the amount of the deferred taxes for the year ($3.4 million in our example).

---

[18]When we were working on this section, we looked at how several companies reported taxes in their financial statements. Three patterns were noted. First, most industrial companies reported income in their annual reports to stockholders as we show in Column 2 of Table 8-5. However, two other situations were found. First, a few extremely strong firms used accelerated depreciation for book and tax purposes. Thus, in effect, such a company would not have a Column 2 and would simply report Column 1 to stockholders. This is a very conservative accounting practice, as it substantially lowers reported net income for any growing company. At the other extreme, some public utilities reported income as shown in Column 2 but *without subtracting the deferred taxes.* In this case, reported income would be $30.0 − $6.8 = $23.2 million. This treatment is very *unconservative,* since it disregards the fact that future taxes will rise as tax depreciation falls. The regulatory commissions of these utilities forced them to report this way to make their profits look higher without the need to raise utility service rates in the short run.

Our main point is that otherwise identical companies can report very different levels of earnings. Security analysts and investors generally need to be aware of the accounting procedures of different companies. A rose is a rose is a rose is a rose, but a dollar of reported profits for one company is not necessarily equal to a dollar reported by another.

ALTERNATIVE APPROACH TO FLOTATION COST ADJUSTMENTS

Throughout this chapter, we have generally incorporated flotation costs into the component costs of capital. Flotation costs raise component costs, hence increasing the firm's WACC. An alternative approach to handling flotation costs is to ignore them when estimating the firm's WACC, but then, in the capital budgeting process, to allocate dollar flotation costs to the firm's new projects, hence increasing project costs rather than capital costs.[19]

When flotation costs are included in project costs, all flotation costs incurred in the current year must be borne by the projects under consideration, whether or not the capital raised will be retained within the firm and used for follow-on projects. When flotation costs are incorporated into the firm's WACC, these costs are assessed against the projects being considered today as well as all future projects. In effect, the alternative method recovers (amortizes) flotation costs over the lives of the projects currently being evaluated, while the conventional method amortizes flotation costs over an infinite life.[20]

SELF-TEST QUESTIONS

What are depreciation-generated funds?

Do depreciation-generated funds have a cost? If so, what is it?

What is the cost of deferred taxes?

How do depreciation-generated funds and deferred taxes affect a firm's WACC and the MCC schedule?

USING THE MCC SCHEDULE IN CAPITAL BUDGETING: A PREVIEW

As noted at the outset of the chapter, the cost of capital is a key element in the capital budgeting process. In essence, capital budgeting consists of these steps:

1. Identify the set of potential investment opportunities.

2. Estimate the future cash flows associated with each project.

3. Find the present value of each future cash flow, discounted at the cost of the capital used to finance the project, and sum these PVs to obtain the total PV of each project.

---

[19]For a more complete discussion of the alternative approach, see Carl M. Hubbard, "Flotation Costs in Capital Budgeting: A Note on the Tax Effect," *Financial Management,* Summer 1984, 38–40; and John P. Ezzell and R. Burr Porter, "Flotation Costs and the Weighted Average Cost of Capital," *Journal of Financial and Quantitative Analysis,* September 1976, 403–413.

[20]For an in-depth comparison of the two methods, see Eugene F. Brigham and Louis C. Gapenski, "Flotation Cost Adjustments," *Journal of Financial Practice and Education,* Winter 1992, 29–34.

4. Compare each project's PV with its cost, and accept a project if the PV of its future cash inflows exceeds its cost.

As you learned in earlier chapters the appropriate discount rate for a given cash flow stream depends on the riskiness of the stream—the riskier the stream (or the riskier the asset), the higher the discount rate. Therefore, the riskier a capital budgeting project, the higher its cost of capital. In this chapter, we were determining the firm's cost of capital for an *average-risk* project. It should be intuitively clear that firms take on different projects with differing degrees of risk. Part of the capital budgeting process involves assessing the riskiness of each project and assigning it a capital cost based on its relative risk. The cost of capital assigned to an average-risk project should be the marginal cost of capital as determined in this chapter. More risky projects should be assigned higher costs of capital, while less risky projects should be evaluated with a lower cost of capital. We will examine procedures for dealing with project risk in Chapter 11. Basically, though, firms first measure the marginal cost of capital as we did in this chapter, and then scale it up or down to reflect the individual division's and project's riskiness.

Another issue that arises relates to picking the appropriate point on the marginal cost of capital schedule for use in capital budgeting. As we have seen, every dollar raised by National Computer Corporation is a weighted average which consists of 30 cents of debt, 10 cents of preferred stock, and 60 cents of common equity (with the equity coming from retained earnings until they have been used up, and then from the issuance of new common stock). Further, we saw that the MCC schedule is constant for a while, but after the firm has exhausted its least expensive sources of capital, the MCC schedule rises. Figure 8-2 gave NCC's MCC schedule with and without depreciation.

Since its cost of capital depends on how much capital the firm raises, just which cost rate should we use in capital budgeting? Put another way, which of the WACC values shown in Figure 8-2 should be used to evaluate an average risk project? We could use 11.8 percent or 12.6 percent, but which one *should* we use? The answer is based on the concept of marginal analysis as developed in economics. In economics you learned that firms should expand output to the point where marginal revenue is equal to marginal cost. At that point, the last unit of output exactly covers its cost—further expansion would reduce profits, but the firm would forego profits at any lower production rate. Therefore, the firm should expand to the point where its marginal revenue equals its marginal cost.

This same type of analysis is applied in capital budgeting. We have already developed the marginal cost curve—it is the MCC schedule. Now we need to develop a schedule that is analogous to the marginal revenue schedule. This is the *Investment Opportunity Schedule (IOS),* which shows the rate of return that is expected on each potential investment opportunity. As you will see in the next chapter, rates of return on capital projects are found in essentially the same way as rates of returns on stocks and bonds. Thus, we can calculate an expected rate of return on each potential project, and we can then plot those returns on the

FIGURE 8-4

COMBINING THE MCC
AND IOS SCHEDULES
TO DETERMINE THE
OPTIMAL CAPITAL
BUDGET

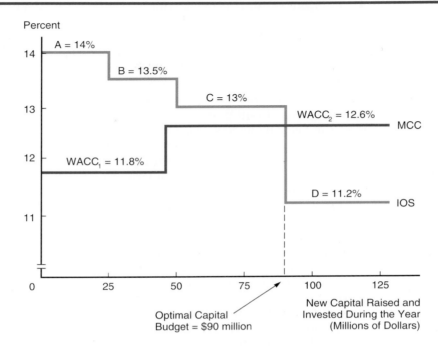

FIGURE 8-4

COMBINING THE MCC
AND IOS SCHEDULES
TO DETERMINE THE
OPTIMAL CAPITAL
BUDGET

Project	Cost (in Millions)	Return of Return
A	$25	14.0%
B	25	13.5
C	40	13.0
D	40	11.2

same graph that shows our marginal cost of capital. Figure 8-4 gives such a graph for NCC. Projects A, B, and C all have expected rates of return which exceed the cost of the capital that will be used to finance them, but the expected return on Project D is less than its cost of capital. Therefore, Projects A, B, and C should be accepted, and Project D should be rejected.

The WACC at the point where the Investment Opportunity Schedule intersects the MCC schedule is defined as "the corporate cost of capital" — this point reflects the marginal cost of capital to the corporation. In our example, NCC's corporate cost of capital is 12.6%, and that is the cost of capital that NCC would use to evaluate average risk projects and as the basing point for developing "risk-adjusted costs of capital" for the firm's other projects. We will return to the MCC and IOS schedules in Chapter 11, after we have seen how IOS schedules are actually developed.

Self-Test Questions

As a general rule, should a firm's cost of capital as determined in this chapter be used to evaluate all of its capital budgeting projects? Explain.

In what respect is marginal analysis in economics analogous to capital budgeting?

Why would it be difficult to identify a firm's cost of capital for use in capital budgeting if you had no idea whatever of how large the capital budget was likely to be?

Summary

This chapter discussed how a firm's cost of capital is estimated. The key concepts covered are listed below:

▶ The cost of capital to be used in capital budgeting decisions is the *weighted average* of the various types of capital the firm uses, typically debt, preferred stock, and common equity.

▶ The *component cost of debt,* which is the *after-tax* cost of new debt, is usually found by multiplying the cost of new debt by $(1 - T)$, where T is the firm's marginal tax rate: $k_d(1 - T)$.

▶ The *component cost of perpetual preferred stock* is calculated as the preferred dividend divided by the net issuance price, where the net issuance price is the price the firm receives after deducting flotation costs: $k_{ps} = D_{ps}/P_n$.

▶ The *cost of common equity* is the cost of retained earnings as long as the firm has retained earnings, but the cost of equity becomes the cost of new common stock once the firm has exhausted its retained earnings.

▶ The *cost of retained earnings* is the rate of return investors require on the firm's common stock, and it can be estimated by three methods: (1) the *CAPM approach,* (2) the *DCF approach,* and (3) the *bond-yield-plus-risk-premium approach.*

▶ To use the *CAPM approach,* we (1) estimate the firm's beta, (2) multiply this beta by the market risk premium to determine the firm's risk premium, and (3) add the firm's risk premium to the risk-free rate to obtain the firm's cost of retained earnings: $k_s = k_{RF} + (k_M - k_{RF})b_i$.

▶ The best proxy for the *risk-free rate* is the yield on long-term T-bonds.

▶ Three types of betas can be used in the CAPM: (1) *historical,* (2) *adjusted,* and (3) *fundamental.*

▶ The market risk premium can be estimated either *historically (ex post)* or *prospectively (ex ante).*

▶ To use the *DCF approach,* we solve for $\hat{k}_s$ in the stock valuation equation. Under constant growth, this is done by adding the firm's expected growth rate to its expected dividend yield: $k_s = \hat{k}_s = D_1/P_0 + g$.

▶ The growth rate can be estimated from historical data by use of the *retention growth model,* g = br, or be based on analysts' forecasts.

▶ The *bond-yield-plus-risk-premium approach* requires one to add a risk premium to the firm's cost of debt: k_s = Company's own bond yield + RP.

▶ The *cost of new common equity* is higher than the cost of retained earnings because the firm must incur *flotation expenses* to sell stock. To find the cost of new common equity by the DCF method, the stock price is first reduced by the flotation expense, then the dividend yield is calculated on the basis of the price the firm will actually receive, and then the expected growth rate is added: $k_e = D_1/[P_0(1 - F)] + g$.

▶ Each firm has a *target capital structure,* and the target weights are used to estimate the firm's *weighted average cost of capital (WACC):*

$$WACC = w_d k_d(1 - T) + w_{ps}k_{ps} + w_{ce}(k_s \text{ or } k_e).$$

▶ The *marginal cost of capital (MCC)* is defined as the cost of the last dollar of new capital the firm raises. The MCC increases as the firm raises more and more capital during a given period. A graph of the MCC plotted against dollars raised is the *MCC schedule.*

The concepts developed in this chapter will be used extensively throughout the book, especially in capital budgeting decisions (Chapters 9 through 11) and capital structure decisions (Chapters 12 and 13).

QUESTIONS

8-1 Define each of the following terms:
  a. Weighted average cost of capital, WACC
  b. After-tax cost of debt, $k_d(1 - T)$
  c. Cost of preferred stock, k_{ps}
  d. Cost of retained earnings, k_s
  e. Historical beta; adjusted beta; fundamental beta
  f. Cost of new common equity, k_e
  g. Flotation cost, F
  h. Target capital structure
  i. MCC schedule
  j. Cost of depreciation-generated funds
  k. Cost of deferred taxes

8-2 In what sense is the WACC an average cost? A marginal cost?

8-3 How would each of the following affect a firm's cost of debt, $k_d(1 - T)$; its cost of equity, k_s; and its average cost of capital, WACC? Indicate by a plus (+), a minus (−), or a zero (0) if the factor would raise, lower, or have an indeterminate effect on the item in question. Assume other things are held constant. Be prepared to justify your answer, but recognize

that several of the parts probably have no single correct answer; these questions are designed to stimulate thought and discussion.

	Effect on		
	$k_d(1 - T)$	k_s	WACC
a. The corporate tax rate is lowered.	_____	_____	_____
b. The Federal Reserve tightens credit.	_____	_____	_____
c. The firm uses more debt.	_____	_____	_____
d. The dividend payout ratio is increased.	_____	_____	_____
e. The firm doubles the amount of capital it raises during the year.	_____	_____	_____
f. The firm expands into a risky new area.	_____	_____	_____
g. The firm merges with another firm whose earnings are countercyclical to those of the first firm and to the stock market.	_____	_____	_____
h. The stock market falls drastically, and our firm's stock price falls along with the rest.	_____	_____	_____
i. Investors become more risk averse.	_____	_____	_____
j. The firm is an electric utility with a large investment in nuclear plants. Several states propose a ban on nuclear power generation.	_____	_____	_____

SELF-TEST PROBLEM (SOLUTION APPEARS IN APPENDIX C)

ST-1 (MCC schedule) Longstreet Communications Inc. (LCI) has the following capital structure, which it considers to be optimal:

Debt	25%
Preferred stock	15
Common stock	60
Total capital	100%

LCI's net income expected this year is $17,142.86; its established dividend payout ratio is 30 percent; its tax rate is 40 percent; and investors expect earnings and dividends to grow at a constant rate of 9 percent in the future. LCI paid a dividend of $3.60 per share last year (D_0), and its stock currently sells at a price of $60 per share. Treasury bonds yield 11 percent; an average stock has a 14 percent expected rate of return; and LCI's beta is 1.51. These terms would apply to new security offerings:

Common: New common stock would have a flotation cost of 10 percent.

Preferred: New preferred could be sold to the public at a price of $100 per share, with a dividend of $11. Flotation costs of $5 per share would be incurred.

Debt: Debt could be sold at an interest rate of 12 percent.

a. Find the component costs of debt, preferred stock, retained earnings, and new common stock.

b. How much new capital can be raised before LCI must sell new equity? (In other words, find the retained earnings break point.)

c. What is the WACC when LCI meets its equity requirement with retained earnings? With new common stock?

d. Construct a graph showing LCI's MCC schedule.

e. Assume that LCI has forecasted $10,000 in depreciation expense for the planning period. What impact does this have on the MCC schedule?

PROBLEMS

8-1 (Component cost of debt)   Calculate the after-tax cost of debt under each of the following conditions:

a. Interest rate, 10 percent; tax rate, 0 percent.

b. Interest rate, 10 percent; tax rate, 20 percent.

c. Interest rate, 10 percent; tax rate, 40 percent.

8-2 (Cost of retained earnings)   The Garvin Company's last dividend per share was $1; that is, $D_0 = \$1$. The stock sells for $20 per share. The expected growth rate is a constant 5 percent. Calculate the firm's cost of retained earnings using the DCF method.

8-3 (WACC estimation)   On January 1, the total market value of the Tysseland Company was $60 million. During the year, the company plans to raise and invest $30 million in new projects. The firm's present market value capital structure, shown below, is considered to be optimal. Assume that there is no short-term debt.

Debt	$30,000,000
Common equity	30,000,000
Total capital	$60,000,000

New bonds will have an 8 percent coupon rate, and they will be sold at par. Common stock, currently selling at $30 a share, can be sold to net the company $27 a share. Stockholders' required rate of return is estimated to be 12 percent, consisting of a dividend yield of 4 percent and an expected constant growth rate of 8 percent. (The next expected dividend is $1.20, so $1.20/$30 = 4%.) Retained earnings for the year are estimated to be $3 million. The marginal corporate tax rate is 40 percent. (Assume no depreciation cash flow.)

a. To maintain the present capital structure, how much of the new investment must be financed by common equity?

b. How much of the needed new common equity funds must be generated internally? Externally?

c. Calculate the cost of each of the common equity components.

d. At what level of capital expenditures will the firm's WACC increase?

e. Calculate the firm's WACC using (1) the cost of retained earnings and (2) the cost of new equity.

8-4   **(WACC estimation)**   The following tabulation gives earnings per share figures for Pappas Manufacturing during the preceding ten years. The firm's common stock, 140,000 shares outstanding, is now selling for $50 a share, and the expected dividend for the coming year (1994) is 50 percent of EPS for the year. Investors expect past trends to continue, so g may be based on the historical earnings growth rate.

Year	EPS
1984	$2.00
1985	2.16
1986	2.33
1987	2.52
1988	2.72
1989	2.94
1990	3.18
1991	3.43
1992	3.70
1993	4.00

The current interest rate on new debt is 8 percent. The firm's marginal federal-plus-state tax rate is 40 percent. The firm's market value capital structure, considered to be optimal, is as follows:

Debt	$ 3,000,000
Common equity	7,000,000
Total capital	$10,000,000

a.   Calculate the firm's after-tax cost of new debt and of common equity, assuming new equity comes only from retained earnings. Calculate the cost of equity assuming constant growth; that is, $\hat{k}_s = D_1/P_0 + g = k_s$.

b.   Find the firm's WACC, assuming no common stock is sold.

c.   How much can be spent for net new capital investments before external equity must be sold? (Assume no depreciation cash flow.)

d.   What is the WACC beyond the retained earnings break point if new common stock can be sold to the public at $50 a share to net the firm $45 a share?

8-5   **(Market value capital structure)**   Suppose the Schoof Company has this *book value* balance sheet:

Current assets	$30,000,000	Current liabilities	$10,000,000
Fixed assets	50,000,000	Long-term debt	30,000,000
		Common equity:	
		Common stock	
		(1 million shares)	1,000,000
		Retained earnings	39,000,000
Total assets	$80,000,000	Total claims	$80,000,000

The current liabilities consist entirely of notes payable to banks, and the interest rate on this debt is 10 percent, the same as the rate on new bank loans. The long-term debt consists of 30,000 bonds, each of which has a par value of $1,000, carries an annual coupon interest rate of 6 percent, and matures in 20 years. The going rate of interest on new long-term debt, k_d, is 10 percent, and this is the present yield to maturity on the bonds. The common stock sells at a price of $60 per share. Calculate the firm's market value capital structure.

8-6   **(Cost of equity)**   The Tallman Tractor Company's EPS in 1993 was $2.00. EPS in 1988 was $1.3612. The company pays out 40 percent of its earnings as dividends, and the stock currently sells for $21.60. The company expects earnings of $10 million in 1994. Its optimal market value debt/assets ratio is 60 percent, and the firm has no preferred stock outstanding.

   a.   Calculate the firm's growth rate in earnings.

   b.   Calculate the firm's dividend per share expected in 1994. Assume that the growth rate calculated in Part a will continue.

   c.   What is the firm's cost of retained earnings, k_s?

   d.   What amount of retained earnings is expected in 1994?

   e.   At what amount of total financing will the firm's cost of equity increase? (Assume no depreciation cash flow.)

   f.   The sale of new stock would net the company $18.36 per share. What is the firm's percentage flotation cost, F? What is the cost of new common stock, k_e?

8-7   **(Cost of equity estimation methods)**   You have just estimated the cost of equity for Shrieves Shipping Company using all three estimation techniques. The results are summarized in the following table:

Method	k_s Estimate
CAPM	12.1%
DCF	14.0
Bond yield plus risk premium	15.4

The inconsistency of the results is worrisome, but you must still develop your equity cost estimate. What factors might you consider as you attempt to place confidence in the above estimates?

8-8   **(WACC estimation)**   A summary of the balance sheet of Travellers Inn Inc. (TII), a company which was formed by merging a number of regional motel chains and which hopes to rival Holiday Inn on the national scene, is shown in the table:

Travellers Inn: December 31, 1993
(Millions of Dollars)

Cash	$ 10	Accounts payable		$ 10
Accounts receivable	20	Accruals		10
Inventories	20	Short-term debt		5
Current assets	$ 50	Current liabilities		$ 25
Net fixed assets	50	Long-term debt		30
		Preferred stock		5
		Common equity:		
		Common stock	$10	
		Retained earnings	30	
		Total common equity		40
Total assets	$100	Total liabilities and equity		$100

These facts are also given for TII:

   (1)   Short-term debt consists of bank loans which currently cost 10 percent, with interest payable quarterly. These loans are used to finance receivables and inventories on a seasonal basis, so in the off-season, bank loans are zero.

(2) The long-term debt consists of 20-year, semiannual payment mortgage bonds with a coupon rate of 8 percent. Currently, these bonds provide a yield to investors of $k_d = 12\%$. If new bonds were sold, they would yield investors 12 percent, but a flotation cost of 5 percent would be required to sell new bonds.

(3) TII's perpetual preferred stock has a $100 par value, pays a quarterly dividend of $2, and has a yield to investors of 11 percent. New perpetual preferred would have to provide the same yield to investors, and the company would incur a 5 percent flotation cost to sell it.

(4) The company has 4 million shares of common stock outstanding. $P_0 = \$20$, but the stock has recently traded in a range of $17 to $23. $D_0 = \$1$ and $EPS_0 = \$2$. ROE based on average equity was 24 percent in 1993, but management expects to increase this return on equity to 30 percent; however, security analysts are not aware of management's optimism in this regard.

(5) Betas, as reported by security analysts, range from 1.3 to 1.7; the T-bond rate is 10 percent; and k_M is estimated by various brokerage houses to be in the range of 14.5 to 15.5 percent. Brokerage house reports forecast growth rates in the range of 10 to 15 percent over the foreseeable future. However, some analysts do not explicitly forecast growth rates, but they indicate to their clients that they expect TII's historical trends as shown in the table below to continue.

(6) At a recent conference, TII's financial vice president polled some pension fund investment managers on the minimum rate of return they would have to expect on TII's common to make them willing to buy the common rather than TII bonds, when the bonds yielded 12 percent. The responses suggested a risk premium over TII bonds of 4 to 6 percentage points.

(7) TII is in the 40 percent federal-plus-state tax bracket. Its dominant stockholders are in the 28 percent bracket.

(8) New common stock would have a 10 percent flotation cost.

(9) TII's principal investment banker, Henry, Kaufman & Company, predicts a decline in interest rates, with k_d falling to 10 percent and the T-bond rate to 8 percent, although Henry, Kaufman & Company acknowledges that an increase in the expected inflation rate could lead to an increase rather than a decrease in rates.

(10) The firm expects depreciation expenses of $5 million for the coming year.

(11) Here is the historical record of EPS and DPS:

Year	EPS[a]	DPS[a]	Year	EPS[a]	DPS[a]
1979	$0.09	$0.00	1987	$0.78	$0.00
1980	−0.20	0.00	1988	0.80	0.00
1981	0.40	0.00	1989	1.20	0.20
1982	0.52	0.00	1990	0.95	0.40
1983	0.10	0.00	1991	1.30	0.60
1984	0.57	0.00	1992	1.60	0.80
1985	0.61	0.00	1993	2.00	1.00
1986	0.70	0.00			

[a]Adjusted for a 2:1 stock split in 1983, a 3:1 split in 1991, and 10 percent stock dividends in 1980 and 1988.

Assume that you are a recently hired financial analyst, and your boss, the treasurer, has asked you to estimate the company's WACC for both retained earnings and new common stock sales. Your cost of capital figures at each level should be appropriate for use in evaluating projects which are in the same risk class as the firm's average assets now on the books.

**M I N I
C A S E**

You have just been hired as a financial analyst by Harry Davis Industries Inc. Your first assignment is to estimate the firm's cost of capital. To get you started, the CFO assembled the following information:

(1) The firm's federal-plus-state tax rate is 40 percent.

(2) The firm has outstanding an issue of 12 percent, semiannual coupon, noncallable bonds with 15 years remaining to maturity. They sell at a price of $1,153.72. The firm does not use short-term debt on a permanent basis.

(3) The current price of the firm's perpetual preferred stock (10 percent, $100 par value, quarterly payment) is $113.10. New perpetual preferred could be sold to the public at this price, but Davis would incur flotation costs of $2.00 per share.

(4) The firm's common stock is currently selling at $50 per share. Its last dividend (D_0) was $4.19, and investors expect the dividend to grow at a constant 5 percent rate into the foreseeable future. The firm's beta is 1.2; the current yield on T-bonds is 7 percent; and the market risk premium is estimated to be 6 percent. When using the bond-yield-plus-risk-premium approach, the managers assume a risk premium of 4 percentage points.

(5) New common stock would involve flotation costs, including market pressure, of 15 percent.

(6) The firm's target capital structure is 30 percent long-term debt, 10 percent preferred stock, and 60 percent common equity.

(7) The company forecasts retained earnings of $300,000 for the coming year.

(8) Depreciation expenses for the coming year are expected to be $500,000.

To structure the task a bit, the CFO asked you to answer the following questions:

a. (1) What sources of capital should be included in the estimate of Davis's WACC?

(2) Should the component cost estimates be on a before-tax or an after-tax basis?

(3) Should the cost estimates reflect historical (embedded) costs or new (marginal) costs?

b. (1) What is the firm's component cost of debt?

(2) Should flotation costs be considered?

(3) Should you use the nominal cost of debt or the effective annual cost?

(4) Would a cost of debt estimate based on 15-year bonds be a valid estimate of k_d if the firm actually planned to issue 30-year bonds?

c. (1) What is the firm's cost of preferred stock?

(2) Is the firm's preferred stock more or less risky to investors than its debt? Why is the yield to investors on the preferred lower than the yield to maturity on the debt?

(3) Now suppose you discovered that the firm's preferred stock had a mandatory redemption provision which specified that the firm must redeem the issue in five years at a price of $110 per share. What would the firm's cost of preferred be in this situation? (Ignore this part in the remainder of the case.)

d. (1) Why is there a cost associated with retained earnings?

(2) What is the firm's estimated cost of retained earnings based on the CAPM approach?

(3) Why is the T-bond rate a better estimate of the risk-free rate than is the T-bill rate?

(4) What is the difference among historical betas, adjusted betas, and fundamental betas?

(5) Describe two methods which can be used to estimate the market risk premium.

e. (1) What is the estimate of the firm's discounted cash flow (DCF) cost of retained earnings, k_s?

(2) Suppose the firm has historically earned 15 percent on equity (ROE) and retained 35 percent of earnings, and investors expect this situation to continue in the future. How could you use this information to estimate the future dividend growth rate, and what growth rate would you get? Is this growth rate consistent with the 5 percent given earlier?

(3) Could DCF methodology be applied if the growth rate was not constant? How?

f. What is the firm's cost of retained earnings based on the bond-yield-plus-risk-premium method?

g. What is your final estimate for k_s?

h. (1) What is the firm's cost of new common stock, k_e?

(2) Explain in words why new common stock has a higher percentage cost than retained earnings.

i. (1) What is the firm's overall, or weighted average, cost of capital (WACC) when only retained earnings are used as the equity component?

(2) What is the WACC when new common stock is used as the equity component?

j. (1) At what amount of new investment would the firm be forced to issue new common stock? (For now, ignore the depreciation cash flow.)

(2) Construct the firm's MCC schedule. Is it reasonable to assume that the firm's MCC schedule would remain constant beyond the retained earnings break point regardless of the amount of capital required? Would what the company planned to do with the money it raised have any effect on the WACC?

k. We know that a firm's annual cash flows are equal to net income plus noncash expenses, typically net income plus depreciation, yet the analysis thus far has ignored the depreciation cash flow. What impact does depreciation have on Davis's MCC schedule? Would a consideration of depreciation affect the acceptability of proposed capital budgeting projects and the size of the total capital budget? Explain.

SELECTED ADDITIONAL REFERENCES AND CASES

The following articles provide some valuable insights into the CAPM approach to estimating the cost of equity:

Beaver, William H., Paul Kettler, and Myron Scholes, "The Association between Market Determined and Accounting Determined Risk Measures," *Accounting Review,* October 1970, 654–682.

Bowman, Robert G., "The Theoretical Relationship between Systematic Risk and Financial (Accounting) Variables," *Journal of Finance,* June 1979, 617–630.

Chen, Carl R., "Time-Series Analysis of Beta Stationarity and Its Determinants: A Case of Public Utilities," *Financial Management,* Autumn 1982, 64–70.

Cooley, Philip L., "A Review of the Use of Beta in Regulatory Proceedings," *Financial Management,* Winter 1981, 75–81.

The weighted average cost of capital as described in this chapter is widely used in both industry and academic circles. It has been criticized on several counts, but to date it has withstood the challenges. See the following articles:

Arditti, Fred D., and Haim Levy, "The Weighted Average Cost of Capital as a Cutoff Rate: A Critical Examination of the Classical Textbook Weighted Average," *Financial Management,* Fall 1977, 24–34.

Beranek, William, "The Weighted Average Cost of Capital and Shareholder Wealth Maximization," *Journal of Financial and Quantitative Analysis,* March 1977, 17–32.

Finally, Nucor, a steel maker, recently spent $500 million on new mills, including one that turned an experimental German slab-making process into a profitable plant. There is excess capacity in the steel industry, and most companies are losing money, but Nucor is the lowest-cost producer and the most profitable U.S. steel company. "If you want to grow in this environment, you must use technology to curb costs," maintains CEO Kenneth Iverson. The investment paid off handsomely; the new mill can produce a ton of steel in 1.5 man-hours versus 4.5 hours in a conventional steel-making plant.

Borden, Intel, and Nucor were all well aware of the recession, but the economic slump did not deter them and many other companies from continuing with their capital expenditure programs. Taking advantage of the weak dollar, which has turned many U.S. firms into low-cost producers and boosted their export potential, these and other companies have allocated large sums to new products, plant, and equipment in order to extend their global reach. Other firms have invested heavily in automation to cut costs, and an opportunistic handful have capitalized on their rivals' financial weakness to increase market share.

Corporate decisions to spend millions, or even billions, of dollars are not made casually, so the managers of Borden, Intel, and Nucor conducted comprehensive analyses to ensure that their capital investments were in the best interests of their firms' shareholders. As you read this chapter, think about the techniques being discussed and how they could be applied to the companies described here.

In the last chapter, we discussed the cost of capital. Now we turn to investment decisions involving fixed assets, or *capital budgeting*. Here the term *capital* refers to fixed assets used in production, while a *budget* is a plan which details projected inflows and outflows during some future period. Thus, the *capital budget* is an outline of planned expenditures on fixed assets, and *capital budgeting* is the whole process of analyzing projects and deciding which ones to include in the capital budget.

Our treatment of capital budgeting is divided into three chapters. First, Chapter 9 explains the basic techniques used in capital budgeting analysis. Chapter 10 goes on to consider how cash flows are estimated, while Chapter 11 discusses risk analysis in capital budgeting and explains how the optimal capital budget is established.

IMPORTANCE OF CAPITAL BUDGETING

A number of factors combine to make capital budgeting extremely important. First, since the effects of capital budgeting decisions continue over many years, the decision maker loses some of his or her flexibility. For example, the purchase of an

asset with an economic life of 10 years often "locks in" the firm for a 10-year period. Further, because asset expansion is fundamentally related to expected future sales, a decision to buy a fixed asset that is expected to last 10 years involves an implicit 10-year sales forecast.

An erroneous forecast of asset requirements can have serious consequences. If the firm invests too much, it will incur unnecessarily heavy expenses. If it does not spend enough, two problems will arise. First, the firm's equipment will not be sufficiently modern to enable it to produce competitively. Second, if it has inadequate capacity, it will lose a portion of its market share to rival firms, and regaining lost customers typically requires heavy selling expenses, price reductions, or product improvements, all of which are costly.

Another aspect of capital budgeting is timing—capital assets must be available when they are needed. Edward Ford, executive vice-president of Western Design, a decorative tile company, gave the authors an illustration of the importance of capital budgeting. His firm tried to operate near capacity most of the time. During a four-year period, Western experienced intermittent spurts in the demand for its products, which forced it to turn away orders. After a sharp increase in demand, the firm would add capacity by renting an additional building, then purchasing and installing the appropriate equipment. It would take six to eight months to get the additional capacity ready, and frequently by that time there was no demand for the increased output—other firms had already expanded their operations and had taken a larger share of the market. If Western had properly forecasted demand and had planned its new capacity six months to a year in advance, it would have been able to maintain or perhaps even increase its market share.

Effective capital budgeting will improve both the timing and the quality of asset additions. A firm which forecasts its needs for capital assets in advance can purchase and install the assets before its sales are at capacity. In practice, though, most firms do not order new plant and equipment until they have approached full capacity, need to replace worn-out equipment, or are adding new product lines. If sales increase because of an increase in general market demand, all firms in the industry will tend to order capital assets at about the same time. This often results in backlogs, long waiting times for machinery, a deterioration in the quality of the capital assets, and an increase in equipment costs. The firm which anticipates its needs can avoid these problems. Note, though, that if a firm forecasts an increase in demand and expands to meet the anticipated demand, and if sales then do not expand, it will be saddled with excess capacity and abnormally high costs. This can lead to losses or even bankruptcy. Thus, the sales forecast is critical.

Finally, capital budgeting is also important because asset expansion typically involves substantial expenditures, and before a firm spends a large amount of money, it must make the proper plans—large amounts of funds are not available automatically. A firm contemplating a major capital expenditure program may need to arrange its financing several years in advance to be sure of having the funds required for the expansion.

SELF-TEST QUESTIONS

Why are capital budgeting decisions so important to the success of a firm?

Why is the sales forecast a key element in capital budgeting decisions?

PROJECT CLASSIFICATIONS

Analyzing capital expenditure proposals is not a costless operation—benefits can be gained from a careful analysis, but such an investigation does have a cost. For certain types of projects, a relatively detailed analysis may be warranted; for others, cost/benefit studies suggest that simpler procedures should be used. Accordingly, firms generally classify projects into the following categories, and they analyze projects in each category somewhat differently:

1. **Replacement: maintenance of business.** Category 1 consists of expenditures necessary to replace worn-out or damaged equipment used to produce profitable products. These projects are necessary if the firm is to continue in its current businesses. The only issues here are (a) should we continue to produce these products or services, and (b) should we continue to use our existing plant and equipment? Usually, the answers are "yes," so maintenance decisions are normally made without going through an elaborate decision process.

2. **Replacement: cost reduction.** This category includes expenditures to replace serviceable but obsolete equipment. The purpose of these expenditures is to lower the costs of labor, materials, or other inputs such as electricity. These decisions are somewhat more discretionary, so a more detailed analysis is generally required to support the expenditure.

3. **Expansion of existing products or markets.** Expenditures to increase output of existing products, or to expand outlets or distribution facilities in markets now being served, are included here. These decisions are more complex, because they require an explicit consideration of future demand in the firm's product markets. Mistakes are more likely, so a still more detailed analysis is required, and the final decision is made at a higher level within the firm.

4. **Expansion into new products or markets.** These are expenditures necessary to produce a new product or to expand into a geographic area not currently being served. These projects involve strategic decisions that could change the fundamental nature of the business, and they normally require the expenditure of large sums of money over long periods. Invariably, a very detailed analysis is required, and final decisions on new products or markets are generally made by the board of directors as a part of the firm's strategic plan.

5. **Safety and/or environmental projects.** Expenditures necessary to comply with government orders, labor agreements, or insurance policy terms fall into this category. These expenditures are often called *mandatory investments,* or *non-revenue-producing projects.* How they are handled depends on their size, with small ones being treated much like the Category 1 projects described previously.

6.   Other. This catch-all includes office buildings, parking lots, executive aircraft, and so on. How they are handled also depends on their size.

In general, relatively simple calculations and only a few supporting documents are required for replacement decisions, especially maintenance-type investments in profitable plants. More detailed analysis is required for cost-reduction replacements, for expansion of existing product lines, and especially for investments in new products or areas. Also, within each category, projects are broken down by their dollar costs: The larger the required investment, the more detailed the analysis, and the higher the level of the officer who must authorize the expenditure. Thus, although a plant manager may be authorized to approve maintenance expenditures up to $10,000 on the basis of a relatively unsophisticated analysis, the full board of directors may have to approve decisions which involve either amounts over $1 million or expansions into new products or markets. Statistical data are generally lacking for new-product decisions, so here judgments, as opposed to detailed cost data, are a key element in the decision process.

SELF-TEST QUESTION

Identify and briefly explain how capital project classification categories are used.

SIMILARITIES BETWEEN CAPITAL BUDGETING AND SECURITY VALUATION

Conceptually, capital budgeting involves exactly the same six steps that are used in security analysis:

1. First, the cost of the project must be determined. This is similar to finding the price that must be paid for a stock or bond.

2. Next, management must estimate the expected cash flows from the project, including the value of the asset at a specified terminal date. This is similar to estimating the future dividend or interest payment stream on a stock or bond.

3. Third, the riskiness of the projected cash flows must be estimated. To do this, management needs information about the probability distributions (uncertainty) of the cash flows.

4. Then, given the riskiness of the projected cash flows, management determines the appropriate cost of capital at which the project's cash flows are to be discounted.

5. Next, the expected cash inflows are put on a present value basis to obtain an estimate of the asset's value to the firm. This is equivalent to finding the present value of expected future dividends or interest payments.

6. Finally, the present value of the expected cash inflows is compared to the required outlay, or cost, of the project; if the asset's value exceeds its cost, the project should be accepted. Otherwise, the project should be rejected. (Alterna-

tively, the expected rate of return on the project can be calculated, and if this rate of return exceeds the project's required rate of return, the project is accepted.)

If an individual investor identifies and then invests in a stock or bond whose market price is less than its true value, the value of the investor's portfolio will increase. Similarly, if a firm identifies (or creates) an investment opportunity with a present value greater than its cost, the value of the firm will increase. Thus, there is a direct link between capital budgeting and stock values: The more effective the firm's capital budgeting procedures, the higher the price of its stock.

SELF-TEST QUESTION

List the six steps of the capital budgeting process, and relate them to security valuation.

CAPITAL BUDGETING DECISION RULES

Five primary methods are currently used to rank projects and to decide whether or not they should be accepted for inclusion in the capital budget: (1) payback period, (2) accounting rate of return (ARR), (3) net present value (NPV), (4) internal rate of return (IRR), and (5) profitability index (PI). We first explain how each ranking criterion is calculated, and then we evaluate how well each performs in terms of identifying those projects which will maximize the firm's stock price. Then, in a later section, we discuss a sixth method, the modified IRR (MIRR), which is a better indicator of percentage profitability than the IRR.

We use the cash flow data shown in Table 9-1 for Projects S and L to illustrate each method, and throughout this chapter we assume that the projects are equally risky. Note that the cash flows in each year, CF_t, are expected values, and that they are adjusted to reflect taxes, depreciation, and salvage values. Also, since many projects require an investment in both fixed assets and working capital, the invest-

TABLE 9-1 CASH FLOWS FOR PROJECTS S AND L	Year (t)	Expected After-Tax Net Cash Flow, CF_t	
		Project S	Project L
	0	($1,000)[a]	($1,000)[a]
	1	500	100
	2	400	300
	3	300	400
	4	100	600

[a]Represents the net investment outlay, or initial cost. The parentheses indicate a negative number, or cash outflow.

ment outlays shown as CF_0 include any necessary changes in net working capital.[1] Finally, we assume that all cash flows occur at the end of the designated year. Incidentally, the S stands for *short* and the L for *long:* Project S is a short-term project in the sense that its cash inflows tend to come in sooner than L's.

PAYBACK PERIOD

The *payback period,* defined as the expected number of years required to recover the original investment in the project, was the first formal method used to evaluate capital budgeting projects. When applied to Projects S and L, the payback period is 2⅓ years for S and 3⅓ years for L.[2]

$$\text{Payback}_S: 2⅓ \text{ years.}$$

$$\text{Payback}_L: 3⅓ \text{ years.}$$

If the firm required a payback of three years or less, Project S would be accepted, but Project L would be rejected. If the projects were *mutually exclusive,* S would be ranked over L because S has the shorter payback.[3]

Some firms use a variant of the regular payback, the *discounted payback period,* which is similar to the regular payback period except that the expected cash

---

[1]Perhaps the most difficult part of the capital budgeting process is the estimation of the relevant cash flows. For simplicity, the net cash flows are treated as a given in this chapter, which allows us to focus on our main area of concern, the capital budgeting decision rules. However, in Chapter 10 we will discuss cash flow estimation in detail. Also, note that *working capital* is defined as the firm's current assets, and that *net working capital* is current assets minus current liabilities.

[2]The easiest way to calculate the payback period is to accumulate the project's net cash flows and see when they sum to zero. For example, the annual and cumulative net cash flows of Project S are shown below:

Year	Net Cash Flow	
	Annual	Cumulative
0	($1,000)	($1,000)
1	500	(500)
2	400	(100)
3	300	200
4	100	300

Thus, the investment is recovered by the end of Year 3. If the cash flows occur evenly during the year, the recovery occurs one-third of the way into Year 3: $100 remains to be recovered at the end of Year 2, and since Year 3 produces $300 in net cash flow, the payback period for Project S is 2⅓ years. As a formula, Payback = Year before complete recovery + (Unrecovered investment/Cash flow during the year in which complete recovery occurs) = 2 + ($100/$300) = 2⅓ years.

[3]*Mutually exclusive* means that if one project is taken on, the other must be rejected. For example, the installation of a conveyor-belt system in a warehouse and the purchase of a fleet of forklift trucks for the same warehouse would be mutually exclusive projects—accepting one implies rejection of the other. *Independent* projects are projects whose cash flows are independent of one another.

		Discounted Net Cash Flow			
	Year	**Project S**		**Project L**	
	(t)	**Annual**	**Cumulative**	**Annual**	**Cumulative**
	0	($1,000)	($1,000)	($1,000)	($1,000)
	1	455	(545)	91	(909)
	2	331	(214)	248	(661)
	3	225	11	301	(360)
	4	68	79	410	50

TABLE 9-2
DISCOUNTED CASH
FLOWS FOR PROJECTS
S AND L

flows are discounted by the project's cost of capital.[4] Thus, the discounted payback period is defined as the number of years required to recover the investment from *discounted* net cash flows. Table 9-2 contains the discounted net cash flows for Projects S and L, assuming both projects have a cost of capital of 10 percent. To construct Table 9-2, each cash inflow in Table 9-1 is divided by $(1 + k)^t = (1.10)^t$, where t is the year in which the cash flow occurs and k is the project's cost of capital. After 3 years, Project S will have generated $1,011 in discounted cash inflows. Since the cost is $1,000, the discounted payback is just under 3 years, or, to be precise, $2 + (\$214/\$225) = 2.95$ years. Project L's discounted payback is 3.88 years:

$$\text{Discounted payback}_S = 2.0 + \$214/\$225 = 2.95 \text{ years.}$$

$$\text{Discounted payback}_L = 3.0 + \$360/\$410 = 3.88 \text{ years.}$$

For Projects S and L, the rankings are the same regardless of which payback method is used; that is, Project S is preferred to Project L, and Project S would still be selected if the firm were to require a discounted payback of three years or less. Sometimes, however, the regular and the discounted paybacks produce conflicting rankings.

Note that the payback is a type of "breakeven" calculation in the sense that if cash flows come in at the expected rate until the payback year, then the project will return its initial investment. However, the regular payback does not take account of the cost of capital—no cost for the debt or equity used to undertake the project is reflected in the cash flows or the calculation. The discounted payback does take account of capital costs—it shows the breakeven year after covering debt and equity costs. Still, both payback methods have serious deficiencies—especially the fact that they ignore all cash flows that occur after the payback period—and other procedures are less likely to lead to errors in project selection. Therefore, we will not dwell on the finer points of payback analysis.

---

[4]A project's cost of capital reflects (1) the overall cost of capital to the firm and (2) the differential risk between the firm's existing projects and the project being evaluated. Risk adjustments will be discussed in detail in Chapter 11.

Although the payback method has some serious faults as a project ranking criterion, it does provide information on how long funds will be tied up in a project. Thus, the shorter the payback period, other things held constant, the greater is the project's *liquidity*. Also, since cash flows expected in the distant future are generally regarded as being riskier than near-term cash flows, the payback period is often used as a rough measure of a project's *riskiness*.

ACCOUNTING RATE OF RETURN (ARR)

The *accounting rate of return (ARR)*, which focuses on a project's contribution to the firm's net income rather than on its cash flows, is the second-oldest evaluation technique. In its most commonly used form, the ARR is measured as the ratio of the project's average annual expected net income to its average investment. If we assume that Projects S and L will both be depreciated by the straight line method to a book value of zero, then each will have a depreciation expense of $1,000/4 = $250 per year. The average cash flow minus the average depreciation charge is the average annual income. For Project S, average annual income is $75:

$$\text{Average annual income} = \text{Average cash flow} - \text{Average annual depreciation}$$
$$= (\$1,300/4) - \$250 = \$75.$$

The average investment is the beginning investment plus the ending investment (the salvage value), divided by 2, or $500:

$$\text{Average investment} = (\text{Cost} + \text{Salvage value})/2$$
$$= (\$1,000 + \$0)/2 = \$500.$$

This $500 is the book value of the asset halfway through its life. Dividing the average annual income by the average investment, we obtain an ARR for Project S of 15 percent:

$$\text{ARR}_S = \frac{\text{Average annual income}}{\text{Average investment}} = \frac{\$75}{\$500} = 15\%.$$

By a similar calculation, we determine ARR_L to be 20 percent. Thus, the ARR method ranks Project L over Project S. If the firm accepts projects with an ARR of 16 percent or more, Project L would be accepted, but Project S would be rejected. Note also that for these two projects the rankings under the ARR method are the opposite of those based on either payback method. One could argue about which method is better, and hence which set of rankings should be used. However, this would really be a hollow argument, because both the payback and ARR methods are badly flawed. The discounted payback ignores cash flows that are expected after the payback year, and the regular payback and the ARR both ignore the time

value of money. Since none of these procedures provides adequate information on the project's contribution to the firm's value, they could all lead to incorrect capital budgeting decisions.[5]

NET PRESENT VALUE (NPV)

As the flaws in the payback and the ARR were recognized, people began to search for ways to improve the effectiveness of project evaluations. One such method is the *net present value (NPV)* method, which relies on *discounted cash flow* (DCF) methodology. To implement this approach, we proceed as follows:

1. Find the present value of each period's net cash flow, including both inflows and outflows, discounted at the project's cost of capital.

2. Sum these discounted net cash flows; this sum is defined as the project's NPV.

3. If the NPV is positive, the project should be accepted; if the NPV is negative, it should be rejected; and if two projects are mutually exclusive, the one with the higher positive NPV should be chosen.

The NPV can be expressed as follows:

$$NPV = \sum_{t=0}^{n} \frac{CF_t}{(1 + k)^t}. \tag{9-1}$$

Here CF_t is the expected net cash flow at Period t, and k is the project's cost of capital.[6] Cash outflows (expenditures on the project, such as the cost of buying equipment or building factories) are treated as *negative* cash flows. In evaluating Projects S and L, only CF_0 is negative, but for many large projects such as Boeing's 777 aircraft project, an electric generating plant, or Nucor's new steel mill, outflows occur for several years before operations begin and cash flows turn positive. Also, note that Equation 9-1 is quite general, so inflows and outflows could occur on any time basis, say, quarterly or monthly, in which case t would represent quarters or months rather than years.[7]

At a 10 percent cost of capital, the NPV of Project S is $78.82:

---

[5]Actually, there are many ways to calculate ARRs. Since all of them have major deficiencies, we see no point in extending the discussion. Also, we should note that many firms use the ARR in one form or another to measure divisional performance. Use of the ARR in this way — as opposed to capital budgeting decision making — makes sense.

[6]In Equation 9-1, we assume that the project's cost of capital, k, is constant across all periods. Since future capital cost changes are difficult, if not impossible, to forecast, the constant capital cost assumption is almost always used in practice.

[7]If t represents any period other than years, then the cost of capital must be adjusted to reflect the periodic rate. For example, if the annual cost of capital were 10 percent, but we were evaluating a project on the basis of quarterly cash flows, the periodic rate would be $10\%/4 = 2.5\%$.

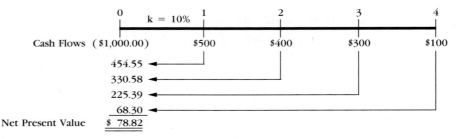

By a similar process, we find $NPV_L = \$49.18$. On this basis, both projects should be accepted if they are independent, but S should be the one chosen if they are mutually exclusive.

When using a financial calculator, enter the cash flows, in order, into the cash flow register, then enter $k = I = 10$, and finally push the NPV key (or compute NPV). When entering the cash flows, note that many calculators have a register labelled CF_0 for the initial cash flow, which is usually an outflow, and then registers labelled CF_j for the succeeding cash flows.[8]

---

[8]The precise steps for two popular calculators, the HP 10B and the HP 17B, are shown below. If you have another type of financial calculator, see its manual.

HP 10B:

1. Clear the memory.

2. Enter CF_0 as follows: 1000 [+/−] [CF$_j$].

3. Enter CF_1 as follows: 500 [CF$_j$].

4. Repeat the process to enter the other cash flows. Note that CF 0, CF 1, and so forth flash on the screen as you press the [CF$_j$] key. If you hold the key down, CF 0 and so forth will remain on the screen until you release it.

5. Once the CFs have been entered, enter $k = I = 10\%$: 10 [I/YR].

6. Now that all of the inputs have been entered, you can press ■ [NPV] to get the answer, NPV = $78.82.

7. If a cash flow is repeated for several years, you can avoid having to enter the CFs for each year. For example, if the $500 cash flow for Year 1 had also been the CF for Years 2 through 10, making 10 of these $500 cash flows, then after entering 500 [CF$_j$] the first time, you could enter 10 ■ [N$_j$]. This would automatically enter 10 CFs of 500.

HP 17B:

1. Go to the cash flow (CFLO) menu, clear if FLOW(0) = ? does not appear on the screen.

2. Enter CF_0 as follows: 1000 [+/−] [INPUT].

3. Enter CF_1 as follows: 500 [INPUT].

4. Now the calculator will ask you if the 500 is for Period 1 only or if it is also used for several following periods. Since it is only used for Period 1, press [INPUT] to answer "1." Alternatively, you could press [EXIT] and then [#T?] to turn off the prompt for the remainder of the problem. For some problems you will want to use the repeat feature.

5. Enter the remaining CFs, being sure to turn off the prompt or else to specify "1" for each entry.

6. Once the CFs have all been entered, press [EXIT] and then [CALC].

7. Now enter $k = I = 10\%$ as follows: 10 [I%].

8. Now press [NPV] to get the answer, NPV = $78.82.

RATIONALE FOR THE NPV METHOD

The rationale for the NPV method is straightforward. An NPV of zero signifies that the project's cash flows are exactly sufficient to (1) repay the invested capital and (2) provide the required rate of return on that capital. If a project has a positive NPV, then its cash flows are generating an excess return, and, since the return to bondholders is fixed, the excess return accrues solely to the firm's stockholders. Therefore, if a firm takes on a zero-NPV project, the position of the stockholders remains constant—the firm becomes larger, but the price of its stock remains unchanged. However, if the firm takes on a project with a positive NPV, the position of the stockholders is improved. In our example, shareholders' wealth would increase by $78.82 if the firm takes on Project S, but it would increase by only $49.18 if it takes on Project L. Viewed in this manner, it is easy to see why S is preferred to L, and it is also easy to see the logic of the NPV approach.[9]

INTERNAL RATE OF RETURN (IRR)

In Chapter 7 we presented procedures for finding the yield to maturity, or rate of return, on a bond—if you invest in the bond and hold it to maturity, you can expect to earn the YTM on the money you invested. Exactly the same concepts are employed in capital budgeting when the IRR method is used. The IRR is defined as that discount rate which equates the present value of a project's expected cash inflows to the present value of the project's expected costs:

$$PV(\text{Inflows}) = PV(\text{Investment costs}),$$

or, equivalently,

$$\sum_{t=0}^{n} \frac{CF_t}{(1 + IRR)^t} = 0. \qquad (9\text{-}2)$$

---

[9]This description of the process is somewhat oversimplified. Both analysts and investors anticipate that firms will identify and accept positive NPV projects, and current stock prices reflect these expectations. Thus, stock prices react to announcements of new capital projects only to the extent that such projects were not already expected. In this sense, we may think of a firm's value as consisting of two parts: (1) the value of its existing assets and (2) the value of its "growth opportunities," or projects with positive NPVs. AT&T is a good example of this: The company has the world's largest long-distance network plus telephone manufacturing facilities, both of which provide current earnings and cash flows, and it has Bell Labs, which has the *potential* for developing new products in the computer/telecommunications area that could be extremely profitable. Security analysts (and investors) thus analyze AT&T as a company with a set of cash-producing assets plus a set of growth opportunities that will materialize if and only if it can come up with a number of positive NPV projects through its capital budgeting process.

For our Project S, here is the setup:

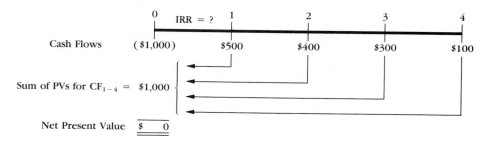

$$IRR_s = 14.5\% = \text{Discount rate which forces the sum of the PVs}$$
$$\text{of } CF_{1-4} \text{ to equal the project's cost, \$1,000.}$$

Internal rates of return can be calculated with financial calculators and computers, and most firms have computerized their capital budgeting processes and can quickly generate IRRs, NPVs, and paybacks for all projects. Thus, business firms have no difficulty whatsoever with the mechanical side of capital budgeting, and a serious business student should have a financial calculator capable of finding IRRs. All IRRs reported in this and the following chapters were obtained by using a financial calculator or a computer. By keying in the cash flows and then pressing the IRR button, we used a financial calculator to find that Project S has $IRR_S = 14.5\%$, while $IRR_L = 11.8\%$.[10] If both projects have a cost of capital, or *hurdle rate*, of 10 percent, then the internal rate of return rule indicates that if the projects are independent, both should be accepted—they both are expected to earn more than the cost of the capital needed to finance them. If they are mutually exclusive, S ranks higher and should be accepted, while L should be rejected. If the cost of capital is more than 14.5 percent, both projects should be rejected.

Notice that the IRR formula, Equation 9-2, is simply the NPV formula, Equation 9-1, solved for the particular discount rate that forces the NPV to equal zero. Thus, the same basic equation is used for both methods, but in the NPV method the discount rate, k, is specified and the NPV is found, whereas in the IRR method the NPV is specified to equal zero, and the value of IRR that forces this equality is determined.

RATIONALE FOR THE IRR METHOD

Why is the particular discount rate that equates a project's cost with the present value of its receipts (the IRR) so special? In effect, the IRR on a project is its

---

[10]To find the IRR with an HP 10B or HP 17B, repeat the steps given in footnote 8. Then, with an HP 10B, press ■ IRR/YR , and after a pause, 14.49, Project S's IRR, will appear. With the HP 17B, simply press IRR% to get the IRR. With both calculators, you would always want to calculate both the NPV and the IRR after entering the input data, before clearing the cash flow register.

expected rate of return. If the internal rate of return exceeds the cost of the funds used to finance the project, a surplus remains after paying for the capital, and this surplus accrues to the firm's stockholders. Therefore, taking on a project whose IRR exceeds its cost of capital increases shareholders' wealth. On the other hand, if the internal rate of return is less than the cost of capital, then taking on the project imposes a cost on current stockholders. It is this "breakeven" characteristic that makes the IRR useful in evaluating capital projects.

PROFITABILITY INDEX

Another method used to evaluate projects is the *profitability index (PI)*, or the *benefit/cost ratio*, as it is sometimes called:

$$PI = \frac{PV \text{ benefits}}{PV \text{ costs}} = \frac{\sum_{t=0}^{n} \dfrac{CIF_t}{(1 + k)^t}}{\sum_{t=0}^{n} \dfrac{COF_t}{(1 + k)^t}}. \tag{9-3}$$

Here CIF_t represents the expected cash inflows, or benefits, and COF_t represents the expected cash outflows, or costs. The PI shows the *relative* profitability of any project, or the present value of benefits per present value dollar of costs. The PI for Project S, based on a 10 percent cost of capital, is 1.079:

$$PI_S = \frac{\$1,078.82}{\$1,000} = 1.079.$$

Similarly, $PI_L = 1.049$. A project is acceptable if its PI is greater than 1.0, and the higher the PI, the higher the project's ranking. Therefore, both S and L would be accepted by the PI criterion if they were independent, and S would be ranked ahead of L if they were mutually exclusive.

Mathematically, the NPV, the IRR, and the PI methods will always lead to the same accept/reject decisions for independent projects: If a project's NPV is positive, its IRR will always exceed k and its PI will always be greater than 1.0. However, NPV, IRR, and PI can give conflicting rankings for mutually exclusive projects. This point will be discussed in more detail in later sections.

SELF-TEST QUESTIONS

What are the five capital budgeting ranking methods discussed in this section?

Briefly describe each method, and explain the rationale for its use.

What three methods always lead to the same accept/reject decision for independent projects?

pronounced if t is larger. To understand this point more clearly, consider the following data:

What two pieces of information does the payback period provide that are not provided by the other methods?

COMPARISON OF THE NPV AND IRR METHODS

As we will demonstrate later, the NPV method is better than the IRR and PI methods. Therefore, we were tempted to explain only the NPV method, to state that it should be used as the acceptance criterion, and to go on to the next topic. However, the IRR and PI methods are familiar to many corporate executives, they are widely entrenched in industry, and they do have some unique virtues. Therefore, it is important that finance students thoroughly understand the IRR and PI methods and be prepared to explain why, at times, a project with a lower IRR or PI may be preferable to one with a higher IRR or PI.

NPV PROFILES

A graph which relates a project's NPV to the discount rate used to calculate the NPV is defined as the project's *net present value profile;* profiles for Projects L and S are shown in Figure 9-1. To construct the profiles, first note that at a zero discount rate, the NPV is simply the total of the undiscounted cash flows of the project; thus, at a zero discount rate, $NPV_S = \$300$ and $NPV_L = \$400$. These values are plotted as the vertical axis intercepts in Figure 9-1. Next, calculate the projects' NPVs at three discount rates, say, 5, 10, and 15 percent, and plot these values. The four points plotted on our graph for each project are shown at the bottom of the figure.

Finally, recall that the IRR is defined as the discount rate at which a project's NPV equals zero. Therefore, *the point where its net present value profile crosses the horizontal axis indicates a project's internal rate of return.* Therefore, since we calculated IRR_S and IRR_L in an earlier section, we have two other points which we can use in plotting the projects' NPV profiles.

When we connect the plot points, we have the net present value profiles.[11] NPV profiles can be very useful in project analysis, and we will use them often in the remainder of the chapter.

NPV RANKINGS DEPEND ON THE DISCOUNT RATE

Figure 9-1 shows that the NPV profiles of both Project L and Project S decline as the discount rate increases. But notice in the figure that Project L has the higher

---

[11]Notice that the NPV profiles are curved—they are *not* straight lines. Also, the NPV profiles approach the $t = 0$ cash flow value (the cost of the project) as the discount rate increases without limit. The reason is that, at an infinitely high discount rate, the PVs of the inflows would be zero, so $NPV (k = \infty) = CF_0$, which in our example is $-\$1,000$. We should also note that under certain conditions the NPV profiles can cross the horizontal axis several times, or never cross it. This point is discussed later in the chapter.

correct? Logic suggests that the NPV method is better, since it selects that project which adds the most to shareholder wealth.[12]

Conditions That Lead to Conflict.   Two basic conditions can cause NPV profiles to cross, and thus can lead to conflicts between NPV and IRR: (1) when *project size (or scale) differences* exist, meaning that the cost of one project is larger than that of the other, or (2) when *timing differences* exist, meaning that the timing of cash flows from the two projects differs such that most of the cash flows from one project come in the early years and most of the cash flows from the other project come in the later years, as occurred with Projects L and S.[13]

When either size or timing differences occur, the firm will have different amounts of funds to invest in the various years, depending on which of the two mutually exclusive projects it chooses. For example, if one project costs more than the other, then the firm will have more money at t = 0 to invest elsewhere if it selects the smaller project. Similarly, for projects of equal size, the one with the larger early cash inflows provides more funds for reinvestment in the early years. Given this situation, the assumed rate of return at which differential cash flows can be invested is an important consideration.

Causes of Conflict.   The critical issue in resolving conflicts between mutually exclusive projects is this: What is the value of generating the cash flows earlier rather than later? The value of the cash flows depends on the opportunity cost rate at which we can reinvest differential early years' cash flows. *The use of the NPV method implicitly assumes that the opportunity rate at which cash flows can be reinvested is the cost of capital, whereas use of the IRR method implies that the firm has the opportunity to reinvest at the IRR.* These assumptions are inherent in the mathematics of the discounting process. Thus, the NPV method discounts cash flows at the cost of capital, while the IRR method discounts cash flows at the project's IRR. The cash flows may actually be withdrawn as dividends by the stock-holders and spent on beer and pizza, but the assumption of a reinvestment opportunity is still implicit in the NPV and IRR calculations.

Resolution of Conflict.   Which is the better assumption, reinvestment of each project's cash flows at the cost of capital or reinvestment at the project's IRR? We can answer the question as follows:

1.   Assume that the firm's cost of capital is 10 percent. Management can obtain all the funds it wants at this rate. This condition is expected to hold in the foreseeable

---

[12]The crossover point is important, and it is easy to calculate. Simply go back to Table 9-1, where we set forth the two projects' cash flows, and calculate the difference in those flows in each year. The differences are $CF_S - CF_L = \$0, +\$400, +\$100, -\$100,$ and $-\$500$, respectively. Enter these values in the cash flow register of a financial calculator, press the IRR button, and the crossover rate, $7.17 \approx 7.2$, appears.

[13]Of course, it is possible for mutually exclusive projects to differ with respect to both scale and timing. Also, if mutually exclusive projects have different lives (as opposed to different cash flow patterns over a common life), this introduces further complications, and for meaningful comparisons, some mutually exclusive projects must be evaluated over a common life. This point will be discussed in detail in the next chapter.

$$\frac{}{(1 + k)^0} \quad \frac{}{(1 + k)^1} \quad \frac{}{(1 + k)^2} \quad \frac{}{(1 + k)^3} \quad \frac{}{(1 + k)^4}$$

Now notice that the denominators of the terms in this equation increase as k and t increase, and the increase is exponential; that is, the effect of a higher k is more

future. Further, assume that all potential projects have the same risk as the firm's current projects.

2. The capital budgeting process calls for all potential projects to be evaluated at $k = 10\%$. All projects with NPV > 0 are accepted. An unlimited supply of capital is available at this rate to finance these projects, both now and in the future.

3. As cash flows come in from past investments, what will be done with them? These cash flows can either (a) be paid out to the equity and debt investors who, on average, require a 10 percent rate of return, or (b) be used as a substitute for outside capital that costs 10 percent. Thus, since the cash flows are expected to save the firm 10 percent, this is their value to the firm, and hence their opportunity cost reinvestment rate.

4. The IRR method implicitly assumes reinvestment at the internal rate of return itself. Given (a) ready access to capital markets and (b) a constant expected future cost of capital, the appropriate reinvestment rate is the opportunity cost of capital, or 10 percent. Even if the firm takes on projects in the future whose IRRs average some high rate, say, 30 percent, this is irrelevant—those projects could always be financed with new external capital costing 10 percent, so cash flows from past projects have an opportunity cost reinvestment rate which is only equal to the cost of capital.

Therefore, we come to the conclusion that *the correct reinvestment rate assumption is the cost of capital, which is built into the NPV method.* This, in turn, leads us to prefer the NPV method, at least for firms willing and able to obtain capital at a cost reasonably close to their current cost of capital. In Chapter 10, when we discuss capital rationing, we will see that under certain conditions the NPV rule may be questionable, but for most firms at most times, NPV is conceptually better than IRR.

We should reiterate that, when projects are independent, the NPV and IRR methods both lead to exactly the same accept/reject decisions. However, *when evaluating mutually exclusive projects, especially those that differ in scale and/ or timing, the NPV method should be used.*

MULTIPLE IRRs

There is one other situation in which the IRR approach may not be usable—this is when non-normal cash flows are involved. A capital project has normal cash flows when one or more cash outflows (costs) are followed by a series of cash inflows. If, however, a project calls for a large cash outflow either sometime during or at the end of its life, then it has *non-normal* cash flows. Non-normal cash flows can present unique difficulties when evaluated by the IRR method. The most common problem encountered when evaluating non-normal projects is multiple IRRs.

Consider again Equation 9-2, which is solved to find the IRR:

$$\sum_{t=0}^{n} \frac{CF_t}{(1 + IRR)^t} = 0. \qquad (9\text{-}2)$$

cision. In all such cases, the NPV criterion could be easily applied, and this method leads to conceptually correct capital budgeting decisions.

SELF-TEST QUESTIONS

Describe how NPV profiles are constructed.

What is a crossover point, and how does it affect the choice when mutually exclusive projects are being considered?

What are the two basic conditions that can lead to conflicts between the NPV and IRR methods?

What are the underlying assumptions which lead to conflicts between the NPV and IRR methods?

If a conflict exists, should the capital budgeting decision be made on the basis of the NPV or the IRR ranking? Why?

Explain the difference between normal and non-normal cash flows.

What is the "multiple IRR problem," and what condition is necessary for its occurrence?

MODIFIED INTERNAL RATE OF RETURN (MIRR)

In spite of a strong academic preference for the NPV method, surveys indicate that business executives prefer IRR over NPV by a margin of 3 to 1. Apparently, managers find it easier to analyze investments in terms of percentage rates of return than dollars of NPV. Given this fact, can we devise a percentage evaluator that is better than the regular IRR? The answer is yes—we can modify the IRR and make it a better indicator of relative profitability, hence better for use in capital budgeting. The new measure is called the *modified IRR,* or *MIRR,* and it is defined as follows:

$$
\text{PV costs} = \text{PV terminal value}
$$

$$
\sum_{t=0}^{n} \frac{COF_t}{(1 + k)^t} = \frac{\displaystyle\sum_{t=0}^{n} CIF_t(1 + k)^{n-t}}{(1 + MIRR)^n} \tag{9-2a}
$$

$$
\text{PV costs} = \frac{TV}{(1 + MIRR)^n}.
$$

Here COF refers to cash outflows, or the costs of the project, and CIF refers to cash inflows. The left term is simply the PV of the investment outlays when dis-

counted at the cost of capital, and the numerator of the right term is the future value of the inflows, assuming that the cash inflows are reinvested at the cost of capital. The future value of the cash inflows is also called the *terminal value,* or *TV.* The discount rate that forces the PV of the TV to equal the PV of the costs is defined as the MIRR.[17]

If the investment costs are all incurred at t = 0, and if the first operating inflow occurs at t = 1, as is true for our illustrative Projects S and L in Table 9-1, then this equation may be used:

$$\text{Cost} = \frac{\text{TV}}{(1 + \text{MIRR})^n} = \frac{\sum_{t=1}^{n} \text{CIF}_t(1 + k)^{n-t}}{(1 + \text{MIRR})^n}. \tag{9-2b}$$

We can illustrate the calculation with Project S:

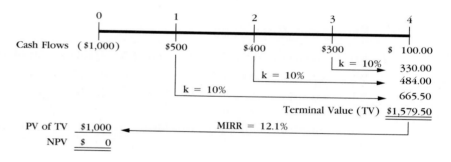

Using a financial calculator, enter PV = 1,000, FV = 1,579.5 (or −1,579.5), and n = 4, and press the i button to find MIRR$_S$ = 12.1%. Similarly, we find MIRR$_L$ = 11.3%.

The modified IRR has a significant advantage over the regular IRR. MIRR assumes that cash flows from all projects are reinvested at the cost of capital, while the regular IRR assumes that the cash flows from each project are reinvested at the project's own IRR. Since reinvestment at k is generally more correct, the modified IRR is a better indicator of a project's true profitability. MIRR also solves the multiple IRR problem. To illustrate, with k = 10%, Project M (the strip mine project) has MIRR = 5.6%, and hence it should be rejected. This is consistent with the decision based on the NPV method, because NPV = − $0.77 million.

---

[17]There are several alternative definitions for the MIRR. The one we present here is effective and relatively simple to use. For a complete discussion, see William R. McDaniel, Daniel E. McCarty, and Kenneth A. Jessell, "Discounted Cash Flow with Explicit Reinvestment Rates: Tutorial and Extension," *The Financial Review,* August 1988, 369–385.

Is MIRR as good as NPV for selecting among competing (mutually exclusive) projects? If the two projects are of equal size and have the same life, then NPV and MIRR will always lead to the same project selection decision. Thus, for any projects like our Projects S and L, if $NPV_S > NPV_L$, then $MIRR_S > MIRR_L$, and the kinds of conflicts we encountered between NPV and the regular IRR will not occur. Also, if the projects are of equal size, but differ in lives, the MIRR will always lead to the same decision as the NPV when the MIRRs are both calculated on the basis of the longer project's life. (Just fill in zeros for the shorter project's missing cash flows.) *However, if the projects differ in scale (or size), then conflicts can still occur— if we were comparing a large project with a small mutually exclusive one, then we might find $NPV_L > NPV_S$, but $MIRR_S > MIRR_L$.*

Our conclusion is that the modified IRR is superior to the regular IRR as an indicator of a project's "true" rate of return, or "expected long-term rate of return," but the NPV method is still better for choosing among competing projects that differ in scale, because it provides a better indicator of how much each project contributes to the value of the firm.[18]

SELF-TEST QUESTIONS

Briefly describe how the modified IRR (MIRR) is calculated.

What is the primary difference between the MIRR and the regular IRR?

What advantages does the MIRR have over the regular IRR in capital budgeting?

What condition can cause the MIRR and NPV methods to lead to different decisions?

COMPARISON OF THE NPV AND PI METHODS

The PI method, where PI equals the PV of cash inflows divided by the PV of cash outflows, measures the present value of benefits per dollar of investment, whereas the NPV measures the total dollars of net present value. These two methods can lead to conflicts when used to evaluate mutually exclusive projects. To illustrate, suppose a firm is comparing Project L (for large), which requires a $5 million investment and returns $6 million after one year, with Project S (for small), which requires an outlay of $100,000 and returns $130,000 at the end of one year. Both

---

[18]Note that some financial calculators, for example the HP 17B, make it relatively easy to calculate MIRR. With the 17B, you enter two cash flow streams: (1) an outflow stream with zeros in place of inflows and (2) an inflow stream with zeros for costs. Then, the 17B calculates the terminal value of the inflow stream and the present value of the outflow stream. The final step is merely finding the MIRR.

projects have average risk and hence will be evaluated at the firm's 10 percent cost of capital. Here are the projects' NPVs and PIs:

$$NPV_L = -\$5,000,000 + \frac{\$6,000,000}{(1.10)^1} = \$454,545.$$

$$NPV_S = -\$100,000 + \frac{\$130,000}{(1.10)^1} = \$18,182.$$

$$PI_L = \frac{\dfrac{\$6,000,000}{(1.10)^1}}{\$5,000,000} = 1.09.$$

$$PI_S = \frac{\dfrac{\$130,000}{(1.10)^1}}{\$100,000} = 1.18.$$

Thus, the NPV method indicates that we should accept Project L because $NPV_L > NPV_S$, but the PI method indicates that Project S is preferable, because $PI_S > PI_L$.

Given this conflict, which project should be accepted? Remembering that shareholders' wealth increases by the NPV of a project, it is clear that Project L contributes more to shareholder wealth, so L should be selected over S. Thus, for a firm that seeks to maximize stockholders' wealth, the NPV method is better. Of course, if the projects were independent, both would be chosen, since both projects have positive NPVs and hence PIs greater than 1.0.

In general, the NPV method leads to better decisions than does the PI method. However, the PI may be useful when capital rationing exists. We explore this topic in Appendix 11A.

SELF-TEST QUESTIONS

What condition can lead to conflicts between the NPV and PI methods?

If a conflict exists, should the NPV or the PI method be used to make the decision? Explain.

PRESENT VALUE OF FUTURE COSTS

Firms often choose between mutually exclusive projects on the basis of the present value of future costs rather than on the basis of the projects' NPVs. For example, Moët & Chandon, a French champagne producer, recently evaluated several different methods for disposing of grape pulp at its California winery. The disposal system chosen would have no effect on either the prices or the quantity of sparkling wine produced by the plant—these would be set in the competitive market-

		Expected Net Cost	
Table 9-3 Production Costs for Processes A and B	**Year**	**Process A**	**Process B**
	0	($50,000)	($100,000)
	1	(22,000)	(10,000)
	2	(22,000)	(10,000)
	3	(22,000)	(10,000)
	4	(22,000)	(10,000)
	5	(22,000)	(10,000)
	PV(12%)	($129,305)	($136,048)

place. Therefore, the revenue stream would be the same regardless of which disposal process is used, so revenues are irrelevant to this capital budgeting decision.

Since the revenue stream will be the same, Moët & Chandon could make the decision on the basis of expected future costs alone, choosing the process that does the job for the lowest cost. Table 9-3 contains the expected net costs for the best two processes over their 5-year expected lives. Process A requires a lower expenditure on capital equipment than B, but A is more labor intensive. Therefore, A's Year 0 cost is relatively low, but its operating costs are relatively high.

The company's analysts judged the processes to both have the same risk as the company's average project, and thus they used the firm's overall cost of capital, 12 percent, to discount the flows of each project. As shown in Table 9-3, Process A has a lower present value of future costs, so it was chosen. We will have more to say about discounting costs (or outflows) in Chapter 11, where we discuss risk adjustments.

Self-Test Questions

Explain the procedure for evaluating two mutually exclusive projects on the basis of costs alone.

What condition is necessary to use the cost analysis approach? (Hint: Think about revenues, but explain.)

Our View of the Capital Budgeting Decision Methods

Ignoring the accounting rate of return, we have presented five potential capital budgeting decision methods in this chapter, and each has its own set of advantages and disadvantages. In the course of our discussion, we purposely compared the methods against one another to highlight their relative strengths and weaknesses. However, in the process we probably created the impression that "sophisticated" firms would use only one method in the decision process, NPV. Today, virtually all

capital budgeting decisions of importance are analyzed by computer, hence it is easy to calculate and list all the relevant decision measures: (1) payback and discounted payback, (2) NPV, (3) IRR, (4) profitability index (PI), and (5) modified IRR (MIRR). In making the accept/reject decision, most large, sophisticated firms such as IBM, GE, and Royal Dutch Petroleum, calculate and consider all five measures because each provides decision makers with a somewhat different piece of relevant information.

Payback and discounted payback provide an indication of both the risk and the liquidity of a project—a long payback means (1) that the investment dollars will be locked up for many years, hence the project is relatively illiquid, and (2) that the project's cash flows must be forecast far out into the future, hence the project is probably quite risky. A good analogy for this is the bond valuation process. You would never compare the yields to maturity on two bonds without considering their terms to maturity (or durations), because a bond's riskiness is significantly influenced by its maturity.

NPV is important because it gives a direct measure of the dollar benefit (on a present value basis) of the project to the firm's shareholders. Therefore, we regard NPV as the best single measure of *profitability*. IRR also measures profitability, but expressed as a percentage rate of return, which many decision makers, especially nonfinancial managers, seem to prefer. Further, IRR contains information concerning a project's "safety margin" which is not inherent in NPV. To illustrate, consider the following two projects: Project S (for small) which costs $10,000 at t = 0 and returns $16,500 at the end of one year, and Project L (for large) which costs $100,000 and has a payoff of $115,500 after one year. At a 10 percent cost of capital, both projects have an NPV of $5,000, and, if they were mutually exclusive, the NPV method indicates that we should be indifferent between the two. However, Project S actually provides a much larger margin for error. The realized cash inflow could be almost 40 percent below the $16,500 forecast, and the firm would still recover its $10,000 investment. On the other hand, if the actual inflow from Project L fell by only 14 percent from the forecasted $115,500, the firm would fall short of recovering its investment. Further, if no revenues were generated at all, the firm would lose only $10,000 on Project S, compared with $100,000 on Project L. The NPV contains no information about either the "safety margin" inherent in a project's cash flow forecasts or the amount of capital at risk; however, the IRR does provide "safety margin" information—Project S's IRR is a whopping 65.0 percent, while Project L's IRR is only 15.5 percent, so even if its realized return fell substantially, Project S would still be a money-maker.

The profitability index also provides a measure of a project's "safety margin," because it measures the profitability per dollar of investment, or the "bang for the buck." Project S's PI is 1.50 while Project L's PI is 1.05, and thus the PI, like the IRR, indicates that Project S has a greater tolerance for cash flow uncertainty than Project L.[19] Finally, the modified IRR has all the virtues of the IRR, but it also

---

[19]For an interesting article which supports the use of the profitability index in capital budgeting decision making, see Edward M. Miller, "The Competitive Market Assumption and Capital Budgeting Criteria," *Financial Management,* Winter 1987, 22–28.

incorporates the correct reinvestment rate assumption and avoids the problems that the IRR can have when applied to non-normal projects.

In summary, the different evaluation methods provide different types of information to decision makers, and since it is so easy to generate the values for all the methods, all should be considered in the decision process. For any specific decision, more weight might be given to one method than another, but it would be foolish to ignore the information inherent in any of the methods.

SELF-TEST QUESTIONS

Describe the advantages and disadvantages of the five capital budgeting methods described in this chapter. (Ignore accounting rate of return.)

Should capital budgeting decisions be made solely on the basis of a project's NPV?

THE POST-AUDIT

An important aspect of the capital budgeting process is the *post-audit,* which involves (1) comparing actual results with those predicted by the project's sponsors and (2) explaining why any differences occurred. For example, many firms require that the operating divisions send a monthly report for the first six months after a project goes into operation, and a quarterly report thereafter, until the project's results are up to expectations. From then on, reports on the project are handled like those of other operations.

The post-audit has several purposes, including the following:

1. Improve forecasts. When decision makers are forced to compare their projections to actual outcomes, there is a tendency for estimates to improve. Conscious or unconscious biases are observed and eliminated; new forecasting methods are sought as the need for them becomes apparent; and people simply tend to do everything better, including forecasting, if they know that their actions are being monitored.

2. Improve operations. Businesses are run by people, and people can perform at higher or lower levels of efficiency. When a divisional team has made a forecast about an investment, its members are, in a sense, putting their reputations on the line. If costs are above predicted levels, sales below expectations, and so on, executives in production, sales, and other areas will strive to improve operations and to bring results into line with forecasts. In a discussion related to this point, an IBM executive made this statement: "You academicians worry only about making good decisions. In business, we also worry about making decisions good."

The post-audit is not a simple process. There are a number of factors that can cause complications. First, we must recognize that each element of the cash flow forecast is subject to uncertainty, so a percentage of all projects undertaken by any reason-

ably venturesome firm will necessarily go awry. This fact must be considered when appraising the performances of the operating executives who submit capital expenditure requests. Second, projects sometimes fail to meet expectations for reasons beyond the control of the operating executives and for reasons that no one could realistically be expected to anticipate. For example, the decline in oil prices in the mid-1980s adversely affected many energy-related projects, as well as real estate projects in Texas and other oil-producing areas. Third, it is often difficult to separate the operating results of one investment from those of a larger system. Although some projects stand alone and permit ready identification of costs and revenues, the actual cost savings that result from a new computer system, for example, may be very hard to measure. Fourth, it is often hard to hand out blame or praise, because the executives who were actually responsible for a given decision may have moved on by the time the results of a long-term investment are known.

Because of these difficulties, some firms tend to play down the importance of the post-audit. However, observations of both businesses and governmental units suggest that the best-run and most successful organizations are the ones that put the greatest emphasis on post-audits. Accordingly, we regard the post-audit as being one of the most important elements in a good capital budgeting system.

SELF-TEST QUESTIONS

What is done in the post-audit?

Identify several purposes of the post-audit.

What factors can cause complications in the post-audit?

SUMMARY

This chapter discussed the capital budgeting process, and the key concepts covered are listed below:

▶ *Capital budgeting* is the process of analyzing potential capital expenditures and deciding which investments the firm should undertake. Capital budgeting decisions are probably the most important ones financial managers must make.

▶ The capital budgeting process requires that the firm (1) determine the *cost of the project,* (2) estimate the *expected cash inflows* from the project and the riskiness of those cash flows, (3) determine the appropriate *cost of capital* at which to discount the cash flows, and (4) determine the sum of the *present values* of the expected cash flows.

▶ The *payback period* is defined as the expected number of years required to recover the original investment. The payback method ignores cash flows beyond the payback period, and it does not consider the time value of money. The payback does, however, provide an indication of a project's risk and liquidity, because it shows how long the original capital will be "at risk."

▶ The *discounted payback* is similar to the regular payback except that it discounts cash flows at the project's cost of capital. Like the regular payback, it ignores cash flows beyond the discounted payback period.

▶ The *accounting rate of return (ARR)* looks at a project's contribution to net income. Although it is useful in measuring performance, it is not a good capital budgeting decision method.

▶ The *net present value (NPV)* is found by discounting all cash flows (positive and negative) at the project's cost of capital and then summing those cash flows. The project is accepted if the NPV is positive.

▶ The *profitability index (PI)* is the ratio of the present value of cash inflows to the present value of cash outflows. The PI shows the profitability of a project per dollar of investment.

▶ The *internal rate of return (IRR)* is defined as the discount rate which forces the present value of a project's future cash inflows to equal the present value of the project's cash outflows (costs). The project is accepted if the IRR is greater than the project's cost of capital.

▶ The NPV, PI, and IRR methods make the same accept/reject decisions for *independent projects,* but if projects are *mutually exclusive,* then ranking conflicts can arise. If conflicts arise, the NPV method should be used. The NPV, PI, and IRR methods are all superior to the payback, but NPV is the single best measure of a project's profitability because it shows how much the project adds to shareholder wealth.

▶ The NPV method assumes that cash flows will be reinvested at the firm's cost of capital, while the IRR method assumes reinvestment at the project's IRR. Because *reinvestment at the cost of capital is the better assumption,* the NPV is superior to the IRR.

▶ The *modified IRR (MIRR) method* corrects some of the problems with the regular IRR. MIRR involves finding the terminal value (TV) of the cash inflows compounded at the firm's cost of capital and then determining the rate (MIRR) which forces the present value of the TV to equal the present value of the outflows. Still, conflicts can arise between MIRR and NPV if projects differ in size, and where conflicts arise, the decision should generally be based on the NPV.

▶ Firms often choose among mutually exclusive projects on the basis of the *present value of future costs.*

▶ Sophisticated managers consider all of the project evaluation measures, because the different measures provide different elements of information. In particular, if the NPV of Project A is only slightly higher than that of Project B, but B's IRR and/or PI is significantly higher than A's, then B should probably be chosen because of risk considerations.

Although this chapter has presented the basic elements of the capital budgeting process, there are many other aspects of this crucial topic. Some of the more important ones are discussed in the following two chapters.

QUESTIONS

9-1 Define each of the following terms:

   a. Capital budget

   b. Regular payback; discounted payback

   c. Accounting rate of return (ARR)

   d. Mutually exclusive projects; independent projects

   e. DCF techniques; net present value (NPV)

   f. Internal rate of return (IRR)

   g. Modified internal rate of return (MIRR)

   h. Profitability index (PI)

   i. NPV profile; crossover rate

   j. Non-normal cash flows; multiple IRRs

   k. Project cost of capital, or discount rate

   l. Reinvestment rate assumption

   m. Post-audit

9-2 How is a project classification scheme (for example, replacement or expansion into new markets) used in the capital budgeting process?

9-3 Explain why the NPV of a relatively long-term project, defined as one where a high percentage of its cash flows is expected in the distant future, is more sensitive to changes in the cost of capital than is the NPV of a short-term project.

9-4 Explain why, if two mutually exclusive projects are being compared, the short-term project might have the higher ranking under the NPV criterion if the cost of capital is high, but the long-term project might be deemed better if the cost of capital is low. Would changes in the cost of capital ever cause a change in the IRR ranking of two such projects?

9-5 For independent projects, is it true that if PI > 1.0, then NPV > 0 and IRR > k? Prove it.

9-6 In what sense is a reinvestment rate assumption embodied in the NPV, IRR, and MIRR methods? What is the implicitly assumed reinvestment rate of each method?

SELF-TEST PROBLEM (SOLUTION APPEARS IN APPENDIX C)

ST-1 (Project analysis) You are a financial analyst for the Hittle Company. The director of capital budgeting has asked you to analyze two proposed capital investments, Projects X and Y. Each project has a cost of $10,000, and the cost of capital for both projects is 12 percent. The projects' expected net cash flows are as follows:

	Expected Net Cash Flow	
Year	Project X	Project Y
0	($10,000)	($10,000)
1	6,500	3,500
2	3,000	3,500
3	3,000	3,500
4	1,000	3,500

   a. Calculate each project's payback, net present value (NPV), internal rate of return (IRR), modified internal rate of return (MIRR), and profitability index (PI).

b. Which project, or projects, should be accepted if they are independent?

c. Which project should be accepted if they are mutually exclusive?

d. How might a change in the cost of capital produce a conflict between the NPV and IRR rankings of these two projects? At what values of k would this conflict exist? Plot the NPV profiles.

e. Why does the conflict exist?

PROBLEMS

9-1 **(Capital budgeting methods)**   Project S has a cost of $10,000 and is expected to produce benefits (cash flows) of $3,000 per year for five years. Project L costs $25,000 and is expected to produce cash flows of $7,400 per year for five years. Calculate the two projects' NPVs, IRRs, MIRRs, and PIs, assuming a cost of capital of 12 percent. Which project would be selected, assuming they are mutually exclusive, using each ranking method? Which should actually be selected?

9-2 **(NPV and IRR analysis)**   Midwest Manufacturing Company is considering two mutually exclusive investments. The projects' expected net cash flows are as follows:

	Expected Net Cash Flow	
Year	**Project A**	**Project B**
0	($300)	($405)
1	(387)	134
2	(193)	134
3	(100)	134
4	600	134
5	600	134
6	850	134
7	(180)	0

a. Construct NPV profiles for Projects A and B.

b. What is each project's IRR?

c. If you were told that each project's cost of capital is 10 percent, which project should be selected? If the cost of capital were 17 percent, what would the proper choice be?

d. What is each project's MIRR at a cost of capital of 10 percent? At k = 17%?

e. What is the crossover rate, and what is its significance?

(Do Parts f and g only if you are using the computer problem diskette.)

f. The firm's management is confident of the projects' cash flows in Years 0 to 6 but is uncertain as to what the Year 7 cash flows will be for the two projects. Under a worst-case scenario, Project A's Year 7 cash flow will be − $300 and B's will be − $150, while under a best-case scenario, the cash flows will be − $70 and + $120 for Projects A and B, respectively. Answer Parts b through d using these new cash flows. Which project should be selected under each scenario?

g. Put the Year 7 cash flows back to − $180 for A and zero for B. Now change the cost of capital and observe what happens to NPV at k = 0%, 5%, 20%, and 400% (input as 4.0).

9-3 **(Timing differences)**   The Ewert Exploration Company is considering two mutually exclusive plans for extracting oil on property for which it has mineral rights. Both plans call

for the expenditure of $10,000,000 to drill development wells. Under Plan A, all the oil will be extracted in one year, producing a cash flow at t = 1 of $12,000,000, while under Plan B, cash flows will be $1,750,000 per year for 20 years.

a. What are the annual incremental cash flows that will be available to Ewert Exploration if it undertakes Plan B rather than Plan A? (Hint: Subtract Plan A's flows from B's.)

b. If the firm accepts Plan A, then invests the extra cash generated at the end of Year 1, what rate of return (reinvestment rate) would cause the cash flows from reinvestment to equal the cash flows from Plan B?

c. Suppose a company has a cost of capital of 10 percent. Is it logical to assume that it would take on all available independent projects (of average risk) with returns greater than 10 percent? Further, if all available projects with returns greater than 10 percent have been taken, would this mean that cash flows from past investments would have an opportunity cost of only 10 percent, because all the firm could do with these cash flows would be to replace money that has a cost of 10 percent? Finally, does this imply that the cost of capital is the correct rate to assume for the reinvestment of a project's cash flows?

d. Construct NPV profiles for Plans A and B, identify each project's IRR, and indicate the crossover rate of return.

9-4 **(Scale differences)** The Pinkerton Publishing Company is considering two mutually exclusive expansion plans. Plan A calls for the expenditure of $50 million on a large-scale, integrated plant which will provide an expected cash flow stream of $8 million per year for 20 years. Plan B calls for the expenditure of $15 million to build a somewhat less efficient, more labor-intensive plant which has an expected cash flow stream of $3.4 million per year for 20 years. The firm's cost of capital is 10 percent.

a. Calculate each project's NPV and IRR.

b. Set up a Project Δ by showing the cash flows that will exist if the firm goes with the large plant rather than the smaller plant. What are the NPV and the IRR for this Project Δ?

c. Graph the NPV profiles for Plan A, Plan B, and Project Δ.

d. Give a logical explanation, based on reinvestment rates and opportunity costs, as to why the NPV method is better than the IRR method when the firm's cost of capital is constant at some value such as 10 percent.

9-5 **(Multiple rates of return)** The Ulmer Uranium Company is deciding whether or not it should open a strip mine, the net cost of which is $4.4 million. Net cash inflows are expected to be $27.7 million, all coming at the end of Year 1. The land must be returned to its natural state at a cost of $25 million, payable at the end of Year 2.

a. Plot the project's NPV profile.

b. Should the project be accepted if k = 8%? If k = 14%? Explain your reasoning.

c. Can you think of some other capital budgeting situations where negative cash flows during or at the end of the project's life might lead to multiple IRRs?

d. What is the project's MIRR at k = 8%? At k = 14%? Does the MIRR method lead to the same accept/reject decision as the NPV method?

9-6 **(Multiple rates of return)** The Durst Development Company (DDC) has many excellent investment opportunities, but it has insufficient cash to undertake them all. Now DDC is offered the chance to borrow $2 million from the Rancho Palisades Retirement Fund at 10 percent, the loan to be repaid at the end of one year. Also, a "consulting fee" of $700,000

will be paid to Rancho Palisades' mayor at the end of one year for helping to arrange the credit. Of the $2 million received, $1 million will be used immediately to buy an old city-owned hotel and to convert it into a gambling casino. The other $1 million will be invested in other lucrative DDC projects that otherwise would have to be foregone because of a lack of capital. For two years, all cash generated by the casino will be plowed back into the casino project. At the end of the two years, the casino will be sold for $2 million.

Assuming that (1) the deal has been worked out in the sunshine and is completely legal and (2) cash from other DDC Company operations will be available to make the required payments at the end of Year 1, under what rate of return conditions should DDC accept the offer? Disregard taxes.

9-7 **(Present value of costs)** The Aubey Coffee Company is evaluating the within-plant distribution system for its new roasting, grinding, and packing plant. The two alternatives are (1) a conveyor system with a high initial cost, but low annual operating costs, and (2) several forklift trucks, which cost less, but have considerably higher operating costs. The decision to construct the plant has already been made, and the choice here will have no effect on the overall revenues of the project. The cost of capital for the plant is 8 percent, and the projects' expected net costs are listed in the table:

	Expected Net Cost	
Year	Conveyor	Forklift
0	($500,000)	($200,000)
1	(120,000)	(160,000)
2	(120,000)	(160,000)
3	(120,000)	(160,000)
4	(120,000)	(160,000)
5	(20,000)	(160,000)

a. What is the IRR of each alternative?

b. What is the present value of costs of each alternative? Which method should be chosen?

**M I N I
C A S E**

Your boss, the chief financial officer (CFO) for the Palmer Company, has just handed you the estimated cash flows for two proposed projects. Project L involves adding a new item to the firm's frozen foods line; it would take some time to build up the market for this product, so the cash inflows would increase over time. Project S involves an add-on to an existing line, and its cash flows would decrease over time. Both projects have 3-year lives, because Palmer is planning to introduce an entirely new frozen foods line at that time.

Here are the net cash flow estimates (in thousands of dollars):

	Expected Net Cash Flow	
Year	Project L	Project S
0	($100)	($100)
1	10	70
2	60	50
3	80	20

Depreciation, salvage values, net working capital requirements, and tax effects are all included in these flows.

The CFO also made subjective risk assessments of each project, and he concluded that the projects both have risk characteristics which are similar to the firm's average project.

Palmer's overall cost of capital is 10 percent. You must now determine whether one or both of the projects should be accepted.

a. What is capital budgeting? Are there any similarities between a firm's capital budgeting decisions and an individual's investment decisions?

b. What is the difference between independent and mutually exclusive projects? Between normal and non-normal cash flows?

c. (1) What is the payback period? Find the paybacks for Projects L and S.

(2) What is the rationale for the payback? According to the payback criterion, which project or projects should be accepted if the firm's maximum acceptable payback is two years, and Projects L and S were independent? Mutually exclusive?

(3) What is the difference between the regular payback and the discounted payback?

(4) What is the main disadvantage of discounted payback? Is the payback method of any real usefulness in capital budgeting decisions?

d. (1) Define the net present value (NPV). What is each project's NPV?

(2) What is the rationale behind the NPV method? According to NPV, which project or projects should be accepted if they are independent? Mutually exclusive?

(3) Would the NPVs change if the cost of capital changed?

e. (1) Define the internal rate of return (IRR). What is each project's IRR?

(2) How is the IRR on a project related to the YTM on a bond?

(3) What is the logic behind the IRR method? According to IRR, which projects should be accepted if they are independent? Mutually exclusive?

(4) Would the projects' IRRs change if the cost of capital changed?

f. (1) Define the profitability index (PI). What is each project's PI?

(2) What is the rationale behind the PI method? According to the PI, which project or projects should be accepted if they are independent? Mutually exclusive?

g. (1) Draw the NPV profiles for Projects L and S. At what discount rate do the profiles cross?

(2) Look at the NPV profile graph without referring to the actual NPVs and IRRs. Which project or projects should be accepted if they are independent? Mutually exclusive? Explain. Do your answers here apply for all discount rates less than 23.6 percent?

h. (1) What is the underlying cause of ranking conflicts between NPV and IRR?

(2) Under what conditions can conflicts occur?

(3) Which method is best? Why?

i. (1) Define the modified IRR (MIRR). Find the MIRR for Projects L and S.

(2) What are the MIRR's advantages and disadvantages vis-à-vis the regular IRR? What are the MIRR's advantages and disadvantages vis-à-vis the NPV?

j. As a separate project (Project P), the firm is considering sponsoring a pavilion at the upcoming World's Fair. The pavilion would cost $800,000, and it is expected to result in $5 million of incremental cash inflows during its one year of operation. However, it would then take another year, and $5 million of costs, to demolish the site and return it to its original condition. Thus, Project P's expected net cash flows look like this (in millions of dollars):

Year	Cash Flow
0	($0.8)
1	5
2	(5)

The project is estimated to be of average risk, so its cost of capital is 10 percent.

(1) What is Project P's NPV? What is its IRR? Its MIRR?

(2) Draw Project P's NPV profile. Does Project P have normal or nonnormal cash flows? Should this project be accepted?

Selected Additional References and Cases

For an in-depth treatment of capital budgeting techniques, see

Bierman, Harold, Jr., and Seymour Smidt, *The Capital Budgeting Decision* (New York: Macmillan, 1988).

Grant, Eugene L., William G. Ireson, and Richard S. Leavenworth, *Principles of Engineering Economy* (New York: Ronald, 1976).

Levy, Haim, and Marshall Sarnat, *Capital Investment and Financial Decisions* (Englewood Cliffs, N.J.: Prentice-Hall, 1982).

Osteryoung, Jerome S., *Capital Budgeting: Long-Term Asset Selection* (Columbus, Ohio: Grid, 1979).

Seitz, Niel E., *Capital Budgeting and Long-Term Financing Decisions* (Hinsdale, Ill.: Dryden Press, 1990).

For a discussion of strategic considerations in capital budgeting, see

Crum, Roy L., and Frans G. J. Derkinderen, eds., *Readings in Strategies for Corporate Investments* (New York: Pitman, 1981).

The following articles present interesting comparisons of four different approaches to finding NPV:

Brick, Ivan E., and Daniel G. Weaver, "A Comparison of Capital Budgeting Techniques in Identifying Profitable Investments," *Financial Management,* Winter 1984, 29–39.

Greenfield, Robert L., Maury R. Randall, and John C. Woods, "Financial Leverage and Use of the Net Present Value Investment Criterion," *Financial Management,* Autumn 1983, 40–44.

Five articles related directly to the topics in Chapter 9 are

Bacon, Peter W., "The Evaluation of Mutually Exclusive Investments," *Financial Management,* Summer 1977, 55–58.

Chaney, Paul K., "Moral Hazard and Capital Budgeting," *Journal of Financial Research,* Summer 1989, 113–128.

Lewellen, Wilbur G., Howard P. Lanser, and John J. McConnell, "Payback Substitutes for Discounted Cash Flow," *Financial Management,* Summer 1973, 17–23.

Miller, Edward M., "Safety Margins and Capital Budgeting Criteria," *Managerial Finance,* Number 2/3, 1988, 1–8.

Woods, John C., and Maury R. Randall, "The Net Present Value of Future Investment Opportunities: Its Impact on Shareholder Wealth and Implications for Capital Budgeting Theory," *Financial Management,* Summer 1989, 85–92.

For five recent articles which discuss the capital budgeting methods actually used in practice, see

Kim, Suk H., Trevor Krick, and Seung H. Kim, "Do Executives Practice What Academics Preach?" *Management Accounting,* November 1986, 49–52.

Mukherjee, Tarun K., "Capital Budgeting Surveys: The Past and the Future," *Review of Business and Economic Research,* Spring, 1987, 37–56.

———, "The Capital Budgeting Process of Large U.S. Firms: An Analysis of Capital Budgeting Manuals," *Managerial Finance,* Number 2/3, 1988, 28–35.

Ross, Marc, "Capital Budgeting Practices of Twelve Large Manufacturers," *Financial Management,* Winter 1986, 15–22.

Weaver, Samuel C., Donald Peters, Roger Cason, and Joe Daleiden, "Capital Budgeting," *Financial Management*, Spring 1989, 10–17.

Additional capital budgeting references are provided in Chapters 10 and 11.

For a case which focuses on capital budgeting decision methods, see
Case 11, "Chicago Valve Company," in the Brigham-Gapenski casebook.

PROJECT CASH FLOW ANALYSIS

ordPerfect Corporation, developer of the most widely used word processing program, recently held an interesting contest—it offered a $25,000 prize to the person who could come the closest to estimating the number of copies of WordPerfect for Windows *shipped during the month following its introduction. Here is an extract from WordPerfect's advertisement:*

While we're confident WordPerfect for Windows *will live up to our standards as the industry leader, we are much less confident about our sales projections. Our vice-president of marketing, Clive Winn, is having trouble predicting how many copies we should produce to meet our first month's orders.*

Here are some questions he must consider:

1. Of the more than 150,000 people who purchase a copy of WordPerfect for DOS *each month, how many will prefer a Windows product?*

2. Of the more than 6 million WordPerfect for DOS *users worldwide, how many will take advantage of our $125 trade-up to* WordPerfect for Windows *during the first month?*

3. Of the 40,000 people who purchase a new personal computer with Windows software included, how many will prefer WordPerfect for Windows *over competing word processing programs?*

4. Of the 2 million or so Windows owners who have not purchased a word processor, how many are waiting for WordPerfect to be released?

The more we look at all the variables, the more we realize we need your help. So, we're going to do what we do best—listen to what you, our current and potential customers, have to say. Give us your best guess and we'll make

it worth your while. Get out your calculator, some paper and pencils, and possibly your algebra book, and call us with your estimate.

Although the contest was clearly designed more to sell WordPerfect than to gather information, it does illustrate that sales forecasting can be quite difficult. Further, sales are but one component—albeit the most important one—in a project cash flow analysis. Also, WordPerfect's contest focused on the first month, but in its internal planning, WordPerfect must worry about a much longer time frame. In addition, the firm must consider the impact of the Windows product on sales of its other products. For example, some WordPerfect for Windows sales will undoubtedly be to customers who would otherwise have bought Word-Perfect for DOS. On the other hand, sales of WordPerfect for Windows will likely stimulate sales of some of WordPerfect's other products.

As you study this chapter, think about the difficulties involved in forecasting each of the cash flow elements associated with new projects—unit sales, sales price, operating costs, and plant and equipment costs. Clearly, for many types of projects the forecasting task is daunting, yet good cash flow forecasts are essential for good capital budgeting decisions. Learning the principles and concepts discussed in this chapter will not guarantee that you will be a top-notch forecaster, but they can help you avoid many of the pitfalls that get companies into trouble.

The basic methods used to evaluate capital budgeting decisions were covered in Chapter 9. However, we assumed that the cash flows were known, so we ignored the most difficult step in capital budgeting—estimating projects' cash flows. Now we examine some key issues, including (1) cash flow estimation, (2) replacement decisions, (3) cash flow estimation bias, (4) managerial options, (5) mutually exclusive projects with unequal lives, (6) abandonment value, and (7) the effects of inflation on capital budgeting analysis. We will see that a thorough understanding of these issues is essential to good capital budgeting decisions.

CASH FLOW ESTIMATION

The most important step in analyzing a potential project is estimating its cash flows—the investment outlays that will be required along with the annual net cash inflows after the project goes into operation. Many variables are involved in cash flow forecasting, and many individuals and departments participate in the process. For example, the forecasts of unit sales and sales prices are normally made by the marketing department, based on its knowledge of price elasticity, advertising effects, the state of the economy, competitors' reactions, and trends in consumers' tastes. Similarly, the capital outlays associated with a new product are generally obtained from the engineering and product development staffs, while operating costs are estimated by cost accountants, production experts, personnel specialists, purchasing agents, and so forth.

It is difficult to make accurate forecasts of the costs and revenues associated with a large, complex project, so forecast errors can be quite large. For example, when several major oil companies decided to build the Alaska Pipeline, the original cost forecasts were in the neighborhood of $700 million, but the final cost was closer to $7 billion. Similar, or even worse, miscalculations are common in forecasts of product design costs, such as the costs to develop a new personal computer. Further, as difficult as plant and equipment costs are to estimate, sales revenues and operating costs over the life of the project are generally even more uncertain.

The financial staff's role in the forecasting process includes (1) coordinating the efforts of the other departments, such as engineering and marketing, (2) ensuring that everyone involved with the forecast uses a consistent set of economic assumptions, and (3) making sure that no biases are inherent in the forecasts. This last point is extremely important, because division managers often become emotionally involved with pet projects, leading to cash flow forecasting biases which make bad projects look good—on paper.

Note also that obtaining unbiased point estimates of the key variables is only one part of the forecasting process. As we shall see in the next chapter, data on probability distributions or other indications of the likely range of variable values are also essential.

It is almost impossible to overstate the difficulties one can encounter when forecasting cash flows. It is also difficult to overstate the importance of these forecasts. However, if the principles discussed in the next several sections are observed, forecast errors can be minimized.

SELF-TEST QUESTIONS

What is the most important step in the capital budgeting process?

Within a firm, what departments are involved in estimating a project's cash flows?

What is the financial staff's role in cash flow estimation?

IDENTIFYING THE RELEVANT CASH FLOWS

Cash flows for a project are defined as the differences in the firm's cash flows for each period if the project is undertaken versus if it is not undertaken:

$$\text{Project CF}_t = \frac{\text{CF}_t \text{ for corporation}}{\text{with project}} - \frac{\text{CF}_t \text{ for corporation}}{\text{without project}}. \qquad \textbf{(10-1)}$$

Defined in this way, we see that project cash flows are *incremental cash flows*. In this section, we discuss how to measure the incremental cash flows attributable to a project.

CASH FLOW VERSUS ACCOUNTING INCOME

Accounting income statements are in some respects a mix of apples and oranges. For example, accountants deduct labor costs, which are cash outflows, from revenues, which may or may not be entirely cash (some sales may be on credit). At the same time, accountants do not deduct capital outlays, which are cash outflows, but they do deduct depreciation expenses, which are not cash outflows. In capital budgeting, it is critical that we base decisions strictly on cash flows, the actual dollars that flow into and out of the company during each time period.

As noted above, the relevant cash flows for capital budgeting purposes are the incremental cash flows attributable to a project. Theoretically, it is possible to construct a firm's pro forma cash flow statements with and without a project for each year of the project's life, and then to measure the annual project cash flows as the differences in cash flows between the two sets of statements. When this is done for operating flows, the following formula results:

$$CF_t = [(R_{1t} - R_{0t}) - (C_{1t} - C_{0t}) \\ - (D_{1t} - D_{0t})](1 - T) + (D_{1t} - D_{0t}). \qquad (10\text{-}2)$$

Here CF_t is the project's net operating cash flow in Period t; R_1 is the corporation's cash sales revenue if the project is undertaken, while R_0 is the cash sales revenue if it is not accepted; C_1 and C_0 are the cash operating costs with and without the project; and D_1 and D_0 are the respective depreciation charges.[1]

To illustrate, suppose a firm is considering a new project that has a cost of $1,000 and a 10-year life. If the project is undertaken, the operating cash flow statement in the left column of the following table is expected to result in each year, while if the project is not undertaken, the firm's cash flows will be as shown in the middle column. The third column shows the changes resulting from the project, so the incremental projected net operating cash flow is $280 per year for 10 years:

	With Project	**Without Project**	**Change**
Sales (R)	$1,600	$1,000	$600
Cash operating costs (C)	600	400	200
Depreciation (D)	200	100	100
Pre-tax income	$ 800	$ 500	$300
Taxes (40%)	320	200	120
Net operating income (NOI)	$ 480	$ 300	$180
CF = NOI + D	$ 680	$ 400	$280

---

[1]Note that we are concentrating solely on operating cash flows. Financing flows (interest expense) are not included in a project's cash flows because financing costs are incorporated in the firm's WACC. When we use the WACC as a discount rate to obtain a project's NPV, we are effectively reducing the values of the cash flows to account for capital costs, so we would be double counting if we reduced the cash flows directly by deducting interest expenses and then discounted these after-interest expense flows.

Equation 10-2 would show exactly the same incremental cash flow, $280:[2]

$$CF_t = [(\$1,600 - \$1,000) - (\$600 - \$400) - (\$200 - \$100)](1 - 0.40) + (\$200 - \$100)$$

$$= [\$600 - \$200 - \$100]\,0.60 + \$100$$

$$= [\$300]\,0.60 + \$100 = \$180 + \$100 = \$280.$$

CASH FLOW TIMING

In financial analysis, we must be careful to account properly for the timing of cash flows. Accounting income statements are for periods such as years or months, so they do not reflect exactly when, during the period, cash revenues or expenses occur. Because of the time value of money, capital budgeting cash flows should in theory be analyzed exactly as they occur. Of course, there must be a compromise between accuracy and simplicity. A time line with daily cash flows would in theory provide the most accuracy, but daily cash flow estimates would be costly to construct, unwieldy to use, and probably no more accurate than annual cash flow estimates because we cannot forecast well enough to warrant this degree of detail. Therefore, in most cases, we simply assume that all cash flows occur at the end of every year. However, for some projects, it may be useful to assume that cash flows occur semiannually, or even to forecast quarterly or monthly cash flows.

INCREMENTAL CASH FLOWS

As noted previously, in capital budgeting our concern is with those cash flows that result directly from the project, or the project's *incremental cash flows.* Three

---

[2]There are times when a new project affects the sales and costs associated with the firm's original assets, and in such cases it is essential to think in terms of either Equation 10-2 or comparative cash flow statements as shown on the previous page. However, new projects often do not affect the firm's existing cash flows, and in such cases we can use a short-cut cash flow formula:

$$CF_t = [R_t - C_t - D_t](1 - T) + D_t. \qquad (10\text{-}3)$$

Here R, C, and D represent the cash sales, cash operating costs, and depreciation of the project itself, and T is the firm's marginal tax rate. To illustrate, suppose a project has a cost of $1,000, will increase sales by $600 per year for ten years, will have operating costs of $200 per year, and will be depreciated by the straight line method toward a zero salvage value over ten years. If the firm's marginal tax rate is 40 percent, then Equation 10-3 may be solved as follows:

$$CF_t = [\$600 - \$200 - \$100](0.60) + \$100 = \$280.$$

Going through some algebra, we can transform Equation 10-3 as follows:

$$CF_t = (R_t - C_t)(1 - T) + TD_t. \qquad (10\text{-}3a)$$

Equation 10-3a shows that the net operating cash flow, CF_t, consists of two components: (1) cash revenues minus cash costs, reduced by taxes, and (2) a depreciation cash flow equal to the amount of depreciation taken during the period times the tax rate. In this form, we see that depreciation affects cash flows because it reduces taxes, and the higher the firm's tax rate, the greater the benefits from depreciation. Equations 10-3 and 10-3a are equivalent methods for calculating a project's net operating cash flows, and either can be used in capital budgeting analysis.

special problems can occur when estimating incremental cash flows; they are discussed next.

Sunk Costs. Sunk costs are *not* incremental costs, so they should *not* be included in a capital budgeting analysis. A *sunk cost* refers to an outlay that has already occurred (or been committed), so it is an outlay that is not affected by the accept/reject decision under consideration. Suppose, for example, that in 1994 Classic Video Rentals was evaluating a new retail outlet in a newly developed section of Albuquerque. As a part of the analysis, Classic had, back in 1993, hired a consulting firm to perform a site analysis at a cost of $100,000, and this $100,000 was expensed for tax purposes in 1993. Is this 1993 expenditure a relevant cost with respect to the 1994 capital budgeting decision? The answer is no. The $100,000 is a sunk cost; Classic cannot recover the $100,000 regardless of whether or not the new outlet is built. It often turns out that a particular project looks bad (that is, has a negative NPV, or an IRR less than its cost of capital) when all the associated costs, including sunk costs, are considered. However, on an incremental basis, the project may be a good one, because the incremental cash inflows may be large enough to produce a positive NPV on the incremental investment. Thus, the correct treatment of sunk costs is critical to a proper capital budgeting analysis.[3]

Opportunity Costs. The second potential problem relates to *opportunity costs:* All relevant opportunity costs should be included in a capital budgeting analysis. For example, suppose Classic Video Rentals already owns a piece of land that is suitable for the outlet. When evaluating the prospective project, should the cost of the land be disregarded because no additional cash outlay would be required? The answer is "no," because there is an opportunity cost inherent in the use of the property for a new outlet. For example, suppose the land could be sold to net $150,000 after commissions and taxes. Use of the site for the outlet would require foregoing this inflow, so $150,000 should be charged as an opportunity cost against the project. Note, though, that the proper land cost in this example would be the $150,000 market-determined value, which is net of any taxes and fees, irrespective of whether Classic had paid $50,000 or $500,000 for the property when it was acquired.

Effects on Other Projects. The third potential problem involves the effects of the project being considered on the firm's other projects. For example, suppose some of the customers that Classic predicts will use the new outlet are already renting videotapes from Classic's downtown store. The profits generated by these customers would not be new to the company, but, rather, they would represent a transfer from the downtown store to the new outlet. Thus, the net revenues pro-

---

[3]For an old but still excellent example of the improper treatment of sunk costs by a major corporation, see U. E. Reinhardt, "Break-Even Analysis for Lockheed's TriStar: An Application of Financial Theory," *Journal of Finance,* September 1973, 821–838.

duced by these customers should not be treated as incremental income in the capital budgeting analysis. On the other hand, having a suburban outlet might actually attract new customers to the downtown store because some potential customers would like to be able to rent videos close to work and then return them close to home over the weekend. In this case, the additional revenues projected to flow to the downtown store should be attributed to the new outlet.

Although often difficult to determine, effects on other projects must be considered. They should, if possible, be quantified, or at least noted, so whoever makes the final decision will be aware of their existence.

SELF-TEST QUESTIONS

Define the term "incremental cash flow."

Within the framework of capital budgeting cash flow estimation, briefly describe the meaning and treatment of (1) sunk costs, (2) opportunity costs, and (3) effects on other projects.

TAX EFFECTS

Taxes can have a major impact on cash flows, and in many cases tax effects can make or break a project. Therefore, it is critical that taxes be dealt with correctly in capital budgeting decisions. However, as financial analysts, we encounter two problems: (1) the tax laws are extremely complex, and (2) these laws are subject to interpretation and to change. The financial staff can get assistance from the firm's accountants and tax lawyers, but even so, it is necessary for financial analysts to have a working knowledge of the current tax laws and their effects on cash flows.

AN OVERVIEW OF DEPRECIATION

Suppose Classic Videos buys a computerized inventory system for $100,000 and plans to use it for five years, after which it will be scrapped. The cost of the video rentals supported by the system must include a charge for the system, and this charge is called *depreciation*. Because depreciation reduces profits as calculated by the accountants, the higher a firm's depreciation charges, the lower its reported net income. However, depreciation is not a cash charge, so higher depreciation levels do not reduce cash flows. Indeed, higher depreciation levels *increase* cash flows, because the greater a firm's depreciation, the lower its tax bill.

Companies generally calculate depreciation one way when figuring taxes and another way when reporting income to investors: Most use the *straight line* method for stockholder reporting (or "book" purposes), but they use the fastest rate permitted by law for tax purposes. Under the straight line method as used for reporting purposes, one normally takes the cost of the asset, subtracts its estimated salvage value, and divides the net amount by the asset's economic life. For an

asset with a 5-year economic life that costs $100,000 and has a $15,000 estimated salvage value, the annual straight line depreciation charge is ($100,000 − $15,000)/5 = $17,000.

For tax purposes, Congress changes the permissible depreciation methods from time to time. Prior to 1954 the straight line method was required for tax purposes, but in 1954 *accelerated* methods (double declining balance and sum-of-years'-digits) were permitted. Then, in 1981, the old accelerated methods were replaced by a simpler procedure known as the *Accelerated Cost Recovery System* (*ACRS,* which is pronounced "acres"). The ACRS system was changed in 1986 as a part of the Tax Reform Act, and it is now called the *Modified Accelerated Cost Recovery System (MACRS)*.

Note that U.S. tax laws are very complicated. Therefore, in this text we can only provide an overview of MACRS in order to give you a basic understanding of the impact of depreciation on capital budgeting decisions. Note also that the tax laws change so often that the numbers we present here may be outdated before the book is even used in class. Thus, when dealing with tax depreciation in real-world situations, current Internal Revenue Service (IRS) publications or individuals with expertise in tax matters should be consulted.

TAX DEPRECIATION CALCULATIONS

For tax purposes, the cost of an asset is expensed over its depreciable life. Historically, an asset's depreciable life for tax purposes was closely related to its estimated useful economic life; it was intended that an asset would be fully depreciated at approximately the same time that it reached the end of its useful economic life. However, MACRS sets simple guidelines which create several classes of assets, each with a more or less arbitrarily prescribed life called a *recovery period* or *class life,* which bears only a rough relationship to the expected economic life.

A major effect of the MACRS system has been to shorten the depreciable lives of assets, thus giving businesses larger tax deductions and thereby increasing their cash flows available for new investment. Table 10-1 describes the types of property that fit into the different class life groups, and Table 10-2 sets forth the MACRS

TABLE 10-1 MAJOR CLASSES AND ASSET LIVES FOR MACRS	Class	Type of Property
	3-year	Specially designated tools and devices, and tractor units.
	5-year	Automobiles, trucks, computers, typewriters, copiers, and other designated equipment.
	7-year	Most industrial equipment, office furniture, and fixtures.
	10-year	Certain longer-lived types of equipment.
	27.5-year	Residential rental real property such as apartment buildings.
	31.5-year	All nonresidential real property, including commercial and industrial buildings.

Ownership Year	Class of Investment			
	3-Year	5-Year	7-Year	10-Year
1	33%	20%	14%	10%
2	45	32	25	18
3	15	19	17	14
4	7	12	13	12
5		11	9	9
6		6	9	7
7			9	7
8			4	7
9				7
10				6
11				3
	100%	100%	100%	100%

Notes:

a. We developed these recovery allowance percentages based on the 200 percent declining balance method prescribed in the 1986 Tax Act, with a switch to straight line depreciation at some point in the asset's life. For example, consider the 5-year recovery allowance percentages. The straight line percentage would be 20 percent per year, so the 200 percent declining balance mutliplier is $2.0(20\%) = 40\% = 0.4$. However, because the half-year convention applies, the MACRS percentage for Year 1 is only 20 percent. For Year 2, there is 80 percent of the depreciable basis remaining to be depreciated, so the recovery allowance percentage is $0.40(80\%) = 32\%$. In Year 3, $20\% + 32\% = 52\%$ of the depreciation has been taken, leaving 48%, so the percentage is $0.4(48\%) \approx 19\%$. In Year 4, the percentage is $0.4(29\%) \approx 12\%$. After 4 years, straight line depreciation exceeds the declining balance depreciation, so a switch is made to straight line (this is permitted under the law). However, the half-year convention must also be applied at the end of the class life, and hence the remaining 17 percent of depreciation must be taken (amortized) over 1.5 years. Thus, the percentage in Year 5 is $17\%/1.5 \approx 11\%$, and in Year 6, $17\% - 11\% = 6\%$. We rounded to the nearest whole number for ease of illustration.

b. Residential rental property (apartments) is depreciated over a 27.5-year life, whereas commercial and industrial structures are depreciated over 31.5 years. In both cases, straight line depreciation must be used. The depreciation allowance for the first year is based, pro rata, on the month the asset was placed in service, with the remainder of the first year's depreciation being taken in the 28th or 32nd year.

recovery allowances (depreciation rates) for the various classes of investment property.

The first column of Table 10-1 gives the MACRS class life, while the second column describes the types of assets which fall into each category. Property in the 27.5- and 31.5-year categories (real estate) must be depreciated by an alternate MACRS straight line method, but 3-, 5-, 7-, and 10-year property can be depreciated either by the alternate straight line method or by an accelerated method which uses the rates shown in Table 10-2.[4]

As we noted earlier in the chapter, higher depreciation expenses result in lower taxes and hence higher cash flows. Therefore, when a firm has the option of

---

[4]As a benefit to very small companies, the Tax Code permits companies to *expense,* which is equivalent to depreciating over one year, up to $10,000 of equipment. Thus, if a small company bought one asset worth up to $10,000, it could write the asset off in the year it was acquired. This is called "Section 179 expensing." We shall disregard this provision throughout the book.

using the MACRS straight line method or the accelerated rates shown in Table 10-2, it should generally elect to use the MACRS accelerated rates. The yearly recovery allowance, or depreciation expense, is determined by multiplying each asset's *depreciable basis* by the applicable recovery percentage, as shown in Table 10-2. Calculations are discussed in the following sections.

HALF-YEAR CONVENTION

Under MACRS, the assumption is generally made that property is placed in service in the middle of the first year. Thus, for 3-year class life property, the recovery period begins in the middle of the year the asset is placed in service and ends three years later. The effect of the *half-year convention* is to extend the recovery period out one more year, so 3-year class life property is depreciated over four calendar years, 5-year property is depreciated over six calendar years, and so on. This convention is incorporated into Table 10-2's recovery allowance percentages.[5]

DEPRECIABLE BASIS

The *depreciable basis* is a critical element of MACRS, because each year's allowance (depreciation expense) depends jointly on the asset's depreciable basis and its MACRS class life. The depreciable basis under MACRS is equal to the purchase price of the asset plus any shipping and installation costs. The basis is *not* adjusted for *salvage value* (which is the estimated market value of the asset at the end of its useful life) regardless of whether MACRS accelerated depreciation or the alternative straight line method is used.

INVESTMENT TAX CREDIT

An *investment tax credit (ITC)* provides for a direct reduction of taxes, and its purpose is to stimulate business investment. ITCs were first introduced during the Kennedy administration in 1961, and they have subsequently been put in and taken out of the tax system, depending on how Congress feels about the need to stimulate business investment versus the need for federal revenues. Immediately prior to the 1986 Tax Reform Act, ITCs applied to depreciable personal property with a life of three or more years, and the credit amounted to 6 percent for short-lived assets and 10 percent for longer-lived assets. The credit was determined by multiplying the cost of the asset by the applicable percentage. However, ITCs were

---

[5]The half-year convention also applies if the straight line alternative is used, with half of one year's depreciation taken in the first year, a full year's depreciation taken in each of the remaining years of the asset's class life, and the remaining half-year's depreciation taken in the year following the end of the class life. You should recognize that virtually all companies have computerized depreciation systems. Each asset's depreciation pattern is programmed into the system at the time of its acquisition, and the computer aggregates the depreciation allowances for all assets when the accountants close the books and prepare the financial statements and tax returns.

eliminated by the 1986 tax revision. Nevertheless, you should be aware of what ITCs are, because there is a chance that they will be reinstated at some future date if Congress deems that they are needed to stimulate investment.[6]

SALE OF A DEPRECIABLE ASSET

If a depreciable asset is sold, the sale price (realized salvage value) minus the then-existing undepreciated tax book value is added to operating income and taxed at the firm's marginal tax rate. For example, suppose a firm buys a 5-year class life asset for $100,000 and sells it at the end of the fourth year for $32,000. After four years, the asset's tax book value is equal to $100,000(0.11 + 0.06) = $100,000(0.17) = $17,000, so $32,000 − $17,000 = $15,000 is added to the firm's operating income and is taxed.[7]

MACRS ILLUSTRATION

Assume that Classic's $100,000 computerized inventory control system, which falls into the MACRS 5-year class life, is placed into service on March 15, 1994. Classic must pay an additional $20,000 for delivery and installation. Salvage value is not considered, so the system's depreciable basis is $120,000. (Delivery and installation charges must be included in the depreciable basis rather than expensed in the year incurred.) Each year's recovery allowance (tax depreciation expense) is determined by multiplying the depreciable basis by the applicable recovery allowance percentage in Table 10-2. Thus, the depreciation expense for 1994 is 0.20($120,000) = $24,000, and for 1995 it is 0.32($120,000) = $38,400. Similarly, the depreciation expense is $22,800 for 1996, $14,400 for 1997, $13,200 for 1998, and $7,200 for 1999. The total depreciation expense over the 6-year recovery period is $120,000, which is equal to the depreciable basis of the system.

SELF-TEST QUESTIONS

What do the acronyms ACRS and MACRS stand for?

Briefly describe the tax depreciation system under MACRS.

What is the effect of the sale of a depreciable asset on a firm's cash flows?

---

[6]As we write this book in mid-1993, there are several congressional proposals to reinstate the ITC. The motivation is to stimulate the economy, which has been recovering slowly from the last recession.

[7]In this case, the tax depreciation charges over the four years exceeded "true" depreciation, and the excess tax depreciation is "recaptured." Since depreciation reduces ordinary income, its recapture is treated as ordinary income. Occasionally, the salvage value is less than the book value, and a loss is reported. In such cases, the sale produces a tax cash inflow, because the firm's taxable income and hence its taxes are reduced by the loss.

CHANGES IN NET WORKING CAPITAL

Normally, additional inventories are required to support a new operation, and the new sales will also produce additional accounts receivable. Thus, both inventories and receivables will increase as a result of capital budgeting decisions, so the "investment outlay" of a new project must include the associated current assets as well as the fixed assets involved. However, accounts payable and accruals will also increase spontaneously as a result of the expansion, and this will reduce the need to raise capital to finance the project. The difference between the projected increase in current assets and that in current liabilities is defined as the *change in net working capital (ΔNWC)*. The change associated with a project is normally positive, so some additional investment, over and above the cost of the fixed assets, is required.[8] (In the unlikely event that the change in net working capital is negative, then the project would be generating an initial cash inflow from the change in net working capital.)

Net working capital changes may occur over several periods, so the increase (or decrease) could be reflected in cash flows for several periods. However, once the operation has stabilized, working capital will also stabilize at the new level, and beyond this time no changes will occur until the project is terminated. At the end of the project's life, the firm's total working capital requirements should revert to prior levels, so it will receive an end-of-project cash inflow equal to the net investment in working capital. This point is illustrated in the next section.

SELF-TEST QUESTIONS

What is net working capital (NWC)?

How do changes in NWC affect a project's cash flow estimates?

CASH FLOW ANALYSIS EXAMPLE

Up to this point, we have discussed several important aspects of cash flow analysis, but we have not seen how they relate to one another and affect the capital budgeting decision. In this section, we illustrate all this by examining a capital budgeting decision that faces RIC Technologies, a Minneapolis-based microcomputer controls company. RIC's research and development department has

---

[8]Actually, the entire change in net working capital does not require additional investment, because some of the increase in receivables represents profits, and hence do not require financing. However, profit margins are normally just a few percentage points, so ignoring this factor does not lead to serious errors. This topic is discussed further in Chapter 18.

been applying its expertise in microprocessor technology to develop a very small computer specifically designed to control commercial landscape watering systems. Once programmed, the computer would automatically sense the need for watering in each separate watering zone and then provide just the right amount of water to each zone. By eliminating excess watering, the system can save enough to pay for itself in a few years. This project has now reached the stage where a decision on whether to go forward with production must be made.

The marketing vice-president believes that annual sales would be 25,000 units if the computers were priced at $2,200 each. The firm would need a new plant, which could be built and made ready for production in two years after the "go" decision is made. The plant would require a 25-acre site, and RIC currently has an option to purchase a suitable tract of land for $1.2 million; the option could be exercised in late 1994. Building construction would begin in early 1995 and would continue through 1996. The building, which would fall into the MACRS 31.5-year class, would cost an estimated $8 million; a $4 million payment would be made on December 31, 1995, and the remaining $4 million would be paid on December 31, 1996.

The necessary equipment would be installed late in 1996, and it would be paid for on December 31, 1996. The equipment, which falls into the MACRS 5-year class, would have a cost of $9.5 million, plus an additional $500,000 for installation.

The project would also require an initial investment in net working capital equal to 12 percent of the estimated sales in the first year. The initial working capital investment would be made on December 31, 1996, and on December 31 of each following year, net working capital would be increased by an amount equal to 12 percent of any sales increase expected during the coming year. The project's estimated economic life is six years. At that time, the land is expected to have a market value of $1.7 million, the building a value of $1.0 million, and the equipment a value of $2 million. The production department has estimated that variable manufacturing costs would total 65 percent of dollar sales, and that fixed overhead costs, excluding depreciation, would be $8 million for the first year of operations. Sales prices and fixed overhead costs, other than depreciation, are projected to increase with inflation, which is expected to average 6 percent per year over the 6-year life of the project.

RIC's marginal federal-plus-state tax rate is 40 percent; its weighted average cost of capital is 11.5 percent; and the company's policy, for capital budgeting purposes, is to assume that cash flows occur at the end of each year. Since the plant would begin operations on January 1, 1997, the first operating cash flows would thus constructively occur on December 31, 1997.

As one of the company's financial analysts, you have been assigned the task of supervising the capital budgeting analysis. For now, you may assume that the project has the same risk as the firm's current average project, hence you may use the corporate WACC, 11.5 percent, for this project. Later on, we will examine additional information concerning the riskiness of the project, but at this point assume that the project has average risk.

ANALYSIS OF THE CASH FLOWS

The first step in the analysis is to summarize the investment outlays required for the project; this is done in Table 10-3. Note that land cannot be depreciated, hence we show its depreciable basis to be $0. Also, since the project will require an increase in net working capital during 1996, this is shown as an investment outlay for that year.

Having estimated the capital requirements, we must now forecast the cash flows that will occur once production begins; these are set forth in Table 10-4. The operating cash flow estimates are based on information provided by RIC's various departments. Note that the sales price and fixed overhead costs are projected to increase each year by the 6 percent inflation rate, and since variable costs are 65 percent of dollar sales, they too will rise by 6 percent each year. The changes in net working capital (NWC) represent the additional investments required to support sales increases (12 percent of the next year's sales increase, which in this case results only from inflation) during 1997–2001, and the recovery of the cumulative net working capital investment in 2002. The depreciation amounts were obtained by multiplying each asset's depreciable basis by the MACRS recovery allowance rates set forth in Note c to Table 10-4.

The analysis also requires an estimation of the cash flows generated by salvage values; Table 10-5 summarizes this analysis. First, we compare the projected 2002 market values against the 2002 book values. The land cannot be depreciated, and it is expected to have an estimated 2002 salvage value greater than the initial purchase price. Thus, RIC would have to pay taxes on the profit. The building is expected to have an estimated salvage value less than the book value — it will be sold at a loss for tax purposes. The loss would reduce the company's taxable income and thus generate a tax savings; in effect, the company would be depreciating the building too slowly, so it would write off the loss against ordinary income. On the other hand, the equipment would be sold for more than book value, so the company would have to pay ordinary taxes on the $2 million difference. In all cases, the book value is the depreciable cost less accumulated depreciation, and the total cash flow from salvage is merely the sum of the land, building, and equipment components.

TABLE 10-3 INVESTMENT OUTLAYS, 1994–1996	Fixed Assets	1994	1995	1996	Total Costs, 1994–1996	Depreciable Basis
	Land	$1,200,000	$ 0	$ 0	$ 1,200,000	$ 0
	Building	0	4,000,000	4,000,000	8,000,000	8,000,000
	Equipment	0	0	10,000,000	10,000,000	10,000,000
	Total fixed assets	$1,200,000	$4,000,000	$14,000,000	$19,200,000	
	Net working capital[a]	0	0	6,600,000	6,600,000	
	Total investment	$1,200,000	$4,000,000	$20,600,000	$25,800,000	

[a]12 percent of first year's sales, or 0.12($55,000,000) = $6,600,000.

TABLE 10-4 NET CASH FLOWS, 1997–2002

	1997	1998	1999	2000	2001	2002
Unit sales	25,000	25,000	25,000	25,000	25,000	25,000
Sale price[a]	$ 2,200	$ 2,332	$ 2,472	$ 2,620	$ 2,777	$ 2,944
Net sales[a]	$55,000,000	$58,300,000	$61,800,000	$65,500,000	$69,425,000	$73,600,000
Variable costs[b]	35,750,000	37,895,000	40,170,000	42,575,000	45,126,250	47,840,000
Fixed costs (overhead)[a]	8,000,000	8,480,000	8,988,800	9,528,128	10,099,816	10,705,805
Depreciation (building)[c]	120,000	240,000	240,000	240,000	240,000	240,000
Depreciation (equipment)[c]	2,000,000	3,200,000	1,900,000	1,200,000	1,100,000	600,000
Earnings before taxes	$ 9,130,000	$ 8,485,000	$10,501,200	$11,956,872	$12,858,934	$14,214,195
Taxes (40%)	3,652,000	3,394,000	4,200,480	4,782,749	5,143,574	5,685,678
Net operating income	$ 5,478,000	$ 5,091,000	$ 6,300,720	$ 7,174,123	$ 7,715,360	$ 8,528,517
Add back noncash expenses[d]	2,120,000	3,440,000	2,140,000	1,440,000	1,340,000	840,000
Net operating cash flow[e]	$ 7,598,000	$ 8,531,000	$ 8,440,720	$ 8,614,123	$ 9,055,360	$ 9,368,517
Investment in NWC[f]	(396,000)	(420,000)	(444,000)	(471,000)	(501,000)	
Net salvage value[g]						5,972,000
Total projected cash flow	$ 7,202,000	$ 8,111,000	$ 7,996,720	$ 8,143,123	$ 8,554,360	$24,172,517

[a]1997 estimate increased by the assumed 6 percent inflation rate.

[b]65 percent of net sales.

[c]MACRS depreciation rates are as follows:

Year	1	2	3	4	5	6
Building	1.5%	3%	3%	3%	3%	3%
Equipment	20	32	19	12	11	6

These percentages are multiplied by each asset's depreciable basis to get the depreciation expense for each year. Note that the allowances have been rounded for ease of computation.

[d]In this case, depreciation on building and equipment.

[e]Net operating income plus noncash expenses.

[f]12 percent of next year's increase in sales. For example, 1998 sales are $3.3 million over 1997 sales, so the addition to NWC in 1997 required to support 1998 sales is (0.12)($3,300,000) = $396,000. The cumulative working capital investment is recovered when the project ends in 2002.

[g]See Table 10-5 for the net salvage value calculation.

TABLE 10-5		Land	Building	Equipment
AFTER-TAX SALVAGE VALUES, 2002	Salvage (ending market) value	$1,700,000	$1,000,000	$ 2,000,000
	Initial cost	1,200,000	8,000,000	10,000,000
	Depreciable basis (1996)	0	8,000,000	10,000,000
	Book value (2002)[a]	1,200,000	6,680,000	0
	Capital gains income	$ 500,000	$ 0	$ 0
	Ordinary income (loss)[b]	0	(5,680,000)	2,000,000
	Taxes[c]	$ 200,000	($2,272,000)	$ 800,000
	Net salvage value (Salvage value − Taxes)	$1,500,000	$3,272,000	$ 1,200,000

Net cash flow from salvage value = $1,500,000 + $3,272,000 + $1,200,000 = $5,972,000.

[a]Book value for the building in 2002 equals depreciable cost minus accumulated MACRS depreciation of $1,320,000. The accumulated depreciation on the equipment is $10,000,000. See Table 10-4.

[b]Building: $1,000,000 market value − $6,680,000 book value = $5,680,000 depreciation shortfall, which is treated as an operating expense in 2002.

Equipment: $2,000,000 market value − $0 book value = $2,000,000 depreciation recapture, which is treated as ordinary income in 2002.

[c]Since corporate capital gains are now taxed at the ordinary income rate, all taxes are based on RIC's 40 percent marginal federal-plus-state rate. The table is set up to differentiate ordinary income from capital gains because Congress may reinstate differential tax rates on those two corporate income sources.

MAKING THE DECISION

To summarize the data and get it ready for evaluation, it is useful to combine all of the net cash flows on a time line such as the one shown in Table 10-6. The table also shows the payback period, IRR, MIRR, and NPV (at the 11.5 percent cost of capital). The project appears to be acceptable using the NPV, IRR, or MIRR methods, and it would also be acceptable if RIC required a payback of six years or less. Note, however, that the analysis thus far has been based on the assumption that the project has the same degree of risk as the company's average project. If the project is riskier than an average project, then it would be necessary to increase the cost of capital, which in turn might cause the NPV to become negative and the IRR and MIRR to fall below k. In Chapter 11, we will extend the evaluation of this project to include the necessary risk analysis.

TABLE 10-6	1994	1995	1996	1997	1998
CONSOLIDATED END-OF-YEAR NET CASH FLOWS, 1994–2002	($1,200,000)	($4,000,000)	($20,600,000)	$7,202,000	$8,111,000

Payback period: 5.3 years from first outflow.
IRR: 25.1% versus an 11.5% cost of capital.
MIRR: 17.9% versus an 11.5% cost of capital.
NPV: $12,075,384.

SELF-TEST QUESTIONS

How does RIC account for inflation in the cash flow estimation process?

Why was it necessary to include changes in net working capital in the analysis?

Describe how depreciation tax effects were included in the Table 10-4 operating cash flows.

Explain the meaning of the negative taxes shown for the building in the net salvage value analysis in Table 10-5.

REPLACEMENT ANALYSIS

We used RIC's watering system computer project to show how an expansion project is analyzed. All companies, including RIC, also make *replacement decisions,* where cash flows from both the old asset and the new asset must be considered. Replacement analysis is illustrated with another RIC example, this time from the company's research and development (R&D) division.

A lathe for trimming molded plastics was purchased 10 years ago at a cost of $7,500. The machine had an expected life of 15 years at the time it was purchased, and management originally estimated, and still believes, that the salvage value will be zero at the end of the 15-year life. The machine is being depreciated on a straight line basis; therefore, its annual depreciation charge is $500, and its current book value is $2,500.[9]

The R&D manager reports that a new special-purpose machine can be purchased for $12,000 (including freight and installation) which, over its 5-year life, will sufficiently reduce labor and raw materials usage to cut operating costs from $7,000 to $4,000. This reduction in costs will cause before-tax profits to rise by $7,000 − $4,000 = $3,000 per year.

---

[9]Since the company had excess tax shelters at the time, it chose to depreciate the lathe by the MACRS alternative straight line method.

TABLE 10-6 continued	1999	2000	2001	2002
	$7,996,720	$8,143,123	$8,554,360	$24,172,517

Line 9. The depreciation expense on the old machine as shown on Line 8 can no longer be taken if the replacement is made, but the new machine's depreciation will be available. Therefore, the $500 depreciation on the old machine is subtracted from that on the new machine to show the incremental change in annual depreciation. The change is positive in Years 1–4, but negative in Year 5. The Year 5 negative net change in annual depreciation signifies that the purchase of the replacement machine results in a *decrease* in depreciation expense in that year.

Line 10. The net change in depreciation results in tax savings which are equal to the change in depreciation multiplied by the tax rate: Depreciation savings = T(Change in depreciation) = 0.40($3,460) = $1,384 for Year 1. Note that the relevant cash flow is the tax savings on the *net change* in depreciation, rather than on only the depreciation on the new equipment. Capital budgeting decisions are based on *incremental* cash flows, and since we lose $500 of depreciation if we replace the old machine, that fact must be taken into account.

Line 11. Here we show the net operating cash flows over the project's 5-year life. These flows are found by adding the after-tax cost decrease to the depreciation tax savings, or Line 6 + Line 10.

Line 12. Part III shows the cash flows associated with the termination of the project. To begin, Line 12 shows the estimated salvage value of the new machine at the end of its 5-year life, $2,000.[11]

Line 13. Since the book value of the new machine at the end of Year 5 is zero, the company will have to pay taxes of $2,000(0.4) = $800.

Line 14. An investment of $1,000 in net working capital was shown as an outflow at t = 0. This investment, like the new machine's salvage value, will be recovered when the project is terminated at the end of Year 5. Accounts receivable will be collected, inventories will be drawn down and not replaced, and the result will be an inflow of $1,000 at t = 5.

Line 15. Here we show the total cash flows resulting from terminating the project.

Line 16. Part IV shows, on Line 16, the total net cash flows in a time line format suitable for capital budgeting evaluation.

Part V of the table, "Results," shows the replacement project's payback, IRR, MIRR, and NPV. The project is assumed to be of similar risk to the old project, and the old project is assumed to be about as risky as the company's average project. Therefore, an 11.5 percent project cost of capital is appropriate. At this cost of capital, the project is not acceptable, so the old lathe should not be replaced.

---

[11]In this analysis, the estimated salvage value of the old machine is zero. However, if the old machine could be sold at the end of five years, then replacing the old machine now would eliminate this cash flow. Thus, the after-tax salvage value of the old machine would represent an opportunity cost to the firm, and it would be included as a Year 5 cash outflow in the terminal cash flow section of the worksheet.

SELF-TEST QUESTIONS

What are the primary differences between cash flow analyses for a new project and those for a replacement project?

Why is the depreciation tax savings negative in Year 5 in Table 10-7?

CASH FLOW ESTIMATION BIAS

As noted at the beginning of the chapter, estimating cash flows is the most critical, but also the most difficult, part of the capital budgeting process. Cash flows must be forecasted many years into the future, and estimation errors are bound to occur.[12] To illustrate, at the end of 1993, RIC's managers had to estimate unit sales and other cash flows for the watering system computer out to 2002. Clearly, large errors can and do occur. However, large firms evaluate and accept many projects every year, and if the cash flow estimates are unbiased and hence errors are random, then estimation errors will tend to cancel each other out. That is, some projects will have NPV estimates that are too high and some will have estimates that are too low, but the total realized NPV on all the projects accepted should be relatively close to the aggregate NPV estimate.

Unfortunately, studies indicate that capital budgeting cash flow forecasts are not unbiased—rather, managers tend to be overly optimistic in their forecasts, and, as a result, revenues tend to be overstated and costs tend to be understated.[13] The end result is an upward bias in estimated net operating cash flows and thus an upward bias in estimated NPVs. Often, this occurs because managers are paid on the basis of the size of the company, so they are motivated to maximize size rather than profitability. Even when this is not the case, managers often become emotionally attached to their projects and thus fail to objectively assess a project's potential negative factors.

If this bias exists at a particular firm, then accepting a project with a zero estimated NPV will likely result in a loss, hence in a decrease in shareholders' wealth. Recognizing that biases may exist, senior managers at many firms now develop data on divisional managers' forecasting accuracies and then consider this information in the capital budgeting decision process. Some companies lower the cash flow estimates of managers whose track records suggest that their forecasts are too rosy, while other companies increase the cost of capital, or hurdle rate, applied to such project submissions.

---

[12]For a discussion of the cash flow estimation practices of some large firms, as well as some estimates of the inaccuracies involved, see Randolph A. Pohlman, Emmanuel S. Santiago, and F. Lynn Markel, "Cash Flow Estimation Practices of Large Firms," *Financial Management,* Summer 1988, 71–79.

[13]For a discussion of cash flow estimation bias, see Stephen W. Pruitt and Lawrence J. Gitman, "Capital Budgeting Forecast Biases: Evidence from the *Fortune* 500," *Financial Management,* Spring 1987, 46–51.

A first step in identifying cash flow estimation bias, especially for projects that are estimated to be highly profitable, is to ask this question: What is the underlying cause of this project's profitability? If the firm has some inherent advantage, such as patent protection, unique manufacturing or marketing expertise, or even a well-known brand name, then projects which utilize such an advantage may truly be extraordinarily profitable. However, in the long run, above-normal profits will probably be eroded by competition. If there is reason to believe that competition is likely to increase, and if division managers cannot identify any unique factors which could support a project's continued high profitability, then senior management should be concerned about estimation bias.

RIC's top management considered the possibility of estimation bias when they reviewed the watering system computer project. With an IRR of 25.1 percent and an MIRR of 17.9 percent versus a cost of capital of 11.5 percent, the project is projected to earn above-normal profits. These high profits might attract other firms into the market, and new entry might cause the actual cash inflows to fall below those forecast in Table 10-4. However, RIC's top management concluded that competitors would not be able to develop and produce a competing product within the next several years. Further, they noted that the unit sales forecasts were held constant over the life of the project, which is probably conservative. Finally, as we will see in Chapter 11, the project is actually quite risky, and the forecasted returns are not all that spectacular in view of the risks involved.

SELF-TEST QUESTIONS

Why might cash flow estimation bias exist in the capital budgeting decision process?

What can be done to deal with such bias?

MANAGERIAL OPTIONS

In the previous section, we discussed the problem of cash flow estimation bias, which can result in overstating a project's profitability. Another problem that can arise in cash flow analysis is understating a project's true profitability by not recognizing the value that stems from *managerial options*. To illustrate, many investments have the potential to lead to investment opportunities (or options) that are beyond the scope of the original proposal. These options include (1) the opportunity to develop follow-up products, (2) the opportunity to expand product markets, (3) the opportunity to expand or retool manufacturing plants, (4) the opportunity to delay a project, (5) the opportunity to abandon a project, and so on. Note that some managerial options involve a company's strategic entry into new products or markets, and such an option is said to have *strategic value*. Since managerial options are many and diverse, and since the timing of their use is un-

certain, it is usually not feasible to incorporate them directly into a project's cash flow estimates. Conceptually, the true NPV of a project can be thought of as the sum of the traditional DCF NPV and the values of inherent managerial options:

$$\text{True NPV} = \text{Traditional NPV} + \text{NPVs of managerial options}.$$

In some situations, it is possible to quantify the value of managerial options. To illustrate an explicit valuation, consider the situation recently faced by American Semiconductor Industries, a leading producer of computer chips. The firm was evaluating a project to build a new semiconductor fabrication plant, with a 10,000-chips-per-week capacity, that had a conventional NPV of $10 million. Additionally, American's managers were able to identify two inherent managerial options for the project: (1) The new plant would create the option to close an older plant and then consolidate its activities with the more up-to-date facility. (2) The new plant would also create the opportunity to easily expand production to 20,000 chips per week should demand warrant expansion.

Here's how American handled the analysis. First, consider the option to consolidate manufacturing activities. American estimated that a consolidation would result in a $2 million value due to labor savings and a $3 million value due to increased equipment efficiency, for a total NPV of $5 million. Further, American estimated that there is an 80 percent chance that this option would be exercised. Thus, the expected NPV of the consolidation option is 0.8($5) = $4 million. Regarding the expansion option, American estimated that the probability of expanding the plant to a 20,000-chips-per-week capacity using the new technology is 20 percent, and the value of the expansion would be $10 million, resulting in an expected NPV of 0.2($10) = $2 million.

Thus, after considering the value of the managerial options, American valued the new plant project at $16 million:

$$\text{True NPV} = \text{Traditional NPV} + \text{NPVs of managerial options}$$
$$= \$10 + \$4 + \$2 = \$16 \text{ million}.$$

Further, the range of potential NPVs runs from $10 million, assuming that no options are exercised, to $10 + $5 + $10 = $25 million, assuming that both the consolidation and the expansion take place. In this situation, managerial options provided an added bonus to an already positive project, but in other situations the traditional NPV might be negative, in which case failure to recognize the value of managerial options could result in rejecting a project that should be accepted.

We should note that option pricing methods (which we will discuss in Chapter 22) are now being used by financial managers in certain industries, such as mining, to value managerial options. In the future, we expect more and more companies to attempt to quantify the value inherent in managerial options. For now, however, managers should recognize that some projects have true NPVs that

exceed their DCF NPVs because of managerial options, and these values should, at a minimum, be subjectively considered when making capital budgeting decisions.[14]

Self-Test Questions

What is meant by a project's managerial options?

How should projects with managerial options be valued?

Evaluating Projects with Unequal Lives

Note that a replacement decision involves two mutually exclusive projects: retaining the old asset versus buying a new one. To simplify matters, in our replacement example we assumed that the new machine had a life equal to the remaining life of the old machine. However, if we were choosing between two mutually exclusive alternatives with significantly different lives, an adjustment would be necessary. We now discuss two procedures — (1) the replacement chain method and (2) the equivalent annual annuity method — to illustrate the problem and to show how to deal with it.

Suppose RIC Technologies is planning to modernize its production facilities, and as a part of the process, it is considering either a conveyor system (Project C) or a fleet of forklift trucks (Project F) for moving materials from the parts department to the main assembly line. Table 10-8 shows both the expected net cash flows and the NPVs for these two mutually exclusive alternatives. We see that Project C, when discounted at an 11.5 percent cost of capital, has the higher NPV and thus appears to be the better project. Project F's IRR is higher, but since C's NPV is higher, we might still judge C to be the better choice.

Replacement Chain (Common Life) Approach

Although the analysis in Table 10-8 suggests that Project C should be selected, this analysis is incomplete, and the decision to choose Project C is actually incorrect. If we choose Project F, we will have the opportunity to make a similar investment in 3 years, and if costs and revenues continue at the Table 10-8 levels, this second investment will also be profitable. However, if we choose Project C, we will not have this second investment opportunity. To make a proper comparison of Projects C and F, we could apply the *replacement chain (common life)* approach. This involves finding the NPV of Project F over a 6-year period and then comparing this extended NPV with the NPV of Project C over the same 6 years.

---

[14]For more information on managerial options, see Nalin Kulatilaka and Alan J. Marcus, "Project Valuation under Uncertainty: When Does DCF Fail?" *Journal of Applied Corporate Finance,* Fall 1992, 92–100. Also, the spring 1987 edition of the *Midland Corporate Finance Journal* contains several articles related to the use of option concepts in capital budgeting analyses. For an overview, see Stewart C. Myers, "Finance Theory and Financial Strategy," 6–13.

	Year	Project C	Project F
TABLE 10-8	0	($40,000)	($20,000)
EXPECTED NET CASH	1	8,000	7,000
FLOWS FOR PROJECTS	2	14,000	13,000
C AND F	3	13,000	12,000
	4	12,000	—
	5	11,000	—
	6	10,000	—
	NPV at 11.5%	$7,165	$5,391
	IRR	17.5%	25.2%

The NPV for Project C, as calculated in Table 10-8, is already over the 6-year common life. For Project F, however, we must create a second project that extends the overall life of the combined projects to 6 years. Here we assume (1) that Project F's cost and annual cash inflows will not change if the project is replicated in three years and (2) that RIC's cost of capital will remain at 11.5 percent:

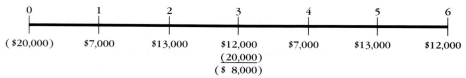

NPV = $9,281.
IRR = 25.2%.

The NPV of this extended Project F is $9,281, and its IRR is 25.2 percent. (The IRR of two Project Fs is the same as the IRR for one Project F.) Since the $9,281 extended NPV of Project F over the common life of 6 years is greater than the $7,165 NPV of Project C, Project F should be selected.

Alternatively, we could recognize that the value of the cash flow stream of two consecutive Project Fs can be summarized by two NPVs: one at Year 0 representing the value of the initial project, and one at Year 3 representing the value of the replication project:

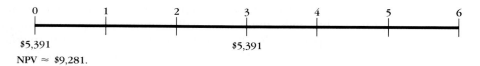

NPV ≈ $9,281.

Ignoring rounding differences, the present value of these two flows, when discounted at 11.5 percent, is $9,281, so we again come to the conclusion that Project F should be selected.

Briefly describe the equivalent annual annuity (EAA) approach.

Under what circumstances do the two approaches lead to the same conclusions?

ABANDONMENT VALUE

Projects are normally analyzed assuming the firm will operate the project over its full physical life. However, this may not be the best course of action—it may be best to abandon a project before the end of its potential life, and this possibility can materially affect the project's estimated profitability.[15] The situation in Table 10-9 can be used to illustrate the abandonment value concept and its effects on capital budgeting. The abandonment values are equivalent to net salvage values, except that they have been estimated for each year of Project A's life.

Using a 10 percent cost of capital, the expected NPV based on operating cash flows as shown in the second column is $-\$117$:

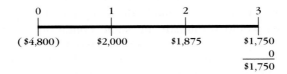

$$NPV = -\$4,800 + \$2,000/(1.10)^1 + \$1,875/(1.10)^2 + \$1,750/(1.10)^3$$

$$= -\$117.$$

Thus, Project A would not be accepted if we considered the single alternative of a 3-year life with a zero salvage (abandonment) value. However, what would its NPV be if the project were abandoned after two years? In this case, we would receive operating cash flows in Years 1 and 2 plus the abandonment value at the end of Year 2, and the project's NPV would be $138:

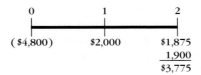

$$NPV = -\$4,800 + \$2,000/(1.10)^1 + \$3,775/(1.10)^2$$

$$= \$138.$$

---

[15] An old but still useful discussion can be found in Alexander A. Robichek and James C. Van Horne, "Abandonment Value and Capital Budgeting," *Journal of Finance,* December 1967, 577–589.

TABLE 10-9 PROJECT A: INVESTMENT, OPERATING, AND ABANDONMENT CASH FLOWS	Year (t)	Initial (Year 0) Investment and Operating Cash Flows	Net Abandonment Value at End of Year t
	0	($4,800)	$4,800
	1	2,000	3,000
	2	1,875	1,900
	3	1,750	0

Thus, Project A becomes acceptable if we plan to operate it for only two years and then dispose of it. To complete the analysis, we note that if the project were abandoned after one year, its NPV would be $-$255. Thus, the optimal life for this project is two years.

As a general rule, any project should be abandoned when its net abandonment value is greater than the present value of all cash flows beyond the abandonment year, discounted to the abandonment decision point. For example, if we accept Project A and operate it for one year, then its abandonment value would be $3,000, but the present value at Year 1 of cash flows beyond Year 1 would be $1,875/(1.10)^1 + $1,750/(1.10)^2 = $3,151$, assuming the project continues through Year 3; and $3,775/(1.10)^1 = $3,432$, assuming abandonment at the end of Year 2. Thus, the Year 1 abandonment value is less than the Year 1 present values of the expected future cash flows under either of the two alternative longer lives, so the project should not be abandoned at this point. However, a similar analysis at Year 2 would show that the abandonment value of $1,900 is greater than the discounted value of future cash flows of $1,750/(1.10)^1 = $1,591$, so our decision rule would tell us to abandon the project in Year 2. This is, of course, the same conclusion that we reached from the NPV calculations.

Abandonment value should be considered in the capital budgeting process because, as our example illustrates, there are cases in which recognition of abandonment can make an otherwise unacceptable project acceptable. Indeed, this type of analysis is required to determine a project's economic life, which is defined as that project life which maximizes the project's NPV and thus maximizes shareholder wealth. For Project A, the *economic life* is actually two years, as opposed to the three-year *physical*, or *engineering, life*.

Two very different types of abandonment occur: (1) sale by the original user of a still-valuable asset to some other party who can obtain greater cash flows from the asset and (2) abandonment of an asset because the project is losing money. The first type of situation can be illustrated by IBM's sale of its typewriter and low-end printer operations to a New York investment firm that rechristened the business Lexmark International. Since IBM had over the years moved into very high-tech businesses, the typewriter and low-end printer lines were simply worth more if they were operated independently rather than remain a poor cousin of IBM's core computer businesses.

The second type of abandonment—closing down money-losing operations—can cut losses and thus reduce the riskiness of a project. This aspect of abandon-

ment is illustrated by RJR's termination of its smokeless cigarette after it became apparent that the cigarette would never become the money-maker the firm had anticipated. We will have more to say about the impact of abandonment on project risk in Chapter 11. The main point to understand now is that the cash flows from a project can be materially different if it is abandoned (or sold off) rather than operated to the end of its initially projected life, and if abandonment possibilities are not considered, then the project's cash flows may be badly misspecified.

SELF-TEST QUESTIONS

Define the economic life of a project (as opposed to its physical life).

Should projects be viewed as having only one life, or should alternative lives be considered in the capital budgeting process?

What are the two main situations where abandonment may be desirable?

ADJUSTING FOR INFLATION

Inflation is a fact of life in the United States and most other nations, so it must be considered in any sound capital budgeting analysis.[16]

INFLATION-INDUCED BIAS

Note that *in the absence of inflation,* the real rate, k_r, and the nominal rate, k_n, are equal, as are the real and nominal expected net cash flows—RCF_t and NCF_t, respectively. (Remember that *real* interest rates and cash flows do not include inflation effects, while *nominal* rates and flows do reflect the effects of inflation.) In the absence of inflation, a project's NPV would be calculated as follows:[17]

$$\text{NPV (no inflation)} = \sum_{t=0}^{n} \frac{RCF_t}{(1 + k_r)^t} = \sum_{t=0}^{n} \frac{NCF_t}{(1 + k)^t}. \qquad (10\text{-}4)$$

Now suppose the expected rate of inflation is positive, and we expect *all* of the project's cash flows, including depreciation, to rise at the rate i. Further, assume

---

[16]For a formal discussion of this subject, see James C. Van Horne, "A Note on Biases in Capital Budgeting Introduced by Inflation," *Journal of Financial and Quantitative Analysis,* January 1971, 653–658; Philip L. Cooley, Rodney L. Roenfeldt, and It-Keong Chew, "Capital Budgeting Procedures under Inflation," *Financial Management,* Winter 1975, 18–27; and "Cooley, Roenfeldt, and Chew vs. Findlay and Frankle," *Financial Management,* Autumn 1976, 83–90.

[17]Note that the nominal rate of return includes an inflation premium that reflects investors' expectations about future inflation rates, while the real rate of return does not. If expected inflation is zero, then the inflation premium is also zero, and real and nominal rates are equal.

that this same inflation rate, i, is built into the market cost of capital as an inflation premium, $IP = i$, so $k_n = k_n + i$. In this situation, the nominal net cash flow, NCF_t, will increase annually at the rate of i percent, producing this result:

$$NCF_t = RCF_t(1 + i)^t.$$

For example, if we expected a net cash flow of $100 in Year 5 in the absence of inflation, then with a 5 percent annual rate of inflation, $NCF_5 = \$100(1.05)^5 = \$127.63$.

Now if net cash flows increase at the rate of i percent per year, and if this same inflation factor is built into the firm's cost of capital, then the NPV would be calculated as follows:

$$\text{NPV (with inflation)} = \sum_{t=0}^{n} \frac{NCF_t}{(1 + k_n)^t} = \sum_{t=0}^{n} \frac{RCF_t (1 + i)^t}{(1 + k_r)^t (1 + i)^t}. \quad \textbf{(10-5)}$$

Since the $(1 + i)^t$ terms in the numerator and denominator cancel, we are left with Equation 10-4:

$$\text{NPV} = \sum_{t=0}^{n} \frac{RCF_t}{(1 + k_r)^t}.$$

Thus, if all costs and sales prices, hence annual cash flows, are expected to rise at the same inflation rate that investors have built into the cost of capital, then the inflation-adjusted NPV determined using Equation 10-5 is identical to the inflation-free NPV found using Equation 10-4.[18]

However, firms occasionally use unadjusted base year dollars throughout the analysis—say, 1993 dollars if the analysis is done in 1993—along with a cost of capital as determined in the marketplace as we described in Chapter 8. This is wrong: *If the cost of capital includes an inflation premium, as it typically does, but the cash flows are all stated in base year dollars, then the calculated NPV will be downward biased.* The denominator will reflect inflation, but the numerator will not, and this will cause a downward bias in the NPV.

ADJUSTING FOR INFLATION

There are two ways to adjust for inflation. First, all project cash flows can be expressed as real (unadjusted) flows, with no consideration of inflation, and then the cost of capital can be adjusted to a real rate by removing the inflation premiums

---

[18]To focus on inflation effects, we have simplified the situation somewhat. The precise nominal cost of capital is $k_n = w_d(k_{dr} + i)(1 - T) + w_{ce}(k_{sr} + i)$ rather than $k_n = k_r + i$. Thus, we have ignored the impact of the tax deductibility of interest payments on the nominal cost of capital.

from the component costs. (See Footnote 18.) This approach is relatively simple, but to produce an unbiased NPV it requires (1) that all project cash flows, including depreciation, be affected identically by inflation, and (2) that this rate of increase equals the inflation rate built into investors' required returns. Since these assumptions generally do not hold in practice, this method is not commonly used.

The second method involves leaving the cost of capital in its nominal form, and then adjusting the individual cash flows to reflect the impact of inflation. This is what we did earlier in our RIC computer project example as summarized in Table 10-4. There we assumed that sales prices, variable costs, and fixed overhead costs would all increase at a rate of 6 percent per year, but that depreciation charges would not be affected by inflation. Of course, we could have assumed different rates of inflation for sales prices, for variable costs, and for fixed overheads. For example, RIC might have long-term labor contracts which cause wage rates to rise with the Consumer Price Index (CPI), but its raw materials might be purchased under a fixed price contract, with the net result that variable costs are expected to rise by a smaller percentage than sales prices. In any event, one should build inflation into the cash flow analysis, with the specific adjustment reflecting as accurately as possible the most likely set of circumstances.

Our conclusions about inflation may be summarized as follows. First, inflation is critically important, for it can and does have major effects on businesses. Therefore, it must be recognized and dealt with. Second, the most effective way of dealing with inflation in capital budgeting analyses is to build inflation estimates into each cash flow element, using the best available information on how each element will be affected. Third, since we cannot estimate future inflation rates with precision, errors are bound to be made. Thus, inflation adds to the uncertainty, or riskiness, of capital budgeting as well as to its complexity. Fortunately, computers are available to help with inflation analysis, but an awareness of the nature of the problem is essential for good capital budgeting analyses.

SELF-TEST QUESTIONS

In what situation does inflation cause a downward bias in a project's estimated NPV? Explain.

What is the best way of handling inflation in a capital budgeting analysis, and how does this procedure eliminate the potential bias?

SUMMARY

This chapter discussed several issues in project cash flow analysis. The key concepts covered are listed below:

▶ The most important, but also the most difficult, step in capital budgeting is *estimating the incremental after-tax cash flows* a project will produce.

▶ *Net operating cash flows* consist of (1) sales revenues minus cash operating costs, reduced by taxes, plus (2) a depreciation cash flow equal to the amount of depreciation taken during the period multiplied by the tax rate. In most situations, net operating cash flows are estimated by constructing cash flow statements.

▶ In determining incremental cash flows, *opportunity costs* (the cash flows foregone by using an asset the company already owns) must be included, but *sunk costs* (cash outlays that have been made and that cannot be recouped) are not included. Any effects of a project on other parts of the firm should also be included in the analysis.

▶ *Tax laws* affect project cash flow analyses in two ways: (1) They reduce project operating cash flows and (2) they determine the depreciation expense that can be taken in each year.

▶ Capital projects often require an additional investment in *net working capital (NWC).* An increase in NWC must be included in the project's cost and then shown as a cash inflow at the end of the project's life.

▶ *Replacement analysis* is slightly different from that for *expansion projects* because the cash flows from the old asset must be considered in replacement decisions.

▶ Cash flow *estimation bias* can result if managers are overly optimistic in their forecasts.

▶ A project may have a *managerial option* value that is not accounted for in a conventional discounted cash flow analysis.

▶ If mutually exclusive projects have *unequal lives,* it may be necessary to adjust the analysis to place the projects on an equal life basis. This can be done using either the *replacement chain* approach or the *equivalent annual annuity* approach.

▶ A project's value may be greater than the NPV of its physical life if it can be *abandoned* at some earlier time.

▶ *Inflation effects* must be considered in project analysis. The best procedure is to build inflation directly into the cash flow estimates.

We continue our discussion of capital budgeting analysis in Chapter 11, where we discuss risk analysis and the optimal capital budget.

QUESTIONS

10-1 Define each of the following terms:

   a. Cash flow; accounting income

   b. Incremental cash flow; sunk cost; opportunity cost

   c. Net working capital changes

   d. Salvage value

   e. Replacement decision

f. Replacement chain

g. Equivalent annual annuity

h. Abandonment value

i. Real rate of return, k_r, versus nominal rate of return, k_n

j. Cash flow estimation bias

k. Managerial options

10-2 Operating cash flows, rather than accounting profits, are listed in Table 10-4. What is the basis for this emphasis on cash flows as opposed to net income?

10-3 Why is it true, in general, that a failure to adjust expected cash flows for expected inflation biases the calculated NPV downward?

10-4 Suppose a firm is considering two mutually exclusive projects. One has a life of six years and the other a life of ten years. Would the failure to employ some type of replacement chain analysis bias an NPV analysis against one of the projects? Explain.

10-5 Look at Table 10-7 and answer these questions:

a. Why is the salvage value shown on Line 12 reduced for taxes on Line 13?

b. Why is depreciation on the old machine deducted on Line 8 to get Line 9?

c. What would happen if the new machine permitted a *reduction* in net working capital?

d. Why are the cost savings on Line 6 reduced by multiplying the before-tax figure by $(1 - T)$, whereas the change in depreciation figure on Line 9 is multiplied by T?

SELF-TEST PROBLEMS   (SOLUTIONS APPEAR IN APPENDIX C)

ST-1 (New project analysis) You have been asked by the president of the Farr Construction Company to evaluate the proposed acquisition of a new earth mover. The mover's basic price is $50,000, and it would cost another $10,000 to modify it for special use. Assume that the mover falls into the MACRS 3-year class, it would be sold after 3 years for $20,000, and it would require an increase in net working capital (spare parts inventory) of $2,000. The earth mover would have no effect on revenues, but it is expected to save the firm $20,000 per year in before-tax operating costs, mainly labor. The firm's marginal federal-plus-state tax rate is 40 percent.

a. What is the net cost of the earth mover? (That is, what are the Year 0 cash flows?)

b. What are the operating cash flows in Years 1, 2, and 3?

c. What are the additional (nonoperating) cash flows in Year 3?

d. If the project's cost of capital is 10 percent, should the earth mover be purchased?

ST-2 (Replacement project analysis) The Erickson Toy Corporation currently uses an injection molding machine that was purchased 2 years ago. This machine is being depreciated on a straight line basis toward a $500 salvage value, and it has 6 years of remaining life. Its current book value is $2,600, and it can be sold for $3,000 at this time. Assume, for ease of calculation, that the annual depreciation expense is $350 per year.

The firm is offered a replacement machine which has a cost of $8,000, an estimated useful life of 6 years, and an estimated salvage value of $800. This machine falls into the MACRS 5-year class. The replacement machine would permit an output expansion, so sales would rise by $1,000 per year; even so, the new machine's much greater efficiency would still cause operating expenses to decline by $1,500 per year. The new machine would

require that inventories be increased by $2,000, but accounts payable would simultaneously increase by $500.

The firm's marginal federal-plus-state tax rate is 40 percent, and its cost of capital is 15 percent. Should it replace the old machine?

PROBLEMS

10-1 (Depreciation effects)   Susan Fischer, great-granddaughter of the founder of Taussig Tile Products and current president of the company, believes in simple, conservative accounting. In keeping with her philosophy, she has decreed that the company shall use alternative straight line depreciation, based on the MACRS class lives, for all newly acquired assets. Your boss, the financial vice president and the only non-family officer, has asked you to develop an exhibit which shows how much this policy costs the company in terms of market value. Ms. Fischer is interested in increasing the value of the firm's stock because she fears a family stockholder revolt which might remove her from office. For your exhibit, assume that the company spends $50 million each year on new capital projects, that the projects have on average a 10-year class life, that the company has a 10 percent cost of debt, and that its tax rate is 34 percent. (Hint: Show how much the NPV of projects in an average year would increase if Taussig used the standard MACRS recovery allowances. Also, ignore the half-year convention on the straight line calculation.)

10-2 (New project analysis)   You have been asked by the president of your company to evaluate the proposed acquisition of a new spectrometer for the firm's R&D department. The equipment's basic price is $70,000, and it would cost another $15,000 to modify it for special use by your firm. The spectrometer, which falls into the MACRS 3-year class, would be sold after 3 years for $30,000. Use of the equipment would require an increase in net working capital (spare parts inventory) of $4,000. The spectrometer would have no effect on revenues, but it is expected to save the firm $25,000 per year in before-tax operating costs, mainly labor. The firm's marginal federal-plus-state tax rate is 40 percent.

a.   What is the net cost of the spectrometer? (That is, what is the Year 0 net cash flow?)

b.   What are the net operating cash flows in Years 1, 2, and 3?

c.   What is the additional (nonoperating) cash flow in Year 3?

d.   If the project's cost of capital is 10 percent, should the spectrometer be purchased?

10-3 (New project analysis)   McLaughlin Mills is evaluating the proposed acquisition of a new milling machine. The machine's base price is $180,000, and it would cost another $25,000 to modify it for special use by your firm. The machine falls into the MACRS 3-year class, and it would be sold after 3 years for $80,000. The machine would require an increase in net working capital (inventory) of $7,500. The machine would have no effect on revenues, but it is expected to save the firm $75,000 per year in before-tax operating costs, mainly labor. McLaughlin's marginal tax rate is 34 percent.

a.   What is the net cost of the machine for capital budgeting purposes? (That is, what is the Year 0 net cash flow?)

b.   What are the operating cash flows in Years 1, 2, and 3?

c.   What is the additional (nonoperating) cash flow in Year 3?

d.   If the project's cost of capital is 10 percent, should the machine be purchased?

(Do Parts e, f, g, and h only if you are using the computer problem diskette.)

e. Determine the NPV if the cost of capital were (1) to rise to 12 percent or (2) to fall to 8 percent.

f. There is some uncertainty about the salvage value. It could be as low as $50,000 or as high as $90,000. What would the NPV be at those two salvage value levels? (Assume k = 10 percent.) Should this uncertainty affect the decision to invest? What salvage value (to the nearest thousand) would make you indifferent to the project?

g. Return to the original salvage value of $80,000. What would be the project's NPV if the corporate tax rate were increased to 46 percent?

h. Return the tax rate to 34 percent. Now assume that the manufacturer of the machine calls you with bad news: The base price of the machine has increased to $200,000. What does this do to the project's NPV? At what cost (to the nearest hundred) would McLaughlin be indifferent to the project?

10-4 (Replacement analysis) The Wingler Equipment Company purchased a machine 5 years ago at a cost of $100,000. It had an expected life of 10 years at the time of purchase and an expected salvage value of $10,000 at the end of the 10 years. It is being depreciated by the straight line method toward a salvage value of $10,000, or by $9,000 per year.

A new machine can be purchased for $150,000, including installation costs. Over its 5-year life, it will reduce cash operating expenses by $50,000 per year. Sales are not expected to change. At the end of its useful life, the machine is estimated to be worthless. MACRS depreciation will be used, and it will be depreciated over its 3-year class life rather than its 5-year economic life.

The old machine can be sold today for $65,000. The firm's tax rate is 34 percent. The appropriate discount rate is 15 percent.

a. If the new machine is purchased, what is the amount of the initial cash flow at Year 0?

b. What incremental operating cash flows will occur at the end of Years 1 through 5 as a result of replacing the old machine?

c. What incremental nonoperating cash flow will occur at the end of Year 5 if the new machine is purchased?

d. What is the NPV of this project? Should the firm replace the old machine?

10-5 (Replacement analysis) The Orange Fizz Company is contemplating the replacement of one of its bottling machines with a newer and more efficient one. The old machine has a book value of $500,000 and a remaining useful life of 5 years. The firm does not expect to realize any return from scrapping the old machine in 5 years, but it can sell it now to another firm in the industry for $200,000. The old machine is being depreciated toward a zero salvage value, or by $100,000 per year, using the straight line method.

The new machine has a purchase price of $1.2 million, an estimated useful life and MACRS class life of 5 years, and an estimated salvage value of $175,000. It is expected to economize on electric power usage, labor, and repair costs, and also to reduce the number of defective bottles. In total, an annual savings of $275,000 will be realized if it is installed. The company is in the 40 percent federal-plus-state tax bracket, and it has a 10 percent cost of capital.

a. What is the initial cash outlay required for the new machine?

b. Calculate the annual depreciation allowances for both machines, and compute the change in the annual depreciation expense if the replacement is made.

c. What are the operating cash flows in Years 1 to 5?

d. What is the cash flow from the salvage value in Year 5?

e. Should the firm purchase the new machine? Support your answer.

f. In general, how would each of the following factors affect the investment decision, and how should each be treated?

    (1) The expected life of the existing machine decreases.

    (2) The cost of capital is not constant but is increasing.

(Do Parts g, h, and i only if you are using the computer problem diskette.)

g. The firm may be able to purchase an alternative new bottling machine from another supplier. Its purchase price would be $1,050,000, and its salvage value would be $250,000. This machine has a lower annual operating savings of $210,000. Should the firm purchase this machine?

h. If the salvage value on the alternative new machine were $200,000 rather than $250,000, how would this affect the decision?

i. With everything as in Part h, assume that the cost of capital declined from 10 percent to 8 percent. How would this affect the decision?

10-6 (Unequal lives) Filkins Fabric Company is considering the replacement of its old, fully depreciated knitting machine. Two new models are available: Machine 190-3, which has a cost of $190,000, a 3-year expected life, and after-tax cash flows (labor savings and depreciation) of $87,000 per year; and Machine 360-6, which has a cost of $360,000, a 6-year life, and after-tax cash flows of $98,300 per year. Knitting machine prices are not expected to rise, because inflation will be offset by cheaper components (microprocessors) used in the machines. Assume that Filkins' cost of capital is 14 percent.

a. Should the firm replace its old knitting machine, and, if so, which new machine should it use?

b. Suppose the firm's basic patents will expire in 9 years, and the company expects to go out of business at that time. Assume further that the firm depreciates its assets using the straight line method, that its marginal federal-plus-state tax rate is 40 percent, and that the used machines can be sold at their book values. Under these circumstances, should the company replace the old machine and, if so, which new model should the company purchase?

10-7 (Abandonment value) The Scampini Supplies Company recently purchased a new delivery truck. The new truck cost $22,500, and it is expected to generate net after-tax operating cash flows, including depreciation, of $6,250 per year. The truck has a 5-year expected life. The expected abandonment values (salvage values after tax adjustments) for the truck are given below. The company's cost of capital is 10 percent.

Year	Annual Operating Cash Flow	Abandonment Value
0	($22,500)	$22,500
1	6,250	17,500
2	6,250	14,000
3	6,250	11,000
4	6,250	5,000
5	6,250	0

a. Should the firm operate the truck until the end of its 5-year physical life, or, if not, what is its optimal economic life?

b. Would the introduction of abandonment values, in addition to operating cash flows, ever *reduce* the expected NPV and/or IRR of a project?

10-8 (Inflation adjustments)   The Rodriguez Company is considering an average-risk investment in a mineral water spring project that has a cost of $150,000. The project will produce 1,000 cases of mineral water per year indefinitely. The current sales price is $138 per case, and the current cost per case (all variable) is $105. The firm is taxed at a rate of 34 percent. Both prices and costs are expected to rise at a rate of 6 percent per year. The firm uses only equity, and it has a cost of capital of 15 percent. Assume that cash flows consist only of after-tax profits, since the spring has an indefinite life and will not be depreciated.

a. Should the firm accept the project? (Hint: The project is a perpetuity, so you must use the formula for a perpetuity to find its NPV.)

b. If total costs consisted of a fixed cost of $10,000 per year and variable costs of $95 per unit, and if only the variable costs were expected to increase with inflation, would this make the project better or worse? Continue with the assumption that the sales price will rise with inflation.

10-9 (Inflation adjustments)   The Dalrymple Company is evaluating an average-risk capital project having both a 3-year economic and MACRS class life. The net investment outlay at Time 0 is $18,800. The expected end-of-year cash flows, expressed in Time 0 dollars, are listed below: (Ignore salvage value and Year 4 depreciation.)

	Year 1	Year 2	Year 3
Revenues	$30,000	$30,000	$30,000
Variable costs	15,000	15,000	15,000
Fixed costs	6,500	6,500	6,500
Depreciation	6,204	8,460	2,820

The firm has a marginal federal-plus-state tax rate of 40 percent. Dalrymple's current cost of debt is 12 percent, and its cost of equity is 16 percent. These costs include an estimated inflation premium of 6 percent. The firm's target capital structure is 50 percent debt and 50 percent equity.

a. What is the firm's nominal WACC? Its real WACC?

b. What are the project's relevant real cash flows? What discount rate should be utilized when calculating a project's NPV based upon real cash flows? Why?

c. What is the NPV for this project? Should this project be accepted? What might have occurred if you had used the *nominal* WACC with *real* cash flows?

d. Now assume that all revenues and costs, except depreciation, are expected to increase at the inflation rate of 6 percent. What are the project's nominal cash flows and NPV based on these flows? Why is this NPV different from the NPV calculated in Part c?

(Do Part e only if you are using the computer problem diskette.)

e. Assume that the firm's management anticipates a rate of inflation resulting in a 6 percent inflation premium for Year 1 through Year 3. Based upon this assumption, the firm accepts the project. However, suppose the firm actually experiences nonneutral inflation such that revenues increase by only 6 percent, while variable and fixed costs increase by 7.5 percent. What are the actual after-tax cash flows in this case? What effect would the acceptance of the project, coupled with unanticipated nonneutral inflation, have had upon the value of the firm?

f. If a company, in its capital budgeting process, bases its cash flows on sales prices and unit costs at the time it analyzes the project, (1) would this tend to produce systematic

errors in its capital budgeting evaluations, (2) would any such error be more serious for long-term or short-term projects, and (3) if you do think that systematic errors are likely to occur, how could they be corrected?

M I N I   C A S E

John Crockett Furniture Company is considering adding a new line to its product mix, and the capital budgeting analysis is being conducted by Joan Samuels, a recently graduated finance MBA. The production line would be set up in unused space in Crockett's main plant. The machinery's invoice price would be approximately $200,000; another $10,000 in shipping charges would be required; and it would cost an additional $30,000 to install the equipment. Further, the firm's inventories would have to be increased by $25,000 to handle the new line, but its accounts payable would rise by $5,000. The machinery has an economic life of 4 years, and Crockett has obtained a special tax ruling which places the equipment in the MACRS 3-year class. The machinery is expected to have a salvage value of $25,000 after 4 years of use.

The new line would generate $125,000 in incremental net revenues (before taxes and excluding depreciation) in each of the next 4 years. The firm's tax rate is 40 percent, and its overall weighted average cost of capital is 10 percent.

a. Set up, without numbers, a time line for the project's cash flows.

b. (1) Construct incremental operating cash flow statements for the project's 4 years of operations.

   (2) Does your cash flow statement include any financial flows such as interest expense or dividends? Why or why not?

c. (1) Suppose the firm had spent $100,000 last year to rehabilitate the production line site. Should this cost be included in the analysis? Explain.

   (2) Now assume that the plant space could be leased out to another firm at $25,000 a year. Should this be included in the analysis? If so, how?

   (3) Finally, assume that the new product line is expected to decrease sales of the firm's other lines by $50,000 per year. Should this be considered in the analysis? If so, how?

d. Disregard the assumptions in Part c. What is Crockett's net investment outlay on this project? What is the net nonoperating cash flow at the time the project is terminated? Based on these cash flows, what are the project's NPV, IRR, MIRR, and payback? Do these indicators suggest that the project should be undertaken?

e. Assume now that the project is a replacement project rather than a new, or expansion, project. Describe how the analysis would differ for a replacement project.

f. Explain what is meant by cash flow estimation bias. What are some steps that Crockett's management could take to eliminate the incentives for bias in the decision process?

g. Do you think it likely that the project being considered here might have managerial option value over and above the indicated NPV? If so, how might this be handled?

h. Assume that inflation is expected to average 5 percent over the next 4 years. Does it appear that Crockett's cash flow estimates are real or nominal? That is, are all the cash flows stated in the Time 0 dollars or have the cash flows been increased to account for expected inflation? Further, would it appear that the 10 percent cost of capital is a nominal or real interest rate? Does it appear that the current NPV is biased because of inflation effects? If so, in what direction, and how could any bias be removed?

i.   In an unrelated analysis, Joan was asked to choose between the following two mutually exclusive projects:

	Expected Net Cash Flow	
Year	**Project S**	**Project L**
0	($100,000)	($100,000)
1	60,000	33,500
2	60,000	33,500
3	—	33,500
4	—	33,500

The projects provide a necessary service, so whichever one is selected is expected to be repeated into the foreseeable future. Both projects have a 10 percent cost of capital.
(1) What is each project's initial NPV without replication?
(2) Now apply the replacement chain approach to determine the projects' extended NPVs. Which project should be chosen?
(3) Repeat the analysis using the equivalent annual annuity approach.
(4) Now assume that the cost to replicate Project S in 2 years will increase to $105,000 because of inflationary pressures. How should the analysis be handled now, and which project should be chosen?

j.   Crockett is also considering another project which has a physical life of 3 years; that is, the machinery will be totally worn-out after 3 years. However, if the project were abandoned prior to the end of 3 years, the machinery would have a positive salvage (or abandonment) value. Here are the project's estimated cash flows:

Year	Initial Investment and Operating Cash Flows	End-of-Year Net Abandonment Value
0	($5,000)	$5,000
1	2,100	3,100
2	2,000	2,000
3	1,750	0

Using the 10 percent cost of capital, what is the project's NPV if it is operated for the full 3 years? Would the NPV change if the company planned to abandon the project at the end of Year 2? At the end of Year 1? What is the project's optimal (economic) life?

SELECTED ADDITIONAL REFERENCES AND CASES

Several articles have been written regarding the implications of the Accelerated Cost Recovery System (ACRS). Among them are the following:

Angell, Robert J., and Tony R. Wingler, "A Note on Expensing versus Depreciating Under the Accelerated Cost Recovery System," *Financial Management,* Winter 1982, 34–35.

McCarty, Daniel E., and William R. McDaniel, "A Note on Expensing versus Depreciating Under the Accelerated Cost Recovery System: Comment," *Financial Management,* Summer 1983, 37–39.

For further information on replacement analysis, as well as other aspects of capital budgeting, see the texts by Bierman and Smidt; by Grant, Ireson, and Leavenworth; by Levy and Sarnat; and by Seitz referenced in Chapter 9.

Three additional papers on the impact of inflation on capital budgeting are the following:

Bailey, Andrew D., and Daniel L. Jensen, "General Price Level Adjustments in the Capital Budgeting Decision," *Financial Management,* Spring 1977, 26–32.

Mehta, Dileep R., Michael D. Curley, and Hung-Gay Fung, "Inflation, Cost of Capital, and Capital Budgeting Procedures," *Financial Management,* Winter 1984, 48–54.

Rappaport, Alfred, and Robert A. Taggart, Jr., "Evaluation of Capital Expenditure Proposals Under Inflation," *Financial Management,* Spring 1982, 5–13.

For additional insights into unequal life analysis, see

Emery, Gary W., "Some Guidelines for Evaluating Capital Investment Alternatives with Unequal Lives," *Financial Management,* Spring 1982, 15–19.

For an interesting discussion on cash flow estimation and abandonment biases, see

Statman, Meir, and David Caldwell, "Applying Behavioral Finance to Capital Budgeting: Project Terminations," *Financial Management,* Winter 1987, 7–13.

Statman, Meir, and Tyzoon T. Tyebjee, "Optimistic Capital Budgeting Forecasts: An Experiment," *Financial Management,* Autumn 1985, 27–33.

The following articles pertain to other topics in this chapter:

Bjerksund, Petter, and Steinar Ekern, "Managing Investment Opportunities Under Price Uncertainty: From 'Last Chance' to 'Wait and See' Strategies," *Financial Management,* Autumn 1990, 65–83.

Chen, Son-Nan, "Optimal Asset Abandonment and Replacement: Tax and Replacement Considerations," *Financial Review,* May 1991, 157–177.

Kroll, Yoram, "On the Differences beween Accrual Accounting Figures and Cash Flows: The Case of Working Capital," *Financial Management,* Spring 1985, 75–82.

Kulatilaka, Nalin, and Alan J. Marcus, "Project Valuation under Uncertainty: When Does DCF Fail," *Journal of Applied Corporate Finance,* Fall 1992, 92–100.

Mukherjee, Tarun K., "Reducing the Uncertainty-Induced Bias in Capital Budgeting Decisions — A Hurdle Rate Approach," *Journal of Business Finance & Accounting,* September 1991, 747–753.

Triantis, Alexander J., and James E. Hodder, "Valuing Flexibility as a Complex Option," *Journal of Finance,* June 1990, 549–565.

The Brigham-Gapenski casebook contains the following cases which focus on Chapter 9 and 10 material:

Case 12, "Indian River Citrus Compnay (A)" and Case 14, "Robert Montoya, Inc. (A)," which focus on cash flow estimation but also include capital budgeting decision methods.

RISK ANALYSIS AND THE OPTIMAL CAPITAL BUDGET

S implesse, the touted fake fat from NutraSweet, was supposed to ensure the company's success and usher in an era of guilt-free gluttony for America's calorie counters and cholesterol watchers, or so Nutra-Sweet executives predicted. It promised all the taste virtues of real fat but with none of the associated vices. It almost seemed too good to be true for both the company and consumers.

Simplesse, a highly processed mixture of whipped egg whites and skim milk, was intended to simulate not only the taste of fat but also its rich texture, its so-called "mouthfeel." Fat is what makes mayonnaise slippery and potato chips crunchy; it is the creaminess in Häagen-Dazs ice cream and the gratifying greasiness in a Big Mac. Nowadays, however, consumers see the dark side of fat: It tastes great, but it can cause "spare tires" and heart disease.

As an ingredient, Simplesse is temperamental. It curdles when heated to a high temperature, which makes it hard to use in baked goods. In the refrigerator, its shelf life is short. Simplesse consists of microparticulated beadlets so tiny that 50 billion of them will fit in a teaspoon. After a few weeks, the beadlets begin to adhere to one another, and when the clumps get big enough, the silky-smooth, fatlike texture of Simplesse begins to have a distinctly gritty feel on the tongue.

In all, about $100 million went into the development of Simplesse. To justify the expenditure, NutraSweet's managers estimated that Simplesse would be a $444 million business and would provide the company with $20 million in annual profits. Although most of the profits were expected to come from sales of Simplesse to other food companies for use in various food products, the first

Simplesse product to be developed was Simple Pleasures, an imitation ice cream produced by NutraSweet.

During Simple Pleasures' development, the research team tried to produce a product that rivaled Häagen-Dazs's vanilla flavor. During in-house testing, senior managers would feed samples to junior managers and ask, "Doesn't it taste like Häagen-Dazs?" Needless to say, everyone replied, "Yes, it tastes just like Häagen-Dazs." In reality, it tasted more like chalk, and early versions of Simple Pleasures melted too slowly and left a scummy ring around the bowl. To add to the problems, NutraSweet's managers badly underestimated how much it would cost to make and market a product mimicking ice cream, how much manufacturing capacity would be needed, and how difficult it would be to move from making small batches in the lab to large-scale production runs.

In the end, Simple Pleasures has captured about 8 percent of the nonfat ice cream market. Furthermore, the company has signed several contracts with other food producers to use Simplesse in their products. The consensus among consumers seems to be that although Simple Pleasures isn't dreadful, it isn't like real ice cream. It compares favorably in taste and texture with other nonfat ice creams, but it is considerably more expensive.

What do NutraSweet's problems with Simplesse have to do with capital budgeting? It is clear that the cash flows associated with new projects are not known with certainty. Indeed, for most projects, there is a great deal of uncertainty, and this uncertainty creates risk for the firm. In this chapter, we discuss procedures that can be used to assess the riskiness of proposed projects and ways to incorporate the results in the decision process. As you read the chapter, consider how NutraSweet might have used these procedures in its analysis of the Simplesse/Simple Pleasures project.

Risk analysis is important in all financial decisions, especially those relating to capital budgeting. As we saw in Chapter 5, the higher the risk associated with a security, the higher the rate of return needed to compensate for the risk, and this situation is as true for capital projects as it is for securities. Since capital projects within a firm can have widely differing risk, it is essential that capital budgeting decisions include risk analysis. In this chapter, we discuss procedures for assessing risk in a capital budgeting context and for incorporating risk into capital budgeting decisions. Also, we discuss how a firm determines its optimal capital budget.

INTRODUCTION TO PROJECT RISK

Three separate and distinct types of project risk can be defined: (1) *stand-alone risk*, which views the risk of a project in isolation, hence without regard to portfolio effects; (2) *within-firm risk*, also called *corporate risk*, which views the risk

of a project within the context of the firm's portfolio of projects; and (3) *market risk*, which views a project's risk within the context of the firm's stockholders' diversification in the general stock market. As we shall see, a particular project might have highly uncertain returns, thus have high stand-alone risk, yet taking it on might not have much effect on either the firm's corporate risk or the risk of its owners, once diversification is taken into account.

Figure 11-1 provides a framework for analyzing the riskiness of a project. In the remainder of this section, we discuss the figure, and in following sections, we discuss how the different types of risk may be quantified and used in actual capital budgeting decisions. Here are nine points related to the figure:

1. Risk in Figure 11-1 and throughout the chapter relates to uncertainty about *future* events, and in capital budgeting, this means the *future* profitability of a project. For certain types of projects, it is possible to look back at historical data and to analyze statistically the riskiness of the investment. This is often true when the investment involves an expansion decision — for example, if Sears were opening a new store, if Citibank were opening a new branch, or if GM were expanding a Chevrolet plant, then past experience could be used as a starting point for assessing future risk. Similarly, a company that is considering going into a new business might be able to look at historical data on existing firms in that industry to get an idea about the riskiness of its proposed investment. However, there are times when it is impossible to obtain historical data regarding proposed investments; for example, if GM were considering the production of an electric auto, not much relevant historical data for assessing the riskiness of the project would be available. Rather, GM would have to rely primarily on the judgment of its executives, and they, in turn, would have to rely on their experience in developing, manufacturing, and marketing new products. *We will try to quantify risk analysis, but you must recognize at the outset that some of the data used in the analysis will necessarily be based on subjective judgments rather than on hard statistical observations.*

2. In Figure 11-1, and in risk analysis generally, we shall use the terms which are defined below. Note that these terms and concepts are drawn directly from security risk and return analysis as set forth back in Chapters 4 and 5, so you should refer back to those chapters if you are hazy on portfolio concepts. Here are the key terms:

σ_P = standard deviation of the profitability of the project in question, measured as the standard deviation of the project's IRR. σ_P is a measure of the project's *stand-alone risk*.

$r_{P,F}$ = correlation coefficient between the rate of return on the project and the rate of return on the firm's other assets. What we want to know here is this: Will this project be profitable at the same time the firm's other assets are also profitable, or are its returns likely to be independent of (or even negatively correlated with) returns on the firm's other assets? This correlation can be determined statistically for certain types of projects, but for many others it must be assessed subjectively.

FIGURE 11-1 PROJECT RISK ANALYSIS

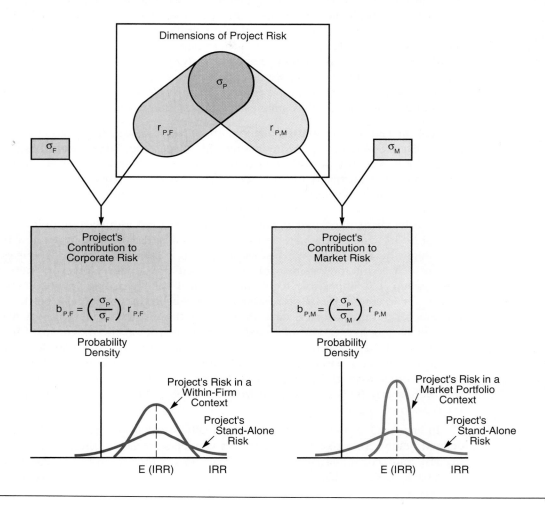

$r_{P,M}$ = correlation coefficient between the rate of return on the project and returns on a stock market index, or "the market." If this correlation, which generally must be assessed subjectively on the basis of judgment and experience, is positive, then the project will tend to produce low returns when the economy, and most stocks, are also doing badly.

σ_F = standard deviation of the rate of return on the firm's assets before it takes on the project in question, measured as [EBIT $(1 - T)$ + Depreciation] / (Debt + Equity). Note that the firm's average rate of return is, in effect, an

average of realized IRRs on past projects. If σ_F is low, then the firm is stable, and its *corporate risk* is relatively low, while if σ_F is high, then the firm has a high degree of corporate risk, and its chances of going bankrupt are higher than if σ_F were low. The value of σ_F for past years can be measured statistically, but changes in the firm's situation may make its *expected future corporate riskiness* different from its past risk, in which case a subjectively estimated σ_F would be preferable for use in the analysis.

σ_M = standard deviation of the market's returns. This value is measured using historical data, and it is about 15 percent.

$b_{P,F}$ = *within-firm beta coefficient* of the project, which is found (conceptually) by regressing the project's returns against returns on the firm excluding the project. If you think of the project as a stock, and the firm as the market, then $b_{P,F}$ is found (conceptually) the same way stock betas were found back in Chapter 5. Note also that we can use the following formula, which was developed in Chapter 5, to calculate the within-firm beta:

$$b_{P,F} = \left(\frac{\sigma_P}{\sigma_F}\right) r_{P,F}.$$

Here we see that the project's within-firm beta is a function of its stand-alone risk, σ_P, the riskiness of the firm's other assets, σ_F, and the correlation coefficient between the returns on the project and those on the firm's other assets. The within-firm beta is a measure of the project's contribution to the firm's *corporate risk*, just as a stock's market beta is a measure of its contribution to the risk faced by a well-diversified investor who holds a broad portfolio of stocks.

$b_{P,M}$ = beta coefficient of the project within the context of the market portfolio of stocks, which could (conceptually) be found by regressing the project's returns against returns on the market. Again, we can express $b_{P,M}$ as an equation:

$$b_{P,M} = \left(\frac{\sigma_P}{\sigma_M}\right) r_{P,M}.$$

This is the project's *market beta*, and it is a measure of the contribution of the project to the risk borne by the firm's stockholders, who are assumed to hold well-diversified portfolios.

3. Now look carefully at Figure 11-1. The upper box shows that there are three attributes to a project's risk: (1) the standard deviation of the project's forecasted returns, σ_P, (2) the correlation of those returns with the firm's other assets, $r_{P,F}$, and (3) the correlation of the project's returns with the stock market, $r_{P,M}$. As shown in the center-left panel, two of the project's risk attributes, σ_P and $r_{P,F}$,

combine with the standard deviation of returns on the firm's other assets, σ_F, to determine the project's contribution to the firm's corporate risk, or its *within-firm risk*. Also, as shown in the center-right panel, two of the project's risk attributes, σ_P and $r_{P,M}$, combine with the riskiness of the market, σ_M, to determine the project's contribution to the riskiness of a well-diversified investor's portfolio, or the project's *market risk*.

4. We see that it is especially important, when assessing a project's riskiness, to measure the project's stand-alone risk, σ_P, because that element is used in all aspects of capital budgeting risk analysis, along with the project's correlation with either the rest of the firm or with the market, or both correlations, depending on whether we want to measure corporate risk, market risk, or both types of risk.

5. Most projects are positively correlated with the firm's other assets, with the correlation being highest for projects in the firm's core business and less high (but still positive) for projects outside the core. However, the correlation coefficient is rarely + 1.0. This being the case, some of most projects' stand-alone risk will be diversified away, and the larger the firm, the greater this effect is likely to be. Therefore, in the probability distribution graph shown at the lower-left corner of Figure 11-1, we show a flatter distribution for the illustrative project's stand-alone risk than for its risk within the context of the firm's portfolio of assets; this shows that the project's within-firm risk is smaller than its stand-alone risk.

6. Most projects are also positively correlated with other assets in the economy —most corporate assets have high returns when the economy is strong, and vice versa—but again, the correlation is usually not perfect, so the typical project's stand-alone risk is also greater than its market risk. Hence, in the lower-right graph the probability distribution curve for the project's stand-alone risk is flatter than its distribution within a market portfolio context.

7. If a project's within-firm beta, $b_{P,F}$, is equal to 1.0, then the project has the same degree of corporate risk as an average project, while if $b_{P,F}$ is greater than 1.0, the project has more than average corporate risk, and vice versa if $b_{P,F}$ is less than 1.0. A higher than average corporate risk would probably lead to a higher than average project cost of capital, but there is no precise formula for specifying how much higher—the adjustment is a matter of judgment.

8. If the project's market beta, $b_{P,M}$, is equal to the firm's market beta, then the project has the same degree of market risk as an average project, while if $b_{P,M}$ is greater than the firm's beta, then the project has more than average market risk, and vice versa if $b_{P,M}$ is less than the firm's beta. A higher than average project beta, where "average" is defined as the firm's market beta, would lead to an upward adjustment in the project's cost of capital, and the CAPM sometimes can be used to make the adjustment. We discuss this adjustment process later in the chapter.

9. People occasionally argue that stand-alone and corporate risk as we have defined them are not important—if a firm seeks to maximize shareholders' wealth, the only relevant risk is market risk. This position is not correct for the following reasons:

    a. Undiversified stockholders, including the owners of small businesses, are more concerned about corporate risk than about market risk.

b. Many financial theorists argue that investors, even those who are well diversified, consider factors other than market risk when setting required returns. One such factor is the risk of financial distress, which depends on a firm's corporate risk. Empirical studies of the determinants of required rates of return generally find both market and corporate risk to be important.

c. The firm's stability is important to all the firm's stakeholders, including its managers, workers, customers, suppliers, creditors, and the community in which it operates. Firms that are in serious danger of bankruptcy, or even of suffering low profits and reduced output, have difficulty attracting and retaining good managers and workers. Also, both suppliers and customers are reluctant to depend on weak firms, and such firms have difficulty borrowing money except at high interest rates. These factors will tend to reduce risky firms' profitability, hence the prices of their stocks.

For these reasons, corporate risk is also important, even to well-diversified stockholders.

SELF-TEST QUESTIONS

What are the three types of project risk, and how are they measured?

How are the three types of risk related?

Why should managers be concerned with a project's corporate risk as well as its market risk?

STAND-ALONE RISK

A project's stand-alone risk is of little interest in and of itself. It is relevant only to single-project firms with undiversified shareholders. However, as we saw earlier, stand-alone risk is an important determinant (along with the correlation coefficients) of both within-firm and market risk. Therefore, firms spend a great deal of time and effort assessing stand-alone risk.

The starting point for analyzing a project's stand-alone risk involves determining the uncertainty inherent in the project's cash flows. This analysis can be handled in a number of ways, ranging from informal judgments to complex economic and statistical analyses involving large-scale computer models. To illustrate what is involved, let's refer back to RIC Technologies' watering system computer project that we discussed in Chapter 10. Most of the individual cash flows in Tables 10-3, 10-4, and 10-5, which produced the expected net cash flows for the project as set forth in Table 10-6, are subject to uncertainty. For example, sales for 1997 were projected at 25,000 units to be sold at a net price of $2,200 per unit, or $55 million in total. However, unit sales would almost certainly be somewhat higher or lower than 25,000, and the sales price would probably be different from $2,200 per unit. In effect, the sales quantity and price estimates are really expected values taken from probability distributions, as are many of the other values listed in Tables 10-3 through 10-5. The distributions could be relatively "tight," reflecting

small standard deviations and low risk, or they could be "flat," denoting a great deal of uncertainty about the variable in question, hence a high degree of stand-alone risk.

The nature of the individual cash flow distributions, and their correlations with one another, determine the nature of the project's NPV and IRR distributions, and thus the project's stand-alone risk. In the following sections, we discuss four techniques for assessing a project's stand-alone risk: (1) sensitivity analysis, (2) scenario analysis, (3) Monte Carlo simulation, and (4) decision tree analysis.

SENSITIVITY ANALYSIS

Intuitively, we know that many of the variables which determine a project's cash flows are subject to some type of probability distribution rather than known with certainty. We also know that if a key input variable such as units sold changes, so will the project's NPV and IRR. *Sensitivity analysis is a technique which indicates exactly how much the NPV or IRR will change in response to a given change in a single input variable, other things held constant.*

Sensitivity analysis begins with a *base case* situation developed using the expected input values. To illustrate, consider the data given in Table 10-4 in Chapter 10, where projected cash flow statements for RIC's computer project are shown. The values for unit sales, sales price, fixed costs, and variable costs are the *expected*, or *base case, values,* and the resulting $12,075,384 NPV shown in Table 10-6 is called the *base case NPV.* Now we ask a series of "what if" questions: "What if unit sales fall 20 percent below the expected level?" "What if the sales price per unit falls?" "What if variable costs are 70 percent of dollar sales rather than the expected 65 percent?" *Sensitivity analysis is designed to provide the decision maker with answers to questions such as these.*

In a sensitivity analysis, we usually change each variable by several specific percentages above and below the expected value (holding other things constant), then calculate new NPVs, and finally plot the derived NPVs against the variable that was changed. Figure 11-2 shows the computer project's sensitivity graphs for three of the key input variables. The table below the graphs gives the NPVs that were used to construct the graphs. The slopes of the lines in the graphs show how sensitive the project's NPV is to changes in each of the inputs: the steeper the slope, the more sensitive the NPV is to a change in the variable. Here we see that the project's NPV is very sensitive to changes in variable costs, fairly sensitive to changes in sales volume, and relatively insensitive to changes in the cost of capital.

If we were comparing two projects, the one with the steeper sensitivity lines would be regarded as riskier because a relatively small error in estimating a variable such as the variable cost per unit would produce a large error in the project's projected NPV. Thus, sensitivity analysis can provide useful insights into the riskiness of a project.

Before we move on, note these two additional points about sensitivity analysis. First, computer spreadsheet models are ideally suited for performing sensitivity analyses, because such models automatically recalculate NPV when an input value

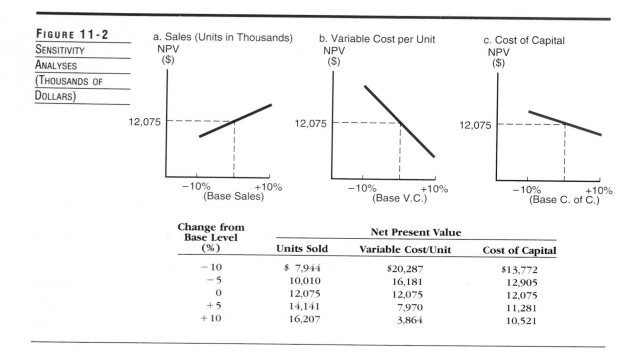

FIGURE 11-2
SENSITIVITY
ANALYSES
(THOUSANDS OF
DOLLARS)

Change from Base Level (%)	Net Present Value		
	Units Sold	Variable Cost/Unit	Cost of Capital
−10	$ 7,944	$20,287	$13,772
−5	10,010	16,181	12,905
0	12,075	12,075	12,075
+5	14,141	7,970	11,281
+10	16,207	3,864	10,521

is changed. We used a *Lotus 1-2-3* model to conduct the analyses represented in Figure 11-2, both the tabular data and the graphs. Second, we could have plotted all of the sensitivity lines on one graph; this would have facilitated direct comparisons of the sensitivities among different input variables.

SCENARIO ANALYSIS

Although sensitivity analysis is probably the most widely used risk analysis technique, it does have some limitations. Consider, for example, a proposed coal mine whose NPV is highly sensitive to changes in output and sales prices. However, if a utility company has contracted to buy a fixed amount of coal at a fixed price per ton, plus inflation adjustments, then the mining venture may be quite safe in spite of its steep sensitivity lines. *In general, a project's stand-alone risk depends on both (1) the sensitivity of its NPV to changes in key variables and (2) the range of likely values of these variables as reflected in their probability distributions.* Because sensitivity analysis considers only the first factor, it is incomplete.

One risk analysis technique that considers both the sensitivity of NPV to changes in key variables and the range of likely variable values is *scenario analysis.* Here the financial analyst asks operating managers to pick a "bad" set of circumstances (low unit sales, low sales price, high variable cost per unit, high construction cost, and so on), an average, or "most likely" set, and a "good" set. The

TABLE 11-1 SCENARIO ANALYSIS	Scenario	Sales Volume (Units)	Sales Price	NPV (Thousands) ×	Probability of Outcome =	Product
	Worst case	15,000	$1,700	($10,079)	0.25	($ 2,520)
	Most likely case	25,000	2,200	12,075	0.50	6,038
	Best case	35,000	2,700	41,752	0.25	10,438
					Expected NPV =	$13,956
					σ_{NPV} =	$18,421

Note: Variables other than unit sales and sales price were set at their expected values.

NPVs under the "bad" and "good" conditions are then calculated and compared with the "most likely" NPV.

As an example, let us return to the watering system computer project. Assume that RIC's managers are fairly confident of their estimates of all the project's cash flow variables except price and unit sales. Further, suppose they regard a drop in unit sales below 15,000 or a rise above 35,000 units as being extremely unlikely, and they expect the sales price as set in the marketplace to fall within the range of $1,700 to $2,700. Thus, 15,000 units at a price of $1,700 defines the lower bound, or the *worst-case scenario,* while 35,000 units at a price of $2,700 defines the upper bound, or the *best-case scenario.* Remember that the most likely values (which are the same as the base case values in this example) are 25,000 units at a price of $2,200. Also, note that the indicated sales prices are for 1997, with future years' prices expected to rise because of inflation.

To complete the scenario analysis, we use the worst-case variable values to obtain the worst-case NPV and the best-case variable values to obtain the best-case NPV.[1] We performed the analysis using a *Lotus* model, and Table 11-1 summarizes the results. We see that the most likely case forecasts a positive NPV; the worst case produces a negative NPV; and the best case results in a very large positive NPV. We can now use these results to determine the expected NPV, standard deviation of NPV, and coefficient of variation of NPV. For this, we need an estimate of the probabilities of occurrence of the three scenarios. Suppose management estimates that there is a 25 percent probability of the worst case occurring, a 50 percent probability of the most likely case, and a 25 percent probability of the best case. Of course, it is *very difficult* to estimate scenario probabilities accurately.

Table 11-1 contains a discrete probability distribution of returns just like those we dealt with in Chapter 4, except that the returns are measured in dollars (NPV)

---

[1]We could have included worst- and best-case values for fixed and variable costs, the inflation rate, salvage values, and so on. For illustrative purposes, we limited the changes to only two variables. Also, note that we are treating sales price and quantity as independent variables; that is, a low sales price could occur when unit sales were low, and a high sales price could be coupled with high unit sales, or vice versa. As we discuss in the next section, it is relatively easy to vary these assumptions if the facts of the situation suggest a different set of conditions.

rather than in percentages (rate of return). The expected NPV (in thousands of dollars) is

$$0.25(-\$10{,}079) + 0.50(\$12{,}075) + 0.25(\$41{,}752) = \$13{,}956.$$

Note that the expected NPV is *not* the same as the base case NPV, $12,075 (in thousands). This is because the two uncertain variables, sales volume and sales price, are multiplied together to get dollar sales, and this process causes the NPV distribution to be skewed to the right. (A big number times another big number produces a very big number, which in turn causes the average, or expected value, to be increased.) The standard deviation of NPV is $18,421 (in thousands of dollars):[2]

$$\sigma_{NPV} = [0.25(-\$10{,}079 - \$13{,}956)^2 + 0.50(\$12{,}075 - \$13{,}956)^2$$
$$+ 0.25(\$41{,}752 - \$13{,}956)^2]^{1/2} = \$18{,}421.$$

Finally, the project's coefficient of variation of NPV is 1.3:

$$CV_{NPV} = \frac{\sigma_{NPV}}{E(NPV)} = \frac{\$18{,}421}{\$13{,}956} = 1.3.$$

---

[2]If we had a probability distribution for the net cash flows for each year of a project's life, then we could calculate the expected net cash flow for each year, CF_t, and the variance of that cash flow, σ_t^2. We could then calculate the expected NPV as

$$E(NPV) = \sum_{t=0}^{n} \frac{CF_t}{(1 + k)^t}. \qquad (11\text{-}1)$$

If the net cash flow distributions across time were normal and were not correlated with one another (intertemporally independent), then the standard deviation of the NPV would be calculated as follows:

$$\text{Independent cash flow case: } \sigma_{NPV} = \left[\sum_{t=0}^{n} \frac{\sigma_t^2}{(1 + k)^{2t}}\right]^{1/2}. \qquad (11\text{-}2)$$

If the net cash flow distributions from one year to the next were normal and were completely dependent on one another (intertemporally dependent) such that the correlation coefficient between them is 1.0, then σ_{NPV} would be calculated as

$$\text{Dependent cash flow case: } \sigma_{NPV} = \sum_{t=0}^{n} \frac{\sigma_t}{(1 + k)^t}. \qquad (11\text{-}3)$$

See Frederick S. Hillier, "The Derivation of Probabilistic Information for the Evaluation of Risky Investments," *Management Science*, April 1963, 443–457. Although Hillier's approach to finding projects' standard deviations is relatively simple, it is rarely used in practice because (1) many project cash flow distributions are not normal and (2) most project cash flow distributions over time are neither totally independent nor perfectly positively correlated. Still, Hillier's model does show that if a project's cash flows are independent across time (that is, fluctuate randomly from year to year), the project is less risky than if cash flows are dependent, because for a given set of σ_t, Equation 11-2 produces a lower σ_{NPV} than Equation 11-3.

The project's coefficient of variation of NPV can be compared with the coefficient of variation of RIC's "average" asset to get an idea of the relative stand-alone riskiness of the project. RIC's existing assets have an aggregate coefficient of variation of about 1.0. Thus, on the basis of this stand-alone total risk measure, RIC's managers would conclude that the computer project is riskier than the firm's "average" project.

While scenario analysis provides useful information about a project's standalone risk, it is limited in that it only considers a few discrete outcomes (NPVs) for the project, although there are in reality an infinite number of possibilities. In the next section, we describe a method of assessing a project's stand-alone risk which deals with this problem.

MONTE CARLO SIMULATION

Monte Carlo simulation, so named because this type of analysis grew out of work on the mathematics of casino gambling, ties together sensitivities and input variable probabilities.[3] The first step in a computer simulation is to specify the probability distribution of each uncertain cash flow variable such as sales price and sales quantity. Continuous distributions, which allow analysts to specify only a mean and standard deviation, or a lower limit, most likely value, and upper limit, are usually used for this purpose. Once this has been done, the simulation proceeds as follows:

1. The simulation software chooses at random a value for each uncertain variable, based on its specified probability distribution. For example, a value for unit sales, for variable costs per unit, and so forth would be chosen.

2. The value selected for each uncertain variable, along with values for the certain variables such as the tax rate and depreciation charges, is then used by the model to determine the net cash flows for each year, and these cash flows are then used to determine the project's NPV for this particular computer run.

3. Steps 1 and 2 are repeated many times, say 1,000, resulting in 1,000 NPVs, which make up a probability distribution with its own expected value and standard deviation.

Using this procedure, we can perform a simulation analysis on RIC's computer project. As in our scenario analysis, we have simplified the illustration by specifying the distributions for only two key variables, unit sales and sales price. For all the other variables, we merely specified their expected values.

In our simulation analysis, we assumed that sales price can be represented by a continuous normal distribution. Suppose the expected value is $2,200, and sup-

---

[3]The use of simulation analysis in capital budgeting was first reported by David B. Hertz, "Risk Analysis in Capital Investments," *Harvard Business Review,* January-February 1964, 95–106.

TABLE 11-2	Probability of NPV Being Greater than the Indicated Value (Thousands of Dollars)								
SUMMARY OF									
SIMULATION RESULTS **Probability**	0.90	0.80	0.70	0.60	0.50	0.40	0.30	0.20	0.10
NPV	($2,114)	$2,577	$6,153	$8,993	$11,637	$14,740	$17,797	$21,417	$26,424

NPV Distribution Statistics
(Thousands of Dollars)

Expected NPV	$12,096
Maximum NPV	$46,755
Minimum NPV	($13,888)
NPV range	$60,643
Probability of NPV > 0	85.7%
Probability of NPV < 0	14.3%
Standard deviation	$10,724
Skewness	0.15[a]

[a]Positive skewness indicates that the NPV distribution is skewed to the right.

pose further that the actual sales price is not likely to vary by more than $500 from the expected value, that is, to fall below $1,700 or rise above $2,700. We know that in a normal distribution, the expected value plus or minus three standard deviations will encompass virtually the entire distribution, which implies that three standard deviations of the sales price would be about $500. Therefore, as a reasonable approximation, we assumed that $\sigma_{Sales\ price} = \$500/3 = \$166.67 \approx \$167$, so we tell the computer to assume that the sales price distribution is normal, with an expected value of $2,200 and a standard deviation of $167.

Next, we assumed that the estimated distribution of unit sales is also symmetric, that it has an expected value of 25,000 units, and that sales could be as high as 40,000 units, given our production capacity, if demand is strong, but that if public acceptance is poor, sales could be as low as 10,000 units. We could have again specified a normal distribution, but in the case of unit sales, we felt that a triangular distribution, with a most likely (and expected) value of 25,000, a lower limit of 10,000, and an upper limit of 40,000, is most appropriate.

We used these data plus a *Lotus* add-in program called *@RISK* to conduct the simulation. The output is summarized in Table 11-2, and the resulting NPV probability distribution is plotted in Figure 11-3. Reading across the top of the table, we see that there is a 90 percent probability that NPV will exceed − $2,114,000. Thus, there is a 10 percent probability of NPV being equal to or less than − $2,114,000. In the lower part of the table, we see that there is a 14.3 percent chance that the project would have a negative NPV, hence an 85.7 percent probability of an NPV greater than zero. Also, note that the simulation output includes the NPV's expected value (mean) and standard deviation. Thus, the project's coefficient of

FIGURE 11-3

NPV PROBABILITY
DISTRIBUTION
(THOUSANDS OF
DOLLARS)

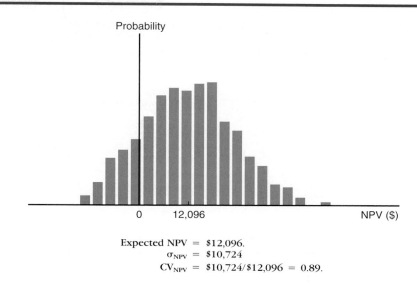

Expected NPV = $12,096.

σ_{NPV} = $10,724

CV_{NPV} = $10,724/$12,096 = 0.89.

variation of NPV can be calculated, and the project's stand-alone risk can be esti-mated in the same way as in our discussion of scenario analysis.[4]

In spite of its obvious appeal, simulation analysis has not been as widely used in industry as one might expect. One of the major problems is specifying each uncertain variable's probability distribution and the correlations among the distri-butions. Mechanically, it is easy to incorporate any type of correlation among var-iables into a simulation analysis; for example, *@RISK* permits us to specify both intervariable and intertemporal correlations. However, it is *not* easy to specify what the correlations should be. Indeed, people who have tried to obtain such relationships from the operating managers who must estimate them have elo-quently emphasized the difficulties involved. Clearly, the problem is not insur-mountable, and simulation is being used in business with increasing frequency.

---

[4]Note that the standard deviation of NPV in the simulation is much smaller than the standard deviation we obtained in the scenario analysis. In the scenario analysis, we assumed that the low unit sales figure would be coupled with the low sales price for the worst case, and high values for each for the best case. That is, we assumed that these variables were *dependent* on one another, so high unit sales would mean high price, and vice versa. Thus, we ended up with only three NPVs, and a 25 percent probability of the worst (or best) case occurring.

In the simulation, we assumed that unit sales and price are *independent* of one another. Thus, in the simulation a high unit sales number could be picked, and in the same run the computer could choose a low sales price. When the two variables are independent, the probability of a very low unit sales coupled with a very low sales price, hence an extremely low revenue and a large loss, is remote. Further, in a simulation there are many possible values for each uncertain variable, while in a scenario analysis there is a discrete number (3 in our example). These two differences led to a lower standard deviation in the simulation analysis.

Still, it is important not to underestimate the difficulty of obtaining valid estimates of variables' probability distributions, and correlations among the distributions.[5]

Another problem with both scenario and simulation analyses is that even when the analysis has been completed, no clear-cut decision rule emerges. We end up with an expected NPV and a distribution about this expected value, which we can use to judge the project's stand-alone risk. However, the analysis provides no mechanism to indicate whether a project's profitability as measured by its expected NPV is sufficient to compensate for its risk as measured by σ_{NPV} or CV_{NPV}.

Finally, since scenario and simulation analyses focus on a project's stand-alone risk, they ignore the effects of diversification, both among projects within the firm and by investors in their personal investment portfolios. Thus, an individual project may have highly uncertain returns when evaluated on a "stand-alone" basis, but if those returns are not correlated with the returns on the firm's other assets or with the returns on a stock portfolio, then the project may not be very risky in terms of either within-firm or market risk. Indeed, if the project's returns are negatively correlated with the returns on the firm's other assets, then it may decrease the firm's corporate risk, and the larger its σ_{NPV}, the more it will reduce the firm's overall risk. Similarly, if a project's returns are not positively correlated with the stock market, then even a project with highly variable returns might not be regarded as risky by well-diversified stockholders, who are normally more concerned with market risk than with stand-alone or within-firm risk.

DECISION TREE ANALYSIS

Up to this point, we have focused primarily on techniques for estimating a project's stand-alone riskiness. Although this is an integral part of capital budgeting, managers are much more concerned about *reducing* risk than they are about *measuring* it. Often, project expenditures are not made at one point in time, but, rather, are made over a period of years, which gives managers the opportunity to reevaluate decisions and either invest additional funds or cancel (abandon) the project. Projects that are structured to permit capital outlays to be made over several years are often evaluated using *decision trees.*

For example, suppose the U.S. subsidiary of Advanced Robotics Ltd., is considering the production of industrial robots for the television manufacturing industry. The net investment for this project will be broken down into three stages, as set forth in Figure 11-4 and described below.

Stage 1.   At t = 0, which in this case is sometime in the near future, conduct a $500,000 study of the market potential for using robots in television assembly lines.

---

[5]For an interesting discussion of the pros and cons of simulation analysis, see Wilbur G. Lewellen and Michael S. Long, "Simulation versus Single-Value Estimates in Capital Expenditure Analysis," *Decision Sciences,* October 1972, 19–33. For more insight into the difficulties involved in estimating probability distributions and correlations in practice, see K. Larry Hastie, "One Businessman's View of Capital Budgeting," *Financial Management,* Winter 1974, 36–43. Hastie was treasurer of Bendix Corporation.

SELF-TEST QUESTIONS

Define stand-alone risk.

Briefly describe the mechanics of sensitivity analysis, scenario analysis, Monte Carlo simulation, and decision tree analysis.

What are the advantages and disadvantages of each type of stand-alone risk analysis?

THE IMPACT OF ABANDONMENT ON NPV AND STAND-ALONE RISK

In Chapter 10 we introduced the concept of abandonment value. We now show how the possibility of abandonment can affect a project's risk as well as its expected NPV. Suppose Advanced Robotics is not contractually bound to continue the industrial robot project once operations have begun. Thus, if sales are poor and cash flows amount to only − $2,000 during Year 3, the first year of operations, and a similar cash flow situation is expected for the remainder of the project's life, the firm can abandon the project at the beginning of Year 4 rather than continue to suffer losses over the next 3 years. (In this case, low first-year cash flows signify that the product is not well received in the market, hence that future sales will be poor. In other cases, the cash flows could vary from year to year depending on economic conditions, in which case low first-year sales and cash flows might be followed by high cash flows in subsequent years.)

The ability to abandon the project changes the branch of the decision tree in Figure 11-4 that contains the series of $2,000 losses. It now looks like this:

	Joint Probability	NPV	Product: Prob. × NPV
	0.144	(10,883)	(1,567)

Changing this branch to reflect abandonment eliminates the $2 million cash losses in Years 4, 5, and 6, and thus causes the NPV for the branch to be less negative. This increases the project's expected NPV from − $338,000 to about $166,000, and also lowers its standard deviation from $7,991,000 to $7,157,000. Thus, abandonment changes the project's NPV from negative to positive and also lowers its stand-alone risk as measured by either the standard deviation or the coefficient of variation.

Here are some additional points to note concerning decision tree analysis and abandonment possibilities:

1. Managers can reduce project risk if they can structure the decision process to include several decision points rather than just one. To illustrate, if Advanced Robotics were to make a total commitment at t = 0, signing contracts that would in effect require completion of the project, it might save some money and accelerate the project, but in doing so it would substantially increase the project's riskiness.

2. Once production begins, the ability to shut down or spin off the project can also dramatically reduce its risk. Indeed, firms do this frequently. To illustrate,

General Motors, IBM, and other companies have been closing plants to cut their losses in recent years.

3. The cost of abandonment is generally reduced if the firm has alternative uses for the project's assets. If Advanced Robotics could use its TV robot production equipment for a planned expansion of its auto robot production facilities, then the TV robot project could be more easily abandoned, hence its riskiness would be reduced.

4. Finally, note that capital budgeting is a dynamic process. Virtually all inputs to a capital budgeting decision change over time, so firms must periodically review both their capital expenditure plans and their ongoing projects. In the Advanced Robotics example, conditions might change between Decision Points 1 and 2, and if so, this new information should be used to develop revised probability and cash flow estimates.

A dramatic example of both good and bad abandonment decisions is nuclear power plant construction. When the demand for electric power dropped sharply in the late 1970s, and construction costs rose in the aftermath of the Three Mile Island accident, some utilities reexamined their nuclear plant construction plans and decided to cancel plants. This required write-offs amounting to millions of dollars. Other companies decided to keep building, and they ended up losing literally billions of dollars.

The key concept to remember is that decisions can often be structured with multiple decision points; if so, and if the company has the willpower to admit it when a project is not working out as initially planned, then risks can be reduced, and expected cash flows can be increased.

SELF-TEST QUESTIONS

How can the possibility of abandonment affect a project's profitability and stand-alone risk?

What are the costs and benefits of structuring large capital budgeting decisions in stages rather than as a single go/no-go decision?

CORPORATE, OR WITHIN-FIRM, RISK

In a previous section, we described four methods for measuring a project's stand-alone risk. However, we know that the type of risk that is generally most relevant to managers, employees, creditors, and suppliers is the project's corporate, or within-firm, risk, while a project's market risk is most relevant to well-diversified stockholders. A project's corporate risk is the contribution of the project to the firm's overall total risk, or, put another way, the way the project affects the variability of the firm's consolidated cash flows. Corporate risk is a function of both the project's standard deviation and its correlation with the returns on the firm's

This suggests that debt and equity investors should be willing to give RIC Technologies money to invest in average-risk projects that are financed in the usual manner if the company could earn 11.5 percent or more on this money. In this case, the term "average risk" means projects which have *market* risk — which is the risk that concerns the investors who supply capital to the company — similar to that of the firm's existing assets.

Now recall that a firm is a portfolio of assets, and its beta as established in the equity market is an average of the betas of each of the firm's projects. Therefore, if taking on a particular project will cause a change in RIC's 1.8 beta coefficient, then taking on the project will also cause a change in the company's cost of equity.[7] For example, the watering system computer project might have a beta, if financed at the target capital structure, of 2.5, so taking it on would cause RIC's stock beta to rise, and it will end up somewhere between its original value of 1.8 and the new project's beta of 2.5. RIC's new beta will depend on the relative size of the investment in the computer project versus the company's investment in other assets. If 80 percent of RIC's equity would be invested in other assets with an average beta of 1.8, and 20 percent in the new project with a beta of 2.5, then the firm's new beta would be 1.94, up from 1.8:

$$\text{New } b = 0.8(1.8) + 0.2(2.5) = 1.94.$$

This increase in RIC's equity risk would cause the stock price to decline *unless the increased beta were offset by a higher expected overall rate of return on equity.* Specifically, taking on the new project would cause the required rate of return on equity to rise from 17.0 to 17.7 percent,

$$k_s = 8\% + (5\%)1.94 = 17.7\%,$$

and RIC's overall cost of capital would rise from 11.5 to 11.85 percent:

$$\text{WACC} = 0.5(10\%)(0.60) + 0.5(17.7\%) = 11.85\%.$$

Therefore, to keep the computer project from lowering the value of the firm, RIC's expected rate of return on assets would have to rise from 11.5 to 11.85 percent.

If RIC's original assets must earn 11.5 percent, how much must the new project earn in order for the new overall rate of return to equal 11.85 percent? We know that if it completes the new project, RIC would have 80 percent of its assets invested in other assets which must earn 11.5 percent, that 20 percent of its assets would be in the new project which must earn X percent, and that the average required rate of return would be 11.85 percent. Therefore,

---

[7]Acceptance of the project would probably also change the firm's cost of debt. However, since debt represents a contractual obligation, while equity is a claim on residual cash flows, the impact on the cost of equity is typically much greater than the impact on the cost of debt. We will ignore any impact on the cost of debt in this section.

$$0.8(11.5\%) + 0.2X = 11.85\%$$
$$0.2X = 11.85\% - 9.20\%$$
$$X = 2.65\%/0.2 = 13.25\%.$$

Thus, the computer project must have an expected return on assets (IRR) of 13.25 percent if the corporation is to earn its new cost of capital.

In summary, if RIC takes on the new project, its beta would rise from 1.8 to 1.94; its cost of equity would increase from 17.0 to 17.7 percent; its weighted average cost of capital would rise from 11.5 to 11.85 percent; and the new project would have to earn at least 13.25 percent for RIC to earn its overall cost of capital.

This line of reasoning leads to the conclusion that if the beta coefficient for each project, b_i, could be estimated, then an individual project's weighted average cost of capital, $WACC_i$, could be found as follows:

1. Find Project i's required rate of return on equity, k_{si}:

$$k_{si} = k_{RF} + (k_M - k_{RF})b_i.$$

2. Use k_{si} to find the project's overall required rate of return, $WACC_i$:

$$WACC_i = w_d k_d(1 - T) + w_{ce}k_{si}.$$

Applying these two steps to RIC's new project gives this result:

$$k_{si} = 8\% + (5\%)2.5 = 20.5\%,$$

and

$$WACC_i = 0.5(10\%)(0.60) + 0.5(20.5\%) = 13.25\%.$$

We see that the required rate of return on the watering system computer project is the same using this "short-cut" method as it was when we developed the project's cost of capital by solving for X in the equation $11.85\% = 0.8(11.5) + 0.2X$. Note, however, that both solutions disregard any effects of the new project on either the firm's capital structure or its cost of debt; implicitly, we assumed that the cost of the debt used to support the new project, and the financing mix, would be the same as for the firm's existing assets.

TECHNIQUES FOR MEASURING MARKET RISK

In Chapter 8, when we discussed the estimation of firms' betas, we indicated that it is difficult to estimate "true future betas" for common stocks. The estimation of *project* betas is even more difficult and more fraught with uncertainty, primarily because individual operating assets pay no dividends and have no quoted market

prices, and hence we cannot calculate historical market-return betas for use in the analysis. However, two approaches have been used for estimating the betas of individual assets: (1) the pure play method and (2) the accounting beta method.

The Pure Play Method. In the *pure play method,* the company tries to find one or more single-product companies in the same line of business as the project being evaluated.[8] For example, suppose RIC could find several existing single-product firms that produced lawn watering computer systems. Further, suppose RIC believes that its new project would be subject to the same risks as those of the other firms. It could then determine the betas of these firms by the regular regression process, average them, and use this average as a proxy for the project's beta.

To illustrate, assume that RIC's analysts have identified three publicly owned companies engaged only in the production and distribution of watering system computers. Further, assume that the average beta of these firms is 2.5. Then, the computer project's cost of equity and its WACC would be:

$$k_{si} = 8\% + (13\% - 8\%)2.50 = 20.5\%.$$

$$WACC_i = 0.5(10\%)(0.60) + 0.5(20.5\%) = 13.25\%.$$

These values are consistent with those we calculated earlier.[9]

The pure play approach is often difficult to implement because it is difficult to find pure play proxy firms. For our illustration, we assumed the existence of three pure play proxies. In reality, there is no pure play manufacturer of watering system computers. In fact, most systems are made by GE, Honeywell, and other large, multidivisional firms, and their control systems' operations are combined with their other operations in a manner that makes it impossible to ascertain market betas for a product such as a watering system computer. However, there are times when the method is feasible. For example, when IBM was considering going into personal computers, it was able to get data on Apple Computer and several other essentially pure play personal computer companies. Similarly, Pillsbury is able to employ this technique when it is considering capital budgeting decisions in its Burger King, Godfather's Pizza, Steak and Ale, and Bennigan's divisions.

The Accounting Beta Method. As previously noted, it is often not possible to find single-product, publicly traded firms suitable for the pure play approach. When this is the case, companies sometimes use the *accounting beta method.* As you know, betas are normally found by regressing the returns on a particular compa-

---

[8]One important article on this subject is Russell J. Fuller and Halbert S. Kerr, "Estimating the Divisional Cost of Capital: An Analysis of the Pure-Play Technique," *Journal of Finance,* December 1981, 997–1009. Fuller and Kerr used the method to estimate divisional betas and then tested the results empirically. They concluded that the pure play method is a valid technique for estimating the betas of major subparts of a firm.

[9]Our discussion here is somewhat simplified. The proxy betas reflect each proxy firm's capital structure and tax rate. If the proxy firms' average capital structure or tax rate is different from the financing mix that the evaluating firm would use, then the proxy beta must be adjusted to account for this difference. We will discuss a procedure for making this adjustment in Chapter 12.

ny's stock against returns on a stock market index. However, one could run a regression of the company's basic earning power (Earnings before interest and taxes/Total assets) against the average basic earning power for a large sample of stocks such as the NYSE or the S&P 500. Such data are readily available from Standard & Poor's Compustat tapes. Betas determined in this manner, using accounting data rather than stock market data, are called *accounting betas.*

Historical accounting betas can be calculated for all types of companies (publicly owned or privately held, or even not-for-profit), for divisions, or even for certain types of large projects. But how good are accounting betas as proxies for market betas? Many studies have addressed this issue.[10] Although the results vary, most studies do support the conclusion that firms with high accounting betas tend to have high market betas, whereas firms with low accounting betas tend to have low market betas. However, the correlations are generally only in the 0.5 to 0.6 range, so accounting-determined betas provide only rough approximations for market-determined betas, market risk, and consequently the cost of capital.

Note that the accounting beta method described here is similar to the procedure discussed earlier to estimate a project's within-firm, or corporate, risk. The only difference is that when measuring corporate risk, the regression is run on the firm's returns rather than on the average return of firms in a stock market index. Also, the accounting beta technique can be used to estimate different divisions' within-firm risk. Here the firm's overall accounting rate of return would be used as the benchmark, and the results would reflect the degree of correlation between different divisions.

SELF-TEST QUESTIONS

What is the difference between corporate risk and market risk?

Briefly describe two techniques that can be used to estimate a project's market risk.

Summarize your views regarding both the relevance and the ease of determining a project's stand-alone risk, corporate risk, and market risk.

RISK-ADJUSTED DISCOUNT RATES VERSUS CERTAINTY EQUIVALENTS

Thus far, we have seen that capital budgeting can affect a firm's market risk, its corporate risk, or both. We have also seen that it is exceedingly difficult to quantify either type of risk. In other words, it may be possible to reach the general conclusion that one project is riskier than another (in either the market, the corporate,

---

[10]One key work on this subject was William H. Beaver and James Manegold, "The Association between Market-Determined Measures of Systematic Risk: Some Further Evidence," *Journal of Financial and Quantitative Analysis,* June 1975, 231–284. That study, and many subsequent ones, are summarized in George Foster, *Financial Statement Analysis* (Englewood Cliffs, N.J.: Prentice-Hall, 1986).

or the stand-alone sense), but it is difficult to develop a really good *measure* of project risk. Further, this lack of precision in measuring project risk makes it difficult to incorporate differential risk into capital budgeting decisions.

Still, two methods have been developed for incorporating project risk into the capital budgeting decision process. One is the *certainty equivalent* method, in which the expected cash flows in each year are adjusted to reflect project risk—risky cash flows are reduced, and the riskier the flows, the greater the reduction. Then, the stream of "certainty equivalent cash flows" is discounted by the risk-free rate. The second procedure is the *risk-adjusted discount rate* method, in which riskier projects are evaluated using a higher discount rate—average-risk projects are discounted at the firm's WACC, above-average risk projects are discounted at a higher cost of capital, and below-average risk projects are discounted at a rate below the firm's WACC.

Risk-adjusted discount rates lump together the time value of money as represented by the risk-free rate and risk as represented by a risk premium: $k = k_{RF} + RP$. On the other hand, the certainty equivalent approach keeps risk and time value separate because risk is incorporated in the numerator of the NPV equation rather than in the denominator. This separation gives a theoretical advantage to certainty equivalents.[11] However, the risk-adjusted discount rate method is more frequently used in practice.

A firm using the risk-adjusted discount rate approach for its capital budgeting decisions will have an overall cost of capital that reflects its overall market-determined riskiness. This rate should be used for "average" projects, that is, projects which have the same risk as the firm's existing assets. Lower rates should be used for less risky projects, and higher rates should be used for riskier projects. Further, as typically applied in practice, the risk-adjusted discount rate approach uses a constant discount rate.

Consciously or unconsciously, the use of a constant k assumes that risk increases with time, and it therefore imposes a relatively severe burden on long-term projects.[12] This means that short-payoff alternatives will tend to be selected over those with longer payoffs when, for example, there are alternative ways of performing a given task.

However, there may be a substantial number of projects for which distant returns are *not* more risky than short-term returns. For example, the estimated returns on a water pipeline serving a developing community may be quite uncertain in the short run, because the rate of growth of the community is uncertain. However, the water company may be quite sure that in time the community will be fully developed and will utilize the full capacity of the pipeline. Similar situ-

---

[11]See Alexander A. Robichek and Stewart C. Myers, "Conceptual Problems in the Use of Risk-Adjusted Discount Rates," *Journal of Finance,* December 1966, 727–730.

[12]The denominator of the NPV equation is, in effect, $(1 + k_{RF} + RP)^t$, where k_{RF} is the risk-free rate and RP is the risk premium for the cash flow in period t. Therefore, the RP term is compounded—as t gets larger, that is, as the cash flows are more distant, the denominator increases exponentially. The net result of compounding the risk premium over time is to impose an ever higher risk penalty as t gets larger and larger.

ations could exist in many public projects—sewer projects, highway programs, schools, and so forth; in public utility investment decisions; and when industrial firms are building plants, or retailers are building stores, to serve growing geographic markets.

To the extent that the implicit assumption of rising risk over time reflects the facts, then a constant discount rate may be appropriate. Indeed, in the majority of business situations, risk undoubtedly is an increasing function of time, so a constant risk-adjusted discount rate is generally reasonable. However, one should be aware of the relationships described in this section and avoid the pitfall of unwittingly penalizing long-term projects when they are not, in fact, more risky than short-term projects.

SELF-TEST QUESTIONS

Describe how the certainty equivalent approach can be used to incorporate risk into the capital budgeting decision.

Describe how the risk-adjusted discount rate approach is used.

What risk assumption is embedded in the use of a constant discount rate?

INCORPORATING RISK AND CAPITAL STRUCTURE INTO CAPITAL BUDGETING DECISIONS

Because of implementation problems with the certainty equivalent approach, firms generally use the risk-adjusted discount rate method to incorporate risk into the capital budgeting process—average-risk projects are discounted at the firm's WACC, above-average-risk projects are discounted at a higher cost of capital, and below-average-risk projects are discounted at a rate below the firm's WACC. Unfortunately, unless projects' betas can be estimated, there is no good way of specifying exactly *how much* higher or lower these discount rates should be—given the present state of the art, risk adjustments are necessarily judgmental, and somewhat arbitrary.

Capital structure should also be taken into account if a firm finances different assets in different ways. For example, one division might have a lot of real estate, which is well suited as collateral for loans, whereas some other division might have most of its capital tied up in special-purpose machinery, which is not good collateral. As a result, the division with the real estate might have a higher *debt capacity* than the machinery division, and thus an optimal capital structure which contains a higher percentage of debt. In this case, the division with more real estate contributes more to the overall debt capacity of the firm, and management might calculate its WACC using a higher debt ratio than for the other division.

Although the process is not exact, many companies use a two-step procedure to develop risk-adjusted discount rates for use in capital budgeting: (1) *Divisional costs of capital* are established for each of the major operating divisions on the

plant, with a PV cost of $3,016 million versus $3,090 million for the nuclear plant, would be chosen. This example illustrates both the problem that a negative out-flow can cause and an approach for dealing with the problem.[13]

SELF-TEST QUESTIONS

Describe some real-world situations in which risk adjustments must be applied to cash outflows.

How does the risk-adjustment process differ for cash outflows as compared to the process for cash inflows?

OUR VIEW OF PROJECT RISK ANALYSIS

It should be apparent that project risk analysis is far from precise. First, there are three types of risk that can be considered, and a project can be highly risky in one sense, say, corporate risk, but not very risky in another, say, market risk. Second, none of these risks can be measured very precisely. To help place all the issues in perspective, we present our view of the process in this section.

To begin, should managers place most emphasis on a project's stand-alone, corporate, or market, risk? First, note that stand-alone risk is truly relevant only to a start-up firm with one undiversified owner which is evaluating its first project. Thus, in most situations, a project's riskiness is measured better by its corporate risk, which takes into account the firm's whole portfolio of assets, than by its stand-alone risk. Second, well-diversified investors should be concerned primarily with market risk, and managers should be concerned primarily with stock price max-imization, and these two factors lead to the conclusion that market risk should be given the most weight in capital budgeting decisions. However, stockholders are concerned about costs resulting from financial distress, and these costs are not captured by market risk. Further, managers should be and are concerned about the firm's other stakeholders (bondholders, suppliers, employees, customers, and so on), and this implies that corporate risk should be taken into account. Thus, man-agers should consider both a project's corporate risk and its market risk when making capital budgeting decisions.

---

[13]The negative outflow problem could arise in a conventional NPV analysis as well as a PV of future costs analysis. For example, in the Toronto Development Company illustration, if the cash outflow at the end of the project's life was judged to be more risky than the cash inflows during the project's life, and if the outflow was discounted at a high risk-adjusted discount rate, then this would incorrectly bias the evaluation toward acceptance of the project. For more on the effects of negative cash flows, see Wilbur G. Lewellen, "Some Observations on Risk-Adjusted Discount Rates," *Journal of Finance,* September 1977, 1331–1337; and a comment on that paper by Stephen E. Celec and Richard H. Pettway, plus a reply by Lewellen, in the September 1979 issue of the *Journal,* 1061–1066. Pettway and Celec's analysis leads to a risk-adjustment process similar to the one contained in this section. Lewellen points out that even though an outflow may be risky in the stand-alone risk sense, this outflow may have correlations with the firm's other cash flows and/or the returns on the market such that its within-firm and/or market risk is equal to, or even less than, the firm's average risk.

In many cases it is impossible to quantify a project's market risk, or even its corporate risk, which leaves managers with only an assessment of the project's stand-alone risk. In most situations, the project being evaluated will be in the same line of business as the firm's other projects, and most firms' profitability is highly correlated with the national economy. Thus, stand-alone, corporate, and market risk are usually highly correlated, and in this case, a project with a high degree of stand-alone risk as measured by the coefficient of variation of NPV will also have high corporate and market risk. This suggests that managers can get a feel for the relative risk of most projects on the basis of such stand-alone risk measurement procedures as sensitivity analysis, scenario analysis, or simulation analysis.

The firm's overall WACC provides the starting point for estimating a project's risk-adjusted discount rate. If all projects were equally risky and had the same debt capacity, then they would all be evaluated using the firm's WACC. However, larger firms typically have several divisions that vary in risk, and projects within divisions can also have risk differences. The first step in developing a project's cost of capital calls for adjusting the firm's WACC to reflect divisional risk and debt capacity. Divisions with above-average risk or below-average debt capacity would be assigned a divisional WACC above the firm's overall WACC, while divisions with below-average risk or above-average debt capacity would be given a lower than average WACC. (Of course, the combined divisional WACCs must equal the firm's overall WACC.) A project is then assigned to a risk category on the basis of its own risk relative to the division's average risk. If a project is riskier than average for the division, then its risk-adjusted discount rate is set above the divisional WACC, and the opposite holds true if the project has below-average risk. Also, adjustments should be made when projects have debt capacities which differ widely from the divisional average. The most difficult part of this process is judging how large the divisional and project adjustments should be. If it is possible to assess the project's market risk, then the project's beta and the CAPM can be used to estimate the size of the adjustment. However, in most situations the adjustment is judgmental, and often a range of two to five percentage points is used.

The end result is a project discount rate and an NPV which incorporates, to the extent possible, the project's debt capacity and a judgment regarding the project's relative riskiness. Managers also must consider other possible risk factors that may not have been included in the analysis. For example, if the project could lead to litigation against the firm, then the project may have additional riskiness that should be taken into account—a number of drug and asbestos companies have learned this, to their regret. Conversely, if the project can easily be abandoned, or if the assets can easily be converted to other uses within the firm, then there might be less risk than appears in a standard analysis. Such additional factors must be considered subjectively in making the final accept/reject decision. Typically, if the project involves new products and is large relative to the firm's average project, then this factor will be very important to the final decision—one large mistake can bankrupt a firm, and bet-the-company decisions are not made lightly. On the other hand, if the project being considered is a small replacement project, then the decision would be made almost exclusively on the basis of a straight numerical analysis.

Ultimately, capital budgeting decisions require an analysis of the objective and subjective factors that determine a project's risk. The process is not precise, and often there is a temptation to ignore risk considerations because they are so nebulous. However, despite the imprecision and subjectiveness, a project's risk should be assessed and incorporated into the capital budgeting process. Not considering risk would be tantamount to ignoring one of the basic principles of finance — projects with higher risk require higher expected returns.

SELF-TEST QUESTIONS

Is project risk analysis a precise process?

Describe the process by which a project's risk and debt capacity are considered in capital budgeting decisions.

Describe some qualitative risk factors that managers should consider in the capital budgeting decision process that may not be included in the quantitative risk analysis.

THE OPTIMAL CAPITAL BUDGET

In Chapter 8, we developed the concept of the weighted average cost of capital (WACC). Then, in Chapters 9 and 10 and up to this point in Chapter 11, we have discussed how the cost of capital is used in project evaluations. However, capital budgeting and the cost of capital are actually interrelated — we cannot specify the cost of capital until we know the size of the capital budget, and we cannot determine the size of the capital budget until we specify the cost of capital. Therefore, as we show in the next sections, *the cost of capital and the capital budget must be determined simultaneously.* Swift Foods, a Midwestern grocery wholesaler, is used to illustrate the concepts involved.

THE INVESTMENT OPPORTUNITY SCHEDULE (IOS)

Consider first Figure 11-5, which gives some information on Swift's potential capital projects for next year. The tabular data show each project's cash flows, IRR, and payback. The graph is defined as the firm's *investment opportunity schedule (IOS),* which is a plot of each project's IRR, in descending order, versus the dollars of new capital required to finance it (the cash flow at t = 0). For example, Project B has an IRR of 38.5 percent, shown on the vertical axis, and a cost of $100,000, shown on the horizontal axis.[14] Notice also that Projects A and B are mutually

---

[14]Do not be concerned at this point by the fact that we use IRR in this analysis rather than MIRR or NPV. The fact is, we cannot calculate either MIRR or NPV until we know k, and we are using this analysis to develop a first-approximation estimate of k. Later on, we could switch to MIRR or NPV, but such a switch is not necessary for this type of analysis.

FIGURE 11-5

SWIFT FOODS: IOS
SCHEDULES

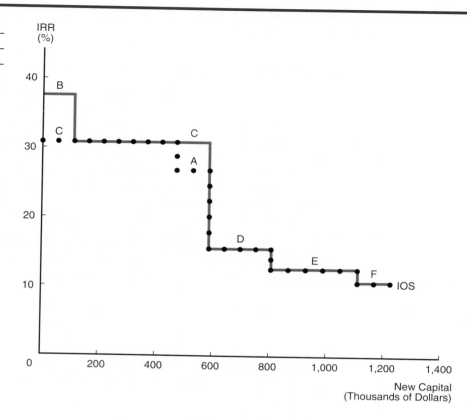

Potential Capital Projects

Year	Aª	Bª	C	D	E	F
0	($100,000)	($100,000)	($500,000)	($200,000)	($300,000)	($100,000)
1	10,000	90,000	190,000	52,800	98,800	58,781
2	70,000	60,000	190,000	52,800	98,800	58,781
3	100,000	10,000	190,000	52,800	98,800	—
4	—	—	190,000	52,800	98,800	—
5	—	—	190,000	52,800	—	—
6	—	—	190,000	52,800	—	—
IRR	27.0%	38.5%	30.2%	15.2%	12.0%	11.5%
Payback	2.2	1.2	2.6	3.8	3.0	1.7

ªProjects A and B are mutually exclusive.

exclusive. Thus, Swift has two possible IOS schedules: the one defined by the solid line, which contains Project B plus C, D, E, and F, and the one defined by the dotted line, which contains Project A plus C, D, E, and F. Beyond $600,000, the two IOS schedules are identical. Thus, the two alternative schedules differ only in that one contains B and has C ranked second, while the other contains A, in which

case C ranks first because $IRR_C > IRR_A$. For now, we assume that all six projects have the same risk as Swift's "average" project.

The Marginal Cost of Capital (MCC) Schedule

In Chapter 8, we discussed the concept of the weighted average cost of capital (WACC). However, the value of the WACC depends on the amount of new capital raised—the WACC will, at some point, rise if more and more capital is raised during a given year. This increase occurs because (1) flotation costs (including any "signaling" costs and supply/demand imbalance costs associated with stock issues) cause the cost of new equity to be higher than the cost of retained earnings, and (2) higher rates of return on debt, preferred stock, and common stock may be required to induce additional investors to supply capital to the firm.

Suppose Swift's cost of retained earnings is 15.0 percent, while its cost of new common stock is 16.8 percent. The company's target capital structure calls for 40 percent debt and 60 percent common equity; its marginal federal-plus-state tax rate is 40 percent; and its before-tax cost of debt is 10 percent. Thus, Swift's WACC using retained earnings as the common equity component is 11.4 percent:

$$WACC_1 = w_d(k_d)(1 - T) + w_{ce}k_s$$

$$= 0.4(10\%)(0.6) + 0.6(15\%) = 11.4\%.$$

Swift is forecasting $240,000 of retained earnings plus $300,000 in depreciation cash flow during the planning period, hence the firm's retained earnings break point is $700,000:

$$\text{Break point} = \$240,000/0.6 + \$300,000 = \$400,000 + \$300,000 = \$700,000.$$

After $700,000 of new capital has been raised, Swift's WACC increases to 12.5 percent:

$$WACC_2 = 0.4(10\%)(0.6) + 0.6(16.8\%) \approx 12.5\%.$$

Thus, each dollar has a weighted average cost of 11.4 percent until the company has raised a total of $700,000. This $700,000 will consist of $300,000 of depreciation cash flow with a cost of 11.4 percent, $160,000 of new debt with an after-tax cost of 6 percent, and $240,000 of retained earnings with a cost of 15 percent. However, if the company raises $700,001 or more, each additional dollar will contain 60 cents of equity obtained by selling new common stock, so $k_a = $ WACC rises from 11.4 to 12.5 percent.

Combining the MCC and IOS Schedules

Now that we have estimated the MCC schedule, we can use it to determine the base discount rate for the capital budgeting process; *that is, we can use the MCC*

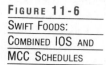

FIGURE 11-6

SWIFT FOODS:
COMBINED IOS AND
MCC SCHEDULES

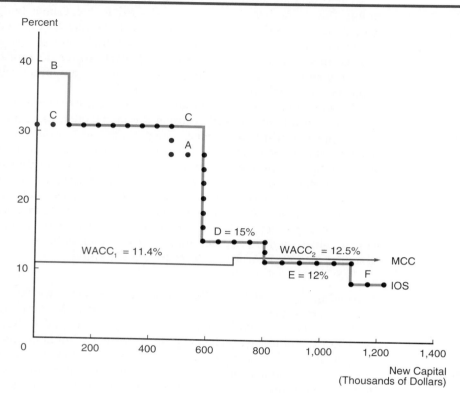

schedule to find the cost of capital for use in determining an average-risk project's net present value. To do this, we combine the IOS and MCC schedules on the same graph, as in Figure 11-6, and then analyze this consolidated figure.

Finding the Marginal Cost of Capital.   Just how far down its IOS curve should Swift go? That is, which of the firm's available projects should it accept? *First, Swift should accept all independent projects that have rates of return in excess of the cost of the capital that will be used to finance them, and it should reject all others.* Projects E and F should be rejected, because they would have to be financed with capital that has a cost of 12.5 percent, and at that cost of capital, we know that these projects must have negative NPVs since their IRRs are below their costs of capital. Therefore, Swift's capital budget should consist of either A or B, plus C and D, and the firm should thus raise and invest a total of $800,000.[15]

---

[15]Note that if the MCC schedule cuts through a project, and if that project must be accepted in total or else rejected, then we can calculate the average cost of the capital that will be used to finance the project (some at the higher WACC and some at the lower WACC) and compare that average WACC to the project's IRR.

The preceding analysis, as summarized in Figure 11-6, reveals a very important point: The average-risk cost of capital used in the capital budgeting process is actually determined at the intersection of the IOS and MCC schedules. This cost is called the firm's *marginal cost of capital (MCC)*, and if it is used as the firm's WACC, then the firm will make correct accept/reject decisions, and its level of financing and investment will be optimal. If it uses any other rate for average-risk projects, its capital budget will not be optimal.

If Swift had fewer good investment opportunities, then its IOS schedule would be shifted to the left, possibly causing the intersection to occur at the $WACC_1 = 11.4\%$ portion of the MCC curve. Then, Swift's MCC would be 11.4 percent, and average-risk projects would be evaluated at that rate. Conversely, if the firm had more and better investment opportunities, its IOS would be shifted to the right, and if the shift is very far to the right, then Swift might have to raise its MCC above 12.5 percent, because its higher capital requirements could lead to further increases in capital costs. Thus, we see that the discount rate used for evaluating average-risk projects is influenced by the set of projects available. We have, of course, abstracted from differential project riskiness in this section, because we assumed that all of Swift's projects are equally risky.

Choosing between Mutually Exclusive Projects.   We have not, at this point, actually determined Swift's optimal capital budget. We know that it should total $800,000, and that Projects C and D should be included, but we do not know which of the mutually exclusive projects, A or B, should be made part of the final budget. How can we choose between A and B? We know that in general the final set of projects should be the one which has the highest total NPV, as this set will increase the value of the firm by the largest amount. We also know that Projects C and D should be included in the final set, so their contributions to the total NPV will be the same regardless of whether we choose Project A or Project B. This narrows our analysis to the NPVs of A and B. The project with the higher NPV should be chosen.

Notice that Figure 11-5 contained the projects' paybacks and IRRs, but no NPVs or MIRRs. We were not able to determine the NPVs or MIRRs at that point, because we did not know Swift's marginal cost of capital. Now, in Figure 11-6, we see that the last dollar raised will cost 12.5 percent, so Swift's marginal cost of capital is 12.5 percent. Therefore, assuming the projects both have average risk, we can use a 12.5 percent discount rate to find $NPV_A = \$34{,}431$ and $NPV_B = \$34{,}431$. Thus, in our example, Swift should be indifferent between the two mutually exclusive projects, according to the NPV criterion. Given a tie, Project B would probably be selected because of its faster payback and higher IRR.

SELF-TEST QUESTIONS

Define a firm's marginal cost of capital.

On what basis is the choice made between mutually exclusive projects?

CAPITAL RATIONING

Under ordinary circumstances, capital budgeting is, in essence, an application of a classic economic principle: A firm should expand to the point where its marginal return is just equal to its marginal cost. However, under some circumstances, a firm may deviate from this principle and place an absolute limit on the size of its capital budget. This is called *capital rationing*, which we discuss in Appendix 11A.

SELF-TEST QUESTION

Define capital rationing.

ESTABLISHING THE OPTIMAL CAPITAL BUDGET IN PRACTICE

The procedures set forth in the preceding sections are conceptually correct, and it is important that you understand the logic of this process. However, Swift Foods (and most other companies) actually uses a more judgmental, less quantitative process for establishing its final capital budget:

Step 1. The financial vice president obtains a reasonably good idea of the firm's IOS schedule from the director of capital budgeting, and a reasonably good estimate of the MCC schedule from the treasurer. These two schedules are then combined, as in Figure 11-6, to get a reasonably good estimate of the corporation's marginal cost of capital (the cost of capital at the intersection of the IOS and MCC schedules).

Step 2. The corporate MCC is scaled up or down for each division to reflect the division's capital structure and risk characteristics. Swift assigns a factor of 0.9 to its stable, low-risk canned vegetables division but a factor of 1.1 to its more risky gourmet frozen foods group. Therefore, if the corporate MCC is determined to be 12.5 percent, the cost for the canned vegetables division is 0.9(12.5%) = 11.25%, while that for the gourmet frozen foods division is 1.1(12.5%) = 13.75%.

Step 3. Each project within each division is classified into one of three groups—high risk, average risk, and low risk—and the same 0.9 and 1.1 factors are used to adjust the divisional MCCs. For example, a low-risk project in the canned vegetables division would have a cost of capital of 0.9(11.25%) = 10.13%, rounded to 10 percent, if the corporate cost of capital were 12.5 percent, while a high-risk project in the gourmet frozen foods division would have a cost of 1.1(13.75%) = 15.13%, rounded to 15 percent.

Step 4. Each project's NPV is then determined, using its risk-adjusted project cost of capital. The optimal capital budget consists of all independent projects with positive risk-adjusted NPVs plus those mutually exclusive projects with the highest positive risk-adjusted NPVs.

These steps implicitly assume that the projects taken on have, on average, about the same debt capacity and risk characteristics, and consequently the same weighted average cost of capital, as the firm's existing assets. If this were not true, then the corporate MCC determined in Step 1 would not be correct, and it would have to be adjusted. However, given all the measurement errors and uncertainties inherent in the entire cost of capital/capital budgeting process, it would be unrealistic to push the adjustment process very far.

This type of analysis may seem more precise than the data warrant. Nevertheless, the procedure does force the firm to think carefully about each division's relative risk, about the risk of each project within the divisions, and about the relationship between the total amount of capital raised and the cost of that capital. Further, the procedure forces the firm to adjust its capital budget to reflect capital market conditions — if the cost of debt and equity rise, this fact will be reflected in the cost of capital used to evaluate projects, and projects that would be marginally acceptable when capital costs were low would (correctly) be ruled unacceptable when capital costs were high.

Self-Test Questions

Describe the general procedures that most firms follow when establishing optimal capital budgets.

What key assumption is implicit in these procedures?

Summary

This chapter discussed three issues in capital budgeting: (1) assessing risk, (2) incorporating risk into the capital budgeting decision process, and (3) determining the optimal capital budget. The key concepts covered are summarized below.

▶ A project's *stand-alone risk* is the risk the project would have if it were the firm's only asset and if the firm's stockholders held only that one stock. Stand-alone risk is measured by the variability of the asset's expected returns. Stand-alone risk is often used as a proxy for both market and corporate risk, because (1) market and corporate risk are difficult to measure and (2) the three types of risk are usually highly correlated.

▶ *Within-firm,* or *corporate, risk* reflects the effects of a project on the firm's risk, and it is measured by the project's effect on the firm's earnings variability. Stockholder diversification is not taken into account.

▶ *Market risk* reflects the effects of a project on the riskiness of a well-diversified stockholder's portfolio. In theory, market risk should be the most relevant type of risk.

▶ *Corporate risk* is important because it influences the firm's ability to use low-cost debt, to maintain smooth operations over time, and to avoid crises that might consume management's energy and also disrupt employees, customers, suppliers, and the community.

▶ *Sensitivity analysis* is a technique which shows how much an output variable such as NPV will change in response to a given change in an input variable such as sales, other things held constant.

▶ *Scenario analysis* is a risk analysis technique in which the best- and worst-case NPVs are compared with the project's expected NPV.

▶ *Monte Carlo simulation* is a risk analysis technique in which a computer is used to simulate all probable future events and thus to estimate the profitability distribution and riskiness of a project.

▶ Projects that require capital outlays in stages over several years are often evaluated using *decision trees*. Sensitivity analysis, scenario analysis, Monte Carlo simulation, and decision trees all measure stand-alone risk.

▶ The ability to *abandon* a project can increase the project's return and decrease its riskiness.

▶ The *pure play method* and the *accounting beta method* can be used to estimate betas for large projects or for divisions.

▶ Either *certainty equivalents* or *risk-adjusted discount rates* can be used to incorporate risk into the decision process. In practice, firms normally use risk-adjusted discount rates.

▶ The *risk-adjusted discount rate* is that rate which is used to evaluate a particular project. The discount rate is increased for projects which are riskier than the firm's average project, and it is decreased for less risky projects.

▶ When evaluating *risky cash outflows,* the risk-adjustment process is generally reversed, that is, lower rates are used to discount more risky outflows.

▶ *Capital rationing* occurs when management places a constraint on the size of the firm's capital budget during a particular period.

▶ The *investment opportunity schedule (IOS)* is a graph of the firm's investment opportunities, listed in descending order of IRR.

▶ The *marginal cost of capital (MCC) schedule* is a graph of the firm's weighted average cost of capital versus the amount of funds raised.

▶ The MCC schedule is combined with the IOS schedule, and the intersection defines the firm's *marginal cost of capital.*

This chapter completes our discussion of capital budgeting decisions. In the next chapter, we begin our discussion of capital structure decisions.

QUESTIONS

11-1 Define each of the following terms:
   a. Stand-alone risk; within-firm (corporate) risk; market risk
   b. Sensitivity analysis
   c. Simulation analysis
   d. Scenario analysis
   e. Decision tree analysis

e. The problem stated that the firm pays out 50 percent of its earnings as dividends. How would the analysis change if the payout ratio were changed to 0 percent? To 100 percent?

PROBLEMS

11-1 (Risky cash outflows)   Suwannee Electric and Gas Company is deciding if it should build an oil or a coal generating plant. Its MCC is 8 percent for low-risk projects, 10 percent for projects of average risk, and 12 percent for high-risk projects. Management believes that an oil plant is of average risk, but that a coal plant is of high risk due to the problem of acid rain. The cash *outflows* required to construct each plant are listed here. The revenues, fuel costs, and other operating costs are expected to be the same under both plans:

	Construction Costs (Thousands of Dollars)	
Year	Coal Plant	Oil Plant
0	($ 100)	($ 400)
1	(500)	(1,000)
2	(1,500)	(1,000)
3	(1,500)	(1,000)
4	(1,500)	(1,500)
5	(1,000)	(1,000)
6	(500)	(200)

Which type of plant should be constructed?

11-2 (Sequential decisions)   The Yoran Yacht Company (YYC), a prominent sailboat builder in Newport, may design a new 30-foot sailboat based on the "winged" keels first introduced on the 12-meter yachts that raced for the America's Cup.

First, YYC would have to invest $10,000 at $t = 0$ for the design and model tank testing of the new boat. YYC's managers believe that there is a 60 percent probability that this phase will be successful and the project will continue. If Stage 1 is not successful, the project will be abandoned with zero salvage value.

The next stage, if undertaken, would consist of making the molds and producing two prototype boats. This would cost $500,000 at $t = 1$. If the boats test well, YYC would go into production. If they do not, the molds and prototypes could be sold for $100,000. The managers estimate that the probability is 80 percent that the boats will pass testing, and that Stage 3 will be undertaken.

Stage 3 consists of converting an unused production line to produce the new design. This would cost $1,000,000 at $t = 2$. If the economy is strong at this point, the net value of sales would be $3,000,000, while if the economy is weak, the net value would be $1,500,000. Both net values occur at $t = 3$, and each state of the economy has a probability of 0.5. YYC's marginal cost of capital is 12 percent.

a. Assume that this project has average risk. Construct a decision tree and determine the project's expected NPV.

b. Find the project's standard deviation of NPV and coefficient of variation (CV) of NPV. If YYC's average project had a CV of between 1.0 and 2.0, would this project be of high, low, or average stand-alone risk?

11-3 (Divisional market risk adjustments)   SureGrip Rubber Company has two divisions: (1) the tire division, which manufactures tires for new autos; and (2) the recap division,

5*	0	20,000	30,000

which manufactures recapping materials that are sold to independent tire recapping shops throughout the United States. Since auto manufacturing fluctuates with the general economy, the tire division's earnings contribution to SureGrip's stock price is highly correlated with returns on most other stocks. If the tire division were operated as a separate company, its beta coefficient would be about 1.60. The sales and profits of the recap division, on the other hand, tend to be countercyclical, since recap sales boom when people cannot afford to buy new tires. The recap division's beta is estimated to be 0.40. Approximately 75 percent of SureGrip's corporate assets are invested in the tire division and 25 percent are in the recap division.

Currently, the rate of interest on Treasury bonds is 10 percent, and the expected rate of return on an average share of stock is 15 percent. SureGrip uses only common equity capital, hence it has no debt outstanding.

a. What is the required rate of return on SureGrip's stock?

b. What discount rate should be used to evaluate capital budgeting projects? Explain your answer fully, and in the process, illustrate your answer with a project which costs $100,000, has a 10-year life, and provides expected after-tax net cash flows of $20,000 per year.

11-4 (Scenario and sensitivity analysis) Your firm, Agrico, is considering the purchase of a tractor which will have a net cost of $30,000, will increase pre-tax operating cash flows exclusive of depreciation effects by $10,000 per year, and will be depreciated on a straight line basis to zero over 5 years at the rate of $6,000 per year, beginning the first year. (Annual cash flows will be $10,000, reduced by taxes, plus the tax savings that result from $6,000 of depreciation.) The board of directors, however, is having a heated debate as to whether the tractor will actually last 5 years. Specifically, Hugo Phillips insists that he knows of some that have lasted only 4 years. Joe Copeland agrees with Phillips, but he argues that most tractors do give 5 years of service. Kate Brown, on the other hand, says she has seen some last as long as 8 years.

a. Given this discussion, the board asks you to prepare a scenario analysis to ascertain the importance of the uncertainty about the tractor's life. Assume a 40 percent marginal federal-plus-state tax rate, a zero salvage value, and a marginal cost of capital of 10 percent. (Hint: The MACRS alternate straight line depreciation is based on the class life of the tractor and is not affected by the actual life. Also, ignore the half-year convention for this problem.)

(Do Parts b and c only if you are using the computer problem diskette.)

b. The board would also like to know how changes in the cost of capital affect the analysis. Assume that the machine's life is 5 years, and analyze the effects of a change in the cost of capital to 8 percent or to 12 percent. Is the project very sensitive to changes in the cost of capital?

c. The board would like to determine the sensitivity of the project's NPV to changes in certain variables. First, they would like to examine the effect of changes in pre-tax operating revenues upon NPV. Calculate the project's NPV at plus 10, 20, and 30 percent of the estimated $10,000 pre-tax revenues, as well as minus 10, 20, and 30 percent of this figure. (Hold all other variables constant.) Second, calculate the effect upon NPV of various project lives. (Hint: Hold all other variables constant, and try lives ranging from 1 to 10 years.) Finally, examine NPV while changing the cost of capital. (Once again, hold all other variables constant at their original levels.) Plot a separate sensitivity diagram for each variable examined.

11-5   (Simulation)   Singleton Supplies Corporation (SSC) manufactures medical products for hospitals, clinics, and nursing homes. SSC may introduce a new type of X-ray scanner designed to identify certain types of cancers in their early stages. There are a number of uncertainties about the proposed project, but the following data are believed to be reasonably accurate.

	Probability	Value	Random Numbers
Developmental costs	0.3	$2,000,000	00–29
	0.4	4,000,000	30–69
	0.3	6,000,000	70–99
Project life	0.2	3 years	00–19
	0.6	8 years	20–79
	0.2	13 years	80–99
Sales in units	0.2	100	00–19
	0.6	200	20–79
	0.2	300	80–99
Sales price	0.1	$13,000	00–09
	0.8	13,500	10–89
	0.1	14,000	90–99
Cost per unit (excluding	0.3	$5,000	00–29
developmental costs)	0.4	6,000	30–69
	0.3	7,000	70–99

SSC uses a cost of capital of 15 percent to analyze average-risk projects, 12 percent for low-risk projects, and 18 percent for high-risk projects. These risk adjustments reflect primarily the uncertainty about each project's NPV and IRR as measured by the coefficients of variation of NPV and IRR. SSC is in the 40 percent federal-plus-state income tax bracket.

a.   What is the expected IRR for the X-ray scanner project? Base your answer on the expected values of the variables. Also, assume the after-tax "profits" figure you develop is equal to annual cash flows. All facilities are leased, so depreciation may be disregarded. Can you determine the value of σ_{IRR} short of actual simulation or a fairly complex statistical analysis?

b.   Assume that SSC uses a 15 percent cost of capital for this project. What is the project's NPV? Could you estimate σ_{NPV} without either simulation or a complex statistical analysis?

c.   Show the process by which a computer would perform a simulation analysis for this project. Use the random numbers 44, 17, 16, 58, 1; 79, 83, 86; and 19, 62, 6 to illustrate the process with the first computer run. Actually calculate the first-run NPV and IRR. Assume that the cash flows for each year are independent of cash flows for other years. Also, assume that the computer operates as follows: (1) A developmental cost and a project life are estimated for the first run. (2) Next, sales volume, sales price, and cost per unit are estimated and used to derive a cash flow for the first year. (3) Then, the next three random numbers are used to estimate sales volume, sales price, and cost per unit for the second year, hence the cash flow for the second year. (4) Cash flows for other years are developed similarly, on out to the first run's estimated life. (5) With the developmental cost and the cash flow stream established, NPV and IRR for the first run are derived and stored in the computer's memory. (6) The process is repeated to generate perhaps 500 other NPVs and IRRs. (7) Frequency distributions for NPV and IRR are plotted by the computer, and the distributions' means and standard deviations are calculated.

d. Does it seem a little strange to conduct a risk analysis such as the one here *after* having already established a cost of capital for use in the analysis? What might be done to improve this situation?

e. In this problem, we assumed that the probability distributions were all independent of one another. It would have been possible to use conditional probabilities where, for example, the probability distribution for cost per unit would vary from trial to trial, depending on the unit sales for the trial. Also, it would be possible to construct a simulation model such that the sales distribution in Year t would depend on the sales level attained in Year t − 1. Had these modifications been made in this problem, do you think the standard deviation of the NPV distribution would have been larger (riskier) or smaller (less risky) than where complete independence is assumed?

f. Name two *major* difficulties not mentioned earlier that occur in the kind of analysis discussed in this problem.

11-6 (Simple optimal capital budget) The Teague Corporation's present capital structure, which is also its target capital structure, calls for 50 percent debt and 50 percent common equity. The firm has only one potential project, an expansion program with a 10.2 percent IRR and a cost of $20 million but which is completely divisible; that is, Teague can invest any amount up to $20 million. The firm expects to retain $2 million of earnings next year and to generate $2 million in depreciation cash flow. It can raise up to $5 million in new debt at a before-tax cost of 8 percent, and all debt after the first $5 million will have a cost of 10 percent. The cost of retained earnings is 12 percent and the firm can sell any amount of new common stock desired at a constant cost of new equity of 15 percent. The firm's marginal federal-plus-state tax rate is 40 percent. What is the firm's optimal capital budget?

11-7 (Optimal capital budget) The management of Flannigan Phosphate Industries (FPI) is planning next year's capital budget. FPI projects its net income at $7,500, and its payout ratio is 40 percent. Depreciation is forecasted at $3,000. The company's earnings and dividends are growing at a constant rate of 5 percent; the last dividend, D_0, was $0.90; and the current stock price is $8.59. FPI's new debt will cost 14 percent. If FPI issues new common stock, flotation costs will be 20 percent. FPI is at its optimal capital structure, which is 40 percent debt and 60 percent equity, and the firm's marginal tax rate is 40 percent. FPI has the following independent, indivisible, and equally risky investment opportunities:

Project	Cost	IRR
A	$15,000	17%
B	20,000	14
C	15,000	16
D	12,000	15

What is FPI's optimal capital budget?

11-8 (Risk-adjusted optimal capital budget) Refer to Problem 11-7. Management neglected to incorporate project risk differentials into the analysis. FPI's policy is to add 2 percentage points to the cost of capital of those projects significantly more risky than average and to subtract 2 percentage points from the cost of capital of those which are substantially less risky than average. Management judges Project A to be of high risk, Projects C and D to be of average risk, and Project B to be of low risk. No projects are divisible. What is the optimal capital budget after adjustment for project risk?

MINI CASE 1

(Risk analysis) The Chapter 10 Mini Case contains the details of a new-project capital budgeting evaluation being conducted by Joan Samuels at the John Crockett Furniture Company. However, in the initial analysis the riskiness of the project was not considered. The base case, or expected, cash flow estimates as they were estimated in Chapter 10 (in thousands of dollars) are given next. Crockett's overall cost of capital (WACC) is 10 percent.

			Year		
	0	**1**	**2**	**3**	**4**
Investment in:					
Fixed assets	($240)				
Net working capital	(20)				
Unit sales		1,250	1,250	1,250	1,250
Sales price (dollars)		$200	$200	$200	$200
Gross revenue		$250	$250	$250	$250
Cash operating costs (50%)		125	125	125	125
Operating profit		$125	$125	$125	$125
Depreciation		79	108	36	17
EBIT		$ 46	$ 17	$ 89	$108
Taxes (40%)		18	7	36	43
Net operating income		$ 28	$ 10	$ 53	$ 65
Add back depreciation		79	108	36	17
Net operating cash flow		$107	$118	$ 89	$ 82
Salvage value					25
Tax on SV (40%)					(10)
Recovery of NWC					20
Net cash flow	($260)	$107	$118	$ 89	$117

NPV at 10% cost of capital = $82
IRR = 23.8%
MIRR = 17.8%

As Joan's assistant, you have been directed to answer the following questions:

a. What does the term "risk" mean in the context of capital budgeting, to what extent can risk be quantified, and when risk is quantified, is the quantification based primarily on statistical analysis of historical data or on subjective, judgmental estimates?

b. (1) What are the three types of risk that are relevant in capital budgeting?
(2) How is each of these risk types measured, and how do they relate to one another?
(3) How is each type of risk used in the capital budgeting process?

c. (1) What is sensitivity analysis?
(2) Perform a sensitivity analysis on the unit sales, salvage value, and cost of capital for the project. Assume that each of these variables can vary from its base case, or expected, value by plus and minus 10, 20, and 30 percent. Include a sensitivity diagram, and discuss the results.
(3) What is the primary weakness of sensitivity analysis? What is its primary usefulness?

d. Assume that Joan Samuels is confident of her estimates of all the variables that affect the project's cash flows except unit sales: If product acceptance is poor, unit sales would be only 900 units a year, while a strong consumer response would produce sales of 1,600 units. In either case, cash costs would still amount to 50 percent of revenues.

Joan believes that there is a 25 percent chance of poor acceptance, a 25 percent chance of excellent acceptance, and a 50 percent chance of average acceptance (the base case).

(1) What is the worst-case NPV? The best-case NPV?

(2) Use the worst-, most likely, and best-case NPVs and probabilities of occurrence to find the project's expected NPV, standard deviation, and coefficient of variation.

e. (1) Assume that Crockett's average project has a coefficient of variation in the range of 0.2–0.4. Would the new furniture line be classified as high risk, average risk, or low risk? What type of risk is being measured here?

(2) Based on common sense, how highly correlated do you think that the project would be to the firm's other assets? (Give a correlation coefficient, or range of coefficients, based on your judgment.)

(3) How would this correlation coefficient and the previously calculated σ combine to affect the project's contribution to corporate, or within-firm, risk? Explain.

f. (1) Based on your judgment, what do you think the project's correlation coefficient would be with the general economy and thus with returns on "the market"?

(2) How would this correlation affect the project's market risk?

g. (1) Crockett typically adds or subtracts 3 percentage points to the overall cost of capital to adjust for risk. Should the new furniture line be accepted?

(2) Are there any subjective risk factors that should be considered before the final decision is made?

h. Define scenario analysis and simulation analysis, and discuss their principal advantages and disadvantages.

i. (1) Crockett's target capital structure is 50 percent debt and 50 percent common equity; its cost of debt is 12 percent; the risk-free rate is 10 percent; the market risk premium is 6 percent; and the firm's tax rate is 40 percent. If Joan's estimate of the new project's beta is 1.2, what is the project's market risk, and what is its cost of capital based on the CAPM?

(2) How does the project's market risk compare with the firm's overall market risk?

(3) How does the project's market risk compare with its stand-alone risk?

(4) Briefly describe two methods that Joan could conceivably have used to estimate the project's market beta. How feasible do you think those procedures would actually be in this case?

(5) What are the advantages and disadvantages of focusing on a project's market risk?

j. As a completely different project, Crockett is also evaluating two different production line systems for its overstuffed furniture line. Plan W requires more workers but less capital, while Plan C requires more capital but fewer workers. Both systems have estimated 3-year lives. Since the production line choice has no impact on revenues, Joan will base her decision on the relative costs of the two systems as set forth next:

| | Expected Net Costs | |
Year	Plan W	Plan C
0	($500)	($1,000)
1	(500)	(300)
2	(500)	(300)
3	(500)	(300)

(1) Assume initially that the two systems are both of average risk. Which one should be chosen?

CAPITAL RATIONING

As we discussed in Chapter 11, under ordinary circumstances a firm should expand to the point where its marginal return is just equal to its marginal cost. A simplified view of the concept is shown in Figure 11A-1. Here we assume that the firm has five equally risky and independent investment opportunities which would cost a total of $23 million. Its cost of capital is assumed to be constant at 10 percent, implying that the firm can raise all the money it wants at a cost of 10 percent. Under these conditions, the firm would accept Projects V, W, and X, since they all have IRRs greater than the cost of capital, hence NPVs greater than zero. It would reject Y and Z because they have IRRs less than k, indicating negative NPVs. This decision would maximize the value of the firm and the wealth of its stockholders.

Firms ordinarily operate in the manner depicted in the graph—they accept all independent projects having positive NPVs, reject those with negative NPVs, and choose between mutually exclusive investments on the basis of the higher NPV. However, some firms set an absolute limit on the size of their capital budgets such that the size of the budget is less than the level of investment called for by the NPV (or IRR) criterion. This is called *capital rationing,* and it is the topic of this appendix.

REASONS FOR CAPITAL RATIONING

The principal reason for capital rationing is that some firms are reluctant to engage in external financing (either borrowing or selling stock). One management, recalling the plight of firms with substantial amounts of debt during recent credit crunches, may simply refuse to use debt. Another management, which has no objection to selling debt, may not want to sell equity capital for fear of losing some measure of voting control. Still others may refuse to use any form of outside financing, considering safety and control to be more important than additional profits. These are all cases of capital rationing, and they result in limiting the rate of expansion to a slower pace than would be dictated by "purely rational wealth-maximizing behavior."

We should make three points here. First, a decision to hold back on expansion is not necessarily irrational. If the owners/managers of a privately held firm have what they consider to be plenty of income and wealth, then it might be quite rational for them to "trim their sails," relax, and concentrate on enjoying what they have already earned rather than on earning still more. Such behavior would not, however, be appropriate for a publicly owned firm.

Second, it is not correct to interpret as capital rationing a situation where the firm is willing to sell additional securities at the going market price but finds that it cannot because the market simply will not absorb more of its issues. Rather, such a situation indicates that the weighted average cost of capital is rising. If more acceptable investments are indicated than can be financed, then the marginal cost of capital being used is too low and should be raised.

Third, firms sometimes set a limit on capital expenditures, not because of a shortage of funds, but because of limitations on other resources, especially managerial talent. A firm might, for example, feel that its personnel development program is sufficient to handle an expansion of no more than 10 percent a year, and then set a limit on the capital budget to ensure that expansion is held to that rate. This is not capital rationing—

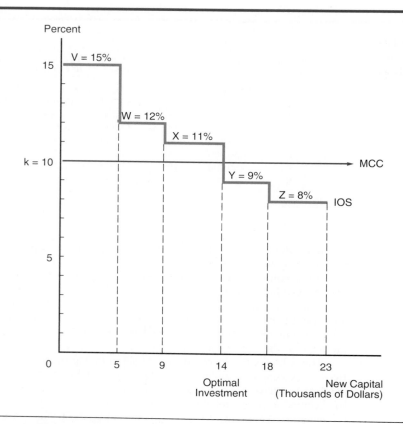

FIGURE 11A-1
THE TYPICAL CAPITAL
BUDGETING SITUATION

Note: If IRR > 10%, NPV is positive. Therefore, Projects V, W, and X have NPV > 0, while Y and Z have NPV < 0.

rather, it involves a downward reevaluation of project returns if growth exceeds some limit; that is, expected rates of return are, after some point, a decreasing function of the level of expenditures.

PROJECT SELECTION UNDER CAPITAL RATIONING

How should projects be selected under conditions of true capital rationing? First, note that if a firm truly rations capital, its value is not being maximized: If management were maximizing, then they would move to the point where the marginal project's NPV was zero, and capital rationing as defined would not exist. So, if a firm uses capital rationing, it has ruled out value maximization. The firm may, however, want to maximize value *subject to the constraint that the capital ceiling not be exceeded.* Constrained maximization behavior will, in general, result in a lower value than following unconstrained maximization, but some type of constrained maximization may produce reasonably satisfactory results. *Linear programming* is one method of constrained maximization that has been applied to capital

TABLE 11A-1	Project Number	Project Cost, or Outlay, at t = 0	Project Life (Years)	Cash Flow per Year	NPV at the 10% Cost of Capital	IRR	Profitability Index
ILLUSTRATION OF CAPITAL RATIONING	1	$400,000	20	$58,600	$98,894	13.5%	1.25
	2	250,000	10	55,000	87,951	17.7	1.35
	3	100,000	8	24,000	28,038	17.3	1.28
	4	75,000	15	12,000	16,273	13.7	1.22
	5	75,000	6	18,000	3,395	11.5	1.05
	6	50,000	5	14,000	3,071	12.4	1.06
	7	250,000	10	41,000	1,927	10.2	1.01
	8	250,000	3	99,000	(3,802)	9.1	0.98

rationing. Much work has been done in this area, and linear programming may, in the future, be widely applied in capital budgeting.[1]

If the firm does face capital rationing, and if the constraint cannot be lifted, what can the financial manager do? The objective should be to select projects, subject to the capital rationing constraint, such that the sum of the projects' NPVs is maximized. Linear programming can be used, or if there are not too many projects involved, the financial manager can simply enumerate all the sets of projects that meet the budget constraint and then select the set with the largest total NPV.

The complexities involved in a capital rationing situation are indicated in Table 11A-1. Here we assume that the firm is considering a total of eight potential projects; all are independent and have average risk. The firm has a 10 percent cost of capital, but management has decided to limit capital expenditures during the year to the amount of money that can be generated internally, $500,000. In the table, the projects are listed in the descending order of their NPVs, but their IRRs and profitability indices (PIs) are also shown.

If it is to maximize the value of the firm, management must choose the set of projects with the greatest total NPV, subject to the constraint that total expenditures must not exceed $500,000. With only eight projects in total, we can try all different combinations and, by "brute force," determine the set which maximizes NPV. This set is optimal:[2]

Project	Cost	NPV
2	$250,000	$87,951
3	100,000	28,038
4	75,000	16,273
5	75,000	3,395
	$500,000	$135,657

---

[1]For further information on mathematical programming solutions to capital rationing, and for a review and analysis of the literature on this issue, see H. Martin Weingarten, "Capital Rationing: n Authors in Search of a Plot," *Journal of Finance*, December 1977, 1403–1431; and Stephen P. Bradley and Sherwood C. Frey, Jr., "Equivalent Mathematical Programming Models of Pure Capital Rationing," *Journal of Financial and Quantitative Analysis*, June 1978, 345–361.

[2]Note that in capital rationing the goal in project selection is to get the "biggest bang for the buck." Since this is measured by the profitability index (PI), one way to determine the optimal set is by accepting projects in descending order of PIs, but recognizing that some high-PI projects might have to be rejected because insufficient funds are available.

This analysis seems simple enough, but there are three factors which complicate it greatly in realistic situations:

1.   **Number of projects.**   In the example, we have only eight projects, so it is easy to simply list all the combinations whose costs do not exceed $500,000 and then see which combination provides the greatest total NPV. For a large firm with thousands of projects, this would be a tedious process, although computer programs are available to solve such problems. However, the other problems listed next are more serious.

2.   **Project risk.**   In our example, we assumed that the eight projects are equally risky, hence have the same cost of capital. If this was not the case, and if the number of projects was so large as to preclude hand analysis, then it would be difficult, if not impossible, to reach an optimal solution, because the computer programs currently available cannot deal efficiently with projects having differential risks.

3.   **Multiple time constraints.**   Our example also assumed a single-time-period capital constraint. Yet, realistically, when capital rationing is practiced, the constraints usually extend for several years. However, the funds available in future years depend on cash throwoffs from investments made in earlier years. Thus, the constraint in Year 2 depends on the investments made in Year 1, and so on. For example, we might have investment funds of $500,000 per year available from external sources for 1991 through 1995 plus the cash flows from investments made in previous years. To solve this type of multiperiod problem, we need information on both investment opportunities and funds availability in future years, and not just on the situation in the current year. Also, the NPV we seek to maximize is the sum of the present values of the NPVs in each year over the time horizon being analyzed, say, 1991 to 1995. In such a situation, we might even choose Project 8 in Table 11A-1, in spite of its negative NPV, because it has rapid cash throw-offs. In fact, if excellent investment opportunities are expected to be available in 1992, 1993, and 1994, taking Project 8 might be part of the best long-run strategy.

A BETTER APPROACH TO CAPITAL RATIONING

Our main conclusion thus far about capital rationing—which means deliberately foregoing projects with positive NPVs—is that practicing it is irrational for any firm which seeks to maximize its stockholders' wealth. Also, while mathematical programming methods are available to help solve the simpler cases of capital rationing so that management can make the best of a bad situation, programming methods are really not capable of dealing with all the complexities encountered in the real world.

Fortunately, there is a better method for handling the types of situations that give rise to capital rationing. Usually, capital rationing occurs when the firm believes that it will encounter severe problems if it attempts to raise capital beyond some specified amount. For example, the interest rate it would have to pay would rise sharply if it attempted to increase its existing lines of credit. Such situations can be rationally handled by increasing the firm's WACC as the amount of capital raised increases. In effect, in terms of Figure 11A-1, the MCC schedule would begin to rise beyond some amount of capital, resulting in a higher MCC, and this higher MCC should be used as the discount rate when determining a project's NPV.

CAPITAL STRUCTURE AND DIVIDEND POLICY

517

CAPITAL STRUCTURE DECISIONS: PART 1

I n 1992, U.S. stock and bond issues totaled $851.2 billion, surpassing the previous record set in 1991 by 44 percent and nearly tripling the amount of corporate capital raised in 1990. The factors that produced 1992's underwriting frenzy include (1) low interest rates, (2) high stock prices, and (3) a move by corporations to slash their debt burdens.

Although some companies used the proceeds from bond and stock sales to buy new plant and equipment, many others used the funds to pay off high-cost debt incurred in the 1980s, thereby slashing their interest charges and raising their credit ratings. "What's going on now is creating a very strong base for the rest of the century," said Mickey D. Levy, chief economist at CRT Government Securities Ltd. "It's setting the stage for a healthy and sustained expansion."

During the past three years, American companies' average debt-to-capital ratio (long-term debt divided by long-term debt plus equity) has decreased from 46.8 percent to 43.0 percent, while their interest expenses have decreased by more than 10 percent. This has lowered breakeven points, putting companies in a better position to post big profits as the economy rebounds.

For example, AT&T recently raised $2.18 billion with four bond offerings. These funds, along with $580 million of equity capital, were used to redeem 11 debt issues totaling $2.76 billion. The ends results were an overall annual interest savings of more than $50 million and a drop in AT&T's debt-to-capital ratio from 35 percent to 27 percent. Similarly, since 1990, RJR Nabisco has used nearly $4 billion from several debt deals, plus $3.3 billion from two stock offerings, to lessen its total debt by one-third, to $14 billion. As a result, the tobacco and

food company's $1.5 billion annual interest expense decreased by about 30 percent. RJR, which was taken private in a record $25 billion leveraged buyout in 1989, is now able to negotiate less restrictive loan terms and, with the added funds flowing to its bottom line, to be more aggressive in expanding its overseas operations.

It is clear that firms have the choice of using either debt or equity financing. Is one form of capital better than the other? If so, shouldn't firms be financed either with all debt or all equity? What are the costs and benefits associated with each type of capital? A consideration of these questions can help managers decide how to finance their firms. The preceding examples might lead you to believe that debt is not advantageous, because most companies are currently reducing their interest burdens. However, companies raise huge amounts of debt capital each year, so there must be some benefit to this source of financing. In the next two chapters, we discuss many facets of the debt versus equity, or capital structure, decision. As you read through these chapters, think about AT&T and RJR and the ways the theory and concepts we discuss might aid their managers in making capital structure decisions.

One of the most perplexing issues facing financial managers is the relationship between *capital structure,* which is the mix of debt and equity financing, and stock prices. Should different industries and different firms within industries have different capital structures, and, if so, what are the factors that lead to these differences? In Chapters 12 and 13, we will discuss both the theories that underlie capital structure decisions and some more pragmatic approaches to the problem. Although the optimal capital structure decision is generally not crystal clear, an understanding of these chapters will help you deal with the issues involved.

Business and Financial Risk

In Chapters 4 and 5, when we examined risk from the viewpoint of the individual investor, we distinguished between *market risk,* which is measured by the firm's beta coefficient, and *total risk,* which includes both market risk and an element of risk which can be eliminated by diversification. Now we introduce two new dimensions of risk: (1) *business risk,* or the riskiness of the firm's assets if it uses no debt, and (2) *financial risk,* which is the additional risk placed on the common stockholders as a result of the firm's decision to use debt.[1] Conceptually, the firm has a certain amount of risk inherent in its operations: this is its business risk. If

---

[1]Using preferred stock also adds to financial risk. To simplify matters somewhat, we concentrate on debt and common equity in this chapter.

the firm uses debt, then in effect it partitions its investors into two groups and concentrates most of its business risk on one class of investors—the common stockholders. However, the common stockholders generally demand compensation for assuming more risk in the form of a higher expected return. We examine business and financial risk both within a total risk framework, which ignores the benefits of stockholder diversification, and within a market risk framework, where part of the business and financial risk is eliminated by diversification.

SELF-TEST QUESTION

Explain the difference between business risk and financial risk.

BUSINESS AND FINANCIAL RISK: A TOTAL RISK PERSPECTIVE

We begin our discussion of business risk and financial risk with a focus on total risk. A market risk perspective is provided later in the chapter.

BUSINESS RISK

Business risk, in a total risk sense, is measured by the uncertainty inherent in projections of a firm's future rate of return on assets (ROA). We could measure ROA in several ways, but for purposes of capital structure analysis, the following definition is most appropriate:

$$\frac{\text{Return on assets}}{(\text{ROA})} = \frac{\text{Return to investors}}{\text{Assets}} = \frac{\text{Net income to}}{\text{common stockholders} + \text{Interest payments}}{\text{Assets}}.$$

Further, since a firm's assets must be equal to the capital that has been invested in the form of debt and equity, we can rewrite the rate of return equation as the return on investment, ROI:

$$\frac{\text{Return on}}{\substack{\text{invested capital} \\ (\text{ROI})}} = \frac{\text{Net income to common stockholders} + \text{Interest payments}}{\text{Invested capital}}.$$

Thus, business risk can be measured by the standard deviation of either ROA or ROI.

Note also that if a firm uses no debt, then its interest payments will be zero, its assets will be all-equity financed, and its return on invested capital will equal its return on equity, ROE:

$$\text{ROI (zero debt)} = \text{ROE} = \frac{\text{Net income to common stockholders}}{\text{Common equity}}.$$

FIGURE 12-1

STRASBURG

ELECTRONICS:

TREND IN ROE,

1983–1993, AND

SUBJECTIVE

PROBABILITY

DISTRIBUTION OF

ROE, 1993

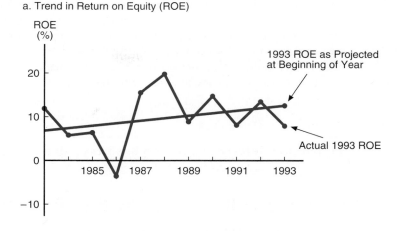

a. Trend in Return on Equity (ROE)

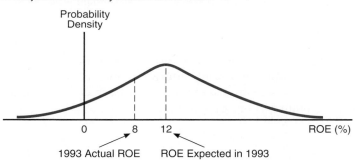

b. Subjective Probability Distribution of ROE

Therefore, the business risk of a *leverage-free* firm can be measured by the standard deviation of its expected ROE, σ_{ROE}.

To illustrate, consider Strasburg Electronics Company, a *debt-free (unlevered)* firm. Figure 12-1 gives some clues about the company's business risk. The top graph shows the trend in the firm's ROE from 1983 through 1993; this graph gives both security analysts and Strasburg's management an idea of the degree to which ROE has varied in the past and consequently might vary in the future. This graph also shows that Strasburg's ROE is growing slowly, so the relevant variability of ROE is the dispersion about the trend line.

The lower graph shows the beginning-of-year subjectively estimated probability distribution of Strasburg's ROE for 1993, based on the trend line in the top section of Figure 12-1. As both graphs indicate, Strasburg's actual ROE in 1993 was only 8 percent, well below the expected value of 12 percent—1993 was a bad year.

Strasburg's past fluctuations in ROE were caused by many factors—booms and recessions in the national economy, successful new products introduced both by Strasburg and by its competitors, labor strikes, price controls, a fire in Strasburg's main plant, and so on. Similar events will doubtless occur in the future, and when they do, the realized ROE will be higher or lower than the projected level. Further, there is always the possibility that a long-term disaster might strike, permanently depressing the company's earning power; for example, a competitor might introduce a new product that would permanently lower Strasburg's earnings. This uncertainty regarding Strasburg's future ROE, assuming the firm uses no debt financing, is defined as the company's *basic business risk.*

Business risk varies not only from industry to industry but also among firms in a given industry. Further, business risk can change over time. For example, the electric utilities were regarded for years as having little business risk, but a combination of events in the 1970s and 1980s altered the utilities' situation, producing sharp declines in their ROEs and greatly increasing the industry's business risk. Now, food processors and grocery retailers are frequently given as examples of industries with low business risk, while cyclical manufacturing industries such as autos and steel are regarded as having especially high business risk. Also, smaller companies, and those that are dependent on a single product, are often regarded as having a high degree of business risk.[2]

Business risk depends on a number of factors; the more important ones are listed below:

1. **Demand variability.** The more stable the demand for a firm's products, other things held constant, the lower its business risk.

2. **Sales price variability.** Firms whose products are sold in highly volatile markets are exposed to more business risk than similar firms whose output prices are more stable.

3. **Input cost variability.** Firms whose input costs are highly uncertain are exposed to a high degree of business risk.

4. **Ability to adjust output prices for changes in input costs.** Some firms are better able than others to raise their own output prices when input costs rise. The greater the ability to adjust output prices to reflect cost conditions, the lower the degree of business risk, other things held constant.

5. **Ability to develop new products in a timely, cost-effective manner.** Firms in such high-tech industries as drugs and computers depend on a constant stream of new products. The faster its products become obsolete, the greater a firm's business risk.

---

[2]We have avoided any discussion of market versus company-specific risk in this section. We note now (1) that any action which increases business risk in the total risk sense will generally also increase a firm's beta coefficient, and (2) that a part of business risk as we define it here will generally be company-specific, hence subject to elimination by diversification by the firm's stockholders. This point is discussed at some length later in the chapter.

6. The extent to which costs are fixed: operating leverage. If a high percentage of a firm's costs are fixed, hence do not decline when demand falls off, then the firm is exposed to a relatively high degree of business risk. This factor is called *operating leverage,* and it is discussed at length in the next section.

Each of these factors is determined partly by the firm's industry characteristics, but each of them is also controllable to some extent by management. For example, most firms can, through their marketing policies, take actions to stabilize both unit sales and sales prices. However, this stabilization may require firms to spend a great deal on advertising and/or price concessions in order to get commitments from their customers to purchase fixed quantities at fixed prices in the future. Similarly, firms such as Strasburg Electronics can reduce the volatility of future input costs by negotiating long-term labor and materials supply contracts, but they may have to agree to pay prices above the current spot price level to obtain these contracts.[3]

OPERATING LEVERAGE

As noted above, business risk depends in part on the extent to which a firm builds fixed costs into its operations — if fixed costs are high, even a small decline in sales can lead to a large decline in ROE, so, other things held constant, the higher a firm's fixed costs, the greater its business risk. Higher fixed costs are generally associated with more highly automated, capital intensive firms and industries. Also, businesses that employ highly skilled workers who must be retained and paid even during recessions have relatively high fixed costs, as do firms with high product development costs, because the amortization of development costs is an element of fixed costs.

If a high percentage of a firm's total costs are fixed, then the firm is said to have a high degree of *operating leverage.* In physics, leverage implies the use of a lever to raise a heavy object with a small force. In politics, if people have leverage, their smallest word or action can accomplish a lot. *In business terminology, a high degree of operating leverage, other factors held constant, implies that a relatively small change in sales results in a large change in ROE.*

Figure 12-2 illustrates the concept of operating leverage by comparing the results that Strasburg could expect if it used different degrees of operating leverage. Plan A calls for a relatively small amount of fixed costs, $20,000. Here the firm would not have much automated equipment, so its depreciation, maintenance, property taxes, and so on would be low, but the total operating costs line has a relatively steep slope, indicating that variable costs per unit are higher than they would be if the firm used more operating leverage. Plan B calls for a higher level of fixed costs, $60,000. Here the firm uses automated equipment (with which one operator can turn out a few or many units at the same labor cost) to a much larger extent. The breakeven point is higher under Plan B: Breakeven occurs at 60,000 units under Plan B versus only 40,000 units under Plan A.

---

[3]For example, in 1993 utilities could buy coal in the spot market for about $30 per ton. Under a 5-year contract, coal costs about $50 per ton. Clearly, the price for reducing uncertainty was high!

FIGURE 12-2   STRASBURG ELECTRONICS: ILLUSTRATION OF OPERATING LEVERAGE

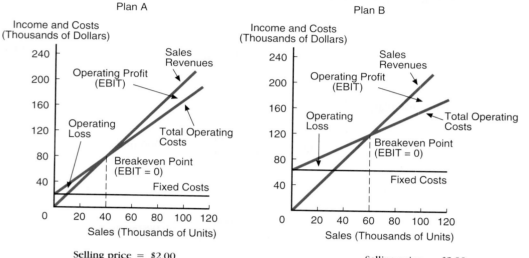

Plan A

Selling price = $2.00
Fixed costs = $20,000
Variable costs = $1.50 per unit

Plan B

Selling price = $2.00
Fixed costs = $60,000
Variable costs = $1.00 per unit

Prob-ability	Units Sold, Q	Sales	Plan A Operating Costs	EBIT	NI	ROE	Plan B Operating Costs	EBIT	NI	ROE
0.03	0	$ 0	$ 20,000	($20,000)	($12,000)	(6.9%)	$ 60,000	($ 60,000)	($36,000)	(20.6%)
0.07	40,000	80,000	80,000	0	0	0.0	100,000	(20,000)	(12,000)	(6.9)
0.15	60,000	120,000	110,000	10,000	6,000	3.4	120,000	0	0	0.0
0.50	110,000	220,000	185,000	35,000	21,000	12.0	170,000	50,000	30,000	17.1
0.15	160,000	320,000	260,000	60,000	36,000	20.6	220,000	100,000	60,000	34.3
0.07	180,000	360,000	290,000	70,000	42,000	24.0	240,000	120,000	72,000	41.1
0.03	220,000	440,000	350,000	90,000	54,000	30.9	280,000	160,000	96,000	54.9
Expected value				$35,000	$21,000	12.0%		$50,000	$30,000	17.1%
Standard deviation				$23,249	$13,949	8.0%		$46,497	$27,898	15.9%

Notes:
a. Strasburg Electronics has a 40 percent federal-plus-state tax rate.
b. The firm uses no debt financing.
c. For simplicity, we assume assets = equity = $175,000 under both plans.

We can calculate the breakeven quantity by recognizing that breakeven occurs when ROE = 0, and, hence, when earnings before interest and taxes (EBIT) = 0:

$$EBIT = 0 = PQ - VQ - F. \qquad (12\text{-}1)$$

this is its business risk, which is defined as the uncertainty inherent in projections of future ROE, assuming the firm is financed solely with common stock. If a firm uses debt and preferred stock (financial leverage), this concentrates its business risk on the common stockholders. To illustrate, suppose ten people decide to form a corporation to manufacture steel roof trusses. There is a certain amount of business risk in the operation. If the firm is capitalized only with common equity, and if each person buys 10 percent of the stock, then each investor shares equally in the business risk. However, suppose the firm is capitalized with 50 percent debt and 50 percent equity, with five of the investors putting up their capital as debt and the other five putting up their money as equity. In this case, the five investors who put up the equity will have to bear all of the business risk, so the common stock will be twice as risky as it would have been had the firm been financed only with equity. Thus, the use of debt, or *financial leverage,* concentrates the firm's business risk on its stockholders.

To illustrate the concentration of business risk, again consider Strasburg Electronics. Strasburg has $175,000 in assets and is all-equity financed.[5] If the firm were using Plan A from Figure 12-2, then its expected ROE would be 12.0 percent with a standard deviation of 8.0 percent. Now suppose the firm decides to change its capital structure by issuing $87,500 of debt at $k_d = 10\%$ and using these funds to replace $87,500 of equity. Its expected return on equity (which would now be only $87,500) would rise from 12 to 18 percent:

	New (Leveraged) Situation	Old (Unleveraged) Situation (See Table 12-2)
Expected EBIT (unchanged)	$35,000	$35,000
Interest (10% on $87,500 of debt)	8,750	0
Earnings before taxes	$26,250	$35,000
Taxes (40%)	10,500	14,000
Net income	$15,750	$21,000
Expected ROE = $15,750/$87,500 =	18% $21,000/$175,000 =	12%

Thus, the use of debt would "leverage up" the expected ROE from 12 percent to 18 percent.

However, financial leverage also increases risk to the equity investors. For example, suppose EBIT actually turned out to be $5,000 rather than the expected $35,000. If the firm used no debt, then ROE would decline from 12.0 percent to

---

[5] A firm in business for at least ten years would likely have far more than $175,000 in assets. We are purposely keeping Strasburg Electronics small so that we may focus on the concepts without being overwhelmed by the numbers. Also note that, to be consistent with capital structure theory, we should be working with market values of securities rather than book values of assets. We are using book values at this point to simplify the illustration, but we will discuss market value relationships later in the chapter. In this regard, see Haim Levy and Robert Brooks, "Financial Break-Even Analysis and the Value of the Firm," *Financial Management,* Autumn 1986, 22–26.

1.7 percent. However, with debt financing, ROE would fall from 18.0 to -2.6 percent:

	$87,500 of Debt	Zero Debt
Actual EBIT	$5,000	$5,000
Interest (10%)	8,750	0
Earnings before taxes	$-$ $3,750	$5,000
Taxes (40%)	$-$ 1,500	2,000
Net income	$-$ $2,250	$3,000
Actual ROE	-2.6%	1.7%
Expected ROE	18.0%	12.0%

A more complete analysis of the effects of leverage on Strasburg's ROE is illustrated in Figure 12-4. The two lines in the top graph show the level of ROE that would exist at different levels of EBIT under the two different capital structures. The lines were plotted from data developed as described previously, and they show that the greater the use of financial leverage, the more sensitive ROE is to changes in EBIT.

The lower panel of Figure 12-4 shows the effects of leverage on the firm's ROE probability distribution. With zero debt, the company would have an expected ROE of 12 percent, and a relatively tight distribution. With 50 percent debt, the expected ROE would rise to 18 percent, but the ROE distribution would be flatter, indicating a larger standard deviation of returns (σ_{ROE}) and a more risky situation for the equity investors. In fact, the standard deviation of ROE is 8.0 percent at zero debt, but exactly twice as high, 16.0 percent, at 50 percent debt.

Our conclusions from this total risk analysis may be stated as follows:

1. The use of debt generally increases a firm's expected ROE; this situation occurs whenever the expected return on assets (measured by EBIT/Total assets) exceeds the cost of debt.

2. The standard deviation of ROE if the firm uses zero financial leverage, $\sigma_{ROE(U)}$, is a measure of the firm's business risk, and σ_{ROE} at any debt level is a measure of the total risk borne by stockholders. $\sigma_{ROE} = \sigma_{ROE(U)}$ if the firm does not use any financial leverage. However, if the firm does use debt, then $\sigma_{ROE} > \sigma_{ROE(U)}$, because business risk is being concentrated on the stockholders.

3. The difference between σ_{ROE} and $\sigma_{ROE(U)}$ is a measure of the risk-increasing effects of financial leverage:

$$\text{Total risk} = \sigma_{ROE}.$$

$$\text{Business risk} = \sigma_{ROE(U)}.$$

$$\text{Financial risk} = \sigma_{ROE} - \sigma_{ROE(U)}.$$

In our example,

$$\text{Financial risk} = 16.0\% - 8.0\% = 8.0\%.$$

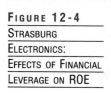

FIGURE 12-4
STRASBURG
ELECTRONICS:
EFFECTS OF FINANCIAL
LEVERAGE ON ROE

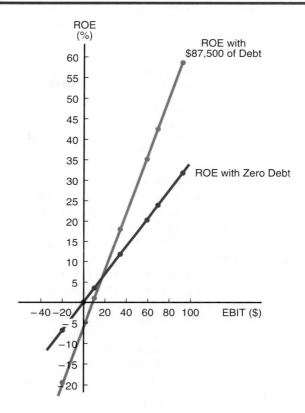

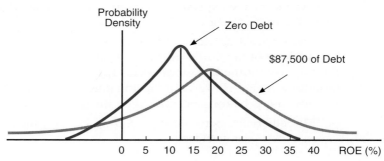

4. Operating leverage and financial leverage normally work in the same way; they both increase expected ROE, but they also increase the risk borne by stockholders.[6] Operating leverage affects the firm's business risk, financial leverage affects the firm's financial risk, and they both affect the firm's total risk.

SELF-TEST QUESTIONS

How can business risk be measured in a total risk context?

What are some determinants of business risk?

How can financial risk be measured within a total risk framework?

What is operating leverage? What are the similarities between operating leverage and financial leverage?

CAPITAL STRUCTURE THEORY: THE MODIGLIANI-MILLER MODELS

In the previous section, we demonstrated that the use of financial leverage typically increases both stockholders' risk and their expected return. But, is the increase in return sufficient to compensate stockholders for the increase in risk? To answer this question, we must turn our attention to capital structure theory. Although capital structure theory does not provide a complete answer to the question of optimal capital structure, it does provide many insights into the value of debt versus equity financing. Thus, an understanding of capital structure theory will aid a manager in establishing his or her firm's target capital structure.

Until 1958, capital structure theory consisted of loose assertions about investor behavior rather than carefully constructed models which could be tested by formal statistical studies. In what has been called the most influential set of financial papers ever published, Franco Modigliani and Merton Miller (MM) addressed the capital structure issue in a rigorous, scientific fashion, and they set off a chain of research that continues to this day.[7]

---

[6]Note that for operating leverage to benefit shareholders, the firm must be operating at a sales level above the breakeven point, and for financial leverage to be of benefit, the cost of debt must be less than the return on assets as measured by EBIT/Total assets. Normally, when managers make operating and financing decisions, they expect the firm to be operating above the breakeven point, and they expect the return on assets to exceed the cost of debt.

[7]See Franco Modigliani and Merton H. Miller, "The Cost of Capital, Corporation Finance and the Theory of Investment," *American Economic Review,* June 1958, 261–297; "The Cost of Capital, Corporation Finance and the Theory of Investment: Reply," *American Economic Review,* September 1958, 655–669; "Taxes and the Cost of Capital: A Correction," *American Economic Review,* June 1963, 433–443; and "Reply," *American Economic Review,* June 1965, 524–527. In a 1979 survey of Financial Management Association members, the original MM article was judged to have had the greatest impact on the field of finance of any work ever published. See Philip L. Cooley and J. Louis Heck, "Significant Contributions to Finance Literature," *Financial Management,* Tenth Anniversary Issue 1981, 23–33. Note that both Modigliani and Miller won Nobel prizes—Modigliani in 1985 and Miller in 1990.

Assumptions

To begin, MM made the following assumptions, some of which were later relaxed:

1. Business risk can be measured by σ_{EBIT}, and firms with the same degree of business risk are said to be in a *homogeneous risk class.*

2. All present and prospective investors have identical estimates of each firm's future EBIT; that is, investors have *homogeneous expectations* about expected future corporate earnings and the riskiness of those earnings. This assumption is comparable to our use of the "marginal investor" in earlier chapters when we discussed the DCF model and market equilibrium ($\hat{k}_s = k_s$).

3. Stocks and bonds are traded in *perfect capital markets.* This assumption implies, among other things, (a) that there are no brokerage costs and (b) that investors (both individuals and institutions) can borrow at the same rate as corporations.

4. The debt of firms and individuals is riskless, so the interest rate on debt is the risk-free rate. Further, this situation holds regardless of how much debt a firm (or an individual) uses.

5. All cash flows are perpetuities; that is, the firm is a zero-growth firm with an "expectationally constant" EBIT, and its bonds are perpetuities. "Expectationally constant" means that investors expect EBIT to be constant, but, after the fact, the realized level could be different from the expected level.

MM without Taxes

MM first performed their analysis under the assumption that there are no corporate or personal income taxes. On the basis of the preceding assumptions, and in the absence of corporate taxes, MM stated and algebraically proved two propositions:[8]

Proposition I. The value of any firm is established by capitalizing its expected net operating income (EBIT when T = 0) at a constant rate which is appropriate for the firm's risk class:

$$V_L = V_U = \frac{EBIT}{WACC} = \frac{EBIT}{k_{sU}}. \tag{12-2}$$

Here the subscript L designates a levered firm, which uses debt financing, and U designates an unlevered firm, which uses no debt financing. Both firms are assumed to be in the same risk class, and k_{sU} is the required rate of return for an unlevered,

---

[8]MM actually stated and proved three propositions, but the third one is not material to our discussion here.

or all-equity, firm. (For our purposes, it is easiest to think in terms of a single firm that has the option of either financing with all equity or using some combination of debt and equity.)

Since V as established by Equation 12-2 is a constant, *then under the MM model, when there are no taxes, the value of the firm is independent of its leverage.* As we shall show, this also implies (1) that the weighted average cost of capital to any firm is completely independent of its capital structure, and (2) that the WACC for any firm, regardless of the amount of debt financing it uses, is equal to the cost of equity it would have if it used no debt.

Proposition II. The cost of equity to a levered firm, k_{sL}, is equal to (1) the cost of equity to an unlevered firm in the same risk class, k_{sU}, plus (2) a risk premium whose size depends on both the differential between the costs of equity and debt to an unlevered firm and the amount of leverage used:

$$k_{sL} = k_{sU} + \text{Risk premium} = k_{sU} + (k_{sU} - k_d)(D/S). \qquad \text{(12-3)}$$

Here D = market value of the firm's debt, S = market value of the firm's equity, and k_d = constant cost of debt. *Proposition II states that as the firm's use of debt increases, its cost of equity also rises, and in a mathematically precise manner.*

Taken together, the two MM propositions imply that the inclusion of more debt in the capital structure will not increase the value of the firm, because the benefits of cheaper debt will be exactly offset by an increase in the riskiness, hence in the cost, of its equity. *Thus, the MM theory implies that in a world without taxes, both the value of a firm and its overall cost of capital are unaffected by its capital structure.*

MM'S ARBITRAGE PROOF

MM used an *arbitrage proof* to support their propositions.[9] They showed that, under their assumptions, if two companies differed only (1) in the way they are financed and (2) in their total market values, then investors would sell shares of the higher-valued firm, buy those of the lower-valued firm, and continue this process until the companies had exactly the same market value. To illustrate, assume that two firms, Firm L (for levered) and Firm U (for unlevered), are identical in all important respects except financial structure. Firm L has $4,000,000 of 7.5 percent debt, while Firm U uses only equity. Both firms have EBIT = $900,000, and σ_{EBIT} is the same for both firms, so they are in the same risk class.

---

[9]By *arbitrage* we mean the simultaneous buying and selling of essentially identical assets at different prices. The buying increases the price of the undervalued asset, and the selling decreases the price of the overvalued asset. Arbitrage operations will continue until prices have been adjusted to the point where the arbitrageur can no longer earn a profit, at which point the markets are in equilibrium.

MM assumed that all firms are in a zero-growth situation; that is, EBIT is expected to remain constant, and all earnings are paid out as dividends. Under this assumption, the total market value of a firm's common stock, S, is the present value of a perpetuity, which is found as follows:

$$S = \frac{\text{Dividends}}{k_s} = \frac{\text{Net income}}{k_s} = \frac{(\text{EBIT} - k_d D)(1 - T)}{k_s}. \qquad (12\text{-}4)$$

Equation 12-4 is merely the value of a perpetuity whose numerator is the net income available to common stockholders, which is all paid out as dividends, and whose denominator is the cost of common equity. In MM's zero-tax world, the tax rate, T, is zero, so Equation 12-4 becomes simply $(\text{EBIT} - k_d D)/k_s$.

Assume that in the initial situation, before any arbitrage occurs, both firms have the same equity capitalization rate: $k_{sU} = k_{sL} = 10\%$. Under this condition, according to Equation 12-4, the following situation would exist:

Firm U:

$$\begin{array}{l}\text{Value of} \\ \text{Firm U's} \\ \text{stock}\end{array} = S_U = \frac{\text{EBIT} - k_d D}{k_{sU}} = \frac{\$900,000 - \$0}{0.10} = \$9,000,000.$$

$$\begin{array}{l}\text{Total market} \\ \text{value of} \\ \text{Firm U}\end{array} = V_U = D_U + S_U = \$0 + \$9,000,000 = \$9,000,000.$$

Firm L:

$$\begin{array}{l}\text{Value of} \\ \text{Firm L's} \\ \text{stock}\end{array} = S_L = \frac{\text{EBIT} - k_d D}{k_{sL}}$$

$$= \frac{\$900,000 - 0.075(\$4,000,000)}{0.10} = \$6,000,000.$$

$$\begin{array}{l}\text{Total market} \\ \text{value of} \\ \text{Firm L}\end{array} = V_L = D_L + S_L = \$4,000,000 + \$6,000,000 = \$10,000,000.$$

Thus, before arbitrage, and assuming that $k_{sU} = k_{sL}$, the value of the levered Firm L exceeds that of unlevered Firm U.

MM argued that this is a disequilibrium situation which cannot persist. To see why, suppose you owned 10 percent of L's stock, so the market value of your investment was 0.10($6,000,000) = $600,000. According to MM, you could increase your total investment income without increasing your exposure to risk. For example, suppose you (1) sold your stock in L for $600,000, (2) borrowed an

amount equal to 10 percent of L's debt ($400,000), and then (3) bought 10 percent of U's stock for $900,000. Notice that you would receive $1,000,000 from the sale of your 10 percent of L's stock plus your borrowing, and you would be spending only $900,000 on U's stock, so you would have an extra $100,000, which MM assumed you would invest in riskless debt to yield 7.5 percent, or $7,500 annually.

Now consider your income positions:

Old Income:	10% of L's $600,000 equity income		$60,000
New Income:	10% of U's $900,000 equity income	$90,000	
	Less 7.5% interest on $400,000 loan	(30,000)	$60,000
	Plus 7.5% interest on extra $100,000		7,500
	Total new investment income		$67,500

Thus, your net investment income from common stock would be exactly the same as before, $60,000, but you would have $100,000 left over for investment in riskless debt, which would increase your income by $7,500. Therefore, the total return on your $600,000 net worth would rise to $67,500. Further, your risk, according to MM, would be the same as before; you would have simply substituted $400,000 of "homemade" leverage for your 10 percent share of Firm L's $4 million of corporate leverage, hence neither your "effective" debt nor your risk would have changed. Thus, you would have increased your income without raising your risk, which is obviously a desirable thing to do.

MM argued that this arbitrage process would actually occur, with sales of L's stock driving its price down, and purchases of U's stock driving its price up, until the market values of the two firms were equal. Until this equality was established, gains could be obtained by switching from one stock to the other, so the profit motive would force the equality to be reached. When equilibrium was established, the values of Firms L and U, and their weighted average costs of capital, would be equal. Thus, according to Modigliani and Miller, both a firm's value and its WACC must be independent of capital structure under equilibrium conditions.

Note that each of the assumptions listed at the beginning of this section is necessary for the arbitrage proof to work. For example, if the companies are not identical in business risk, then the arbitrage process cannot be invoked. We will discuss further implications of the assumptions later in the chapter.

MM WITH CORPORATE TAXES

MM's original work, published in 1958, assumed zero taxes. In 1963, they published a second article which included corporate tax effects. With corporate income taxes, they concluded that leverage will increase a firm's value, because interest on debt is a tax-deductible expense, hence more of a leveraged firm's operating income flows through to investors. Here are the MM propositions when corporations are subject to income taxes:

Proposition I.   The value of a levered firm is equal to (1) the value of an unlevered firm in the same risk class plus (2) the gain from leverage, which is the value of the tax savings and which equals the corporate tax rate times the amount of debt the firm uses:

$$V_L = V_U + TD. \tag{12-2a}$$

The important point here is that when corporate taxes are introduced, the value of the levered firm exceeds that of the unlevered firm by the amount TD. Note also that the differential increases as the use of debt increases, so a firm's value is maximized at virtually 100 percent debt financing.

The value of the unlevered firm can be found by using Equation 12-5. With zero debt, then D = \$0, and the value of the firm is its equity value. Thus,

$$S = V_U = \frac{EBIT(1 - T)}{k_{sU}}. \tag{12-5}$$

Proposition II.   The cost of equity to a levered firm is equal to (1) the cost of equity to an unlevered firm in the same risk class plus (2) a risk premium whose size depends on the differential between the costs of equity and debt to an unlevered firm, the amount of financial leverage used, and the corporate tax rate:

$$k_{sL} = k_{sU} + (k_{sU} - k_d)(1 - T)(D/S). \tag{12-3a}$$

Notice that Equation 12-3a is identical to the corresponding without-tax equation, 12-3, except for the term $(1 - T)$ in 12-3a. Since $(1 - T)$ is less than 1.0, the imposition of corporate taxes causes the cost of equity to rise at a slower rate than it did in the absence of taxes. It is this characteristic, along with the fact that the taxes reduce the effective cost of debt, that produces the Proposition I result, namely, the increase in firm value as leverage increases.

ILLUSTRATION OF THE MM MODELS

To illustrate the MM models, assume that the following data and conditions hold for Fredrickson Water Company, an old, established firm that supplies water to business and residential customers in several no-growth upstate New York metropolitan areas.

1. Fredrickson currently has no debt; it is an all-equity company.

2. Expected EBIT = $2,400,000. EBIT is not expected to increase over time, so Fredrickson is in a no-growth situation.

3. Fredrickson pays out all of its income as dividends.

4. If Fredrickson begins to use debt, it can borrow at a rate $k_d = 8\%$. This borrowing rate is constant, and it is independent of the amount of debt used. Any money raised by selling debt would be used to retire common stock, so Fredrickson's assets would remain constant.

5. The risk of Fredrickson's assets, and thus its EBIT, is such that its shareholders require a rate of return, k_{sU}, of 12 percent if no debt is used.

With Zero Taxes. To begin, assume that there are no taxes, so T = 0%. At any level of debt, Proposition I (Equation 12-2) can be used to find Fredrickson's value, $20 million:

$$V_L = V_U = \frac{\text{EBIT}}{k_{sU}} = \frac{\$2.4 \text{ million}}{0.12} = \$20.0 \text{ million.}$$

If Fredrickson uses $10 million of debt, its stock value must be $10 million:

$$S = V - D = \$20 \text{ million} - \$10 \text{ million} = \$10 \text{ million.}$$

We can also find Fredrickson's cost of equity, k_{sL}, and its WACC at a debt level of $10 million. First, we use Proposition II (Equation 12-3) to find k_{sL}, Fredrickson's leveraged cost of equity:

$$k_{sL} = k_{sU} + (k_{sU} - k_d)(D/S)$$

$$= 12\% + (12\% - 8\%)(\$10 \text{ million}/\$10 \text{ million})$$

$$= 12\% + 4.0\% = 16.0\%.$$

Now we can find the company's weighted average cost of capital:

$$\text{WACC} = (D/V)(k_d)(1 - T) + (S/V)k_s$$

$$= (\$10/\$20)(8\%)(1.0) + (\$10/\$20)(16.0\%) = 12.0\%.$$

Fredrickson's value and cost of capital based on the MM model with zero taxes at various debt levels are shown in Panel a of Figure 12-5. Here we see that in an MM world without taxes, financial leverage does not matter: The value of the firm and its overall cost of capital are independent of the amount of debt financing.

FIGURE 12-5 EFFECTS OF LEVERAGE: MM MODELS (MILLIONS OF DOLLARS)

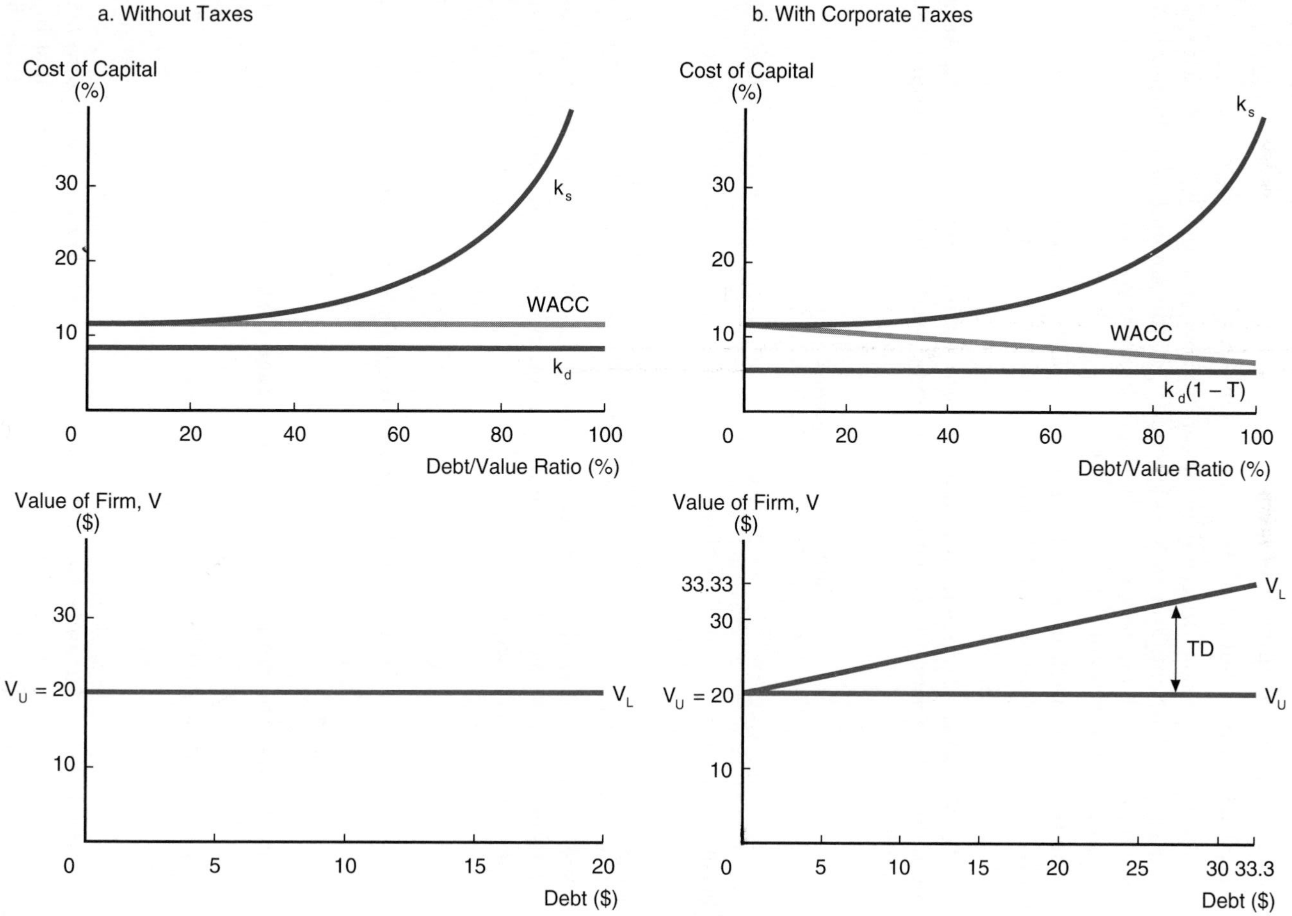

a. Without Taxes
Cost of Capital (%)
30
20
10
0
20
40
60
80
100
Debt/Value Ratio (%)
k_s
WACC
k_d
Value of Firm, V ($)
30
V_U = 20
10
0
5
10
15
20
Debt ($)
V_L
b. With Corporate Taxes
Cost of Capital (%)
k_s
WACC
$k_d(1 - T)$
Debt/Value Ratio (%)
Value of Firm, V ($)
33.33
30
V_U = 20
10
25
30 33.3
Debt ($)
V_L
TD
V_U

Without Taxes

D	V	S	D/V	k_d	k_s	WACC
$ 0	$20.00	$20.00	0.00%	8.0%	12.00%	12.00%
5	20.00	15.00	25.00	8.0	13.33	12.00
10	20.00	10.00	50.00	8.0	16.00	12.00
15	20.00	5.00	75.00	8.0	24.00	12.00
20	20.00	0.00	100.00	12.0	—	12.00

With Corporate Taxes

D	V	S	D/V	k_d	k_s	WACC
$ 0	$20.00	$20.00	0.00%	8.0%	12.00%	12.00%
5	22.00	17.00	22.73	8.0	12.71	10.91
10	24.00	14.00	41.67	8.0	13.71	10.00
15	26.00	11.00	57.69	8.0	15.27	9.23
20	28.00	8.00	71.43	8.0	18.00	8.57
25	30.00	5.00	83.33	8.0	24.00	8.00
30	32.00	2.00	93.75	8.0	48.00	7.50
33.33	33.33	0.00	100.00	12.0	—	12.00

With Corporate Taxes. To illustrate the MM model with corporate taxes, assume that all of the previous assumptions hold except these two:

1. Expected EBIT = $4,000,000.

2. Fredrickson has a 40 percent federal-plus-state tax rate, so T = 40%.

Note that, other things held constant, the introduction of corporate taxes would lower Fredrickson's value, so we increased its EBIT from $2.4 million to $4 million to make the comparison between the two models easier.

When Fredrickson has zero debt but pays taxes, Equation 12-5 can be used to find its value, $20 million:[10]

$$V_U = \frac{EBIT(1 - T)}{k_{sU}} = \frac{\$4 \text{ million}(0.6)}{0.12} = \$20.0 \text{ million}.$$

With $10 million of debt in a world with taxes, we see by Proposition I (Equation 12-2a) that Fredrickson's total market value rises to $24 million:

$$V_L = V_U + TD = \$20 \text{ million} + 0.4(\$10 \text{ million}) = \$24 \text{ million}.$$

Therefore, the value of Fredrickson's stock must be $14 million:

$$S = V - D = \$24 \text{ million} - \$10 \text{ million} = \$14 \text{ million}.$$

We can also find Fredrickson's cost of equity, k_{sL}, and its WACC at a debt level of $10 million. First, we use Proposition II (Equation 12-3a) to find k_{sL}, the leveraged cost of equity:

$$
\begin{aligned}
k_{sL} &= k_{sU} + (k_{sU} - k_d)(1 - T)(D/S) \\
&= 12\% + (12\% - 8\%)(0.6)(\$10 \text{ million}/\$14 \text{ million}) \\
&= 12\% + 1.71\% = 13.71\%.
\end{aligned}
$$

Now we can find the company's weighted average cost of capital:

$$
\begin{aligned}
WACC &= (D/V)(k_d)(1 - T) + (S/V)k_s \\
&= (\$10/\$24)(8\%)(0.6) + (\$14/\$24)(13.71\%) = 10.0\%.
\end{aligned}
$$

---

[10]Note that we increased Fredrickson's EBIT to $4.0 million. If we had left its EBIT at $2.4 million, the introduction of corporate taxes would have reduced the firm's value from $20 million to $12 million:

$$V_U = \frac{EBIT (1 - T)}{k_{sU}} = \frac{\$2.4 \text{ million } (0.6)}{0.12} = \$12.0 \text{ million}.$$

Corporate taxes reduce the amount of operating income available to investors by the factor $(1 - T)$, so the value of the firm is reduced by a like amount.

Fredrickson's value and cost of capital at various debt levels with corporate taxes are shown in Panel b of Figure 12-5. Here we see that in an MM world with corporate taxes, financial leverage does matter: The value of the firm is maximized, and its overall cost of capital is minimized, if it uses virtually 100 percent debt financing. Further, we see that the increase in value is due solely to the tax deductibility of interest payments, which lowers both the cost of debt and the increase in the cost of equity with leverage by $(1 - T)$.[11]

Self-Test Questions

What is the single most important conclusion of the MM zero-tax model?

What is the single most important conclusion of the MM model with corporate taxes?

How does Proposition I differ in the two models?

How does Proposition II differ in the two models?

What is the underlying cause of the "gain from leverage" in the MM with corporate taxes model?

Business and Financial Risk: A Market Risk Perspective

In our earlier discussion of business and financial risk, we focused on total risk, using $\sigma_{ROE(U)}$ as the measure of business risk and σ_{ROE} as the measure of the total risk borne by the stockholders in a leveraged firm. Thus, in the total risk sense, $\sigma_{ROE} - \sigma_{ROE(U)}$ is a measure of financial risk. Recall, though, that part of total risk can be eliminated if stockholders diversify their own portfolios. This point is ad-

---

[11]In the limiting case, where the firm used 100 percent debt financing, the bondholders would own the entire company; thus, they would have to bear all the business risk. (Up until this point, MM assume that the stockholders bear all the risk.) If the bondholders bear all the risk, then the capitalization rate on the debt should be equal to the equity capitalization rate at zero debt, $k_d = k_{sU} = 12\%$.

The income stream to the stockholders in the all-equity case was $CF_U = \$4,000,000(1 - T) = \$2,400,000$, and the value of the firm was

$$V_U = \frac{\$2,400,000}{0.12} = \$20,000,000.$$

With all debt, the entire $4,000,000 of EBIT would be used to pay interest charges—k_d would be 12 percent, so $I = 0.12(\text{Debt}) = \$4,000,000$. Taxes would be zero, and investors (bondholders) would get the entire $4,000,000 of operating income; they would not have to share it with the government. Thus, at 100 percent debt, the value of the firm would be

$$V_L = \frac{\$4,000,000}{0.12} = \$33,333,333 = D.$$

There is, of course, a transition problem in all this—MM assume that $k_d = 8\%$ regardless of how much debt the firm has until debt reaches 100 percent, at which point k_d jumps to 12 percent, the cost of equity. As we shall see later in the chapter, k_d realistically rises as the use of financial leverage increases.

dressed in this section, where we consider business and financial risk from a *market,* or *beta, risk* standpoint.

Robert Hamada combined the Capital Asset Pricing Model (CAPM) that we presented in Chapter 5 with the MM after-tax model that we discussed in the last section to obtain this expression for k_{sL}, the cost of equity to a leveraged firm:[12]

$$k_{sL} = \frac{\text{Risk-free}}{\text{rate}} + \frac{\text{Business risk}}{\text{premium}} + \frac{\text{Financial risk}}{\text{premium}} \quad (12\text{-}6)$$

$$= k_{RF} + (k_M - k_{RF})b_U + (k_M - k_{RF})b_U(1 - T)(D/S).$$

Here b_U is the beta coefficient the firm would have if it used no financial leverage, and the other terms are as defined in previous chapters. In effect, Equation 12-6 partitions the required rate of return on the stock into three components: k_{RF}, the risk-free rate, which compensates shareholders for the time value of money; a premium for business risk as reflected by the term $(k_M - k_{RF})b_U$; and a premium for financial risk as reflected by the third term, $(k_M - k_{RF})b_U (1 - T)(D/S)$. If a firm has no financial leverage (D = $0), then the financial risk premium term would be zero (the third term would drop out) and equity investors would be compensated only for business risk.

As we will see, the MM model with corporate taxes does not hold exactly, and we also know that the CAPM does not fully describe investor behavior. Therefore, Equation 12-6 must be regarded as an approximation. Nevertheless, Equation 12-6 can provide financial managers with some useful insights. As an illustration, assume that Firm U, an unlevered company with b_U = 1.5 and $100,000 of equity (S = $100,000), is considering replacing $20,000 of equity with debt. Assuming also that k_{RF} = 10%, k_M = 15%, and T = 34%, then Firm U's current unlevered required rate of return on equity would be 17.5 percent:

$$k_{sU} = 10\% + (15\% - 10\%)1.5$$

$$= 10\% + 7.5\% = 17.5\%.$$

This shows that the business risk premium is 7.5 percentage points. If the firm were to add $20,000 of debt to its capital structure, then its new value, according to MM, would be $V_L = V_U + TD = \$100,000 + 0.34(\$20,000) = \$106,800$, and its k_s, using Equation 12-6, would rise to 18.64 percent:

$$k_{sL} = 10\% + (15\% - 10\%)1.5 + (15\% - 10\%)1.5(1 - 0.34)(\$20,000/\$86,800)$$

$$= 10\% + 7.5\% + 1.14\% = 18.64\%.$$

---

[12]See Robert S. Hamada, "Portfolio Analysis, Market Equilibrium, and Corporation Finance," *Journal of Finance,* March 1969, 13–31. Note that Thomas Conine and Maurry Tamarkin have extended Hamada's work to include risky debt. See "Divisional Cost of Capital Estimation: Adjusting for Leverage," *Financial Management,* Spring 1985, 54–58.

Thus, adding $20,000 of debt to the capital structure would result in a financial risk premium on the stock of 1.14 percentage points, which would be added to the business risk premium of 7.5 percentage points.

Hamada also showed that Equation 12-6 can be used to analyze the effect of financial leverage on beta. We know that the SML can be used to estimate any firm's required rate of return on equity:

$$\text{SML: } k_s = k_{RF} + (k_M - k_{RF})b.$$

Now, by equating the SML equation with Equation 12-6, we obtain:

$$k_{RF} + (k_M - k_{RF})b = k_{RF} + (k_M - k_{RF})b_U + (k_M - k_{RF})b_U(1 - T)(D/S)$$

$$(k_M - k_{RF})b = (k_M - k_{RF})b_U + (k_M - k_{RF})b_U(1 - T)(D/S)$$

$$b = b_U + b_U(1 - T)(D/S), \qquad \text{(12-7)}$$

or

$$b = b_U[1 + (1 - T)(D/S)]. \qquad \text{(12-7a)}$$

Thus, under the MM and CAPM assumptions, the beta of any firm is equal to the beta the firm would have if it used zero debt, adjusted upward by a factor that depends on (1) the corporate tax rate and (2) the amount of financial leverage employed.[13] Therefore, the firm's market risk, which is measured by b, depends on both the firm's business risk as measured by b_U and its financial risk as measured by $b - b_U = b_U(1 - T)(D/S)$.

To continue our illustration, if Firm U were to replace $20,000 of equity with debt, its beta would increase from 1.5 to 1.728, according to Equation 12-7a:

$$b = b_U[1 + (1 - T)(D/S)]$$

$$= 1.5[1 + (1 - 0.34)(20,000/\$86,800)]$$

$$= 1.5(1.152) = 1.728.$$

---

[13]If a firm uses preferred stock financing, then Equation 12-7 becomes

$$b = b_U + b_U(P/S) + b_U(1 - T)(D/S),$$

where P = market value of preferred stock. Here the unlevered beta is adjusted upward by the preferred stock as well as the debt.

We can confirm the Equation 12-6 value of $k_{sL} = 18.64\%$ by using $b = 1.728$ in the SML:

$$k_s = k_{RF} + (k_M - k_{RF})b$$

$$= 10\% + (15\% - 10\%)1.728 = 18.64\%.$$

These relationships can be used to help estimate a company's or a division's cost of equity. In both instances, we proceed by obtaining betas for similar publicly traded firms and then "lever them up or down" to make them consistent with our own firm's (or division's) capital structure and tax rate. The result is an estimate of our firm's (or division's) beta, given (1) its business risk as measured by the betas of other firms in the same line of business and (2) its financial risk as measured by its own capital structure and tax rate.

SELF-TEST QUESTIONS

According to Hamada, the required rate of return on a stock consists of three elements. What are they?

How is business risk measured within a market risk framework?

How is financial risk measured within a market risk framework?

What is the relationship between levered and unlevered betas according to Hamada?

CAPITAL STRUCTURE THEORY: THE MILLER MODEL

Although MM included *corporate* taxes in the second version of their model, they did not extend the model to analyze the effects of *personal* taxes. However, in his 1976 presidential address to the American Finance Association, Merton Miller did introduce a model designed to show how leverage affects firms' values when both personal and corporate taxes are taken into account.[14] To explain Miller's model, let us begin by defining T_c as the corporate tax rate, T_s as the personal tax rate on income from stocks, and T_d as the personal tax rate on income from debt. Note that stock returns come partly as dividends and partly as capital gains, so T_s is a weighted average of the effective tax rates on dividends and capital gains, while essentially all debt income comes from interest, which is effectively taxed at an investor's top rate.

With personal taxes included, *and under the same set of assumptions used in the earlier MM models,* the value of an unlevered firm is found as follows on page 544:

---

[14]See Merton H. Miller, "Debt and Taxes," *Journal of Finance,* May 1977, 261–275.

$$V_U = \frac{EBIT(1 - T_c)(1 - T_s)}{k_{sU}}. \qquad (12\text{-}8)$$

The $(1 - T_s)$ term adjusts for personal taxes. Therefore, the numerator shows how much of the firm's operating income is left after the unlevered firm itself pays corporate income taxes and its investors subsequently pay personal taxes on their equity income. Since the introduction of personal taxes lowers the usable income to investors, personal taxes reduce the value of the unlevered firm, other things held constant.

Miller's results can be obtained from an arbitrage proof similar to the one we presented earlier. However, the alternative proof shown below is easier to follow. To begin, we partition the levered firm's annual cash flows, CF_L, into those going to the stockholders and those going to the bondholders, considering both corporate and personal taxes:

$$
\begin{aligned}
CF_L &= \quad \text{Net CF to stockholders} \quad + \text{ Net CF to bondholders} \\
&= (EBIT - I)(1 - T_c)(1 - T_s) + \qquad I(1 - T_d).
\end{aligned}
\qquad (12\text{-}9)
$$

Here I is the annual interest payment. Equation 12-9 can be rearranged as follows:

$$CF_L = [EBIT(1 - T_c)(1 - T_s)] - [I(1 - T_c)(1 - T_s)] + [I(1 - T_d)]. \qquad (12\text{-}9a)$$

The first term in Equation 12-9a is identical to the after-tax cash flow of an unlevered firm as shown in Equation 12-8, and its present value is found by discounting the perpetual cash flow by k_{sU}. The second and third terms, which reflect leverage, result from the cash flows associated with interest payments, and these two cash flows are assumed to have a risk equal to that of the basic interest payment stream, hence their present values are obtained by discounting at the cost of debt, k_d. (Remember, these are all perpetual cash flows, so the basic perpetuity valuation model, $V = CF/k$, applies.) Combining the present values of the three terms, we obtain this value for the levered firm:

$$V_L = \frac{EBIT(1 - T_c)(1 - T_s)}{k_{sU}} - \frac{I(1 - T_c)(1 - T_s)}{k_d} + \frac{I(1 - T_d)}{k_d}. \qquad (12\text{-}10)$$

The first term in Equation 12-10 is identical to V_U as set forth in Equation 12-8, and when we consolidate the second two terms we obtain this equation:

$$V_L = V_U + \frac{I(1 - T_d)}{k_d}\left[1 - \frac{(1 - T_c)(1 - T_s)}{(1 - T_d)}\right].\qquad \text{(12-10a)}$$

Now recognize that the after-tax perpetual interest payment divided by the required rate of return on debt, $I(1 - T_d)/k_d$, equals the market value of the debt, D. Substituting D into the preceding equation, and rearranging, we obtain this very important expression, called the Miller model:

$$\text{Miller model: } V_L = V_U + \left[1 - \frac{(1 - T_c)(1 - T_s)}{(1 - T_d)}\right]D.\qquad \text{(12-11)}$$

The Miller model estimates the value of a levered firm in a world with both corporate and personal taxes.

The Miller model has several important implications:

1. The term in brackets,

$$\left[1 - \frac{(1 - T_c)(1 - T_s)}{(1 - T_d)}\right],$$

when multiplied by D, represents the gain from leverage. The bracketed term replaces the factor $T = T_c$ in the earlier MM model with corporate taxes, $V_L = V_U + TD$.

2. If we ignore all taxes, that is, if $T_c = T_s = T_d = 0$, then the bracketed term reduces to zero, so in that case Equation 12-11 is the same as the original MM model without taxes.

3. If we ignore personal taxes, that is, if $T_s = T_d = 0$, then the bracketed term reduces to $[1 - (1 - T_c)] = T_c$, so Equation 12-11 is the same as the MM model with corporate taxes.

4. If the effective personal tax rates on stock and bond incomes were equal, that is, if $T_s = T_d$, then $(1 - T_s)$ and $(1 - T_d)$ would cancel, and the bracketed term would again reduce to T_c.

5. If $(1 - T_c)(1 - T_s) = (1 - T_d)$, then the bracketed term would go to zero, and the value of using leverage would also be zero. This implies that the tax advantage of debt to the firm would be exactly offset by the personal tax advantage of equity. Under this condition, capital structure would have no effect on a firm's value or its cost of capital, so we would be back to MM's original zero-tax theory.

6. Because taxes on capital gains are both lower at the top personal rate and deferred, the effective tax rate on stock income is normally less than on bond income. This being the case, what would the Miller model predict as the gain from

leverage? To answer this question, assume that the tax rate on corporate income is $T_c = 34\%$, the effective rate on bond income is $T_d = 28\%$, and the effective rate on stock income is $T_s = 20\%$.[15] Using these values in the Miller model, we find that a levered firm's value increases over that of an unlevered firm by 27 percent of the market value of corporate debt:

$$\text{Gain from leverage} = \left[1 - \frac{(1 - T_c)(1 - T_s)}{(1 - T_d)}\right]D$$

$$= \left[1 - \frac{(1 - 0.34)(1 - 0.20)}{(1 - 0.28)}\right]D$$

$$= [1 - 0.73]D = 0.27(D).$$

Note that the MM model with corporate taxes would indicate a gain from leverage of $T_c(D) = 0.34D$, or 34 percent of the amount of corporate debt. Thus, with these assumed tax rates, adding personal taxes to the model lowers the benefit from corporate debt financing. In general, whenever the effective tax rate on stock income is less than the effective rate on bond income, the Miller model produces a lower gain from leverage than is produced by the MM with-tax model.

In his paper, Miller argued that firms in the aggregate would issue a mix of debt and equity securities such that the before-tax yields on corporate securities and the personal tax rates of the investors who bought these securities would adjust until an equilibrium was reached. At the equilibrium, $(1 - T_d)$ would equal $(1 - T_c)(1 - T_s)$, so, as we noted earlier in Point 5, the tax advantage of debt to the firm would be exactly offset by personal taxation, and capital structure would have no effect on a firm's value or its cost of capital. Thus, according to Miller, the conclusions derived from the original Modigliani-Miller zero-tax model are correct!

Others have extended and tested Miller's 1977 analysis. Generally, these extensions disagree with Miller's conclusion that there is no advantage to the use of corporate debt. In the United States, the effective tax rate on income from stock is less than on income from bonds. Thus, it appears that $(1 - T_c)(1 - T_s)$ is less than $(1 - T_d)$, and there is an advantage to the use of corporate debt. However, Miller's work does show that personal taxes offset some of the benefits of corporate debt, so the tax advantages of corporate debt are less than were implied by the earlier MM model that considered only corporate taxes.

As we note in the next section, there are a number of problems with both the MM and the Miller models, so one should not put great trust in results such as those in our examples.

---

[15]In a 1978 article, Miller and Scholes described how investors could, theoretically, shelter or delay income from stock to the point where the effective personal tax rate on such income is essentially zero. See Merton H. Miller and Myron S. Scholes, "Dividends and Taxes," *Journal of Financial Economics,* December 1978, 333–364. However, the 1986 changes in the tax law eliminated most of the shelters Miller and Scholes discussed.

SELF-TEST QUESTIONS

How does the Miller model differ from the MM model with corporate taxes?

What are the implications of the Miller model if $T_c = T_s = T_d = 0$?

What are the implications if $T_s = T_d = 0$?

Considering the current tax structure in the United States, what is the primary implication of the Miller model?

CRITICISMS OF THE MM AND MILLER MODELS

The conclusions of the MM and Miller models followed logically from their initial assumptions. However, both academicians and financial executives have voiced concern over the validity of the MM and Miller models, and virtually no firms adhere strictly to their recommendations. The MM zero-tax model leads to the conclusion that capital structure doesn't matter, yet we observe some regularities in structure within industries. Further, when used with "reasonable" tax rates, both the MM model with corporate taxes and the Miller model lead to the conclusion that firms should use 100 percent debt financing, a condition found only for firms whose equity has been eroded by operating losses. People who disagree with the MM and Miller theories generally attack them on the grounds that their assumptions are not correct. Some of the main objections include the following:

1. Both MM and Miller assume that personal and corporate leverage are perfect substitutes. However, an individual investing in a levered firm has less loss exposure, which means a more *limited liability,* than if he or she used "homemade" leverage. For example, in our earlier illustration of the MM arbitrage argument, it should be noted that only the $600,000 our investor had in Firm L would be lost if that firm went bankrupt. However, if the investor engaged in arbitrage transactions and employed "homemade" leverage to invest in Firm U, then he or she could lose $900,000—the original $600,000 investment plus the $400,000 loan less the $100,000 investment in riskless bonds. This increased personal risk exposure would tend to restrain investors from engaging in arbitrage, and that could cause the equilibrium values of V_L, V_U, k_{sL}, and k_{sU} to be different from those specified by the models. Restrictions on institutional investors, who dominate capital markets today, may also retard the arbitrage process, because most institutional investors cannot legally borrow to buy stocks, hence they are prohibited from engaging in homemade leverage.

2. Brokerage costs were assumed away by MM and Miller, making the switch from L to U costless. However, brokerage and other transaction costs do exist, and they too impede the arbitrage process.

3. MM initially assumed that corporations and investors can borrow at the risk-free rate. Although risky debt has been introduced into the analysis by others, to reach the MM and Miller conclusions it is still necessary to assume that both corporations and investors can borrow at the same rate. While major institutional

investors probably can borrow at the corporate rate, many institutions are not allowed to borrow to buy securities. Further, most individual investors probably must borrow at higher rates than those paid by large corporations.

4. In his article, Miller concluded that an equilibrium would be reached, but to reach his equilibrium the tax benefit from corporate debt (a) must be the same for all firms, and (b) it must be constant for an individual firm regardless of the amount of leverage used. However, we know that tax benefits vary from firm to firm: Highly profitable companies gain the maximum tax benefit from leverage, while the benefits to firms that are struggling are much smaller. Further, some firms have other tax shields such as high depreciation, pension plan contributions, and operating loss carry-forwards, and these shields reduce the tax savings value of interest payments.[16] It also appears simplistic to assume that the expected tax shield is unaffected by the amount of debt financing used. Higher leverage increases the probability that the firm cannot effectively use the full tax shield in the future, because higher leverage increases the probability of future unprofitability and consequently lower tax rates. All things considered, it appears likely that the interest tax shield from corporate debt is more valuable to some firms than to others.

5. MM and Miller assume that there are no costs associated with financial distress. Further, they ignore agency costs. These topics are discussed in the next section.

SELF-TEST QUESTIONS

Should we accept one of the models presented thus far (MM with zero taxes, MM with corporate taxes, or Miller) as being correct? Why or why not?

Which of the assumptions used in the models is most worrisome to you, and what does "worrisome" mean in this context?

FINANCIAL DISTRESS AND AGENCY COSTS

Some of the assumptions inherent in the MM and Miller models can be relaxed, and when this is done, their basic conclusions remain unchanged.[17] However, as we discuss next, when financial distress and agency costs are added, the MM and Miller results are altered significantly.

---

[16]For a discussion of the impact of tax shields other than debt financing, see Harry DeAngelo and Ronald W. Masulis, "Optimal Capital Structure under Corporate and Personal Taxation," *Journal of Financial Economics,* March 1980, 3–30.

[17]For example, see Robert A. Haugen and James L. Pappas, "Equilibrium in the Pricing of Capital Assets, Risk-Bearing Debt Instruments, and the Question of Optimal Capital Structure," *Journal of Financial and Quantitative Analysis,* June 1971, 943–954; Joseph Stiglitz, "A Re-Examination of the Modigliani-Miller Theorem," *American Economic Review,* December 1969, 784–793; and Mark E. Rubenstein, "A Mean-Variance Synthesis of Corporate Financial Theory," *Journal of Finance,* March 1973, 167–181.

COSTS OF FINANCIAL DISTRESS

Financial distress includes, but is not restricted to, bankruptcy, and when distress occurs, several things can happen:

1. Arguments between claimants often delay the liquidation of assets. Bankruptcy cases can take many years to settle, and during this time machinery rusts, buildings are vandalized, inventories become obsolete, and the like.

2. Lawyer's fees, court costs, and administrative expenses can absorb a large part of the firm's value. Together, the costs of physical deterioration plus legal fees and administrative expenses are called the *direct costs* of financial distress.

3. Managers and other employees generally lose their jobs when a firm fails. Knowing this, the management of a firm that is in financial distress may take actions which keep it alive in the short run but which also dilute long-run value. For example, the firm may defer maintenance of machinery, sell off valuable assets at bargain prices to raise cash, or cut costs so much that the quality of its products or services is impaired and the firm's long-run market position is eroded.

4. Both customers and suppliers are aware of the problems that can arise, and they often take "evasive action" that further damages the troubled firm. For example, Eastern Airlines, as it struggled to deal with its unions and to avoid liquidation in 1990, was having trouble selling tickets because potential customers were worried about buying a seat for a future flight and then having the company shut down before they could take the trip. Some potential customers were also worried that the company might cut back on maintenance, and its suppliers were reluctant to grant normal credit terms or to gear up to supply Eastern with parts and other materials on a long-term basis. Finally, Eastern had trouble attracting and retaining the highest-quality workers, as most workers with a choice prefer employment with a more stable airline to one that could go out of business at any time.

Nonoptimal managerial actions associated with financial distress, as well as the costs imposed by customers, suppliers, and capital providers, are called the *indirect costs* of financial distress. Of course, these costs may be incurred by a firm in financial distress even if it does not go into bankruptcy: Bankruptcy is just one point on the continuum of financial distress.

All things considered, the direct and indirect costs associated with financial distress are high.[18] Further, financial distress typically occurs only if a firm has debts — debt-free firms do not usually experience financial distress. *Therefore, the greater the use of debt financing, and the larger the fixed interest charges, the greater the probability that a decline in earnings will lead to financial distress, hence the higher the probability that the costs of financial distress will be incurred.*

---

[18]See Edward I. Altman, "A Further Empirical Investigation of the Bankruptcy Cost Question," *Journal of Finance,* September 1984, 1067–1089. On the basis of a sample of 26 bankrupt companies, Altman found that bankruptcy costs often exceed 20 percent of firm value.

TABLE 12-1		Amount of Debt				
FREDRICKSON WATER COMPANY: EXPECTED COSTS OF FINANCIAL DISTRESS		$0	$5 Million	$10 Million	$20 Million	$30 Million
	Probability of financial distress	0.0	0.05	0.15	0.50	0.95
	PV of expected costs of financial distress[a]	$0	$250,000	$750,000	$2,500,000	$4,750,000

[a]$5 million times the indicated probability.

An increase in the probability of future financial distress lowers the current value of a firm and raises its cost of capital. To see why, suppose we estimate that Fredrickson Water will incur financial distress costs of $7 million if it fails at some future date, and that the *present value* of this possible future cost is $5 million. Further, the probability of financial distress increases with leverage, causing the expected present value cost of financial distress to rise from zero at zero debt to $4.75 million at $30 million of debt as shown in Table 12-1.

These expected costs of financial distress must be subtracted from the values we previously calculated in Part b of Figure 12-5 to find the firm's value at various amounts of leverage: They would reduce the values of V and S and, as a result, would raise k_s and the WACC. For example, at $20 million of debt, we would obtain the values in Table 12-2.[19] These changes would, of course, then have carry-through effects on the graphs in Panel b of Figure 12-5—most important, they would (1) reduce the decline of the WACC line and (2) reduce the slope of the V_L line.

The effects of financial distress are also felt by a firm's bondholders. Firms experiencing financial distress have a higher probability of defaulting on debt payments, so the higher the probability of financial distress, the higher the required return on debt. Thus, as a firm uses more and more debt, hence increasing the probability of distress, the value of k_d also increases, causing several elements in Panel b of Figure 12-5 to change.

AGENCY COSTS

We introduced the concept of agency costs in Chapter 1. One type of agency cost is associated with the use of debt, and it involves the relationship between a firm's

---

[19]To find k_s and the WACC in Table 12-2, simply transpose Equation 12-4 and then apply the definition for the WACC:

$$k_s = \frac{(EBIT - k_d D)(1 - T)}{S} = \frac{[\$4 - 0.08(\$20)](1 - 0.4)}{\$5.5} = 26.18\%.$$

$$WACC = (D/V)(k_d)(1 - T) + (S/V)(k_s)$$
$$= (\$20/\$25.5)(8\%)(0.6) + (\$5.5/\$25.5)(26.18\%)$$
$$= 3.76\% + 5.65\% = 9.41\%.$$

TABLE 12-2 FREDRICKSON WATER COMPANY: EFFECTS OF FINANCIAL DISTRESS (MILLIONS OF DOLLARS)		Values at D = $20 Million with Financial Distress Effects Ignored: Pure MM	Values at D = $20 Million with Financial Distress Effects Considered: Modified MM
	V	$28.00	$28.00 − $2.5 = $25.5
	S	$8.00	$8.00 − $2.5 = $5.5
	k_s	18.00%	26.18%
	WACC	8.57%	9.41%

stockholders and its bondholders. In the absence of any restrictions, a firm's management would be tempted to take actions that would benefit stockholders at the expense of bondholders. For example, if Fredrickson Water were to sell only a small amount of debt, then this debt would have relatively little risk, hence a high bond rating and a low interest rate. Yet, after it sold the low-risk debt, Fredrickson could issue more debt secured by the same assets as the original debt. This would raise the risks faced by *all bondholders,* cause k_d to rise, and consequently cause the original bondholders to suffer capital losses. Similarly, suppose that after issuing a substantial amount of debt, Fredrickson decided to restructure its assets, selling off assets with low business risk and acquiring assets that were more risky but that also had higher expected rates of return. If things worked out well, the stockholders would benefit. If things went sour, most of the loss in a highly leveraged firm would fall on the bondholders. So, stockholders would be playing a game of "heads, I win; tails, you lose" with bondholders.

Because of the possibility that stockholders might try to take advantage of bondholders in these and other ways, bonds are protected by restrictive covenants. These covenants hamper the corporation's legitimate operations to some extent. Further, the company must be monitored to ensure that the covenants are being obeyed, and the costs of monitoring are passed on to the stockholders in the form of higher debt costs. The costs of lost efficiency plus monitoring are an important type of *agency cost,* which increases the cost of debt and reduces the value of the equity, and thus reduces the advantage of debt.[20]

VALUE OF THE FIRM AND COST OF CAPITAL CONSIDERING FINANCIAL DISTRESS AND AGENCY COSTS

If the MM model with corporate taxes were correct, a firm's value would rise continuously as it moved from zero debt toward 100 percent debt: The equation $V_L = V_U + TD$ shows that TD, hence V_L, is maximized if D is at a maximum. Recall

---

[20]Jensen and Meckling point out that there are also agency costs between outside equity holders and management. See "Theory of the Firm: Managerial Behavior, Agency Costs, and Ownership Structure," *Journal of Financial Economics,* October 1976, 305–360. Their study further suggests that (1) bondholder agency costs increase as the debt ratio increases, but (2) outside stockholder agency costs move in reverse fashion, falling with increased use of debt.

FIGURE 12-6

NET EFFECTS OF

LEVERAGE ON THE

VALUE OF THE FIRM

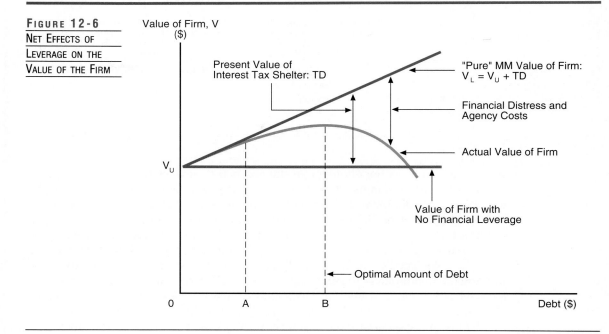

FIGURE 12-6
NET EFFECTS OF
LEVERAGE ON THE
VALUE OF THE FIRM

that the increasing component of value, TD, arises as a direct result of the tax shelter provided by interest on the debt. However, two factors which are not reflected in the MM model could cause V_L to decline as the level of debt rises: (1) costs associated with potential future financial distress, and (2) agency costs. Therefore, the relationship between a firm's value and its use of leverage should look like this:

$$V_L = V_U + TD - \begin{pmatrix} \text{PV of} \\ \text{expected} \\ \text{financial} \\ \text{distress costs} \end{pmatrix} - \begin{pmatrix} \text{PV of} \\ \text{agency} \\ \text{costs} \end{pmatrix}. \qquad (12\text{-}12)$$

The relationship expressed in Equation 12-12 is graphed in Figure 12-6. The tax shelter effect totally dominates until the amount of debt reaches Point A. After Point A, financial distress and agency costs become increasingly important, offsetting some of the tax advantages. At Point B, the marginal tax shelter benefit of additional debt is exactly offset by the disadvantages of debt, and beyond Point B, the disadvantages outweigh the tax benefit.

Equation 12-11, the Miller model, can also be modified to reflect financial distress and agency costs. The equation would be identical to Equation 12-12, except

that the gain from leverage term, TD, would reflect the addition of personal taxes. In either the MM or Miller models, the gain from leverage can at least be roughly estimated, but the value reduction resulting from potential financial distress and agency costs is almost entirely subjective. We know that these costs must increase as leverage rises, but we simply do not know the specific functional relationships.

The addition of financial distress and agency costs to either the MM tax model or the Miller model results in a *trade-off model* of capital structure. In such a model, the optimal capital structure can be visualized as a trade-off between the benefit of debt financing (the interest tax shelter) and the costs of debt financing (financial distress and agency costs). In the next chapter, we will continue our discussion of the trade-off model and examine its implications.

SELF-TEST QUESTIONS

Describe some types of financial distress and agency costs.

How are these costs related to the use of financial leverage?

How are the basic MM with corporate taxes and Miller models affected by the inclusion of financial distress and agency costs?

SUMMARY

This chapter began our discussion of capital structure decisions. The key concepts covered are listed below:

▶ *Business risk* is the inherent riskiness in a firm's operations if it uses no debt. *Financial risk* is the additional risk that is concentrated on the shareholders when debt financing is used. Business and financial risk can be viewed from either a *total risk* or *market risk* perspective.

▶ Within a *total risk framework*, business risk can be measured by $\sigma_{ROE(U)}$, total risk can be measured by σ_{ROE}, and financial risk can be measured by Total risk − Business risk = $\sigma_{ROE} - \sigma_{ROE(U)}$.

▶ The *Hamada model* combines the CAPM with MM (with corporate taxes) to produce the following equation:

$$k_{sL} = k_{RF} + (k_M - k_{RF})b_U + (k_M - k_{RF})b_U(1 - T)(D/S).$$

This equation shows that the required rate of return on a levered company's stock is equal to the risk-free rate, which compensates investors for the time value of money, plus a premium for business risk, plus another premium for financial risk.

▶ Within a *market risk framework*, business risk can be measured by b_U, market risk can be measured by b, and financial risk can be measured by $b - b_U = b_U(1 - T)(D/S)$.

▶ In 1958, *Franco Modigliani and Merton Miller (MM)* startled the academic community by proving, under a restrictive set of assumptions including zero taxes, that capital structure is irrelevant; that is, according to the original MM article, a firm's value is not affected by its financing mix.

▶ *MM* later added *corporate taxes* to their model, leading to the conclusion that capital structure does matter, and that firms should use almost 100 percent debt financing in order to maximize value.

▶ MM's model with corporate taxes demonstrated that the benefits of debt financing stem solely from the *tax deductibility of interest payments.*

▶ Much later, Miller extended the theory to include *personal taxes.* The introduction of personal taxes reduces, but does not eliminate, the benefits of debt financing. Thus, the *Miller model* also leads to 100 percent debt financing.

▶ The addition of financial distress and agency costs to either the MM corporate tax model or the Miller model results in a *trade-off model.* Here the marginal costs and benefits of debt financing are balanced against one another, and the result is an optimal capital structure that falls somewhere between zero and 100 percent debt.

In the next chapter, we will examine some additional issues which provide further insights into the capital structure decision.

QUESTIONS

12-1 Define each of the following terms:

    a. Capital structure

    b. Business risk

    c. Financial risk

    d. Operating leverage

    e. Financial leverage

    f. Breakeven point

    g. Hamada equation

    h. Leverage

    i. MM Proposition I without taxes; with corporate taxes

    j. MM Proposition II without taxes; with corporate taxes

    k. Miller model

    l. Financial distress costs; agency costs

12-2 What term refers to the uncertainty inherent in projections of future ROE(U)?

12-3 Firms with relatively high nonfinancial fixed costs are said to have a high degree of what?

12-4 "One type of leverage affects both EBIT and EPS. The other type affects only EPS." Explain this statement.

12-5 What is the relationship between market risk and leverage?

12-6 Explain why agency costs would probably be more of a problem for a large, publicly owned firm that uses both debt and equity capital than for a small, unleveraged, owner-managed firm.

12-7 Explain, verbally, how MM use the arbitrage process to prove the validity of Proposition I. Also, list the major MM assumptions and explain why each of these assumptions is necessary in the arbitrage proof.

12-8 A utility company is supposed to be allowed to charge prices high enough to cover all costs, including its cost of capital. Public service commissions are supposed to take actions to stimulate companies to operate as efficiently as possible in order to keep costs, hence prices, as low as possible. Some time ago, AT&T's debt ratio was about 33 percent. Some people (Myron J. Gordon in particular) argued that a higher debt ratio would lower AT&T's cost of capital and permit it to charge lower rates for telephone service. Gordon thought an optimal debt ratio for AT&T was about 50 percent. Do the theories presented in the chapter support or refute Gordon's position?

SELF-TEST PROBLEM   (SOLUTION APPEARS IN APPENDIX C)

ST-1 **(MM with financial distress costs)**   B. Gibbs Inc. is an unleveraged firm, and it has constant expected operating earnings (EBIT) of $2 million per year. The firm's tax rate is 40 percent, and its market value is V = S = $12 million. Management is considering the use of some debt financing. (Debt would be issued and used to buy back stock, so the size of the firm would remain constant.) Since interest expense is tax deductible, the value of the firm would tend to increase as debt is added to the capital structure, but there would be an offset in the form of a rising risk of financial distress. The firm's analysts have estimated, as an approximation, that the present value of any future financial distress costs is $8 million, and that the probability of distress would increase with leverage according to the following schedule:

Value of Debt	Probability of Financial Distress
$ 2,500,000	0.00%
5,000,000	1.25
7,500,000	2.50
10,000,000	6.25
12,500,000	12.50
15,000,000	31.25
20,000,000	75.00

a. What is the firm's cost of equity and weighted average cost of capital at this time?

b. According to the "pure" MM with-tax model, what is the optimal level of debt?

c. What is the optimal capital structure when financial distress costs are included?

d. Plot the value of the firm, with and without distress costs, as a function of the level of debt.

PROBLEMS

12-1 **(Operating leverage and breakeven)**   Schweser Satellites Inc. produces satellite earth stations which sell for $100,000 each. The firm's fixed costs, F, are $2 million; 50 earth stations are produced and sold each year; profits total $500,000; and the firm's assets (all

equity financed) are $5 million. The firm estimates that it can change its production process, adding $4 million to investment and $500,000 to fixed operating costs. This change will (1) reduce variable costs per unit by $10,000 and (2) increase output by 20 units, but (3) the sales price on all units will have to be lowered to $95,000 to permit sales of the additional output. The firm has tax loss carry-forwards that cause its tax rate to be zero, its cost of equity is 15 percent, and it uses no debt.

a. Should the firm make the change?

b. Would the firm's operating leverage increase or decrease if it made the change? What about its breakeven point?

c. Would the new situation expose the firm to more or less business risk than the old one?

12-2 (Business and financial risk: total)   Here are the estimated ROE distributions for Firms A, B, and C:

	Probability				
	0.1	**0.2**	**0.4**	**0.2**	**0.1**
Firm A: ROE_A	0.0%	5.0%	10.0%	15.0%	20.0%
Firm B: ROE_B	(2.0)	5.0	12.0	19.0	26.0
Firm C: ROE_C	(5.0)	5.0	15.0	25.0	35.0

a. Calculate the expected value and standard deviation for Firm C's ROE. $ROE_A = 10.0\%$, $\sigma_A = 5.5\%$; $ROE_B = 12.0\%$, $\sigma_B = 7.7\%$.

b. Discuss the relative riskiness of the three firms' returns. (Assume that these distributions are expected to remain constant over time.)

c. Now suppose all three firms have the same standard deviation of basic earning power (EBIT/Total assets), $\sigma_A = \sigma_B = \sigma_C = 5.5\%$. What can we tell about the financial risk of each firm?

12-3 (Business and financial risk: market)   Air Tampa has just been incorporated, and its board of directors is currently grappling with the question of optimal capital structure. The company plans to offer commuter air services between Tampa and smaller surrounding cities. Jaxair has been around for a few years, and it has about the same basic business risk as Air Tampa would have. Jaxair's market-determined beta is 1.8, and it has a current market value debt ratio (total debt/total assets) of 50 percent and a federal-plus-state tax rate of 40 percent. Air Tampa expects only to be marginally profitable at start up, hence its tax rate would only be 25 percent. Air Tampa's owners expect that the total book and market value of the firm's stock, if it uses zero debt, would be $10 million.

a. Estimate the beta of an unleveraged firm in the commuter airline business based on Jaxair's market-determined beta. (Hint: Jaxair's market-determined beta is a leveraged beta. Use Equation 12-7a and solve for b_U.)

b. Now assume that $k_{RF} = 10\%$ and $k_M = 15\%$. Find the required rate of return on equity for an unleveraged commuter airline. What is the business risk premium for this industry?

c. Air Tampa is considering three capital structures: (1) $2 million debt, (2) $4 million debt, and (3) $6 million debt. Estimate Air Tampa's k_s for these debt levels. What is the financial risk premium at each level?

d. Calculate Air Tampa's k_s and financial risk premium at $6 million debt assuming its federal-plus-state tax rate is now 40 percent. Compare this with your corresponding answer to Part c. (Hint: The increase in the tax rate causes V_U to drop to $8 million.)

12-4 (MM without taxes) Companies U and L are identical in every respect except that U is unleveraged while L has $10 million of 5 percent bonds outstanding. Assume (1) that all of the MM assumptions are met, (2) that there are no corporate or personal taxes, (3) that EBIT is $2 million, and (4) that the cost of equity to Company U is 10 percent.

a. What value would MM estimate for each firm?

b. What is k_s for Firm U? For Firm L?

c. Find S_L, and then show that $S_L + D = V_L = \$20$ million.

d. What is the WACC for Firm U? For Firm L?

e. Suppose $V_U = \$20$ million and $V_L = \$22$ million. According to MM, do these values represent an equilibrium? If not, explain the process by which equilibrium would be restored.

12-5 (MM with corporate taxes) Refer to Problem 12-4. Assume that all the facts hold, except that both firms are subject to a 40 percent federal-plus-state corporate tax rate.

a. What value would MM now estimate for each firm? (Use Proposition I.)

b. What is k_s for Firm U? Firm L?

c. Find S_L, and then show that $S_L + D = V_L$ results in the same value as obtained in Part a.

d. What is the WACC for Firm U? For Firm L?

12-6 (Miller model) Refer to Problems 12-4 and 12-5. Assume that all facts hold, except that both corporate and personal taxes apply. Assume that both firms must pay a federal-plus-state corporate tax rate of $T_c = 40\%$, and that investors in both firms face a tax rate of $T_d = 28\%$ on debt income and $T_s = 20\%$, on average, on stock income.

a. What is the value of the unleveraged firm, V_U? (Note that V_U is now reduced by the personal tax on stock income, hence $V_U \neq \$12$ million as in Problem 12-5.)

b. What is the value of V_L?

c. What is the gain from leverage in this situation? Compare this with the gain from leverage in Problem 12-5.

d. Set $T_c = T_s = T_d = 0$. What is the value of the leveraged firm? The gain from leverage?

e. Now suppose $T_s = T_d = 0$. What are the value of the leveraged firm and the gain from leverage?

f. Assume that $T_d = 28\%$, $T_s = 28\%$, and $T_c = 40\%$. Now what are the value of the leveraged firm and the gain from leverage?

12-7 (MM with and without taxes) International Associates (IA) is just about to commence operations as an international trading company. The firm will have book assets of $10 million, and it expects to earn a 16 percent return on these assets before taxes. However, because of certain tax arrangements with foreign governments, IA will not pay any taxes; that is, its tax rate will be zero. Management is trying to decide how to raise the required $10 million. It is known that the capitalization rate for an all-equity firm in this business is 11 percent, that is, $k_{sU} = 11\%$. Further, IA can borrow at a rate $k_d = 6\%$. Assume that the MM assumptions apply.

a. According to MM, what will be the value of IA if it uses no debt? If it uses $6 million of 6 percent debt?

b. What are the values of the WACC and k_s at debt levels of D = $0, D = $6 million, and D = $10 million? What effect does leverage have on firm value? Why?

c. Assume the initial facts of the problem ($k_d = 6\%$, EBIT $= \$1.6$ million, $k_{sU} = 11\%$), but now assume that a 40 percent federal-plus-state corporate tax rate exists. Find the new market values for IA with zero debt and with $6 million of debt, using the MM formulas.

d. What are the values of the WACC and k_s at debt levels of D $= \$0$, D $= \$6$ million, and D $= \$10$ million, assuming a 40 percent corporate tax rate? Plot the relationships between the value of the firm and the debt ratio, and between capital costs and the debt ratio.

e. What is the maximum dollar amount of debt financing that can be used? What is the value of the firm at this debt level? What is the cost of this debt?

f. How would each of the following factors tend to change the values you plotted in your graph?
    (1) The interest rate on debt increases as the debt ratio rises.
    (2) At higher levels of debt, the probability of financial distress rises.

12-8 (Agency costs)   Until recently, the Prestopino Company carried a triple-A bond rating and was strong in every respect. However, a series of problems has afflicted the firm: It is currently in severe financial distress, and its ability to make future payments on outstanding debt is questionable. If the firm were forced into bankruptcy at this time, the common stockholders would almost certainly be wiped out. Although the firm has limited financial resources, its cash flows (primarily from depreciation) are sufficient to support one of two mutually exclusive investments, each costing $150 million and having a 10-year expected life. These projects have the same market risk, but different total risk as measured by the variance of returns. Each project has the following after-tax cash inflows for 10 years:

	Annual Cash Inflows	
Probability	**Project A**	**Project B**
0.5	$30,000,000	$10,000,000
0.5	35,000,000	50,000,000

Assume that both projects have the same market risk as the firm's "average" project. The firm's weighted average cost of capital is 15 percent.

a. What is the expected annual cash inflow from each project?

b. Which project has the greater total risk?

c. Which project would you choose if you were a stockholder? Why?

d. Which project would the bondholders prefer to see management select? Why?

e. If the choices conflict, what "protection" do the bondholders have against the firm's making a decision that is contrary to their interests?

f. Who bears the cost of this "protection"? How is this cost related to leverage and the optimal capital structure?

12-9 (MM with financial distress costs)   The Boisjoly Company currently has no debt. An in-house research group has just been assigned the job of determining whether the firm should change its capital structure. Because of the importance of the decision, management has also hired the investment banking firm of Stanley Morgan & Company to conduct a parallel analysis of the situation. Mr. Harris, the in-house analyst, who is well versed in modern finance theory, has decided to carry out the analysis using the MM framework. Ms. Broske, the Stanley Morgan consultant, who has a good knowledge of capital market conditions and is confident of her ability to predict the firm's debt and equity costs at various levels of

debt, has decided to estimate the optimal capital structure as that structure which minimizes the firm's weighted average cost of capital. The following data are relevant to both analyses:

$$\text{EBIT} = \$4 \text{ million per year, in perpetuity.}$$
$$\text{Federal-plus-state tax rate} = 40\%.$$
$$\text{Dividend payout ratio} = 100\%.$$
$$\text{Current required rate of return on equity} = 12\%.$$

The cost of capital schedule predicted by Mr. Harris follows:

	At a Debt Level of (Millions of Dollars)							
	$0	$2	$4	$6	$8	$10	$12	$14
Interest rate (%)	—	8.0	8.3	9.0	10.0	11.0	13.0	16.0
Cost of equity (%)	12.0	12.25	12.75	13.0	13.15	13.4	14.65	17.0

Ms. Broske estimated the present value of financial distress costs at $8 million. Additionally, she estimated the following probabilities of financial distress:

	At a Debt Level of (Millions of Dollars)							
	$0	$2	$4	$6	$8	$10	$12	$14
Probability of financial distress	0	0	0.05	0.07	0.10	0.17	0.47	0.90

a. What level of debt would Mr. Harris and Ms. Broske recommend as optimal?

b. Comment on the similarities and differences in their recommendations.

12-10 (MM with financial distress costs)   The Brandt Corporation is an unleveraged firm, and it has constant expected operating earnings (EBIT) of $2 million per year. Brandt's federal-plus-state tax rate is 40 percent, its cost of equity is 10 percent, and its market value is $V = S = \$12$ million. Management is considering the use of debt which would cost the firm 8 percent regardless of the amount used. (Debt would be issued and used to buy back stock, so the size of the firm would remain constant.) Since interest expense is tax deductible, the value of the firm would tend to increase as debt is added to the capital structure, but there would be an offset in the form of rising risk of financial distress. The firm's analysts have estimated, as an approximation, that the present value of any future financial distress costs is $8 million, and that the probability of distress would increase with leverage according to the following schedule:

Value of Debt	Probability of Distress
$ 0	0.0%
2,500,000	2.5
5,000,000	5.0
7,500,000	10.0
10,000,000	25.0
12,500,000	50.0
15,000,000	75.0

a. According to the "pure" MM with corporate taxes model, what is the optimal level of debt? (Consider only those debt values listed in the table.)

b. What is the optimal capital structure when financial distress costs are included?

(Do Parts c, d, e, and f only if you are using the computer problem diskette.)

c. Plot the value of the firm, with and without financial distress costs, as a function of the level of debt.

d. Assume that the firm's unleveraged cost of equity is 8 percent. What is the firm's optimal capital structure now? (From this point on, include financial distress costs in all your analyses.)

e. Return to the base case k_{sU} of 10 percent. Now assume that the firm's tax rate increases to 60 percent. What effect does this change have on the firm's optimal capital structure?

f. Return to the base case tax rate of 40 percent. Assume that the estimated present value of financial distress costs is only $5 million. Now what is the firm's optimal capital structure?

**M I N I
C A S E**

Donald Cheney, the CEO of Cheney Electronics, is concerned about his firm's level of debt financing. The company uses short-term debt to finance its temporary working capital needs, but it does not use any permanent (long-term) debt. Other electronics companies average about 30 percent debt, and Mr. Cheney wonders why the difference occurs, and what its effects are on stock prices. To gain some insights into the matter, he poses the following questions to you, his recently hired assistant:

a. (1) What is business risk? What factors influence a firm's business risk?
    (2) What is operating leverage, and how does it affect a firm's business risk?

b. (1) What is meant by financial leverage and financial risk?
    (2) How does financial risk differ from business risk?

c. How are financial and business risk measured in a total risk framework? In a market risk framework?

d. Now, to develop an example which can be presented to Cheney Electronics' management as an illustration, consider two hypothetical firms: Firm U, which uses no debt, and Firm L, which uses $10,000 of 12 percent debt. Both firms have $20,000 in assets and a 40 percent tax rate, and the following EBIT probability distribution applies to both for the coming year:

Probability	EBIT
0.25	$2,000
0.50	3,000
0.25	4,000

(1) Construct partial income statements, which start with EBIT, for the two firms at each level of EBIT.
(2) Now calculate the ratio of EBIT to total assets, which is the *basic earning power* ratio; the ROI, which is (net income + interest) divided by (debt + equity); the ROE; and the times-interest-earned (TIE) ratio for both firms at each level of EBIT.
(3) What does this example illustrate concerning the impact of financial leverage on risk and expected rate of return?

e. *Business Week* recently ran an article on companies' debt policies, and the names Modigliani and Miller (MM) were mentioned several times as leading researchers on the

theory of capital structure. Briefly, who are MM, and what assumptions are embedded in the MM and Miller models?

f. Assume that Firms U and L are in the same risk class, and that both have EBIT = $500,000. Firm U uses no debt financing, and its cost of equity is $k_{sU} = 14\%$. Firm L has $1 million of debt outstanding at a cost of $k_d = 8\%$. There are no taxes. Assume that the MM assumptions hold, and then:

(1) Find V, S, k_s, and WACC for Firms U and L.

(2) Graph (a) the relationships between capital costs and leverage as measured by D/V, and (b) the relationship between value and D.

g. Using the data given in Part f, but now assuming that firms L and U are both subject to a 40 percent corporate tax rate, repeat the analysis called for in f(1) and f(2) under the MM with-tax model.

h. Now suppose investors are subject to the following tax rates: $T_d = 30\%$ and $T_s = 25\%$.

(1) What is the gain from leverage according to the Miller model?

(2) How does this gain compare to the gain in the MM model with corporate taxes?

(3) What does the Miller model imply about the effect of corporate debt on the value of the firm, that is, how do personal taxes affect the situation?

i. What capital structure policy recommendations do the three theories (MM without taxes, MM with corporate taxes, and Miller) suggest to financial managers? Empirically, do firms appear to follow any one of these guidelines?

j. What are financial distress and agency costs? How does the addition of these costs change the MM and Miller models? (Express your answer in words, in equation form, and in graphical form.)

SELECTED ADDITIONAL REFERENCES AND CASES

The body of literature on capital structure—and the number of potential references—is huge. Therefore, only a sampling can be given here. For an extensive review of the recent literature, as well as a detailed bibliography, see

Beranek, William, "Research Directions in Finance," *Quarterly Review of Business and Economics,* Spring 1981, 6–24.

The major theoretical works on capital structure theory are discussed in an integrated framework in

Copeland, Thomas E., and J. Fred Weston, *Financial Theory and Corporate Policy* (Reading, Mass.: Addison-Wesley, 1988).

Harris, Milton, and Artur Raviv, "The Theory of Capital Structure," *Journal of Finance,* March 1991, 297–355.

The Fall 1988 issue of The Journal of Economic Perspectives *and the Summer 1989 issue of* Financial Management *each contain several interesting and very readable articles which review the MM propositions after 30 years of debate and testing.*

In addition to Miller's work, the effect of personal taxes on capital structure decisions has been addressed by

Gordon, Myron J., and Lawrence I. Gould, "The Cost of Equity Capital with Personal Income Taxes and Flotation Costs," *Journal of Finance,* September 1978, 1201–1212.

Some other references of relevance include the following:

Ben-Horim, Moshe, Shalom Hockman, and Oded Palmon, "The Impact of the 1986 Tax Reform Act on Corporate Financial Policy," *Financial Management,* Autumn 1987, 29–35.

Bradley, Michael, Gregg A. Jarrell, and E. Han Kim, "On the Existence of an Optimal Capital Structure: Theory and Evidence," *Journal of Finance,* July 1984, 857–878.

Conine, Thomas E., Jr., "Debt Capacity and the Capital Budgeting Decision: Comment," *Financial Management,* Spring 1980, 20–22.

Crutchley, Claire E., and Robert S. Hansen, "A Test of the Agency Theory of Managerial Ownership, Corporate Leverage, and Corporate Dividends," *Financial Management,* Winter 1989, 36–46.

Dugan, Michael T., and Keith A. Shriver, "An Empirical Comparison of Alternative Methods for Estimating the Degree of Operating Leverage," *Financial Review,* May 1992, 309–321.

Ferri, Michael, and Wesley H. Jones, "Determinants of Financial Structure: A New Methodological Approach," *Journal of Finance,* June 1979, 631–644.

Flath, David, and Charles R. Knoeber, "Taxes, Failure Costs, and Optimal Industry Capital Structure," *Journal of Finance,* March 1980, 89–117.

Ghosh, Dilip K., "Optimum Capital Structure Redefined," *Financial Review,* August 1992, 411–429.

Kelly, William A., Jr., and James A. Miles, "Capital Structure Theory and the Fisher Effect," *The Financial Review,* February 1989, 53–73.

Lee, Wayne Y., and Henry H. Barker, "Bankruptcy Costs and the Firm's Optimal Debt Capacity: A Positive Theory of Capital Structure," *Southern Economic Journal,* April 1977, 1453–1465.

Mackie-Mason, Jeffrey K., "Do Taxes Affect Corporate Financing Decisions," *Journal of Finance,* December 1990, 1471–1493.

Martin, John D., and David F. Scott, "Debt Capacity and the Capital Budgeting Decision: A Revisitation," *Financial Management,* Spring 1980, 23–26.

Miller, Merton H., "The Modigliani-Miller Propositions after Thirty Years," *Journal of Applied Corporate Finance,* Spring 1989, 6–18.

————, "Leverage," *Journal of Finance,* June 1991, 479–488.

Pinegar, J. Michael, and Lisa Wilbricht, "What Managers Think of Capital Structure Theory: A Survey," *Financial Management,* Winter 1989, 82–91.

Scherr, Frederick C., "A Multiperiod Mean-Variance Model of Optimal Capital Structure," *The Financial Review,* February 1987, 1–31.

Schneller, Meir I., "Taxes and the Optimal Capital Structure of the Firm," *Journal of Finance,* March 1980, 119–127.

Taggart, Robert A., Jr., "Taxes and Corporate Capital Structure in an Incomplete Market," *Journal of Finance,* June 1980, 645–659.

Thakor, Anjan V., "Strategic Issues in Financial Contracting: An Overview," *Financial Management,* Summer 1989, 39–58.

There has been considerable discussion in the literature concerning a financial leverage clientele effect. Many theorists postulate that firms with low leverage are favored by high-tax-bracket investors and vice versa. Two articles on this subject are

Harris, John M., Jr., Rodney L. Roenfeldt, and Philip L. Cooley, "Evidence of Financial Leverage Clienteles," *Journal of Finance,* September 1983, 1125–1132.

Kim, E. Han, "Miller's Equilibrium, Shareholder Leverage Clienteles, and Optimal Capital Leverage," *Journal of Finance,* May 1982, 301–319.

For a very readable discussion of the many issues involved in capital structure theory, see

"A Discussion of Corporate Capital Structure," *Midland Corporate Finance Journal,* Fall 1985, 19–48.

The Brigham-Gapenski casebook has the following cases that apply to this chapter:

Case 7, "Seattle Steel Products," focuses on capital structure theory.

Case 8, "Johnson Window Company," covers operating and financial leverage.

CAPITAL STRUCTURE DECISIONS: PART 2

A t the 1993 meeting of the Financial Management Association, a professional organization that includes both academics and practitioners, a panel session focused on how several firms actually set their optimal, or target, capital structures. The participants included financial managers from Hershey Foods, Bell Atlantic, EG&G (a high-tech firm), and a number of other firms in various industries. Although there were minor differences in philosophy and procedures among the companies, several themes dominated.

First, in practice it is impossible to specify a point value for a firm's optimal capital structure—indeed, managers even feel uncomfortable about specifying an optimal capital structure range. Thus, financial managers worry primarily about whether their firms are using too little or too much debt, and not about the precise optimal amount of debt. Second, even if a firm's actual capital structure varies widely from the theoretical optimum, this may have little impact on the firm's value, and hence on its stock price. Thus, financial managers believe that capital structure decisions are secondary in importance to other decisions, especially those relating to capital budgeting and to the strategic direction of the firm.

In general, financial managers focus more on identifying a "prudent" level of debt than on setting a precise optimal level. A prudent level of debt should capture most of the benefits of debt financing yet (1) keep financial risk at a manageable level, (2) ensure future financing flexibility, and (3) allow the firm to maintain a desirable credit rating. Thus, a prudent level of debt will protect the company against financial distress under all but the most unlikely pessimistic economic scenarios, will ensure access to money and capital markets, and

will maintain a bond rating consistent with the firm's financing plans. For example, a minimum bond rating of A may be required for the firm to issue commercial paper.

As you read this chapter, think about how you would make capital structure decisions if you were the financial manager at Hershey, Bell Atlantic, or EG&G. At the same time, don't forget the very important message from the panel session: Establishing the right capital structure is an imprecise process at best, and it should blend informed judgment with quantitative analyses.

We began our discussion of capital structure decisions in Chapter 12. We discovered that using debt concentrates a firm's business risk on its stockholders, but it also increases the expected return on equity. We discussed three important capital structure theories: MM with zero taxes, MM with corporate taxes, and Miller (corporate and personal taxes). Although these models provide insights into the value of debt financing, their prescriptions (either that debt does not matter or that 100 percent debt is optimal) are simply not followed by managers. However, when financial distress and agency costs are considered along with taxes, the models lead to the more reasonable conclusion that some debt is good, but too much debt is bad. Now, in Chapter 13, we expand our discussion and consider how capital structure decisions are made in practice.

CAPITAL STRUCTURE THEORY: REVIEW OF THE TRADE-OFF MODELS

In Chapter 12, we discussed MM with corporate taxes and the Miller model. Both of these models have been modified to reflect financial distress and agency costs, and the modified models are called *trade-off models* — the optimal capital structure is found by balancing the tax shield benefits provided by leverage against the costs of financial distress and agency, so the costs and benefits of leverage are "traded off" against one another.

IMPLICATIONS OF THE MODELS

The trade-off models cannot be used to specify a firm's precise optimal capital structure, but they can enable us to make three statements about debt usage:

1. Higher-risk firms, as measured by the variability of returns on the firm's assets, ought to borrow less than lower-risk firms, other things being equal. The greater the earnings variability, the greater the probability of financial distress at any level of debt, hence the greater the expected costs of distress. Thus, firms with lower business risk can borrow more without having the expected costs of distress offset the tax advantages of borrowing.

2. Firms that have tangible, marketable assets such as real estate should be able to use more debt than firms whose value is derived primarily from intangible assets such as patents and goodwill. The costs of financial distress depend not only on the probability of incurring distress, but also on what happens if distress occurs. Specialized assets and intangible assets are more likely to lose value if financial distress occurs than are standardized, tangible assets.

3. Firms that are currently paying taxes at the highest rate, and that are likely to continue to do so in the future, should carry more debt than firms with lower current and/or prospective tax rates. High corporate taxes lead to greater benefits from debt financing, hence high-tax-rate firms can carry more debt, other factors held constant, before the tax shield is offset by financial distress and agency costs.

According to the trade-off models, each firm should set its target capital structure such that its costs and benefits of leverage are balanced at the margin, because such a structure will maximize its value. If the trade-off models are correct, we would expect to find actual target structures that are consistent with the three points just noted. Further, we would generally expect to find that firms within an industry have similar capital structures, because such firms have roughly the same types of assets, business risk, and profitability.

THE EMPIRICAL EVIDENCE

The trade-off models have intuitive appeal because they lead to the conclusion that both no-debt and all-debt are bad, while a "moderate" debt level is good. However, we must ask ourselves whether these models explain actual behavior. If they do not, then we must search for other explanations.

The trade-off models do have some empirical support.[1] For example, firms that have primarily tangible assets tend to borrow more heavily than firms whose value stems from intangibles. However, there is other empirical evidence which refutes the trade-off models. First, several studies have examined models of financing behavior to see if firms' financing decisions reflect adjustment toward a target capital structure. These studies provide some evidence that this occurs, but the explanatory power of the models is very low, suggesting that trade-off models capture only a part of actual behavior. Second, only a handful of studies have demonstrated that a firm's tax rate has a predictable, material effect on its capital structure. Also, firms used about as much debt financing before corporate income taxes even existed as they do today. Finally, actual debt ratios tend to vary widely across apparently similar firms, whereas the trade-off models suggest that debt ratios should be clustered within industries.

All in all, the empirical support for the trade-off models is quite weak, which suggests that other factors not incorporated into these models are also at work. In other words, the trade-off models do not tell the full story.

---

[1]For examples of the empirical research in this area, see Robert A. Taggart, Jr., "A Model of Corporate Financing Decisions," *Journal of Finance,* December 1977, 1467–1484; and Paul Marsh, "The Choice between Equity and Debt: An Empirical Study," *Journal of Finance,* March 1982, 121–144.

Self-Test Questions

What is a trade-off model of capital structure?

What implications do the trade-off models have regarding capital structure?

Does the empirical evidence fully support the trade-off models?

Capital Structure Theory:
the Impact of Asymmetric Information

In the early 1960s, Professor Gordon Donaldson of Harvard University conducted an extensive survey of how corporations actually establish their capital structures.[2] Here is a summary of his findings:

1. Firms prefer to finance with internally generated funds, that is, with retained earnings and depreciation cash flow.

2. Firms set their target dividend payout ratios based on (a) their expected future investment opportunities and (b) their expected future cash flows. The target payout ratio is set at a level such that retained earnings plus depreciation will meet capital expenditure requirements under normal conditions.

3. Dividends are "sticky" in the short run—firms are reluctant to make major changes in the dollar dividend, and they are especially reluctant to cut the dividend. Thus, in any given year, depending on realized cash flows and actual investment opportunities, a firm may or may not have sufficient internally generated funds to cover its capital expenditures.

4. If the firm has more internal cash flow than is needed for expansion purposes, then it will invest in marketable securities, use the funds to retire debt, or increase dividends. If it has insufficient internal cash flow to finance non-postponable new projects, then it will first draw down its marketable securities portfolio, and if still more funds are needed, it will go to the external capital markets, first issuing debt, then convertible bonds, and then common stock as a last resort. *Thus, Donaldson observed that there is a "pecking order" of financing, not the balanced approach that would result if the trade-off models accurately described real-world behavior.*

Professor Stewart Myers noted the inconsistency between Donaldson's findings and the trade-off models, and that inconsistency led Myers to propose a new theory.[3] First, Myers noted that Donaldson's pecking-order findings led away from, rather than toward, a well-defined capital structure. Equity is raised in two forms,

---

[2]Gordon Donaldson, *Corporate Debt Capacity: A Study of Corporate Debt Policy and the Determination of Corporate Debt Capacity* (Boston: Harvard Graduate School of Business Administration, 1961).

[3]Stewart C. Myers, "The Capital Structure Puzzle," *Journal of Finance,* July 1984, 575–592. It is interesting to note that, like the Miller model, Myers's paper was first presented as a presidential address to the American Finance Association.

and one form, retained earnings, is at the top of the pecking order, while the other, new common stock, is at the bottom. The trade-off models, on the other hand, regarded equity from the sale of stock as being identical to that from retained earnings.

Next, Myers noted that the trade-off models assume that all market participants have homogeneous expectations, which implies (1) that all participants have the same information set and (2) that any changes in operating income are purely random as opposed to being anticipated by some parties. Myers had the insight to see that if the homogeneous expectations assumption is relaxed, and asymmetric (or different) information by different groups of market participants is admitted, Donaldson's results could be explained in a logical manner. Myers's work resulted in what is now called the *asymmetric information theory* of capital structure.

To illustrate Myers's theory, assume that a firm has 10,000 common shares outstanding at a current price of $19 per share, so the market value of its equity is $190,000. However, its managers have better information about the firm's prospects than stockholders, and the managers believe that the actual value per share based on existing assets is $21, giving the equity a total "true" market value of $210,000. Such information asymmetry could easily exist, for managers often know more about their firms' prospects than do current and potential investors.[4]

Suppose further that the firm now identifies a new project which requires external financing of $100,000 and which has an estimated net present value (NPV) of $5,000. (Remember that a project's NPV is a residual value over its costs, and that this residual accrues to the shareholders.) This project is unanticipated by the firm's investors, so the $5,000 NPV has not been incorporated into the firm's $190,000 equity market value. Should the firm accept the project? To begin, assume that the firm plans to sell new equity to raise the $100,000 to finance the project. Several possibilities are set forth next:

1. Symmetric information. First, as a point of departure, consider the situation where management can convey its information to the public, hence all investors *do* have the same information as management regarding existing asset values. Under these conditions, the stock would be selling at $21 per share, so the firm would have to sell $100,000/$21 = 4,762 new shares to finance the project. Acceptance of the project would result in a new stock price of $21.34:

$$\text{New stock price} = \frac{\text{Original market value} + \text{New money raised} + \text{NPV}}{\text{Original shares} + \text{New shares}}$$

$$= \frac{\$210,000 + \$100,000 + \$5,000}{10,000 + 4,762} = \$21.34.$$

Clearly, both old and new shareholders would benefit if the project were accepted.

---

[4]This assumption is contrary to the strong-form efficient markets hypothesis (EMH) presented in Chapter 7, but few observers — including people who believe ardently in weak-form and semistrong-form efficiency — are willing to accept strong-form efficiency.

2. Asymmetric information prior to stock issue. Now consider the situation where our firm's management is unable to inform investors about the stock's "true" value. Perhaps it is necessary to hold back such information to maintain a competitive edge, or perhaps SEC regulations cause management to refrain from "touting" the stock price prior to the new issue (if things did not work out as expected, new shareholders might sue the managers who had provided the rosy forecast). In this situation, new stock would fetch the current price, $19 per share, so the company would have to sell $100,000/$19 = 5,263 shares in order to raise the required $100,000. If this were done, this new price would result after the project was accepted and the information asymmetry was removed:

$$\text{New stock price} = \frac{\text{New market value} + \text{New money raised} + \text{NPV}}{\text{Original shares} + \text{New shares}}$$

$$= \frac{\$210,000 + \$100,000 + \$5,000}{10,000 + 5,263} = \$20.64.$$

Under this condition, the project should not be undertaken. If the project were not accepted, so no new shares were sold, then the price of the stock would rise to $21 when the information asymmetry was removed. The sale of new stock at $19 per share would lead to a $0.36 per share loss to the firm's existing shareholders and to a $1.64 gain to the new shareholders.

3. A more profitable project. Suppose now that the project had an NPV of $20,000, the stock sold for $19, and other conditions in section 2 were unchanged. Now the firm's stock price would rise to $21.62 if it undertook the project:

$$\text{New stock price} = \frac{\$210,000 + \$100,000 + \$20,000}{10,000 + 5,263} = \$21.62.$$

Under these conditions, the firm should take on the project. Note, though, that most of the positive NPV would go to the new stockholders, who would pay $19 per share and thus would enjoy a capital gain of $2.62 versus a gain of only $0.62 for the original stockholders.

4. Dark clouds on the horizon. Now suppose an entirely different—and bad—situation faced the firm. Stockholders think the firm is worth $19 per share, but the firm's managers think (a) that outside investors are entirely too optimistic about the firm's growth opportunities, (b) that investors have not factored in proposed legislation which will require large, nonearning investments in pollution control equipment, and (c) that the current stock price does not reflect the need for new R&D expenditures which will be required to keep the firm's products competitive. If all of these bad events materialize, profit margins will be under pressure, cash flows will be down, and the company will not be able to carry safely its present level of debt. This will cause the stock price to fall sharply, and it will be extremely difficult to raise the capital that will be necessary to assure the firm's survival.

Faced with these conditions, management might well conclude that the "true" value of the firm's stock is only $17 per share, and further decide to sell a new issue of 10,000 shares at the current price of $19, raising $190,000 and using the funds to retire debt or to support this year's capital budget. This action would increase the "true" value of the stock from $17 to $18:

$$\text{New "true" value} = \frac{\text{Old "true" market value} + \text{New money}}{\text{Original shares} + \text{New shares}}$$

$$= \frac{\$170,000 + \$190,000}{10,000 + 10,000} = \$18.00.$$

Current stockholders will, if management's expectations come true, suffer a loss when the bad news becomes known, but the sale of new stock would reduce that loss. (Note: Management would have to carefully word the prospectus for the new issue, pointing out the potential problems. However, virtually all prospectuses are filled with cautionary language, so investors cannot tell from them what management really expects.)

5. Finance the original $5,000 NPV project with debt. If the firm used debt to finance the original $100,000 project, *and then the information asymmetry were removed,* the new stock price would be $21.50 versus the $20.64 we found under Scenario 2:

$$\text{New stock price} = \frac{\text{New market value} + \text{NPV}}{\text{Original shares}}$$

$$= \frac{\$210,000 + \$5,000}{10,000} = \$21.50.$$

Thus, if debt financing were used, all of the "true" value of the firm's existing assets, plus the NPV of the new project, would accrue to the original shareholders. If stock financing were used, we saw that the value of the original stock would end up at $20.64 rather than $21, the true value without the new investment.

What does all this suggest about corporate financial policy? First, in a world where asymmetric information exists, corporations should issue new shares only (1) in the unlikely event that they have extraordinarily profitable investments that cannot be postponed, signaled to investors, or financed by debt or (2) if management thinks the shares are overvalued. Second, investors recognize this and tend to mark down a company's share prices when it announces plans to issue new shares, because chances are good that the announcement is signaling bad news, not good news. Third, the financing pecking order that Donaldson observed is rational when asymmetric information exists — it pays to retain a large fraction of earnings, and to keep the equity ratio up and the debt ratio down, so as to maintain some "reserve borrowing capacity" which can be used to support the capital

budget if and when an unusually large number of positive NPV projects come along, or if problems arise which require outside capital.[5]

Note that the degree of information asymmetry, and its impact on investors' perceptions, differ substantially across firms. To illustrate, the degree of asymmetry is typically much greater in the drug and semiconductor industries than in the retailing and trucking industries, because success in the drug and semiconductor industries depends on secretive proprietary research and development. Thus, managers in these industries have significantly more information about their firms' prospects than do outside analysts and investors. Also, emerging firms with limited capital but good growth opportunities are recognized as having to use external financing, so the announcement of new stock offerings is not viewed with as much concern by investors as is new offerings by a mature firm with limited growth opportunities. Thus, although the asymmetric information theory is applicable to all firms, its impact on managerial decisions varies from firm to firm and over time.

SELF-TEST QUESTIONS

Briefly explain the asymmetric information theory.

What does this theory suggest about capital structure decisions?

Is the asymmetric information theory equally applicable to all firms at all times?

CAPITAL STRUCTURE THEORY: OUR VIEW

The great contribution of the trade-off models developed by MM, Miller, and their followers is that these models identified the specific benefits and costs of using debt — the tax effects, financial distress costs, and so on. Prior to MM, no capital structure theory existed, and we had no systematic way of analyzing the effects of debt financing.

The trade-off models are summarized graphically in Figure 13-1. The top graph shows the relationships between the debt ratio and the cost of debt, the cost of equity, and the WACC. Both k_s and $k_d(1 - T_c)$ rise steadily with increases in leverage, but the rate of increase accelerates at higher debt levels, reflecting agency costs and the increased probability of financial distress and its attendant costs. The WACC first declines, then hits a minimum at D/V*, and then begins to rise. Note that the value of D in D/V* in the upper graph is D*, the level of debt in the lower graph that maximizes the firm's value. Thus, a firm's WACC is minimized, and its value is maximized, at the same capital structure. Note also that the general shapes of the curves apply regardless of whether we are using the modified MM with corporate taxes model, the Miller model, or a variant of these models.

---

[5]Flotation costs also play a role in capital structure theory. In general, flotation costs are smaller on debt issues than on equity issues, and this provides an additional rationale for using debt rather than outside equity. We will discuss this issue in more detail in Chapter 19.

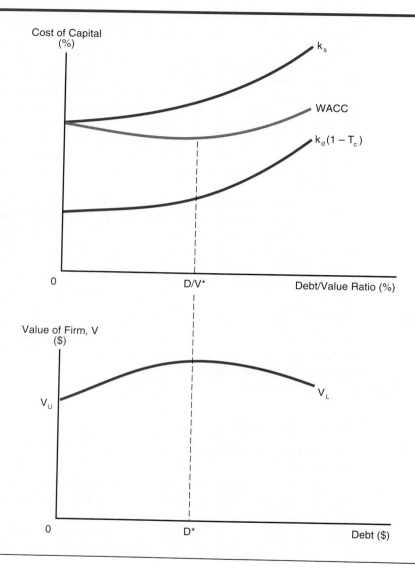

FIGURE 13-1

EFFECTS OF
LEVERAGE: THE
TRADE-OFF MODELS

Unfortunately, it is extremely difficult for financial managers to quantify the costs and benefits of debt financing to their firms, so it is virtually impossible to pinpoint D/V*, the capital structure that truly maximizes a firm's value. Most experts believe such a structure exists for every firm, but that it changes substantially over time as firms' operations and investors' preferences change. Most experts also believe that, as shown in Figure 13-1, the relationship between firm value and leverage is relatively flat, so relatively large deviations from the optimal capital structure can occur without materially affecting a firm's value.

Now consider the asymmetric information theory. Because of asymmetric information, investors know less about a firm's prospects than do its managers. Further, managers try to maximize value for current stockholders, not new ones, so if the firm has excellent prospects, management will not want to issue new shares, but if things look bleak, then a new stock offering would benefit current stockholders. Therefore, investors take a stock offering to be a signal of bad news, so stock prices tend to decline when new issues are announced. As a result, new equity financings can be very expensive, and this fact must be incorporated into the capital structure decision. The net effect of the asymmetric information situation is to motivate firms to maintain a reserve borrowing capacity, which permits future investment opportunities to be financed by debt when internal funds are insufficient.

By combining the two theories, we obtain this explanation for firms' behavior: (1) Debt financing provides benefits because of the tax deductibility of interest, so firms should have some debt in their capital structures. (2) However, financial distress and agency costs place limits on debt usage — beyond some point, these costs offset the tax advantage of debt. (3) Finally, because of asymmetric information, firms maintain a reserve borrowing capacity in order to be able to take advantage of good investment opportunities without having to issue stock at distressed prices.

All this may sound reasonable, but how should financial decisions actually be made in practice? The answer is somewhat fuzzy, and many factors must be considered when choosing a capital structure. This topic will be discussed in the remainder of the chapter.

SELF-TEST QUESTIONS

Summarize the trade-off and asymmetric information theories of capital structure.

Can the trade-off theory and the asymmetric information theory coexist; that is, can they both help explain capital structure choices, or are they mutually exclusive? Explain.

Does capital structure theory provide managers with a model that can be used to set a precise optimal capital structure for each firm?

ESTIMATING THE TARGET CAPITAL STRUCTURE: A SIMPLIFIED EXAMPLE

We know that the tax benefit/financial distress trade-off theory leads to the conclusion that each firm has an optimal capital structure, one which maximizes its value and minimizes its weighted average cost of capital. In this section, we present an illustration which demonstrates many of these points.

TABLE 13-1	**Balance Sheet as of December 31, 1993**				
DATA ON HILL	Current assets	$ 500,000	Debt	$	0
SOFTWARE SYSTEMS	Net fixed assets	500,000	Common equity (1.0 million		
			shares outstanding)		1,000,000
	Total assets	$1,000,000	Total claims		$1,000,000

Income Statement for 1993

Sales		$20,000,000
Fixed operating costs	$ 4,000,000	
Variable operating costs	12,000,000	16,000,000
Earnings before interest and taxes (EBIT)		$ 4,000,000
Interest		0
Taxable income		$ 4,000,000
Taxes (40% federal-plus-state)		1,600,000
Net income		$ 2,400,000

Other Data

1. Earnings per share = EPS = $2,400,000/1,000,000 shares = $2.40.
2. Dividends per share = DPS = $2,400,000/1,000,000 shares = $2.40. Thus, the company has a 100 percent payout ratio.
3. Book value per share = $1,000,000/1,000,000 shares = $1.
4. Market price per share = P_0 = $20. Thus, the stock sells at 20 times its book value.
5. Price/earnings ratio = P/E = $20/2.40 = 8.33 times.
6. Dividend yield = DPS/P_0 = $2.40/$20 = 12%.

HILL SOFTWARE SYSTEMS

Hill Software Systems (HSS) was founded in 1987 to develop and market a new type of operating system for personal computers. The basic program was written and patented by Mark Hill, HSS's founder. Hill owns a majority of the stock, although a significant portion is held by institutional investors. The company has no debt, and HSS's key financial data are shown in Table 13-1. Assets are carried at a book value of $1 million; hence, the common equity also has a balance sheet value of $1 million. However, these balance sheet figures are not very meaningful because (1) the asset figures do not include the value of patents and (2) the fixed assets were purchased several years ago at prices lower than today's.

Mark Hill will retire shortly, and he is planning to sell a major part of his interest in the company to the public, using the proceeds of the sale to diversify his personal portfolio. As a part of the planning process, the question of capital structure has arisen. Should the firm continue its policy of using no debt, or should it recapitalize? And if it does decide to substitute debt for equity, how far should it go? As in all such decisions, the correct answer is that *it should choose that capital structure which maximizes the value of the company.* If the company's

TABLE 13-2 HSS'S VALUE, STOCK PRICE, AND COST OF CAPITAL AT DIFFERENT DEBT LEVELS	Value of Debt, D (in Millions) (1)	k_d (2)	k_s (3)	Value of Stock, S (in Millions) (4)	Value of Firm, V (in Millions) (1) + (4) = (5)	Stock Price, P_0 (6)	D/V (7)	WACC (8)
	$ 0.0	—	12.0%	$20.000	$20.000	$20.00	0.0%	12.0%
	2.0	8.0%	12.2	18.885	20.885	20.89	9.6	11.5
	4.0	8.3	12.6	17.467	21.467	21.47	18.6	11.2
	6.0	**9.0**	**13.2**	**15.727**	**21.727**	**21.73**	**27.6**	**11.0**
	8.0	10.0	14.0	13.714	21.714	21.71	36.8	11.1
	10.0	12.0	15.2	11.053	21.053	21.05	47.5	11.4
	12.0	15.0	16.8	7.857	19.857	19.86	60.4	12.1
	14.0	18.0	19.0	3.158	17.158	17.16	81.6	12.3

Notes:

a. The data in Columns 1 through 3 were taken from Figure 13-2.

b. The values for S in Column 4 were found by use of Equation 13-2.

$$S = \frac{\text{Net income}}{k_s} = \frac{(\text{EBIT} - k_d D)(1 - T)}{k_s}.$$

For example, at D = $0,

$$S = \frac{(\$4.0 - 0)(0.6)}{0.12} = \frac{\$2.4}{0.12} = \$20.0 \text{ million,}$$

and at D = $6.0,

$$S = \frac{[\$4.0 - 0.09(\$6.0)](0.6)}{0.132} = \frac{\$2.076}{0.132} = \$15.727 \text{ million.}$$

c. The values for V in Column 5 were obtained as the sum of D + S. For example, at D = $6.0, V = $6.0 + $15.727 = $21.727 million.

d. The stock prices shown in Column 6 are equal to the value of the firm as shown in Column 5 divided by the original number of shares outstanding, which, in this case, is 1 million. The logic behind this procedure is explained in the text.

e. Column 7 is found by dividing Column 1 by Column 5. For example, at D = $6.0, D/V = $6.0/$21.727 = 27.6%.

f. Column 8 is found by use of Equation 13-4. For example, at D = $6.0,

$$\text{WACC} = (\text{D/V})(k_d)(1 - T) + (\text{S/V})(k_s)$$
$$= (0.276)(9\%)(0.6) + (0.724)(13.2\%) = 11.0\%.$$

g. At $14.0 million of debt, EBIT declines from $4 million to $3.52 million.

h. The row in boldface indicates the optimal amount of debt.

3. The values shown in Columns 1 through 5 of Table 13-2 are estimated as described previously. The major institutional investors, and the large brokerage companies which advise individual investors, have analysts just as capable of making these estimates as the firm's management. These analysts would start making their own estimates as soon as HSS announced the planned change in leverage, and they would presumably reach conclusions similar to those of the HSS analysts.

FIGURE 13-3

RELATIONSHIP
BETWEEN HSS'S
CAPITAL STRUCTURE,
COST OF CAPITAL,
AND STOCK PRICE

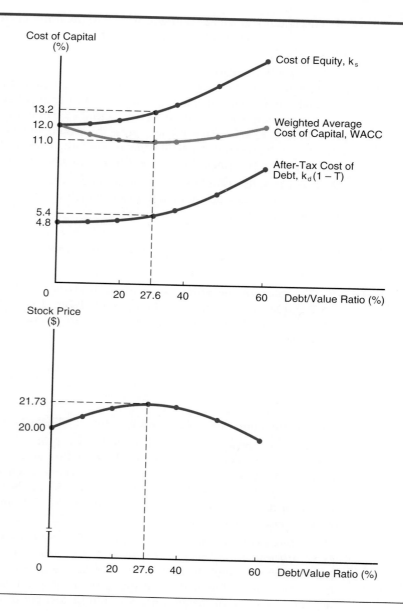

FIGURE 13-3

RELATIONSHIP BETWEEN HSS'S CAPITAL STRUCTURE, COST OF CAPITAL, AND STOCK PRICE

4. HSS's stockholders initially own the entire company. (There are not yet any bondholders.) They see, or are told by their advisor-analysts, that very shortly the value of the enterprise will rise from $20 million to some higher amount, presumably the maximum attainable, or $21,727,000. Thus, they anticipate that the value of the firm will increase by $1,727,000.

5. This additional $1,727,000 will accrue to the firm's current stockholders. Since there are 1 million shares of stock, each share will rise in value by $1.73, or from $20 to $21.73.

6. This price increase will occur *before* the transaction is completed. Suppose, for example, that the stock price remained at $20 after the announcement of the recapitalization plan. Shrewd investors would immediately recognize that the stock's price will soon go up to $21.73, and they would place orders to buy at any price below $21.73. This buying pressure would quickly run the price up to $21.73, at which point it would remain constant. Thus, $21.73 is the *equilibrium stock price* for HSS once the decision to recapitalize is announced.

7. The firm sells $6 million of bonds at an interest rate of 9 percent. This money is used to buy stock at the market price, which is now $21.73, so 276,116 shares are repurchased:

$$\text{Shares repurchased} = \frac{\$6,000,000}{\$21.73} = 276,116.$$

8. The value of the equity after the 276,116 shares have been repurchased is $15,727,000, as shown in Column 4 of Table 13-2. There are 1,000,000 − 276,116 = 723,884 shares still outstanding, so the value per share of the remaining stock is

$$\text{Value per share} = \frac{\$15,727,000}{723,884} = \$21.73.$$

This confirms our earlier calculation of the equilibrium stock price.

9. The same process was used to find stock prices at other capital structures; these prices are given in Column 6 of Table 13-2 and plotted in the lower graph of Figure 13-3. *Since the maximum price occurs when HSS uses $6 million of debt, its optimal capital structure calls for $6 million of debt.* Note that $6 million of debt corresponds to a firm value of $21.727 million. Thus, the optimal market value capital structure, D/V*, is $6/$21.727 = 27.6%.

10. *In this example, we assumed that EBIT would decline from $4 million to $3.52 million if the firm's debt rose to $14 million.* The reason for the decline is that, at this very high level of debt, managers and employees would be worried about the firm's failing and about losing their jobs; suppliers would not sell to the firm on normal credit terms; orders would be lost because of customers' fears that the company might go bankrupt and thus be unable to deliver; and so on. EBIT is independent of financial leverage at "reasonable" debt levels, but at extreme degrees of leverage, EBIT is adversely affected.

11. Quite obviously, the situation in the real world is much more complex, and less exact, than this example suggests. Most important, different investors will have different estimates for EBIT and k_s; hence, they will form different expectations about the equilibrium stock price. This means that HSS might have to pay more

than $21.73 to repurchase its shares, or perhaps that the shares could be bought at a lower price. These changes would cause the optimal amount of debt to be somewhat higher or lower than $6 million. Still, $6 million represents our best estimate of the optimal debt level, so it is the level we should use as our target capital structure.

12. The WACC for the various levels of debt is shown in Column 8 of Table 13-2. It can be seen that the minimum cost of capital, 11.0 percent, corresponds to the level of debt at which the value of the firm and its stock price are maximized, $6.0 million.

The stock price and cost of capital relationships developed in Table 13-2 are graphed in Figure 13-3. Here we see that HSS's stock price is maximized, and its weighted average cost of capital is minimized, at the same D/V ratio, 27.6 percent.

EXTENSIONS OF THE EXAMPLE

In the preceding section, we examined the effects of debt financing on its stock price if HSS went from zero debt to some positive level of debt. Now we will examine the general effects of a change from one debt level to some other level, using this equation:

$$P_1 = \frac{\text{Ending value of firm} - \text{Beginning value of debt}}{\text{Beginning number of shares}}. \quad \text{(13-5)}$$

Note that the beginning value of debt could be zero, so Equation 13-5 is general in the sense that it could apply to any analysis, zero initial debt or not. In this section, we explain the logic of Equation 13-5, and we illustrate it with three different cases.

Example 1: Zero Initial Debt.   Suppose we want to determine what would happen to HSS's stock price if it went from zero debt to $4 million of debt. This requires us to find new values of V and P, V_1 and P_1, with $4 million of debt:

$$V_1 = D_1 + S_1 = D_1 + \frac{(\text{EBIT} - k_d D)(1 - T)}{k_s}$$

$$= \$4,000,000 + \frac{(\$4,000,000 - \$332,000)(0.6)}{0.126}$$

$$= \$4,000,000 + \$17,466,667 = \$21,466,667.$$

$$P_1 = \frac{\text{Ending value} - \text{Beginning debt}}{\text{Beginning shares}} = \frac{\$21,466,667 - \$0}{1,000,000}$$

$$= \$21.47, \text{ versus } P_0 = \$20 \text{ with zero debt.}$$

As explained previously, this stock price would exist *as soon as investors learned of the recapitalization plan, before the plan was actually carried out.* Stockholders would recognize that the company will have a value of $21,466,667 very shortly, and this value will belong entirely to them because they will receive the $4,000,000 brought in by the sale of bonds as payment for shares repurchased. Note also that management must inform all stockholders of the planned recapitalization. If you were a stockholder, you would certainly not be willing to sell your stock back to the company at $20 per share if you expected to see the stock price rise to $21.47. You and the other stockholders would insist on receiving as much if you sold your stock back to the company as you would end up with if you chose not to sell it.[8]

Once the plan had been carried out, the shares outstanding would decline from 1,000,000 to 813,694:

$$\text{New shares} = \text{Old shares} - \text{Shares repurchased}$$

$$n_1 = n_0 - \text{Shares repurchased}$$

$$= n_0 - \frac{\text{Incremental debt}}{\text{Price per share}}$$

$$= 1,000,000 - \frac{\$4,000,000}{\$21.47}$$

$$= 1,000,000 - 186,306$$

$$= 813,694 \text{ shares after repurchase.}$$

Check on stock price:

$$P_1 = \frac{\text{New value of equity}}{\text{New shares outstanding}} = \frac{S_1}{n_1} = \frac{\$17,466,667}{813,694} = \$21.47.$$

Had we made similar calculations, but used $6 million of debt, the resulting stock price would have been $21.73 as shown in Table 13-2.

Example 2: $4 Million Initial Debt. Now assume that HSS had actually made the move to $4 million of debt, and management is now considering another in-

---

[8] Indeed, if you and other stockholders were silly enough to sell at $20 per share, then the $4 million of debt could be used to buy and retire even more shares, so the remaining shares would be worth even more than $21.47. In fact, the stock would, under these conditions, be worth $21.83:

$$P_1 = \frac{S_1}{n_1} = \frac{\$17,466,667}{1,000,000 - (\$4,000,000/\$20)} = \$21.83.$$

Of course, you might be afraid that the recapitalization plan would fall through, so you might be willing to sell out for slightly less than $21.47, say, for $21, figuring that $21 in the hand is better than $21.47 in the bush.

crease in leverage. What would happen to HSS's stock price if it increased its leverage from $4 million to $6 million of debt? *Assume that the old debt must be retired if new debt is issued, so the entire $6 million will be new debt having a cost of 9 percent (from Figure 13-2).* Now the analysis will begin with these initial values:

$$\text{Initial debt value} = D_0 = \$4,000,000.$$

$$\text{Initial stock value} = S_0 = \$17,466,667.$$

$$\text{Initial total value} = V_0 = \$21,466,667.$$

$$\text{Initial stock price} = P_0 = \$21.47.$$

$$\text{Initial number of shares} = n_0 = 813,694.$$

The new equilibrium total value will be

$$V_1 = D_1 + S_1$$

$$= \$6,000,000 + \frac{(\$4,000,000 - \$540,000)(0.6)}{0.132}$$

$$= \$6,000,000 + \$15,727,273 = \$21,727,273,$$

and the new equilibrium stock price will be

$$P_1 = \frac{V_1 - D_0}{n_0} = \frac{\$21,727,273 - \$4,000,000}{813,694}$$

$$= \frac{\$17,727,273}{813,694} = \$21.79.$$

Thus, HSS could increase the value of its stock from $21.47 to $21.79 by increasing its leverage from $4 million to $6 million.[9] This second round of debt financing would increase the stockholders' gain by ($21.79 − $21.47)813,694 = $260,382.

Example 3: Nonreplacement of Old Debt.   Now assume that HSS again plans to increase its leverage from $4 million to $6 million, *but that the old debt need not be retired.* Here the $4 million in old debt would remain outstanding, carrying a coupon rate of 8.3 percent. As before, assume that the new debt issue of $2

---

[9]Notice the slight difference in equilibrium stock prices at $6 million of debt: $21.73 in the first example versus $21.79 now. This difference demonstrates two points: (1) If HSS could move to its optimal capital structure in stages, it could repurchase shares at a lower average price than the equilibrium price of $21.73, and (2) if it could buy back shares at a lower price, its final price would be higher because more shares could be repurchased for a given expenditure (debt raised), hence fewer shares would be outstanding in the end.

million would have a cost of 9 percent. Assuming the same initial values as in Example 2, the new equilibrium values are calculated as follows:

1.
$$S_1 = \frac{\left[EBIT - \left(\begin{array}{c} Cost\ of \\ old\ debt \end{array}\right)\left(\begin{array}{c} Amount\ of \\ old\ debt \end{array}\right) - \left(\begin{array}{c} Cost\ of \\ new\ debt \end{array}\right)\left(\begin{array}{c} Amount\ of \\ new\ debt \end{array}\right)\right](1 - T)}{k_s}$$

$$= \frac{[\$4,000,000 - (0.083)(\$4,000,000) - (0.09)(\$2,000,000)](0.6)}{0.132}$$

$$= \frac{(\$3,488,000)(0.6)}{0.132} = \$15,854,545.$$

2. The old debt has a book value of $4,000,000. However, because more debt is to be issued, the risk of the old debt will rise and consequently its market value will fall. The old debt's new market value, D_0', is $3,688,889:

$$D_0' = \frac{0.083(\$4,000,000)}{0.09}$$

$$= \$3,688,889 \text{ versus } \$4,000,000 \text{ before the recapitalization announcement.}$$

3. The loss suffered by the old bondholders is $311,111:

$$D_0 - D_0' = \$4,000,000 - \$3,688,889 = \$311,111.$$

4. The new value of the firm will be

$$V_1 = D_1 + S_1 = D_0' + \text{New debt value} + S_1$$

$$= \$3,688,889 + \$2,000,000 + \$15,854,545 = \$21,543,434.$$

5. The new equilibrium stock price will be

$$P_1 = \frac{\$21,543,434 - \$3,688,889}{813,694} = \$21.943.$$

6. The stockholders will have an aggregate gain calculated as follows:

$$\text{Stockholders' gain} = (P_1 - P_0)n_0$$

$$= (\$21.943 - \$21.467)(813,694) = \$387,318.$$

7. Of the stockholders' $387,318 gain, $311,111 will have "come out of the hides of the old bondholders," while $76,207 will have come as a "true gain from leverage" as a result of tax savings net of costs associated with financial distress:[10]

$$\text{True gain from leverage} = V_1 - V_0$$

$$= \$21,543,434 - \$21,466,667 = \$76,767.$$

Thus, HSS could increase the value of its stock from $21.47 to $21.94 by increasing its leverage from $4 million to $6 million if it did not have to refund its initial lower-cost debt. Of course, this gain to stockholders would come mostly at the expense of the old bondholders. The addition of $2 million of new debt would increase the riskiness of all the firm's securities. The stockholders would be compensated, as would the new bondholders, but the old bondholders would still be receiving coupon payments of only 8.3 percent, even though the new debt increased the riskiness of HSS's bonds to the point where $k_d = 9\%$.[11] Therefore, the value of the old debt would fall, and there would be a transfer of wealth from the old bondholders to HSS's stockholders. Because of the possibility of such events, bond indentures generally limit the amount of debt a firm can issue.

THE EFFECT OF FINANCIAL LEVERAGE ON EPS

Thus far we have focused on the impact of leverage on a firm's total value and its stock price. Before we leave the HSS illustration, we should also take a look at how leverage affects earnings per share (EPS); this is done in Table 13-3. The top third of the table gives operating income data. It begins by recognizing that HSS's future EBIT is not known with certainty. Expected EBIT is $4 million, but the realized EBIT could be less than or greater than $4 million. To simplify matters, we have assumed a discrete distribution of sales, so EBIT has only three possible outcomes. Notice also that EBIT is assumed not to depend on financial leverage.[12]

---

[10]Rounding differences occur in these calculations, primarily in Steps 6 and 7.

[11]The $2 million of additional debt might actually have a cost somewhat below 9 percent. This is because retention of the old debt at 8.3 percent would result in lower total interest payments at the new debt level than if the entire $6 million of debt had cost 9 percent. Given equal business risk, the lower interest payments would lower the probability of financial distress, and thus lower the riskiness of the new debt. Additionally, lower distress risk would mean that equity holders might have a required return somewhat less than the 13.2 percent indicated in Table 13-2. However, these gains all come at the expense of the existing bondholders—the addition of new debt makes the old debt more risky, yet the old debtholders will not be compensated for the additional risk. Our analysis does not include these effects; they would, of course, be extremely hard to measure with any degree of confidence.
　　Note, too, that bondholders would be concerned that the company, having "stuck it to bondholders" once, might issue still more debt in the future. This fear could keep the cost of the new debt issue at or even above 9 percent.

[12]As we discussed earlier, capital structure does affect EBIT at very high debt levels. For example, we assumed that HSS's EBIT would fall from $4 million to $3.52 million if the level of debt rose to $14 million. However, debt in Table 13-3 is limited to $10 million, so the "excessive leverage effect on EBIT" is not present in this particular example.

TABLE 13-3	*Operating Income (EBIT)*			
HSS's EPS AT DIFFERENT AMOUNTS OF DEBT (MILLIONS OF DOLLARS EXCEPT PER-SHARE FIGURES)	Probability of indicated sales	0.2	0.6	0.2
	Sales	$10.00	$20.00	$30.00
	Fixed operating costs	4.00	4.00	4.00
	Variable costs (60% of sales)	6.00	12.00	18.00
	Total costs (except interest)	$10.00	$16.00	$22.00
	Earnings before interest and taxes (EBIT)	$ 0.00	$ 4.00	$ 8.00
	Zero Debt			
	Less interest	0.00	0.00	0.00
	Earnings before taxes	$ 0.00	$ 4.00	$ 8.00
	Less taxes (40%)	0.00	1.60	3.20
	Net income	$ 0.00	$ 2.40	$ 4.80
	Earnings per share on 1 million shares (EPS)	$ 0.00	$ 2.40	$ 4.80
	Expected EPS		$ 2.40	
	Standard deviation of EPS[a]		$ 1.52	
	Coefficient of variation of EPS[a]		0.63	
	$10 Million of Debt			
	Less interest (0.12 × $10,000,000)	1.20	1.20	1.20
	Earnings before taxes	($1.20)	$ 2.80	$ 6.80
	Less taxes (40%)[b]	(0.48)	1.12	2.72
	Net income	($0.72)	$ 1.68	$ 4.08
	Earnings per share on 524,940 shares (EPS)[c]	($1.37)	$ 3.20	$ 7.77
	Expected EPS		$ 3.20	
	Standard deviation of EPS[a]		$ 2.90	
	Coefficient of variation of EPS[a]		0.91	

[a]Procedures for calculating the standard deviation and the coefficient of variation were discussed in Chapter 4.
[b]Assume tax credit on losses. If credits were not available, expected EPS would be lower, and risk higher, at high debt levels.
[c]Shares outstanding is determined as follows:

$$\text{Shares} = \text{Original shares} - \frac{\text{Debt}}{\text{Stock price}} = 1,000,000 - \frac{\text{Debt}}{\text{Stock price}},$$

where the stock price is taken from Table 13-2, Column 6. With $10 million of debt, P = $21.05. After the recapitalization, 524,940 shares will remain outstanding:

$$\text{Shares} = 1,000,000 - \frac{\$10,000,000}{\$21.05} = 524,940.$$

EPS figures can also be calculated using this formula:

$$EPS = \frac{(EBIT - k_dD)(1 - T)}{\text{Original shares} - \text{Debt/Price}}.$$

For example, at D = $10 million,

$$EPS = \frac{[\$4,000,000 - (0.12)(\$10,000,000)](0.6)}{1,000,000 - \$10,000,000/\$21.05} = \frac{\$1,680,000}{524,940} = \$3.20.$$

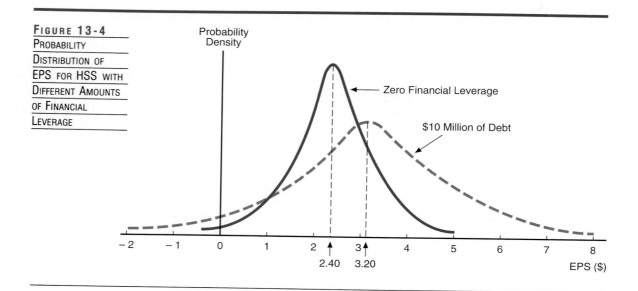

FIGURE 13-4

PROBABILITY DISTRIBUTION OF EPS FOR HSS WITH DIFFERENT AMOUNTS OF FINANCIAL LEVERAGE

The middle third of Table 13-3 shows the situation that would exist if HSS continues to use no debt. Net income after taxes is divided by the 1 million shares outstanding to calculate EPS. If sales were as low as $10 million, EPS would be zero, but EPS would rise to $4.80 at sales of $30 million.

The EPS at each sales level is next multiplied by the probability of that sales level to obtain the expected EPS, which is $2.40 if HSS uses no debt. We also calculate the standard deviation of EPS and its coefficient of variation to get an idea of the firm's total risk at a zero debt ratio: $\sigma_{EPS} = \$1.52$, and $CV_{EPS} = 0.63$.

The lower third of Table 13-3 shows the financial results that would occur if the company decided to use $10 million of debt. The interest rate on the debt, 12 percent, is taken from Figure 13-2. With $10 million of 12 percent debt outstanding, the company's interest expense is $1.2 million per year. This is a fixed cost, and it is deducted from EBIT as calculated in the top section. Next, taxes are taken out, and we work on down to the EPS figures that would result at each sales level. With $10 million of debt, EPS would be − $1.37 if sales were as low as $10 million; it would rise to $3.20 if sales were $20 million; and it would soar to $7.77 if sales were as high as $30 million.

Continuous approximations of the EPS distributions under the two financial structures are graphed in Figure 13-4. Although expected EPS is much higher if the firm uses financial leverage, the graph makes it clear that the risk of low, or even negative, EPS is also higher if debt is used. Figure 13-4 shows that using leverage involves a risk/return trade-off—higher leverage increases expected earnings per share, but using more leverage also increases the firm's risk. It is this

increasing risk that causes k_s and k_d to increase at higher amounts of financial leverage.[13]

The relationship between expected EPS and financial leverage is plotted in the top section of Figure 13-5. Here we see that expected EPS first rises as the use of debt increases—interest charges rise, but the decreasing number of shares outstanding as debt is substituted for equity still causes EPS to increase. However, EPS peaks when $12 million of debt is used. Beyond this amount, interest rates rise rapidly, and EBIT begins to fall, so EPS is depressed in spite of the falling number of shares outstanding. Risk as measured by the coefficient of variation of EPS shown in the fourth column of the data in Figure 13-5 rises continuously, and at an increasing rate, as debt is substituted for equity.

Does the same amount of debt maximize both price and EPS? The answer is *no*. As we can see from the lower graph in Figure 13-5, HSS's stock price is maximized with $6 million of debt, while the upper graph shows that expected EPS is maximized by using $12 million of debt. *Since management is primarily interested in maximizing the value of the stock, the optimal capital structure calls for the use of $6 million of debt.*

PROBLEMS WITH THE HSS ANALYSIS

The Hill Software Systems example illustrated the effects of leverage on firm value, stock prices, earnings per share, and debt values. However, the example was obviously simplified to facilitate the discussion, and we cannot overemphasize the difficulties that are encountered when one attempts to use this type of analysis in practice. First, the capitalization rates (k_d and especially k_s) are very difficult to estimate. The cost of debt at different debt levels can generally be estimated with some degree of confidence, but cost of equity estimates must be viewed as very rough approximations.[14]

Second, the mathematics of the valuation process make the outcomes very sensitive to the input estimates. Thus, fairly small errors in the estimates of k_d, k_s, and EBIT can lead to large errors in estimated EPS and stock price.

Third, our example was restricted to the case of a no-growth firm. In view of the input requirements to model even a simple no-growth situation, and the still greater requirements for the growth model, it is unrealistic to think that a precise optimal capital structure can really be identified.

---

[13]Note that financial leverage has similar effects on the risk of both EPS and ROE. Thus, Figure 13-4 is similar in appearance to the lower part of Figure 12-4 in Chapter 12.

[14]The statistical relationship between k_s and financial leverage has been studied extensively by using both cross-sectional and time series data. In the cross-sectional studies, a sample of firms is analyzed, with multiple regression techniques used in an attempt to "hold constant" all factors other than financial leverage that might influence k_s. The general conclusion of the cross-sectional studies is that k_s rises as leverage increases, but statistical problems preclude us from specifying the functional relationship with much confidence.

In the time series studies, a single firm's k_s is analyzed over time in an attempt to see how k_s changes in response to changes in its debt ratio. Here again, "other factors" do not remain constant, so it is impossible to specify exactly how k_s is affected by financial leverage.

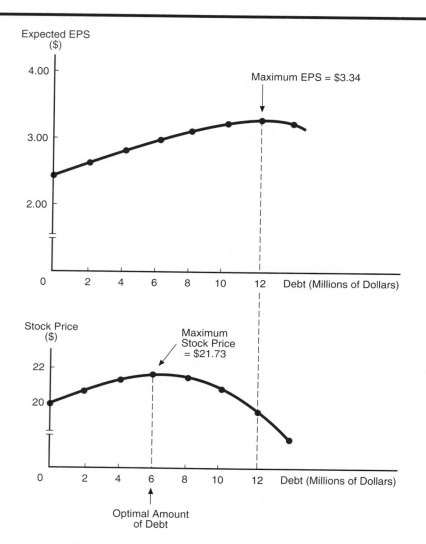

FIGURE 13-5

RELATIONSHIP BETWEEN HSS'S EXPECTED EPS AND STOCK PRICE

Debt	Expected EPS	Standard Deviation of EPS	Coefficient of Variation	Stock Price[b]
$ 0	$2.40[a]	$1.52[a]	0.63[a]	$20.00
2,000,000	2.55	1.68	0.66	20.89
4,000,000	2.70	1.87	0.69	21.47
6,000,000	2.87	2.09	0.73	21.73
8,000,000	3.04	2.40	0.80	21.71
10,000,000	3.20[a]	2.90[a]	0.91[a]	21.05
12,000,000	3.34	3.83	1.15	19.86
14,000,000	3.26	5.20	1.60	17.16

[a]These values are taken from Table 13-3. Values at other debt levels were calculated similarly.
[b]Stock prices are from Table 13-2.

Finally, many firms are not publicly owned, and that causes still more difficulties. If a privately held firm's owner never plans to have his or her firm go public, then potential market value data are really irrelevant. However, an analysis based on market values for a privately owned firm is useful if the owner is interested in knowing how the firm's market value would be affected by leverage should the decision be made to go public.

SELF-TEST QUESTIONS

What are the key assumptions used in the Hill Software Systems example?

Briefly describe the steps involved in finding Hill's optimal capital structure.

Why is the stock price higher when the firm adds debt in increments rather than a single step, even when the existing issue is retired?

Why is the stock price higher when the existing issue remains outstanding rather than being refunded?

What problems occur when the Hill example procedures are used to estimate real-world optimal capital structures?

SOME CONSIDERATIONS IN THE CAPITAL STRUCTURE DECISION

Since one cannot determine a precise optimal capital structure, managers must apply judgment to their quantitative analyses. The judgmental analysis involves several different factors, and in one situation a particular factor might have great importance, while the same factor might be relatively unimportant in another situation. This section discusses some of the more important judgmental issues that should be taken into account.

LONG-RUN VIABILITY

Managers of large firms, especially those providing vital services such as electricity or telephone service, have a responsibility to provide *continuous* service, so they must refrain from using leverage to the point where the firm's long-run viability is endangered. Long-run viability may conflict with stock price maximization and cost of capital minimization.[15]

---

[15]Recognizing this fact, most public service commissions require utilities to obtain their approval before issuing long-term securities, and Congress has empowered the SEC to supervise the capital structures of public utility holding companies. However, in addition to concern over the firms' safety, which suggests low debt ratios, both managers and regulators recognize a need to keep all costs as low as possible, including the cost of capital. Since a firm's capital structure affects its cost of capital, regulatory commissions and utility managers try to select capital structures that minimize utilities' cost of capital, subject to the constraint that a firm's ability to finance needed construction projects is not endangered.

MANAGERIAL CONSERVATISM

Well-diversified investors have eliminated most, if not all, of the diversifiable risk from their portfolios. Therefore, the typical investor can tolerate some chance of financial distress, because a loss on one stock would probably be offset by random gains on other stocks in his or her portfolio. However, managers often view financial distress with more concern—they are typically not well diversified, and their careers, and thus the present value of their expected earnings, can be seriously affected by the onset of financial distress. Thus, it is not difficult to imagine that managers might be more "conservative" in their use of leverage than the average stockholder would desire. If this is true, then managers would set somewhat lower target capital structures than the ones which maximize expected stock prices. The managers of a publicly owned firm would never admit this, for unless they owned voting control, they would quickly be removed from office. However, in view of the uncertainties about what constitutes the value-maximizing structure, management could always say that the target capital structure employed is, in its judgment, the value-maximizing structure, and it would be difficult to prove otherwise.[16]

LENDER AND RATING AGENCY ATTITUDES

Regardless of a manager's own analysis of the proper leverage for his or her firm, there is no question but that lenders' and rating agencies' attitudes are frequently important determinants of financial structures. Generally, management will discuss the firm's financial structure with lenders and rating agencies and give much weight to their advice. However, if a particular firm's management is so confident of the future that it seeks to use leverage beyond the norms for its industry, its lenders may be unwilling to accept such debt increases, or may do so only at a high price.

Coverage ratios are often used by lenders and rating agencies to measure the risk of financial distress. Accordingly, managements give considerable weight to such ratios as the *times-interest-earned (TIE) ratio,* which is defined as EBIT divided by total interest charges. The lower this ratio, the higher the probability that a firm will encounter financial distress.

Table 13-4 shows how HSS's expected TIE ratio declines as its use of debt increases. At zero debt, the TIE ratio is undefined, but it is almost infinitely high at very low debt levels. When $2 million of debt is used, the expected TIE is a high 25 times, but the interest coverage ratio declines rapidly as debt rises. Note, however, that these coverages are expected values—the actual TIE will be higher if

---

[16]It is, of course, possible for a particular manager to be less conservative than his or her firm's average stockholder. However, this condition is less likely to occur than is excessive managerial conservatism, which is just another manifestation of the agency problem. If excessive conservatism exists, then managers, as agents of the stockholders, are not acting in the best interests of their principals. However, when managers become the primary owners of a company, such as in managerial buyouts (MBOs), they often become very aggressive in their use of financial leverage. By using extreme amounts of debt, they take on a great deal of risk, but, in the process, they open the door for big payoffs.

TABLE 13-4	Amount of Debt (in Millions)	Expected TIE[a]
HSS's Expected	$ 0	Undefined
Times-Interest-	2	25.0
Earned Ratio at	4	12.1
Different Amounts	6	7.4
of Debt	8	5.0
	10	3.3
	12	2.2

[a]TIE = EBIT/Interest. Example: TIE = $4,000,000/$1,200,000 = 3.3 at $10 million of debt. Data are from Table 13-1 and Figure 13-2.

sales exceed the expected $20 million level, but lower if sales fall below $20 million.

The variability of the TIE ratio is highlighted in Figure 13-6, which shows the probability distributions of the ratio at $8 million and $12 million of debt. The expected TIE is much higher if only $8 million of debt is used. Even more important, with less debt there is a much lower probability of a TIE of less than 1.0, the level at which the firm is not earning enough to meet its required interest payments and thus is seriously exposed to the threat of bankruptcy.

Another coverage ratio that is often used by lenders and rating agencies is the *fixed charge coverage (FCC) ratio.* This is a better measure than the TIE ratio because it recognizes that there are fixed financial charges other than interest payments which could lead to financial distress. The FCC ratio is defined as follows:

$$FCC = \frac{EBIT + \text{Lease payments}}{\text{Interest} + \left(\begin{array}{c}\text{Lease}\\\text{payments}\end{array}\right) + \left(\dfrac{\text{Sinking fund payments}}{1 - T}\right)}.$$

Note that the sinking fund (debt principal) payments are "grossed up" in recognition of the fact that these payments must be made with after-tax dollars (net income) because they are not tax deductible.

If HSS had $1 million of lease payments and $1 million of sinking fund payments, its FCC ratio at a debt level of $10 million would be 1.3:

$$FCC = \frac{\$4,000,000 + \$1,000,000}{\$1,200,000 + \$1,000,000 + \dfrac{\$1,000,000}{0.6}}$$

$$= \frac{\$5,000,000}{\$3,866,667} = 1.3.$$

Thus, the coverage of total fixed charges is considerably less than the 3.3 times-interest-earned coverage at the same $10 million debt level.

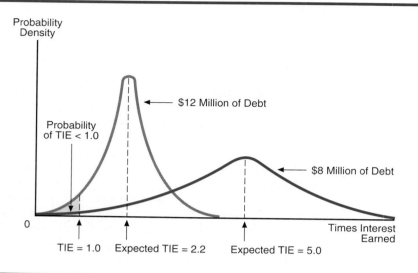

FIGURE 13-6

PROBABILITY DISTRIBUTIONS OF TIMES-INTEREST-EARNED RATIO FOR HSS WITH DIFFERENT CAPITAL STRUCTURES

RESERVE BORROWING CAPACITY AND FINANCING FLEXIBILITY

When we discussed the asymmetric information theory, we noted that firms should maintain a borrowing capacity reserve, which preserves the ability to issue debt on favorable terms. For example, suppose Advanced Biotechnics had just successfully completed an R&D program, and its internal projections forecasted much higher earnings in the immediate future. However, the new earnings are not yet anticipated by investors, hence are not reflected in the price of its stock. Advanced Biotechnics would not want to issue stock—it would prefer to finance with debt until the higher earnings materialized and were reflected in the stock price, at which time it could sell an issue of common stock, retire the debt, and return to its target capital structure. Similarly, if the financial manager felt that interest rates were temporarily low, but were likely to rise fairly soon, he or she might want to issue long-term bonds and thus "lock in" the low rates for many years. To maintain this reserve borrowing capacity, firms generally use less debt under "normal" conditions, thus presenting a stronger financial picture than they otherwise would. This is not suboptimal from a long-run standpoint, although it might appear so if viewed strictly on a short-run basis.

Note too that firms' debt contracts often specify that no new debt can be issued unless certain ratios exceed minimum levels. Very frequently, the TIE ratio is required to exceed 2 or 2.5 times as a condition for the issuance of additional debt. With this in mind, look back at Figure 13-6 and note that, if it used $12 million of debt, HSS's TIE would be less than 2.0 almost half the time, whereas the probability of a coverage less than 2.0 would be quite small if it used only $8 million of debt. Thus, if HSS sets a relatively high target debt ratio, its *financing flexibility* would be reduced in the sense that it could not count on using whatever type of capital it wanted to use at all times.

Control

The effect of its choice of securities on a management's control position may also influence the capital structure decision. If a firm's management just barely has majority control (just over 50 percent of the stock), but it is not in a position to buy any more stock, debt may be the choice for new financings. On the other hand, a management group that is not concerned about voting control may decide to use equity rather than debt if the firm's financial situation is so weak that the use of debt might subject the company to serious risk of default. If the firm gets into serious difficulties, the creditors (through covenants in the debt agreements) may assume control and perhaps force a management change. This has happened to Chrysler, Navistar International (formerly International Harvester), Braniff, Continental Illinois Bank, and a number of other companies in recent years. However, if too little debt is used, management runs the risk of a takeover, where some other company or management group tries to persuade stockholders to turn over control to the new group, which may plan to boost earnings and stock prices by using financial leverage. This happened to Lenox, the china company, and to many other firms in the 1980s. In general, control considerations do not necessarily suggest the use of debt or of equity, but if management does not have majority control, the effects of capital structure on control will certainly be taken into account.

Additional Considerations

In addition to those factors just listed, the following considerations are also relevant to the capital structure decision:

Asset Structure. Firms whose assets are suitable as security for loans tend to use debt rather heavily. Thus, real estate companies tend to be highly leveraged. However, companies involved in technological research employ relatively little debt. Also, if the firm's assets are subject to high business risk, then the firm will be less able to use financial leverage than a firm with low business risk. Accordingly, factors such as sales stability and operating leverage, which influence business risk, also influence firms' optimal capital structures.

Growth Rate. Other factors being the same, faster-growing firms must rely more heavily on external capital—slow growth can be financed with retained earnings, but rapid growth generally requires the use of external funds. For reasons set forth in our discussion of information asymmetry theory, and also because the flotation costs involved in selling common stock exceed those incurred when selling debt, firms first turn to debt financing to meet external funding needs. Thus, rapidly growing firms tend to use somewhat more debt than slower-growth companies.

Profitability. One often observes that firms with very high rates of return on investment use relatively little debt. This behavior is consistent with the information asymmetry theory, and the practical reason seems to be that highly profitable firms such as Merck, 3M, and Microsoft simply do not need to do much debt

financing—their high rates of return enable them to do most of their financing with retained earnings.

Taxes. Interest is a deductible expense, while dividends are not deductible, so the higher a firm's corporate tax rate, the greater the advantage of using corporate debt.

SELF-TEST QUESTIONS

Is the capital structure decision mostly objective (made on the basis of numerical analysis) or mostly subjective (judgmental, with many factors considered)?

Briefly discuss some of the factors that managers consider when setting the firm's target capital structure.

AN APPROACH TO SETTING THE TARGET CAPITAL STRUCTURE

Thus far in Chapters 12 and 13, we have discussed (1) several theories of capital structure, (2) a method of analysis based on these theories (including a discussion of the very severe problems one encounters when attempting to apply the theory), and (3) a number of factors which influence the capital structure decisions of most firms. In this section, we describe a pragmatic approach to setting the target capital structure. Our approach requires judgmental assumptions, but it also allows managers to consider how alternative capital structures would affect future profitability, coverage, and external financing requirements under a variety of assumptions.

The starting point for the analysis is a forecasting model that is set up to test the effects of capital structure changes. Here is a brief description of a *Lotus 1-2-3* model and how it has been used. Basically, the model generates forecasted data based on inputs supplied by the financial manager. Each data item can be fixed, or it can be allowed to vary from year to year. The required data include the most recent balance sheet and income statement, plus the following items, all of which represent either expectations or management-determined policy variables:

1. Annual growth rates in unit sales
2. Annual inflation rates
3. Corporate tax rate
4. Variable costs as a percentage of sales
5. Fixed costs
6. Interest rates on already outstanding (or embedded) debt
7. Marginal component costs of capital
8. Capital structure percentages
9. Dividend growth rate
10. Long-term dividend payout ratio

The model uses the input data to forecast balance sheets and income statements for five years, and it calculates and displays other information such as external financing requirements, ROE, EPS, DPS, times interest earned, stock price, and WACC for projected future years.

The financial manager begins by entering base year values plus data on expected unit sales growth rates, expected inflation rates, and so on. These inputs are used by the model to forecast operating income and asset requirements which, in general, will *not* depend on the financing decision. In addition, the financial manager must consider the financing mix. Our model uses as inputs both the debt/equity mix and the debt maturity mix. By debt maturity mix, we mean the proportion of short-term versus long-term debt. Further, the manager must estimate as best he or she can the effects of the capital structure on the component costs—a higher debt ratio will lead to increases in the costs of all components, and vice versa if less debt is used. With all inputs entered, the model then completes the forecasted financial statements and generates projected stock prices.

The model is then used to analyze alternative scenarios. This analysis takes two forms: (1) changing the financing inputs to get some idea of how the financing mix affects the key outputs and (2) changing the operating inputs to see how the basic business risk of the firm affects the key outputs under various financing strategies. Finally, the model's output must be reviewed and analyzed, and a decision must be made as to the best capital structure. Since we are focusing on the capital structure decision, we would pay particular attention to the forecasted EPS, coverage, and external funding requirements, as well as the projected stock price.

The model can generate the output "answers" quite easily, but it remains up to the financial manager to assign input values, to interpret the output, and, finally, to set the target capital structure. The final decision is based on all the factors we have discussed in Chapters 12 and 13, and the decision maker must judge which factors are most relevant to his or her firm. Reaching a decision is not easy, but a capital structure forecasting model such as the one we use at least permits managers to analyze the effects of alternative courses of action, which is an essential element of good decision making.

It should be noted again that, although capital structure decisions do affect the prices of companies' stocks, those effects are relatively small in comparison to the effects of operating decisions. A company's ability to identify (or create) market opportunities, and to produce and sell products efficiently, is the primary determinant of success. Financial arrangements can facilitate or hamper operations, but the best of financial plans cannot overcome deficiencies in the operations area. These statements are supported by empirical studies, which generally find a weak statistical relationship between capital structure and stock price. Our opinions are also supported by runs of the computer model, which show stock price to be affected significantly by changes in unit sales, sales prices, fixed costs, and variable costs, but not to be affected much by changes in capital structure. This last point can also be seen from the HSS example discussed earlier. Refer again to Table 13-2. Hill Software Systems' stock price is maximized at a D/V ratio of 27.6 percent. However, at a D/V of 18.6 percent, which is one-third lower, the firm's stock price drops only from $21.73 to $21.47, or by a slight 1.2 percent, while if D/V rises to

36.8 percent, HSS's stock price hardly drops at all. Thus, HSS could set its target D/V ratio anywhere in the range from 18.6 to 36.8 percent and still come very close to maximizing the stock price.

SELF-TEST QUESTIONS

Briefly describe the elements of a financial forecasting model designed to help set the target capital structure.

How critical is the optimal capital structure decision to the financial performance of the firm; that is, how important are small deviations from the optimal structure?

Should the target capital structure be thought of as a single point or as a range?

SOME ADDITIONAL INSIGHTS INTO CAPITAL STRUCTURE DECISIONS

At this point, one might have an uneasy feeling regarding both how to establish an optimal capital structure and its effect on risk, profitability, and stock prices. We know that we can construct models which generate projected earnings, stock prices, coverage ratios, and so on under different capital structures. However, our confidence in these results is limited, because we do not know for sure how k_d and k_s, and hence stock price, will really change with changes in the capital structure. We also know that in practice a myriad of more or less subjective factors also influence the decision. Therefore, to gain more insights into capital structure decisions, it seems appropriate to take a look at how managers say they actually establish target capital structures.

Professors David Scott and Dana Johnson surveyed a group of large firms to find out how managers attempt to estimate the optimal capital structure, and whether managers really believe that one can be determined.[17] Scott and Johnson sent questionnaires to the chief financial officer (CFO) of each Fortune 1000 firm. Although only 212 financial managers replied, the sample was still large enough to provide useful insights into the operational decision process.

First, the respondents reported a belief that capital structure decisions do matter—in general, financial managers believe that the prudent use of debt can lower the firm's overall cost of capital, and that excessive use of debt will increase the required rate of return on equity. Second, the most popular measures of financial leverage are (1) the long-term debt to total capitalization ratio,[18] (2) the times-interest-earned (TIE) ratio, and (3) the long-term debt to common equity

---

[17]See David F. Scott and Dana J. Johnson, "Financing Policies and Practices in Large Corporations," *Financial Management,* Summer 1982, 51–59.

[18]Total capitalization is defined as long-term debt plus preferred stock plus common equity. Therefore, current liabilities and deferred taxes are excluded.

ratio. However, when computing these ratios, accounting (or book) values rather than market values were virtually always used. Third, 64 percent of the responding managers indicated that their firms' target long-term debt to total capitalization ratios were in the range of 26 to 40 percent, and the most popular reported target range was 26 to 30 percent. (Because stock market values generally exceed book values, the debt ratio measured in market value terms would be quite a bit lower than the reported book value figures.)

The survey also gathered data on how various parties influence the capital structure decision. The data indicate that managers give the greatest weight to their own internal analyses, but that investment bankers and bond rating agencies also have a significant influence. Additionally, firms consider industry averages when setting their target capital structures, but they are willing to depart from these averages if their own conditions suggest that a departure is warranted.

Self-Test Questions

Do practicing financial managers believe that capital structure matters?

Do investment bankers and rating agencies influence the capital structure decision?

Variations in Capital Structures among Firms

As might be expected, wide variations in the use of financial leverage occur both across industries and among the individual firms in each industry. Table 13-5 illustrates differences for four industries, ranked in descending order of the percentage of common equity as shown in Column 1.[19]

The drug and steel companies do not use much debt (their common equity ratios are high), because uncertainties inherent in industries that are cyclical, oriented toward research, or subject to huge product liability suits render the heavy use of leverage unwise. Retailers and utility companies, on the other hand, use debt relatively heavily, but for different reasons. Retailers use short-term debt to finance inventories and long-term debt secured by mortgages on their stores. The utilities have traditionally used large amounts of debt, particularly long-term debt — their fixed assets make good security for mortgage bonds, and their relatively stable sales make it safe for them to carry more debt than would be true for firms with more business risk.

Particular attention should be given to the times-interest-earned (TIE) ratio, because it provides a measure of how safe the debt is and how vulnerable the company is to financial distress. TIE depends on three factors: (1) the percentage of debt, (2) the interest rate on the debt, and (3) the company's profitability.

---

[19]Information on capital structures and financial strength is available from a multitude of sources. We used the *Compustat* Industrial Data Tapes to develop Table 13-5, but other published sources include *The Value Line Investment Survey, Robert Morris Associates Annual Studies,* and *Dun & Bradstreet Key Business Ratios.*

TABLE 13-5   CAPITAL STRUCTURE PERCENTAGES: FOUR INDUSTRIES RANKED BY COMMON EQUITY RATIO

Industry	Common Equity (1)	Preferred Stock (2)	Total Debt (3)	Long-Term Debt (4)	Short-Term Debt (5)	Times-Interest-Earned Ratio (6)	Return on Equity
Steel	72.4%	0.0%	27.6%	23.7%	3.9%	5.0×	6.0
Drugs	69.1	0.9	30.0	15.6	14.4	10.2	27.4
Retailing	44.9	1.5	53.6	35.3	18.3	2.6	12.0
Utilities	43.4	5.6	51.0	47.0	4.0	2.4	8.3
Composite (average of all industries, not just those listed above)	40.5%	1.7%	57.8%	35.4%	22.4%	1.9×	10.7%

Note: These ratios are based on accounting (or book) values. Stated on a market value basis, the equity percentages would rise because most stocks sell at prices that are much higher than their book values.

Source: *Compustat* Industrial Data Tape, 1992.

Embedded interest rates are fairly similar across the firms in the four industries, but the ROEs and amounts of debt are quite different. Thus, the drug industry, with its low debt and high profitability, has the highest TIE by far.

Wide variations in capital structures also exist among firms within given industries—for example, although the average steel company used 28 percent debt, Birmingham Steel used 41 percent, while Nucor used only 4 percent. Thus, factors unique to individual firms, including managerial attitudes, play an important role in setting target capital structures.

SELF-TEST QUESTIONS

Why does the average capital structure vary from industry to industry?

Do all firms within an industry have roughly the same capital structure and debt maturity mix?

BOOK WEIGHTS VERSUS MARKET WEIGHTS

In Chapter 8, we calculated the weighted average cost of capital with market value rather than book value weights. Further, in our discussions of capital structure thus far in Chapters 12 and 13, we continued to focus on market value, not book value. However, survey data indicate that financial managers generally focus on book value structures. Thus, there seems to be a conflict between academic theory and business practice. Here are some thoughts on this issue:

1. If stocks and bonds do not sell exactly at book value—and they almost never do—then it would be impossible for a growing firm to establish and maintain at constant levels a target book value and a target market value capital structure. The firm could stay on its book value target or on its market value target, but not on

both. To illustrate, assume that a company has, at book value, $50 million of debt and $50 million of equity, for a total book value of $100 million. However, its stock sells at twice book. Here is the capital structure situation, with dollars in millions:

	Book Value		Market Value	
Debt	$ 50	50%	$ 50	33%
Equity	50	50	100	67
Total	$100	100%	$150	100%

Now suppose the company needs to raise an additional $100 million. If it sells $50 million of debt and $50 million of common stock, it will add these amounts to its balance sheet, so its book value capital structure will remain constant. However, adding $50 million to both debt and equity will cause its market value capital structure to change. On the other hand, if it raises $33 million as debt and $67 million as equity, its market value capital structure will remain constant, but its book value structure will change. Thus, it can maintain either its book value or its market value capital structure, but not both.

2. Book values as reported on balance sheets reflect the historical costs of assets. At times, historical costs have little to do with the actual value of these assets or with their ability to produce cash flows which can be used to service debt. Market values would almost always better reflect cash generation and debt service ability.

3. As we have repeatedly noted throughout this chapter and the last one, the point of capital structure analysis is to find that capital structure which maximizes the firm's market value, and hence its stock price. Since this optimum is defined in terms of stock prices, it can only be determined by an analysis of market values.

4. Now suppose a firm found its optimal market value structure, but then financed so as to maintain a constant book value structure. This would lead to a departure from value maximization. Therefore, if a firm is growing, it must finance so as to hold constant its market value structure. That will, as we saw above, normally lead to a change in the book value structure.

5. Since the firm should, to keep its value at a maximum, finance so as to hold its market value structure constant, the weighted average cost of capital, WACC, should be found using market value weights.

6. Business executives prefer stability and predictability to volatility and uncertainty. Book values are far more predictable than market values. Further, a financial manager can set a target book value capital structure and then attain it, right on the money. It would be virtually impossible to stay at a target market value structure because of bond and stock price fluctuations. This is one reason why executives focus on book value structures rather than on the more logical market value structures. Also, many financial executives have accounting backgrounds, and accountants focus on accounting numbers. However, as financial executives gain a knowledge of financial (as opposed to accounting) theory, the focus should shift more toward market values.

7. For purposes of developing the weighted average cost of capital, we strongly recommend the use of market value weights. However, if a company focuses on a

book value capital structure, seeks to maintain that structure, and finances in accordance with book value weights, then its weighted average cost of capital should be based on book weights.

8. Some executives have argued against the use of market value weights on the grounds that as stock prices change, so would capital structure weights, with the result being a volatile cost of capital. This argument is incorrect. The cost of capital should be based on *target* weights, not on the actual capital structure, and there is no reason to think that a target market value structure would be any less stable than a target book value structure. In fact, as we discuss in Point 9 below, target market value weights are probably more stable than target book weights.

9. Now consider a fairly typical situation. Firm X currently has a 50/50 debt/equity ratio at book, and a 33/67 ratio at market. It targets on the book value ratio. Several years go by. Inflation occurs, so new assets cost more. Output prices are based on marginal costs, which have risen because of inflation. With the new, higher prices, the rate of return on old assets increases, as does the value of the old assets, and the firm's stock price rises. Book values per share are relatively stable, so the increasing stock price leads to an increase in the market/book ratio. Debt values, on the other hand, remain close to book. Rising stock prices, when combined with stable bond prices, could cause the market value debt/equity ratio to remain constant at the 33/67 level, or even to increase, even though the firm finances on a 50/50 book basis.

10. Note also that, under our scenario, the rising ROE will lead to improved coverages. This fact, together with analysts' knowledge that the firm's book asset values are understated, will support an increase in the debt ratio measured at book.

What can we conclude from all this? We are absolutely convinced that the procedures we recommend are correct—namely, firms should focus on market value capital structures and base their cost of capital calculations on market value weights. Because market values do change, it would be impossible to keep the actual capital structure on target at all times, but this fact in no way detracts from the validity of market value targets.

SELF-TEST QUESTIONS

Should the target capital structure be expressed in book value or market value weights?

Why do practicing financial managers prefer to work with book weights?

SUMMARY

In this chapter, we discussed a variety of topics related to capital structure decisions. The key concepts covered are listed below:

▶ Incorporating financial distress and agency costs into either the MM tax model or the Miller model results in a *tradeoff model*. Here the marginal costs and benefits of debt financing are balanced against one another, and the result is

an optimal capital structure that falls somewhere between zero and 100 percent debt.

▶   The *asymmetric information theory,* which is based on the assumption that managers have better information than investors, postulates that there is a preferred "pecking order" of financing: first retained earnings (and depreciation), then debt, and finally, as a last resort only, new common stock.

▶   The asymmetric information theory leads to the conclusion that firms should maintain a *borrowing capacity reserve* so that they can always issue debt on reasonable terms rather than have to issue new equity at the wrong time.

▶   There is clearly some value to debt financing, and firms use different amounts of debt depending on their tax rates, their asset structures, and their inherent riskiness.

▶   Unfortunately, capital structure theory does not provide neat, clean answers to the question of the optimal capital structure. Thus, many factors must be considered when actually choosing a firm's target capital structure, and the final decision will be based on both analysis and judgment.

▶   If a firm has *perpetual cash flows*, then a relatively simple model can be used to value the firm at different capital structures. In theory, this model can be used to find the capital structure that maximizes stock price. However, the inputs to the model are very difficult, if not impossible, to estimate. Further, most firms are growing, so they do not have constant cash flows.

▶   Since one cannot determine the optimal capital structure with quantitative models, managers must also consider *qualitative factors* including long-run viability, managerial conservatism, lender and rating agency attitudes, reserve borrowing capacity, control, asset structure, profitability, and taxes.

▶   Firms generally have *computerized planning models* which are used in the financial planning process. These models can be used to get a feel for the impact of capital structure changes on a firm's financial condition.

▶   Wide variations in capital structure exist, both across industries and among individual firms within industries. The variations across industries can be explained to a large extent by the economic fundamentals of the industry.

▶   The optimal capital structure should be thought of in market value rather than book value terms, even though managers often seem to focus on book values.

QUESTIONS

13-1 Define each of the following terms:

    a.   Optimal capital structure; target capital structure

    b.   Tradeoff model

    c.   Asymmetric information theory

    d.   Perpetual cash flow analysis

    e.   Market value versus book value

    f.   Reserve borrowing capacity

13-2 Why is the following statement true? "Other things being the same, firms with relatively stable sales are able to carry relatively high debt ratios."

13-3 Why do public utility companies usually have capital structures that are different from those of retail firms?

13-4 Some economists believe that swings in business cycles will not be as wide in the future as they have been in the past. Assuming that they are correct, what effect might this added stability have on the types of financing used by firms in the United States? Would your answer be true for all firms?

13-5 Why is EBIT generally considered to be independent of financial leverage? Why might EBIT actually be influenced by financial leverage at high debt levels?

13-6 If a firm with no debt could buy back and retire its stock at the pre-announcement price, would its final stock price be higher than that resulting from the procedure outlined in the chapter? Would it be fair for a firm to buy back its stock without telling stockholders that stock was being repurchased?

13-7 How might increasingly volatile inflation rates, interest rates, and bond prices affect the optimal capital structure for corporations?

13-8 If a firm went from zero debt to successively higher levels of debt, why would you expect its stock price to first rise, then hit a peak, and then begin to decline?

13-9 The stock of Gentech Company is currently selling at its low for the year, but management feels that the stock price is only temporarily depressed because of investor pessimism. The firm's capital budget this year is so large that the use of new outside equity is contemplated. However, management does not want to sell new stock at the current low price and is therefore considering a temporary departure from the firm's "optimal" capital structure by borrowing the funds it would otherwise have raised in the equity markets. Does this seem to be a wise move? Does this action conform to any of the theories presented in the chapter?

13-10 Briefly describe the asymmetric information theory of capital structure. What implications does this theory have for capital structure decision making?

13-11 Why is the debt level that maximizes a firm's expected EPS generally higher than the debt level that maximizes its stock price?

SELF-TEST PROBLEM (SOLUTION APPEARS IN APPENDIX C)

ST-1 (Optimal capital structure) The Rogers Company is currently in this situation: (1) EBIT = $4 million; (2) tax rate, $T = 35\%$; (3) value of debt, $D = \$2$ million; (4) $k_d = 10\%$; (5) $k_s = 15\%$; and (6) shares of stock outstanding, $n = 600{,}000$. The firm's market is stable, and it expects no growth, so all earnings are paid out as dividends. The debt consists of perpetual bonds.

    a. What is the total market value of the firm's stock, S, its price per share, P_0, and the firm's total market value, V?

    b. What is the firm's weighted average cost of capital?

    c. The firm can increase its debt by $8 million, to a total of $10 million, using the new debt to buy back and retire some of its shares. Its interest rate on all debt will be 12 percent (it will have to call and refund the old debt), and its cost of equity will rise from 15 to 17 percent. EBIT will remain constant. Should the firm change its capital structure?

what are (1) expected EPS and σ_{EPS} and (2) expected TIE and σ_{TIE}, assuming an increase in book value of debt to $70 million?

13-4 (Pro forma analysis) The Norman Corporation is currently all-equity financed, but the firm is considering a change to 50 percent debt financing. The debt would cost 12 percent, and would be used to repurchase shares currently selling at $25 per share. Norman now has 40,000 shares outstanding and $1,000,000 in total assets. Its pro forma income statement for 1994, assuming zero debt usage, is as follows:

Sales	$900,000
Operating costs	750,000
EBIT	$150,000
Taxes (40%)	60,000
Net income	$ 90,000

a. What is the firm's expected EPS for 1993 using zero debt? At a debt level of $500,000?

b. Assume that operating costs remain at 83.33 percent of sales over a wide range of sales levels. Further, the 1993 pro forma income statement is based on expected sales of $900,000, but the actual sales distribution is as follows:

Probability	Sales
0.10	$ 500,000
0.15	700,000
0.50	900,000
0.15	1,100,000
0.10	1,300,000

Find the EPS at each sales level for both zero debt and 50 percent debt financing.

c. Make a plot of EPS versus sales level for both financing alternatives. Place the plots on the same set of axes. Interpret this graph.

(Do Parts d and e only if you are using the computer problem diskette.)

d. At a zero debt level, Norman's expected ROE = $90,000/$1,000,000 = 9.0%, while at $500,000 of debt, expected ROE = $54,000/$500,000 = 10.8%. Determine the firm's ROE at each debt level for every possible sales level. Plot the two ROE distributions.

e. Now, assume that the $500,000 debt financing would cost 15 percent. Repeat the Part d analysis. Is there a significant difference? Why?

13-5 (Subjective analysis) You have been hired as a financial consultant by two firms, Alpha Industries (Firm A) and Zed Corporation (Firm Z). Firm A is in the fast-growing microcomputer retail sales industry, while Firm Z manufactures office equipment such as pencil sharpeners, staplers, and tape dispensers. Your task is to recommend the optimal capital structure for the two firms. Discuss the factors that would influence your decision, and specifically how each of these factors apply to each firm. Here are some additional points about the two firms:

(1) Firm A generally leases its stores, while Firm Z purchases its plants.

(2) Firm A's stock is widely held, while the family of Firm Z's founder holds 40 percent of its stock.

(3) Firm Z has a significant amount of accelerated depreciation expense each year, while Firm A has almost none.

(4) Firm A has demonstrated high growth and profitability over the last few years. On the other hand, Firm Z's growth has averaged a modest 5 percent per year, and its profit margins and ROEs have been unspectacular.

MINI
CASE

Assume you have just been hired as business manager of PizzaPalace, a pizza restaurant located adjacent to campus. The company's EBIT was $500,000 last year, and since the university's enrollment is capped, EBIT is expected to remain constant (in real terms) over time. Since no expansion capital will be required, PizzaPalace plans to pay out all earnings as dividends. The management group owns about 50 percent of the stock, and the stock is traded in the over-the-counter market.

The firm is currently financed with all equity; it has 100,000 shares outstanding; and $P_0 = \$20$ per share. When you took your MBA corporate finance course, your instructor stated that most firms' owners would be financially better off if the firms used some debt. When you suggested this to your new boss, he encouraged you to pursue the idea. As a first step, assume that you obtained from the firm's investment banker the following estimated costs of debt and equity for the firm at different debt levels (in thousands of dollars):

Amount Borrowed	k_d	k_s
$ 0	—	15.0%
250	10.0%	15.5
500	11.0	16.5
750	13.0	18.0
1,000	16.0	20.0

If the company were to recapitalize, debt would be issued, and the funds received would be used to repurchase stock. PizzaPalace is in the 40 percent state-plus-federal corporate tax bracket.

a. Briefly describe the tradeoff theory of capital structure.

b. Briefly describe the asymmetric information theory of capital structure.

c. Are the tradeoff and asymmetric information theories mutually exclusive? What do you believe that capital structure theory prescribes for financial managers? What insights does capital structure theory provide regarding the factors that influence firms' optimal capital structures?

d. With the above points in mind, now consider the optimal capital structure for Pizza-Palace.
   (1) What valuation equations can you use in the analysis?
   (2) Could either the MM or the Miller capital structure theories be applied directly in this analysis, and if you presented an analysis based on these theories, how do you think the owners would respond?

e. (1) Describe briefly, without using any numbers, the sequence of events that would take place if PizzaPalace does recapitalize.
   (2) What would be the new stock price if PizzaPalace recapitalized and used these amounts of debt: $250,000; $500,000; $750,000?
   (3) How many shares would remain outstanding after recapitalization under each debt scenario?
   (4) Considering only the levels of debt discussed, what is PizzaPalace's optimal capital structure?

f. (1) Assume now that the firm has recapitalized with $250,000 of debt, and that currently $S = \$1,839,000$, $D = \$250,000$, $P = \$20.89$, and $n = 88,030$. The debt has a "poison put" which requires that it be paid off if additional debt is issued. What would PizzaPalace's stock price be if it now increased its debt to $500,000 by issuing $500,000 of new debt and using half to refund the old issue and half to repurchase stock?

(2) Now assume that PizzaPalace issues an additional $250,000 of debt, but it does not have to refund the old issue. What would happen to its stock price? Assume also that the new and old issues have the same priority of claims.

g. It is also useful to determine the effect of any proposed recapitalization on EPS. Calculate the EPS at debt levels of $0, $250,000, $500,000, and $750,000, assuming that the firm begins at zero debt and recapitalizes to each level in a single step. Is EPS maximized at the same level that maximizes stock price?

h. Calculate the firm's WACC at each debt level. What is the relationship between the WACC and the stock price?

i. Suppose you discovered that PizzaPalace had more business risk than you originally estimated. Describe how this would affect the analysis. What if the firm had less business risk than originally estimated?

j. Would it make sense to do an analysis similar to the PizzaPalace analysis for most firms? Why or why not? What type of analysis do you think a firm should actually use to help set its optimal, or target, capital structure? What other factors should managers consider when setting the target capital structure?

SELECTED ADDITIONAL REFERENCES AND CASES

Chapter 11 provided references that focus on the theory of capital structure; the references listed here are oriented more toward applications than theory.

Donaldson's work on the setting of debt targets is old but still relevant:

Donaldson, Gordon, "New Framework for Corporate Debt Capacity," *Harvard Business Review,* March-April 1962, 117–131.

———, "Strategy for Financial Emergencies," *Harvard Business Review,* November-December 1969, 67–79.

For a recent article on the asymmetric information theory, see

Baskin, Jonathon, "An Empirical Investigation of the Pecking Order Hypothesis," *Financial Management,* Spring 1989, 26–35.

Definitive references on the empirical relationships between capital structure and (1) the cost of debt, (2) the cost of equity, (3) earnings, and (4) the price of a firm's stock are virtually nonexistent — statistical problems make the precise estimation of these relationships extraordinarily difficult, if not impossible. One good way to get a feel for the issues involved is to obtain a set of the cost of capital testimonies filed in a major utility rate case — such testimony is available from state public utility commissions, the Federal Communications Commission, the Federal Energy Regulatory Commission, and utility companies themselves. For an academic discussion of the issues, see

Caks, John, "Corporate Debt Decisions: A New Analytical Framework," *Journal of Finance,* December 1978, 1297–1315.

Gordon, Myron J., *The Cost of Capital to a Public Utility* (East Lansing, Mich.: Division of Research, Graduate School of Business Administration, Michigan State University, 1974).

Hamada, Robert S., "The Effect of the Firm's Capital Structure on the Systematic Risk of Common Stocks," *Journal of Finance,* May 1972, 435–452.

Masulis, Ronald W., "The Impact of Capital Structure Change on Firm Value: Some Estimates," *Journal of Finance,* March 1983, 107–126.

Piper, Thomas R., and Wolf A. Weinhold, "How Much Debt is Right for Your Company," *Harvard Business Review,* July-August 1982, 106–114.

Shalit, Sol S., "On the Mathematics of Financial Leverage," *Financial Management,* Spring 1975, 57–66.

Shiller, Robert J., and Franco Modigliani, "Coupon and Tax Effects on New and Seasoned Bond Yields and the Measurement of the Cost of Debt Capital," *Journal of Financial Economics,* September 1979, 297–318.

For some insights into how practicing financial managers view the capital structure decision, see

Norton, Edgar, "Factors Affecting Capital Structure Decisions," *Financial Review,* August 1991, 431–446.

Pinegar, J. Michael, and Lisa Wilbricht, "What Managers Think of Capital Structure Theory: A Survey," *Financial Management,* Winter 1989, 82–91.

Scott, David F., and Dana J. Johnson, "Financing Policies and Practices in Large Corporations," *Financial Management,* Summer 1982, 51–59.

To learn more about the link between market risk and operating and financial leverage, see

Callahan, Carolyn M., and Rosanne M. Mohr, "The Determinants of Systematic Risk: A Synthesis," *The Financial Review,* May 1989, 157–181.

Gahlon, James M., and James A. Gentry, "On the Relationship between Systematic Risk and the Degrees of Operating and Financial Leverage," *Financial Management,* Summer 1982, 15–23.

Prezas, Alexandros P., "Effects of Debt on the Degrees of Operating and Financial Leverage," *Financial Management,* Summer 1987, 39–44.

Here are some recent articles which relate to this chapter:

Easterwood, John C., and Palani-Rajan Kadapakkam, "The Role of Private and Public Debt in Corporate Capital Structures," *Financial Management,* Autumn 1991, 49–57.

Garvey, Gerald T., "Leveraging the Underinvestment Problem: How High Debt and Management Shareholdings Solve the Agency Costs of Free Cash Flow," *Journal of Financial Research,* Summer 1992, 149–166.

Harris, Milton, and Artur Raviv, "Capital Structure and the Informational Role of Debt," *Journal of Finance,* June 1990, 321–349.

Israel, Ronen, "Capital Structure and the Market for Corporate Control: The Defensive Role of Debt Financing," *Journal of Finance,* September 1991, 1391–1409.

See the following three articles for additional insights into the relationship between industry characteristics and financial leverage:

Bowen, Robert M., Lane A. Daley, and Charles C. Huber, Jr., "Evidence on the Existence and Determinants of Inter-Industry Differences in Leverage," *Financial Management,* Winter 1982, 10–20.

Long, Michael, and Ileen Malitz, "The Investment-Financing Nexus: Some Empirical Evidence," *Midland Corporate Finance Journal,* Fall 1985, 53–59.

Scott, David F., Jr., and John D. Martin, "Industry Influence on Financial Structure," *Financial Management,* Spring 1975, 67–73.

For a more thorough discussion of the international implications of capital structure, see

Rutterford, Janette, "An International Perspective on the Capital Structure Puzzle," *Midland Corporate Finance Journal,* Fall 1985, 60–72.

The following Brigham-Gapenski cases contain many of the concepts we present in Chapters 11 and 12.

Case 9, "Home Security Systems, Inc.," and Case 10, "Kleen Kar, Inc.," which present a situation similar to the Hill Software Systems example in the text.

DIVIDEND POLICY

T *he financial news wire carried this one-sentence announcement at 9:02 on the morning of January 26, 1993: "IBM slashes the quarterly dividend on its common from $1.21 to 54¢." A later story provided the following additional information:*

> *The Board of Directors took this action only after serious deliberation and careful consideration of both IBM's earnings and the investment required for the long-term development of the Company's businesses, as well as IBM's intention to pay an appropriate return to shareholders. After weighing all factors, and taking into account the need to maintain IBM's strong financial position, the Board decided to act now in the best long-term interests of the Company and its shareholders.*

IBM's dividend cut—the first ever for the company—reduced the annual dividend from $4.84 to $2.16. The $4.84 amount had been established in 1989, and the dividend growth rate prior to 1989 had averaged 7 percent per year.

Many analysts and investors had been expecting a dividend cut because IBM had not adequately anticipated the shift from mainframe computing to personal computers, and it was not prepared for the near collapse of the mainframe computer market. In spite of seven large-scale restructurings and tens of thousands of managerial and employee layoffs, IBM was still trapped with massive resources devoted to poor-selling products. Meanwhile, nimbler companies such as Microsoft and Intel earned record-breaking profits derived from software and microchip businesses that IBM, in effect, ceded to them in the 1980s. The end result for IBM was a record U.S. corporate loss in 1992, a 60 percent drop in stock price, and, finally, a 53 percent dividend reduction.

At the same time the dividend cut was announced, IBM's board of directors announced the resignation of John F. Akers, the company's chairman and chief executive officer. Although analysts' opinions were equally divided on whether it was realistic to think that someone else could have done better at the company's helm, there was near-unanimous agreement that someone new must be brought in to reshape the enterprise.

When the markets first responded to the dividend cut and management change, IBM's stock price shot up by $3, but it retreated later in the day as investors concluded that the management shake-up would not produce a quick fix for IBM's problems. By the end of the day, IBM was selling at $49 on the New York Stock Exchange, up just 12.5¢.

This chapter discusses the many facets of dividend policy. As you read the material, put yourself in the shoes of an IBM board member. If the board saw the company's problems on the horizon a few years earlier, why didn't it cut the dividend then? Also, if things looked so bleak, why didn't the board eliminate the dividend instead of just cutting it? By the end of the chapter, you should have a good idea of how dividend policy decisions are made and a better appreciation of the dilemma faced by IBM's board.

Dividend policy, which is the decision to pay out earnings as dividends or to retain and reinvest them in the firm, has three key elements: (1) What fraction of earnings should be paid out, on average, over time? This is the *target payout policy* decision. (2) Should the firm attempt to maintain a steady, stable dividend growth rate, or should it vary its dividend payments from year to year depending on its internal needs for funds and on its cash flows? (3) What dollar amount should the firm pay in current dividends? These three elements are the primary focus of this chapter, but we also examine two related issues, stock repurchases and stock splits.

DIVIDENDS VERSUS CAPITAL GAINS: WHAT DO INVESTORS PREFER?

The target payout ratio should be based in large part on investors' preferences for dividends versus capital gains—do investors prefer to have the firm distribute its income as dividends or plow earnings back into the business to produce capital gains? This preference can be considered in terms of the constant growth stock valuation model:

$$\hat{P}_0 = \frac{D_1}{k_s - g}.$$

This equation shows that if the company increases the payout ratio and thus raises D_1, this increase in the numerator, taken alone, would cause the stock price to rise. However, if D_1 is raised, then less money will be available for reinvestment, the expected growth rate will decline, and that would tend to depress the stock's price. Thus, any change in payout policy will have two opposing effects, and the firm should strike that balance between current dividends and future growth which maximizes the price of the stock.

In this section we examine three theories of investor preference: (1) the dividend irrelevance theory, (2) the "bird-in-the-hand" theory, and (3) the tax differential theory.

DIVIDEND IRRELEVANCE: MODIGLIANI AND MILLER

In an important theoretical article on dividend policy, Merton Miller and Franco Modigliani (MM) argued that dividend policy has no effect on either the price of a firm's stock or its cost of capital—MM argued that dividend policy is *irrelevant*.[1] They reasoned that the value of a firm is determined by its basic earning power and its risk class, and, therefore, that a firm's value depends on its asset investment policy rather than on how earnings are split between dividends and retained earnings. MM demonstrated, under a specific set of assumptions, that if a firm pays higher dividends, then it must sell more stock to new investors, and that the share of the value of the company given up to new investors is exactly equal to the dividends paid out. For example, if Boeing's capital budget calls for $1 billion of equity financing in 1994, and if the company expects $1 billion of earnings, then (1) it could pay all of its earnings out as dividends and finance the equity requirement by selling $1 billion of new stock; (2) it could retain the entire $1 billion of earnings, pay no dividends, sell no new stock, and provide stockholders with a capital gain having a present value of $1 billion; or (3) it could pick a payout anywhere between 0 and 100 percent and thus provide stockholders with a total of $1 billion in dividends and capital gains.

MM proved that their proposition holds in theory, but only under these five assumptions: (1) There are no personal or corporate income taxes. (2) There are no stock flotation or transaction costs. (3) Investors are indifferent between dividends and capital gains. (4) The firm's capital investment policy is independent of its dividend policy. (5) Investors and managers have the same set of information (symmetric information) regarding future investment opportunities.

The MM assumptions are not realistic, and they obviously do not hold precisely. Firms and investors do pay income taxes, firms do incur flotation costs, and investors do incur transactions costs. Further, managers often have better information than outside investors. Thus, MM's theoretical conclusions on dividend irrelevance may not be valid under real-world conditions.

---

[1] See Merton H. Miller and Franco Modigliani, "Dividend Policy, Growth, and the Valuation of Shares," *Journal of Business,* October 1961, 411–433.

"Bird-in-the-Hand" Theory: Gordon and Lintner

In some respects, the most critical facet of MM's dividend irrelevance theory is that investors are indifferent between dividends and capital gains. This issue has been hotly debated in academic circles. Myron Gordon and John Lintner, on the one hand, argued that k_s increases as the dividend payout is reduced, because investors can be more sure of receiving dividend payments than the income from capital gains which are expected to result from retaining earnings.[2] They say, in effect, that investors value a dollar of expected dividends more highly than a dollar of expected capital gains because the dividend yield component, D_1/P_0, is less risky than the g component in the total expected return equation, $\hat{k}_s = D_1/P_0 + g$.

On the other hand, MM argued that investors are indifferent between D_1/P_0 and g, hence k_s is not affected by dividend policy. MM called the Gordon-Lintner argument the "bird-in-the-hand fallacy" because, in MM's view, many, if not most, investors are going to reinvest their dividends in the same or similar firms anyway, and, in any event, the riskiness of the firm's cash flows to investors in the long run is determined only by the riskiness of its cash flows from operating assets, and not by its dividend payout policy.[3]

Tax Preference Theory: Litzenberger and Ramaswamy

A third theory, based on tax effects, was supported by Litzenberger and Ramaswamy.[4] In 1993, the maximum tax rate on long-term capital gains was 28 percent, while the proposed top marginal rate on dividend income was 39.6 percent (and over 40 percent when limitations on deductions and personal exemptions are considered). Thus, an investor in the 40 percent marginal tax bracket would pay a 40 percent tax rate on his or her dividend income, but only 28 percent on long-term capital gains. Further, by not selling stock, the investor could defer realization of the capital gains and thus payment of the tax, and since a dollar paid in the future is less valuable than a dollar paid today, the tax deferral feature provides yet another advantage to capital gains.

To illustrate the tax advantage of capital gains, suppose an individual investor in the 40 percent tax bracket is considering the purchase of two stocks: Stock G, which is a "growth stock" with a 10 percent capital gains yield and a 5 percent dividend yield, and Stock I, which is an "income stock" with a 5 percent capital gains yield and a 10 percent dividend yield. Both stocks sell for $10, have the same

[2]See Myron J. Gordon, "Optimal Investment and Financing Policy," *Journal of Finance,* May 1963, 264–272; John Lintner, "Dividends, Earnings, Leverage, Stock Prices, and the Supply of Capital to Corporations," *Review of Economics and Statistics,* August 1962, 243–269; and Myron J. Gordon and Lawrence I. Gould, "The Cost of Equity Capital: A Reconsideration," *Journal of Finance,* June 1979, 849–861.

[3]Academicians other than MM have also rebutted the "bird-in-the-hand" theory. For example, see Michael Brennan, "A Note on Dividend Irrelevance and the Gordon Valuation Model," *Journal of Finance,* December 1971, 1115–1121.

[4]Robert H. Litzenberger and Krishna Ramaswamy, "The Effects of Personal Taxes and Dividends on Capital Asset Prices," *Journal of Financial Economics,* June 1979, 163–196.

risk, and are constant-growth stocks; thus, $\hat{k}_G = \hat{k}_I$ = Dividend yield + Capital gains yield = 15% on a before-tax basis.

If the investor holds the stocks for a year and thus is subject to the long-term capital gains tax, the after-tax returns on the two stocks would be as follows:

		Dividend Yield	+	Capital Gain	=	Total Return
Stock I:	Before-tax return	10.0%		5.0%		15.0%
	Tax (40% and 28%)	− 4.0		− 1.4		− 5.4
	After-tax return	6.0%		3.6%		9.6%
Stock G:	Before-tax return	5.0%		10.0%		15.0%
	Tax (40% and 28%)	− 2.0		− 2.8		− 4.8
	After-tax return	3.0%		7.2%		10.2%

Thus, the after-tax return on the growth stock is significantly higher than that on the high-dividend (income) stock.

Note too that the after-tax return differential on these two stocks would increase as the holding period increased, because taxes on capital gains are not paid until the gains are realized. At the extreme, when the stocks are kept (in the family) forever, hence capital gains taxes are never paid, the return differential is 2.0 percentage points:

	After-Tax Dividend Yield	+	After-Tax Capital Gains Yield	=	After-Tax Total Return
Stock I	6.0%		5.0%		11.0%
Stock G	3.0%		10.0%		13.0%
			Difference: Advantage to G =		2.0%

Tax-paying investors would recognize that Stock G offers a higher after-tax return than Stock I, and thus would bid up the price of G relative to I. For example, Stock G's price might rise to $10.25, while Stock I's might fall to $9.75. The end result would be a higher before-tax yield on Stock I than on Stock G, but equal after-tax returns to the marginal investor. If investors in the aggregate behave as described in this section, the result would be higher pre-tax required rates of return on high dividend yield stocks than on low dividend yield stocks.

ILLUSTRATION OF DIVIDEND POLICY THEORIES

Figure 14-1 can be used to explain the three dividend policy theories: (1) Miller and Modigliani's dividend irrelevance theory, (2) Gordon and Lintner's bird-in-the-hand theory, and (3) Litzenberger and Ramaswamy's tax preference theory. To illustrate the three theories, consider the case of Hardin Electronics, which has, from its inception, plowed all of its earnings back into the business, and consequently has never paid a dividend. Hardin's management is now considering a change in policy, and it wants to adopt the policy that will maximize its stock price.

Figure 14-1   Dividend Irrelevance, Bird-in-the-Hand, and Tax Preference Dividend Theories

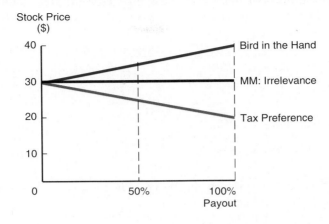

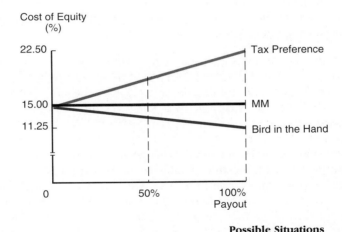

Percent Payout (1)	Percent Retained (2)	DPS (3)	g (4)	MM			Bird-in-the-Hand			Tax Preference		
				P_0 (5)	D/P_0 (6)	k_s (7)	P_0 (8)	D/P_0 (9)	k_s (10)	P_0 (11)	D/P_0 (12)	k_s (13)
0%	100%	$0.00	15.0%	$30	0.0%	15.0%	$30	0.00%	15.00%	$30	0.0%	15.0%
50	50	2.25	7.5	30	7.5	15.0	35	6.43	13.93	25	9.0	16.5
100	0	4.50	0.0	30	15.0	15.0	40	11.25	11.25	20	22.5	22.5

Notes:

1. Book value = Initial market value = $30 per share.

2. ROE = 15%.

3. EPS = $30(0.15) = $4.50.

4. g = b(ROE) = (% retained)(ROE).

5. k_s = Dividend yield + Growth rate.

Consider first the data presented below the graph. Columns 1 and 2 show three alternative dividend policies: (1) Retain all earnings and pay out zero, which is the present policy, (2) pay out 50 percent of earnings, and (3) pay out 100 percent of earnings. In the example, we assume that the company will have a 15 percent ROE regardless of which payout policy it follows, so with a book value per share of $30, EPS will be 0.15($30) = $4.50 under all payout policies.[5] Given an EPS of $4.50, dividends per share are shown in Column 3 under each payout policy.

Under the assumption of a constant ROE, the growth rate shown in Column 4 will be g = b(ROE) = (% Retained)(ROE), and it will vary from 15 percent at a zero payout to zero at a 100 percent payout. If Hardin pays out 50 percent of its earnings, then its dividend growth rate will be 7.5 percent.

Columns 5, 6, and 7 show how the situation would look if MM's irrelevance theory were correct. Under this theory, neither the stock price nor the cost of equity would be affected by the payout policy—the stock price would remain constant at $30, and k_s would be stable at 15 percent. Note that k_s is found as the sum of the growth rate in Column 4 plus the dividend yield in Column 6.

Columns 8, 9, and 10 show how the situation would look if the bird-in-the-hand theory were true. Under this theory, investors prefer dividends, and the more dividends the company pays out, the higher its stock price and the lower its cost of equity. In this example, the bird-in-the-hand argument indicates that adopting a 100 percent payout policy would cause the stock price to rise from $30 to $40, and the cost of equity would decline from 15 percent to 11.25 percent.

Finally, Columns 11, 12, and 13 show the situation that would exist if the tax preference theory were correct. Under this theory, investors want companies to retain earnings and thus provide returns in the form of lower-taxed capital gains rather than heavily taxed dividends. If the tax preference theory were correct, then an increase in the dividend payout ratio would cause the stock price to decline and the cost of equity to rise.

The data in the table can be plotted to produce the two graphs shown in Figure 14-1. The top panel shows how the stock price reacts to dividend policy under each of the theories, and the bottom panel shows how the cost of equity is affected. Thus, the three theories lead to very different conclusions, and we cannot at this point say which theory is most correct. Before reaching any conclusions, we must examine the available empirical evidence.

SELF-TEST QUESTIONS

Differentiate between the dividend irrelevance theory, the bird-in-the-hand theory, and the tax preference theory. Use a graph such as Figure 14-1 to illustrate your answer.

---

[5]When the three theories were developed, it was assumed that a company's investment opportunities would be held constant and that if the company increased its dividends, its capital budget could be funded by selling common stock. Conversely, if a high-payout company lowered its payout to the point where retained earnings exceeded good investment opportunities, it was assumed that the company would repurchase shares. Transactions costs were assumed to be zero. We maintain those assumptions in our example.

List the assumptions of Modigliani and Miller concerning the dividend irrelevance theory.

How did the bird-in-the-hand theory get its name?

In what sense does MM's theory represent a middle ground position between the other two theories?

TESTS OF THE DIVIDEND THEORIES

In the preceding section, we presented three dividend theories:

1. MM argued that dividend policy is irrelevant; that is, it does not affect a firm's value or its cost of capital. Thus, according to MM, there is no optimal dividend policy—one dividend policy is as good as any other.

2. Gordon and Lintner disagreed with MM, arguing that dividends are less risky than capital gains, so a firm should set a high dividend payout ratio and offer a high dividend yield in order to maximize its stock price. MM called this the bird-in-the-hand fallacy.

3. A third position is that investors prefer retained earnings to dividends because of the tax preference given to capital gains. This theory suggests that companies should hold dividend payments to low levels if they want to maximize stock prices.

These three theories offer contradictory advice to corporate managers, so which, if any, should we believe? Two primary types of empirical tests have been conducted in an attempt to determine the true relationship between dividend policy and required equity returns. In the DCF type of test, empirical data on dividend yields and growth rates are plotted for different companies, and the slope of the plot is examined. If the slope were -1.0, this would indicate that investors were indifferent between dividends and capital gains, and hence support MM. Unfortunately, the DCF tests have been inconclusive for two reasons: (1) For a valid statistical test, things other than dividend policy must be held constant; that is, the sample companies must differ only in their dividend policies, and (2) we must be able to measure accurately the expected growth rates for the sample firms. Neither of these two conditions holds: We cannot find a set of publicly owned firms that differ only in their dividend policies, and we cannot obtain precise estimates of growth rates. Therefore, DCF tests cannot determine what effect dividend policy has on the cost of equity, and, hence, cannot resolve the dividend policy controversy.

Academic researchers have also studied the dividend policy issue from a CAPM perspective. These studies hypothesize that required returns are a function of both market risk, as measured by beta, and dividend yield. If so, then a stock's required return, k_i, could be expressed as follows:

$$k_i = k_{RF} + (k_M - k_{RF})b_i + (D_i - D_M)\lambda_i. \qquad \text{(14-1)}$$

Here D_i is the dividend yield of Stock i, D_M is the dividend yield of an average stock, and λ_i is the dividend impact coefficient. Researchers have tested Equation 14-1 by regressing historical values of k_{RF}, k_M, D_i, and D_M against historical values of k_i. If the coefficient of λ_i turns out to be zero, dividend yield would not appear to affect required returns, and MM would be supported. If λ_i were positive, then investors would appear to require a higher return on stocks with high dividend yields, as the tax preference theory predicts. If λ_i were negative, this would support Gordon-Lintner.

The results of this line of research have been mixed. Litzenberger and Ramaswamy showed, using NYSE data from 1936 through 1977, that stocks with high dividend yields did have higher total returns than did stocks with low dividend yields, after adjusting for market risk.[6] Their study indicated that investors' required rates of return increased about 0.24 percentage points for every percentage point increase in dividend yield. However, other studies have reached contradictory conclusions; namely, that the λ_i term is zero and consequently that dividend yield has no effect on required returns.[7] (Note that when these studies were conducted, the capital gains and dividend income tax differential was greater than it is today.)

The major problem with the CAPM studies is that they used historical earned rates of return as proxies for expected future returns, and with such a poor proxy, the tests are almost bound to have mixed results. Thus, these CAPM empirical tests, like the DCF-based tests, have not led to definitive conclusions as to which dividend theory is most correct. The issue is still unresolved.

SELF-TEST QUESTIONS

What are the two types of empirical tests that have been used to try to identify the correct dividend policy theory?

What are the general results of the empirical tests?

OTHER DIVIDEND POLICY ISSUES

Before we discuss dividend policy in practice, we need to examine three other issues that could affect our views toward the three theories presented above. These issues are (1) the information content, or signaling, hypothesis, (2) the clientele effect, and (3) the relationship between dividend policy and agency costs.

---

[6]See Litzenberger and Ramaswamy, "Effects of Personal Taxes," 163–196.

[7]For example, see Fischer Black and Myron Scholes, "The Effects of Dividend Yield and Dividend Policy on Common Stock Prices and Returns," *Journal of Financial Economics,* May 1974, 1–22.

INFORMATION CONTENT, OR SIGNALING, HYPOTHESIS

When MM set forth their dividend irrelevance theory, they assumed, among other things, that everyone—investors and managers alike—have identical expectations about the firm's future earnings and dividend stream. In reality, however, investors have conflicting opinions regarding both the level of future dividend payments and the degree of uncertainty inherent in those payments, and managers often have better information about future prospects than public stockholders. This is the same sort of *asymmetric information* situation that we discussed in Chapter 13 in connection with the announcement of new stock issues.

It has been observed that an increase in the dividend is often accompanied by an increase in the price of the stock, while a dividend cut generally leads to a stock price decline. This could indicate that investors, in the aggregate, prefer dividends to capital gains. However, MM argued differently. They noted the well-established fact that corporations are reluctant to cut dividends, hence do not raise dividends unless they anticipate equal or higher earnings in the future. Thus, MM argued that a higher-than-expected dividend increase is a "signal" to investors that the firm's management forecasts good future earnings.[8] Conversely, a dividend reduction, or a smaller-than-expected increase, is a signal that management is forecasting poor earnings in the future. Thus, MM claimed that investors' reactions to changes in dividend policy do not necessarily show that investors prefer dividends to retained earnings. Rather, the fact that price changes follow dividend actions simply indicated to MM that there is an important *information, or signaling, content* in dividend announcements.

To illustrate the signaling content of dividend announcements, consider the case of Clabir Corporation, a conglomerate with an odd mixture of businesses ranging from the manufacture of tank ammunition to the production of food products such as the Klondike ice cream bar. Clabir had been troubled by losses in its defense business, and the firm recently announced an annual dividend cut from 72 cents to only 16 cents a share. After this bad news had been digested, the stock was selling for about $3.00 a share. Then, Clabir announced that it planned to completely omit dividends for the coming year. Although the near-term cash flow loss to stockholders was relatively small, only 16 cents in annual dividends, the firm's stock price dropped almost immediately from $3.00 to $1.00. Clearly, investors viewed the dividend announcement as a signal that the company was in for very rough times ahead, and this caused them to lower their expectations about Clabir's future profitability, and hence to cut the value of its stock.

---

[8]Stephen Ross has suggested that managers can use capital structure as well as dividends to give signals concerning firms' future prospects. For example, a firm with good earnings prospects can carry more debt than a similar firm with poor earnings prospects. This theory, called *incentive-signaling,* rests on the premise that signals with cash-based variables (either debt interest or dividends) cannot be mimicked by unsuccessful firms because such firms do not have the future cash-generating power to maintain the announced interest or dividend payment. Thus, investors are more likely to believe a glowing verbal report when it is accompanied by a dividend increase or a debt-financed expansion program. See Stephen A. Ross, "The Determination of Financial Structure: The Incentive-Signaling Approach," *The Bell Journal of Economics,* Spring 1977, 23–40.

At this point, you might make this observation: When IBM cut its dividend, as we noted at the beginning of the chapter, its stock price closed slightly up. Isn't this incident contrary to the signaling hypothesis? The answer is no! The fact that IBM was in serious trouble was well known by the markets; in fact, this was so well known that its stock price had been pushed down by more than 60 percent in the preceding year. Analysts and investors were expecting a substantial dividend cut, so the announcement confirmed the expectations that were already embedded in IBM's stock price. If the $4.84 dividend had been maintained, or if it had been eliminated entirely, the announcement would likely have triggered a much greater market response, positive in the first case, negative in the second. Also, the dividend cut was accompanied by the news of a management change. Thus, the market had to digest two events simultaneously, and the resulting stock price increase of 12.5¢ reflected investors' joint reaction to the two signaling events.

Like most other aspects of dividend policy, empirical studies of signaling effects have had mixed results. There clearly is some information content in dividend announcements. However, it is difficult to tell whether stock price changes that follow increases or decreases in dividends reflect only signaling effects or both signaling and dividend preference effects, because major dividend policy changes typically include both a change in the percentage payout ratio and a change in the dollars of dividends paid.

Signaling effects must be considered when a firm is contemplating a change in dividend policy as a result of changed economic conditions. Later in the chapter we will look at a method for determining a firm's target payout ratio. If that analysis suggests that a change in the payout ratio is desirable, signaling effects might constrain the firm's ability to move quickly to the new policy.

CLIENTELE EFFECT

Different groups, or *clienteles,* of stockholders prefer different dividend payout policies. For example, retired individuals and university endowment funds generally prefer current income, so they would want the firm to pay out a high percentage of its earnings. Such investors are often in a low or even zero tax bracket, so taxes are of no concern. On the other hand, stockholders in their peak earning years prefer reinvestment, because they have no need for current investment income and would simply reinvest any dividends received, after first paying income taxes on the dividend income.

If the firm retains and reinvests income, rather than paying dividends, those stockholders who need current income would be disadvantaged. The value of their stock would increase, but they would be forced to go to the trouble and expense of selling off some of their shares to obtain cash. Also, some institutional investors (or trustees for individuals) would be precluded from selling stock and then "spending capital." The other group, the stockholders who are saving rather than spending dividends, would favor the low dividend policy, for the more the firm pays out in dividends, the more these stockholders will have to pay in current taxes, and the more trouble and expense they will have to go through to reinvest

their after-tax dividends. Therefore, investors who want current investment income should own shares in high dividend payout firms, while investors with no need for current investment income should own shares in low dividend payout firms. For example, investors seeking high current income might invest in electric utilities, which averaged a 78 percent payout from 1988 through 1992, while those favoring growth could invest in the semiconductor industry, which averaged a low 14 percent payout.

To the extent that stockholders can shift their investments among firms, a firm can change from one dividend payout policy to another and then let stockholders who do not like the new policy sell to other investors who do. However, switching may be inefficient because of (1) brokerage costs, (2) the likelihood that stockholders who are selling will have to pay capital gains taxes (the "lock-in effect"), and (3) a possible shortage of investors who like the firm's newly adopted dividend policy. Thus, management might be reluctant to change its dividend policy, because such changes might cause current shareholders to sell their stock, forcing the stock price down. Such a price decline might be temporary, but it might also be permanent—if few new investors are attracted by the new dividend policy, then the stock price would remain depressed. Of course, it is possible that the new policy would attract an even larger clientele than the firm had previously, in which case the stock price would rise.

Evidence from several studies suggests that there is in fact a clientele effect.[9] MM and others have argued that one clientele is as good as any other, so the existence of a clientele effect does not necessarily imply that one dividend policy is better than any other. MM may be wrong, though, and neither they nor anyone else has offered proof that the aggregate makeup of investors permits firms to disregard clientele effects. This issue, like most others in the dividend arena, is still up in the air.

DIVIDEND POLICY AND AGENCY COSTS

One of the most perplexing issues in dividend policy is why firms pay dividends and then issue new securities. Since the cost of issuing new securities can be substantial, total corporate costs would be minimized by paying dividends only when investment opportunities are so poor that the full amount of net income cannot be productively reinvested within the firm.[10]

One potential answer to this puzzle is the signaling value inherent in dividends. However, it is hard to imagine that the value that arises from signaling is greater than the costs associated with new security issues. A second potential explanation for paying dividends relates to agency costs.[11] As we discussed in Chap-

---

[9]For example, see R. Richardson Pettit, "Taxes, Transactions Costs and the Clientele Effect of Dividends," *The Journal of Financial Economics,* December 1977, 419–436.

[10]We will discuss this concept, called the *residual dividend model,* in a later section.

[11]For an example of this literature, see Frank H. Easterbrook, "Two Agency-Cost Explanations of Dividends," *American Economic Review,* September 1984, 650–659.

ter 1, an agency conflict exists between stockholders and managers—stockholders, as owners of the firm, want managers to maximize shareholders' value, but managers may be more motivated to act in their own best interests.

Because of this potential agency conflict, stockholders are willing to incur agency costs to monitor managerial actions. However, for large, publicly held corporations, it is difficult for stockholders to act collectively to monitor managerial actions, hence it is likely that too little monitoring will take place. In this situation, the most efficient way to monitor managerial actions is to have some other party, similar to the trustee who monitors managerial actions on behalf of bondholders, act on shareholders' behalf. Of course, the board of directors is supposed to be this entity, but board members often side with managers when conflicts arise.

The monitoring problem is substantially reduced when firms must consistently raise external capital. When a firm issues stocks or bonds, its operating and financial decisions are scrutinized by the investment bankers who underwrite the issue, analysts at rating agencies, security analysts at retail brokerage houses, and, ultimately, by investors who will purchase the new securities. Whereas the firm's existing investors can influence managerial actions only by voting or selling their securities, new investors can examine managerial behavior, and they can refuse to buy the firm's securities if they detect improper managerial actions. In effect, new investors are more efficient than old investors in monitoring managerial behavior; hence, agency problems are reduced when firms must continuously raise external capital.

The role of dividend policy in capital market monitoring should be apparent. For any given level of investment, the higher the dividend payout, the more frequently the firm must issue new securities. A higher payout policy thus forces firms to undergo the frequent scrutiny of the capital markets, and this appraisal process mitigates the agency problem. If the costs involved in paying dividends, including the flotation costs associated with additional security issues, are less than the value inherent in the additional monitoring, then large dividend payouts make sense.

SELF-TEST QUESTIONS

Briefly describe the information content, or signaling, hypothesis.

What is the clientele effect?

How could the signaling hypothesis and the presence of dividend clienteles affect the dividend policy decision?

How might agency costs justify a high dividend payout policy?

DIVIDEND STABILITY

As we noted at the beginning of the chapter, the decision as to how stable a firm's dividend should be is important. Profits and cash flows vary over time, as do investment opportunities. Taken alone, this suggests that corporations should vary

their dividends over time, increasing them when cash flows are large and the need for funds is low, and lowering them when cash is in short supply relative to investment opportunities. However, many stockholders rely on dividends to meet expenses, and they would be seriously inconvenienced if the dividend stream were unstable. Further, reducing dividends to make funds available for investment could send incorrect signals, and that could drive down stock prices. Thus, maximizing its stock price requires a firm to balance its internal needs for funds against the needs and desires of its stockholders.

How should this balance be struck; that is, how stable and dependable should a firm attempt to make its dividends? It is impossible to give a definitive answer to this question, but the following points are relevant:

1. Virtually every publicly owned company makes a 5- to 10-year financial forecast of earnings and dividends. Such forecasts are not made public—they are used for internal planning purposes. However, security analysts construct similar forecasts and make them available to investors; see *Value Line* for an example. Further, every internal 5- to 10-year corporate forecast we have seen for a "normal" company projects a trend of higher earnings and dividends. Both managers and investors know that economic conditions may cause actual results to differ from forecasted results, but "normal" companies are expected to grow.

2. Years ago, when inflation was not persistent, the term "stable dividend policy" meant a policy of paying the same dollar dividend year after year. AT&T was a prime example of a company with a stable dividend policy—it paid $9 per year ($2.25 per quarter) for 25 straight years. Today, most companies and stockholders expect earnings to grow over time as a result of earnings retention and inflation. Further, dividends are normally expected to grow more or less in line with earnings. Thus, today a "stable dividend policy" generally means increasing the dividend at a reasonably steady rate. For example, Rubbermaid made this statement in a recent annual report:

> *Dividends per share were increased . . . for the 34th consecutive year. . . . Our goal is to increase sales, earnings, and earnings per share by 15% per year, while achieving a 21% return on beginning shareholders' equity. It is also the Company's objective to pay approximately 30% of current year's earnings as dividends, which will permit us to retain sufficient capital to provide for future growth.*

Rubbermaid used the word "approximately" in discussing its payout ratio, because even if earnings vary a bit from the target level, the company still plans to increase the dividend by the target growth rate, thus forcing the payout ratio to vary from the target level. Note also that even though the dividend growth rate is not specified directly in the statement, analysts can calculate the growth rate and see that it is the same 15 percent as indicated for sales and earnings:

$$g = b\,(\text{ROE})$$
$$= (1 - \text{Payout})\,(\text{ROE})$$
$$= 0.7(21\%) \approx 15\%.$$

Companies with volatile earnings and cash flows would be reluctant to make a commitment to increase the dividend each year, so they would not make such a detailed statement. Even so, most companies would like to be able to exhibit the kind of stability Rubbermaid has shown, and they try to come as close to it as they can.

Dividend stability has two components: (1) How dependable is the growth rate, and (2) how dependable is the current dividend, that is, can we count on at least receiving the current dividend in the future? The most stable policy, from an investor's standpoint, is that of a firm whose dividend growth rate is predictable —such a company's total return (dividend yield plus capital gains yield) should be relatively stable over the long run, and its stock should be a good hedge against inflation. The second most stable policy is one of a firm whose investors can be reasonably sure that the current dividend will not be reduced—it may not grow at a steady rate, but management will probably be able and willing to avoid cutting the current dividend. The least stable dividend policy is one of a firm whose earnings and cash flows are so volatile that investors cannot count on the company to maintain the current dividend over the typical business cycle.

3. Most observers believe that dividend stability is desirable, even though statistical problems prevent empirical tests from proving the point. If this position is correct, then investors would prefer a stock that pays more predictable dividends to one expected to pay the same average amount of dividends but to pay them in a more erratic manner. This means that the cost of equity will be minimized, and the stock price maximized, if a firm stabilizes its dividends as much as possible, given its own cash flows and requirements for capital.

SELF-TEST QUESTIONS

What does the term "stable dividend policy" mean?

Has this meaning changed over time?

What are the two components of dividend stability?

ESTABLISHING THE DIVIDEND POLICY IN PRACTICE

In the preceding sections we have seen that investors may or may not prefer dividends to capital gains but that they do prefer predictable to unpredictable dividends. Given this situation, how should firms set their basic dividend policies? For example, how should a company like Rubbermaid establish the specific percentage of earnings which it will pay out? Rubbermaid's target is 30 percent, but why not 40 percent, 50 percent, or some other percentage? In this section, we describe how firms actually set their dividend policies.

SETTING THE TARGET PAYOUT RATIO: THE RESIDUAL DIVIDEND MODEL

The optimal payout ratio is a function of four factors: (1) investors' preferences for dividends versus capital gains, (2) the firm's investment opportunities, (3) the firm's target capital structure, and (4) the availability and cost of external capital. The last three elements are combined in what we call the *residual dividend model,* under which a firm follows these four steps when deciding its target payout ratio: (1) It determines the optimal capital budget; (2) it determines the amount of equity needed to finance that budget given its target capital structure; (3) it uses retained earnings to supply this equity to the extent possible; and (4) it pays dividends only if more earnings are available than are needed to support the optimal capital budget. The word *residual* implies "leftover," and the residual policy implies that dividends are paid out of "leftover" earnings.

We saw in Chapter 8 that the cost of retained earnings is an *opportunity cost* which reflects rates of return available to equity investors. If a firm's stockholders could buy other stocks of equal risk and obtain a 12 percent dividend-plus-capital-gains yield, then 12 percent is the firm's cost of retained earnings. The cost of new outside equity raised by selling common stock is higher because of the costs of floating the issue, including both underwriting costs and any downward price pressure resulting from "negative signals" investors might get from the announcement of the stock offering.

Also, most firms have a target capital structure that calls for at least some debt, so new financing is done partly with debt and partly with equity. As long as the firm finances with the optimal mix, using the proper amounts of debt and equity, and provided it uses only internally generated equity (retained earnings), then its marginal cost of each new dollar of capital will be minimized. Internally generated equity is available for financing a certain amount of new investment, but beyond that amount, the firm must turn to more expensive new common stock. At the point where new stock must be sold, the cost of equity, and consequently the weighted average cost of capital (WACC), rises.

These concepts, which were developed in Chapters 8 and 11, are illustrated in Figure 14-2 with data from the Dallas Oil Company (DOC). DOC has a WACC of 10 percent as long as its equity is from retained earnings, but its MCC schedule begins to rise at the point where new stock must be sold. DOC has $60 million of earnings and a 40 percent optimal debt ratio. Provided it does not pay any cash dividends, DOC can make net investments (investments in addition to asset replacements financed from depreciation) of $100 million, consisting of $60 million from retained earnings plus $40 million of new debt supported by the retained earnings, at a 10 percent cost of capital. Therefore, its WACC is *potentially* constant at 10 percent up to $100 million of capital. Beyond $100 million, the WACC must increase because the firm must use more expensive new common stock.

Of course, if DOC does not retain all of its earnings, its WACC will begin to rise before $100 million. For example, if DOC retained only $30 million, then its WACC would begin to rise at $30 million retained earnings + $20 million debt = $50 million.

FIGURE 14-2   DALLAS OIL COMPANY: MARGINAL COST OF CAPITAL (MCC) SCHEDULE

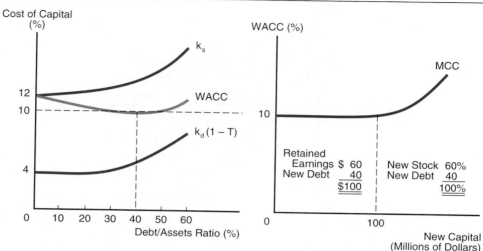

Now suppose DOC's director of capital budgeting constructs several investment opportunity schedules and plots them on a graph. In Figure 14-3, we combine these investment opportunity schedules with the cost of capital schedule. The point where the relevant IOS curve cuts the MCC curve defines the firm's marginal cost of capital and its optimal level of new investment. When investment opportunities are relatively bad (IOS_B), the optimal level of investment is $40 million; when opportunities are normal (IOS_N), $70 million should be invested; and when opportunities are relatively good (IOS_G), DOC should make new investments in the amount of $150 million.

If IOS_G is the appropriate schedule, the company should raise and invest $150 million. DOC has $60 million in earnings and a 40 percent target debt ratio. Thus, it can finance $100 million, consisting of $60 million of retained earnings plus $40 million of new debt, at an average cost of 10 percent if it retains all of its earnings. The remaining $50 million will include external equity and thus have a higher cost. If DOC pays out part of its earnings in dividends, it will have to begin to use costly new common stock earlier than need be, so its MCC schedule will rise earlier than it otherwise would. *This suggests that, under the conditions of IOS_G, DOC should retain all of its earnings. According to the residual policy, DOC's payout ratio should be zero if IOS_G applies.*

Under the normal conditions of IOS_N, however, DOC should invest only $70 million. How should this investment be financed? First, notice that if DOC retained all of its earnings, $60 million, it would need to sell only $10 million of new debt. However, if DOC retained $60 million and sold only $10 million of new debt, it would move away from its target capital structure. To stay on target, DOC must

FIGURE 14-3

DALLAS OIL
COMPANY: COMBINED
IOS AND MCC
SCHEDULES

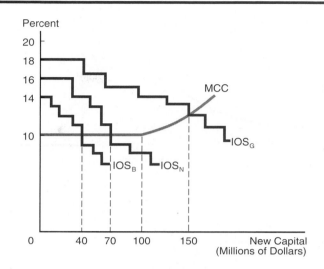

finance 60 percent of the required $70 million by equity—retained earnings—and 40 percent by debt; this means DOC must retain $42 million and sell $28 million of new debt. If DOC retains only $42 million of its $60 million total earnings, it must distribute the residual, $18 million, to its stockholders. Thus, its optimal payout ratio under IOS_N is $18/$60 = 30%.

Under the conditions shown in IOS_B, DOC should invest only $40 million. Because it has $60 million in earnings, it could finance the entire $40 million out of retained earnings and still have $20 million available for dividends. Should this be done? Under our assumptions, this would not be a good decision, because DOC would move away from its optimal capital structure. To stay at the 40 percent target debt/assets ratio, DOC must retain $24 million of earnings and sell $16 million of debt. When the $24 million of retained earnings is subtracted from the $60 million total earnings, DOC is left with a residual of $36 million, the amount that should be paid out in dividends. Thus, the payout ratio as prescribed by the residual policy is $36/$60 = 60%.

Since both the IOS schedule and the earnings level will surely vary from year to year, strict adherence to the residual dividend policy would result in dividend variability—one year the firm might declare zero dividends because investment opportunities were good, but the next year it might pay a large dividend because investment opportunities were poor. Similarly, fluctuating earnings would also lead to variable dividends even if investment opportunities were stable over time. As we noted earlier, variable dividend payments are less desirable than stable dividends, and varying the dividend payments could also lead to false signals and a loss of investor confidence in the firm. *Therefore, the residual model can be used as a guide for establishing the long-run target payout ratio, but the model should not be adhered to strictly on a year-to-year basis.*

Companies use the residual dividend model as presented to gain an understanding of the determinants of an optimal dividend policy, but they typically use a financial forecasting model as the basis for the target payout ratio. Most larger corporations have a corporate model which is used to forecast their financial statements over the next 5 or 10 years. Information on projected capital expenditures and working capital requirements is programmed into the model, along with sales forecasts, profit margins, depreciation, and the other elements required to forecast corporate cash flows. The target capital structure is also specified, and the model is designed to show the amount of debt and equity that will be required to meet the forecasted capital requirements while maintaining the target capital structure.

Then, dividend payments are introduced. Naturally, the larger the payout ratio, the greater the required external equity. Most companies then use the model to find a dividend pattern over the forecast period (generally 5 years) that will provide sufficient equity to support the capital budget without having to sell new common stock or to move the capital structure ratios outside the optimal range. The end result might include a statement, in a memo from the financial vice-president to the chairman of the board, such as the following:

We have forecasted the total market demand for our products, what our share of the market is likely to be, and our required investments in capital assets and working capital if we are to meet our forecasted demand. Using this information, we have developed projected balance sheets and income statements for the period 1994–1998.

Our 1993 dividends totaled $50 million, or $2 per share. On the basis of our projected earnings, cash flows, and capital requirements, we can increase the dividend by 8 percent per year. This is consistent with a payout ratio of 42 percent, on average, over the forecast period. Any faster dividend growth rate (or higher payout) would require us to sell common stock, cut the capital budget, or raise the debt ratio. Any slower growth rate would lead to a buildup of the common equity ratio. Therefore, I recommend that the Board increase the dividend for 1994 to $2.16, and that it plan for similar 8 percent increases in the future.

Events will undoubtedly occur over the next 5 years that lead to differences between our forecasts and actual results. If and when changes occur, we will want to reexamine our position. However, I am confident that we can meet any random cash shortfalls by increasing our borrowings — we have some unused debt capacity which gives us flexibility in this regard.

We ran the corporate model under several recession scenarios. If the economy really crashes, our earnings will not cover the dividend. However, in all "reasonable" scenarios cash flows do cover the dividend. I know you do not want to get the dividend up to a level where we would have to cut it under bad economic conditions, and I share this concern. Our model runs indicate, though, that the $2.16 dividend can be maintained under any reasonable set of forecasts — only if we increased the dividend to over $3 would we really be exposed to the danger of having to cut the dividend.

> *I might also note that* Value Line *and most other analysts' reports are forecasting that our dividends will grow in the 6 to 8 percent range. Thus, if we go to $2.16, we will be at the high end of the range, which should give our stock a boost. With takeover rumors so widespread, getting the stock price up a bit would make us all breathe a little easier.*

This company, like Rubbermaid, has very stable operations, so it can plan its dividends with a fairly high degree of confidence. Other companies, especially those in cyclical industries, have difficulty maintaining in bad times a dividend that is really too low in good times. Such companies set a very low "regular" dividend and then supplement it with an "extra" dividend when times are good. General Motor, Ford, and other auto companies have followed this *low-regular-dividend-plus-extras* policy in the past. Each company announced a low regular dividend that it was sure could be maintained "through hell or high water," and stockholders could count on receiving this dividend under all conditions. Then, when times were good and profits and cash flows were high, each company paid a clearly noted extra dividend. Investors recognized that the extras might not be maintained in the future, so they did not interpret them as a signal that the companies' earnings were going up permanently, nor did they take the elimination of the extra as a negative signal. In recent years, however, the "low-regular-dividend-plus-extras" policy has been replaced in those firms by the stable policy.

EARNINGS, CASH FLOWS, AND DIVIDENDS

We normally think of earnings as being the primary determinant of dividends, but in reality cash flows are even more important. This situation is revealed in Figure 14-4, which gives data for Chevron Corporation from 1972 through 1993. Chevron's dividends increased steadily from 1972 to 1981; during that period both earnings and cash flows were rising, as was the price of oil. After 1981, oil prices declined sharply, pulling earnings down. Cash flows, though, remained relatively high.

Chevron acquired Gulf Oil in 1984, and it issued over $10 billion of debt to finance the acquisition. Interest on the debt immediately hurt earnings after the merger, as did certain write-offs connected with the merger. Further, Chevron's management wanted to pay off the new debt as fast as possible. All of this influenced the company's decision to hold the dividend constant from 1982 through 1987. Earnings improved dramatically in 1988, and the dividend has increased more or less steadily since then. Note that the dividend was increased in 1991 in spite of the weak earnings and cash flow resulting from the Persian Gulf War.

Now look at Columns 4 and 6, which show payout ratios based on earnings and on cash flows. The earnings payout is quite volatile—dividends ranged from 26 percent to 113 percent of earnings. The cash flow payout, on the other hand, is much more stable—it ranged from 19 percent to 33 percent of cash flows. Further, the correlation between dividends and cash flows was 0.93 versus only 0.48 between dividends and earnings. Thus, dividends clearly depend more on cash flows, which reflect the company's *ability* to pay dividends, than on current

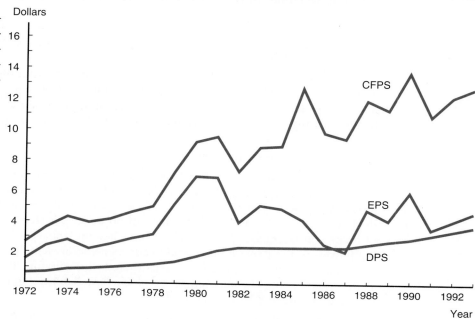

FIGURE 14-4
CHEVRON: EARNINGS, CASH FLOWS, AND DIVIDENDS, 1972–1993

Year (1)	Dividends per Share (2)	Earnings per Share (3)	Earnings Payout (4)	Cash Flow per Share (5)	Cash Flow Payout (6)
1972	$0.73	$1.61	45%	$ 2.72	27%
1973	0.78	2.49	31	3.68	21
1974	0.96	2.86	34	4.36	22
1975	1.00	2.28	44	4.00	25
1976	1.08	2.59	42	4.22	26
1977	1.18	2.98	40	4.68	25
1978	1.28	3.24	40	5.06	25
1979	1.45	5.22	28	7.29	20
1980	1.80	7.02	26	9.26	19
1981	2.20	6.96	32	9.61	23
1982	2.40	4.03	60	7.35	33
1983	2.40	5.15	47	8.93	27
1984	2.40	4.94	49	9.00	27
1985	2.40	4.19	57	12.76	19
1986	2.40	2.63	91	9.86	24
1987	2.40	2.13	113	9.47	25
1988	2.55	4.86	52	11.97	21
1989	2.80	4.16	67	11.33	25
1990	2.95	6.02	49	13.75	21
1991	3.25	3.69	88	11.14	29
1992	3.30	4.35	76	12.30	27
1993 (est.)	3.50	4.80	73	13.00	27

earnings, which are heavily influenced by accounting practices and which do not necessarily reflect the ability to pay dividends.

PAYMENT PROCEDURES

Dividends are normally paid quarterly, and, if conditions permit, the dividend is increased once each year. For example, Randolph Controls paid $0.50 per quarter in 1993, or at an annual rate of $2.00. In common financial parlance, we say that Randolph's *regular quarterly dividend* was $0.50, and its *annual dividend* was $2.00.

The actual payment procedure is as follows:

1. Declaration date.   On the declaration date—say, on November 15—the directors meet and declare the regular dividend, issuing a statement similar to the following: "On November 15, 1993, the directors of Randolph Controls met and declared the regular quarterly dividend of 50 cents per share, payable to holders of record on December 10, payment to be made on January 4, 1994." For accounting purposes, the declared dividend becomes an actual liability on the declaration date, and if a balance sheet were constructed, the amount $0.50 × (Number of shares outstanding) would appear as a current liability, and retained earnings would be reduced by a like amount.

2. Holder-of-record date.   At the close of business on the holder-of-record date, December 10, the company closes its stock transfer books and makes up a list of shareholders as of that date. If Randolph Controls is notified of the sale and transfer of some stock before 5 P.M. on December 10, then the new owner receives the dividend. However, if notification is received on or after December 11, the previous owner of the stock gets the dividend check.

3. Ex-dividend date.   Suppose Jean Buyer buys 100 shares of stock from John Seller on December 8. Will the company be notified of the transfer in time to list Buyer as the new owner and thus pay the dividend to her? To avoid conflict, the securities industry has set up a convention of declaring that the right to the dividend remains with the stock until four business days prior to the holder-of-record date; on the fourth day before that date, the right to the dividend no longer goes with the shares. The date when the right to the dividend leaves the stock is called the *ex-dividend date.* In this case, the ex-dividend date is December 6:

	Friday,	December 3, Buyer would receive dividend
Ex-dividend date:	Monday,	December 6, Seller will receive dividend
	Tuesday,	December 7
	Wednesday,	December 8
	Thursday,	December 9
Holder-of-record date:	Friday,	December 10

Therefore, if Buyer is to receive the dividend, she must buy the stock on or before December 3. If she buys it on December 6 or later, Seller will receive the dividend because he will be the official holder of record.

The Randolph Controls dividend amounts to $0.50, so the ex-dividend date is important. Barring fluctuations in the stock market, one would normally expect the price of a stock to drop by approximately the amount of the dividend on the ex-dividend date. Thus, if Randolph Controls closed at $30½ on Friday, December 3, it would probably open at about $30 on Monday, December 6.

4. Payment date. The company actually mails the checks to the holders of record on January 4, the payment date.

SELF-TEST QUESTIONS

Explain the residual dividend model.

How do firms use planning models to help set dividend policy?

Which are more critical to the dividend decision: earnings or cash flows?

Explain the procedures used to actually pay the dividend.

DIVIDEND REINVESTMENT PLANS

During the 1970s, most large companies instituted *dividend reinvestment plans (DRPs or DRIPs)*, whereby stockholders can automatically reinvest their dividends in the stock of the paying corporation.[12] Today it is estimated that about 1,000 companies offer DRPs, and, although participation rates vary considerably, about 25 percent of an average firm's shareholders are enrolled. There are two types of DRPs: (1) plans which involve only "old stock" that is already outstanding, and (2) plans which involve newly issued stock. In either case, the stockholder must pay income taxes on the amount of the dividends, even though stock rather than cash is received.

Under both types of DRP, the stockholder must choose between continuing to receive dividend checks or using the dividends to buy more stock in the corporation. Under the "old stock" type of plan, if the stockholder elects reinvestment, a bank, acting as trustee, takes the total funds available for reinvestment (less a fee), purchases the corporation's stock on the open market, and allocates the shares purchased to the participating stockholders' accounts on a pro rata basis. The transactions costs of buying shares (brokerage costs) are low because of volume purchases, so these plans benefit small stockholders who do not need cash dividends for current consumption.

The "new stock" type of DRP provides for dividends to be invested in newly issued stock; hence, these plans raise new capital for the firm. AT&T, Xerox, Union Carbide, and many other companies have had new stock plans in effect in recent years, using them to raise substantial amounts of new equity capital. No fees are

---

[12]See Richard H. Pettway and R. Phil Malone, "Automatic Dividend Reinvestment Plans," *Financial Management,* Winter 1973, 11–18, for an excellent discussion of the subject.

charged to stockholders, and some companies offer stock at a discount of 3 to 5 percent below the actual market price. The companies absorb these costs as a trade-off against flotation costs that would be incurred if stocks were sold through investment bankers rather than through the dividend reinvestment plans. Discussions with corporate treasurers suggest that many other companies are seriously considering establishing or switching to new-stock DRPs.[13]

SELF-TEST QUESTIONS

What are dividend reinvestment plans?

What are their advantages and disadvantages from both the stockholders' and the firm's perspectives?

OTHER FACTORS THAT INFLUENCE DIVIDEND POLICY

In earlier sections, we described both the major theories of investor preference and some issues concerning the effect of dividend policy on the value of a firm. We also discussed the residual dividend model for setting a firm's long-run target payout ratio. In this section, we discuss several other factors that affect the dividend decision.

1. Bond indentures. Debt contracts often restrict dividend payments to earnings generated after the loan was granted. Also, debt contracts frequently stipulate that no dividends can be paid unless the current ratio, the times-interest-earned ratio, and other safety ratios exceed stated minimums.

2. Preferred stock restrictions. Typically, common dividends cannot be paid if the company has omitted (passed) its preferred dividend. The preferred arrearages must be satisfied before common dividends can be resumed.

3. Impairment of capital rule. Dividend payments cannot exceed the balance sheet item "retained earnings." This legal restriction, known as the "impairment of

---

[13]One interesting aspect of DRPs is that they are forcing corporations to reexamine their basic dividend policies. A high participation rate in a DRP suggests that stockholders might be better off if the firm simply reduced cash dividends to save stockholders some personal income taxes. Quite a few firms are surveying their stockholders to learn more about their preferences and to find out how they would react to a change in dividend policy. A more rational approach to basic dividend policy decisions may emerge from this research.

Note that companies use or stop the use of new-stock DRPs depending on their need for equity capital. Thus, both Union Carbide and AT&T recently stopped offering a new-stock DRP with a 5 percent discount because their needs for equity capital declined, but Xerox recently began such a plan. Other companies have continued their DRPs, but eliminated the price discount. For example, Travellers Corporation, a diversified insurance company, recently eliminated its 5 percent discount. The discount was halted because the DRP had become a "relatively expensive source of capital," a spokeswoman said.

capital rule," is designed to protect creditors. (*Liquidating dividends* can be paid out of capital, but they must be indicated as such and they must not reduce capital below limits stated in the firm's debt contracts.)

4. Availability of cash. Cash dividends can only be paid with cash. Thus, a shortage of cash in the bank can restrict dividend payments. However, unused borrowing capacity can offset this factor.

5. Penalty tax on improperly accumulated earnings. To prevent wealthy individuals from using corporations to avoid personal taxes, the Tax Code provides for a special surtax on improperly accumulated income. Thus, if the IRS can demonstrate that the dividend payout ratio is being deliberately held down to help stockholders avoid personal taxes, heavy penalties will be imposed on the firm. However, as a practical matter, the penalty has been applied only to privately owned firms.

6. Control. If management is concerned about maintaining control, it may be reluctant to sell new stock, hence it may retain more earnings than it otherwise would. This factor is especially important for small, closely held firms.

SELF-TEST QUESTION

What are some factors that influence a firm's dividend policy decision?

OUR VIEW OF THE DIVIDEND POLICY DECISION

In many ways, our discussion of dividend policy parallels our discussion of capital structure: We have presented the relevant theories and issues, and have listed some additional factors that influence dividend policy, but we have not come up with any hard-and-fast guidelines that managers should follow. It should be apparent from our discussion that dividend policy decisions are truly exercises in informed judgment, not decisions that can be made on the basis of a precise mathematical model.

In practice, dividend policy is not an independent decision—the dividend decision is made jointly with capital structure and capital expenditure decisions. The underlying reason for this joint decision process is asymmetric information, which influences managerial actions in two ways:

1. In general, managers do not want to issue new common stock. First, new common stock involves issuance costs—commissions, fees, and so on—that may be avoided by using retained earnings to finance the firm's equity needs. Also, as we discussed in Chapter 13, the potential for asymmetric information causes investors to view new common stock sales as negative signals, causing investors to lower their expectations regarding the firm's future prospects. The end result is that the announcement of a new stock issue is usually followed by a decrease in the firm's

stock price. Considering the total costs involved, including both issuance and asymmetric information costs, managers strongly prefer to use retained earnings as their primary source of equity financing.

2. Because of asymmetric information, analysts and investors view dividend changes as an important means for a manager to signal his or her beliefs about the firm's future prospects. Thus, dividend reductions, or worse yet, omissions, generally have a significant negative effect on a firm's stock price. Since managers recognize this, they try to set dollar dividends low enough so that there is only a remote chance that the payment will have to be reduced in the future.

The effects of asymmetric information on dividend policy are clear. To the extent possible, managers should avoid both new common stock sales and dividend cuts, because both actions tend to lower stock prices. Thus, in setting dividend policy, managers should first consider the firm's future investment opportunities relative to its projected internal sources of funds, because the amount of capital required for new investment dictates the firm's future equity requirements. The firm's target capital structure also plays a part, but because the optimal capital structure is a *range,* firms can vary the actual capital structure somewhat from year to year. Since it is best to avoid issuing new common stock, a long-term payout ratio is set which, for planning purposes, will permit the firm to meet all its equity capital requirements with retentions. In effect, managers use the residual dividend model to set dividends, but in a long-term framework. Finally, the current dollar dividend is set so that there is an extremely low probability that the dividend, once set, will ever have to be lowered or omitted.

Of course, the dividend decision is made during the planning process, so there is uncertainty about future investment opportunities and operating cash flows. Thus, the actual payout ratio in any year may be above or below the firm's long-range target, but the dollar dividend will be maintained, or increased as planned, unless the firm's financial condition deteriorates to the point where the planned policy simply cannot be maintained. A steady or increasing stream of dividends over the long run signals that the firm's financial condition is under control. Further, investor uncertainty is decreased by stable dividends, so a steady dividend stream reduces the negative effect of a new stock issue, should one become absolutely necessary.

In general, firms with superior investment opportunities set lower payouts than firms with poor investment opportunities, because firms with strong growth opportunities require more equity capital to support growth. The degree of uncertainty also influences the decision. If there is a great deal of uncertainty in the forecasts of *free cash flows,* which are defined here as the firm's operating cash flows minus mandatory equity investment requirements, then it is best to be conservative and to set a lower current dollar dividend. Also, firms with postponable investment opportunities can afford to set a higher dollar dividend, because, in times of stress, investments can be postponed for a year or two, thus increasing the cash available for dividends. Finally, firms which have a flat WACC curve, when WACC is plotted against the debt ratio as in the left panel of Figure 14-2, can also

afford to set a higher payout ratio, because they can, in times of stress, more easily issue additional debt to maintain the capital budgeting program without having to cut dividends or issue stock.

In practice, dividend policy is a dynamic process, because most firms have only a single opportunity to set the dividend payment from scratch. Therefore, for the average firm, today's dividend policy decision is constrained by the policies that have been followed in the past, so setting a policy for the next 5-year planning period necessarily begins with a review of the current dividend situation.

Although we have outlined a rational process which managers can use to set their firms' dividend policies, dividend policy still remains one of the most judgmental decisions that a manager must make. For this reason, dividend policy is always set by the board of directors — the financial staff does various types of analyses, and the financial vice-president makes a recommendation, but the board makes the final dividend policy decision.

SELF-TEST QUESTION

Describe the dividend policy decision process. Be sure to discuss all the factors that influence the decision.

STOCK REPURCHASES

As an alternative to paying cash dividends, a firm may distribute income to stockholders by *repurchasing its own stock*. Stock that has been repurchased by a firm is called *treasury stock*. If some of the outstanding stock is repurchased and held as treasury stock, fewer shares will remain outstanding. Assuming the repurchase does not adversely affect the firm's earnings, the earnings per share on the remaining shares will increase, resulting in a higher market price per share, which means that capital gains will have been substituted for dividends.

Most large repurchase programs are part of a general corporate restructuring, wherein certain major assets, such as whole divisions or subsidiaries, are sold off, or where the debt ratio is increased substantially. Asset sales and the issuance of new debt both bring in additional capital, and this capital can then be distributed to stockholders through a major, one-time stock repurchase. A repurchase that is part of a corporate restructuring is quite different from a "regular" repurchase, where the repurchase is merely a substitute for cash dividends as a method for distributing operating cash flow to shareholders.

The effects of a "regular" repurchase can be illustrated with data on American Development Corporation (ADC). The company expects to earn $4.4 million in 1994, and 50 percent of this amount, or $2.2 million, will be available for distribution to common shareholders. There are 1,100,000 shares outstanding. ADC could use the $2.2 million to repurchase 100,000 of its shares through a tender

offer for $22 a share, or it could pay a cash dividend of $2 a share.[14] The current stock price is $20 per share.

The effect of the repurchase on ADC's EPS and stock price can be determined in the following way:

1. Current EPS $= \dfrac{\text{Total earnings}}{\text{Number of shares}} = \dfrac{\$4.4 \text{ million}}{1.1 \text{ million}} = \$4$ per share.

2. Current P/E ratio $= \dfrac{\$20}{\$4} = 5$, assumed to remain constant.

3. EPS after repurchase of 100,000 shares $= \dfrac{\$4.4 \text{ million}}{1 \text{ million}} = \$4.40$ per share.

4. Expected stock price after repurchase $= (\text{P/E})(\text{EPS}) = (5)(\$4.40) = \$22$ per share.

5. Expected capital gains per remaining share $= \$22 - \$20 = \$2.00$.

It should be noticed from this example that investors will receive benefits of $2 per share, either in the form of a $2 cash dividend or a $2 increase in the stock price. This result occurs because we assumed (1) that shares could be repurchased at exactly $22 a share and (2) that the P/E ratio would remain constant. If shares could be bought for less than $22, the repurchase would be even better for *remaining* stockholders, but the reverse would hold if ADC paid more than $22 a share. Furthermore, the P/E ratio might change as a result of the repurchase, rising if investors viewed the repurchase favorably and falling if they viewed it unfavorably. Some factors that might affect P/E ratios are considered next.

ADVANTAGES OF REPURCHASES

The advantages of repurchases are as follows:

1. Repurchase announcements are viewed as positive signals by investors because the repurchase is often motivated by management's belief that the firm's shares are undervalued.

2. The stockholders have a choice when the firm repurchases stock—to sell or not to sell. However, stockholders must accept a dividend payment and pay the

---

[14]Stock repurchases are commonly made in three ways. First, a publicly owned firm can simply buy its own stock through a broker on the open market. Second, it can issue a *fixed price tender,* under which it permits stockholders to send in (that is, "tender") their shares to the firm in exchange for a specified price per share. When tender offers are made, the firm generally indicates that it will buy up a specified number of shares within a particular time period (usually one month); if more shares are tendered than the company wishes to purchase, then purchases are made on a pro rata basis. Third, the firm can use a *Dutch-auction tender,* where it announces that it will spend, say, $10 million to repurchase stock, and it then sets a range of prices at which shares can be tendered, say, from $20 to $25 per share if

tax. Thus, those stockholders who need cash can sell back some of their shares, while those who do not want additional cash can simply retain their stock. From a tax standpoint, in a repurchase both types of stockholders get what they want.

3. A third advantage is that a repurchase can remove a large block of stock that is overhanging the market and keeping the price per share down.

4. Dividends are "sticky" in the short run because managements are reluctant to raise the dividend if the increase cannot be maintained in the future—managements dislike cutting cash dividends. Hence, if the excess cash flow is thought to be only temporary, management may prefer to make the distribution in the form of a share repurchase rather than to declare an increased cash dividend that cannot be maintained.

5. Repurchases can be used to produce large-scale changes in capital structures. For example, Consolidated Edison recently decided to repurchase $400 million of its common stock in order to increase its debt ratio. The repurchase was necessary because even if the company financed its capital budget only with debt, it would still have taken years to get the debt ratio up to the target level. Con Ed used repurchases to produce an instantaneous change in its capital structure.

DISADVANTAGES OF REPURCHASES

Disadvantages of repurchases include the following:

1. Stockholders may not be indifferent between dividends and capital gains, and the price of the stock might benefit more from cash dividends than from repurchases. Cash dividends are generally dependable, but repurchases are not. Further, if a firm announced a regular, dependable repurchase program, the improper accumulation tax would become more of a threat.

2. The *selling* stockholders may not be fully aware of all the implications of a repurchase, or they may not have all pertinent information about the corporation's present and future activities. However, firms generally announce repurchase programs before embarking on them to avoid potential stockholder suits.

3. The corporation may pay too high a price for the repurchased stock, to the disadvantage of remaining stockholders. If its shares are inactively traded, and if the firm seeks to acquire a relatively large amount of the stock, then the price may be bid above its equilibrium level and then fall after the firm ceases its repurchase operations.

---

the stock currently sells for $20. Stockholders who elect to tender can choose a price anywhere in the specified range, but the lower the price chosen, the higher the probability of getting cash. The company completes the Dutch-auction tender by using the lowest price which spends the allocated money. All stockholders who tendered at or below the selected price will get cash for their shares, while all others will have their shares returned. Finally, the firm can purchase a block of shares from one or more large holders on a negotiated basis. If a negotiated purchase is employed, care should be taken to ensure that these stockholders do not receive preferential treatment not available to other stockholders.

CONCLUSIONS ON STOCK REPURCHASES

When all the pros and cons on stock repurchases have been totaled, where do we stand? Our conclusions may be summarized as follows:

1. Because of uncertainties about their tax treatment, repurchases on a regular, systematic, dependable basis are probably not a good idea.

2. However, repurchases do offer investors an opportunity to save taxes, and, for this reason, they should be given careful consideration.

3. Repurchases can be especially valuable to a firm that wants to make a large shift in its capital structure within a short period of time.

On balance, companies probably ought to be doing more repurchasing and distributing less cash as dividends than they are. However, increases in the size and frequency of repurchases in recent years suggest that companies are rapidly reaching this same conclusion.

SELF-TEST QUESTIONS

Explain how repurchases can (1) help stockholders hold down taxes and (2) help firms change their capital structures.

What is treasury stock?

What are the three ways a firm can make repurchases?

What are the key advantages and disadvantages of stock repurchases?

STOCK DIVIDENDS AND STOCK SPLITS

Stock dividends and stock splits are related to the firm's cash dividend policy. The rationale for stock dividends and splits can best be explained through an example; we will use the Nashville Company, a large multimedia entertainment company specializing in country and western music, in our illustrations.

Nashville's markets are expanding, and as the company continues to grow and to retain earnings, its book value per share should also grow. More important, its earnings per share and stock price should also rise. The company began its life with only a few thousand shares outstanding. After some years of growth, each share had a very high EPS and DPS. When a "normal" P/E ratio was applied to the stock, the derived market price was so high that few people could afford to buy a "round lot" of 100 shares. This limited demand for the stock, thus keeping the total market value of the firm below what it would have been if more shares, at lower prices, were outstanding. To correct this situation, Nashville "split its stock" as described next.

STOCK SPLITS

Although there is little empirical evidence to support the contention, there is nevertheless a widespread belief in financial circles that an *optimal price range* exists

for stocks. "Optimal" means that if the price is in this range, the price/earnings ratio, hence the value of the firm, will be maximized. Many observers, including Nashville's management, believe that the best range for most New York Stock Exchange stocks is from $20 to $80 per share. Companies whose shares are owned largely by institutions tend to move toward the high end of the range, while those owned largely by individuals, such as the public utilities, generally operate in the lower end of the range. Companies with average institutional ownership, like Nashville Company, cluster in the $30 to $50 range. Accordingly, if the price of Nashville's stock rose to $80, management would probably declare a two-for-one stock split, thus doubling the number of shares outstanding, halving the earnings and dividends per share, and thereby lowering the price of the stock. Each stockholder would have more shares, but each share would be worth less. If the post-split price were $40, Nashville's stockholders would be exactly as well off as they were before the split. If the price of the stock were to stabilize above $40, stockholders would be better off. Stock splits can be of any size. For example, the stock could be split two-for-one, three-for-one, 1.5-for-one, or in any other way.[15]

Ford Motor Company, in late 1987, announced the largest quarterly dividend increase in the firm's history, along with a two-for-one stock split. At the time of the announcement, Ford's stock was selling at about $94 a share. Wall Street analysts said they had expected Ford to take these actions in view of the stock's soaring price and relatively modest dividend. "I thought it was overdue," said David Healy, a well-known security analyst. "Generally, they split the stock when it gets into the $50 to $70 range." Individual investors "would rather buy two shares for $47 each than one for $94," Healy said. The quarterly dividend on the old shares was increased 33 percent to $1.00 a share, up from 75 cents. After the split, which occurred in January 1988, the quarterly dividend was readjusted to 50 cents, producing a $2.00 annual dividend, up from $1.50. Ford raised its quarterly dividend two more times—to $0.60 and then to $0.75—before it was forced to cut it to $0.40 a share in 1991. In announcing the cut, Harold A. Poling, Ford's chairman, said this: "Ford's policy is to sustain the dividend during normal cyclical downturns, but the situation we face today is much more than a normal trough in the business cycle."

Stock splits can also be used to increase the "float," or the number of shares held by outsiders. For example, Care Corporation, a nursing home operator, recently declared a 4-for-1 split, in large part because about 60 percent of the company's 500,000 shares outstanding were controlled by insiders and relatives, leaving only 200,000 shares for trading by others. The split increased the float to 800,000 which, according to the firm's management, increased the trading activity in the stock. Note, though, that academic studies have suggested that stock splits

---

[15]*Reverse splits,* which reduce the shares outstanding, can even be used. For example, a company whose stock sells for $5 might employ a one-for-five reverse split, exchanging one new share for five old shares and raising the value of the shares to about $25, which is within the "acceptable" range. LTV Corporation did this after several years of losses had driven its stock price down below the optimal range.

actually lower trading volume when measured on a proportional basis, primarily because brokerage commissions are increased.[16]

Stock Dividends

Stock dividends are similar to stock splits in that they divide the pie into smaller slices without affecting the fundamental position of the current stockholders. On a 5 percent stock dividend, the holder of 100 shares would receive an additional 5 shares (without cost); on a 20 percent stock dividend, the same holder would receive 20 new shares; and so on. Again, the total number of shares is increased, so earnings, dividends, and price per share all decline.

If a firm wants to reduce the price of its stock, should a stock split or a stock dividend be used? Stock splits and large stock dividends are generally used after a sharp price run-up, when a large price reduction is sought. Small stock dividends are occasionally used on a regular annual basis to keep the stock price more or less constrained. For example, if a firm's earnings and dividends are growing at about 10 percent per year, the price would tend to go up at about that same rate, and the price would soon be outside the desired trading range. For this company, a 10 percent annual stock dividend would maintain the stock price within the optimal trading range.

Although the economic effects of stock splits and stock dividends are virtually identical, accountants treat them somewhat differently. For a discussion of the accounting treatment, see any financial accounting text.

Price Effects

If a company splits its stock or declares a stock dividend, will this action increase the market value of its stock? Several empirical studies have sought to answer this question, and here is a summary of their findings.[17]

1. On average, the price of a company's stock rises shortly after it announces a stock split or dividend.

2. However, these price increases are more the result of the fact that investors take stock splits/dividends as signals of higher future earnings and dividends than of a desire for stock dividends/splits per se. Since only those companies whose managements think things look good tend to use stock splits/dividends, the an-

---

[16]Commissions are generally higher on a trade of, say, 500 shares at $10 per share than on a trade of 100 shares at $50 a share, even though the dollar value of the trades is the same. For a further discussion of the effects of stock splits on market liquidity, see Thomas E. Copeland, "Liquidity Changes Following Stock Splits," *Journal of Finance,* March 1979, 115–141.

[17]See Eugene F. Fama, Lawrence Fisher, Michael C. Jensen, and Richard Roll, "The Adjustment of Stock Prices to New Information," *International Economic Review,* February 1969, 1–21; Mark S. Grinblatt, Ronald M. Masulis, and Sheridan Titman, "The Valuation Effects of Stock Splits and Stock Dividends," *Journal of Financial Economics,* December 1984, 461–490; C. Austin Barker, "Evaluation of Stock Dividends," *Harvard Business Review,* July-August 1958, 99–114; and Copeland, "Liquidty Changes," 115–141.

nouncement of a stock split is taken as a signal that earnings and cash dividends are likely to rise. Thus, the price increases that are associated with stock splits/dividends are probably the result of signals of favorable prospects for earnings and dividends, not a desire for stock splits/dividends per se.

3. It has been observed that if a company announces a stock split or dividend, its price will tend to rise. However, if during the next few months it does not announce an increase in earnings and dividends, then its stock price will drop back to the earlier level.

4. As we noted earlier, brokerage commissions are higher in percentage terms on lower-priced stocks. This means that it is more expensive to trade low-priced than high-priced stocks, and this in turn means that stock splits reduce the liquidity of a company's shares. This particular piece of evidence suggests that stock splits/dividends are actually harmful, although a lower price does mean that more investors can afford to make round lot (100 shares) purchases, which carry lower commissions than do odd lot (less than 100 shares) purchases.

What do we conclude from all this? From a pure economic standpoint, stock dividends and splits are just additional pieces of paper. However, they do provide management with a relatively low-cost way of signaling that the firm's prospects look good. Further, we should note that since few large, publicly owned stocks sell at prices above several hundred dollars, we simply do not know what the effect would be if Microsoft, Xerox, Hewlett-Packard, and other highly successful firms had never split their stocks, and consequently had sold at prices in the thousands or even tens of thousands of dollars. All in all, it probably makes sense to employ stock dividends/splits when a firm's prospects are favorable, especially if the price of its stock has gone beyond the normal trading range.[18]

SELF-TEST QUESTIONS

What are stock dividends and stock splits?

What impact do stock dividends and splits have on stock price? Why?

In what situations should managers consider the use of stock dividends? In what situations should they consider the use of stock splits?

SUMMARY

Dividend policy involves the decision to pay out earnings versus retaining them for reinvestment in the firm, and dividend policy decisions can have either favorable or unfavorable effects on the price of the firm's stock. The key factors influencing a firm's dividend policy are listed below:

---

[18]It is interesting to note that Berkshire Hathaway, which is controlled by billionaire Warren Buffett, one of the most successful financiers of the twentieth century, has never had a stock split, and its stock sold on the NYSE for more than $12,000 per share in early 1993. Perhaps Berkshire Hathaway's total market value would be even higher if it had a 200:1 split, but we would not want to debate Buffett on the point!

▶ The *dividend policy decision* involves three questions: (1) What fraction of earnings should be paid out, on average, over time? (2) Should the firm maintain a steady, stable dividend growth rate? (3) What dollar amount should the firm pay in current dividends?

▶ Miller and Modigliani developed the *dividend irrelevance theory,* which holds that a firm's dividend policy has no effect either on the value of the firm or on its cost of capital.

▶ The *"bird-in-the-hand" theory,* advocated by Gordon and Lintner, holds that the value of the firm will be maximized by a high dividend payout ratio, because investors regard actual dividends as being less risky than potential capital gains.

▶ The *tax preference theory,* advocated by Litzenberger and Ramaswamy, holds that the value of the firm will be maximized by a low dividend payout, because investors pay lower effective taxes on capital gains than on dividends.

▶ Because *empirical tests* of the three theories *have been inconclusive,* academicians simply cannot tell corporate managers with any degree of precision how a change in dividend policy will affect stock prices and capital costs. Thus, actually determining the optimal dividend policy is extremely difficult.

▶ Dividend policy should also reflect the *information content of dividends (signaling)* and the *clientele effect.* The information content, or signaling, hypothesis states that investors regard dividend changes as a signal of management's forecast of future earnings. The clientele effect suggests that a firm will attract investors who like the firm's dividend policy, hence a change in dividend policy will lead to a change in the set of stockholders.

▶ A high dividend payout policy may reduce *agency costs,* because it forces firms to go to the capital markets more often, hence to undergo periodic outside scrutiny.

▶ In practice, most firms try to follow a policy of paying a *steadily increasing dividend.* This policy provides investors with a stable, dependable income, and, if the signaling theory is correct, it also gives investors information about management's expectations for earnings growth.

▶ Most firms use the *residual dividend model* to set a long-run target payout ratio which permits the firm to satisfy its equity requirements with retained earnings.

▶ Other factors, such as *legal constraints, investment opportunities, availability and cost of funds from other sources,* and *taxes,* are considered by managers when they establish dividend policies.

▶ A *dividend reinvestment plan (DRP or DRIP)* allows stockholders to have the company automatically use their dividends to purchase additional shares of the firm's stock. DRPs are popular with investors who do not need current income because the plans allow stockholders to acquire additional shares without incurring normal brokerage fees.

▶ Under a *stock repurchase plan,* a firm buys back some of its outstanding stock, thereby decreasing the number of shares, which in turn increases both EPS

and the stock price. Repurchases are useful for making major changes in a firm's capital structure, as well as for allowing stockholders to delay paying taxes on their share of the firm's profits.

▶ A *stock split* is an action taken by a firm to increase the number of shares outstanding. Normally, splits reduce the price per share in proportion to the increase in shares because splits merely "divide the pie into smaller slices." A *stock dividend* is a dividend paid in additional shares of stock rather than in cash. Both stock dividends and splits are used to keep stock prices within an "optimal" range.

QUESTIONS

14-1 Define each of the following terms:

   a. Dividend policy

   b. Dividend irrelevance theory

   c. "Bird-in-the-hand" theory

   d. Tax preference theory

   e. Residual dividend model

   f. Constraints on dividend policy

   g. Clientele effect

   h. Information content of dividends; signaling

   i. Extra dividend

   j. Ex-dividend date

   k. Dividend reinvestment plans (each of two types)

   l. Stock split; stock dividend

   m. Stock repurchase

14-2 As an investor, would you rather invest in a firm that has a policy of maintaining (a) a constant payout ratio, (b) a constant dollar dividend per share, (c) a target dividend growth rate, or (d) a constant regular quarterly dividend plus a year-end extra when earnings are sufficiently high or corporate investment needs are sufficiently low? Explain your answer, stating how these policies would affect your k_s.

14-3 How would each of the following changes probably affect aggregate (that is, the average for all corporations) payout ratios? Explain your answers.

   a. An increase in the personal income tax rate. An increase in the corporate tax rate.

   b. A liberalization in depreciation for federal income tax purposes, that is, faster tax write-offs.

   c. A rise in interest rates.

   d. An increase in corporate profits.

   e. A decline in investment opportunities.

   f. Reinstatement of a differential (lower) capital gains tax rate.

14-4 Discuss the pros and cons of having the directors formally announce what a firm's dividend policy will be in the future.

14-5 Most firms would like to have their stock selling at a high P/E ratio and also have an extensive public ownership (many different shareholders). Explain how stock dividends or stock splits may help achieve these goals.

14-6 What is the difference between a stock dividend and a stock split? As a stockholder, would you prefer to see your company declare a 100 percent stock dividend or a two-for-one split? Assume that either action is feasible.

14-7 "The cost of retained earnings is less than the cost of new outside equity capital. Consequently, it is totally irrational for a firm to sell a new issue of stock and to pay dividends during the same year." Discuss this statement.

14-8 Would it ever be rational for a firm to borrow money in order to pay dividends? Explain.

14-9 Union representatives have presented arguments similar to the following: "Corporations such as General Motors retain about half of their profits for financing needs. If they financed by selling stock instead of by retaining earnings, they could substantially raise wages and still earn enough to pay the same dividend to their shareholders. Therefore, their profits are too high." Evaluate this statement.

14-10 "Executive salaries have been shown to be more closely correlated to the size of the firm than to its profitability. If a firm's board of directors is controlled by management instead of by outside directors, this might result in the firm's retaining more earnings than can be justified from the stockholders' point of view." Discuss the statement, being sure (a) to use Figure 14-3 in your answer and (b) to explain the implied relationship between dividend policy and stock prices.

14-11 Explain why a high dividend payout policy might encourage managers to act in the best interests of the firm's investors.

PROBLEMS

14-1 **(Dividend theories)** Modigliani and Miller (MM), on the one hand, and Gordon and Lintner (GL), on the other, have expressed strong views regarding the effect of dividend policy on a firm's cost of capital and value.

    a. In essence, what are the MM and the GL views regarding the effect of dividend policy on cost of capital and value? Illustrate your answer with a graph.

    b. How does the tax preference model differ from the views of MM and GL?

    c. According to the text, which position (MM, GL, or tax preference) has received statistical confirmation from empirical tests?

    d. How could GL use the fact that dividend increase announcements are often followed by stock price increases to support their "bird-in-the-hand" theory? How could MM use the information content, or signaling, hypothesis to counter these arguments?

    e. How could MM's opponents use the clientele effect concept to counter MM's arguments? If you were debating MM's opponents, how would you counter them?

14-2 **(Residual dividend model)** One position expressed in the literature is that firms should set their dividends as a residual, after using income to support new investment.

    a. Explain what the residual dividend model implies, illustrating your answer with a graph showing how different conditions could lead to different dividend payout ratios.

    b. Could the residual dividend model be consistent with (1) a constant dividend growth rate policy, (2) a constant payout policy, and/or (3) a low-regular-plus-extras policy? Explain.

c. In Chapters 12 and 13, we considered the relationship between capital structure and the cost of capital. If the WACC versus debt ratio plot were shaped like a sharp V, would this have a different implication for the importance of setting dividends according to the residual model than if the ratio relationship were shaped like a shallow bowl (or a U)?

d. Companies A and B both have IOS schedules which intersect their MCC schedules at a point which, under the residual policy, calls for a 20 percent payout. In both cases, a 20 percent payout would require a cut in the annual dividend from $2 to $1. One company cut its dividend and accepted all projects, while the other did not cut its dividend and accepted less than the optimal number of projects. One company had a relatively steep IOS curve, while the other had a relatively flat IOS. Explain which company had the steep, and which the flat, IOS.

14-3 (Stock dividends and splits) More NYSE companies had stock dividends and stock splits during 1983 and 1984 than ever before. What events in these years could have made stock splits and dividends so popular? Explain the rationale that a financial vice-president might give the board of directors to support a stock split/dividend recommendation.

14-4 (Residual dividend model) Magee Manufacturing Corporation (MMC) has an all-equity capital structure which includes no preferred stock. It has 200,000 shares of $2 par value common stock outstanding.

When MMC's founder, who was also its research director and most successful inventor, died unexpectedly in early 1994, MMC was left suddenly and permanently with materially lower growth expectations and relatively few attractive new investment opportunities. Unfortunately, there was no way to replace the founder's contributions to the firm. Previously, MMC had found it necessary to plow back most of its earnings to finance growth, which has been averaging 12 percent per year. Future growth at a 5 percent rate is considered realistic, but that level would call for an increase in the dividend payout. Further, it now appears that new investment projects with at least the 14 percent rate of return required by MMC's stockholders (k_s = 14%) would amount to only $800,000 for 1994 in comparison to a projected $2,000,000 of net income. If the existing 20 percent dividend payout were continued, retained earnings would be $1.6 million in 1994, but as noted, investments which yield the 14 percent cost of capital amount to only $800,000.

The one encouraging thing is that the high earnings from existing assets are expected to continue and net income of $2 million is still expected for 1994. Given the dramatically changed circumstances, MMC's management is reviewing the firm's dividend policy.

a. Assuming that the acceptable 1994 investment projects would be financed entirely by earnings retained during the year, calculate DPS in 1994 assuming MMC uses the residual payment model.

b. What payout ratio does this imply for 1994?

c. If the increased payout ratio is maintained for the foreseeable future, what should be the present intrinsic value of the common stock? How does this compare with the price that should have prevailed under the assumptions existing just prior to the news about the death of the founder? If the two values of $\hat{P}_0$ are different, comment on why.

14-5 (Dividend policy and capital structure) The Tennessee Bourbon Company (TBC) has for many years enjoyed a moderate but stable growth in sales and earnings. However, bourbon consumption has been falling recently, primarily because of an increasing use of lighter alcoholic beverages such as vodka and wines. Anticipating further declines in sales for the future, TBC's management hopes eventually to move almost entirely out of the liquor business and into a newly developed, diversified product line in growth-oriented industries. The company is especially interested in the prospects for pollution-control devices, because its

research department has already done much work in this area. Right now the company estimates that an investment of $24 million is necessary to purchase new facilities and to begin operations on these products, but the investment could be earning a return of about 18 percent within a short time. The only other available investment opportunity totals $9.6 million, is expected to return about 11.2 percent, and is indivisible, that is, it must be accepted in its entirety or else be rejected.

The company is expected to pay a $2.00 dividend on its 7 million outstanding shares, the same as its dividend last year. The directors might, however, change the dividend if there are good reasons for doing so. Net income for the year is expected to be $22.5 million; the common stock is currently selling for $45; the firm's target debt ratio (debt/assets ratio) is 45 percent; and its tax rate is 34 percent. The costs of various forms of financing are listed below:

New bonds: $k_d = 11\%$. This is a before-tax rate.

New common stock sold at $45 per share will net $41.

Required rate of return on retained earnings: $k_s = 14\%$.

a. Calculate TBC's expected payout ratio, the break point where its MCC schedule rises, and its marginal cost of capital above and below the point of exhaustion of retained earnings at the current payout. (Hint: k_s is given, and D_1/P_0 can be found. Then, knowing k_s and D_1/P_0, and assuming constant growth, g can be determined.)

b. How large should TBC's capital budget be for the year?

c. What is an appropriate dividend policy for the firm? How should the capital budget be financed?

d. How might risk factors influence TBC's cost of capital, capital structure, and dividend policy?

e. What assumptions, if any, do your answers to Questions a-d make about investors' preferences for dividends versus capital gains, that is, their preferences regarding the D_1/P_0 and g components of k_s?

(Do Part f only if you are using the computer problem diskette.)

f. Assume that TBC's management is considering a change in its capital structure to include more debt, and thus it would like to analyze the effects of an increase in the debt ratio to 60 percent. However, the treasurer believes that such a move would cause lenders to increase the required rate of return on new bonds to 12 percent and k_s would rise to 14.5 percent. How would this change affect the optimal capital budget? If k_s rose to 16 percent, would the low-return project be acceptable? Would the project selection be affected if the dividend were reduced to $1.25 from $2.00, still assuming $k_s = 16$ percent?

14-6 **(Stock repurchases)** Sure Thing Inc. has earnings this year of $16.5 million, 50 percent of which is required to take advantage of the firm's excellent investment opportunities. The firm has 2,062,500 shares outstanding, selling currently at $32 per share. Susan Long, a major stockholder (187,500 shares), has expressed displeasure with a great deal of managerial policy. Management has approached her about selling her holdings back to the firm, and she has expressed a willingness to do this at a price of $32 a share. Assuming that the market uses a constant P/E ratio of 4 in valuing the stock, should the firm buy Long's shares? Assume that dividends will not be paid on Long's shares if they are repurchased. (Hint: Calculate the ex-dividend price of the stock with and without the repurchase, and add to these values the dividends received to determine the remaining shareholders' value per share.)

MINI CASE

Information Systems Inc. (ISI) was founded five years ago by Michael Taylor and Karen Black, who are still its only stockholders. ISI has now reached the stage where outside equity capital is necessary if the firm is to grow with the industry and still maintain its target capital structure of 60 percent equity and 40 percent debt. Therefore, Taylor and Black have decided to take the company public. Until now, Taylor and Black have routinely invested all earnings in the firm, so dividend policy had not been an issue. However, since ISI will soon be a publicly owned firm, they will have to decide on a dividend policy.

Assume that you were recently hired by Arthur Adamson & Company, a national consulting firm which has been asked to help ISI prepare its public offering. Tom Nickols, the senior consultant in your group, has asked you to make a presentation to Taylor and Black in which you review the theory of dividend policy and discuss the following questions.

a. (1) What is meant by the term "dividend policy"?
    (2) What are the three elements of dividend policy?

b. (1) What are the three major theories regarding stockholders' preferences for dividends versus capital gains?
    (2) What do the three theories indicate regarding the actions management should take regarding dividend policy?

c. Explain the relationships between dividend policy and (1) stock price and (2) the cost of equity under each dividend policy theory by constructing two graphs, such as those shown in Figure 14-1. Dividend policy should be placed on the X axis. Assume, for purposes of this part only, that if the company paid out all earnings as dividends, it would have a required rate of return of 15 percent and a stock price of $30.

d. Has empirical testing been able to prove which theory, if any, is most correct?

e. What is the information content, or signaling, hypothesis, and how does it constrain dividend policy?

f. What is the clientele effect, and how does it constrain dividend policy?

g. What impact might dividend policy have on agency costs?

h. (1) What is the residual dividend model? Assume that ISI plans to spend $800,000 on capital investments during the coming year; its optimal capital structure calls for 60 percent equity and 40 percent debt; and its net income is forecasted at $600,000. Construct a graph which shows what the total dollar dividend and the payout ratio would be if the firm used the residual model.
    (2) How would a change in net income affect the dividend?
    (3) How would a change in investment opportunities affect the dividend?
    (4) Assume that the firm also forecasts $100,000 of depreciation cash flow. How would these funds impact the residual analysis, still assuming $600,000 in net income?
    (5) What are the advantages and disadvantages of the residual model? (Hint: Think about both signaling and the clientele effect.)

i. What is a dividend reinvestment plan? What are the two major types of plans, and when should each type be used?

j. Describe how most firms set their dividend policies in practice.

k. What is a stock repurchase? Discuss the advantages and disadvantages of stock repurchases.

l. What is a stock dividend, and how does it differ from a stock split? When should a firm consider issuing a stock dividend? When should a firm consider splitting its stock?

Selected Additional References and Cases

Dividend policy has been studied extensively by academicians. The first major academic work, and still a classic that we recommend highly, is Lintner's analysis of the way corporations actually set their dividend payment policies:

Lintner, John, "Distribution of Incomes of Corporations among Dividends, Retained Earnings, and Taxes," *American Economic Review,* May 1956, 97–113.

The effects of dividend policy on stock prices and capital costs have been examined by many researchers. The classic theoretical argument that dividend policy is important, and that stockholders like dividends, was set forth by Gordon, while Miller and Modigliani (MM) developed the notion that dividend policy is not important. Many researchers have extended both Gordon's and MM's theoretical arguments, and have attempted to test the effects of dividend policy in a variety of ways. Although statistical problems have precluded definitive conclusions, the following articles, among others, have helped to clarify the issues:

Brennan, Michael, "Taxes, Market Valuation, and Corporate Financial Policy," *National Tax Journal,* Spring 1975, 417–427.

Hayes, Linda S., "Fresh Evidence That Dividends Don't Matter," *Fortune,* May 4, 1981, 351–354.

Lewellen, Wilbur G., Kenneth L. Stanley, Ronald C. Lease, and Gary G. Schlarbaum, "Some Direct Evidence on the Dividend Clientele Phenomenon," *Journal of Finance,* December 1978, 1385–1399.

Mukherjee, Tarun, and Larry M. Austin, "An Empirical Investigation of Small Bank Stock Valuation and Dividend Policy," *Financial Management,* Spring 1980, 27–31.

On stock dividends and stock splits, see

Baker, H. Kent, and Patricia L. Gallagher, "Management's View of Stock Splits," *Financial Management,* Summer 1980, 73–77.

Copeland, Thomas E., "Liquidity Changes Following Stock Splits," *Journal of Finance,* March 1979, 115–141.

McNichols, Maureen, and Ajay Dravid, "Stock Dividends, Stock Splits, and Signaling," *Journal of Finance,* July 1990, 857–879.

On repurchases, see

Denis, David J., "Defensive Changes in Corporate Payout Policy: Share Repurchases and Special Dividends," *Journal of Finance,* December 1990, 1433–1456.

Finnerty, Joseph E., "Corporate Stock Issue and Repurchase," *Financial Management,* Autumn 1975, 62–71.

Gay, Gerold D., Jayant R. Kale, and Thomas H. Noe, "Shareholder Repurchase Mechanisms: A Comparative Analysis of Efficacy, Shareholder Wealth and Corporate Control Effects," *Financial Management,* Spring 1991, 44–59.

Klein, April, and James Rosenfeld, "The Impact of Targeted Share Repurchases on the Wealth of Non-Participating Shareholders," *Journal of Financial Research,* Summer 1988, 89–97.

Netter, Jeffry M., and Mark L. Mitchell, "Stock-Repurchase Announcements and Insider Transactions after the October 1987 Stock Market Crash," *Financial Management,* Autumn 1989, 84–96.

Pugh, William, and John S. Jahera, Jr., "Stock Repurchases and Excess Returns: An Empirical Examination," *The Financial Review,* February 1990, 127–142.

Stewart, Samuel S., Jr., "Should a Corporation Repurchase Its Own Stock?" *Journal of Finance,* June 1976, 911–921.

Wansley, James W., William R. Lane, and Salil Sarkar, "Managements' View on Share Repurchase and Tender Offer Premiums," *Financial Management,* Autumn 1989, 97–110.

Woolridge, J. Randall, and Donald R. Chambers, "Reverse Splits and Shareholder Wealth," *Financial Management,* Autumn 1983, 5–15.

For surveys of managers' views on dividend policy, see

Baker, H. Kent, Gail E. Farrelly, and Richard B. Edelman, "A Survey of Management Views on Dividend Policy," *Financial Management,* Autumn 1985, 78–84.

Pruitt, Stephen W., and Lawrence J. Gitman, "The Interactions between the Investment, Financing, and Dividend Decisions of Major U.S. Firms," *Financial Review,* August 1991, 409–430.

Other pertinent articles include

Asquith, Paul, and David W. Mullins, Jr., "Signalling with Dividends, Stock Repurchases, and Equity Issues," *Financial Management,* Autumn 1986, 27–44.

Born, Jeffrey A., "Insider Ownership and Signals — Evidence from Dividend Initiation Announcement Effects," *Financial Management,* Spring 1988, 38–45.

Brealey, Richard A., "Does Dividend Policy Matter?" *Midland Corporate Finance Journal,* Spring 1983, 17–25.

Brennan, Michael J., and Anjan V. Thakor, "Shareholder Preferences and Dividend Policy," *Journal of Finance,* September 1990, 993–1018.

Chang, Rosita P., and S. Ghon Rhee, "The Impact of Personal Taxes on Corporate Dividend Policy and Capital Structure Decisions," *Financial Management,* Summer 1990, 21–31.

DeAngelo, Harry, and Linda DeAngelo, "Dividend Policy and Financial Distress: An Empirical Investigation of Troubled NYSE Firms," *Journal of Finance,* December 1990, 1415–1432.

DeAngelo, Harry, Linda DeAngelo, and Douglas J. Skinner, "Dividends and Losses," *Journal of Finance,* December 1992, 1837–1863.

Dempsey, Stephen J., and Gene Laber, "Effects of Agency and Transactions Costs on Dividend Payout Ratios: Further Evidence of the Agency-Transaction Cost Hypothesis," *Journal of Financial Research,* Winter 1992, 317–321.

Fehrs, Donald H., Gary A. Benesh, and David R. Peterson, "Evidence of a Relation between Stock Price Reactions Around Cash Dividend Changes and Yields," *Journal of Financial Research,* Summer 1988, 111–123.

Ghosh, Chinmoy, and J. Randall Woolridge, "An Analysis of Shareholder Reaction to Dividend Cuts and Omissions," *Journal of Financial Research,* Winter 1988, 281–294.

Healy, Paul M., and Krishna G. Palepu, "How Investors Interpret Changes in Corporate Financial Policy," *Journal of Applied Corporate Finance,* Fall 1989, 59–64.

Impson, C. Michael, and Imre Karafiath, "A Note on the Stock Market Reaction to Dividend Announcements," *The Financial Review,* May 1992, 259–271.

Kale, Jayant R., and Thomas H. Noe, "Dividends, Uncertainty, and Underwriting Costs Under Asymmetric Information," *Journal of Financial Research,* Winter 1990, 265–277.

Manakyan, Herman, and Carolyn Carroll, "An Empirical Examination of the Existence of a Signaling Value Function for Dividends," *Journal of Financial Research,* Fall 1990, 201–210.

Miller, Merton H., "Behavioral Rationality in Finance: The Case of Dividends," *Midland Corporate Finance Journal,* Winter 1987, 6–15.

Peterson, David R., and Pamela P. Peterson, "A Further Understanding of Stock Distributions: The Case of Reverse Stock Splits," *Journal of Financial Research,* Fall 1992, 189–205.

Peterson, Pamela P., David R. Peterson, and Norman H. Moore, "The Adoption of New-Issue Dividend Reinvestment Plans and Shareholder Wealth," *Financial Review,* May 1987, 221–232.

Talmor, Eli, and Sheridan Titman, "Taxes and Dividend Policy," *Financial Management,* Summer 1990, 32–35.

Wansley, James W., C. F. Sirmans, James D. Shilling, and Young-jin Lee, "Dividend Change Announcement Effects and Earnings Volatility and Timing," *Journal of Financial Research,* Spring 1991, 37–49.

Woolridge, J. Randall, and Chinmoy Ghosh, "Dividend Cuts: Do They Always Signal Bad News?" *Midland Corporate Finance Journal,* Summer 1985, 20–32.

The following cases from the Brigham-Gapenski casebook focus on the issues contained in this chapter:

Case 19, "Georgia Atlantic Company," which examines many dividend policy issues.

Case 20, "Bessemer Steel Products, Inc.," which illustrates the dividend policy decision.

PLANNING AND BUDGETING

Long-Term Planning and Forecasting

*M*itch Leibovitz, CEO of Pep Boys—Manny, Moe, and Jack, the auto parts and service chain, wants to annihilate the competition. When intense competition from Pep Boys forces chains such as Auto Zone, Western Auto, or Genuine Parts to abandon a location, Leibovitz adds a snapshot of the closed store to his collection. "I don't believe in friendly competition. I want to put them out of business," he says. Consolidation is under way in the $125-billion-a-year aftermarket for automotive parts and servicing, so survival demands that Pep Boys be "a killer."

Alone among its competitors, Pep Boys can install what it sells. If customers don't want to do the work themselves, Pep Boys will do everything except body work or replacing engines and transmissions for them. Nearly all of its 358 stores have ten or more service bays that keep long hours. They stay open 13 hours a day Monday through Saturday, 9 hours on Sunday, and no appointment is needed. The company can perform repairs more cheaply than dealers can, largely because it charges no markup on parts. Mechanics get paid 32 to 38 percent of the service charge instead of an hourly wage, but, contrary to common practice, no share of the price of the parts they install. If work has to be redone, mechanics must do it at their own expense.

Pep Boys was founded in 1921 by Emmanuel Rosenfield ("Manny"), Maurice Strauss ("Moe"), and W. Graham Jackson ("Jack"). The company grew to more than 100 stores by the early 1960s, after which conservative family management slowed expansion. Pep Boys went public in 1946, but the families kept control until the mid-1980s.

However, when Leibovitz took the helm in 1986, the company embarked on a major expansion program which has accelerated in the 1990s. Since 1986, the company has more than doubled the number of its stores and doubled sales to more than $1.1 billion. Pep Boys's success demonstrates that unswerving dedication to a single concept, no matter how mundane, can create a dynamic, growing business.

In 1992, the firm decided not to take on any new debt, so it added only 30 stores—all that could be financed from internal cash flow. Now that interest rates have declined, Leibovitz plans to add 40 stores in 1993 as part of a 270-store expansion by 1997. Pep Boys has plenty of room to grow: It is currently concentrated in 20 Sunbelt states, and it had no outlets in Florida or New York until 1992. From the planned expansion, the firm hopes to double sales again and to triple profits. According to Leibovitz, "If you want to have ho-hum results, have ho-hum goals."

Pep Boys will have to do a lot of planning to complete its expansion program; it will have to locate unserved markets, select sites, and line up the funds necessary to build the new outlets on schedule. In this chapter, we discuss financial forecasting, with an emphasis on how firms estimate the amount of capital needed to meet their growth targets. As you read the chapter, think about how Mitch Leibovitz might use the concepts presented to plan Pep Boys's expansion program. When you consider the potential impact of incorrect forecasting, you will quickly realize how important financial planning is to the success of any firm.

Thus far, we have focused on financial decisions. We began with some background information on financial statement analysis, financial markets, risk measurement, discounted cash flow analysis, and valuation. Then we proceeded to cost of capital, capital budgeting, capital structure, and dividend policy.

Parts I through IV dealt to a large extent with theory and strategic decision making. However, investment and financing decisions are not made in a vacuum; rather, they are made within the guidelines set down by firms' operating and financial plans. Now, in Part V, we discuss firms' planning processes, with emphasis on financial planning, forecasting, and budgeting. In this chapter, we discuss long-term planning and forecasting, which provides managers with a "road map" for some future period, usually the next five years.

STRATEGIC PLANS

Financial plans are developed within the framework of the firm's overall strategic and operating plans. Thus, we begin our discussion of financial planning with an overview of the strategic planning process.[1]

CORPORATE PURPOSE

The long-run strategic plan should begin with a statement of the *corporate purpose,* which defines the overall mission of the firm. The purpose can be defined either specifically or in general terms. For example, one firm might state that its corporate purpose is "to increase the intrinsic value of our common stock." Another might say that its purpose is "to maximize the growth rate in earnings and dividends per share while avoiding excessive risk." Yet another might state that its principal goal is "to provide our customers with state-of-the-art computing systems at the lowest attainable cost, which, in our opinion, will also maximize benefits to our employees and stockholders."

There should be no conflict between a firm's corporate purpose and stockholders' benefits, but occasionally there is. For example, Varian Associates, Inc., an NYSE company with 1993 sales of over $1 billion, was for years regarded as one of the most technologically advanced companies in the electronics devices and semiconductor fields. However, Varian's management was reputed to be more concerned with developing new technology than with marketing it, and the stock price was lower than it had been 10 years earlier. Some of the larger stockholders were intensely unhappy with the state of affairs, and management was faced with the threat of a proxy fight or a forced merger. At that point, management announced a conscious change in policy and stated that it would, in the future, emphasize both technological excellence *and* profitability, rather than focusing primarily on technology. Earnings improved dramatically, and the stock price rose from $6.75 to over $60 in only four years.

The Varian example illustrates both the importance of the corporate purpose as viewed by management and the discipline imposed by the financial markets. Well-run companies need to define an area and become competent at meeting the needs of their customers, but they will be forced by the market to translate that competence into earnings.

CORPORATE SCOPE

The *corporate scope* defines a firm's lines of business and geographic area of operations. Again, the corporate scope can be spelled out in great detail or put merely in general terms. The steel industry provides a study in contrasts: Some

---

[1]One can take many approaches to corporate planning. For more insights into the corporate planning process, see Benton E. Gup, *Guide to Strategic Planning* (New York: McGraw-Hill, 1980).

companies such as U.S. Steel (now USX Corporation) have diversified widely, from oil to financial services, while other companies have stuck closely to their basic business. Nucor Corporation, an NYSE-listed specialty steel producer, is one which has stuck to its basic business:

> *We are a manufacturing company producing primarily steel products. Nucor's major strength is constructing plants economically and operating them efficiently.*

A $1,000 investment in Nucor's stock in 1977 would be worth over $18,000 in 1993, while a similar investment in U.S. Steel would be worth $700. Factors other than scope of operations affected these results, but scope was surely an important factor.

CORPORATE OBJECTIVES

The corporate purpose and scope outline the general philosophy of the business, but they do not provide managers with operational objectives. The *corporate objectives* set forth specific goals that management strives to attain. Corporate objectives can be quantitative, such as specifying a target market share, a target ROE, or a target earnings per share growth rate, or they can be qualitative, such as "keeping the firm's research and development efforts at the cutting edge of the industry." Multiple goals are often established, and these goals are not static—they are changed as conditions change. The goals should be challenging, yet realistically attainable, and management compensation should be based on the extent to which objectives are met.

CORPORATE STRATEGIES

Once a firm has defined its purpose, scope, and objectives, it should develop a strategy to achieve its stated objectives. *Corporate strategies* are broad approaches rather than detailed plans. For example, one airline may have a strategy of offering no-frills service between a limited number of cities, while another may plan to offer "staterooms in the sky." Strategies must be attainable and compatible with the firm's purpose, scope, and objectives.

Perhaps the most interesting and important set of strategies that has been developed in recent years is that of AT&T and the Bell operating companies in the wake of the breakup of AT&T. The seven regional telephone holding companies which emerged from the breakup all provide basic local telephone service, but beyond that, they have been developing different strategies which will take them in different directions. Some now sell a broad array of telecommunications equipment, while others have more limited offerings. Some are rapidly diversifying into nonregulated lines of business—Bell Atlantic has spent over $2 billion for this purpose—while others are diversifying at a much slower pace. Others are moving

abroad; for example, BellSouth recently won a $220 million contract to build a mobile phone system in Argentina.

The surviving AT&T faces perhaps even greater challenges in setting its corporate strategy. On the one hand, it faces increasing competition in its two major markets, long-distance transmission and telephone equipment manufacturing. Currently, AT&T has most of the industry's capacity in these areas, so to some extent, it can set high prices and enjoy high short-run profits, but at the expense of an erosion of its share of the business. Alternatively, it can price low and maintain a large market share, but at the expense of short-run (and perhaps also long-run) profits. Also, AT&T must decide on the extent of its foray into the computer business. Its PC6300 clone of the IBM PC did poorly, and its other computer ventures, such as its Unix operating system, have started slow, but are now beginning to show promise. IBM, meanwhile, has invested heavily in the telecommunications business (both manufacturing and satellite transmissions), and is thus attacking AT&T on its own turf. At the same time, the new Bell companies are all trying to get permission to compete with their former parent in the businesses of long-distance service and equipment manufacturing. The AT&T/Bell companies' strategic decisions are more dramatic than most, but they do illustrate the kinds of issues that arise when companies develop their strategic plans.

SELF-TEST QUESTIONS

Briefly describe the nature and use of the following corporate planning tools:
   (1) Corporate purpose
   (2) Corporate scope
   (3) Corporate objectives
   (4) Corporate strategies

Why do financial planners need to be familiar with the company's overall strategic plan?

OPERATING PLANS

Operating plans can be developed for any time horizon, but most companies use a 5-year horizon. In a 5-year plan, the plan is most detailed for the first year, with each succeeding year's plan becoming less specific. The plan is intended to provide detailed implementation guidance, based on the corporate strategy, in order to meet the corporate objectives. The plan explains in considerable detail who is responsible for what particular function, and when specific tasks are to be accomplished.

Table 15-1 contains the annual planning schedule of Century Electronics Corporation, a leading manufacturer of telecommunications equipment. This schedule illustrates the fact that for larger companies, the planning process is essentially continuous. Next, Table 15-2 outlines the key elements of Century's 5-year plan. A

TABLE 15-1	Months	Action
CENTURY ELECTRONICS CORPORATION: ANNUAL PLANNING SCHEDULE	April–May	Planning department analyzes environmental and industry factors. Marketing department prepares sales forecast for each product group.
	June–July	Engineering department prepares cost estimates for new manufacturing facilities and plant modernization programs.
	August–September	Financial analysts evaluate proposed capital expenditures, divisional operating plans, and proposed sources and uses of funds.
	October–November	Five-year plan is finalized by planning department, reviewed by divisional officers, and put into "semifinal" form.
	December	Five-year plan is approved by the executive committee and then submitted to the board of directors for final approval.

full outline would require several pages, but Table 15-2 does at least provide insights into the format and content of a 5-year plan. It should be noted that Century, like other large, multidivisional companies, breaks down its operating plan by divisions. Thus, each division has its own goals, mission, and plan for meeting its objectives, and these plans are then consolidated to form the corporate plan.

TABLE 15-2
CENTURY ELECTRONICS CORPORATION: 5-YEAR OPERATING PLAN OUTLINE

Part 1.   Corporate purpose
Part 2.   Corporate scope
Part 3.   Corporate objectives
Part 4.   Projected business environment
Part 5.   Corporate strategies
Part 6.   Summary of projected business results
Part 7.   Product line plans and policies
    a.   Marketing
    b.   Manufacturing
    c.   Finance
       1.   Working capital
          (a)   Overall working capital policy
          (b)   Cash and marketable securities management
          (c)   Inventory management
          (d)   Credit policy and receivables management
       2.   Dividend policy
       3.   Financial forecast
          (a)   Capital budget
          (b)   Cash budget
          (c)   Pro forma financial statements
          (d)   External financing requirements
          (e)   Financial condition analysis
       4.   Accounting plan
       5.   Control plan
    d.   Administrative and personnel
    e.   Research and development
    f.   New products
Part 8.   Consolidated corporate plan

SELF-TEST QUESTIONS

What is the purpose of a firm's operating plan?

What is the most common time horizon for operating plans?

Briefly describe the contents of a typical operating plan.

THE FINANCIAL PLAN

The financial planning process can be broken down into five steps:

1. Set up a system of projected financial statements which can be used to analyze the effects of the operating plan on projected profits and other financial indicators. This system can also be used to monitor operations after the plan has been finalized and put into effect. Rapid awareness of deviations from plans is essential to a good control system, which in turn is essential to corporate success in a changing world.

2. Determine the funds needed to support the five-year plan. This includes funds for plant and equipment as well as for inventory and receivables buildups, for R&D programs, and for major advertising campaigns.

3. Forecast funds availability over the next five years. This involves estimating the funds generated internally as well as those which must be obtained from external sources. Any constraints on operating plans imposed by financial restrictions which would limit the use of total and/or short-term debt should be incorporated into the plan; examples include restrictions on the debt ratio, the current ratio, and the coverage ratios.

4. Establish and maintain a system of controls governing the allocation and use of funds within the firm. In essence, this involves making sure that the basic plan is carried out properly.

5. Develop procedures for adjusting the basic plan if the economic forecasts upon which the plan was based do not materialize. For example, if the economy turns out to be stronger than was forecasted, then these new conditions must be recognized and reflected in higher production budgets, larger marketing quotas, and the like, and as rapidly as possible. Thus, Step 5 is really a "feedback loop" which triggers modifications to the financial plan.

The principal components of the financial plan are (1) an analysis of the firm's current financial condition as indicated by an analysis of its most recent statements, (2) a sales forecast, (3) the capital budget, (4) the cash budget, (5) a set of pro forma (or projected) financial statements, and (6) the external financing plan. We have in previous chapters discussed the capital budget and financial statement analysis. In the remainder of this chapter, we focus on the plan's other elements — the sales forecast, the pro forma financial statements, and the external financing plan. Then, in Chapter 16, we will discuss the cash budget.

SELF-TEST QUESTIONS

What are the five steps of the financial planning process?
What are the principal components of the financial plan?

SALES FORECASTS

The *sales forecast* generally starts with a review of sales during the past five to ten years, expressed in a graph such as that in Figure 15-1. The graph shows five years of historical sales for Allied Food Products, a diversified food processor and distributor. The graph could have contained 10 years of sales data, but Allied typically focuses on sales figures for the latest 5 years because the firm's studies have shown that future growth is more closely related to the recent than to the distant past.

Allied had its ups and downs during the period from 1989 to 1993. In 1991, poor weather in California's fruit-producing regions resulted in low production, which caused 1991 sales to fall below the 1990 level. Then, a bumper crop in 1992 pushed sales up by 15 percent, an unusually high growth rate for a mature food processor. Based on a regression analysis, Allied's forecasters determined that the average annual growth rate in sales over the past 5 years was 9.1 percent. On the basis of this historical sales trend, on new product and market introductions, and on Allied's forecast for the economy, the firm's planning committee projects a 10 percent sales growth rate during 1994, to sales of $3,300 million. Here are some of the factors that Allied considered in developing its sales forecast:

1. Allied Food Products is divided into three divisions: canned foods, frozen foods, and packaged foods, such as dried fruits. Sales growth is seldom the same for each of the divisions, so to begin the forecasting process, divisional projections are made on the basis of historical growth, and then the divisional forecasts are combined to produce a "first approximation" corporate sales forecast.

2. Next, the level of economic activity in each of the company's marketing areas is forecasted — for example, how strong will the economies be in each of Allied's six domestic and two foreign distribution territories, and what population changes are forecasted in each area?

3. Allied's planning committee also looks at the firm's probable market share in each distribution territory. Consideration is given to such factors as the firm's production and distribution capacity, its competitors' capacities, new product introductions that are planned by Allied or its competitors, and potential changes in shelf-space allocations, which are vital for food sales. Pricing strategies are also considered — for example, does the company have plans to raise prices to boost margins, or to lower prices to increase market share and take advantage of economies of scale in purchasing and processing raw foods? Obviously, such factors would affect future sales. In addition, Allied's export sales are affected by exchange rates, governmental policies, and the like.

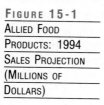

FIGURE 15-1
ALLIED FOOD
PRODUCTS: 1994
SALES PROJECTION
(MILLIONS OF
DOLLARS)

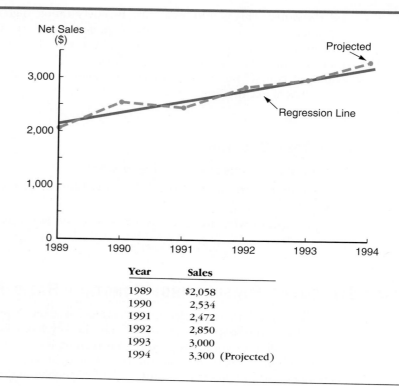

Year	Sales
1989	$2,058
1990	2,534
1991	2,472
1992	2,850
1993	3,000
1994	3,300 (Projected)

4. Allied's planners must also consider the effects of inflation on the firm's prices. Over the next five years, the inflation rate is expected to average 4 to 5 percent, and Allied plans to increase prices, on average, by a like amount. In addition, the firm expects to expand its market share in certain products, resulting in a 4 percent growth rate in unit sales. The combination of unit sales growth and increases in sales prices has resulted in historical revenue growth rates in the 8 to 10 percent range, and this same situation is expected in the future.

5. Advertising campaigns, promotional discounts, credit terms, and the like also affect sales, so probable developments in these areas are factored in.

6. Forecasts are made for each division both in total and on an individual product basis. The individual product sales forecasts are summed, and this sum is compared with the overall divisional forecasts. Differences are reconciled, and the end result is a sales forecast for the company as a whole but with breakdowns by the three divisions and by individual products.

If the sales forecast is off, the consequences can be serious. First, if the market expands *more* than Allied has geared up for, the company will not be able to meet demand. Its customers will end up buying competitors' products, and Allied will lose market share, which will be hard to regain. On the other hand, if its projections are overly optimistic, Allied could end up with too much plant, equipment,

and inventory. This would mean low turnover ratios, high costs for depreciation and storage, and, possibly, write-offs of spoiled inventory. All of this would result in a low rate of return on equity, which in turn would depress the company's stock price. If Allied had financed an unnecessary expansion with debt, its problems would, of course, be compounded. Thus, an accurate sales forecast is critical to the well-being of the firm.[2]

SELF-TEST QUESTIONS

How do past trends affect a sales forecast?

List some factors that should be considered when developing a sales forecast.

Briefly explain why an accurate sales forecast is critical to profitability.

FINANCIAL STATEMENT FORECASTING: CONSTANT RATIO METHOD

The first step in the financial plan is to develop a set of projected financial statements. As we discussed in the last section, the key input variable is the sales forecast. Once sales are forecasted, numerous techniques can be used to forecast financial statement balance sheet accounts and income statement items. The simplest technique, and the one that is most useful for explaining the mechanics of financial statement forecasting, is the *constant ratio method*. The steps in this procedure are described below, using data from Allied Food Products.

STEP 1. FORECAST THE INCOME STATEMENT

The income statement for the coming year is forecasted in order to obtain an estimate of the amount of retained earnings the company will generate during the year. This requires assumptions about the operating cost ratio, the tax rate, interest charges, and the dividend payout ratio. In the simplest case, the assumption is made that costs will increase at the same rate as sales; in more complicated situations, cost changes will be forecasted separately. Still, the primary objective of this part of the forecast is to determine how much income the company will earn and then retain for reinvestment in the business during the forecasted year.

Table 15-3 shows Allied's actual 1993 and forecasted 1994 income statements. To begin, we assume that sales and costs grow by 10 percent in 1994 over the 1993 levels. Therefore, we show the factor $(1 + g) = 1.10$ in the first three rows

---

[2]A sales forecast is actually the *expected value of a probability distribution* with many possible levels of sales. Because any sales forecast is subject to a greater or lesser degree of uncertainty, for financial planning we are often just as interested in the degree of uncertainty inherent in the sales forecast, as measured by standard deviation, as we are in the expected value of sales.

TABLE 15-3 ALLIED FOOD PRODUCTS: ACTUAL 1993 AND PROJECTED 1994 INCOME STATEMENTS (MILLIONS OF DOLLARS)

	Actual 1993 (1)	Forecast Basis (2)	1994 Forecast			
			First Pass (3)	Feedback (4)	Second Pass (5)	Final (6)
1. Sales	$3,000	× 1.10[a]	$3,300		$3,300	$3,300
2. Costs except depreciation	$2,616	× 1.10	$2,878		$2,878	$2,878
3. Depreciation	100	× 1.10	110		110	110
4. Total operating costs	$2,716		$2,988		$2,988	$2,988
5. EBIT	$ 284		$ 312		$ 312	$ 312
6. Less interest	88		88[b]	+5	93	93
7. Earnings before taxes (EBT)	$ 196		$ 224		$ 219	$ 219
8. Taxes (40%)	78		89	−1	88	88
9. NI before preferred dividends	$ 118		$ 135		$ 131	$ 131
10. Dividends to preferred	4		4[b]		4	4
11. NI available to common	$ 114		$ 131		$ 127	$ 127
12. Dividends to common	$ 58		$ 63[c]	+3	$ 66	$ 66
13. Addition to retained earnings	$ 56		$ 68	−7	$ 61	$ 61

[a] × 1.10 indicates "times 1 + g"; used for items which grow proportionally with sales.
[b] Indicates a 1993 amount carried over for first-pass forecast.
[c] Indicates a projected figure. See text for explanation.

of Column 2, and in the same rows of Column 3 we show the forecasted 1994 sales, operating costs, and depreciation. EBIT is found by subtraction, while the interest charges in Column 3 are simply carried over from Column 1. Note, though, that interest charges could change once we know whether additional debt will be required.

Earnings before taxes (EBT) are then calculated, as is net income before preferred dividends. Preferred dividends are carried over from the 1993 column, and they will remain constant unless Allied decides to issue additional preferred stock in 1994. Net income available to common is calculated, and then the 1994 initial dividends are forecasted as follows: The 1993 dividend per share is $1.15, and this dividend is expected to be increased by about 8 percent, to $1.25. Since there are 50 million shares outstanding, the initially projected dividends are $1.25(50,000,000) = $62.5 million, rounded to $63 million. (Again, like interest, this figure will be increased later in the analysis if additional shares are sold.)

As the last part of the first-pass forecasted income statement, the $63 million projected dividends are subtracted from the $131 million projected net income to common shareholders to determine the first-pass projection of funds available from retained earnings, $131 − $63 = $68 million. *Note, though, that this $68 million forecast for retained earnings will turn out to be too high because it understates the actual amount of interest and common stock dividends for 1993. Allied will have to borrow as well as sell additional shares of common stock to finance its asset requirements, and these actions will change the first pass forecasted income statement.* Those modifications will be made after we know how much additional financing will be required.

STEP 2. FORECAST THE BALANCE SHEET

If Allied's sales are to increase, then its assets must also grow. Since the company was operating at full capacity in 1993, each asset account must increase if the higher sales level is to be attained: More cash will be needed for transactions, higher sales will lead to higher receivables, additional inventory will have to be stocked, and new plant and equipment must be added.

Further, if Allied's assets are to increase, its liabilities and equity must also increase—the additional assets must be financed in some manner. *Spontaneously generated funds* will be provided by accounts payable and accruals. For example, as sales increase, so will Allied's purchases of raw materials, and these larger purchases will spontaneously lead to higher levels of accounts payable. Similarly, a higher level of operations will require more labor, while higher sales will result in higher taxable income. Therefore, both accrued wages and accrued taxes will increase. In general, these spontaneous liability accounts will increase at the same rate as sales.

Retained earnings will also increase, but not at the same rate as sales: The new level of retained earnings will be the old level plus the addition to retained earnings, and the new retained earnings must be calculated by working down through the projected income statement as we did in Step 1. Also, notes payable, long-term bonds, preferred stock, and common stock will not rise spontaneously with sales —rather, the projected levels of these accounts will depend on financing decisions that will be made later.

In summary, (1) higher sales must be supported by higher asset levels, (2) some of the asset increases can be financed by spontaneous increases in accounts payable and accruals and by retained earnings, and (3) any shortfall must be financed from external sources, either by borrowing or by selling new common or preferred stock.

Table 15-4 contains Allied's 1993 actual and its projected 1994 balance sheets. The mechanics of the balance sheet forecast are similar to those used to develop the forecasted income statement. First, those balance sheet accounts that are expected to increase directly with sales are multiplied by 1.10 to obtain the initial 1994 forecasts. Thus, 1994 cash is projected to be $10(1.10) = $11 million, accounts receivable are projected to be $375(1.10) ≈ $412 million, and so on. Note that Allied was operating its fixed assets at full capacity in 1993, so its net plant and equipment must also increase by the 10 percent sales growth rate.

Once the individual asset levels have been forecasted, they can be summed to complete the asset side of the forecasted balance sheet. For example, the total current assets forecasted for 1994 are $11 + $412 + $677 = $1,100 million, and total assets equal $2,200 million.

Next, the spontaneously increasing liabilities (accounts payable and accruals) are forecasted and shown in Column 3, the first pass forecast. Then those liability accounts whose values reflect conscious management decisions—notes payable, long-term bonds, preferred stock, and common stock—are initially set at their 1993 levels. Thus, 1994 notes payable are initially set at $110 million, the long-term bond account is forecasted at $754 million, and so on. The 1994 value for

TABLE 15-4

ALLIED FOOD PRODUCTS: ACTUAL 1993 AND PROJECTED 1994 BALANCE SHEETS (MILLIONS OF DOLLARS)

| | Actual 1993 (1) | Forecast Basis (2) | 1994 Forecast | | | |
			First Pass (3)	AFN[a] (4)	Second Pass (5)	Final (6)
Cash	$ 10	×1.10[b]	$ 11			
Accounts receivable	375	×1.10	412			
Inventories	615	×1.10	677			
Total current assets	$1,000		$1,100			
Net plant and equipment	1,000	×1.10	1,100			
Total assets	$2,000		$2,200		$2,200	$2,200
Accounts payable	$ 60	×1.10	$ 66		$ 66	$ 66
Notes payable	110		110[c]	+ 28	138	140
Accruals	140	×1.10	154		154	154
Total current liabilities	$ 310		$ 330		$ 358	$ 360
Long-term bonds	754		754[c]	+ 28	782	784
Total debt	$1,064		$1,084		$1,140	$1,144
Preferred stock	$ 40		$ 40[c]		$ 40	$ 40
Common stock	$ 130		$ 130[c]	+ 56	$ 186	$ 189
Retained earnings	766		834		827	827
Total common equity	$ 896		$ 964		$1,013	$1,016
Total liabilities and equity	$2,000		$2,088	+112	$2,193	$2,200
Additional funds needed (AFN) this pass			$ 112		$ 7	$ 0
Cumulative AFN			$ 112		$ 119	$ 119

[a]AFN stands for "Additional Funds Needed." This figure is determined at the bottom of Column 3, and Column 4 shows how the required $112 of AFN will be raised.

[b]×1.10 indicates "times 1 + g"; used for items which grow proportionally with sales.

[c]Indicates a 1993 amount carried over as the first-pass forecast.

the retained earnings (RE) account is obtained by adding the projected addition to retained earnings as developed in the 1994 income statement (see Table 15-3) to the 1993 ending balance:

$$1994 \text{ RE} = 1993 \text{ RE} + 1994 \text{ forecasted addition to RE}$$

$$= \$766 + \$68 = \$834 \text{ million.}$$

The forecast of total assets as shown in the first-pass forecast of Table 15-4 is $2,200 million, which indicates that Allied must add $200 million of new assets in 1994 to support the higher sales level. However, the forecasted liability and equity accounts as shown in the lower portion of Column 3 total to only $2,088 million. Since the balance sheet must balance, Allied must raise an additional $2,200 − $2,088 = $112 million, which we designate as *Additional Funds Needed (AFN)*. The AFN will be raised by borrowing from the bank as notes payable, by issuing long-term bonds, by selling new common stock, or by some combination of these actions.

STEP 3. RAISING THE ADDITIONAL FUNDS NEEDED

Allied's financial manager will base the financing decision on several factors, including the firm's target capital structure, conditions in the debt and equity markets, and restrictions imposed by existing debt agreements. Allied's financial manager, after considering all of the relevant factors, decided on the following financing mix to raise the $112 million of additional funds:

Type of Capital	Amount of New Capital		Interest Rate
	Percent	Dollars (Millions)	
Notes payable	25%	$ 28	8%
Long-term bonds	25	28	10
Common stock	50	56	—
	100%	$112	

These amounts, which are shown in Column 4 of Table 15-4, are added to the initially forecasted account totals as shown in Column 3 to generate the second-pass balance sheet. Thus, in Column 5, the notes payable account increases to $110 + $28 = $138 million, long-term bonds rise to $754 + $28 = $782 million, and common stock increases to $130 + $56 = $186 million.

If there were no changes in any other income statement item or balance sheet account, the forecast would be complete—the initial shortfall was $112 million, and Allied would raise that amount as shown above. However, when Allied takes on new debt, its interest expenses will rise, and the additional shares of common stock will cause the total dividend payment to increase. These changes will affect the amount of retained earnings, as we discuss in the next section.

STEP 4. FINANCING FEEDBACKS

One complexity that arises in financial forecasting relates to *financing feedbacks*. The external funds raised to pay for new assets create additional expenses which must be reflected in the income statement, and that lowers the initially forecasted addition to retained earnings. To handle the financing feedback process, we first forecast the additional interest expense and any additional dividends that will be paid as a result of the external financings. New short-term debt costs 8 percent, so the $28 million of new notes payable will increase Allied's projected 1994 interest expense by 0.08($28) = $2.24 million. Similarly, the new long-term bonds will add 0.10($28) = $2.80 million in interest expense, so the total increase in interest expense will be $5.04 million. When these feedbacks are considered, interest expense as shown in the projected 1994 second-pass income statement in Column 5 of Table 15-3 increases to $88 + $5 = $93 million. The higher interest charges will, of course, also affect the remainder of the income statement.

The financing plan also calls for $56 million of new common stock to be sold. Allied's stock price was $23 per share at the end of 1993, and if we assume that

new shares would be sold at this price, then $56/$23 = 2.4 million shares of new stock will have to be sold. Further, Allied's 1994 dividend payment is projected to be $1.25 per share, so the 2.4 million shares of new stock will require 2.4($1.25) = $3 million of additional dividend payments. Thus, dividends to common stockholders as shown in the second-pass income statement increase to $63 + $3 = $66 million.

The net effect of the financing feedbacks on the income statement is to reduce the addition to retained earnings by $7 million, from $68 million to $61 million. This reduction in the addition to retained earnings reduces the balance sheet forecast of retained earnings by a like amount, so in Table 15-4 the second-pass 1994 balance sheet projection for retained earnings becomes $766 + $61 = $827 million, or $7 million less than in the initial forecast. Thus, a shortfall of $7 million will still exist as a direct result of financing feedback effects — the additional interest and dividend payments reduce the projected retained earnings account by $7 million from the initial forecast, so an additional shortfall exists. This amount is shown at the bottom of Column 5 in Table 15-4.

How would the second-pass shortfall be financed? In Allied's case, 25 percent of the $7 million would be obtained as short-term debt, 25 percent as long-term bonds, and 50 percent as new common stock.

We could create a third-pass balance sheet by using this financing mix to add another $7 million to the liabilities and equity side. Would the third pass balance? No, because the additional $7 million in capital would require another increase in interest and dividend payments, and this would affect the third-pass income statement. There would still be a shortfall, although it would be much smaller than the $7 million shortfall on the second pass. We could then construct a fourth-pass forecasted income statement and balance sheet, fifth-pass statements, and so on. In each iteration, the additional financing needed would become smaller and smaller, and after about five iterations, the AFN would become so small that we could consider the forecast to be completed. We do not show the additional iterations, but the final results are shown in Column 6 of Tables 15-3 and 15-4.[3]

ANALYSIS OF THE FORECAST

The 1994 forecast as developed above is only the first part of Allied's total forecasting process. Next, the projected statements must be analyzed to determine whether the forecast meets the firm's financial targets as laid down in the 5-year financial plan. If the statements do not meet the targets, then elements of the forecast must be changed.

Table 15-5 shows Allied's key ratios for 1993, plus the projected 1994 ratios and the latest industry average ratios. (The table also shows some "Revised" data which we will discuss later.) The firm's financial condition at the close of 1993

---

[3]It is rather tedious to make financial forecasts by hand. Fortunately, it is easy to make a model using *Lotus 1-2-3* or some other spreadsheet program which can be used to do the iterations and arrive at the final forecast.

	1993	Preliminary 1994[a]	Industry Average	Revised 1994[a]
TABLE 15-5				
PROJECTED AFN AND				
KEY RATIOS				
AFN		$112		($64)
Current ratio	3.2	3.1	4.2	3.6
Inventory turnover	4.9	4.9	9.0	6.0
Days sales outstanding	45.0	45.0	36.0	42.5
Total assets turnover	1.5	1.5	1.8	1.6
Debt ratio[b]	55.2%	53.8%	40.0%	51.6%
Profit margin	3.8%	3.8%	5.0%	4.8%
Return on assets	5.7%	5.8%	9.0%	7.7%
Return on equity	12.7%	12.5%	15.0%	15.9%

[a]The revised data reflect all financing feedback effects.
[b]Includes preferred stock.

was weak, with many ratios being well below the industry averages. The preliminary forecast for 1994 (after financing feedbacks are considered), which assumes that Allied's past practices will continue into the future, also shows a relatively weak financial condition—naturally, this condition will persist unless management takes some actions to improve things.

Allied's management actually plans to take three steps to improve its financial condition: (1) Management plans to lay off some workers and to close certain operations. These steps should lower operating costs (excluding depreciation) from the current 87.2 percent of sales to 86 percent. (2) By screening credit customers more closely and by being more aggressive in collecting past due accounts, the days sales outstanding on receivables can be reduced from 45 to 42.5 days. (3) Finally, management thinks that the inventory turnover ratio can be raised from 4.9 to 6 times through the use of tighter inventory controls.[4]

These proposed operational changes were then used to create a revised set of forecasted statements for 1994. We do not show the new financial statements, but their impact on the key ratios is shown in Table 15-5 in the Revised 1994 column. Here are the highlights:

1.   By decreasing operating costs from 87.2 to 86 percent of sales, Allied's forecasted cost figures on Rows 2 and 4 of Table 15-3 were changed. These changes worked on through the statement, and as a result the profit margin improved from 3.8 to 4.8 percent, which is closer to the industry average.

2.   The increase in the profit margin resulted in an increase in projected retained earnings. Further, by tightening inventory controls and reducing the days sales outstanding, Allied projected a reduction in the forecasted levels of inventories

---

[4]We will discuss receivables and inventory management in detail in Chapter 18.

and receivables. Taken together, these actions resulted in a *negative* AFN of $64 million, which means that Allied would actually generate $64 million more from internal operations than it needs to spend on new assets. This $64 million of surplus funds would be used to reduce short-term debt, which would lead to a decrease in the forecasted debt ratio from 53.8 to 51.6 percent. The debt ratio would still be well above the industry average, but this would be a step in the right direction.

3. The indicated changes would also affect Allied's current ratio, which would improve from 3.1 to 3.6.

4. These actions also resulted in a forecasted improvement in the rate of return on assets from 5.8 to 7.7 percent, and they gave a boost to the return on equity from 12.5 to 15.9 percent, which even exceeds the industry average.

Although Allied's managers believe that the revised forecast is achievable, they cannot be sure of this. Accordingly, they also want to know how variations in sales would affect the forecast. Therefore, a *Lotus 1-2-3* model was run using alternative sales growth rates, and the results were analyzed to see how the firm's financial condition would change under alternative growth scenarios. To illustrate, if the sales growth rate forecast increased from 10 to 20 percent, the additional funding requirement would change dramatically, from a $64 million surplus to an $83 million shortfall.

The *Lotus 1-2-3* model was then used to evaluate dividend policy. If Allied decided to reduce its dividend growth rate, then additional funds would be generated, and these funds could be invested in plant, equipment, and inventories, used to reduce debt, or, possibly, used to repurchase stock.

The model was also used to evaluate financing alternatives. For example, Allied could use the forecasted $64 million of surplus funds to retire long-term bonds rather than to reduce short-term debt. Under this financing alternative, the current ratio would drop from 3.6 to 2.9, but the total debt ratio would still decline, and the interest coverage ratio would also improve.

Forecasting is an iterative process, both in the way the financial statements are generated and in the way the financial plan is developed. For planning purposes, the financial staff develops a preliminary forecast based on a continuation of past policies and trends. This provides the executives with a starting point, or "straw man" forecast. Next, the model is modified to see what effects alternative operating plans would have on the firm's earnings and financial condition. This results in a revised forecast. In addition, alternative operating plans are examined under different sales growth rate scenarios, and the model is used to evaluate both dividend policy and capital structure decisions.

The model can also be used to analyze alternative short-term policies — that is, to determine the effects of changes in cash management, credit policy, inventory policy, and the use of different types of short-term credit. We will examine Allied's short-term policy within the model framework in Chapter 16, but in the remainder of this chapter we consider some other aspects of the financial forecasting process.

F IGURE 1 5 - 2

A LLIED F OOD
P RODUCTS:
R ELATIONSHIP
BETWEEN G ROWTH IN
S ALES AND F INANCIAL
R EQUIREMENTS,
A SSUMING S_0 =
$3,000 (M ILLIONS
OF D OLLARS)

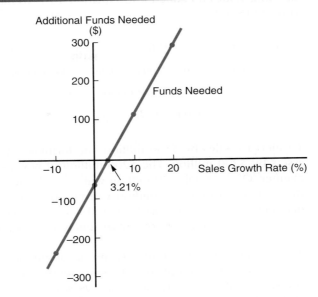

Growth Rate in Sales (1)	Increase (Decrease) in Sales, ΔS (2)	Forecasted Sales, S_1 (3)	Additional Funds Needed (4)
20%	$600	$3,600	$293
10	300	3,300	118
3.21	96	3,096	0
0	0	3,000	(56)
(10)	(300)	2,700	(230)

Explanation of Columns:
Column 1: Assumed growth rate in sales, g.
Column 2: Increase (decrease) in sales, $\Delta S = g(S_0) = g(\$3,000)$.
Column 3: Forecasted sales, $S_1 = S_0 + g(S_0) = S_0(1 + g) = \$3,000(1 + g)$.
Column 4: Additional funds needed = $0.667(\Delta S) - 0.067(\Delta S) - 0.019(S_1)$.

earnings, hence the greater the requirements for external capital. Therefore, if Allied foresees difficulties in raising capital, it might want to consider a reduction in the dividend payout ratio. This would lower (or shift to the right) the line in Figure 15-2, indicating smaller external capital requirements at all growth rates. However, before changing its dividend policy, management should consider the effects of such a decision on stock prices. These effects were considered in Chapter 14.

Notice that the line in Figure 15-2 does *not* pass through the origin; thus, at low growth rates (below 3.21 percent), surplus funds will be produced, because

new retained earnings plus spontaneous funds will exceed the required asset increases. Only if the dividend payout ratio were 100 percent, meaning that the firm did not retain any of its earnings, would the "funds needed" line pass through the origin.

3. **Capital intensity.** The amount of assets required per dollar of sales, A*/S in Equation 15-1, is often called the *capital intensity ratio.* This ratio has a major effect on capital requirements per unit of sales growth. If the capital intensity ratio is low, sales can grow rapidly without much outside capital. However, if the firm is capital intensive, even a small growth in output will require a great deal of new outside capital.

4. **Profit margin.** The profit margin, M, is also an important determinant of the funds-required equation—the higher the margin, the lower the funds requirements, other things held constant. In terms of the graph, an increase in the profit margin would cause the line to shift down, and its slope would also become less steep. Because of the relationship between profit margins and additional capital requirements, some very rapidly growing firms do not need much external capital. For example, for many years Xerox grew at a rapid rate with very little borrowing or stock sales. However, as the company lost patent protection and as competition intensified in the copier industry, Xerox's profit margin declined, its needs for external capital rose, and it began to borrow from banks and other sources. IBM has had a similar experience.

SELF-TEST QUESTIONS

Under certain conditions a simple formula can be used to forecast AFN. Give the formula and briefly explain it.

How do the following factors affect external capital requirements?
   (1) Dividend policy
   (2) Capital intensity
   (3) Profit margin

FORECASTING FINANCIAL REQUIREMENTS WHEN THE BALANCE SHEET RATIOS ARE SUBJECT TO CHANGE

Both the AFN formula and the constant ratio forecasting method assume that the balance sheet ratios of assets and spontaneous liabilities to sales (A*/S and L*/S) remain constant over time, which in turn requires the assumption that each "spontaneous" asset and liability item increases at the same rate as sales. In graph form, this implies the type of relationship shown in Panel a of Figure 15-3, a relationship that is (1) linear and (2) passes through the origin. Under those conditions, if the company's sales increase from $200 million to $400 million, inventory must increase at the same rate, or proportionately, from $100 million to $200 million.

FIGURE 15-3   FOUR POSSIBLE RATIO RELATIONSHIPS (MILLIONS OF DOLLARS)

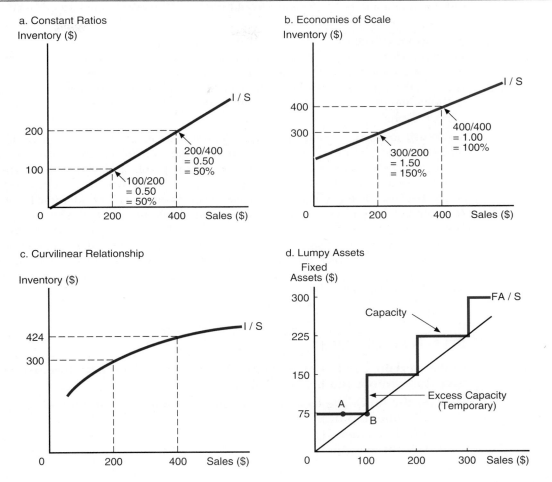

The assumption of constant ratios, which implies identical growth rates, is appropriate at times, but there are times when it is incorrect. Three such conditions are described in the following sections.

ECONOMIES OF SCALE

There are economies of scale in the use of many kinds of assets, and when economies occur, the ratios are likely to change over time as the size of the firm increases. For example, firms often need to maintain base stocks of different inventory items even if current sales levels are quite low. As sales expand, inventories

grow less rapidly than sales, so the ratio of inventory to sales declines. This situation is depicted in Panel b of Figure 15-3. Here we see that the inventory/sales ratio is 1.5, or 150 percent, when sales are $200 million, but the ratio declines to 1.0 when sales climb to $400 million.

The relationship used to illustrate economies of scale is linear, but nonlinear relationships often exist. Indeed, as we shall see in Chapter 18, if the firm uses the most popular model for establishing inventory levels, the EOQ model, its inventories will rise with the square root of sales. In this type of situation, which is shown in Panel c, the graph is a curved line whose slope decreases at higher sales levels.

LUMPY ASSETS

In many industries, technological considerations dictate that if a firm is to be competitive, it must add fixed assets in large, discrete units; such assets are often referred to as *lumpy assets*. In the paper industry, for example, there are strong economies of scale in basic paper mill equipment, so when a paper company expands capacity, it must do so in large, lumpy increments. This type of situation is depicted in Panel d of Figure 15-3. Here we assume that the minimum economically efficient plant has a cost of $75 million and that such a plant can produce enough output to attain a sales level of $100 million. If the firm is to be competitive, it simply must have at least $75 million of fixed assets.

Lumpy assets have a major effect on the fixed assets/sales ratio at different sales levels and, consequently, on financial requirements. At Point A in Figure 15-3d, which represents a sales level of $50 million, the fixed assets are $75 million, so the ratio FA/S = $75/$50 = 1.5. Sales can expand by $50 million, out to $100 million, with no additions to fixed assets. At that point, represented by Point B, the ratio FA/S = $75/$100 = 0.75. However, if the firm is operating at capacity (sales of $100 million), even a small increase in sales would require a doubling of plant capacity, so a small projected sales increase would bring with it a very large financial requirement.[6]

NONOPTIMAL STARTING RATIOS

Panels a, b, c, and d of Figure 15-3 all focus on target, or projected, relationships between sales and assets. Actual sales, however, are often different from projected

---

[6]Several other points should be noted about Panel d of Figure 15-3. First, if the firm is operating at a sales level of $100 million or less, any expansion that calls for a sales increase above $100 million will require a *doubling* of the firm's fixed assets. A much smaller percentage increase would be involved if the firm were large enough to be operating a number of plants. Second, firms generally go to multiple shifts and take other actions to minimize the need for new fixed asset capacity as they approach Point B. However, these efforts can go only so far, and eventually a fixed asset expansion will be required. Third, firms often make arrangements to share excess capacity with other firms in their industry. For example, consider the situation in the electric utility industry, which is very much like that depicted in Panel c. Electric companies often build jointly owned plants, or else they "take turns" building plants, and then they buy power from or sell power to other utilities to avoid building new plants that may be underutilized.

sales, and the actual asset/sales ratio for a given period may thus be quite different from the planned ratio. To illustrate, the firm depicted in Panel b of Figure 15-3 might, when its sales are at $200 million and its inventories at $300 million, project a sales expansion to $400 million and then increase its inventories to $400 million in anticipation of the sales expansion. However, suppose an unforeseen economic downturn were to hold sales to only $300 million. Actual inventories would then be $400 million, but inventories of only $350 million would be needed to support actual sales of $300 million. Thus, inventories would be $50 million larger than needed. In this situation, if the firm were making its forecast for the following year, it would need to recognize that sales could expand by $100 million with no increase whatever in inventories but that any sales expansion beyond $100 million would require additional financing to build inventories.

SELF-TEST QUESTION

Describe three conditions under which the assumption that each "spontaneous" asset and liability item increases at the same rate as sales is *not* correct.

OTHER TECHNIQUES FOR FORECASTING FINANCIAL STATEMENTS

If any of the conditions noted above applies (economies of scale, excess capacity, or lumpy assets), the A*/S ratio will not be a constant, and the constant ratio technique should not be used. Rather, other techniques must be used to forecast income statement items and balance sheet accounts, and hence additional financing requirements. Two of these methods—linear regression and excess capacity adjustments—are discussed in the following sections.

SIMPLE LINEAR REGRESSION

If we assume that the relationship between a certain item or account and sales is linear, then we can use simple linear regression techniques to estimate the item or account level for any given sales increase. For example, Allied's levels of sales, inventories, and receivables during the last 5 years are shown in the lower section of Figure 15-4, and each current asset item is plotted in the upper section as a scatter diagram versus sales. Estimated regression equations determined using a financial calculator are also shown with each graph. For example, the estimated relationship between inventories and sales (in millions of dollars) is

$$\text{Inventories} = -\$35.7 + 0.186(\text{Sales}).$$

The plotted points are not very close to the regression line, which indicates a low degree of correlation. In fact, the correlation coefficient between inventories and

FIGURE 15-4   ALLIED FOOD PRODUCTS: LINEAR REGRESSION MODELS (MILLIONS OF DOLLARS)

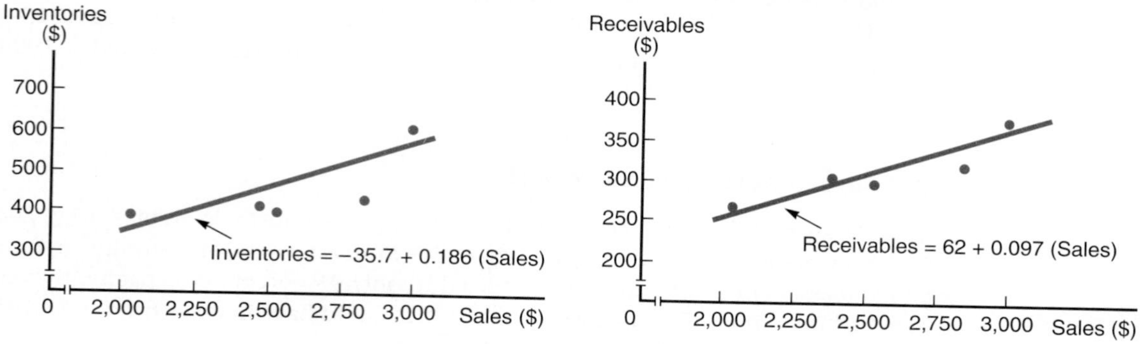

Year	Sales	Inventories	Accounts Receivable
1989	$2,058	$387	$268
1990	2,534	398	297
1991	2,472	409	304
1992	2,850	415	315
1993	3,000	615	375

sales is 0.71, indicating that there is only a moderate linear relationship between these two variables. Still, management regards the regression relationship as providing a reasonable basis for forecasting target inventory levels, and they have more confidence in it than they do in the constant ratio forecast.

We can use the estimated relationship between inventories and sales to forecast 1994 inventory levels. Since 1994 sales are projected at $3,300 million, 1994 inventories should be $578 million:

$$\text{Inventories} = -\$35.7 + 0.186(\$3,300) = \$578 \text{ million.}$$

This is $99 million less than the preliminary forecast based on the projected balance sheet method as shown in Table 15-4. The difference occurs because the projected balance sheet method assumed that the ratio of inventories to sales would remain constant, when in fact it will probably decline. Note also that although our graphs show linear relationships, we could have easily used a nonlinear regression model had such a relationship been indicated.

After analyzing the regression results, Allied's managers directed that a new forecast of AFN be developed in which a lower days sales outstanding and a higher inventory turnover ratio are assumed. Management recognized that the 1993 levels of these accounts were above the industry averages, hence that the preliminary results projected for 1994 were also too high. When simple linear regression was used to forecast the receivables and inventories accounts, the 1994 levels reflect

both the average relationships of these accounts to sales over the 5-year period and the trend in the variables' values. The initial projected balance sheet method assumed that the nonoptimal 1993 levels would remain constant in 1994 and beyond. The new preliminary 1994 forecast for Allied, based on the Figure 15-4 linear regression relationships for receivables and inventories, projected a 1994 funds surplus of $17 million.

EXCESS CAPACITY ADJUSTMENTS

Consider again the Allied Food Products example set forth in Tables 15-3 and 15-4. Now assume that excess capacity exists in fixed assets. Specifically, assume that fixed assets in 1993 were being utilized to only 96 percent of capacity. If fixed assets had been used to full capacity, 1993 sales could have been as high as $3,125 million, versus the $3,000 million in actual sales.

$$\begin{matrix} \text{Full} \\ \text{capacity} \\ \text{sales} \end{matrix} = \frac{\text{Actual sales}}{\begin{matrix}\text{Percentage of capacity} \\ \text{at which fixed assets} \\ \text{were operated}\end{matrix}} = \frac{\$3,000 \text{ million}}{0.96} = \$3,125 \text{ million.}$$

$$(15\text{-}2)$$

This suggests that Allied's Fixed assets/Sales ratio should be 32 percent:

$$\text{Target fixed assets/Sales ratio} = \frac{\text{Actual fixed assets}}{\text{Full capacity sales}} \qquad (15\text{-}3)$$

$$= \frac{\$1,000}{\$3,125} = 0.32 = 32\%.$$

Therefore, if sales are to increase to $3,300 million, then fixed assets would have to increase to $1,056 million:

$$\begin{matrix}\text{Required level} \\ \text{of fixed assets}\end{matrix} = \text{Target fixed assets/Sales ratio (Projected sales)} \quad (15\text{-}4)$$

$$= 0.32(\$3,300) = \$1,056 \text{ million.}$$

We had previously forecasted that Allied would need to increase fixed assets at the same rate as sales, or by 10 percent, which meant an increase from $1,000

million to $1,100 million, or by $100 million. Now we see that the actual required increase is only from $1,000 million to $1,056 million, or by $56 million. Thus, the capacity-adjusted forecast is $100 million − $56 million = $44 million less than the earlier forecast. Therefore, the projected AFN would decline from an estimated $112 million (before financing feedback effects) to $112 million − $44 million = $68 million.

Note also that when excess capacity exists, sales growth up to the capacity sales as determined above can occur with no increase whatever in fixed assets and that sales beyond that growth will require fixed asset additions as calculated in our example. The same situation could occur with respect to inventories, and the required additions would be determined in exactly the same manner as for fixed assets. Theoretically, the same situation could occur with other types of assets, but as a practical matter, excess capacity normally exists primarily with respect to fixed assets and inventories.

SELF-TEST QUESTION

Identify two methods which can be used to forecast asset levels when the assets-to-sales ratio is not constant.

COMPUTERIZED FINANCIAL PLANNING MODELS

Although the types of financial forecasting described in this chapter can be done with a hand calculator, virtually all corporate forecasts are made using computerized forecasting models. Many computerized financial forecasting models are based on a spreadsheet program such as *Lotus 1-2-3*. Spreadsheet models have two major advantages over pencil-and-paper calculations. First, it is much faster to construct a spreadsheet model than to make a "by hand" forecast if the forecast period extends beyond two or three years. Second, and more important, a spreadsheet model can almost instantaneously recompute the projected financial statements and ratios when one of the input variables is changed, thus making it feasible for managers to determine the effects of changes in variables such as sales.

We developed forecasts for Allied using a 5-year financial planning model based on *Lotus 1-2-3*. The model begins with 5 years of historical data, which are used to establish basic relationships. Other input data include forecasted sales growth rates, the financing mix to apply to any additional funds needed, the cost rates on incremental debt financing, and the tax rate. The model calculates projected financial statements for 5 years, including financing feedback effects, along with some key financial ratios. We used *Lotus*'s linear regression capability to develop Allied's historical sales growth rate and the historical relationships between

accounts receivable, inventories, and sales. Thus, it was quite easy to examine the effects of alternative assumptions on Allied's forecasts.[7]

SELF-TEST QUESTION

Why are computerized planning models playing an increasingly important role in corporate management?

FINANCIAL CONTROLS

Financial forecasting and planning is vital to corporate success, but planning is for nought unless the firm has a control system (1) that ensures implementation of the planned policies and (2) that provides an information feedback loop which permits rapid adjustments if the market conditions upon which the plan is based change. In a financial control system, the key question is not "How is the firm doing in 1994 as compared with 1993?" Rather, it is "How is the firm doing in 1994 as compared with our forecasts, and if actual results differ from the budget, what can we do to get back on track?"

The basic tools of financial control are *budgets* and *pro forma financial statements*. These documents set forth expected performance, and, hence, they express management's targets. These targets are then compared with actual corporate performance—on a daily, weekly, or monthly basis—to determine the variances, which are defined here as the difference between actual values and target values. Thus, the control system identifies those areas where performance is not meeting target levels. If a division's actuals are better than its targets, this could signify that its manager should be given a raise, but it could also mean that the targets were

---

[7]It is becoming increasingly easy for companies to develop planning models as a result of the dramatic improvements that have been made in computer hardware and software in recent years. *Lotus 1-2-3* is the most widely used system, although many companies also employ more complex and elaborate modeling systems. Increasingly, a knowledge of *Lotus 1-2-3* or some similar spreadsheet program is becoming a requirement for getting even an entry-level job in many corporations. Indeed, surveys indicate that the probability of a business student getting an attractive job offer increases dramatically if he or she has a working knowledge of *Lotus 1-2-3*. In addition, starting salaries are materially higher for those students who have such a knowledge.

Note also that we have concentrated on long-run, or strategic, financial planning. Within the framework of the long-run strategic plan, firms also develop short-run financial plans. For example, in Table 15-4 we saw that Allied Food Products expects to need $112 million by the end of 1994, and that it plans to raise this capital by using short-term debt, long-term debt, and common stock. However, we do not know when during the year the funds will be needed or when Allied will obtain each of its different types of capital. To address these issues, the firm must develop a short-run financial plan, the centerpiece of which is the *cash budget*, which is a projection of cash inflows and outflows on a daily, weekly, or monthly basis during the coming year (or other budget period). We will discuss cash budgeting in Chapter 16, where we continue our discussion of financial planning and control.

set too low and thus should be raised in the future. Conversely, failure to meet the financial targets could mean that market conditions are changing, that some managers are not performing up to par, or that the targets were set initially at unrealistic, unattainable levels. In any event, some action should be taken, and perhaps quickly, if the situation is deteriorating rapidly. By focusing on variances, managers can "manage by exception," concentrating on those variables that are most in need of improvement and leaving alone those operations that are running smoothly.[8]

SELF-TEST QUESTIONS

What are the purposes of a financial control system?

What are the basic financial control tools and how do they work?

SUMMARY

This chapter described in broad outline how firms project their financial statements and determine their capital requirements. The key concepts covered are listed below.

▶ The primary planning documents are *strategic plans, operating plans,* and *financial plans.*

▶ *Financial forecasting* generally begins with a forecast of the firm's sales, in terms of both units and dollars, for some future period.

▶ *Projected,* or *pro forma, financial statements* are used to forecast financial requirements.

▶ A firm can determine the amount of *additional funds needed (AFN)* by estimating the amount of new assets necessary to support the forecasted level of sales and then subtracting from that amount the spontaneous funds that will be generated from operations. The firm can then plan to raise the AFN through bank borrowing, by issuing securities, or both.

▶ The *higher a firm's sales growth rate,* the *greater* will be its need for additional financing. Similarly, the *larger a firm's dividend payout ratio,* the *greater* its need for additional funds.

▶ Adjustments must be made if *economies of scale* exist in the use of assets, if *excess capacity exists,* or if assets must be added in *lumpy increments.*

---

[8]Of course, entire textbooks have been written on financial controls, and much of the subject of financial control overlaps with managerial, or cost, accounting. Here, we want only to emphasize that financial controls are as critical to financial performance as is financial planning and forecasting. We must also add that financial control systems are not costless. Thus, managers must balance the cost of a control system against the savings it is intended to produce.

▶ Many balance sheet accounts and income statement items can be projected using the *constant ratio method,* which assumes that the accounts and items will grow at the same rate as sales.

▶ *Linear regression* can be used to forecast accounts and items in situations where they cannot be expected to grow at the same rate as sales.

▶ Even the smallest firms now use *computerized financial planning models* to forecast both their financial statements and their external financing needs.

The type of forecasting described in this chapter is important for several reasons. First, if the projected operating results are unsatisfactory, management can "go back to the drawing board," reformulate its plans, and develop more reasonable targets for the coming year. Second, it is possible that the funds required to meet the sales forecast simply cannot be obtained; if so, it is obviously better to know this in advance and to scale back the projected level of operations than to suddenly run out of cash and have operations grind to a halt. And third, even if the required funds can be raised, it is desirable to plan for their acquisition well in advance.

Questions

15-1 Define each of the following terms:

   a. Operating plan; 5-year plan

   b. Financial plan

   c. Sales forecast

   d. Constant ratio method

   e. Spontaneously generated funds

   f. Dividend payout ratio

   g. Pro forma financial statement

   h. Additional funds needed (AFN); AFN formula

   i. Capital intensity ratio

   j. Lumpy assets

   k. Financing feedback

   l. Simple linear regression

   m. Computerized financial planning model

15-2 Certain liability and net worth items generally increase spontaneously with increases in sales. Put a check (√) by those items that typically increase spontaneously:

Accounts payable	_____
Notes payable to banks	_____
Accrued wages	_____
Accrued taxes	_____
Mortgage bonds	_____
Common stock	_____
Retained earnings	_____

15-3 The following equation can, under certain assumptions, be used to forecast financial requirements:

$$AFN = (A^*/S)(\Delta S) - (L^*/S)(\Delta S) - MS_1(1 - d).$$

Under what conditions does the equation give satisfactory predictions, and when should it not be used?

15-4 Assume that an average firm in the office supply business has a 6 percent after-tax profit margin, a 40 percent debt/assets ratio, a total assets turnover of 2 times, and a dividend payout ratio of 40 percent. Is it true that if such a firm is to have *any* sales growth (g > 0), it will be forced either to borrow or to sell common stock (that is, it will need some nonspontaneous, external capital even if g is very small)?

15-5 Is it true that computerized corporate planning models were a fad during the 1980s but, because of a need for flexibility in corporate planning, they have been dropped by most firms?

15-6 Suppose a firm makes the following policy changes. If the change means that external, nonspontaneous financial requirements (AFN) will increase, indicate this by a (+); indicate a decrease by a (−); and indicate indeterminate or no effect by a (0). Think in terms of the immediate, short-run effect on funds requirements.

a. The dividend payout ratio is increased.   _____

b. The firm contracts to buy, rather than make, certain components used in its products.   _____

c. The firm decides to pay all suppliers on delivery, rather than after a 30-day delay, to take advantage of discounts for rapid payment.   _____

d. The firm begins to sell on credit (previously all sales had been on a cash basis).   _____

e. The firm's profit margin is eroded by increased competition; sales are steady.   _____

f. Advertising expenditures are stepped up.   _____

g. A decision is made to substitute long-term mortgage bonds for short-term bank loans.   _____

h. The firm begins to pay employees on a weekly basis (previously it had paid at the end of each month).   _____

SELF-TEST PROBLEMS (SOLUTIONS APPEAR IN APPENDIX C)

ST-1 (Maximum growth rate) Weatherford Industries Inc. has the following ratios: $A^*/S = 1.6$; $L^*/S = 0.4$; profit margin $= 0.10$; and dividend payout ratio $= 0.45$, or 45 percent. Sales last year were $100 million. Assuming that these ratios will remain constant, use the AFN formula to determine the maximum growth rate Weatherford can achieve without having to employ nonspontaneous external funds.

ST-2 (Additional funds needed) Suppose Weatherford's financial consultants report (1) that the inventory turnover ratio is sales/inventory $= 3$ times versus an industry average of 4 times, and (2) that Weatherford could reduce inventories and thus raise its turnover to 4 without affecting sales, the profit margin, or the other asset turnover ratios. Under these conditions, use the AFN formula to determine the amount of additional funds Weatherford would require during each of the next 2 years if sales grew at a rate of 20 percent per year.

ST-3 **(Excess capacity)** Van Auken Lumber's 1993 financial statements are shown below.

Van Auken Lumber:
Balance Sheet as of December 31, 1993
(Thousands of Dollars)

Cash	$ 1,800	Accounts payable	$ 7,200
Receivables	10,800	Notes payable	3,472
Inventories	12,600	Accruals	2,520
Total current assets	$25,200	Total current liabilities	$13,192
Net fixed assets	21,600	Mortgage bonds	5,000
		Common stock	2,000
		Retained earnings	26,608
Total assets	$46,800	Total liabilities and equity	$46,800

Van Auken Lumber:
Income Statement for December 31, 1993
(Thousands of Dollars)

Sales	$36,000
Operating costs	30,783
Earnings before interest and taxes	$ 5,217
Interest	1,017
Earnings before taxes	$ 4,200
Taxes (40%)	1,680
Net Income	$ 2,520
Dividends (60%)	$1,512
Addition to retained earnings	$1,008

a. Assume that the company was operating at full capacity in 1993 with regard to all items *except* fixed assets; fixed assets in 1993 were being utilized to only 75 percent of capacity. By what percentage could 1994 sales increase over 1993 sales without the need for an increase in fixed assets?

b. Now suppose 1994 sales increase by 25 percent over 1993 sales. How much additional external capital will be required? Assume that Van Auken cannot sell any fixed assets. (Hint: Use the constant ratio method to develop a pro forma balance sheet and income statement as in Tables 15-3 and 15-4.) Assume that any required financing is borrowed as notes payable. Do not include any financing feedbacks, and use a pro forma income statement to determine the addition to retained earnings. (Another hint: Notes payable = $6,021.)

c. Use the financial statements developed in Part b to incorporate the financing feedback which results from the addition to notes payable. (That is, do the next financial statement iteration.) For purposes of this part, assume that the notes payable interest rate is 12 percent. What is the AFN for this iteration?

d. Suppose the industry average DSO and inventory turnover ratio are 90 days and 3.33, respectively, and that Van Auken Lumber matches these figures in 1994 and then uses the funds released to reduce equity. (It pays a special dividend out of retained earnings.) What would this do to the rate of return on year-end 1994 equity? Use the second-pass balance sheet and income statement as developed in Part c, and assume that the additional AFN amount calculated in that iteration is added to notes payable. (Hint: Notes payable is now $6,094.)

PROBLEMS

15-1 (Pro forma statements and ratios) Upton Computers makes bulk purchases of small computers, stocks them in conveniently located warehouses, and ships them to its chain of retail stores. Upton's balance sheet as of December 31, 1993, is shown here (millions of dollars):

Cash	$ 3.5	Accounts payable	$ 9.0
Receivables	26.0	Notes payable	18.0
Inventories	58.0	Accruals	8.5
Total current assets	$ 87.5	Total current liabilities	$ 35.5
Net fixed assets	35.0	Mortgage loan	6.0
		Common stock	15.0
		Retained earnings	66.0
Total assets	$122.5	Total liabilities and equity	$122.5

Sales for 1993 were $350 million, while net income for the year was $10.5 million. Upton paid dividends of $4.2 million to common stockholders. The firm is operating at full capacity. Assume that all ratios remain constant.

a. If sales are projected to increase by $70 million, or 20 percent, during 1994, use the AFN equation to determine Upton's projected external capital requirements.

b. Construct Upton's pro forma balance sheet for December 31, 1994. Assume that all external capital requirements are met by bank loans and are reflected in notes payable. Do not consider any financing feedback effects.

c. Now calculate the following ratios, based on your projected December 31, 1994, balance sheet. Upton's 1993 ratios and industry average ratios are shown here for comparison:

	Upton Computers		Industry Average
	12/31/94	12/31/93	12/31/93
Current ratio	_____	2.5×	3×
Debt/total assets	_____	33.9%	30%
Rate of return on equity	_____	13%	12%

d. Now assume that Upton grows by the same $70 million but that the growth is spread over 5 years—that is, that sales grow by $14 million each year. Do not consider any financing feedback effects.

(1) Calculate total additional financial requirements over the 5-year period. (Hint: Use 1993 ratios, $\Delta S = \$70$, but *total* sales for the 5-year period.)

(2) Construct a pro forma balance sheet as of December 31, 1998, using notes payable as the balancing item.

(3) Calculate the current ratio, total debt/total assets ratio, and rate of return on equity as of December 31, 1998. [Hint: Be sure to use *total sales*, which amount to $1,960 million, to calculate retained earnings but 1998 profits to calculate the rate of return on equity—that is, return on equity = (1998 profits)/(12/31/97 equity).]

e. Do the plans outlined in Parts b and/or d seem feasible to you? That is, do you think Upton could borrow the required capital, and would the company be raising the odds on its bankruptcy to an excessive level in the event of some temporary misfortune?

15-2 **(Additional funds needed)** Stevens Textile's 1993 financial statements are shown below.

Stevens Textile:
Balance Sheet as of December 31, 1993
(Thousands of Dollars)

Cash	$ 1,080	Accounts payable	$ 4,320
Receivables	6,480	Accruals	2,880
Inventories	9,000	Notes payable	2,100
Total current assets	$16,560	Total current liabilities	$ 9,300
Net fixed assets	12,600	Mortgage bonds	3,500
		Common stock	3,500
		Retained earnings	12,860
Total assets	$29,160	Total liabilities and equity	$29,160

Stevens Textile:
Income Statement for December 31, 1993
(Thousands of Dollars)

Sales	$36,000
Operating costs	32,440
Earnings before interest and taxes	$ 3,560
Interest	560
Earnings before taxes	$ 3,000
Taxes (40%)	1,200
Net Income	$ 1,800
Dividends (45%)	$810
Addition to retained earnings	$990

a. Suppose 1994 sales are projected to increase by 15 percent over 1993 sales. Determine the additional funds needed. Assume that the company was operating at full capacity in 1993, that it cannot sell off any of its fixed assets, and that any required financing will be borrowed as notes payable. Also, assume that assets, spontaneous liabilities, and operating costs are expected to increase by the same percentage as sales. Use the constant ratio method to develop a pro forma balance sheet and income statement for December 31, 1994. (Do not incorporate any financing feedback effects. Use the pro forma income statement to determine the addition to retained earnings.)

b. Use the financial statements developed in Part a to incorporate the financing feedback as a result of the addition to notes payable. (That is, do the next financial statement iteration.) For the purpose of this part, assume that the notes payable interest rate is 10 percent. What is the AFN for this iteration?

15-3 **(Additional funds needed)** Garlington Technologies Inc.'s 1993 financial statements are shown below.

Garlington Technologies Inc.:
Balance Sheet as of December 31, 1993

Cash	$ 180,000	Accounts payable	$ 360,000
Receivables	360,000	Notes payable	156,000
Inventories	720,000	Accruals	180,000
Total current assets	$1,260,000	Total current liabilities	$ 696,000
Fixed assets	1,440,000	Common stock	1,800,000
		Retained earnings	204,000
Total assets	$2,700,000	Total liabilities and equity	$2,700,000

Garlington Technologies Inc.:
Income Statement for
December 31, 1993

Sales		$3,600,000
Operating costs		3,279,720
EBIT		$ 320,280
Interest		20,280
EBT		$ 300,000
Taxes (40%)		120,000
Net Income		$ 180,000

Per Share Data:

Common stock price	$24.00
Earnings per share (EPS)	$1.80
Dividends per share (DPS)	$1.08

a. Suppose that in 1994 sales increase by 10 percent over 1993 sales and that 1994 DPS will increase to $1.12. Construct the pro forma financial statements using the constant ratio method. How much additional capital will be required? Assume the firm operated at full capacity in 1993. Do not include any financing feedbacks.

b. Now assume that 50 percent of the additional capital required will be financed by selling common stock and the remainder by borrowing as notes payable. Assume that the interest rate on notes payable is 13 percent. Do the next iteration of financial statements incorporating financing feedbacks. What is the AFN for this iteration?

c. If the profit margin were to remain at 5 percent and the dividend payout rate were to remain at 60 percent, at what growth rate in sales would the additional financing requirements be exactly zero? (Hint: Set AFN equal to zero and solve for g.)

15-4 (External financing requirements) The 1993 balance sheet and income statement for the Damon Company are shown below.

Damon Company:
Balance Sheet as of
December 31, 1993
(Thousands of Dollars)

Cash	$ 80		Accounts payable	$ 160
Accounts receivable	240		Accruals	40
Inventories	720		Notes payable	252
Total current assets	$1,040		Total current liabilities	$ 452
Fixed assets	3,200		Long-term debt	1,244
			Total debt	$1,696
			Common stock	1,605
			Retained earnings	939
Total assets	$4,240		Total liabilities and equity	$4,240

Damon Company: Income Statement for December 31, 1993 (Thousands of Dollars)

Sales	$8,000
Operating costs	7,450
EBIT	$ 550
Interest	150
EBT	$ 400
Taxes (40%)	160
Net income	$ 240

Per Share Data

Common stock price	$16.96
Earnings per share (EPS)	$1.60
Dividends per share (DPS)	$1.04

a.   The firm operated at full capacity in 1993. It expects sales to increase by 20 percent during 1994 and expects 1994 dividends per share to increase to $1.10. Use the constant ratio method to determine how much outside financing is required, developing the firm's pro forma balance sheet and income statement, and use AFN as the balancing item.

b.   If the firm must maintain a current ratio of 2.3 and a debt ratio of 40 percent, how much financing, after the first pass, will be obtained using notes payable, long-term debt, and common stock?

c.   Make the second-pass financial statements incorporating financing feedbacks, using the ratios in Part b. Assume that the interest rate on debt averages 10 percent.

15-5   **(Long-term financing needed)**   At year-end 1993, total assets for Bertin Inc. were $1.2 million and accounts payable were $375,000. Sales, which in 1993 were $2.5 million, are expected to increase by 25 percent in 1994. Total assets and accounts payable are proportional to sales and that relationship will be maintained. Bertin typically uses no current liabilities other than accounts payable. Common stock amounted to $425,000 in 1993, and retained earnings were $295,000. Bertin plans to sell new common stock in the amount of $75,000. The firm's profit margin on sales is 6 percent; 40 percent of earnings will be paid out as dividends.

a.   What was Bertin's total debt in 1993?

b.   How much new, long-term debt financing will be needed in 1994? (Hint: AFN − New stock = New long-term debt.) Do not consider any financing feedback effects.

15-6   **(Additional funds needed)**   The Booth Company's sales are forecasted to increase from $1,000 in 1993 to $2,000 in 1994. Here is the December 31, 1993, balance sheet:

Cash	$ 100	Accounts payable	$ 50
Accounts receivable	200	Notes payable	150
Inventories	200	Accruals	50
Net fixed assets	500	Long-term debt	400
		Common stock	100
		Retained earnings	250
Total assets	$1,000	Total liabilities and equity	$1,000

Booth's fixed assets were used to only 50 percent of capacity during 1993, but its current assets were at their proper levels. All assets except fixed assets increase at the same rate as sales, and fixed assets would also increase at the same rate if the current excess capacity did not exist. Booth's after-tax profit margin is forecasted to be 5 percent, and its payout

ratio will be 60 percent. What is Booth's additional funds needed (AFN) for the coming year? Ignore financing feedback effects.

Work problem 15-7 only if you are using the computer problem diskette.

15-7 (Forecasting)   Roussakis Industries' 1993 financial statements are shown below.

Roussakis Industries:
Balance Sheet as of December 31, 1993
(Millions of Dollars)

Cash	$ 4.0	Accounts payable	$ 8.0
Receivables	12.0	Notes payable	5.0
Inventories	16.0	Total current liabilities	$13.0
Total current assets	$32.0	Long-term debt	12.0
Net fixed assets	40.0	Common stock	20.0
		Retained earnings	27.0
Total assets	$72.0	Total liabilities and equity	$72.0

Roussakis Industries:
Income Statement for December 31, 1993
(Millions of Dollars)

Sales	$80.0
Operating costs	71.3
EBIT	$ 8.7
Interest	2.0
EBT	$ 6.7
Taxes (40%)	2.7
Net income	$ 4.0
Dividends (40%)	$1.60
Addition to retained earnings	$2.40

Assume that the firm has no excess capacity in fixed assets, that the average interest rate for debt is 12 percent, and that the projected annual sales growth rate for the next 5 years is 15 percent.

a.   Roussakis plans to finance its additional funds needed with 50 percent short-term debt and 50 percent long-term debt. Using the constant ratio method, prepare the pro forma financial statements for 1994 through 1998, and then determine (1) additional funds needed, (2) the current ratio, (3) the debt ratio, and (4) the return on equity.

b.   Sales growth could be 5 percentage points above or below the projected 15 percent. Determine the effect of such variances on AFN and the key ratios.

c.   Perform an analysis to determine the sensitivity of AFN and the key ratios for 1998 to changes in the dividend payout ratio as specified in the following, assuming sales grow at a constant 15 percent. What happens to AFN if the dividend payout ratio (1) is raised from 40 to 70 percent or (2) is lowered from 40 to 20 percent?

M I N I
C A S E

(Financial forecasting)   Sue Wilson, the new financial manager of Northwest Chemicals (NWC), an Oregon producer of specialized chemicals for use in fruit orchards, must prepare a financial forecast for 1994. NWC's 1993 sales were $2 billion, and the marketing department is forecasting a 25 percent increase for 1994. Sue thinks the company was operating

at full capacity in 1993, but she is not sure about this. The 1993 financial statements, plus some other data, are given in Table MC15-1.

Assume that you were recently hired as Sue's assistant, and your first major task is to help her develop the forecast. She asked you to begin by answering the following set of questions.

a. Assume (1) that NWC was operating at full capacity in 1993 with respect to all assets, (2) that all assets must grow proportionally with sales, (3) that accounts payable and accruals will also grow in proportion to sales, and (4) that the 1993 profit margin and dividend payout will be maintained. Under these conditions, what will the company's financial requirements be for the coming year? Use the AFN equation to answer this question.

b. Now estimate the 1994 financial requirements using the constant ratio approach, making an initial forecast plus one additional "pass" to determine the effects of "financing feedbacks." Assume (1) that each type of asset, as well as payables, accruals, and fixed and variable costs, grow at the same rate as sales; (2) that the payout ratio is held constant at 30 percent; (3) that external funds needed are financed 50 percent by notes payable and 50 percent by long-term debt (no new common stock will be issued); and (4) that all debt carries an interest rate of 8 percent.

c. Why do the two methods produce somewhat different AFN forecasts? Which method provides the more accurate forecast?

d. Calculate NWC's forecasted ratios, and compare them with the company's 1993 ratios and with the industry averages. How does NWC compare with the average firm in its industry, and is the company expected to improve during the coming year?

e. Suppose you now learn that NWC's 1993 receivables and inventories were in line with required levels, given the firm's credit and inventory policies, but that excess capacity existed with regard to fixed assets. Specifically, fixed assets were operated at only 75 percent of capacity.

   (1) What level of sales could have existed in 1993 with the available fixed assets? What would the fixed assets/sales ratio have been if NWC had been operating at full capacity?

   (2) How would the existence of excess capacity in fixed assets affect the additional funds needed during 1994?

f. Without actually working out the numbers, how would you expect the ratios to change in the situation where excess capacity in fixed assets exists? Explain your reasoning.

g. Based on comparisons between NWC's days sales outstanding (DSO) and inventory turnover ratios with the industry average figures, does it appear that NWC is operating efficiently with respect to its inventories and accounts receivable? If the company were able to bring these ratios into line with the industry averages, what effect would this have on its AFN and its financial ratios? (Note: Inventories and receivables will be discussed in detail in Chapter 18.)

h. The relationship between sales and the various types of assets is important in financial forecasting. The constant ratio approach, under the assumption that each asset item grows at the same rate as sales, leads to an AFN forecast that is reasonably close to the forecast using the AFN equation. Explain how each of the following factors would affect the accuracy of financial forecasts based on the AFN equation: (1) excess capacity, (2) base stocks of assets, such as shoes in a shoe store, (3) economies of scale in the use of assets, and (4) lumpy assets.

TABLE MC15-1

FINANCIAL
STATEMENTS AND
OTHER DATA ON
NWC (MILLIONS OF
DOLLARS)

A. 1993 Balance Sheet

Cash and securities	$ 20	Accounts payable and accruals	$ 100
Accounts receivable	240	Notes payable	100
Inventories	240	Total current liabilities	$ 200
Total current assets	$ 500	Long-term debt	100
Net fixed assets	500	Common stock	500
		Retained earnings	200
Total assets	$ 1,000	Total liabilities and equity	$1,000

B. 1993 Income Statement

Sales	$2,000.00
Less: Variable costs	1,200.00
Fixed costs	700.00
Earnings before interest and taxes	$ 100.00
Interest	16.00
Earnings before taxes	$ 84.00
Taxes (40%)	33.60
Net income	$ 50.40
Dividends (30%)	15.12
Addition to retained earnings	$ 35.28

C. Key Ratios

	NWC	Industry
Basic earning power	10.00%	20.00%
Profit margin	2.52	4.00
Return on equity	7.20	15.60
Days sales outstanding (360 days)	43.20 days	32.00 days
Inventory turnover	8.33×	11.00×
Fixed assets turnover	4.00	5.00
Total assets turnover	2.00	2.50
Debt/assets	30.00%	36.00%
Times interest earned	6.25×	9.40×
Current ratio	2.50	3.00
Payout ratio	30.00%	30.00%

i. (1) How could regression analysis be used to detect the presence of the situations described above and then to improve the financial forecasts? Plot a graph of the following data, which is for a typical well-managed company in NWC's industry, to illustrate your answer.

Year	Sales	Inventories
1991	$1,280	$118
1992	1,600	138
1993	2,000	162
1994 (est.)	2,500	192

(2) On the same graph that plots the above data, draw a line which shows how the regression line must appear to justify the use of the AFN formula and the constant ratio forecasting procedure. As a part of your answer, show the growth rate in inventories that results from a 10 percent increase in sales from a sales level of (a) $200 and (b) $2,000 based on both the actual regression line and a *hypothetical* regression line which is linear and which goes through the origin.

j. How would changes in these items affect the AFN? (1) The dividend payout ratio, (2) the profit margin, (3) the capital intensity ratio, and (4) NWC begins buying from its suppliers on terms which permit it to pay after 60 days rather than after 30 days. (Consider each item separately and hold all other things constant.)

SELECTED ADDITIONAL REFERENCES AND CASES

The heart of successful financial planning is the sales forecast. On this key subject, see

Pan, Judy, Donald R. Nichols, and O. Maurice Joy, "Sales Forecasting Practices of Large U.S. Industrial Firms," *Financial Management,* Fall 1977, 72–77.

Pappas, James L., and Mark Hirschey, *Managerial Economics* (Hinsdale, Ill.: Dryden Press, 1989).

Computer modeling is becoming increasingly important. For general references, see

Carleton, Willard T., Charles L. Dick, Jr., and David H. Downes, "Financial Policy Models: Theory and Practice," *Journal of Finance,* December 1973, 691–709.

Francis, Jack Clark, and Dexter R. Rowell, "A Simultaneous Equation Model of the Firm for Financial Analysis and Planning," *Financial Management,* Spring 1978, 29–44.

Grinyer, P. H., and J. Wooller, *Corporate Models Today—A New Tool for Financial Management* (London: Institute of Chartered Accountants, 1978).

Pappas, James L., and George P. Huber, "Probabilistic Short-Term Financial Planning," *Financial Management,* Autumn 1973, 36–44.

Traenkle, J. W., E. B. Cox, and J. A. Bullard, *The Use of Financial Models in Business* (New York: Financial Executives' Research Foundation, 1975).

Considerable effort has been expended to develop integrated financial planning models that identify optimal policies. For one example, see

Myers, Stewart C., and Gerald A. Pogue, "A Programming Approach to Corporate Financial Management," *Journal of Finance,* May 1974, 579–599.

For a recent article on control, see

Bierman, Harold, "Beyond Cash Flow ROI," *Midland Corporate Finance Journal,* Winter 1988, 36–39.

The Brigham-Gapenski casebook contains the following applicable cases:

Case 37, "Space-Age Materials, Inc.," which focuses on using the percentage of sales forecasting method to forecast future financing requirements.

Case 38, "Automated Banking Management, Inc.," which is similar to Case 37.

SHORT-TERM PLANNING AND BUDGETING

O range Springs, near Ocala, has perhaps the best water in Florida, and it is also one of the largest privately owned springs in the state. Recognizing the spring's potential as a source of bottled water, Roger Wood, a real estate developer, purchased the property in 1986, founded Florida Orange Springs Inc. (FOS) in 1989, and entered the rapidly growing bottled-water business.

FOS targeted three market segments: (1) bulk sales to large, established bottlers for bottling under those bottlers' own labels, (2) retail sales in 5-gallon containers to offices and homes in the north central Florida area, and (3) wholesale sales to supermarkets and convenience stores. Bulk sales were neither very profitable nor very dependable, but they provided badly needed cash flow, and they could be made without much capital investment. Retail sales, on the other hand, were both profitable and stable, and FOS's business plan called for "locking up" that segment of the market in the Jacksonville-Gainesville-Ocala area before the "majors" could move in and preempt it. FOS was counting on the wholesale market for additional growth, which was where most industry growth was occurring.

Wood purchased the spring and 85 surrounding acres with his own funds (and a mortgage from the people who sold him the property), and he obtained additional capital from 10 private investors. That money was sufficient to construct a bottling plant and to get the company started. However, FOS experienced an unexpected capital shortage that delayed full implementation of its business plan and even threatened the company's future.

The marketing program was successful—FOS was signing up doctors, lawyers, and homeowners for its retail business, and it was close to closing deals

with such major supermarkets as Publix, the largest grocery chain in Florida. The deal with Publix stipulated that FOS bottle water for Publix under Publix's own label, and the company was seeking other private-label business as well as promoting its own brand name. But instead of solving the cash flow problem, new business was making FOS's financial problem worse!

First, every time a new retail customer signed on, FOS had to buy and install a water cooler in the customer's office and provide a supply of full 5-gallon bottles at an out-of-pocket cost of about $300 per new customer. This money would be returned, plus a profit, over time as the customer paid monthly bills, but in the meantime the sale caused FOS to experience a cash shortfall. Sales to Publix and other potentially large-scale customers created a similar problem. Such customers dealt only with suppliers that could provide large quantities of product on short notice. This meant that FOS had to carry a large inventory of bottled water, and this required an investment in labor and materials (bottles and cases) long before sales were made and even longer before receivables created by sales were collected.

So, although FOS thought it was adequately financed, it was not, because it had not recognized fully the investment in working capital needed to support growing sales. FOS was eventually able to obtain the capital it needed, but its financing difficulties delayed implementation of the business plan by a full year. Many other businesses are less fortunate and are literally pulled under by the combination of working capital requirements and inadequate capital.

In the next three chapters, we will discuss short-term planning, budgeting, and management. At the end, you will have an appreciation of how firms plan for, manage, and finance their working capital needs. As you read these chapters, remember the situation faced by Florida Orange Springs. In particular, recall the importance of short-term planning and how good planning can contribute significantly to the success of a company.

In Chapter 15 we discussed long-term financial planning, which is how firms chart their strategic directions and plan for the long run. Although long-term financial planning is an essential part of good management, such planning does not include the detail necessary for businesses to operate efficiently in the short run. Thus, it is possible for a firm with an excellent long-term plan to go bankrupt before it gets the chance to implement its plan. In this chapter, we discuss short-term planning and budgeting. In essence, short-term planning involves making sure that the firm has the short-term assets—primarily cash and inventories—to conduct day-to-day operations. If cash is not available to pay employees, suppliers, and tax collectors, or if inventories are not on hand to make or sell products, the company will grind to a halt.

SHORT-TERM PLANNING TERMINOLOGY

It is useful to begin our discussion by reviewing some basic definitions and concepts:

1. *Working capital,* sometimes called *gross working capital,* simply refers to current assets.

2. *Net working capital* is defined as current assets minus current liabilities.

3. The *current ratio,* which was discussed in Chapter 2, is calculated by dividing current assets by current liabilities, and it is intended to measure a firm's liquidity. However, a high current ratio does not ensure that a firm will have the cash required to meet its needs. If inventories cannot be sold, or if receivables cannot be collected in a timely manner, then the apparent safety reflected in a high current ratio could be illusory.

4. The *quick ratio,* or *acid test,* also attempts to measure liquidity, and it is found by subtracting inventories from current assets and then dividing by current liabilities. The quick ratio removes inventories from current assets because they are the least liquid of current assets, so it is an "acid test" of a company's ability to meet its current obligations.

5. The best and most comprehensive picture of a firm's liquidity position is obtained by examining its *cash budget.* This statement, which forecasts cash inflows and outflows, focuses on what really counts, the firm's ability to generate sufficient cash inflows to meet its required cash outflows. Cash budgeting will be discussed in detail later in the chapter.

6. *Working capital policy* refers to the firm's basic policies regarding (1) target levels for each category of current assets and (2) how current assets will be financed.

7. *Working capital management* involves the administration, within policy guidelines, of current assets and current liabilities.

The term *working capital* originated with the old Yankee peddler, who would load up his wagon with goods and then go off on his route to peddle his wares. The merchandise was called working capital because it was what he actually sold, or "turned over," to produce his profits. The wagon and horse were his fixed assets. He generally owned the horse and wagon, so they were financed with "equity" capital, but he borrowed the funds to buy the merchandise. These borrowings were called *working capital loans,* and they had to be repaid after each trip to demonstrate to the bank that the credit was sound. If the peddler was able to repay the loan, then the bank would make another loan, and banks that followed this procedure were said to be employing sound banking practices.

Table 16-1 contains three balance sheets for Allied Food Products. According to the definitions given above, Allied's December 31, 1993, working capital was $1,000 million, and its net working capital was $1,000 − $310 = $690 million. Also, Allied's year-end 1993 current ratio was 3.23 and its quick ratio was 1.24.

TABLE 16-1		12/31/93 (Historical)	9/30/94 (Projected)	12/31/94 (Projected)
ALLIED FOOD				
PRODUCTS:	Cash	$ 10	$ 15	$ 11
HISTORICAL AND	Accounts receivable	375	562	412
PROJECTED BALANCE	Inventories	615	922	677
SHEETS (MILLIONS OF	Total current assets	$1,000	$1,499	$1,100
DOLLARS)	Net plant and equipment	1,000	1,075	1,100
	Total assets	$2,000	$2,574	$2,200
	Accounts payable	$ 60	$ 90	$ 66
	Notes payable	110	451	140
	Accruals	140	210	154
	Total current liabilities	$ 310	$ 751	$ 360
	Long-term bonds	754	784	784
	Total debt	$1,064	$1,535	$1,144
	Preferred stock	$ 40	$ 40	$ 40
	Common stock	$ 130	$ 189	$ 189
	Retained earnings	766	810	827
	Total common equity	$ 896	$ 999	$1,016
	Total liabilities and equity	$2,000	$2,574	$2,200
	Current ratio	3.23	2.00	3.06
	Quick ratio	1.24	0.77	1.18

It is useful to distinguish between those current liabilities which are specifically used to finance current assets and those current liabilities which represent (1) current maturities of long-term debt; (2) financing associated with a construction program which will, after the project is completed, be funded with the proceeds of a long-term security issue; or (3) the use of short-term debt to finance fixed assets. Note that the total current liabilities of $310 million at the end of 1993 includes the current portion of long-term debt, which was $20 million. This account is unaffected by changes in working capital policy because it is a function of past long-term debt financing decisions. Thus, even though we define long-term debt coming due in the next accounting period as a current liability, it is not a working capital decision variable. Similarly, if Allied were building a new canning factory and initially financed the construction with a short-term loan which would be replaced later with mortgage bonds, the construction loan would not be considered part of working capital management. Although such accounts are not part of Allied's working capital decision process, they cannot be ignored, and they must be taken into account when Allied's managers construct the cash budget and appraise the firm's liquidity.

SELF-TEST QUESTIONS

Why is the quick ratio also called an acid test?

Where did the term "working capital" originate?

THE REQUIREMENT FOR EXTERNAL WORKING CAPITAL FINANCING

Food processing is a seasonal business. Most of Allied's output consists of noncitrus fruits and vegetables, and the harvest season for these crops generally runs from May through September. Thus, at the end of September Allied's inventories are significantly higher than they are at the end of the calendar year. Allied offers significant sales incentives to wholesalers during August and September in an effort to move inventories out of its warehouses and into those of its customers; otherwise, inventories would be even higher than shown in Table 16-1. Because of this sales surge, Allied's receivables are also much higher at the end of September than at the end of December.

Consider what will happen to Allied's current assets and current liabilities from December 31, 1993, to September 30, 1994. Current assets increase from $1,000 million to $1,499 million, or by $499 million. Since increases on the asset side of the balance sheet must be financed by identical increases on the liabilities and equity side, the firm must raise $499 million to meet its increase in working capital over the period. However, the higher volume of purchases, plus labor expenditures associated with increased production, will cause accounts payable and accruals to increase spontaneously from $60 + $140 = $200 million to $90 + $210 = $300 million, or by $100 million. This leaves a projected $499 − $100 = $399 million current asset financing requirement, which Allied will finance primarily by a $341 million increase in notes payable. Therefore, for September 30, 1994, notes payable are projected to rise to $451 million. Note that Allied's current ratio falls from 3.23 to 2.00, and its quick ratio declines from 1.24 to 0.77, from December to September because most of the funds invested in current assets come from current liabilities.

The fluctuations in Allied's working capital position shown in Table 16-1 result from seasonal variations. Similar fluctuations in working capital requirements, and hence in financing needs, also occur during business cycles—working capital needs typically decline during recessions but increase during booms. For food companies, seasonal fluctuations are much greater than business cycle fluctuations, but for other companies—for example, appliance manufacturers—cyclical fluctuations are larger.

SELF-TEST QUESTION

Describe how both seasonal and cyclical sales fluctuations influence current asset levels and financing requirements.

THE CASH CONVERSION CYCLE

As we noted above, the concept of working capital management originated with the old Yankee peddler, who would borrow to buy inventory, sell the inventory to pay off the bank loan, and then repeat the cycle. That general concept has been applied to more complex businesses, and the cash flow cycle concept is used for analyzing the effectiveness of a firm's working capital management.

We can illustrate the concept with data from Real Time Computer Corporation (RTC), which in early 1993 introduced a new super-minicomputer that can perform 500 million instructions per second and that will sell for $250,000. The effects of this new product on RTC's working capital position were analyzed in terms of the following five steps:

1. RTC will order and then receive the materials it needs to produce the 100 computers that are expected to be sold. Because RTC and most other firms purchase materials on credit, this transaction will create an account payable. However, the purchase will have no immediate cash flow effect.

2. Labor will be used to convert the materials into finished computers. However, wages will not be fully paid at the time the work is done, so accrued wages will build up.

3. The finished computers will be sold, but on credit, so sales will create receivables, not immediate cash inflows.

4. At some point during the cycle, RTC must pay off its accounts payable and accrued wages. Because these payments will be made before RTC has collected cash from its receivables, a net cash outflow will occur, and this outflow must be financed.

5. The cycle will be completed when RTC's receivables have been collected. At that time, the company will be in a position to pay off the credit that was used to finance production, and it can then repeat the cycle.

The *cash conversion cycle* model, which focuses on the length of time between when the company makes payments and when it receives cash inflows, formalizes the steps outlined above.[1] The following terms are used in the model:

1. *Inventory conversion period,* which is the average length of time required to convert materials into finished goods and then to sell those goods. Note that the inventory conversion period is calculated by dividing inventory by sales per day. For example, if average inventories are $2 million and annual sales are $10 million, then the inventory conversion period is 72 days:

$$\text{Inventory conversion period} = \frac{\text{Inventory}}{\text{Sales per day}}$$

$$= \frac{\$2,000,000}{\$10,000,000/360}$$

$$= 72 \text{ days.}$$

---

[1]See Verlyn D. Richards and Eugene J. Laughlin, "A Cash Conversion Cycle Approach to Liquidity Analysis," *Financial Management,* Spring 1980, 32–38. A similar approach was set forth earlier by Lawrence J. Gitman, "Estimating Corporate Liquidity Requirements: A Simplified Approach," *The Financial Review,* 1974, 79–88.

Thus, it takes an average of 72 days to convert materials into finished goods and then to sell those goods.

2. *Receivables collection period,* which is the average length of time required to convert the firm's receivables into cash, that is, to collect cash following a sale. The receivables collection period is also called the days sales outstanding (DSO), and it is calculated by dividing accounts receivable by the average credit sales per day. If receivables are $666,667 and sales are $10 million, the receivables collection period is

$$\frac{\text{Receivables}}{\text{collection period}} = \text{DSO} = \frac{\text{Receivables}}{\text{Sales}/360}$$

$$= \frac{\$666,667}{\$10 \text{ million}/360} = 24 \text{ days.}$$

Thus, it takes 24 days after a sale to convert the receivables into cash.

3. *Payables deferral period,* which is the average length of time between the purchase of materials and labor and the payment of cash for them. For example, if the firm on average has 30 days to pay for labor and materials, if its cost of goods sold are $8 million per year, and if its accounts payable average $666,667, then its payables deferral period can be calculated as follows:

$$\text{Payables deferral period} = \text{Payables}/\text{Credit purchases per day}$$
$$= \text{Payables}/(\text{Cost of goods sold}/360)$$

$$= \$666,667/(\$8,000,000/360)$$
$$= 30 \text{ days.}$$

The calculated figure is consistent with the stated 30 day payment period.

4. *Cash conversion cycle,* which nets out the three periods just defined and thus equals the length of time between the firm's actual cash expenditures to pay for productive resources and its own cash receipts from the sale of products. The cash conversion cycle thus equals the average length of time a dollar is tied up in current assets.

We can now use these definitions to analyze the cash conversion cycle. First, the concept is diagrammed in Figure 16-1. Each component is given a number, and the cash conversion cycle can be expressed by the following equation:

F I G U R E   1 6 - 1   T H E   C A S H   C O N V E R S I O N   C Y C L E   M O D E L

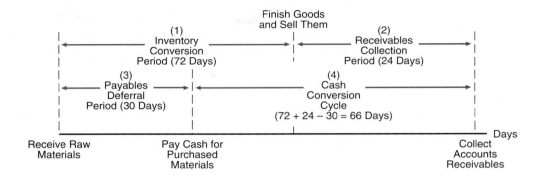

$$
\begin{array}{ccccccc}
(1) & + & (2) & - & (3) & = & (4) \\
\text{Inventory} & & \text{Receivables} & & \text{Payables} & & \text{Cash} \\
\text{conversion} & + & \text{collection} & - & \text{deferral} & = & \text{conversion.} \\
\text{period} & & \text{period} & & \text{period} & & \text{cycle}
\end{array}
\qquad \text{(16-1)}
$$

To illustrate, suppose it takes Real Time an average of 72 days to convert raw materials to computers and then sell them, and another 24 days to collect on receivables. However, 30 days normally elapse between receipt of raw materials and payment for them. In this case, the cash conversion cycle would be 66 days:

$$72 \text{ days} + 24 \text{ days} - 30 \text{ days} = 66 \text{ days}.$$

To look at it another way,

$$
\begin{array}{ccc}
\text{Receipts delay} & - \text{ Payment delay} & = \text{ Net delay} \\
(72 \text{ days} + 24 \text{ days}) - & 30 \text{ days} & = \ \ 66 \text{ days}.
\end{array}
$$

Given these data, RTC knows when it starts producing a computer that it will have to finance the manufacturing costs for a 66-day period. The firm's goal should be to shorten its cash conversion cycle as much as possible without hurting operations. This would improve profits, because the longer the cash conversion cycle, the greater the need for external financing, and such financing has a cost.

The cash conversion cycle can be shortened (1) by reducing the inventory conversion period by processing and selling goods more quickly, (2) by reducing the receivables collection period by speeding up collections, or (3) by lengthening

the payables deferral period by slowing down its own payments. To the extent that these actions can be taken *without increasing costs or depressing sales,* they should be carried out.

We can illustrate the benefits of shortening the cash conversion cycle by looking again at Real Time Computer Corporation. Suppose RTC must spend $200,000 on materials and labor to produce one computer, and it takes 3 days to produce a computer. Thus, it must invest $200,000/3 = $66,667 for each day's production. This investment must be financed for 66 days—the length of the cash conversion cycle—so the company's working capital financing needs will be 66 × $66,667 = $4.4 million. If RTC could reduce the cash conversion cycle to 56 days by deferring payment of its accounts payable an additional 10 days, or by speeding up either the production process or the collection of its receivables, it could reduce its working capital financing requirements by about $667,000. We see, then, that actions which affect the inventory conversion period, the receivables collection period, and the payables deferral period all affect the cash conversion cycle, hence they influence the firm's need for current assets and current asset financing. You should keep the cash conversion cycle concept in mind as you go through the remainder of this chapter and the other chapters on working capital management.

SELF-TEST QUESTIONS

What steps are involved in estimating the cash conversion cycle?

What do the following terms mean?
    (1) Inventory conversion period.
    (2) Receivables collection period.
    (3) Payables deferral period.

What is the cash conversion cycle model? How can it be used to improve current asset management?

WORKING CAPITAL INVESTMENT AND FINANCING POLICIES

Working capital policy involves two basic questions: (1) What is the appropriate level for current assets, both in total and by specific accounts, and (2) how should current assets be financed?

ALTERNATIVE CURRENT ASSET INVESTMENT POLICIES

Figure 16-2 shows three alternative policies regarding the total amount of current assets carried. Essentially, these policies differ in that different amounts of current assets are carried to support any given level of sales. The line with the steepest slope represents a *relaxed current asset investment (or "fat cat") policy,* where relatively large amounts of cash, marketable securities, and inventories are carried

FIGURE 16-2

ALTERNATIVE
CURRENT ASSET
INVESTMENT POLICIES
(MILLIONS OF
DOLLARS)

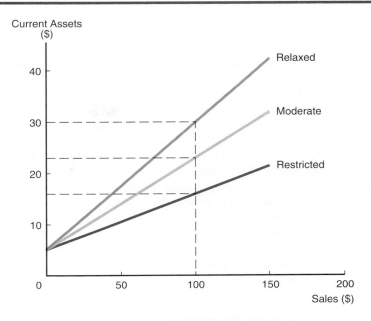

Policy	Current Assets to Support Sales of $100
Relaxed	$30
Moderate	23
Restricted	16

Note: The sales/current assets relationship is shown here as being linear, but the relationship is often curvilinear.

and where sales are stimulated by the use of a credit policy that provides liberal financing to customers and a corresponding high level of receivables. Conversely, with the *restricted current asset investment (or "lean-and-mean") policy*, the holdings of cash, securities, inventories, and receivables are minimized. The *moderate current asset investment policy* is between the two extremes.

Under conditions of certainty—when sales, costs, lead times, payment periods, and so on, are known for sure—all firms would hold only minimal levels of current assets. Any larger amounts would increase the need for working capital financing without a corresponding increase in profits, while any smaller holdings would involve late payments to labor and suppliers and lost sales due to inventory shortages and an overly restrictive credit policy.

However, the picture changes when uncertainty is introduced. Here the firm requires some minimum amount of cash and inventories based on expected payments, expected sales, expected order lead times, and so on, plus additional amounts, or *safety stocks,* which enable it to deal with departures from the expected values. Similarly, accounts receivable levels are determined by credit terms,

and the tougher the credit terms, the lower the receivables for any given level of sales. With a restricted current asset investment policy, the firm would hold minimal levels of safety stocks for cash and inventories, and it would have a tight credit policy even though this meant running the risk of losing sales. A restricted, lean-and-mean current asset investment policy generally provides the highest expected return on investment, but it entails the greatest risk, while the reverse is true under a relaxed policy. The moderate policy falls in between the two extremes in terms of expected risk and return.

In terms of the cash conversion cycle, a restricted investment policy would tend to reduce the inventory conversion and receivables collection periods, hence resulting in a relatively short cash conversion cycle. Conversely, a relaxed policy would create higher levels of inventories and receivables, longer inventory conversion and receivables collection periods, and a relatively long cash conversion cycle. A moderate policy would produce a cash conversion cycle which falls between the two extremes.

As we will see in the next two chapters, which focus on working capital management and financing, companies can often reduce current assets without adversely affecting sales or operating costs by using just-in-time inventory procedures and the like. Also, the profit penalty for holding current assets is dependent on how they are financed and the prevailing level of interest rates. Therefore, current asset investment policy is never set in isolation — it is always established jointly with the firm's current asset financing policy, which we consider next.

ALTERNATIVE CURRENT ASSET FINANCING POLICIES

Most businesses experience seasonal and/or cyclical fluctuations. For example, construction firms have peaks in the spring and summer, retailers peak around Christmas, and the manufacturers that supply both construction companies and retailers follow similar patterns. Similarly, virtually all businesses must build up current assets when the economy is strong, but they then sell off inventories and have net reductions of receivables when the economy slacks off. Still, current assets rarely drop to zero, and this realization has led to the development of the idea of *permanent current assets*. Applying this idea to Allied Food Products, Table 16-1 (presented earlier) suggests that, at this stage in its life, Allied's total assets are growing at a 10 percent rate, from $2,000 million to $2,200 million, but seasonal fluctuations push total assets up to $2,574 million during the firm's peak season. Thus, at the end of September, Allied's total assets of $2,574 million consist of about $2,150 million of permanent assets (9/12ths of the increase from $2,000 to $2,200 million) and $2,574 − $2,150 = $424 million of seasonal, or *temporary, current assets*. Allied's temporary current assets fluctuate from zero during the slow season in March to $424 million during the peak season in September. The manner in which the permanent and temporary current assets are financed is called the firm's *current asset financing policy.*

Maturity Matching, or "Self-Liquidating," Approach. The *maturity matching,* or *"self-liquidating," approach* calls for matching asset and liability maturities

as shown in Panel a of Figure 16-3. This strategy minimizes the risk that the firm will be unable to pay off its maturing obligations. To illustrate, suppose Allied borrows on a 1-year basis and uses the funds obtained to build and equip a plant. Cash flows from the plant (profits plus depreciation) would not be sufficient to pay off the loan at the end of only one year, so the loan would have to be renewed. If for some reason the lender refused to renew the loan, then Allied would have problems. Had the plant been financed with long-term debt, however, the required loan payments would have been better matched with cash flows from profits and depreciation, and the problem of renewal would not have arisen.

At the limit, a firm could attempt to match exactly the maturity structure of its assets and liabilities. Inventory expected to be sold in 30 days could be financed with a 30-day bank loan; a machine expected to last for 5 years could be financed by a 5-year loan; a 20-year building could be financed by a 20-year mortgage bond; and so forth. Actually, of course, two factors prevent this exact maturity matching: (1) there is uncertainty about the lives of assets, and (2) some common equity must be used, and common equity has no maturity. To illustrate the uncertainty factor, Allied might finance inventories with a 30-day loan, expecting to sell the inventories and to use the cash generated to retire the loan. But if sales were slow, the cash would not be forthcoming, and the use of short-term credit could end up causing a problem. Still, if Allied makes an attempt to match asset and liability maturities, we would define this as a maturity matching current asset financing policy.

Aggressive Approach.   Panel b of Figure 16-3 illustrates the situation for a relatively aggressive firm which finances all of its fixed assets with long-term capital but part of its permanent current assets with short-term, nonspontaneous credit. A look back at Table 16-1 will show that Allied actually follows this strategy. Allied has $1,075 million in permanent current assets projected for September 1994, so its temporary current assets must be $1,499 − $1,075 = $424 million.[2] However, the firm has $451 million in notes payable as well as some temporary financing from peak levels of accounts payable and accruals. Thus, Allied's level of temporary financing exceeds its level of temporary current assets, so some part of its permanent assets are financed with temporary capital.

Returning to Figure 16-3, note that we used the term "relatively" in the title for Panel b, because there can be different *degrees* of aggressiveness. For example, the dashed line in Panel b could have been drawn *below* the line designating fixed assets, indicating that all of the permanent current assets and part of the fixed assets were financed with short-term credit; this would be a highly aggressive, extremely nonconservative position, and the firm would be very much subject to dangers from rising interest rates as well as to loan renewal problems. However, short-term debt is often cheaper than long-term debt, and some firms are willing to sacrifice safety for the chance of higher profits.

---

[2]We estimated in an earlier section that as of September, Allied Food Products had $2,150 million of permanent assets, and of that amount, $1,075 million is fixed assets. Therefore, permanent current assets = $2,150 million − $1,075 million = $1,075 million.

FIGURE 16-3

ALTERNATIVE
CURRENT ASSET
FINANCING POLICIES

a. Maturity Matching Approach

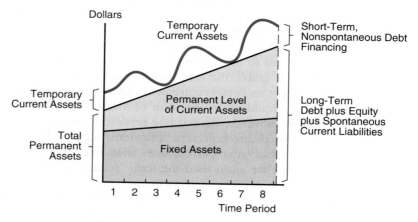

Dollars

Temporary
Current Assets

Short-Term,
Nonspontaneous Debt
Financing

Temporary
Current Assets

Permanent Level
of Current Assets

Long-Term
Debt plus Equity
plus Spontaneous
Current Liabilities

Total
Permanent
Assets

Fixed Assets

1 2 3 4 5 6 7 8

Time Period

b. Relatively Aggressive Approach

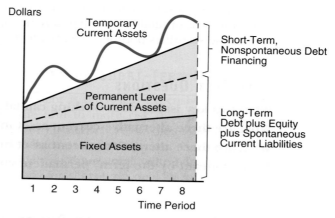

Dollars

Temporary
Current Assets

Short-Term,
Nonspontaneous Debt
Financing

Permanent Level
of Current Assets

Long-Term
Debt plus Equity
plus Spontaneous
Current Liabilities

Fixed Assets

1 2 3 4 5 6 7 8

Time Period

c. Relatively Conservative Approach

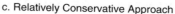
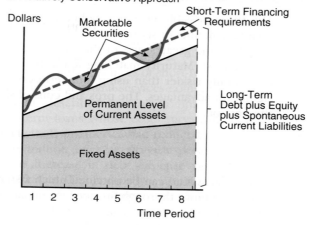

Dollars

Short-Term Financing
Requirements

Marketable
Securities

Permanent Level
of Current Assets

Long-Term
Debt plus Equity
plus Spontaneous
Current Liabilities

Fixed Assets

1 2 3 4 5 6 7 8

Time Period

depressed by the increase in short-term rates, but other companies were even less fortunate — they simply could not pay the rising interest charges, and this forced them into bankruptcy.

SELF-TEST QUESTIONS

Which of the three alternative current asset financing policies uses the most short-term debt?

What are some advantages of short-term debt over long-term debt as a source of capital?

What are some disadvantages of short-term debt?

THE CASH BUDGET

Perhaps the most important element of short-term planning is the estimate of the firm's cash requirements. To begin, the firm forecasts both fixed asset and inventory requirements, along with the times when payments must be made. This information is combined with projections about the delay in collecting accounts receivable, tax payment dates, dividend and interest payment dates, and so on. All of this information is summarized in the *cash budget,* which shows the firm's projected cash inflows and outflows over some specified period. Generally, firms use a monthly cash budget forecasted over the next year plus a more detailed daily or weekly cash budget for the coming month. The monthly cash budgets are used for planning purposes and the daily or weekly budgets for actual cash control.

The cash budget provides much more detailed information concerning a firm's future cash flows than do the forecasted financial statements. In Chapter 15, we developed Allied Food Products' 1994 forecasted financial statements. Allied's projected 1994 sales were $3,300 million, resulting in a net cash flow from operations of $162 million. When all expenditures and financing flows are considered, Allied's cash account is projected to increase by $1 million in 1994. Does this mean that Allied will not have to worry about cash shortages during 1994? To answer this question, we must construct Allied's cash budget for 1994.

To simplify the example, we will only consider Allied's cash budget for the last half of 1994. Further, we will not list every cash flow that is expected to occur but rather focus on the operating flows. Allied's sales peak is in September, shortly after the majority of its raw food inputs have been harvested. All sales are made on terms that allow a 2 percent cash discount for payments made within 10 days, and, if the discount is not taken, the full amount is due in 40 days. However, like most companies, Allied finds that some of its customers delay payment up to 90 days. Experience has shown that payment on 20 percent of Allied's dollar sales is made during the month in which the sale is made — these are the discount sales. On 70 percent of sales, payment is made during the month immediately following the month of sale, and payment is made on 10 percent of sales in the second month following the month of sale.

The costs to Allied of foodstuffs, spices, preservatives, and packaging materials average 70 percent of the sales prices of the finished products. These purchases are generally made one month before the firm expects to sell the finished products, but Allied's purchase terms with its suppliers allow it to delay payments for 30 days. Accordingly, if July sales are forecasted at $300 million, then purchases during June will amount to $210 million, and this amount will actually be paid in July.

Such other cash expenditures as wages and rent are also built into the cash budget, and Allied must make estimated tax payments of $30 million on September 15 and $20 million on December 15, while a $100 million payment for a new plant must be made in October. Assuming that Allied's *target cash balance* is $10 million and that it projects $15 million to be on hand on July 1, 1994, what will the firm's monthly cash surpluses or shortfalls be for the period from July to December?[3]

The monthly cash flows are shown in Table 16-2. Section I of the table provides a worksheet for calculating both collections on sales and payments on purchases. Line 1 gives the sales forecast for the period from May through December. (May and June sales are necessary to determine collections for July and August.) Next, Lines 2 through 5 show cash collections. Line 2 shows that 20 percent of the sales during any given month are collected during that month. Customers who pay in the first month, however, typically take the discount, so the cash collected in the month of sale is reduced by 2 percent; for example, collections during July for the $300 million of sales in that month will be 20 percent times sales less the 2 percent discount $= (0.2)(0.98)(\$300) \approx \$59$ million. Line 3 shows the collections on the previous month's sales, or 70 percent of sales in the preceding month; for example, in July, 70 percent of the $250 million June sales, or $175 million, will be collected. Line 4 gives collections from sales two months earlier, or 10 percent of sales in that month; for example, the July collections for May sales are $(0.10)(\$200) = \$20$ million. The collections during each month are summed and shown on Line 5; thus, the July collections represent 20 percent of July sales (minus the discount) plus 70 percent of June sales plus 10 percent of May sales, or $254 million in total.

Next, payments for purchases of raw materials are shown. July sales are forecasted at $300 million, so Allied will purchase $210 million of materials in June (Line 6) and pay for these purchases in July (Line 7). Similarly, Allied will purchase $280 million of materials in July to meet August's forecasted sales of $400 million.

With Section I completed, Section II can be constructed. Cash from collections is shown on Line 8. Lines 9 through 14 list payments made during each month, and these payments are summed on Line 15. The difference between cash receipts and cash payments (Line 8 minus Line 15) is the net cash gain or loss during the month; for July there is a net cash loss of $11 million, as shown on Line 16.

In Section III, we first determine Allied's cash balance at the start of each month, assuming no borrowing is done; this is shown on Line 17. We assume that Allied will have $15 million on hand on July 1. The beginning cash balance

---

[3]Setting the target cash balance is an important part of cash management. We will discuss this topic later, in Chapter 17.

TABLE 16-2   ALLIED FOOD PRODUCTS: CASH BUDGET (MILLIONS OF DOLLARS)

	May	Jun	Jul	Aug	Sep	Oct	Nov	Dec
I. Collections and Purchases Worksheet								
(1) Sales (gross)[a]	$200	$250	$300	$400	$500	$350	$250	$200
Collections:								
(2) During month of sale: (0.2)(0.98)(month's sales)			$ 59	$ 78	$ 98	$ 69	$ 49	$ 39
(3) During first month after sale: 0.7 (previous month's sales)			175	210	280	350	245	175
(4) During second month after sale: 0.1 (sales 2 months ago)			20	25	30	40	50	35
(5) Total collections (2 + 3 + 4)			$254	$313	$408	$459	$344	$249
Purchases:								
(6) 0.7 (next month's sales)		$210	$280	$350	$245	$175	$140	
(7) Payments (1-month lag)			$210	$280	$350	$245	$175	$140
II. Cash Gain or Loss for Month								
(8) Collections (from Section I)			$254	$313	$408	$459	$344	$249
(9) Payments for purchases (from Section I)			$210	$280	$350	$245	$175	$140
(10) Wages and salaries			30	40	50	40	30	30
(11) Rent			15	15	15	15	15	15
(12) Other expenses			10	15	20	15	10	10
(13) Taxes					30			20
(14) Payment for plant construction						100		
(15) Total payments			$265	$350	$465	$415	$230	$215
(16) Net cash gain (loss) during month (Line 8 − Line 15)			($ 11)	($ 37)	($ 57)	$ 44	$114	$ 34
III. Cash Surplus or Loan Requirement								
(17) Cash at start of month if no borrowing is done[b]			$ 15	$ 4	($ 33)	($ 90)	($ 46)	$ 68
(18) Cumulative cash (cash at start, +gain or −loss = Line 16 + Line 17)			$ 4	($ 33)	($ 90)	($ 46)	$ 68	$102
(19) Target cash balance			10	10	10	10	10	10
(20) Cumulative surplus cash or loans outstanding to maintain $10 target cash balance: (Line 18 − Line 19)[c]			($ 6)	($ 43)	($100)	($ 56)	$ 58	$ 92

[a]Although the budget period is July through December, sales and purchases data for May and June are needed to determine collections and payments during July and August.

[b]The amount shown on Line 17 for July, the $15 balance (in millions), is assumed to be on hand initially. The values shown for each of the following months on Line 17 are equal to the cumulative cash as shown on Line 18 for the preceding month; for example, the $4 shown on Line 17 for August is taken from Line 18 in the July column.

[c]When the target cash balance of $10 (Line 19) is deducted from the cumulative cash balance (Line 18), a resulting negative figure on Line 20 represents a required loan, whereas a positive figure represents surplus cash. Loans are required from July through October, and surpluses are expected during November and December. Note also that firms can borrow or pay off loans on a daily basis, so the $6 borrowed during July would be done on a daily basis, as needed, and during October the $100 loan that existed at the beginning of the month would be reduced daily to the $56 ending balance, which in turn would be completely paid off during November.

(Line 17) is then added to the net cash gain or loss during the month (Line 16) to obtain the cumulative cash that would be on hand if no financing were done (Line 18); at the end of July, Allied forecasts a cumulative cash balance of $4 million in the absence of borrowing.

The target cash balance, $10 million, is then subtracted from the cumulative cash balance to determine the firm's borrowing requirements, shown in parentheses, or its surplus cash. Because Allied expects to have cumulative cash, as shown on Line 18, of only $4 million in July, it will have to borrow $6 million to bring the cash account up to the target balance of $10 million. Assuming that this amount is indeed borrowed, loans outstanding will total $6 million at the end of July. (We assume that Allied did not have any loans outstanding on July 1 because its beginning cash balance exceeded the target balance.) The cash surplus or required loan balance is given on Line 20; a positive value indicates a cash surplus, whereas a negative value indicates a loan requirement. Note that the surplus cash or loan requirement shown on Line 20 is a *cumulative amount.* Thus, Allied must borrow $6 million in July; it has a cash shortfall during August of $37 million as reported on Line 16, so its total loan requirement at the end of August is $6 + $37 = $43 million, as reported on Line 20. Allied's arrangement with the bank permits it to increase its outstanding loans on a daily basis, up to a prearranged maximum, just as you could increase the amount you owe on a credit card. Allied will use any surplus funds it generates to pay off its loans, and because the loan can be paid down at any time, on a daily basis, the firm will never have both a cash surplus and an outstanding loan balance.

This same procedure is used in the following months. Sales will peak in September, accompanied by increased payments for purchases, wages, and other items. Receipts from sales will also go up, but the firm will still be left with a $57 million net cash outflow during the month. The total loan requirement at the end of September will hit a peak of $100 million, the cumulative cash plus the target cash balance. This amount is also equal to the $43 million needed at the end of August plus the $57 million cash deficit for September.

Sales, purchases, and payments for past purchases will fall sharply in October, but collections will be the highest of any month because they will reflect the high September sales. As a result, Allied will enjoy a healthy $44 million net cash gain during October. This net gain can be used to pay off borrowings, so loans outstanding will decline by $44 million, to $56 million.

Allied will have an even larger cash surplus in November, which will permit it to pay off all of its loans. In fact, the company is expected to have $58 million in surplus cash by the month's end, and another cash surplus in December will swell the excess cash to $92 million. With such a large amount of unneeded funds, Allied's treasurer will certainly want to invest in interest-bearing securities or to put the funds to use in some other way. Various types of temporary investments into which Allied might put its excess funds are discussed in Chapter 17.

Before concluding our discussion of the cash budget, we should make some additional points:

1. For simplicity, our illustrative budget for Allied omitted many important cash flows that are anticipated for 1994, such as dividends, proceeds from stock and

bond sales, and additional fixed asset additions. Some of these are projected to occur in the first half of the year, but those that are projected for the July–December period could easily be added to the example. The final cash budget should contain all projected cash inflows and outflows.

2. Our cash budget example does not reflect interest expense on loans or income from investing surplus cash. This refinement could easily be added.

3. If cash inflows and outflows are not uniform during the month, we could seriously understate the firm's peak financing requirements. The data in Table 16-2 show the situation expected on the last day of each month, but on any given day during the month it could be quite different. For example, if all payments had to be made on the fifth of each month, but collections came in uniformly throughout the month, the firm would need to borrow much larger amounts than those shown in Table 16-2. In this case, we would have to prepare a cash budget identifying requirements on a daily basis.

4. Since depreciation is a noncash charge, it does not appear on the cash budget other than through its effect on taxable income, hence on taxes paid.

5. Since the cash budget represents a forecast, all the values in the table are *expected* values. If actual sales, purchases, and so on are different from the forecasted levels, then the projected cash deficits and surpluses will also be incorrect. Thus, Allied might end up needing to borrow larger amounts than are indicated on Line 20, so it should arrange a line of credit in excess of that amount. For example, if Allied's monthly sales are only 80 percent of their forecasted levels, the firm's maximum cumulative borrowing requirement will turn out to be $126 million, a 26 percent increase from the expected cash budget.

6. Computerized spreadsheet programs such as *Lotus 1-2-3* are particularly well suited for constructing and analyzing cash budgets, especially with respect to the sensitivity of cash flows to changes in sales levels, collection periods, and the like. We could change any assumption, say the projected monthly sales or the time that customers pay, and the cash budget would automatically and instantly be recalculated. This would show us exactly how the firm's borrowing requirements would change if various other things changed. Also, with a computer model, it is easy to add features like interest paid on loans, interest earned on marketable securities, and so on. We have written such a model for the spreadsheet problem at the end of the chapter.

7. Finally, we should note that the target cash balance probably will be adjusted over time, rising and falling with seasonal patterns and with long-term changes in the scale of the firm's operations. Thus, Allied will probably plan to maintain larger cash balances during August and September than at other times, and, as the company grows, so will its required cash balance. Also, the firm might even set the target cash balance at zero — this could be done if it carried a portfolio of marketable securities which could be sold to replenish the cash account or if it had an arrangement with its bank that permitted it to borrow any funds needed on a daily basis. In that event, the cash budget would simply stop with Line 18, and the amounts on that line would represent projected loans outstanding or surplus cash.

Note, though, that most firms would find it difficult to operate with a zero-balance bank account, just as you would, and the costs of such an operation would in most instances offset the costs associated with maintaining a positive cash balance. Therefore, most firms do set a positive target cash balance. Factors that influence the target cash balance are discussed in Chapter 17.

SELF-TEST QUESTIONS

What is the purpose of a cash budget?

What are the three major sections of a cash budget?

Suppose a firm's cash flows do not occur uniformly throughout the month. What impact might this have on the accuracy of the forecasted borrowing requirements?

How is uncertainty handled in a cash budget?

Is depreciation reflected in a cash budget? Explain.

SUMMARY

This chapter examined short-term planning, including the cash budget. The key concepts covered are listed below.

▶ *Working capital* refers to current assets, and *net working capital* is defined as current assets minus current liabilities. *Working capital policy* refers to decisions relating to the level of current assets and the way they are financed.

▶ The *inventory conversion period* is the average length of time required to convert raw materials into finished goods and then to sell them.

▶ The *receivables collection period* is the average length of time required to convert the firm's receivables into cash, and it is equal to the days sales outstanding.

▶ The *payables deferral period* is the average length of time between the purchase of raw materials and labor and paying for them.

▶ The *cash conversion cycle* is the length of time between paying for purchases and receiving cash from the sale of finished goods. The cash conversion cycle can be calculated as follows:

$$\begin{matrix} \text{Inventory} \\ \text{conversion} \\ \text{period} \end{matrix} + \begin{matrix} \text{Receivables} \\ \text{collection} \\ \text{period} \end{matrix} - \begin{matrix} \text{Payables} \\ \text{deferral} \\ \text{period} \end{matrix} = \begin{matrix} \text{Cash} \\ \text{conversion.} \\ \text{cycle} \end{matrix}$$

▶ Under a *relaxed current asset investment policy,* a firm holds relatively large amounts of each type of current asset. Under a *restricted current asset investment policy,* the firm holds minimal amounts of these items.

▶ *Permanent current assets* are those current assets that the firm holds even during slack times, whereas *temporary current assets* are the additional current assets that are needed during seasonal or cyclical peaks. The methods used to finance permanent and temporary current assets constitute the firm's *current asset financing policy.*

▶ A *moderate* approach to current asset financing involves matching, to the extent possible, the maturities of assets and liabilities, so that temporary current assets are financed with short-term nonspontaneous debt and permanent current assets, and fixed assets are financed with long-term debt or equity plus spontaneous debt. Under an *aggressive* approach, some permanent current assets and perhaps even some fixed assets are financed with short-term debt. A *conservative* approach would be to use long-term capital to finance all permanent assets and some of the temporary current assets.

▶ The advantages of short-term credit are (1) the *speed* with which short-term loans can be arranged, (2) increased *flexibility,* and (3) the fact that short-term *interest rates* are generally *lower* than long-term rates. The principal disadvantage of short-term credit is the *extra risk* that the borrower must bear because (1) the lender can demand payment on short notice and (2) the cost of the loan will increase if interest rates rise.

▶ A *cash budget* is a schedule showing projected cash inflows and outflows over some period. It is used to predict cash surpluses and shortages and thus is the most important short-term planning tool.

QUESTIONS

16-1 Define each of the following terms:
  a. Working capital; net working capital; working capital policy
  b. Permanent current assets; temporary current assets
  c. Cash conversion cycle; inventory conversion period; receivables collection period; payables deferral period
  d. Relaxed current asset investment policy; restricted current asset investment policy; moderate current asset investment policy
  e. Moderate current asset financing policy; aggressive current asset financing policy; conservative current asset financing policy
  f. Maturity matching, or "self-liquidating," approach
  g. Cash budget; net cash gain (loss)
  h. Target cash balance.

16-2 How does the seasonal nature of a firm's sales influence its decision regarding the amount of short-term credit to use in its financial structure?

16-3 Assuming the firm's sales volume remained constant, would you expect it to have a higher cash balance during a tight-money period or during an easy-money period? Why?

16-4 What are the advantages of matching the maturities of assets and liabilities? What are the disadvantages?

16-5 From the standpoint of the borrower, is long-term or short-term credit riskier? Explain. Would it ever make sense to borrow on a short-term basis if short-term rates were above long-term rates?

16-6 If long-term credit exposes a borrower to less risk, why would people or firms ever borrow on a short-term basis?

16-7 Why is a cash budget important even when a company has plenty of cash in the bank?

SELF-TEST PROBLEMS (SOLUTIONS APPEAR IN APPENDIX C)

ST-1 (Current asset financing) Vanderheiden Press Inc. and the Herrenhouse Publishing Company had the following balance sheets as of December 31, 1993 (thousands of dollars):

	Vanderheiden Press	Herrenhouse Publishing
Current assets	$100,000	$ 80,000
Fixed assets (net)	100,000	120,000
Total assets	$200,000	$200,000
Current liabilities	$ 20,000	$ 80,000
Long-term debt	80,000	20,000
Common stock	50,000	50,000
Retained earnings	50,000	50,000
Total liabilities and equity	$200,000	$200,000

Earnings before interest and taxes (EBIT) for both firms are $30 million, and the federal-plus-state tax rate is 40 percent.

a. What is the return on equity for each firm if the interest rate on current liabilities is 10 percent and the rate on long-term debt is 13 percent?

b. Assume that the short-term rate rises to 20 percent. While the rate on new long-term debt rises to 16 percent, the rate on existing long-term debt remains unchanged. What would be the return on equity for Vanderheiden Press and Herrenhouse Publishing under these conditions?

c. Which company is in a riskier position? Why?

ST-2 (Working capital policy) The Calgary Company is attempting to establish a current assets policy. Fixed assets are $600,000, and the firm plans to maintain a 50 percent debt to assets ratio. The interest rate is 10 percent on all debt. Three alternative current asset policies are under consideration: 40, 50, and 60 percent of projected sales. The company expects to earn 15 percent before interest and taxes on sales of $3 million. Calgary's federal-plus-state tax rate is 40 percent. What is the expected return on equity under each alternative?

PROBLEMS

16-1 (Cash conversion cycle) Look back in the chapter to Table 16-1, which showed the balance sheets for Allied Food Products on three different dates. Allied's sales fluctuate during the year due to the seasonal nature of its business; however, we can calculate its sales on an average day as total sales divided by 360, recognizing that daily sales will be much higher than this value during its peak selling season and much lower during its slack

time. Assume Allied's sales for 1994 totaled $3,300 million, so an average day's sales were $9.167 million.

a. Calculate Allied's inventory conversion period as of January 1 and September 30. (Hint: The inventory conversion period is equal to the number of average days' sales held in inventory, and it is calculated as inventory divided by an average day's sales.)

b. Calculate Allied's receivables collection period as of January 1 and September 30.

c. Assume Allied's purchases are 50 percent of sales and all purchases are made on credit. Using this information, calculate the payables deferral period as of January 1 and September 30 as accounts payable divided by average daily purchases.

d. Using the values calculated in Parts a through c, calculate the length of Allied's cash conversion cycle on the two balance sheet dates.

e. In Part d, you should have found that the cash conversion cycle was longer on September 30 than on January 1. Why did these results occur?

f. Can you think of any reason why the cash conversion cycle of a firm with seasonal sales might be different during the slack selling season than during the peak selling season?

16-2 (Working capital investment)   Niendorf Corporation is a leading U.S. producer of automobile batteries. Niendorf turns out 1,500 batteries a day at a cost of $6 per battery for materials and labor. It takes the firm 22 days to convert raw materials into a battery. Niendorf allows its customers 40 days in which to pay for the batteries, and the firm generally pays its suppliers in 30 days.

a. What is the length of Niendorf's cash conversion cycle?

b. At a steady state in which Niendorf produces 1,500 batteries a day, what amount of working capital must it finance?

c. By what amount could Niendorf reduce its working capital financing needs if it was able to stretch its payables deferral period to 35 days?

d. Niendorf's management is trying to analyze the effect of a proposed new production process on the working capital investment. The new production process would allow Niendorf to decrease its inventory conversion period to 20 days and to increase its daily production to 1,800 batteries. However, the new process would cause the cost of materials and labor to increase to $7. Assuming the change does not affect the receivables collection period (40 days) or the payables deferral period (30 days), what will be the length of the cash conversion cycle and the working capital financing requirement if the new production process is implemented?

16-3 (Working capital policy)   The Sorenson Corporation is attempting to determine the optimal level of current assets for the coming year. Management expects sales to increase to approximately $2 million as a result of an asset expansion presently being undertaken. Fixed assets total $1 million, and the firm wishes to maintain a 60 percent debt ratio. Sorenson's interest cost is currently 8 percent on both short-term and longer-term debt (which the firm uses in its permanent structure). Three alternatives regarding the projected current asset level are available to the firm: (1) a tight policy requiring current assets of only 45 percent of projected sales, (2) a moderate policy of 50 percent of sales in current assets, and (3) a relaxed policy requiring current assets of 60 percent of sales. The firm expects to generate earnings before interest and taxes (EBIT) at a rate of 12 percent on total sales.

a. What is the expected return on equity under each current asset level? (Assume a 40 percent federal-plus-state tax rate.)

b. In this problem we have assumed that the level of expected sales is independent of current asset policy. Is this a valid assumption?

c. How would the overall riskiness of the firm vary under each policy?

16-4 (Cash conversion cycle) The Boudreaux Corporation has an inventory conversion period of 75 days, a receivables collection period of 38 days, and a payables deferral period of 30 days.

a. What is the length of the firm's cash conversion cycle?

b. If Boudreaux's annual sales are $3,375,000 and all sales are on credit, what is the firm's investment in accounts receivable?

c. How many times per year does Boudreaux turn over its inventory?

16-5 (Working capital cash flow cycle) The Howe Corporation is trying to determine the effect of its inventory turnover ratio and days sales outstanding (DSO) on its cash flow cycle. Howe's 1993 sales (all on credit) were $150,000, and it earned a net profit of 6 percent, or $9,000. It turned over its inventory 6 times during the year, and its DSO was 36 days. The firm had fixed assets totaling $40,000. Howe's payables deferral period is 40 days.

a. Calculate Howe's cash conversion cycle.

b. Assuming Howe holds negligible amounts of cash and marketable securities, calculate its total assets turnover and ROA.

c. Suppose Howe's managers believe that the inventory turnover can be raised to 8 times. What would Howe's cash conversion cycle, total assets turnover, and ROA have been if the inventory turnover had been 8 for 1993?

16-6 (Working capital financing) Three companies—Aggressive, Moderate, and Conservative—have different working capital management policies as implied by their names. For example, Aggressive employs only minimal current assets, and it finances almost entirely with current liabilities plus equity. This restricted approach has a dual effect. It keeps total assets low, which tends to increase return on assets; but because of stock-outs and credit rejections, total sales are reduced, and because inventory is ordered more frequently and in smaller quantities, variable costs are increased. Condensed balance sheets for the three companies follow:

	Aggressive	Moderate	Conservative
Current assets	$225,000	$300,000	$450,000
Fixed assets	300,000	300,000	300,000
Total assets	$525,000	$600,000	$750,000
Current liabilities (cost = 12%)	$300,000	$150,000	$ 75,000
Long-term debt (cost = 10%)	0	150,000	300,000
Total debt	$300,000	$300,000	$375,000
Equity	225,000	300,000	375,000
Total liabilities and equity	$525,000	$600,000	$750,000
Current ratio	0.75:1	2:1	6:1

The cost of goods sold functions for the three firms are as follows:

Cost of goods sold = Fixed costs + Variable costs.
Aggressive: Cost of goods sold = $300,000 + 0.70(Sales).
Moderate: Cost of goods sold = $405,000 + 0.65(Sales).
Conservative: Cost of goods sold = $577,500 + 0.60(Sales).

Because of the working capital differences, sales for the three firms under different economic conditions are expected to vary as follows:

	Aggressive	Moderate	Conservative
Strong economy	$1,800,000	$1,875,000	$1,950,000
Average economy	1,350,000	1,500,000	1,725,000
Weak economy	1,050,000	1,200,000	1,575,000

a. Construct income statements for each company for strong, average, and weak economies using the following format:

> Sales
> Less cost of goods sold
>   Earnings before interest and taxes (EBIT)
> Less interest expense
>   Earnings before taxes (EBT)
> Less taxes (at 40%)
> Net income (NI)

b. Compare the basic earning power (EBIT/assets) and return on equity for the companies. Which company is best in a strong economy? In an average economy? In a weak economy?

Work the following parts only if you are using the computer problem diskette.

c. Suppose that, with sales at the average-economy level, short-term interest rates rose to 20 percent. How would this affect the three firms?

d. Suppose that because of production slowdowns caused by inventory shortages, the aggressive company's variable cost ratio rose to 80 percent. What would happen to its ROE? Assume a short-term interest rate of 12 percent.

e. What considerations for the management of working capital are indicated by this problem?

16-7 **(Cash budgeting)**   Ilene Malitz recently leased space in the Southside Mall and opened a new business, Ilene's Dress Shop. Business has been good, but Ilene has frequently run out of cash. This has necessitated late payment on certain orders, which in turn is beginning to cause a problem with suppliers. Ilene plans to borrow from the bank to have cash ready as needed, but first she needs a forecast of just how much she must borrow. Accordingly, she has asked you to prepare a cash budget for the critical period around Christmas, when needs will be especially high.

Sales are made on a cash basis only. Ilene's purchases must be paid for during the following month. Ilene pays herself a salary of $4,800 per month, and the rent is $2,000 per month. In addition, she must make a tax payment of $12,000 in December. The current cash on hand (on December 1) is $400, but Ilene has agreed to maintain an average bank balance of $6,000—this is her target cash balance. (Disregard till cash, which is insignificant because Ilene keeps only a small amount on hand in order to lessen the chances of robbery.)

The estimated sales and purchases for December, January, and February are shown below. Purchases during November amounted to $140,000.

	Sales	Purchases
December	$160,000	$40,000
January	40,000	40,000
February	60,000	40,000

a.   Prepare a cash budget for December, January, and February.

b.   Now suppose Ilene were to start selling on a credit basis on December 1, giving customers 30 days to pay. All customers accept these terms, and all other facts in the problem are unchanged. What would the company's loan requirements be at the end of December in this case? (Hint: The calculations required to answer this question are minimal.)

16-8 (Cash budgeting)   Susan Long, owner of Susan's Fashion Designs Inc., is planning to request a line of credit from her bank. She has estimated the following sales forecasts for the firm for parts of 1994 and 1995:

May 1994	$180,000
June	180,000
July	360,000
August	540,000
September	720,000
October	360,000
November	360,000
December	90,000
January 1995	180,000

Collection estimates obtained from the credit and collection department are as follows: collections within the month of sale, 10 percent; collections the month following the sale, 75 percent; collections the second month following the sale, 15 percent. Payments for labor and raw materials are typically made during the month following the one in which these costs have been incurred. Total labor and raw materials costs are estimated for each month as follows:

May 1994	$ 90,000
June	90,000
July	126,000
August	882,000
September	306,000
October	234,000
November	162,000
December	90,000

General and administrative salaries will amount to approximately $27,000 a month; lease payments under long-term lease contracts will be $9,000 a month; depreciation charges will be $36,000 a month; miscellaneous expenses will be $2,700 a month; income tax payments of $63,000 will be due in both September and December; and a progress payment of $180,000 on a new design studio must be paid in October. Cash on hand on July 1 will amount to $132,000, and a minimum cash balance of $90,000 will be maintained throughout the cash budget period.

a.   Prepare a monthly cash budget for the last six months of 1994.

b.   Prepare an estimate of the required financing (or excess funds)—that is, the amount of money Susan will need to borrow (or will have available to invest)—for each month during that period.

c.   Assume that receipts from sales come in uniformly during the month (that is, cash receipts come in at the rate of ⅟₃₀ each day), but all outflows are paid on the fifth of the month. Will this have an effect on the cash budget—in other words, would the cash budget you have prepared be valid under these assumptions? If not, what can be done

to make a valid estimate of peak financing requirements? No calculations are required, although calculations can be used to illustrate the effects.

d. Susan produces on a seasonal basis, just ahead of sales. Without making any calculations, discuss how the company's current ratio and debt ratio would vary during the year assuming all financial requirements were met by short-term bank loans. Could changes in these ratios affect the firm's ability to obtain bank credit?

Work the following parts only if you are using the computer problem diskette.

e. Suppose that by offering a 2 percent cash discount for paying within the month of sale, the credit manager of Susan's Fashion Designs Inc. has revised the collection percentages to 50 percent, 35 percent, and 15 percent, respectively. How will this affect the loan requirements?

f. Return the payment percentages to their base case values: 10 percent, 75 percent, and 15 percent, respectively, and the discount to zero percent. Now suppose sales fall to only 70 percent of the forecasted level. Production is maintained, so cash outflows are unchanged. How does this affect Susan's financial requirements?

g. Return sales to the forecasted level (100%), and suppose collections slow down to 3 percent, 10 percent, and 87 percent for the three months, respectively. How does this affect financial requirements? If Susan went to a cash-only sales policy, how would that affect requirements, other things held constant?

**M I N I
C A S E**

(Part I: Working capital policy and financing)   Daniel Barnes, financial manager of New York Fuels (NYF), a heating oil distributor, is concerned about the company's working capital policy, and he is considering three alternative policies: (1) a "restrictive" ("lean-and-mean" or "tight") policy, which calls for reducing receivables by $100,000 and inventories by $200,000; (2) a "relaxed" ("loose" or "fat cat") policy, which calls for increasing receivables by $100,000 and inventories by $200,000; and (3) a "moderate" policy, which would mean leaving receivables and inventories at their current levels. NYF's 1993 financial statements and key ratios, plus some industry average data, are given in Table MC16-1.

The cost of long-term debt is 12 percent versus only 8 percent for short-term notes payable. Variable costs as a percentage of sales (74 percent) would not be affected by the firm's working capital policy, but fixed costs would be affected due to the storage, handling, and insurance costs associated with inventory. Here are the assumed fixed costs under the three policies:

Policy	Fixed Costs
Restrictive	$ 950,000
Moderate	1,000,000
Relaxed	1,100,000

Sales would also be affected by the policy chosen: Carrying larger inventories and using easier credit terms would stimulate sales, so sales would be highest under the relaxed policy and lowest under the restrictive policy. Also, these effects would vary depending on the strength of the economy. Here are the relationships Barnes assumes would have held in 1993:

TABLE MC16-1

FINANCIAL
STATEMENTS AND
OTHER DATA ON NYF
(THOUSANDS OF
DOLLARS)

A. 1993 Balance Sheet

Cash and securities	$ 100	Accounts payable and accruals	$ 300
Accounts receivable	600	Notes payable (8%)	500
Inventories	1,000	Total current liabilities	$ 800
Total current assets	$1,700	Long-term debt (12%)	600
Net fixed assets	800	Common equity	1,100
Total assets	$2,500	Total liabilities and equity	$2,500

B. 1993 Income Statement

Sales	$5,000.00
Variable costs	3,700.00
Fixed costs	1,000.00
EBIT	$ 300.00
Interest	112.00
Earnings before taxes (EBT)	$ 188.00
Taxes (40%)	75.20
Net income	$ 112.80
Dividends (30% payout)	$ 33.84
Addition to retained earnings	$ 78.96

C. Key Ratios

	NYF	Industry
Basic earning power	12.0%	15.8%
Profit margin	2.3	3.0
Return on equity	10.3	15.0
Days sales outstanding (360 days)	43.2	30.0
Accounts receivable turnover	8.3×	12.0×
Inventory turnover	5.0	7.5
Fixed assets turnover	6.3	6.0
Total assets turnover	2.0	2.5
Debt/assets	56.0%	50.0%
Times interest earned	2.7×	4.8×
Current ratio	2.1	2.3
Quick ratio	0.9	1.3

	Sales (Millions of Dollars)		
State of the Economy	Restrictive	Moderate	Relaxed
Weak	$4.3	$4.5	$5.0
Average	4.7	5.0	5.5
Strong	5.3	5.5	6.0

Barnes considers the 1993 economy to be average.

You have been asked to answer the following questions to help determine NYF's optimal working capital policy.

a. How does NYF's current working capital policy, as reflected in its financial statements, compare with an average firm's policy? Do the differences suggest that NYF's policy is better or worse than that of the average firm in its industry?

TABLE MC16-2		Working Capital Policy		
ROEs UNDER THE	State of the Economy	Tight	Moderate	Easy
ALTERNATIVE POLICIES	Weak	4.2%	3.2%	3.8%
	Average	12.0	10.3	9.3
	Strong	23.7	17.3	14.9
	Average	13.3%	10.3%	9.3%

b. Based on the 1993 ratios and financial statements, what were the company's inventory conversion period, its receivables collection period, and, assuming a 29-day payables deferral period, its cash conversion cycle? How could the cash conversion cycle concept be used to help improve the firm's working capital management?

c. Barnes has asked you to recast the 1993 financial statements, and calculate some key ratios, assuming an average economy and a restrictive (tight) working capital policy, and to check some calculations he has made. Construct these statements, and then calculate the new current ratio and ROE. Assume that common stock is used to make the balance sheet balance, but do not get into financing feedbacks. (Hint: You need to change sales, fixed costs, receivables, inventories, and common equity, plus items affected by those changes, and then calculate new ratios.)

d. Barnes himself has actually analyzed the situation for each of the policies under each economic scenario; the ROEs he has calculated are shown in Table MC16-2. What are the implications of these data for the working capital policy decision?

e. The working capital policy discussion thus far has focused entirely on current assets, and not at all on the current asset financing policy. How would you bring financing policy into the analysis?

(Part II: Cash Budget)   Betty Rose, financial manager of Golf World Inc. (GWI), a Washington, D.C.-based chain of golf supply stores, was asked by Kitty Barton, the president, to consider the company's cash and marketable securities position. Currently, GWI has $300,000 of cash and no marketable securities, and Barton wonders if the company needs that much cash, given that cash earns no return.

GWI's business is highly seasonal. Here is a forecast of sales for the last two months of 1993 and the first eight months of 1994, in thousands:

November 1993	$ 500	April	$5,800
December	500	May	3,300
January 1994	200	June	1,000
February	200	July	800
March	3,200	August	1,000

GWI's credit terms allow customers to take a 2 percent discount if they pay within 10 days of the purchase date; otherwise, the full invoice amount is due within 30 days. In the past, 40 percent of the customers have taken the discount and thus paid in the month of the sale, 50 percent have paid the following month, and 10 percent have paid during the second month after the sale. These percentages are expected to continue. Also, GWI purchases goods for resale two months prior to when they should be sold and pays for them the month after receipt, and purchases amount to 75 percent of sales. Thus, the $3,200,000 of goods to be sold in March will be purchased in January at a cost of $3,200,000 (0.75) = $2,400,000, and this amount will be paid in February.

Wages, administrative, and selling expenses are projected at $140,000 per month, and depreciation expenses at $42,500 per month. Quarterly income tax payments of $125,000 must be made in March and June, and $250,000 will be needed in April to pay for the spring advertising campaign. Betty Rose estimates that there will be $300,000 of cash in the bank on January 1.

As Rose's assistant, you have been asked to answer the following questions.

a. What is a cash budget?

b. Prepare a cash budget for the first six months of 1994. Assume that $300,000 of cash will be on hand on January 1 and that Rose wants to begin each subsequent month with $200,000 of cash on hand. What is the maximum cash surplus GWI will enjoy during the period studied? The maximum cash shortfall?

c. (1) Should depreciation expense be explicitly included in the cash budget? Why or why not?

(2) Suppose the outflows all occur on the 5th day of each month, but the inflows all occur on the 25th day. This situation occurs because of the credit terms used by GWI and its suppliers. How would this affect March's cash budget? What could be done to incorporate such nonuniform flows into the cash budget?

(3) GWI's only receipts are collections. What are some other types of inflows that could occur? List both fairly regular cash inflows and also some cash inflows that could be forecasted, but which would have to be planned for (negotiated with someone).

(4) Rose plans to "sweep" any excess cash balances into marketable securities. Further, GWI would have to pay interest on its short-term borrowings. Explain how these flows could be incorporated into the cash budget.

d. We have assumed that all sales are collected and thus that GWI has no bad debts. Is this realistic? If not, how would bad debts be dealt with in a cash budgeting sense? For purposes of this question, assume that 3 percent of sales end up as bad debts. (Hint: Bad debts will affect collections but not purchases.)

e. The cash budget is a *forecast,* so many of the flows are expected values rather than amounts known with certainty. If actual sales, hence collections and production, were different from the forecasted levels, then the forecasted surpluses and deficits would also be incorrect. In words, how would you expect the funds needed or surplus cash position to be affected if sales were to rise or fall 15 percent above or below the levels originally forecasted? How would the company's ability to react in a timely manner to falling sales affect the outcome? How could scenario analysis be used to help forecast the net cash inflows and required beginning-of-month cash balances? Assume zero bad debt losses.

SELECTED ADDITIONAL REFERENCES AND CASES

The following books focus on short-term financial management:

Gallinger, George W., and P. Basil Healy, *Liquidity Analysis and Management* (Reading, Mass.: Addison-Wesley, 1991).

Hill, Ned C., and William L. Sartoris, *Short-Term Financial Management* (New York: Macmillan, 1988).

Maness, Terry S., and John T. Zietlow, *Short-Term Financial Management: Text, Cases, and Readings* (Minneapolis/St. Paul: West, 1993).

Smith, Keith V., and George W. Gallinger, *Readings on Short-term Financial Management* (St. Paul: West, 1988).

The following articles provide more information on short-term financial management:

Gentry, James A., "State of the Art of Short-Run Financial Management," *Financial Management,* Summer 1988, 41–57.

Gentry, James A., and Jesus M. De La Garza, "Monitoring Accounts Payables," *Financial Review,* November 1990, 559–576.

Gentry, James A., R. Vaidyanathan, and Hei Wai Lee, "A Weighted Cash Conversion Cycle," *Financial Management,* Spring 1990, 90–99.

Lambrix, R. J., and S. S. Singhvi, "Managing the Working Capital Cycle," *Financial Executive,* June 1979, 32–41.

Maier, Steven F., and James H. Vander Weide, "A Practical Approach to Short-Run Financial Planning," *Financial Management,* Winter 1978, 10–16.

Merville, Larry J., and Lee A. Tavis, "Optimal Working Capital Policies: A Chance-Constrained Programming Approach," *Journal of Financial and Quantitative Analysis,* January 1973, 47–60.

Smith, Keith V., and Brian Belt, "Working Capital Management in Practice: An Update," Krannert Graduate School of Management Working Paper Number 951, March 1989.

Yardini, Edward E., "A Portfolio-Balance Model of Corporate Working Capital," *Journal of Finance,* May 1979, 535–552.

The following cases are appropriate for use with this chapter:

Case 29, "Office Mates, Inc.," in the Brigham-Gapenski casebook, which illustrates how changes in current asset policy affect expected profitability and risk.

Case 32, "Alpine Wear, Inc.," which illustrates the mechanics of the cash budget and the rationale behind its use.

WORKING CAPITAL MANAGEMENT AND FINANCING

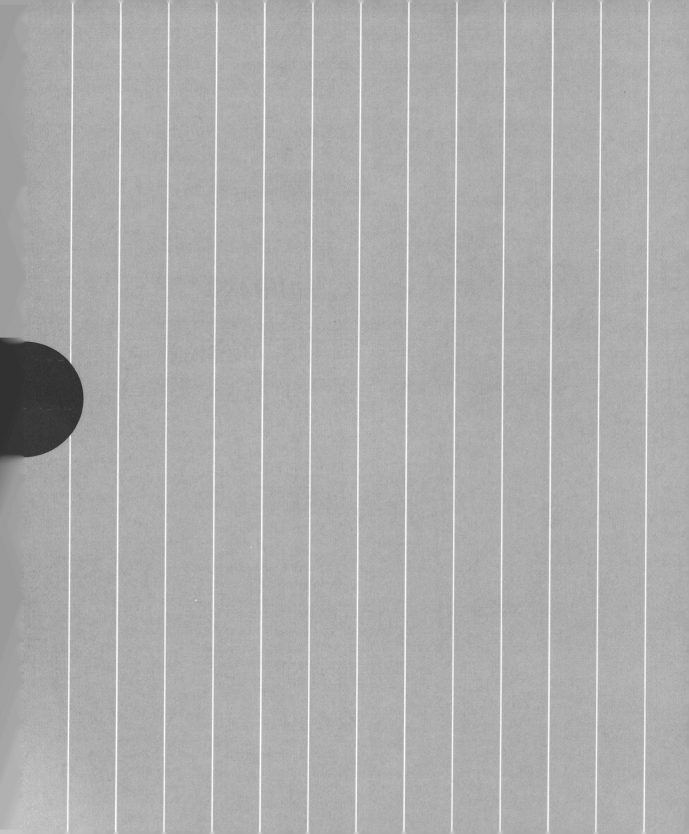

CASH MANAGEMENT AND SHORT-TERM FINANCING

Cash management as we know it today began in 1947, the year that lockbox services were introduced. Even so, during the 1950s, there was little incentive for corporations to aggressively manage their cash balances, because low interest rates minimized the cost of poor cash management. In general, companies relied on large bank deposits both for liquidity and to compensate banks for providing credit lines and other services. However, as interest rates rose in the 1960s and 1970s, corporations paid more attention to cash management. Furthermore, computers provided the means to develop what is now known as electronic banking services. These services offered corporate bank customers a way to optimize their use of cash, thus bringing efficiency to corporate cash management.

Another factor that influenced bank cash management services was the dramatic expansion of the commercial paper market in the 1970s, which enabled large companies to rely less on banks for short-term financing. In addition, new competition—both at home and abroad—brought considerable pressure on the concept of compensating balances as a way of paying for bank services, and banks began to unbundle services and to charge fees for noncredit services to bolster their own profitability.

By the 1980s, cash management had moved to the forefront of corporate banking services, because noncredit services had the potential to provide banks with more income than traditional lending activities. Furthermore, the return on assets for nonloan services was particularly attractive. Even the meaning of the term "lead bank" had changed. When once it meant exclusively the primary lender among a group of banks, it now just as frequently means "lead operating

bank," which is the bank that directs a group of banks in providing cash management services for a company. Surveys of the Fortune 1,000 companies confirm that one of the major reasons for choosing a lead bank, or for changing a lead bank, is its cash management capabilities.

Truly, cash management has come of age. Providers of cash management services now see them as a key to revenue growth, so more and more banks are providing such services. The number of committed cash management banks increased from fewer than 10 in 1960 to more than 200 today. And what was once a "freebie," compensated by a corporate customer's cash balances, has turned into a $5.5 billion industry.

The trend among the largest banks has been to put all operating services under a single umbrella. For example, Manufacturers Hanover Bank (now Chemical Banking Corporation) created Geoserve, which groups five key corporate services: cash management, corporate and institutional trusts, electronic funds transfer services, trade services, and global custody and safekeeping. Each business line is run as a profit center with its own production, product management, systems development, and sales organizations.

The explosion in bank cash management services was slowed by the recession of the early 1990s, which both lowered interest rates and caused corporations to be more frugal in contracting for cash management services. By 1993, the typical large corporate customer was using about six banks for cash management, down from about nine in 1986 — the profit squeeze on corporations caused buyers of cash management services to examine and cost-justify their banking networks, and to drop some banks. And as customers drop banks, some banks will undoubtedly drop their cash management services.

As you read this chapter, think about the relationship between banks and their corporate customers. What services might banks offer, and how should corporations analyze these services to choose the most cost-effective ones? By the end of the chapter, you will have a better understanding of both cash management and the role of banks in providing cash management services.

Approximately 1.5 percent of the average industrial firm's assets are held in the form of cash, which is defined as demand deposits plus currency. In addition, sizable holdings of such near-cash items as short-term marketable securities such as U.S. Treasury bills (T-bills), bank certificates of deposit (CDs), money market funds, and floating rate preferred stock are often reported on corporations' financial statements. However, cash and marketable securities balances vary widely across industries, between firms within a given industry, and within a given firm over time. Moreover, firms often use short-term financing as a cash management

tool when they need to supplement cash from operations. In this chapter, we analyze the factors that determine how much cash and marketable securities firms hold, describe the most commonly held types of marketable securities, and discuss the use and sources of short-term financing.

CASH MANAGEMENT

Cash is often called a "nonearning asset." It is needed to pay for labor and raw materials, to buy fixed assets, to pay taxes, to service debt, to pay dividends, and so on. However, cash itself (and also commercial checking accounts) earns no interest. Thus, the goal of the cash manager is to minimize the amount of cash the firm must hold for use in conducting its normal business activities, yet, at the same time, maintain sufficient cash balances (1) to take trade discounts, (2) to maintain its credit rating, and (3) to meet unexpected cash needs. We begin our analysis with a discussion of the reasons for holding cash.

RATIONALE FOR HOLDING CASH

Firms hold cash for two primary reasons:

1. **Transactions.** Cash balances are necessary in business operations. Payments must be made in cash, and receipts are deposited in the cash account. Cash balances associated with routine payments and collections are known as *transactions balances*.

2. **Compensation to banks for providing loans and services.** A bank makes money by lending out funds that have been deposited with it, so the larger its deposits, the better the bank's profit position. In addition, if a bank is providing services to a customer, it may require the customer to leave a minimum balance on deposit to help offset the costs of providing the services. This type of balance, defined as a *compensating balance,* is discussed in detail later in this chapter.

Two other reasons for holding cash have been noted in the finance and economics literature: for *precaution* and for *speculation*. Cash inflows and outflows are somewhat unpredictable, with the degree of predictability varying among firms and industries. Therefore, firms need to hold some cash in reserve for random, unforeseen fluctuations in cash inflows and outflows. These "safety stocks" are called *precautionary balances*, and the less predictable the firm's cash flows, the larger such balances should be. However, if the firm has easy access to borrowed funds —that is, if it can borrow on short notice—its need for precautionary balances is reduced. Also, as we note later in this chapter, firms that would otherwise need large precautionary balances tend to hold highly liquid marketable securities rather than cash per se; marketable securities serve many of the purposes of cash, but they provide interest or dividends, whereas banks are prohibited by law from paying interest on commercial checking accounts.

Some cash balances may be held to enable the firm to take advantage of bargain purchases that might arise; these funds are called *speculative balances*. However, as with precautionary balances, firms today are more likely to rely on reserve borrowing capacity and/or marketable securities portfolios than on cash per se for speculative purposes.

Although the cash accounts of most firms can be thought of as consisting of transactions, compensating, precautionary, and speculative balances, we cannot calculate the amount needed for each purpose, sum them, and produce a total desired cash balance, because the same money often serves more than one purpose. For instance, precautionary and speculative balances can also be used to satisfy compensating balance requirements. Firms do, however, consider all four factors when establishing their target cash positions.

ADVANTAGES OF HOLDING ADEQUATE CASH AND NEAR-CASH ASSETS

In addition to the four motives just discussed, sound cash management requires that an ample supply of cash be maintained for several specific reasons:

1. It is essential that the firm have sufficient cash and near-cash assets to take *discounts*. Suppliers frequently offer customers discounts for early payment of bills. As we will see later in this chapter, the cost of not taking discounts is very high, so firms should have enough cash and near-cash assets to permit payment of bills in time to take discounts.

2. Adequate holdings of cash and near-cash assets can help the firm maintain its credit rating by keeping its current and acid test (quick) ratios in line with those of other firms in its industry. A strong credit rating enables the firm both to purchase goods from suppliers on favorable terms and to maintain an ample line of credit with its bank.

3. Cash and near-cash assets are useful for taking advantage of favorable business opportunities, such as special offers from suppliers or the chance to acquire another firm.

4. The firm should have sufficient cash and near-cash assets to meet such emergencies as strikes, fires, or competitors' marketing campaigns and to weather seasonal and cyclical downturns.

SELF-TEST QUESTIONS

Why is cash management important?

What are the two primary motives for holding cash?

What are the two secondary motives for holding cash as noted in the finance and economics literature?

CASH MANAGEMENT TECHNIQUES

Cash management has changed significantly over the last 20 years as a result of two factors. First, interest rates were relatively high during most of the 1980s, which both increased the opportunity cost of holding cash and encouraged financial managers to search for more efficient ways of managing the firm's cash. Second, new technologies, particularly computerized electronic funds transfer mechanisms, have made improved cash management possible.

Most cash management activities are performed jointly by the firm and its primary (or lead) bank, but the financial manager is responsible for the effectiveness of the cash management program. Effective cash management encompasses proper management of both the cash inflows and the cash outflows of a firm. More specifically, managing cash inflows and cash outflows entails (1) synchronizing cash flows, (2) using float, (3) accelerating collections, (4) getting available funds to where they are needed, and (5) controlling disbursements. Most business is conducted by large firms, many of which operate regionally, nationally, or even worldwide. They collect cash from many sources and make payments from a number of different cities. For example, companies like IBM, General Motors, and Hewlett-Packard have manufacturing plants all around the world, even more sales offices, and bank accounts in virtually every city where they do business. Their collection points are typically spread out, following sales patterns. Some disbursements are made from local offices, but most disbursements (dividend and interest payments, taxes, debt repayments, and the like) are made in the areas where manufacturing occurs or else from the home office. Thus, a major corporation might have hundreds or even thousands of bank accounts, and since there is no reason to think that inflows and outflows will balance in each account, a system must be in place to transfer funds from where they currently are to where they are needed, to arrange loans to cover net corporate shortfalls, and to invest net corporate surpluses without delay. We discuss the most commonly used techniques for accomplishing these tasks in the following sections.

CASH FLOW SYNCHRONIZATION

If you as an individual were to receive income once a year, you would probably put it in the bank, periodically draw down your account, and have an average balance during the year equal to about half your annual income. If you received income monthly instead of once a year, you would operate similarly, but now your average balance would be much smaller. If you could arrange to receive income daily and to pay rent, tuition, and other charges on a daily basis, and if you were quite confident of your forecasted inflows and outflows, then you could hold a very small average cash balance.

Exactly the same situation holds for business firms—by improving their forecasts and by arranging events so that cash receipts coincide with required cash outflows, firms can reduce their transactions balances to a minimum. Recognizing

this point, utility companies, oil companies, credit card companies, and so on arrange to bill customers, and to pay their own bills, on regular "billing cycles" throughout the month. This improves the *synchronization of cash flows,* which in turn enables a firm to reduce its cash balances, decrease its bank loans, lower interest expenses, and boost profits.

CHECK-CLEARING PROCESS

When a customer writes and mails a check, this does *not* mean that the funds are immediately available to the receiving firm. Most of us have been told by someone that "the check is in the mail," and we have also deposited a check in our account and then been told that we cannot write our own checks against this deposit until the *check-clearing* process has been completed. Our bank must first make sure that the check we deposited is good and then receive funds itself from the customer's bank before it will give us cash.

As shown on the left side of Figure 17-1, quite a bit of time may be required for a firm to process incoming checks and obtain the use of the money. A check must first be delivered through the mail and then be cleared through the banking system before the money can be put to use. Checks received from customers in distant cities are especially subject to delays because of mail time and also because more parties are involved. For example, assume that we receive a check and deposit it in our bank. Our bank must send the check to the bank on which it was drawn. Only when this latter bank transfers funds to our bank are the funds available for us to use. Checks are generally cleared through the Federal Reserve System or through a clearinghouse set up by the banks in a particular city. Of course, if the check is deposited in the same bank on which it was drawn, that bank merely transfers funds by bookkeeping entries from one of its depositors to another. The length of time required for checks to clear is thus a function of the distance between the payer's and the payee's banks. In the case of private clearinghouses, it can range from one to three days. The maximum time required for checks to clear through the Federal Reserve System is two days, but mail delays can slow down things on each end of the Fed's involvement in the process.

USING FLOAT

Float is defined as the difference between the balance shown in a firm's (or individual's) checkbook and the balance on the bank's records. Suppose a firm writes, on the average, checks in the amount of $5,000 each day, and it takes six days for these checks to clear and to be deducted from the firm's bank account. This will cause the firm's own checkbook to show a balance $30,000 smaller than the balance on the bank's records; this difference is called *disbursement float.* Now suppose the firm also receives checks in the amount of $5,000 daily, but it loses four days while they are being deposited and cleared. This will result in $20,000 of *collections float.* In total, the firm's *net float*—the difference between $30,000

FIGURE 17-1   DIAGRAM OF THE CHECK-CLEARING PROCESS

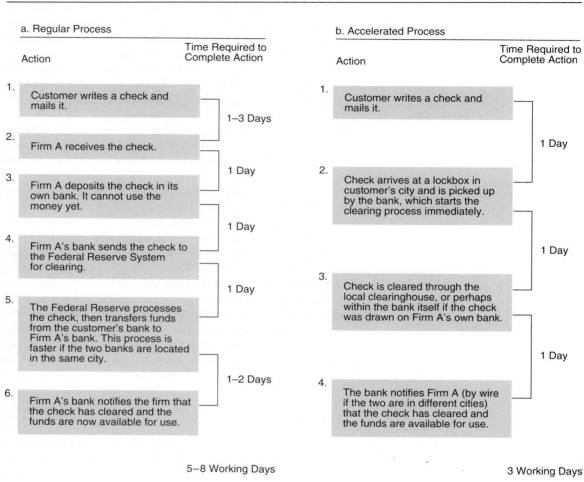

a. Regular Process

Action	Time Required to Complete Action
1. Customer writes a check and mails it.	
	1–3 Days
2. Firm A receives the check.	
	1 Day
3. Firm A deposits the check in its own bank. It cannot use the money yet.	
	1 Day
4. Firm A's bank sends the check to the Federal Reserve System for clearing.	
	1 Day
5. The Federal Reserve processes the check, then transfers funds from the customer's bank to Firm A's bank. This process is faster if the two banks are located in the same city.	
	1–2 Days
6. Firm A's bank notifies the firm that the check has cleared and the funds are now available for use.	

5–8 Working Days

b. Accelerated Process

Action	Time Required to Complete Action
1. Customer writes a check and mails it.	
	1 Day
2. Check arrives at a lockbox in customer's city and is picked up by the bank, which starts the clearing process immediately.	
	1 Day
3. Check is cleared through the local clearinghouse, or perhaps within the bank itself if the check was drawn on Firm A's own bank.	
	1 Day
4. The bank notifies Firm A (by wire if the two are in different cities) that the check has cleared and the funds are available for use.	

3 Working Days

positive disbursement float and the $20,000 negative collections float—will be $10,000.

Delays that cause float can be broken down into the time it takes for checks (1) to travel through the mail (mail float), (2) to be processed by the receiving firm (processing float), and (3) to clear through the banking system (clearing, or availability, float). Basically, the size of a firm's net float is a function of its ability to speed up collections on checks received and to slow down collections on checks written. Efficient firms go to great lengths to speed up the processing of incoming checks, thus putting the funds to work faster, and they try to stretch their own payments out as long as possible.

If the firm's own collection and clearing process is more efficient than that of the recipients of its checks—which is generally true of larger, more efficient firms—then the firm could actually show a *negative* balance on its own books but have a *positive* balance on the records of its bank. Some firms indicate that they *never* have positive book cash balances. One large manufacturer of construction equipment stated that while its account, according to its bank's records, shows an average cash balance of about $20 million, its *book* cash balance is *minus* $20 million—it has $40 million of net float. Obviously, the firm must be able to forecast its disbursements and collections accurately in order to make such heavy use of float.

E. F. Hutton provides an example of pushing cash management too far. Hutton, a leading brokerage firm at the time, did business with banks all across the country, and it had to keep compensating balances in these banks. The sizes of the required compensating balances were known, and any excess funds in these banks were sent electronically, on a daily basis, to concentration banks, where they were immediately invested in interest-bearing securities. However, rather than waiting to see what the end-of-day balances actually were, Hutton began estimating inflows and outflows, and it transferred out for investment the *estimated* end-of-day excess. But then Hutton got greedy, and it deliberately overestimated its deposits and underestimated clearings of its own checks, thereby deliberately overstating the estimated end-of-day balances. As a result, Hutton was chronically overdrawn at its local banks, and it was in effect earning interest on funds which really belonged to those local banks. It is entirely proper to forecast what your bank will have recorded as your balance and then to make decisions based on the estimate, even if that balance is different from the balance your own books show. However, it is illegal to forecast an overdrawn situation but then to tell the bank that you expect to have a positive balance.[1]

ACCELERATION OF RECEIPTS

Financial managers have been searching for ways to collect receivables faster since credit transactions began. Although cash collection is the financial manager's responsibility, the speed with which checks are cleared is dependent on the banking system. Several techniques are now used both to speed collections and to get funds where they are needed. Included are lockbox plans, pre-authorized debits, and concentration banking.

---

[1]A question raised during the Hutton investigation was this: "Why didn't the banks recognize that Hutton was systematically overdrawing its account and call the company to task?" The answer is that some banks, with tight controls, did exactly that—they refused to let Hutton get away with the practice. Other banks were lax. Still other banks apparently let Hutton get away with being chronically overdrawn out of fear of losing its business: Hutton used its economic muscle to force the banks to let it get away with an illegal act. In many people's opinion, the banks were as much at fault as Hutton. Still, in business dealings, honesty is presumed, and Hutton was dishonest in its dealings with the banks. This dishonesty severely damaged Hutton's reputation, cost the company profits totaling hundreds of millions of dollars, cost its top managers their jobs, and contributed to the ultimate demise of the company.

Lockboxes. A *lockbox plan* is one of the oldest cash management tools. In a lockbox system, incoming checks are sent to post office boxes rather than to corporate headquarters. For example, a firm headquartered in New York City might have its West Coast customers send their payments to a box in San Francisco, its customers in the Southwest send their checks to Dallas, and so on, rather than having all checks sent to New York City. Several times a day a local bank will collect the contents of the lockbox and deposit the checks into the company's local account. The bank would then provide the firm with a daily record of the receipts collected, usually via an electronic data transmission system in a format that permits on-line updating of the firm's receivables accounts.

A lockbox system reduces the time required for a firm to receive incoming checks, to deposit them, and to get them cleared through the banking system so that the funds are available for use. As shown on the right side of Figure 17-1, this time reduction occurs because mail time and check collection time are both reduced if the lockbox is located in the geographic area where the customer is located. Lockbox services can often increase the availability of funds by two to five days over the "regular" system.

Pre-Authorized Debits. A *pre-authorized debit* allows funds to be automatically transferred from a customer's account to the firm's account on specified dates. These transactions are also called "checkless" or "paperless" transactions since they are accomplished without using traditional paper checks. However, a record of payment does appear on both parties' bank statements. Pre-authorized debiting accelerates the transfer of funds because mail and check-clearing time are totally eliminated. Although pre-authorized debits are efficient in that the paperwork of both parties is reduced, and they appear to be the trend of the future, the pace of acceptance by payers has been much slower than originally predicted. Of course, a payer who agrees to a pre-authorized debit system loses the disbursement float that is inherent in the paper-based system. Currently, the biggest users of pre-authorized debits are insurance companies, which encourage policy holders to use them to pay periodic insurance premiums.

Concentration Banking. Lockbox systems and pre-authorized debits, although efficient in speeding up collections, result in the firm's cash being spread around among many banks. The primary purpose of *concentration banking* is to mobilize funds from decentralized receiving locations, whether they be lockboxes or decentralized company locations, into one or more central cash pools. The cash manager then uses these pools for short-term investing or reallocation among the firm's banks.

In a typical concentration system, the firm's collection banks record deposits received each day. Then, based on disbursement needs, the corporate cash manager transfers the funds from these collection points to a *concentration bank*. Concentration accounts allow firms to take maximum advantage of economies of scale in cash management and investment.

One of the keys to concentration banking is the ability to quickly transfer funds from collecting banks to concentration banks. One commonly used transfer

tool is the *depository transfer check (DTC)*. Here's how it works: Collection (lock-box) banks report the amounts on hand daily to the firm's concentration bank. The concentration bank, based on preset cash balance targets for the collection accounts, automatically writes DTCs that transfer funds to the concentration bank.

A relatively new development in funds transfer is the *electronic depository transfer,* sometimes called an *ACH-DTC.* The ACH stands for *automated clearing-house,* which is an electronic communications network that provides a means of sending data from one bank to another. Instead of using paper checks, magnetic tape files are processed by the ACH, and all entries for a particular bank are placed on a single file which is sent to that bank. Previously, banks sent and received their data on tapes, but today most have direct computer links to their ACH.

The ACH system is actually composed of 42 ACH associations, which have as members more than 17,500 financial institutions and nearly 40,000 corporations and government agencies. Four of the ACH associations are operated by private companies, while the remainder are operated by the Federal Reserve. Thus far, the primary users of electronic depository transfers are corporations and the federal government, which use the system for direct deposit of salary and social security checks.

To illustrate electronic transfers, consider the payroll of New England Ship-yards, a Boston company with 5,000 employees who are paid every two weeks. Before the ACH system was used, the company had to print and process 5,000 checks $\times$ 26 paydays = 130,000 checks each year. Now the company creates a data file with electronic payroll entries for each employee every payday and trans-mits it electronically to its lead bank, Boston National Bank (the originating depos-itory financial institution, or ODFI). Boston National removes any records for em-ployees with accounts there, merges the file with electronic payrolls from other companies, and sends the data to the local ACH. The ACH then divides the file into several parts: Transfers on banks belonging to the ACH (called local banks) are put into one file, and transfers to banks outside the ACH are put into other files. The ACH credits the employees' local banks with the aggregate payroll for each bank (the receiving depository financial institution, or RDFI), and sends the nonlocal records to other ACHs for further processing. At the same time, Boston National's account is charged for the total amount of payroll being processed by the ACH, so New England Shipyards must have the funds in its account to cover its payroll. Finally, the ACH will electronically transmit to each RDFI a file that contains the account numbers and amounts being transferred, so each bank can deposit the funds into each employee's checking account.

Electronic depository transfers have serveral advantages over paper checks, the primary ones being a significant savings in processing costs, greater reliability, and quicker access to funds by payees. On the other hand, the use of electronic depository transfers requires a large initial investment by banks to obtain the re-quired hardware and software, and it virtually eliminates disbursement float.

In addition to the automated clearinghouses, the Federal Reserve wire system can be used for cash concentration or other cash transfers. This system is typically used to move large sums that occur on a sporadic basis, such as would occur if a firm borrowed $10 million in the commercial paper market.

DISBURSEMENT CONTROL

Efficient cash management requires that both inflows and outflows be effectively managed. Accelerating collections represents one side of cash management, and controlling funds outflows is the flip side.

Payables Centralization. No single action controls cash outflows more effectively than the centralized processing of payables. This permits the financial manager to evaluate the payments coming due for the entire firm and to schedule the availability of funds to meet these needs on a companywide basis. Centralizing disbursements also permits more efficient monitoring of payables and float balances. Of course, there are also disadvantages to a centralized disbursement system—regional offices may not be able to make prompt payment for services rendered, which can create ill will and raise the company's operating costs. More than one firm has saved a few pennies by using a more cost-effective check-disbursing system but lost far more as a result of higher operating costs caused by ill will.

Zero-Balance Accounts. *Zero-balance accounts (ZBAs)* are special disbursement accounts having a zero-dollar balance on which checks are written. Typically, a firm establishes several ZBAs in the concentration bank and funds them from a master account. As checks are presented to a ZBA for payment, funds are automatically transferred from the master account. If the master account goes negative, it is replenished by borrowing from the bank against a line of credit, by borrowing in the commercial paper market, or by selling some T-bills from the marketable securities portfolio. Zero-balance accounts simplify the control of disbursements and cash balances, hence reduce the amount of idle (non-interest-bearing) cash.

Controlled Disbursement Accounts. Whereas zero-balance accounts are typically established at concentration banks, *controlled disbursement accounts* can be set up at any bank. In fact, controlled disbursement accounts were initially used only in relatively remote banks, hence this technique was originally called *remote disbursement.* The basic technique is simple: Controlled disbursement accounts are not funded until the day's checks are presented against the account. The key to controlled disbursement is the ability of the bank having the account to report the total daily amount of checks received for clearance by 11 A.M., New York time. This early notification gives financial managers sufficient time (1) to wire funds to the controlled disbursement account to cover the checks presented for payment or (2) to invest excess cash at midday, when money market trading is at a peak.

CASH MANAGEMENT IN THE MULTIDIVISIONAL FIRM

The concepts, techniques, and procedures described thus far in the chapter must be extended when applied to large, national firms. Such corporations have plants and sales offices all across the nation (or around the world), and they deal with

banks in all of their operating territories. These companies must maintain compensating balances in each of their banks, and they must be sure that no bank account becomes overdrawn. (After E. F. Hutton's problems, this has become especially important.) Cash inflows and outflows are subject to random fluctuations, so in the absence of close control and coordination, there would be a tendency for some accounts to have shortages while others had excess balances.

An example of such a firm is General Motors, which has extended the electronic transfer system for use in paying its suppliers. GM's electronic system utilizes eight banks across the nation, and it not only speeds up the payment process but also decreases uncertainty about the timing of the payment. This system benefits both GM and its suppliers because it reduces the required level of each firms' transactions and precautionary cash balances. GM's suppliers especially like the electronic system because overdue bills from GM have been reduced considerably, and suppliers take this into account when they bid for GM's business.

SELF-TEST QUESTIONS

What is float? How do firms use float to increase cash management efficiency?

What are some methods firms can use to accelerate receipts?

What are some techniques for controlling disbursements?

Explain how an ACH processes electronic depository transfers.

COMPENSATING BANKS FOR SERVICES

In addition to lending firms money, banks provide a great many services—they clear checks, provide full cash management services, operate lockbox plans, supply credit information, and the like. Because these services cost the bank money, the bank must be compensated for rendering them.

COMPENSATING BALANCES

Banks earn most of their income by lending money at interest, and most of the funds they lend are obtained in the form of deposits. If a firm maintains a deposit account with an average balance of $100,000, and if the bank can lend these funds at a net return of $8,000, then the account is, in a sense, worth $8,000 to the bank. Thus, it is to the bank's advantage to provide services worth up to $8,000 to attract and hold the account.

Banks first determine the costs of the services rendered to their larger customers, and then they estimate the average account balances necessary to provide enough income to compensate for these costs. Firms can make direct fee payments

for these services, but they often find it more convenient to maintain compensating balances rather than to pay monthly cash service charges to the bank.[2]

Compensating balances are also required by some banks under loan agreements. During periods when the supply of credit is restricted and interest rates are high, banks frequently require that borrowers maintain accounts which average a specified percentage of the loan amount as a condition for granting a loan; 10 percent is a typical figure. If the required balance is larger than the firm would otherwise maintain, the effective cost of the loan is increased; the excess balance presumably "compensates" the bank for making a loan at a rate below what it could earn on the funds if they were invested elsewhere.[3]

Compensating balances can be established (1) as an *absolute minimum*— say, $100,000—below which the actual balance must never fall or (2) as a *minimum average balance*—perhaps $100,000—over some period, generally a month. The absolute minimum is a much more restrictive requirement, because the total amount of cash held during the month must exceed $100,000 by the amount of the firm's transactions balances. The $100,000 in this case is "dead money" from the firm's standpoint. With a minimum average balance, however, the account could fall to zero on one day provided it was $200,000 on some other day, with the average working out to $100,000. Thus, the $100,000 in this case would be available for transactions.

Statistics on compensating balance requirements are not available, but average balances are typical and absolute minimums rare for business accounts. Discussions with bankers, however, indicate that absolute balance requirements are less rare during times of extremely tight money.

FEES FOR SERVICES

In general, compensating balance requirements were used to compensate banks for a generic "bundle" of cash management services. However, as the number of services increased, some firms wanted to choose only certain services from among the set offered. To accommodate their customers, many banks "unbundled" their cash management services, and instead of compensating balances, they now charge fees for each service rendered.

From a company's point of view, fees for services are generally favored over compensating balances. First, fees are a tax-deductible expense, while interest foregone on compensating balances is not. Second, fees are generally fixed over some period, often a year, so they can be easily budgeted and monitored. The costs associated with compensating balances, on the other hand, are much more uncertain, especially if interest rates are volatile. Finally, it is more practical for compa-

---

[2]Compensating balance arrangements apply to individuals as well as to business firms. Thus, you might get "free" checking services if you maintain a minimum balance of $500 but be charged 25 cents per check if your balance falls below that amount during the month.

[3]The effect of compensating balances on loan costs will be discussed later in the chapter.

nies to "shop" for cash management services when fees are charged, because it is easier to compare the fees of competing banks than to compare compensating balance requirements, which may be structured quite differently from bank to bank.

From a bank's point of view, compensating balances are often preferred. First, compensating balances increase the bank's total deposits, which is one benchmark of a bank's success. Second, compensating balances create additional security for the bank if the company defaults on a bank loan. Finally, compensating balances are available to banks to relend to another customer, so, to some extent, the same funds can be loaned to two customers.

Regardless of whether a bank uses compensating balances, fees, or some combination of the two, companies must assess the costs of the cash managment services provided. We will have more to say on this issue in the next section.

SELF-TEST QUESTIONS

What are compensating balances, and why are they used?

Differentiate between an absolute minimum and a minimum average compensating balance.

If you were a corporate treasurer, would you prefer to pay fees or meet compensating balance requirements to pay for cash management services? Why?

MATCHING THE COSTS AND BENEFITS OF CASH MANAGEMENT

Although a number of techniques have been discussed to reduce cash balance requirements, implementing these procedures is not a costless operation. How far should a firm go in making its cash operations more efficient? As a general rule, the firm should incur these expenses as long as the marginal returns exceed the marginal costs.

For example, suppose that by establishing a lockbox system a firm can reduce its investment in cash by $1 million without increasing the risk of running short of cash. Further, suppose the firm borrows at a cost of 12 percent. The lockbox system will release $1 million, which can be used to reduce bank loans and thus save $120,000 per year. If the costs of setting up and operating the lockbox system are less than $120,000, the move is a good one, but if the costs exceed $120,000, the improvement in efficiency is not worth the cost. It is clear that larger firms, with larger cash balances, can better afford to hire the personnel necessary to maintain tight control over their cash positions. Cash management is one element of business operations in which economies of scale are present.

Very clearly, the value of careful cash management depends upon the costs of funds invested in cash, which in turn depend upon the current rate of interest. In the 1980s, with interest rates at relatively high levels, firms devoted a great deal

of care to cash management.[4] As we write this in mid-1993, interest rates are lower, but the importance of cash management remains high due to the need to maintain profits in a weak economic environment.

SELF-TEST QUESTION

How far should a firm go in its cash management effort; that is, how much should be spent on cash management?

MARKETABLE SECURITIES

Since *marketable securities* represent cash that has been turned into earning assets, cash management is interrelated to marketable securities management. In this section, we discuss marketable securities and then, in the next section, we present a model for balancing a firm's holdings of cash and marketable securities.

RATIONALE FOR HOLDING MARKETABLE SECURITIES

Marketable securities typically provide much lower yields than operating assets; for example, Procter & Gamble holds a $1.5 billion portfolio of marketable securities that yields about 4 percent, while its operating assets provide a return of about 14 percent. Why would a company such as Procter & Gamble have such large holdings of low-yielding assets? There are two basic reasons for these holdings: (1) They serve as a substitute for cash balances, and (2) they are used as a temporary investment. These points are considered next.

Marketable Securities as a Substitute for Cash.   Some firms hold portfolios of marketable securities in lieu of larger cash balances, liquidating part of the portfolio to increase the cash account when cash outflows exceed inflows. In such situations, the marketable securities could be used as a substitute for transactions balances, for precautionary balances, for speculative balances, or for all three. In most cases, the securities are held primarily for precautionary purposes — most firms prefer to rely on bank credit to make temporary transactions or to meet speculative needs, but they may still hold some liquid assets to guard against a possible shortage of bank credit.

A few years ago, IBM had substantially more marketable securities than the $4 billion it has today. Those large liquid balances had been built up primarily as a reserve for possible damage payments resulting from pending antitrust suits. When it became clear that IBM would win most of the suits, its liquidity needs declined,

---

[4]Banks have also placed considerable emphasis on developing and marketing cash management services. Because of scale economies, banks can generally provide these services to smaller companies at lower costs than the companies could achieve by operating in-house cash management systems.

and the company spent some of the funds on other assets, including repurchases of its own stock. This is a good example of a firm's building up its precautionary balances to handle possible emergencies.

Marketable Securities Held as a Temporary Investment. Temporary investments in marketable securities generally occur in one of the following two situations:

1. To finance seasonal or cyclical operations. If the firm has a conservative financing policy as we defined it back in Panel c of Figure 16-3 in Chapter 16, then its long-term capital will exceed its permanent assets, and marketable securities will be held when inventories and receivables are low. On the other hand, with a highly aggressive policy it will never carry any securities, and it will borrow heavily to meet peak needs. With a moderate policy, where maturities are matched, permanent assets will be matched with long-term financing, most seasonal increases in inventories and receivables will be met by short-term loans, but the firm may also carry marketable securities at certain times.

2. To meet known financial requirements. Marketable securities are frequently built up immediately preceding quarterly corporate tax or dividend payment dates. Further, if a major plant construction program is planned for the near future, if an acquisition is planned, or if a bond issue is about to mature, a firm may build up its marketable securities portfolio to provide the required funds. For example, Commonwealth Edison, the electric utility serving Chicago, has a permanent, ongoing construction program, generating a continuous need for new capital. Since there are substantial fixed costs involved in stock or bond flotations, these securities are issued infrequently and in large amounts.

During the 1970s, Edison followed the practice of selling bonds and stock *before* the capital was needed, investing the proceeds in marketable securities, and then liquidating the securities to finance plant construction. Plan A in Figure 17-2 illustrates this procedure. However, during the 1980s, Edison encountered financial stress. It was forced to use up its liquid assets and to switch to its present policy of financing plant construction with short-term bank loans and then selling long-term securities to retire the bank loans when they had built up to some target level. This policy is illustrated by Plan B of Figure 17-2.

Plan A is the more conservative, less risky one. First, the company is minimizing its liquidity problems because it has no short-term debt hanging over its head. Second, it is sure of having the funds available to meet construction payments as they come due. On the other hand, firms generally have to pay higher interest rates when they borrow than the return they receive on marketable securities, so following the less risky strategy has a cost.

FACTORS INFLUENCING THE CHOICE OF MARKETABLE SECURITIES

A wide variety of securities, differing in terms of default risk, interest rate price risk, liquidity risk, and expected rate of return, are available to firms that choose to hold marketable securities. In this section we first consider the different types

FIGURE 17-2   ALTERNATIVE METHODS OF FINANCING A CONTINUOUS CONSTRUCTION PROGRAM

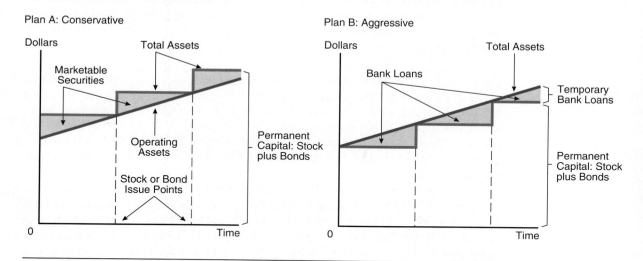

of risk, then we look at the extent to which each type of risk is found in different securities, and, finally, we look at some specific instruments which are suitable investments for temporary excess cash.

Default Risk.   The risk that a borrower will be unable to make interest payments, or to repay the principal amount on schedule, is known as *default risk*. If the issuer is the U.S. Treasury, default risk is negligible, so Treasury securities are regarded as being default-free. (Treasury securities are not completely free of risk, since U.S. government bonds are subject to price risk caused by interest rate fluctuations, and they are also subject to loss of purchasing power due to inflation.) Recall that in Chapter 3 we developed this equation for determining the nominal interest rate:

$$k_{Nom} = k^* + IP + DRP + LP + MRP.$$

Here k^* is the real risk-free rate, IP is a premium for expected inflation, DRP is the default risk premium, LP is the liquidity (or marketability) risk premium, and MRP is the maturity risk (or price risk) premium. Also, remember from Chapter 3 that the risk-free rate, k_{RF}, is equal to $k^* + IP$. As we learned in Chapter 3, a U.S. Treasury bill comes closest to being risk free, while a U.S. Treasury bond has no default or liquidity risk premiums, but it is exposed to interest rate price risk, so a maturity risk premium is included in its nominal interest rate. Corporate securities, as well as bonds issued by state and local governments, are subject to some degree

of default risk, so these securities' returns include a default risk premium. Several organizations (for example, Moody's Investment Service and Standard & Poor's Corporation) rate bonds on the basis of their default risk. They classify them on a scale that ranges from very high quality to highly speculative, with a definite chance of going into default. Ratings change from time to time as the issuer's situation changes.

Event Risk.   The probability that some event (such as a recapitalization or a leveraged buyout) will occur and suddenly increase a firm's default risk is called *event risk*. Bonds issued by industrial and service companies generally have more event risk than bonds issued by regulated companies such as banks or electric utilities. Also, long-term securities are affected more by unfavorable events than are short-term securities. Treasury securities do not carry any event risk, barring national disaster.

Price Risk.   We saw in Chapter 7 that bond prices vary with changes in interest rates. Also, the prices of long-term bonds are much more sensitive to changes in interest rates than are prices of short-term securities — long-term bonds have more *price risk*. Thus, if Allied's treasurer purchased at par $1 million of 25-year U.S. government bonds paying 9 percent interest, and if interest rates then rose to 14.5 percent, the market value of the bonds would fall from $1 million to just below $635,000 — a loss of almost 40 percent. (This actually happened from 1980 to 1982) If 90-day Treasury bills had been held, however, the loss would have been negligible. Thus, the Treasury bill would have a zero maturity risk premium, but the long-term Treasury bond would have a positive maturity risk premium included in its nominal interest rate.

Inflation Risk.   Another type of risk is *inflation*, or *purchasing power, risk*, which is the risk that inflation will reduce the purchasing power of a given sum of money. Inflation risk, which is important both to firms and to individual investors during times of rising prices, is lower on assets whose returns tend to rise with inflation than on assets whose returns are fixed. Thus, real estate and common stocks are generally better hedges against inflation than are bonds and other fixed-income securities. You should recall from our discussion in Chapter 3 that a security's interest rate reflects the average rate of inflation expected over the security's life. Therefore, a 90-day Treasury bill would include the average rate of inflation expected over the 90-day period, while a 30-year Treasury bond would include the average rate of inflation expected over a 30-year period. Thus, if a high rate of inflation is expected in the future, that expectation is built into interest rates. Accordingly, the primary risk of inflation to bondholders is the possibility that actual inflation will exceed the expected level.

Liquidity Risk.   An asset that can be sold on short notice for close to its quoted market price is considered to be highly liquid. If Allied Food Products purchased $1 million of infrequently traded bonds of a relatively obscure company like

Bigham Pork Products, it would probably have to accept a price reduction in order to sell the bonds on short notice. On the other hand, if Allied invested in U.S. Treasury bonds, or in bonds issued by AT&T, DuPont, or Exxon, it would be able to dispose of them almost instantaneously at close to the quoted market price. These latter bonds are therefore said to have very little *liquidity,* or *marketability, risk.* If we go back to the nominal interest rate equation discussed earlier, the required return for any bond includes a premium for inflation, default, maturity, and liquidity risk. Therefore, the bonds of Bigham Pork Products would have a greater liquidity premium than the bonds of AT&T, DuPont, or Exxon.

Of course, long-term bonds are exposed to significantly more interest rate price risk than are short-term instruments. There are many types of safe, highly liquid short-term securities in which a company can invest temporary excess cash. These instruments will be discussed shortly.

Returns on Securities (Yields).   As we know from earlier chapters, the higher a security's risk, the higher its required return. Thus, corporate treasurers, like other investors, must make a trade-off between risk and return when choosing marketable securities. Because these securities are generally held either for a specific known need or for use in emergencies, the firm might be financially embarrassed should the portfolio decline in value. Also, most corporations do not have investment departments specializing in appraising securities and determining the probability of their going into default. Accordingly, the marketable securities portfolio is generally composed of highly liquid short-term securities issued either by the U.S. government or by the very strongest corporations. Given the purpose of the portfolio, treasurers should not sacrifice safety for higher rates of return.

TYPES OF MARKETABLE SECURITIES

Table 17-1 lists the major types of securities available for investment, with yields as of June 10, 1977, February 10, 1982, and March 1, 1993. Depending on how long they will be held, the financial manager decides upon a suitable set of securities, and a suitable maturity pattern, to hold as *near-cash reserves.*

It should be noted that larger corporations, with large amounts of surplus cash, tend to own directly Treasury bills, commercial paper, and CDs, as well as Euromarket securities. Smaller firms, on the other hand, are more likely to invest through a money market or preferred stock mutual fund because the small firm's volume of investment simply does not warrant the hiring of specialists who can manage the portfolio and make sure that the securities held mature (or can be sold) at the same time cash is required. Firms can use a mutual fund and then literally write checks on the fund to meet cash needs as they arise. Interest rates on money funds are somewhat lower than rates on direct investments of equivalent risk because of management fees, but for smaller companies the net returns may well be higher on money funds.

TABLE 17-1

SECURITIES AVAILABLE FOR INVESTMENT OF SURPLUS CASH

Security	Typical Maturity at Time of Issue	Approximate Yields 6/10/77	2/10/82	3/1/93
Generally Suitable to Hold as Near-Cash Reserves				
U.S. Treasury bills[a]	91 days to 1 year	4.8%	15.1%	3.1%
Commercial paper[a]	Up to 270 days	5.5	15.3	3.3
Negotiable certificates of deposit (CDs) of U.S. banks	Up to 1 year	6.0	15.5	2.8
Money market mutual funds	Instant liquidity	5.1	14.0	3.3
Floating rate and market auction preferred stock[b]	Instant liquidity	N.A.	N.A.	3.0
Eurodollar time deposits	Up to 1 year	6.1	16.2	3.2
Generally Not Suitable to Hold as Near-Cash Reserves				
U.S. Treasury notes	3 to 10 years	6.8	14.8	5.1
U.S. Treasury bonds	Up to 30 years	7.6	14.6	6.8
Corporate bonds (AAA)[c]	Up to 40 years	8.2	16.0	7.6
State and local government bonds (AAA)[c,d]	Up to 30 years	5.7	12.8	6.0
Preferred stocks (AAA)[c,d]	30 years to perpetual	7.5	14.0	7.1
Common stocks of other corporations	Unlimited	Variable	Variable	Variable
Common stock of the firm in question	Unlimited	Variable	Variable	Variable

[a]Treasury bills and commercial paper are sold at a discount but are paid off at par upon maturity, so their returns are quoted on a *discount basis rate*. To obtain an interest rate which can be compared to quoted yields on coupon bonds — called a *yield basis rate* — we use the following formula:

$$\text{Yield basis rate} = \frac{365(\text{Discount basis rate})}{360 - (\text{Discount basis rate})(\text{Days to maturity})}.$$

To illustrate, if we assume a 3-month (91-day) maturity, the T-bills' 3.1 percent discount basis rate on March 1, 1993, translates into a yield basis rate (or effective annual rate) of 3.17 percent:

$$\text{Yield basis rate} = \frac{365(0.031)}{360 - 0.031(91)}$$

$$= 0.0317 = 3.17\%.$$

See Robert C. Radcliffe, *Investment Concepts, Analysis, and Strategy* (Glenview, Ill.: Scott, Foresman, 1993), for a further discussion.

[b]Floating rate and market auction preferred stocks are recent innovations in near-cash securities. They are held by corporations (often through money funds designed for this purpose) because of the 70 percent dividend tax exclusion.

[c]Rates shown for corporate and state/local government bonds, and for preferred stock, are for longer maturities rated AAA. Lower-rated securities have higher yields. The slope of the yield curve determines whether shorter- or longer-term securities of a given rating would have higher yields.

[d]Rates are lower on state/municipal government bonds because the interest they pay is exempt from federal income taxes, and the rate on preferred stocks is low because 70 percent of the dividends paid on them is exempt from federal taxes for corporate owners, who own most preferred stocks.

SELF-TEST QUESTIONS

Why do firms hold marketable securities?

What criteria are applied when selecting securities for a firm's liquid asset portfolio?

What are some securities commonly held as marketable securities?

THE BAUMOL MODEL FOR BALANCING CASH AND MARKETABLE SECURITIES

In Chapter 16, when we discussed Allied's cash budget, we took as a given the $10 million target cash balance. In this chapter, we have discussed how lockboxes, synchronizing inflows and outflows, and float can reduce the required cash balance. Now we consider a formal model which can be used for establishing the target cash balance.

William Baumol first noted that cash balances are in many respects similar to inventories, and that the EOQ inventory model, which will be developed in Chapter 18, can be used to establish a target cash balance.[5] Baumol's model assumes that the firm uses cash at a steady, predictable rate—say, $1 million per week—and that the firm's cash inflows from operations also occur at a steady, predictable rate—say, $900,000 per week. Therefore, the firm's net cash outflows, or net need for cash, also occur at a steady rate—in this case, $100,000 per week.[6] Under these steady-state assumptions, the firm's cash position will resemble the situation shown in Figure 17-3.

If our illustrative firm started at Time 0 with a cash balance of C = $300,000, and if its outflows exceeded its inflows by $100,000 per week, then its cash balance would drop to zero at the end of Week 3, and its average cash balance would be C/2 = $300,000/2 = $150,000. Therefore, at the end of Week 3 the firm would have to replenish its cash balance, either by selling marketable securities, if it had any, or by borrowing.

If C were set at a higher level, say, $600,000, then the cash supply would last longer (6 weeks), and the firm would have to sell securities (or borrow) less frequently, but its average cash balance would rise from $150,000 to $300,000. Brokerage or some other type of transactions cost must be incurred to sell securities (or to borrow), so holding larger cash balances will lower the transactions

---

[5]William J. Baumol, "The Transactions Demand for Cash: An Inventory Theoretic Approach," *Quarterly Journal of Economics,* November 1952, 545–556.

[6]Our hypothetical firm is experiencing a $100,000 weekly cash shortfall, but this does not necessarily imply that it is headed for bankruptcy. The firm could, for example, be highly profitable and be enjoying high earnings, but be expanding so rapidly that it is experiencing chronic cash shortages that must be made up by borrowing or by selling common stock. Or the firm could be in the construction business and therefore receive major cash inflows at wide intervals but have net cash outflows of $100,000 per week between major inflows.

FIGURE 17-3

CASH BALANCES
UNDER THE BAUMOL
MODEL'S
ASSUMPTIONS

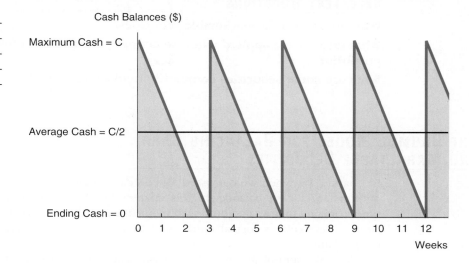

costs associated with obtaining cash. On the other hand, cash provides no income, so the larger the average cash balance, the higher the opportunity cost, which is the return that could have been earned on securities or other assets held in lieu of cash. Thus, we have the situation that is graphed in Figure 17-4. The optimal cash balance is found by using the following variables and equations:

C = amount of cash raised by selling marketable securities or by borrowing. $C/2$ = average cash balance.

C^* = optimal amount of cash to be raised by selling marketable securities or by borrowing. $C^*/2$ = optimal average cash balance.

F = fixed costs of making a securities trade or of obtaining a loan.

T = total amount of net new cash needed for transactions during the entire period (usually a year).

k = opportunity cost of holding cash, set equal to the rate of return foregone on marketable securities or the cost of borrowing to hold cash.

The total costs of cash balances consist of holding (or opportunity) costs plus transactions costs:[7]

---

[7]Total costs can be expressed on either a before-tax or an after-tax basis. Both methods lead to the same conclusions regarding target cash balances and comparative costs. For simplicity, we present the model here on a before-tax basis.

FIGURE 17-4

DETERMINATION OF
THE TARGET CASH
BALANCE

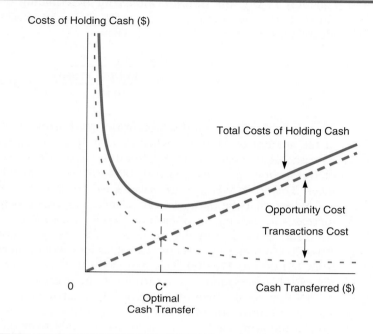

Costs of Holding Cash ($)

Total Costs of Holding Cash

Opportunity Cost

Transactions Cost

0

C*
Optimal
Cash Transfer

Cash Transferred ($)

$$
\begin{aligned}
\frac{\text{Total}}{\text{costs}} &= \qquad \text{Holding costs} \qquad + \qquad \text{Transactions costs} \\
&= \left(\begin{array}{c}\text{Average cash} \\ \text{balance}\end{array}\right)\left(\begin{array}{c}\text{Opportunity} \\ \text{cost}\end{array}\right) + \left(\begin{array}{c}\text{Number of} \\ \text{transactions}\end{array}\right)\left(\begin{array}{c}\text{Cost per} \\ \text{transaction}\end{array}\right) \\
&= \qquad\quad \frac{C}{2}(k) \qquad\qquad + \qquad\qquad \frac{T}{C}(F).
\end{aligned}
$$
(17-1)

The minimum total costs are achieved when C is set equal to C*, the optimal cash transfer. C* is found as follows:[8]

$$
C^* = \sqrt{\frac{2(F)(T)}{k}}.
$$
(17-2)

[8]Equation 17-1 is differentiated with respect to C. The derivative is set equal to zero, and we then solve for C = C* to derive Equation 17-2. This model, applied to inventories and called the EOQ model, is discussed further in Chapter 18.

Equation 17-2 is the *Baumol model* for determining optimal cash balances. To illustrate its use, suppose F = $150; T = 52 weeks × $100,000/week = $5,200,000; and k = 15% = 0.15. Then

$$C^* = \sqrt{\frac{2(\$150)(\$5,200,000)}{0.15}} = \$101,980.$$

Therefore, the firm should sell securities (or borrow if it does not hold securities) in the amount of $101,980 when its cash balance approaches zero, thus building its cash balance back up to $101,980. If we divide T by C*, we have the number of transactions per year: $5,200,000/$101,980 = 50.99 ≈ 51, or about once a week. The firm's average cash balance is $101,980/2 = $50,990 ≈ $51,000.

Notice that the optimal cash balance increases less than proportionately with increases in the amount of cash needed for transactions. For example, if the firm's size, and consequently its net new cash needs, doubled from $5,200,000 to $10,400,000 per year, average cash balances would increase by only 41 percent, from $51,000 to $72,000. This suggests that there are economies of scale in holding cash balances, and this in turn gives larger firms an edge over smaller ones.[9]

Of course, the firm would probably want to hold a safety stock of cash designed to reduce the probability of a cash shortage to some specified level. However, if the firm is able to sell securities or to borrow on short notice — and most larger firms can do so in a matter of just a couple of hours simply by making a telephone call — the safety stock of cash can be quite low.

The Baumol model is obviously simplistic in many respects. Most important, it assumes relatively stable, predictable cash inflows and outflows, and it does not take into account any seasonal or cyclical trends. Other models have been developed to deal both with uncertainty in the cash flows and with trends. Any of these models, including the Baumol model, can provide a useful starting point for establishing a target cash balance, but all of them have limitations and must be applied with judgment.

SELF-TEST QUESTIONS

What is the purpose of the Baumol model?

Write out the equation for the model and then list its key assumptions.

SHORT-TERM FINANCING

If a firm does not have the cash and marketable securities to meet its cash budget shortfalls, it must raise the funds externally. As we discussed in Chapter 16, most firms use short-term financing to meet temporary shortfalls, while permanent cap-

---

[9]This edge may, of course, be more than offset by other factors — after all, cash management is only one aspect of running a business.

ital (long-term debt and equity) is used to meet long-term capital requirements. In the remainder of this chapter, we discuss the four primary sources of short-term financing: (1) accruals, (2) accounts payable, (3) bank loans, and (4) commercial paper. In addition, we discuss the cost of bank loans and the factors that influence a firm's choice of a bank.

ACCRUALS

Firms generally pay employees on a weekly, biweekly, or monthly basis, so the balance sheet will typically show some accrued wages. Similarly, the firm's own estimated income taxes, the social security and income taxes withheld from employee payrolls, and the sales taxes collected are generally paid on a weekly, monthly, or quarterly basis, so the balance sheet will typically show some accrued taxes along with accrued wages.

Accruals increase automatically, or spontaneously, as a firm's operations expand. Further, this type of debt is "free" in the sense that no explicit interest is paid on funds raised through accruals. However, a firm cannot ordinarily control its accruals: The timing of wage payments is set by economic forces and industry custom, while tax payment dates are established by law. Thus, firms use all the accruals they can, but they have little control over the levels of these accounts.

SELF-TEST QUESTIONS

What types of short-term credits are classified as accruals?

What is the cost of accruals?

How much control do financial managers have over the dollar amount of accruals?

ACCOUNTS PAYABLE (TRADE CREDIT)

Firms generally make purchases from other firms on credit, recording the debt as an *account payable.* Accounts payable, or *trade credit,* is the largest single category of short-term debt, representing about 40 percent of the current liabilities of the average nonfinancial corporation. The percentage is somewhat larger for smaller firms: Because small companies often do not qualify for financing from other sources, they rely especially heavily on trade credit.[10]

---

[10]In a credit sale, the seller records the transaction as a receivable; the buyer, as a payable. We will examine accounts receivable as an asset investment in Chapter 18. Our focus in this chapter is on accounts payable, a liability item. We might also note that if a firm's accounts payable exceed its receivables, it is said to be *receiving net trade credit,* whereas if its receivables exceed its payables, it is *extending net trade credit.* Smaller firms frequently receive net credit; larger firms generally extend it.

Trade credit is a spontaneous source of financing in the sense that it arises from ordinary business transactions. For example, suppose a firm makes average purchases of $2,000 a day on terms of net 30, meaning that it must pay for goods 30 days after the invoice date. On average, it will owe $30 \times \$2,000 = \$60,000$, to its suppliers. If its sales, and consequently its purchases, were to double, then its accounts payable would also double, to $120,000. So, simply by growing, the firm would have spontaneously generated an additional $60,000 of financing. Similarly, if the terms under which it bought were extended from 30 to 40 days, its accounts payable would expand from $60,000 to $80,000. Thus, lengthening the credit period, as well as expanding sales and purchases, generates additional financing.

THE COST OF TRADE CREDIT

Firms that sell on credit have a *credit policy* that includes certain *terms of credit*. For example, Microchip Electronics sells on terms of 2/10, net 30, meaning that a 2 percent discount is given if payment is made within 10 days of the invoice date, with the full invoice amount being due and payable within 30 days if the discount is not taken.

Note that the true price of Microchip's products is the net price, or 0.98 (list price), because any customer can purchase an item at a 2 percent "discount" as long as the customer pays within 10 days. Consider Personal Computer Company (PCC), which buys its memory chips from Microchip. One commonly used memory chip is listed at $100, so the true cost to PCC, or to any other Microchip customer, is $98. Now if PCC wants an additional 20 days of credit beyond the 10-day discount period, it must incur a finance charge of $2 per chip for that credit. Thus, the $100 list price can be thought of as follows:

$$\text{List price} = \$100 = \$98 \text{ true price} + \$2 \text{ finance charge.}$$

The question that PCC must ask before it pays the $2 and takes the additional 20 days of credit from Microchip is whether the firm could obtain similar credit under better terms from some other lender, say, a bank. In other words, could 20 days of credit be obtained for less than $2 per item?

PCC buys an average of $11,760,000 of memory chips from Microchip each year at the net or true price, which amounts to $11,760,000/360 = $32,666.67 per day. For simplicity, assume that Microchip is PCC's only supplier. If PCC declines the additional trade credit offered by Microchip—that is, if it pays on the 10th day and takes the discount—its payables will average 10($32,666.67) = $326,667. Thus, PCC will be receiving $326,667 of credit from its only supplier, Microchip Electronics.

Now suppose PCC decides to take the additional 20 days credit and thus must pay the finance charge. Since PCC will now pay on the 30th day, its accounts

payable will increase to 30($32,666.67) = $980,000.[11] Microchip will now be supplying PCC with an additional $653,333 of credit, which it could use to build up its cash account, to pay off debt, to expand inventories, or even to extend more credit to its own customers and hence to increase its own accounts receivable.

The additional credit offered by Microchip has a cost — PCC must pay the finance charge by foregoing the 2 percent discount on its purchases. Since PCC buys $11,760,000 of chips at the true price of 0.98 (list price), the added finance charge increases the total cost to PCC to $11,760,000/0.98 = $12 million, so the annual financing cost is $12,000,000 − $11,760,000 = $240,000. (Alternatively, the financing cost, or discount lost, can be calculated as 0.02 [List price] = 0.02 [$12,000,000] = $240,000.) Dividing the $240,000 financing cost by the $653,333 in average annual additional credit, we find the approximate cost of the additional trade credit to be 36.7 percent:

$$\text{Approximate percentage cost} = \frac{\$240,000}{\$653,333} = 36.7\%.$$

Assuming that PCC can borrow from its bank (or from other sources) at an interest rate less than 36.7 percent, it should not obtain credit in the form of accounts payable by foregoing discounts.

The following equation can be used to calculate the approximate percentage cost, on an annual basis, of not taking discounts:

$$\begin{array}{c}\text{Approximate} \\ \text{percentage} \\ \text{cost}\end{array} = \frac{\text{Discount percent}}{100 - \begin{array}{c}\text{Discount} \\ \text{percent}\end{array}} \times \frac{360}{\begin{array}{c}\text{Days credit is} \\ \text{outstanding}\end{array} - \begin{array}{c}\text{Discount} \\ \text{period}\end{array}}. \quad \text{(17-3)}$$

The numerator of the first term, Discount percent, is the cost per dollar of credit, while the denominator in this term, 100 − Discount percent, represents the funds made available by not taking the discount. Thus, the first term is the periodic cost of the trade credit. The denominator of the second term is the number of days of extra credit obtained by not taking the discount, so the entire second term shows how many times each year the cost is incurred. To illustrate the equation, the approximate cost of not taking a discount when the terms are 2/10, net 30, is calculated as follows:

---

[11] A question arises here: Should accounts payable reflect gross purchases or purchases net of discounts? Although generally accepted accounting principles permit either treatment on the grounds that the difference is not material, most accountants prefer to record payables net of discounts, or at "true" prices, and then to report the higher payments that result from not taking discounts as an additional expense, called "discounts lost." *Thus, we show accounts payable net of discounts even if the company does not expect to take the discount.*

$$\text{Approximate percentage cost} = \frac{2}{98} \times \frac{360}{20} = 2.04\% \times 18 = 36.7\%.$$

The approximation formula does not take account of compounding, and in effective annual interest terms, the cost of trade credit is seen to be much higher. The discount amounts to interest, and with terms of 2/10, net 30, the firm gains use of the funds for $30 - 10 = 20$ days, so there are $360/20 = 18$ "interest periods" per year. Remember that the first term in Equation 17-3, (Discount percent)/(100 − Discount percent) = 0.02/0.98 = 0.0204, is the periodic interest rate. This rate is paid 18 times each year, so the effective annual cost rate of trade credit is

$$\text{Effective annual rate} = (1.0204)^{18} - 1.0 = 1.439 - 1.0 = 43.9\%.$$

Thus, the 36.7 percent approximate cost calculated with Equation 17-3 understates the true cost of trade credit.

Notice, however, that the cost of trade credit can be reduced by paying late. Thus, if PCC could get away with paying in 60 days rather than in the specified 30, then the effective credit period would become $60 - 10 = 50$ days, the number of times the discount would be lost would fall to $360/50 = 7.2$, and the approximate cost would drop from 36.7 percent to $2.04\% \times 7.2 = 14.7\%$. The effective annual rate would drop from 43.9 to 15.7 percent:

$$\text{Effective annual rate} = (1.0204)^{7.2} - 1.0 = 1.157 - 1.0 = 15.7\%.$$

In periods of excess capacity, firms may be able to get away with late payments, but they will also suffer a variety of problems associated with *stretching accounts payable* and being branded a "slow payer." These problems are discussed later in the chapter.

The cost of the additional trade credit that is incurred by not taking discounts can be worked out for other purchase terms. Some illustrative costs are shown below:

	Cost of Additional Credit If the Cash Discount Is Not Taken	
Credit Terms	Approximate Cost	Effective Cost
1/10, net 20	36%	44%
1/10, net 30	18	20
2/10, net 20	73	107
3/15, net 45	37	44

As these figures show, the cost of not taking discounts can be substantial. Incidentally, throughout the chapter, we assume that payments are made either on the *last day* for taking discounts or on the *last day* of the credit period, unless otherwise noted. It would be foolish to pay, say, on the fifth day or on the twentieth day if the credit terms were 2/10, net 30.

EFFECTS OF TRADE CREDIT ON THE FINANCIAL STATEMENTS

A firm's policy with regard to taking or not taking discounts can have a significant effect on its financial statements. To illustrate, let us assume that PCC is just beginning its operations. On the first day, it makes net purchases of $32,666.67. This amount is recorded on its balance sheet under accounts payable.[12] The second day it buys another $32,666.67. The first day's purchases are not yet paid for, so at the end of the second day, accounts payable total $65,333.34. Accounts payable increase by another $32,666.67 on the third day, for a total of $98,000, and after 10 days, accounts payable are up to $326,667.

If PCC takes discounts, then on the 11th day it will have to pay for the $32,666.67 of purchases made on the first day, which will reduce accounts payable. However, it will buy another $32,666.67, which will increase payables. Thus, after the 10th day of operations, PCC's balance sheet will level off, showing a balance of $326,667 in accounts payable, assuming that the company pays on the 10th day in order to take discounts.

Now suppose PCC decides not to take discounts. In this case, on the 11th day it will add another $32,666.67 to payables, but it will not pay for the purchases made on the 1st day. Thus, the balance sheet figure for accounts payable will rise to 11($32,666.67) = $359,333.37. This buildup will continue through the 30th day, at which point payables will total 30($32,666.67) = $980,000. On the 31st day, PCC will buy another $32,666.67 of goods, which will increase accounts payable, but it will also pay for the purchases made the 1st day, which will reduce payables. Thus, the balance sheet item accounts payable will stabilize at $980,000 after 30 days, assuming PCC does not take discounts.

The upper section of Table 17-2 shows PCC's balance sheet, after it reaches a steady state, under the two trade credit policies. Total assets are unchanged by this policy decision, and we also assume that the accruals and common equity accounts are unchanged. The differences show up in accounts payable and notes payable; when PCC elects to take discounts and thus gives up some of the trade credit it otherwise could have obtained, it will have to raise $653,333 from some other source. It could have sold more common stock, or it could have used long-term bonds, but it chose to use bank credit, which has a 10 percent cost and is reflected in the notes payable account.

The lower section of Table 17-2 shows PCC's income statement under the two policies. If the company does not take discounts, then its interest expense will be zero, but it will have a $240,000 expense for discounts lost. On the other hand, if it does take discounts, it will incur an interest expense of $65,333, but it will avoid the cost of discounts lost. Since discounts lost exceed the interest expense, the take-discounts policy results in a higher net income and, thus, in a higher stock price.

---

[12]Inventories also increase by $32,666.67, but we are not now concerned with inventories. Again note that both inventories and receivables are recorded net of discounts regardless of whether discounts are taken.

TABLE 17-2 PCC'S FINANCIAL STATEMENTS WITH DIFFERENT TRADE CREDIT POLICIES		Take Discounts; Borrow from Bank (1)	Do Not Take Discounts; Use Maximum Trade Credit (2)	Difference (1) − (2)
I. Balance Sheets				
	Cash	$ 500,000	$ 500,000	$ 0
	Receivables	1,000,000	1,000,000	0
	Inventories	2,000,000	2,000,000	0
	Fixed assets	2,980,000	2,980,000	0
	Total assets	$ 6,480,000	$ 6,480,000	$ 0
	Accounts payable	$ 326,667	$ 980,000	$ − 653,333
	Notes payable (10%)	653,333	0	+ 653,333
	Accruals	500,000	500,000	0
	Common equity	5,000,000	5,000,000	0
	Total claims	$ 6,480,000	$ 6,480,000	$ 0
II. Income Statements				
	Sales	$15,000,000	$15,000,000	$ 0
	Less: Purchases	11,760,000	11,760,000	0
	Labor	2,000,000	2,000,000	0
	Interest	65,333	0	+ 65,333
	Discounts lost	0	240,000	− 240,000
	Earnings before taxes (EBT)	$ 1,174,667	$ 1,000,000	$ + 174,667
	Taxes (40%)	469,867	400,000	+ 69,867
	Net income	$ 704,800	$ 600,000	$ + 104,800

COMPONENTS OF TRADE CREDIT: FREE VERSUS COSTLY

On the basis of the preceding discussion, trade credit can be divided into two components: (1) *free trade credit,* which involves credit received during the discount period and which for PCC amounts to 10 days' net purchases, or $326,667, and (2) *costly trade credit,* which involves credit in excess of the free trade credit and whose cost is an implicit one based on the foregone discounts.[13] PCC could obtain $653,333, or 20 days' net purchases, of nonfree trade credit at a cost of approximately 37 percent. *Financial managers should always use the free component, but they should use the costly component only after analyzing the cost of this capital to make sure that it is less than the cost of funds which could be obtained from other sources.* Under the terms of trade found in most industries, the costly component will involve a relatively high percentage cost, so stronger firms will avoid using it.

---

[13]There is some question as to whether any credit is really "free," because the supplier will have a cost of carrying receivables which must be passed on to the customer in the form of higher prices. Still, if suppliers sell on standard terms such as 2/10, net 30, and if the base price cannot be negotiated downward for early payment, then for all intents and purposes the 10 days of trade credit is indeed "free."

We noted earlier that firms sometimes can and do deviate from the stated credit terms, thus altering the percentage cost figures cited earlier. For example, a California manufacturing firm that buys on terms of 2/10, net 30, makes a practice of paying in 15 days (rather than 10), but it still takes discounts. Its treasurer simply waits until 15 days after receipt of the goods to pay, and then writes a check for the invoiced amount less the 2 percent discount. The company's suppliers want its business, so they tolerate this practice. Similarly, a Wisconsin firm that also buys on terms of 2/10, net 30, does not take discounts, but it pays in 60 rather than in 30 days, thus "stretching" its trade credit. As we saw earlier, both practices reduce the cost of trade credit. Neither of these firms is "loved" by its suppliers, and neither could continue these practices in times when suppliers were operating at full capacity and had order backlogs, but these practices can and do reduce the costs of trade credit during times when suppliers have excess capacity.

SELF-TEST QUESTIONS

What is trade credit?

What is the difference between free trade credit and costly trade credit?

What is the formula for finding the approximate cost of trade credit? What is the formula for the effective annual cost rate of trade credit?

How does the cost of costly trade credit generally compare with the cost of short-term bank loans?

SHORT-TERM BANK LOANS

Commercial banks, whose loans generally appear on firms' balance sheets as notes payable, are second in importance to trade credit as a source of short-term financing.[14] The banks' influence is actually greater than it appears from the dollar amounts they lend because banks provide *nonspontaneous* funds. As a firm's financing needs increase, it requests additional funds from its bank. If the request is denied, the firm may be forced to abandon attractive growth opportunities. The key features of bank loans are discussed in the following paragraphs.

MATURITY

Although banks do make longer-term loans, *the bulk of their lending is on a short-term basis*—about two-thirds of all bank loans mature in a year or less. Bank loans to businesses are frequently written as 90-day notes, so the loan must be repaid or

---

[14]Although commercial banks remain the primary source of short-term loans, other sources are available. For example, in 1993 GE Capital Corporation (GECC) had several billion dollars in commercial loans outstanding. Firms such as GECC, which was initially established to finance consumers' purchases of GE's durable goods, often find business loans to be more profitable than consumer loans.

renewed at the end of 90 days. Of course, if a borrower's financial position has deteriorated, the bank may well refuse to renew the loan. This can mean serious trouble for the borrower.

PROMISSORY NOTE

When a bank loan is approved, the agreement is executed by signing a *promissory note.* The note specifies (1) the amount borrowed; (2) the percentage interest rate; (3) the repayment schedule, which can call for either a lump sum or a series of installments; (4) any collateral that might have to be put up as security for the loan; and (5) any other terms and conditions to which the bank and the borrower may have agreed. When the note is signed, the bank credits the borrower's checking account with the amount of the loan, so on the borrower's balance sheet both cash and notes payable increase.

COMPENSATING BALANCES

Banks sometimes require borrowers to maintain an average demand deposit (checking account) balance equal to from 10 to 20 percent of the face amount of the loan. This is called a *compensating balance (CB),* and such balances raise the effective interest rate on the loans.[15] We will discuss the impact of compensating balances on loan costs in the next major section.

LINE OF CREDIT

A *line of credit* is an agreement between a bank and a borrower indicating the maximum credit the bank will extend to the borrower. For example, on December 31 a bank loan officer might indicate to a financial manager that the bank regards the firm as being "good" for up to $80,000 during the forthcoming year. If on January 10 the financial manager signs a promissory note for $15,000 for 90 days, this would be called "taking down" $15,000 of the total line of credit. This amount would be credited to the firm's checking account at the bank, and before repayment of the $15,000, the firm could borrow additional amounts up to a total of $80,000 outstanding at any one time.

REVOLVING CREDIT AGREEMENT

A *revolving credit agreement* is a formal line of credit often used by large firms. To illustrate, in 1993 Texas Petroleum Company negotiated a revolving credit agreement for $100 million with a group of banks. The banks were formally com-

---

[15]Note that compensating balances may be set as a minimum monthly *average,* and if the firm would maintain this average anyway, the compensating balance requirement would not raise the effective interest rate. Also, note that these *loan* compensating balances are added to any compensating balances that the firm's bank may require for *services performed,* such as clearing checks.

mitted for 4 years to lend the firm up to $100 million if the funds were needed. Texas Petroleum, in turn, paid an annual commitment fee of one-quarter of 1 percent on the unused balance of the commitment to compensate the banks for making the commitment. Thus, if Texas Petroleum did not take down any of the $100 million commitment during a year, it would still be required to pay a $250,000 annual fee, normally in monthly installments of $20,833.33. If it borrowed $50 million on the first day of the agreement, the unused portion of the line of credit would fall to $50 million, and the annual fee would fall to $125,000. Of course, interest would also have to be paid on the money Texas Petroleum actually borrowed. As a general rule, the rate of interest on "revolvers" is pegged to the prime rate, so the cost of the loan varies over time as interest rates change.[16] Texas Petroleum's rate was set at prime plus 0.5 percentage points.

Note that a revolving credit agreement is very similar to a regular line of credit. However, there is an important distinguishing feature: The bank has a *legal obligation* to honor a revolving credit agreement, and it receives a commitment fee. Neither the legal obligation nor the fee exists under the typical line of credit.

SELF-TEST QUESTION

Explain how a firm that expects to need funds during the coming year might make sure the needed funds will be available.

THE COST OF BANK LOANS

The cost of bank loans varies for different types of borrowers at any given point in time, and for all borrowers over time. Interest rates are higher for riskier borrowers, and rates are also higher on smaller loans because of the fixed costs involved

---

[16]Each bank sets its own prime rate, but, because of competitive forces, most banks' prime rates are identical. Further, most banks follow the rate set by the large New York City banks, and they, in turn, generally follow the rate set by Citibank, the largest bank in the United States. Citibank formerly set the prime rate each week at 1¼ to 1½ percentage points above the average rate on certificates of deposit (CDs) during the three weeks immediately preceding. CD rates represent the "price" of money in the open market, and they rise and fall with the supply and demand of money, so CD rates are "market-clearing" rates. By tying the prime rate to CD rates, the banking system ensured that the prime rate would also clear the market.

Except for the cut in the prime rate from 7.5 percent to 6.5 percent in late December 1991, which was the immediate result of the Federal Reserve Board's actions to lower the discount and federal funds rates in order to spur the economy, in recent years the prime rate has been held relatively constant even during periods when open market rates fluctuated. Also, in recent years many banks have been lending to the very strongest companies at rates below the prime rate. As we discuss later in this chapter, larger firms have ready access to the commercial paper market, and if banks want to do business with these larger companies, they must match or at least come close to the commercial paper rate. As competition in financial markets increases, as it has been doing because of the deregulation of banks and other financial institutions, "administered" rates such as the prime rate are giving way to flexible, negotiated rates based on market conditions.

in making and servicing loans. If a firm can qualify as a "prime credit" because of its size and financial strength, it can borrow at the *prime rate,* which has traditionally been the lowest rate banks charge. Rates on other loans are generally scaled up from the prime rate, but they can be scaled down.

Bank rates vary widely over time, depending on economic conditions and Federal Reserve policy. When the economy is weak, then (1) loan demand is usually slack, (2) inflation is low, and (3) the Fed also makes plenty of money available to the system. As a result, rates on all types of loans are relatively low. Conversely, when the economy is booming, loan demand is typically strong, and the Fed restricts the money supply; the result is high interest rates. As an indication of the kinds of fluctuations that can occur, the prime rate during 1980 rose from 11 percent to 21 percent in just four months. Interest rates on other bank loans also vary, generally moving with the prime rate, which is currently 6 percent.

Interest rates on bank loans are calculated in three ways: (1) *simple interest,* (2) *discount interest,* and (3) *add-on interest.* These three methods are explained in the following sections.

REGULAR, OR SIMPLE, INTEREST

In a *simple interest* loan, the borrower receives the face value of the loan and repays both the principal and interest at maturity. For example, in a simple interest loan of $10,000 at 12 percent for one year, the borrower receives the $10,000 upon approval of the loan and pays back the $10,000 principal plus $10,000(0.12) = $1,200 in interest at maturity (one year later). The 12 percent is the quoted, or nominal, rate. On this 1-year loan, the effective annual rate is also 12 percent:

$$\text{Effective annual rate}_{\text{Simple}} = \frac{\text{Interest}}{\text{Amount received}} \qquad (17\text{-}4)$$

$$= \frac{\$1,200}{\$10,000} = 12\%.$$

Here is the time line set up:

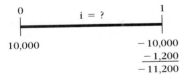

To solve with a financial calculator, enter PV = 10000, FV = −11200, and N = 1, and then press I to obtain 12.0.

On a simple interest loan of one year or more, the nominal rate equals the effective rate. However, if the loan had a term of less than one year, say, 90 days, then the effective annual rate would be calculated as follows:

$$\text{Effective annual rate}_{\text{simple}} = \left(1 + \frac{k_{\text{Nom}}}{m}\right)^m - 1.0 \qquad \textbf{(17-5)}$$

$$= (1 + 0.12/4)^4 - 1.0 = 12.55\%.$$

Here k_{Nom} is the nominal, or quoted, rate and m is the number of loan periods per year, or $360/90 = 4$. The bank gets the interest sooner than under a 1-year loan, hence the effective rate is higher.

Note that the interest payment on a $10,000 90-day loan is $10,000(0.12)$ $(90/360) = \$300$, so the time line looks like this:

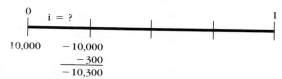

To solve with a financial calculator, enter PV = 10000, FV = -10300, and N = 1, and then press I to obtain 3.0. But this is a quarterly rate, so the effective annual rate = $(1.03)^4 - 1.0 = 12.55\%$.

An alternative way to calculate the effective rate is to enter PV = 10000, FV = -10300, and N = 0.25, and then press I to obtain 12.55%.

DISCOUNT INTEREST

In a *discount interest* loan, the bank deducts the interest in advance (*discounts the loan*). Thus, the borrower receives less than the face value of the loan. On a 1-year, $10,000 loan with a 12 percent (nominal) rate, discount basis, the interest is $10,000(0.12) = \$1,200$, so the borrower obtains the use of only $10,000 - \$1,200 = \$8,800$. The effective annual rate is 13.64 percent versus 12 percent on a 1-year simple interest loan:[17]

---

[17]Note that the firm actually receives less than the face amount of the loan:

$$\text{Funds received} = \text{Face amount of loan}(1.0 - \text{Nominal interest rate}).$$

We can solve for the face amount that would provide the needed $10,000 as follows:

$$\text{Face amount of loan} = \frac{\text{Funds received}}{1.0 - \text{Nominal rate (fraction)}}.$$

Therefore, if the borrowing firm actually requires $10,000 of cash, it must borrow $11,363.64:

$$\text{Face value} = \frac{\$10,000}{1.0 - 0.12} = \frac{\$10,000}{0.88} = \$11,363.64.$$

Now, the borrower will receive $11,363.64 - 0.12(\$11,363.64) = \$10,000$. Increasing the face value of the loan does not change the effective rate of 13.64 percent on the $10,000 of usable funds.

$$\frac{\text{Effective}}{\text{annual rate}_{\text{Discount}}} = \frac{\text{Interest}}{\text{Amount received}} = \frac{\text{Interest}}{\text{Face value} - \text{Interest}} \quad \text{(17-6)}$$

$$= \frac{\$1,200}{\$10,000 - \$1,200} = 13.64\%.$$

An alternative procedure for finding the effective annual rate on a discount interest loan is

$$\text{Effective annual rate}_{\text{Discount}} = \frac{\text{Nominal rate (\%)}}{1.0 - \text{Nominal rate (fraction)}} \quad \text{(17-6a)}$$

$$= \frac{12\%}{1.0 - 0.12} = \frac{12\%}{0.88} = 13.64\%.$$

Here's how the loan looks on a time line:

$$
\begin{array}{ccc}
0 & i = ? & 1 \\
\vert & & \vert \\
8,800 & & -10,000
\end{array}
$$

With a financial calculator, enter PV = 8800, FV = −10000, and N = 1, and then press I to obtain 13.64.

If the discount loan is for a period of less than one year, its effective annual rate is found as follows:

$$\frac{\text{Effective}}{\text{annual rate}_{\text{Discount}}} = \left(1.0 + \frac{\text{Interest}}{\text{Face value} - \text{Interest}}\right)^{m} - 1.0. \quad \text{(17-6b)}$$

For example, if we borrow $10,000 face value at a nominal rate of 12 percent, discount interest, for 3 months, then m = 12/3 = 4, and the interest payment is (0.12/4)($10,000) = $300, so

$$\text{Effective annual rate}_{\text{Discount}} = \left(1.0 + \frac{\$300}{\$10,000 - \$300}\right)^{4} - 1.0$$

$$= 0.1296 = 12.96\%.$$

Thus, discount interest imposes less of a penalty on shorter-term than on longer-term loans.

Here's the time line situation:

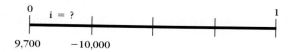

With a financial calculator, enter PV = 9700, FV = -10000, and N = 1, and then press I to obtain 3.0928. Then, the effective annual rate is $(1.030928)^4 - 1.0 = 12.96\%$.

An alternative way to calculate the effective rate is to enter PV = 9700, FV = -10000, and N = 0.25, and then press I to obtain 12.96%.

INSTALLMENT LOANS: ADD-ON INTEREST

Lenders typically charge *add-on interest* on automobile and other types of installment loans. The term "add-on" means that the interest is calculated and then added to the amount received to obtain the loan's face value. To illustrate, suppose you borrow $10,000 on an add-on basis at a nominal rate of 12 percent to buy a car, with the loan to be repaid in 12 monthly installments. At a 12 percent add-on rate, you will pay a total interest charge of $10,000(0.12) = $1,200. However, since the loan is paid off in monthly installments, you have the use of the full $10,000 for only the first month, and the outstanding balance declines until, during the last month, only $\frac{1}{12}$ of the original loan will still be outstanding. Thus, you are paying $1,200 for the use of only about half the loan's face amount, as the average outstanding balance of the loan is only about $5,000. Therefore, we can approximate the effective rate as follows:

$$\text{Approximate effective annual rate}_{\text{Add-on}} = \frac{\text{Interest}}{(\text{Amount received})/2} \quad (17\text{-}7)$$

$$= \frac{\$1,200}{\$10,000/2} = 24.0\%.$$

To determine the precise effective rate of an add-on loan, we proceed as follows:

1. The total amount to be repaid is $10,000 of principal, plus $1,200 of interest, or $11,200.

2. The monthly payment is $11,200/12 = $933.33.

3. The bank is, in effect, buying a 12-period annuity of $933.33 for $10,000, so $10,000 is the present value of the annuity. Here is the time line:

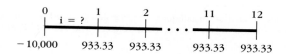

4. With a financial calculator, enter PV $= -10000$, PMT $= 933.33$, N $= 12$, and then press I to obtain 1.7880. However, this is a monthly rate.

5. The effective annual rate is found as follows:[18]

$$\text{Effective annual rate}_{\text{Add-on}} = (1 + k_d)^{12} - 1.0$$
$$= (1.01788)^{12} - 1.0$$
$$= 1.2370 - 1.0 = 23.7\%.$$

SIMPLE INTEREST WITH COMPENSATING BALANCES

Compensating balances tend to raise the effective rate on a loan. To illustrate, suppose a firm needs $10,000 to pay for some equipment that it recently purchased. A bank offers to lend the company money for one year at a 12 percent simple rate, but the company must maintain a *compensating balance (CB)* equal to 20 percent of the loan amount. If the firm did not take the loan, it would keep no deposits with the bank. What is the effective annual rate on the loan?

First, note that if the firm requires $10,000, it must, assuming it does not currently have cash balances that can be used as all or part of the compensating balance, borrow $12,500:

$$\text{Face value} = \frac{\text{Funds required}}{1.0 - \text{CB (fraction)}} \qquad \text{(17-8)}$$

$$= \frac{\$10,000}{1.0 - 0.20} = \$12,500.$$

The interest paid at the end of the year will be $12,500(0.12) = $1,500, but the firm will only get the use of $10,000. Therefore, the effective annual rate is 15 percent:

$$\text{Effective annual rate}_{\text{Simple/CB}} = \frac{\text{Interest}}{\text{Amount received}} \qquad \text{(17-9)}$$

$$= \frac{\$1,500}{\$10,000} = 15\%.$$

---

[18]Note that if an installment loan is paid off ahead of schedule, additional complications arise. For a discussion of this point, see Dick Bonker, "The Rule of 78," *Journal of Finance,* June 1976, 877–888.

An alternative formula is

$$\text{Effective annual rate}_{\text{Simple/CB}} = \frac{\text{Nominal rate (\%)}}{1.0 - \text{CB (fraction)}} \qquad \textbf{(17-9a)}$$

$$= \frac{12\%}{1.0 - 0.2} = 15\%.$$

Here's the time line solution:

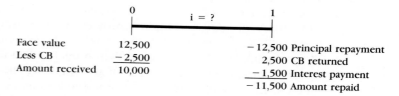

	0	i = ?	1	
Face value	12,500		−12,500	Principal repayment
Less CB	−2,500		2,500	CB returned
Amount received	10,000		−1,500	Interest payment
			−11,500	Amount repaid

With a financial calculator, enter PV = 10000, FV = −11500, and N = 1, and then press I to obtain 15.0.

Note that if a firm normally carries cash balances with the bank, then those balances can be used to meet all or part of the compensating balance requirement, and this will reduce the effective cost of the loan. In this case, the calculations required to determine the effective annual rate are a bit more complicated, and we must go through the following three-step process:

1. $\begin{pmatrix}\text{Additional funds} \\ \text{needed to meet} \\ \text{compensating balance} \\ \text{requirement}\end{pmatrix} = \begin{pmatrix}\text{Compensating} \\ \text{balance} \\ \text{percentage}\end{pmatrix} \times \text{Loan} - \begin{pmatrix}\text{Cash available} \\ \text{for compensating} \\ \text{balance}\end{pmatrix}.$

2. $\text{Loan} = \begin{pmatrix}\text{Funds} \\ \text{needed}\end{pmatrix} + \begin{pmatrix}\text{Required additional funds} \\ \text{for compensating balance}\end{pmatrix}$

$= \begin{pmatrix}\text{Funds} \\ \text{needed}\end{pmatrix} + \begin{pmatrix}\text{Compensating} \\ \text{balance percentage} \times \text{Loan}\end{pmatrix} - \begin{pmatrix}\text{Available} \\ \text{cash}\end{pmatrix}.$

3. $\text{Effective annual rate} = \dfrac{\text{Interest rate (Loan)}}{\text{Funds needed}}.$

To illustrate, if our firm normally carried a working balance of $1,000, then the effective annual cost of a $10,000 loan requiring a 20 percent compensating balance would be found as follows:

Step 1. $\begin{array}{l}\text{Additional funds to meet} \\ \text{compensating balance}\end{array} = 0.2(\text{Loan}) - \$1,000.$

Step 2. $\begin{array}{l}\text{Loan} = \$10,000 + 0.2(\text{Loan}) - \$1,000 \\ 0.8(\text{Loan}) = \$9,000 \\ \text{Loan} = \$11,250.\end{array}$

Step 3.

$$\text{Effective interest rate} = \frac{\text{Nominal rate(Loan)}}{\text{Funds needed}}$$

$$= \frac{0.12(\$11,250)}{\$10,000} = 13.5\%.$$

Thus, the firm will borrow $11,250, use $10,000 of this amount to meet its obligations, leave $1,250 on deposit as part of the compensating balance requirement, meet the remainder of the compensating balance requirement with the currently available $1,000, and pay an effective interest rate of 13.5 percent for the $10,000 net usable funds it received.

We can confirm the interest cost with a financial calculator. Note that when the loan matures at year end, the firm must pay the $11,250 loan amount plus interest of 0.12($11,250) = $1,350, or $12,600 in total, but it can use the $11,250 − $10,000 = $1,250 borrowed compensating balance, so its net repayment will be $12,600 − $1,250 = $11,350. Therefore, we can enter N = 1, PV = 10000, FV = −11350 and then press I to find the effective rate, 13.5%.

In our experience, most firms that require significant bank loans do not have much in the way of cash balances available for compensating balances. Therefore, in most situations Equation 17-9a can be used to find the cost of a bank loan with compensating balance requirements. However, if cash balances are available, it is easy enough to go through the three-step process described.

DISCOUNT INTEREST WITH COMPENSATING BALANCES

The analysis can be extended to the case where compensating balances are required and the loan is on a discount basis. In this situation, if a firm needs $10,000 for one year and a 20 percent compensating balance (CB) is required on a 12 percent discount loan, it must borrow $14,705.88:

$$\text{Face value} = \frac{\text{Funds required}}{1.0 - \text{Nominal rate (fraction)} - \text{CB (fraction)}} \qquad \textbf{(17-10)}$$

$$= \frac{\$10,000}{1.0 - 0.12 - 0.2} = \$10,000/0.68 = \$14,705.88.$$

The firm would record this $14,705.88 as a note payable offset by these asset accounts (note that a small rounding error occurs):

To cash account	$10,000.00
Prepaid interest (12% of $14,705.88)	1,764.71
Compensating balance (20% of $14,705.88)	2,941.18
	$14,705.89

Now the effective annual rate is 17.65 percent:

$$\text{Effective annual rate}_{\text{Discount/CB}} = \frac{\text{Nominal rate (\%)}}{1.0 - \text{Nominal rate (fraction)} - \text{CB (fraction)}} \qquad \text{(17-11)}$$

$$= \frac{12\%}{1.0 - 0.12 - 0.2} = 12\%/0.68 = 17.65\%.$$

On a time line, the situation looks like this:

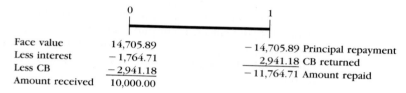

	0	1
Face value	14,705.89	−14,705.89 Principal repayment
Less interest	−1,764.71	2,941.18 CB returned
Less CB	−2,941.18	−11,764.71 Amount repaid
Amount received	10,000.00	

With a financial calculator, enter PV = 10000, FV = −11764.71, and N = 1, and then press I to obtain 17.65.

In our example, compensating balances and discount interest combined to push the effective rate of interest up from 12 to 17.65 percent. Note, however, that in this analysis we assumed that the compensating balance requirement forced the firm to increase its bank deposits. If the company normally carried cash balances which could be used to supply all or part of the compensating balances, we would have to adjust the calculations along the lines discussed in the preceding section, and the effective annual rate would have been less than 17.65 percent. Also, if the firm earns interest on its bank deposits, including the compensating balance, then the effective annual rate would be further decreased.

SELF-TEST QUESTIONS

What are some different ways that banks can calculate interest on loans?

What is a compensating balance? What effect does a compensating balance requirement have on the effective interest rate on a loan?

CHOOSING A BANK

Individuals whose only contact with their bank is through the use of its checking services generally choose a bank for the convenience of its location and the competitive cost of its services. However, a business that borrows from banks must look at other criteria, and a potential borrower seeking banking relations should

recognize that important differences exist among banks. Some of these differences are considered next.

WILLINGNESS TO ASSUME RISKS

Banks have different basic policies toward risk. Some banks are inclined to follow relatively conservative lending practices, while others engage in what are sometimes termed "creative banking practices." These policies reflect partly the personalities of officers of the bank and partly the characteristics of the bank's deposit liabilities. Thus, a bank with fluctuating deposit liabilities in a static community will tend to be a conservative lender, while a bank whose deposits are growing with little interruption may follow more liberal credit policies. Similarly, a large bank with broad diversification over geographic regions or across industries can obtain the benefit of combining and averaging risks. Thus, marginal credit risks that might be unacceptable to a small bank or specialized bank can be pooled by a large branch banking system to reduce the overall risk of a group of marginal accounts.

ADVICE AND COUNSEL

Some bank loan officers are active in providing counsel and in stimulating development loans to firms in their early and formative years. Certain banks have specialized departments which make loans to firms expected to grow and thus to become more important customers. The personnel of these departments can provide valuable counseling to customers: The bankers' experience with other firms in growth situations may enable them to spot, and then to warn their customers about, developing problems.

LOYALTY TO CUSTOMERS

Banks differ in the extent to which they will support the activities of borrowers in bad times. This characteristic is referred to as the degree of *loyalty* of the bank. Some banks may put great pressure on a business to liquidate its loans when the firm's outlook becomes clouded, whereas others will stand by the firm and work diligently to help it get back on its feet. An especially dramatic illustration of this point was Bank of America's bailout of Memorex Corporation. The bank could have forced Memorex into bankruptcy, but instead it loaned the company additional capital and helped it survive a bad period. Memorex's stock price subsequently rose on the New York Stock Exchange from $1.50 to $68, so Bank of America's help was indeed beneficial.

SPECIALIZATION

Banks differ greatly in their degrees of loan specialization. Larger banks have separate departments that specialize in different kinds of loans—for example, real estate loans, farm loans, and commercial loans. Within these broad categories,

there may be a specialization by line of business, such as steel, machinery, cattle, or textiles. The strengths of banks are also likely to reflect the nature of the business and the economic environment in which they operate. For example, some California banks have become specialists in lending to electronics companies, while many Midwestern banks are agricultural specialists. A sound firm can obtain more creative cooperation and more active support by going to a bank that has experience and familiarity with its particular type of business. Therefore, a bank that is excellent for one firm may be unsatisfactory for another.

MAXIMUM LOAN SIZE

The size of a bank can be an important factor. Since the maximum loan a bank can make to any one customer is limited to 15 percent of the bank's capital accounts (capital stock plus retained earnings), it is generally not appropriate for large firms to develop borrowing relationships with small banks.

MERCHANT BANKING

The term "merchant bank" was originally applied to banks which not only loaned depositors' money but also provided customers with equity capital and financial advice. Prior to 1933, U.S. commercial banks performed all types of merchant banking functions. However, about one-third of the U.S. banks failed during the Great Depression, in part because of these activities, so in 1933 the Glass-Steagall Act was passed in an effort to reduce banks' exposure to risk. In recent years, commercial banks have been attempting to get back into merchant banking, in part because their foreign competitors offer such services, and U.S. banks need to be able to compete with their foreign counterparts for multinational corporations' business. Currently, the larger banks, often through holding companies, are being permitted to get back into merchant banking, at least to a limited extent. This trend will probably continue, and, if it does, corporations will need to consider a bank's ability to provide a full range of commercial and merchant banking services when choosing a bank.

OTHER SERVICES

Banks can also provide cash management services, assist with electronic funds transfers, help firms obtain foreign exchange, and the like, and the availability of such services should be taken into account when selecting a bank. Also, if the firm is a small business whose manager owns most of its stock, the bank's willingness and ability to provide trust and estate services should also be considered.

SELF-TEST QUESTION

What are some of the factors that should be considered when choosing a bank?

COMMERCIAL PAPER

Commercial paper is a type of unsecured promissory note issued by large, strong firms, and it is sold primarily to other business firms, to insurance companies, to pension funds, to money market mutual funds, and to banks. The amount of commercial paper outstanding has grown rapidly in recent years, and it now exceeds the amount of commercial bank loans. In early 1993, there was approximately $550 billion of commercial paper outstanding, versus about $540 billion of regular business loans.

MATURITY AND COST

Maturities of commercial paper generally vary from one to nine months, with an average of about five months.[19] The rate on commercial paper fluctuates with supply and demand conditions—it is determined in the marketplace, varying daily as conditions change. Recently, commercial paper rates have ranged from 1½ to 3 percentage points below the stated prime rate, and about ⅛ to ½ of a percentage point above the T-bill rate. For example, on March 1, 1993, the average rate on 3-month commercial paper was 3.1 percent, the stated prime rate was 6.0 percent, and the 3-month T-bill rate was 2.9 percent.

USE OF COMMERCIAL PAPER

The use of commercial paper is restricted to a comparatively small number of concerns that are exceptionally good credit risks. Dealers prefer to handle the paper of firms whose net worth is $100 million or more and whose annual borrowing exceeds $10 million. One potential problem with commercial paper is that a debtor who is in temporary financial difficulty may receive little help because commercial paper dealings are generally less personal than are bank relationships. Thus, banks are generally more able and willing to help a good customer weather a temporary storm than is a commercial paper dealer. On the other hand, using commercial paper permits a corporation to tap a wide range of credit sources, including financial institutions outside its own area and industrial corporations across the country, and this can reduce interest costs.

SELF-TEST QUESTIONS

What is commercial paper?

What types of companies can use commercial paper to meet their short-term financing needs?

---

[19]The maximum maturity without SEC registration is 270 days. Also, commercial paper can only be sold to "sophisticated" investors; otherwise, SEC registration would be required even for maturities of 270 days or less.

How does the cost of commercial paper compare to the cost of short-term bank loans? To the cost of Treasury bills?

USE OF SECURITY IN SHORT-TERM FINANCING

Thus far we have not addressed the question of whether or not loans should be secured. Commercial paper is rarely secured, but all other types of loans are often secured if this is deemed necessary or desirable. Given a choice, it is ordinarily better to borrow on an unsecured basis, because the bookkeeping costs of *secured loans* are often high. However, weak firms may find that they can borrow only if they put up some type of security to protect the lender, or that by using security they can borrow at a lower rate.

Several different kinds of collateral can be employed, including marketable stocks or bonds, land or buildings, equipment, inventory, and accounts receivable. Marketable securities make excellent collateral, but few firms that need loans also hold portfolios of stocks and bonds. Similarly, real property (land and buildings) and equipment are good forms of collateral, but they are generally used as security for long-term loans rather than for working capital loans. Therefore, most secured short-term business borrowing involves the use of accounts receivable and inventories as collateral.

To understand the use of security, consider the case of a Chicago hardware dealer who wanted to modernize and expand his store. He requested a $200,000 bank loan. After examining his business's financial statements, the bank indicated that it would lend him a maximum of $100,000 and that the interest rate would be 12 percent, discount interest, for an effective rate of 13.6 percent. The owner had a substantial personal portfolio of stocks, and he offered to put up $300,000 of high-quality stocks to support the $200,000 loan. The bank then granted the full $200,000 loan, and at a rate of only 10 percent, simple interest. The store owner might also have used his inventories or receivables as security for the loan, but processing costs would have been high.[20]

In the past, state laws varied greatly with regard to the use of security in financing. Today, however, all states except Louisiana operate under the *Uniform Commercial Code,* which standardized and simplified the procedures for establishing loan security. The heart of the Uniform Commercial Code is the *Security Agreement,* a standardized document on which the specific pledged assets are listed. The assets can be items of equipment, accounts receivable, or inventories. Procedures under the Uniform Commercial Code for using accounts receivable and inventories as security for short-term credit are described in the following sections.

---

[20]The term "asset-based financing" is often used as a synonym for "secured financing." In recent years accounts receivable have been used as security for long-term bonds, and this permits corporations to borrow from lenders such as pension funds rather than being restricted to banks and other traditional short-term lenders.

ACCOUNTS RECEIVABLE FINANCING

Accounts receivable financing involves either the pledging of receivables or the selling of receivables (called factoring). The *pledging of accounts receivable* is characterized by the fact that the lender not only has a claim against the receivables but also has *recourse* to the borrower, so if the person or firm that bought the goods does not pay, the selling firm must take the loss. Therefore, the risk of default on the pledged accounts receivable remains with the borrower. The buyer of the goods is not ordinarily notified about the pledging of the receivables, and the financial institution that lends on the security of accounts receivable is generally either a commercial bank or one of the large industrial finance companies.

Factoring, or *selling accounts receivable,* involves the purchase of accounts receivable by the lender, generally without recourse to the borrower, which means that if the purchaser of the goods does not pay for them, the lender rather than the seller of the goods takes the loss. Under factoring, the buyer of the goods is typically notified of the transfer and is asked to make payment directly to the financial institution. Since the factoring firm assumes the risk of default on bad accounts, the factor must make the credit check. Accordingly, factors provide not only money but also a credit department for the borrower. Incidentally, the same financial institutions that make loans against pledged receivables also serve as factors. Thus, depending on the circumstances and the wishes of the borrower, a financial institution will provide either form of receivables financing.

INVENTORY FINANCING

A substantial amount of credit is secured by business inventories. If a firm is a relatively good credit risk, the mere existence of the inventory may be a sufficient basis for an unsecured loan. However, if the firm is a relatively poor risk, the lending institution may insist upon security, which can take the form of a blanket lien against all inventory or either trust receipts or warehouse receipts against specific inventory items.

The *inventory blanket lien* gives the lending institution a lien against all the borrower's inventories. However, the borrower is free to sell inventories, so the value of the collateral can be reduced below the level that existed when the loan was granted. Because of the inherent weakness of the blanket lien, another procedure for inventory financing was developed—the *security instrument* (also called a *trust receipt*), which is an instrument acknowledging that the goods are held in trust for the lender. When trust receipts are used, the borrowing firm, upon receiving funds from the lender, signs and delivers a trust receipt for the goods. The goods can be stored in a public warehouse or held on the premises of the borrower. The trust receipt acknowledges that the goods are held in trust for the lender and that any proceeds from the sale of trust goods must be transmitted to the lender at the end of each day. Automobile dealer financing is one of the best examples of trust receipt financing.

Like trust receipts, *warehouse receipt* financing uses inventory as security. A *public warehouse* is an independent third-party operation engaged in the business

of storing goods. Items which must age, such as tobacco and liquor, are often financed and stored in public warehouses. The borrower cannot remove the goods until the lender has been repaid, so the warehouse operation protects the lender. However, at times a public warehouse is not practical because of the bulkiness of goods and the expense of transporting them to and from the borrower's premises. In such cases, a *field warehouse* may be established at the borrower's place of business. To provide inventory supervision, the lending institution employs a third party, a field warehouse company, which acts as an agent for the lending institution.

SELF-TEST QUESTIONS

What are some types of current assets that are pledged as a security for short-term loans?

What is the difference between pledging receivables and factoring receivables?

Explain the differences among blanket liens, trust receipts, and warehouse receipts.

SUMMARY

In this chapter, we discussed cash management, including marketable securities and short-term financing. The key concepts covered are listed below.

▶ The *primary goal of cash management* is to reduce the amount of cash held to the minimum necessary to conduct business.

▶ The *transactions balance* is the cash necessary to conduct day-to-day business, whereas the *precautionary balance* is a cash reserve held to meet random, unforeseen needs. A *compensating balance* is a minimum checking account balance that a bank requires as compensation either for services provided or as part of a loan agreement. Firms also hold *speculative balances,* which allow them to take advantage of bargain purchases. Note, though, that borrowing capacity and marketable security holdings reduce the need for both precautionary and speculative balances.

▶ *Effective cash management* encompasses the proper management of cash inflows and outflows, which entails (1) synchronizing cash flows, (2) using float, (3) accelerating collections, (4) determining where and when funds will be needed and then ensuring that they are available at the right place at the right time, and (5) controlling disbursements.

▶ *Disbursement float* is the amount of funds associated with checks written by our firm that are still in process and hence have not yet been deducted by the bank from our account.

▶ *Collections float* is the amount of funds associated with checks written to our firm that have not been cleared and hence are not yet available for our use.

▶ *Net float* is the difference between disbursement float and collections float, and it also is equal to the difference between the balance in our firm's checkbook and the balance on the bank's records. The larger the net float, the smaller the cash balances we must maintain, so net float is good.

▶ Two techniques that can be used to speed up collections are (1) *lockboxes* and (2) *pre-authorized debits*. Also, a *concentration banking system* consolidates cash into a centralized pool that can be managed more efficiently than a large number of individual accounts.

▶ Three techniques for controlling disbursements are (1) *payables centralization*, (2) *zero-balance accounts*, and (3) *controlled disbursement accounts*.

▶ The implementation of a sophisticated cash management system is costly, so all cash management actions must be evaluated to ensure that *benefits exceed costs*.

▶ Firms can reduce their cash balances by holding *marketable securities*, which can be easily sold on short notice at close to their quoted market values. Marketable securities serve both as a substitute for cash and as a temporary investment for funds that will be needed in the near future. Safety is the primary consideration when selecting marketable securities.

▶ The *Baumol model* is used to help determine the optimal cash balance. This model balances the opportunity cost of holding cash against the transactions costs associated with replenishing the cash account by selling off marketable securities or by borrowing.

$$\text{Optimal cash transfer} = C^* = \sqrt{\frac{2(F)(T)}{k}}.$$

▶ *Short-term credit* is defined as any liability originally scheduled for payment within one year. The four major sources of short-term credit are (1) accruals, (2) accounts payable, (3) bank loans, and (4) commercial paper.

▶ *Accruals,* which are continually recurring short-term liabilities, represent free, spontaneous credit.

▶ *Accounts payable,* or *trade credit,* is the largest category of short-term debt. This credit arises spontaneously as a result of purchases on credit. Firms should use all the *free trade credit* they can obtain, but they should use *costly trade credit* only if it is less expensive than other forms of short-term debt. Suppliers often offer discounts to customers who pay within a stated discount period. The following equation may be used to calculate the approximate percentage cost, on an annual basis, of not taking discounts:

$$\frac{\text{Approximate}}{\text{percentage}} = \frac{\text{Discount percent}}{100 - \text{Discount percent}} \times \frac{360}{\frac{\text{Days credit}}{\text{is outstanding}} - \frac{\text{Discount}}{\text{period}}}.$$

▶ *Bank loans* are an important source of short-term credit. Interest on bank loans may be quoted as *simple interest, discount interest,* or *add-on interest.*

The effective rate on a discount or add-on loan always exceeds the quoted nominal rate.

▶ When a bank loan is approved, a *promissory note* is signed. It specifies: (1) the amount borrowed, (2) the percentage interest rate, (3) the repayment schedule, (4) the collateral, and (5) any other conditions to which the parties have agreed.

▶ Banks sometimes require borrowers to maintain *compensating balances,* which are deposit requirements set at between 10 and 20 percent of the loan amount. Compensating balances raise the effective rate of interest on bank loans.

▶ A *line of credit* is an understanding between the bank and the borrower indicating the maximum amount of credit the bank will extend to the borrower.

▶ A *revolving credit agreement* is a formal line of credit which involves a *commitment fee.*

▶ *Commercial paper* is unsecured short-term debt issued by a large, financially strong corporation. Although the cost of commercial paper is lower than the cost of bank loans, commercial paper's maturity is limited to 270 days, and it can be used only by large firms with exceptionally strong credit ratings.

▶ Sometimes a borrower will find it necessary to borrow on a *secured basis,* in which case the borrower pledges assets such as real estate, securities, equipment, inventories, or accounts receivable as collateral for the loan.

▶ Accounts receivable financing involves either *pledging* or *factoring receivables.* Under a pledging arrangement the lender not only gets a claim against the receivables but also has recourse to the borrower. Factoring involves the purchase of accounts receivable by the lender, generally without recourse to the borrower.

▶ There are three primary methods of inventory financing: (1) An *inventory blanket lien* gives the lender a lien against all of the borrower's inventories. (2) A *trust receipt* is an instrument that acknowledges that goods are held in trust for the lender. (3) *Warehouse receipt financing* is an arrangement under which the lender employs a third party to exercise control over the borrower's inventory and to act as the lender's agent.

QUESTIONS

17-1 Define each of the following terms:

a. Transactions balance; compensating balance; precautionary balance; speculative balance

b. Trade discounts

c. Synchronized cash flows

d. Check clearing; net float; disbursement float; collections float

e. Lockbox plan; pre-authorized debit

f. Depository transfer check (DTC); electronic depository transfer; concentration bank

    g. Zero-balance accounts; controlled disbursement accounts

    h. Marketable securities; near-cash reserves

    i. Default risk; price risk; inflation (purchasing power) risk; marketability risk; event risk

    j. Baumol model

    k. Accruals

    l. Trade credit; stretching accounts payable; free trade credit; costly trade credit

    m. Promissory note; line of credit; revolving credit agreement

    n. Prime rate

    o. Simple interest; discount interest; add-on interest

    p. Commercial paper

    q. Secured loan

    r. Uniform Commercial Code

    s. Pledging receivables; factoring

    t. Recourse

    u. Inventory blanket lien; trust receipt; warehouse receipt financing; field warehouse

17-2 What are the two principal reasons for holding cash? Can a firm estimate its target cash balance by summing the cash held to satisfy each of the two?

17-3 Explain how each of the following factors would probably affect a firm's target cash balance if all other factors were held constant.

    a. The firm institutes a new billing procedure which better synchronizes its cash inflows and outflows.

    b. The firm develops a new sales forecasting technique which improves its forecasts.

    c. The firm reduces its portfolio of U.S. Treasury bills.

    d. The firm borrows a large amount of money from its bank and also begins to write far more checks than it did in the past.

    e. Interest rates on Treasury bills rise from 5 percent to 10 percent.

17-4 Why would a lockbox plan make more sense for a firm that makes sales all over the United States than for a firm with the same volume of business but concentrated in its home city?

17-5 Would a corporate treasurer be more tempted to invest the firm's liquidity portfolio in long-term as opposed to short-term securities when the yield curve was upward sloping or downward sloping?

17-6 What does the term "liquidity" mean? Which would be more important to a firm that held a portfolio of marketable securities as precautionary balances against the possibility of losing a major lawsuit—liquidity or rate of return? Explain.

17-7 Firm A's management is very conservative whereas Firm B's is more aggressive. Is it true that, other things the same, Firm B would probably have larger holdings of marketable securities? Explain.

17-8 Is it true that price risk refers to the risk that a firm will be unable to pay the interest on its bonds? Explain.

17-9 When selecting securities for portfolio investments, corporate treasurers must make a trade-off between risk and returns. Is it true that most treasurers are willing to assume a fairly high exposure to risk to gain higher expected returns?

17-10 "Firms can control their accruals within fairly wide limits; depending on the cost of accruals, financing from this source will be increased or decreased." Discuss.

17-11 Is it true that both trade credit and accruals represent a spontaneous source of capital for financing growth? Explain.

17-12 Is it true that most firms are able to obtain some free trade credit and that additional trade credit is often available, but at a cost? Explain.

17-13 The availability of bank credit is often more important to a small firm than to a large one. Why?

17-14 What kinds of firms use commercial paper? Could Mama and Papa Gus's Corner Grocery borrow using this form of credit?

17-15 Given that commercial paper interest rates are generally lower than bank loan rates to a given borrower, why might firms which are capable of selling commercial paper also use bank credit?

17-16 Suppose a firm can obtain funds by borrowing at the prime rate or by selling commercial paper.

    a. If the prime rate is 6 percent, what is a reasonable estimate for the cost of commercial paper?

    b. If a substantial cost differential exists, why might a firm like this one actually borrow some of its funds in each market?

SELF-TEST PROBLEMS (SOLUTIONS APPEAR IN APPENDIX C)

ST-1 (Float) The Upton Company is setting up a new checking account with Howe National Bank. Upton plans to issue checks in the amount of $1 million each day and to deduct them from its own records at the close of business on the day they are written. On average, the bank will receive and clear the checks at 5 P.M. the third day after they are written; for example, a check written on Monday will be cleared on Thursday afternoon. The firm's agreement with the bank requires it to maintain a $500,000 average compensating balance; this is $250,000 greater than the cash balance the firm would otherwise have on deposit. It makes a $500,000 deposit at the time it opens the account.

    a. Assuming that the firm makes deposits at 4 P.M. each day (and the bank includes them in that day's transactions), how much must it deposit daily in order to maintain a sufficient balance once it reaches a steady state? (To do this, set up a table which shows the daily balance recorded on the company's books and the daily balance at the bank until a steady state is reached.) Indicate the required deposit on Day 1, Day 2, Day 3, if any, and each day thereafter, assuming that the company will write checks for $1 million on Day 1 and each day thereafter.

    b. How many days of float does Upton have?

    c. What ending daily balance should the firm try to maintain (1) on the bank's records and (2) on its own records?

ST-2 (Comparison of transfer methods) Kroncke Inc. has grown from a small Boston firm with customers concentrated in New England to a large, national firm serving customers throughout the United States. It has, however, kept its central billing system in Boston. On average, 5 days elapse from the time customers mail payments until Kroncke is able to receive, process, and deposit them. To shorten the collection period, Kroncke is considering the installation of a lockbox system consisting of 30 local depository banks, or lockbox

operators, and 8 regional concentration banks. The fixed costs of operating the system are estimated to be $14,000 per month. Under this system, customers' checks would be received by the lockbox operator 1 day after they are mailed, and daily collections should average $30,000 at each location. The collections would be transferred daily to the regional concentration banks. One transfer mechanism involves having the local depository banks use "mail depository transfer checks," or DTCs, to move the funds to the concentration banks; the alternative would be to use electronic (wire) transfers. A DTC would cost only 75 cents, but it would take 2 days before funds were in the concentration bank and thus available to Kroncke. Therefore, float time under the DTC system would be 1 day for mail plus 2 days for transfers, or 3 days total, down from 5 days. A wire transfer would cost $11, but funds would be available immediately, so float time would be only 1 day. If Kroncke's opportunity cost is 11 percent, should it initiate the lockbox system? If so, which transfer method should be used? (Assume that there are $52 \times 5 = 260$ working days in a year.)

ST-3 **(Receivables financing)** The Naylor Corporation is considering two methods of raising working capital: (1) a commercial bank loan secured by accounts receivable and (2) factoring accounts receivable. Naylor's bank has agreed to lend the firm 75 percent of its average monthly accounts receivable balance of $250,000 at an annual interest rate of 9 percent. The bank loan is in the form of a series of 30-day loans. The loan would be discounted, and a 20 percent compensating balance would also be required.

A factor has agreed to purchase Naylor's accounts receivable and to advance 85 percent of the balance to the firm. The 15 percent of receivables not loaned to the firm under the factoring arrangement is held in a reserve account. The factor would charge a 3.5 percent factoring commission and annual interest of 9 percent on the invoice price, less both the factoring commission and the reserve account. The monthly interest payment would be deducted from the advance. If Naylor chooses the factoring arrangement, it can eliminate its credit department and reduce operating expenses by $4,000 per month. In addition, bad debt losses of 2 percent of the monthly receivables will be avoided.

a. What is the annual cost associated with each financing arrangement?

b. Discuss some considerations other than cost that may influence management's decision between factoring and a commercial bank loan.

PROBLEMS

17-1 **(Net float)** The Sirmans Company is setting up a new checking account with Ritchie National Bank. Sirmans plans to issue checks in the amount of $1.6 million each day and to deduct them from its own records at the close of business on the day they are written. On average, the bank will receive and clear (that is, deduct from the firm's bank balance) the checks at 5 P.M. the fourth day after they are written; for example, a check written on Monday will be cleared on Friday afternoon. The firm's agreement with the bank requires it to maintain a $1.2 million average compensating balance; this is $400,000 greater than the cash balance the firm would otherwise have on deposit. It makes a $1.2 million deposit at the time it opens the account.

a. Assuming that the firm makes deposits at 4 P.M. each day (and the bank includes them in that day's transactions), how much must it deposit daily in order to maintain a sufficient balance once it reaches a steady state? (To do this, set up a table which shows the daily balance recorded on the company's books and the daily balance at the bank until a steady state is reached.) Indicate the required deposit on Day 1, Day 2, Day 3,

Day 4, if any, and each day thereafter, assuming that the company will write checks for $1.6 million on Day 1 and each day thereafter.

b. How many days of float does Sirmans carry?

c. What ending daily balance should the firm try to maintain (1) on the bank's records and (2) on its own records?

d. Explain how net float can help increase the value of the firm's common stock.

17-2 (Lockbox system) Bahnsen Corporation began operations 5 years ago as a small firm serving customers in the Denver area. However, its reputation and market area grew quickly, so that today Bahnsen has customers throughout the entire United States. Despite its broad customer base, Bahnsen has maintained its headquarters in Denver and keeps its central billing system there. Bahnsen's management is considering an alternative collection procedure to reduce its mail time and processing float. On average, it takes 5 days from the time customers mail payments until Bahnsen is able to receive, process, and deposit them. Bahnsen would like to set up a lockbox collection system, which it estimates would reduce the time lag from customer mailing to deposit by 3 days—bringing it down to 2 days. Bahnsen receives an average of $1,400,000 in payments per day.

a. How many days of collection float now exist (Bahnsen's customers' disbursement float) and what would it be under the lockbox system? What reduction in cash balances could Bahnsen achieve by initiating the lockbox system?

b. If Bahnsen has an opportunity cost of 10 percent, how much is the lockbox system worth on an annual basis?

c. What is the maximum monthly charge Bahnsen should pay for the lockbox system?

17-3 (Comparison of transfer mechanisms) The San Francisco field office of the Metallux Corporation has sold a quantity of silver ingots for $22,500. Metallux wants to transfer this amount to its concentration bank in New York as economically as possible. Two means of transfer are being considered:

(1) A mail depository transfer check (DTC), which costs $0.75 and takes three days.

(2) A wire transfer, which costs $8.00 and for which funds are immediately available in New York.

a. Metallux earns 12 percent annual interest on funds in its concentration bank. Which transfer method should Metallux use to minimize the total cost of the transfer?

b. At what dollar transfer amount would Metallux be indifferent to the two transfer procedures? (Hint: Set the cost of the two methods equal.)

c. What other factors might influence the decision?

17-4 (Optimal cash transfer) Barenbaum Industries projects that cash outlays of $4.5 million will occur uniformly throughout the year. Barenbaum plans to meet its cash requirements by periodically selling marketable securities from its portfolio. The firm's marketable securities are invested to earn 12 percent, and the cost per transaction of converting securities to cash is $27.

a. Use the Baumol model to determine the optimal transaction size for transfers from marketable securities to cash.

b. What will be Barenbaum's average cash balance?

c. How many transfers per year will be required?

d. What will be Barenbaum's total annual cost of maintaining cash balances? What would the total cost be if the company maintained an average cash balance of $50,000 or of $0 (it deposits funds daily to meet cash requirements)?

17-5 (Lockbox system) Brannigan and Daughters Inc. operates a mail-order firm doing business on the East Coast. Brannigan receives an average of $325,000 in payments per day. On average it takes 4 days from the time customers mail checks until Brannigan receives and processes them. Brannigan is considering the use of a lockbox system to reduce collection and processing float. The system will cost $6,500 per month and will consist of 10 local depository banks and a concentration bank located in Philadelphia. Under this system, customers' checks should be received at the lockbox locations 1 day after they are mailed, and daily totals will be transferred to Philadelphia using wire transfers costing $9.75 each. Assume that Brannigan has an opportunity cost of 10 percent and that there are $52 \times 5 = 260$ working days, hence 260 transfers from each lockbox location, in a year.

a. What is the total annual cost of operating the lockbox system?

b. What is the annual benefit of the lockbox system to Brannigan?

c. Should Brannigan initiate the system?

Work Parts d and e only if you are using the computer problem diskette.

d. Would the lockbox system be beneficial if Brannigan could operate it with only 8 lockbox locations while achieving the same reduction in float?

e. Suppose that interest rates rise so that Brannigan can now earn 11 percent on its invested funds. What will be the benefit (or loss) of operating the lockbox system with 8 lockbox locations?

17-6 (Cash discounts) Suppose a firm makes purchases of $3.6 million per year under terms of 2/10, net 30 and takes discounts.

a. What is the average amount of accounts payable net of discounts? (Assume that the $3.6 million of purchases is net of discounts—that is, gross purchases are $3,673,469, discounts are $73,469, and net purchases are $3.6 million. Also, use 360 days in a year.)

b. Is there a cost of the trade credit the firm uses?

c. If the firm did not take discounts but it did pay on the due date, what would be its average payables and the approximate and effective annual costs of this nonfree trade credit? Assume the firm records accounts payable net of discounts.

d. What would its approximate and effective annual costs of not taking discounts be if it could stretch its payments to 40 days?

17-7 (Trade credit versus bank credit) Jarvis Corporation projects an increase in sales from $1.5 million to $2 million, but it needs an additional $300,000 of current assets to support this expansion. The money can be obtained from the bank at an interest rate of 13 percent, discount interest; no compensating balance is required. Alternatively, Jarvis can finance the expansion by no longer taking discounts, thus increasing accounts payable. Jarvis purchases under terms of 2/10, net 30, but it can delay payment for an additional 35 days—paying in 65 days and thus becoming 35 days past due—without a penalty because of its suppliers' current excess capacity problems.

a. Based strictly on effective annual interest rate comparisons, how should Jarvis finance its expansion?

b. What additional qualitative factors should Jarvis consider before reaching a decision?

17-8 (Bank financing) The Vanderburg Corporation had sales of $3.5 million last year, and it earned a 5 percent return, after taxes, on sales. Recently the company has fallen behind in its accounts payable. Although its terms of purchase are net 30 days, its accounts payable represent 60 days' purchases. The company's treasurer is seeking to increase bank borrow-

ings in order to become current in meeting its trade obligations (that is, to have 30 days' payables outstanding). The company's balance sheet is as follows (thousands of dollars):

Cash	$ 100	Accounts payable	$ 600
Accounts receivable	300	Bank loans	700
Inventories	1,400	Accruals	200
Current assets	$1,800	Current liabilities	$1,500
Land and buildings	600	Mortgage on real estate	700
Equipment	600	Common stock, $0.10 par	300
		Retained earnings	500
Total assets	$3,000	Total liabilities and equity	$3,000

a. How much bank financing is needed to eliminate the past-due accounts payable?

b. Would you, as a bank loan officer, make the loan? Why?

17-9 (Cost of bank loans) Gifts Galore Inc. borrowed $1.5 million from National City Bank. The loan was made at a simple annual interest rate of 9 percent a year for three months. A 20 percent compensating balance requirement raised the effective interest rate.

a. The approximate interest rate on the loan was 11.25 percent. What is the true effective rate?

b. What would be the effective cost of the loan if the note required discount interest?

c. What would be the approximate annual interest rate on the loan if National City Bank required Gifts Galore to repay the loan and interest in three equal monthly installments?

17-10 (Short-term financing analysis) Kiernan Feed and Supply Company buys on terms of 1/10, net 30, but it has not been taking discounts and has actually been paying in 60 rather than 30 days. Kiernan's balance sheet follows (thousands of dollars):

Cash	$ 50	Accounts payable[a]	$ 500
Accounts receivable	450	Notes payable	50
Inventories	750	Accruals	50
Current assets	$1,250	Current liabilities	$ 600
Fixed assets	750	Long-term debt	150
		Common equity	1,250
Total assets	$2,000	Total liabilities and equity	$2,000

[a]Stated net of discounts.

Now Kiernan's suppliers are threatening to stop shipments unless the company begins making prompt payments (that is, paying in 30 days or less). The firm can borrow on a 1-year note (call this a current liability) from its bank at a rate of 15 percent, discount interest, with a 20 percent compensating balance required. (Kiernan's $50,000 of cash is needed for transactions; it cannot be used as part of the compensating balance.)

a. Determine what action Kiernan should take by calculating (1) the cost of nonfree trade credit and (2) the cost of the bank loan.

b. Assume that Kiernan foregoes discounts and then borrows the amount needed to become current on its payables from the bank. How large will the bank loan be?

c. Based on your conclusion in Part b, construct a pro forma balance sheet. (Hint: Remember that the interest for a discount loan is paid "up front"; therefore, you will need to include an account entitled "prepaid interest" under current assets.)

17-11 (Alternative financing arrangements) Sail Boats Limited estimates that because of the seasonal nature of its business, it will require an additional $2 million of cash for the month

of July. Sail Boats Limited has the following four options available for raising the needed funds:

(1) Establish a one-year line of credit for $2 million with a commercial bank. The commitment fee will be 0.5 percent per year on the unused portion, and the interest charge on the used funds will be 11 percent per annum. Assume that the funds are needed only in July and that there are 30 days in July and 360 days in the year.

(2) Forego the trade discount of 2/10, net 40 on $2 million of purchases during July.

(3) Issue $2 million of 30-day commercial paper at a 9.5 percent per annum interest rate. The total transactions fee, including the cost of a backup credit line, on using commercial paper is 0.5 percent of the amount of the issue.

(4) Issue $2 million of 60-day commercial paper at a 9 percent per annum interest rate, plus a transactions fee of 0.5 percent. Since the funds are required for only 30 days, the excess funds ($2 million) can be invested in 9.4 percent per annum marketable securities for the month of August. The total transactions cost of purchasing and selling the marketable securities is 0.4 percent of the amount of the issue.

a.   What is the dollar cost of each financing arrangement?

b.   Is the source with the lowest expected cost necessarily the one to select? Why or why not?

17-12 (Receivables financing)   Finnerty's Funtime Company manufactures plastic toys. It buys raw materials, manufactures the toys in the spring and summer, and ships them to department stores and toy stores by late summer or early fall. Funtime factors its receivables; if it did not, its October 1993 balance sheet would appear as follows (thousands of dollars):

Cash	$ 40	Accounts payable	$1,200
Receivables	1,200	Notes payable	800
Inventories	800	Accruals	80
Current assets	$2,040	Current liabilities	$2,080
Fixed assets	800	Mortgages	200
		Common stock	400
		Retained earnings	160
Total assets	$2,840	Total liabilities and equity	$2,840

Funtime provides extended credit to its customers, so its receivables are not due for payment until January 31, 1994. Also, Funtime would have been overdue on some $800,000 of its accounts payable if the preceding situation had actually existed.

Funtime has an agreement with a finance company to factor the receivables for the period October 31 through January 31 of each selling season. The factoring company charges a flat commission of 2 percent of the invoice price, plus 6 percent per year interest on the outstanding balance; it deducts a reserve of 8 percent for returned and damaged materials. Interest and commissions are paid in advance. Note, however, that interest is not recognized as an expense until the end of the 90-day period. No interest is charged on the reserved funds or on the commission.

a.   Show Funtime's balance sheet on October 31, 1993, including the purchase of all the receivables by the factoring company and the use of the funds to pay accounts payable. Ignore tax effects, and assume all proceeds from receivables factored are applied to accounts payable.

b.   If the $1.2 million is the average level of outstanding receivables, and if they turn over four times a year (hence the commission is paid four times a year), what are the total dollar costs of receivables financing (factoring) and the effective annual interest rate?

M I N I C A S E

(Part I: Cash and marketable securities management) Ray Smith, a retired librarian, recently opened a sportsman's shop called Ray's Camping & Fishing Gear, Unlimited. Ray decided at age 62 that he wasn't quite ready to stay at home, living the life of leisure. It had always been his dream to open a sportsman's shop, so his friends convinced him to go ahead. Because Ray's educational background was in literature and not in business, he hired you, a finance expert, to help him with the store's cash management. Ray is very eager to learn, so he asked you to develop a set of questions to help him understand cash management. Now answer the following questions:

a. What is the goal of cash management?

b. For what two primary reasons do firms hold cash?

c. What is meant by the terms "precautionary" and "speculative" balances?

d. What are some specific advantages for a firm holding adequate cash balances?

e. How can a firm synchronize its cash flows, and what good would this do?

f. You have been going through the store's checkbook and bank balances. In the process, you discovered that Ray, on average, writes checks in the amount of $500 each day and that it takes about 5 days for these checks to clear. Also, the firm receives checks in the amount of $500 daily, but loses 4 days while they are being deposited and cleared. What is the firm's disbursement float, collections float, and net float?

g. How can a firm speed up collections and slow down disbursements?

h. Identify two funds transfer "tools" and explain how they work. Would they be appropriate for Ray's business?

i. Define compensating balances, zero-balance accounts, and controlled disbursement accounts, and explain how each is used.

j. Why would a firm hold marketable securities?

k. What factors should a firm consider in building its marketable securities portfolio? What are some securities which should and which should not be held?

l. What is the Baumol model, and what are its major assumptions? How might the firm use the Baumol model? Assume that Ray's opportunity cost of holding cash is 9.5 percent, the fixed cost of obtaining a loan is $75, and the total amount of cash needed for transactions during the year is $200,000. What is the optimal cash balance, and what is the total cost associated with the average cash balance? If Ray tries to use the Baumol model to determine his cash balances, what could go wrong? Should Ray hold a "safety stock" of cash?

(Part II: Short-term financing) C. Charles Smith was recently hired as president of Dellvoe Office Equipment Inc., a small manufacturer of metal office equipment. As his assistant, you have been asked to review the company's short-term financing policies and to prepare a report for Smith and the board of directors. To help you get started, Smith has prepared some questions which, when answered, will give him a better idea of the company's short-term financing policies.

a. What is short-term credit, and what are the four major sources of this credit?

b. Is there a cost to accruals, and do firms have much control over them?

c. What is trade credit?

d. Like most small companies, Dellvoe has two primary sources of short-term debt: trade credit and bank loans. One supplier, which supplies Dellvoe with $50,000 of materials a year, offers Dellvoe terms of 2/10, net 50.

(1) What are Dellvoe's net daily purchases from this supplier?

(2) What is the average level of Dellvoe's accounts payable to this supplier if the discount is taken? What is the average level if the discount is not taken? What are the amounts of free credit and costly credit under both discount policies?

(3) What is the approximate cost of the costly trade credit? What is its effective annual cost?

e. In discussing a possible loan with the firm's banker, Smith has found that the bank is willing to lend Dellvoe up to $800,000 for 1 year at a 9 percent nominal, or quoted, rate. However, he forgot to ask what the specific terms would be.

(1) Assume the firm will borrow $800,000. What would be the effective interest rate if the loan were based on simple interest? If the loan had been a 9 percent simple interest loan for 6 months rather than for a year, would that have affected the effective annual rate?

(2) What would be the effective rate if the loan were a discount interest loan? What would be the face amount of a loan large enough to net the firm $800,000 of usable funds?

(3) Assume now that the terms call for an installment (or add-on) loan with equal monthly payments. The add-on loan is for a period of one year. What would be Dellvoe's monthly payment? What would be the approximate cost of the loan? What would be the effective annual rate?

(4) Now assume that the bank charges simple interest, but it requires the firm to maintain a 20 percent compensating balance. How much must Dellvoe borrow to obtain its needed $800,000 and to meet the compensating balance requirement? What is the effective annual rate on the loan?

(5) Now assume that the bank charges discount interest of 9 percent and also requires a compensating balance of 20 percent. How much must Dellvoe borrow, and what is the effective annual rate under these terms?

(6) Now assume all the conditions in Part 4, that is, a 20 percent compensating balance and a 9 percent simple interest loan, but assume also that Dellvoe has $100,000 of cash balances which it normally holds for transactions purposes and which can be used as part of the required compensating balance. How does this affect (a) the size of the required loan and (b) the effective cost of the loan?

f. Dellvoe is considering using secured short-term financing. What is a secured loan? What two types of current assets can be used to secure loans?

g. What are the differences between pledging receivables and factoring receivables? Is one type generally considered better?

h. What are the differences among the three forms of inventory financing? Is one type generally considered best?

i. Dellvoe had expected a really strong market for office equipment for the year just ended, and in anticipation of strong sales, the firm increased its inventory purchases. However, sales for the last quarter of the year did not meet its expectations, and now Dellvoe finds itself short on cash. The firm expects that its cash shortage will be temporary, only lasting 3 months. (The inventory has been paid for and cannot be returned to suppliers. The office equipment market is one where designs change nearly every two years, and Dellvoe's inventory reflects the new design changes, so its inventory is not obsolete.) Dellvoe has decided to use inventory financing to meet its short-term cash needs. It estimates that it will require $800,000 for inventory financing during this three-month period. Dellvoe has negotiated with the bank for a three-month, $1,000,000 line of credit with terms of 10 percent annual interest on the used portion,

a 1 percent annual commitment fee on the unused portion, and a $125,000 compensating balance at all times. Expected inventory levels to be financed are as follows:

Month	Amount
January 1994	$800,000
February	500,000
March	300,000

Calculate the cost of funds from this source, including interest charges and commitment fees. (Hint: Each month's borrowings will be $125,000 greater than the inventory level to be financed because of the compensating balance requirement.)

SELECTED ADDITIONAL REFERENCES AND CASES

Perhaps the best way to get a good feel for the current state of the art in cash management is to look through recent issues of The Journal of Cash Management, *a relatively new publication aimed at professionals in the field.*

For more information on cash management in general, see

Beehler, Paul J., *Contemporary Cash Management* (New York: Wiley, 1983).

Driscoll, Mary C., *Cash Management: Corporate Strategies for Profit* (New York: Wiley, 1983).

Key references on cash balance models include the following:

Daellenbach, Hans G., "Are Cash Management Optimization Models Worthwhile?" *Journal of Financial and Quantitative Analysis,* September 1974, 607–626.

Miller, Merton H., and Daniel Orr, "The Demand for Money by Firms: Extension of Analytic Results," *Journal of Finance,* December 1968, 735–759.

Mullins, David Wiley, Jr., and Richard B. Homonoff, "Applications of Inventory Cash Management Models," in *Modern Developments in Financial Management,* Stewart C. Myers, ed. (New York: Praeger, 1976).

Stone, Bernell K., "The Use of Forecasts for Smoothing in Control-Limit Models for Cash Management," *Financial Management,* Spring 1972, 72–84.

For more information on transfer systems, see

Summers, Bruce J., "Clearing and Payment Systems: The Role of the Central Bank," *Federal Reserve Bulletin,* February 1991, 81–91.

Wood, John C., and Dolores D. Smith, "Electronic Transfer of Government Benefits," *Federal Reserve Bulletin,* April 1991, 204–207.

For more information on float management, see

Batlin, C. A., and Susan Hinko, "Lockbox Management and Value Maximization," *Financial Management,* Winter 1981, 39–44.

Gitman, Lawrence J., D. Keith Forrester, and John R. Forrester, Jr., "Maximizing Cash Disbursement Float," *Financial Management,* Summer 1976, 32–41.

Nauss, Robert M., and Robert E. Markland, "Solving Lockbox Location Problems," *Financial Management,* Spring 1979, 21–31.

The following articles provide more information on cash concentration systems:

Stone, Bernell K., and Ned C. Hill, "Cash Transfer Scheduling for Efficient Cash Concentration," *Financial Management,* Autumn 1980, 35–43.

————, "The Design of a Cash Concentration System," *Journal of Financial and Quantitative Analysis,* September 1981, 301–322.

Stone, Bernell K., and Tom W. Miller, "Daily Cash Forecasting with Multiplicative Models of Cash Flow Patterns," *Financial Management,* Winter 1987, 45–54.

For greater insights into compensating balance requirements, see

Campbell, Tim S., and Leland Brendsel, "The Impact of Compensating Balance Requirements on the Cash Balances of Manufacturing Corporations," *Journal of Finance,* March 1977, 31–40.

Frost, Peter A., "Banking Services, Minimum Cash Balances, and the Firm's Demand for Money," *Journal of Finance,* December 1970, 1029–1039.

For more information on marketable securities, see any of the investment textbooks referenced in Chapter 4, or see

Brown, Keith C., and Scott L. Lummer, "A Reexamination of the Covered Call Option Strategy for Corporate Cash Management," *Financial Management,* Summer 1986, 13–17.

Kamath, Ravindra R., et al., "Management of Excess Cash: Practices and Developments," *Financial Management,* Autumn 1985, 70–77.

Stigum, M., *The Money Market: Myth, Reality, and Practice* (Homewood, Ill.: Dow Jones-Irwin, 1978).

Van Horne, J. C., *Financial Market Rates and Flows* (Englewood Cliffs, N.J.: Prentice-Hall, 1984).

Zivney, Terry L., and Michael J. Alderson, "Hedged Dividend Capture with Stock Index Options," *Financial Management,* Summer 1986, 5–12.

For more on trade credit, see

Adams, Paul D., Steve R. Wyatt, and Yong H. Kim, "A Contingent Claims Analysis of Trade Credit," *Financial Management,* Autumn 1992, 104–112.

Brosky, John J., *The Implicit Cost of Trade Credit and Theory of Optimal Terms of Sale* (New York: Credit Research Foundation, 1969).

Schwartz, Robert A., "An Economic Analysis of Trade," *Journal of Financial and Quantitative Analysis,* September 1974, 643–658.

For more on bank lending and commercial credit in general, see

Campbell, Tim S., "A Model of the Market for Lines of Credit," *Journal of Finance,* March 1978, 231–243.

Stone, Bernell K., "Allocating Credit Lines, Planned Borrowing, and Tangible Services over a Company's Banking System," *Financial Management,* Summer 1975, 65–78.

For a discussion of effective yeilds, see

Finnerty, John D., "Bank Discount, Coupon Equivalent, and Compound Yields: Comment," *Financial Management,* Summer 1983, 40–44.

Glasgo, Philip W., William J. Landes, and A. Frank Thompson, "Bank Discount, Coupon Equivalent, and Compound Yields," *Financial Management,* Autumn 1982, 82–84.

The following cases from the Brigham-Gapenski casebook focus on cash management:

Case 31, "Elite Manufacturing Company," which focuses on the target cash balance decision.

Case 32, "Alpine Wear, Inc.," which illustrates the mechanics of the cash budget and the rationale behind its use.

ACCOUNTS RECEIVABLE AND INVENTORY MANAGEMENT

*F*or many Americans, the mention of baseball cards brings to mind the name of Topps Company, the father of the sports card industry. For many years, Topps had the sports card market to itself, but competitors rushed into the market in the 1980s, when news of collectors' paying thousands of dollars for old baseball cards helped create new interest in sports cards. Today, about 100 companies vie for a share of the $1.4 billion (annual retail sales) sports and entertainment card market.

With a 32 percent share, Topps remains the biggest player in the market. Its current line includes the traditional 55-cents-a-pack cards covering baseball and three other sports, plus premium packs with fancier pictures and more statistics that sell for $1.75 per pack. Topps's sales in 1992 were $300 million, up 4.5 percent for the year, which was in line with its competitors.

The sports card business is inherently risky because any sales to wholesalers and retailers — which account for about 70 percent of the business — can be returned to manufacturers. Thus, sales can be "undone" by merely returning the merchandise. Topps records its sales, minus a reserve for returns, when it ships its products. Customers have 21 days to pay for the cards they receive, but Topps must refund the sales price of all cards returned. At the end of the year (not at the end of each quarter), Topps compares the dollar amount of returns with the reserve amount. If the actual dollar amount of cards returned is higher than the reserve, the loss is charged against earnings. If returns are less than the reserve, the difference is added to earnings.

For four consecutive quarters in 1992, Topps's accounts receivable rose steadily. In the last two quarters, receivables rose at 50 percent, while sales ac-

tually fell. In general, when receivables rise much faster than sales, there is a good chance that trouble is brewing.

Is Topps having trouble collecting from its customers? Are some customers waiting to see if the cards will sell and, if they don't, returning them to Topps without paying? If this is the case, Topps will have to write off the sales and will potentially end up with unwanted inventory. According to John Perillo, Topps's chief financial officer, the problem is in timing, not in fictitious sales. He says that customers are still paying in 21 days, and the real problem is that Topps ships nearly 50 percent of its cards in the final few weeks of each quarter. Thus, when the firm's books are closed, most of the sales have not yet been collected, so they appear as receivables.

In this chapter, we discuss both receivables management and inventory management. While reading the first part of the chapter, think about how Topps might set up a receivables control system to help it with its admittedly difficult task. By the end of the chapter, you should have an appreciation for the importance of receivables and inventory management to a firm's financial well-being, as well as some techniques for making the task easier.

RECEIVABLES MANAGEMENT

Firms would, in general, rather sell for cash than on credit, but competitive pressures force most firms to offer credit. Thus, goods are shipped, inventories are reduced, and an account receivable is created. Eventually, the customer will pay the account, at which time (1) the firm will receive cash and (2) its receivables will decline. Carrying receivables results in both direct and indirect costs, but it also provides an important benefit—it increases sales. The optimal credit policy is the one which maximizes the firm's net cash flows over time, giving consideration to the risk assumed.

Receivables management begins with the decision of whether or not to grant credit. In this section, we discuss the manner in which a firm's receivables build up, and we also present several alternative means of monitoring receivables. A monitoring system is important, because without it, receivables will build up to excessive levels, cash flows will decline, and bad debts will offset the profits on sales. Corrective action is often needed, and the only way to know whether the situation is getting out of hand is to set up and then follow a good receivables control system.

THE ACCUMULATION OF RECEIVABLES

The total amount of accounts receivable outstanding at any given time is determined by two factors: (1) the volume of credit sales and (2) the average length of time between sales and collections. For example, suppose the Boston Lumber

Company (BLC), a wholesale distributor of lumber products, opens a warehouse on January 1 and, starting the first day, makes sales of $1,000 each day. (For simplicity, we assume that all sales are on credit.) Customers are given 10 days in which to pay. At the end of the first day, accounts receivable will be $1,000; they will rise to $2,000 by the end of the second day; and by January 10, they will have risen to 10($1,000) = $10,000. On January 11, another $1,000 will be added to receivables, but payments for sales made on January 1 will reduce receivables by $1,000, so total accounts receivable will remain constant at $10,000. Once the firm's operations have stabilized, this situation will exist:

$$\frac{\text{Accounts}}{\text{receivable}} = \frac{\text{Credit sales}}{\text{per day}} \times \frac{\text{Length of}}{\text{collection period}}$$

$$= \quad \$1,000 \quad \times \quad 10 \text{ days} \quad = \$10,000.$$

If either credit sales or the collection period changes, such changes will be reflected in accounts receivable.

Notice that the $10,000 investment in receivables must be financed. To illustrate, suppose that when the store opened on January 1, BLC's shareholders had put up $800 as common stock and used this money to buy the goods sold the first day. The $800 worth of inventory will be sold for $1,000; thus, BLC's gross profit on the $800 investment is $200, or 25 percent. In this situation, the initial balance sheet would be as follows:[1]

Inventories	$800	Common equity	$800
Total assets	$800	Total claims	$800

At the end of the day, the balance sheet would look like this:

Accounts receivable	$1,000	Common equity	$ 800
Inventories	0	Retained earnings	200
Total assets	$1,000	Total claims	$1,000

In order to remain in business, BLC must replenish inventories. To do so requires that $800 of goods be purchased, and this requires $800 in cash. Assuming that BLC borrows the $800 from the bank, the balance sheet at the start of the second day will be as follows:

Accounts receivable	$1,000	Notes payable to bank	$ 800
Inventories	800	Common equity	800
		Retained earnings	200
Total assets	$1,800	Total claims	$1,800

---

[1]Note that the firm would need other assets such as cash, fixed assets, and a permanent stock of inventory. Also, overhead costs and taxes would have to be deducted, so retained earnings would be less than the figures shown here. We abstract from these details here so that we may focus on receivables.

At the end of the second day, the inventories will have been converted to receivables, and the firm will have to borrow another $800 to restock for the third day.

This process will continue, provided the bank is willing to lend the necessary funds, until the beginning of the eleventh day, when the balance sheet reads as follows:

Accounts receivable	$10,000	Notes payable to bank	$ 8,000
Inventories	800	Common equity	800
		Retained earnings	2,000
Total assets	$10,800	Total claims	$10,800

From this point on, $1,000 of receivables will be collected every day, and $800 of these funds can be used to purchase new inventories.

This example should make it clear (1) that accounts receivable depend jointly on the level of credit sales and the collection period, (2) that any increase in receivables must be financed in some manner, but (3) that the entire amount of receivables does not have to be financed because the profit portion ($200 of each $1,000 of sales in this example) does not represent a cash outflow. In this example, we assumed bank financing, but there are many alternative ways to finance current assets. For most firms, the permanent level of receivables would be financed with long-term capital such as stocks and bonds. Then, any seasonal or cyclical increases in receivables would be financed with short-term credit.

MONITORING THE RECEIVABLES POSITION

The optimal credit policy, hence the optimal level of accounts receivable, depends on the firm's own unique operating conditions. For example, a firm with excess capacity and low variable production costs should extend credit more liberally, and carry a higher level of receivables, than a firm operating at full capacity on a slim profit margin. However, even though optimal credit policies vary among firms, or even for a single firm over time, it is still useful to analyze the effectiveness of the firm's credit policy in an overall, aggregate sense. Investors—both stockholders and bank loan officers—should pay close attention to accounts receivable management, for, as we shall see, one can be misled by reported financial statements and later suffer serious losses on an investment.

When a credit sale is made, the following events occur: (1) Inventories are reduced by the cost of goods sold, (2) accounts receivable are increased by the sales price, and (3) the difference is profit, which is added to retained earnings. If the sale is for cash, the profit is definitely earned, but if the sale is on credit, the profit is not actually earned unless and until the account is collected. Firms have been known to encourage "sales" to very weak customers in order to report high profits. This could boost the firm's stock price, at least until credit losses begin to lower earnings, at which time the stock price will fall. Analyses along the lines suggested in the following sections will detect any such questionable practice, as

well as any unconscious deterioration in the quality of accounts receivable. Such early detection could help both investors and bankers avoid losses.[2]

Days Sales Outstanding (DSO).   Suppose Super Sets, Inc., a television manufacturer, sells 200,000 television sets a year at a sales price of $198 each. Further, assume that all sales are on credit, with terms of 2/10, net 30. Finally, assume that 70 percent of the customers take discounts and pay on Day 10, while the other 30 percent pay on Day 30.

Super Sets's *days sales outstanding (DSO),* sometimes called the *average collection period (ACP),* is 16 days:

$$DSO = ACP = 0.7(10 \text{ days}) + 0.3(30 \text{ days}) = 16 \text{ days}.$$

Super Sets's *average daily sales (ADS),* assuming a 360-day year, is $110,000:

$$ADS = \frac{\text{Annual sales}}{360} = \frac{(\text{Units sold})(\text{Sales price})}{360} = \frac{200,000(\$198)}{360}$$

$$= \frac{\$39,600,000}{360} = \$110,000.$$

If the company had made cash as well as credit sales, we would have concentrated on credit sales only, and calculated average daily *credit* sales.

Super Sets's accounts receivable, assuming a constant, uniform rate of sales all during the year, will at any point in time be $1,760,000:

$$\text{Receivables} = (ADS)(DSO) = (\$110,000)(16) = \$1,760,000.$$

Finally, note that its DSO is a measure of the average length of time it takes Super Sets's customers to pay off their credit purchases, and the DSO is often compared with the industry average DSO. For example, if all television manufacturers sell on the same credit terms, and if the industry average DSO is 25 days versus Super Sets's 16-day DSO, then Super Sets either has a higher percentage of discount customers or else its credit department is exceptionally good at ensuring prompt payment.[3]

---

[2]Accountants are increasingly interested in these matters. Investors have sued several of the major accounting firms for substantial damages when (1) profits were overstated and (2) it could be shown that the auditors should have conducted an analysis along the lines described here and then should have reported the results to stockholders in their audit opinion letter.

[3]Note that the DSO can be calculated, given a firm's accounts receivable balance and its average daily credit sales, as follows:

$$DSO = \frac{\text{Receivables}}{ADS} = \frac{\$1,760,000}{\$110,000} = 16 \text{ days}.$$

TABLE 18-1 AGING SCHEDULES		Super Sets		Wonder Vision	
Age of Account (Days)	Value of Account	Percentage of Total Value	Value of Account	Percentage of Total Value
0–10	$1,232,000	70%	$ 825,000	47%
11–30	528,000	30	460,000	26
31–45	0	0	265,000	15
46–60	0	0	179,000	10
Over 60	0	0	31,000	2
Total receivables	$1,760,000	100%	$1,760,000	100%

The DSO can also be compared with the firm's own credit terms. For example, suppose Super Sets's DSO had been running at a level of 35 days versus its 2/10, net 30 credit terms. With a 35-day DSO, some customers would obviously be taking more than 30 days to pay their bills. In fact, if some customers were paying within 10 days to take advantage of the discount, the others would, on average, have to be taking much longer than 35 days. One way to check this possibility is to use an aging schedule as described in the next section.

Aging Schedules.   An *aging schedule* breaks down a firm's receivables by age of account. Table 18-1 contains the December 31, 1993, aging schedules of two television manufacturers, Super Sets and Wonder Vision. Both firms offer the same credit terms, 2/10, net 30, and both show the same total receivables. However, Super Sets's aging schedule indicates that all of its customers pay on time — 70 percent pay on Day 10 while 30 percent pay on Day 30. Wonder Vision's schedule, which is more typical, shows that many of its customers are not abiding by its credit terms — some 27 percent of its receivables are more than 30 days old, even though Wonder Vision's credit terms call for full payment by Day 30.

Aging schedules cannot be constructed from the type of summary data that are reported in financial statements; they must be developed from the firm's accounts receivable ledger. However, well-run firms have computerized their accounts receivable records, so it is easy to determine the age of each invoice, to sort categories electronically by age, and thus to generate an aging schedule. Although changes in aging schedules over time do provide more information than does the corporate DSO taken alone, and although aging schedules are valuable for monitoring individual accounts, there is a better way to monitor the aggregate quality of a firm's receivables, as we demonstrate in the next section.

The Payments Pattern Approach.   The primary point in analyzing the aggregate accounts receivable situation is to see if customers are slowing down their payments. If so, the firm will have to increase its receivables financing, which will increase its dollar cost of carrying receivables. Further, the payment slowdown may signal a decrease in the quality of the firm's receivables, and hence an increase in bad debt losses down the road. The DSO and aging schedules are useful in

TABLE 18-2 HANOVER COMPANY: RECEIVABLES DATA (THOUSANDS OF DOLLARS)			Based on Quarterly Data		Based on Year-to-Date Data	
Month (1)	Credit Sales (2)	Receivables (3)	ADS[a] (4)	DSO[b] (5)	ADS (6)	DSO (7)
January	$ 60	$ 54				
February	60	90				
March	60	102	$2.00	51 days	$2.00	51 days
April	60	102				
May	90	129				
June	120	174	3.00	58	2.50	70
July	120	198				
August	90	177				
September	60	132	3.00	44	2.67	49
October	60	108				
November	60	102				
December	60	102	2.00	51	2.50	41

[a]ADS = Average daily sales.
[b]DSO = Days sales outstanding.

monitoring credit operations, but both are affected by increases and decreases in a firm's level of sales. Thus, changes in sales levels, including normal seasonal or cyclical changes, can change a firm's DSO and aging schedule even though its customers' payment behavior has not changed at all. For this reason, a procedure called the *payments pattern approach* has been developed to measure any changes that might be occurring in customers' payment behavior.[4] To illustrate the payments pattern approach, consider the credit sales of the Hanover Company, a small manufacturer of hand tools which commenced operations in January 1993. Table 18-2 contains Hanover's credit sales and receivables data for 1993. Column 2 shows that Hanover's credit sales are seasonal, with the lowest sales in the fall and winter months and the highest sales during the summer.

Now assume that 10 percent of Hanover's customers pay in the same month the sale is made, that 30 percent pay in the first month following the sale, that 40 percent pay in the second month, and that the remaining 20 percent pay in the third month. Further, assume that Hanover's customers have the same payment behavior throughout the year; that is, they always take the same length of time to pay. On the basis of this payment pattern, Column 3 of Table 18-2 contains Hanover's receivables balance at the end of each month. For example, during January, Hanover has $60,000 in sales. Ten percent of the customers paid during the month

---

[4]See Wilbur G. Lewellen and Robert W. Johnson, "A Better Way to Monitor Accounts Receivable," *Harvard Business Review,* May-June 1972, 101–109; and Bernell Stone, "The Payments-Pattern Approach to the Forecasting and Control of Accounts Receivable," *Financial Management,* Autumn 1976, 65–82.

of sale, so the receivables balance at the end of January was $60,000 − 0.1($60,000) = (1.0 − 0.1)($60,000) = 0.9($60,000) = $54,000. By the end of February, 10% + 30% = 40% of the customers had paid for January's sales, and 10 percent had paid for February's sales. Thus, the receivables balance at the end of February was 0.6($60,000) + 0.9($60,000) = $90,000. By the end of March, 80 percent of January's sales had been paid, 40 percent of February's had been paid, and 10 percent of March's sales had been paid, so the receivables balance was 0.2($60,000) + 0.6($60,000) + 0.9($60,000) = $102,000; and so on.

Columns 4 and 5 give Hanover's average daily sales (ADS) and days sales outstanding (DSO), respectively, as these measures would be calculated from quarterly financial statements. For example, in the April-June quarter, ADS = ($60,000 + $90,000 + $120,000)/90 = $3,000, and the end-of-quarter (June 30) DSO = $174,000/$3,000 = 58 days. Columns 6 and 7 also show ADS and DSO, but here they are calculated on the basis of accumulated sales throughout the year. For example, at the end of June, ADS = $450,000/180 = $2,500 and DSO = $174,000/$2,500 = 70 days. (For the entire year, sales are $900,000; ADS = $2,500, and DSO at year end = 41 days. These last two figures are shown in the lower right corner of the table.)

The data in Table 18-2 illustrate two major points. First, when the level of sales changes, this leads to changes in the DSO, which suggests that customers are paying faster or slower, even though in this case we know that customers' payment patterns are actually not changing at all. The rising monthly sales trend causes the calculated DSO to rise, whereas falling sales (as in the third quarter) cause the calculated DSO to fall, even though nothing is changing with regard to when customers pay. Second, we see that the DSO depends on an averaging procedure, but regardless of whether quarterly, semiannual, or annual data are used, the DSO is still unstable even though payment patterns are *not* changing. Therefore, it is difficult to use the DSO as a monitoring device if the firm's sales exhibit seasonal or cyclical patterns.

Seasonal or cyclical variations also make it difficult to interpret aging schedules. Table 18-3 contains Hanover's aging schedules at the end of each quarter of 1993. At the end of June, Table 18-2 showed that Hanover's receivables balance was $174,000. Eighty percent of April's $60,000 of sales had been collected, 40 percent of May's $90,000 of sales had been collected, and 10 percent of June's $120,000 of sales had been collected. Thus, the end-of-June receivables balance consisted of 0.2($60,000) = $12,000 of April sales, 0.6($90,000) = $54,000 of May sales, and 0.9($120,000) = $108,000 of June sales. Note again that Hanover's customers had not changed their payment patterns. However, rising sales during the second quarter created the impression of faster payments when judged by the percentage aging schedule, and falling sales after July created the opposite appearance. Thus, neither the DSO nor the aging schedule provides the financial manager with an accurate picture of customers' payment patterns if sales fluctuate during the year, or if sales are trending up or down.

With this background, we can now examine another basic tool, the *uncollected balances schedule,* as shown in Table 18-4. At the end of each quarter, the dollar amount of receivables remaining from each of the three month's sales is

TABLE 18-3

HANOVER COMPANY: AGING SCHEDULES (THOUSANDS OF DOLLARS)

Age of Accounts (Days)	Value and Percentage of Total Value of Accounts Receivable at the End of Quarter Ending							
	March 31		June 30		September 30		December 31	
0–30	$ 54	53%	$108	62%	$ 54	41%	$ 54	53%
31–60	36	35	54	31	54	41	36	35
61–90	12	12	12	7	24	18	12	12
	$102	100%	$174	100%	$132	100%	$102	100%

TABLE 18-4

HANOVER COMPANY: UNCOLLECTED BALANCES SCHEDULES (THOUSANDS OF DOLLARS)

Quarter	Sales	Remaining Receivables	Receivables/Sales
Quarter 1:			
January	$ 60	$ 12	20%
February	60	36	60
March	60	54	90
		$102	170%
Quarter 2:			
April	$ 60	$ 12	20%
May	90	54	60
June	120	108	90
		$174	170%
Quarter 3:			
July	$120	$ 24	20%
August	90	54	60
September	60	54	90
		$132	170%
Quarter 4:			
October	$ 60	$ 12	20%
November	60	36	60
December	60	54	90
		$102	170%

divided by that month's sales to obtain three receivables-to-sales ratios. For example, at the end of the first quarter, $12,000 of the $60,000 January sales, or 20 percent, are still outstanding; 60 percent of February sales are still out; and 90 percent of March sales are uncollected. Exactly the same situation is revealed at the end of each of the next three quarters. Thus, Table 18-4 shows that Hanover's customers' payment behavior has remained constant.

Recall that at the beginning of the example we assumed the existence of a constant payments pattern. In a normal situation, the firm's customers' payments pattern would probably vary somewhat over time. Such variations would be shown in the last column of the uncollected balances schedule. For example, suppose

customers began, in the second quarter, to pay their accounts slower. That might cause the second quarter uncollected balances schedule to look like this (in thousands of dollars):

Quarter 2, 1993	Sales	Remaining Receivables	Receivables/Sales
April	$ 60	$ 16	27%
May	90	70	78
June	120	110	92
		$196	197%

We see that the receivables-to-sales ratios are now higher than in the corresponding months of the first quarter. This causes the total uncollected balances percentage to rise from 170 to 197 percent, which in turn should alert Hanover's managers that customers are paying slower than they did earlier in the year.

The uncollected balances schedule permits a firm to monitor its receivables better, and it can also be used to forecast future receivables balances. When Hanover's pro forma 1994 quarterly balance sheets are constructed, management can use the receivables-to-sales ratios, coupled with 1994 sales estimates, to project each quarter's receivables balance. For example, with projected sales as given below, and using the same payments pattern as in 1993, Hanover's projected end-of-June 1994 receivables balance would be as follows:

Quarter 2, 1994	Projected Sales	Receivables/Sales	Projected Receivables
April	$ 70,000	20%	$ 14,000
May	100,000	60	60,000
June	140,000	90	126,000
		Total projected receivables =	$200,000

The payments pattern approach permits us to remove the effects of seasonal and/or cyclical sales variation and to construct an accurate measure of customers' payments patterns. Thus, it provides financial managers with better aggregate information than such crude measures as the days sales outstanding or the aging schedule. Managers should use the payments pattern approach to monitor collection performance as well as to project future receivables requirements.

USE OF COMPUTERS IN RECEIVABLES MANAGEMENT

Except possibly in the inventory and cash management areas, nowhere in the typical firm have computers had more of an impact than in accounts receivable management. A well-run business will use a computer system to record sales, to send out bills, to keep track of when payments are made, to alert the credit manager when an account becomes past due, and to ensure that actions are taken to collect past due accounts (for example, to prepare form letters requesting payment) automatically. Additionally, the payment history of each customer can be summarized and used to help establish credit limits for customers and classes of customers, and the data on each account can be aggregated and used for the firm's accounts re-

ceivable monitoring system. Finally, historical data can be stored in the firm's data base and used to develop inputs for studies related to credit policy changes, as we discuss in the next section.

SELF-TEST QUESTIONS

Explain how a new firm's receivables balance is built up over time.

Define days sales outstanding (DSO). What can be learned from it? Does it have any deficiencies when used to monitor collections over time?

What is an aging schedule? What can be learned from it? Does it have any deficiencies when used to monitor collections over time?

What is the uncollected balances schedule? What advantages does it have over the DSO and the aging schedule for monitoring receivables? How can it be used to forecast a firm's receivables balance?

CREDIT POLICY

The success or failure of a business depends primarily on the demand for its products—as a rule, the higher its sales, the larger its profits and the higher the value of its stock. Sales, in turn, depend on a number of factors, some exogenous but others under the control of the firm. The major controllable variables which affect demand are sales prices, product quality, advertising, and *the firm's credit policy.* Credit policy, in turn, consists of these four variables:

1. The *credit period,* which is the length of time buyers are given to pay for their purchases.

2. The *credit standards,* which refer to the minimum financial strength of acceptable credit customers, and the amount of credit available to different customers.

3. The firm's *collection policy,* which is measured by its toughness or laxity in following up on slow-paying accounts.

4. Any *discounts* given for early payment, including the discount amount and period.

The credit manager has the responsibility for administering the firm's credit policy. However, because of the pervasive importance of credit, the credit policy itself is normally established by the executive committee, which usually consists of the president and the vice-presidents in charge of finance, marketing, and production.

SELF-TEST QUESTION

What are the four credit policy variables?

Setting the Credit Period and Standards

A firm's regular credit terms, which include the *credit period,* might call for sales on a 2/10, net 30 basis to all "acceptable" customers. Its *credit standards* would be applied to determine which customers are qualified for the regular credit terms, and the amount of credit available to each customer. The focal point when considering credit standards is the likelihood that a given customer will pay slowly, or end up as a bad debt loss. This requires a measurement of *credit quality,* which is defined in terms of the probability of default. The probability estimate for a given customer is, for the most part, a subjective judgment, but credit evaluation is a well-established practice, and a good credit manager can make reasonably accurate judgments regarding the probability of default by different classes of customers.

Credit-Scoring Systems

Although most credit decisions are subjective, many firms now use a sophisticated statistical method called *multiple discriminant analysis (MDA)* to assess credit quality. MDA is similar to multiple regression analysis. The dependent variable is, in essence, the probability of default, and the independent variables are factors associated with financial strength and the ability to pay off the debt if credit is granted. For example, if a firm such as Sears evaluated consumers' credit quality, then the independent variables in the credit scoring system would be such factors as these: (1) Does the credit applicant own his or her own home? (2) How long has the applicant worked on his or her current job? (3) What is the applicant's outstanding debt in relation to his or her annual income? (4) Does the potential customer have a history of paying his or her debts on time?

One major advantage of an MDA credit-scoring system is that a customer's credit quality is expressed in a single numerical value, rather than as a subjective assessment of various factors. This is a tremendous advantage for a large firm which must evaluate many customers in many different locations using many different credit analysts, for without an automated procedure, the firm would have a hard time applying equal standards to all credit applicants. Therefore, most credit card companies, department stores, oil companies, and the like use credit-scoring systems to determine who gets how much credit, as do the larger building supply chains and manufacturers of electrical products, machinery, and so on.

Multiple discriminant analysis will be discussed in detail in Chapter 23 in connection with bankruptcy prediction. For now, we will briefly describe the concept. Suppose the Hanover Company has historical information on 500 of its customers, all of whom are retail businesses. Of these 500, assume that 400 have always paid on time, but the other 100 either paid late or, in some cases, went bankrupt and did not pay at all. Further, the firm has historical data on each customer's quick ratio, times-interest-earned ratio, debt ratio, years in existence, and so on. Multiple discriminant analysis relates the experienced record (or historical probability) of late payment or nonpayment with various measures of a firm's financial condition, and MDA assigns weights for the critical factors. In effect, MDA produces an equa-

tion that looks much like a regression equation, and when data on a customer are plugged into the equation, then a credit score for that customer is produced.

For example, suppose Hanover's multiple discriminant analysis indicates that the critical factors affecting prompt payment are its customer's times-interest-earned ratio (TIE), quick ratio, debt/assets ratio, and number of years in business. Here is the discriminant function:

$$\text{Score} = 3.5(\text{TIE}) + 10.0(\text{Quick ratio}) - 25.0(\text{Debt/assets}) + 1.3(\text{Years in business}).$$

Further, assume that a score less than 40 indicates a poor credit risk, 40–50 indicates an average credit risk, and a score above 50 signifies a good credit risk. Now, suppose a firm with the following conditions applies for credit:

$$\text{TIE} = 4.2$$

$$\text{Quick ratio} = 3.1$$

$$\text{Debt/assets} = 0.30$$

$$\text{Years in business} = 10$$

This firm's credit score would be $3.5(4.2) + 10.0(3.1) - 25.0(0.30) + 1.3(10) = 51.2$. Therefore, it would be considered a good credit risk, and consequently it would be offered favorable credit terms.

SOURCES OF CREDIT INFORMATION

Two major sources of credit information are available. The first is a set of *credit associations,* which are local groups that meet frequently and which correspond with one another to exchange information on credit customers. These local groups have also banded together to create Credit Interchange, a system developed by the National Association of Credit Management for assembling and distributing information about debtors' past performance. The interchange reports show the paying records of different debtors, the industries from which they are buying, and the geographic areas in which they are making purchases. The second source of external information is the work of the *credit-reporting agencies,* which collect credit information and sell it for a fee. The best known of these agencies are Dun & Bradstreet (D&B), TRW, Equifax, and Trans Union, which provide factual data that can be used in credit analysis as well as credit ratings similar to those available on corporate bonds.[5]

The main problem with credit-reporting agencies, especially those that deal in consumer credit reports, is the accuracy of the credit data. Recently, TRW settled

---

[5]For additional information, see *Credit Management,* a publication of the National Association of Credit Management; and also see Peter Nulty, "An Upstart Takes on Dun & Bradstreet," *Fortune,* April 9, 1979, 98–100.

lawsuits with 19 states and the Federal Trade Commission by consenting to sweeping changes in its procedures to make credit reporting fairer to consumers. This agreement, which is expected ultimately to affect all consumer credit-reporting companies, should go a long way toward removing the red tape that has engulfed consumer credit reports. Such reports play a vital role in virtually every American's ability to get a loan, a credit card, and sometimes even a job. In the past, these reports were filled with errors, and it seemed almost impossible to get an error corrected once it was made. TRW agreed to take several steps to be more responsive to consumers, even though credit-reporting agencies' customers are typically banks and retailers, not the consumers that are carried on the companies' data bases. TRW agreed (1) to set up a toll-free number for consumers to call with any questions regarding their credit reports; (2) to make its reports easier to read; (3) to adopt a strict set of new rules for handling consumer complaints about credit-reporting errors; and (4) to offer consumers a free annual copy of their credit reports and to supply additional copies for $7.50 each, well below current charges. All in all, the trend among consumer credit-reporting companies is to be much more user friendly to the consumer, which should allow these companies to offer better reports to their customers.

Whereas TRW, Equifax, and Trans Union specialize in consumer credit reporting, Dun & Bradstreet specializes in business credit reports. Like the consumer credit-reporting companies, Dun & Bradstreet has an electronic system that provides preliminary reports, plus another service that provides more detailed, hard-copy reports.

A typical business credit report would include the following pieces of information:

1. A summary balance sheet and income statement.

2. A number of key ratios, with trend information.

3. Information obtained from the firm's suppliers telling whether it has been paying promptly or slowly, and whether it has recently failed to make any payments.

4. A verbal description of the physical condition of the firm's operations.

5. A verbal description of the backgrounds of the firm's owners, including any previous bankruptcies, lawsuits, divorce settlement problems, and the like.

6. A summary rating, ranging from A for the best credit risks down to F for those that are deemed likely to default.

Although a great deal of credit information is available, it must still be processed in a judgmental manner. Computerized information systems can assist in making better credit decisions, but, in the final analysis, most credit decisions are really exercises in informed judgment. Even credit-scoring systems require judgment in deciding where to draw the lines, given the set of derived scores.

SELF-TEST QUESTIONS

What is a credit-scoring system?

What are some sources of credit information?

SETTING THE COLLECTION POLICY

Collection policy refers to the procedures the firm follows to collect past-due accounts. For example, a letter may be sent to customers when a bill is 10 days past due; a more severe letter, followed by a telephone call, may be used if payment is not received within 30 days; and the account may be turned over to a collection agency after 90 days.

The collection process can be expensive in terms of both out-of-pocket expenditures and lost goodwill, but at least some firmness is needed to prevent an undue lengthening of the collection period and to minimize outright losses. Again, a balance must be struck between the costs and benefits of different collection policies.

Changes in collection policy influence sales, the collection period, the bad debt loss percentage, and the percentage of customers who take discounts. The effects of a change in collection policy, along with changes in the other credit policy variables, will be analyzed later in the chapter.

SELF-TEST QUESTION

What does the term "collection policy" mean, and what impact does it have on sales and profitability?

CASH DISCOUNTS

The last element in the credit policy decision, the use of *cash discounts* for early payment, is analyzed by balancing the costs and benefits of different cash discounts. For example, a firm might decide to change its credit terms from "net 30," which means that customers must pay within 30 days, to "2/10, net 30," which means that it will allow a 2 percent discount if payment is received within 10 days, while the full invoice price must otherwise be paid within 30 days. This change should produce two benefits: (1) It should attract new customers who consider discounts to be a type of price reduction, and (2) the discounts should cause a reduction in the days sales outstanding, since some established customers will pay more promptly in order to take advantage of the discount. Offsetting these benefits is the dollar cost of the discounts taken.[6] The optimal discount is established at the point where the marginal costs and benefits are exactly offsetting. The methodology for analyzing changes in the discount is developed in a later section.

If sales are seasonal, a firm may use *seasonal dating* on discounts. For example, Slimware Inc., a swimsuit manufacturer, sells on terms of 2/10, net 30, May 1 dating. This means that the effective invoice date is May 1, even if the sale was made back in January. The discount may be taken up to May 10; otherwise the full amount must be paid on May 30. Slimware produces throughout the year, but

---

[6]Note that some firms offer discounts only to customers who pay cash on the spot, because the cost of giving such discounts is offset by the reduction in receivables processing costs.

retail sales of bathing suits are concentrated in the spring and early summer, and by offering seasonal dating, the company induces some of its customers to stock up early, saving Slimware storage costs and also nailing down sales.

SELF-TEST QUESTIONS

How can cash discounts be used to influence sales volume and collections? What is seasonal dating?

OTHER FACTORS INFLUENCING CREDIT POLICY

In addition to the factors discussed in the previous sections, several other conditions also influence a firm's overall credit policy.

PROFIT POTENTIAL

Thus far, we have emphasized the costs of granting credit. *However, if it is possible to sell on credit and also to assess a carrying charge on the receivables that are outstanding, then credit sales can actually be more profitable than cash sales.* This is especially true for consumer durables (autos, appliances, clothing, and so on), but it is also true for certain types of industrial equipment. Thus, GM's General Motors Acceptance Corporation (GMAC) unit, which finances automobiles, is highly profitable, as is Sears, Roebuck's credit subsidiary.[7] Some encyclopedia companies are even reported to lose money on cash sales but to more than make up these losses from the carrying charges on their credit sales; obviously, such companies would rather sell on credit than for cash!

The carrying charges on outstanding credit have generally been about 18 percent on a nominal interest rate basis: 1.5 percent per month, so $1.5\% \times 12 = 18\%$. This is equivalent to an effective annual rate of $(1.015)^{12} - 1.0 = 19.6\%$. Except in the type of situation that occurred in the early 1980s, when short-term interest rates rose to unprecedented levels, having receivables outstanding that earn over 18 percent is highly profitable. Although consumer carrying charges have fallen somewhat in the last few years, they remain considerably above the cost of receivables financing.

LEGAL CONSIDERATIONS

It is illegal, under the Robinson-Patman Act, for a firm to charge prices that discriminate between customers unless these differential prices are cost-justified. The same holds true for credit — it is illegal to offer more favorable credit terms to one

---

[7]Companies that do a large volume of sales financing typically set up subsidiary companies called *captive finance companies* to do the actual financing. Thus, General Motors, Chrysler, and Ford all have captive finance companies, as do Sears and Montgomery Ward.

customer or class of customers than to another, unless the differences are cost-justified.

CREDIT INSTRUMENTS

Most credit is offered on *open account,* which means that the only formal evidence of credit is an invoice which accompanies the shipment and which the buyer signs to indicate that goods have been received. Then, the buyer and the seller each record the purchase on their books of account. Under certain circumstances, the selling firm may require the buyer to sign a *promissory note* evidencing the credit obligation. Promissory notes are useful (1) if the order is very large; (2) if the seller anticipates the possibility of having trouble collecting, because a note is a stronger legal claim than a simple signed invoice; or (3) if the buyer wants a longer-than-usual time in which to pay for the order, because in that case interest should be charged, and interest charges can be built into a promissory note.

Another instrument used in trade credit, especially in international trade, is the *commercial draft.* Here the seller draws up a draft—which is a sort of combination check and a promissory note—calling for the buyer to pay a specific amount to the seller by a specified date. This draft is then sent to the buyer's bank, along with the shipping invoices necessary to take possession of the goods. The bank forwards the draft to the buyer, who signs it and returns it to the bank. The bank then delivers the shipping documents to its customer, who at this point can claim the goods. If the draft is a *sight draft,* then upon delivery of the shipping documents and acceptance of the draft by the buyer, the bank actually withdraws money from the buyer's account and forwards it to the selling firm. If the draft is a *time draft,* payable on a specific future date, then the bank returns it to the selling firm. In this case, the draft is called a *trade acceptance,* and it amounts to a promissory note that the seller can hold for future payment or use as collateral for a loan. The bank, in such a situation, has served as an intermediary, making sure that the buyer does not receive the goods until the note (or draft) has been executed for the benefit of the seller.

A seller who lacks confidence in the ability or willingness of the buyer to pay off a time draft may refuse to ship without a guarantee of payment by the buyer's bank. Presumably, the bank knows its customer, and, for a fee, the bank will guarantee payment of the draft. In this instance, the draft is called a *banker's acceptance.* Such instruments are widely used, especially in foreign trade. They have a low degree of risk if guaranteed by a strong bank, and there is a ready market for acceptances, making it easy for the seller of the goods to sell the instrument to raise immediate cash. (Banker's acceptances are sold at a discount below face value, and then paid off at face value when they mature, so the discount amounts to interest on the acceptance. The effective interest rate on a strong banker's acceptance is a little above the Treasury bill rate of interest.)

Another type of credit instrument is the *conditional sales contract,* under which the seller retains legal ownership of the goods until the buyer has completed payment. Conditional sales contracts are used primarily for such items as

machinery, dental equipment, and the like, which are often purchased on an installment basis over a period of two or three years. The significant advantage of a conditional sales contract is that it is easier for the seller to repossess the equipment in the event of default than it would be if title had passed. This feature makes possible some credit sales that otherwise would not be feasible. Conditional sales contracts generally have a market interest rate built into their payment schedules.

SELF-TEST QUESTIONS

How do profit potential and legal considerations affect a firm's credit policy?

Define and illustrate the following credit instruments:
  (1) Open account invoice
  (2) Promissory note
  (3) Commercial draft
  (4) Sight draft
  (5) Trade acceptance
  (6) Conditional sales contract

ANALYZING PROPOSED CHANGES IN CREDIT POLICY

If the firm's credit policy is *eased* by such actions as lengthening the credit period, relaxing credit standards, following a less tough collection policy, or offering cash discounts, then sales should increase: *Easing the credit policy stimulates sales.* Of course, if credit policy is eased and sales rise, then costs will also rise because more labor, materials, and so on will be required to produce the additional goods. Additionally, receivables outstanding will also increase, which will increase carrying costs, and bad debt and/or discount expenses may also rise. Thus, the key question when deciding on a proposed credit policy change is this: Will sales revenues rise more than costs, including credit-related costs, causing cash flow to increase, or will the increase in sales revenues be more than offset by the higher costs?

Table 18-5 illustrates the general idea behind the analysis of credit policy changes. Column 1 shows the projected 1994 income statement for Monroe Manufacturing under the assumption that the firm's current credit policy is maintained throughout the year. Column 2 shows the expected effects of easing the credit policy by extending the credit period, offering larger discounts, relaxing credit standards, and easing collection efforts. Specifically, Monroe is analyzing the effects of changing its credit terms from 1/10, net 30, to 2/10, net 40, relaxing its credit standards, and putting less pressure on slow-paying customers. Column 3 shows the projected 1994 income statement incorporating the expected effects of an easing in credit policy. The generally looser policy is expected to increase sales and lower collection costs, but discounts and several other types of costs would

TABLE 18-5		Projected 1994 Net Income under Current Credit Policy (1)	Effect of Credit Policy Change (2)	Projected 1994 Net Income under New Credit Policy (3)
MONROE MANUFACTURING COMPANY: ANALYSIS OF CHANGING CREDIT POLICY (MILLIONS OF DOLLARS)	Gross sales	$400	+ $130	$530
	Less discounts	2	+ 4	6
	Net sales	$398	+ $126	$524
	Production costs, including overhead	280	+ 91	371
	Profit before credit costs and taxes	$118	+ $ 35	$153
	Credit-related costs:			
	Cost of carrying receivables	3	+ 2	5
	Credit analysis and collection expenses	5	− 3	2
	Bad debt losses	10	+ 22	32
	Profit before taxes	$100	+ $ 14	$114
	State-plus-federal taxes (50%)	50	+ 7	57
	Net income	$ 50	+ $ 7	$ 57

Note: The above statements include only those cash flows incremental to the credit policy decision. Also, since the items in the statements are basically cash flows, the "bottom line" net income is actually a net cash flow.

rise. The overall, bottom-line effect is a $7 million increase in projected net income. In the following paragraphs, we explain how the numbers in the table were calculated.

Monroe's annual sales are $400 million. Under its current credit policy, 50 percent of those customers who pay do so on Day 10 and take the discount, 40 percent pay on Day 30, and 10 percent pay late, on Day 40. Thus, Monroe's days sales outstanding is $(0.5)(10) + (0.4)(30) + (0.1)(40) = 21$ days, and discounts total $(0.01)($400,000,000)(0.5) = $2,000,000$.

The cost of carrying receivables is equal to the average receivables balance times the variable cost percentage times the cost of money used to carry receivables. The firm's variable cost ratio is 70 percent, and its pre-tax cost of capital invested in receivables is 20 percent. Thus, its cost of carrying receivables is $3 million:

$$(DSO)\begin{pmatrix} \text{Sales} \\ \text{per} \\ \text{day} \end{pmatrix}\begin{pmatrix} \text{Variable} \\ \text{cost} \\ \text{ratio} \end{pmatrix}\begin{pmatrix} \text{Cost} \\ \text{of} \\ \text{funds} \end{pmatrix} = \text{Cost of carrying receivables}$$

$$(21)($400,000,000/360)(0.70)(0.20) = $3,266,667 \approx $3 \text{ million.}$$

Only variable costs enter this calculation because this is the only cost element in receivables that must be financed. We are seeking the cost of carrying receivables, and variable costs represent the firm's investment in the cost of goods sold.

Even though Monroe spends $5 million annually to analyze accounts and to collect bad debts, 2.5 percent of sales will never be collected. Bad debt losses therefore amount to $(0.025)($400,000,000) = $10,000,000$.

Monroe's new credit policy would be 2/10, net 40 versus the old policy of 1/10, net 30, so it would call for a larger discount and a longer payment period, as well as a relaxed collection effort and lower credit standards. The company believes that these changes will lead to a $130 million increase in sales, to $530 million per year. Under the new terms, management believes that 60 percent of the customers who pay will take the 2 percent discount, so discounts will increase to $(0.02)(\$530,000,000)(0.60) = \$6,360,000 \approx \$6$ million. Half of the nondiscount customers will pay on Day 40, and the remainder on Day 50. The new DSO is thus estimated to be 24 days:

$$(0.6)(10) + (0.2)(40) + (0.2)(50) = 24 \text{ days.}$$

Also, the cost of carrying receivables will increase to $5 million:

$$(24)(\$530,000,000/360)(0.70)(0.20) = \$4,946,667 \approx \$5 \text{ million.}[8]$$

The company plans to reduce its annual credit analysis and collection expenditures to $2 million. The reduced credit standards and the relaxed collection effort are expected to raise bad debt losses to about 6 percent of sales, or to $(0.06)(\$530,000,000) = \$31,800,000 \approx \$32,000,000$, which is an increase of $22 million from the previous level.

The combined effect of all the changes in credit policy is a projected $7 million annual increase in net income. There would, of course, be corresponding changes on the projected balance sheet—the higher sales would necessitate somewhat larger cash balances, inventories, and, depending on the capacity situation, perhaps more fixed assets. Accounts receivable would, of course, also increase. Since these asset increases would have to be financed, certain liabilities and/or equity would have to be increased.

The $7 million expected increase in net income is, of course, an estimate, and the actual effects of the change could be quite different. In the first place, there is uncertainty—perhaps quite a lot—about the projected $130 million increase in sales. Conceivably, if the firm's competitors matched its changes, sales would not

---

[8]Since the credit policy change will result in a longer DSO, the firm will have to wait longer to receive its profit on the goods it sells. Therefore, the firm will incur an opportunity cost due to not having the cash from these profits available for investment. The dollar amount of this opportunity cost is equal to the old sales per day times the change in DSO times the contribution margin $(1 - \text{Variable cost ratio})$ times the firm's cost of carrying receivables, or

$$\begin{aligned} \text{Opportunity cost} &= (\text{Old sales}/360)(\Delta DSO)(1 - v)(k) \\ &= (\$400/360)(3)(0.3)(0.20) \\ &= \$0.2 = \$200,000. \end{aligned}$$

For simplicity, we have ignored this opportunity cost in our analysis. For a more complete discussion of credit policy change analysis, see Eugene F. Brigham and Louis C. Gapenski, *Intermediate Financial Management,* 4th ed. (Fort Worth, Tex.: Dryden Press, 1993), Chapter 23.

rise at all. Similar uncertainties must be attached to the number of customers who would take discounts, to production costs at higher or lower sales levels, to the costs of carrying additional receivables, and to bad debt losses. In the final analysis, the decision will be based on judgment, especially concerning the risks involved, but the type of quantitative analysis set forth above is essential to the process.

SELF-TEST QUESTIONS

Describe the procedure for evaluating a change in credit policy using the income statement approach.

Do you think that credit policy decisions are made more on the basis of numerical analyses or on judgmental factors?

INVENTORY MANAGEMENT

Although our discussion of inventory management will focus on the finance perspective, it is important to understand that good inventory management is vital to the success of virtually all firms. In fact, inventory management is the key to being a top player in many industries today, including both retailing and manufacturing. Because of its importance, managers at all levels, and in all functional areas, are involved in inventory management.

To illustrate the importance of inventory management, consider two companies, Wal-Mart and Boeing. To Wal-Mart, the world's largest retailer, inventory control is its business. Wal-Mart cannot succeed if its stores do not have the items that its customers want, at the time they want them, and at the price to make a sale. To ensure that its customers are satisfied, Wal-Mart uses a sophisticated point-of-sale inventory management system to record each sale and to automatically reduce that item's inventory balance. Then, when each item's inventory balance reaches a predetermined level, the item is automatically reordered. The system depends on unique bar codes that are scanned and recognized at the check-out cash register, but the real key is a sophisticated computer system that combines purchasing, inventory, and administrative functions.

It is not enough for Wal-Mart just to reorder inventory when stocks are low. The company's managers need to know what items are selling at what time of year and at what prices. This information, which is available almost instantaneously, permits Wal-Mart constantly to reassess its inventory and pricing policies. In addition, the real-time sales data, along with the advantage of having significant buying clout because of its size, allows the firm to purchase the right quantities of the right items at the right price. It is obvious that for Wal-Mart, inventory management is not just another working capital function; rather, it is truly the heart and soul of the company.

To Boeing, the world's largest commercial aircraft manufacturer, inventory management means something totally different. In manufacturing, the inventory system is integrated with the production system, so firms must strive for joint

inventory-production efficiency. A low-cost inventory system is not optimal if it leads to a high-cost production system, while a high-cost inventory system is not necessarily bad if it contributes to an efficient, and hence low-cost, production system.

Boeing, which was flying high in the airline expansion years following deregulation, has encountered two major problems. First, it is having trouble matching the government-subsidized prices set by its leading competitor, Europe's Airbus Industrie. Second, and more important, at today's prices for airplanes and jet fuel, it is not cost-effective for airlines to retire older, less-efficient aircraft and replace them with more efficient, but much more expensive, new aircraft. In the past, commercial aircraft were retired after 20 years or so of service, but the balance between capital costs and operating costs has swung decisively in favor of retaining older planes. Now, because of the relatively low price of jet fuel and the high cost of new aircraft, fully depreciated older planes are bargains for the airlines, even though they require more maintenance, burn more fuel, and need larger flight crews. Boeing has recently estimated that it must reduce its costs by 25 to 30 percent to be competitive with Airbus and to encourage airlines to retire their older planes.

Where is Boeing going to find savings of this magnitude? To start, it is closely examining its inventory and production systems. Boeing's commercial aircraft operation holds nearly $8 billion in inventories. It turns its inventory over a little more than twice a year, compared with more than ten times or more for world-class manufacturers in other industries. By streamlining work flow and eliminating excesses, Boeing hopes to decrease the time needed to manufacture a plane from more than a year to just six months by 1998. If inventories fall by just half as a result, the company will save an estimated $400 million annually in inventory financing costs, and even more—perhaps as much as $600 million—in storage, handling, and transportation costs.

In the past, Boeing rationalized its bulging inventories by pointing to the incredible complexity of its products. For example, each 747 has more than 3 million parts, not counting fasteners. In addition, no two orders are exactly alike, because each airline insists on its own designs for seats, galleys, and lavatories, and each has its own preferences for engines and avionics equipment. Boeing prided itself on being able to satisfy every buyer, but all that flexibility added to costs. According to one manager, "In the past, the idea was not to delay a $100 million plane for a $2,000 part. It was just-in-case inventory management instead of just-in-time." Furthermore, inventory costs were billed to corporate headquarters, not to divisions or plants, so production managers had no incentive to hold down inventories. If their plants were well run otherwise, managers with overstuffed warehouses often pocketed bonuses for good performance.

Those days are long gone. Inventory management is now a major factor in gauging plant performance, and managers have become inventory hawks. But their concern goes beyond inventory to the entire production process. By streamlining both inventory and production, Boeing will be able to make the greatest gains. For the company that launched the jet age, the key to the future is on the factory floor.

Inventories are often classified as (1) *raw materials,* (2) *work-in-process,* and (3) *finished goods.* As in the case of accounts receivable, inventory levels depend heavily on sales. However, whereas receivables build up after sales have been made, inventories must be acquired ahead of sales. This is a critical difference, and the necessity of forecasting sales before establishing inventory levels makes inventory management a difficult task. Also, as we pointed out in the Wal-Mart and Boeing examples, errors in inventory management can lead either to lost sales or to excessive costs, and either can quickly sink an otherwise good company.

Inventory management techniques are covered in depth in production and management courses. Further, most inventory management is actually carried out by production engineers, marketing managers, plant managers, and the like. Thus, you may be wondering why we include inventory management in a financial management text. Although the details of inventory management are generally left to other departments, financial managers can assist in inventory management by tracking the firm's inventories, by establishing benchmarks (typically the inventory turnovers of major competitors), and by making sure that operating managers know when inventories appear to be getting out of line.

Inventory management focuses on five basic questions: (1) How many units should be ordered (or produced) at a given time? (2) At which point should inventory be ordered (or produced)? (3) What inventory items warrant special attention? (4) How does our firm's inventory management compare with other firms'? (5) Can changing prices which affect inventory costs be hedged? The remainder of this chapter is devoted to answering these questions.

SELF-TEST QUESTIONS

Why is good inventory management essential to a firm's success?

What functional areas should be involved in inventory management?

What five basic questions does inventory management address?

INVENTORY COSTS

The goal of inventory management is to provide, at the lowest total cost, the inventories required to sustain efficient operations. The first step in inventory management is to identify all the costs involved in purchasing and maintaining inventories. Table 18-6 gives a listing of the typical costs that are associated with inventories. In the table, we have broken down costs into three categories: those associated with carrying inventories, those associated with ordering, shipping and receiving inventories, and those associated with running short of inventories.

Although they may well be the most important element, we shall at this point disregard the third category of costs—the costs of running short. These costs are dealt with by adding safety stocks, as we will discuss later. Similarly, we shall dis-

TABLE 18-6		Approximate Annual Cost as a Percentage of Inventory Value
COSTS ASSOCIATED WITH INVENTORIES		
	I. Carrying Costs	
	Cost of capital tied up	12.0%
	Storage and handling costs	0.5
	Insurance	0.5
	Property taxes	1.0
	Depreciation and obsolescence	12.0
	Total	26.0%
	II. Ordering, Shipping, and Receiving Costs	
	Cost of placing orders, including production and set-up costs	Varies
	Shipping and handling costs	2.5%
	III. Costs of Running Short	
	Loss of sales	Varies
	Loss of customer goodwill	Varies
	Disruption of production schedules	Varies

Note: These costs vary from firm to firm, from item to item, and also over time. The figures shown are U.S. Department of Commerce estimates for an average manufacturing firm. Where costs vary so widely that no meaningful numbers can be assigned, we simply report "Varies."

cuss quantity discounts in a later section. The costs that remain for consideration at this stage, then, are carrying costs and ordering, shipping, and receiving costs.

CARRYING COSTS

Carrying costs generally rise in direct proportion to the average amount of inventory carried. Inventories carried, in turn, depend on the frequency with which orders are placed. To illustrate, if a firm sells S units per year, and if it places equal-sized orders N times per year, then S/N units will be purchased with each order. If the inventory is used evenly over the year, and if no safety stocks are carried, then the average inventory, A, will be:

$$\text{Average inventory} = A = \frac{\text{Units per order}}{2} = \frac{S/N}{2}. \qquad (18\text{-}1)$$

For example, if S = 120,000 units in a year and N = 4, then the firm will order 30,000 units at a time, and its average inventory will be 15,000 units:

$$A = \frac{S/N}{2} = \frac{120,000/4}{2} = \frac{30,000}{2} = 15,000 \text{ units.}$$

Just after a shipment arrives, the inventory will be 30,000 units; just before the next shipment arrives, it will be zero; and on average, 15,000 units will be carried.

Now assume the firm purchases its inventory at a price P = $2 per unit. The average inventory value is thus (P)(A) = $2(15,000) = $30,000. If the firm has a cost of capital of 10 percent, it will incur $3,000 in financing charges to carry the inventory for one year. Further, assume that each year the firm incurs $2,000 of storage costs (space, utilities, security, taxes, and so forth), that its inventory insurance costs are $500, and that it must mark down inventories by $1,000 because of depreciation and obsolescence. The firm's total costs of carrying the $30,000 average inventory is thus $3,000 + $2,000 + $500 + $1,000 = $6,500, and the annual percentage cost of carrying the inventory is $6,500/$30,000 = 0.217 = 21.7%.

Defining the annual percentage carrying cost as C, we can, in general, find the annual total carrying cost, TCC, as the percentage carrying cost, C, times the purchase price per unit, P, times the average number of units, A:

$$\text{TCC} = \text{Total carrying cost} = (C)(P)(A). \qquad \text{(18-2)}$$

In our example,

$$\text{TCC} = (0.217)(\$2)(15,000) \approx \$6,500.$$

ORDERING COSTS

Although carrying costs are generally entirely variable and thus rise in direct proportion to the average size of inventories, ordering costs are often fixed. For example, the costs of placing and receiving an order—interoffice memos, long-distance telephone calls, setting up a production run, and taking delivery—are essentially fixed regardless of the size of an order, so this part of inventory cost is simply the fixed cost of placing and receiving an order times the number of orders placed per year.[9] We define the fixed costs associated with ordering inventories as

---

[9]Note that, in reality, both carrying and ordering costs can have variable and fixed cost elements, at least over certain ranges of average inventory. For example, security and utilities charges are probably fixed in the short run over a wide range of inventory levels. Similarly, labor costs in receiving inventory could be tied to the quantity received, and hence could be variable. To simplify matters, we treat all carrying costs as variable and all ordering costs as fixed. However, if these assumptions do not fit the situation at hand, the cost definitions can be changed. For example, one could add another term for shipping costs if there are economies of scale in shipping, such that the cost of shipping a unit is smaller if shipments are larger. However, in most situations, shipping costs are not sensitive to order size, so total shipping costs are simply the shipping cost per unit times the units ordered (and sold) during the year. Under this condition, shipping costs are not influenced by inventory policy, hence they may be disregarded for purposes of determining the optimal inventory level and the optimal order size.

F, and if we place N orders per year, the total ordering cost is given by Equation 18-3:

$$\text{Total ordering cost} = \text{TOC} = (F)(N). \tag{18-3}$$

Here TOC = total ordering cost, F = fixed costs per order, and N = number of orders placed per year.

Equation 18-1 may be rewritten as N = S/2A, and then substituted into Equation 18-3:

$$\text{Total ordering cost} = \text{TOC} = (F)\left(\frac{S}{2A}\right). \tag{18-4}$$

To illustrate the use of Equation 18-4, if F = \$100, S = 120,000 units, and A = 15,000 units, then TOC, the total annual ordering cost, is \$400:

$$\text{TOC} = \$100\left(\frac{120,000}{30,000}\right) = \$100(4) = \$400.$$

TOTAL INVENTORY COSTS

Total carrying cost, TCC as defined in Equation 18-2, and total ordering cost, TOC as defined in Equation 18-4, may be combined to find total inventory costs, TIC, as follows:

$$\begin{aligned}\text{Total inventory costs} = \text{TIC} &= \text{TCC} + \text{TOC} \\ &= (C)(P)(A) + (F)\left(\frac{S}{2A}\right). \end{aligned} \tag{18-5}$$

Recognizing that the average inventory carried is A = Q/2, or one-half the size of each order quantity, Q, we may rewrite Equation 18-5 as follows:

$$\begin{aligned}\text{TIC} &= \text{TCC} + \text{TOC} \\ &= (C)(P)\left(\frac{Q}{2}\right) + (F)\left(\frac{S}{Q}\right). \end{aligned} \tag{18-6}$$

Here we see that total carrying cost equals average inventory in units, Q/2, multiplied by unit price, P, times the percentage annual carrying cost, C. Total ordering cost equals the number of orders placed per year, S/Q, multiplied by the fixed cost of placing and receiving an order, F. Finally, total inventory costs equal the sum of total carrying cost plus total ordering cost. We will use this equation in the next section to develop the optimal inventory ordering quantity model.

SELF-TEST QUESTIONS

What are the three categories of inventory costs?

What are some specific inventory carrying costs? As defined here, are these costs fixed or variable?

What are some inventory ordering costs? As defined here, are these costs fixed or variable?

What are the components of total inventory costs?

THE ECONOMIC ORDERING QUANTITY (EOQ) MODEL

Inventories are obviously necessary, but it is equally obvious that a firm's profitability will suffer if it has too much or too little inventory. How can we determine the optimal inventory level? One commonly used approach is based on the *economic ordering quantity (EOQ)* model, which is described next.

DERIVATION OF THE EOQ MODEL

Figure 18-1 illustrates the basic premise on which the EOQ model is built, namely, that some costs rise with larger inventories while other costs decline, and there is an optimal order size (and associated average inventory) which minimizes the total costs of inventories. First, as noted earlier, the average investment in inventories depends on how frequently orders are placed and the size of each order — if we order every day, average inventories will be much smaller than if we order once a year. Further, as Figure 18-1 shows, the firm's carrying costs rise with larger orders: Larger orders mean larger average inventories, so warehousing costs, interest on funds tied up in inventory, insurance, and obsolescence costs will all increase. However, ordering costs decline with larger orders and inventories: The cost of placing orders, suppliers' production setup costs, and order handling costs will all decline if we order infrequently and consequently hold larger quantities.

If the carrying and ordering cost curves in Figure 18-1 are added, the sum represents total inventory costs, TIC. The point where the TIC is minimized represents the *economic ordering quantity (EOQ),* and this, in turn, determines the optimal average inventory level.

FIGURE 18-1

DETERMINATION OF
THE OPTIMAL ORDER
QUANTITY

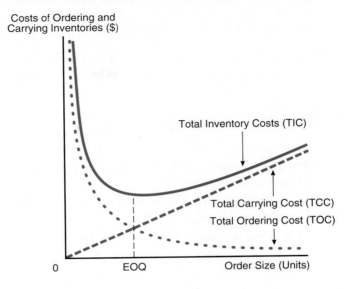

The EOQ is found by differentiating Equation 18-6 with respect to ordering quantity, Q, and setting the derivative equal to zero:

$$\frac{d(TIC)}{dQ} = \frac{(C)(P)}{2} - \frac{(F)(S)}{Q^2} = 0.$$

Now, solving for Q, we obtain:

$$\frac{(C)(P)}{2} = \frac{(F)(S)}{Q^2}$$

$$Q^2 = \frac{2(F)(S)}{(C)(P)}$$

$$EOQ = \sqrt{\frac{2(F)(S)}{(C)(P)}}. \qquad (18\text{-}7)$$

Here

EOQ = economic ordering quantity, or the optimal quantity to be ordered each time an order is placed.

F = fixed costs of placing and receiving an order.

S = annual sales in units.

C = annual carrying costs expressed as a percentage of average inventory value.

P = purchase price the firm must pay per unit of inventory.

Equation 18-7 is the EOQ model.[10] The assumptions of the model, which will be relaxed shortly, include the following: (1) sales can be forecasted perfectly, (2) sales are evenly distributed throughout the year, and (3) orders are received when expected.

EOQ MODEL ILLUSTRATION

To illustrate the EOQ model, consider the following data supplied by Cotton Tops Inc., a distributor of custom-designed T-shirts, which sells to concessionaires at various theme parks in the United States:

S = annual sales = 26,000 shirts per year.

C = percentage carrying cost = 25 percent of inventory value.

P = purchase price per shirt = $4.92 per shirt. (The sales price is $9, but this is irrelevant for our purposes here.)

F = fixed cost per order = $1,000. Cotton Tops designs and distributes the shirts, but the actual production is done by another company. The bulk of this $1,000 cost is the labor cost for setting up the equipment for the production run, which the manufacturer bills separately from the $4.92 cost per shirt.

Substituting these data into Equation 18-7, we obtain an EOQ of 6,500 units:

$$EOQ = \sqrt{\frac{2(F)(S)}{(C)(P)}} = \sqrt{\frac{(2)(\$1,000)(26,000)}{(0.25)(\$4.92)}}$$
$$= \sqrt{42,276,423} \approx 6,500 \text{ units.}$$

---

[10]The EOQ model can also be written as

$$EOQ = \sqrt{\frac{2(F)(S)}{C^*}},$$

where C^* is the annual carrying cost per unit expressed in *dollars*.

Figure 18-2

Inventory Position
without Safety
Stock

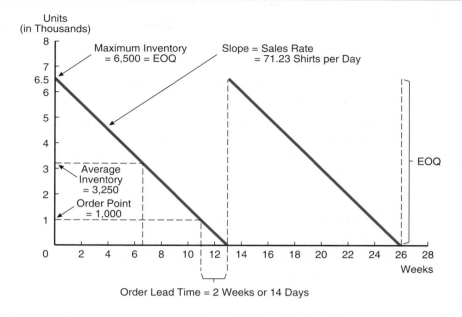

Order Lead Time = 2 Weeks or 14 Days

With an EOQ of 6,500 shirts and annual usage of 26,000 shirts, Cotton Tops will place 26,000/6,500 = 4 orders per year. Notice that average inventory holdings depend directly on the EOQ. This relationship is illustrated graphically in Figure 18-2, where we see that average inventory = EOQ/2. Immediately after an order is received, 6,500 shirts are in stock. The usage rate, or sales rate, is 500 shirts per week (26,000/52 weeks), so inventories are drawn down by this amount each week. Thus, the actual number of units held in inventory will vary from 6,500 shirts just after an order is received to zero just before a new order arrives. With a 6,500 beginning balance, a zero ending balance, and a uniform sales rate, inventories will average one-half the EOQ, or 3,250 shirts, during the year. At a cost of $4.92 per shirt, the average investment in inventories will be (3,250)($4.92) ≈ $16,000. If inventories are financed by bank loans, the loan will vary from a high of $32,000 to a low of $0, but the average amount outstanding over the course of a year will be $16,000.

Notice that the EOQ, hence average inventory holdings, rises with the square root of sales. Therefore, a given increase in sales will result in a less-than-proportionate increase in inventories, so the inventory/sales ratio will tend to decline as a firm grows. For example, Cotton Tops's EOQ is 6,500 shirts at an annual sales level of 26,000, and the average inventory is 3,250 shirts, or $16,000. However, if sales were to increase by 100 percent, to 52,000 shirts per year, the EOQ would

rise only to 9,195 units, or by 41 percent, and the average inventory would rise by this same percentage. This suggests that there are economies of scale in holding inventories.[11]

Finally, look at Cotton Tops's total inventory costs for the year, assuming that the EOQ is ordered each time. Using Equation 18-6, we find that total inventory costs are $8,000:

$$
\begin{aligned}
\text{TIC} &= \quad\quad \text{TCC} \quad\quad + \quad\quad \text{TOC} \\
&= \quad (C)(P)\left(\frac{Q}{2}\right) \quad + \quad (F)\left(\frac{S}{Q}\right) \\
&= 0.25(\$4.92)\left(\frac{6,500}{2}\right) + (\$1,000)\left(\frac{26,000}{6,500}\right) \\
&\approx \quad\quad \$4,000 \quad\quad + \quad\quad \$4,000 \quad = \$8,000.
\end{aligned}
$$

Note these two points: (1) The $8,000 total inventory cost represents the total of carrying costs and ordering costs, but this amount does *not* include the 26,000($4.92) = $127,920 paid to the supplier for the inventory itself. (2) As we see both in Figure 18-1 and in the calculation above, at the EOQ, total carrying cost (TCC) equals total ordering cost (TOC). This property is not unique to our Cotton Tops illustration—it always holds.

SETTING THE ORDER POINT

If a 2-week lead time is required for production and shipping, what is Cotton Tops's order point level? If we use a 52-week year, Cotton Tops sells 26,000/52 = 500 shirts per week. Thus, if a 2-week lag occurs between placing an order and receiving goods, Cotton Tops must place the order when there are 2(500) = 1,000 shirts on hand. During the 2-week production and shipping period, the inventory balance will continue to decline at the rate of 500 shirts per week, and the inventory balance will hit zero just as the order of new shirts arrives.

If Cotton Tops knew for certain that both the sales rate and the order lead time would never vary, it could operate exactly as shown in Figure 18-2. However, sales do change, and production and/or shipping delays are frequently encountered; to guard against these events, the firm must carry additional inventories, or safety stocks, as discussed in the next section.

---

[11]Note, however, that these scale economies relate to each particular item, not to the entire firm. Thus, a large distributor with $500 million of sales might have a higher inventory/sales ratio than a much smaller distributor if the small firm has only a few high-sales-volume items while the large firm distributes a great many low-volume items.

SELF-TEST QUESTIONS

What is the concept behind the EOQ model?

What is the relationship between total carrying cost and total ordering cost at the EOQ?

What assumptions are inherent in the EOQ model as presented here?

EOQ MODEL EXTENSIONS

The basic EOQ model was derived under several restrictive assumptions. In this section, we relax some of these assumptions and, in the process, extend the model to make it more useful.

THE CONCEPT OF SAFETY STOCKS

The concept of a *safety stock* is illustrated in Figure 18-3. First, note that the slope of the sales line measures the expected rate of sales. The company *expects* to sell 500 shirts per week, but let us assume that the maximum likely sales rate is twice this amount, or 1,000 units each week. Further, assume that Cotton Tops sets the safety stock at 1,000 shirts, so it initially orders 7,500 shirts, the EOQ of 6,500 plus the 1,000-unit safety stock. Subsequently, it reorders the EOQ whenever the inventory level falls to 2,000 shirts, the safety stock of 1,000 shirts plus the 1,000 shirts expected to be sold while awaiting delivery of the order.

Notice that the company could, over the 2-week delivery period, sell 1,000 units a week, or double its normal expected sales. This maximum rate of sales is shown by the steeper dashed line in Figure 18-3. The condition that makes possible this higher maximum sales rate is the safety stock of 1,000 shirts.

The safety stock is also useful to guard against delays in receiving orders. The expected delivery time is 2 weeks, but with a 1,000-unit safety stock, the company could maintain sales at the expected rate of 500 units per week for an additional 2 weeks if production or shipping delays held up an order.

However, carrying a safety stock has a cost. The average inventory is now EOQ/2 plus the safety stock, or 6,500/2 + 1,000 = 3,250 + 1,000 = 4,250 shirts, and the average inventory value is now (4,250)($4.92) = $20,910. This increase in average inventory causes an increase in annual inventory carrying costs equal to (Safety stock)(P)(C) = 1,000($4.92)(0.25) = $1,230.

The optimal safety stock varies from situation to situation, but, in general, it *increases* (1) with the uncertainty of demand forecasts, (2) with the costs (in terms of lost sales and lost goodwill) that result from inventory shortages, and (3) with the probability that delays will occur in receiving shipments. The optimal safety stock *decreases* as the cost of carrying this additional inventory increases.[12]

---

[12]For a more detailed discussion of safety stocks, see Arthur Snyder, "Principles of Inventory Management," *Financial Executive,* April 1964, 13–21.

FIGURE 18-3

INVENTORY POSITION
WITH SAFETY STOCK
INCLUDED

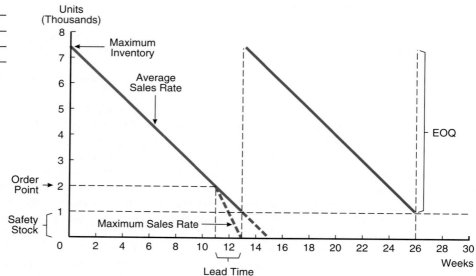

QUANTITY DISCOUNTS

Now suppose the T-shirt manufacturer offered Cotton Tops a *quantity discount* of 2 percent on large orders. If the quantity discount applied to orders of 5,000 or more, then Cotton Tops would continue to place the EOQ order of 6,500 shirts and take the quantity discount. However, if the quantity discount required orders of 10,000 or more, then Cotton Tops's inventory manager would have to compare the savings in purchase price that would result if its ordering quantity were increased to 10,000 units with the increase in total inventory costs caused by the departure from the 6,500-unit EOQ.

First, consider the total costs associated with Cotton Tops's EOQ of 6,500 units. We found earlier that total inventory costs are $8,000:

$$\text{TIC} = \qquad \text{TCC} \qquad + \qquad \text{TOC}$$

$$= \qquad (\text{C})(\text{P})\left(\frac{Q}{2}\right) \qquad + \qquad (\text{F})\left(\frac{S}{Q}\right)$$

$$= \quad 0.25(\$4.92)\left(\frac{6,500}{2}\right) \quad + \quad (\$1,000)\left(\frac{26,000}{6,500}\right)$$

$$\approx \qquad \$4,000 \qquad + \qquad \$4,000 \qquad = \$8,000.$$

Now, what would the total inventory costs be if Cotton Tops ordered 10,000 units instead of 6,500? The answer is $8,625:

$$\text{TIC} = 0.25(\$4.82)\left(\frac{10,000}{2}\right) + (\$1,000)\left(\frac{26,000}{10,000}\right)$$

$$= \$6,025 + \$2,600 = \$8,625.$$

Notice that when the discount is taken, the price, P, is reduced by the amount of the discount; the new price per unit would be $0.98(\$4.92) = \$4.82$. Also note that when the ordering quantity is increased, carrying costs increase because the firm is carrying a larger average inventory, but ordering costs decrease since the number of orders per year decreases. If we were to calculate total inventory costs at an ordering quantity of 5,000, we would find that carrying costs would be less than $4,000, and ordering costs would be more than $4,000, but the total inventory costs would be more than $8,000, since they are at a minimum when 6,500 units are ordered.[13]

Thus, inventory costs would increase by $8,625 − $8,000 = $625 if Cotton Tops were to increase its order size to 10,000 shirts. *However, this cost increase must be compared with Cotton Tops's savings if it takes the discount.* Taking the discount would save $0.02(\$4.92) = \$0.0984$ per unit. Over the year, Cotton Tops orders 26,000 shirts, so the annual savings is $\$0.0984(26,000) \approx \$2,558$. Here is a summary:

Reduction in purchase price = $0.02(\$4.92)(26,000)$ = $2,558
Less: Increase in total inventory cost = 625
Net savings from taking discounts $1,933

Obviously, the company should order 10,000 units at a time and take advantage of the quantity discount.

INFLATION

Moderate inflation—say, 3 percent per year—can largely be ignored for purposes of inventory management, but higher rates of inflation must be explicitly considered. If the rate of inflation in the types of goods the firm stocks tends to be relatively constant, it can be dealt with quite easily—simply deduct the expected annual rate of inflation from the carrying cost percentage, C, in Equation 18-7, and

---

[13]At an ordering quantity of 5,000 units, total inventory costs are $8,275:

$$\text{TIC} = (0.25)(\$4.92)\left(\frac{5,000}{2}\right) + (\$1,000)\left(\frac{26,000}{5,000}\right)$$

$$= \$3,075 + \$5,200 = \$8,275.$$

use this modified version of the EOQ model to establish the working stock. The reason for making this deduction is that inflation causes the value of the inventory to rise, thus offsetting somewhat the effects of depreciation and other carrying costs factors. Since C will now be smaller, the calculated EOQ, and the average inventory, will increase. However, the higher the rate of inflation, the higher are interest rates, and this factor will cause C to increase, thus lowering the EOQ and average inventories.

On balance, there is no evidence that inflation either raises or lowers the optimal inventories of firms in the aggregate. Inflation should still be explicitly considered, however, for it will raise the individual firm's optimal holdings if the rate of inflation for its own inventories is above average (and is greater than the effects of inflation on interest rates), and vice versa.

SEASONAL DEMAND

For most firms, it is unrealistic to assume that the demand for an inventory item is uniform throughout the year. What happens when there is seasonal demand, as would hold true for an ice cream company? Here the standard annual EOQ model is obviously not appropriate. However, it does provide a point of departure for setting inventory parameters, which are then modified to fit the particular seasonal pattern. The procedure here is to divide the year into the seasons in which annualized sales are relatively constant, say, the summer, the spring and fall, and the winter. Then, the EOQ model can be applied separately to each period. During the transitions between seasons, inventories would be either run down or else built up with special seasonal orders.

EOQ RANGE

Thus far, we have interpreted the EOQ, and the resulting inventory variables, as single-point estimates. It can be easily demonstrated that small deviations from the EOQ do not appreciably affect total inventory costs, and, consequently, that the optimal ordering quantity should be viewed more as a range than as a single value.[14]

To illustrate this point, we can examine the sensitivity of total inventory costs to ordering quantity for Cotton Tops Inc. Table 18-7 contains the results of our sensitivity analysis. We conclude that the ordering quantity could range from 5,000 to 8,000 units without affecting total inventory costs by more than 3.4 percent. Thus, we see that managers can adjust the ordering quantity within a fairly wide range without fear of significantly increasing total inventory costs.

---

[14]This is somewhat analogous to the optimal capital structure in that small changes in capital structure around the optimum do not have much effect on the firm's weighted average cost of capital.

TABLE 18-7

EOQ SENSITIVITY

ANALYSIS

Ordering Quantity	Total Inventory Costs	Percentage Deviation from Optimum
3,000	$10,512	+31.4%
4,000	8,960	+12.0
5,000	8,275	+3.4
6,000	8,023	+0.3
6,500	8,000	0.0
7,000	8,019	+0.2
8,000	8,170	+2.1
9,000	8,423	+5.3
10,000	8,750	+9.4

SELF-TEST QUESTIONS

Why are inventory safety stocks required?

Conceptually, how would you evaluate a quantity discount offer from a supplier?

What impact does inflation have on the EOQ?

Can the EOQ model be used when a company faces seasonal demand fluctuations?

What is the impact of minor deviations from the EOQ on total inventory costs?

INVENTORY CONTROL SYSTEMS

The EOQ model, together with safety stock analysis, can be used to help establish the proper inventory level, but inventory management also involves the establishment of an *inventory control system.* Inventory control systems run the gamut from very simple to extremely complex, depending on the size of the firm and the nature of its inventories. For example, one simple control procedure is the *red-line method*—inventory items are stocked in a bin, a red line is drawn around the inside of the bin at the level of the order point, and the inventory clerk places an order when the red line shows. The *two-bin method* has inventory items stocked in two bins. When the working bin is empty, an order is placed and inventory is drawn from the second bin. These procedures work well for parts such as bolts in a manufacturing process and for many items in retail businesses.

COMPUTERIZED SYSTEMS

Larger companies employ *computerized inventory control systems.* The computer starts with an inventory count in memory. As withdrawals are made, they are recorded by the computer, and the inventory balance is revised. When the order point is reached, the computer automatically places an order, and when the order

is received, the recorded balance is increased. As we discussed earlier, retailers such as Wal-Mart have carried this system quite far.

A good inventory control system is dynamic, not static. A company such as IBM or General Motors stocks hundreds of thousands of different items. The sales (or use) of these various items can rise or fall quite separately from rising or falling overall corporate sales. As the usage rate for an individual item begins to rise or fall, the inventory manager must adjust its balance to avoid running short or ending up with obsolete items. If the change in the usage rate appears to be permanent, then the EOQ should be recomputed, the safety stock level should be reconsidered, and the computer model used in the control process should be reprogrammed.

JUST-IN-TIME SYSTEMS

A relatively new approach to inventory control called *just-in-time* has been developed by Japanese firms and is gaining popularity throughout the world. Toyota provides a good example of the just-in-time system. Eight of Toyota's ten domestic factories, along with most of Toyota's suppliers, dot the countryside around Toyota City, Japan. Delivery of components is tied to the speed of the assembly line, and parts are generally delivered no more than a few hours before they are used. The just-in-time system reduces the need for Toyota and other manufacturers to carry large inventories, but it requires a great deal of coordination between the manufacturer and its suppliers, both in the timing of deliveries and the quality of the parts.

Not surprisingly, U.S. automobile manufacturers were among the first domestic firms to move toward just-in-time systems. Ford has been restructuring its production system with a goal of increasing its inventory turnover from 20 times a year to 30 or 40 times. Of course, just-in-time systems place considerable pressure on suppliers. GM used to keep a 10-day supply of seats and other parts made by Lear Siegler; now GM sends in orders at four- to eight-hour intervals and expects immediate shipment. A Lear Siegler spokesman stated, "We can't afford to keep things sitting around either," so Lear Siegler has had to be tougher on its own suppliers.

Just-in-time systems are also being adopted by smaller firms. In fact, some production experts say that small companies are better positioned than large ones to use just-in-time methods, because it is easier to redefine job functions and to educate people in small firms. One small-firm example is Fireplace Manufacturers, a manufacturer of prefabricated fireplaces. The company was recently having cash flow problems, and it was carrying $1.1 million in inventories to support annual sales of about $8 million. The company used just-in-time methods to trim its raw material and work-in-process inventories to $750,000, freeing up $350,000 of cash, even though sales were doubling.

OUT-SOURCING

Another important development related to inventories is *out-sourcing,* which is the practice of purchasing components rather than making them in-house. Thus, if General Motors arranged to buy radiators, axles, and other parts from suppliers

rather than making them itself, it would be increasing its use of out-sourcing. Out-sourcing is often combined with just-in-time systems to reduce inventory levels. However, perhaps the major reason for out-sourcing has nothing to do with inventory policy—a heavily unionized company like GM can often buy parts from a nonunionized supplier at a lower cost than it would take to make them because of wage-rate and fringe-benefit differentials, and work rules.

THE RELATIONSHIP BETWEEN PRODUCTION SCHEDULING AND INVENTORY LEVELS

Another point relating to inventory levels is *the relationship between production scheduling and inventory levels.* A firm like a greeting card manufacturer has highly seasonal sales. Such a firm could produce on a steady, year-round basis, or it could let production rise and fall with sales. If it established a level production schedule, its inventories would rise sharply during periods when sales were low and then would decline during peak sales periods, but the average inventory held would be substantially higher than if production were geared to rise and fall with sales.

Our discussions of just-in-time systems, out-sourcing, and production scheduling all point out the necessity of coordinating inventory policy with manufacturing policies. Companies try to minimize *total production costs,* and inventory costs are just one part of total costs. Still, they are an important cost, and financial managers should be aware of the determinants of inventory costs and how they can be minimized.

MONITORING INVENTORY

We stated earlier that the primary inventory management function of the financial manager is to monitor inventory levels to ensure that they are, at a minimum, consistent with those of the firm's major competitors. One useful tool for accomplishing this is the *inventory turnover ratio,* which is defined as sales (or better yet, cost of goods sold) divided by inventory (or better yet, average inventory). For example, suppose that Boston Lumber Company (BLC) has annual cost of goods sold of $288,000 and an average inventory over the year of $36,000. In this situation, BLC's inventory turnover is $288,000/$36,000 = 8.0 times.

Another common measure for monitoring inventory is the *number of days in inventory,* which is defined as inventory divided by average daily cost of goods sold. BLC, with an average daily cost of goods sold of $288,000/360 = $800, has $36,000/$800 = 45.0 days in inventory. In general, the higher the inventory turnover the better, while the lower the number of days in inventory the better.[15]

---

[15]Note that the number of days in inventory is related to the inventory turnover ratio:

$$\text{Number of days in inventory} = \frac{360}{\text{Inventory turnover ratio}}$$

$$= \frac{360}{8.0} = 45 \text{ days.}$$

TABLE 18-8	Month (1)	Average Daily Cost of Goods Sold (2)	Average Inventory (3)	Days in Inventory (4) = (3)/(2)
BOSTON LUMBER	January	$ 600	$32,000	53.3
COMPANY: INVENTORY	February	650	33,000	50.8
MONITORING CHART	March	700	34,000	48.6
	April	800	36,000	45.0
	May	900	38,000	42.2
	June	1,000	40,000	40.0

Monitoring inventory on an annual basis does not give managers timely feedback, so most firms monitor inventory on a quarterly, monthly, or even weekly basis. For example, BLC monitors its inventory situation monthly, and it uses the format shown in Table 18-8. Here we see that BLC's inventory usage, as measured by days in inventory, becomes more efficient as the firm moves from January to June. Note, however, that monitoring inventories by this method has the same problem as monitoring receivables by days sales outstanding—both measures are biased when sales change. What Table 18-8 is really telling BLC's managers is that sales are growing faster over the period (roughly 11 percent monthly) than are inventories (roughly 5 percent monthly). The fact that inventories are being used more efficiently is real, but the cause may be seasonal variations rather than improved inventory management. Of course, the addition of data from BLC's leading competitors would greatly increase the value of the Table 18-8 analysis.

There are several other methods that can be used to monitor inventories—monitoring inventories is analogous to monitoring receivables, so many of the same techniques apply. We will leave additional detail to books that specialize in inventory management. However, we do want to reiterate that, for most firms, good inventory management is necessary for survival, so all facets of inventory management, including monitoring, are executed properly by top firms.

SELF-TEST QUESTIONS

Describe some inventory control systems used in practice.

What are just-in-time systems? What advantages do these inventory systems offer?

What is out-sourcing?

Describe the dependency between production scheduling and inventory levels.

How might firms monitor their inventory position?

INVENTORY COST HEDGING

In Chapter 22, we will discuss the use of financial futures to hedge against changes in interest rate levels. Actually, futures markets were established for many industrial and agricultural commodities long before they began to be used for financial instruments. We can use Porter Electronics, which uses large quantities of copper as well as several precious metals, to illustrate inventory hedging. Suppose that in March 1993, Porter foresaw a need for 100,000 pounds of copper in September 1993 for use in fulfilling a fixed-price contract to supply solar power cells to the U.S. Government. Porter's managers are concerned that a strike by the copper mineworkers' union will occur when the union contract expires in June 1993. A strike would significantly raise the price of copper and possibly turn the expected profit on the solar cell contract into a loss.

Porter could, of course, go ahead and buy the copper now that it will need to fulfill the contract, but if it does, it will incur substantial carrying costs. As an alternative, the company could hedge against increasing copper prices in the futures market. The New York Commodity Exchange trades standard copper futures contracts of 25,000 pounds each. Thus, Porter could buy four contracts (go long) for delivery in September 1993. These contracts were trading in March for about $0.97 per pound. The spot price at that date was about $0.95 per pound. If copper prices do rise appreciably over the next 6 months, the value of Porter's long position in copper futures would increase, thus offsetting some of the price increase in the commodity itself. Of course, if copper prices fall, Porter would lose money on its futures contract, but the company would be buying the copper on the spot market at a cheaper price, so it would make a higher-than-anticipated profit on its sale of solar cells. Thus, hedging in the copper futures market locks in the cost of raw materials and removes some uncertainties, or risks, to which the firm would otherwise be exposed but at a cost.

Some firms have been using the futures markets for speculation, rather than hedging, and this can lead to disastrous results. For example, when the once-stable aluminum ingot market began fluctuating wildly in the early 1980s, aluminum fabricators did what mining companies had been doing for years — they turned to the futures market to lock in prices. That worked well, but then some companies started speculating. One company, National Aluminum Corporation, lost $41.4 million in futures trading. Basically, National Aluminum bought forward contracts to buy 100,000 tons of ingot for 80 cents a pound, which was far in excess of its planned production needs. When the contracts were near expiration, the price of ingots had dropped below 60 cents a pound, resulting in a huge loss.

SELF-TEST QUESTION

Discuss how futures markets can be used to hedge against increasing raw material prices.

SUMMARY

This chapter discussed both receivables and inventories. The key concepts covered are listed below.

▶ When a firm sells goods to a customer on credit, an *account receivable* is created.

▶ Firms can use an *aging schedule* and the *days sales outstanding (DSO)* to help keep track of their receivables position and to help avoid the buildup of possible bad debts.

▶ The *payments pattern approach* is the best way to monitor receivables. The primary tool in this approach is the *uncollected balances schedule*.

▶ A firm's *credit policy* consists of four elements: (1) credit period, (2) discounts given for early payment, (3) credit standards, and (4) collection policy. The first two, when combined, are called the *credit terms*.

▶ Two major sources of external credit information are available: *credit associations*, which are local groups that meet frequently and correspond with one another to exchange information on credit customers, and *credit reporting agencies*, which collect credit information and sell it for a fee.

▶ Additional factors that influence a firm's overall credit policy are (1) *profit potential*, (2) *legal considerations*, and (3) the type of *credit instruments* offered.

▶ The basic objective of the credit manager is to increase profitable sales by extending credit to worthy customers and therefore adding value to the firm.

▶ If a firm *eases its credit policy*, its sales should increase. Actions which ease the credit policy include lengthening the credit period, relaxing credit standards and collection policy, and offering cash discounts. Each of these actions, however, increases costs. A firm should ease its credit policy only if the costs of doing so will be more than offset by higher sales revenues.

▶ *Inventory management* involves determining how much inventory to hold, when to place orders, and how many units to order at a time. Because the cost of holding inventory is high, inventory management is important.

▶ *Inventory* can be grouped into three categories: (1) raw materials, (2) work-in-process, and (3) finished goods.

▶ *Inventory costs* can also be divided into three types: carrying costs, ordering costs, and stock-out costs. In general, carrying costs increase as the level of inventory rises, but ordering costs and stock-out costs decline with larger inventory holdings.

▶ *Total carrying cost (TCC)* is equal to the percentage cost of carrying inventory (C) times the purchase price per unit of inventory (P) times the average number of units held (A): $TCC = (C)(P)(A)$.

▶ *Total ordering cost (TOC)* is equal to the fixed cost of placing an order (F) times the number of orders placed per year (N): $TOC = (F)(N)$.

▶ *Total inventory costs (TIC)* are equal to carrying costs plus ordering costs.

▶ The *economic ordering quantity (EOQ) model* is a formula for determining the order quantity that will minimize total inventory costs:

$$EOQ = \sqrt{\frac{2(F)(S)}{(C)(P)}}.$$

Here F is the fixed cost per order, S is annual sales in units, C is the percentage cost of carrying inventory, and P is the purchase price per unit.

▶ The *reorder point* is the inventory level at which new items must be ordered.

▶ *Safety stocks* are held to avoid shortages (1) if demand becomes greater than expected or (2) if shipping delays are encountered. The cost of carrying safety stocks is equal to the percentage cost of carrying inventories times the purchase price per unit times the number of units held as the safety stock. These costs are separate from those used in the EOQ model.

▶ Firms use inventory control systems, such as the *red-line method* and the *two-bin method,* as well as *computerized inventory control systems,* to help them keep track of actual inventory levels and to ensure that inventory levels are adjusted as sales change. *Just-in-time (JIT)* systems are also used to hold down inventory costs and, simultaneously, to improve the production process.

QUESTIONS

18-1 Define each of the following terms:
  a. Account receivable
  b. Aging schedule; days sales outstanding (DSO)
  c. Payments pattern approach; uncollected balances schedule
  d. Credit policy; credit period; credit standards; collection policy
  e. Cash discounts
  f. Seasonal dating
  g. Open account; promissory note; commercial draft; sight draft; time draft; trade acceptance; banker's acceptance; conditional sales contract
  h. Carrying costs; ordering costs; total inventory costs
  i. Economic ordering quantity (EOQ); EOQ model; EOQ range
  j. Reorder point; safety stock
  k. Red-line method; two-bin method; computerized inventory control system
  l. Just-in-time systems

18-2 Is it true that when one firm sells to another on credit, the seller records the transaction as an account receivable while the buyer records it as an account payable and that, disregarding discounts, the receivable typically exceeds the payable by the amount of profit on the sale?

18-3 What are the four elements in a firm's credit policy? To what extent can firms set their own credit policies as opposed to having to accept policies that are dictated by "the competition"?

18-4 Suppose a firm makes a purchase and receives the shipment on February 1. The terms of trade as stated on the invoice read "2/10, net 40, May 1 dating." What is the latest date on which payment can be made and the discount still be taken? What is the date on which payment must be made if the discount is not taken?

18-5 What is the days sales outstanding (DSO) for a firm whose sales are $2,880,000 per year and whose accounts receivable are $312,000? (Use 360 days per year.) Is it true that if this firm sells on terms of 3/10, net 40, its customers probably all pay on time?

18-6 Is it true that if a firm calculates its days sales outstanding (DSO) it has no need for an aging schedule?

18-7 Firm A had no credit losses last year, but 1 percent of Firm B's accounts receivable proved to be uncollectible and resulted in losses. Should Firm B fire its credit manager and hire A's?

18-8 Indicate by a +, −, or 0 whether each of the following events would probably cause accounts receivable (A/R), sales, and profits to increase, decrease, or be affected in an indeterminate manner:

	A/R	Sales	Profits
a. The firm tightens its credit standards.	_____	_____	_____
b. The terms of trade are changed from 2/10, net 30, to 3/10, net 30.	_____	_____	_____
c. The terms are changed from 2/10, net 30, to 3/10, net 40.	_____	_____	_____
d. The credit manager gets tough with past-due accounts.	_____	_____	_____

18-9 Indicate by a +, −, or 0 whether each of the following events would probably cause average annual inventories (the sum of the inventories held at the end of each month of the year divided by 12) to rise, fall, or be affected in an indeterminate manner:

a. Our suppliers switch from delivering by train to air freight. _____

b. We change from producing just in time to meet seasonal sales to steady, year-round production. (Sales peak at Christmas.) _____

c. Competition increases in the markets in which we sell. _____

d. The rate of general inflation increases. _____

e. Interest rates rise; other things are constant. _____

SELF-TEST PROBLEMS (SOLUTIONS APPEAR IN APPENDIX C)

ST-1 **(Credit policy)** The McCue Company expects to have sales of $10 million this year under its current operating policies. Its variable costs as a percentage of sales are 80 percent, and its cost of capital is 16 percent. Currently the firm's credit policy is net 25 (no discount for early payment). However, its DSO is 30 days, and its bad debt loss percentage is 2 percent. McCue spends $50,000 per year to collect bad debts, and its federal-plus-state-plus-local tax rate is 50 percent.

The credit manager is considering two alternative proposals, given below, for changing the firm's credit policy. Find the expected change in net income, taking into consideration anticipated changes in carrying costs for accounts receivable, the probable bad debt losses,

and the discounts likely to be taken, for each proposal. Should a change in credit policy be made?

Proposal 1: Lengthen the credit period by going from net 25 to net 30. The bad debt collection expenditures will remain constant. Under this proposal, sales are expected to increase by $1 million annually, and the bad debt loss percentage on *new* sales is expected to rise to 4 percent (the loss percentage on old sales should not change). In addition, the DSO is expected to increase from 30 to 45 days on all sales.

Proposal 2: Shorten the credit period by going from net 25 to net 20. Again, collection expenses will remain constant. The anticipated effects of this change are (1) a decrease in sales of $1 million per year, (2) a decline in the DSO from 30 to 22 days, and (3) a decline in the bad debt loss percentage to 1 percent on all sales.

ST-2 (EOQ model)   The Bertin Breads Company buys and then sells (as bread) 2.6 million bushels of wheat annually. The wheat must be purchased in multiples of 2,000 bushels. Ordering costs, which include grain elevator removal charges of $3,500, are $5,000 per order. Annual carrying costs are 2 percent of the purchase price per bushel of $5. The company maintains a safety stock of 200,000 bushels. The delivery time is 6 weeks.

a.   What is the EOQ?

b.   At what inventory level should a reorder be placed to prevent having to draw on the safety stock?

c.   What are the total inventory costs?

d.   The wheat processor agrees to pay the elevator removal charges if Bertin Breads will purchase wheat in quantities of 650,000 bushels. Would it be to the firm's advantage to order under this alternative?

PROBLEMS

18-1 (Receivables investment)   Wendt Inc. sells on terms of 2/10, net 30. Total sales for the year are $600,000. Forty percent of the customers pay on the tenth day and take discounts; the other 60 percent pay, on average, 40 days after their purchases.

a.   What is the days sales outstanding?

b.   What is the average amount of receivables?

c.   What would happen to the average amount of receivables if Wendt toughened up on its collection policy with the result that all nondiscount customers paid on the thirtieth day?

18-2 (Easing credit terms)   Altman Auto Parts is considering changing its credit terms from 2/15, net 30, to 3/10, net 30, in order to speed collections. At present, 60 percent of the firm's customers take the 2 percent discount. Under the new terms, discount customers are expected to rise to 70 percent. Regardless of the credit terms, half of the customers who do not take the discount are expected to pay on time, while the remainder will pay 10 days late. The change does not involve a relaxation of credit standards; therefore, bad debt losses are not expected to rise above their present 2 percent level. However, the more generous cash discount terms are expected to increase sales from $1 million to $1.2 million per year. The firm's variable cost ratio is 75 percent, the interest rate on funds invested in accounts receivable is 12 percent, and its tax rate is 40 percent.

a.   What is the days sales outstanding before and after the change?

b.   Calculate the discount costs before and after the change.

c. Calculate the dollar cost of carrying receivables before and after the change.

d. Calculate the bad debt losses before and after the change.

e. What is the incremental profit from the change in credit terms? Should the firm change its credit terms?

(Do Part f only if you are using the computer problem diskette.)

f. (1) Suppose the sales forecast is lowered to $1,100,000. Should the firm change its credit policy? What if the sales forecast dropped to $1,036,310?

(2) Suppose the payment pattern of customers remains unchanged with the new credit plan; that is, 60 percent still take the discount, 20 percent pay on time, and 20 percent pay late. Also, the variable cost ratio rises to 78 percent. How does all this affect the decision, assuming the sales forecast remains at $1,200,000?

18-3 (Credit analysis) Dill Distributors makes all sales on a credit basis, selling on terms of 2/10, net 30. Once a year it evaluates the creditworthiness of all its customers. The evaluation procedure ranks customers from 1 to 5, with 1 indicating the "best" customers. Results of the ranking are as follows:

Customer Category	Percentage of Bad Debts	Days Sales Outstanding	Credit Decision	Annual Sales Lost Due to Credit Restrictions
1	None	10	Unlimited credit	None
2	1.0	12	Unlimited credit	None
3	3.0	20	Limited credit	$365,000
4	9.0	60	Limited credit	$182,500
5	16.0	90	Limited credit	$230,000

The variable cost ratio is 75 percent. The cost of capital invested in receivables is 15 percent. What would be the effect on the profitability of extending unlimited credit to each of the Categories 3, 4, and 5? (Hint: Determine the effect of changing each policy separately on the income statement. In other words, find the change in sales, change in production costs, change in receivables and cost of carrying receivables, change in bad debt costs, and so forth, down to the change in net profits. Assume a tax rate of 40 percent.)

18-4 (Tightening credit terms) Helen Bowers, the new credit manager of the Vinson Corporation, was alarmed to find that Vinson sells on credit terms of net 90 days while industry-wide credit terms have recently been lowered to net 30 days. On annual credit sales of $2.5 million, Vinson currently averages 95 days of sales in accounts receivable. Bowers estimates that tightening the credit terms to 30 days would reduce annual sales to $2,375,000, but accounts receivable would drop to 35 days of sales and the savings on investment in them should more than overcome any loss in profit.

Vinson's variable cost ratio is 85 percent, and taxes are 40 percent. If the interest rate on funds invested in receivables is 18 percent, should the change in credit terms be made?

18-5 (Monitoring of receivables) The Russ Fogler Company, a small manufacturer of cordless telephones, began operations on January 1, 1993. Its credit sales for the first 6 months of operations were as follows:

Month	Credit Sales
January	$ 50,000
February	100,000
March	120,000
April	105,000
May	140,000
June	160,000

Throughout this entire period, the firm's credit customers maintained a constant payments pattern: 20 percent paid in the month of sale, 30 percent paid in the month following the sale, and 50 percent paid in the second month following the sale.

a. What was Fogler's receivables balance at the end of March and at the end of June?

b. Assume 90 days per calendar quarter. What were the average daily sales (ADS) and days sales outstanding (DSO) for the first quarter and for the second quarter? What were the cumulative ADS and DSO for the first half-year?

c. Construct an aging schedule as of June 30. Use 0-30, 31-60, and 61-90 day account ages.

d. Construct the uncollected balances schedule for the second quarter as of June 30.

18-6 (Relaxing collection efforts)   The Boyd Corporation has annual credit sales of $1.6 million. Current expenses for the collection department are $35,000, bad debt losses are 1.5 percent, and the days sales outstanding is 30 days. The firm is considering easing its collection efforts such that collection expenses will be reduced to $22,000 per year. The change is expected to increase bad debt losses to 2.5 percent and to increase the days sales outstanding to 45 days. In addition, sales are expected to increase to $1,625,000 per year.

Should the firm relax collection efforts if the opportunity cost of funds is 16 percent, the variable cost ratio is 75 percent, and taxes are 40 percent?

18-7 (Economic ordering quantity)   The Gentry Garden Center sells 90,000 bags of lawn fertilizer annually. The optimal safety stock (which is on hand initially) is 1,000 bags. Each bag costs the firm $1.50, inventory carrying costs are 20 percent, and the cost of placing an order with its supplier is $15.

a. What is the economic ordering quantity?

b. What is the maximum inventory of fertilizer?

c. What will be the firm's average inventory?

d. How often must the company order?

18-8 (EOQ and total ordering costs)   The following inventory data have been established for the Adler Corporation:

1. Orders must be placed in multiples of 100 units.

2. Annual sales are 338,000 units.

3. The purchase price per unit is $3.

4. Carrying cost is 20 percent of the purchase price of goods.

5. Cost per order placed is $24.

6. Desired safety stock is 14,000 units; this amount is on hand initially.

7. Two weeks are required for delivery.

   a. What is the EOQ?

   b. How many orders should the firm place each year?

   c. At what inventory level should a reorder be made? (Hint: Reorder point = Safety stock + (Weeks to deliver × Weekly usage) − Goods in transit.)

   d. Calculate the total costs of ordering and carrying inventories if the order quantity is (1) 4,000 units, (2) 4,800 units, or (3) 6,000 units. What are the total costs if the order quantity is the EOQ?

(Do Part e only if you are using the computer problem diskette.)

e. What are the EOQ and total inventory costs if
    (1) Sales increase to 500,000 units?
    (2) Fixed order costs increase to $30? Sales remain at 338,000 units.
    (3) Purchase price increases to $4? Leave sales and fixed costs at original values.

MINI CASE

(Part I: Receivables management) Rich Jackson, a recent finance graduate, is planning to go into the wholesale building supply business with his brother, Jim, who majored in building construction. The firm would sell primarily to general contractors, and it would start operating next January. Sales would be slow during the cold months, rise during the spring, and then fall off again in the summer, when new construction in the area slows. Sales estimates for the first 6 months are as follows (in thousands of dollars):

January	$100	March	$300	May	$200
February	200	April	300	June	100

The terms of sale are net 30, but because of special incentives, the brothers expect 30 percent of the customers (by dollar value) to pay on the 10th day following the sale, 50 percent to pay on the 40th day, and the remaining 20 percent to pay on the 70th day. No bad debt losses are expected, because Jim, the building construction expert, knows which contractors are having financial problems.

a. Assume that, on average, the brothers expect annual sales of 18,000 items at an average price of $100 per item. (Use a 360-day year.)
    (1) What is the firm's expected days sales outstanding (DSO)?
    (2) What is its expected average daily sales (ADS)?
    (3) What is its expected average accounts receivable level?
    (4) Assume that the firm's profit margin is 25 percent. How much of the receivables balance must be financed? What would the firm's balance sheet figures for accounts receivable, notes payable, and retained earnings be at the end of one year if notes payable are used to finance the investment in receivables? Assume that the cost of carrying receivables had been deducted when the 25 percent profit margin was calculated.
    (5) If bank loans cost 12 percent, what is the annual dollar cost of carrying the receivables?

b. What are some factors which influence (1) a firm's receivables level and (2) the dollar cost of carrying receivables?

c. Assuming that the monthly sales forecasts given previously are accurate, and that customers pay exactly as was predicted, what would the receivables level be at the end of each month? *To reduce calculations, assume that 30 percent of the firm's customers pay in the month of sale, 50 percent pay in the month following the sale, and the remaining 20 percent pay in the second month following the sale. Note that this is a different assumption than was made earlier.* Use the following format to answer Parts c and d:

Month	Sales	End-of-Month Receivables	Quarterly Sales	ADS	DSO = (A/R)/(ADS)
Jan	$100	$ 70			
Feb	200	160			
Mar	300	250	$600	$6.67	37.5
Apr	$300				
May	200				
Jun	100				

d. What is the firm's forecasted average daily sales for the first 3 months? For the entire half-year? The days sales outstanding is commonly used to measure receivables performance. What DSO is expected at the end of March? At the end of June? What does the DSO indicate about customers' payments? Is DSO a good management tool in this situation? If not, why not?

e. Construct aging schedules for the end of March and the end of June (use the format given below). Do these schedules properly measure customers' payment patterns? If not, why not?

	Mar		Jun	
Age of Account (Days)	A/R	%	A/R	%
0–30	$210	84%		
31–60	40	16		
61–90	0	0	___	___
	$250	100%		

f. Construct the uncollected balances schedules for the end of March and the end of June. Use the format given below. Do these schedules properly measure customers' payment patterns?

Month	Sales	Contribution to A/R	A/R-to-Sales Ratio	Month	Sales	Contribution to A/R	A/R-to-Sales Ratio
Jan	$100	$ 0	0%	Apr			
Feb	200	40	20	May			
Mar	300	210	70	Jun			

g. Assume that it is now July of Year 1, and the brothers are developing pro forma financial statements for the following year. Further, assume that sales and collections in the first half-year matched the predicted levels. Using the Year 2 sales forecasts as shown next, what are next year's pro forma receivables levels for the end of March and for the end of June?

Month	Predicted Sales	Predicted A/R-to-Sales Ratio	Predicted Contribution to Receivables
Jan	$150	0%	$ 0
Feb	300	20	60
Mar	500	70	350
	Projected March 31 A/R balance =		$410
Apr	$400		
May	300		
Jun	200		
	Projected June 30 A/R balance =		___

h. Assume now that it is several years later. The brothers are concerned about the firm's current credit terms, which are now net 30, which means that contractors buying building products from the firm are not offered a discount, and they are supposed to pay the full amount in 30 days. Gross sales are now running $1,000,000 a year, and 80 percent (by dollar volume) of the firm's *paying* customers generally pay the full amount on Day 30, while the other 20 percent pay, on average, on Day 40. Two percent of the firm's gross sales end up as bad debt losses.

The brothers are now considering a change in the firm's credit policy. The change would entail (1) changing the credit terms to 2/10, net 20, (2) employing stricter credit standards before granting credit, and (3) enforcing collections with greater vigor than in the past. Thus, cash customers and those paying within 10 days would receive a 2 percent discount, but all others would have to pay the full amount after only 20 days. The brothers believe that the discount would both attract additional customers and encourage some existing customers to purchase more from the firm — after all, the discount amounts to a price reduction. Of course, these customers would take the discount and, hence, would pay in only 10 days. The net expected result is for sales to increase to $1,100,000; for 60 percent of the paying customers to take the discount and pay on the 10th day; for 30 percent to pay the full amount on Day 20; for 10 percent to pay late on Day 30; and for bad debt losses to fall from 2 percent to 1 percent of gross sales. The firm's operating cost ratio will remain unchanged at 75 percent, and its cost of carrying receivables will remain unchanged at 12 percent.

To begin the analysis, describe the four variables which make up a firm's credit policy, and explain how each of them affects sales and collections. Then use the information given in Part h to answer Parts i through n.

i. Under the current credit policy, what is the firm's days sales outstanding (DSO)? What would the expected DSO be if the credit policy change were made?

j. What is the dollar amount of the firm's current bad debt losses? What losses would be expected under the new policy?

k. What would be the firm's expected dollar cost of granting discounts under the new policy?

l. What is the firm's current dollar cost of carrying receivables? What would it be after the proposed change?

m. What is the incremental after-tax profit associated with the change in credit terms? Should the company make the change? (Assume a tax rate of 40 percent.)

	New	Old	Difference
Gross sales		$1,000,000	
Less discounts		0	
Net sales		$1,000,000	
Production costs		750,000	
Profit before credit costs and taxes		$ 250,000	
Credit-related costs:			
Carrying costs		8,000	
Bad debt losses		20,000	
Profit before taxes		$ 222,000	
Taxes (40%)		88,800	
Net income		$ 133,200	

n. Suppose the firm makes the change, but its competitors react by making similar changes to their own credit terms, with the net result being that gross sales remain at the current $1,000,000 level. What would the impact be on the firm's post-tax profitability?

(Part II: Inventory management) Andria Mullins, financial manager of Webster Electronics, has been asked by the firm's CEO, Fred Weygandt, to evaluate the company's inventory control techniques and to lead a discussion of the subject with the senior executives. Andria plans to use as an example one of Webster's "big ticket" items, a customized computer microchip which the firm uses in its laptop computer. Each chip costs Webster $200, and in addition it must pay its supplier a $1,000 setup fee on each order. Further, the minimum order size is 250 units; Webster's annual usage forecast is 5,000 units; and the annual carrying cost of this item is estimated to be 20 percent of the average inventory value.

Andria plans to begin her session with the senior executives by reviewing some basic inventory concepts, after which she will apply the EOQ model to Webster's microchip inventory. As her assistant, she has asked you to help her by answering the following questions:

a. Why is inventory management vital to the financial health of most firms?

b. What assumptions underlie the EOQ model?

c. Write out the formula for the total costs of carrying and ordering inventory, and then use the formula to derive the EOQ model.

d. What is the EOQ for custom microchips? What are total inventory costs if the EOQ is ordered?

e. What is Webster's added cost if it orders 400 units at a time rather than the EOQ quantity? What if it orders 600 per order?

f. Suppose it takes 2 weeks for Webster's supplier to set up production, make and test the chips, and deliver them to Webster's plant. Assuming certainty in delivery times and usage, at what inventory level should Webster reorder? (Assume a 52-week year, and assume that Webster orders the EOQ amount.)

g. Of course, there is uncertainty in Webster's usage rate as well as in delivery times, so the company must carry a safety stock to avoid running out of chips and having to halt production. If a 200-unit safety stock is carried, what effect would this have on total inventory costs? What is the new reorder point? What protection does the safety stock provide if usage increases, or if delivery is delayed?

h. Now suppose Webster's supplier offers a discount of 1 percent on orders of 1,000 or more. Should Webster take the discount? Why or why not?

i. For many firms, inventory usage is not uniform throughout the year, but, rather, follows some seasonal pattern. Can the EOQ model be used in this situation? If so, how?

j. How would these factors affect an EOQ analysis?

(1) The use of just-in-time procedures.

(2) The use of air freight for deliveries.

(3) The use of a computerized inventory control system, wherein as units were removed from stock, an electronic system automatically reduced the inventory account and, when the order point was hit, automatically sent an electronic message to the supplier placing an order. The electronic system ensures that inventory records are accurate, and that orders are placed promptly.

(4) The manufacturing plant is redesigned and automated. Computerized process equipment and state-of-the-art robotics are installed, making the plant highly flexible in the sense that the company can switch from the production of one item to

another at a minimum cost and quite quickly. This makes short production runs more feasible than under the old plant setup.

SELECTED ADDITIONAL REFERENCES AND CASES

Recent articles which address credit policy and receivables management include the following:

Atkins, Joseph C., and Yong H. Kim, "Comment and Correction: Opportunity Cost in the Evaluation of Investment in Accounts Receivable," *Financial Management,* Winter 1977, 71–74.

Ben-Horim, Moshe, and Haim Levy, "Management of Accounts Receivable under Inflation," *Financial Management,* Spring 1983, 42–48.

Dyl, Edward A., "Another Look at the Evaluation of Interest in Accounts Receivable," *Financial Management,* Winter 1977, 67–70.

Gallinger, George W., and A. James Ifflander, "Monitoring Accounts Receivable Using Variance Analysis," *Financial Management,* Winter 1986, 69–76.

Gentry, James A., and Jesus M. De La Garza, "A Generalized Model for Monitoring Accounts Receivable," *Financial Management,* Winter 1985, 28–38.

Hill, Ned C., and Kenneth D. Riener, "Determining the Cash Discount in the Firm's Credit Policy," *Financial Management,* Spring 1979, 68–73.

Kim, Yong H., and Joseph C. Atkins, "Evaluating Investments in Accounts Receivable: A Wealth Maximizing Framework," *Journal of Finance,* May 1978, 403–412.

Oh, John S., "Opportunity Cost in the Evaluation of Investment in Accounts Receivable," *Financial Management,* Summer 1976, 32–36.

Roberts, Gordon S., and Jeremy A. Viscione, "Captive Finance Subsidiaries: The Manager's View," *Financial Management,* Spring 1981, 36–42.

Sachdeva, Kanwal S., and Lawrence J. Gitman, "Accounts Receivable Decisions in a Capital Budgeting Framework," *Financial Management,* Winter 1981, 45–49.

Walia, Tinlochan S., "Explicit and Implicit Cost of Changes in the Level of Accounts Receivable and the Credit Policy Decision of the Firm," *Financial Management,* Winter 1977, 75–78.

Weston, J. Fred, and Pham D. Tuan, "Comment on Analysis of Credit Policy Changes," *Financial Management,* Winter 1980, 59–63.

The textbooks referenced in Chapter 16 include detailed discussions of inventory management.

The following articles and books provide additional insights into the problems of inventory management:

Arvan, L., and L. N. Moses, "Inventory Management and the Theory of the Firm," *American Economic Review,* March 1982, 186–193.

Bierman, H., Jr., C. P. Bonini, and W. H. Hausman, *Quantitative Analysis for Business Decisions* (Homewood, Ill.: Irwin, 1977).

Brooks, L. D., "Risk-Return Criteria and Optimal Inventory Stocks," *Engineering Economist,* Summer 1980, 275–299.

Followill, Richard A., Michael Schellenger, and Patrick H. Marchand, "Economic Order Quantities, Volume Discounts, and Wealth Maximization," *The Financial Review,* February 1990, 143–152.

Kallberg, Jarl G., and Kenneth L. Parkinson, *Current Asset Management: Cash, Credit, and Inventory* (New York: Wiley, 1984).

Magee, John F., "Guides to Inventory Policy, I," *Harvard Business Review,* January-February 1956, 49–60.

———, "Guides to Inventory Policy, II," *Harvard Business Review,* March-April 1956, 103–116.

———, "Guides to Inventory Policy, III," *Harvard Business Review,* May-June 1956, 57–70.

Mehta, Dileep R., *Working Capital Management* (Englewood Cliffs, N.J.: Prentice-Hall, 1974).

Shapiro, A., "Optimal Inventory and Credit Granting Strategies under Inflation and Devaluation," *Journal of Financial and Quantitative Analysis,* January 1973, 37–46.

Smith, Keith V., *Guide to Working Capital Management* (New York: McGraw-Hill, 1979).

The Brigham-Gapenski casebook has a useful case on inventory management:
Case 30, "Narragansett Yacht Corporation," which focuses on the EOQ model and safety stocks.

The following cases from the Brigham-Gapenski casebook focus on the credit policy decision:
Case 33, "Upscale Toddlers, Inc.," which deals with credit policy changes.
Case 34, "Texas Rose Company," which focuses on receivables management.

LONG-TERM FINANCING

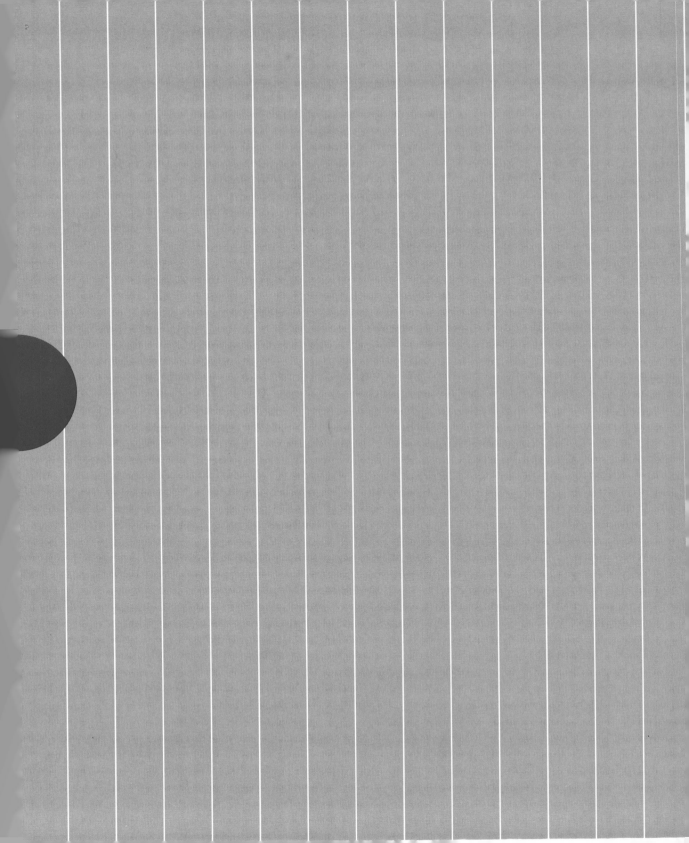

COMMON STOCK, PREFERRED STOCK, AND THE INVESTMENT BANKING PROCESS

I n early 1993 Chrysler announced plans to sell 40 million new shares of common stock, which would raise about $1.46 billion. With its shares selling at about $36, Chrysler's stock price had more than tripled from its 1992 low of $11.50. The major reason for the sale was to bolster the balance sheet, which had been weakened by low sales caused by the poor economy. Chrysler planned to use some of the funds to beef up its pension fund, which had about $4 billion in unfunded liabilities. In addition, some of the proceeds would be used to help fund the company's planned 1993–1997 $17.5 billion capital investment program and to pay down some of Chrysler's $3.8 billion debt.

The decision to issue new stock came at the crest of a wave of good news for Chrysler, which just two years before had been one of industrial America's walking wounded. Because of its ongoing cost-cutting efforts, Chrysler had lowered its breakeven point to about 1.7 million vehicles in 1992, down from 1.9 million in 1991. Also, initial sales of the company's trio of new LH sedans — the Chrysler Concorde, Dodge Intrepid, and Eagle Vision — had been so strong that Chrysler had announced that it would increase production.

"The best time to ask people for more money is when they like you," said analyst John Casesa of Wertheim Schroder & Co. "Right now the market feels that Chrysler can do no wrong." Apparently the rating agencies liked the announcement. Both Moody's and Standard & Poor's upgraded Chrysler's debt rating, and both firms cited the equity issue as well as Chrysler's line of profitable new products as keys to their decision. Despite the upgrades, Chrysler's debt is still rated below investment grade. However, in its upgrade statement, Standard

& Poor's stated that Chrysler plans to achieve investment-grade ratings by paying down its pension liability and accumulating a large cash position.

As you read this chapter, place yourself in the shoes of Chrysler's executives, and think about the pros and cons of its new equity issue. In particular, consider the impact of the stock issue on the firm's debt rating and the signals the issue announcement might be sending to the market. When you finish this chapter, you should have a better appreciation of the advantages and disadvantages of new equity sales, the various ways that firms can issue new equity, including preferred stock, and the investment banking process.

In Part III we examined the analysis financial managers employ when making decisions regarding the investment in long-term (or fixed) assets, and in Part IV we discussed capital structure and dividend decisions. Then in Part V we examined the planning and budgeting process, and in Part VI we discussed short-term management and financing. With this background, we now turn our attention to specific types of long-term capital. Any decision to acquire new assets necessitates the raising of new capital, and, generally, long-term assets are financed with long-term capital. In this chapter, we consider in some detail the decisions financial managers must make regarding stock financings. As a part of this analysis, we also examine in detail the procedures used to raise new long-term capital, or the investment banking process.

BALANCE SHEET ACCOUNTS AND DEFINITIONS

Legal and accounting terminology is vital to both investors and financial managers if they are to avoid misinterpretations and possibly costly mistakes. Therefore, we begin our analysis of common stock with a discussion of accounting and legal issues. Consider first Table 19-1, which shows the common equity section of American Chemical Company's balance sheet. American's owners, its stockholders, have authorized management to issue a total of 30 million shares, and management has thus far actually issued (or sold) 25 million shares. Each share has a *par value* of $1; this is the minimum amount for which new shares can be issued.[1]

---

[1]A stock's par value is an arbitrary figure that indicates the minimum amount of money stockholders have put up, or must put up, in the event of bankruptcy. Actually, the firm could legally sell new shares at below par, but any purchaser would be liable for the difference between the issue price and the par value in the event the company went bankrupt. Thus, if American sold an investor 10,000 shares at 40 cents per share, for $4,000, then the investor would have to put up an additional $6,000 if the company later went bankrupt. This contingent liability effectively precludes the sale of new common stock at prices below par.

Also, we should point out that firms are not required to establish a par value for their stock. Thus, American could have elected to use "no par" stock, in which case the common stock and additional paid-in capital accounts could have been consolidated under one account called *common stock,* which would show a 1993 balance of $75 million.

TABLE 19-1	Common stock (30 million shares authorized,
AMERICAN CHEMICAL	25 million shares outstanding, $1 par) $ 25,000,000
COMPANY:	Additional paid-in capital 50,000,000
STOCKHOLDERS'	Retained earnings 375,000,000
EQUITY ACCOUNTS AS	Total common stockholders' equity (or common net worth) $450,000,000
OF DECEMBER 31,	
1993	Book value per share $= \dfrac{\text{Total common stockholders' equity}}{\text{Shares outstanding}} = \dfrac{\$450,000,000}{25,000,000} = \$18.$

American Chemical is an old company—it was established back in 1920. Its initial equity capital consisted of 3,000 shares sold at the $1 par value, so on its first balance sheet the total stockholders' equity was $3,000. The initial paid-in capital and retained earnings accounts showed zero balances. Over the years American has retained some of its earnings, and the firm has issued new stock to raise capital from time to time. During 1993, American earned $60 million, paid $50 million in dividends, and retained $10 million. The $10 million was added to the $365 million accumulated *retained earnings,* shown on the year-end 1992 balance sheet, to produce the $375 million retained earnings at year-end 1993. Thus, since its inception in 1920, American has retained, or plowed back, a total of $375 million. This is money that belongs to the stockholders and that they could have received in the form of dividends. Instead, the stockholders chose to let management reinvest the $375 million in the business.

Now consider the $50 million *additional paid-in capital.* This account shows the difference between the stock's par value and what new stockholders paid when they bought newly issued shares. As we noted, American was formed in 1920 with 3,000 shares issued at the $1 par value; thus, the first balance sheet showed a zero balance for additional paid-in capital. By 1925, the company had demonstrated its profitability and was earning 50 cents per share. Further, it had built up the retained earnings account to a total of $6,000, so the total stockholders' equity was $3,000 of par value plus $6,000 of retained earnings = $9,000, and the *book value per share* was $9,000/3,000 shares = $3. American had also borrowed heavily, and, even though it had retained most of its earnings, the company's debt ratio had risen to an unacceptable level, precluding further use of debt without an infusion of equity.

The company had profitable investment opportunities, so in order to take advantage of them, management decided to issue another 2,000 shares of stock. The market price at the time was $4 per share, which was eight times the 50 cents earnings per share (the price/earnings ratio was 8×). This $4 market value per share was well in excess of the $1 par value and also higher than the $3 book value per share, demonstrating that par value, book value, and market value are not necessarily equal. Had the company lost money since its inception, it would have had negative retained earnings, the book value would have been below par, and the market price might well have been below book.

Table 19-2 shows how the 1925 stock sale affected American's common equity accounts. A total of 2,000 new shares were sold to investors at the market price

TABLE 19-2		
EFFECTS OF 1925	**Before Sale of Stock**	
STOCK SALE ON	Common stock (3,000 shares outstanding, $1 par)	$ 3,000
AMERICAN	Additional paid-in capital	0
CHEMICAL'S EQUITY	Retained earnings	6,000
ACCOUNTS	Total stockholders' equity	$ 9,000
	Book value per share = $9,000/3,000 =	$ 3.00
	After Sale of Stock	
	Common stock (5,000 shares outstanding, $1 par)	$ 5,000
	Additional paid-in capital ($4 − $1) × 2,000 shares	6,000
	Retained earnings	6,000
	Total stockholders' equity	$17,000
	Book value per share = $17,000/5,000 =	$ 3.40

of $4 per share. Each share brought in $4, of which $1 represented the par value, and $3 represented the excess of the sale price above par. Since 2,000 shares were involved, a total of $2,000 was added to common stock, and $6,000 was entered in additional paid-in capital. Notice also that book value per share rose from $3 to $3.40; whenever stock is sold at a price above book, the book value increases, and vice versa if stock is sold below book.[2] Similar transactions have taken place down through the years to produce the current situation, as shown earlier in Table 19-1.[3]

SELF-TEST QUESTIONS

Explain how the balance sheet is affected when a company issues new common stock.

Does it really matter if new common stock is sold for more or less than its par value? Than its book value?

---

[2]The effects of stock sales on book value are not important for industrial firms, but they are *very* important for utility companies, whose allowable earnings per share are in effect determined by regulators as a percentage of book value. Thus, if a utility's stock is selling below book and the company sells stock to raise new equity, this will dilute the book value per share of its existing stockholders and drive down their allowable earnings per share, which in turn will drive down the market price. Most U.S. electric utilities' stocks sold below book value during the late 1970s and early 1980s. The firms needed to raise large amounts of capital, including equity, since they had to keep their capital structures in balance. This meant selling stock at prices below book, which tended to depress the market value of the stock still further.

[3]Stock dividends, stock splits, and stock repurchases (the reverse of stock issues) also affect the capital accounts. These topics were discussed in Chapter 14.

LEGAL RIGHTS AND PRIVILEGES OF COMMON STOCKHOLDERS

The common stockholders are the owners of a corporation, and as such they have certain rights and privileges. The most important of these rights are discussed in this section.

CONTROL OF THE FIRM

The stockholders have the right to elect the firm's directors, who in turn elect the officers who will manage the business. In a small firm, the major stockholder typically assumes the positions of president and chairman of the board of directors. In a large, publicly owned firm, the managers typically have some stock, but their personal holdings are insufficient to allow them to exercise voting control. Thus, the managements of most publicly owned firms can be removed by the stockholders if they decide a management team is not effective.

Various state and federal laws stipulate how stockholder control is to be exercised. First, corporations must periodically hold an election of directors, usually once a year, with the vote taken at the annual meeting. Frequently, one-third of the directors are elected each year for a three-year term. Each share of stock has one vote; thus, the owner of 1,000 shares has 1,000 votes. Stockholders can appear at the annual meeting and vote in person, but typically they transfer their right to vote to a second party by means of a *proxy.* Management always solicits stockholders' proxies and usually gets them. However, if earnings are poor and stockholders are dissatisfied, an outside group may solicit the proxies in an effort to overthrow management and take control of the business. This is known as a *proxy fight.*

The question of control has become a central issue in finance in recent years. The frequency of proxy fights has increased, as have attempts by one corporation to take over another by purchasing a majority of the outstanding stock. This latter action, which is called a *takeover,* is discussed in detail in Chapter 24. Managers who do not have majority control (over 50 percent) of their firms' stocks are very concerned about proxy fights and takeovers, and many of them are attempting to get stockholder approval for changes in their corporate charters that would make takeovers more difficult. Managements seeking such changes generally cite a fear that the firm will be picked up at a bargain price, but it often appears that managers' concern over their own positions is an even more important consideration.

THE PREEMPTIVE RIGHT

Common stockholders often have the right, called the *preemptive right,* to purchase any new shares sold by the firm. In some states the preemptive right is mandatory; in others it is necessary to specifically insert it into the charter.

The purpose of the preemptive right is twofold. First, it protects the present stockholders' power of control. If it were not for this safeguard, the management of a corporation under criticism from stockholders could secure its position by issuing a large number of additional shares and purchasing these shares itself or

getting a group of "friendly" investors to purchase the new shares. Management would thereby gain effective control of the corporation and frustrate the current stockholders.

The second, and by far the more important, reason for the preemptive right is that it protects stockholders against a dilution of value. For example, suppose 1,000 shares of common stock, each with a price of $100, were outstanding, making the total market value of the firm $100,000. If an additional 1,000 shares were sold at $50 a share, or for $50,000, this would raise the total market value of the firm to $150,000. When the total market value is divided by the new total shares outstanding, a value of $75 a share is obtained. The old stockholders thus lose $25 per share, and the new stockholders have an instant profit of $25 per share. Thus, selling common stock at a price below the market value would dilute its price and would transfer wealth from the present stockholders to those who purchase the new shares. The preemptive right prevents such wealth transfers.

SELF-TEST QUESTIONS

How do shareholders exercise their right of control?

What is the preemptive right, and what is its purpose?

TYPES OF COMMON STOCK

Although most firms have only one type of common stock, in some instances *classified stock* is used to meet the special needs of the company. Generally, when special classifications of stock are used, one type is designated *Class A,* another *Class B,* and so on. Small, new companies seeking to obtain funds from outside sources frequently use different types of common stock. For example, when Genetic Research went public in 1993, its Class A stock was sold to the public and paid a dividend, but carried no voting rights for five years. Its Class B stock was retained by the organizers of the company and carried full voting rights for five years, but dividends could not be paid on the Class B stock until the company had established its earning power by building up retained earnings to a designated level. Because of the use of classified stock, the public was able to take a position in a conservatively financed growth company without sacrificing income, while the founders retained absolute control during the crucial early stages of the firm's development. At the same time, outside investors were protected against excessive withdrawals of funds by the original owners. As is often the case in such situations, the Class B stock was also called *founders' shares.*

Note that "Class A," "Class B," and so on, have no standard meanings. Most firms have no classified shares, but a firm that does could designate its Class B shares as founders' shares and its Class A shares as those sold to the public, while another could reverse these designations. Other firms could use the A and B designations for entirely different purposes.

General Motors recently introduced yet another type of common stock. When GM acquired Hughes Aircraft for $5 billion, it paid in part with a new Class H common, GMH, which had limited voting rights and whose dividends were tied to Hughes's performance as a GM subsidiary. The reasons for the new stock were reported to be that: (1) GM wanted to limit voting privileges on the new classified stock because of management's concern about a possible takeover, and (2) Hughes employees wanted to participate more directly in Hughes's own performance than would have been possible through regular GM stock.

GM's deal posed a problem for the NYSE, which had a rule against listing any company's common stock if the company had any nonvoting common stock outstanding. GM made it clear that it was willing to delist if the NYSE did not change its rules. The NYSE concluded that such arrangements as GM had made were logical and were likely to be made by other companies in the future, so it changed its rules to accommodate GM. In reality, the NYSE had little choice. In recent years the over-the-counter (OTC) market has proven that it could provide a deep, liquid market for common stocks, and the defection of GM would have severely crippled the NYSE's reputation.

SELF-TEST QUESTION

Name several types of common stock, and explain their uses.

THE MARKET FOR COMMON STOCK

Some companies are so small that their common stock is not actively traded — it is owned by only a few people, usually the companies' managers. Such companies are said to be *privately held,* or *closely held,* and the stock is said to be *closely held stock.* On the other hand, the stocks of most larger companies are owned by many investors, most of whom are not active in management. Such companies are said to be *publicly owned,* and their stock is said to be *publicly held stock.*

The stocks of smaller, publicly owned firms are not listed on an exchange; they trade in the *over-the-counter (OTC)* market. The companies and their stocks are said to be *unlisted.* However, most larger, publicly owned companies apply for listing on an exchange. These companies and their stocks are said to be *listed.* As a general rule, companies are first listed on a regional exchange, such as the Pacific Coast or Midwest, then they move up to the American (AMEX), and finally, if they grow large enough, to the "Big Board," the New York Stock Exchange (NYSE). Thousands of stocks are traded in the OTC market, but in terms of market value of both outstanding and daily transactions, the NYSE dominates, with about 60 percent of the business. However, as we discuss next, electronic communication links between OTC market participants are giving them many of the advantages formerly enjoyed solely by the organized exchanges, so the OTC market has been growing more rapidly than the exchanges in recent years.

Institutional investors such as pension trusts, insurance companies, and mutual funds own about 55 percent of all common stocks. However, the institutions buy and sell relatively actively, so they account for more than 80 percent of all transactions. Thus, the institutions have a heavy influence on the prices of individual stocks — in a real sense, institutional investors determine the price levels of individual stocks.

We can classify stock market transactions into three distinct categories:

1.   Initial public offerings by privately held firms: the new issue market. In 1992, Hat Brands Inc., the largest hat maker in the United States (Stetson is one of its brand names), sold 2.2 million shares to the general public. At the time, the company was owned by its management and a small group of corporate investors. Of the 2.2 million shares sold, 1.8 million were newly issued by the company, while the remaining 400,000 were sold by existing shareholders. Hat Brands's action is defined as *going public*—whenever stock in a closely held corporation is offered to the public, the company is said to be going public. The market for stock that is in the process of going public is often called the *new issue market,* and the issue is called an *initial public offering (IPO).* After going public, Hat Brands's shares were traded on the over-the-counter market. Note that Hat Brands's IPO served two functions: (1) It raised new capital for the company, and (2) it put cash into the hands of the private owners.

The market for IPOs varies widely from year to year. For example, new public issues totaled 550 in 1987 but fell to under 300 in 1988 and 1989. The large decline in the number of new issues was attributed to the stock market crash of October 1987, which led to lower equity prices, fear of further losses, and a reduced investor demand for stocks. Companies that had planned to go public were turned off by the depressed valuations and sluggish market conditions. For example, ComputerLand Corporation, one of the leading computer retailers, cancelled its planned 1988 initial public offering because of poor market conditions. Said a company spokesman, "We realized the stock wasn't going to command the price we thought it deserved." A surging stock market and strong demand for IPOs pushed the number of IPOs up to 595 in 1992.

Firms can go public without raising any additional capital. For example, in its early days the Ford Motor Company was owned exclusively by the Ford family. When Henry Ford died, he left a substantial part of his stock to the Ford Foundation. When the Foundation later sold some of this stock to the general public, the Ford Motor Company went public, even though the company raised no capital in the transaction.

2.   Additional shares sold by established, publicly owned companies: the primary market.   In 1992, General Motors raised $2.1 billion by issuing new common stock. Since the shares sold were newly created, GM's issue was defined as a *primary market* offering, but since the firm was already publicly held, the offering was not an IPO. As we discussed in Chapters 13 and 14, firms prefer to obtain equity by retaining earnings because of the flotation costs and market pressure associated with the sale of new common stock. Thus, only 9 percent of the new securities issued in 1992 were common stock. Still, if a company requires

more equity funds than can be generated from retained earnings, a stock sale may be required.

3.   Outstanding shares of established, publicly owned companies: the secondary market.   If the owner of 100 shares of GM sells his or her stock, the trade is said to have occurred in the *secondary market.* Thus, the market for outstanding shares, or *used shares,* is defined as the secondary market. Over 153 million shares of GM were bought and sold on the NYSE in 1992, and GM did not receive a dime from these transactions.

SELF-TEST QUESTIONS

What is an initial public offering (IPO)?

What are some differences in the situation when GM sells shares in the primary market and when its shares are sold in the secondary market?

THE DECISION TO GO PUBLIC

Most businesses begin life as proprietorships or partnerships, and then, as the more successful ones grow, at some point they find it desirable to convert into corporations. Initially, these new corporations' stocks are generally owned by the firm's officers, key employees, and/or a very few investors who are not actively involved in management. However, if growth continues, at some point the company may decide to go public. As described earlier, Hat Brands decided to take this step in 1992. The advantages and disadvantages of public ownership are discussed next.

ADVANTAGES OF GOING PUBLIC

1.   Permits founder diversification.   As a company grows and becomes more valuable, its founders often have most of their wealth tied up in the company. By selling some of their stock in a public offering, they can diversify their holdings, thereby reducing somewhat the riskiness of their personal portfolios.

2.   Increases liquidity.   The stock of a closely held firm is illiquid: it has no ready market. If one of the owners wants to sell some shares to raise cash, it is hard to find a ready buyer, and even if a buyer is located, there is no established price on which to base the transaction. These problems do not exist with publicly owned firms.

3.   Facilitates raising new corporate cash.   If a privately held company wants to raise cash by a sale of new stock, it must either go to its existing owners, who may not have any money or not want to put any more eggs in this particular basket, or else shop around for wealthy investors. However, it is usually quite difficult to get outsiders to put money into a closely held company, because if the outsiders do not have voting control (over 50 percent of the stock), the inside

stockholders/managers can run roughshod over them. The insiders can pay or not pay dividends, pay themselves exorbitant salaries, have private deals with the company, and so on. For example, the president might buy a warehouse and lease it to the company at a high rental, get the use of a Rolls Royce, and enjoy frequent "all-the-frills" travel to conventions. The insiders can even keep the outsiders from knowing the company's actual earnings, or its real worth. There are not many positions more vulnerable than that of an outside stockholder in a closely held company, and for this reason, it is hard for closely held companies to raise new equity capital. Going public, which brings with it both public disclosure of information and regulation by the Securities and Exchange Commission (SEC), greatly reduces these problems, making people more willing to invest in the company, and thus making it easier for the firm to raise capital.

4. Establishes a value for the firm.   For a number of reasons, it is often useful to establish a firm's value in the marketplace. For one thing, when the owner of a privately owned business dies, state and federal tax appraisers must set a value on the company for estate tax purposes. Often, these appraisers set too high a value, which creates an obvious problem. However, a company that is publicly owned has its value established with little room for argument. Similarly, if a company wants to give incentive stock options to key employees, it is useful to know the exact value of those options. Finally, for a number of reasons, employees much prefer to own stock, or options on stock, that is publicly traded.

DISADVANTAGES OF GOING PUBLIC

1. Cost of reporting.   A publicly owned company must file quarterly and annual reports with the SEC and/or with various state agencies. These reports can be costly, especially for small firms.

2. Disclosure.   Management may not like the idea of reporting operating data, because such data will then be available to competitors. Similarly, the owners of the company may not want people to know their net worth, and since a publicly owned company must disclose the number of shares owned by its officers, directors, and major stockholders, it is easy enough for anyone to multiply shares held by price per share to estimate the net worth of the insiders.

3. Self-dealings.   The owners/managers of closely held companies have many opportunities for various types of questionable but legal self-dealings, including the payment of high salaries, nepotism, personal transactions with the business (such as a leasing arrangement), and not-truly-necessary fringe benefits. Such self-dealings, which are often designed to minimize taxes, are much harder to arrange if a company is publicly owned.

4. Inactive market/low price.   If the firm is very small, and if its shares are not traded with much frequency, its stock will not really be liquid, and the market price may not be representative of the stock's true value. Security analysts and stockbrokers simply will not follow the stock, because there will just not be sufficient trading activity to generate sufficient sales commissions to cover the costs of following the stock.

5. Control. Because of the recent dramatic increase in tender offers and proxy fights, the managers of publicly owned firms who do not have voting control must be concerned about maintaining control. Further, there is pressure on such managers to produce annual earnings gains, even when it might be in the shareholders' best long-term interests to adopt a strategy that might penalize short-term earnings but benefit earnings in future years. These factors have led a number of public companies to "go private" in "leveraged buyout" deals where the managers borrow the money to buy out the nonmanagement stockholders. We discuss the decision to go private in a later section.

CONCLUSIONS ON GOING PUBLIC

It should be obvious from this discussion that there are no hard-and-fast rules regarding if or when a company should go public. This is an individual decision that should be made on the basis of the company's and stockholders' own unique circumstances.

If a company does decide to go public, either by selling newly issued stock to raise new capital or by the sale of stock by the current owners, the key issue is setting the price at which shares will be offered to the public. The company and its current owners want to set the price as high as possible—the higher the offering price, the smaller the fraction of the company the current owners will have to give up to obtain any specified amount of money. On the other hand, potential buyers will want the price set as low as possible. We will return to the establishment of the offering price later in the chapter, after we have described some other aspects of common stock financing.

SELF-TEST QUESTIONS

What are the major advantages of going public?

What are the major disadvantages?

THE DECISION TO LIST

The decision to go public is truly a milestone in a company's life—it marks a major transition in the relationship between the firm and its owners. The decision to *list* the stock and have it trade on an exchange rather than in the over-the-counter market, on the other hand, is not a major event. The company will have to file a few new reports with an exchange and to abide by the rules of the exchange; stockholders will generally purchase or sell shares through a stockbroker who acts as an *agent* rather than a *dealer;* and the stock's price will be quoted in the newspaper under a stock exchange rather than in the over-the-counter section. These are not very significant differences.

In order to have its stock listed, a company must apply to an exchange, pay a relatively small fee, and meet the exchange's minimum requirements. These requirements relate to the size of the company's net income as well as to the number of shares outstanding and in the hands of outsiders (as opposed to the number held by insiders, who generally do not trade their stock very actively). Also, the company must agree to disclose certain information to the exchange; this information is designed to help the exchange track trading patterns and thus to try to ensure that no one is attempting to manipulate the price of the stock.[4] The size qualifications increase as one moves from the regional exchanges to the AMEX and on to the NYSE.

Assuming a company qualifies, many people believe that listing is beneficial both to it and to its stockholders. Listed companies receive a certain amount of free advertising and publicity, and their status as a listed company may enhance their prestige and reputation. This may have a beneficial effect on the sales of the firm's products. Investors respond favorably to increased information, increased liquidity, and confidence that the quoted price is not being manipulated. By providing investors with these benefits in the form of listing their companies' stocks, financial managers may be able to lower their firms' cost of equity and increase the value of their stock. However, due to improvements in telecommunications and computer technologies, the differences between the OTC and the exchanges have become less distinct. As a result, some very large companies such as MCI and Apple, which almost certainly would have been listed on the NYSE in earlier days, have elected to remain in the OTC market.

Self-Test Question

What are the major advantages and disadvantages to a company listing its stock on an exchange?

Procedures for Selling New Common Stock

If stock is to be sold to raise new capital, the new shares may be sold in one of five ways: (1) on a pro rata basis to existing stockholders through a rights offering, (2) through investment bankers to the general public in a public offering, (3) to a single buyer (or a very small number of buyers) in a private placement, (4) to employees through employee stock purchase plans, or (5) through a dividend reinvestment plan. We discussed dividend reinvestment plans in Chapter 14; the other methods of selling stock are considered in the following sections.

---

[4]It is illegal for anyone to attempt to manipulate the price of a stock. During the 1920s, and earlier, syndicates would buy and sell stocks back and forth at rigged prices so the public would believe that a particular stock was worth more or less than its true value. The exchanges, with the encouragement and support of the SEC, utilize sophisticated computer programs to help spot any irregularities that suggest manipulation, and they require disclosures to help identify manipulators. This same system helps to identify illegal insider trading.

RIGHTS OFFERINGS

As discussed earlier, common stockholders often have the *preemptive right* to purchase any additional shares sold by the firm. If the preemptive right is contained in a particular firm's charter, the company must offer any newly issued common stock to existing stockholders. If the charter does not prescribe a preemptive right, the firm can choose to sell to its existing stockholders or to the public at large. If it sells to the existing stockholders, the stock flotation is called a *rights offering*. Each stockholder is issued an option to buy a certain number of new shares, and the terms of the option are listed on a certificate called a *stock purchase right*, or simply a *right*. If a stockholder does not wish to purchase any additional shares in the company, then he or she can sell the rights to some other person who does want to buy the stock.[5]

PUBLIC OFFERINGS

If the preemptive right exists in a company's charter, it must sell new stock through a rights offering. If the preemptive right does not exist, the company can choose between a rights offering and a *public offering*. We discuss procedures for public offerings later in the chapter.

PRIVATE PLACEMENTS

In a *private placement,* securities are sold to one or a few investors, generally institutional investors. Private placements are most common with bonds, but they also occur with stocks. The primary advantages of private placements are (1) lower flotation costs and (2) greater speed, since the shares do not have to go through the SEC registration process.

The most common type of private placement occurs when a company places securities directly with a financial institution, usually an insurance company. In fact, Prudential has begun sending salespeople to call on businesses — not to sell them policies, but to sell them on borrowing privately from Prudential. To illustrate a private placement, AT&T recently sold 6.3 million shares of common stock worth about $650 million directly to Capital Group, Inc., a Los Angeles institutional investor that manages both mutual and pension funds. The transaction was a blow to three Wall Street firms, Morgan Stanley, Dillon Reed, and Goldman Sachs, which had planned to sell the stock in a conventional public offering. AT&T treasurer Lawrence Prendergast said selling the stock in a private placement would save about 2.5 percent, or $16.3 million, in underwriting expenses.

One particular type of private stock placement that is occurring with increasing frequency is the situation in which a large company makes an equity investment in a smaller supplier. For example, IBM invested close to $500 million in

---

[5]For more details on the mechanics of a rights offering, see Eugene F. Brigham and Louis C. Gapenski, *Intermediate Financial Management,* 4th Ed. (Forth Worth, Tex.: Dryden Press, 1993), Chapter 14.

Rolm, a telecommunications equipment manufacturer, and a similar amount in Intel, a semiconductor manufacturer. In both instances, (1) the companies needed capital for expansion, (2) IBM was engaged in joint development ventures with the companies, and thus wanted them to be financially strong, and (3) the companies had strong, independent managements, who would probably have resisted an attempt by IBM to take full control. So, IBM (1) bought stock that gave it an ownership in the 15 to 25 percent range, (2) agreed to limit its ownership to no more than 30 percent, and (3) simultaneously executed operating contracts for joint ventures with Rolm and Intel. Similar arrangements are quite common, and some of them go back many years. For example, Sears, Roebuck has for many years supplied equity capital to some of its major suppliers, including Johnson Controls, which furnishes Sears with "Die-Hard" batteries, and with DeSoto Chemical, which supplies most of the paints that Sears sells.

The primary disadvantage of a private placement is that the securities generally will not have gone through the SEC registration process, so they cannot be sold except to another large, "sophisticated" purchaser in the event the original buyer wants to sell them. However, the SEC has recently ruled that any institution with a portfolio of $100 million or more can buy and sell private placement securities. Since there are many institutions with assets that exceed this limit, private placements are expected to boom in the 1990s. Today, private placements constitute almost 40 percent of all nonbank debt financing.

EMPLOYEE PURCHASE PLANS AND ESOPs

Many companies have plans that allow employees to purchase stock on favorable terms. First, under executive incentive stock option plans, key managers are given options to purchase stock. These managers generally have a direct, material influence on the company's fortunes, so if they perform well, the stock will go up, and the options will become valuable. Second, there are plans for lower-level employees. For example, IBM permits employees who are not participants in its stock option plan to allocate up to 10 percent of their salaries to its stock purchase plan, and the funds are then used to buy newly issued shares at 85 percent of the market value on the purchase date. Often, the company's contribution (in IBM's case, the 15 percent discount) is not vested in an employee until five years after the purchase date. This type of plan is designed both to improve employee performance and to reduce turnover.

A third type of plan is related to the second one, but here the stock bought for employees is purchased out of a share of the company's profits. Congress has sought to encourage such plans through tax policy—under an *Employee Stock Ownership Plan (ESOP),* companies can claim a tax credit equal to a percentage of wages, provided that the funds are used to buy newly issued stock for the benefit of employees. The amount of the credit varies from year to year, depending on the whims of Congress: currently it is ½ of 1 percent of total wages.

ESOPs have been hailed by some as a miracle tonic that will invigorate a tiring manufacturing economy, but critics claim that ESOPs represent a desperate move by managers who would rather give the company to employees than succumb to

raiders. Others call ESOPs tax dodges, some call them socialistic, and some call them "people's capitalism." All parties can muster some evidence to support their claims, but the ESOP trend is still too new for anyone to be sure who is right.

In a typical ESOP start-up, a company borrows money to buy its own stock, either from treasury stock or on the open market, and places the stock in the hands of the ESOP trustee, who then allocates the stock ownership to the firm's employees on the basis of relative salaries. Then, after the ESOP is initially funded, stock contributions are made out of annual earnings. Often, ESOPs are set up to supplement or to replace entirely the employees' retirement programs. ESOPs often have one thing in common with leveraged buyouts (LBOs)—more debt and hence higher financial leverage. However, the similarity ends there. While an LBO usually makes owners out of a small group of managers, an ESOP makes an owner out of practically everyone on the payroll.

The advantages of ESOPs are as follows:

1. **Tax breaks.** Companies get a triple tax deduction on ESOPs—they can deduct (1) the interest on the debt used to buy the stock for the ESOP, (2) some of the principal payments on the ESOP-funding debt, and (3) the dividends they pay on the ESOP-held shares.

2. **Anti-takeover defense.** The more of a company's stock the ESOP holds, the better equipped a company is to fend off a raider, because the ESOP's trustee is presumably inclined to support current management over a raider who may fire many of the current employees.

3. **Pension cost control.** When a company uses an ESOP to reduce or even replace its conventional pension plan, it can save heavily. Some companies drop their retirement medical benefits, telling employees that they can dip into their ESOP accounts to buy medical coverage.

4. **Productivity enhancement.** Once the employees are owners as well as workers, they are presumably motivated to become more productive and concerned about product quality. However, studies have shown that ESOPs help little toward increased productivity unless executives are willing to give workers a strong and genuine role in running the company.

Although their advantages are very real, ESOPs do have some potential disadvantages:

1. **Balance of power.** ESOPs transform workers into a large bloc of shareholders with intimate knowledge about the company. If a firm's managers alienate the employee-owners, workers could vote their shares in favor of a raider.

2. **Legal considerations.** The Labor Department and the courts are on the lookout for ESOP abuses. If they perceive an ESOP to be a hastily constructed takeover defense, designed primarily to protect current management, they could reject the ESOP plan. Also, ESOP laws could be changed by Congress at any time to make them less favorable to the firm.

3. **Retiree benefits.** The more that retirees' benefits are tied to an ESOP, the more dependent retirees become on the price of the company's stock. That leaves retirees vulnerable to the whims of Wall Street as well as to management mistakes.

Although employee purchase plans are designed more to provide incentives to help improve employee performance than to raise capital, the fact is that these plans can produce a surprisingly large amount of new equity. Note, though, that companies may choose to repurchase shares for its ESOP on the open market rather than issue new shares. The decision to use newly issued shares or repurchased shares depends upon the company's need for funds in a given year. Still, employee purchase plans provide the potential for raising equity regardless of whether they are actually used for this purpose each and every year.

SELF-TEST QUESTIONS

What is a rights offering?

What is a private placement? What are its primary advantages over a public offering?

Briefly describe employee purchase plans.

What is an Employee Stock Ownership Plan (ESOP)? What are its major advantages and disadvantages?

ADVANTAGES AND DISADVANTAGES OF COMMON STOCK FINANCING

In this section we briefly discuss the advantages and disadvantages of common stock financing.

ADVANTAGES OF COMMON STOCK FINANCING

1. Common stock does not entail fixed charges. If the company generates the earnings, it can pay common stock dividends. This is very much in contrast to interest on debt, which must be paid regardless of the level of earnings.

2. Common stock carries no fixed maturity date — it is permanent capital which does not have to be "paid back."

3. Since common stock provides a cushion against losses to the firm's creditors, its use helps bond ratings and lowers the cost of debt.

4. Common stock can, at times, be sold more easily than debt. It appeals to certain investor groups because (1) it typically carries a higher expected return than does preferred stock or debt, (2) it provides investors with a better hedge against inflation than does preferred stock or bonds, and (3) returns from capital gains on common stock are not taxed until the gains are realized.

DISADVANTAGES OF COMMON STOCK FINANCING

1. The sale of common stock normally extends voting rights, or even control, to the additional stock owners who are brought into the company. For this reason, additional equity financing is often avoided by small firms, whose owner-managers

may be unwilling to share control of their companies with outsiders. Note, though, that firms can use special classes of common stock that do not carry voting rights.

2. The use of debt enables the firm to acquire funds at a fixed cost, whereas the use of common stock means that more stockholders will share in the firm's future profits.

3. The costs of underwriting and distributing common stock are usually higher than the costs of underwriting and distributing preferred stock or debt.

4. As we discussed in Chapters 13 and 14, the sale of new common stock may be perceived by investors as a negative signal, hence may cause the stock price to fall.

SELF-TEST QUESTIONS

What are the advantages of common stock financing?

What are some disadvantages of common stock financing?

THE DECISION TO GO PRIVATE

In a *going private* transaction, the entire equity of a publicly held firm is purchased by a small group of investors which usually includes the firm's current senior management.[6] In some of these transactions, the current management group acquires all of the equity of the new company. In others, current management participates in the ownership with a small group of outside investors who typically place directors on the now private firm's board and arrange for the financing needed to purchase the publicly held stock. Such deals almost always involve substantial borrowing, often up to 90 percent, and thus are commonly known as *leveraged buyouts (LBOs)* or *leveraged managerial buyouts (MBOs)*.

Regardless of the structure of the deal, going private initially affects the right-hand side of the balance sheet, the liabilities and capital, and not the assets—going private simply rearranges the ownership structure. Thus, going private involves no obvious operating economies, yet the new owners are generally willing to pay a large premium over the stock's current price in order to take the firm private. For example, the managers of Hospital Corporation of America (HCA) recently paid $51 a share to outside (public) shareholders although the stock was only selling for about $31 before the LBO offer was made. It is hard to believe that the managers of a company, who have the best information about the firm's potential profitability, would knowingly pay too much for the firm. Thus, HCA's management must have regarded the firm as being grossly undervalued or else thought that it could significantly boost the firm's value under private ownership. This suggests

---

[6]See Harry DeAngelo, Linda DeAngelo, and Edward M. Rice, "Going Private: The Effects of a Change in Corporate Ownership," *Midland Corporate Finance Journal,* Summer 1984, 35–43, for a more complete discussion of going private. The discussion in this section draws heavily from their work.

that going private can sufficiently increase the value of some firms to enrich both managers and public stockholders. The primary advantages to going private are (1) administrative cost savings, (2) increased managerial incentives, (3) increased managerial flexibility, (4) increased shareholder participation, and (5) increased use of financial leverage, which of course reduces taxes. We will discuss each of these advantages in more detail in the following paragraphs.

1. **Administrative cost savings.** Because going private takes the stock of a firm out of public hands, it saves on costs associated with securities registration, annual reports, SEC and exchange reporting, responding to stockholder inquiries, and so on. More important, the top management of private firms are free from meetings with security analysts, government bodies, and other outside parties. Byron C. Radaker, CEO of Congoleum Corporation, a company that went private in the early 1980s, estimated the cost savings to his company from going private at between $6 million and $8 million per year.

2. **Increased managerial incentives.** An even larger potential gain comes from the improvement in the incentives for high-level managerial performance. Their increased ownership means that the firm's managers will benefit more directly from their own efforts, hence managerial efficiency tends to increase after going private. If the firm is highly successful, its managers can easily see their personal net worth increase 10 or 20 fold, while if the firm fails, its managers will end up with nothing. Further, a highly leveraged position will tend to drive the firm toward the extremes—large losses or large profits. The managers of companies that have gone through an LBO tell us that heavy interest payments, combined with a knowledge that success will bring large wealth, do a lot to improve both decisions and effort levels.

3. **Increased managerial flexibility.** Another source of value stems from the increased flexibility available to managers of private firms. These managers do not have to worry about what a drop in next quarter's earnings will do to the firm's stock price, hence they can focus on long-term, strategic actions that ultimately will have the greatest positive impact on the firm's value. Managerial flexibility concerning asset sales is also greater in a private firm, since such sales do not have to be justified to a large number of shareholders with potentially diverse interests.

4. **Increased shareholder participation.** Going private typically results in replacing a dispersed, largely passive group of public shareholders with a small group of new investors who play a much more active role in managing the firm. These new equity investors take a substantial position in the private firm, hence have a greater motivation to monitor management and to provide incentives to management than do the typical stockholders of a public corporation. Further, the new nonmanagement equity investors, such as KKR, are typically represented on the board, and they bring both sophisticated financial expertise and hard-nosed attitudes to the new firm. These outsiders don't have old buddies running money-losing operations, so they are more willing to force major operating changes than is an entrenched management. For example, within a few weeks after KKR won the battle for RJR Nabisco, the much touted but unprofitable Premier "smokeless" cigarette project was abandoned.

5. Increased financial leverage. Going private usually entails a drastic increase in the firm's use of debt financing, which has two effects. First, the firm's taxes are reduced because interest payments are tax deductible, so more of the operating income flows through to investors. Second, the increased debt servicing requirements force managers to increase revenues and/or reduce costs to insure that the firm has sufficient cash flow to meet its obligations—a highly leveraged firm simply cannot afford any fat.

One might ask why all firms are not privately held. The answer is that, while there are real benefits to private ownership, there are also benefits to being publicly owned. Most notably, public corporations have access to large amounts of equity capital on advantageous terms, and for most companies, the advantage of access to public capital markets dominates the advantages of going private. Also, note that most companies which go private end up going public again after several years of operation as private firms. During the private phase, management typically sheds inefficient businesses, cuts costs throughout the corporation, and, generally, rationalizes operations. These actions increase the value of the firm to investors. Once the company has been "straightened up," going public allows the private equityholders to recover their investment, take their profit, and move on to new ventures.

Note too that the examples set by LBO companies are not lost on companies that maintain their publicly owned status. Thus, companies such as Phillips Petroleum and Union Carbide have changed their operations to the point where they resemble LBO companies. This has increased their value and thus made them less attractive to KKR and other LBO specialists, and this has benefitted both managements and shareholders. Thus far, LBOs seem to have provided a net advantage to the economy. However, the final chapter has not been written, and the high degree of leverage inherent in LBOs has proved fatal to many.

SELF-TEST QUESTIONS

What is meant by the term "going private"?

What are the main benefits of going private?

Why don't all firms go private to capture these benefits?

PREFERRED STOCK

Preferred stock is a hybrid—it is similar to bonds in some respects and to common stock in other ways. Accountants generally view preferred stock as equity and show it on the balance sheet as an equity account. However, financial managers view preferred stock as being somewhere between debt and common equity—it imposes a fixed charge and thus increases the firm's financial leverage, yet if the preferred dividend is not paid, the company cannot be forced into bankruptcy. We first describe the basic features of preferred, after which we describe some recent innovations in preferred stock financing.

Basic Features

Preferred stock generally has a par (or liquidating) value, usually either $25 or $100. The dividend is indicated as a percentage of par, as so many dollars per share, or sometimes both ways. For example, several years ago Mississippi Power Company sold 150,000 shares of $100 par value perpetual preferred stock for a total of $15 million. This preferred had a stated annual dividend of $12 per share, so the preferred dividend yield was $12/$100 = 0.12, or 12 percent, at the time of issue. The dividend was set when the stock was issued; it will not be changed in the future. Therefore, if the required rate of return on preferred, k_p, changes from 12 percent after the issue date—as it did—then the market price of the preferred stock will go up or down. Currently, k_p for Mississippi Power's preferred is 7.5 percent, and the price of the preferred has risen to $12/0.075 = $160.00.

If the preferred dividend is not earned, the company does not have to pay it. However, most preferred issues are *cumulative,* meaning that the cumulative total of all unpaid preferred dividends must be paid before dividends can be paid on the common stock. Unpaid preferred dividends are called *arrearages.*[7]

Preferred stock normally has no voting rights. However, most preferred issues stipulate that the preferred stockholders can elect a minority of the directors— say, 3 out of 10—if the preferred dividend is passed (omitted). Jersey Central Power & Light, one of the companies that owned a share of the Three Mile Island (TMI) nuclear plant, has preferred stock outstanding which can even elect a *majority* of the directors if the preferred dividend is passed for four successive quarters. Jersey Central kept paying its preferred dividends even during the dark days following the TMI accident. Had the preferred only been entitled to elect a minority of the directors, the dividend would probably have been passed.

Even though nonpayment of preferred dividends will not bankrupt a company, corporations issue preferred with every intention of paying the dividends. Even if passing the dividend does not give the preferred stockholders control of the company, failure to pay a preferred dividend precludes payment of common dividends and, in addition, makes it difficult for a firm to raise capital by selling bonds, and virtually impossible to sell more preferred or common stock. However, having preferred stock outstanding does give the firm that experiences temporary problems a chance to overcome its difficulties; had bonds been used instead of preferred stock, the company might have been forced into bankruptcy before it could straighten out its problems. Thus, from the viewpoint of the issuing corporation, preferred stock is less risky than bonds.

Investors, on the other hand, regard preferred stock as being riskier than bonds for two reasons: (1) Preferred stockholders' claims are subordinated to

---

[7]Dividends in arrears do not earn interest; thus, arrearages do not increase in a compound interest sense. They only grow from continued nonpayment of the preferred dividend. Also, many preferred stocks accrue arrearages for only a limited number of years, not indefinitely. Often, only three years of arrearages accrue; the cumulative feature ceases after three years, but the dividends in arrears until that point continue in force.

those of bondholders in the event of liquidation, and (2) bondholders are more likely to continue receiving income during hard times than are preferred stockholders. Accordingly, investors require a higher after-tax rate of return on a given firm's preferred stock than on its bonds. However, recall that 70 percent of preferred dividends are exempt from corporate income taxes; this makes preferred stock attractive to corporate investors. In recent years, high-grade preferred stock, on average, has sold on a lower pre-tax yield basis than have high-grade bonds. As an example, in March 1993, GM's preferred stock had a market yield of about 7.5 percent, whereas its bonds provided a yield of 8.0 percent, or 0.5 percentage points *more* than its preferred. The tax treatment accounted for this differential; the *after-tax yield* to corporate investors was greater on the preferred stock than on the bonds.[8]

About half of all preferred stock issued in recent years has been convertible into common stock. For example, Enron Corporation issued preferred stock which stipulated that one share of preferred could be converted into three shares of common, at the option of the preferred stockholder. Convertibles are discussed at length in Chapter 22.

Some preferred stocks are similar to perpetual bonds in that they have no maturity date. However, many preferred shares do have a sinking fund provision, often one which calls for the retirement of 2 percent of the issue each year, meaning that the issue will "mature" in a maximum of 50 years. Also, many preferred issues are callable by the issuing corporation. This feature, if exercised, can also limit the life of the preferred.[9]

Nonconvertible preferred stock is virtually all owned by corporations, which can take advantage of the 70 percent dividend exclusion to obtain a higher after-tax yield on preferred stock than on bonds. Individuals should not own preferred stocks (except convertible preferreds)—they can get higher yields on safer bonds, so it is not logical for them to hold preferreds. As a result of this ownership pattern, the volume of preferred stock financing is geared to the supply of money in the hands of insurance companies and other corporate investors who are looking for tax-favored investments. When the supply of such money is plentiful, the prices of preferred stocks are bid up, their yields fall, and investment bankers suggest to companies that they consider issuing preferred stock.

---

[8]The after-tax yield on a 8.0 percent bond to a corporate investor that is paying a 34 percent marginal tax rate is $8.0\%(1 - T) = 8.0\%(0.66) = 5.28\%$. The after-tax yield on an 7.5 percent preferred stock is $7.5\%(1 - \text{Effective } T) = 7.5\%[1 - (0.30)(0.34)] = 6.74\%$. Also, note that the tax law prohibits firms from issuing debt and then using the proceeds to purchase another firm's preferred or common stock. If debt financing is used for stock purchases, then the 70 percent dividend exclusion is reduced. This provision is designed to prevent firms from engaging in "tax arbitrage," or the use of tax-deductible debt to purchase largely tax-exempt preferred stock.

[9]Prior to the late 1970s, virtually all preferred stock was perpetual, and almost no issues had sinking funds or call provisions. Then, insurance company regulators, worried about the unrealized losses the companies had been incurring on preferred holdings as a result of rising interest rates, put into effect some regulatory changes which essentially mandated that insurance companies buy only limited life preferreds. From that time on, virtually no new issues have been perpetuities. This example illustrates the way the nature of securities changes as a result of changes in the economic environment.

RECENT INNOVATIONS

Several important innovations in preferred stock financing have occurred in recent years. We will discuss two of these here: (1) floating, or adjustable rate, preferred and (2) money market, or market auction, preferred.

Adjustable-rate preferred stocks (ARPs) were introduced in 1982. These stocks, instead of paying fixed dividends, have their dividends tied to the rate on Treasury securities. The ARPs, which are issued mainly by large commercial banks, were touted as nearly perfect short-term corporate investments since (1) only 30 percent of the dividends are taxable to corporations, and (2) the floating rate feature was supposed to keep the issue trading at near par. The new security proved to be so popular as a short-term investment for firms with idle cash that mutual funds which invest in these securities sprouted like weeds (the funds, in turn, were purchased by corporations). However, the ARPs still had some price volatility due (1) to changes in the riskiness of the issues (some big banks which had issued ARPs, such as Continental Illinois, ran into serious loan default problems) and (2) to the fact that Treasury yields exhibited significant fluctuations between dividend rate adjustments dates. Thus, the ARPs had too much price instability for the liquid asset portfolios of many corporate investors.

In 1984, Shearson Lehman Brothers introduced *money market,* or *market auction, preferred.* Here is how they work: The underwriter conducts an auction on the issue every 7 weeks (to get the 70 percent exclusion from taxable income, buyers must hold the stock at least 46 days). Any holders who want to sell their shares can put them up for auction at par value. Buyers then submit bids in the form of the yields they are willing to accept over the next 7-week period. The yield that is set on the issue for the next period is the lowest yield necessary to sell all the shares being offered at that auction. The buyers pay the sellers the par value, hence holders are virtually assured that their shares can be sold at par. The issuer then has to pay the dividend rate over the next 7-week period as determined by the auction. From the holder's standpoint, market auction preferred is a low-risk, largely tax-exempt, 7-week maturity security which can be sold between auction dates at close to par value. However, if there are not enough buyers to match the sellers, then the auction can fail. This has occurred several times recently. For example, an auction of MCorp, a Texas bank holding company, preferred stock recently failed. Analysts attributed the failure to the downgrading of MCorp's preferred stock by major rating agencies.

Adjustable-rate and market auction preferreds, although initially issued exclusively by banks, are also now being issued by nonfinancial corporations. For example, Texas Instruments recently issued $225 million of market auction preferred. About the only thing investors do not seem to like about ARPs and auction market preferreds is that, as stock, they are more vulnerable to an issuer's financial problems than debt would be, as evidenced by the MCorp example.

ADVANTAGES AND DISADVANTAGES OF PREFERRED STOCK FINANCING

There are both advantages and disadvantages to selling preferred stock. Here are the major advantages from the issuers' standpoint:

1. In contrast to bonds, the obligation to make preferred dividend payments is not contractual in nature, and the passing (omission) of preferred dividends cannot force a firm into bankruptcy.

2. By selling preferred stock, the firm avoids the dilution of common equity that occurs when common stock is sold.

3. Since preferred stock often has no maturity, and since preferred sinking fund payments, if present, are typically spread over a long period, preferred issues avoid the cash flow drain from repayment of principal that is inherent in debt issues.

These are the major disadvantages:

1. Preferred stock dividends are not deductible as a tax expense to the issuer, hence the after-tax cost of preferred is typically higher than the after-tax cost of debt.

2. Although preferred dividends can be passed, investors expect them to be paid, and firms intend to pay the dividends if conditions permit. Thus, preferred dividends are truly a fixed payment, and the use of preferred stock, like debt, increases the financial risk of the firm and thus increases the cost of debt and equity.

SELF-TEST QUESTIONS

Should preferred stock be considered as equity or debt financing? Explain.

Who are the major purchasers of nonconvertible preferred stock? Why?

Briefly explain the mechanics of adjustable-rate and market auction preferred stock.

What are the advantages and disadvantages of preferred stock financing to the issuer?

REGULATION AND THE INVESTMENT BANKING PROCESS

In this section, we describe the regulation of securities markets, the way securities are issued, and the role of investment bankers in the process.

REGULATION OF SECURITIES MARKETS

Sales of new securities, and also sales in the secondary markets, are regulated by the *Securities and Exchange Commission (SEC)* and, to a lesser extent, by each of the 50 states. Here are the primary elements of SEC regulation:

1. The SEC has jurisdiction over all interstate offerings of new securities to the public in amounts of $1.5 million or more.

2. Newly issued securities must be registered with the SEC at least 20 days before they are publicly offered. The *registration statement* provides financial, legal, and

technical information about the company to the SEC, and the *prospectus* summarizes this information for investors. SEC lawyers and accountants analyze both the registration statement and the prospectus; if the information is inadequate or misleading, the SEC will delay or stop the public offering.

3. After the registration has become effective, new securities may be offered, but any sales solicitation must be accompanied by the prospectus. Preliminary, or *"red herring," prospectuses* may be distributed to potential buyers during the 20-day waiting period, but no sales may be finalized during this time. The "red herring" prospectus contains all the key information that will appear in the final prospectus except the price, which is generally set after the market closes the day before the new securities are actually offered to the public.

4. If the registration statement or prospectus contains misrepresentations or omissions of material facts, any purchaser who suffers a loss may sue for damages. Severe penalties may be imposed on the issuer or its officers, directors, accountants, engineers, appraisers, underwriters, and all others who participated in the preparation of the registration statement or prospectus.

5. The SEC also regulates all national stock exchanges, and companies whose securities are listed on an exchange must file annual reports similar to the registration statement with both the SEC and the exchange.

6. The SEC has control over corporate *insiders.* Officers, directors, and major stockholders must file monthly reports of changes in their holdings of the stock of the corporation. Any short-term profits from such transactions must be turned over to the corporation.

7. The SEC has the power to prohibit manipulation by such devices as pools (large amounts of money used to buy or sell stocks to artificially affect prices) or wash sales (sales between members of the same group to record artificial transaction prices).

8. The SEC has control over the form of the proxy and the way the company uses it to solicit votes.

Control over the flow of credit into security transactions is exercised by the Board of Governors of the Federal Reserve System. The Fed exercises this control through *margin requirements,* which specify the maximum percentage of the purchase price of a security that can be borrowed. If a great deal of margin borrowing has been going on, then a decline in stock prices can result in inadequate coverages; this forces the stockbrokers to issue *margin calls,* which in turn require investors either to put up more money or to have their margined stock sold to pay off their loans. Such forced sales further depress the stock market and can set off a downward spiral. The margin requirement has been 50 percent since 1974.

States also have some control over the issuance of new securities within their boundaries. This control is usually exercised by a "corporation commissioner" or someone with a similar title. State laws relating to security sales are called *blue sky laws,* because they were put into effect to keep unscrupulous promoters from selling securities that offered the "blue sky" but which actually had little or no asset backing.

The securities industry itself realizes the importance of stable markets, sound brokerage firms, and the absence of stock manipulation. Therefore, the various exchanges work closely with the SEC to police transactions on the exchanges and to maintain the integrity and credibility of the system. Similarly, the *National Association of Securities Dealers (NASD)* cooperates with the SEC to police trading in the OTC market. These industry groups also cooperate with regulatory authorities to set net worth and other standards for securities firms, to develop insurance programs to protect the customers of brokerage houses, and the like.

In general, government regulation of securities trading, as well as industry self-regulation, is designed to ensure that investors receive information that is as accurate as possible, that no one artificially manipulates the market price of a given stock, and that corporate insiders do not take advantage of their position to profit in their companies' stocks at the expense of other stockholders. Neither the SEC, the state regulators, nor the industry itself can prevent investors from making foolish decisions or from having "bad luck," but they can and do help investors obtain the best data possible for making sound investment decisions.

THE INVESTMENT BANKING PROCESS

The investment banking process takes place in two stages.

Stage I Decisions. At Stage I, the firm itself makes some initial, preliminary decisions, including the following:

1. **Dollars to be raised.** How much new capital is needed?
2. **Type of securities used.** Should common, preferred, bonds, or hybrid securities, or a combination, be used? Further, if common stock is to be issued, should it be done as a rights offering or by a direct sale to the general public?
3. **Competitive bid versus a negotiated deal.** Should the company simply offer a block of its securities for sale to the highest bidder, or should it negotiate a deal with an investment banker? These two procedures are called *competitive bids* and *negotiated deals,* respectively. Only about 100 of the largest firms listed on the NYSE, whose securities are already well known to the investment banking community, are in a position to use the competitive bidding process. The investment banks must do a large amount of investigative work in order to bid on an issue unless they are already quite familiar with the firm, and such costs would be too high to make it worthwhile unless the banker were sure of getting the deal. Therefore, except for the largest firms, offerings of stock or bonds are generally on a negotiated basis.
4. **Selection of an investment banker.** If the issue is to be negotiated, the firm must select an investment banker. This can be an important decision for a firm that is going public. On the other hand, an older firm that has already "been to market" will have an established relationship with an investment banker. However, it is easy to change bankers if the firm is dissatisfied. Different investment

Table 19-3

Top Ten Global

Underwriters

	Total Amount Managed (In Billions of Dollars)
1. Merrill Lynch	150.7
2. Goldman Sachs	119.6
3. Lehman Brothers	106.2
4. CS First Boston	98.7
5. Kidder Peabody	81.0
6. Salomon Brothers	80.3
7. Morgan Stanley	72.5
8. Bear Stearns	53.4
9. J. P. Morgan	29.2
10. Prudential Securities	28.6

Source: *The Wall Street Journal*, January 4, 1993.

banking houses are better suited for different companies. The older, larger "establishment houses" such as Morgan Stanley deal mainly with companies such as AT&T, IBM, and Exxon. Other bankers handle more speculative issues. Some houses specialize in new issues, while others are not well suited to handle such issues because their brokerage clients are relatively conservative. (Investment banking firms sell new issues largely to their own regular brokerage customers, so the nature of these customers has a major effect on the ability of the house to do a good job for a corporate client.) Table 19-3 lists the top ten global underwriters for 1992 as measured by the dollar amount of securities underwritten.

Stage II Decisions. Stage II decisions, which are made jointly by the firm and its selected investment banker, include the following:

1. Reevaluating the initial decisions. The firm and its banker will reevaluate the initial decisions regarding the size of the issue and the type of securities to use. For example, the firm may have decided initially to raise $50 million by selling common stock, but the investment banker may convince management that it would be better off, in view of current market conditions, to limit the stock issue to $25 million and to raise the other $25 million as debt.

2. Best efforts or underwritten issues. The firm and its investment banker must decide whether the banker will work on a *best efforts* basis or will *underwrite* the issue. In a best efforts sale, the banker does not guarantee that the securities will be sold or that the company will get the cash it needs, only that it will put forth its best efforts to sell the issue. On an underwritten issue, the company does get a guarantee, because the banker agrees to buy the entire issue and then resell the stock to its customers. Therefore, the banker bears significant risks in underwritten offerings. For example, on one IBM bond issue, interest rates rose sharply, and bond prices fell, after the deal had been set but before the investment bankers could sell the bonds to ultimate purchasers. The bankers lost somewhere

between $10 million and $20 million. Had the offering been on a best efforts basis, IBM would have been the loser.

3. Banker's compensation and other expenses. The investment banker's compensation must be negotiated. Also, the firm must estimate the other underwriting expenses it will incur in connection with the issue — lawyers' fees, accountants' costs, printing and engraving, and so on. In an underwritten issue, the banker will buy the issue from the company at a discount below the price at which the securities are to be offered to the public, with this "spread" being set to cover the banker's costs and to provide a profit.

Table 19-4 gives an indication of the issuance costs associated with public issues of bonds, preferred stock, and common stock. As the table shows, costs as a percentage of the proceeds are higher for stocks than for bonds, and costs are higher for small than for large issues. The relationship between size of issue and flotation cost is due primarily to the existence of fixed costs — certain costs must be incurred regardless of the size of the issue, so the percentage flotation cost is quite high for small issues.

Also, it should be noted that when companies go public to raise new capital, the new shares are typically underpriced. Thus, the stock closes on the first day of trading at a price above the issue price. Underpricing represents a potentially large cost to existing shareholders, as shown in the initial public offerings section of Table 19-4. Further, the investment bankers frequently take part of their compensation in the form of options to buy stock in the firm. For example, Glasgo Technologies recently went public with a $10 million issue by selling 1 million shares at a price of $10 per share. Its investment bankers bought the stock from the company at a price of $9.75 per share, so the direct underwriting fee was only 1,000,000($10.00 − $9.75) = $250,000, or 2.5 percent, but they also received a 5-year option to buy 200,000 shares at a price of $10 per share. If the stock should go up to $15 per share, which the bankers expected it to do, then the investment banking firm would make a $1 million profit, which would in effect be an additional underwriting fee.

4. Setting the offering price. If the company is already publicly owned, the offering price will be based upon the existing market price of the stock or the yield on the bonds. Typically, for common stock, the investment banker buys the securities at a prescribed number of points below the closing price on the last day of registration. For example, suppose that in October 1993, the stock of Microwave Telecommunications Inc. (MTI) had a current price of $28.50 per share, and the stock had traded between $25 and $30 per share during the previous three months. Suppose further that MTI and its underwriter agreed that the investment banker would buy 10 million new shares at $1 per share below the closing price on the last day of registration. If the stock closed at $25 on the day the SEC released the issue, MTI would receive $24 per share. Typically, such agreements have an escape clause that provides for the contract to be voided if the price of the securities drops below some predetermined figure. In the illustrative case, this "upset" price might be set at $24 per share. Thus, if the closing price of the shares on the last day of registration had been $23.50, MTI would have had the option of withdrawing from the agreement.

TABLE 19-4	Size of Issue (Millions of Dollars)	Bonds			Preferred Stock		
ISSUANCE COSTS FOR UNDERWRITTEN, NONRIGHTS OFFERINGS (EXPRESSED AS PERCENTAGE OF GROSS PROCEEDS)		Underwriting Commission	Other Expenses	Total Costs	Underwriting Commission	Other Expenses	Total Costs
	Under 1.0	10.0%	4.0%	14.0%	—	—	—
	1.0–1.9	8.0	3.0	11.0	—	—	—
	2.0–4.9	4.0	2.2	6.2	—	—	—
	5.0–9.9	2.4	0.8	3.2	1.9%	0.7%	2.6%
	10.0–19.9	1.2	0.7	1.9	1.4	0.4	1.8
	20.0–49.9	1.0	0.4	1.4	1.4	0.3	1.7
	50.0 and over	0.9	0.2	1.1	1.4	0.2	1.6

Notes:

a. Small issues of preferred are rare, so no data on issues below $5 million are given.

b. Flotation costs tend to rise somewhat when interest rates are cyclically high, indicating that money is in relatively tight supply, hence investment bankers will have a relatively hard time placing issues with permanent investors. Thus, the figures shown in this table represent averages, as flotation costs actually vary somewhat over time.

c. Underpricing is shown as a separate cost component for initial public offerings because it has been measured and is reasonably predictable. Underpricing also exists for common stock offerings by companies that already have publicly traded stock, but the effects are unstable and difficult to measure; these effects are discussed later in the chapter.

The investment banker will have an easier job if the issue is priced relatively low, but the issuer of the securities naturally wants as high a price as possible. Some conflict of interest on price therefore arises between the investment banker and the issuer. If the issuer is financially sophisticated and makes comparisons with similar security issues, the investment banker will be forced to price close to the market.

As we discussed in Chapter 13, the announcement of a new stock offering by a mature firm is often taken as a negative signal — if the firm's prospects were very good, management would not want to issue new stock and thus share the rosy future with new stockholders, so the announcement of a new offering is taken as bad news. Consequently, the price will probably fall when the announcement is made, so the offering price will probably have to be set at a price substantially below the pre-announcement market price. Consider Figure 19-1, in which d_0 is the estimated market demand curve for MTI's stock and S_0 is the number of shares currently outstanding. Initially, there are 50 million shares outstanding, and the equilibrium price of the stock is $28.60 per share, determined as follows:

$$\hat{P}_0 = \frac{D_1}{k_s - g} = \frac{\$2.00}{0.12 - 0.05} \approx \$28.60.$$

The values shown for D_1, k_s, and g are the *estimates of the marginal investor.* Investors who do not now own MTI's stock probably, on average, regard the stock as being more risky, thus assign it a higher value for k_s, or perhaps they estimate

TABLE 19-4
continued

Common Stock: Additional Shares			Common Stock: Initial Public Offerings			
Underwriting Commission	Other Expenses	Total Costs	Underwriting Commission	Other Expenses	Underpricing Costs	Total Costs
13.0%	9.0%	22.0%	9.8%	9.6%	12.3%	31.7%
11.0	5.9	16.9	9.8	9.6	12.3	31.7
8.6	3.8	12.4	9.4	6.6	6.9	22.9
6.3	1.9	8.1	8.0	4.3	5.5	17.8
5.1	0.9	6.0	7.2	2.1	7.0	16.3
4.1	0.5	4.6	7.2	2.1	7.0	16.3
3.3	0.2	3.5	7.2	2.1	7.0	16.3

Sources: Securities and Exchange Commission, *Cost of Flotation of Registered Equity Issues* (Washington, D.C.: U.S. Government Printing Office, December 1974); Richard H. Pettway, "A Note on the Flotation Costs of New Equity Capital Issues of Electric Companies," *Public Utilities Fortnightly,* March 18, 1982; Robert Hansen, "Evaluating the Costs of a New Equity Issue," *Midland Corporate Finance Journal,* Spring 1986; Jay R. Ritter, "The Costs of Going Public," *Journal of Financial Economics,* December 1987; and informal surveys of common stock, preferred stock, and bond issues conducted by the authors.

FIGURE 19-1

MICROWAVE TELECOMMUNICATIONS INC.: ESTIMATED COMMON STOCK DEMAND CURVES

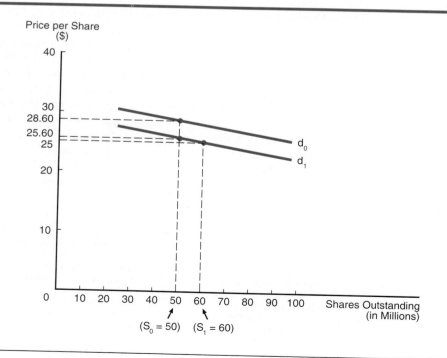

the company's growth rate as being lower than do people who now own the stock, and so they use g < 5 percent when calculating the stock's intrinsic value. In any event, people who do not now own the stock think the stock is worth less than $28.60.

When MTI announces that it is going to sell another 10 million shares, this is taken as a negative signal. Consequently, the demand curve for the stock drops from d_0 to d_1, and the price falls. The new equilibrium price, if 50 million shares were outstanding, and if the marginal investor now expects MTI's growth rate to be 4.2 percent, would be about $25.60:

$$\hat{P}_0 = \frac{\$2.00}{0.12 - 0.042} \approx \$25.60.$$

However, if MTI is to sell another 10 million shares of stock, it will either have to attract investors who would not be willing to own the stock at the $25.60 per share price or else induce present stockholders to buy additional shares. There are two ways this can be accomplished: (1) by reducing the offering price of the stock or (2) by "promoting" or "advertising" the company and thus shifting the demand curve for its stock back to the right.[10] If the demand curve does not shift at all from d_1, we see from Figure 19-1 that the only way the 10 million additional shares could be sold would be by setting the offering price at about $25 per share. However, if the investment banker could sufficiently promote the stock to shift the demand curve back up to d_0, then the offering price could be set much closer to the preannouncement equilibrium price of $28.60 per share.[11]

The extent to which the demand curve can be shifted depends primarily on two factors: (1) what investors think the company can do with the money brought in by the stock sale and (2) how effectively the brokers promote the issue. If investors can be convinced that the new money will be invested in highly profitable projects that will substantially raise earnings and the earnings growth rate, then the demand curve shift will occur, and the stock price might actually go above $28.60. Even if investors do not radically change their expectations about the company's fundamental factors, the fact that MTI's stock is brought to their attention may shift the demand curve. The extent to which this promotion campaign is successful in shifting the demand curve depends, of course, upon the

---

[10]It should be noted that investors can buy newly issued stock without paying normal brokerage commissions, and brokers are quick to point this out to potential purchasers. Thus, if an investor were to buy MTI's stock at $28 per share in the regular market, the commission would be about 1 percent, or 28 cents per share. If the stock were purchased in an underwriting, this commission would be avoided.

It should also be noted that for years many academicians argued that the demand curve for a firm's stock is either horizontal or has an extremely slight downward slope, and that signaling effects are minimal. Most corporate treasurers, on the other hand, have long felt that both effects exist for mature companies, and recent empirical studies confirm the treasurers' position. For example, see Andrei Shleifer, "Do Demand Curves for Stocks Slope Down?" *Journal of Finance,* July 1986, 579–590.

[11]Note that the supply curve is a vertical line, first at 50 million and then, after the new issue, at 60 million.

effectiveness of the investment banking firm. Therefore, the effectiveness of different investment bankers, as perceived by MTI's financial manager, will be an important factor in the choice of an underwriter.

One final point is that *if pressure from the new shares and/or negative signaling effects drives down the price of the stock, all shares outstanding, not just the new shares, are affected.* Thus, if MTI's stock should fall from $28.60 to $25 per share as a result of the financing, and if the price should remain at that new level, then the company would incur a loss of $3.60 on each of the 50 million shares previously outstanding, or a total market value loss of $180 million. This loss, like underwriting expenses, is a flotation cost, and it should be considered as a cost associated with the stock issue. However, if the company's prospects really were poorer than investors thought, then the price decline would have occurred sooner or later anyway. On the other hand, if the company's prospects are really not all that bad (the signal was incorrect), then over time MTI's demand curve will move back to d_0, or even above d_0, so the company would not suffer a permanent loss anywhere close to $180 million.

If the company is "going public," there will be no established price or demand curve, so the bankers will have to estimate the *equilibrium price* at which the stock will sell after issue. Note that if the offering price is set below the true equilibrium price, the stock will rise sharply after the issue, and the company and its selling stockholders will have given away too much stock to raise the required capital. If the offering price is set above the true equilibrium price, either the issue will fail or, if the bankers succeed in selling the stock to their retail clients, these clients will be unhappy when the stock subsequently falls to its equilibrium level. Therefore, it is important that the equilibrium price be closely approximated, although it is hard to estimate this price.

Selling Procedures.   Once the company and its investment banker have decided how much money to raise, the types of securities to issue, and the basis for pricing the issue, they will prepare and file an SEC *registration statement* and a *prospectus.* It generally takes about 20 days for the issue to be approved by the SEC. The final price of the stock (or the interest rate on a bond issue) is set at the close of business the day the issue clears the SEC, and the securities are offered to the public the following day.

Investors are required to pay for securities within 10 days, and the investment banker must pay the issuing firm within four days of the official commencement of the offering. Typically, the banker sells the stock within a day or two after the offering begins, but on occasion, the banker miscalculates, sets the offering price too high, and thus is unable to move the issue. At other times, the market declines during the offering period, forcing the banker to reduce the price of the stock or bonds. In either instance, on an underwritten offering the firm receives the price that was agreed upon, so the banker must absorb any losses that are incurred.

Because they are exposed to large potential losses, investment bankers typically do not handle the purchase and distribution of issues single-handedly unless the issue is a very small one. If the sum of money involved is large, investment bankers form *underwriting syndicates* in an effort to minimize the risk each

banker carries. The banking house which sets up the deal is called the *lead,* or *managing, underwriter.*

In addition to the underwriting syndicate, on larger offerings still more investment bankers are included in a *selling group,* which handles the distribution of securities to individual investors. The selling group includes all members of the underwriting syndicate plus additional dealers who take relatively small percentages of the total issue from the members of the underwriting syndicate. Thus, the underwriters act as *wholesalers,* while members of the selling group act as *retailers.* The number of houses in a selling group depends partly upon the size of the issue. For example, the one set up when Communications Satellite Corporation (Comsat) went public consisted of 385 members.

A new selling procedure has recently emerged which does not require an underwriting syndicate. In this type of sale, called an *unsyndicated stock offering,* the managing underwriter, acting alone, sells the issue entirely to institutional investors, thus bypassing both retail stockbrokers and individual investors. In recent years, about 50 percent of all stock sold has been by unsyndicated offerings. Behind this phenomenon is a simple motivating force: money. The fees that issuers pay on a syndicated offering, which includes commissions paid to retail brokers, can run at least a full percentage point higher than those on unsyndicated offerings. Further, although total fees are lower if there is no syndicate, managing underwriters usually come out ahead because they do not have to share the fees with an underwriting syndicate. Recent issuers of unsyndicated stock include Transamerica Corporation and Public Service Company of New Mexico. However, some types of stock do not appeal to institutional investors, so not all firms can use unsyndicated offers.

Shelf Registrations.   The selling procedures described previously, including the 20-day waiting period between registration with the SEC and sale of the issue, apply to most security sales. However, under the SEC's Rule 415, large, well-known public companies which issue securities frequently may file a *master registration statement* with the SEC and then update it with a *short-form statement* just prior to each individual offering. Under this procedure, the company can decide at 10 A.M. to sell securities and have the sale completed before noon. This procedure is known as *shelf registration* because, in effect, the company puts its new securities "on the shelf" and then sells them to investors when it feels the market is "right." Firms with less than $150 million in stock held by outside investors cannot use shelf registrations. The rationale for this distinction is to protect investors who may not be able to get adequate financial data about a little-known company in the short time between announcement of a shelf issue and its sale. Shelf registrations have two advantages over standard registrations: (1) lower flotation costs and (2) more control over the timing of the issue.

Maintenance of the Secondary Market.   In the case of a large, established firm such as IBM or GM, the investment banking firm's job is finished after it has disposed of the stock and turned the net proceeds over to the issuing firm. However, in the case of a small company going public for the first time, the investment banker is under some obligation to maintain a market in the shares after the issue

has been completed. Such stocks are typically traded in the over-the-counter market, and the lead underwriter generally agrees to "make a market" in the stock so as to keep it reasonably liquid. The company wants a good market to exist for its stock, as do the stockholders. Therefore, if the banking house wants to do business with the company in the future, to keep its own brokerage customers happy, and to have future referral business, it will hold an inventory and help to maintain an active secondary market in the stock.

SELF-TEST QUESTIONS

What are the key features of securities markets regulation?

What is the difference between Stage I and Stage II decisions?

What is the difference between a best efforts and an underwritten issue?

What are some potential problems encountered when setting the offering price on a stock issue?

Briefly explain the selling procedures used on a new securities issue.

What is a shelf registration? What are the advantages of shelf registrations over standard registrations?

SUMMARY

This chapter is more descriptive than analytical, but a knowledge of the issues discussed here is essential to an understanding of corporate finance. The key concepts covered are listed below.

▶ *Stockholders' equity* consists of the firm's common stock, additional paid-in capital (funds received in excess of the par value), and retained earnings (earnings not paid out as dividends).

▶ *Book value per share* is equal to stockholders' equity divided by the number of shares of stock outstanding. A stock's book value is often different from its par value and its market value.

▶ A *proxy* is a document which gives one person the power to act for another person, typically the power to vote shares of common stock. A *proxy fight* occurs when an outside group solicits stockholders' proxies in order to vote a new management team into office.

▶ Stockholders often have the right to purchase any additional shares sold by the firm. This right, called the *preemptive right,* protects the control of the present stockholders and prevents dilution of the value of their stock.

▶ Although most firms use only one type of common stock, in some instances several *classes of stock* are issued.

▶ The major *advantages of common stock financing* are as follows: (1) there is no obligation to make fixed payments, (2) common stock never matures,

(3) the use of common stock increases the creditworthiness of the firm, (4) stock can often be sold more easily than debt, and (5) using stock helps the firm maintain its reserve borrowing capacity.

▶ The major *disadvantages of common stock financing* are (1) it extends voting privileges to new stockholders, (2) new stockholders share in the firm's profits, (3) the costs of issuing stock are high, (4) using stock can raise the firm's cost of capital, and (5) dividends paid on common stock are not tax deductible.

▶ A *closely held corporation* is one that is owned by a few individuals who are typically associated with the firm's management.

▶ A *publicly owned corporation* is one that is owned by a relatively large number of individuals who are not actively involved in its management.

▶ *Going public* facilitates stockholder diversification, increases liquidity of the firm's stock, makes it easier for the firm to raise capital, and establishes a value for the firm. However, reporting costs are high, operating data must be disclosed, management self-dealings are harder to arrange, the price may sink to a low level if the stock is not traded actively, and public ownership may make it harder for management to maintain control of the firm.

▶ The decision to *list* the stock on a major exchange is not as critical as the decision to go public.

▶ New common stock may be sold in five ways: (1) on a pro rata basis to existing stockholders through a *rights offering,* (2) through investment bankers to the general public in a *public offering,* (3) to a single buyer, or a small number of buyers, in a *private placement,* (4) to employees through an *employee purchase plan,* and (5) to shareholders through a *dividend reinvestment plan.*

▶ Securities markets are regulated by the *Securities and Exchange Commission (SEC).*

▶ An *investment banker* assists in the issuing of securities by helping the firm determine the size of the issue and the type of securities to be used, by establishing the selling price, by selling the issue, and, in some cases, by maintaining an after-market for the stock.

▶ *Preferred stock* is a hybrid—it is similar to bonds in some respects and to common stock in other ways.

▶ The 1980s spawned two innovations in preferred stock financing: (1) *floating rate preferred* and (2) *money market, or market auction, preferred.*

QUESTIONS

19-1 Define each of the following terms:
   a. Common equity; additional paid-in capital; retained earnings
   b. Par value; book value per share; market value per share

    c. Proxy; proxy fight

    d. Preemptive right

    e. Classified stock; founders' shares

    f. Closely held corporation; publicly owned corporation

    g. Over-the-counter (OTC) market; organized security exchange

    h. Primary market; secondary market

    i. Going public; new issue market; initial public offering (IPO)

    j. Rights offering

    k. Public offering; private placement

    l. Employee purchase plan; ESOP

    m. Securities and Exchange Commission (SEC); registration statement; shelf registration; "blue sky" laws; margin requirement; insiders

    n. Prospectus; "red herring" prospectus

    o. National Association of Securities Dealers (NASD)

    p. Cumulative dividends; arrearages

    q. Floating rate preferred stock

    r. Best efforts arrangement; underwritten arrangement

    s. Spread; flotation costs; offering price

    t. Underwriting syndicate; lead, or managing, underwriter; selling group

19-2 Examine Table 19-1. Suppose American Chemical sold 2 million shares, with the company netting $25 per share. Construct a pro forma statement of the equity accounts to reflect this sale.

19-3 Is it true that the "flatter," or more nearly horizontal, the demand curve for a particular firm's stock, and the less important investors regard the signaling effect of the offering, the more important the role of investment bankers when the company sells a new issue of stock?

19-4 The SEC attempts to protect investors who are purchasing newly issued securities by making sure that the information put out by a company and its investment bankers is correct and is not misleading. However, the SEC does not provide an opinion about the real value of the securities; hence, an investor might pay too much for some new stock and consequently lose heavily. Do you think the SEC should, as a part of every new stock or bond offering, render an opinion to investors on the proper value of the securities being offered? Explain.

19-5 How do you think each of the following items would affect a company's ability to attract new capital and the flotation costs involved in doing so?

    a. A decision to list a company's stock; the stock now trades in the over-the-counter market.

    b. A decision of a privately held company to go public.

    c. The increasing institutionalization of the "buy side" of the stock and bond markets.

    d. The trend toward "financial conglomerates" as opposed to stand-alone investment banking houses.

    e. Elimination of the preemptive right.

    f. The introduction of "shelf registrations" in 1981.

19-6 Before entering a formal agreement, investment bankers carefully investigate the companies whose securities they underwrite; this is especially true of the issues of firms going public for the first time. Since the bankers do not themselves plan to hold the securities but intend to sell them to others as soon as possible, why are they so concerned about making careful investigations?

19-7 It is frequently stated that the primary purpose of the preemptive right is to allow individuals to maintain their proportionate share of the ownership and control of a corporation.

    a. How important do you suppose this consideration is for the average stockholder of a firm whose shares are traded on the New York or American Stock Exchanges?

    b. Is the preemptive right likely to be of more importance to stockholders of publicly owned or closely held firms? Explain.

    c. Is a firm likely to get a wider distribution of shares if it sells new stock through a preemptive rights offering to existing stockholders or directly to underwriters?

    d. Why would management be interested in getting a wider distribution of its shares?

PROBLEMS

19-1 (Book value per share) The Morrissey Music Company had the following balance sheet at the end of 1993.

Morrissey Music Company:
Balance Sheet as of
December 31, 1993

		Accounts payable	$ 48,000
		Notes payable	54,000
		Long-term debt	108,000
		Common stock (30,000 shares authorized, 20,000 shares outstanding)	270,000
		Retained earnings	225,000
Total assets	$705,000	Total liabilities and equity	$705,000

    a. What is the book value per share of the firm's common stock?

    b. Suppose the firm sold the remaining authorized shares and netted $22.50 per share from the sale. What would be the new book value per share?

19-2 (Profit or loss on new stock issue) Security Brokers Inc. specializes in underwriting new issues by small firms. On a recent offering of Beedles Inc., the terms were as follows:

Price to public:	$5 per share
Number of shares:	3 million
Proceeds to Beedles:	$14,000,000

The out-of-pocket expenses incurred by Security Brokers in the design and distribution of the issue were $300,000. What profit or loss would Security Brokers incur if the issue were sold to the public at an average price of

    a. $5 per share?

    b. $6 per share?

    c. $4 per share?

19-3 (Underwriting and flotation expenses) The Beranek Company, whose stock price is now $25, needs to raise $20 million in common stock. Underwriters have informed the firm's management that they must price the new issue to the public at $22 per share be-

cause of a downward-sloping demand curve. The underwriters' compensation will be 5 percent of the issue price, so Beranek will net $20.90 per share. The firm will also incur expenses in the amount of $150,000.

How many shares must the firm sell to net $20 million after underwriting and flotation expenses?

19-4 **(New stock issue)** The Edelman Gem Company, a small jewelry manufacturer, has been successful and has enjoyed a good growth trend. Now Edelman is planning to go public with an issue of common stock, and it faces the problem of setting an appropriate price on the stock. The company and its investment bankers believe that the proper procedure is to select several similar firms with publicly traded common stock and to make relevant comparisons.

Several jewelry manufacturers are reasonably similar to Edelman with respect to product mix, asset composition, and debt/equity proportions. Of these companies, Kennedy Jewelers and Strasburg Fashions are most similar. When analyzing the following data, assume that 1988 and 1993 were reasonably "normal" years for all three companies—that is, these years were neither especially good nor especially bad in terms of sales, earnings, and dividends. At the time of the analysis, k_{RF} was 8 percent and k_M was 12 percent. Kennedy is listed on the AMEX and Strasburg on the NYSE, while Edelman will be traded in the OTC market.

	Kennedy	Strasburg	Edelman (Totals)
Earnings per share			
1993	$ 4.50	$ 7.50	$1,200,000
1988	3.00	5.50	816,000
Price per share			
1993	$36.00	$65.00	—
Dividends per share			
1993	$ 2.25	$ 3.75	$ 600,000
1988	1.50	2.75	420,000
Book value per share, 1993	$30.00	$55.00	$ 9 million
Market/book ratio, 1993	120%	118%	—
Total assets, 1993	$28 million	$ 82 million	$20 million
Total debt, 1993	$12 million	$ 30 million	$11 million
Sales, 1993	$41 million	$140 million	$37 million

a. Assume that Edelman has 100 shares of stock outstanding. Use this information to calculate earnings per share (EPS), dividends per share (DPS), and book value per share for Edelman. (Hint: Edelman's 1993 EPS = $12,000.)

b. Calculate earnings and dividend growth rates for the three companies. (Hint: Edelman's EPS growth rate is 8 percent.)

c. On the basis of your answer to Part a, do you think Edelman's stock would sell at a price in the same "ballpark" as that of Kennedy and Strasburg, that is, in the range of $25 to $100 per share?

d. Assuming that Edelman's management can split the stock so that the 100 shares could be changed to 1,000 shares, 100,000 shares, or any other number, would such an action make sense in this case? Why?

e. Now assume that Edelman did split its stock and has 400,000 shares. Calculate new values for EPS, DPS, and book value per share. (Hint: Edelman's new 1993 EPS is $3.00.)

f. Return on equity (ROE) can be measured as EPS/book value per share or as total earnings/total equity. Calculate ROEs for the three companies for 1993. (Hint: Edelman's 1993 ROE = 13.3%.)

g. Calculate dividend payout ratios for the three companies for both years. (Hint: Edelman's 1993 payout ratio is 50%.)

h. Calculate debt/total assets ratios for the three companies for 1993. (Hint: Edelman's 1993 debt ratio is 55%.)

i. Calculate the P/E ratios for Kennedy and Strasburg for 1993. Are these P/Es reasonable in view of relative growth, payout, and ROE data? If not, what other factors might explain them? (Hint: Kennedy's P/E = 8×.)

j. Now determine a range of values for Edelman's stock price, with 400,000 shares outstanding, by applying Kennedy's and Strasburg's P/E ratios, price/dividends ratios, and price/book value ratios to your data for Edelman. For example, one possible price for Edelman's stock is (P/E Kennedy)(EPS Edelman) = 8($3) = $24 per share. Similar calculations would produce a range of prices based on both Kennedy's and Strasburg's data. (Hint: Our range was $24 to $27.)

k. Using the equation $k = D_1/P_0 + g$, find approximate k values for Kennedy and Strasburg. Then use these values in the constant growth stock price model to find a price for Edelman's stock. (Hint: We averaged the EPS and DPS g's for Edelman.)

l. At what price do you think Edelman's shares should be offered to the public? You will want to select a price that will be low enough to induce investors to buy the stock but not so low that it will rise sharply immediately after it is issued. Think about relative growth rates, ROEs, dividend yields, and total returns ($k_s = D_1/P_0 + g$).

M I N I C A S E

Randy's, a family-owned restaurant chain operating in Alabama, has grown to the point where expansion throughout the entire Southeast is feasible. The proposed expansion would require the firm to raise about $15 million in new capital. Because Randy's currently has a debt ratio of 50 percent, and also because the family members already have all their personal wealth invested in the company, the family would like to sell common stock to the public to raise the $15 million. However, the family does want to retain voting control. You have been asked to brief the family members on the issues involved by answering the following questions:

a. What are the primary advantages of financing with stock rather than bonds? What are the disadvantages to financing with stock?

b. Is the stock of Randy's currently publicly held or privately owned? Would this situation change if the stock sale were made?

c. What is classified stock? Would there be any advantages to the family in designating the stock currently outstanding as "founders' shares"? What type of common stock should Randy's sell to the public to allow the family to retain control of the business?

d. Would the stock sale be an initial public offering (IPO)? What would be the advantages to the family members of having the firm go public? Would there be any disadvantages? If you were a key employee, but not a family member, or a potential key employee being interviewed as a part of the expansion process, how would the decision affect you?

e. What does it mean for a stock to be listed? Do you think that Randy's stock would be listed shortly after the company goes public? If not, where would the stock trade?

f.   What is a rights offering? Would it make sense for Randy's to use a rights offering to raise the $15 million? Even if you do not think a rights offering should be employed, could one be used?

g.   What is the difference between a private placement and a public offering? What are the advantages and disadvantages of each type of placement? Which type would be most suitable for Randy's?

h.   What is meant by going private? Assume for the sake of this question that Randy's previously went public. What are the advantages and disadvantages of the firm's going private?

i.   How does preferred stock differ from both common equity and debt? Briefly describe the features of floating rate (or adjustable rate) preferred stock.

j.   (1) Would Randy's be likely to sell the $15 million of stock by itself or through an investment banker?
     (2) If an investment banker were used, would the sale most likely be on the basis of a competitive bid or a negotiated deal?
     (3) If it were a negotiated deal, would it most likely be done on a best efforts or an underwritten basis? In each case, explain your answer.

k.   Without doing any calculations, describe the procedure by which the company and its investment banker would determine the price at which the stock would be offered to the public.

l.   Suppose the decision were made to issue 1.5 million shares at $10 per share. What would be the approximate flotation cost on the issue? Would the cost be higher or lower if the firm were already publicly owned? Would there be a difference in costs between a best efforts and an underwritten offering?

m.   If some of the family members wanted to sell some of their own shares in order to diversify their holdings at the same time the company was selling new shares to raise capital, would this be feasible?

SELECTED ADDITIONAL REFERENCES AND CASES

For a wealth of facts and figures on a major segment of the stock market, see New York Stock Exchange, Fact Book (New York: published annually).

For both a description of the stock markets and some further facts and figures, see the investment textbooks referenced in Chapter 3. For a discussion of the current state of investment banking and trends in the industry, see

Auerbach, Joseph, and Samuel L. Hayes III, *Investment Banking and Diligence: What Price Deregulation* (Boston: HBS Press, 1986).

Eccles, Robert G., and Dwight B. Crane, *Doing Deals: Investment Bankers at Work* (Boston: HBS Press, 1988).

Hayes, S. L., "The Transformation of Investment Banking," *Harvard Business Review,* January-February 1979, 153–170.

Rogowski, Robert, and Eric Sorensen, "The New Competitive Environment of Investment Banking: Transactional Finance and Concession Pricing of New Issues," *Midland Corporate Finance Journal,* Spring 1986, 64–71.

For additional insights on the benefits of listing, see

Baker, H. Kent, and Richard B. Edelman, "AMEX-to-NYSE Transfers, Market Microstructure, and Shareholder Wealth," *Financial Management,* Winter 1992, 60–72.

Edelman, Richard B., and H. Kent Baker, "Liquidity and Stock Exchange Listing," *The Financial Review,* May 1990, 231–249.

Other good references on specific aspects of equity financing include the following:

Aggarwal, Reena, and Pietra Rivoli, "Fads in the Initial Public Offering Market?" *Financial Management,* Winter 1990, 45–57.

Block, Stanley, and Marjorie Stanley, "The Financial Characteristics and Price Movement Patterns of Companies Approaching the Unseasoned Securities Market in the Late 1970s," *Financial Management,* Winter 1980, 30–36.

Bowyer, John W., and Jess B. Yawitz, "Effect of New Equity Issues on Utility Stock Prices," *Public Utilities Fortnightly,* May 22, 1980, 25–28.

Brickley, James A., and Kathleen T. Hevert, "Direct Employee Stock Ownership: An Empirical Investigation," *Financial Management,* Summer 1991, 70–84.

Carter, Richard, and Steven Manaster, "Initial Public Offerings and Underwriter Reputation," *Journal of Finance,* September 1990, 1045–1067.

Denis, David J., "The Costs of Equity Issues Since Rule 415: A Closer Look," *Journal of Financial Research,* Spring 1993, 77–88.

Fabozzi, Frank J., "Does Listing on the AMEX Increase the Value of Equity?" *Financial Management,* Spring 1981, 43–50.

Hansen, Robert S., and John M. Pinkerton, "Direct Equity Financing: A Resolution to a Paradox," *Journal of Finance,* June 1982, 651–665.

Ibbotson, Roger G., Jody L. Sindelar, and Jay R. Ritter, "Initial Public Offerings," *Journal of Applied Corporate Finance,* Summer 1988, 37–45.

Jurin, Bruce, "Raising Equity in an Efficient Market," *Midland Corporate Finance Journal,* Winter 1988, 53–60.

Loderer, Claudio, John W. Cooney, and Leonard D. Van Drunen, "The Price Elasticity of Demand for Common Stock," *Journal of Finance,* June 1991, 621–651.

Logue, Dennis, and Robert A. Jarrow, "Negotiation versus Competitive Bidding in the Sale of Securities by Public Utilities," *Financial Management,* Autumn 1978, 31–39.

Lucas, Deborah, J., and Robert L. McDonald, "Equity Issues and Stock Price Dynamics," *Journal of Finance,* September 1990, 1019–1043.

Muscarella, Chris J., and Michael R. Vetsuypens, "The Underpricing of 'Second' Initial Public Offerings," *Journal of Financial Research,* Fall 1989, 183–192.

Ritter, Jay R., "The Long-Run Performance of Initial Public Offerings," *Journal of Finance,* March 1991, 3–27.

For more information on shelf registration, see

Bhagat, Sanjai, "The Evidence on Shelf Registration," *Midland Corporate Finance Journal,* Spring 1984, 6–12.

For an excellent discussion of the various procedures used to raise capital, see

Smith, Clifford W., Jr., "Raising Capital: Theory and Evidence," *Midland Corporate Finance Journal,* Spring 1986, 6–22. Also, Pages 72–76 of the Spring 1986 issue of the *Midland Corporate Finance Journal* contain a bibliography of recent articles pertaining to investment banking and capital acquisition.

For additional discussions on preferred stock, see

Alderson, Michael J., Keith C. Brown, and Scott L. Lummer, "Dutch Auction Rate Preferred Stock," *Financial Management,* Summer 1987, 68–73.

Fooladi, Iraj, and Gordon S. Roberts, "On Preferred Stock," *Journal of Financial Research,* Winter 1986, 319–324.

Wansley, James W., Fayez A. Elayan, and Brian A. Maris, "Preferred Stock Returns, CreditWatch, and Preferred Stock Rating Changes," *The Financial Review,* May 1990, 265–285.

Winger, Bernard J., et al., "Adjustable Rate Preferred Stock," *Financial Management,* Spring 1986, 48–57.

The Spring 1990 issue of Financial Management *is devoted to Employee Stock Ownership Plans (ESOPs).*

The Spring 1993 issue of Financial Management *contains several articles on IPOs and LBOs.*

The Winter 1993 issue of the Journal of Applied Corporate Finance *is devoted to the SEC and securities regulation.*

The following cases from the Brigham-Gapenski casebook focus on the issues contained in this chapter:

Case 21, "Sun Coast Savings Bank," which illustrates the decision to go public.

Case 22, "Precision Tool Company," which emphasizes the investment banking process.

Case 23, "Art Deco Reproductions, Inc.," which focuses on the analysis of a rights offering.

LONG-TERM DEBT

O n any given day, corporations go to the markets for vast amounts of debt capital—in 1992, $779 billion of bonds alone were issued, and bonds are only one of many forms of debt financing. One good way to become familiar with the many facets of debt financing is to read the debt announcements in The Wall Street Journal. *The following debt-related actions are among the thousands that occurred during one week in March 1993:*

1. *Georgia Power Company issued $100 million of 7³⁄₈ percent first mortgage bonds due March 1, 2023. The 30-year bonds were priced at 99.2 ($992 per $1,000 par value) to yield 7.69 percent. These A-rated bonds, which are callable after 5 years, yielded 95 basis points above the 30-year T-bond.*

2. *Pacific Bell issued $625 million of 7¼ percent debentures due March 15, 2026. These 33-year bonds were priced at 98.11 to yield 7.28 percent. The AA-rated bonds, which are noncallable, yielded 55 basis points above the nearest (30-year) Treasury issue.*

3. *Scotia Pacific Holdings, a subsidiary of Pacific Lumber Company, issued $385 million of timber-collateralized notes due July 2015. Due to early principal payments, the notes have a weighted average life of less than 10 years. The issue, which is rated BBB, was priced at par to yield 7.95 percent, a spread of 188 basis points above the 10-year T-note.*

4. *General Motors Acceptance Corporation issued $1.3 billion of automobile loan asset-backed one-year certificates. The certificates, which are rated AAA and have a coupon rate of 4.15 percent, were priced at 97⅞ to yield 4.28 percent.*

5. *Standard & Poor's Corporation downgraded its rating on the debt of K-III Communications, a closely held publisher of magazines and reference materials,*

from BB to BB−. S&P cited lackluster advertising sales and weaker-than-expected debt coverage.

6. *ABN Bank of the Netherlands issued $100 million of subordinated collared floating rate Euronotes due 2005. Interest on the notes floats at ⅛ percent below the London Interbank Offered Rate with a minimum of 5⅛ percent and a maximum of 8 percent.*

7. *Navajo County Arizona announced the sinking fund call of randomly selected bonds from its 1977 Series A Pollution Control Revenue Bond issue. The selected bonds will be redeemed at 100 percent (par value) on April 15, 1993. Interest will cease to accrue after the redemption date.*

8. *Keisei Electric Railway Company of Japan issued $200 million of 1⅝ percent Eurobonds due April 2, 1997. The bonds, which were priced at par, contained warrants which permit bondholders to purchase the company's stock at a stated price until March 19, 1997. Because investors expect the firm's stock price to increase above the price stated in the warrants, the company was able to issue the bonds at a very low coupon rate.*

Why did these companies use so many different types of debt? Are there still other types? How are bond ratings determined, and how do they affect a firm's cost of debt? How does a company decide when to call a bond, or, at time of issue, whether to make a bond callable? After you read this chapter, you will have a good understanding of these issues, and many others related to debt financing.

As noted in Chapters 12 and 13, the use of debt financing is generally required to maximize the value of a firm. In this chapter, we discuss long-term debt, including its different forms, typical provisions in debt contracts, swaps, securitization, bond ratings, refunding operations, and the various factors that influence a firm's decision to use debt financing at a particular point in time.

TRADITIONAL DEBT INSTRUMENTS

There are many types of long-term debt: amortized and nonamortized, publicly issued and privately placed, secured and unsecured, marketable and nonmarketable, callable and noncallable, and so on. In this section, we review briefly the traditional long-term debt instruments and then, in the next section, we discuss some important recent innovations in long-term debt financing.

TERM LOANS

A *term loan* is a contract under which a borrower agrees to make a series of interest and principal payments, on specific dates, to a lender.[1] Investment bankers are generally not involved: Term loans are negotiated directly between the borrowing firm and a financial institution—generally a bank, an insurance company, or a pension fund. Although the maturities of term loans vary from 2 to 30 years, most are for periods in the 3- to 15-year range.

Term loans have three major advantages over public offerings—*speed, flexibility,* and *low issuance costs.* Also, because they are negotiated directly between the lender and the borrower, formal documentation is minimized. The key provisions of the loan can be worked out much more quickly, and with more flexibility, than can those for a public issue, and it is not necessary for a term loan to go through the Securities and Exchange Commission registration process. A further advantage of term loans over publicly held debt has to do with future flexibility: If a bond issue is held by many different bondholders, it is virtually impossible to alter the terms of the agreement, even though new economic conditions may make such changes desirable. With a term loan, the borrower can generally negotiate with the lender to work out modifications in the contract.

The interest rate on a term loan can be either fixed for the life of the loan or variable (floating). If it is fixed, the rate used will be close to the rate on bonds of equivalent maturity for companies of comparable risk. If the rate is variable, it is usually set at a certain number of percentage points over the prime rate, the commercial paper rate, the T-bill rate, or the London Interbank Offered Rate (LIBOR). Then, when the index rate goes up or down, so does the rate on the outstanding balance of the term loan. In 1993, about 60 percent of the dollar amount of term loans made by banks had floating rates, up from virtually zero in 1970. Most of the money banks lend to corporations is "bought" in the certificate of deposit market, and if CD rates rise along with other market rates, banks need to raise the rates they earn in order to meet their own interest costs. With the increased volatility of interest rates in recent years, banks have rightly become reluctant to make long-term, fixed rate loans.

Term loans are actually private placements of debt (as we discussed in Chapter 19), as opposed to public offerings of bonds. Typically, bonds are sold by large, well-known companies with strong financial positions. Thus, bond buyers do not need to spend much time and effort gathering information about the issuer since buyers are well aware of the company and its bond rating. Further, most bonds are not amortized, that is, no principal payments are made during the life of the issue. On the other hand, private placements usually involve smaller companies whose credit conditions must be analyzed. Credit assessment can be done easily by large banks, insurance companies, and the like, but individual investors and small institutional investors do not have this capability. Also, private placements (term loans)

---

[1] If the interest and maturity payments required under a term loan agreement are not met on schedule, the borrowing firm is said to have *defaulted,* and it can then be forced into bankruptcy.

are usually amortized in equal installments over the life of the loan. Private placements are often called *story credit*, because each placement has a "story" which explains the company's need for funds.

BONDS

Like a term loan, a bond is a long-term contract under which a borrower agrees to make payments of interest and principal, on specific dates, to the holder of the bond. Although bonds are similar to term loans, a bond issue is generally advertised, offered to the public, and actually sold to many different investors. Indeed, thousands of individual and institutional investors may participate when a firm such as New York Telephone sells a bond issue, while there is generally only one lender in the case of a term loan.[2] Although bonds are generally issued with maturities in the range of 20 to 30 years, shorter maturities, such as 7 to 10 years, are sometimes used, and Disney recently sold a 100-year issue. Unlike term loans, a bond's interest rate is generally fixed, although in recent years there has been an increase in the use of various types of floating rate bonds.

Mortgage Bonds.   Under a *mortgage bond*, the corporation pledges certain real assets as security for the bond. To illustrate, suppose McLaughlin Container Company needs $10 million in 1993 to purchase land and to build a plant. Bonds in the amount of $4 million, secured by a mortgage on the property, are issued. If McLaughlin defaults on the bonds, the bondholders could foreclose on the plant and sell it to satisfy their claims.

McLaughlin could, if it so chose, also issue *second mortgage bonds* secured by the same $10 million plant. In the event of liquidation, the holders of these second mortgage bonds would have a claim against the property only after the first mortgage bondholders had been paid off in full. Thus, second mortgages are sometimes called *junior mortgages,* or *junior liens,* because they are junior in priority to claims of *senior mortgages,* or *first mortgage bonds.*

Most major corporations' first mortgage indentures (discussed in detail later in the chapter) were written 20, 30, 40, or more years ago. These indentures are generally "open ended," meaning that new bonds may be issued from time to time under the existing indenture. However, the amount of new bonds that can be issued is virtually always limited to a specified percentage of the firm's total "bondable property," which generally includes all plant and equipment. For example, Savannah Electric Company can issue first mortgage bonds which total up to 60 percent of its fixed assets. If fixed assets totaled $100 million, and if Savannah Electric had $50 million of first mortgage bonds outstanding, then it could, by the 60 percent of property test, issue another $10 million of bonds.

---

[2]However, for very large term loans, 20 or more financial institutions may form a syndicate to grant the credit. Also, it should be noted that a bond issue can be sold to one lender (or to just a few); in this case, the issue would be a private placement.

At times, Savannah Electric has been unable to issue any new first mortgage bonds because of another indenture provision: Its times-interest-earned (TIE) ratio was below 2.5, the minimum coverage that it must maintain in order to sell new bonds. Thus, Savannah Electric passed the property test but failed the coverage test; hence, it could not issue first mortgage bonds, and it had to finance with other securities. Since first mortgage bonds carry lower rates of interest than junior long-term debt, this restriction was a costly one.

Savannah Electric's neighbor, Georgia Power Company, has more flexibility under its indenture; its interest coverage requirement is only 2.0 versus Savannah's 2.5 requirement. In hearings before the Georgia Public Service Commission, it was suggested that Savannah Electric should change its indenture coverage to 2.0 so that it could issue more first mortgage bonds. However, this was simply not possible — the holders of the outstanding bonds would have to approve the change, and it is inconceivable that they would vote for a change that would seriously weaken their position.

Debentures.   A *debenture* is an unsecured bond, and as such it has no lien against specific property as security for the obligation. Debenture holders are, therefore, general creditors whose claims are protected by property not otherwise pledged. In practice, the use of debentures depends on the nature of the firm's assets and its general credit strength. If its credit position is exceptionally strong, the firm can issue debentures — it simply does not need specific security. AT&T and General Electric have both financed mainly through debentures; they are such strong corporations that they do not have to put up property as security for their debt issues. Debentures are also issued by companies in industries where it would not be practical to provide security through a mortgage on fixed assets. Examples of such industries are the large mail-order houses and commercial banks, which characteristically hold most of their assets in the form of inventory or loans, neither of which is satisfactory security for a mortgage bond. Finally, companies that have used up their capacity to borrow in the mortgage market may be forced to use debentures. These companies' debentures will be quite risky, and their interest rates will be correspondingly high.

Subordinated Debentures.   The term *subordinate* means "below," or "inferior." Thus, *subordinated debt* has a claim on assets in the event of bankruptcy only after senior debt has been paid off. Debentures may be subordinated either to designated notes payable — usually bank loans — or to all other debt. In the event of liquidation or reorganization, holders of subordinated debentures cannot be paid until senior debt, as named in the debentures' indenture, has been paid. The subordinated debenture of a company that has used up its ability to employ mortgage bonds is normally quite risky, and these debentures carry interest rates that are up to six percentage points above the rate on top quality debt. Precisely how subordination works, and how it strengthens the position of senior debtholders, is discussed in Chapter 23.

Other Types of Bonds.   Several other types of bonds are used often enough to warrant mention. First, *convertible bonds* are securities that are convertible into shares of common stock, at a fixed price, at the option of the bondholder. Basically, convertibles provide their holders with a chance for capital gains in exchange for a lower coupon rate, while the issuing firm gets the advantage of the low coupon rate. Bonds issued with *warrants* are similar to convertibles. Warrants are options which permit the holder to buy stock for a stated price. Therefore, if the price of the stock rises, the holder of the warrant will earn a capital gain. Bonds that are issued with warrants, like convertibles, carry lower coupon rates than straight bonds. Both warrants and convertibles are discussed in detail in Chapter 22.

Income bonds pay interest only when the interest is earned. Thus, these securities cannot bankrupt a company, so from a corporation's standpoint, they are less risky than "regular" bonds. However, from an investor's standpoint, they are riskier than regular bonds. Another type of bond that has been discussed in the United States, but which has not yet been used here to any extent, is the *indexed*, or *purchasing power, bond*, which is popular in Brazil, Israel, and a few other countries long plagued by high inflation. The interest rate paid on these bonds is based on an inflation index such as the Consumer Price Index, and the interest paid rises when the inflation rate rises, thus protecting bondholders against inflation. Mexico has used bonds whose interest rate is pegged to the price of oil to finance the development of its huge petroleum reserves; since oil prices and inflation are correlated, these bonds offer some protection to investors against inflation.

Some companies may be in a position to benefit from the sale of either *development bonds* or *pollution control bonds*. State and local governments may set up both *industrial development agencies* and *pollution control agencies*. These agencies are allowed, under certain circumstances, to sell *tax-exempt bonds*, then to make the proceeds available to corporations for specific uses deemed (by Congress) to be in the public interest. Thus, an industrial development agency in Florida might sell bonds to provide funds for a paper company to build a plant in the Florida Panhandle, where unemployment is high. Similarly, a Detroit pollution control agency might sell bonds to provide Ford with funds to be used to purchase pollution control equipment. In both cases, the income from the bonds would be tax exempt to the holders, so the bonds would sell at relatively low interest rates. Note, however, that these bonds are guaranteed by the corporation that will use the funds, not by a governmental unit, so their rating reflects the credit strength of the corporation obtaining the funds.

Self-Test Question

Describe the primary features of the following debt instruments:
  (1) **Term loan; bond**
  (2) **Mortgage bond; first mortgage bond; junior mortgage**
  (3) **Debenture; subordinated debenture**
  (4) **Convertible bond; bond with warrants; income bond**
  (5) **Indexed bond; development bond; pollution control bond**

RECENT INNOVATIONS IN BOND FINANCING

The last 15 years witnessed many innovations in long-term debt financing. We will discuss seven in this section. The first three — zero coupon bonds, floating rate bonds, and bonds that are redeemable at par — are a result of the extreme volatility in interest rates which has characterized the period. The fourth, so called "junk bonds," gained popularity (some observers might say notoriety) as a source of takeover financing. The fifth and sixth, project financing and securitization, permit a firm to tie a debt issue to a specific asset. The final innovation, swaps, permits firms to change the nature of their debt obligations by trading them with other firms.

ZERO (OR VERY LOW) COUPON BONDS

Some bonds pay no interest but are offered at a substantial discount below their par values and hence provide capital appreciation rather than interest income. These securities are called *zero coupon bonds ("zeros"),* or *original issue discount bonds (OIDs).* Corporations first used zeros in a major way in 1981. In recent years IBM, Alcoa, J. C. Penney, ITT, Cities Service, GMAC, Martin-Marietta, and many other companies have used them to raise billions of dollars. Municipal governments also sell "zero munis," and investment bankers have in effect created zero coupon Treasury bonds.

To understand how zeros are used and analyzed, consider the zeros that are going to be issued by Vandenberg Corporation, a shopping center developer. Vandenberg is developing a new shopping center in Orange County, California, and it needs $50 million. The company does not anticipate major cash flows from the project for about 5 years. However, Pieter Vandenberg, the president, plans to sell the center once it is fully developed and rented, which should take about 5 years. Therefore, Vandenberg wants to use a financing vehicle that will not require cash outflows for 5 years, and he has decided on a 5-year zero coupon bond, with a maturity value of $1,000.

Vandenberg Corporation is an A-rated company, and A-rated zeros with 5-year maturities yield 9 percent at this time (5-year coupon bonds also yield 9 percent). The company is in the 40 percent federal-plus-state tax bracket. Pieter Vandenberg wants to know the firm's after-tax cost of capital if it uses 9 percent, 5-year maturity zeros, and he also wants to know what the bond's cash flows will be. Table 20-1 provides an analysis of the situation, and the following numbered paragraphs explain the table itself.

1. The information in the "Basic Data" section, except the issue price, was given in the preceding paragraph, and the information in the "Analysis" section was calculated using the known data. The maturity value of the bond is always set at $1,000 or some multiple thereof.

2. The issue price is the PV of $1,000, discounted back 5 years at the rate $k_d = 9\%$. Using a financial calculator, we input N = 5, I = 9, and FV = 1000, then press the PV key to find PV = $649.93. Note that $649.93, compounded

TABLE 20-1

ANALYSIS OF A ZERO COUPON BOND

Basic Data

Maturity value	$1,000
k_d	9.00%
Maturity	5 years
Corporate tax rate	40.00%
Issue price	$649.93

Analysis

	Years					
	0	1	2	3	4	5
(1) Year-end accrued value	649.93	708.42	772.18	841.68	917.43	1,000.00
(2) Interest deduction		58.49	63.76	69.50	75.75	82.57
(3) Tax savings (40%)		23.40	25.50	27.80	30.30	33.03
(4) Cash flow	+649.93	+23.40	+25.50	+27.80	+30.30	−966.97

After-tax cost of debt = 5.40%.

Number of $1,000 zeros the company must issue to raise $50 million = Amount needed/Price per bond

= $50,000,000/$649.93

= 76,931 bonds.

annually for 5 years at 9 percent, will grow to $1,000 as shown on the time line in Table 20-1.

3.   The accrued values as shown on Line 1 in the analysis section represent the compounded value of the bond at the end of each year. The accrued value for Year 0 is the issue price; the accrued value for Year 1 is found as $649.93(1.09)^1 = $708.42; the accrued value at the end of Year 2 is $649.93(1.09)^2 = $772.18; and, in general, the value at the end of any Year n is

$$\text{Accrued value at the end of Year n} = \text{Issue price} \times (1 + k_d)^n.$$

4.   The interest deduction as shown on Line 2 represents the increase in accrued value during the year. Thus, interest in Year 1 = $708.42 − $649.93 = $58.49. In general,

$$\text{Interest in Year n} = \text{Accrued value}_n - \text{Accrued value}_{n-1}.$$

This method of calculating taxable interest is specified in the Tax Code.

5.   The company can deduct interest each year, even though the payment is not made in cash. This deduction lowers the taxes that would otherwise be paid, producing the following savings:

> Tax savings = (Interest deduction)(T)

$$= \$58.49(0.4)$$

$$= \$23.40 \text{ in Year } 1.$$

6. Line 4 represents cash flows on a time line; it shows the cash flow at the end of Years 0 through 5. At Year 0, the company receives the $649.93 issue price. The company also has positive cash inflows equal to the tax savings during Years 1 through 4. Finally, in Year 5, it must pay the $1,000 maturity value, but it gets one more interest tax saving for the year. Therefore, the net cash flow in Year 5 is $-\$1,000 + \$33.03 = -\$966.97$.

7. We can find the IRR of the cash flows shown on Line 4 using the IRR function of a financial calculator by simply inputting the annual cash flows in the cash flow register; the IRR is the after-tax cost of zero coupon debt to the company. Conceptually, here is the situation:

$$\sum_{t=0}^{n} \frac{CF_n}{(1 + k_{d(AT)})^n} = 0.$$

$$\frac{\$649.93}{(1 + k_{d(AT)})^0} + \frac{\$23.40}{(1 + k_{d(AT)})^1} + \frac{\$25.50}{(1 + k_{d(AT)})^2} + \frac{\$27.80}{(1 + k_{d(AT)})^3} + \frac{\$30.30}{(1 + k_{d(AT)})^4} + \frac{-\$966.97}{(1 + k_{d(AT)})^5} = 0.$$

The value $k_{d(AT)} = 0.054 = 5.4\%$, found with a financial calculator, produces the equality, and it is the after-tax cost of the zero coupon bond.

8. Note that $k_d(1 - T) = 9\%(0.6) = 5.4\%$. As we saw in Chapter 8, the cost of capital for regular coupon debt is found using the formula $k_d(1 - T)$. Thus, there is symmetrical treatment for tax purposes for zero coupon and regular coupon debt; that is, both types of debt have the same after-tax cost effects. This was Congress's intent, and it is why the Tax Code specifies the treatment set forth in Table 20-1.[3]

---

[3]The purchaser of a zero coupon bond must calculate interest income on the bond in the same manner as the issuer calculates the interest deduction. Thus, in Year 1, a buyer of a bond would report interest income of $58.49 and would pay taxes in the amount of T(Interest income), even though no cash was received. T, of course, would be the bondholder's personal tax rate. Because of the tax situation, most zero coupon bonds are bought by pension funds and other tax-exempt entities. Individuals do, however, buy taxable zeros for their Individual Retirement Accounts (IRAs). Also, state and local governments issue "tax exempt muni zeros," which are purchased by individuals in high tax brackets.

Note too that we have analyzed the bond as if the cash flows accrued annually. Generally, to facilitate comparisons with semiannual payment coupon bonds, the analysis is conducted on a semiannual basis.

Not all original issue discount bonds (OIDs) have zero coupons. For example, Vandenberg might have sold an issue of 5-year bonds with a 5 percent coupon at a time when other bonds with similar ratings and maturities were yielding 9 percent. Such a bond would have had a value of $844.41:

$$\text{Bond value} = \sum_{t=1}^{5} \frac{\$50}{(1.09)^t} + \frac{\$1,000}{(1.09)^5} = \$844.41.$$

If an investor had purchased these bonds at a price of $844.41, the yield to maturity would have been 9 percent. The discount of $1,000 − $844.41 = $155.59 would have been amortized over the bond's 5-year life, and it would have been handled by both Vandenberg and the bondholders exactly as the discount on the zeros was handled.

Thus, zero coupon bonds are just one type of original issue discount bond. Any nonconvertible bond whose coupon rate is set below the going market rate at the time of its issue will sell at a discount, and it will be classified (for tax and other purposes) as an OID bond.

Shortly after corporations began to issue zeros, investment bankers figured out a way to create zeros from U.S. Treasury bonds, which are issued only in coupon form. In 1983 Salomon Brothers bought $1 billion of 7 percent, 30-year Treasuries. Each bond had 60 coupons worth $35 each, which represented the interest payments due every 6 months. Salomon then in effect clipped the coupons and placed them in 60 piles; the last pile also contained the now "stripped" bond itself, which represented a promise of $1,000 in the year 2013. These 60 piles of U.S. Treasury promises were then placed with the trust department of a bank and used as collateral for "zero coupon U.S. Treasury Trust Certificates," which are, in essence, zero coupon Treasury bonds. A pension fund that expected to need money in 2004 could have bought 11-year certificates backed by the interest the Treasury will pay in 2004. Treasury zeros are, of course, safer than corporate zeros, so they are very popular with pension fund managers.

Corporate (and municipal) zeros are generally callable at the option of the issuer, just like coupon bonds, after some stated call protection period. The call price is set at a premium over the accrued value at the time of the call. Stripped U.S. Treasury bonds (Treasury zeros) generally are not callable because the Treasury normally sells noncallable bonds. Thus, Treasury zeros are completely protected against reinvestment risk (the risk of having to invest cash flows from a bond at a lower rate because of a decline in interest rates).

Floating Rate Debt

In the early 1980s, inflation pushed interest rates up to unprecedented levels, causing sharp declines in the prices of long-term bonds. Even some supposedly "risk-free" U.S. Treasury bonds lost fully half their value, and a similar situation occurred with corporate bonds, mortgages, and other fixed-rate, long-term securities. As a

result, many lenders became reluctant to lend money at fixed rates on a long-term basis, and they would do so only at extraordinarily high rates.

There is normally a *maturity risk premium* embodied in long-term interest rates; this premium is designed to offset the risk of declining bond prices if interest rates rise. Prior to the 1970s, the maturity risk premium on 30-year bonds was about one percentage point, meaning that under normal conditions, a firm might expect to pay about one percentage point more to borrow on a long-term than on a short-term basis. However, in the early 1980s, the maturity risk premium is estimated to have jumped to about three percentage points, which made long-term debt very expensive relative to short-term debt. Lenders were able and willing to lend on a short-term basis, but corporations were correctly reluctant to borrow on a short-term basis to finance long-term assets — such action is extremely dangerous. Therefore, there was a situation in which lenders did not want to lend on a long-term basis, but corporations needed long-term money. The problem was solved by the introduction of long-term, floating rate debt.

A typical *floating rate bond* works as follows. The coupon rate is set for, say, the initial six-month period, after which it is adjusted every six months based on some market rate. Some corporate issues have been tied to the Treasury bond rate, while other issues have been tied to short-term rates. Many additional provisions can be included in floating rate issues; for example, some are convertible to fixed rate debt, whereas others have limits ("caps," "floors," and "collars") on how high or low the yield can go.

Floating rate debt is advantageous to investors because the interest rate moves up if market rates rise. This causes the market value of the debt to be stabilized, and it also provides lenders such as banks with income which is better geared to their own obligations. (Banks' deposit costs rise with interest rates, so the income on floating rate loans rises just when banks' deposit costs are rising.) Moreover, floating rate debt is advantageous to corporations because by using it, firms can issue debt with a long maturity without committing themselves to paying a historically high rate of interest for the entire life of the loan. Of course, if interest rates were to move even higher after a floating rate note had been signed, the borrower would have been better off issuing conventional, fixed rate debt.

BONDS THAT ARE REDEEMABLE AT PAR

Bonds that are *redeemable at par* at the holder's option also protect the holder against a rise in interest rates. If rates rise, the price of fixed-rate debt declines. However, if the holders have the option of turning their bonds in and having them redeemed at par, they are protected against rising rates. Examples of such debt include Transamerica's $50 million issue of 25-year, 8½ percent bonds. The bonds are not callable by the company, but holders can turn them in for redemption at par five years after the date of issue. If interest rates have risen, holders will turn in the bonds and reinvest the proceeds at a higher rate. This feature enabled Transamerica to sell the bonds with an 8½ percent coupon at a time when other similarly rated bonds had yields of 9 percent.

In late 1988, the corporate bond markets were sent into turmoil by a leveraged buyout of RJR Nabisco. RJR's bonds dropped in value by 20 percent within days of the LBO announcement, and the prices of many industrial corporate bonds also plunged, because investors feared that a boom in LBOs would load up many companies with excessive debt, leading to lower bond ratings and declining bond prices. All this led to a resurgence of concern about *event risk,* which is the risk that some sudden action, such as an LBO, will occur and increase the credit risk of the company, hence lower the firm's bond rating and the value of its outstanding bonds. Investors' concern over event risk meant that those firms deemed most likely to face events that could harm bondholders suddenly had to pay dearly to raise new debt capital, if they could raise it at all. In an attempt to control debt costs, a new type of protective covenant devised to minimize event risk was developed. This covenant, called a *super poison put,* enables a bondholder to turn in, or "put" a bond back to the issuer at par in the event of a takeover, merger, or major recapitalization.

Poison puts had actually been around since 1986, when the leveraged buyout trend took off. However, the earlier puts proved to be almost worthless because they allowed investors to "put" their bonds back to the issuer at par value only in the event of an *unfriendly* takeover, but almost all takeovers were eventually approved by the target firm's board, hence what started as a hostile takeover generally ended up as a friendly takeover. Also, the earlier poison puts failed to protect investors from voluntary recapitalizations, in which a company loads up on debt to pay a big, one-time dividend to stockholders or to buy back its own stock. The "super" poison puts that were used following the RJR buyout announcement protected against both of these actions. It is too early to say whether super poison puts are here to stay, but their use does provide a good illustration of how quickly the financial community reacts to changes in the marketplace.

JUNK BONDS

Prior to the 1980s, fixed income investors such as pension funds and insurance companies were generally unwilling to buy risky bonds, so it was almost impossible for risky companies to raise capital in the public bond markets. These companies, if they could raise debt capital at all, had to do so in the term loan market, where the loan could be tailored to satisfy the lender. Then, in the late 1970s, Michael Milken of the investment banking firm Drexel Burnham Lambert, relying on historical studies which showed that risky bonds yielded more than enough to compensate for their risk, began to convince certain institutional investors of the merits of purchasing risky debt. Thus was born the *junk bond,* a high-risk, high-yield bond issued to finance a leveraged buyout, a merger, or a troubled company.[4] For example, when Ted Turner attempted to buy CBS, he planned to finance the

---

[4]For an excellent discussion of junk bonds, see Kevin J. Perry and Robert A. Taggart, Jr., "The Growing Role of Junk Bonds in Corporate Finance," *Journal of Applied Corporate Finance,* Spring 1988, 37–45. This section draws heavily from their work.

acquisition by issuing junk bonds to CBS's stockholders in exchange for their shares. Similarly, Public Service of New Hampshire financed construction of its troubled Seabrook nuclear plant with junk bonds, and junk bonds were used in the RJR Nabisco LBO. In junk bond deals, the debt ratio is generally extremely high, so the bondholders must bear as much risk as stockholders normally would. The bonds' yields reflect this fact—a coupon rate of 25 percent per annum was required to sell the Public Service of New Hampshire bonds.

The emergence of junk bonds as an important type of debt is another example of how the investment banking industry adjusts to and facilitates new developments in capital markets. In the 1980s, mergers and takeovers increased dramatically. People like T. Boone Pickens and Ted Turner thought that certain old-line, established companies were run inefficiently and were financed too conservatively, and they wanted to take these companies over and restructure them. Michael Milken and his staff at Drexel Burnham Lambert began an active campaign to persuade certain institutions (often S&Ls) to purchase high-yield bonds. Milken developed expertise in putting together deals that were attractive to the institutions yet apparently feasible in the sense that projected cash flows were sufficient to meet the required interest payments. The fact that interest on the bonds was tax deductible, combined with the much higher debt ratios of the restructured firms, also increased after-tax cash flows and helped make the deals appear feasible.

The development of junk bond financing has done as much as any single factor to reshape the U.S. financial scene. The existence of these securities led directly to the loss of independence of Gulf Oil and hundreds of other companies, and it led to major shake-ups in such companies as CBS, Union Carbide, and USX (formerly U.S. Steel). It also caused Drexel Burnham Lambert to leap from essentially nowhere in the 1970s to become the most profitable investment banking firm during the 1980s.

The phenomenal growth of the junk bond market was impressive, but controversial. In early 1989, Drexel Burnham Lambert was forced into bankruptcy, and "junk bond king" Michael Milken was jailed. These events badly tarnished the junk bond market, which also came under severe criticism for fueling takeover fires and adding to the cost of the S&L bailout. Additionally, the realization that high leverage can spell trouble—as when Campeau, with $3 billion in junk financing, filed for bankruptcy in early 1990—has slowed the growth in the junk bond market.

Do junk bonds have a future role in corporate finance aside from takeovers and LBOs? In Chapter 13, we discussed the signaling theory of capital structure, which implies that companies should first use retained earnings plus debt supported by retained earnings, then use "reserve borrowing capacity" debt, and only issue new common stock as a last resort, after all the debt capacity has been exhausted. The development of the junk bond market has effectively extended the limits of firms' debt capacities beyond the earlier limits, and in spite of all the publicity surrounding the use of junk bonds in mergers and acquisitions, statistics show that well over half of the junk bond issues in recent years have been used for normal expansion purposes.

The final verdict on junk bonds is not yet in. However, at this point it appears that junk bonds will play a smaller role in corporate financings in the 1990s than

they did in the 1980s, but that they will remain an important part of the financial scene.

PROJECT FINANCING

In recent years, many large projects such as the Alaska pipeline have been financed by what is called *project financing.*[5] We can only present an overview of the concept, for in practice it involves very complicated provisions and can take many forms.

Project financing has been used to finance energy explorations, oil tankers, refineries, and utility power plants. Generally, one or more firms will sponsor the project, putting up the required equity capital, while the remainder of the financing is furnished by lenders or lessors.[6] Most often, a separate legal entity is formed to operate the project. The single most important feature of project financing is that normally the project's creditors do not have full recourse against the sponsors. In other words, the lenders and lessors must be paid from the project's cash flows, plus the sponsors' equity in the project, for the creditors have no claims against the sponsors' other assets or cash flows. Often the sponsors write "comfort" letters, giving general assurances that they will strive diligently to make the project successful, but these letters are not legally binding and therefore represent only a moral commitment. Therefore, in project financing the lenders and lessors must focus their analysis on the inherent merits of the project plus the equity cushion provided by the sponsors.[7]

Project financing is not a new development. Indeed, back in 1299, the English Crown negotiated a loan with Florentine merchant bankers that was repaid with one year's output from the Devon silver mines. Essentially, the Italians were allowed to operate the mines for one year, paying all the operating costs and mining as much ore as they could. The Crown made no guarantes as to how much ore could be mined, or the value of the refined silver. A more current example involved GE Capital, the credit arm of General Electric, which recently arranged a $72 million project financing to build an aluminum can plant. The plant is owned by several beverage makers, but it is operated independently, and GE Capital must depend on the cash flows from the plant to repay the loan. About half of all project

---

[5]For an excellent discussion of project financing, see John W. Kensinger and John D. Martin, "Project Finance: Raising Money the Old-Fashioned Way," *Journal of Applied Corporate Finance,* Fall 1988, 69–81.

[6]A lessor is an individual or firm that owns buildings and equipment and then leases them to another firm. Leasing is discussed in Chapter 21.

[7]In another type of project financing, each sponsor guarantees its share of the project's debt obligations. Here the creditors would also consider the creditworthiness of the sponsors in addition to the project's own prospects. It should be noted that project financing with multiple sponsors in the electric utility industry has led to problems when one or more of the sponsors has gotten into financial trouble. For example, Long Island Lighting, one of the sponsors in the Nine Mile Point nuclear project, became unable to meet its commitments to the project, which forced other sponsors to shoulder an additional burden or else see the project cancelled and lose all their investment up to that point. Utility executives have stated that this default, and others, will make companies reluctant to enter into similar projects in the future.

financings in recent years have been for electric generating plants, including both plants owned by electric utilities and cogeneration plants operated by industrial companies. Project financings are generally characterized by large size and a high degree of complexity. However, since project financing is tied to a specific project, it can be tailored to meet the specific needs of both the creditors and the sponsors. In particular, the financing can be structured so that both the funds provided during the construction phase and the subsequent repayments match the timing of the project's projected cash outflows and inflows.

Project financing offers several potential benefits over conventional debt financing. For one, project financing usually restricts the usage of the project's cash flows, which means that the lenders, rather than the managers, can decide whether to reinvest excess cash flows or to use them to reduce the loan balance by more than the minimum required. Conferring this power on the lenders reduces their risks. Project financings also have advantages for borrowers. First, because risks to the lenders are reduced, the interest rate built into a project financing deal may be relatively low. Second, since suppliers of project financing capital have no recourse against the sponsoring firms' other assets and cash flows, project financings insulate the firm's other assets from risks associated with the project being financed. Managers may be more willing to take on a very large, risky project if they know that the company's existence would not be threatened if it fails.

Project financings increase the number and type of investment opportunities, hence they make capital markets "more complete." At the same time, project financings reduce the costs to investors of obtaining information and monitoring the borrower's operations. To illustrate, consider an oil and gas exploration project that is funded using project financing. If the project were financed as an integral part of the firm's normal operations, investors in all the firm's outstanding securities would need information on the project. By isolating the project, the need for information is confined to the investors in the project financing, and they need to monitor only the project's operations, and not those of the entire firm.

Project financings also permit firms whose earnings are below the minimum requirements specified in their existing bond indentures to obtain additional debt financing. In such situations, lenders look only at the merits of the new project, and its cash flows may support additional debt even though the firm's existing assets would not. Project financings also permit managers to reveal proprietary information to a smaller group of investors, hence project financings increase the ability of a firm to maintain confidentiality. Finally, project financings can improve incentives for key managers by enabling them to take direct ownership stakes in the operations under their control. By establishing separate projects, companies can provide incentives that are much more directly based upon individual performance than is typically possible within a large corporation.

SECURITIZATION

As the term is generally used, a *security* refers to a publicly traded financial instrument, as opposed to a privately placed instrument. Thus, securities have greater liquidity than otherwise similar instruments that are not traded in an open market.

In recent years, procedures have been developed to *securitize* various types of debt instruments, thus increasing their liquidity, lowering the cost of capital to borrowers, and generally increasing the efficiency of the financial markets.[8]

Securitization has occurred in two major ways. First, some debt instruments that were formerly never traded in a broad market are now widely traded, with the change being due to decisions by certain financial institutions to "make a market," which means to stand willing to buy or sell the security, and to hold an inventory of the security in order to balance buy and sell orders. This occurred many years ago in the case of common stocks and investment-grade bonds. More recently, it occurred in the commercial paper market, in which large, financially strong firms issue short-term, unsecured debt in lieu of obtaining bank loans. The commercial paper market has grown from about $50 billion outstanding in the mid-1970s to over $350 billion today, and this market permits borrowers to finance working capital needs at lower cost than bank loans.

Another example of securitization is the junk bond market. Before this market developed, firms with high credit risk were forced to obtain debt financing on a private placement basis, typically supplied by the firm's commercial bank. It was difficult for firms to shop around for the best rate, because lenders who were not familiar with them were unwilling to spend the time and money necessary to determine the feasibility of the loan, and lenders were also reluctant (and hence charged a higher rate) because of the illiquidity of privately placed debt. Then, Michael Milken developed procedures for analyzing the repayment feasibility of junk bonds, and Drexel Burnham Lambert put its reputation and credibility behind these issues and made a market for them in case a purchaser needed to cash out. Subsequently, Morgan Stanley, Merrill Lynch, Salomon Brothers, and the other major investment bankers entered the junk bond market, and today it has "securitized" much of the old private placement market for below-investment-grade debt.

The second major development in securitization involves the pledging of specific assets, *asset securitization,* or the creation of *asset-backed securities.* The oldest type of asset securitization is the mortgage-backed security. Here, individual home mortgages are combined into pools, and then bonds are created which use the pool of mortgages as collateral. The financial institution that originated the mortgage generally continues to act as collection agent, but the mortgage itself is sold to other investors. The securitization of mortgages has created a national mortgage market with many players, hence it has benefited borrowers. The development has also benefited lenders, for the original lending institution, often a savings and loan, no longer owns the relatively long-term mortgage, hence it is better able to match the maturity of its assets (loans) with its liabilities (savings accounts and certificates of deposit). Today, many different types of assets are being used as collateral for securitization, including auto loans and credit card balances.

The asset securitization process involves the pooling and repackaging of loans secured by relatively homogeneous, small-dollar assets into liquid securities. In the

---

[8]The Fall 1988 issue of the *Journal of Applied Corporate Finance* is devoted to securitization. For additional discussion, see any of its excellent articles.

past, such financing was provided by a single lending institution, which would write the loan, structure the terms, absorb the credit and interest rate risk, provide the capital, and service the collections. Under securitization, several different institutions are involved, with each playing a different functional role. A savings and loan might originate the loan, an investment banker might pool the loans and structure the security, a federal agency might insure against credit risk, a second investment banker might sell the securities, and a pension fund might be the investor which supplies the final capital.

In early 1992, the Resolution Trust Corporation (RTC), the federal government's savings and loan cleanup agency, announced it was selling $528 million of debt securities backed by mortgages on small office buildings and stores. The deal —the first of its kind for the RTC—not only rid the government of more assets from failed thrift institutions but also blazed the trail for a new type of security. More than $1 trillion in home mortgages had been securitized through agencies such as the Federal National Mortgage Association (FNMA, or Fannie Mae), but this was the first effort in securitizing commercial mortgages. Since commercial mortgages are more varied in size and terms than home mortgages, they are more difficult to pool and sell as uniform securities. To be rated highly by the rating agencies, the RTC had to create a $150 million reserve fund—about 30 percent of the offering—which was used to cover any defaults that occured on the original loans. Moreover, the securities offered were in three classes, each with a specific degree of risk. The agency likes such deals, because they permit the government to quickly liquidate assets, and they limit risk to the amount of funds put into reserve.

The process of securitization has, in general, lowered costs and increased the availability of funds to borrowers, decreased risks to lenders, and created new investment opportunities for many investors. With these potential benefits, we predict that securitization will continue to expand in the future.

SWAPS

As its name implies, a *swap* is an exchange.[9] In finance, a swap is an exchange of cash payment obligations, in which each party to the swap, often called a "counterparty," prefers the payment type or pattern of the other party. In other words, swaps occur because the parties involved prefer the terms of someone else's debt contract, and the swap enables each party to obtain a more desirable payment obligation. Generally, one party has a fixed rate obligation and the other a floating rate obligation, or else one obligation is denominated in one currency and the other in another.

The earliest swaps were *currency swaps,* in which one company, say, with a debt obligation in British pounds, trades its interest payment obligation with another company that had dollar-denominated debt. To illustrate, suppose a U.S. firm

---

[9]For more information on swaps, see Clifford W. Smith, Jr., Charles W. Smithson, and Lee Macdonald Wakeman, "The Evolving Market for Swaps," *Midland Corporate Finance Journal,* Winter 1986, 20–32; and Mary E. Ruth and Steve R. Vinson, "Managing Interest Rate Uncertainty Amidst Change," *Public Utilities Fortnightly,* December 22, 1988, 28–31.

is expanding into England. It might prefer to issue debt denominated in pounds to fund the venture—this would remove any currency risk, since the cash flows generated by the project and available to service the debt would be in pounds. However, the firm may not be well known in England, and thus it might have trouble placing debt there at a reasonable cost because of the time and effort English lenders would have to expend to gather the necessary credit information. In this case, it might be cheaper for the firm to issue debt denominated in dollars in the United States to fund the British effort, and then to arrange a currency swap. In the swap, the U.S. firm would agree to make interest payments in pounds to a counterparty who, in return, would agree to pay the firm a series of interest payments in dollars, which would then be used to service the original dollar-denominated debt. The firm would, in effect, have converted dollar-denominated debt to pound-denominated debt, and the exchange rate risk would have been removed, because the source of the cash flows for the interest payments would be the firm's British operation, whose cash flows would be denominated in pounds. If the firm had not engaged in the swap, then the pounds generated by the British operation would have to be converted to dollars to make the interest payments to the U.S. bondholders, and a change in the exchange rate could increase the effective cost of the debt, and perhaps render the entire operation unprofitable. The motivation for the counterparty would be similar, but a mirror image of the first party; for example, the counterparty might be a British firm expanding into the United States.

The earliest currency swaps were custom-tailored products which involved matching two firms that wanted to trade a given principal amount of debt denominated in two different currencies. The swaps were typically arranged by a financial intermediary, usually a commercial or investment banker, and a great deal of time was spent matching the counterparties and developing terms that were mutually agreeable to the participants. The intermediaries themselves typically were not counterparties in the early deals—they merely arranged the swap and were paid a fee for their efforts. However, the swap market has evolved considerably over the last decade, and now there are several different types of swaps. In addition to currency swaps, some of the more common types are (1) interest rate swaps, in which the counterparties trade fixed rate debt for floating rate debt; (2) basis rate swaps, in which the counterparties both hold floating rate debt, but the basis differs, say, with one being tied to the T-bill rate and the other tied to the commercial paper rate; and (3) timing swaps, where, for example, one party would trade a stream of quarterly payments to a counterparty which makes annual payments.

Other major changes have occurred in the swaps market. First, standardized contracts have been developed for the most common types of swaps, and this had two effects: (1) Standardized contracts lower the time and effort involved in arranging swaps, and thus lower transactions costs. (2) The development of standardized contracts has led to a secondary market for swaps, which increased the liquidity and efficiency of the swaps market. Thus, swaps are becoming a commodity-type item, and a number of international banks now make markets in swaps and offer quotes on several standard types. Finally, the intermediaries now take counterparty positions in swaps, and thus it is not necessary to find another firm with matching needs before a swap transaction can be completed. The intermediary

would generally find a final counterparty for the swap at a later date, so intermediary positioning helps make the swap market more operationally efficient.

To further illustrate a swap transaction, consider the following situation. An electric utility currently has outstanding a 5-year floating rate note tied to the prime rate. The prime rate could rise significantly over the period, so the note carries a high degree of interest rate risk to the utility. The utility could, however, enter into a swap with a counterparty, say, Citibank, wherein the utility would pay Citibank a fixed series of interest payments over the 5-year period, and Citibank would make the company's required floating rate payments. As a result, the utility would have converted a floating rate loan to a fixed rate loan, and the risk of rising interest rates would have been passed from the utility to Citibank. Note, though, that a bank's income tends to rise as interest rates rise, so Citibank's risk is actually lower if it has floating as opposed to fixed rate obligations.

Longer-term swaps can also be made. Recently, Citibank entered into a 17-year swap in an electricity cogeneration project financing deal. The project's sponsors were unable to obtain fixed rate financing on reasonable terms, and they were afraid that interest rates might rise to the point where the project would be unprofitable. The project's sponsors were, however, able to borrow from local banks on a floating rate basis and to arrange a simultaneous swap with Citibank for a fixed rate obligation.

SELF-TEST QUESTIONS

What are zero coupon bonds? What are their advantages and disadvantages for issuers and purchasers?

What is the difference between fixed rate and floating rate debt? What are the advantages and disadvantages of floating rate debt for issuers and purchasers?

What are super poison puts, and how do they lower event risk?

Briefly describe the characteristics and role of junk bonds.

What is project financing? What are its advantages and disadvantages?

What is meant by securitization? What are the advantages of securitization to borrowers? What are the advantages to lenders?

What is a swap? Briefly describe the mechanics of (1) a fixed rate to floating rate swap and (2) a currency swap.

DEBT CONTRACT PROVISIONS

When they take on debt, a firm's managers are most concerned about (1) the effective cost of the debt and (2) any provisions which might restrict the firm's future actions. In this section, we discuss features which could have an effect either on the cost of the firm's debt or on its future flexibility.

BOND INDENTURES

An *indenture* is a legal document that spells out the rights of both bondholders and the issuing corporation, and a *trustee* is an official (usually of a bank) who represents the bondholders and makes sure that the terms of the indenture are carried out. The indenture may be several hundred pages in length, and it will include *restrictive covenants* that cover such points as the conditions under which the issuer can pay off the bonds prior to maturity, the level at which the issuer's times-interest-earned ratio must be maintained if the company is to issue additional debt, and restrictions against the payment of dividends unless earnings meet certain specifications. Overall, these covenants relate to the agency problem first discussed in Chapter 1, and they are designed to ensure, insofar as possible, that the firm does not change its financial policies in a way that would cause the quality of its bonds to deteriorate after they have been issued.

The trustee is responsible for trying to keep the covenants from being violated and for taking appropriate action if a violation does occur. What constitutes "appropriate action" varies with the circumstances. It might be that to insist on immediate compliance would result in bankruptcy and possibly large losses on the bonds. In such a case, the trustee might decide that the bondholders would be better served by giving the company a chance to work out its problems and thus avoid forcing it into bankruptcy.

The Securities and Exchange Commission (1) approves indentures and (2) makes sure that all indenture provisions are met before allowing a company to sell new securities to the public. Also, it should be noted that the indentures of most larger corporations were actually written in the 1930s or 1940s, and that many issues of new bonds sold since then were covered by the same indenture. The interest rates on the bonds, and perhaps also the maturities, varies depending on market conditions at the time of each issue, but bondholders' protection as spelled out in the indenture is the same for all bonds of the same type.[10]

CALL PROVISIONS

A *call provision* gives the issuing corporation the right to call a bond (or preferred stock) for redemption. If it is used, the call provision generally states that the company must pay an amount greater than the par value for the bond. The additional sum required, defined as the *call premium,* is typically set equal to one year's interest if the bond is called during the first year, with the premium declining at a constant rate of I/n each year thereafter, where I = annual interest and n = original maturity in years. For example, the call premium on a $1,000 par value, 20-year, 10 percent bond would generally be $100 if it were called during the first year, $95 during the second year (calculated by reducing the $100, or 10 percent, premium by one-twentieth), and so on.

The call privilege is valuable to the firm but potentially detrimental to the investor, especially if the bond is issued in a period when interest rates are cycli-

---

[10]A firm will have different indentures for each of the major types of bonds it issues. For example, one indenture will cover its first mortgage bonds, another its debentures, and a third its convertible bonds.

cally high. This point was illustrated in Chapter 7, and it causes the interest rate on a new issue of callable bonds to exceed that on a new issue of noncallable bonds. For example, on February 1, 1993, Great Falls Timber Company sold an issue of A-rated bonds to yield 8.375 percent. These bonds were callable immediately. On the same day, Midwest Milling Company sold an issue of A-rated bonds to yield 8 percent. Midwest's bonds were noncallable for 10 years. (This is known as a *deferred call.*) Investors were apparently willing to accept a 0.375 percent lower interest rate on Midwest's bonds for the assurance that the rate of interest would be earned for at least 10 years. Great Falls, on the other hand, had to incur a 0.375 percent higher annual interest rate to obtain the option of calling the bonds in the event of a subsequent decline in interest rates. We discuss the analysis for determining when to call an issue in Appendix 20A.

SINKING FUNDS

A *sinking fund* is a provision that provides for the systematic retirement of a bond issue (or an issue of preferred stock). Typically, the sinking fund provision requires a firm to call and retire a portion of its bonds each year. On some occasions, the firm may be required to deposit money with a trustee, who invests the funds and then uses the accumulated sum to retire the entire bond issue when it matures. Sometimes the stipulated sinking fund payment is tied to the sales or earnings of the current year, but usually it is a mandatory fixed amount. If it is mandatory, a failure to meet the sinking fund requirement causes the bond issue to be thrown into default, which may force the company into bankruptcy.

In most cases, the firm is given the right to handle the sinking fund in either of two ways:

1. It may call in for redemption (at par value) a certain percentage of the bonds each year—for example, it might be able to call 2 percent of the total original amount of the issue at a price of $1,000 per bond. The bonds are numbered serially, and the ones called for redemption are determined by a lottery. (For bonds issued in denominations of $100,000 or more, the specified percentage of the holder's par value is called.)

2. It may buy the required amount of bonds on the open market.

The firm will choose the least cost method. Therefore, if interest rates have risen, causing bond prices to fall, the company will elect to use the option of buying bonds in the open market at a discount. Otherwise, it will call them. Note that a call for sinking fund purposes is quite different from a refunding call. A sinking fund call requires no call premium, but only a small percentage of the issue is callable in any one year.

Although the sinking fund is designed to protect the bondholders by assuring that the issue is retired in an orderly fashion, it must be recognized that the sinking fund may at times work to the detriment of bondholders. If, for example, the bond carries a 10 percent interest rate, and if yields on similar securities have fallen to 8 percent, then the bond will sell above par. A sinking fund call at par would thus greatly disadvantage those bondholders whose bonds were called. On balance,

however, securities that provide for a sinking fund and continuing redemption are regarded as being safer than bonds without sinking funds, so adding a sinking fund provision to a bond issue will lower the interest rate on the bond.

SELF-TEST QUESTIONS

What is a bond indenture? A restrictive covenant?

What is a call provision? What impact does a call provision have on an issue's required rate of return?

What is a sinking fund? How are bonds retired for sinking fund purposes?

What impact does a sinking fund have on an issue's required rate of return? How do sinking funds differ from call provisions?

BOND RATINGS

Since the early 1900s, bonds have been assigned quality ratings that reflect their probability of going into default. The two major rating agencies are Moody's Investors Service (Moody's) and Standard & Poor's Corporation (S&P). These agencies' rating designations are shown in Table 20-2.[11]

The triple and double A bonds are extremely safe. Single A and triple B bonds are strong enough to be called "investment grade," and they are the lowest rated bonds that many banks and other institutional investors are permitted by law to hold. Double B and lower bonds are speculations; they are junk bonds with a fairly high probability of going into default, and many financial institutions are prohibited from buying them.

BOND RATING CRITERIA

Although the rating assignments are subjective, they are based on both qualitative characteristics such as "quality of management" and quantitative factors such as the debt ratio, the coverage ratio, and so forth. Analysts at the rating agencies have consistently stated that no precise formula is used to set a firm's rating—many factors are taken into account, but not in a mathematically precise manner. Statistical studies have borne out this contention. Researchers who have tried to predict bond ratings on the basis of quantitative data have had only limited success, indicating that the agencies do indeed use a good deal of subjective judgment to establish a firm's rating.[12]

---

[11]In the discussion to follow, reference to the S&P code is intended to imply the Moody's code as well. Thus, for example, triple B bonds means both BBB and Baa bonds; double B bonds, both BB and Ba bonds.

[12]See Robert S. Kaplan and Gabriel Urwitz, "Statistical Models of Bond Ratings: A Methodological Inquiry," *Journal of Business,* April 1979, 231–261; and Ahmed Belkaoui, *Industrial Bonds and the Rating Process* (London: Quorum Books, 1983).

TABLE 20-2	Moody's	S&P	
COMPARISON OF	Aaa	AAA	Highest quality
BOND RATINGS	Aa	AA	High quality
	A	A	Upper medium grade
	Baa	BBB	Medium grade
	Ba	BB	Lower medium grade/some speculative elements
	B	B	Speculative
	Caa	CCC	
	Ca	CC	More speculative/in or high risk of default
	C	C	
	—	D	In default

Note: Both Moody's and S&P use "modifiers" for bonds rated below triple A. S&P uses a plus and minus system; thus, A+ designates the strongest A rated bonds and A− the weakest. Moody's uses a 1, 2, or 3 designation, with 1 denoting the strongest and 3 the weakest; thus, within the double A category, Aa1 is the best, Aa2 is average, and Aa3 is the weakest. Triple A bonds have no modifiers in either system.

IMPORTANCE OF BOND RATINGS

Bond ratings are important both to firms and to investors. First, a bond's rating is an indicator of its default risk, so the rating has a direct, measurable influence on the bond's interest rate and the firm's cost of debt capital. Second, most bonds are purchased by institutional investors, not by individuals, and many of these institutions are restricted to investment-grade securities. Thus, if a firm's bonds fall below BBB, it will have a hard time selling new bonds, since many potential purchasers will not be allowed to buy them.

As a result of their higher risk and more restricted market, lower-grade bonds have much higher required rates of return, k_d, than do high-grade bonds. This point is highlighted in Figure 20-1, which gives the yields on three types of bonds, and the risk premiums for AAA and BBB bonds, in June 1963, in June 1975, and again in April 1989.[13] Note first that the riskless rate, or vertical axis intercept, rose 5.17 percentage points from 1963 to 1989, reflecting the increase in realized and anticipated inflation. Second, the slope of the line also rose, indicating increased investor risk aversion from 1963 to 1989, but risk aversion declined from 1975 to 1989.

---

[13]The term *risk premium* ought to reflect only the difference in the expected (and required) returns between two securities that results from differences in their risk. However, the difference between *yields to maturity* on different types of bonds consists of (1) a true risk premium; (2) a liquidity premium, which reflects the fact that U.S. Treasury bonds are more readily marketable than most corporate bonds; (3) a call premium, because most Treasury bonds are not callable, while corporate bonds are; and (4) an expected loss differential, which reflects the probability of loss on the corporate bonds. As an example of the latter point, suppose the yield to maturity on a BBB bond were 10 percent versus 7 percent on government bonds, but there is a 5 percent probability of total default loss on the corporate bond. In this case, the expected return on the BBB bond would be 0.95(10%) + 0.05(0%) = 9.5%, and the risk premium would be 2.5 percent, not the full 3.0 percentage point difference in "promised" yields to maturity. Therefore, the risk premiums given in Figure 20-1 overstate somewhat the true (but unmeasurable) risk premiums.

FIGURE 20-1

RELATIONSHIP
BETWEEN BOND
RATINGS AND BOND
YIELDS, 1963,
1975, AND 1989

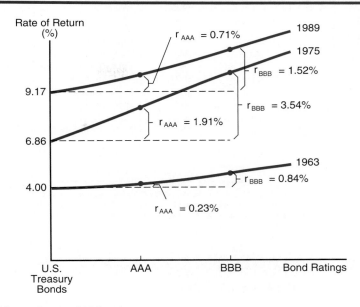

r_{AAA} = risk premium on AAA bonds.
r_{BBB} = risk premium on BBB bonds.

	Long-Term Government Bonds (Default-Free) (1)	AAA Corporate Bonds (2)	BBB Corporate Bonds (3)	Risk Premiums	
				AAA (4) = (2) − (1)	BBB (5) = (3) − (1)
June 1963	4.00%	4.23%	4.84%	0.23%	0.84%
June 1975	6.86	8.77	10.40	1.91	3.54
April 1989	9.17	9.88	10.69	0.71	1.52

Sources: *Federal Reserve Bulletin,* December 1963 and December 1975; *Federal Reserve Statistical Release,* April 1989.

Thus, the penalty for having a low credit rating varies over time. Occasionally, as in 1963, it is not too severe, but at other times, as in 1975, it is quite large.[14]

---

[14]The relationship graphed here is akin to the Security Market Line developed in Chapter 5, although bond ratings rather than beta coefficients are used to measure risk. A word about the scaling of the horizontal axis and about the placement of the points is in order. (1) We have shown a linear fit, although there is no theoretical reason to think that yields plotted against bond ratings are necessarily linear. (2) We have shown the interval on the horizontal axis between AAA and BBB to be equal to that between U.S. Government bonds and AAA, but this is an arbitrary scaling. (3) Finally, on an accurate, large-scale graph, it would be clear that the plotted points for the AAA and BBB bonds are not precisely on straight lines as they appear in the graph; however, they are sufficiently close to warrant our analysis.

Attempts have been made to calculate beta coefficients for bonds and to plot bonds on the same SML that is used for common stocks. However, these results have not been successful—bonds do not plot on the same linear SML as stocks.

CHANGES IN RATINGS

A change in a firm's bond rating will have a significant effect on its ability to borrow long-term capital, and on the cost of that capital. Rating agencies review outstanding bonds on a periodic basis, occasionally upgrading or downgrading a bond as a result of its issuer's changed circumstances. Also, an announcement that a company plans to sell a new debt issue, or to merge with another company and to pay for the acquisition by exchanging bonds for the stock of the acquired company, will trigger an agency review and possibly lead to a rating change. For example, in January 1989, when Texaco and financier Carl Icahn reached an agreement which precluded him from making a bid for Texaco, S&P placed Texaco's bonds on "CreditWatch" with "positive implications." CreditWatch is an S&P publication which lists bonds that it is actively reviewing for a possible rating change in response to some development, and investors are warned that the rating may be changed upon completion of the review. CreditWatch listings are published in *The Wall Street Journal,* and the publication itself may be subscribed to or read in many libraries. It spells out in detail what S&P sees as going on, and it is updated frequently.[15]

If a firm's situation has deteriorated somewhat, but its bonds have not been reviewed and downgraded, then it may choose to use a term loan or short-term debt rather than to finance through a public bond issue. This will perhaps postpone a rating agency review until the situation has improved. For example, a number of public utilities delayed bond issues in the early 1980s, financing with short-term debt until electric rate increases could be obtained to raise interest coverage ratios to acceptable levels. After rate increases were put into effect and coverages improved, the companies sold bonds and used the proceeds to retire the excess short-term debt.

SELF-TEST QUESTIONS

What are the two major rating agencies?

What are some criteria the rating agencies use when they assign ratings?

What impact does its bond rating have on the cost of debt to the issuing firm?

---

[15]Rating agencies do review ratings without being prompted by the company. However, most reviews associated with new issues are actually requested by the company, not because the company wants a review but because the investment bankers make such a review a condition of their handling the offering. Note also that a company must pay the agency to have its bonds rated. It has been suggested that such payments might lead to a favorable bias in ratings. However, there is no evidence whatever of any bias on the part of the major rating agencies. The value of their service, hence the rating agencies' incomes, depends almost entirely on their credibility, so there is every reason to expect the agencies to maintain strict objectivity.

ADVANTAGES AND DISADVANTAGES OF LONG-TERM DEBT FINANCING

From the issuer's viewpoint, there are several advantages and disadvantages to long-term debt financing. The major advantages are as follows:

1. The cost of debt is independent of earnings, so debtholders do not participate if profits soar. There is, however, a flip side to this argument—if profits fall, the company must still pay the interest on its debt.

2. Because of tax deductibility of interest payments, the risk-adjusted component cost of debt is lower than that of common stock.

3. The owners of the corporation do not have to share control when debt financing is used.

The major disadvantages are as follows:

1. Since debt service (interest plus scheduled principal repayments) is a fixed charge, a reduction in revenues may result in insufficient cash flow to meet debt service requirements. This can lead to bankruptcy.

2. As discussed in Chapters 12 and 13, financial leverage increases the firm's riskiness, hence increases its cost of both debt and equity.

3. Debt normally has a fixed maturity, hence the firm must repay the principal at some future time.

4. In a long-term contractual relationship, it is necessary for the indenture provisions to be much more stringent than in a short-term credit agreement. Thus, the firm will be subject to more restrictions than if it had borrowed on a short-term basis or had issued common stock.

5. There is a limit to the amount of funds which can be raised at a "reasonable" rate. Widely accepted lending standards dictate that the debt ratio should not exceed certain limits (which vary from industry), and when debt goes beyond these limits, its cost becomes exhorbitant.

SELF-TEST QUESTIONS

What are the major advantages to long-term debt financing?

What are the major disadvantages?

FACTORS THAT INFLUENCE LONG-TERM FINANCING DECISIONS

As we show in this section, many factors influence a firm's long-term financing decisions. It is impossible to rank the factors in order of importance, because their relative importance varies among firms at any point in time and also for any given firm over time.

CAPITAL STRUCTURE CONSIDERATIONS

One of the most important considerations in any financing decision is the relationship between the firm's actual capital structure and its target capital structure. Remember that firms establish an optimal, or target, capital structure (or at least a range) and, over time, finance in accordance with this target. Of course, in any one year, few firms finance exactly in accordance with their target capital structures, primarily because of flotation costs: Smaller issues of new securities have proportionally larger flotation costs, so firms tend to issue common stock and long-term debt sporadically, while retained earnings are generated continuously.

Note that making fewer, but larger, security offerings causes a firm's capital structure to fluctuate about its optimal level rather than stay right on target. However, (1) small fluctuations about the optimal capital structure have little effect on a firm's weighted average cost of capital, (2) investors recognize that this action is prudent, and (3) the firm saves substantial amounts of flotation costs by financing in this manner. So, firms tend, over the long haul, to finance in accordance with their target capital structures, but flotation costs plus the factors discussed in the following sections do influence the specific financing decisions in any given year.

We should also point out that firms can, and often do, arrange financings in advance. Thus, if a firm concluded that it would need $8 million of debt over a 2-year period, it might arrange with one or more pension funds to lend it $4 million in each of the next 2 years, with the second $4 million being firmly committed by the lenders at the time the first $4 million is borrowed. Such financings can reduce flotation costs, because the lenders need to make only one detailed credit analysis. Similarly, larger firms can use shelf registrations, which we discussed in Chapter 19, to hold down financing costs even while they sell relatively small blocks of securities. Both commitment financings and shelf registrations make it possible for firms to adhere reasonably closely to their optimal capital structures without incurring unduly high flotation costs.

MATURITY MATCHING

Assume that Consolidated Tools, a Cincinnati machine tool manufacturer, made the decision to float a single $25 million nonconvertible bond issue to help finance its 1994 capital budget. It must next choose a maturity for the issue, taking into consideration both the shape of the yield curve, management's own expectations about future interest rates, and the maturity of the assets being financed. To illustrate how asset maturities affect the choice of debt maturities, suppose Consolidated's capital projects consist primarily of new, automated milling and stamping machinery for its Cincinnati plant. This machinery has an expected economic life of 10 years (even though it falls into the MACRS 5-year class life). Should Consolidated finance the debt portion of this equipment with 5-year, 10-year, 20-year, or 30-year debt, or some other maturity?

Note that some of the new capital for the machinery will come from common and perhaps preferred stock, both of which are generally considered to be permanent capital. Of course, preferred stock can have a sinking fund or be redeemable, and common stock can always be repurchased on the open market or by a tender offer, so the effective maturity of preferred and common stock can be reduced significantly. On the other hand, debt maturities can be specified at the time of issue. If Consolidated financed its capital budget with 10-year sinking fund bonds, it would be matching asset and liability maturities. The cash flows resulting from the new machinery could be used to make the interest and sinking fund payments on the issue, so the bonds would be retired as the machinery wore out. If Consolidated had used one-year debt, it would have to pay off this debt with cash flows derived from assets other than the machinery in question. Conversely, if it used 20-year or 30-year debt, it would have to service the debt long after the assets that were purchased with the funds raised had been scrapped and had ceased providing cash flows. This would worry the lenders.

Of course, the one-year debt could probably be rolled over year after year, out to the 10-year asset maturity. However, if interest rates rose, Consolidated would have to pay a higher rate when it rolled over its debt, or if the company experienced difficulties, it might not be able to refund the debt at any reasonable rate. On the other hand, if Consolidated financed 10-year assets with 20-year or 30-year bonds, it would still have (1) a liability after the 10-year life of the asset, but (2) it would have generated some excess cash from the assets over their 10-year life. The question then would be this: Can we reinvest the accumulated cash flows at a rate which will enable us to pay off the bonds over their remaining 20-year or 30-year life? This strategy clearly imposes uncertainty on the firm, since it cannot know at the time it sells the bonds if profitable capital investment opportunities will be available 10 years later.

For all these reasons, the best all-around financing strategy is to match debt maturities with asset maturities. In recognition of this fact, firms generally do place great emphasis on maturity matching, and this factor often dominates the debt portion of the financing decision.

EFFECTS OF INTEREST RATE LEVELS AND FORECASTS

Financial managers also consider interest rate levels and forecasts, both absolute and relative, when making financing decisions. For example, if long-term interest rates are high by historical standards and are expected to fall, managers will be reluctant to issue long-term debt and thus lock in those costs for long periods. We already know that one solution to this problem is for firms to use a call provision — callability permits refunding of the issue should interest rates drop, but there is a cost, because the firm must pay more for callable debt. Alternatively, the firm could finance with short-term debt whenever long-term rates were historically high, and then, assuming that interest rates subsequently fall, sell a long-term issue to replace the short-term debt. Of course, this strategy has its risks: If interest rates move even higher, the firm will be forced to renew its short-term debt at higher

and higher rates, or to replace the short-term debt with a long-term bond which costs even more than it would have when the original decision was made.

One could argue, and many do, that capital markets are efficient. If so — and most evidence supports the efficient markets hypothesis — then it is impossible to predict what future interest rates will be because these rates will be determined by information which is not now known. Thus, under the efficient markets hypothesis, it would be unproductive for firms to try to "beat the market" by forecasting future capital costs and then acting on these forecasts. According to this view, financial managers ought to arrange their capital structures in such a manner that they can ride out almost any economic storm, and this generally calls for (1) using some "reasonable" mix of debt and equity and (2) using debt with maturities which more or less match the maturities of the assets being financed.

Although we personally support the view dictated by the efficient markets hypothesis, there is no question that many managers disagree. They are influenced by current cost levels and forecasts, and they act accordingly. One manifestation of this behavior is the heavy use of shelf registrations. Some firms use shelf registrations because managers believe that financing "windows" exist. In the volatile interest rate environment that has characterized recent years, a company might decide to issue bonds when the rate is 8 percent but then find, 6 weeks later when it has SEC approval to go ahead with the issue, that rates are up to 9 percent. If it had "bonds on the shelf," it could have gone ahead and sold the issue while the low-cost window was open. (Another way to protect against rising rates is to hedge against this possibility by use of interest rate futures. We discuss futures markets and the use of futures in Chapter 22.)

A few years ago, the interest rate on AAA corporate bonds was about 12.5 percent. Exxon's investment bankers advised the company to tap the Eurobond market for relatively cheap fixed-rate financing.[16] At the time, Exxon could issue its bonds in London at 0.4 percentage points *below* comparable maturity U.S. Treasury bonds. However, one of Exxon's officers was quoted as saying, "I say so what. The absolute level of rates is too high. Our people would rather wait." The managers of Exxon, as well as many other companies, were betting that the next move in interest rates would be down. This belief was also openly expressed by executives of ITT, Ontario Hydro, and RCA, among others. Since interest rates are now much lower, it turned out that these executives were right.

These attitudes confirm that many firms base their financing decisions on expectations about future interest rates. It is easy to be right on one interest rate call — if you predict a decline in interest rates, you have a 50-50 chance of being correct. However, the success of a strategy based on forecasting rates requires that those forecasts be right more often than they are wrong, and it is very difficult to find someone with a long-term track record which is better than 50-50. Finance would be easy if we could accurately predict future interest rates. Unfortunately, predicting future interest rates with consistent accuracy is somewhere between

---

[16]See Chapter 25 for a discussion of Eurobonds.

difficult and impossible—people who make a living selling interest rate forecasts say it is difficult; many others say it is impossible.

INFORMATION ASYMMETRIES

Earlier in the chapter, we discussed bond ratings and the effects of changes in ratings on the cost and availability of capital. If a firm's current financial condition is poor, its managers may be reluctant to issue new long-term debt because (1) a new debt issue would probably trigger a review by the rating agencies, and (2) debt issued when a firm is in poor financial condition would probably cost more and have more severe restrictive covenants than debt issued from strength. Further, in Chapter 13, we pointed out that firms are reluctant to use new common stock financing, especially when this might be taken as a negative signal. Thus, a firm that is in a weakened condition, but which is forecasting a better time in the future, would be inclined to delay permanent financing of any type until things improved. Conversely, a firm that is strong now, but which forecasts a potentially bad time in the period just ahead, would be motivated to finance long term now rather than to wait. Each of these scenarios implies that the capital markets are either inefficient or that investors do not have the same information regarding the firm's future as does its financial manager. The second situation is undoubtedly true at times, and possibly the first one is also true in rare cases.

The firm's earnings outlook, and the extent to which forecasted higher earnings per share are reflected in stock prices, also has an effect on the choice of securities. If a successful R&D program has just been concluded, and as a result management forecasts higher earnings than do most investors, then the firm would not want to issue common stock. It would use debt and then, once earnings rise and push up the stock price, sell common to restore the capital structure to its target level.

AMOUNT OF FINANCING REQUIRED

Obviously, the amount of financing required will influence the financing decision. This is mainly due to flotation costs. A $5 million debt financing would most likely be done with a term loan or a privately placed bond issue, while a firm seeking $100 million of new debt would most likely use a public offering.

AVAILABILITY OF COLLATERAL

Generally, secured debt will be less costly than unsecured debt. Thus, firms with large amounts of fixed assets which have a ready resale value are likely to use a relatively large amount of debt, especially mortgage bonds. Additionally, each year's financing decision would be influenced by the amount of qualified assets available as security for new bonds.

SELF-TEST QUESTIONS

What are some factors that financial managers should consider when making long-term financing decisions?

How do information asymmetries affect financing decisions?

SUMMARY

This chapter described the characteristics, advantages, and disadvantages of the major types of long-term debt securities. The key concepts covered are listed next.

▶ *Term loans* and *bonds* are long-term debt contracts under which a borrower agrees to make a series of interest and principal payments on specific dates to the lender. A term loan is generally sold to one (or a few) lenders, while a bond is typically offered to the public and sold to many different investors.

▶ There are many different types of bonds, including *mortgage bonds, debentures, convertibles, bonds with warrants, income bonds, putable bonds,* and *purchasing power (indexed) bonds.* The return required on each type of bond is determined by the bond's riskiness.

▶ A bond's *indenture* is a legal document that spells out the rights of the bondholders and of the issuing corporation. A *trustee* is assigned to make sure that the terms of the indenture are carried out.

▶ A *call provision* gives the issuing corporation the right to redeem the bonds prior to maturity under specified terms, usually at a price greater than the maturity value (the difference is a *call premium*). A firm will typically call a bond and refund it if interest rates fall substantially.

▶ A *sinking fund* is a provision which requires the corporation to retire a portion of the bond issue each year. The purpose of the sinking fund is to provide for the orderly retirement of the issue. No call premium is paid to the holders of bonds called for sinking fund purposes.

▶ Some recent innovations in long-term financing include *zero coupon bonds,* which pay no annual interest but which are issued at a discount; *floating rate debt,* whose interest payments fluctuate with changes in the general level of interest rates; and *junk bonds,* which are high-risk, high-yield instruments used by firms which are poor credit risks. Other innovations include *project financing, bonds that are redeemable at par, securitization,* and *swaps.*

▶ Bonds are assigned *ratings* which reflect the probability of their going into default. The higher a bond's rating, the lower its interest rate.

▶ A firm's long-term financing decisions are influenced by its *target capital structure,* the *maturity of its assets,* current and forecasted *interest rate levels,* the firm's current and forecasted *financial condition,* and the suitability of its *assets for use as collateral.*

If a bond has a call provision, the issuer may refund (call) the bond prior to maturity. We discuss refunding analysis in detail in Appendix 20A. Also, firms may

issue bonds (or preferred stocks) that are convertible into the firm's common stock. Convertible bonds are discussed in detail in Chapter 22.

QUESTIONS

20-1 Define each of the following terms:

a. Story credit

b. Term loan; bond

c. Mortgage bond

d. Debenture; subordinated debenture

e. Convertible bond; warrant; income bond; indexed, or purchasing power, bond

f. Indenture; restrictive covenant

g. Trustee

h. Call provision; sinking fund

i. Zero coupon bond; original issue discount bond (OID)

j. Floating rate bond

k. Junk bond

l. Project financing

m. Securitization

n. Swaps

o. Poison put; super poison put

p. Bond rating; rating agency; investment-grade bonds

q. Maturity matching

20-2 What effect would each of the following items have on the interest rate a firm must pay on a new issue of long-term debt? Indicate whether each factor would tend to raise, lower, or have an indeterminate effect on the interest rate, and then explain *why*.

a. The firm uses bonds rather than a term loan.

b. The firm uses nonsubordinated debentures rather than first mortgage bonds.

c. The firm makes its bonds convertible into common stock.

d. The firm makes its debentures subordinate to its bank debt. What will the effect be
(1) On the cost of the debentures?
(2) On the cost of the bank debt?
(3) On the average cost of total debt?

e. The firm sells income bonds rather than debentures.

f. The firm must raise $100 million, all of which will be used to construct a new plant, and is debating the sale of first mortgage bonds or debentures. If it decides to issue $50 million of each type, as opposed to $75 million of first mortgage bonds and $25 million of debentures, how will this affect
(1) The cost of debentures?
(2) The cost of mortgage bonds?
(3) The average cost of the $100 million?

g. The firm puts a call provision on its new issue of bonds.

h. The firm uses zero coupon bonds rather than coupon bonds.

i. The firm includes a sinking fund on its new issue of bonds.

j. The firm's bonds are downgraded from A to BBB.

k. The firm adds a super poison put provision on its new bond issue.

20-3 Rank the following securities from lowest (1) to highest (9) in terms of their riskiness for an investor. All securities (except the government bond) are for a given firm. If you think two or more securities are equally risky, indicate so.

a. Income bond _____

b. Subordinated debentures — noncallable _____

c. First mortgage bond — no sinking fund _____

d. Common stock _____

e. U.S. Treasury bond _____

f. First mortgage bond — with sinking fund _____

g. Subordinated debentures — callable _____

h. Amortized term loan _____

i. Nonamortized term loan _____

20-4 A sinking fund can be set up in one of two ways:

(1) The corporation makes annual payments to the trustee, who invests the proceeds in securities (frequently government bonds) and uses the accumulated total to retire the bond issue at maturity.

(2) The trustee uses the annual payments to retire a portion of the issue each year, either calling a given percentage of the issue by a lottery and paying a specified price per bond or buying bonds on the open market, whichever is cheaper.

Discuss the advantages and disadvantages of each procedure from the viewpoint of both the firm and the bondholders.

20-5 Draw an SML graph. Put dots on the graph to show (approximately) where you think a particular company's (a) common stock and (b) bonds would lie. Now put on dots to represent a riskier company's stock and bonds.

20-6 Suppose you work for the treasurer of a large, profitable corporation. Your company has some surplus funds to invest. You can buy these securities:

(1) Aaa-rated Exxon 20-year bonds which sell at par and yield 9 percent.

(2) Aa-rated Exxon preferred stock which yields 7 percent.

(3) Ca-rated Continental Airlines bonds which yield 13 percent.

(4) C-rated Continental Airlines preferred stock which yields 14 percent.

(5) A-rated Alabama Power floating rate preferred stock which currently yields 5 percent.

(6) Treasury bills which yield 4 percent.

a. Does it appear that these securities are in equilibrium?

b. If these were your only choices, which would you recommend? Why?

SELF-TEST PROBLEM (SOLUTION APPEARS IN APPENDIX C)

ST-1 (Sinking funds) The California Development Commission has just issued a $100 million, 10-year, 12 percent bond with semiannual coupon payments. A sinking fund will retire the issue over its life. Sinking fund payments are of equal amounts and will be made *semiannually,* and the proceeds will be used to retire bonds as the payments are made. Assume that the bonds will be called at par for sinking fund purposes.

a. How large must each semiannual sinking fund payment be?

b. What will happen, under the conditions of the problem thus far, to the company's debt service requirements per year for this issue over time?

c. Now suppose the Commission had set its sinking fund so that *equal annual amounts,* payable at the end of each year, were paid into a sinking fund trust held by a bank, with the proceeds being used to buy government bonds that pay 9 percent interest. The payments, plus accumulated interest, must total $100 million at the end of 10 years, and the proceeds will be used to retire the bonds at that time. How large must the annual sinking fund payment now be?

d. What are the annual cash requirements for covering bond service costs under the trusteeship arrangement described in Part c? (Note: Interest must be paid on the outstanding bonds but not on bonds that have been retired.)

e. Now assume that the Commission has the option of buying the bonds on the open market. What would have to happen to interest rates to cause the company to buy bonds on the open market rather than call them under the original sinking fund plan?

PROBLEMS

20-1 (Loan amortization) Suppose a firm is setting up an amortized term loan. What are the annual payments for a $10 million loan under the following terms:

a. 9 percent, 5 years?

b. 9 percent, 10 years?

c. 12 percent, 5 years?

d. 12 percent, 10 years?

20-2 (Amortization schedule) Set up an amortization schedule for a $1 million, 3-year, 10 percent loan.

20-3 (Yield to call) Five years ago Wachowicz Company sold a 20-year bond issue with a 17 percent coupon rate and a 10 percent constant call premium. Today the firm called the bonds. The bonds originally were sold at their face value of $1,000. Compute the realized rate of return for investors who purchased the bonds when they were issued and will surrender them today in exchange for the call price.

20-4 (Perpetual bond analysis) In 1936 the Canadian government raised $55 million by issuing bonds at a 3 percent annual rate of interest. Unlike most bonds issued today, which have a specific maturity date, these bonds can remain outstanding forever; they are, in fact, perpetuities.

At the time of issue, the Canadian government stated in the bond indenture that cash redemption was possible at face value ($100) on or after September 1966; in other words, the bonds were callable at par after September 1966. Believing that the bonds would in fact be called, many investors purchased these bonds in 1965 with expectations of receiving

$100 in 1966 for each perpetual bond they had. In 1965 the bonds sold for $55, but a rush of buyers drove the price to just below the $100 par value by 1966. Prices fell dramatically, however, when the Canadian government announced that these perpetual bonds were indeed perpetual and would not be paid off. A new, 30-year supply of coupons was sent to each bondholder.

The bonds' market price declined to $42 in December 1966. Because of their severe losses, hundreds of Canadian bondholders formed the Perpetual Bond Association to lobby for face value redemption of the bonds, claiming that the government had reneged on an implied promise to redeem the bonds. Government officials in Ottawa insisted that claims for face value payment were nonsense, for the bonds were and always had been clearly identified as perpetuals. One Ottawa official stated, "Our job is to protect the taxpayer. Why should we pay $55 million for less than $25 million worth of bonds?"

The issue heats up again every few years, and it recently resurfaced once more. Here are some questions relating to the Canadian issue that will test your understanding of bonds in general:

a. Would it make sense for a business firm to issue bonds such as the Canadian bonds described here? Would it matter whether the firm were a proprietorship or a corporation?

b. Suppose the U.S. government today sold $100 million each of these four types of bonds: 5-year bonds, 50-year bonds, "regular" perpetuities, and Canadian-type (callable) perpetuities. What do you think the relative order of interest rates would be? In other words, rank the bonds from the one with the lowest to the one with the highest rate of interest. Explain your answer.

c. (1) Suppose that because of pressure by the Perpetual Bond Association you believe that the Canadian government will redeem this particular perpetual bond issue in 3 years. Which course of action would be more advantageous to you if you owned the bonds: (a) sell your bonds today at $42, or (b) wait 3 years and have them redeemed? Assume that similar-risk bonds earn 8 percent today and that interest rates are expected to remain at this level for the next 3 years.

(2) If you had the opportunity to invest your money in bonds of similar risk, at what rate of return would you be indifferent to the choice of selling your perpetuals today or having them redeemed in 3 years — that is, what is the expected yield to maturity on the Canadian bonds?

d. Show mathematically the perpetuities' value if they yield 7.15 percent, pay $3 interest annually, and are considered "regular" perpetuities. Show what would happen to the price of bonds if the going interest rate fell to 2 percent.

e. Are the Canadian bonds more likely to be valued as "regular" perpetuities if the going rate of interest is above or below 3 percent? Why?

f. Do you think the Canadian government would have taken the same action with regard to retiring the bonds if the interest rate had fallen rather than risen after they were issued?

g. Do you think the Canadian government was "fair" or "unfair" in its actions? Give the pros and cons, and justify your reason for thinking that one outweighs the other. Would it matter if the bonds had been sold to "sophisticated" as opposed to "naive" purchasers?

20-5 (Zero coupon bond) Suppose Southern States Insurance Company needs to raise $400 million, and its investment bankers have indicated that 10-year zero coupon bonds could be sold at a YTM of 12 percent while a 14 percent yield would be required on *annual*

payment coupon bonds sold at par. Southern States's tax rate is 34 percent. (Assume that the discount can be amortized by the issuer using the straight line method. This cannot be done under current tax laws, but assume it anyway.)

a.   How many $1,000 par value bonds would Southern States have to sell under each plan?

b.   What would be the after-tax YTM on each type of bond (1) to a holder who is tax exempt and (2) to a taxpayer in the 50 percent federal-plus-state bracket?

c.   What would be the after-tax cost of each type of bond to Southern States?

d.   Why would investors be willing to buy the zero coupon bonds?

e.   Why might Southern States turn down the offer to issue zero coupon bonds?

(Do Part f only if you are using the computer problem diskette.)

f.   Redo Parts a, b, and c assuming that the YTM on zero coupon bonds falls to 10 percent and that on annual coupon bonds falls to 12 percent. As in the previous analysis, the after-tax yield to investors on the annual coupon bond exceeds that of the zero coupon bond. Has the differential between the annual and zero coupon bond yields changed? Would investors be more willing to purchase the zero coupon bond under the original assumptions or under the new assumptions? If the before-tax YTM were 10 percent on each type of bond, what would the after-tax YTMs be to zero and to 50 percent taxpayers, what would the after-tax cost be to the company, and what type of investors would be likely to hold the zeros and what type the regular coupon bonds?

**M I N I
C A S E**

Hospital Development Corporation (HDC) needs $10 million to build a regional testing laboratory in Birmingham, Alabama. Once the lab is completed and fully operational, which should take about 5 years, HDC will sell it to a health maintenance organization (HMO). HDC tentatively plans to raise the $10 million by selling 5-year bonds, and its investment bankers have stated that either regular or zero coupon bonds can be used. Regular coupon bonds would have annual payment coupons of 12 percent, and zero coupon bonds would also be priced to yield 12 percent. Either bond would be callable after 3 years, on the anniversary date of the issue, at a premium of 6 months' interest for regular bonds or 5 percent over the accrued value on the call date for zero coupon bonds. HDC's federal-plus-state tax rate is 40 percent.

As assistant to HDC's treasurer, you have been assigned the task of making a recommendation as to which type of bonds to issue. As part of your analysis, you have been asked to answer the following questions.

a.   What is the difference between a bond and a term loan? What are the advantages of a term loan over a bond?

b.   Suppose HDC issues bonds and uses the medical center as collateral for the issue. What type of bond would this be? Suppose that instead of using a secured bond, HDC had decided to sell debentures. How would this affect the interest rate that HDC would have to pay on the debt?

c.   What is a bond indenture? What are some examples of provisions the bondholders would probably require HDC to include in its indenture?

d.   HDC's bonds will be callable after 3 years. If the bonds were not callable, would the interest rate required be higher or lower than 12 percent? What would be the effect

on the rate if the bonds were callable immediately? What are the advantages to HDC of making the bonds callable?

e. (1) If its indenture included a sinking fund provision which required HDC to retire one-fifth of the bonds each year, would this provision raise or lower the interest rate required on the bonds?

  (2) How would the sinking fund operate?

  (3) Why might HDC's investors require it to use a sinking fund? For this particular issue, would it make sense to include a sinking fund?

f. If HDC were to issue zero coupon bonds, what initial price would cause the zeros to yield 12 percent? How many $1,000 par value zeros would HDC have to sell to raise the needed $10 million? How many regular 12 percent coupon bonds would HDC have to sell?

g. Set up a time line which shows the accrued value of the zeros at the end of each year, along with the annual after-tax cash flows from the zeros to an investor in the 28 percent tax bracket and to HDC.

h. What would the after-tax yield to maturity be on each type of bond to an investor in the 28 percent tax bracket? What would be the after-tax cost of debt be to HDC?

i. If interest rates were to fall, causing HDC to call the bonds (either the coupon or the zero) at the end of Year 3, what would be the after-tax yield to call on each type of bond to an investor in the 28 percent tax bracket?

j. HDC is an A-rated firm. Suppose HDC's bond rating was (1) lowered to triple B or (2) raised to double A. What would be the effect of these changes on the interest rate required on HDC's new long-term debt and on the market value of the company's outstanding debt?

k. What are some of the factors a firm such as HDC should consider when deciding whether to issue long-term debt, short-term debt, or equity? Why might long-term debt be HDC's best choice in this situation?

l. Describe the key features of the following securities and transactions:

  (1) Junk bonds

  (2) Project financing

  (3) Swaps

  (4) Securitization

  (5) Bonds that are redeemable at par

SELECTED ADDITIONAL REFERENCES AND CASES

The investment textbooks listed in the Chapter 5 references provide useful information on bonds, as well as the markets in which they are traded. In addition, the following articles offer useful insights:

Allen, David S., Robert E. Lamy, and G. Rodney Thompson, "Agency Costs and Alternative Call Provisions: An Empirical Investigation," *Financial Management,* Winter 1987, 37–44.

Altman, Edward I., "Revisiting the High-Yield Bond Market," *Financial Management,* Summer 1992, 78–92.

Arak, Marcelle, Arturo Estrella, Laurie Goodman, and Andrew Silver, "Interest Rate Swaps: An Alternative Explanation," *Financial Management,* Summer 1988, 12–18.

Backer, Morton, and Martin L. Gosman, "The Use of Financial Ratios in Credit Downgrade Decisions," *Financial Management,* Spring 1980, 53–56.

Barrett, W. Brian, Andrea J. Heuson, and Robert W. Kolb, "The Differential Effects of Sinking Funds on Bond Risk Premia," *Journal of Financial Research,* Winter 1986, 303–312.

Chen, Chao, and Philip Fanara, Jr., "The Choice Among Long-Term Financing Instruments for Public Utilities," *The Financial Review,* August 1992, 431–465.

Clark, John J., with Brenton W. Harries, "Some Recent Trends in Municipal and Corporate Securities Markets: An Interview with Brenton W. Harries, President of Standard & Poor's Corporation," *Financial Management,* Spring 1976, 9–17.

Crabbe, Leland, "Event Risk: An Analysis of Losses to Bondholders and 'Super Poison Put' Bond Covenants," *Journal of Finance,* June 1991, 689–706.

Easterwood, John C., and Palani-Rajan Kadapakkam, "The Role of Private and Public Debt in Corporate Capital Structures," *Financial Management,* Autumn 1991, 49–57.

Emerick, Dennis, and William White, "The Case for Private Placements: How Sophisticated Investors Add Value to Corporate Debt Issuers," *Journal of Applied Corporate Finance,* Fall 1992, 83–91.

Ferri, Michael G., "An Empirical Examination of the Determinants of Bond Yield Spreads," *Financial Management,* Autumn 1978, 40–46.

Gentry, James A., David T. Whitford, and Paul Newbold, "Predicting Industrial Bond Ratings with a Probit Model and Funds Flow Components," *The Financial Review,* August 1988, 269–286.

Hand, John R. M., Robert W. Holthausen, and Richard W. Leftwich, "The Effect of Bond Rating Agency Announcements on Bond and Stock Prices," *Journal of Finance,* June 1992, 733–752.

Hsueh, L. Paul, and David S. Kidwell, "Bond Ratings: Are Two Better than One?" *Financial Management,* Spring 1988, 46–53.

Johnson, James M., Robert A. Pari, and Leonard Rosenthal, "The Impact of In-Substance Defeasance on Bondholder and Shareholder Wealth," *Journal of Finance,* September 1989, 1049–1057.

Kalotay, Andrew J. "Sinking Funds and the Realized Cost of Debt," *Financial Management,* Spring 1982, 43–54.

———, "Innovations in Corporation Finance: Deep Discount Private Placements," *Financial Management,* Spring 1982, 55–57.

Kao, Chihwa, and Chunchi Wu, "Sinking Funds and the Agency Costs of Corporate Debt," *The Financial Review,* February 1990, 95–113.

Laber, Gene, "Bond Covenants and Foregone Opportunities: The Case of Burlington Northern Railroad Company," *Financial Management,* Summer 1992, 71–77.

Litzenberger, Robert H., "Swaps: Plain and Fanciful," *Journal of Finance,* July 1992, 831–850.

Pinches, George E., J. Clay Singleton, and Ali Jahankhani, "Fixed Coverage as a Determinant of Electric Utility Bond Ratings," *Financial Management,* Summer 1978, 45–55.

Roach, Stephen S., "Living with Corporate Debt," *Journal of Applied Corporate Finance,* Spring 1989, 19–29.

Smith, Clifford W., and J. B. Warner, "On Financial Contracting: An Analysis of Bond Covenants," *Journal of Financial Economics,* June 1979, 117–161.

Szewczyk, Samuel H., and Raj Varma, "Raising Capital with Private Placements of Debt," *Journal of Financial Research,* Spring 1991, 1–13.

Thompson, G. Rodney, and Peter Vaz, "Dual Bond Ratings: A Test of the Certification Function of Rating Agencies," *Financial Review,* August 1990, 457–471.

Weinsten, Mark I., "The Seasoning Process of New Corporate Bond Issues," *Journal of Finance,* December 1978, 1343–1354.

Zwick, Burton, "Yields on Privately Placed Corporate Bonds," *Journal of Finance,* March 1980, 23–29.

References on bond refunding include the following:

Ang, James S., "The Two Faces of Bond Refunding," *Journal of Finance,* June 1975, 869–874.

———, "The Two Faces of Bond Refunding: Reply," *Journal of Finance,* March 1978, 354–356.

Chiang, Raymond C., and M. P. Narayanan, "Bond Refunding in Efficient Markets: A Dynamic Analysis with Tax Effects," *Journal of Financial Research,* Winter 1991, 287–302.

Dyl, Edward A. and Michael D. Joehnk, "Refunding Tax Exempt Bonds," *Financial Management,* Summer 1976, 59–66.

Emery, Douglas R., "Overlapping Interest in Bond Refunding: A Reconsideration," *Financial Management,* Summer 1978, 19–20.

Finnerty, John D., "Refunding High-Coupon Debt," *Midland Corporate Finance Journal,* Winter 1986, 59–74.

Harris, Robert S., "The Refunding of Discounted Debt: An Adjusted Present Value Analysis," *Financial Management,* Winter 1980, 7–12.

Kalotay, Andrew J., "On the Advanced Refunding of Discounted Debt," *Financial Management,* Summer 1978, 14–18.

———, "On the Structure and Valuation of Debt Refundings," *Financial Management,* Spring 1982, 41–42.

Kraus, Alan, "An Analysis of Call Provisions and the Corporate Refunding Decision," *Midland Corporate Finance Journal,* Spring 1983, 46–60.

Laber, Gene, "The Effect of Bond Refunding of Discounted Debt," *Financial Management,* June 1979, 795–799.

———, "Implications of Discount Rates and Financing Assumptions for Bond Refunding Decisions," *Financial Management,* Spring 1979, 7–12.

———, "Repurchases of Bonds through Tender Offers: Implications for Shareholder Wealth," *Financial Management,* Summer 1978, 7–13.

Livingston, Miles, "The Effect of Bond Refunding on Shareholder Wealth: Comment," *Journal of Finance,* June 1979, 801–804.

———, "Bond Refunding Reconsidered: Comment," *Journal of Finance,* March 1980, 191–196.

Mauer, David C., "Optimal Bond Call Policies under Transactions Costs," *Journal of Financial Research,* Spring 1993, 23–37.

Mayor, Thomas H., and Kenneth G. McCoin, "Bond Refunding: One or Two Faces?" *Journal of Finance,* March 1978, 349–353.

Ofer, Ahron R., and Robert A. Taggart, Jr., "Bond Refunding: Reconsidered: Reply," *Journal of Finance,* March 1980, 197–200.

Riener, Kenneth D., "Financial Structure Effects of Bond Refunding," *Financial Management,* Summer 1980, 18–23.

Thatcher, Janet S., and John G. Thatcher, "An Empirical Test of the Timing of Bond-Refunding Decisions," *Journal of Financial Research,* Fall 1992, 219–230.

Yawitz, Jess B., and James A. Anderson, "The Effect of Bond Refunding on Shareholder Wealth," *Journal of Finance,* December 1977, 1738–1746.

———, "The Effect of Bond Refunding on Shareholder Wealth: Reply," *Journal of Finance,* June 1979, 805–809.

Zeise, Charles H., and Roger K. Taylor, "Advance Refunding: A Practitioner's Perspective," *Financial Management,* Summer 1977, 73–76.

The following Brigham-Gapenski case focuses on the topic covered in Appendix 20A:

Case 24, "Bay Area Telephone Company," which illustrates the bond refunding decision.

REFUNDING OPERATIONS

APPENDIX
20A

A great deal of long-term debt was sold during the period from 1979 through 1984 at interest rates going up to 18 percent for double A companies. Because the period of call protection on much of this debt is ending, many companies are analyzing the pros and cons of bond refundings. Refunding decisions actually involve two separate questions: (1) Is it profitable to call an outstanding issue in the current period and replace it with a new issue; and (2) even if refunding is currently profitable, would the value of the firm be increased even more if the refunding were postponed to a later date? We consider both questions in this section.

Note that the decision to refund a security is analyzed in much the same way as a capital budgeting expenditure. The costs of refunding (the investment outlays) are (1) the call premium paid for the privilege of calling the old issue, (2) the tax savings from writing off the unexpensed flotation costs on the old issue, and (3) the net interest that must be paid while both issues are outstanding (the new issue is often sold one month before the refunding to ensure that the funds will be available). The annual cash flows, in a capital budgeting sense, are the interest payments that are saved each year plus the net tax savings which the firm receives for amortizing the flotation expenses. For example, if the interest expense on the old issue is $1,000,000 whereas that on the new issue is $700,000, the $300,000 reduction in interest savings constitutes an annual benefit.[1]

The net present value method is used to analyze the advantages of refunding: the future cash flows are discounted back to the present, and then this discounted value is compared with the cash outlays associated with the refunding. The firm should refund the bond if the present value of the savings exceeds the cost—that is, if the NPV of the refunding operation is positive.

In the discounting process, the after-tax cost of the new debt should be used as the discount rate. The reasons for this are (1) there is relatively little risk to the savings—cash flows in a refunding are known with relative certainty, which is quite unlike the situation with cash flows in most capital budgeting decisions, and (2) the cash outlay required to refund the old issue is generally obtained by increasing the amount of the new issue (see Footnote 4).

The easiest way to examine the refunding decision is through an example. Microchip Computer Company has outstanding a $60 million bond issue which has a 15 percent annual coupon and 20 years remaining to maturity. This issue, which was sold 5 years ago, had flotation costs of $3 million, which the firm has been amortizing on a straight line basis over the 25-year original life of the issue. The bond has a call provision which makes it possible for the company to retire the bonds at this time by calling them in at a 10 percent call premium. Investment bankers have assured the company that it could sell an additional $60 million to $70 million worth of new annual coupon 20-year bonds at an interest rate

---

[1]During the early 1980s, there was a flurry of work on the pros and cons of refunding bond issues that had fallen to deep discounts as a result of rising interest rates. At such times, the company could go into the market, buy its debt at a low price, and retire it. The difference between the bonds' par value and the price the company paid would be reported as income, and taxes would have to be paid on it. The results of the research on the refunding of discount issues suggest that bonds should not, in general, be refunded after a rise in rates. See Andrew J. Kalotay, "On the Structure and Valuation of Debt Refundings," *Financial Management,* Spring 1982, 41–42; and Robert S. Harris, "The Refunding of Discounted Debt: An Adjusted Present Value Analysis," *Financial Management,* Winter 1980, 7–12.

TABLE 20A-1

BOND REFUNDING DECISION WORKSHEET

Investment Outlay: t = 0	Amount before Tax	Amount after Tax	Present Value at 7.92%
1. Call premium on old issue	($6,000,000)	($3,960,000)	($ 3,960,000)
2. Flotation costs on new issue	(2,650,000)	(2,650,000)	(2,650,000)
3. Tax savings on old issue flotation costs	2,400,000	816,000	816,000
4. Extra interest cost on old issue	(750,000)	(495,000)	(495,000)
5. Interest earned on short-term investment	550,000	363,000	363,000
6. Net investment outlay at t = 0			($ 5,926,000)
Annual Flotation Cost Tax Effects: t = 1 – 20			
7. Annual benefit from new issue flotation costs	$132,500	$45,050	$ 444,953
8. Annual lost benefit from old issue flotation costs	(120,000)	(40,800)	(402,976)
9. PV of amortization tax effects			$ 41,977
Savings Due to Refunding: t = 1 – 20			
10. Interest payment on old issue	$9,000,000	$5,940,000	
11. Interest payment on new issue	7,200,000	4,752,000	
12. Net interest savings		$1,188,000	$11,733,727
NPV of Refunding Decision			$ 5,849,704

of 12 percent. To ensure that the funds required to pay off the old debt will be available, the new bonds would be sold one month before the old issue is called, so for one month, interest would have to be paid on both issues. Current short-term interest rates are 11 percent; for the one-month overlap period, proceeds from the new issue will be invested in short-term securities. Predictions are that long-term interest rates are unlikely to fall below 12 percent.[2] Flotation costs on a new refunding issue would amount to $2,650,000. Microchip's marginal tax rate is 34 percent. Should the company refund the $60 million of 15 percent bonds?

The following steps outline the decision process; the steps are summarized in worksheet form in Table 20A-1.

Step 1. Determine the investment outlay required to refund the issue.
a. Call premium

$$\text{Before tax: } 0.10(\$60,000,000) = \$6,000,000.$$
$$\text{After tax: } \$6,000,000(1 - T) = \$6,000,000(0.66)$$
$$= \$3,960,000.$$

---

[2]The firm's management has estimated that there is a 75 percent probability that interest rates will remain at their present level of 12 percent or else rise; there is only a 25 percent probability that they will fall further.

Although Microchip must expend $6 million on the call premium, this is a tax deductible expense in the year the call is made. Since the company is in the 34 percent tax bracket, it saves $6,000,000 − $3,960,000 = $2,040,000 in taxes. Therefore, the after-tax cost of the call is only $3.96 million. This amount is shown as a cost, or outflow, on Line 1 of Table 20A-1.

b. Flotation costs on new issue

Flotation costs on the new issue are $2,650,000, as shown on Line 2 of the worksheet. For tax purposes, flotation costs must be amortized over the life of the new bond, or 20 years. Therefore, the annual tax deduction is

$$\frac{\$2,650,000}{20} = \$132,500.$$

Since Microchip is in the 34 percent tax bracket, it has a tax savings of $132,500(0.34) = $45,050 a year for 20 years. This is an annuity of $45,050 for 20 years. In a refunding analysis, all cash flows should be discounted at the after-tax cost of new debt, in this case 12%(1 − T) = 12%(0.66) = 7.92%. The present value of the tax savings, discounted at 7.92 percent, is $444,953, which is shown on Line 7 as an inflow.

c. Flotation costs on old issue

The old issue has an unamortized flotation cost of (20/25)($3,000,000) = $2.4 million at this time. If the issue is retired, the unamortized flotation cost may be recognized immediately as an expense, thus creating an after-tax savings of $2,400,000(0.34) = $816,000, which is shown on Line 3 of the worksheet. The firm will, however, no longer receive a tax deduction of $120,000 a year for 20 years, or an after-tax benefit of $40,800 a year. The present value of this tax savings, discounted at 7.92 percent, is $402,976, which is shown on Line 8 as an opportunity cost of the refunding. It is important to note that because of the refunding, the old flotation costs provide an immediate tax saving rather than annual savings over the next 20 years. Thus, the $816,000 − $402,976 = $413,024 net savings simply reflects the difference between the present value of benefits received in the future without the refunding versus an immediate benefit if the refunding occurs.

d. Additional interest

One month "extra" interest on the old issue, after taxes, costs $495,000:

$$(\text{Dollar amount})(1/12 \text{ of } 15\%)(1 − T) = \text{Interest cost}$$
$$(\$60,000,000)(0.0125)(0.66) = \$495,000.$$

However, the proceeds from the new issue can be invested in short-term securities for one month. Thus, $60 million invested at a rate of 11 percent will return $363,000 in after-tax interest:

$$(\$60,000,000)(1/12 \text{ of } 11\%)(1 − T) = \text{Interest earned}$$
$$(\$60,000,000)(0.009167)(0.66) = \$363,000.$$

These figures are reflected in Lines 4 and 5.

e. Total after-tax investment outlay

The total investment outlay required to refund the bond issue, which will be financed by debt, is thus $5,926,000.[3] This is shown on Line 6 of Table 20A-1.

Step 2. Calculate the PV of the flotation cost tax effects.

The net effect of the amortization of the flotation costs on the old and new issues is $41,977 in savings on a present value basis. This amount is shown on Line 9.

Step 3. Calculate the PV of the annual interest savings.

a. Interest on old bond, after tax

The annual after-tax interest on the old issue is $5,940,000:

$$(\$60,000,000)(0.15)(0.66) = \$5,940,000.$$

This is shown on Line 10.

b. Interest on new bond, after tax

The new issue has an annual after-tax cost of $4,752,000:

$$(\$60,000,000)(0.12)(0.66) = \$4,752,000.$$

This is shown on Line 11.

c. Annual savings

Thus, the annual after-tax savings is $1,188,000:

Interest on old bond, after tax	$5,940,000
Interest on new bond, after tax	(4,752,000)
Annual net savings	$1,188,000

This is shown on Line 12.

d. PV of annual savings

The PV of $1,188,000 per year at 7.92 percent for 20 years is $11,733,727. This is also shown on Line 12.

Step 4. Determine the NPV of the refunding.

Net investment outlay	($ 5,926,000)
Amortization tax effects	41,977
Interest savings	11,733,727
NPV from refunding	$ 5,849,704

Since the net present value of the refunding is positive, it would benefit stockholders to refund the old bond issue.

---

[3]The net cash investment outlay (in this case, about $6 million) is usually obtained by increasing the amount of the new bond issue. Thus, the new issue would be about $66 million. However, the interest on the additional debt *should not* be deducted at Step 2 because the net investment outlay itself will be deducted at Step 3. If additional interest on the $6 million were deducted at Step 2, then interest would, in effect, be deducted twice. The situation here is exactly like that in regular capital budgeting decisions. Even though some debt may be used to finance a project, interest on that debt is not subtracted when developing the annual cash flows. Rather, the annual cash flows are discounted by the project's cost of capital.

Several other points should be noted. First, since the cash flows are based on differences between contractual obligations, their risk is the same as that of the underlying obligations. Therefore, the present values of the cash flows should be found by discounting at the firm's least risky rate—its after-tax cost of marginal debt. Second, since the refunding operation is advantageous to the firm, it must be disadvantageous to bondholders; they must give up their 15 percent bonds and reinvest in new ones that yield 12 percent. This points out the danger of the call provision to bondholders, and it also explains why bonds without a call provision command higher prices than callable bonds. Third, although it is not emphasized in the example, we assumed that the firm raises the investment required to undertake the refunding operation (the $5,926,000 shown on Line 6 of Table 20A-1) as debt. This should be feasible, since the refunding operation will improve the interest coverage ratio even though, if the investment outlay is raised as debt, a larger amount of debt will be outstanding.[4] Fourth, we set up our example in such a way that the new issue had the same maturity as the remaining life of the old issue. Often, the old bonds have only a relatively short time to maturity (say, 5 to 10 years), while the new bonds would have a longer maturity (say, 25 to 30 years). In this situation, a replacement chain analysis is required. Although the interest savings benefit occurs over a much shorter period, refunding now pushes future flotation costs out further into the future, and this value can most easily be captured by a replacement chain analysis. Fifth, refunding decisions are well suited for analysis with a spreadsheet program such as *Lotus 1-2-3*. The spreadsheet is easy to set up, and once it is, it is easy to vary the assumptions, especially the assumption about the interest rate on the new issue, and to see the way such changes affect the NPV.

One final point should be addressed: Although our analysis shows that the refunding would increase the value of the firm, would refunding *at this time* truly maximize the firm's expected value? Note that if interest rates continue to fall, then the company might be better off waiting, for this could increase the NPV of the refunding operation even more. The mechanics of calculating the NPV of a refunding are simple, but the decision on *when* to refund is not a simple one at all, because it requires a forecast of future interest rates. Thus, refund now versus waiting for a possibly more favorable future refunding is a judgmental decision.

To illustrate the timing decision, assume that Microchip's managers forecast that long-term interest rates have a 50 percent probability of remaining at their present level of 12 percent over the next year. However, there is a 25 percent probability that rates could fall to 10 percent, and a 25 percent probability that they could rise to 14 percent. Further, assume that short-term rates are expected to remain one percentage point below long-term rates, and that the call premium would be reduced by one-twentieth if the call were delayed for one year.

The refunding analysis could then be repeated, as previously, but assuming it would take place one year from now. Thus, the old bonds would have only 19 years remaining to

---

[4]See Ahron R. Ofer and Robert A. Taggart, Jr., "Bond Refunding: A Clarifying Analysis," *Journal of Finance,* March 1977, 21–30, for a discussion of how the method of financing the refunding affects the analysis. Ofer and Taggart prove that (1) if the refunding investment outlay is to be raised as debt, the after-tax cost of debt is the proper discount rate, while (2) if these funds are to be raised as common equity, then the before-tax cost of debt is the proper rate. Since a profitable refunding will virtually always raise the firm's debt-carrying capacity (because total interest charges after the refunding will be lower than before the refunding), it is more logical to use debt than either equity or a combination of debt and equity to finance the operation. Therefore, firms generally do use additional debt to finance refunding operations, so we assume debt financing for the costs of refunding and discount at the after-tax cost of debt.

maturity. We performed the analysis and found the NPV distribution of refunding one year from now:

Probability	Long-Term Interest Rate	NPV of Refunding One Year from Now
25%	10%	$15,328,674
50	12	5,770,191
25	14	(2,158,208)

At first blush, it would seem reasonable to calculate the expected NPV of refunding next year in terms of the probability distribution. However, that would not be correct. If interest rates did rise to 14 percent, Microchip would not refund the issue; therefore, the actual NPV if rates rise to 14 percent would be zero. The expected NPV from refunding one year hence is, therefore, $0.25(\$15,328,674) + 0.50(\$5,770,191) + 0.25(\$0) = \$6,717,264$ versus $5,849,704 if refunding occurred today.

Even though the expected NPV of refunding in one year is higher, Microchip's managers would probably decide to refund today. The $5,849,704 represents a certain increase in firm value, whereas the $6,717,264 is only an expected increase, plus proper comparison requires that the $6,717,264 be discounted back one year to today. Microchip's managers should opt to delay refunding only if the expected NPV from later refunding is sufficiently above today's certain NPV to compensate for the risk and time value involved.

The refunding analysis could be extended by (1) including possible refunding at more than one future point in time, and (2) specifying future interest rates by a continuous rather than a discrete distribution. However, the essence of the timing decision would remain the same.

LEASE FINANCING

S ome of the biggest players in the airline business have never issued a ticket, lost a passenger's luggage, or landed a plane in bad weather. They are the aircraft lease companies — the merchant bankers of aviation — whose role in financing aircraft sales has helped cash-strapped airlines respond more quickly to market changes. Among the major players in aircraft leasing are GPA Group, a closely held company based in Shannon, Ireland, and International Lease Finance of Beverly Hills.

Aircraft leasing companies purchase airplanes from manufacturers such as Boeing, Airbus Industrie, and McDonnell Douglas and then lease them, often on a relatively short-term basis, to carriers such as American, British Airways, Delta, Lufthansa, and United. Currently, leasing companies buy about 50 percent of all new commercial aircraft sold. For years, banks, insurance companies, and aircraft manufacturers offered long-term financial leases to airlines, but in recent years, aircraft lease companies have offered short-term operating leases. Such leases, with terms that range from a few months to five years, separate the risks and rewards of owning aircraft from those of operating them.

The airline industry is currently undergoing major changes due to deregulation. The highly competitive nature of the industry has placed TWA and Continental in bankruptcy and has caused many airlines to cease operations, including Braniff, Eastern, Midway, and Pan Am. Furthermore, airlines are scrambling to find international partners — British Airways just made a $300 million investment in USAir, and there have been rumors of a possible merger between KLM, SAS, Swissair, and Austrian Airlines. In the days of regulation, airlines knew precisely the routes they would serve and also that prices could be

raised to cover whatever costs were incurred. Thus, airlines could buy planes with every confidence that route structures served would be relatively stable and revenues would cover financing costs. Now, airlines are constantly dropping and adding routes in response to competitive conditions and changing travel patterns. Because different types of aircraft are better suited for some routes than others, airlines now need to restructure their fleets routinely to optimize their aircraft mix for the routes being flown. Leasing provides airlines with this needed flexibility. If an airline had purchased all of its aircraft, it would be hampered in its ability to respond quickly to changing conditions. The leasing companies, on the other hand, lease all types of aircraft to all types of airlines, so there is usually some airline interested in leasing an aircraft when its lease is dropped by another airline.

Interestingly, Airbus Industrie, the European aircraft consortium, has adopted short-term leases as a sales tool. In 1992 alone, Delta and United "bought" aircraft from Airbus on "walkaway" leases, whereby the aircraft could be returned to the manufacturer in less than a year. U.S. manufacturers complain that Airbus can offer such terms only because it is subsidized by the four European countries that back the consortium. The Clinton administration is reportedly lobbying for Airbus to discontinue its short-term lease program, which would help Boeing and McDonnell Douglas but would potentially hurt U.S. airlines.

As you read this chapter, think about the airline industry and the reason leasing can be more attractive than buying, at least for some portion of an airline's fleet. Also, think about the leasing companies and manufacturers and why they may be able to offer lease rates that are attractive to the airlines. When you finish the chapter, you should have a good appreciation of how leases are analyzed and, just as important, in what situations leasing is likely to be attractive to both the user of the equipment and the leasing firm.

Firms generally own fixed assets and report them on their balance sheets, but it is the *use* of buildings and equipment that is important, not their ownership per se. One way of obtaining the use of facilities and equipment is to buy them, but an alternative is to lease them. Prior to the 1950s, leasing was generally associated with real estate — land and buildings. Today, however, it is possible to lease virtually any kind of fixed asset, and currently about 30 percent of all new capital equipment acquired by businesses is financed through lease arrangements.

TYPES OF LEASES

Leasing takes several different forms, the four most important being (1) operating leases, (2) financial, or capital, leases, (3) sale-and-leaseback arrangements, and (4) combination leases.

OPERATING LEASES

Operating leases, sometimes called *service leases,* generally provide for both *financing* and *maintenance.* IBM was one of the pioneers of the operating lease contract, and computers and office copying machines, together with automobiles and trucks, are the primary types of equipment involved in operating leases. The owner of the property is called the *lessor,* while the user is called the *lessee.*[1] Ordinarily, operating leases require the lessor to maintain and service the leased equipment, and the cost of the maintenance is built into the lease payments.

Another important characteristic of operating leases is the fact that they are *not fully amortized.* In other words, the payments required under the lease contract are not sufficient to recover the full cost of the equipment. However, the lease contract is written for a period considerably less than the expected economic life of the leased equipment, and the lessor expects to recover all costs either by subsequent renewal payments, by re-leasing the equipment to other lessees, or by sale of the equipment.

A final feature of operating leases is that they often contain a *cancellation clause* which gives the lessee the right to cancel the lease and to return the equipment before the expiration of the basic lease agreement. This is an important consideration to the lessee, for it means that the equipment can be returned if it is rendered obsolete by technological developments or if it is no longer needed because of a change in the lessee's business.

FINANCIAL, OR CAPITAL, LEASES

Financial leases, sometimes called *capital leases,* are differentiated from operating leases in that (1) they *do not* provide for maintenance service, (2) they *are not* cancellable, and (3) they *are* fully amortized (that is, the lessor receives rental payments equal to the full price of the leased equipment plus a return on investment). In a typical arrangement, the firm that will use the equipment (the lessee) selects the specific items it requires, and then it negotiates the price and delivery terms with the manufacturer. The user firm then arranges to have a leasing company (the lessor) buy the equipment from the manufacturer or the distributor, and the user firm simultaneously executes an agreement to lease the equipment from the financial institution. The terms of the lease call for full amortization of the

---

[1]The term *lessee* is pronounced "less-ee," not "lease-ee," and *lessor* is pronounced "less-or."

lessor's investment, plus a rate of return on the unamortized balance which is close to the percentage rate the lessee would have paid on a secured term loan. For example, if the lessee would have to pay 10 percent for a term loan, then a rate of about 10 percent would be built into the lease contract.

The lessee is generally given an option to renew the lease at a reduced rate upon expiration of the basic lease. However, the basic lease usually cannot be cancelled unless the lessor is completely paid off. Also, the lessee generally pays the property taxes and insurance on the leased property. Since the lessor receives a return *after,* or *net of,* these payments, this type of lease is often called a "net, net" lease.

SALE-AND-LEASEBACK ARRANGEMENTS

Under a *sale-and-leaseback arrangement,* a firm that owns land, buildings, or equipment sells the property to another firm and simultaneously executes an agreement to lease the property back for a stated period under specific terms. The capital supplier could be an insurance company, a commercial bank, a specialized leasing company, the finance arm of an industrial firm, or an individual investor. The sale-and-leaseback plan is an alternative to a mortgage.

Note that the seller immediately receives the purchase price put up by the buyer. At the same time, the seller-lessee retains the use of the property. The parallel to borrowing is carried over to the lease payment schedule. Under a mortgage loan arrangement, the lender would normally receive a series of equal payments just sufficient to amortize the loan and to provide a specified rate of return on the outstanding loan balance. Under a sale-and-leaseback arrangement, the lease payments are set up exactly the same way—the payments are just sufficient to return the full purchase price to the investor, plus a stated return on the lessor's investment.

Sale-and-leaseback arrangements are almost the same as financial leases, the major difference being that the leased equipment is used and the lessor buys it from the user-lessee instead of from a manufacturer or a distributor. A sale and leaseback may, then, be thought of as a special type of financial lease.

COMBINATION LEASES

Many lessors now offer leases under a wide variety of terms. Therefore, in practice, leases often do not fit exactly into the operating lease or financial lease category, but, rather, combine some features of each. Such leases are called *combination leases.* To illustrate, cancellation clauses are normally associated with operating leases, but many of today's financial leases also contain cancellation clauses. However, in financial leases these clauses generally include prepayment provisions whereby the lessee must make penalty payments sufficient to enable the lessor to recover the unamortized cost of the leased property.

SELF-TEST QUESTIONS

What is the difference between an operating lease and a financial, or capital, lease?

What is a sale-and-leaseback transaction?

What is a combination lease?

TAX EFFECTS

The full amount of the lease payments is a tax-deductible expense for the lessee *provided that the Internal Revenue Service agrees that a particular contract is a genuine lease and not simply an installment loan called a lease.* This makes it important that a lease contract be written in a form acceptable to the IRS. A lease that complies with all of the IRS requirements is called a *guideline,* or *tax-oriented, lease,* and the tax benefits of ownership (depreciation and investment tax credits when they are available) belong to the lessor. The main provisions of the tax guidelines are as follows:

1. The lease term (including any extensions or renewals at a fixed rental rate) must not exceed 80 percent of the estimated useful life of the equipment at the commencement of the lease transaction. Thus, at the end of the lease the equipment must have an estimated remaining life equal to at least 20 percent of its original life. Further, the remaining useful life must not be less than one year. This requirement limits the maximum term of a guideline lease to 80 percent of the asset's useful life. Note that an asset's useful life is normally much longer than its MACRS depreciation class life.

2. The equipment's estimated residual value (in constant dollars without adjustment for inflation) at the expiration of the lease must equal at least 20 percent of its value at the start of the lease. This requirement can have the effect of limiting the maximum lease term.

3. Neither the lessee nor any related party can have the right to purchase the property from the lessor at a fixed price predetermined at the lease's inception. However, the lessee can be given a fair market value purchase option.

4. Neither the lessee nor any related party can pay or guarantee payment of any part of the price of the leased equipment. Simply put, the lessee cannot make any investment in the equipment, other than through the lease payments.

5. The leased equipment must not be "limited use" property, defined as equipment that can only be used by the lessee or a related party at the end of the lease.

The reason for the IRS's concern about lease terms is that, without restrictions, a company could set up a "lease" transaction calling for very rapid payments, which would be tax deductions. The effect would be to depreciate the equipment over a much shorter period than its MACRS class life. For example, suppose a firm planned to acquire a $2,000,000 computer which had a 3-year MACRS class life.

The annual depreciation allowances would be $660,000 in Year 1, $900,000 in Year 2, $300,000 in Year 3, and $140,000 in Year 4. If the firm were in the 40 percent federal-plus-state tax bracket, the depreciation would provide a tax saving of $264,000 in Year 1, $360,000 in Year 2, $120,000 in Year 3, and $56,000 in Year 4, for a total savings of $800,000. At a 6 percent discount rate, the present value of these tax savings would be $757,441.

Now suppose the firm could acquire the computer through a 1-year lease arrangement with a leasing company for a payment of $2 million, with a 1-dollar purchase option. If the $2,000,000 payment were treated as a lease payment, it would be fully deductible, so it would provide a tax savings of 0.4($2,000,000) = $800,000 versus a present value of only $757,441 for the depreciation shelters. Thus, the lease payment and the depreciation would both provide the same total amount of tax savings (40% of $2,000,000, or $800,000), but the savings would come in faster, hence have a higher present value, with the 1-year lease. Therefore, if just any type of contract could be called a lease and given tax treatment as a lease, then the timing of the tax shelters could be speeded up as compared with ownership depreciation tax shelters. This speedup would benefit companies, but it would be costly to the government. For this reason, the IRS has established the rules described above for defining a lease for tax purposes.

Even though leasing can be used only within limits to speed up the effective depreciation schedule, there are still times when very substantial tax benefits can be derived from a leasing arrangement. For example, if a firm like Tucson Electric has a very large construction program which has generated so many investment tax credits and so much accelerated depreciation that it has no current tax liabilities, then depreciation shelters are not very useful. In this case, a leasing company set up by profitable companies like GE or Philip Morris can buy the equipment, receive the depreciation shelters, and then share these benefits with the lessee by charging lower lease payments. This point will be discussed in detail later in the chapter, but the point to be made now is that if firms are to obtain tax benefits from leasing, the lease contract must be written in a manner that will qualify it as a true lease under IRS guidelines. If there is any question about the legal status of the contract, the financial manager must be sure to have the firm's lawyers and accountants check the latest IRS regulations.[2]

Note that a lease which does not meet the tax guidelines is called a *non-tax-oriented lease.* For this type of lease, the lessee can only deduct the interest portion of each lease payment. However, the lessee is effectively the owner of the leased equipment; thus the lessee can take the tax depreciation.

---

[2]In 1981, Congress relaxed the normal IRS rules to permit *safe harbor leases,* which had virtually no IRS restrictions and which were explicitly designed to permit the transfer of tax benefits from low-profit companies which could not use them to high-profit companies which could. The point of safe harbor leases was to provide incentives for capital investment to companies which had little or no tax liability—under safe harbor leasing, companies with a low tax liability could sell the benefit to companies in a high marginal tax bracket. In 1981 and 1982, literally billions of dollars were paid by such profitable firms as IBM and Philip Morris for the tax shelters of such unprofitable ones as Ford and Eastern Airlines. However, in 1983, Congress sharply curtailed the use of safe harbor leases.

TABLE 21-1   BALANCE SHEET EFFECTS OF LEASING

Before Asset Increase				After Asset Increase							
Firms B and L				Firm B, which Borrows and Buys				Firm L, which Leases			
Current assets	$ 50	Debt	$ 50	Current assets	$ 50	Debt	$150	Current assets	$ 50	Debt	$ 50
Fixed assets	50	Equity	50	Fixed assets	150	Equity	50	Fixed assets	50	Equity	50
	$100		$100		$200		$200		$100		$100
Debt/assets ratio:			50%				75%				50%

SELF-TEST QUESTIONS

What is the difference between a tax-oriented lease and a non-tax-oriented lease?

What are some lease provisions that would cause a lease to be classified as a non-tax-oriented lease?

Why is it necessary for the IRS to place limits on lease provisions?

FINANCIAL STATEMENT EFFECTS

Under certain conditions, neither the leased assets nor the liabilities under the lease contract appear on the firm's balance sheet. For this reason, leasing is often called *off-balance sheet* financing. This point is illustrated in Table 21-1 by the balance sheets of two hypothetical firms, B and L. Initially, the balance sheets of both firms are identical, and they both have debt ratios of 50 percent. Next, each firm decides to acquire a fixed asset costing $100. Firm B borrows $100 and buys the asset, so both an asset and a liability go on its balance sheet, and its debt ratio rises from 50 to 75 percent. Firm L leases the equipment. The lease may call for fixed charges as high or even higher than the loan, and the obligations assumed under the lease may be equally or more dangerous from the standpoint of potential bankruptcy, but the firm's debt ratio remains at only 50 percent.

To correct this problem, the Financial Accounting Standards Board issued FASB Statement 13, which requires that, for an unqualified audit report, firms that enter into financial (or capital) leases must restate their balance sheets to report the leased asset as a fixed asset and the present value of the future lease payments as a liability. This process is called *capitalizing the lease,* and its net effect is to cause Firms B and L to have similar balance sheets, both of which will, in essence, resemble the one shown for Firm B.[3]

---

[3]FASB Statement 13, "Accounting for Leases," spells out in detail both the conditions under which the lease must be capitalized and the procedures for capitalizing it.

The logic behind Statement 13 is as follows. If a firm signs a financial lease contract, its obligation to make lease payments is just as binding as if it had signed a loan agreement—the failure to make lease payments can bankrupt a firm just as fast as the failure to make principal and interest payments on a loan. Therefore, for all intents and purposes, a financial lease is identical to a loan.[4] This being the case, if a firm signs a financial lease agreement, this has the effect of raising its true debt ratio, and thus its true capital structure is changed. Therefore, if the firm had previously established a target capital structure, and if there is no reason to think that the optimal capital structure has changed, then using lease financing requires additional equity support exactly like debt financing.

If disclosure of the lease in our Table 21-1 example were not made, then Firm L's investors could be deceived into thinking that its financial position is stronger than it really is. Thus, even before FASB Statement 13 was issued in 1976, firms were required to disclose the existence of long-term leases in footnotes to their financial statements. At that time, it was debated as to whether or not investors recognized fully the impact of leases and, in effect, would see that Firms B and L were in essentially the same financial position. Some people argued that leases were not fully recognized, even by sophisticated investors. If this were the case, then leasing could alter the capital structure decision in a really significant manner—a firm could increase its true leverage through a lease arrangement, and this procedure would have a smaller effect on its cost of conventional debt, k_d, and on its cost of equity, k_s, than if it had borrowed directly and reflected this fact on its balance sheet. These benefits of leasing would accrue to existing investors at the expense of new investors who would, in effect, be deceived by the fact that the firm's balance sheet did not reflect its true liability situation.

The question of whether investors were truly deceived was debated but never resolved. Those who believed strongly in efficient markets thought that investors were not deceived and that footnotes were sufficient, while those who questioned market efficiency thought that all leases should be capitalized. Statement 13 represents a compromise between these two positions, though one that is tilted heavily toward those who favor capitalization.

A lease is classified as a capital lease, and hence is capitalized and shown directly on the balance sheet, if one or more of the following conditions exist:

1. Under the terms of the lease, ownership of the property is effectively transferred from the lessor to the lessee.

2. The lessee can purchase the property at less than its true market value when the lease expires.

---

[4]There are, however, certain legal differences between loans and leases. In the event of liquidation in bankruptcy, a lessor is entitled to take possession of the leased asset, and if the value of the asset is less than the required payments under the lease, the lessor can enter a claim (as a general creditor) for one year's lease payments. In a reorganization, the lessor receives the asset plus three years' lease payments if needed to cover the value of the lease. The lender under a secured loan arrangement has a security interest in the asset, meaning that if it is sold, the lender will be given the proceeds, and the full unsatisfied portion of the lender's claim will be treated as a general creditor obligation. It is not possible to state, as a general rule, whether a supplier of capital is in a stronger position as a secured creditor or as a lessor. Usually, one position is regarded as being about as good as the other at the time the financial arrangements are being made.

3. The lease runs for a period equal to or greater than 75 percent of the asset's life. Thus, if an asset has a 10-year life and the lease is written for 8 years, the lease must be capitalized.

4. The present value of the lease payments is equal to or greater than 90 percent of the initial value of the asset.[5]

These rules, together with strong footnote disclosure rules for operating leases, are sufficient to ensure that no one will be fooled by lease financing; thus, leases are regarded as debt for capital structure purposes, and they have the same effects as debt on k_d and k_s. Therefore, leasing is not likely to permit a firm to use more financial leverage than could be obtained with conventional debt.

SELF-TEST QUESTIONS

Why is lease financing sometimes referred to as off-balance sheet financing?

What is the intent of FASB Statement 13?

What is the difference in the balance sheet treatment of a lease that is capitalized and one that is not?

EVALUATION BY THE LESSEE

Leases are evaluated by both the lessee and the lessor. The lessee must determine whether leasing an asset is less costly than buying the asset, and the lessor must decide what the lease payments must be to produce a target rate of return on invested funds. This section focuses on the analysis by the lessee.

In the typical case, the events leading to a lease arrangement follow the sequence described next. We should note that a degree of uncertainty exists regarding the theoretically correct way to evaluate lease-versus-purchase decisions, and some very complex decision models have been developed to aid in the analysis. However, the simple analysis given here leads to the correct decision in all the cases we have ever encountered.

1. The firm decides to acquire a particular building or piece of equipment; this decision is based on regular capital budgeting procedures. The decision to acquire the machine is not at issue in the typical lease analysis—this decision was made previously as part of the capital budgeting process. In a lease analysis, we are concerned simply with whether to obtain the use of the machine by lease or by purchase. However, if the effective cost of capital obtained by leasing is substan-

---

[5]The discount rate used to calculate the present value of the lease payments must be the lower of (1) the rate used by the lessor to establish the lease payments (this rate is discussed later in the chapter) or (2) the rate of interest which the lessee would have to pay for new debt with a maturity equal to that of the lease. Also, note that any maintenance payments embedded in the lease payment must be stripped out prior to checking this condition.

tially lower than the cost of debt, then the cost of capital used in capital budgeting would have to be recalculated, and perhaps projects formerly deemed unacceptable might become acceptable.

2. Once the firm has decided to acquire the asset, the next question is how to finance its acquisition. Well-run businesses do not have excess cash lying around, so capital to finance new assets must be obtained from some source.

3. Funds to purchase the asset could be obtained by borrowing, by retaining earnings, or by selling new equity. Alternatively, the asset could be leased. Because of the capitalization/disclosure provision for leases, leasing normally has the same capital structure effect as borrowing.

As indicated earlier, a lease is comparable to a loan in the sense that the firm is required to make a specified series of payments and that a failure to meet these payments could result in bankruptcy. Thus, the most appropriate comparison is the cost of lease financing versus the cost of debt financing.[6]

To illustrate the basic elements of lease analysis, consider this simplified example. The Thompson-Grammatikos Company (TGC) requires the use of a 2-year asset that costs $100, and the company must choose between leasing and buying the asset. If the asset is purchased, the bank would lend TGC the $100 at a rate of 10 percent on a 2-year, simple interest loan. Thus, the firm would have to pay the bank $10 in interest at the end of each year, plus return the $100 of principal at the end of Year 2. For simplicity, assume that TGC could depreciate the asset over 2 years for tax purposes by the straight line method if it is purchased, resulting in tax depreciation of $50 in each year. Also for simplicity, assume the asset's value at the end of 2 years (the residual value) is estimated to be $0.

Alternatively, assume the firm could lease the asset under a guideline lease for 2 years for a payment of $55 at the end of each year. TGC's tax rate is 40 percent. The analysis for the lease-versus-borrow decision consists of (1) estimating the cash flows associated with borrowing and buying the asset, that is, the flows associated with debt financing, (2) estimating the cash flows associated with leasing the asset, and (3) comparing the two financing methods to determine which has the lower cost. Here are the borrow-and-buy flows:

Cash Flows if TGC Buys	Year 0	Year 1	Year 2
Equipment cost	($100)		
Loan amount	100		
Interest expense		($10)	($ 10)
Tax savings from interest		4	4
Principal repayment			(100)
Tax savings from depreciation		20	20
Net cash flow	$ 0	$14	($ 86)

---

[6]Note that the analysis should compare the cost of leasing with the cost of debt financing *regardless* of how the asset purchase is actually financed. The asset may be purchased with available cash if not leased, but since leasing is a substitute for debt financing, the appropriate comparison would still be with debt financing.

The net cash flow is zero in Year 0, positive in Year 1, and negative in Year 2. The operating cash flows are not shown, but they must, of course, be positive or else TGC would not want to acquire the asset. Since the operating cash flows will be the same regardless of whether the asset is leased or purchased, they can be ignored.

Here are the cash flows associated with the lease:

Cash Flows if TGC Leases	Year 0	Year 1	Year 2
Lease payment		($55)	($55)
Tax savings from payment	__	22	22
Net cash flow	$0	($33)	($33)

Note that the two sets of cash flows reflect the tax deductibility of interest expense, depreciation, and lease payments, as appropriate. Thus, the net cash flows include the tax savings from these items. If the lease had not met IRS guidelines, then ownership would effectively reside with the lessee, and TGC would depreciate the asset for tax purposes whether it was leased or purchased. In this case, only the implied interest portion of the lease payment would be tax deductible. Thus, the analysis for a nonguideline lease would consist of simply comparing the after-tax financing flows on the loan with the after-tax lease payment stream.

To compare the cost streams of buying and leasing, we must put them on a present value basis. As we explain later, the correct discount rate is the after-tax cost of debt, which for TGC is $10\%(1 - 0.4) = 6.0\%$. Applying this rate, we find the present value cost of buying to be $63.33, and the present value cost of leasing to be $60.50. Since leasing has the lower present value of costs, the company should lease this particular asset.

The example shows the general approach that we use in lease analysis, and it also illustrates a concept that can simplify the cash flow estimation process. Look back at the loan-related cash flows if TGC buys the asset. The after-tax principal and interest payments are − $6 in Year 1 and − $106 in Year 2. When these flows are discounted to Year 0 at the 6.0 percent after-tax cost rate, their present value is − $100, the negative of the loan amount. This equality results because we first used the cost of debt to estimate the future financing flows, and we then used this same rate to discount the flows back to the present, all on an after-tax basis. The net result is that the financing flows cancel one another out.

Here is the cash flow stream after the Year 0 loan amount and the related Year 1 and Year 2 flows have been removed:

Cash Flows if TGC Buys	Year 0	Year 1	Year 2
Cost of asset	($100)		
Tax savings from depreciation	__	$20	$20
Net cash flow	($100)	$20	$20

The present value cost of buying here is, of course, $63.33, the same number we found earlier. This result will always occur regardless of the specific terms of the

debt financing—as long as the discount rate is the after-tax cost of debt, the cash flows associated with the loan can be ignored.

Now we examine a more realistic example, one for the Anderson Equipment Company, which is conducting a lease analysis on some assembly line equipment that it will procure in the coming year. The following data have been developed:

1. Anderson plans to acquire automated assembly line equipment with a 10-year life and a cost of $10 million, delivered and installed. However, Anderson plans to use the equipment for only 5 years, for it will discontinue the product line at that time.

2. Anderson can borrow the required $10 million at a before-tax cost of 10 percent.

3. The equipment's estimated scrap value is $50,000 after 10 years of use, but its estimated salvage value after only 5 years of use is $1,000,000. Thus, if Anderson buys the equipment, it would expect to receive $1,000,000 before taxes when the equipment is sold in 5 years. Note that in leasing, the asset's value at the end of the lease period is generally called its *residual value*.

4. Anderson can lease the equipment for 5 years at a rental charge of $2,750,000, payable at the beginning of each year, but the lessor will own the equipment upon the expiration of the lease. (The lease payment schedule is established by the potential lessor, as described in the next major section, and Anderson can accept it, reject it, or negotiate.)

5. The lease contract stipulates that the lessor will maintain the equipment at no additional charge to Anderson. However, if Anderson borrows and buys, it will have to bear the cost of maintenance, which will be performed by the equipment manufacturer at a fixed contract rate of $500,000 per year, payable at the beginning of each year.

6. The equipment falls in the MACRS 5-year class life, Anderson's marginal tax rate is 40 percent, and the lease qualifies as a guideline lease.

NPV ANALYSIS

Table 21-2 shows the steps involved in a complete NPV lease analysis. Part I of the table is devoted to the costs of borrowing and buying. Line 1 gives the equipment's cost; Line 2 shows the maintenance expense; Line 3 gives the maintenance tax savings; Line 4 contains the depreciation tax savings, which is the depreciation expense times the tax rate; Lines 5 and 6 contain the residual value cash flows; Line 7 contains the net cash flows; and Line 8 shows the net present value of these flows, discounted at 6 percent.

Part II of Table 21-2 contains an analysis of the cost of leasing. The lease payments, shown on Line 9, are $2,750,000 per year; this rate, which includes maintenance, was established by the prospective lessor and offered to Anderson Equipment. If Anderson accepts the lease, the full amount will be a deductible expense, so the tax savings, shown on Line 10, is 0.40(Lease payment) = 0.40($2,750,000) = $1,100,000. Thus, the after-tax cost of the lease payment is Lease payment − Tax savings = $2,750,000 − $1,100,000 = $1,650,000. This amount is shown on Line 11, Years 0 through 4.

TABLE 21-2   ANDERSON EQUIPMENT COMPANY: NPV ANALYSIS (THOUSANDS OF DOLLARS)

I. Cost of Owning (Borrowing and Buying)

	Year 0	Year 1	Year 2	Year 3	Year 4	Year 5
1. Net purchase price	($10,000)					
2. Maintenance cost	(500)	($500)	($ 500)	($500)	($500)	
3. Maintenance tax savings	200	200	200	200	200	
4. Depreciation tax savings		800	1,280	760	480	$ 440
5. Residual value						1,000
6. Residual value tax						(160)
7. Net cash flow	($10,300)	$500	$ 980	$460	$180	$1,280
8. PV cost of owning = ($7,471)						

II. Cost of Leasing

	Year 0	Year 1	Year 2	Year 3	Year 4	Year 5
9. Lease payment	($2,750)	($2,750)	($2,750)	($2,750)	($2,750)	
10. Payment tax savings	1,100	1,100	1,100	1,100	1,100	
11. Net cash flow	($1,650)	($1,650)	($1,650)	($1,650)	($1,650)	$0
12. PV cost of leasing = ($7,367)						

III. Cost Comparison

13. Net advantage to leasing (NAL) = PV cost of owning − PV cost of leasing = $7,471 − $7,367 = $104.

Notes:

a. The net cash flows shown in Lines 7 and 11 are discounted at the lessee's after-tax cost of debt, 6.0 percent.

b. The MACRS depreciation allowances are 0.20, 0.32, 0.19, 0.12, and 0.11 in Years 1 through 5, respectively. Thus, the depreciation expense is 0.20($10,000) = $2,000 in Year 1, and so on. The depreciation tax savings in each year is merely 0.4 (Depreciation).

c. The residual value is $1,000 while the book value is $600. Thus, Anderson would have to pay 0.4($1,000 − $600) = $160 in taxes, producing a net after-tax residual value of $1,000 − $160 = $840. These amounts are shown in Lines 5 and 6 in the cost of owning analysis.

d. In practice, a lease analysis such as this would be done using a spreadsheet program such as *Lotus 1-2-3*.

e. In the NAL equation on Line 13, the PV costs are stated as positive values. If the PV costs are treated as negative values, or outflows, the NAL must be redefined as follows: NAL = PV cost of leasing − PV cost of owning = − $7,367 − (− $7,471) = $104.

The next step is to compare the net cost of owning with the net cost of leasing. However, we must first put the annual cash flows of leasing and borrowing on a common basis. This requires converting them to present values, which brings up the question of the proper rate at which to discount the costs. We know that the riskier the cash flows, the higher will be the discount rate used to find present values. This same principle was observed in our discussion of capital budgeting, and it also applies in lease analysis. Just how risky are the cash flows under consideration here? Most of them are relatively certain, at least when compared with the types of cash flow estimates that were developed in capital budgeting. For example, the loan payment schedule is set by contract, as is the lease payment schedule. The depreciation expenses are also established by law and not subject to change, and the $500,000 annual maintenance cost is fixed by contract as well. The tax

savings are somewhat uncertain, but they will be as projected so long as Anderson's marginal tax rate remains at 40 percent. The residual value is the least certain of the cash flows, but even here, Anderson's management is fairly confident because the estimated residual value distribution is relatively tight.

Since the cash flows under the lease and under the borrow-and-purchase alternatives are both relatively certain, they should be discounted at a relatively low rate. Most analysts recommend that the company's cost of debt be used, and this rate seems reasonable in our example. Further, since the interest on the loan would be tax deductible, *the after-tax cost of debt, which is 6.0 percent, should be used.* Accordingly, we discount the net cash flows on Lines 7 and 11 using a rate of 6.0 percent. The resulting present values are $7,471,000 for the cost of owning and $7,367,000 for the cost of leasing, as shown on Lines 8 and 12. The financing method that produces the smaller present value of costs is the one that should be selected. We define the net advantage to leasing (NAL) as follows (see Note e to Table 21-2):

$$
\begin{aligned}
\text{NAL} &= \text{PV cost of owning} - \text{PV cost of leasing} \\
&= \$7,471,000 \quad - \quad \$7,367,000 \\
&= \$104,000.
\end{aligned}
$$

The PV cost of owning exceeds the PV cost of leasing, so the NAL is positive. Therefore, Anderson should lease the equipment.[7]

---

[7]The more complicated methods which exist for analyzing leasing generally focus on the issue of the discount rate that should be used to discount the cash flows. Conceptually, we could assign a separate discount rate to each individual cash flow component, then find the present values of each of the cash flow components, and finally sum these present values to determine the net advantage or disadvantage to leasing. This approach has been taken by Stewart C. Myers, David A. Dill, and Alberto J. Bautista (MDB) in "Valuation of Financial Lease Contracts," *Journal of Finance,* June 1976, 799–819, among others. MDB correctly note that procedures like the one presented in this chapter are valid only if (1) leases and loans are viewed by investors as being equivalent and (2) all cash flows are equally risky, hence appropriately discounted at the same rate. The first assumption is valid today for virtually all financial leases, and even where it is not, no one knows how to adjust properly for any capital structure effects that leases might have. (MDB, and others, have presented an adjustment formula, but it is based on the assumption that the Modigliani-Miller leverage argument, with no financial distress costs, is correct. Since even MM do not regard the pure MM model as being correct, the MDB formula cannot be correct.) Regarding the second assumption, it is generally believed that all of the cash flows in Table 21-2 except the residual value are of about the same degree of risk, at least to the extent that we are able to evaluate risk. Therefore, the procedures used in Table 21-2 normally meet the MDB assumption; hence, the Table 21-2 analysis is usually correct.

Regarding the residual value, advocates of multiple discount rates often point out that the residual value is more uncertain than are the other cash flows and thus recommend discounting it at a higher rate. However, there is no way of knowing precisely how much to increase the after-tax cost of debt to account for the increased riskiness of the residual value cash flow. Further, in a market risk sense, all cash flows could be equally risky even though individual items such as the residual value might have more or less total variability than others. To complicate matters even more, the market risk of the residual value will usually be different than the firm's market risk. For more on residual value risk, see John J. McConnell and James S. Schallheim, "Valuation of Asset Leasing Contracts," *Journal of Financial Economics,* August 1983, 237–261.

TABLE 21-3   Anderson Equipment Company: IRR Analysis (Thousands of Dollars)

	Year 0	Year 1	Year 2	Year 3	Year 4	Year 5
1. Avoided net purchase price	$10,000					
2. After-tax lease payment	(1,650)	($1,650)	($1,650)	($1,650)	($1,650)	
3. Loss of depreciation tax savings		(800)	(1,280)	(760)	(480)	($ 440)
4. Avoided after-tax maintenance cost	300	300	300	300	300	
5. Loss of after-tax residual value						(840)
6. Net cash flow	$ 8,650	($2,150)	($2,630)	($2,110)	($1,830)	($1,280)

$$\text{NPV} = \sum_{t=0}^{5} \frac{\text{NCF}_t}{(1 + k_L)^t} = 0 \text{ when } k_L = \text{IRR} = 5.5\%.$$

IRR ANALYSIS

Anderson's lease-versus-purchase decision could also be analyzed using the IRR approach. Here we know the after-tax cost of debt, 6.0 percent, so we can find the *after-tax cost rate implied in the lease contract* and compare it with the cost of the loan. Signing a lease is similar to signing a loan contract—the firm has the use of equipment, but it must make a series of payments under either type of contract. We know the rate built into the loan; it is 6.0 percent after taxes for Anderson. There is an equivalent cost rate built into the lease. If the equivalent after-tax cost rate in the lease is less than the after-tax interest rate on the debt, then there is an advantage to leasing.

Table 21-3 sets forth the cash flows needed to determine the equivalent loan cost. Here is an explanation of the table:

1. The net cost to purchase the equipment, which is avoided if Anderson leases, is shown on Line 1 as a positive cash flow (an inflow) at Year 0. If Anderson leases, it avoids having to pay the net purchase price for the equipment—the lessor pays that cost—so Anderson saves $10 million. That is a positive cash flow at Year 0.

2. Next, we must determine what Anderson must give up (or "pay back") if it leases. As we saw in the last section, Anderson must make annual lease payments of $2,750,000, which amount to $1,650,000 on an after-tax basis. These amounts are reported as cash outflows on Line 2, Years 0 through 4.

3. If Anderson elects to lease, it will give up the right to depreciate the asset. The lost depreciation tax savings, which represent an opportunity cost of leasing, are shown as outflows on Line 3, Years 1 through 5.

4. If Anderson decides to lease rather than borrow and buy, it will avoid the maintenance cost of $500,000 per year, or $300,000 after taxes. This is shown on Line 4 as an inflow, or benefit of leasing.

5. Finally, if Anderson leases the equipment, it will give up the net after-tax residual value of $840,000. This is also an opportunity cost of leasing, and it is shown on Line 5 as an outflow in Year 5.

6. Line 6 shows the annual net cash flows. If Anderson leases, there is an inflow at Year 0 followed by outflows in Years 1 to 5. Note that the Line 6 net cash flows are simply the net cash flows of leasing rather than buying, or Line 11 minus Line 7 in Table 21-2.

By entering the cash flows on Line 6 of Table 21-3 into the cash flow register of a calculator and then pressing the IRR button, we can find the IRR for the stream; it is 5.5 percent, and this is the equivalent after-tax cost rate implied in the lease contract. If Anderson leases, it is using up $10 million of its debt capacity, and the implied cost rate is 5.5 percent. Since this cost rate is less than the 6.0 percent after-tax cost of a regular loan, this IRR lease analysis confirms the NPV analysis: Anderson should lease rather than buy the equipment. The NPV and IRR approaches will always lead to the same decision. Thus, one method is as good as the other from a decision standpoint.[8]

FEEDBACK EFFECT ON CAPITAL BUDGETING

Up to now, we have assumed that the potential lessee has already made a firm decision to acquire the new equipment. Thus, the lease analysis was conducted only to determine whether the equipment should be leased or purchased. However, if the cost of leasing is less than the cost of debt, it is possible for projects formerly deemed unacceptable to become acceptable.

To illustrate this point, assume that Anderson's target capital structure calls for 50 percent debt and 50 percent common equity, that Anderson's cost of debt, k_d, is 10 percent, and that its cost of equity, k_s, is 15 percent. Thus, Anderson's weighted average cost of capital is

$$\text{WACC} = 0.5(10\%)(0.60) + 0.5(15\%)$$
$$= 0.5(6.0\%) + 0.5(15\%) = 10.5\%.$$

Further, assume that the firm's initial capital budgeting analysis on this equipment, using a 10.5 percent project cost of capital for average-risk projects, resulted in an NPV of − $50,000. As we saw in the preceding section, the after-tax cost of leasing for this project is 5.5 percent, compared with Anderson's after-tax cost of debt of 6.0 percent. Thus, this project can be financed at a lower cost than other projects which involve equipment that cannot be leased.

What should we do now? There are two possible polar positions, depending on Anderson's opportunity to substitute lease financing for regular debt financing:

1. *The debt component of all projects can be financed by leasing on similar lease terms.* In this case, Anderson should never borrow—all of its "debt" financing

---

[8]Note that the net cash flows shown on Line 6 of Table 21-3 are the incremental cash flows to Anderson if it leases rather than borrows and buys. Thus, the NPV of these flows is the net advantage to leasing. When discounted at a rate of 6.0 percent, the NPV of the Line 6 flows is $103,389, which, except for a rounding difference, is the same as we obtained in the Table 21-2 NPV analysis.

should come from leasing. If it had a capital budget of $100 million, and if its optimal capital structure called for 50 percent debt, then it should lease assets with a cost of $50 million and finance the remainder with equity. All projects, regardless of how they will actually be financed, should be evaluated at a WACC based on the debt cost implied in the lease contracts, 5.5 percent in our example. Thus for all average-risk projects,

$$\begin{array}{c}\text{WACC for use in}\\ \text{capital budgeting}\end{array} = 0.5(5.5\%) + 0.5(15\%) = 10.25\%.$$

Anderson's capital budgeting director should now recalculate the project's NPV using a cost of capital of 10.25 percent versus the average project cost of capital, ignoring leasing, of 10.5 percent. Assume that the project's NPV is now + $20,000. The availability of lease financing has made the project acceptable, whereas the project would have been unacceptable if lease financing were not available.

2. *The project under consideration is unique in that it is the only one for which favorable lease terms are available.* In this case, with the further assumption that the cost of the project does not exceed the company's debt financing for the year (or in total under certain circumstances), then the NPV of the project for capital budgeting purposes should be determined as follows:

$$\text{Adjusted NPV} = \begin{array}{c}\text{NPV based on}\\ \text{``regular'' WACC}\end{array} + \begin{array}{c}\text{NAL from}\\ \text{Table 21-2}\end{array}$$
$$= -\$50,000 + \$104,000 = \$54,000.$$

Here the firm has enough debt capacity to finance the project entirely by leasing, so the firm will get the entire NAL. (If all projects were suitable for leasing, they still could not be leased because of the total debt capacity constraint. Therefore, under the conditions of the preceding paragraph, this procedure is not appropriate.) The entire NAL should be allocated to this project. All other projects should be evaluated on the basis of the WACC with "regular" debt.

If neither polar position holds, or if different projects can be leased on different lease terms with different equivalent loan rates, then no simple rule can be used. Note, though, that as a practical matter we rarely need to go into the feedback effects of leasing on capital budgeting in the first place, because few projects that are not acceptable under one financing method would be acceptable under another. Given all the uncertainties about capital budgeting cash flows, few managers would change their minds about the acceptability of a project as a result of a few basis points change in the WACC. Still, for certain types of businesses, especially those where real estate is an important element, the availability of lease financing could make the difference in the go/no-go decision. Therefore, it is important for financial managers to know how leasing might affect capital budgeting analysis.

EQUIVALENT LOAN ANALYSIS

There is yet another way to think about a lease from the lessee's perspective. Refer back to the net cash flows listed in Line 6 of Table 21-3. These are the incremental cash flows of leasing versus owning. In effect, Anderson would save $8,650,000 at Time 0 if it leases, but it would have to bear the incremental costs shown for Years 1 to 5. Now consider the dollar amount of the loan that Anderson could obtain if it paid the cash flows in Years 1 to 5 to a lender instead of the lessor. At the 6.0 percent after-tax cost of debt, the present value of the cash outflows is $8,547,000. Thus, a lender charging 10.0 percent (6.0 percent after taxes) would lend Anderson $8,547,000 at Time 0 in return for the 5-year payment stream. However, the lessor, in effect, is willing to lend Anderson $8,650,000 at Time 0. Thus, the lessor would provide an additional $8,650,000 − $8,547,000 = $103,000 in financing over that provided by a lender. This amount, of course, is Anderson's net advantage to leasing (except for a rounding difference).

We have looked at three different ways of analyzing a lease from the lessee's perspective: (1) the NPV (or NAL) method, (2) the IRR method, and (3) the equivalent loan method. The three methods are equivalent, and it is only necessary to apply one method in practice. However, all three methods are used in practice, so it is useful to be familiar with all of them.

SELF-TEST QUESTIONS

Explain how the cash flows are structured when estimating the net advantage to leasing.

What discount rate should be used in the lessee's analysis? Why?

Define the term "net advantage to leasing."

What is the economic significance of a lease's IRR?

Can the ability to lease an asset ever affect the capital budgeting decision? Explain.

Briefly describe the concept behind the equivalent loan analysis method.

EVALUATION BY THE LESSOR

Thus far we have considered leasing only from the lessee's viewpoint. It is also useful to analyze the transaction as the lessor sees it: Is the lease a good investment for the party who must put up the money? The lessor will generally be a specialized leasing company, a bank or bank affiliate, an individual or group of individuals, or a manufacturer such as IBM that uses leasing as a sales tool. The specialized leasing companies are often owned by profitable companies such as General Electric, which owns General Electric Capital, the largest leasing company in existence. Investment banking houses such as Merrill Lynch also set up and/or work with specialized leasing companies, where brokerage clients' money is made available

TABLE 21-4		Year 0	Year 1	Year 2	Year 3	Year 4	Year 5
LEASE ANALYSIS	1. Net purchase price	($10,000)					
FROM THE LESSOR'S	2. Maintenance cost	(500)	($ 500)	($ 500)	($ 500)	($ 500)	
VIEWPOINT	3. Maintenance tax savings	200	200	200	200	200	
(THOUSANDS OF	4. Depreciation tax savings		800	1,280	760	480	$ 440
DOLLARS)	5. Lease payment	2,750	2,750	2,750	2,750	2,750	
	6. Tax on lease payment	(1,100)	(1,100)	(1,100)	(1,100)	(1,100)	
	7. Residual value						1,000
	8. Tax on residual value						(160)
	9. Net cash flow	($ 8,650)	$2,150	$2,630	$2,110	$1,830	$1,280

$$\text{NPV} = \sum_{t=0}^{5} \frac{\text{NCF}_t}{(1 + k)^t} = \$26 \text{ when } k = 5.4\%.$$

$$\text{IRR: NPV} = 0 = \sum_{t=0}^{5} \frac{\text{NCF}_t}{(1 + \text{IRR})^t}. \quad \text{IRR} = 5.5\%.$$

to leasing customers in deals which permit the investors to share in the tax shelters provided by the lease.

Any potential lessor needs to know the rate of return on the capital invested in the lease, and this information is also useful to the prospective lessee: Lease terms on large leases are generally negotiated, so the lessor and the lessee should know one another's position. The lessor's analysis involves (1) determining the net cash outlay, which is usually the invoice price of the leased equipment less any lease payments made in advance; (2) determining the periodic cash inflows, which consist of the lease payments minus both income taxes and any maintenance expense the lessor must bear; (3) estimating the after-tax residual value of the property when the lease expires; and (4) determining whether the rate of return on the lease exceeds the lessor's opportunity cost of capital or, equivalently, whether the NPV of the lease exceeds zero.

To illustrate the lessor's analysis, we assume the same facts as for the Anderson Equipment Company lease, as well as this situation: (1) The potential lessor is a wealthy individual whose current income is in the form of interest, and whose marginal federal-plus-state income tax rate, T, is 40 percent. (2) The investor can buy bonds that have a 9 percent yield to maturity, providing an after-tax yield of $(9\%)(1 - T) = (9\%)(0.6) = 5.4\%$. This is the after-tax return that the investor can obtain on alternative investments of similar risk. (3) The before-tax residual value is $1,000,000. Since the asset will be depreciated to a book value of $600,000 at the end of the 5-year lease, $400,000 of this $1 million will be taxable at the 40 percent rate because of the recapture of depreciation rule, so the lessor can expect to receive $840,000 after taxes from the sale of the equipment after the lease expires.

The NPV of the lease from the lessor's standpoint is developed in Table 21-4. Here we see that the lease as an investment has a net present value of $26,000. On a present value basis, the investor who invests in the lease rather than in the

9 percent bonds (5.4 percent after taxes) is better off by $26,000, indicating that the investor should be willing to write the lease. Since we saw earlier that the lease is also advantageous to Anderson Equipment Company, the transaction should be completed.

The investor can also calculate the lease investment's IRR based on the net cash flows shown on Line 9 of Table 21-4. The IRR of the lease, which is that discount rate which forces the NPV of the lease to zero, is 5.5 percent. Thus, the lease provides a 5.5 percent after-tax return to this 40 percent tax rate investor. This exceeds the 5.4 percent after-tax return on 9 percent bonds. So, using either the IRR or the NPV method, the lease would appear to be a satisfactory investment.[9]

SETTING THE LEASE PAYMENT

In the preceding sections we evaluated the lease assuming that the lease payments had already been specified. However, as a general rule, in large leases the parties will sit down and work out an agreement as to the size of the lease payments, with these payments being set so as to provide the lessor with some specific required rate of return. In situations where the lease terms are not negotiated, which is often the case for small leases, the lessor must still go through the same type of analysis, setting terms which provide a target rate of return, and then offering these terms to the potential lessee on a take-it-or-leave-it basis.

Competition among leasing companies forces lessors to build market-related returns into their lease payment schedules. To illustrate all this, suppose the potential lessor described earlier, after examining other alternative investment opportunities, decides that the 5.5 percent return on the Anderson Equipment Company lease is too low, and that the lease should provide an after-tax return of 6.0 percent. What lease payment schedule would provide this return?

To answer this question, note again that Table 21-4 contains the lessor's cash flow analysis. If the basic analysis is computerized, it is very easy to first change the discount rate to 6 percent, and then change the lease payment until the lease's NPV = $0 or, equivalently, its IRR = 6.0 percent. We did this with our *Lotus 1-2-3* lease evaluation model, and found that the lessor must set the lease payment at $2,788,591.50 to obtain an expected after-tax rate of return of 6.0 percent. However, if this lease payment is not acceptable to the lessee, Anderson Equipment Company, then it may not be possible to strike a deal.

Note that a lease payment of $2,788,591.50 would drive Anderson's NAL down to exactly zero. Thus, both the lessee and the lessor would have NAL = NPV = $0. Leasing is not always a zero sum game, but if the inputs to the lessee and the lessor are identical, as in this case, then a positive NAL to the lessee implies an equal but negative NPV to the lessor. However, conditions are often such

---

[9]Note that the lease investment is actually slightly more risky than the alternative bond investment because the residual value cash flow is less certain than a principal repayment. Thus, the lessor might require an expected return somewhat above the 5.4 percent promised on a bond investment.

that leasing can provide net benefits to both parties. This situation arises because of differentials, generally in taxes, in estimated residual values, or in the ability to bear the residual value risk. We will explore this issue in detail in a later section.

LEVERAGED LEASE ANALYSIS

When leasing began, only two parties were involved in a lease transaction—the lessor, who put up the money, and the lessee. In recent years, however, a new type of lease, the *leveraged lease,* has come into widespread use. Under a leveraged lease, the lessor arranges to borrow part of the required funds, generally giving the lender a first mortgage on the plant or equipment being leased. The lessor still receives the tax benefits associated with accelerated depreciation. However, the lessor now has a riskier position, because of the use of financial leverage.

Such leveraged leases, often with syndicates of wealthy individuals seeking tax shelters acting as owner-lessors, are an important part of the financial scene today. Incidentally, whether or not a lease is leveraged is not important to the lessee; from the lessee's standpoint, the method of analyzing a proposed lease is unaffected by whether or not the lessor borrows part of the required capital.

The example in Table 21-4 is not set up as a leveraged lease. However, it would be easy enough to modify the analysis if the lessor borrows all or part of the required $10 million, making the transaction a leveraged lease. First, we would add a set of lines to Table 21-4 to show the financing cash flows. The interest component would represent another tax deduction, while the loan repayments would constitute additional cash outlays. The initial cost of the asset would be reduced by the amount of the loan. With these changes made, a new NPV and IRR could be calculated and used to evaluate whether or not the lease represents a good investment.

To illustrate, assume that the lessor can borrow $5 million of the $10 million net purchase price at a rate of 9 percent on a 5-year simple interest loan. Table 21-5 contains the lessor's leveraged lease NPV analysis. The NPV of the leveraged lease investment based on the net cash flows shown on Line 3 is $26,000, which is the same as the $26,000 NPV for the unleveraged lease. Note, though, that the

TABLE 21-5		Year 0	Year 1	Year 2	Year 3	Year 4	Year 5
LEVERAGED LEASE ANALYSIS (THOUSANDS OF DOLLARS)	1. Net cash flow from Table 21-4	($8,650)	$2,150	$2,630	$2,110	$1,830	$1,280
	2. Leveraging cash flows[a]	5,000	(270)	(270)	(270)	(270)	(5,270)
	3. Net cash flow	($3,650)	$1,880	$2,360	$1,840	$1,560	($3,990)

$$NPV = \sum_{t=0}^{5} \frac{NCF_t}{(1 + k)^t} = \$26 \text{ when } k = 5.4\%.$$

[a]The lessor borrows $5 million at t = 0 and repays it at t = 5. Interest expense, payable at the end of each year, is $0.09(\$5,000) = \$450$, but it is tax deductible, so the after-tax interest cash flow is $-\$450(1 - T) = -\$450(0.6) = -\$270$.

lessor has spent only $3.65 million on this lease. Therefore, the lessor could invest in a total of 2.37 similar leveraged leases for the same $8.65 million investment required to finance a single unleveraged lease, producing a total net present value of 2.37($26,000) = $61,620.

The effect of leverage on the lessor's return is also reflected in the leveraged lease's IRR. The IRR is that discount rate which equates the sum of the present values of the Line 3 cash flows to zero. We find the IRR of the leveraged lease to be about 8.5 percent, which is substantially higher than the 5.5 percent after-tax return on the unleveraged lease.[10]

Typically, leveraged leases provide lessors with higher expected rates of return (IRRs) and higher NPVs per dollar of invested capital than unleveraged leases. However, such leases are also riskier for the same reason that any leveraged investment is riskier. Since leveraged leases are a relatively new development, no standard methodology has been developed for analyzing them in a risk/return framework. However, sophisticated lessors are now developing Monte Carlo simulations similar to those described in Chapter 11. Then, given the apparent riskiness of the lease investment, the lessor can decide whether the returns built into the contract are sufficient to compensate for the risk involved.

SELF-TEST QUESTIONS

What discount rate is used in a lessor's NPV analysis?

What is the economic interpretation of the lessor's IRR?

What is a leveraged lease? What is the usual impact of leveraging on the lessor's expected return? On the lessor's risk?

OTHER ISSUES IN LEASE ANALYSIS

The basic methods of analysis used by lessees and lessors were presented in the previous sections. However, some other issues warrant discussion.

ESTIMATED RESIDUAL VALUE

It is important to note that the lessor owns the property upon expiration of a lease; thus, the lessor has claim to the asset's residual value. Superficially, it would appear that if residual values are expected to be large, owning would have an advantage over leasing. However, this apparent advantage does not hold up. If expected residual values are large—as they may be under inflation for certain types of equip-

---

[10]Note two additional points concerning the leveraged lease analysis. First, in this situation, leveraging had no impact on the lessor's per-lease NPV. This is because the cost of loan to the lessor (5.4 percent after taxes) equals the discount rate, and hence the leveraging cash flows are netted out on a present value basis. Second, the leveraged lease has multiple IRRs, one at 0.0 percent and another at approximately 8.5 percent.

ment and also if real property is involved — competition between leasing companies and other financing sources, as well as competition among leasing companies themselves, will force leasing rates down to the point where potential residual values are fully recognized in the lease contract. Thus, the existence of large residual values on equipment is not likely to result in materially higher costs for leasing.

INCREASED CREDIT AVAILABILITY

As noted earlier, leasing is sometimes said to have an advantage for firms that are seeking the maximum degree of financial leverage. First, it is sometimes argued that firms can obtain more money, and for longer terms, under a lease arrangement than under a loan secured by a specific piece of equipment. Second, since some leases do not appear on the balance sheet, lease financing has been said to give the firm a stronger appearance in a *superficial* credit analysis and thus to permit the firm to use more leverage than would be possible if it did not lease.

There may be some truth to these claims for smaller firms, but now that firms are required to capitalize financial leases and to report them on their balance sheets, this point is of questionable validity for any firm large enough to have audited financial statements. However, leasing can be a way to circumvent existing loan covenants. If restrictive covenants prohibit a firm from issuing more debt but fail to restrict lease payments, then the firm could effectively increase its leverge by leasing additional assets.

COMPUTER MODELS

Lease analysis, like capital budgeting analysis, is particularly well suited for computer analysis. Both the lessee and lessor can create computer models for their analyses. Setting the analysis up on a computer is especially useful when negotiations are under way, and when investment banking houses such as Merrill Lynch are working out a leasing deal between a group of investors and a company, the analysis is always computerized.

LEASING AND TAX LAWS

The ability to structure leases that are advantageous to both lessor and lessee depends in large part on tax laws. The four major tax factors that influence leasing are (1) investment tax credits, (2) depreciation rules, (3) tax rates, and (4) alternative minimum taxes. In this section, we briefly discuss each of these factors and how they influence leasing decisions.

The investment tax credit (ITC) is a direct reduction of taxes that occurs when a firm purchases new capital equipment. For example, prior to 1987 firms could immediately deduct up to 10 percent of the cost of new capital investments from their corporate tax bills. Thus, a company that bought a $1,000,000 mainframe computer system would get a $100,000 reduction in current-year taxes. Since the ITC goes to the owner of the capital asset, low-tax-bracket lessees can pass immediate tax savings to high-tax-bracket lessors when the ITC is in force.

Congress eliminated the ITC in 1986, but there is some chance that Congress will reinstate the ITC. If the ITC is put back into law, leasing would become more attractive to low-tax-bracket firms.

Owners recover their investments in capital assets through depreciation, which is a tax-deductible expense. Because of the time value of money, the faster an asset can be depreciated, the greater the tax advantages of ownership. Recent tax laws have tended to slow depreciation write-offs and, hence, to reduce the value of ownership. This has also reduced the advantage to leasing between low-tax-bracket lessees and high-tax-bracket lessors. Any move to liberalize depreciation rules would tend to make leasing more desirable in many situations. The value of depreciation also depends on the firm's tax rate, because the depreciation tax savings equal the amount of depreciation multiplied by the tax rate. Thus, higher tax rates mean greater ownership tax savings, and hence more incentive for tax-driven leases.

Finally, the alternative minimum tax (AMT) also impacts leasing activity. Corporations are permitted to use accelerated depreciation and other tax shelters on their tax books but then can use straight line depreciation in reporting results to shareholders. Thus, some firms report to the IRS that they are doing poorly and hence owe little or no taxes, while the same firms report high earnings to shareholders. The AMT, which is roughly computed by applying a 20 percent tax rate to the profits reported to shareholders, is designed to force highly profitable companies to pay at least some taxes even if they have tax shelters that push their taxable income to zero. In effect, all firms (and individuals also) must compute the "regular" tax and the AMT and then pay the higher of the two.

Companies that have large AMT liabilities look for ways to reduce their tax bills by lowering reported income. Leasing can be benefical here—a relatively short-term lease with high annual payments will increase reported expenses and hence lower reported profits. Note that the lease does not have to qualify as a guideline lease and be deducted for regular tax purposes—all that is needed is to lower reported income as shown on the income statement.

We see that tax laws and differential tax rates between lessors and lessees can be a motivating force for leasing. However, as we discuss in the next section, there are some other reasons why firms lease plant and equipment.

SELF-TEST QUESTIONS

Does leasing lead to increased credit availability?

What impact do tax laws have on leasing?

WHY FIRMS LEASE

Up to this point, we have noted that tax rate or other differentials are generally necessary to make leasing attractive to both the lessee and lessor. If the lessee and lessor are facing different tax situations, including the alternative minimum tax, then it may be possible to structure a lease that is beneficial to both parties. How-

ever, there are other reasons why firms might want to lease an asset rather than buy it.

For example, over half of the commercial aircraft coming into service today in the United States are leased, and smaller airlines lease an even higher percentage of their planes. One of the reasons for the high lease usage is that airlines can reduce their risks by leasing. If an airline purchases all its aircraft, it would be hampered in its ability to quickly respond to changing market conditions. Because they have become specialists at matching airlines with available aircraft, the aircraft lessors are quite good at managing the changing demand for different types of aircraft. This permits them to offer lease terms that are attractive to the airlines. In this situation leasing provides operating flexibility. Leasing is not necessarily less expensive than buying, but the operating flexibility afforded by leasing is worth the extra costs.

Leasing is also an attractive alternative for many high-technology items that are subject to rapid and unpredictable technological obsolescence. Say a small rural hospital wants to buy a magnetic resonance imaging (MRI) device. If it buys the MRI equipment, it is exposed to the risk of technological obsolescence. In a short time some new technology might make the current system almost worthless, and this large economic depreciation could make the whole project unprofitable. Since it does not use much equipment of this nature, the hospital would bear a great deal of risk if it buys the MRI device. Conversely, a lessor that specializes in state-of-the-art medical equipment would be exposed to significantly less risk. By purchasing and then leasing many different items, the lessor benefits from diversification. Of course, over time some items will probably lose more value than the lessor expected, but this will be offset by other items that retained more value than was expected. Also, since such a leasing company will be especially familiar with the market for used medical equipment, it can get a better price in the resale market than could a remote rural hospital. For these reasons, leasing can reduce the risk of technological obsolescence.

Leasing can also be attractive when a firm is uncertain about the demand for its products or services, and thus about how long the equipment will be needed. Again, consider the hospital industry. Hospitals often offer services that are dependent on a single staff member—for example, a physician who does liver transplants. To support the physician's practice, the hospital might have to invest millions of dollars in equipment that can be used only for this particular procedure. The hospital will charge for the use of the equipment, and if things go as expected, the investment will be profitable. However, if the physician dies or leaves the hospital staff, and if no replacement can be recruited to fill the void, then the project is dead, and the equipment becomes useless to the hospital. In this case, a lease with a cancellation clause would permit the hospital to simply return the equipment. The lessor would charge something for the cancellation clause, and this would lower the expected profitability of the project, but it would provide the hospital with an option to abandon the equipment, and such an option could have a value that exceeds the incremental cost of the cancellation clause. The leasing company would be willing to write this option because it is in a better position to remarket the equipment, either by writing another lease or by selling it outright.

Some companies also find leasing attractive because the lessor is able to provide services on favorable terms. For example, Virco Manufacturing, a company that makes school desks and other furniture, recently leased 25 truck tractors and 140 trailers which it uses to ship furniture from its plant. The lease agreement, with a large leasing company which specializes in purchasing, maintaining, and then reselling trucks, permitted the replacement of an aging fleet that Virco had built up over seven years. "We are pretty good at manufacturing furniture, but we aren't very good at maintaining a truck fleet," said Virco's CFO.

There are other reasons that might influence a firm to lease an asset rather than buy it. Often, these reasons are difficult to quantify, and hence they cannot be easily incorporated into an NPV or IRR analysis. Nevertheless, a sound lease analysis must begin with a quantitative analysis, and then qualitative factors can be considered before making the final lease-or-buy decision.

Self-Test Questions

Describe some economic factors which might provide an advantage to leasing.

Would it ever make sense to lease an asset that has a negative NAL? Explain.

Summary

In this chapter, we discussed the leasing decision from the standpoints of both the lessee and lessor. The key concepts covered are listed below:

▶ The four most important types of lease agreement are (1) *operating lease*, (2) *financial*, or *capital, lease*, (3) *sale and leaseback*, and (4) *combination lease*.

▶ The IRS has specific guidelines that apply to lease arrangements. A lease that meets these guidelines is called a *guideline*, or *tax-oriented, lease*, because the IRS permits the lessor to deduct the asset's depreciation and allows the lessee to deduct the lease payments. A lease that does not meet the IRS guidelines is called a *non-tax-oriented lease*. In these leases, ownership effectively resides with the lessee rather than the lessor.

▶ *FASB Statement 13* spells out the conditions under which a lease must be *capitalized* (shown directly on the balance sheet) as opposed to shown only in the notes to the financial statements. Generally, leases that run for a period equal to or greater than 75 percent of the asset's life must be capitalized.

▶ The lessee's analysis consists basically of a comparison of the costs associated with leasing the asset and the costs associated with owning the asset. There are two analytical techniques that can be used: (1) the *net advantage to leasing (NAL or PV of costs) method*, and (2) the *internal rate of return (IRR) method*.

▶ One of the key issues in the lessee's analysis is the appropriate discount rate. Since the cash flows in a lease analysis are known with relative certainty, the appropriate discount rate is the *lessee's after-tax cost of debt*. A higher discount rate may be used on the *residual value* if it is substantially riskier than the other flows.

▶ The lessor evaluates the lease as an *investment*. If the lease's NPV is greater than zero or its IRR is greater than the lessor's opportunity cost, then the lease should be written.

▶ In a *leveraged lease,* the lessor borrows part of the funds required to buy the asset. Generally, the asset is pledged as collateral for the loan.

▶ Leasing is motivated by differentials between lessees and lessors. Some of the more common reasons for leasing are (1) *tax rate differentials,* (2) leases in which the lessee faces the *alternative minimum tax (AMT),* and (3) leases in which the lessor is better able to bear the *residual value risk* than the lessee.

In the next chapter, the last in our discussion of long-term financing, we discuss options and option-like securities.

QUESTIONS

21-1 Define each of the following terms:
   a. Lessee; lessor
   b. Operating lease; financial lease; sale and leaseback; combination lease; leveraged lease
   c. "Off-balance sheet" financing; capitalizing
   d. FASB Statement 13
   e. Guideline lease
   f. Residual value
   g. Lessee's analysis; lessor's analysis
   h. Alternative minimum tax (AMT)

21-2 Distinguish between operating leases and financial leases. Would you be more likely to find an operating lease employed for a fleet of trucks or for a manufacturing plant?

21-3 Would you be more likely to find that lessees are in high or low income tax brackets as compared with lessors?

21-4 Commercial banks moved heavily into equipment leasing during the early 1970s, acting as lessors. One major reason for this invasion of the leasing industry was to gain the benefits of accelerated depreciation and the investment tax credit on leased equipment. During this same period, commercial banks were investing heavily in municipal securities, and they were also making loans to real estate investment trusts (REITs). In the mid-1970s, these REITs got into such serious difficulty that many banks suffered large losses on their REIT loans. Explain how its investments in municipal bonds and REITs could reduce a bank's willingness to act as a lessor.

21-5 One alleged advantage of leasing voiced in the past is that it kept liabilities off the balance sheet, thus making it possible for a firm to obtain more leverage than it otherwise could have. This raised the question of whether or not both the lease obligation and the asset

involved should be capitalized and shown on the balance sheet. Discuss the pros and cons of capitalizing leases and related assets.

21-6 Suppose there were no IRS restrictions on what constituted a valid lease. Explain, in a manner that a legislator might understand, why some restrictions should be imposed. Illustrate your answer with numbers.

21-7 What are the advantages and disadvantages of leveraged leases from the standpoint of (a) the lessee, (b) the equity investor in the lease, and (c) the supplier of the debt capital?

21-8 Suppose Congress enacted new tax law changes that would (1) permit equipment to be depreciated over a shorter period, (2) lower corporate tax rates, and (3) reinstate the investment tax credit. Discuss how each of these potential changes would affect the relative volume of leasing versus conventional debt in the U.S. economy.

21-9 In our Anderson Equipment Company example, we assumed that the lease could not be cancelled. What effect would a cancellation clause have on the lessee's analysis? On the lessor's analysis?

SELF-TEST PROBLEM   (SOLUTION APPEARS IN APPENDIX C)

ST-1 **(Lease versus buy)**   The Randolph Teweles Company (RTC) has decided to acquire a new truck. One alternative is to lease the truck on a 4-year guideline contract for a lease payment of $10,000 per year, with payments to be made at the *beginning* of each year. The lease would include maintenance. Alternatively, RTC could purchase the truck outright for $40,000, financing the purchase by a bank loan for the net purchase price and amortizing the loan over a 4-year period at an interest rate of 10 percent per year. Under the borrow-to-purchase arrangement, RTC would have to maintain the truck at a cost of $1,000 per year, payable at year end. The truck falls into the MACRS 3-year class. It has a residual value of $10,000, which is the expected market value after 4 years, when RTC plans to replace the truck irrespective of whether it leases or buys. RTC has a marginal federal-plus-state tax rate of 40 percent.

a.   What is RTC's PV cost of leasing?

b.   What is RTC's PV cost of owning? Should the truck be leased or purchased?

c.   The appropriate discount rate for use in the analysis is the firm's after-tax cost of debt. Why?

d.   The residual value is the least certain cash flow in the analysis. How might RTC incorporate differential riskiness on this cash flow into the analysis?

PROBLEMS

21-1 **(Balance sheet effects)**   Two companies, Energen and Hastings Corporation, began operations with identical balance sheets. A year later, both required additional manufacturing capacity at a cost of $50,000. Energen obtained a 5-year, $50,000 loan at an 8 percent interest rate from its bank. Hastings, on the other hand, decided to lease the required $50,000 capacity for 5 years, and an 8 percent return was built into the lease. The balance sheet for each company, before the asset increases, follows:

		Debt	$ 50,000
		Equity	100,000
Total assets	$150,000	Total claims	$150,000

a. Show the balance sheets for both firms after the asset increases and calculate each firm's new debt ratio. (Assume that the lease is not capitalized.)

b. Show how Hastings's balance sheet would look immediately after the financing if it capitalized the lease.

c. Would the rate of return (1) on assets and (2) on equity be affected by the choice of financing? How?

21-2 (Lease versus buy) A. Sadik Industries must install $1 million of new machinery in its Texas plant. It can obtain a bank loan for 100 percent of the required amount. Alternatively, a Texas investment banking firm which represents a group of investors believes that it can arrange for a lease financing plan. *Assume* that these facts apply:

(1) The equipment falls in the MACRS 3-year class.

(2) Estimated maintenance expenses are $50,000 per year.

(3) The firm's tax rate is 34 percent.

(4) If the money is borrowed, the bank loan will be at a rate of 14 percent, amortized in 3 equal installments at the end of each year.

(5) The tentative lease terms call for payments of $320,000 at the end of each year for 3 years. The lease is a guideline lease.

(6) Under the proposed lease terms, the lessee must pay for insurance, property taxes, and maintenance.

(7) Sadik must use the equipment if it is to continue in business, so it will almost certainly want to acquire the property at the end of the lease. If it does, then under the lease terms it can purchase the machinery at its fair market value at that time. The best estimate of this market value is $200,000, but it could be much higher or lower under certain circumstances.

To assist management in making the proper lease-versus-buy decision, you are asked to answer the following questions:

a. Assuming that the lease can be arranged, should the firm lease or borrow and buy the equipment? Explain. (Hint: In this situation, the firm plans to use the asset beyond the term of the lease. Thus, the residual value becomes a *cost* to leasing in Year 3. Also, there is no Year 3 residual value tax consequence, as the firm cannot immediately deduct the Year 3 purchase price from taxable income.)

b. Consider the $200,000 estimated residual value. Is it appropriate to discount it at the same rate as the other cash flows? What about the other cash flows—are they all equally risky? (Hint: Riskier cash flows are normally discounted at higher rates, but when the cash flows are *costs* rather than *inflows,* the normal procedure must be reversed.)

(Do Parts c and d only if you are using the computer problem diskette.)

c. Determine the lease payment at which Sadik would be indifferent to buying or leasing; that is, the lease payment which equates the PV cost of leasing to that of buying. (Hint: Use trial and error.)

d. Using the $320,000 lease payment, what would be the effect if the firm's tax rate fell to zero?

21-3 (Lessor's analysis) The Dorfman Company has decided to acquire some new R&D equipment. One alternative is to lease the equipment on a 4-year guideline contract for a lease payment of $11,500 per year, payments to be made at the *beginning* of each year. The lease, which would include maintenance, is being offered by Bankston Credit Corporation, a local leasing company. Bankston would purchase the equipment outright for $40,000, and

would have to pay the local dealer $1,000 at the beginning of each year to provide maintenance service. The equipment falls into the MACRS 3-year class; and it has a residual value of $10,000, which is the expected market value after 4 years. The lessor's marginal state-plus-federal tax rate is 40 percent. The analysts at Bankston compare the returns on potential leases with returns available on comparable maturity commercial loans which the firm also writes. Currently, Bankston is charging 9 percent on 4-year commercial loans.

a. What is the NPV on the lease investment?

b. Should Bankston write the lease? Why or why not?

(Do the remainder of the problem only if you are using the computer problem diskette.)

c. Assume that interest rates rise, and Bankston can now earn 16 percent (before taxes) on its commercial loans. How does this affect the lease analysis?

d. What lease payment must Bankston charge to be indifferent between writing the lease and loaning at 16 percent?

e. Return to the original situation. Suppose there is a 25 percent chance that the residual value will be only $5,000, and another 25 percent probability that the residual value will be $15,000. There is a 50 percent probability that the residual value will be $10,000. What is Bankston's best-case and worst-case NPV? Suppose that the Bankston analysts account for differential risk by increasing the residual value discount rate. What residual value discount rate forces NPV = $0 when the residual value is $10,000?

f. Now suppose that Bankston can leverage the lease. Bankston could borrow up to $30,000 using the truck as collateral on a term loan at an 8 percent rate. Should Bankston leverage the lease? Should Bankston leverage the lease at 9 percent?

g. Refer back to Part f. Suppose that the loan for $30,000 may only be obtained at a rate of 16 percent. What is the new NPV to the lessor of the leveraged lease? Should Bankston leverage the lease under these circumstances? Why?

h. If Bankston were able to borrow only $15,000 for this project due to restrictive covenants contained in a previous loan agreement, would it be beneficial to leverage the lease at 8 percent? At 9 percent? At 16 percent?

21-4 **(Lessee's analysis)**   As part of its overall plant modernization and cost reduction program, Western Fabrics' management has decided to install a new automated weaving loom. In the capital budgeting analysis of this equipment, the IRR of the project was found to be 29 percent versus a project required return of 14 percent.

The loom has an invoice price of $100,000, including delivery and installation charges. The funds needed could be borrowed from the bank through a 4-year amortized loan at a 15 percent interest rate, with payments to be made at the end of each year. In the event the loom is purchased, the manufacturer will contract to maintain and service it for a fee of $8,000 per year paid at the end of each year. The loom falls in the MACRS 5-year class, and Western's marginal federal-plus-state tax rate is 40 percent.

Aubey Automation Inc., maker of the loom, has offered to lease the loom to Western for $30,500 upon delivery and installation (at t = 0) plus 4 additional annual lease payments of $30,500 to be made at the end of Years 1 to 4. (Note that there are 5 lease payments in total.) The lease agreement includes maintenance and servicing. Actually, the loom has an expected life of 8 years, at which time its expected salvage value is zero; however, after 4 years, its market value is expected to equal its book value. Western plans to build an entirely new plant in 4 years, so it has no interest in either leasing or owning the proposed loom for more than that period.

a. Should the loom be leased or purchased?

(Do the remainder of the problem only if you are using the computer problem diskette.)

b. Western's managers disagree on the appropriate discount rate to be used in the analysis. What effect would a discount rate change have on the lease-versus-purchase decision?

c. The salvage value is clearly the most uncertain cash flow in the analysis. What effect would a salvage value risk adjustment have on the analysis? (Assume that the appropriate salvage value pre-tax discount rate is 18 percent.)

d. The original analysis assumed that the firm would not need the loom after 4 years. Now assume that the firm will continue to use it after the lease expires. Thus, if it leased, Western would have to buy the asset after 4 years at the then existing market value, which is assumed to equal the book value. What effect would this requirement have on the basic analysis?

e. Under the original lease terms, it was to Western's advantage to purchase the loom. However, if you had analyzed the lease from the lessor's viewpoint, you would have found that it was more profitable for Aubey Automation to lease the machine than to sell it — in fact, the manager of Aubey has found that the company can lower the lease payment to $30,000 and still make more by leasing the machine than by selling it. With an annual lease payment of $30,000, should the loom be leased or bought?

f. Perform the lease analysis assuming that Western's marginal tax rate is (1) 0 percent and (2) 50 percent. Assume a lease payment of $30,500 and a 15 percent pre-tax discount rate. What effect, if any, would the lessee's tax rate have on the lease-buy decision?

M I N I
C A S E

Lewis Securities Inc. has decided to acquire a new market data and quotation system for its Richmond home office. The system receives current market prices and other information from several on-line data services, then either displays the information on a screen or stores it for later retrieval by the firm's brokers. The system also permits customers to call up current quotes on terminals in the lobby.

The equipment costs $1,000,000, and, if it were purchased, Lewis could obtain a term loan for the full purchase price at a 10 percent interest rate. The equipment is classified as a special-purpose computer, so it falls into the MACRS 3-year class. If the system were purchased, a 4-year maintenance contract could be obtained at a cost of $20,000 per year, payable at the *beginning* of each year. The equipment would be sold after 4 years, and the best estimate of its residual value at that time is $100,000. However, since real-time display system technology is changing rapidly, the actual residual value is uncertain.

As an alternative to the borrow-and-buy plan, the equipment manufacturer informed Lewis that Consolidated Leasing would be willing to write a 4-year guideline lease on the equipment, including maintenance, for payments of $280,000 at the *beginning* of each year. Lewis's marginal federal-plus-state tax rate is 40 percent. You have been asked to analyze the lease-versus-purchase decision, and in the process to answer the following questions:

a. (1) Why is leasing sometimes referred to as "off-balance sheet" financing?
(2) What is the difference between a capital lease and an operating lease?
(3) What impact does leasing have on a firm's capital structure?

b. (1) What is the present value cost of owning the equipment? (Hint: Set up a time line which shows the net cash flows over the period t = 0 to t = 4, and then find the PV of these net cash flows, or the PV cost of owning.)
(2) Explain the rationale for the discount rate you used to find the PV.

c. What is Lewis's present value cost of leasing the equipment? (Hint: Again, construct a time line.)

d. What is the net advantage to leasing (NAL)? Does your analysis indicate that Lewis should buy or lease the equipment? Explain.

e. What is the IRR of the lease from the lessee's standpoint? What is the economic meaning of this IRR?

f. Now assume that the equipment's residual value could be as low as $0 or as high as $200,000, but that $100,000 is the expected value. Since the residual value is riskier than the other cash flows in the analysis, this differential risk should be incorporated into the analysis. Describe how this could be accomplished. (No calculations are necessary, but explain how you would modify the analysis if calculations were required.) What effect would increased uncertainty about the residual value have on Lewis's lease-versus-purchase decision?

g. The lessee compares the cost of owning the equipment with the cost of leasing it. Now put yourself in the lessor's shoes. In a few sentences, how should you analyze the decision to write or not write the lease?

h. (1) Assume that the lease payments were actually $300,000 per year, that Consolidated Leasing is also in the 40 percent tax bracket, and that it also forecasts a $100,000 residual value. Also, to furnish the maintenance support, Consolidated would have to purchase a maintenance contract from the manufacturer at the same $20,000 annual cost, again paid in advance. Consolidated Leasing can obtain an expected 10 percent pre-tax return on investments of similar risk. What would Consolidated's NPV and IRR of leasing be under these conditions?

(2) What do you think the lessor's NPV would be if the lease payment were set at $280,000 per year? (Hint: The lessor's cash flows would be a "mirror image" of the lessee's cash flows.)

i. Now assume that the lessor can leverage the $300,000 payment lease by borrowing $500,000 of the $1,000,000 purchase price on a 4-year simple interest note having a 10 percent interest rate. The lender requires only interest payments (at the end of each year) during the life of the note, with the full $500,000 principal to be repaid at maturity. What is the NPV of the leveraged lease? What is its rate of return? What factors, besides the NPV and the IRR, should the lessor consider before deciding to leverage the lease? Should it be leveraged?

j. Lewis's management has been considering moving to a new downtown location, and they are concerned that these plans may come to fruition prior to the expiration of the lease. If the move occurs, Lewis would buy or lease an entirely new set of equipment, and hence management would like to include a cancellation clause in the lease contract. What impact would such a clause have on the riskiness of the lease from Lewis's standpoint? From the lessor's standpoint? If you were the lessor, would you insist on changing any of the lease terms if a cancellation clause were added? Should the cancellation clause contain any restrictive covenants and/or penalties of the type contained in bond indentures or provisions similar to call premiums?

SELECTED ADDITIONAL REFERENCES AND CASES

For a description of lease analysis in practice, as well as a comprehensive bibliography of the leasing literature, see

Mukherjee, Tarun K., "A Survey of Corporate Leasing Analysis," *Financial Management*, Autumn 1991, 96–107.

O'Brien, Thomas J., and Bennie H. Nunnally, Jr., "A 1982 Survey of Corporate Leasing Analysis," *Financial Management,* Summer 1983, 30–36.

Many of the theoretical issues surrounding lease analysis are discussed in the following articles:

Finucane, Thomas J., "Some Empirical Evidence on the Use of Financial Leases," *The Journal of Financial Research,* Fall 1988, 321–333.

Hockman, Shalom, and Ramon Rabinovitch, "Financial Leasing under Inflation," *Financial Management,* Spring 1984, 17–26.

Levy, Haim, and Marshall Sarnat, "Leasing, Borrowing, and Financial Risk," *Financial Management,* Winter 1979, 47–54.

Lewellen, Wilbur G., Michael S. Long, and John J. McConnell, "Asset Leasing in Competitive Capital Markets," *Journal of Finance,* June 1976, 787–798.

Miller, Merton H., and Charles W. Upton, "Leasing, Buying, and the Cost of Capital Services," *Journal of Finance,* June 1976, 761–786.

Schall, Lawrence D., "The Evaluation of Lease Financing Opportunities," *Midland Corporate Finance Journal,* Spring 1985, 48–65.

Leveraged lease analysis is discussed in these articles:

Athanasopoulos, Peter J., and Peter W. Bacon, "The Evaluation of Leveraged Leases," *Financial Management,* Spring 1980, 76–80.

Dyl, Edward A., and Stanley A. Martin, Jr., "Setting Terms for Leveraged Leases," *Financial Management,* Winter 1977, 20–27.

Grimlund, Richard A., and Robert Capettini, "A Note on the Evaluation of Leveraged Leases and Other Investments," *Financial Management,* Summer 1982, 68–72.

Perg, Wayne F., "Leveraged Leasing: The Problem of Changing Leverage," *Financial Management,* Autumn 1978, 47–51.

For a discussion of realized returns on lease contracts, see

Lease, Ronald C., John J. McConnell, and James S. Schallheim, "Realized Returns and the Default and Prepayment Experience of Financial Leasing Contracts," *Financial Management,* Summer 1990, 11–20.

The Summer 1987 issue of Financial Management *contains articles by H. Martin Weingartner, Roger L. Cason, and Lawrence D. Schall which focus on the impact of asset life uncertainty on lease analysis.*

The Option Pricing Model (OPM) has recently been used in lease analysis by

Copeland, Thomas E., and J. Fred Weston, "A Note on the Evaluation of Cancellable Operating Leases," *Financial Management,* Summer 1982, 60–67.

Lee, Wayne Y., John D. Martin, and Andrew J. Senchack, "The Case for Using Options to Evaluate Salvage Values in Financial Leases," *Financial Management,* Autumn 1982, 33–41.

For a discussion of the impact of the AMT on lease decisions, see

"The Effect of the Corporate Alternative Minimum Tax: Amount, Duration, and Effect on the Lease versus Buy Decision," *The Journal of Equipment Lease Financing,* Spring 1989, 7–26.

The Brigham-Gapenski casebook contains the following cases which deal with lease analysis:

Case 25, "Environmental Sciences, Inc.," which examines the lease decision from the perspectives of both the lessee and lessor.

Case 26, "Prudent Solutions, Inc.," which examines the same issues as Case 25.

OPTIONS, WARRANTS, CONVERTIBLES, AND FUTURES

*I*n early 1992, Jonathon Goodman, a money manager at Steinhardt Partners, described a little-known security issued by oil and steel giant USX as "the best bargain in the convertible-bond universe." The bond he was referring to was issued in 1990, shortly before USX split its common stock into two classes: USX-U.S. Steel Group and USX-Marathon Group. Each bond could be converted into 1.64 shares of U.S. Steel stock plus 8.21 shares of Marathon Oil stock. In early 1993, the steel shares were selling at about $40 and the oil shares were trading at about $20, so the value of converting the bonds into common stock was 1.64($40) + 8.21($20) ≈ $230. At the time, the bonds were trading for about $400, so it made no sense for investors to make the conversion.

The USX bonds have three features that make them more interesting than other bonds but, at the same time, significantly complicate a valuation analysis of the issue. First, the bond is a zero coupon bond—it pays no interest but, rather, promises to pay $1,000 at maturity in 2005. In early 1993 the issue promised a return of about 8 percent if we consider only its bond value. Second, the bonds contain a provision whereby USX promises to buy back the bonds in 1995 from anyone who wants to sell them at a price of $467. Thus, the bonds have a put provision, which also promised about an 8 percent return if investors sell their bonds back to USX in 1995. However, there is a catch—USX has the option of paying the $467 in cash, common stock, or notes, so investors could receive paper instead of cash. Finally, to complicate matters even more, the bonds contain a call provision. USX can call the bonds in 1995 for $462, but the call price rises gradually to $926 in 2004, one year before maturity.

All in all, the bonds provide USX with a great deal of flexibility, but this flexibility for the issuer translates into risk for investors. Said one bond analyst, "The 8 percent yield to put is a good one, but I don't know if it is compelling enough to make me recommend the bond. The bond is rated BBB, so it has substantial default risk. Also, you're taking call risk, and if you are looking for a put option in a bond, you want cash."

The USX bond raises many issues about convertibles, as well as other bond provisions. As you read this chapter, think about the USX issue and the impact that the bond's provisions have on its riskiness, hence its rate of return, for both the issuer and potential investors. When you finish the chapter, you should have a much better understanding of hybrid securities, how they are valued, and why firms might choose to issue a bond with warrants or a convertible rather than straight debt or common stock.

Thus far our discussion of long-term financing has concentrated on common and preferred stock, on various types of debt, and on lease financing. In this chapter, we shall see how a company can use warrants and convertibles to make its securities attractive to a broader range of investors, thereby increasing the potential supply of capital. We also introduce options and futures markets, and we illustrate how these markets provide a method for locking in future financing costs.

Oᴘᴛɪᴏɴs

Both warrants and convertibles are types of option securities, and options themselves represent an important part of today's financial scene. Therefore, we begin the chapter by discussing option pricing theory and the rapidly growing option markets. An *option* is a contract which gives its holder the right to buy (or sell) an asset at some predetermined price within a specified period of time. *Pure options* are instruments that (1) are created by outsiders (generally exchanges which specialize in options) rather than the firm, (2) are bought and sold primarily by investors and speculators, and (3) are of greater importance to individual investors than to financial managers. However, financial managers should understand option theory, because such an understanding will help them structure warrant and convertible financings. Additionally, option theory provides some useful insights into other facets of corporate finance.

Oᴘᴛɪᴏɴ Tʏᴘᴇs ᴀɴᴅ Mᴀʀᴋᴇᴛs

There are many types of options and option markets.[1] To illustrate how options work, suppose you owned 100 shares of IBM, which, on March 22, 1993, sold for

---

[1] For an in-depth treatment of options, see Robert C. Radcliffe, *Investment Concepts, Analysis, and Strategy* (Glenview, Ill.: Scott, Foresman, 1993).

TABLE 22-1	NYSE Close	Strike Price	Calls—Last Quote			Puts—Last Quote		
MARCH 23, 1993,			April	May	July	April	May	July
LISTED OPTIONS								
QUOTATIONS	**IBM**							
	53½	50	4¼	4¾	5½	⅝	1⅜	2³⁄₁₆
	53½	55	1⁵⁄₁₆	2¹⁄₁₆	3⅛	2⅝	r	4½
	53½	60	⁵⁄₁₆	¹¹⁄₁₆	1½	6⅝	r	8
	U.S. Surgical							
	56⅝	55	4¼	5⅛	7	2¼	3¾	r
	McDonald's							
	53⅛	55	½	1⅛	r	2⅛	r	r

Note: r means not traded on March 22.

$53.50 per share. You could give (or sell) to someone else the right to buy the 100 shares at any time during the next 4 months at a price of, say, $55 per share. The $55 is called the *striking,* or *exercise, price.* Such options exist, and they are traded on a number of exchanges, with the Chicago Board Options Exchange (CBOE) being the oldest and the largest. This type of option is defined as a *call option,* because the purchaser has a "call" on 100 shares of stock. The seller of an option is called the option *writer.* An investor who "writes" call options against stock held in his or her portfolio is said to be selling *covered options.* Options sold without the stock to back them up are called *naked options.* When the exercise price exceeds the current stock price, a call option is said to be *out-of-the-money.* When the exercise price is less than the current price of the underlying stock, a call option is *in-the-money.*

You can also buy an option which gives you the right to *sell* a stock at a specified price within some future period—this is called a *put option.* For example, suppose you think IBM's stock price is likely to decline from its current level of $53.50 sometime during the next 4 months. For $218.75 you could buy a 4-month put option giving you the right to sell 100 shares (which you would not necessarily own) at a price of $50 per share ($50 is the striking price). If you bought a 100-share contract for $218.75 and then IBM's stock actually fell to $45, your put option would be worth ($50 − $45)(100) = $500. After subtracting the $218.75 you paid for the option, your profit (before taxes and commissions) would be $281.25.

Table 22-1 contains an extract from the March 23, 1993, *Wall Street Journal* Listed Options Quotations Table. This extract, which focuses on IBM, U.S. Surgical, and McDonald's options, reflects the trading which occurred on the previous day. On March 22, McDonald's April (1-month), $55 call option sold on the CBOE for $0.50. Thus, for $0.50(100) = $50 you could buy options that would give you the right to purchase 100 shares of McDonald's at a price of $55 per share at any

time during the next month.[2] If the stock price stayed below $55 during that period, you would lose your $50, but if it rose to $65, then your $50 investment would have grown to ($65 − $55)(100) = $500 in less than 30 days. That translates into a very healthy annualized rate of return. Incidentally, if the stock price did go up, you would probably not actually exercise your options and buy the stock—rather, you would sell the options, which would then have a value of at least $500 versus the $50 you paid, to another option buyer.

Option trading is one of the hottest financial activities in the United States. In addition to options on individual stocks, options are also available on several stock indexes such as the NYSE Index and the S&P 100 Index, permitting one to bet on a rise or fall in the general market as well as on individual stocks such as IBM. The leverage involved makes it possible for speculators with just a few dollars to make a fortune almost overnight. Also, investors with sizable portfolios can sell options against their stocks and earn the value of the option (less brokerage commissions), even if the stock's price remains constant. Further, options can be used to create hedges which protect the value of an individual stock or portfolio. We will discuss hedging strategies in more detail later in the chapter.[3]

Corporations such as McDonald's and IBM, on whose stocks options are written, have nothing to do with the option market. The corporations do not raise money in the option market, nor do they have any direct transactions in it, and option holders do not vote for corporate directors (unless they exercise their options to purchase the stock, which few actually do) or receive dividends. There have been studies by the SEC and others as to whether option trading stabilizes or destabilizes the stock market, and whether this activity helps or hinders corporations seeking to raise new capital. The studies have not been conclusive, but option trading does seem to be here to stay, and many regard it as the most exciting game in town.

FACTORS THAT AFFECT THE VALUE OF A CALL OPTION

An analysis of Table 22-1 provides some insights into call option valuation. First, we can see that there are at least three factors which affect a call option's value: (1) For a given striking price, the higher the stock's market price in relation to the strike price, the higher will be the call option price. Thus, McDonald's $55 April call option sells for $0.50, whereas U.S. Surgical's $55 April option sells for $4.25 because U.S. Surgical's current stock price is $56⅝ versus $53⅛ for McDonald's.

---

[2]Actually, the *expiration date,* which is the last date that the option can be exercised, is the Friday before the third Saturday of the exercise month. Thus, the April options actually have a term one day less than four weeks. Also, note that option contracts are generally written in 100-share multiples.

[3]It should be noted that insiders who trade illegally generally buy options rather than stock because options increase the profit potential. Note, though, that it is illegal to use insider information for personal gain, and an insider would be taking advantage of the option seller. Insider trading, in addition to being unfair and essentially equivalent to stealing, hurts the economy: Investors lose confidence in the capital markets and raise their required returns because of an increased element of risk, which raises the cost of capital and thus reduces the level of investment.

(2) For a given stock price, the higher the striking price, the lower will be the call option price. Thus, all of IBM's call options, regardless of exercise month, decline as the striking price increases. (3) The longer the option period, the higher will be the option price, because the longer the time before expiration, the greater the chance that the stock price will climb substantially above the exercise price. Thus, for all striking prices, option prices increase as the expiration date is lengthened.

EXPIRATION VALUE VERSUS OPTION PRICE

How is the actual price of a call option determined in the market? We shall, shortly, present a widely used model (the Black-Scholes model) for pricing call options, but first it is useful to establish some basic concepts. To begin, we define a call option's *expiration value* as follows:

$$\text{Expiration value} = \frac{\text{Current price}}{\text{of the stock}} - \text{Striking price.}$$

For example, if a stock sells for \$50, and its option has a striking price of \$20, then the expiration value is \$30. The expiration value can be thought of as the value of the option if it expired today. Note that the calculated expiration value of a call option could be negative, but realistically the minimum expiration value of an option is zero. Note also that an option's expiration value can be thought of as its first approximation value, because it provides a starting point for finding the actual value of the option.

Now consider Figure 22-1, which presents some data on Space Technology Inc. (STI), a company which recently went public and whose stock price has fluctuated widely during its short history. The third column in the tabular data shows the expiration values for STI's call option when the stock was selling at different prices; the fourth column gives the actual market prices for the option; and the fifth column shows the premium of the actual option price over its expiration value. At any stock price below \$20, the expiration value is zero; above \$20, each \$1 increase in the price of the stock brings with it a \$1 increase in the option's expiration value. Note, however, that the actual market price of the option lies above the expiration value at each price of the common stock, but the premium declines as the price of the common stock increases. For example, when the common stock sold for \$20 and the option had a zero expiration value, its actual price, and the premium, was \$9. Then, as the price of the stock rose, the *expiration value's increase* matched the stock's increase dollar for dollar, but the *market price* of the option climbed less rapidly, so the premium declined. The premium was \$9 when the stock sold for \$20 a share, but it declined to \$1 by the time the stock price had risen to \$73 a share. Beyond this point, the premium virtually disappeared.

Why does this pattern exist? Why should the option ever sell for more than its expiration value, and why does the premium decline as the price of the stock increases? The answer lies in the speculative appeal of options — they enable

FIGURE 22-1

SPACE TECHNOLOGY
INC.: OPTION PRICE
AND EXPIRATION
VALUE

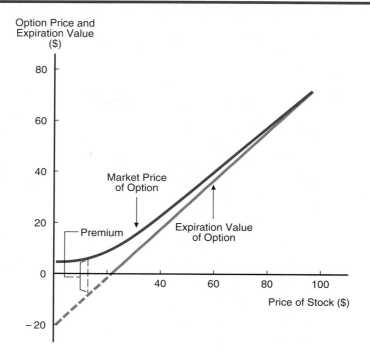

Price of Stock (1)	Striking Price (2)	Expiration Value of Option (1) − (2) = (3)	Market Price of Option (4)	Premium (4) − (3) = (5)
$20.00	$20.00	$ 0.00	$ 9.00	$9.00
21.00	20.00	1.00	9.75	8.75
22.00	20.00	2.00	10.50	8.50
35.00	20.00	15.00	21.00	6.00
42.00	20.00	22.00	26.00	4.00
50.00	20.00	30.00	32.00	2.00
73.00	20.00	53.00	54.00	1.00
98.00	20.00	78.00	78.50	0.50

someone to gain a high degree of personal leverage when buying securities. To illustrate, *suppose STI's option sold for exactly its expiration value.* Now suppose you were thinking of investing in the company's common stock at a time when it was selling for $21 a share. If you bought a share and the price rose to $42, you would have made a 100 percent capital gain. However, had you bought the option at its expiration value ($1 when the stock was selling for $21), your capital gain would have been $22 − $1 = $21 on a $1 investment, or 2,100 percent! At the same time, your total loss potential with the option would be only $1 versus a potential loss of $21 if you purchased the stock. The huge capital gains potential, combined with the loss limitation, is clearly worth something—the exact amount

it is worth to investors is the amount of the premium. Note, however, that buying the option is riskier than buying STI's stock, because there is a higher probability of losing money on the option. If STI's stock price remains at $21, you would break even on the stock (ignoring transaction costs), but you would lose your entire $1 option investment.

Why does the premium decline as the price of the stock rises? Part of the answer is that both the leverage effect and the loss protection feature decline at high stock prices. For example, if you were thinking of buying STI stock when its price was $73 a share, the expiration value of the option would be $53. If the stock price doubled to $146, the expiration value of the option would go from $53 to $126. The percentage capital gain on the stock would still be 100 percent, but the percentage gain on the option would now be only 138 percent versus 2,100 percent in the earlier case. Notice also that the potential loss on the option is much greater when the option is selling at high prices. These two factors, the declining leverage impact and the increasing danger of larger losses, help explain why the premium diminishes as the price of the common stock rises.

In addition to the stock price and the exercise price, the price of an option depends on three other factors: (1) the option's term to maturity, (2) the variability of the stock price, and (3) the risk-free rate. We will explain precisely how these factors affect call option prices later, but for now, note these points:

1. The longer an option has to run, the greater its value and the larger its premium. If an option expires at 4 P.M. today, there is not much chance that the stock price will go way up, so the option must sell at close to its expiration value, and its premium must be small. On the other hand, if the expiration date is a year away, the stock price could rise sharply, pulling the option's value up with it.

2. An option on an extremely volatile stock will be worth more than one on a very stable stock. If the stock price rarely moves, then there is only a small chance of a large gain. However, if the stock price is highly volatile, the option could easily become very valuable. At the same time, losses on options are limited, so large declines in a stock's price do not have a corresponding bad effect on option holders. Therefore, the more volatile a stock, the higher is the value of its options.

Because of Points 1 and 2, in a graph such as Figure 22-1, if everything else were constant, then the longer an option's life, the higher its market price line would be above the expiration value line. Similarly, the more volatile the price of the underlying stock, the higher is the market price line. We will see precisely how these factors, and also the risk-free rate, affect option values when we discuss the option pricing model.

SELF-TEST QUESTIONS

What is an option? A call option? A put option?

Define a call option's expiration value. Why is the actual market price of a call option usually above its expiration value?

What are some factors which affect a call option's value?

INTRODUCTION TO OPTION PRICING

In the next section, we will discuss a well-known option pricing model, but it is useful first to go through a simple example. Assume that 1-year call options are available on Butler Company, a Midwestern firm which produces cellular telephones. Each option has an exercise price of $35, and Butler's stock is now selling for $40 a share. Assume further that when the options expire 1 year hence, Butler's shares will be selling at one of only two possible prices, $30 or $50. Under these simple conditions, what is the value of a call option on Butler's stock?

To answer this question, we proceed as follows:

1. **Examine the payoffs at maturity.** At expiration, the stock price will be either $30 or $50, and the value of the option at expiration will depend on Butler's stock price. Thus, we have the following situation at expiration:

	Stock Price	Option Value	
Low	$30	$ 0	(option is worthless)
High	50	15	(expiration value)
Range	$20	$15	

2. **Create the same range of payoffs.** Note that the range of payoffs as shown in Step 1 is $20 for a stock investment (from a low of $30 to a high of $50) and $15 for an option investment (from $0 to $15). The payoff ranges would be identical on the two investments if you could buy 0.75 shares of Butler's stock. In this situation, the payoff matrix would look like this:

	Stock Price	Value of 0.75 Shares	Option Value
Low	$30	$22.50	$ 0
High	50	37.50	15
Range	$20	$15.00	$15

3. **Create a riskless hedge.** You can now create a riskless portfolio by buying 0.75 shares of Butler's stock and selling 1 call option. The sale of the call option will not affect the final portfolio value if the price of the stock declines, but it will lower the portfolio's value by $50 − $35 = $15 if the price rises. Here is the resulting payoff matrix:

	Stock Price	Value of 0.75 Shares	+	Effect of the Call on Portfolio Value	=	Value of Portfolio
Low	$30	$22.50	+	$ 0	=	$22.50
High	50	37.50	+	(15)	=	22.50

If the stock price at expiration is $30, the stock investment returns $22.50, but the call will not be exercised, hence it will not affect the portfolio's value. On the other hand, if the stock price is $50 at expiration, the value of the stock investment

would be $37.50, but the holder of the call would exercise his or her option. Thus, you must provide one share at the exercise price, $35, which you must purchase at the market price of $50, hence you will incur a $15 loss. Therefore, regardless of what happens to the price of the stock, your portfolio's return is $22.50 — you have created a riskless portfolio by buying the stock and writing (selling) a call option on that stock.

4. Valuing the call option.   To this point, we have not specified what price you would charge to write (sell) the call. However, we have seen that your riskless portfolio will provide a sure $22.50 at option expiration in 1 year. If the risk-free rate is 8 percent, the value of the portfolio today is $22.50/1.08 = $20.83. Since Butler's stock is currently selling at $40 a share, creating the riskless portfolio would require a stock investment of 0.75($40) = $30. Since your total investment outlay to create the riskless portfolio must be equal to or less than $20.83, the present value of the portfolio, you must be able to sell the call option for at least $30 − $20.83 = $9.17 in order to break even. Assuming that competition exists in the options market, $9.17 will be the equilibrium price of the option.

Clearly, this example is unrealistic — Butler's stock price could be almost anything after 1 year, and you cannot purchase 0.75 shares of stock. But the example does illustrate that investors can, in principle, create riskless portfolios by buying stocks and selling call options against those stocks, and the return on such portfolios should be the risk-free rate. If call options are not priced to reflect this condition, arbitrageurs will actively trade stocks and options until option prices do reflect such equilibrium conditions. In the next section, we discuss the Black-Scholes Option Pricing Model, which is based on the general premise we developed here — the creation of a riskless portfolio — but which is much more applicable to "real-world" option pricing because it allows for a wide range of ending stock prices.

SELF-TEST QUESTIONS

Describe how a risk-free portfolio can be created using stocks and options.

How can such a portfolio be used to help estimate a call option's value?

THE BLACK-SCHOLES OPTION PRICING MODEL (OPM)

The *Black-Scholes Option Pricing Model (OPM)* was developed in 1973, just as the rapid growth in options trading began.[4] This model, which has actually been programmed into the permanent memories of some hand-held calculators, is

---

[4]See Fischer Black and Myron Scholes, "The Pricing of Options and Corporate Liabilities," *Journal of Political Economy*, May/June 1973, 637–659.

widely used by option traders. Our interest, however, lies in the insights that option theory provides in valuing all securities subject to contingent claims, including warrants, convertibles, and even the equity of a levered firm.

In deriving their option pricing model, which estimates the value of a call option, Black and Scholes made the following assumptions:

1. The stock underlying the call option provides no dividends or other distributions during the life of the option.

2. There are no transaction costs in buying or selling either the stock or the option.

3. The short-term, risk-free interest rate is known and is constant during the life of the option.

4. Any purchaser of a security may borrow any fraction of the purchase price at the short-term, risk-free interest rate.

5. Short selling is permitted without penalty, and the short seller will receive immediately the full cash proceeds of today's price for a security sold short.[5]

6. The call option can be exercised only on its expiration date.

7. Trading in all securities takes place in continuous time, and the stock price moves randomly in continuous time.

The derivation of the Black-Scholes Option Pricing Model rests on the concept of a riskless hedge such as the one we set up in the last section. By buying shares of a stock and simultaneously selling call options on that stock, an investor can create a risk-free investment position, where gains on the stock will exactly offset losses on the option, and vice versa. This riskless hedged position must earn a rate of return equal to the risk-free rate; otherwise, an arbitrage opportunity would exist, and people trying to take advantage of this opportunity would drive the price of the option to the equilibrium level as specified by the Black-Scholes model.

The Black-Scholes model consists of the following three equations:

$$V = P[N(d_1)] - Xe^{-k_{RF}t}[N(d_2)]. \tag{22-1}$$

$$d_1 = \frac{\ln(P/X) + [k_{RF} + (\sigma^2/2)]t}{\sigma\sqrt{t}}. \tag{22-2}$$

$$d_2 = d_1 - \sigma\sqrt{t}. \tag{22-3}$$

---

[5]Suppose an investor (or speculator) does not now own any IBM stock. If the investor anticipates a rise in the stock price and consequently buys IBM stock, he or she is said to have *gone long* in IBM. On the other hand, if the investor thinks IBM's stock is likely to fall, he or she could *go short,* or *sell IBM short.* Since the short seller has no IBM stock, he or she would have to borrow the shares sold short from a broker. If the stock price falls, the short seller could, later on, buy shares on the open market and pay back the ones borrowed from the broker. The short seller's profit, before commissions and taxes, would be the difference between the price received from the short sale and the price paid later to purchase the replacement stock.

Here

V = current value of a call option with time t until expiration.

P = current price of the underlying stock.

$N(d_i)$ = probability that a deviation less than d_i will occur in a standard normal distribution. Thus, $N(d_1)$ and $N(d_2)$ represent areas under a standard normal distribution function.

X = exercise, or striking, price of the option.

$e \approx 2.7183$.

k_{RF} = risk-free interest rate.

t = time until the option expires (the option period).

$\ln(P/X)$ = natural logarithm of P/X.

σ^2 = variance of the rate of return on the stock.

Note that the value of the option is a function of the variables we discussed earlier: (1) P, the stock's price; (2) t, the option's time to expiration; (3) X, the striking price; (4) σ^2, the variance of the underlying stock; and (5) k_{RF}, the risk-free rate. We do not derive the Black-Scholes model—the derivation involves some extremely complicated mathematics that go far beyond the scope of this text. However, it is not difficult to use the model, and under the assumptions set forth previously, if the option price is different from the one found by Equation 22-1, this would provide the opportunity for arbitrage profits, which would, in turn, force the option price back to the value indicated by the model.[6] As we noted earlier, the Black-Scholes model is widely used by traders, so actual option prices do conform reasonably well to values derived from the model.

In essence, the first term of Equation 22-1, $P[N(d_1)]$, can be thought of as the expected present value of the terminal stock price, while the second term, $Xe^{-k_{RF}t}[N(d_2)]$, can be thought of as the present value of the exercise price. However, rather than try to figure out exactly what the equations mean, it is more productive to work out some values and to see how changes in the inputs affect the value of a call option.

OPM ILLUSTRATION

The current stock price, P, the exercise price, X, and the time to maturity, t, of the option can be obtained from a newspaper such as *The Wall Street Journal*. The risk-free rate, k_{RF}, used in the OPM is the yield on Treasury bills with a

---

[6]*Programmed trading,* in which stocks are bought and options are sold, or vice versa, is an example of arbitrage between stocks and options.

maturity date equal to the option expiration date. The stock price variance, σ^2, can be estimated by calculating the variance of the percentage change in daily stock prices for the past year, that is, the variance of $(P_t - P_{t-1})/P_t$ on a daily basis.

Assume that the following information has been obtained:

P = $20.

X = $20.

t = 3 months or 0.25 years.

k_{RF} = 12% = 0.12.

σ^2 = 0.16.

Given this information, we can now use the OPM by solving Equations 22-1 through 22-3. Since d_1 and d_2 are required inputs for Equation 22-1, we solve Equations 22-2 and 22-3 first:

$$d_1 = \frac{\ln(\$20/\$20) + [0.12 + (0.16/2)](0.25)}{0.40(0.50)}$$

$$= \frac{0 + 0.05}{0.20} = 0.25.$$

$$d_2 = d_1 - 0.20 = 0.05.$$

Note that $N(d_1) = N(0.25)$ and $N(d_2) = N(0.05)$ represent areas under a standard normal distribution function. From Table A-5 in Appendix A at the end of the book, we see that the value $d_1 = 0.25$ implies a probability of $0.0987 + 0.5000 = 0.5987$, so $N(d_1) = 0.5987$. Similarly, $N(d_2) = 0.5199$. We can use those values to solve Equation 22-1:

$$V = \$20[N(d_1)] - \$20e^{-(0.12 \times 0.25)}[N(d_2)]$$

$$= \$20[N(0.25)] - \$20(0.9704)[N(0.05)]$$

$$= \$20(0.5987) - \$19.41(0.5199)$$

$$= \$11.97 - \$10.09 = \$1.88.$$

Thus, the value of the option, under the assumed conditions, is $1.88. Suppose the actual option price were $2.25. Arbitrageurs could simultaneously sell the option and buy the underlying stock, and earn a riskless profit. Such trading would occur until the price of the option was driven to $1.88. The reverse would occur if the option sold for less than $1.88. Thus, investors would be unwilling to pay more than $1.88 for the option, and they could not buy it for less, so $1.88 is the *equilibrium value* of the option.

To see how each of the five OPM factors affects the value of the option, V, consider Table 22-2. Here the top row shows the base case input values and the resulting option value, V = $1.88. The base case input values are those we used

TABLE 22-2
EFFECTS OF OPM
FACTORS ON THE
VALUE OF A CALL
OPTION

Case	Input Factors					
	P	X	t	k_{RF}	σ^2	V
Base case	$20	$20	0.25	12%	0.16	$1.88
Increase P by $5	**25**	20	0.25	12	0.16	5.81
Increase X by $5	20	**25**	0.25	12	0.16	0.39
Increase t to 6 months	20	20	**0.50**	12	0.16	2.81
Increase k_{RF} to 16%	20	20	0.25	**16**	0.16	1.99
Increase σ^2 to 0.25	20	20	0.25	12	**0.25**	2.27

earlier to illustrate how to solve the OPM. In each of the subsequent rows, one factor is increased, while the values of the other four are held constant at their base case levels. The value of the call option is given in the last column. Now consider the effects of a change in each factor:

1. **Current stock price.** As the current stock price, P, increases from $20 to $25, the option value increases from $1.88 to $5.81. Thus, the value of the option increases as the stock price increases, but by less than the stock price increase, $3.93 versus $5.00. Note, though, that the percentage increase in the option value, ($5.81 − $1.88)/$1.88 = 209%, far exceeds the percentage increase in the stock price, ($25 − $20)/$20 = 25%.

2. **Exercise price.** As the exercise price, X, increases from $20 to $25, the value of the option declines. Again, though, the decrease in the option value is less than the exercise price increase, but the percentage change in the option value, ($0.39 − $1.88)/$1.88 = −79%, exceeds the percentage change in the exercise price, ($25 − $20)/$20 = 25%.

3. **Option period.** As time to expiration increases from t = 3 months (or 0.25 years) to t = 6 months (or 0.50 years), the value of the option increases from $1.88 to $2.81. This result occurs because the value of the option depends on the chances for an increase in the price of the underlying stock, and the longer the option has to go, the higher the stock price may climb. Thus, other factors held constant, a 6-month option is worth more than a 3-month option.

4. **Risk-free rate.** The next factor is the risk-free rate, k_{RF}. As the risk-free rate increases from 12 to 16 percent, the value of the option increases slightly, from $1.88 to $1.99. Equations 22-1, 22-2, and 22-3 suggest that the principal effect of an increase in k_{RF} is to reduce the present value of the exercise price, $Xe^{-k_{RF}t}$, hence to increase the current value of the option.[7] The risk-free rate also plays a role in determining the values of the normal distribution functions $N(d_1)$ and

---

[7]At this point, you may be wondering why the first term in Equation 22-1, $P[N(d_1)]$, is not discounted. In fact, it has been, because the current stock price, P, already represents the present value of the expected expiration date stock price. In other words, P is a discounted value, and the discount rate used in the market to determine today's stock price includes the risk-free rate. Thus, Equation 22-1 can be thought of as the present value of the end-of-option-period spread between the stock price and the striking price, adjusted for the probability that the stock price will be higher than the striking price.

$N(d_2)$, but this effect is of secondary importance. Indeed, option prices in general are not very sensitive to interest rate changes, at least not to changes within the ranges normally encountered.

5. Variance. As the variance increases from the base case level of 0.16 to 0.25, the value of the option increases from $1.88 to $2.27. That is, if all other factors are held constant, the riskier the underlying security, the more valuable will be the option. This result is logical. First, if you bought an option to buy a stock that sells at its exercise price, and if $\sigma^2 = 0$, then there would be a zero probability of the stock price going up, hence a zero probability of making any money on the option. On the other hand, if you bought an option on a high-variance stock, there would be a fairly high probability that the stock price would go way up, hence that you would make a large profit on the option. Of course, the price of a high-variance stock could go way down, but as an option holder, your losses would be limited to the price paid to buy the option—only the right-hand side of the stock's probability distribution counts. Put another way, an increase in the price of the stock helps options holders more than a decrease hurts them; thus, the greater the variance, the greater is the value of the option. All of this makes options on risky stocks more valuable than those on safer, low-variance stocks.

This concludes our discussion of options and option pricing theory. The next section discusses how option pricing theory can be used to help think about financial decisions, while the following two major sections describe warrants and convertibles, the primary types of option securities issued by firms.

SELF-TEST QUESTIONS

What is the purpose of the Black-Scholes Option Pricing Model?

Explain what a "riskless hedge" is, and how the riskless hedge concept is used in the Black-Scholes OPM.

Describe the impact that an increase in each of the following factors would have on the value of a call option:
  (1) Stock price
  (2) Exercise price
  (3) Option period
  (4) Risk-free rate
  (5) Stock price variance

OPTION PRICING: IMPLICATIONS FOR CORPORATE FINANCIAL POLICY

The equity of a levered firm can be thought of as a call option: When a firm issues debt, this is, in a sense, equivalent to the shareholders selling the assets of the firm to the debtholders, who pay for the assets with cash but also give the stockholders an implied call option with a striking price equal to the principal value of the debt plus interest. If the company is successful, the stockholders will "buy the company

back" by exercising their call, which means paying the principal and interest on the debt. If the company is not successful, stockholders will default on the loan, which amounts to not exercising their call and thus giving the company to the creditors.

As an illustration, suppose the One-Shot Corporation is just being formed to make a 1-year investment in producing and marketing presidential campaign buttons. The firm requires an investment of $10,000, of which $7,500 will be obtained by selling debt with a 10 percent interest rate, and the other $2,500 will be raised by selling common stock. All cash distributions to debtholders and stockholders are to be made at the end of 1 year. After this year is over, the value of the firm will depend primarily on which candidates make it through the primary elections, plus a small value based on the collector's market. Here is the estimated probability distribution of the firm's value:

Probability	Value
0.7	$20,000
0.2	5,000
0.1	0
1.0	

Thus, the expected value of the firm at the end of the year is 0.7($20,000) + 0.2($5,000) + 0.1($0) = $15,000.

The expected value, if it could be realized, would provide the shareholders with $6,750 before taxes on their $2,500 investment:

Expected value		$15,000
Less:		
Debt principal	$7,500	
Debt interest	750	8,250
Before-tax return		$ 6,750

However, the expected value is not achievable: The value of the firm will be $0 or $5,000 or $20,000. If the value is either $0 or $5,000, the shareholders will not exercise their call option; instead, they will default. The debtholders would then be entitled to the value of the firm, and the equity holders would receive nothing. However, if the firm's value turns out to be $20,000, the shareholders would exercise the call option by paying off the $8,250 principal and interest, and then pocket the remaining $11,750 before taxes. Thus, equity ownership can be viewed as a call option. In this illustration, an equity investment of $2,500 (the current price of the call) entitles the shareholders to purchase the assets of the firm from the debtholders for $8,250 (the exercise price). This insight has been applied to several of the traditional issues of corporate finance.[8] We look at one issue here,

---

[8]For example, see Dan Galai and Ronald Masulis, "The Option Pricing Model and the Risk Factor of Stock," *The Journal of Financial Economics,* January/March 1976, 53–82. Galai and Masulis combine the CAPM with the OPM. Thus, the assumptions of both models underlie their analysis.

investment decisions, and we will examine the implications of option analysis for mergers in Chapter 24.

Start with a levered firm which has a large portfolio of Treasury bills. Suppose management sold the bills (which are riskless) and used the proceeds to purchase a risky asset that increased the firm's earnings variance, yet had no effect on the firm's beta coefficient. Since the firm's equity can be viewed as a call option, the increased variance would increase the market value of the equity without increasing its market risk. The risk of bankruptcy would increase, but shareholders would have increased their chances of greater gains while their losses would still be limited to the amount of their investment. However, any gains to shareholders come at the expense of the debtholders. In general, we can see that increasing a firm's riskiness by changing its asset mix benefits the stockholders at the expense of the debtholders. This point is made clear by applying option pricing theory.

Options are important in the investments area, so students of investments need to have a knowledge of how they are used and priced in the market. Further, option theory helps us understand the nature of option-like securities such as warrants and convertibles. However, the role of option theory in financial management decision making is less clear. As we have seen, it is possible to use option theory to gain insights into the effects of asset investments on the value of the firm's debt and equity. However, these insights are really rather obvious, and one can see the general effects of asset risk changes more easily just by thinking about them than by working through the OPM. Still, it may be that the OPM approach can in the future lead to a more precise quantification of certain effects, which would be useful in structuring contracts and in other types of financial policy decisions. Also, we noted in Chapter 10 that the Black-Scholes OPM is being used in some industries to value the managerial options inherent in some capital projects. In any event, it is safe to predict that option pricing theory will play a greater role in financial management decision making in the future, so students of corporate finance need to be aware of the progress in this area.

SELF-TEST QUESTIONS

Describe how the equity of a levered firm can be thought of as a call option.

What does option pricing theory tell us about how changes in assets might affect the value of a firm's debt and equity?

WARRANTS

A *warrant* is an option issued by a company which gives the warrant's owner the right to buy a stated number of shares of the company's stock at a specified price. Generally, warrants are distributed with debt, and they are used to induce investors to buy a firm's long-term debt at a lower interest rate than would otherwise be required. For example, when Infomatics Corporation, a rapidly growing high-

tech company, wanted to sell $50 million of 20-year bonds in 1993, the company's investment banker informed the financial vice-president that the bonds, which would be B rated, would be difficult to sell, and that an interest rate of 10 percent would be required. However, as an alternative the banker suggested that investors might be willing to buy the bonds with a coupon rate of only 8 percent if the company would offer 20 warrants with each $1,000 bond, each warrant entitling the holder to buy one share of common stock at a price of $22 per share. The stock was selling for $20 per share at the time, and the warrants would expire in the year 2003 if they were not exercised.

Why would investors be willing to buy Infomatics Corporation's bonds at a yield of only 8 percent in a 10 percent market just because warrants were also offered as part of the package? It is because the warrants are long-term call options which have value as discussed earlier, and this value offsets the low interest rate on the bonds and makes the package of low-yield bonds plus warrants attractive to investors.

INITIAL MARKET PRICE OF BOND WITH WARRANTS

The Infomatics bonds, if they had been issued as straight debt, would have carried a 10 percent interest rate. However, with warrants attached, the bonds were sold to yield 8 percent. Someone buying the bonds at their $1,000 initial offering price would thus be receiving a package consisting of an 8 percent, 20-year bond plus 20 warrants. Since the going interest rate on bonds as risky as those of Infomatics was 10 percent, we can find the straight-debt value of the bonds, assuming an annual coupon for ease of illustration, as follows:

$$\text{Value} = \sum_{t=1}^{20} \frac{\$80}{(1.10)^t} + \frac{\$1,000}{(1.10)^{20}}$$

$$= \$681.09 + \$148.64 = \$829.73.$$

Using a financial calculator, enter N = 20, I = 10, PMT = 80, and FV = 1000. Then press PV to obtain the bond's value, $829.73. Thus, a person buying the bonds in the initial underwriting would pay $1,000 and receive in exchange a straight bond worth about $830 plus 20 warrants presumably worth about $1,000 − $830 = $170:

$$\frac{\text{Price paid for}}{\text{bond with warrants}} = \frac{\text{Straight-debt}}{\text{value of bond}} + \frac{\text{Value of}}{\text{warrants}}$$

$$\$1,000 = \$830 + \$170.$$

Since investors receive 20 warrants with each bond, each warrant has an implied value of $170/20 = $8.50.

The key issue in setting the terms of a bond-with-warrants offering is valuing the warrants. The straight-debt value of the bond can be estimated quite accurately. However, it is much more difficult to estimate the value of the warrants.

Even the Black-Scholes OPM provides only a rough estimate because (1) its parameters are not easily estimated; (2) it assumes no dividends on the underlying stock, which is not generally a reasonable assumption for a long-term option; and (3) it assumes that any stock deliveries involve currently outstanding stock, but warrants, when exercised, create new stock, and hence dilute earnings.

If, in setting the terms, the warrants are overvalued relative to their true market value, then it will be difficult to sell the issue at its par value. Conversely, if the warrants are undervalued, then investors who subscribe to the issue will receive a windfall profit, since they can sell the warrants in the market for more than they implicitly paid for them, and this windfall profit would come out of the pockets of Infomatics's stockholders.

USE OF WARRANTS IN FINANCING

In the past, warrants have generally been used by small, rapidly growing firms as "sweeteners" when they were selling either debt or preferred stock. Such firms are frequently regarded by investors as being highly risky. Their bonds could be sold only if they were willing to pay extremely high rates of interest and also to accept very restrictive indenture provisions. To avoid this, firms such as Infomatics often offered warrants along with the bonds. However, some time ago, AT&T raised $1.57 billion by selling bonds with warrants. This was the largest financing of any type ever undertaken by a business firm, and it marked the first use ever of warrants by a large, strong corporation.[9]

Getting warrants along with bonds enables investors to share in the company's growth, if it does in fact grow and prosper; therefore, investors are willing to accept a lower bond interest rate and less restrictive indenture provisions. A bond with warrants has some characteristics of debt and some characteristics of equity. It is a hybrid security that provides the financial manager with an opportunity to expand the firm's mix of securities and to appeal to a broader group of investors.

Virtually all warrants today are *detachable*. Thus, after a bond with attached warrants is sold, the warrants can be detached and traded separately from the bond. Further, when these warrants are exercised, the bond issue (with its low coupon rate) remains outstanding, so the warrants bring in additional funds to the firm while leaving its interest costs relatively low.

---

[9]It is interesting to note that before the AT&T issue, the New York Stock Exchange's stated policy was that warrants could not be listed because they were "speculative" instruments rather than "investment" securities. When AT&T issued warrants, however, the Exchange changed its policy, agreeing to list warrants that met certain requirements. Many other warrants have since been listed.

It is also interesting to note that, prior to the sale, AT&T's treasury staff, working with Morgan Stanley analysts, estimated the value of the warrants as a part of the underwriting decision. The package was supposed to sell for a total price in the neighborhood of $1,000. The bond value could be determined accurately, so the trick was to estimate the equilibrium value of the warrant under different possible exercise prices and years to expiration, and then to use that exercise price and life that caused Bond value + Warrant value ≈ $1,000. Using the option pricing model, the AT&T/Morgan Stanley analysts set terms which caused the warrant to sell on the open market at a price that was only 35¢ away from the estimated price.

The exercise price is generally set at from 10 to 30 percent above the market price of the stock on the date the bond is issued. If the firm does grow and prosper, and if its stock price rises above the exercise price at which shares may be purchased, warrant holders could exercise their warrants and buy stock at the stated price. However, without some incentive, warrants would never be exercised prior to maturity — their value in the market would be greater than their exercise value, hence holders would sell rather than exercise. There are three conditions which encourage holders to exercise their warrants: (1) Warrant holders will surely exercise warrants and buy stock if the warrants are about to expire and the market price of the stock is above the exercise price. (2) Warrant holders will tend to exercise voluntarily and buy stock if the company raises the dividend on the common stock by a sufficient amount. No dividend is earned on the warrant, so it provides no current income. However, if the common stock pays a high dividend, it provides an attractive dividend yield. This induces warrant holders to exercise their option to buy the stock. (3) Warrants sometimes have *stepped-up exercise prices,* which prod owners into exercising them. For example, the Williamson Scientific Company has warrants outstanding with an exercise price of $25 until December 31, 1998, at which time the exercise price rises to $30. If the price of the common stock is over $25 just before December 31, 1998, many warrant holders will exercise their options before the stepped-up price takes effect.

Another desirable feature of warrants is that they generally bring in funds only if funds are needed. If the company grows, it will probably need new equity capital. At the same time, growth will cause the price of the stock to rise, the warrants to be exercised, and the firm to obtain additional cash. If the company is not successful and cannot profitably employ additional money, the price of its stock will probably not rise sufficiently to induce exercise of the warrants.

THE COMPONENT COST OF BONDS WITH WARRANTS

When Infomatics issued its debt with warrants, the firm received $50 million, or $1,000 for each bond. Simultaneously, the company assumed an obligation to pay $80 interest for 20 years plus $1,000 at the end of 20 years. The cost of the money would have been 10 percent if no warrants had been attached, but each Infomatics bond had 20 warrants, each of which entitles its holder to buy one share of Infomatics stock for $22. A cost rate must be assigned to the warrants to determine the total cost of the issue. As we shall see, the total cost is well above 8 percent.

Assume that Infomatics's stock price, which is now $20, is expected to grow, and does grow, at 10 percent per year. When the warrants expire 10 years from now, the stock price will be $20(1.10)^{10} = \$51.87$. Assuming the warrants had not been exercised during the 10-year period, the company would then have to issue one share of stock worth $51.87 for each warrant exercised, and in return, Infomatics would receive the exercise price, $22. Thus, a purchaser of the bonds, if he or she holds the complete package, will make a profit in Year 10 of $51.87 − $22 = $29.87 for each common share issued. Since each bond has 20 warrants attached, investors would have a gain of 20($29.87) = $597.40 per bond at the end of Year 10. Here is a time line of the cash flow stream to an investor:

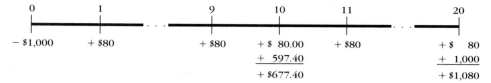

The IRR of this stream is 10.7 percent, which is the investor's overall rate of return on the issue. This return is 70 basis points higher than the return on straight debt, which reflects the fact that the issue is riskier to investors than a straight-debt issue because some of the return is expected to come in the form of stock price appreciation, and that part of the return may not materialize.

The expected rate of return to investors is, of course, also the before-tax cost of the issue to the company—this was true of common stocks, straight bonds, and preferred stocks, and it is also true of bonds sold with warrants. In thinking about this, note that the investor's Year 10 gain of $597.40 does not just appear out of thin air—the company is giving the warrant holders the right to buy for $22 a share of stock with a market value of $51.87. That obviously dilutes the value of the stock, so Infomatics's original shareholders are incurring an opportunity cost which is exactly equal to the warrant holders' gain.

The cost of warrants can also be illustrated in terms of the effect on earnings per share (EPS). Suppose Infomatics had 1,000,000 common shares outstanding just prior to the expiration of the warrants. Further, assume that the company earns 13.5 percent on its market value equity, so earnings per share are $0.135(\$51.87) = \$7$, and total earnings are $1,000,000(\$7) = \$7,000,000$. Now, if there were 100,000 warrants outstanding at expiration, exercise of these warrants would bring in $100,000(\$22) = \$2,200,000$ of new equity funds, and the number of shares would increase by 100,000. Assuming that the earning power of the $2.2 million of new assets was also 13.5 percent, then $0.135(\$2,200,000) = \$297,000$ of new earnings would be produced, making the new total earnings $\$7,000,000 + \$297,000 = \$7,297,000$. When that new total earnings figure is divided by the new total shares outstanding ($1,000,000 + 100,000 = 1,100,000$), we get a new EPS of $6.63:

$$\text{New EPS} = \$7,297,000/1,100,000 = \$6.63.$$

Thus, exercise of the warrants results in a dilution of EPS from $7 to $6.63, or by $0.37. This $0.37 EPS dilution is a real cost, it is borne by Infomatics's original shareholders, and it must be considered when calculating the cost of the bonds with warrants.

A WARRANT ISSUE THAT WENT AWRY

Although warrant issues are bought by investors with the expectation of receiving a total return commensurate with the overall riskiness of the securities package

being purchased, things do not always work out as expected. For example, in November 1989 Sony paid $3.4 billion for Columbia Pictures, a U.S. movie studio. To help finance the deal, in early 1990 Sony sold $470 million of 4-year bonds with warrants at an incredibly low 0.3 percent coupon interest rate. The rate was so low because the warrants, which also had a maturity of 4 years, allowed investors to purchase Sony stock at 7,670 yen per share, only 2.5 percent above the share price at the time the bonds with warrants were issued.

Investors snapped up the issue, and many of the warrants were "peeled off" and sold separately on the open market. The warrant buyers obviously believed that Sony's stock would shortly climb above the exercise price, even though the Tokyo stock market had recently taken a small tumble. From Sony's point of view, the bonds-with-warrants package provided a very low cost "bridge loan" (the bonds) that would be replaced with equity financing when the warrants were exercised, presumably in 4 years when the bonds became due. Sony also issued $2.2 billion in convertible bonds with a coupon rate of only 1.4 percent to help finance the Columbia deal. (We will discuss convertible issues in the next section.) This access to very low-cost capital encouraged Japanese firms to acquire foreign companies and to invest huge amounts in new plant and equipment.

However, the willingness of investors to buy Japanese warrants and convertibles suffered a severe blow when the Japanese stock market fell by about 40 percent. In early 1993, Sony's stock price stood at 4,110 yen, about 46 percent below the exercise price on the warrants, and the warrants that were intended to sweeten the bonds were trading at less than 20 percent of their original price. If the stock price does not rise substantially by 1994 — and the odds are against it — the warrants will not be exercised and Sony will not realize any new equity capital. Thus, the bond issue will have to be refinanced at a cost that is significantly higher than the 0.3 percent rate on the currently outstanding bonds.

Assuming a miraculous recovery in stock prices does not occur, Sony and the investors will both lose on the deal. The investors, other than those who quickly sold off the warrants, will lose because they will not get the return that they expected, and required, on the issue. Sony will lose because it will have to alter its financing plans due to the fact that the warrants will not be exercised. In spite of presumably good planning by both the company and investors, this bond-with-warrants issue, and many like it, did not work out as anticipated.

SELF-TEST QUESTIONS

What is a warrant?

Describe how a new bond issue with warrants is valued.

How are warrants used in corporate financing?

The use of warrants lowers the coupon rate on the corresponding debt issue. Does this mean that the component cost of debt plus warrants is less than the cost of straight debt? Explain.

CONVERTIBLES

Convertible securities are bonds or preferred stocks which, under specified terms and conditions, can be exchanged for common stock at the option of the holder. Unlike the exercise of warrants, which brings in additional funds to the firm, conversion does not bring in additional capital: Debt (or preferred stock) is simply replaced on the balance sheet by common stock. Of course, the reduction of the debt or preferred stock will improve the financial strength of the company and make it easier to raise additional fixed charge capital, but that requires a separate action.

CONVERSION RATIO AND CONVERSION PRICE

One of the most important provisions of a convertible security is the *conversion ratio, CR,* defined as the number of shares of stock a bondholder will receive upon conversion. Related to the conversion ratio is the *conversion price, P_c,* which is the effective price the company will receive for the common stock when conversion occurs. The relationship between the conversion ratio and the conversion price can be illustrated by the Silicon Valley Software Company's convertible debentures, issued at their $1,000 par value in July of 1993. At any time prior to maturity on July 15, 2013, a debenture holder can exchange a bond for 20 shares of common stock; therefore, the conversion ratio, CR, is 20. The bond has a par value of $1,000, so the holder would be relinquishing the right to receive $1,000 at maturity if he or she converts. Dividing the $1,000 par value by the 20 shares received gives a conversion price of P_c = $50 a share:

$$\text{Conversion price} = P_c = \frac{\text{Par value of bond given up}}{\text{Shares received}}$$

$$= \frac{\$1,000}{\text{CR}} = \frac{\$1,000}{20} = \$50.$$

Conversely, by solving for CR, we obtain the conversion ratio:

$$\text{Conversion ratio} = \text{CR} = \frac{\$1,000}{P_c} = \frac{\$1,000}{\$50} = 20 \text{ shares.}$$

Once CR is set, the value of P_c is established, and vice versa.

Like a warrant's exercise price, the conversion price is characteristically set at from 10 to 30 percent above the prevailing market price of the common stock at the time the convertible issue is sold. Exactly how the conversion price is established can best be understood after examining some of the reasons firms use convertibles.

Generally, the conversion price and conversion ratio are fixed for the life of the bond, although sometimes a stepped-up conversion price is used. For example,

the 1993 convertible debentures for Breedon Industries are convertible into 12.5 shares until 2003; into 11.76 shares from 2003 until 2013; and into 11.11 shares from 2013 until maturity in 2023. The conversion price thus starts at $80, rises to $85, and then goes to $90. Breedon's convertibles, like most, become callable after a 10-year call-protection period.

Another factor that may cause a change in the conversion price and ratio is a standard feature of almost all convertibles—the clause protecting the convertible against dilution from stock splits, stock dividends, and the sale of common stock at prices below the conversion price. The typical provision states that if common stock is sold at a price below the conversion price, then the conversion price must be lowered (and the conversion ratio raised) to the price at which the new stock was issued. Also, if the stock is split, or if a stock dividend is declared, the conversion price must be lowered by the percentage amount of the stock dividend or split. For example, if Breedon Industries were to have a two-for-one stock split during the first 10 years of its convertible's life, the conversion ratio would automatically be adjusted from 12.5 to 25, and the conversion price lowered from $80 to $40. If this protection were not contained in the contract, a company could completely thwart conversion by the use of stock splits and stock dividends. Warrants are similarly protected against dilution.

The standard protection against dilution from selling new stock at prices below the conversion price can, however, get a company into trouble. For example, assume that Breedon's stock was selling for $65 per share in 1993 at the time of the convertible issue. Further, suppose the market went sour, and Breedon's stock price dropped to $50 per share. A new common stock sale now would require the company to lower the conversion price on the convertible debentures from $80 to $50. That would raise the value of the convertibles and, in effect, transfer wealth from current shareholders to the convertible holders. Potential problems such as this must be kept in mind by firms considering the use of convertibles or bonds with warrants.

CONVERTIBLE BOND MODEL

In the spring of 1993, Silicon Valley Software was evaluating the use of the convertible bond issue described earlier. The issue would consist of 20-year convertible bonds which would sell at a price of $1,000 per bond; this $1,000 would also be the bond's par (and maturity) value. The bonds would pay a 10 percent annual coupon interest rate, or $100 per year. Each bond would be convertible into 20 shares of stock, so the conversion price would be $1,000/20 = $50. The stock was expected to pay a dividend of $2.80 during the coming year, and it sold at $35 per share. Further, the stock price was expected to grow at a constant rate of 8 percent per year. Therefore, $k_s = \hat{k}_s = D_1/P_0 + g = \$2.80/\$35 + 8\% = 8\% + 8\% = 16\%$. If the bonds were not made convertible, they would have to offer a yield of 13 percent, given their riskiness and the general level of interest rates. The convertible bonds would not be callable for 10 years, after which they could be called at a price of $1,050, with this price declining by $5 per year thereafter.

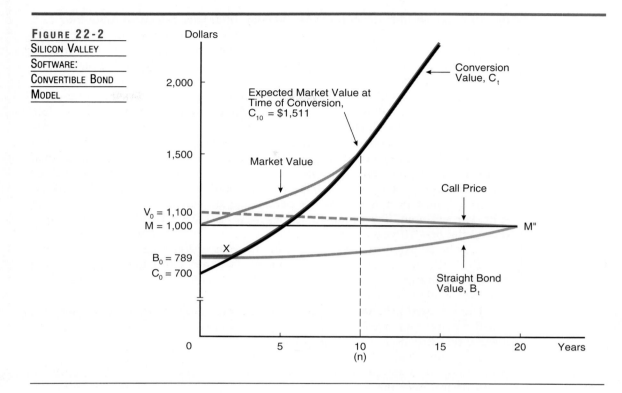

FIGURE 22-2
SILICON VALLEY
SOFTWARE:
CONVERTIBLE BOND
MODEL

If, after 10 years, the conversion value exceeds the call price by at least 20 percent, management would probably call the bonds.

Figure 22-2 shows the expectations of both an average investor and the company:[10]

1. The horizontal line at $M = \$1,000$ represents the par (and maturity) value. Also, $1,000 is the price at which the bond is initially offered to the public.

2. The bond is protected against call for 10 years. It is initially callable at a price of $1,050, and the call price declines thereafter by $5 per year. Thus, the call price is represented by the solid section of the line V_0M''.

3. Since the convertible has a 10 percent coupon rate, and since the yield on a nonconvertible bond of similar risk was stated to be 13 percent, the "straight

---

[10]For a more complete discussion of how this model can be used to structure the terms of a convertible offering, see Eugene F. Brigham, "An Analysis of Convertible Debentures: Theory and Some Empirical Evidence," *Journal of Finance,* March 1966, 35–54; and M. Wayne Marr and G. Rodney Thompson, "The Pricing of New Convertible Bond Issues," *Financial Management,* Summer 1984, 31–37.

bond" value of the convertible, B_t, must be less than par. At the time of issue, assuming an annual coupon, B_0 is $789:

$$B_0 = \sum_{t=1}^{20} \frac{\$100}{(1.13)^t} + \frac{\$1,000}{(1.13)^{20}} = \$789.$$

Note, however, that the bond's straight-debt value must be $1,000 just prior to maturity, so the bond's straight-debt value rises over time. B_t follows the line B_0M'' in the graph.

4. The bond's initial conversion value, or the value of the stock the investor would receive if the bonds were converted at t = 0, is $700: The bond's conversion value is $P_t(CR)$, so at t = 0, conversion value = $P_0(CR)$ = $35(20 shares) = $700. Since the stock's price is expected to grow at an 8 percent rate, the conversion value of the bond should rise over time. For example, in Year 5 it should be $P_5(CR)$ = $35(1.08)^5(20)$ = $1,029. The expected conversion value over time is given by the line C_t in Figure 22-2.

5. The actual market price of the bond can never fall below the higher of its straight-debt value or its conversion value. If the market price were below the straight-bond value, those who wanted bonds would recognize the bargain and buy the convertible as a bond. If the market price were below the conversion value, people would buy the convertibles, turn them in for stock, and sell the stock at a profit. Therefore, the higher of the bond value and conversion value curves in the graph represents a *floor price* for the bond. In Figure 22-2, the floor price is represented by the thicker shaded line B_0XC_t.

6. In fact, the bond's market value will typically exceed its floor value. It will exceed the straight-bond value because the option to convert is worth something —a 10 percent bond with conversion possibilities is worth more than a 10 percent bond without this option. The actual price will also exceed the conversion value because holding the convertible is equivalent to holding a call option, and, prior to expiration, the option's true value is higher than its expiration (or conversion) value. We cannot say exactly where the market value line will lie, but it will typically be above the floor set by the straight bond and conversion value lines.

7. At some point, the market value line will hit the conversion value line. This convergence will occur for two reasons. First, the stock should pay higher and higher dividends as the years go by, but the interest payments on the convertible are fixed. For example, Silicon's convertibles would pay $100 in interest annually, while the dividends on the 20 shares received upon conversion would initially be 20($2.80) = $56. However, at an 8 percent growth rate, the dividends after 10 years would be up to $120.90, while the interest would still be $100. Thus, at some point, rising dividends could be expected to push against the fixed interest payments, causing the premium to disappear and investors to convert voluntarily. Second, once the bond becomes callable, its market value cannot get very far above the higher of the conversion value and the call price without exposing investors to the danger of a call. For example, suppose that 10 years after issue

(when the bonds were callable), the market value of the bonds was $1,600, the conversion value was $1,500, and the call price was $1,050. If the company called the bonds the day after you bought 10 bonds for $16,000, you would be forced to convert into stock worth only $15,000, so you would suffer a loss of $100 per bond, or $1,000, in one day. Recognizing this danger, you and other investors would simply not pay much of a premium over the higher of the call price or the conversion value once the bond becomes callable. Therefore, in Figure 22-2, we assume that the market value line hits the conversion value line in Year 10, when the bond becomes callable.

8. We can let n represent the year when investors expect conversion to occur, either voluntarily because of rising dividends or because the company calls the convertibles to strengthen its balance sheet by substituting equity for debt. In our example, we assume that n = 10, the first call date. Had the company used a lower initial conversion value, or a lower expected growth rate for the stock, such that C_{10} was less than V_{10}, n would have been greater than 10, the first call date.

9. Since n = 10, the expected market value at Year 10 is $35(1.08)^{10}(20)$ = $1,511. An investor can find the expected rate of return on the convertible bond, k_c, by finding the IRR of the following cash flow stream:

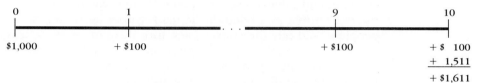

The solution is k_c = IRR = 12.8 percent.

10. The return on a convertible is expected to come partly from interest income and partly from capital gains; in this case, the total return is 12.8 percent, with 10 percent representing interest income and 2.8 percent representing the expected capital gain. The interest component is relatively assured, while the capital gain component is more risky. On a new straight bond, all of the return is in the form of interest. Therefore, a convertible's expected return is more risky than that of a straight bond, so k_c should be larger than the cost of straight debt, k_d. Thus, it would seem that the expected rate of return on Silicon's convertibles, k_c, should lie between its cost of straight debt, k_d = 13%, and its cost of common stock, k_s = 16%.

Investment bankers use the type of model described here, plus a knowledge of the market, to set the terms on convertibles (the conversion ratio and the coupon interest rate) such that the security will just "clear the market" at its $1,000 offering price. In this example, the required conditions do not seem to hold—the calculated rate of return on the convertible is only 12.8 percent, which is less, rather than more, than the 13 percent cost of straight debt. Therefore, it would appear that the terms on the bond must be made more attractive to investors. Silicon Valley Software would have to increase the coupon interest rate on the convertible to a level above 10 percent, raise the conversion ratio above 20 (and thereby lower the conversion price from $50 to a level closer to the current $35

market price of the stock), or use a combination of these two such that the expected rate of return on the convertible ends up between 13 and 16 percent.[11]

USE OF CONVERTIBLES IN FINANCING

Convertibles have two important advantages from the issuer's standpoint. (1) Convertibles, like bonds with warrants, offer a company the chance to sell debt with lower interest rates and less restrictive covenants in exchange for a chance to participate in the company's success if it does well. (2) In a sense, convertibles provide a way to sell common stock at prices higher than those currently prevailing. Some companies actually want to sell common stock, and not debt, but feel that the price of their stock is temporarily depressed. Management may know, for example, that earnings are depressed because of start-up costs associated with a new project, but they expect earnings to rise sharply during the next year or so, pulling the price of the stock up with them. Such a management might think that if it sold stock now, it would be giving up more shares than necessary to raise a given amount of money. However, if it set the conversion price 20 to 30 percent above the present market price of the stock, then 20 to 30 percent fewer shares would be given up when the bonds were converted than would be required if stock were sold directly at the current time. Notice, however, that management is counting on the stock's price to rise above the conversion price to make the bonds attractive in conversion. If earnings do not rise and pull the stock price up, hence conversion does not occur, then the company will be saddled with debt in the face of low earnings, which could be disastrous.

How can the company be sure that conversion will occur if the price of the stock rises above the conversion price? Typically, convertibles contain a call provision that enables the issuing firm to force bondholders to convert. Suppose the conversion price is $50, the conversion ratio is 20, the market price of the common stock has risen to $60, and the call price on the convertible bond is $1,050. If the company calls the bond, bondholders can either convert into common stock with a market value of 20($60) = $1,200 or allow the company to redeem the bond for $1,050. Naturally, bondholders prefer $1,200 to $1,050, so conversion occurs. The call provision therefore gives the company a way to force conversion, provided the market price of the stock is greater than the conversion price. Note, however, that most convertibles have a fairly long period of call protection—10 years is typical. Therefore, if the company wants to be able to force conversion fairly early, then it will have to set a short call protection period. This will, in turn, require that it set a higher coupon rate or a lower conversion price.

From the standpoint of the issuer, convertibles have three important disadvantages. (1) Although the use of a convertible security does give the issuer the opportunity to sell common stock at a price higher than the price at which it could

---

[11]In this discussion, we ignore the tax advantages to investors of the deferral of taxes on capital gains. This factor could explain why k_c is less than k_d.

be sold currently, if the common stock greatly increases in price, the issuing firm would probably find that it would have been better off if it had used straight debt in spite of its higher cost and then later sold common stock and refunded the debt. (2) Convertibles typically have a low coupon interest rate, and the advantage of this low-cost debt will be lost when conversion occurs. (3) If the company truly wants to raise equity capital, and if the price of the stock does not rise sufficiently after the bond is issued, then the company will be stuck with debt. This debt will, however, have a low interest rate.

To illustrate the third disadvantage, consider what happened after the October 1987 stock market crash. Prior to the crash, many firms, especially small technology companies, had issued convertibles because the rising stock market had made convertibles attractive to investors and therefore an inexpensive form of financing. For example, Seagate Technology, which manufactures hard disk drives for personal computers such as the IBM PC, issued $288 million of convertible bonds with a coupon rate of 6.75 percent and a conversion price of $42.50. The stock price at the time of the issue was $30, and straight debt would have cost the company about 11 percent. By mid-November of 1987, the firm's stock price had fallen to only $11.875 per share, and in the spring of 1993, the stock was trading at about $15. As a result, the convertible holders are stuck with low-yielding bonds, while Seagate is saddled with too much long-term debt on its balance sheet, and it cannot issue new common stock without lowering the conversion price and thus giving a tremendous break to the convertible bondholders. At the time of issue, both the company and its investors were anticipating a relatively quick conversion. One investment banker has said that some convertible issuers do so "without a serious consideration of the downside" and that "convertible issuers with depressed stock prices are stuck with a form of debt in sheep's clothing."

SELF-TEST QUESTIONS

What is the difference between a convertible bond and a bond with warrants?

What is a convertible's conversion ratio? Its conversion price? Its straight bond value?

What is meant by a convertible's floor value?

What are the advantages and disadvantages of convertibles to issuers? To investors?

MAKING THE CALL DECISION ON A CONVERTIBLE ISSUE

Most convertible issues have provisions that allow the issuer to call the issue prior to maturity. If such a provision exists, the firm must make the decision when, if at all, to call the convertible. If a convertible is called when its conversion value is less than the stock price, convertible holders will accept the call and receive the call price. In this situation, the firm will have to pay out cash to redeem the issue,

and no new equity will appear on the balance sheet. If the call is made when the conversion value exceeds the stock price, convertible holders will convert their bonds and, if they really wanted cash, sell the shares obtained in the open market. In this case, the firm will not need to use cash to retire the convertibles, and a balance sheet transfer will be made from debt (or preferred) to common equity.

To begin our discussion of the call decision, assume that the issuing firm has done well since the convertible was issued, and the firm's stock price has steadily increased so the convertible's conversion value is approaching the call price. For example, consider the USX convertible bond discussed in the opening section. Assume it is 1995 and the conversion value of the bond is approaching $462, the call price. Remember that a convertible bond consists of a straight bond plus a call option, so the market value of a convertible is the sum of the straight debt and call option values, adjusted for any other provisions such as call and put provisions.

When a convertible is converted into common stock, any conversion price that is less than the stock's current market price results in a wealth transfer from current stockholders to convertible holders. Since managers act in the best interests of the firm's current stockholders, and not of prospective stockholders who hold the convertible, managers have an incentive to minimize the amount of wealth transfer. Thus, in theory and assuming everything else is held constant, the optimal call policy is to call the convertible issue as soon as the issue's conversion value reaches the call price. In the USX example, managers should call the convertible in 1995 if the conversion value reaches $462. (In reality, because of transactions costs, the conversion value should be slightly above the call price.)

Put another way, the total value of a firm is split among all the firm's security holders. As the firm's fortunes rise, so do the values of its common stock and convertibles, which have a call option on the stock. But, the existence of this call option lowers the value of the common stock, and the greater the value of the call option (the convertible), the lower the value of the common stock. By calling the bond as soon as the conversion value equals the call price, managers "kill" the bondholder's conversion option, and hence remove the opportunity for convertible holders to share in future stock price increases. In effect, the call removes a class of potential shareholders that have upside potential and downside (the bond) protection, so the call protects the interest of current stockholders.

Now assume that the conversion value is less than the convertible's call price. In general, there will be no incentive to call the convertible, because the convertible issue will have an interest rate (or preferred dividend yield) that is less than on comparable straight securities. However, if interest rates drop to the point where new straight debt can be sold with a coupon rate less than on the existing convertible issue, the convertible should be called. Here the rationale is the same as for calling a nonconvertible bond.

Interestingly, several studies have examined firms' convertible call policies.[12] In general, these studies find that firms do not call convertibles when conversion

---

[12]For example, see Jonathan Ingersoll, "An Examination of Corporate Call Policies on Convertible Securities," *Journal of Finance,* May 1977, 463–478.

value reaches call price, but, rather, many firms wait until the conversion value is well above the call price. One reason for the delay is to protect against a stock price decline that would cause bondholders to prefer the redemption price to the now lower conversion value. Another reason is to save near-term cash flow—for some firms, the after-tax interest payment on the convertible is less than the dividend payment on common stock, so keeping the convertible on the market saves the firm the difference. A third explanation has to do with signaling—if a firm calls its convertibles at the earliest possible time, then investors will be less interested in future issues of convertibles it might decide to use.

SELF-TEST QUESTIONS

Why would firms ever consider calling a convertible issue?

What is the theoretically optimal point at which to call a convertible bond?

A FINAL COMPARISON OF WARRANTS AND CONVERTIBLES

Convertible debt can be thought of as straight debt with nondetachable warrants. Thus, at first blush, it might appear that debt with warrants and convertible debt are more or less interchangeable. However, a closer examination reveals one major and several minor differences between the two types of option securities.[13] First and foremost, as we discussed previously, the exercise of warrants brings in new equity capital, while the conversion of convertibles results only in an accounting transfer.

A more subtle difference involves flexibility. Most convertible issues contain a call provision that allows the issuer either to refund the debt or to force conversion, depending on the relationship between the conversion value and call price. However, most warrants are not callable, so firms generally must wait until maturity for the warrants to generate new equity capital. Generally, maturities also differ between warrants and convertibles. Warrants typically have much shorter maturities than convertibles, and warrants typically have much shorter maturities than their accompanying debt. Further, warrants typically provide for fewer future common shares than do convertibles. Together, these facts suggest that debt-plus-warrant issuers are actually more interested in selling debt than in selling equity.

In general, firms that issue debt with warrants are smaller and riskier than those that issue convertibles. One possible rationale for the use of option securities by firms, especially the use of debt with warrants by small firms, is the inability of investors to adequately assess the risk of small companies. If a start-up firm with a new, untested product seeks debt financing, it is very difficult for potential lenders

---

[13]For a more detailed comparison of warrants and convertibles, see Michael S. Long and Stephen E. Sefcik, "Participation Financing: A Comparison of the Characteristics of Convertible Debt and Straight Bonds Issued in Conjunction with Warrants," *Financial Management*, Autumn 1990, 23–34.

to assess the riskiness of the venture, and hence it is difficult to set a fair interest rate. Under these circumstances, many potential investors will opt not to invest, so it is often necessary to set very high interest rates to attract debt capital. These high interest rates, and the cash outflows they require, could doom the firm before it can reach its earnings potential. By issuing debt with warrants, investors obtain a package that offers upside potential which compensates for the high risk. If the firm turns out to be successful, the value of the warrant will rise, compensating investors for the fact that they earned a low interest rate on their bonds.

Finally, there is a significant difference in issuance costs between debt with warrants and convertible debt. Bonds with warrants typically require issuance costs that are about 1.2 percent of the issue value more than convertibles. In general, bond-with-warrant financings have underwriting fees that closely reflect the weighted average of the fees associated with debt and equity issues, while underwriting costs for convertibles are substantially below the weighted average issuance costs of debt and equity financings.

SELF-TEST QUESTIONS

What are some of the differences between debt-with-warrant financing and convertible debt?

Explain how bonds with warrants might help firms with uncertain risk sell debt securities.

REPORTING EARNINGS WHEN WARRANTS OR CONVERTIBLES ARE OUTSTANDING

If warrants or convertibles are outstanding, a firm could theoretically report earnings per share in one of three ways:

1. *Simple EPS,* where earnings available to common stockholders are divided by the average number of shares actually outstanding at the end of the period.

2. *Primary EPS,* where earnings available are divided by the average number of shares that would have been outstanding if warrants and convertibles "likely to be converted in the near future" had actually been exercised or converted. Earnings are pro formed by "backing out" the interest on the convertibles. Accountants have a formula which basically compares the conversion or exercise price with the actual market value of the stock to determine the likelihood of conversion when deciding on the need to use this adjustment procedure.

3. *Fully diluted EPS,* which is similar to primary EPS except that *all* warrants and convertibles are assumed to be exercised or converted, regardless of the likelihood of exercise or conversion.

Simple EPS is virtually never reported by firms which have warrants or convertibles likely to be exercised or converted, but the SEC requires that primary

and fully diluted earnings be shown. For firms with large amounts of option securities outstanding, there can be a substantial difference between the primary and fully diluted EPS figures. The purpose of the provision is, of course, to give investors a more accurate picture of the firm's true profit position.

Self-Test Questions

What are the three possible methods for reporting EPS when warrants and convertibles are outstanding?

Which methods are most used in practice?

Why should investors be concerned about a firm's outstanding warrants and convertibles?

FUTURES

Recent years have been characterized by record capital markets volatility. To illustrate, in June 1982, AA bonds were yielding 15.3 percent, while the same bonds yielded 8.9 percent in May 1986, 10.2 percent in April 1989, and 7.6 percent in March 1993. Further, it is not unusual for long-term rates to move by over 100 basis points within a 2- or 3-month period; indeed, a 100 basis point increase occurred during the first quarter of 1990. At the same time, the level of stock prices has bounced around like a rubber ball. All this instability in the capital markets has made corporate financing much more difficult than it was in the 1950s, 1960s, and 1970s.

Although the evidence strongly indicates that managers can forecast their own firms' internal conditions better than outside investors, no one has been able to make consistent forecasts of either interest rates or the general level of stock prices. If one believes that it is impossible to forecast future capital costs, then the major concern should be to minimize the adverse effects of deviations in capital costs from today's "spot" costs. The use of futures contracts can help in this regard.[14]

FUTURES MARKETS AND CONTRACTS

Most financial and real asset transactions occur in what is known as the *spot,* or *cash, market,* where the asset is delivered immediately (or within a few days). *Futures,* or *futures contracts,* on the other hand, call for the purchase or sale of a financial or real asset at some future date, but at a price which is fixed today.

---

[14]Our discussion of futures is necessarily limited in scope. For a more detailed description of futures and their use in financial management, see Daniel R. Siegel and Diane F. Siegel, *Futures Markets* (Hinsdale, Ill.: Dryden Press, 1990).

TABLE 22-3
MAY 6 FUTURES
PRICES

Treasury Bonds (CBT) — $100,000; pts. 32nds of 100%

(1)	Open (2)	High (3)	Low (4)	Settle (5)	Change (6)	Yield Settle (7)	Yield Change (8)	Open Interest (9)
June	100-20	101-11	100-07	100-16	−13	7.950	+.041	188,460
Sept	99-25	100-18	99-16	99-24	−11	8.025	+.034	42,622
Dec	99-00	99-24	98-24	98-30	−10	8.108	+.032	5,207

In 1993, futures contracts were available on more than 30 real and financial assets, and futures are traded on 14 U.S. exchanges, the largest of which are the Chicago Board of Trade (CBT) and the Chicago Mercantile Exchange (CME). Futures contracts are divided into two classes, *commodity futures* and *financial futures.* Commodity futures, which cover various grains, oilseeds, livestock, meats, fibers, metals, and wood, were first traded in the United States in the middle of the 1800s. Financial futures, which were first traded in 1975, include Treasury bills, Treasury notes and bonds, certificates of deposit, Eurodollar deposits, foreign currencies, and stock indexes.

To illustrate how futures contracts work, consider the CBT's contract on Treasury bonds. The basic contract is for $100,000 of a hypothetical 8 percent coupon, semiannual payment, Treasury bond with 20 years to maturity. Table 22-3 shows an extract from the Treasury bond futures prices which appeared in a recent issue of *The Wall Street Journal.*

The first column gives the delivery month; the next three columns give the opening, high, and low prices on that contract for that day. The opening price for the June future, 100-20, means 100 plus 20/32, or 100.625 percent of par. Column 5 gives the settlement price, which is typically the price at the close of trading. Column 6 reports the change in the settlement price from the preceding day — the June contract dropped by 13/32. Column 7 gives the yield on the 8 percent bonds at the settlement price, while Column 8 reports the change in the settlement yield from the previous trading day. Finally, Column 9 shows the "open interest," which is the number of contracts outstanding.

To illustrate, we focus on the Treasury bonds for December delivery. The settlement price on May 6 was 98-30, or 98 plus 30/32 percent of the $100,000 contract value. Thus, the futures price closed at 98.9375 percent, or at 0.989375($100,000) = $98,937.50. The contract price declined by 10/32 of one percent of $100,000, or by $312.50, from the previous day. The settlement yield on the contract was 8.108 percent, and the yield increased by 0.032 percentage points from the previous day. Finally, there were 5,207 contracts outstanding on the December futures, representing a total value of about $520 million. Thus, on May 6, futures contracts for December delivery (7-month futures) of this hypothetical bond sold for $98,937.50 for 100 bonds with a par value of $100,000,

which translates to a yield to maturity of about 8.1 percent.[15] This yield reflects investors' beliefs in May about the interest rate level which will prevail in December. The spot yield on T-bonds on May 6 was about 7.9 percent, so the marginal trader in the futures market was predicting a 20 basis point increase in yields over the next 7 months.

Suppose now that three months later, on August 6, interest rates in the futures market had fallen from the May levels, say, from 8.1 to 7.5 percent. Falling interest rates mean rising bond prices, so the December contract would now be worth about $105,138. Thus, the contract's value would have increased by $105,138 − $98,938 = $6,200.

When futures contracts are purchased, the purchaser does not have to put up the full amount of the purchase price; rather, the purchaser is required to post an initial *margin,* which for CBT Treasury bond contracts is $3,000 per $100,000 contract. However, investors are required to maintain a certain value in the margin account, called a *maintenance margin.* If the value of the contract declines, then the owner may be required to add additional funds to the margin account, and the more the contract value falls, the more money must be added. The value of the contract is checked at the end of every working day, and margin account adjustments are made at that time. If an investor purchased a contract in May, and then sold it in August, he or she would have made a profit of $6,200 on a $3,000 investment, or a return of over 200 percent in only three months. It is clear, therefore, that futures contracts offer a considerable amount of leverage. Of course, if interest rates had risen, then the value of the contract would have declined, and the investor could easily have lost his or her $3,000, or more.

Commodity futures contracts are sometimes settled by the actual delivery of the commodity—for example, a wheat farmer might sell in April a futures contract for 5,000 bushels of wheat for October delivery, and then deliver 5,000 bushels of wheat to satisfy the contract. The purchaser of the contract might be General Mills. The price would have been established in April, so the farmer would know how much he would get for his wheat, and General Mills would know its cost for flour. Financial futures, on the other hand, are virtually never settled by delivery of the securities involved. Rather, the transaction is completed by reversing the trade, which amounts to selling the contract back to the original seller.[16] The actual gains and losses on the contract are realized when the futures contract is closed.

---

[15]The yield is calculated by solving for k_d in the following equation:

$$\$989.375 = \sum_{t=1}^{40} \frac{\$40}{(1 + k_d/2)^t} + \frac{\$1,000}{(1 + k_d/2)^{40}}.$$

Recall that the hypothetical bond is assumed to be a semiannual payment, 8 percent coupon bond with a 20-year maturity.

[16]The buyers and sellers of financial futures contracts do not actually trade with one another, even though a contract cannot be bought without a seller, and vice versa. Each trader's contractual obligation is with the futures exchange. This feature helps to guarantee the fiscal integrity of the trade. Incidentally, commodities futures traded on the exchanges are settled in the same way as financial futures, but in the case of commodities much of the contracting is done off the exchange, between farmers and processors, and there actual deliveries occur.

FUTURES VERSUS OPTIONS

Futures contracts and options are similar to one another—so similar that people often confuse the two. Therefore, it is useful to compare the two instruments.

A *futures contract* is a definite agreement on the part of one party to buy something on a specific date and at a specific price, and the other party agrees to sell on the same terms. No matter how low or how high the price goes, the two parties must settle the contract at the agreed-upon price. An *option,* on the other hand, merely gives someone the right to buy (a call option) or sell (a put option), but the holder of the option does not have to complete the transaction.

Note also that options exist for individual stocks and for "bundles" of stocks such as those in the S&P or Value Line index, whereas futures are used for commodities, debt securities, and stock indexes. The two types of instruments can be used for the same purposes. One is not necessarily better or worse than another —they are simply different.

HEDGING

Futures markets are used for both speculation and hedging. Speculation involves betting on future price movements, and futures are used because the inherent leverage in the contract enhances expected returns. Hedging, on the other hand, is done by a firm or individual engaged in a business where a price change could negatively affect profits. For example, rising interest rates and commodity (raw material) prices can hurt profits, as can adverse currency fluctuations. Of course, one party to a futures contract could be a speculator, the other a hedger. Thus, to the extent that they broaden the market and make hedging possible, speculators decrease risks in the economy.

There are two basic types of hedges: (1) *long hedges,* in which futures contracts are bought in anticipation of (or to guard against) price increases, and (2) *short hedges,* where a firm or individual sells futures contracts to guard against price declines. Recall that rising interest rates lower bond prices and thus the value of bond futures contracts. Therefore, if a firm or individual needs to guard against an *increase* in interest rates, a futures contract that makes money if rates rise should be used. That means selling, or going short, on the futures contract. To illustrate, assume that Carson Foods plans to issue $10,000,000 of 20-year bonds in September to support a capital expenditure program. The interest rate would be 10 percent if the bonds were issued today, May 6, and at that rate, the project being financed has a positive NPV. However, Carson's financial manager fears that interest rates may rise over the next four months, and that, when the issue is actually sold, it may have a cost substantially above 10 percent, which would make the project a bad investment. Carson can protect itself against such a rise in rates by hedging in the futures market.

In this situation, Carson would be hurt by an increase in interest rates, hence Carson would use a short hedge. It would choose a futures contract on the security most similar to the one Carson plans to issue, long-term bonds. In this case, Carson would probably choose to hedge with Treasury bond futures. Since it plans to issue

$10,000,000 of bonds, Carson would sell $10,000,000/$100,000 = 100 Treasury bond contracts for delivery in September. In doing so, Carson would have to put up 100($3,000) = $300,000 in margin money, and also pay brokerage commissions. We can see from Table 22-3 that each September contract has a value of 99 plus 24/32 percent, so the total value of the 100 contracts is 0.9975($100,000)(100) = $9,975,000. Now suppose the interest rate on Carson's debt rises by 100 basis points, to 11 percent, over the next four months. Carson's own 10 percent coupon bonds would bring only about $920 per bond, because investors now require an 11 percent return. Thus, Carson would lose $80 per bond times 10,000 bonds, or $800,000, as a result of delaying the financing. However, the increase in interest rates would also bring about a change in the value of Carson's short position in the futures market. Since interest rates have increased, the futures contract value would fall, and if the interest rate on the futures contract also increased by a full percentage point, from 8.025 to 9.025 percent, the contract value would fall to $9,059,000. Carson would then close its position in the futures market by repurchasing for $9,059,000 the contracts which it sold short for $9,975,000, giving it a profit of $916,000, less commissions.

Thus, Carson has, if we ignore commissions and the opportunity cost of the margin money, offset the loss on the bond issue. In fact, Carson more than offset the loss, pocketing an additional $116,000 in our example. Of course, if in our example interest rates had fallen, Carson would have lost on its futures position. However, this loss would have been offset by the fact that Carson could now sell its bonds at a lower yield. If futures contracts existed on Carson's own debt, then the firm could construct a *perfect hedge,* in which gains on the futures contract would exactly offset losses due to rising interest rates. In reality, it is virtually impossible to construct perfect hedges, because in most cases the underlying asset is not identical to the futures asset.

Similarly, if Carson had been planning an equity offering, and if its stock tended to move fairly closely with one of the stock indexes on which futures are written, the company could have hedged against falling stock prices by selling short the index future. Alternatively, if options on Carson Foods were traded in the option market, then options, rather than futures, could be used to hedge against falling stock prices.

The futures and option markets permit flexibility in the timing of financial transactions, because the firm can be protected, at least partially, against changes that occur between the present and the time when a particular transaction will be completed. There is, however, a cost for this protection, and it is the commissions plus the opportunity cost of the margin money. Whether or not the protection is worth the cost is a matter of judgment, and it depends on management's risk aversion as well as the company's strength and ability to assume the risk of changing interest rates and stock prices. In theory, the reduction in risk resulting from a hedge transaction has a value exactly equal to the cost of the hedge. Thus, a firm should be indifferent to hedging. However, many firms believe that hedging is worthwhile. Trammell Crow, a large Texas real estate developer, recently used T-bill futures to lock in interest costs on floating rate construction loans, while Dart & Kraft used Eurodollar futures to protect its marketable securities portfolio.

Merrill Lynch, Salomon Brothers, and the other investment banking houses hedge in the futures and option markets to protect themselves when they are engaged in major underwritings. Similarly, institutional investors engage in hedging activities to protect their bond portfolios against interest rate increases, their stock portfolios against market declines, and their foreign holdings against adverse exchange rate movements.

SELF-TEST QUESTIONS

What is a futures contract?

What is the difference between futures and options?

Explain how a company can use the futures market to hedge against rising interest rates.

SECURITIES INNOVATION

In recent years an avalanche of new types of securities has hit the markets, and the trend shows no sign of letting up. Each new offering is heralded by the investment bank that developed it as a boon to both issuers and investors. Yet there are critics who contend that the development of new securities has contributed little, if any, economic gain to anyone except the investment banks that sell them.

Two primary factors have fueled the rush to innovation. First, the investment banking business has become increasingly competitive, and the development of a new security usually means increased business and profits, both for the firm and for the individuals who developed it. Second, the last decade has been an era of unprecedented volatility: Interest rates, tax laws, and regulation are now changing much more rapidly than in the past, and new financial products are needed to cope with the changing economic environment. For example, adjustable rate preferred stock was specifically developed to eliminate investors' exposure to losses in principal as interest rates change, and at the same time to provide a tax shelter to corporate investors in high tax brackets.

The development of new securities has presented an almost overwhelming number of financial alternatives to financial managers, and it is necessary for managers to evaluate the merits of each alternative before making a decision. It is not enough that a security be different—it must also enable issuers or investors to do something that they could not previously do, or permit them to do the same things in a more cost-effective way.[17] Value is created in new securities in a number of ways. For example, value can be created if the new security reallocates risk from one class of investors to another class that is less risk sensitive and thus requires a

---

[17]For a more complete discussion of securities innovation, see John D. Finnerty, "Securities Innovation: Where Is the Value Added?" *Financial Management Collection,* Winter 1988, 1–7.

smaller risk premium. Interest rate swaps are an example of this type of value creation. Value can also be created if a new security reduces the transactions costs paid to third parties, or increases the liquidity to investors. The development of the junk bond market illustrates these points. Taxes also present an opportunity for value creation. If taxes can be reduced to investors without increasing the corporate tax liability, or vice versa, then value can be created (or at least transferred). Leasing provides a good example of this point.

Not all innovations are successful. Shearson Lehman Hutton recently unveiled a new product called *unbundled stock units*, which it proposed to create and sell initially for four companies: American Express, Dow Chemical, Pfizer, and Sara Lee. Common stock has traditionally offered investors three sources of value: (1) the current dollar dividend, (2) potential increases in the dollar dividend, and (3) potential capital appreciation in stock price. In the unbundled stock unit concept, a portion of the firm's outstanding common stock, say 20 percent, would be broken into those three parts which would trade separately on the NYSE. To illustrate, consider the offering planned for Pfizer. At the time, Pfizer's stock was trading at about $56 a share and paying $2 in annual dividends. A stockholder who tendered his or her shares would receive the following for each share tendered:

1. A 30-year bond that pays $2 annually in interest and has a maturity value of $150.

2. A share of preferred stock that initially pays no dividend, but which pays a dividend that matches any common stock dividend increases above the $2 current dividend for the next 30 years. For example, if Pfizer paid $3 in common dividends in 1995, the preferred would receive a $3 − $2 = $1 dividend. The preferred stock would be redeemed after 30 years for $250.

3. An equity appreciation certificate that entitles the holder to any rise in stock price above $150 after 30 years. Thus, if Pfizer's stock rose to $200 in 30 years, the appreciation certificate would be worth $200 − $150 = $50.

From an investor's standpoint, the new securities created the same cash flow as the common stock, but without voting rights. However, the new securities in the aggregate would have less risk because, while the common dividend could be cut or omitted, the interest payment on the bond portion of the package could not be lowered. Further, once trading began, an investor need not hold all three securities —he or she could hold only the securities that provided the optimal risk/return combination for him or her.

The initial investor reaction to unbundled stock units was mixed. "This sounds like an interesting way to get the stock price up, and if it works, then it's a good thing to do," said one analyst. However, other analysts were not as supportive. One trader said she would be reluctant to swap her common shares for the new securities. "What happens if you change your opinion on Pfizer?" she asked. "I couldn't be sure that the liquidity would be there." Shearson pushed hard to sell the new product, but a lukewarm response from institutional investors and an adverse ruling by the SEC regarding accounting for the new securities tolled the death knell for the product, and three months later Shearson announced that the idea was dead.

Undoubtedly, many opportunities remain for innovation, and new ones will arise as the economy continues to change. Such innovations will offer opportunities for financial managers to lower their companies' costs of capital, hence to increase their shareholders' wealth. However, the increase in the number of financing possibilities, and the increasing complexity of the new securities, will make it more important than ever that corporate decision makers keep up with developments in the financial world, and learn how to use (or when to avoid using) the new products.

SELF-TEST QUESTIONS

What is meant by securities innovation?

What are some factors that can create value in new types of securities?

SUMMARY

In this chapter, we first discussed options, then warrants and convertibles, and finally futures and how futures can be used to hedge against undesirable market movements. The key concepts covered are listed below.

▸ *Pure options* are financial instruments that (1) are created by exchanges rather than firms, (2) are bought and sold primarily by investors, and (3) are of greater importance to investors than to financial managers. However, an understanding of options will help financial managers understand warrants and convertibles, which are option-type securities issued by firms.

▸ The two primary types of options are (1) *call options,* which give the holder the right to purchase a common stock at a given price (the *exercise* or *striking price*) for a given period of time, and (2) *put options,* which give the holder the right to sell a stock at a given price for a given period of time.

▸ The *Black-Scholes Option Pricing Model (OPM)* can be used to estimate the value of a call option.

▸ A *warrant* is a long-term call option issued along with a bond. Warrants are generally detachable from the bond, and they trade separately in the markets. When warrants are exercised, the firm receives additional equity capital, and the original bonds remain outstanding.

▸ A *convertible* security is a bond or preferred stock which can be exchanged for common stock at the option of the holder. When a security is converted, debt or preferred stock is replaced with common stock, and no money changes hands.

▸ Warrants and convertibles are *"sweeteners"* which are used to make the underlying debt or preferred stock issue more attractive to investors. Although the coupon rate on the debt or dividend yield on the preferred stock is lower when options are part of the issue, the overall cost of the issue is higher than

the cost of straight debt or preferred, because the addition of warrants or convertibility makes the issue riskier to an investor.

▶ *Financial futures* permit firms to create hedge positions to protect themselves against the damage which can be inflicted by fluctuating interest rates, stock prices, and exchange rates.

▶ In recent years, a large number of new securities have been introduced. Such *securities innovation* can provide opportunities for financial managers to lower their firms' costs of capital.

This concludes our discussion of long-term financing. In Part VIII we will discuss selected special topics, beginning with bankruptcy, reorganization, and liquidation.

QUESTIONS

22-1 Define each of the following terms:
a. Option; call option; put option
b. Striking price; exercise price; variance
c. Warrant; detachable warrant
d. Expiration value
e. Stepped-up price
f. Convertible security
g. Conversion ratio; conversion price; conversion value
h. "Sweetener"
i. Simple EPS; primary EPS; fully diluted EPS
j. Futures; hedging
k. Securities innovation

22-2 Why do options typically sell at prices higher than their expiration values?

22-3 What effect does the trend in stock prices (subsequent to issue) have on a firm's ability to raise funds through (a) convertibles and (b) warrants?

22-4 If a firm expects to have additional financial requirements in the future, would you recommend that it use convertibles or bonds with warrants? What factors would influence your decision?

22-5 How does a firm's dividend policy affect each of the following?
a. The value of its long-term warrants.
b. The likelihood that its convertible bonds will be converted.
c. The likelihood that its warrants will be exercised.

22-6 Evaluate the following statement: "Issuing convertible securities represents a means by which a firm can sell common stock at a price above the existing market."

22-7 Why do corporations often sell convertibles on a rights basis?

22-8 Suppose a company simultaneously issues $50 million of convertible bonds with a coupon rate of 10 percent and $50 million of straight bonds with a coupon rate of 14 percent. Both

bonds have the same maturity. Does the fact that the convertible issue has the lower coupon rate suggest that it is less risky than the straight bond? Is the cost of capital lower on the convertible than on the straight bond? Explain.

PROBLEMS

22-1 **(Black-Scholes OPM)** Considine Software Corporation (CSC) options are actively traded on one of the regional exchanges. CSC's current stock price is $10, with a 0.16 instantaneous variance of returns. The current 6-month risk-free rate is 12 percent.

    a. What is the value of CSC's 6-month option with an exercise price of $10 according to the Black-Scholes model?

    b. What would be the effect on the option price if CSC redeployed its assets and thereby reduced its variance of returns to 0.09?

(Do Parts c and d only if you are using the computer problem diskette.)

    c. Assume that CSC returns to its initial asset structure; that is, its stock return variance is 0.16. Now assume that CSC's current stock price is $15. What effect does the stock price increase have on the option value?

    d. Return to base case (Part a) values. Now assume that the striking price is $15. What is the new option value?

22-2 **(Warrants)** O'Donnell Industries Inc. has warrants outstanding that permit the holders to purchase one share of stock per warrant at a price of $25.

    a. Calculate the expiration value of the firm's warrants if the common sells at each of the following prices: (1) $20, (2) $25, (3) $30, (4) $100.

    b. At what approximate price do you think the warrants would actually sell under each condition indicated above? What premium is implied in your price? Your answer is a guess, but your prices and premiums should bear reasonable relationships to one another.

    c. How would each of the following factors affect your estimates of the warrants' prices and premiums in Part b?
        (1) The life of the warrant.
        (2) Expected variability (σ_p) in the stock's price.
        (3) The expected growth rate in the stock's EPS.
        (4) The company announces a change in dividend policy: Whereas it formerly paid no dividends, henceforth it will pay out *all* earnings as dividends.

    d. Assume the firm's stock now sells for $20 per share. The company wants to sell some 20-year, annual interest, $1,000 par value bonds. Each bond will have attached 50 warrants, each exercisable into one share of stock at an exercise price of $25. The firm's straight bonds yield 12 percent. Regardless of your answer to Part b, assume that each warrant will have a market value of $3 when the stock sells at $20. What coupon interest rate, and dollar coupon, must the company set on the bonds with warrants if they are to clear the market?

22-3 **(Convertible premiums)** The Scanlon Company was planning to finance an expansion in the summer of 1993. The principal executives of the company all agreed that an industrial company such as theirs should finance growth by means of common stock rather than by debt. However, they felt that the price of the company's common stock did not reflect its true worth, so they decided to sell a convertible security. They considered a convertible

debenture but feared the burden of fixed interest charges if the common stock did not rise in price to make conversion attractive. They decided on an issue of convertible preferred stock, which would pay a dividend of $2.10 per share.

The common stock was selling for $42 a share at the time. Management projected earnings for 1993 at $3 a share and expected a future growth rate of 10 percent a year in 1994 and beyond. It was agreed by the investment bankers and the management that the common stock would sell at 14 times earnings, the current price/earnings ratio.

a. What conversion price should be set by the issuer? The conversion ratio will be 1.0; that is, each share of convertible preferred can be converted into one share of common. Therefore, the convertible's par value (and also the issue price) will be equal to the conversion price, which in turn will be determined as a percentage over the current market price of the common. Your answer will be a guess, but make it a reasonable one.

b. Should the preferred stock include a call provision? Why?

22-4 **(Convertible bond analysis)** In June 1976, U.S. Steel (now USX Corporation) sold $400 million of convertible bonds, the largest issue on record. The bonds had a 25-year maturity, a 5¾ percent coupon rate, and were sold at their $1,000 par value. The conversion price was set at $62.75 against a current price of $55 per share of common. The bonds were subordinated debentures, and they were given an A rating; straight nonconvertible debentures of the same quality yielded about 8¾ percent at the time.

a. Calculate the premium on the bonds, that is, the percentage excess of the conversion price over the current stock price.

b. What is U.S. Steel's annual interest savings on the convertible issue versus a straight debt issue?

c. Look up U.S. Steel's (USX's) current stock price in the paper. On the basis of this price, do you think it likely that the bonds would have been converted? (Calculate the value of the stock one would receive by converting a bond.)

d. The bonds originally sold for $1,000. If interest rates on A-rated bonds had remained constant at 8¾ percent, what do you think would have happened to the price of the convertible bonds?

e. Now suppose the price of U.S. Steel's common stock had fallen from $55 on the day the bonds were issued to $32.75 at present. (At the time this problem was written, that is exactly what had happened.) Suppose also that the rate of interest had fallen from 8¾ to 5¾ percent. (This had not happened when the problem was being written — the interest rate on A-rated bonds was about 10 percent.) Under these conditions, what do you think would have happened to the price of the bonds?

f. Set up a graphic model to illustrate how investors valued the U.S. Steel convertibles in 1976. How well were these expectations realized?

22-5 **(Warrant/convertible decisions)** The Dunlap Carpet Company has grown rapidly during the past 5 years. Recently its commercial bank urged the company to consider increasing its permanent financing. Its bank loan under a line of credit has risen to $250,000, carrying an 8 percent interest rate. Dunlap has been 30 to 60 days late in paying trade creditors.

Discussions with an investment banker have resulted in the decision to raise $500,000 at this time. Investment bankers have assured the firm that the following alternatives are feasible (flotation costs will be ignored):

▶ *Alternative 1:* Sell common stock at $8.

▶ *Alternative 2:* Sell convertible bonds at an 8 percent coupon, convertible into 100 shares of common stock for each $1,000 bond (that is, the conversion price is $10 per share).

▶ *Alternative 3:* Sell debentures at an 8 percent coupon, each $1,000 bond carrying 100 warrants to buy common stock at $10.

Scott Dunlap, the president, owns 80 percent of the common stock and wishes to maintain control of the company. One hundred thousand shares are outstanding. The following are extracts of Dunlap's latest financial statements:

Balance Sheet

		Current liabilities	$400,000
		Common stock, par $1	100,000
		Retained earnings	50,000
Total assets	$550,000	Total claims	$550,000

Income Statement

Sales	$1,100,000
All costs except interest	990,000
EBIT	$ 110,000
Interest	20,000
EBT	$ 90,000
Taxes (40%)	36,000
Net income	$ 54,000
Shares outstanding	100,000
Earnings per share	$0.54
Price/earnings ratio	15.83 ×
Market price of stock	$8.55

a. Show the new balance sheet under each alternative. For Alternatives 2 and 3, show the balance sheet after conversion of the bonds or exercise of the warrants. Assume that half of the funds raised will be used to pay off the bank loan and half to increase total assets.

b. Show Mr. Dunlap's control position under each alternative, assuming that he does not purchase additional shares.

c. What is the effect on earnings per share of each alternative, if it is assumed that profits before interest and taxes will be 20 percent of total assets?

d. What will be the debt ratio under each alternative?

e. Which of the three alternatives would you recommend to Dunlap, and why?

22-6 (Convertible bond model) Goode Incorporated needs to raise $25 million to construct production facilities for a new model diskette drive. The firm's straight nonconvertible debentures currently yield 14 percent. Its stock sells for $30 per share; the last dividend was $2; and the expected growth rate is a constant 9 percent. Investment bankers have tentatively proposed that the firm raise the $25 million by issuing convertible debentures. These convertibles would have a $1,000 par value, carry a coupon rate of 10 percent, have a 20-year maturity, and be convertible into 20 shares of stock. The bonds would be noncallable for 5 years, after which they would be callable at a price of $1,075; this call price would decline by $5 per year in Year 6 and each year thereafter. Management has called convertibles in the past (and presumably it will call them again in the future), once they were

eligible for call, when the bonds' conversion value was about 20 percent above the bonds' par value (not their call price).

a. Draw an accurate graph similar to Figure 22-2 representing the expectations set forth above. (Assume an annual coupon.)

b. What is the expected rate of return on the proposed convertible issue?

c. Do you think that these bonds could be successfully offered to the public at par? That is, does $1,000 seem to be an equilibrium price in view of the stated terms? If not, suggest the type of change that would have to be made to cause the bonds to trade at $1,000 in the secondary market, assuming no change in capital market conditions.

d. Suppose the projects outlined here work out on schedule for 2 years, but then the firm begins to experience extremely strong competition from Japanese firms. As a result, Goode's expected growth rate drops from 9 percent to zero. Assume that the dividend at the time of the drop is $2.38. The company's credit strength is not impaired, and its value of k_s is also unchanged. What would happen (1) to stock price and (2) to the convertible bond's price? Be as precise as you can.

22-7 (Futures) Refer back to Table 22-3. It is now May 6. The D. J. Masson Company plans to negotiate a 5-year, $100,000 semiannual interest loan in December. However, its managers are concerned about rising interest rates, and plan to use the futures market to hedge against this possibility. Discussions with their lenders indicate that the loan rate would be 10 percent if the loan were negotiated today.

a. Suppose the company planned to use T-bond futures for the hedge. Would the firm buy or sell futures contracts? How many contracts would be involved?

b. Assume that interest rates on all securities increased by 2 percentage points from May to December. What impact would the rate rise have on the value of the firm's loan? On its futures position? Overall?

c. Did the firm create a perfect hedge? Explain.

d. Now assume that interest rates dropped by 2 percentage points. What impact does the hedge now have on the pending financing transaction? Does this imply that firms should not hedge future financings?

M I N I C A S E

Paul Duncan, financial manager of EduSoft Inc., is facing a dilemma. The firm was founded 5 years ago to provide educational software for the rapidly expanding primary and secondary school markets. Although EduSoft has done well, the firm's founder believes that an industry shakeout is imminent. To survive, EduSoft must grab market share now, and this will require a large infusion of new capital.

Because he expects earnings to continue rising sharply and looks for the stock price to follow suit, Mr. Duncan does not think it would be wise to issue new common stock at this time. On the other hand, interest rates are currently high by historical standards, and with the firm's B rating, the interest payments on a new debt issue would be prohibitive. Thus, he has narrowed his choice of financing alternatives to two securities: (1) bonds with warrants or (2) convertible bonds. As Duncan's assistant, you have been asked to help in the decision process by answering the following questions:

a. What is a call option? How can a knowledge of call options help a financial manager to better understand warrants and convertibles?

b. Consolidated Energy Industries (CEI) has options listed on the CBOE. The following table gives the option prices for its 6-month, $20 strike price call option at 3 different stock prices:

Stock Price	Option Price
$20	$ 5
30	13
40	21

(1) What are the option's expiration values, and the premiums, at each stock price? Why do call options sell for more than their expiration values?

(2) Assume that CEI's stock price increased from $20 to $30. What rate of return would this provide to a stock investor? To an option investor? What is the loss potential on the stock and on the option if the stock price remains at $20?

(3) Now assume that CEI's stock price increased from $30 to $40. What rate of return would a stock investor receive? An option investor? What is the loss potential on the stock? On the option? Why does the premium over the expiration value decline as the stock price increases?

c. One of the firm's alternatives is to issue a bond with warrants attached. EduSoft's current stock price is $20, and its investment banker estimates that the cost of a 20-year, annual coupon bond without warrants would be 12 percent. The bankers suggest attaching 50 warrants, each with an exercise price of $25, to each $1,000 bond. It is estimated that each warrant, when detached and traded separately, would have a value of $3.

(1) What coupon rate should be set on the bond with warrants if the total package is to sell for $1,000?

(2) Suppose the bonds were issued and the warrants immediately traded on the open market for $5 each. What would this imply about the terms of the issue? Did the company "win" or "lose"?

(3) When would you expect the warrants to be exercised? Assume they have a 10-year life, that is, they expire 10 years after issue.

(4) Will the warrants bring in additional capital when exercised? If so, how much, and what type of capital?

(5) Since warrants lower the cost of the accompanying debt issue, shouldn't all debt be issued with warrants? What is the expected return to the holders of the bond with warrants (or the expected cost to the company) if the warrants are expected to be exercised in 5 years, when EduSoft's stock price is expected to be $36.75? How would you expect the cost of the bond with warrants to compare with the cost of straight debt? With the cost of common stock?

d. As an alternative to the bond with warrants, Mr. Duncan is considering convertible bonds. The firm's investment bankers estimate that EduSoft could sell a 20-year, 10.5 percent annual coupon, callable convertible bond for its $1,000 par value, whereas a straight debt issue would require a 12 percent coupon. The convertibles would be call protected for 5 years, the call price would be $1,100, and the company would probably call the bonds as soon as possible after their conversion value exceeds $1,200. Note, though, that the call must occur on an issue date anniversary. EduSoft's current stock price is $20, its last dividend was $1.48, and the dividend is expected to grow at a constant 8 percent rate. The convertible could be converted into 40 shares of EduSoft stock at the owner's option.

(1) What conversion price is built into the bond?

(2) What is the convertible's straight debt value? What is the implied value of the convertibility feature?

(3) What is the formula for the bond's expected conversion value in any year? What is its conversion value at Year 0? At Year 10?

(4) What is meant by the "floor value" of a convertible? What is the convertible's expected floor value at Year 0? At Year 10?

(5) Assume that EduSoft intends to force conversion by calling the bond as soon as possible after its conversion value exceeds 20 percent above its par value, or $1.2(\$1,000) = \$1,200$. When is the issue expected to be called? (Hint: Recall that the call must be made on an anniversary date of the issue.)

(6) What is the expected cost of capital for the convertible to EduSoft? Does this cost appear to be consistent with the riskiness of the issue?

e.   EduSoft's market value capital structure is as follows (in millions of dollars):

Debt	$ 50
Equity	50
	$100

If the company raises $20 million in additional capital by selling (1) convertibles or (2) bonds with warrants, what would its WACC be, and how would those figures compare to its current WACC? EduSoft's tax rate is 40 percent.

f.   Mr. Duncan believes that the costs of both the bond with warrants and the convertible bond are close enough to one another to call them even, and also consistent with the risks involved. Thus, he will make his decision based on other factors. What are some of the factors which he should consider?

g.   (Unrelated question) Explain briefly why the equity of a leveraged firm can be thought of as a call option. What does option pricing theory indicate will happen to shareholders' wealth if the firm increases the riskiness of its asset mix? What happens to bondholders' wealth?

h.   (Unrelated question) What is the futures market? Explain how futures contracts can be used to hedge against rising interest rates.

Selected Additional References and Cases

The investment texts listed in Chapter 4 provide extended discussions of options, warrants, convertibles, and futures.

The original Black-Scholes article tested the OPM to see how well predicted prices conformed to market values. For additional empirical tests, see

Galai, Dan, "Tests of Market Efficiency of the Chicago Board Options Exchange," *Journal of Business,* April 1977, 167–197.

Gultekin, N. Bulent, Richard J. Rogalski, and Seha M. Tinic, "Option Pricing Model Estimates: Some Empirical Results," *Financial Management,* Spring 1982, 58–69.

MacBeth, James D., and Larry J. Merville, "An Empirical Examination of the Black-Scholes Call Option Pricing Model," *Journal of Finance,* December 1979, 1173–1186.

Quite a bit of work has been done on warrant pricing. Some of the more prominent articles include

Galai, Dan, and Mier I. Schneller, "The Pricing of Warrants and the Value of the Firm," *Journal of Finance,* December 1978, 1333–1342.

Lauterbach, Beni, and Paul Schultz, "Pricing Warrants: An Empirical Study of the Black-Scholes Model and Its Alternatives," *Journal of Finance,* September 1990, 1181–1209.

Leonard, David C., and Michael E. Solt, "On Using the Black-Scholes Model to Value Warrants," *Journal of Financial Research,* Summer 1990, 81–92.

Phelps, Katherine L., William T. Moore, and Rodney L. Roenfeldt, "Equity Valuation Effects of Warrant-Debt Financing," *Journal of Financial Research,* Summer 1991, 93–103.

Schwartz, Eduardo S., "The Valuation of Warrants: Implementing a New Approach," *Journal of Financial Economics,* January 1977, 79–93.

For more insights into convertible pricing and use, see

Alexander, Gordon J., and Roger D. Stover, "Pricing in the New Issue Convertible Debt Market," *Financial Management,* Fall 1977, 35–39.

Alexander, Gordon J., Roger D. Stover, and D. B. Kuhnau, "Market Timing Strategies in Convertible Debt Financing," *Journal of Finance,* March 1979, 143–155.

Asquith, Paul, and David W. Mullins, Jr., "Convertible Debt: Corporate Call Policy and Voluntary Conversion," *Journal of Finance,* September 1991, 1273–1289.

Brennan, Michael, "The Case for Convertibles," *Issues in Corporate Finance* (New York: Stern Stewart Putnam & Macklis, 1983), 102–111.

Ingersoll, Jonathan E., "A Contingent Claims Valuation of Convertible Securities," *Journal of Financial Economics,* May 1977, 289–322.

Janjigian, Vahan, "The Leverage Changing Consequences of Convertible Debt Financing," *Financial Management,* Autumn 1987, 15–21.

For additional insights into the use of financial futures for hedging, see

Bacon, Peter W., and Richard Williams, "Interest Rate Futures Trading: A New Tool for the Financial Manager," *Financial Management,* Spring 1976, 32–38.

Block, Stanley B., and Timothy J. Gallagher, "The Use of Interest Rate Futures and Options by Corporate Financial Managers," *Financial Management,* Autumn 1986, 73–78.

McCabe, George M., and Charles T. Franckle, "The Effectiveness of Rolling the Hedge Forward in the Treasury Bill Futures Market," *Financial Management,* Summer 1983, 21–29.

The following Brigham-Gapenski case covers many of the issues presented in this chapter:

Case 27, "Virginia May Chocolate Company," which illustrates convertible bond valuation.

SPECIAL TOPICS

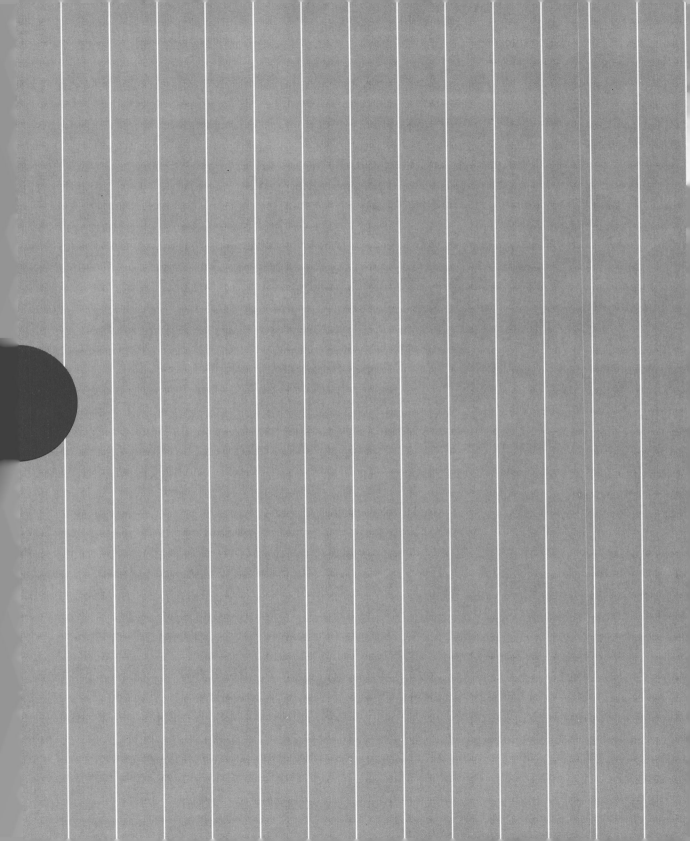

BANKRUPTCY, REORGANIZATION, AND LIQUIDATION

I n June 1993, Continental Airlines performed, for the second time, a feat that few companies do even once—emerge from bankruptcy. (Braniff Airlines went into bankruptcy twice but only came out once.) When Continental Airlines Holdings Inc., along with 53 subsidiaries, filed for bankruptcy court protection in December 1990, it had $3.96 billion dollars in debt. When it emerged from bankruptcy in 1993, the firm was leaner, with only four subsidiaries, and it had shaved its debt to $1.8 billion and had about $635 million in cash. However, with equity of roughly $600 million, the company still had a hefty debt-to-equity ratio of 3.0.

While under court protection, Continental was able to take many actions that other nonbankrupt airlines could not. For example, it was able to suspend its interest payments to creditors without the threat of foreclosure, and it was able to abrogate and renegotiate its labor contracts. The ability to take such actions permitted it to offer very low fares by industry standards and still pare its losses. In 1991, Continental lost more than $300 million, but in 1992, the loss was only $125 million. More important, the lower operating and financing costs make Continental better able to take advantage of any future growth in air travel brought about by the strengthening economy.

However, the operating and financing advantages brought on by bankruptcy were not without costs. The company's reorganization plan, which provided the road map out of bankruptcy, called for paying creditors a fraction of what they were owed. For example, unsecured creditors received about 5 cents to 40 cents per dollar of claims, depending on the exact type of debt. Creditors also received some equity in the "new" Continental. In addition, 55 percent of the equity

went to Air Canada and Air Partners, a Fort Worth investor group, which poured $450 million dollars of new cash into the airline. With new equity going both to existing creditors and new investors, the firm's existing stockholders were wiped out.

Will the bankruptcy turn Continental into a supercompany, ready to take on all comers and make winners out of its investors? "Don't bet on it," says Sam Buttrick, an analyst at Kidder Peabody. "They're still an airline, and leisure travellers don't buy tickets without steep discounts, and businessmen aren't travelling very much." "Besides," he adds, "Continental was never as bad as many people thought, and they won't be magically transformed into a world-leading airline."

After you read this chapter, you will have a good understanding of the basics of bankruptcy. As you go through the material, think about the decisions that Continental's managers had to make regarding bankruptcy and reorganization, and the effects that the firm's bankruptcy has had on all of its stakeholders as well as on competing airlines.

This text has thus far dealt with issues faced by growing, successful enterprises. However, many firms encounter financial difficulties, and some enter bankruptcy, including such big names as Pan American Airlines, Texaco, and Executive Life. Indeed, in 1991 Dun & Bradstreet reported that a record 87,266 businesses with $108.8 billion in liabilities—nearly 2 percent of the gross domestic product—went belly-up. The primary causes of the record number of bankruptcies were the longest recession since the 1930s and the vast amount of debt corporations took on during the 1980s.

The financial manager of a failing firm must know how to ward off his or her firm's total collapse and thereby reduce its losses. The ability to hang on during rough times often means the difference between the firm's forced liquidation versus its rehabilitation and eventual success. At the same time, an understanding of business failures and bankruptcies, their causes, and their possible remedies is also important to financial managers of successful firms, because they must know their firms' rights when their customers or suppliers go bankrupt.

FINANCIAL DISTRESS AND ITS CONSEQUENCES

In this section, we present some background information on financial distress and its consequences.[1] Specifically, we discuss (1) types of financial distress, (2) causes of business failure, and (3) the business failure and bankruptcy record.

---

[1]Much of the current academic work in the area of financial distress and bankruptcy is based on writings by Edward I. Altman. For a summary of his work and that of others, see Edward I. Altman, *Corporate Financial Distress and Bankruptcy* (New York: Wiley, 1983), and *Bankruptcy and Distressed Restructuring* (Homewood, Ill.: Irwin, 1992).

TYPES OF FINANCIAL DISTRESS

Financial distress runs the gamut from a vague uneasiness about future profitability to complete disintegration of the firm. Financially distressed firms can attempt to solve their problems either informally or under the guidance of a bankruptcy court. Some ways in which financial distress is commonly defined include the following:

1. **Economic failure.** Failure in an economic sense signifies that a firm's revenues do not cover its total costs, including its cost of capital. Businesses that are *economic failures* can continue operating as long as investors are willing to provide additional capital and their owners are willing to accept below-market rates of return. Eventually, though, no new capital will be provided, and assets will wear out and not be replaced, so such firms either close or contract to the point where the smaller level of output provides a "normal" return.

2. **Business failure.** The term *business failure* is used by Dun & Bradstreet, which is the major compiler of failure statistics, to define any business that has terminated operations with a resultant loss to creditors. Thus, a business can be classified by Dun & Bradstreet as a failure even though it never enters formal bankruptcy proceedings. Also, a firm can shut down, but if there is no loss to creditors, it would not be counted as a business failure.

3. **Technical insolvency.** A firm is considered *technically insolvent* if 't cannot meet its current obligations as they fall due. Technical insolvency may denote a temporary lack of liquidity; given time, a firm that is technically insolvent may be able to raise cash, pay off its obligations, and survive. On the other hand, if technical insolvency is an early symptom of economic failure, it may be only the first step on the road to financial disaster.

4. **Insolvency in bankruptcy.** A firm is *insolvent in bankruptcy* when its book value of total liabilities exceeds the true market value of its assets. This is a more serious condition than technical insolvency because, generally, it is a sign of economic failure, and it often leads to liquidation of the business. Note that a firm that is insolvent in bankruptcy is not necessarily in legal bankruptcy proceedings.

5. **Legal bankruptcy.** Although many people use the term *bankruptcy* to refer to any firm that has "failed," a firm is not *legally bankrupt* unless it has filed for bankruptcy under federal law.

CAUSES OF BUSINESS FAILURE

The causes of business failure are numerous, and they vary from situation to situation. However, it is useful to understand the major underlying causes to avoid them if possible or to correct them in the event that a reorganization is necessary.

A recent Dun & Bradstreet compilation assigned percentage values to business failure causes, as shown in Table 23-1. Economic factors include industry weakness and poor location, and financial factors include too much debt and insufficient capital. Of course, most business failures occur because a number of factors combine to make the business unsustainable. Further, case studies show that financial

TABLE 23-1	Cause of Failure	Percentage of Total
CAUSES OF BUSINESS FAILURE	Economic factors	55.1%
	Financial factors	36.0
	Neglect, disaster, and fraud	7.1
	Other factors	1.8
		100.0%

Source: Dun & Bradstreet, Inc., *Business Failure Record* (New York, 1990/1991).

difficulties are usually the result of a series of errors, misjudgments, and interrelated weaknesses that can be attributed directly or indirectly to management, and signs of potential financial distress are generally evident before the firm actually fails.

A number of remedies are available to management when it becomes aware of the imminence or occurrence of financial distress. These remedies are described later in the chapter.

THE BUSINESS FAILURE AND BANKRUPTCY RECORD

How widespread is business failure and bankruptcy in the United States? In Table 23-2, we see that a fairly large number of businesses fail each year according to the Dun & Bradstreet definition, although the failures in any one year are not a

TABLE 23-2 HISTORICAL FAILURE RATE OF U.S. BUSINESSES	Years	Average Number of Failures per Year	Average Failure Rate per 10,000 Businesses	Average Liability per Failure
	1950–1959	11,119	42	$ 41,082
	1960–1969	13,110	52	92,271
	1970–1979	9,311	36	296,497
	1980	11,742	42	394,744
	1981	17,041	61	414,147
	1982	24,908	89	626,738
	1983	31,334	110	512,953
	1984	52,078	107	562,016
	1985	57,253	115	645,160
	1986	61,616	120	725,850
	1987	61,111	102	568,209
	1988	57,097	98	693,084
	1989	50,361	65	840,507
	1990	60,747	74	923,996
	1991	87,266	106	1,207,365
	1992	96,857	110	942,516

Note: Due to statistical revision, data prior to 1984 are not directly comparable to data in 1984 and thereafter.
Source: Dun & Bradstreet, Inc., *Business Failure Record* (New York, 1991/1992).

TABLE 23-3	Year	Number of Bankruptcies
HISTORICAL BANKRUPTCY RATE OF U.S. BUSINESSES	1980	43,629
	1981	48,014
	1982	69,207
	1983	59,013
	1984	63,954
	1985	71,242
	1986	81,019
	1987	81,999
	1988	63,775
	1989	63,227
	1990	64,853
	1991	71,549

Source: Administrative Office of the United States Courts, *Bankruptcy Statistical Information* (Washington, D.C., March 1992).

large percentage of the total business population. It is interesting to note that whereas the failure rate per 10,000 businesses fluctuates with the state of the economy, the average liability per failure has tended to increase over time. This is due primarily to inflation, but it also reflects the fact that some very large firms have failed in recent years.

Whereas Table 23-2 focuses on business failures—firms that have terminated operations with a resultant loss to creditors—Table 23-3 presents the number of bankruptcy filings from 1980 to 1991. It is difficult to make direct comparisons between Tables 23-2 and 23-3 because Table 23-2 includes all firms that failed, whether within legal bankruptcy or not, while Table 23-3 includes all firms that filed for bankruptcy, including those that reorganized and avoided failure.

Although bankruptcy is more frequent among smaller firms, it is clear from Table 23-4 that large firms are not immune. In fact, there have been 40 bankruptcies of firms with $1 billion or more in liabilities over the last five years (1988 to 1992). However, some firms are thought to be too big or "too important" to fail, and mergers or governmental intervention are often used as an alternative to outright failure and liquidation. The decision to give federal aid to Chrysler in the early 1980s is an excellent illustration. Also, in recent years federal regulators have arranged the absorption of many large "problem" savings and loan associations and commercial banks by financially sound institutions. In addition, several U.S. government agencies, principally the Defense Department, were able to bail out Lockheed when it otherwise would have failed, and the "shotgun marriage" of Douglas Aircraft and McDonnell was designed to prevent Douglas's failure. Another example of intervention is that of Merrill Lynch taking over Goodbody & Company, which would otherwise have gone bankrupt and would have frozen the accounts of its 225,000 customers while the bankruptcy settlement was being worked out. Goodbody's failure would have panicked investors across the country, so New York Stock Exchange member firms put up $30 million as an inducement to get Merrill

TABLE 23-4

TWELVE LARGEST NONBANK BANKRUPTCIES (BILLIONS OF DOLLARS)

Company	Liabilities	Date
Texaco	$21.6	April 1987
Olympia & York	19.8	May 1992
Executive Life Insurance	14.6	April 1991
Mutual Benefit Life	13.5	July 1991
Campeau (Allied and Federated)	9.9	January 1990
First Capital Holdings	9.3	May 1991
Baldwin United	9.0	September 1983
Continental Airlines	6.2	December 1990
Lomas Financial	6.1	September 1989
Macy's	5.3	January 1992
Columbia Gas	5.0	July 1991
LTV	4.7	July 1986

Note: There are motivations for filing for bankruptcy other than immediate financial distress. For example, Texaco's bankruptcy was the result of a lawsuit, and Continental Airlines' first filing, in 1983, was motivated by a desire to abrogate union contracts.

Source: Data supplied by Edward I. Altman.

Lynch to keep Goodbody from folding. Similar instances in other industries could also be cited.

Why do government and industry sometimes seek to avoid failure among larger firms? There are many reasons. In the case of financial institutions, the main reason is to prevent an erosion of confidence and a consequent run on the banks. With Lockheed and Douglas, the Defense Department wanted not only to maintain viable suppliers but also to avoid disrupting local communities. With Chrysler, the government wanted to preserve jobs as well as a competitor in the U.S. auto industry. Even when the public interest is not at stake, the fact that bankruptcy is a very expensive process gives private industry strong incentives to avoid outright bankruptcy. The costs and complexities of bankruptcy are discussed in subsequent sections of this chapter, but first some less formal and less expensive remedies and legal actions are examined.

SELF-TEST QUESTIONS

Define the following types of financial distress:
    (1) Economic failure
    (2) Business failure
    (3) Technical insolvency
    (4) Insolvency in bankruptcy
    (5) Legal bankruptcy

What are the major causes of business failure?

Do business failures occur evenly over time?

Which size of firm, large or small, is most prone to business failure? Why?

THE FINANCIAL DISTRESS PROCESS

Financial distress begins when a firm is unable to meet scheduled payments to creditors or when the firm's cash flow projections indicate that it will soon be unable to do so. As the situation develops, these central issues arise:

1. Is the firm's inability to meet scheduled debt payments a temporary cash flow problem (technical insolvency), or is it a permanent problem caused by asset values having fallen below debt obligations (insolvency in bankruptcy)?

2. If the problem is a temporary one, then an agreement by creditors that gives the firm time to recover and to satisfy everyone will be worked out. However, if basic long-run asset values have truly declined, then economic losses have occurred. In this event, who should bear the losses?

3. Is the company "worth more dead than alive"? That is, would the business be more valuable if it were maintained and continued in operation or if it were liquidated and sold off in pieces?

4. Should the firm file for bankruptcy, or should it try to use informal procedures? (Both reorganization and liquidation can be accomplished either informally or formally, under the direction of a bankruptcy court.)

5. Who should control the firm while it is being liquidated or rehabilitated? Should the existing management be left in control, or should a trustee be placed in charge of operations?

The answers to these questions effectively chart the course of a company in financial distress. In the remainder of the chapter, we discuss the issues surrounding these questions, beginning with informal solutions to financial distress.

SELF-TEST QUESTION

What are the major issues that must be addressed if a firm is subjected to financial distress?

SETTLEMENTS SHORT OF FORMAL BANKRUPTCY

When a firm experiences financial distress, its managers must first decide whether the problem is temporary and the firm is financially viable or whether a permanent economic problem exists that endangers the life of the firm. Then, the firm's managers must decide whether to tackle the problem informally or under the direction of a bankruptcy court. Because of costs associated with formal bankruptcy, it is often desirable to reorganize or liquidate a firm outside formal bankruptcy. In this section, we discuss informal settlements.

INFORMAL REORGANIZATION

In the case of an economically sound company whose financial difficulties appear to be temporary, creditors are often willing to work directly with the company,

helping it to recover and reestablish itself on a sound financial basis. Such voluntary plans, commonly called *workouts,* usually require some type of *restructuring* of the firm's debt. Restructuring typically involves extension and/or composition. In an *extension,* creditors postpone the dates of required interest or principal payments, or both. In a *composition,* creditors voluntarily reduce their fixed claims on the debtor by accepting a lower principal amount, by reducing the interest rate on the debt, by accepting equity in place of debt, or by accepting some combination of these changes.

A debt restructuring begins with a meeting between the failing firm's managers and creditors. The creditors appoint a committee consisting of four or five of the largest creditors, plus one or two of the smaller ones. This meeting is often arranged and conducted by an *adjustment bureau* associated with and run by the local credit managers' association.[2] Once the decision has been reached that the problems can be worked out, the bureau assigns investigators to make an exhaustive report. Then the bureau and the creditors' committee use the report to formulate a preliminary reorganization plan. Another meeting between the debtor and the creditors is then held in an attempt to craft a plan that can be agreed upon by all parties. At least three conditions are usually necessary to make an informal debt restructuring feasible: (1) The debtor must be a good moral risk, (2) the debtor must show an ability to make a recovery, and (3) general business conditions must be favorable to recovery. Many meetings and a great deal of negotiation may be required to reach a final agreement.

In developing the reorganization plan, creditors prefer an extension because it promises eventual payment in full. In some cases, creditors may agree not only to postpone the date of payment but also to subordinate existing claims to vendors who are willing to extend new credit during the extension period. Similarly, creditors may agree to accept a lower interest rate on loans during the extension, perhaps in exchange for a pledge of collateral. Because of the sacrifices involved, the creditors must have faith that the debtor firm will be able to solve its problems.

In a composition, creditors agree to reduce their claims on the debtor. Typically, creditors receive cash and/or new securities from the debtor that have a combined market value that is less than the amounts owed them. The cash and securities, which might have a value of only 10 percent of the original claim, are taken as full settlement of the original debt. Bargaining will take place between the debtor and the creditors over the savings that result from avoiding the costs associated with legal bankruptcy: administrative costs, legal fees, investigative costs, and so on. In addition to escaping such costs, the debtor gains in that the stigma of bankruptcy may be avoided; as a result, the debtor may be induced to part with most of the savings that result from avoiding a formal bankruptcy.

Often the bargaining process will result in a restructuring which involves both extension and composition. For example, the settlement may provide for a cash

---

[2]There is a nationwide group called the National Association of Credit Management, which consists of bankers and industrial companies' credit managers. This group sponsors research on credit policy and problems, conducts seminars on credit management, and operates local chapters in cities throughout the nation. These local chapters frequently operate adjustment bureaus.

payment of 25 percent of the debt immediately, plus a new note promising six future installments of 10 percent each, for a total payment of 85 percent. In some plans, creditors may end up with more senior (or perhaps secured) claims after the reorganization, which could motivate creditors to agree to the plan even though the amount of the claim had been reduced.

Voluntary settlements are not only informal and simple but also relatively inexpensive because legal and administrative expenses are held to a minimum. Thus, voluntary procedures often result in the largest return to creditors. Although creditors do not obtain immediate payment and may even have to accept less than is owed them, they often recover more money, and sooner, than if the firm were to file for bankruptcy.

In recent years, one factor that has motivated some creditors, especially banks and insurance companies, to agree to voluntary restructurings is the fact that restructurings can sometimes help creditors avoid showing a loss. Thus, banks and other financial institutions that are "in trouble" with their regulators over weak capital ratios may agree to extend new loans which are used to pay the interest on earlier loans and thus keep the bank from having to write down the value of the earlier loans. This particular type of restructuring depends on (1) the willingness of the regulators to go along with the process and (2) whether the bank is likely to recover more in the end by restructuring the debt or by forcing the borrower into bankruptcy immediately.

We should point out that informal voluntary settlements are not reserved for small firms. International Harvester avoided formal bankruptcy proceedings by getting its creditors to agree to restructure some $3.5 billion of debt. Likewise, Chrysler's creditors accepted both an extension and a composition to help it through its bad years. However, there are two potential problems associated with informal reorganizations. First, the debtor firm's managers—the ones who got the firm into trouble in the first place—are often left to manage the business. This situation may result in an erosion of assets and hence loss of creditor value. Note, however, that it is not uncommon for creditors to gain control during severe financial distress, so the problems associated with poor management can be resolved in an informal reorganization. Also, in the past few years, there has been a tendency in the courts to maintain that directors have some responsibility to the creditors in times of financial distress. In effect, directors are supposed to act as trustees, conserving assets to pay the creditors. Perhaps the biggest problem in informal reorganizations is in getting all the parties to agree to the voluntary plan. This problem, called the *holdout problem,* is discussed in a later section.

INFORMAL LIQUIDATION

When it is obvious that a firm is more valuable dead than alive, informal procedures can also be used to *liquidate* the firm. *Assignment* is an informal procedure for liquidating a firm, and it usually yields creditors a larger amount than they would receive in a formal bankruptcy liquidation. However, assignments are feasible only if the firm is small and its affairs are not too complex. An assignment calls

for title to the debtor's assets to be transferred to a third party, known as an *assignee* or *trustee*. The assignee is instructed to liquidate the assets through a private sale or a public auction and then to distribute the proceeds among the creditors on a pro rata basis. The assignment does not automatically discharge the debtor's obligations. However, the debtor may have the assignee write on the check to each creditor the requisite legal language to make endorsement of the check acknowledgment of full settlement of the claim.

Assignment has some advantages over liquidation in bankruptcy, which involves more time, legal formality, and expense. The assignee has more flexibility in disposing of property than does a bankruptcy trustee. Action can be taken sooner, before the inventory becomes obsolete or the machinery rusts, and, since the assignee is often familiar with the channels of trade in the debtor's business, better results may be achieved. However, an assignment does not automatically result in a full and legal discharge of all the debtor's liabilities, nor does it protect the creditors against fraud. Both of these problems can be reduced by formal liquidation in bankruptcy, which we discuss in a later section.

SELF-TEST QUESTIONS

Define the following terms:
  (1) Restructuring
  (2) Extension
  (3) Composition
  (4) Assignment
  (5) Assignee (trustee)

What three conditions are usually necessary to make an informal debt restructuring feasible?

What are the advantages of liquidation by assignment over a formal bankruptcy liquidation?

FEDERAL BANKRUPTCY LAW

U.S. bankruptcy laws were first enacted in 1898. They were modified substantially in 1938, then they were changed substantially again in 1978, and some fine-tuning was done in 1986. The primary purpose of our bankruptcy laws is to avoid the "destructive race to the courthouse." Without a bankruptcy law, firms that are worth more as ongoing concerns could be put out of business by individual creditors that find it in their best interests to force liquidation and receive full payment on their individual claims, without regard to the effects on other parties.

The Bankruptcy Reform Act of 1978 was a major revision designed to streamline and expedite proceedings. Current bankruptcy law consists of nine *nonconsecutively* numbered chapters (for the most part, only odd numbers are used), designated by Arabic numbers. Chapters 1, 3, and 5 contain general provisions applicable to the other chapters. Chapter 7 details the procedures to be followed

when liquidating a firm; generally, Chapter 7 is not used unless it has been determined that reorganization under Chapter 11 is not feasible. Chapter 9 deals with financially distressed municipalities; Chapter 11 is the business reorganization chapter; Chapter 12 deals with family-owned farms; Chapter 13 covers the adjustment of debts for "individuals with regular income"; and Chapter 15 sets up a system of trustees who help administer proceedings under the new act.

A firm is officially bankrupt when it files for bankruptcy with a federal court. When you read that a company, such as Southland (the owner of the 7-Eleven convenience store chain), has "filed for court protection under Chapter 11," this means that the company is attempting to work out a reorganization under the supervision of a bankruptcy court. Formal bankruptcy proceedings are designed to protect both the firm and its creditors. If the problem is technical insolvency, then the firm may use bankruptcy proceedings to gain time to solve its cash flow problems without foreclosure by its creditors. However, if the firm is bankrupt in the sense that liabilities exceed assets, the creditors can use bankruptcy procedures to attempt to ensure that the firm's owners do not siphon off assets which should go to creditors.

Bankruptcy law is flexible, and it provides much scope for negotiations between a company and its creditors and stockholders. A case is opened by filing a petition with one of 291 bankruptcy courts serving 90 judicial districts. The petition may be either *voluntary* or *involuntary*; that is, it may be filed either by the firm's management or by its creditors. A committee of unsecured creditors is then appointed by the court to negotiate with management for a reorganization, which may include the restructuring of debt and other claims against the firm. A *trustee* will be appointed by the court if current management is judged to be incompetent or if fraud is suspected; otherwise, the existing management will retain control. If no fair and feasible reorganization can be worked out, the firm will be liquidated under the procedures spelled out in Chapter 7.

SELF-TEST QUESTIONS

Define the following terms:
  (1) **Bankruptcy law**
  (2) **Chapter 11**
  (3) **Chapter 7**
  (4) **Trustee**
  (5) **Voluntary bankruptcy**
  (6) **Involuntary bankruptcy**

How does a firm formally declare bankruptcy?

REORGANIZATION IN BANKRUPTCY

It might appear that most reorganizations would be handled informally, because they can be accomplished more quickly and at less cost than through formal bankruptcy. However, two problems—the common pool problem and the holdout

problem—often arise to stymie informal reorganizations and thus force debtors into Chapter 11 bankruptcy.[3]

To illustrate the two problems, consider a firm that is having financial difficulties. The firm is worth $9 million as an ongoing concern (this is the present value of its expected operating cash flow) but only $7 million if totally liquidated. The firm's debt totals $10 million face value—ten creditors with equal priority each have a $1 million claim. Now suppose the firm's liquidity deteriorates to the point where it defaults on one of its loans. The holder of the loan in default has the contractual right to *accelerate* the claim, which means the creditor can *foreclose* on the loan and demand payment of the entire balance. Further, since most debt agreements have *cross-default provisions,* defaulting on one loan effectively places all loans in default.

The firm's market value is less than the $10 million face value of debt regardless of whether the firm remains in business or liquidates, so all of the creditors cannot be paid in full under either scenario. However, the creditors in total clearly would be better off as a group if the firm is not shut down, because their collective claims would be worth $9 million if the firm were to remain in business but only $7 million if the firm were liquidated. The problem here, which is called the *common pool problem,* is that individual creditors have an incentive to foreclose on the firm even though the firm is worth more collectively as an ongoing concern.

An individual creditor has the incentive to foreclose because it can force the firm to liquidate a portion of its assets to pay off the creditor's $1 million claim in full. The foreclosure by a single creditor reduces the amount of assets, and hence operating cash flow, so the value of the remaining creditors' claims is reduced by the foreclosure. Of course, all the creditors of the firm recognize the gains to be had from this strategy, so they storm the debtor with foreclosure notices. Even those creditors who understand the merits of keeping the firm alive may be forced to foreclose, because the foreclosures of the other creditors reduce the claims of those who do not. In this example, if seven creditors foreclose and force liquidation, they would be paid in full, and the remaining three creditors would receive nothing.

With many creditors, as soon as a firm defaults on one loan, there is high potential for a disruptive flood of foreclosures that would make the creditors collectively worse off. In our example, the creditors would lose $2 million in value if a flood of foreclosures were to force the firm to liquidate. If the firm had only one creditor, say a single bank loan, the common pool problem would not exist—if a single bank had loaned the company $10 million, it would not likely force liquidation of the firm to get $7 million when it could keep the firm alive and realize $9 million.

Chapter 11 provides a solution to the common pool problem because of its *automatic stay* provision. Automatic stay, which is granted to all debtors in bankruptcy, limits the ability of creditors to foreclose unilaterally on the debtor to

[3]The issues discussed in this section are covered in more detail in Thomas H. Jackson, *The Logic and Limits of Bankruptcy Law* (Cambridge, Mass.: Harvard University Press, 1986).

collect their individual claims. However, the creditors can collectively foreclose on the debtor and force liquidation.

While bankruptcy gives the firm a chance to work out its problems without the threat of creditor foreclosure, it does not give the debtor free reign over the firm's assets. First, bankruptcy law gives creditors the right to petition the bankruptcy court to block almost any action the firm might take while in bankruptcy. Second, *fraudulent conveyance* statutes, which are part of debtor-creditor law in most states, protect creditors from unjustified transfers of property by a firm in financial distress.

To illustrate fraudulent conveyance, suppose a holding company is contemplating bankruptcy protection for one of its subsidiaries. The holding company might be tempted to sell some or all of the subsidiary's assets to itself (the parent company) for less than the true market value. This transaction would reduce the value of the subsidiary by the difference between the true market value of its assets and the amount paid, and the loss would be borne primarily by the subsidiary's creditors. Such a transaction would likely be voided by the courts as a fraudulent conveyance. Note that transactions that favor one creditor at the expense of another can also be voided under the same law. For example, a transaction in which an asset is sold and the proceeds are used to pay one creditor in full at the expense of other creditors could be voided. Thus, fraudulent conveyance laws also protect creditors from each other.[4]

The second problem that bankruptcy law mitigates is the *holdout problem*. To illustrate this problem, consider the previous example. The goal of the firm is to avoid liquidation by *remedying* the default. Outside of bankruptcy, this requires a reorganization plan that is agreed to by each of the ten creditors. Suppose the firm offers each creditor new debt with a face value of $850,000 in exchange for the old $1,000,000 face value debt. If each of the creditors accepted the offer, the firm could be successfully reorganized. The reorganization would leave the equity holders with some value — the market value of the equity would be $9,000,000 − 10($850,000) = $500,000. Further, the creditors would have claims worth $8.5 million, much more than the $7 million value of their claims in liquidation.

Although such an exchange offer seems to benefit all parties, it is unlikely to be accepted by the creditors. Here is why: Suppose that seven creditors tender their bonds; thus, seven creditors each now have claims with a face value of $850,000, while the three creditors that did not tender their bonds each have a claim with a face value of $1 million. The total face value of the debt at this point is $8,950,000, which is less than the $9 million value of the firm. In this situation, none of the three holdout creditors would tender their bonds, because the firm could afford to pay the full face value on this debt. The problem lies in the fact that (1) the creditors are sophisticated enough to realize this will happen and (2) each creditor would want to be one of the three holdouts that gets paid in

---

[4]Note that federal bankruptcy law contains *voidable preference* provisions that are similar to state fraudulent conveyance laws. The bankruptcy code requires that all transactions undertaken by the firm in the six months prior to bankruptcy filing be reviewed by the court for fraudulent conveyance.

full. Thus, it is quite likely that none of the creditors would accept the offer. The holdout problem makes it very difficult to reorganize the firm's debts. Again, if the firm had a single creditor, there would obviously be no holdout problem.

In bankruptcy, it is much easier to gain acceptance of a reorganization plan, because the bankruptcy court will lump the creditors into classes. Each class is considered to have accepted a reorganization plan if a majority of the creditors in the class (holding at least two-thirds of the amount of debt) vote for the plan, and the plan will be approved by the court if it is deemed to be "fair and equitable" to the dissenting parties. This procedure, in which the court mandates a reorganization plan in spite of dissent, is called a *cramdown*. The ability of the court to force acceptance of a reorganization plan greatly reduces the incentive for creditors to hold out. Thus, in our example, if the plan to offer each creditor new claims worth $850,000 in face value were proposed in bankruptcy, it would have a much greater chance of success. Those bondholders who do not vote in favor of the plan will not gain from the willingness of other creditors to scale down their claims—the bondholders who do not vote in favor of the plan will receive the same claim as those who vote in favor of the plan.

Because of the holdout problem, it is easier for a firm with few creditors to informally reorganize than it is for a firm with many creditors. A recent study examined 169 publicly traded firms that experienced severe financial distress from 1978 to 1987.[5] About half of the firms reorganized without filing for bankruptcy; the other half were forced to reorganize in bankruptcy. The firms that reorganized without filing for bankruptcy owed more of their debt to banks and had fewer creditors. Generally, bank debt can be reorganized outside of bankruptcy, while a publicly traded bond issue may be held by hundreds or even thousands of individual bondholders.

Filing for bankruptcy under Chapter 11 has several benefits besides automatic stay and cramdown that are not inherent in informal restructurings.

1. Interest and principal payments, including interest on delayed payments, may be delayed without penalty until a reorganization plan is approved (the plan may call for even further delays). This permits cash generated from operations to be used to sustain operations rather than be siphoned off by creditors.

2. The firm is permitted to issue *debtor in possession (DIP) financing.* DIP financing enhances the ability of the firm to borrow funds for short-term liquidity purposes, because such loans are senior to all other unsecured debt, regardless of the provisions in those contracts. This feature of bankruptcy is particularly useful for retailers, who must use credit to buy new merchandise to create revenue opportunities.

3. The debtor firm's managers are given the exclusive right for 120 days after filing to submit a reorganization plan, plus another 60 days to obtain agreement on

---

[5]See Stuart Gilson, Kose John, and Larry Lang, "Troubled Debt Restructurings: An Empirical Study of Private Reorganization of Firms in Default," *Journal of Financial Economics,* October 1990, 315–354.

the plan from the parties affected. The court may, however, extend these dates. After the first right of plan submission has expired, any party to the proceedings may propose a reorganization plan.

Under earlier bankruptcy laws, most formal reorganization plans were guided by the *absolute priority doctrine*. This doctrine holds that creditors should be compensated for their claims in a rigid hierarchical order, and that senior claims must be paid in full before junior claims can receive even a dime. However, an alternative position, the *relative priority doctrine,* holds that more flexibility should be allowed in a reorganization and that balanced consideration should be given to all claimants. The 1978 law represented a movement away from absolute priority and toward relative priority. As a result, in recent years, bankruptcy reorganizations have moved closer to the relative priority doctrine.

The primary role of the bankruptcy court in a reorganization is to determine the *fairness* and the *feasibility* of proposed plans of reorganization. The basic doctrine of fairness states that claims must be recognized in the order of their legal and contractual priority. Carrying out this concept of fairness in a reorganization involves the following steps:

1. Future sales must be estimated.

2. Operating conditions must be analyzed so that the future earnings and cash flows can be predicted.

3. A capitalization rate to be applied to these future cash flows must be determined.

4. This capitalization rate must then be applied to the estimated cash flows to obtain an estimated value for the company.

5. Provision for distributions to the claimants must then be made.

The primary test of feasiblity in a reorganization is whether the fixed charges after reorganization will be adequately covered by earnings. Adequate coverage generally requires an improvement in earnings or a reduction of fixed charges, or both. Among the actions that must generally be taken are the following:

1. Debt maturities are usually lengthened, and some debt is usually converted into equity.

2. When the quality of management has been substandard, a new team must be given control of the company.

3. If inventories have become obsolete or depleted, they must be replaced.

4. Sometimes the plant and equipment must be modernized before the firm can operate and compete successfully on a cost basis.

5. Reorganization may also require an improvement in production, marketing, advertising, and other functions.

6. It is sometimes necessary to develop new products or markets to enable the firm to move from areas where economic trends are poor into areas with more potential for growth or at least stability.

TABLE 23-5	**Assets**	
COLUMBIA SOFTWARE	Current assets	$ 3.50
COMPANY: BALANCE	Net fixed assets	12.50
SHEET AS OF MARCH	Other assets	0.70
31, 1993	Total assets	$16.70
(MILLIONS OF		
DOLLARS)	**Liabilities and Equity**	
	Accounts payable	$ 1.00
	Accrued taxes	0.25
	Notes payable	0.25
	Other current liabilities	1.75
	7½% first mortgage bonds, due 2004	6.00
	9% subordinated debentures, due 1999[a]	7.00
	Common stock ($1 par)	1.00
	Paid-in capital	3.45
	Retained earnings	(4.00)
	Total liabilities and equity	$16.70

[a]The debentures are subordinated to the notes payable.

REORGANIZATION EXAMPLE

The meaning and content of reorganization procedures may best be shown with an example of reorganization involving the Columbia Software Company, a firm that specializes in accounting software for small businesses.[6] Table 23-5 gives Columbia's balance sheet as of March 31, 1993. The company had been suffering losses running to $2.5 million a year, and, as will be made clear in the following discussion, the asset values in the balance sheet are overstated. Because the firm was insolvent, it filed a petition with a federal court for reorganization under Chapter 11. Management filed a plan of reorganization with the court and the SEC on June 13, 1993.[7]

The plan concluded that the company could not be internally reorganized and that the only feasible solution would be to combine Columbia with a larger, integrated software company. Accordingly, the court solicited the interest of a number of software companies. Late in July 1993, Moreland Software showed an interest in Columbia. On August 3, 1993, Moreland made a formal proposal to take over the payments on Columbia's $6 million of 7½ percent first mortgage bonds, to pay the $250,000 in taxes owed by Columbia, and to pay 40,000 shares of Moreland com-

---

[6]This example is based on an actual reorganization, although the company name has been changed and the numbers have been changed slightly to simplify the analysis.

[7]Reorganization plans must be submitted to the Securities and Exchange Commission (SEC) if (1) the securities of the debtor are publicly held and (2) total indebtedness exceeds $3 million. However, in recent years the only bankruptcy cases that the SEC has become involved in are those that are either precedent setting or that involve issues of national interest.

TABLE 23-6

COLUMBIA SOFTWARE COMPANY: REORGANIZATION PLAN (MILLIONS OF DOLLARS)

Senior Claims:

Taxes	$ 250,000	Paid off by Moreland	
Mortgage bonds	$6,000,000	Assumed by Moreland	

Reorganization plan for the remaining $10 million of liabilities, based on 40,000 shares at a price of $75 per share for a total market value of $3 million, or 30 percent of the remaining liabilities:

Remaining Claims (1)	Original Amount (2)	30% of Claim Amount (3)	Claim after Subordination (4)	Number of Shares of Common Stock (5)	Percentage of Original Claim Received (6)
Notes payable	$ 250,000	$ 75,000	$ 250,000	3,333	100%
Unsecured creditors	2,750,000	825,000	825,000	11,000	30
Subordinated debentures	7,000,000	2,100,000	1,925,000[a]	25,667	28
	$10,000,000	$3,000,000	$3,000,000	40,000	30%

[a]Because the debentures are subordinated to the notes payable, $250,000 − $75,000 = $175,000 must be redistributed from the debentures to the notes payable.

mon stock to Columbia's stockholders. Since the Moreland stock had a market price of $75 per share, the value of the stock was $3 million. Thus, Moreland was offering $3 million of stock plus the takeover of $6 million of loans and $250,000 of taxes—a total of $9.25 million for assets that had a book value of $16.7 million.

Moreland's plan is shown in Table 23-6. As in all Chapter 11 plans, the secured creditors' claims are paid in full (in this case, the mortgage bonds are taken over by Moreland Software). However, the total remaining claims of the unsecured creditors equal $10 million against only $3 million of available funds. Thus, each claimant would be entitled to receive 30 percent before the adjustment for subordination. Before this adjustment, holders of notes payable would receive 30 percent of their $250,000 claim, or $75,000. However, the debentures are subordinated to the notes payable, so an additional $175,000 must be allocated to notes payable from the subordinated debentures. In Column 5, the dollar claims of each class of debt are restated in terms of the number of shares of Moreland common stock received by each class of unsecured creditors. Finally, Column 6 shows the percentage of the original claim each group received. Of course, both the taxes and the secured creditors were paid off in full, while the stockholders received nothing.

The bankruptcy court first evaluated the proposal from the standpoint of fairness. The court began by estimating the value of Columbia Software. After a survey and discussion with various experts, the court arrived at estimated sales of $25 million per year. It further estimated that the profit margin on sales would equal 6 percent, thus giving estimated future annual earnings of $1.5 million.

The court analyzed price/earnings ratios for comparable software companies and arrived at eight times future earnings for a capitalization factor. Multiplying 8 by $1.5 million gave an indicated total value of the company of $12 million. Since

the mortgage bonds assumed and taxes paid by Moreland Software totaled $6,250,000, a net value of $5,750,000 was left for the other claims. This value is almost double that of the 40,000 shares of Moreland stock offered for the remainder of the company. Thus, the court concluded that the plan for reorganization did not meet the test of fairness. Note that under both Moreland's plan and the court evaluation, the holders of common stock were to receive nothing, which is one of the risks of ownership, while the holders of the first mortgage bonds were to be paid in full.

The court also examined Moreland's plan for feasibility, observing that in the reorganization, Moreland Software would take over Columbia's assets and liabilities. The court judged that the direction and aid of Moreland would remedy the deficiencies that had troubled Columbia. Whereas the debt/assets ratio of Columbia Software had become unbalanced, Moreland has only a moderate amount of debt. After consolidation, Moreland would still have a relatively low 27 percent debt ratio.

Moreland's net income before interest and taxes had been running at a level of approximately $15 million. The interest on its long-term debt after the merger would be $1.5 million and, taking short-term borrowings into account, would total a maximum of $2 million per year. The $15 million in earnings before interest and taxes would therefore provide an interest charge coverage of 7.5 times, exceeding the norm of 5 times for the industry.

Notice that the question of feasibility would have been irrelevant had Moreland offered $3 million in cash rather than in stock and had it offered to pay off the bonds rather than take them over. It is the court's function to protect the interests of Columbia's creditors. Since the creditors are being forced to take common stock or bonds guaranteed by another firm, the court felt the need to look into the feasibility of the transaction. If Moreland had made a cash offer, however, the feasibility of its own operation after the transaction was completed would not have been a concern.

Moreland Software was told of the court's conclusions, particularly its concern over the fairness of the plan. Further, Moreland was asked to increase the number of shares it offered. Moreland refused, and no other company offered to acquire Columbia. Because no better offer could be obtained and the only alternative to the plan was liquidation (with an even lower realized value), Moreland's proposal was ultimately accepted by the court despite its disagreement with the valuation.

PREPACKAGED BANKRUPTCIES

In the last few years, a new type of reorganization has become popular that combines the advantages of both the informal workout and formal Chapter 11 reorganization. This new hybrid is called a *prepackaged bankruptcy*.[8]

---

[8]For more information on prepackaged bankruptcies, see John J. McConnell and Henri Servaes, "The Economics of Pre-Packaged Bankruptcy," *Journal of Applied Corporate Finance,* Summer 1991, 93–97.

In a workout, a debtor negotiates a restructuring with its creditors. Even though complex workouts typically involve corporate officers, lenders, lawyers, and investment bankers, workouts are still less expensive and less damaging to reputations than are Chapter 11 reorganizations. In a prepackaged bankruptcy, the debtor firm gets all, or most of, the creditors to agree to the reorganization plan *prior* to filing for bankruptcy. Then, a reorganization plan is filed along with, or shortly after, the bankruptcy petition.

A logical question arises: Why would a firm that can arrange an informal reorganization want to file for bankrupcty? The three primary advantages of a prepackaged bankruptcy are (1) reduction of the holdout problem, (2) preserving creditors' claims, and (3) taxes. Perhaps the biggest benefit of a prepackaged bankruptcy is the reduction of the holdout problem—a bankruptcy filing permits a cramdown that would otherwise be impossible. In addition, by eliminating holdouts, bankruptcy also forces all creditors in each class to participate on a pro rata basis, which preserves the relative value of all claimants. Finally, filing for formal bankruptcy may have positive tax implications. First, in an informal reorganization in which the debtholders trade debt for equity and the original equity holders end up with less than 50 percent ownership, the company loses its accumulated tax losses. In formal bankruptcy, the firm gets to keep its loss carryforwards. Second, in a workout, when debt worth, say, $1,000 is exchanged for debt worth, say, $500, the reduction in debt of $500 is considered to be taxable income to the firm. However, if this same situation occurs in a Chapter 11 reorganization, the difference is not treated as taxable income.[9]

All in all, prepackaged bankruptcies make sense in many situations. If sufficient agreement can be reached among creditors through informal negotiations, a subsequent filing can solve the holdout problem and result in favorable tax treatment. For these reasons, the number of prepackaged bankruptcies has grown dramatically in recent years.

SELF-TEST QUESTIONS

Define the following terms:
   (1) Common pool problem
   (2) Holdout problem
   (3) Automatic stay
   (4) Cramdown
   (5) Fraudulent conveyance
   (6) Absolute priority doctrine
   (7) Relative priority doctrine
   (8) Fairness
   (9) Feasibility

---

[9]Note that in both tax situations—loss carryforwards and debt value reductions—favorable tax treatment is available in workouts if the firm is deemed to be legally insolvent, that is, if the market value of its assets is demonstrated to be less than the face value of its liabilities.

(10) **Debtor in possession financing**

(11) **Prepackaged bankruptcy**

What are the advantages of a formal reorganization under Chapter 11?

What has been the recent trend regarding absolute versus relative priority doctrines?

How do courts assess the fairness of proposed reorganization plans?

How do courts assess the feasibility of proposed reorganization plans?

Why have prepackaged bankruptcies become so popular in recent years?

LIQUIDATION IN BANKRUPTCY

If a company is "too far gone" to be reorganized, then it must be liquidated. Liquidation should occur when the business is worth more dead than alive, or when the possibility of restoring the firm to financial health is so remote that the creditors run a high risk of greater loss if operations are continued. Earlier in the chapter we discussed assignment, which is an informal liquidation procedure. Now, we consider *liquidation in bankruptcy,* which is carried out under the jurisdiction of a federal district bankruptcy court.

Chapter 7 of the Federal Bankruptcy Reform Act addresses three important problems during a liquidation: (1) It provides safeguards against fraud by the debtor; (2) it provides for an equitable distribution of the debtor's assets among the creditors; and (3) it allows insolvent debtors to discharge all their obligations and thus be able to start new businesses unhampered by the burden of prior debt. However, formal liquidation is time-consuming, it can be costly, and it results in the extinction of the business.

The distribution of assets in a liquidation under Chapter 7 of the Bankruptcy Act is governed by the following priority of claims:

1. **Secured creditors, who are entitled to the proceeds of the sale of specific property pledged for a lien or a mortgage.** If the proceeds from the sale of property do not fully satisfy the secured creditors' claims, the remaining balance is treated as a general creditor claim (see Item 9).[10]

2. **Trustee's costs to administer and operate the bankrupt firm.**

3. **Expenses incurred after an involuntary case has begun but before a trustee is appointed.**

---

[10]When a firm or individual who goes bankrupt has a bank loan, the bank will attach any deposit balances. The loan agreement may stipulate that the bank has a first-priority claim on any deposits. If this is the case, the deposits are used to offset all or part of the bank loan; this is called, in legal terms, "the right of offset." In this case, the bank will not have to share the deposits with other creditors. Loan contracts often designate compensating balances as security against a loan. Even if the bank has no explicit claim against deposits, the bank will attach the deposits and hold them for the general body of creditors, including the bank itself. Without an explicit statement in the loan agreement, the bank does not receive preferential treatment with regard to attached deposits.

4. Wages due workers if earned within three months prior to the filing of the petition in bankruptcy. The amount of wages is limited to $2,000 per person.

5. Claims for unpaid contributions to employee benefit plans that should have been paid within six months prior to filing. These claims, plus wages in Item 4, may not exceed the $2,000-per-wage-earner limit.

6. Unsecured claims for customer deposits. These claims are not to exceed a maximum of $900 per individual.

7. Taxes due to federal, state, county, and any other government agency.

8. Unfunded pension plan liabilities. These liabilities have a claim above that of the general creditors for an amount up to 30 percent of the common and preferred equity, and any remaining unfunded pension claims rank with the general creditors.[11]

9. General, or unsecured, creditors. Holders of trade credit, unsecured loans, the unsatisfied portion of secured loans, and debenture bonds are classified as *general creditors*. Holders of subordinated debt also fall into this category, but they must turn over required amounts to the holders of senior debt.

10. Preferred stockholders. These stockholders can receive an amount up to the par value of their stock.

11. Common stockholders. These stockholders receive all remaining funds, if any.[12]

To illustrate how this priority system works, consider the balance sheet of Woldman Inc., shown in Table 23-7. Assets have a book value of $90 million. The claims are indicated on the right-hand side of the balance sheet. Note that the debentures are subordinated to the notes payable to banks. Woldman has filed for bankruptcy under Chapter 11, and since no fair and feasible reorganization could be arranged, the trustee is liquidating the firm under Chapter 7.

---

[11]Pension plan liabilities have a significant bearing on bankruptcy settlements. Pension plans are of two types, *funded* and *unfunded*. Under a funded plan, the firm makes cash payments to an insurance company or to a trustee (generally a bank), which then uses these funds (and interest earned on them) to pay retirees' pensions. Under an unfunded plan, the firm is obligated to make payments to retirees, but it does not provide cash in advance. Many plans are actually partially funded—some money has been paid in advance, but not enough to provide full pension benefits to all employees.

If a firm goes bankrupt, the funded part of the pension plan remains intact and is available for retirees. Prior to 1974, employees had no explicit claims for unfunded pension liabilities, but under the Employees' Retirement Income Security Act of 1974 (ERISA), an amount up to 30 percent of the equity (common and preferred) is earmarked for employees' pension plans and has a priority over the general creditors, with any remaining pension claims having status equal to that of the general creditors. This means, in effect, that the funded portion of a bankrupt firm's pension plan is completely secured but that the unfunded portion ranks somewhat above the general creditors. Obviously, unfunded pension fund liabilities should be of great concern to a firm's unsecured creditors.

[12]Note that if different classes of common stock have been issued, differential priorities may exist in common stockholder claims.

TABLE 23-7	Current assets	$80.0	Accounts payable	$20.0
WOLDMAN INC.:	Net fixed assets	10.0	Notes payable (to banks)	10.0
BALANCE SHEET AT			Accrued wages (1,400 @ $500)	0.7
LIQUIDATION			Federal taxes	1.0
(MILLIONS OF			State and local taxes	0.3
DOLLARS)			Current liabilities	$32.0
			First mortgage	$ 6.0
			Second mortgage	1.0
			Subordinated debentures[a]	8.0
			Total long-term debt	$15.0
			Preferred stock	$ 2.0
			Common stock	26.0
			Paid-in capital	4.0
			Retained earnings	11.0
			Total equity	$43.0
	Total assets	$90.0	Total liabilities and equity	$90.0

[a]The debentures are subordinated to the notes payable.

The assets as reported in the balance sheet are greatly overstated; they are, in fact, worth less than half of the $90 million at which they are carried. The following amounts are realized on liquidation:

From sale of current assets	$28,000,000
From sale of fixed assets	5,000,000
Total receipts	$33,000,000

The distribution of the proceeds from the liquidation is shown in Table 23-8. The first mortgage holders receive the $5 million in net proceeds from the sale of fixed property, leaving $28 million available to the remaining creditors, including a $1 million unsatisfied claim of the first mortgage holders. Next are the fees and expenses of administering the bankruptcy, which are typically about 20 percent of gross proceeds; in this example, they are assumed to be $6 million. Next in priority are wages due workers, which total $700,000, and taxes due, which amount to $1.3 million. Thus far, the total amount of claims paid from the $33 million received from the asset sale is $13 million, leaving $20 million for the general creditors. In this example, we assume that there are no claims for unpaid benefit plans or unfunded pension liabilities.

The claims of the general creditors total $40 million. Since $20 million is available, claimants will initially be allocated 50 percent of their claims, as shown in Column 3, before the subordination adjustment. This adjustment requires that the subordinated debentures turn over to the notes payable all amounts received until the notes are satisfied. In this situation, the claim of the notes payable is $10 million, but only $5 million is available; the deficiency is therefore $5 million. After transfer of $4 million from the subordinated debentures, there remains a deficiency of $1 million on the notes; this amount will remain unsatisfied.

TABLE 23-8

WOLDMAN INC.:
DISTRIBUTION OF
LIQUIDATIONS
PROCEEDS (MILLIONS
OF DOLLARS)

Distribution to Priority Claimants:

Proceeds from the sale of assets	$33.0
Less:	
1. First mortgage (paid from the sale of fixed assets)	5.0
2. Fees and expenses of bankruptcy	6.0
3. Wages due to workers within three months of bankruptcy	0.7
4. Taxes due to federal, state, and local governments	1.3
Funds available for distribution to general creditors	$20.0

Distribution to General Creditors:

General Creditors' Claims (1)	Amount of Claim[a] (2)	Pro Rata Distribution[b] (3)	Distribution after Subordination Adjustment[c] (4)	Percentage of Original Claim Received[d] (5)
Unsatisfied portion of first mortgage	$ 1.0	$ 0.5	$ 0.5	92%
Second mortgage	1.0	0.5	0.5	50
Notes payable	10.0	5.0	9.0	90
Accounts payable	20.0	10.0	10.0	50
Subordinated debentures	8.0	4.0	0.0	
Total	$40.0	$20.0	$20.0	

[a]Column 2 is the claim of each class of general creditor. Total claims equal $40.0 million.

[b]From the top section of the table, we see that $20 million is available for distribution to general creditors. Since there is $40 million in general creditor claims, the pro rata distribution will be $20/$40 = 0.50, or 50 cents on the dollar.

[c]The debentures are subordinate to the notes payable, so up to $5 million could be reallocated from debentures to notes payable. However, only $4 million is available to the debentures, so the entire amount is reallocated.

[d]Column 5 shows the results of dividing the Column 4 final allocation by the original claim shown in Column 2, except for the first mortgage, where the $5 million received from the sale of fixed assets is included in the calculation.

Note that 90 percent of the bank claim is satisfied, whereas a maximum of 50 percent of other unsecured claims will be satisfied. These figures illustrate the usefulness of the subordination provision to the security to which the subordination is made.

Since no other funds remain, the claims of the holders of preferred and common stocks are completely wiped out. Studies of the proceeds in bankruptcy liquidations reveal that unsecured creditors receive, on the average, about 15 cents on the dollar, while common stockholders generally receive nothing.

SELF-TEST QUESTIONS

Describe briefly the priority of claims in a formal liquidation.

What is the impact of subordination on the final allocation of proceeds from liquidation?

In general, how much do creditors receive from a liquidation? How much do stockholders receive?

RECENT BUSINESS FAILURES

This section sketches two of the more prominent recent business failures.

EASTERN AIRLINES

During the 1980s, Eastern Airlines was plagued by seemingly unending woes, from incessant labor strife to occasionally poor service, which caused the airline to lose hundreds of millions of dollars.[13] Finally, under its chairman, Frank Lorenzo, the company filed for Chapter 11 bankruptcy in March 1989 after a showdown with its unions. Lorenzo, who was determined to break the unions' strike, insisted that he could restore Eastern to profitability if given enough time—and money. Every few months, the company would submit projections to the bankruptcy court showing when the airline would turn the corner, while creditors complained that the forecasts were wildly optimistic.

The bankruptcy judge stated early on that keeping Eastern flying was in the "public interest" and that this goal outweighed the "parochial" concerns of the creditors. Thus, the court allowed Lorenzo to sell off assets and use the proceeds to cover operating losses. In early 1990, the unsecured creditors demanded that a trustee be appointed to run Eastern, and Martin Shugrue was appointed by the court in April. By then, however, $1.2 billion in assets had been sold and the funds had been used to keep Eastern in the air. Although analysts gave Eastern almost no chance of surviving, Shugrue launched an expensive program to restore the carrier to health. About $35 million was spent on national TV ads featuring the trustee as the leader of a new Eastern, and millions more were poured into new leather seats and increased flight attendants for first-class passengers to try to steal full-fare passengers away from rival carriers with better reputations for service, such as Delta.

When the Persian Gulf crisis slowed air travel and sent fuel prices upward, it became obvious to all that Eastern would never make it, and the court agreed to shut it down for good on January 18, 1991. By that time, however, Eastern had spent another $530 million in its attempt to stay afloat. Critics say that the almost $2 billion in total spent trying to keep the airline alive was a complete waste, while supporters contend that "Monday morning quarterbacking" is worthless and that the creditors were in line for so little toward the end that it was worth the risk just to save jobs. Shugrue continued to liquidate assets after the shutdown, but the bankruptcy was not officially converted to Chapter 7 until October 29, 1991. Although this last-gasp step might speed up the liquidation process, Eastern could end up as one of the few large bankruptcies in history that won't even have enough money to pay off the $388 million in fees and salaries to lawyers, bankers, and its remaining employees. If that happens, unsecured creditors won't get a penny of the $2.2 billion they are owed.

---

[13]For more information on the Eastern bankruptcy, see "Eastern: The Wings of Greed," which was published in the November 11, 1991, issue of *Business Week*.

REVCO

On December 29, 1986, Revco Drug Stores went private in a leveraged buyout.[14] At the time, Revco was one of the nation's largest retail drug chains, operating over 2,000 stores in 30 states. The buyout increased management's ownership in the company from 3 percent to 31 percent, but it also raised the company's indebtedness from $309 million to $1.3 billion, including $700 million in subordinated notes (junk bonds). Immediately after the buyout, the company only had $35 million in common equity out of $1.7 billion in capital, for a debt ratio (including preferred stock) of 98 percent. Given the company's heavy debt burden, right from the start many analysts viewed bankruptcy as inevitable.

On April 15, 1988, Revco announced that it could not make a $46 million interest payment on its subordinated notes. In a press release issued that day, the company said: "Revco believes that its business is strong and its operations solid; however, our current capitalization is not the appropriate one for the company. After evaluation, Revco's board has determined that a financial restructuring is appropriate." The company and its creditors made several attempts at a workout. For example, in mid-May Revco proposed that bondholders exchange their subordinated notes for a new class of common stock that would leave then-current stockholders with only 5 percent ownership. Such a restructuring was consistent with the argument that the LBO team paid too much for the company and that any equity value remaining after the overpayment was destroyed by poor operating performance. However, this proposal failed because the company's stockholders would not go along with it.

As Revco's fortunes fell, Magten Asset Management, a firm that specializes in investing in distressed companies, began buying Revco's senior subordinated notes at about 50 cents on the dollar. By late June, Magten had accumulated over 25 percent of that particular security, so it had veto power over any reorganization plan, whether private or under court supervision. Such power gave Magten the right to hold out for higher returns before consenting to any reorganization plan. On July 7, 1988, bondholders granted a one-month "standstill," whereby creditors agreed not to take action against Revco for missing its June interest payments. However, the company's cash flow was not improving, and on July 22 Magten demanded full and immediate payment of all principal and interest due. This action triggered cross-default provisions, which put Revco in default on all its borrowings. On July 28, 1988, Revco filed for protection under Chapter 11 of the Bankruptcy Act.

Since the formal bankruptcy filing, numerous reorganization plans have been proposed, but most failed because of arguments among the various claimants. In September 1991, creditors filed the latest plan, in which they would get 100 percent ownership of the company in return for agreeing to lighten Revco's current debt load of $1.5 billion. In addition, the plan called for Salomon Brothers, Revco's

---

[14]For more detail on the Revco buyout and subsequent failure, see Karen H. Wruck, "What Really Went Wrong at Revco," *Journal of Applied Corporate Finance,* Summer 1991, 79–92. For more information on leveraged buyouts in general, see Chapter 24.

advisor which collected almost $40 million in fees on the LBO deal, to pay $9.5 million to the creditors in return for an agreement to drop several proposed suits against the investment bank. In the plan, banks that lent Revco $306 million would receive $205 million of new 12 percent notes due December 31, 1998, a small amount of cash, and some new convertible preferred stock. The value of this package of securities was estimated at about 60 cents on the dollar. Holders of Revco's subordinated notes did not fare as well as the banks under the plan. They would get common stock in the post-bankruptcy Revco, but no cash or notes. The notes had been trading at about 18 cents on the dollar, reflecting investors' beliefs that the final reorganization plan would leave little for bondholders. According to the plan, holders of Revco's stock would receive nothing. There is little that they can do to avoid being wiped out, because creditors with senior claims will be forced to accept far less than their original claims.

Finally, in June 1992, the plan was accepted, and Revco emerged from bankruptcy. With several former creditors now on the board, the first order of business was to fire the chairman, Boake Sells. Then, the board created a committee of five executives to lead the company. In spite of its years of problems, many analysts are predicting a bright future for Revco now that it has shed its onerous debt burden.

SELF-TEST QUESTION

What are the most important points to be learned from the bankruptcy situations of Eastern Airlines and Revco Drug Stores?

OTHER MOTIVATIONS FOR BANKRUPTCY

Normally, bankruptcy proceedings originate after a company has become so financially weak that it cannot meet its current obligations. However, bankruptcy law also permits a company to file for bankruptcy if its financial forecasts indicate that a continuation of current conditions would lead to insolvency. This provision was used by Continental Airlines in 1983 to break its union contract and hence to lower labor costs. Continental demonstrated to a bankruptcy court that operations under the then-current union contract would lead to insolvency in a matter of months. The company then filed a reorganization plan that included major changes in its union contract. The court sided with Continental and allowed the company to abrogate its contract. Continental then reorganized as a nonunion carrier, and that reorganization turned the company from a money loser into a money maker.[15] Congress changed the law after the Continental affair to make it more difficult to

---

[15]In 1990, Continental's fortunes reversed again when it was unable to successfully integrate several acquisitions, including Eastern, and the company filed for bankruptcy a second time. As we discussed in the opening section, Continental is about to reemerge from its second bankruptcy.

use bankruptcy to break union contracts, but this case did set the precedent for using bankruptcy to help prevent financial problems as well as to help solve existing ones.

Bankruptcy law has also been used to hasten settlements in major product liability suits. The Manville asbestos and A. H. Robins dalkon shield cases are examples. In both situations, the companies were being bombarded by thousands of lawsuits, and the very existence of such huge contingent liabilities made normal operations virtually impossible. Further, in both cases it was relatively easy to prove (1) that if the plaintiffs won, the companies would be unable to pay the full amount of the claims, (2) that a larger amount of funds would be available to the claimants if the companies continued to operate rather than liquidate, (3) that continued operations were possible only if the suits were brought to a conclusion, and (4) that a timely resolution of all the suits was impossible because of their vast number and variety. The bankruptcy statutes were used to consolidate all the suits and to reach settlements under which the plaintiffs obtained more money than they otherwise would have received, and the companies were able to stay in business. The stockholders did poorly under these plans, because most of the companies' future cash flows were assigned to the plaintiffs, but, even so, the stockholders probably fared better than they would have if the suits had been concluded through the jury system.

SELF-TEST QUESTION

What are some situations other than immediate financial distress that lead firms to file for bankruptcy?

SOME CRITICISMS OF BANKRUPTCY LAWS

Although bankruptcy laws, for the most part, exist to protect creditors, many critics today claim that current laws are not doing what they were intended to do. Before 1978, most bankruptcies ended quickly in liquidation. Then, Congress rewrote the laws, giving companies more opportunity to stay alive, believing that this was best for managers, employees, creditors, and stockholders. Before the reform, 90 percent of Chapter 11 filers were liquidated, but now that percentage is less than 80 percent. Furthermore, large public corporations with the ability to hire high-priced legal help have a very good chance of avoiding, or at least delaying, liquidation, usually at the expense of the firm's creditors and shareholders.

Critics believe that bankruptcy is great for business these days—great for consultants, lawyers, and investment bankers, who reap hefty fees during bankruptcy proceedings, and for managers, who continue to collect their salaries and bonuses as long as the business is kept alive. The problem, according to critics, is that bankruptcy courts allow cases to drag on for years, depleting assets that could be sold to pay off creditors and shareholders. Too often, quick resolution is impossible because bankruptcy judges are required to deal with issues such as labor disputes,

pension plan funding, and environmental liability—social questions that should be solved by legislative action rather than by bankruptcy courts.

For example, LTV Corporation has been in bankruptcy since 1986, mainly because of a pension dispute among the company, its workers, retirees, and the federal government. During this time, the Dallas-based conglomerate has spent $162 million in legal and consulting fees. Meanwhile, under the latest reorganization plan, creditors would get only 4 to 53 cents on the dollar.

Critics contend that bankruptcy judges have to realize that some sick companies should be allowed to die—and quickly. Maintaining companies on life support does not serve the interests of the parties the bankruptcy laws were meant to protect. One proposal for overhauling the system is to limit the time that companies have to file a reorganization plan. A debtor is supposed to have only 120 days, but the deadline is almost never enforced. It might make more sense to set a deadline of six months or a year and then stick to it. "Bankruptcy is like open-heart surgery—the longer you stay under the knife, the lower the chance of success," says James E. Spiotto, a creditor's lawyer with Chapman & Cutler in Chicago. "We should be shooting for a quick, efficient way to give companies a fresh start."

Other critics think the entire bankruptcy system of judicial protection and supervision needs to be scrapped. Some even have proposed a kind of auction, where shareholders and creditors would have the opportunity to gain control of a bankrupt company by raising the cash needed to pay the bills. The rationale here is that the market is a better judge than a bankruptcy court whether a company is worth more dead or alive.

Self-Test Question

According to critics, what is wrong with the current bankruptcy system?

Using Multiple Discriminant Analysis to Predict Bankruptcy

As we have seen, bankruptcy, or even the possibility of bankruptcy, can cause significant trauma for a firm's managers, investors, suppliers, customers, and community. Thus, it would be beneficial to be able to predict the possibility of bankruptcy so that steps could be taken to avoid it or at least reduce its impact. The most successful approach to bankruptcy prediction is *Multiple Discriminant Analysis (MDA),* a statistical technique similar to regression analysis. We briefly discussed MDA in Chapter 18, in connection with credit-scoring systems. In this section, we discuss MDA in more detail, and we illustrate its application to bankruptcy prediction.[16]

---

[16]This section is based largely on the work of Edward I. Altman, especially these two papers: (1) "Financial Ratios, Discriminant Analysis, and the Prediction of Corporate Bankruptcy," *Journal of Finance,* September 1968, 589–609; and (2) with Robert G. Haldeman and P. Narayanan, "Zeta Analysis: A New Model to Identify Bankruptcy Risk of Corporations," *Journal of Banking and Finance,* June 1977, 29–54.

THE BASICS OF MULTIPLE DISCRIMINANT ANALYSIS

Suppose a bank loan officer wants to segregate corporate loan applications into those likely to default and those not likely to default. Assume that data for some past period are available on a group of firms which includes both companies that went bankrupt and companies that did not. For simplicity, we assume that only the current ratio and the debt/assets ratio are analyzed. These ratios for our sample of firms are given in Columns 2 and 3 at the bottom of Figure 23-1. The Xs in the graph represent firms that went bankrupt, while the dots represent firms that remained solvent. For example, Point A in the upper left section is the point for Firm 2, which had a current ratio of 3.0 and a debt ratio of 20 percent, and a dot to indicate that the firm did not go bankrupt. Point B, in the lower right section, represents Firm 19, which had a current ratio of 1.0, a debt ratio of 60 percent, and an X to indicate that it did go bankrupt.

The objective of discriminant analysis is to construct a boundary line through the graph such that, if the firm is to the left of the line, it is not likely to become insolvent, whereas it is likely to go bankrupt if it falls to the right. This boundary line is called the *discriminant function,* and in our example it takes this form:

$$Z = a + b_1(\text{Current ratio}) + b_2(\text{Debt ratio}).$$

Here Z is called the *Z score,* a is a constant term, and b_1 and b_2 indicate the effect of the current ratio and the debt ratio on the probability of a firm's going bankrupt.

Although a full discussion of discriminant analysis would go well beyond the scope of this book, some useful insights may be gained by observing these points:

1. The discriminant function is fitted (that is, the values of a, b_1, and b_2 are obtained) using historical data for a sample of firms that either went bankrupt or did not during some past period. When the data in the lower part of Figure 23-1 were fed into a "canned" discriminant analysis program (the computing centers of most universities and large corporations have such programs), the following discriminant function was obtained:

$$Z = -0.3877 - 1.0736(\text{Current ratio}) + 0.0579(\text{Debt ratio}).$$

2. This equation was plotted on Figure 23-1 as the locus of points for which $Z = 0$. All combinations of current ratios and debt ratios shown on the line result in $Z = 0$.[17] Companies that lie to the left of the line (and also have Z values less

---

[17]To plot the boundary line, let D/A = 0% and 80%, and then find the current ratio that forces $Z = 0$ at those two values. For example, at D/A = 0,

$$Z = -0.3877 - 1.0736(\text{Current ratio}) + 0.0579(0) = 0$$
$$0.3877 = -1.0736(\text{Current ratio})$$
$$\text{Current ratio} = 0.3877/(-1.0736) = -0.3611.$$

Thus, -0.3611 is the vertical axis intercept. Similarly, the current ratio at D/A = 80% is found to be 3.9533. Plotting these two points on Figure 23-1, and then connecting them, provides the discriminant boundary line, which is the line that best partitions the companies into bankrupt and nonbankrupt. It should be noted that nonlinear discriminant functions may also be used.

FIGURE 23-1

DISCRIMINANT

BOUNDARY BETWEEN

BANKRUPT AND

SOLVENT FIRMS

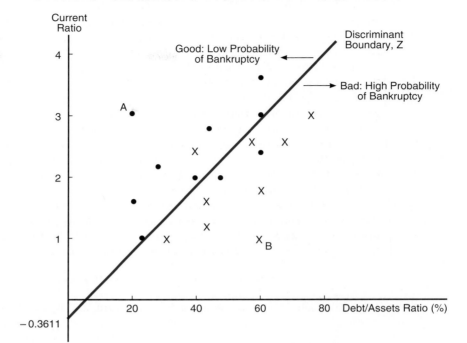

FIGURE 23-1

DISCRIMINANT BOUNDARY BETWEEN BANKRUPT AND SOLVENT FIRMS

Firm Number (1)	Current Ratio (2)	Debt/Assets Ratio (3)	Did Firm Go Bankrupt? (4)	Z Score (5)	Probability of Bankruptcy (6)
1	3.6	60%	No	−0.780	17.2%
2(A)	3.0	20	No	−2.451	0.8
3	3.0	60	No	−0.135	42.0
4	3.0	76	Yes	0.791	81.2
5	2.8	44	No	−0.847	15.5
6	2.6	56	Yes	0.062	51.5
7	2.6	68	Yes	0.757	80.2
8	2.4	40	Yes[a]	−0.649	21.1
9	2.4	60	No[a]	0.509	71.5
10	2.2	28	No	−1.129	9.6
11	2.0	40	No	−0.220	38.1
12	2.0	48	No[a]	0.244	60.1
13	1.8	60	Yes	1.153	89.7
14	1.6	20	No	−0.948	13.1
15	1.6	44	Yes	0.441	68.8
16	1.2	44	Yes	0.871	83.5
17	1.0	24	No	−0.072	45.0
18	1.0	32	Yes	0.391	66.7
19(B)	1.0	60	Yes	2.012	97.9

continued

than zero) are not likely to go bankrupt, while those to the right (and have Z greater than zero) are likely to fail. It can be seen from the graph that one X, indicating a failing company, lies to the left of the line, while two dots, indicating nonbankrupt companies, lie to the right of the line. Thus, the discriminant analysis failed to properly classify three companies.

3. If we have determined the parameters of the discriminant function, then we can calculate the Z scores for other companies, say, loan applicants at a bank. The Z scores for our hypothetical companies, along with their probabilities for going bankrupt, are given in Columns 5 and 6 of Figure 23-1. The higher the Z score, the worse the company looks from the standpoint of bankruptcy. Here is an interpretation:

Z = 0:   50-50 probability of future bankruptcy (say, within two years). The company lies exactly on the boundary line.

Z < 0:   If Z is negative, there is a less than 50 percent probability of bankruptcy. The smaller (more negative) the Z score, the lower the probability of bankruptcy. The computer output from MDA programs gives this probability, and it is shown in Column 6 of Figure 23-1.

Z > 0:   If Z is positive, the probability of bankruptcy is greater than 50 percent, and the larger Z, the greater the probability of bankruptcy.

4. The mean Z score of the companies that did not go bankrupt is -0.583, while that for the bankrupt firms is $+0.648$. These means, along with approximations of the Z score probability distributions of the two groups, are shown in Figure 23-2. We may interpret this graph as indicating that if Z is less than about -0.3, there is a very small probability that the firm will go bankrupt, whereas if Z is greater than $+0.3$, there is only a small probability that it will remain solvent. If Z is in the range ± 0.3, called the *zone of ignorance,* we are uncertain about how the firm should be classified.

5. The signs of the coefficients of the discriminant function are logical. Since its coefficient is negative, the larger the current ratio, the lower a company's Z score, and the lower the Z score, the smaller the probability of failure. Similarly, high

---

Footnote to Figure 23-1

[a]Denotes a misclassification. Firm 8 had Z = -0.649, so MDA predicted no bankruptcy, but it did go bankrupt. Similarly, MDA predicted bankruptcy for Firms 9 and 12, but they did not go bankrupt. The following tabulation shows bankruptcy and solvency predictions versus actual results:

	Z Positive: MDA Predicts Bankruptcy	Z Negative: MDA Predicts Solvency
Went bankrupt	8	1
Remained solvent	2	8

The model did not perform perfectly, as two predicted bankruptcies remained solvent and one firm that was expected to remain solvent went bankrupt. Thus, the model misclassified 3 out of 19 firms, or 16 percent of the sample. Its success rate was 84 percent.

FIGURE 23-2

PROBABILITY

DISTRIBUTIONS OF

Z SCORES

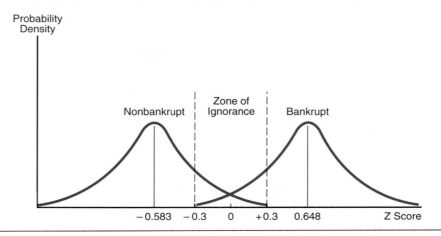

debt ratios produce high Z scores, and this is directly translated into a higher probability of bankruptcy.

6. Our illustrative discriminant function has only two variables, but other characteristics could be introduced. For example, we could add such variables as the rate of return on assets, the times-interest-earned ratio, the days sales outstanding, the quick ratio, and so forth.[18] Had the rate of return on assets been introduced, it might have turned out that Firm 8 (which failed) had a low ROA, while Firm 9 (which did not fail) had a high ROA. A new discriminant function would be calculated:

$$Z = a + b_1(\text{Current ratio}) + b_2(\text{D/A}) + b_3(\text{ROA}).$$

Firm 8 might now have a positive Z, while Firm 9's Z might become negative. Thus, it is likely that by adding more characteristics we would improve the accuracy of our bankruptcy forecasts. We could not draw Figure 23-1, but in Figure 23-2, this would cause each probability distribution to become tighter, narrow the zone of ignorance, and lead to fewer misclassifications.

ALTMAN'S MODEL

In a classic paper, Edward Altman applied MDA to a sample of corporations, and he developed a discriminant function that has seen wide use in actual practice. Altman's function was fitted as follows:

$$Z = 0.012X_1 + 0.014X_2 + 0.033X_3 + 0.006X_4 + 0.999X_5.$$

---

[18]With more than two variables, it is difficult to graph the function, but this presents no problem in actual usage because graphs are only used to explain MDA.

Here

X_1 = net working capital/total assets.

X_2 = retained earnings/total assets.[19]

X_3 = EBIT/total assets.

X_4 = market value of common and preferred stock/book value of debt.[20]

X_5 = sales/total assets.

The first four variables are expressed as percentages rather than as decimals. (For example, if X_3 = 13.3%, then 13.3, *not* 0.133, is used as its value.) Also, Altman's 50-50 point was 2.675, and not 0.0 as in our hypothetical example; his zone of ignorance was from Z = 1.81 to Z = 2.99; and the *larger* the Z score, the less the probability of bankruptcy.[21]

Altman's function can be used to calculate a Z score for MicroDrive Inc. based on the data presented previously in Chapter 2 in Tables 2-1 and 2-2. This calculation, ignoring the small amount of preferred stock, is shown next for 1993:

$$
\begin{array}{llll}
X_1 = & \$690/\$2{,}000 = 0.345 = 34.5\% & 34.5 \times 0.012 = 0.414 \\
X_2 = & \$766/\$2{,}000 = 0.383 = 38.3\% & 38.3 \times 0.014 = 0.536 \\
X_3 = & \$284/\$2{,}000 = 0.142 = 14.2\% & 14.2 \times 0.033 = 0.469 \\
X_4 = & 50(\$23)/\$1{,}064 = 1.081 = 108.1\% & 108.1 \times 0.006 = 0.649 \\
X_5 = & \$3{,}000/\$2{,}000 = 1.5 & 1.5 \times 0.999 = \underline{1.499} \\
& & Z = \underline{\underline{3.567}}
\end{array}
$$

Since MicroDrive's Z score of 3.567 is above the 2.99 upper limit of Altman's zone of ignorance, the data indicate that there is virtually no chance that MicroDrive will go bankrupt within the next two years. (Altman's model predicts bankruptcy reasonably well for about two years into the future.)

Altman and his colleagues' later work updated and improved his original study. In their more recent work, they explicitly considered such factors as capitalized lease obligations, and they applied smoothing techniques to level out random fluctuations in the data. The new model was able to predict bankruptcy with a high degree of accuracy for two years into the future, and with a slightly lower but still reasonable degree of accuracy (70 percent) for about five years.

MDA has been used with success by credit analysts to establish default probabilities for both consumer and corporate loan applicants, and by portfolio managers considering both stock and bond investments. It can also be used to evaluate

---

[19]Retained earnings is the balance sheet figure, not the addition to retained earnings for the year.

[20][(Shares of common outstanding)(Price per share) + (Shares of preferred)(Price per share of preferred)]/Balance sheet value of total debt, including all short-term liabilities.

[21]These differences reflect the software package Altman used to generate the discriminant function. Altman's program operated from a base of 2.675 rather than 0.0, and his program simply reversed the sign of Z from ours. Also, note that the Altman model does not have a constant term — the software program used by Altman suppresses it.

a set of pro forma ratios as developed in Chapter 15, or to gain insights into the feasibility of a reorganization plan filed under the Bankruptcy Act. Altman's model has also been used by Morgan Stanley and other investment banking houses to appraise the quality of junk bonds used to finance takeovers and leveraged buyouts. The technique is described in detail in many statistics texts, while several articles cited at the end of this chapter discuss financial applications of MDA. The interested reader is urged to study this literature, for MDA has many potentially valuable applications in finance.

However, when using MDA in practice it is best to create your own discriminant data using a recent sample from the industry in question. It is not reasonable to assume that the financial characteristics of a steel company facing imminent bankruptcy are the same as for a retail grocery chain in the same dire straits. If both of these firms were analyzed using Z scores calculated with the same equation, it might turn out that the grocery chain had a relatively high score, signifying (incorrectly) a low probability of bankruptcy, while the steel company had a relatively low score, indicating (correctly) a high probability of bankruptcy. The misclassification of the grocery company could result from the fact that it has very high sales for the amount of its book assets, and hence X_5, which has the highest coefficient, is much higher than for an average firm in an average industry facing potential bankruptcy. To remove any such industry-unique bias, the MDA analysis should be based on a sample with characteristics similar to the firm being analyzed. Unfortunately, it is often not possible to find enough firms that have recently gone bankrupt to conduct an industry MDA.

SUMMARY

This chapter discussed the main issues involved in corporate financial distress. The key concepts are listed below:

▶ There are several categories of financial distress: (1) *economic failure,* (2) *business failure,* (3) *technical insolvency,* (4) *insolvency in bankruptcy,* and (5) *legal bankruptcy.*

▶ The most common reasons for business failures are *economic factors* and *financial factors.*

▶ The proportion of businesses that fail fluctuates with the economy, but the average liability per failure has tended to increase over time. This is due both to inflation and to an increase in the number of billion-dollar bankruptcies in recent years.

▶ The fundamental issue that must be addressed when a company encounters financial problems is whether the company is "worth more dead than alive"; that is, would the business be more valuable if it continued in operation or if it were liquidated and sold off in pieces?

▶ In the case of a fundamentally sound company whose financial difficulties appear to be temporary, creditors frequently will work directly with the company, helping it to recover and reestablish itself on a sound financial basis. Such voluntary reorganization plans are called *workouts.*

▶ Reorganization plans usually require some type of *restructuring* of the firm's debt, involving either an *extension,* which postpones the date of required payment of past-due obligations, or a *composition,* by which the creditors voluntarily reduce their claims on the debtor.

▶ When it is obvious that a firm is better off dead than alive, informal procedures can also be used to *liquidate* the firm. *Assignment* is an informal procedure for liquidating a firm, and it usually yields creditors a larger amount than they would receive in a formal bankruptcy liquidation. However, assignments are feasible only if the firm is small and its affairs are not too complex.

▶ Current *bankruptcy law* consists of nine chapters, designated by Arabic numbers. For businesses, the most important chapters are *Chapter 7,* which details the procedures to be followed when liquidating a firm, and *Chapter 11,* which contains procedures for formal reorganizations.

▶ Since the very first bankruptcy laws, most formal reorganization plans have been guided by the *absolute priority doctrine.* This doctrine holds that creditors should be compensated for their claims in a rigid hierarchical order, and that senior claims must be paid in full before junior claims can receive even a dime.

▶ Conversely, the *relative priority doctrine* holds that more flexibility should be allowed in a reorganization, and that balanced consideration should be given to all claimants. In recent years, there has been a shift away from absolute priority toward relative priority.

▶ The primary role of the bankruptcy court in a reorganization is to determine the *fairness* and the *feasibility* of proposed plans of reorganization.

▶ Even if a particular class of creditors or the stockholders dissent and do not accept a reorganization plan, the plan may still be approved by the court if the plan is deemed to be "fair and equitable" to the dissenting parties. This procedure, in which the court mandates a reorganization plan in spite of dissent, is called a *cramdown.*

▶ In the last few years, a new type of reorganization has become popular that combines the advantages of both the informal workout and formal Chapter 11 reorganization. This new hybrid is called a *prepackaged bankruptcy.*

▶ The distribution of assets in a *liquidation* under Chapter 7 of the Bankruptcy Act is governed by a specific priority of claims.

▶ *Multiple Discriminant Analysis (MDA)* is one technique for predicting business failure. MDA uses a set of economic variables, such as the current ratio and debt ratio, to establish the probability of failure.

QUESTIONS

23-1 Define each of the following terms:
  a. Failure; insolvency; legal bankruptcy
  b. Informal restructuring; reorganization in bankruptcy
  c. Assignment; liquidation in bankruptcy

    d. Fairness; feasibility

    e. Absolute priority doctrine; relative priority doctrine

    f. Bankruptcy Reform Act of 1978; Chapter 11; Chapter 7

    g. Priority of claims in liquidation

    h. Extension; composition

    i. Workout; cramdown

    j. Prepackaged bankruptcy

    k. Holdout

    l. Multiple discrimination analysis; Z score

23-2 "A certain number of business failures is a healthy sign. If there are no failures, this is an indication (a) that entrepreneurs are overly cautious, and hence not as inventive and as willing to take risks as a healthy, growing economy requires; (b) that competition is not functioning to weed out inefficient producers; or (c) that both situations exist." Discuss this statement.

23-3 How could financial analysis be used to forecast the probability of a given firm's failure? Assuming that such analysis is properly applied, could it always predict failure?

23-4 Why do creditors usually accept a plan for financial rehabilitation rather than demand liquidation of the business?

23-5 Would it be possible to form a profitable company by merging two companies, both of which are business failures? Explain.

23-6 Would it be a sound rule to liquidate whenever the liquidation value is above the value of the corporation as a going concern? Discuss.

23-7 Why do liquidations usually result in losses for the creditors or the owners, or both? Would partial liquidation or liquidation over a period limit their losses? Explain.

23-8 Are liquidations likely to be more common for public utility, railroad, or industrial corporations? Why?

PROBLEMS

23-1 **(Reorganization)** The Verbrugge Publishing Company's 1993 balance sheet and income statement are as follows (in million of dollars). Verbrugge and its creditors have agreed upon a voluntary reorganization plan. In this plan, each share of the $6 preferred will be exchanged for one share of $2.40 preferred with a par value of $37.50 plus one 8 percent subordinated income debenture with a par value of $75. The $10.50 preferred issue will be retired with cash.

Balance Sheet

Current assets	$168	Current liabilities	$ 42
Net fixed assets	153	Advance payments	78
Goodwill	15	Reserves	6
		$6 preferred stock, $112.50 par value (1,200,000 shares)	135
		$10.50 preferred stock, no par, callable at $150 (60,000 shares)	9
		Common stock, $1.50 par value (6,000,000 shares)	9
		Retained earnings	57
Total assets	$336	Total claims	$336

Income Statement

Net sales	$540.0
Operating expense	516.0
Net operating income	$ 24.0
Other income	3.0
EBT	$ 27.0
Taxes (50%)	13.5
Net income	$ 13.5
Dividends on $6 preferred	7.2
Dividends on $10.50 preferred	0.6
Income available to common stockholders	$ 5.7

a. Construct the pro forma balance sheet assuming that reorganization takes place. Show the new preferred at is par value.

b. Construct the pro forma income statement. How much does the proposed recapitalization increase income available to common shareholders?

c. *Required earnings* is defined as the amount that is just enough to meet fixed charges (debenture interest and/or preferred dividends). What are the required pre-tax earnings before and after the recapitalization?

d. How is the debt ratio affected by the reorganization? If you were a holder of Verbrugge's common stock, would you vote in favor of the reorganization?

23-2 **(Liquidation)** At the time it defaulted on its interest payments and filed for bankruptcy, the McDaniel Mining Company had the following balance sheet (in thousands of dollars). The court, after trying unsuccessfully to reorganize the firm, decided that the only recourse was liquidation under Chapter 7. Sale of the fixed assets, which were pledged as collateral to the mortgage bondholders, brought in $400,000, while the current assets were sold for another $200,000. Thus, the total proceeds from the liquidation sale were $600,000. Trustee's costs amounted to $50,000; no single worker was due more than $2,000 in wages; and there were no unfunded pension plan liabilities.

Current assets	$ 400	Accounts payable	$ 50
Net fixed assets	600	Accrued taxes	40
		Accrued wages	30
		Notes payable	180
		Total current liabilities	$ 300
		First mortgage bonds[a]	300
		Second mortgage bonds[a]	200
		Debentures	200
		Subordinated debentures[b]	100
		Common stock	50
		Retained earnings	(150)
Total assets	$1,000	Total claims	$1,000

[a]All fixed assets are pledged as collateral to the mortgage bonds.
[b]Subordinated to notes payable only.

a. How much will McDaniel's shareholders receive from the liquidation?

b. How much will the mortgage bondholders receive?

c. Who are the other priority claimants in addition to the mortgage bondholders? How much will they receive from the liquidation?

d. Who are the remaining general creditors? How much will each receive from the distribution before subordination adjustment? What is the effect of adjusting for subordination?

23-3 (Bankruptcy prediction)   The balance sheet of the McDaniel Mining Company at the time it filed for bankruptcy is given in Problem 23-2. McDaniel's EBIT was $80,000 based on sales of $1,200,000, and its common stock market value was $200,000. Use the Altman multiple discriminant bankruptcy prediction model in answering the following questions.

  a. What does the Altman model predict about the bankruptcy potential of McDaniel Mining?

  b. Is the Altman model more sensitive to some variables than to others?

23-4 (Liquidation)   The following balance sheet represents Boles Electronics Corporation's position at the time it filed for bankruptcy (in thousands of dollars):

Cash	$ 10	Accounts payable	$ 1,600
Receivables	100	Notes payable	500
Inventories	890	Wages payable	150
		Taxes payable	50
Total current assets	$ 1,000	Total current liabilities	$ 2,300
Net plant	4,000	Mortgage bonds	2,000
Net equipment	5,000	Subordinated debentures	2,500
		Preferred stock	1,500
		Common stock	1,700
Total assets	$10,000	Total claims	$10,000

The mortgage bonds are secured by the plant, but not by the equipment. The subordinated debentures are subordinated to notes payable. The firm was unable to reorganize under Chapter 11; therefore, it was liquidated under Chapter 7. The trustee, whose legal and administrative fees amounted to $200,000, sold off the assets and received the following proceeds (in thousands of dollars):

Asset	Proceeds
Plant	$1,600
Equipment	1,300
Receivables	50
Inventories	240
Total	$3,190

In addition, the firm had $10,000 in cash available for distribution. No single wage earner had over $2,000 in claims, and there were no unfunded pension plan liabilities.

  a. What is the total amount available for distribution to all claimants? What is the total of creditor and trustee claims? Will the preferred and common stockholders receive any distributions?

  b. Determine the dollar distribution to each creditor and to the trustee. What percentage of each claim is satisfied?

- -

M I N I
C A S E

Kimberly MacKenzie, president of Kim's Clothes Inc., a medium-sized manufacturer of women's casual clothing, is worried. Her firm has been selling clothes to Russ Brothers Department Store for over ten years, and she has never experienced any problems in collecting payment for the merchandise sold. Currently, Russ Brothers owes Kim's clothes $65,000 for spring sportswear that was delivered to the store just two weeks ago. Kim's concern was

brought about by an article that appeared in yesterday's *Wall Street Journal* that indicated that Russ Brothers was having serious financial problems. Further, the article stated that Russ Brothers' management was considering filing for reorganization, or even liquidation, with a federal bankruptcy court.

Kim's immediate concern was whether or not her firm would collect its receivables if Russ Brothers went bankrupt. In pondering the situation, Kim also realized that she knew nothing about the process that firms go through when they encounter severe financial distress. To learn more about bankruptcy, reorganization, and liquidation, Kim asked Ron Mitchell, the firm's chief financial officer, to prepare a briefing on the subject for the entire board of directors. In turn, Ron asked you, a newly hired financial analyst, to do the groundwork for the briefing by answering the following questions.

a. What are the various levels, or degrees, of financial distress?

b. (1) What are the major causes of business failure?
   (2) Do business failures occur evenly over time?
   (3) Which size of firm, large or small, is more prone to business failure? Why?

c. What key issues must managers face in the financial distress process?

d. What informal remedies are available to firms in financial distress? In answering this question, define the following terms:
   (1) Workout
   (2) Restructuring
   (3) Extension
   (4) Composition
   (5) Assignment
   (6) Assignee (trustee)

e. Briefly describe U.S. bankruptcy law, including the following terms:
   (1) Chapter 11
   (2) Chapter 7
   (3) Trustee
   (4) Voluntary bankruptcy
   (5) Involuntary bankruptcy

f. What are the major differences between an informal reorganization and reorganization in bankruptcy? In answering this question, be sure to discuss the following items:
   (1) Common pool problem
   (2) Holdout problem
   (3) Automatic stay
   (4) Cramdown
   (5) Fraudulent conveyance

g. What is a prepackaged bankruptcy? Why have prepackaged bankruptcies become more popular in recent years?

h. Briefly describe the priority of claims in a Chapter 7 liquidation.

i. Kendrick Products Inc. had the following balance sheet when it was liquidated (in millions of dollars):

Current assets	$40.0	Accounts payable	$10.0
Net fixed assets	5.0	Notes payable (to banks)	5.0
		Accrued wages	0.3
		Federal taxes	0.5
		State and local taxes	0.2
		Current liabilities	$16.0
		First mortgage	$ 3.0
		Second mortgage	0.5
		Subordinated debentures[a]	4.0
		Total long-term debt	$ 7.5
		Preferred stock	$ 1.0
		Common stock	13.0
		Paid-in capital	2.0
		Retained earnings	5.5
		Total equity	$21.5
Total assets	$45.0	Total claims	$45.0

[a]The debentures are subordinated to the notes payable.

The liquidation sale resulted in the following proceeds:

From sale of current assets	$14,000,000
From sale of fixed assets	2,500,000
Total receipts	$16,500,000

For simplicity, assume that there were no trustee's fees or any other claims against the liquidation proceeds. What would each claimant receive from the liquidation distribution?

SELECTED ADDITIONAL REFERENCES AND CASES

For a better understanding of multiple discriminant analysis and its use to predict corporate bankruptcy, see

Collins, Robert A., "An Empirical Comparison of Bankruptcy Prediction Models," *Financial Management,* Summer 1980, 52–57.

Eisenbeis, Robert A., "Pitfalls in the Application of Discriminant Analysis," *Journal of Finance,* June 1977, 875–900.

Joy, O. Maurice, and John O. Tollefson, "On the Financial Application of Discriminant Analysis," *Journal of Financial and Quantitative Analysis,* December 1975, 723–739.

For more information on bankruptcy costs, see

Altman, Edward I., "A Further Empirical Investigation of the Bankruptcy Cost Question," *Journal of Finance,* September 1984, 1067–1089.

Guffey, Daryl M., and William T. Moore, "Direct Bankruptcy Costs: Evidence from the Trucking Industry," *Financial Review,* May 1991, 223–235.

Warner, Jerold B., "Bankruptcy Costs: Some Evidence," *Journal of Finance,* May 1977, 337–347.

In addition to those articles cited in the chapter, the Summer 1991 issue of the Journal of Applied Corporate Finance *contains the following relevant works:*

Fitts, Peter, et al., "Bankruptcies, Workouts, and Turnarounds: A Roundtable Discussion," 34–61.

Gilson, Stuart C., "Managing Default: Some Evidence on How Firms Choose between Workouts and Chapter 11," 62–70.

Weiss, Lawrence A., "The Bankruptcy Code and Violations of Absolute Priority," 71–78.

The following articles and publications provide insights into various aspects of bankruptcy:

Brown, David T., "Claimholder Incentive Conflicts in Reorganization: The Role of Bankruptcy Law," *Review of Financial Studies,* 1989, 109–123.

Business Failure Record (New York: Dun & Bradstreet, Inc., updated annually).

Eberhart, Allan C., William T. Moore, and Rodney Roenfeldt, "Security Pricing and Deviations from the Absolute Priority Rule in Bankruptcy Proceedings," *Journal of Finance,* December 1990, 1457–1469.

Franks, Julian R., and Walter N. Torous, "An Empirical Investigation of U.S. Firms in Reorganization," *Journal of Finance,* July 1989, 747–769.

Harris, Richard, "The Consequences of Costly Default," *Economic Inquiry,* October 1978, 477–496.

The following bankruptcy case can be found in Cases in Financial Management:

Case 39, "Mark X Company (B)," which examines both liquidation and restructuring alternatives for a firm in financial distress.

MERGERS, LBOs, DIVESTITURES, AND HOLDING COMPANIES

T*he deal that created America's newest defense giant began at a resort —the Homestead in Hot Springs, Virginia—during a meeting of the Business Council, a business group composed of senior executives of the nation's top companies. At the meeting, General Electric Chairman Jack Welch approached his old friend, Martin Marietta Chairman Norman Augustine, with a stunning proposal: Why not buy GE's aerospace division?*

Why would GE's chairman suggest such a deal? GE prefers businesses in which it can be one of the market leaders, especially in global markets. Although GE Aerospace was a world leader in technology, it was not in a position to dominate the defense electronics market. Furthermore, cutbacks in defense spending, especially in the United States, meant that business would be sagging and that an industry consolidation was inevitable. Sale of the subsidiary would provide immediate cash to GE, which could then acquire nondefense assets that troubled companies were eager to dump.

For Martin Marietta, the acquisition would cement its position as one of the top players in the industry. Electronics, which is Martin's primary business, appears to be the safest place for defense contractors. As the armed services shrink and buy fewer ships, tanks, and planes, it will be even more important for them to have a large arsenal of "smart" weapons systems along with the latest surveillance, command-and-control, and computer systems. GE Aerospace was a perfect complement for Martin Marietta: GE Aerospace was a major supplier to the Navy, while Martin dealt mainly with the Army, and GE Aerospace built satellites, while Martin made rockets; the companies combined could supply the

entire system. "There's very little overlap between the two companies," said a defense analyst. "Its almost like two pieces of a jigsaw puzzle."

Often, mergers fail because the two corporate cultures cannot be blended into one, well-functioning team. It appeared that there would be little problem in this regard for GE and Martin; both companies were run by engineers and both had strong reputations for financial discipline.

Intrigued by the offer, Martin's Augustine and GE's Welsh met to thrash out the details. On November 22, 1992, they announced the deal that made Martin Marietta the world's largest maker of defense electronics. Martin agreed to pay about $3 billion for GE Aerospace, including $1.25 billion in cash, $1 billion in convertible preferred stock (which could give GE as much as 23 percent ownership of Martin), and $750 million of debt assumptions. The market loved the deal; both companies' stocks jumped when the sale was announced.

Martin now faces some big challenges. Its debt-to-capital ratio was boosted from 27 to 46 percent by the deal, and successfully merging large enterprises is always a difficult task, even when the cultures are similar. Still, even with defense budgets shrinking, the Pentagon spends $100 billion a year on research and procurement. "Weaker companies will shrink and sink," concedes Augustine. But he adds, "There is room for strong survivors," and he bet that Martin Marietta will be one of them.

The acquisition of GE Aerospace by Martin Marietta poses many interesting questions. For example, why do companies acquire other companies? How are deals valued? And what is the best way to structure a takeover bid? After reading this chapter, you will have an understanding of these issues, as well as many others that pertain to mergers and acquisitions.

Most of the growth in corporations occurs through *internal expansion,* which takes place when the firm's existing divisions grow through normal capital budgeting activities. However, the most dramatic examples of growth, and often the largest increases in firms' stock prices, are the result of *mergers,* the first topic covered in this chapter. *Leveraged buyouts,* or *LBOs,* occur when a firm's stock is acquired by a small group of investors rather than by another operating company. Since LBOs are similar in many respects to mergers, they are also covered in this chapter. The conditions of corporate life do change over time, and, as a result, firms often find it desirable to *divest,* or sell off, major divisions to other firms that can better utilize the divested assets. Divestitures are also discussed in the chapter. Finally, we discuss the *holding company* form of organization, wherein one corporation owns the stock of one or more other companies.

Rationale for Mergers

Many reasons have been proposed by both financial managers and theorists to account for the high level of merger activity in the United States. In this section, we present some of the motives behind corporate mergers.[1]

Synergy

The primary motivation for most mergers is to increase the value of the combined enterprise. If Companies A and B merge to form Company C, and if C's value exceeds that of A and B taken separately, then *synergy* is said to exist. Such a merger should be beneficial to both A's and B's stockholders.[2] Synergistic effects can arise from four sources: (1) *operating economies,* which result from economies of scale in management, marketing, production, or distribution; (2) *financial economies,* including lower transactions costs and better coverage by security analysts; (3) *differential efficiency,* which implies that the management of one firm is inefficient, and that the firm's assets will be more productive after the merger; and (4) *increased market power* due to reduced competition. Operating and financial economies are socially desirable, as are mergers that increase managerial efficiency, but mergers that reduce competition are both undesirable and illegal.[3]

Tax Considerations

Tax considerations have stimulated a number of mergers. For example, a firm which is highly profitable and is therefore in the highest corporate tax bracket could acquire a firm with large accumulated tax losses. These losses could then be turned into immediate tax savings rather than carried forward and presumably used in the future.[4] Also, mergers can provide an outlet for excess cash. If a firm

---

[1]As we use the term, *merger* means any combination that forms one economic unit from two or more previous ones. For legal purposes, there are distinctions among the various ways these combinations can occur, but our focus is on the fundamental business and financial aspects of mergers.

[2]If synergy exists, then the whole is greater than the sum of the parts. Synergy is also called the "2 plus 2 equals 5 effect." The distribution of the synergistic gain between A's and B's stockholders is determined by negotiation. This point is discussed later in the chapter.

[3]In the 1880s and 1890s, many mergers occurred in the United States, and some of them were rather obviously directed toward gaining market power rather than increasing operating efficiency. As a result, Congress passed a series of acts designed to ensure that mergers are not used as a method of reducing competition. The principal acts include the Sherman Act (1890), the Clayton Act (1914), and the Celler Act (1950). These acts make it illegal for firms to combine in any manner if the combination tends to lessen competition. The acts are enforced by the antitrust division of the Justice Department and by the Federal Trade Commission.

[4]Mergers undertaken only to use accumulated tax losses would probably be challenged by the IRS. However, because many factors are present in any given merger, it is hard to prove that a merger was motivated only, or even primarily, by tax considerations.

has a shortage of internal investment opportunities compared with its cash flow, it could (1) pay an extra dividend, (2) invest in marketable securities, (3) repurchase its own stock, or (4) purchase another firm. If the firm pays an extra dividend, the stockholders would have to pay immediate taxes on the distribution. Marketable securities often provide a good temporary parking place for money, but generally the rate of return on such securities is less than that required by stockholders. A stock repurchase would result in a capital gain for the remaining stockholders, but (1) a repurchase might push up the firm's stock price to a level which is temporarily above the equilibrium price, so the company would have to pay too much for the repurchased shares, which would be disadvantageous to remaining stockholders, and (2) a repurchase designed solely to avoid dividend payment might be challenged by the IRS. However, using surplus cash to acquire another firm has no immediate tax consequences to the acquiring firm or its stockholders, and this fact has motivated a number of mergers.

PURCHASE OF ASSETS BELOW THEIR REPLACEMENT COST

Sometimes a firm will be touted as a possible acquisition candidate because the cost of replacing its assets is considerably higher than its market value. For example, in the early 1980s oil companies could acquire reserves cheaper by buying other oil companies than by doing exploratory drilling. Thus, Chevron Corporation acquired Gulf Oil in order to augment its reserves. Similarly, steel companies have stated that it is cheaper to buy an existing steel company than to construct a new mill, and LTV (the fourth largest steel company) acquired Republic Steel (the sixth largest) for $700 million in a merger that created the second largest firm in the industry.

At the time the LTV-Republic merger was announced, Republic was selling for less than one-third of its book value. However, the market value of any firm should be based on its earning power, which sets the economic value of its assets. If a firm is fairly valued (that is, if markets are efficient), then its market value, rather than book value, will reflect the economic value of its assets. The real questions, then, were these: Could LTV operate the merged company more efficiently than the two companies had been operating before the merger, or could LTV break up Republic and sell its assets to other producers which could operate them more efficiently? LTV argued that sufficient economies of scale existed to make the merger synergistic. The least efficient plants of both companies would be closed; plants that make similar products (say, sheet steel for autos or oil drilling pipe) would be consolidated, and distribution systems would be integrated. If these moves resulted in sizable cost savings, then the merger could be successful. Otherwise, the fact that LTV bought Republic's assets at below their replacement value would be immaterial. The merger appears to have done little for LTV—it has consistently reported losses since the merger, and ultimately it filed for protection from its creditors under Chapter 11 of the Bankruptcy Act.

DIVERSIFICATION

Managers often claim that diversification into other lines of business is a reason for mergers. They contend that diversification helps to stabilize the firm's earnings stream and thus benefits its owners. Stabilization of earnings is certainly beneficial to employees, suppliers, and customers, but its value is less certain from the standpoint of stockholders. If a stockholder is worried about the variability of a firm's earnings, he or she could diversify more easily than could the firm. Why should Firms A and B merge to stabilize earnings when a stockholder in Firm A could sell half of his or her stock in A and use the proceeds to purchase stock in Firm B? Stockholders can create diversification more easily than can the firm.

Of course, if you were the owner-manager of a closely held firm, it might be nearly impossible for you to sell part of your stock to diversify, because this would dilute your ownership and perhaps also generate a large capital gains tax liability. In this case, a diversification merger might well be the best way to achieve personal diversification.

We can use option pricing theory to gain some insights into the ways stockholders and debtholders are affected by mergers. In Chapter 22 we discussed the application of option pricing theory to corporate decisions. If we view stock ownership as a call option, then the value of the stock is increased by an increase in earnings variability, but lowered by a decrease in variability. Assume that two firms have the same variability of earnings. If these two firms merge, and their earnings are not perfectly positively correlated, then the earnings of the combined firm will have less variability than the premerger earnings of the separate firms. This decrease in earnings variability would, according to option theory, lower the value of the combined firm's equity. Conversely, the value of the debt would increase, because the probability of default would lessen. According to option theory, using mergers for diversification results in a transfer of wealth from stockholders to debtholders, leaving the total value of the combined firm equal to the sum of the premerger values, assuming no synergistic effects.

However, it is possible for the stockholders to avoid these theoretical losses by financing the merger with debt, or to recoup them by issuing additional debt based on the increased debt capacity of the combined firm, and then using the proceeds to repurchase equity. Also, note that this result depends on the CAPM assumption that only market risk is relevant to stockholders, and that operating income stability has no beneficial effects for shareholders. To the extent that these assumptions are not correct, then corporate diversification could benefit stockholders.

MANAGERS' PERSONAL INCENTIVES

Financial economists like to think that business decisions are based only on economic considerations. However, there can be no question that some business decisions are based more on managers' personal motivations than on economic analyses. Many people, business leaders included, like power, and more power is

attached to running a larger corporation than a smaller one. Obviously, no executive would ever admit that his or her ego was the primary reason behind a series of mergers, but knowledgeable observers are convinced that egos do play a prominent role in many mergers.

It has also been observed that executive salaries are highly correlated with company size—the bigger the company, the higher the salaries of its top officers. This too could play a role in the aggressive acquisition programs of some corporations.

In recent years many hostile takeovers have occurred, and the managers of the target companies generally lost their jobs, or at least their autonomy. Therefore, managers who own less than 51 percent of the stock in their firms look to devices that will lessen the chances of their firms' being taken over. Mergers can serve as such a device. For example, when Enron was under attack, it arranged to buy Houston Natural Gas Company, paying for Houston primarily with debt. That merger made Enron much larger, hence harder for any potential acquirer to "digest." Also, the much higher debt level resulting from the merger made it harder for any acquiring company to use debt to buy Enron. Such *defensive mergers* are hard to defend on economic grounds. The managers involved invariably argue that synergy, not a desire to protect their own jobs, motivated the acquisition, but there can be no question that many mergers today are indeed designed more for the benefit of managers than for that of stockholders.

Managers' personal incentives as a basis for mergers constitute another example of the agency problem. Of course, there is nothing wrong with executives feeling good about increasing the size of their firms, or with their getting paid a higher salary as a result of growth through mergers—provided the mergers make economic sense from the stockholders' viewpoint. There have been quite a few stockholder suits against managers who resisted hostile takeovers. Perhaps there should be a few such suits against managers who paid too high a price for target companies, hence diluted the wealth of their own shareholders.

Breakup Value

Firms can be valued in many ways, such as by book value, economic value, or replacement value. Recently, analysts and takeover specialists have begun to recognize *breakup value* as another basis for valuation. It is now common for analysts to estimate a company's breakup value, and sometimes this value is higher than the firm's current market value. If this situation holds, then a takeover specialist could acquire the firm at or even somewhat above its current market value, sell it off in pieces, and earn a substantial profit.

The breakup rationale for mergers is surrounded by controversy. If a firm's assets can be employed more efficiently when split up and sold to other firms that could gain some type of synergy, including better management, then there is economic justification for such actions. However, the breakup of companies is often associated with the closings of headquarters and plants, the loss of jobs, and a resulting economic disruption to employees, suppliers, customers, and even entire

communities. Although all of this has some economic cost, the cost is not borne by the shareholders who must make the decision on whether or not to sell the company for breakup. If one takes an altruistic view, breakups should only occur when the economic gains outweigh the economic losses. However, the gains can be measured relatively easily whereas the costs are much more elusive.

SELF-TEST QUESTIONS

Define synergy. Is synergy a valid rationale for mergers? Describe several situations that might produce synergistic gains.

Give two examples of how tax considerations can motivate mergers.

Suppose your firm could purchase another firm for only half of its replacement value. Would this be sufficient justification for the acquisition?

Discuss the merits of diversification as a rationale for mergers.

Can managers' personal incentives motivate mergers? Explain.

What is breakup value? Discuss the pros and cons of breakup-motivated acquisitions.

TYPES OF MERGERS

Economists classify mergers into four groups: (1) horizontal, (2) vertical, (3) congeneric, and (4) conglomerate. A *horizontal merger* occurs when one firm combines with another in its same line of business—for example, when one widget manufacturer acquires another, or one retail food chain merges with a second. The merger of Burroughs and Sperry to form Unisys was a horizontal merger, because both firms manufactured computers and electronics products. An example of a *vertical merger* is a steel producer's acquisition of one of its own suppliers, such as an iron or coal mining firm, or an oil producer's acquisition of a petrochemical firm which uses oil as a raw material. *Congeneric* means "allied in nature or action"; hence, a *congeneric merger* involves related enterprises but not producers of the same product (horizontal) or firms in a producer-supplier relationship (vertical). Examples of congeneric mergers would be American Express's takeover of Shearson Hammill, a stock brokerage firm, or Philip Morris's acquisition of General Foods and Kraft. A *conglomerate merger* occurs when unrelated enterprises combine, as illustrated by Mobil Oil's acquisition of Montgomery Ward.

Operating economies (and also anticompetitive effects) are at least partially dependent on the type of merger involved. Vertical and horizontal mergers generally provide the greatest synergistic operating benefits, but they are also the ones most likely to be attacked by the U.S. Department of Justice as anticompetitive. In any event, it is useful to think of these economic classifications when analyzing the feasibility of a prospective merger.

SELF-TEST QUESTIONS

What are the four economic classifications of mergers?

Briefly describe the characteristics of each type of merger.

LEVEL OF MERGER ACTIVITY

Four major "merger waves" have occurred in the United States. The first was in the late 1800s, when consolidations occurred in the oil, steel, tobacco, and other basic industries. The second was in the 1920s, when the stock market boom helped financial promoters consolidate firms in a number of industries, including utilities, communications, and autos. The third was in the 1960s, when conglomerate mergers were the rage. The fourth occurred in the 1980s.

The "merger mania" of the 1980s was sparked by seven factors: (1) the relatively depressed condition of the stock market at the beginning of the decade (for example, the Dow Jones Industrial Index in early 1982 was below its 1968 level); (2) the unprecedented level of inflation that existed during the 1970s and early 1980s, which increased the replacement value of firms' assets even while a weak stock market reduced their market values; (3) the Reagan administration's stated view that "bigness is not necessarily badness," which resulted in a more tolerant attitude toward large mergers; (4) the general belief among the major natural resource companies that it was cheaper to "buy reserves on Wall Street" through mergers than to explore and find them in the field; (5) the development of an active junk bond market, which helped raiders obtain the capital needed to make tender offers for target firms; (6) attempts to ward off raiders by use of defensive mergers; and (7) the decline of the dollar, which made U.S. firms relatively cheap for foreign firms to acquire, combined with huge U.S. trade deficits, which gave foreign firms large pools of funds to invest in the United States.

As seen in Table 24-1, the 1980s witnessed some huge mergers.[5] This wave had its share of successes, such as the General Electric/RCA and Quaker Oats/Stokely-Van Camp mergers, as well as its share of failures, such as the LTV/Republic Steel and Pan Am/National Airlines mergers. Although merger activity has fallen off significantly in the 1990s, the merger wave of the 1980s will likely spawn a great deal of financial activity throughout the current decade, when many companies will be forced to reduce the debt burdens of past mergers and others will shed acquisitions that, for one reason or another, have just not worked out.

---

[5]For detailed reviews of the 1980s merger wave, see Andrei Shleifer and Robert W. Vishny, "The Takeover Wave of the 1980s," *Journal of Applied Corporate Finance,* Fall 1991, 49–56; Edmund Faltermayer, "The Deal Decade: Verdict on the '80s," *Fortune,* August 26, 1991, 58–70; and "The Best and Worst Deals of the '80s: What We Learned from All Those Mergers, Acquisitions, and Takeovers," *Business Week,* January 15, 1990, 52–57.

TABLE 24-1 THE FIVE BIGGEST MERGERS (BILLIONS OF DOLLARS)	Company	Year	Value	Premium Paid over Book Value	Type of Transaction
	Chevron-Gulf	1984	$13.3	136%	Acquisition for cash
	Philip Morris-Kraft	1988	12.9	609	Acquisition for cash
	Bristol-Meyers-Squibb	1989	12.7	852	Acquisition for common stock
	Texaco-Getty	1984	10.1	191	Acquisition for cash and notes
	Beecham Group-Smithkline Beckman	1989	8.3	519	Merger by exchange of stock

SELF-TEST QUESTIONS

What are the four major "merger waves" that have occurred in the United States?

What are some reasons for the 1980s wave?

HOSTILE VERSUS FRIENDLY TAKEOVERS

In the vast majority of merger situations, one firm (generally the larger of the two) simply decides to buy another company, negotiates a price with the management of the target firm, and then acquires the target company. Occasionally, the acquired firm will initiate the action, but it is much more common for a firm to seek acquisitions than to seek to be acquired.[6] Following convention, we shall call a company that seeks to acquire another the *acquiring company* and the one which it seeks to acquire the *target company.*

Once an acquiring company has identified a possible target, it must (1) establish a suitable price, or range of prices, and (2) tentatively set the terms of payment—will it offer cash, its own common stock, bonds, or a mix of securities? Next, the acquiring firm's managers must decide how to approach the target company's managers. If the acquiring firm has reason to believe that the target's management will approve the merger, then it will simply propose a merger and try to work out some suitable terms. If an agreement is reached, then the two management groups will issue statements to their stockholders indicating that they approve the merger, and the target firm's management will recommend to its stockholders that they agree to the merger. Generally, the stockholders are asked to

---

[6]However, if a firm is in financial difficulty, if its managers are elderly and do not think that suitable replacements are on hand, or if it needs the support (often the capital) of a larger company, then it may seek to be acquired. Thus, when a number of Texas, Ohio, and Maryland financial institutions were in trouble in the 1980s, they lobbied to get their state legislatures to pass laws that would make it easier for them to be acquired. Out-of-state banks then moved in to help salvage the situation and minimize depositor losses.

tender (or send in) their shares to a designated financial institution, along with a signed power of attorney which transfers ownership of the shares to the acquiring firm. The target firm's stockholders then receive the specified payment, be it common stock of the acquiring company (in which case the target company's stockholders become stockholders of the acquiring company), cash, bonds, or some mix of cash and securities. This is a *friendly merger,* or a *friendly tender offer.*

The acquisition of RCA by General Electric typifies a friendly merger. First, the boards of directors of the two firms announced that RCA had agreed to be acquired by GE in an all-cash transaction for $66.50 a share. The merger was approved by shareholders, by the Federal Communications Commission, and by the Justice Department, and then the acquisition was completed. Another example of a friendly merger is Federal Express's acquisition of Tiger International, an air freight carrier.

Often, however, the target company's management resists the merger. Perhaps the managers feel that the price offered for the stock is too low, or perhaps they simply want to keep their jobs. In either case, the acquiring firm's offer is said to be *hostile* rather than friendly, and the acquiring firm must make a direct appeal to the target firm's stockholders. In a hostile merger, the acquiring company will again make a tender offer, and again it will ask the stockholders of the target firm to tender their shares in exchange for the offered price. This time, though, the target firm's managers will urge stockholders not to tender their shares, generally stating that the price offered (cash, bonds, or stocks in the acquiring firm) is too low.

The recent battle between Shamrock Holdings and Polaroid illustrates a failed hostile merger attempt. It began in the summer of 1988, when Polaroid's stock was trading in the low $30s. At the time, many analysts had declared that Polaroid was a likely takeover candidate because of its sluggish performance but strong brand name. Also, Polaroid was expected to receive a substantial settlement from its successful suit against Eastman Kodak, which had been found guilty of violating Polaroid's instant camera patents.

Then, Shamrock Holdings, the investment vehicle of the Roy E. Disney family, proposed a friendly takeover, was rebuffed, and made a $45-per-share hostile tender offer. Polaroid responded to the unwanted offer (1) by selling a chunk of its stock to a newly established employee stock ownership plan (ESOP), (2) by selling another chunk to a friendly investor (a *white squire*), and (3) by buying back 22 percent of its outstanding shares at $50 a share. To finance all of this, Polaroid added $536 million in bank debt. Additionally, Polaroid restructured its operations by cutting its work force by 15 percent through a voluntary program of early retirements. Shamrock responded to these actions (1) by initiating a proxy fight to elect a new slate of officers at Polaroid and (2) by filing a court suit challenging the legitimacy of Polaroid's defensive maneuvers.

After nine months of heated exchanges between the companies, an accord was reached in March 1989. Polaroid agreed to pay Shamrock $20 million in compensation for expenses incurred in the battle, and Shamrock signed an agreement promising not to seek control of Polaroid for ten years. Also, Polaroid agreed to spend $5 million in advertising on Shamrock's radio and television stations, and to

distribute to shareholders anywhere between 25 and 50 percent of its pending award from Kodak, depending on the amount of the award. Finally, Shamrock agreed to drop all litigation, as well as its proxy fight. Although defeated, Shamrock ended up making about $35 million before taxes, considering both the cash settlement and the Polaroid shares that it owns. Stanley P. Gold, Shamrock's president, said that the decision to settle was sealed by Delaware court decisions upholding Polaroid's defenses. "It isn't that I went away quietly; I tried as hard as I could," he said. Polaroid ended up with more debt, although it still has a strong balance sheet, and a $36-per-share stock price. Polaroid's president and CEO, I. MacAllister Booth, said "The fundamental changes and initiatives put in place during this period made us stronger, despite the pressure."

The 1988 battle between Campeau Corporation and Federated Department Stores provides a good illustration of a hostile takeover that succeeded—in a sense. On January 25, Campeau, a Toronto-based real estate and department store company which owned such stores as Jordan Marsh, Maas Brothers, Ann Taylor, and Brooks Brothers, made a hostile $47-a-share offer for Federated Department Stores, a Cincinnati-based company that owned Bloomingdale's, Bullock's, Burdine's, Filene's, and I. Magnin, among others. At the same time, Campeau filed suit in a New York federal court challenging Federated's "poison pill" defense, which would allow Federated's shareholders to purchase Campeau's shares at a bargain price should a hostile takeover take place. While waiting for a response from Federated's board, Campeau attempted to coax Federated into a friendly merger by increasing its bid to $61 a share. On February 16, Federated's board rejected the offer, and it also announced that it was weighing various restructuring alternatives.

Under pressure from its shareholders, Federated tentatively accepted Campeau's improved $68-a-share offer on February 29, but this agreement was derailed when R. H. Macy, the large New York–based retailer, made a last-minute bid of $73.80 per share for Federated. On March 2, Federated agreed to be acquired by Macy, but the offer consisted of both cash and securities, and many of Federated's stockholders, who were now dominated by institutional arbitrageurs, were unhappy with the deal. This kept Campeau's interest in Federated alive, even though the Macy deal contained provisions that would make it costly for Federated to back out. Specifically, Federated would be required to pay Macy up to $45 million for expenses incurred in the merger attempt, plus some other penalties. On March 18, the New York court upheld Federated's poison pill, which forced Campeau to seek a friendly merger rather than pushing forward with its hostile tender offer.

During the remainder of March, both Macy and Campeau sweetened their bids, culminating with a $74-a-share all-cash bid from Campeau and a $75.14-a-share cash bid from Macy. Finally, on April 1, Federated agreed to be acquired by Campeau for $74 a share. Macy dropped its bid in return for the right to buy I. Magnin and part of Bullock's for $1.1 billion plus a $60 million payment from Campeau for expenses incurred in the battle. By winning the battle, Robert Campeau, the dynamic head of Campeau Corporation, became the new king of American department stores. However, he had to pay top dollar to do it, and he had to finance the takeover with high-cost junk bonds. The win was costly, for Campeau was unable to meet the debt payments in the relatively slow economy that has been especially

tough on department stores. After struggling through most of 1989, Campeau was forced to declare bankruptcy in early 1990.

The Campeau-Federated battle demonstrates that a resolved buyer, with access to cash and the will to go as high as needed, will usually prevail in a hostile takeover. However, bids that are too high, and that are financed with debt, may spell disaster for the acquiring firm.

Self-Test Questions

What is the difference between a hostile and a friendly merger?

Describe the mechanics of a typical friendly takeover and of a typical hostile takeover.

Merger Regulation

Prior to the mid-1960s, friendly acquisitions generally took place through simple exchange-of-stock mergers, and a proxy fight was the primary weapon used in a hostile control battle. However, in the mid-1960s, corporate raiders began to operate differently. First, they noted that it took a long time to mount a proxy fight — they had to first request a list of the target company's stockholders, be refused, and then get a court order forcing management to turn over the list. During that time, management could think through and then implement a strategy to fend off the raider. As a result, the instigator lost most proxy fights.

Then raiders began saying to themselves, "If we could take an action that would bring the decision to a head quickly, before management could take countermeasures, that would greatly increase the probability of a successful takeover." That led the raiders to turn from proxy fights to tender offers, which had a much shorter response time. For example, the stockholders of a company whose stock was selling for $20 might be offered $27 per share and be given two weeks to accept. The raider, meanwhile, would have accumulated a substantial block of the shares in open market purchases, and additional shares might have been purchased by institutional friends of the raider, who promised to tender their shares in exchange for the tip that a raid was to occur.

Faced with a well-planned raid, managements were generally overwhelmed. The stock might actually still be undervalued at the offered price, but management simply did not have time to get this message across to stockholders, or to find a friendly competing bidder (called a *white knight*), or anything else. This situation was thought to be unfair, and, as a result, Congress passed the Williams Act in 1968. This law had two main objectives: (1) to regulate the way in which acquiring firms can structure takeover offers and (2) to force acquiring firms to disclose more information about their offers. Basically, Congress wanted to put target managements in a better position to defend against hostile offers. Additionally, Congress believed that shareholders needed easy access to information about tender offers — including information on any securities that might be offered in lieu of cash — in order to make rational tender-versus-don't-tender decisions.

The Williams Act placed the following three major restrictions on the activities of acquiring firms: (1) Acquirers must disclose their current holdings and future intentions within 10 days of amassing at least 5 percent of a company's stock, and they must disclose the source of the funds to be used in the acquisition. (2) The target firm's shareholders must be allowed at least 20 days to tender their shares; that is, the offer must be "open" for at least 20 days. (3) If the acquiring firm increases the offer price during the 20-day open period, all shareholders who tendered prior to the new offer must receive the higher price. In total, these restrictions were intended to reduce the ability of the acquiring firm to surprise management and to stampede target shareholders into accepting the offer. Prior to the Williams Act, offers were generally made on a first-come, first-served basis, and they were often accompanied by an implicit threat to lower the bid price after 50 percent of the shares were in hand. The legislation also gave target managements more time to mount a defense, and it gave rival bidders and white knights a chance to enter the fray and thus help a target's stockholders obtain a better price.

Many states have also passed laws designed to protect firms in their states from hostile takeovers. At first, these laws focused on disclosure requirements, but by the late 1970s, several states had enacted takeover statutes so restrictive that they virtually precluded hostile takeovers. In 1979, when MITE Corporation, a Delaware firm, made a hostile tender offer for Chicago Rivet and Machine Co., a publicly held Illinois corporation, Chicago Rivet sought protection under the Illinois Business Takeover Act. The constitutionality of the Illinois act was contested, and the U.S. Supreme Court found the law unconstitutional. The court ruled that the Illinois law put undue burdens on interstate commerce. The opinion also stated that the market for securities is a national market, and even though the issuing firm was incorporated in Illinois, the State of Illinois could not regulate interstate securities transactions.

The Illinois decision effectively eliminated the first generation of state merger regulations. However, the states kept trying to protect their state-headquartered companies, and in 1987 the U.S. Supreme Court upheld an Indiana law which radically changed the rules of the takeover game. Specifically, the Indiana law first defined "control shares" as enough shares to give an investor 20 percent of the vote, and it went on to state that when an investor buys control shares, those shares can be voted only after approval by a majority of "disinterested shareholders," defined as those who are neither officers nor inside directors of the company, nor associates of the raider. The law also gives the buyer of control shares the right to insist that a shareholders' meeting be called within 50 days to decide whether the shares may be voted. The Indiana law dealt a major blow to raiders, mainly because it slows down the action. Delaware (the state in which most large companies are incorporated) later passed a similar bill, and so did New York and a number of other important states.

The new state laws also have some features which protect target stockholders from their own managers. Included are limits on the use of golden parachutes, onerous debt-financing plans, and some types of poison pills. Since these laws do not regulate tender offers per se, but, rather, govern the practices of firms in the state, they have, at least up to this point, withstood all legal challenges.

SELF-TEST QUESTIONS

Is there a need to regulate mergers? Explain.

Do the states play a role in merger regulation, or is it all done at the national level?

MERGER ANALYSIS

In theory, merger analysis is quite simple. The acquiring firm simply performs a capital budgeting analysis to determine whether the present value of the incremental cash flows expected to result from the merger exceeds the price that must be paid for the target company; if the net present value is positive, the acquiring firm should begin the acquisition process. The target company's stockholders, on the other hand, should accept the proposal if the price offered exceeds the present value of the expected future cash flows that would result if it continued to operate independently. Theory aside, however, some difficult issues are involved: (1) the acquiring company must estimate the cash flows that will result from the acquisition; (2) it must also determine what effect, if any, the merger will have on its own required rate of return on equity; (3) it must decide how to pay for the merger—with cash, its own stock, or some other type or package of securities; and (4) having estimated the benefits of the merger, the acquiring and target firms' managers and stockholders must bargain (or fight) over how to share these benefits.

OPERATING VERSUS FINANCIAL MERGERS

From the standpoint of financial analysis, there are two basic types of mergers, operating mergers and financial mergers.

1. An *operating merger* is one in which the operations of two companies are integrated with the expectation of obtaining synergistic effects. To illustrate, Texas Air's 1987 acquisition of People Express resulted in People's planes being repainted and incorporated into Texas Air's Continental Airlines subsidiary.

2. A pure *financial merger* is one in which the merged companies will not be operated as a single unit and from which no significant operating economies are expected. Coca-Cola's acquisition of Columbia Pictures with $748 million of surplus cash is an example of a financial merger.

Of course, mergers may actually combine these two features. For example, some of RCA's electronics and defense operations were merged with similar GE businesses, but other operations, such as RCA's NBC television network, have been maintained as separate lines of business.

VALUING THE TARGET FIRM

To determine the value of the target firm, two key items are needed: (1) a set of pro forma statements which develop the incremental cash flows expected from

TABLE 24-2		1994	1995	1996	1997	1998
HIGHTECH	1. Net sales	$105.0	$126.0	$151.0	$174.0	$191.0
CORPORATION:	2. Cost of goods sold	80.0	94.0	111.0	127.0	137.0
PROJECTED	3. Selling and administrative expenses	10.0	12.0	13.0	15.0	16.0
POSTMERGER CASH	4. Depreciation	8.0	8.0	9.0	9.0	10.0
FLOW STATEMENTS	5. EBIT	$ 7.0	$ 12.0	$ 18.0	$ 23.0	$ 28.0
FOR THE APEX	6. Interest[a]	3.0	4.0	5.0	6.0	6.0
SUBSIDIARY AS OF	7. EBT	$ 4.0	$ 8.0	$ 13.0	$ 17.0	$22.0
DECEMBER 31	8. Taxes[b] (40%)	1.6	3.2	5.2	6.8	8.8
(MILLIONS OF	9. Net income	$ 2.4	$ 4.8	$ 7.8	$ 10.2	$ 13.2
DOLLARS)	10. Plus depreciation	8.0	8.0	9.0	9.0	10.0
	11. Cash flow	$ 10.4	$ 12.8	$ 16.8	$ 19.2	$ 23.2
	12. Less retentions[c]	4.0	4.0	7.0	9.0	12.0
	13. Plus terminal value[d]					150.2
	14. Net cash flow to Hightech[e]	$ 6.4	$ 8.8	$ 9.8	$ 10.2	$161.4

[a]Interest payments are estimates based on Apex's existing debt plus additional debt required to increase the debt ratio to 50 percent, plus additional debt required after the merger to finance asset expansion while maintaining the 50 percent target capital structure.

[b]Hightech will file a consolidated tax return after the merger. Thus, the taxes shown here are the full corporate taxes attributable to Apex's operations: there will be no additional taxes on any cash flows passed from Apex to Hightech.

[c]Some of the cash flow generated by the Apex subsidiary after the merger will be retained to finance Apex's own asset replacement and growth, while some will be transferred to Hightech to pay dividends on its stock or for redeployment within the corporation.

[d]Apex's available cash flows are expected to grow at a constant 10 percent rate after 1998. The value of all post-1998 cash flows as of December 31, 1998, is estimated by use of the constant growth model to be $150.2 million:

$$V_{1998} = \frac{(\$23.2 - \$12.0)(1.10)}{0.182 - 0.10} = \$150.2 \text{ million.}$$

In the next section, we discuss the estimation of the 18.2 percent cost of equity. The $150.2 million is the PV at the end of 1998 of the stream of cash flows for years 1999 and thereafter.

[e]These are the net cash flows projected to be available to Hightech by virtue of the acquisition of Apex. These cash flows could be used for dividend payments to Hightech's stockholders, to finance asset expansion in Hightech's other divisions and subsidiaries, and so on.

the merger and (2) a discount rate, or cost of capital, to apply to these projected cash flows.

Pro Forma Cash Flow Statements. The development of accurate postmerger cash flow forecasts is the most important step in a merger analysis. In a pure financial merger, the incremental postmerger cash flows are simply the expected cash flows of the target firm if it were to continue to operate independently. However, if the two firms' operations are to be integrated, or if the acquiring firm plans to change the target firm's operations in order to get better results, then forecasting future cash flows is a more complex task.

Table 24-2 shows the projected cash flow statements for Apex Corporation, which is being considered as a target by Hightech, a large conglomerate. The projected data are for the postmerger period, so all synergistic effects have been included. Apex currently uses 30 percent debt, but if it were acquired, Hightech

would increase Apex's debt ratio to 50 percent. Both Hightech and Apex have 40 percent marginal federal-plus-state tax rates.

Lines 1 through 4 of Table 24-2 contain the operating and depreciation cash flows that Hightech expects will occur in the Apex subsidiary if the merger takes place, and Line 5 contains the earnings before interest and taxes (EBIT) for each year. Unlike a typical capital budgeting analysis, merger analyses usually incorporate interest expense in the cash flow forecast, which is shown on Line 6. This is done for three reasons: (1) acquiring firms often assume the debt of the target firm, so old debt having different coupon rates is often part of the deal, (2) the acquisition is often partially financed by debt, and (3) if the subsidiary is expected to grow in the future, new debt will have to be issued over time to support the expansion. Thus, debt associated with a merger is typically much more complex than the single issue of new debt associated with a normal capital project, and the easiest way to properly account for the complexities of merger debt is to specifically include each year's expected interest expense in the cash flow forecast. In essence, we are using the *equity residual method* to value the target firm, as the estimated net cash flows will belong solely to the acquiring firm's shareholders.

Line 7 contains the earnings before taxes (EBT), and Line 8 lists the taxes based on Hightech's 40 percent marginal rate. Line 9 lists each year's net income, but depreciation is added back in Line 10 to obtain each year's cash flow, which is shown on Line 11. Since some of Apex's assets are expected to wear out or become obsolete, and since Hightech plans to expand the Apex subsidiary should the acquisition occur, some equity funds must be retained and reinvested in the subsidiary. These retentions, which are not available for transfer from Apex to the parent, are shown on Line 12. Finally, we have projected only five years of cash flows, but Hightech would likely operate the Apex subsidiary for many years, perhaps 20 or 30 or more. We applied the constant growth model to the 1998 cash flow to estimate the value of all cash flows beyond 1998. (See Note d to Table 24-2.) This "terminal value" of the Apex subsidiary, which represents its market value at the end of 1998, is shown on Line 13.

The net cash flows shown on Line 14 are the flows that would be available to Hightech's stockholders, and these are the basis of the valuation.[7] Of course, the postmerger cash flows attributable to the target firm are extremely difficult to estimate, and in a complete merger valuation, just as in a complete capital budgeting analysis, the component cash flow probability distributions should be specified, and sensitivity, scenario, and simulation analyses should be conducted. Indeed, in a friendly merger, the acquiring firm would send a team consisting of literally dozens of accountants, engineers, and so forth, to the target firm's headquarters to go over its books, to estimate required maintenance expenditures, to set values on assets such as real estate and petroleum reserves, and the like.

---

[7]We purposely kept the cash flows relatively simple to help focus on the key issues of the valuation process. In an actual merger valuation, the cash flows would be much more complex, normally including such items as additional capital furnished by the acquiring firm, tax loss carry-forwards, tax effects of plant and equipment valuation adjustments, and cash flows from the sale of some of the subsidiary's assets.

Estimating the Discount Rate. The bottom-line net cash flows shown in Table 24-2 belong to Hightech's stockholders, so they should be discounted at the cost of equity rather than at the company's overall cost of capital. Further, the cost of equity used must reflect the riskiness of the net cash flows in the table, hence the appropriate discount rate is Apex's cost of equity, not that of either Hightech or the consolidated postmerger firm.

Although we will not illustrate it here, Hightech would perform a risk analysis on the Table 24-2 cash flows just as it does on any set of capital budgeting flows. Generally, scenario analysis and Monte Carlo simulation would be used to give Hightech's management some feel for the risks involved with the acquisition. In this situation, we assume that Apex is a publicly traded company, so we can assess directly the firm's market risk. Apex's market-determined premerger beta was 1.28. However, this reflects its premerger 30 percent debt ratio, while its postmerger debt ratio will increase to 50 percent. The Hamada equations, which were developed in Chapter 12, can be used to approximate the effects of the leverage change on beta. First, we obtain the unlevered beta of Apex's assets:

$$b_U = \frac{b_L}{1 + (1 - T)(D/E)} = \frac{1.28}{1 + (1 - 0.40)(0.30/0.70)} = \frac{1.28}{1.26} = 1.02.$$

Next, we relever Apex's asset beta to reflect its new 50 percent debt ratio:

$$b_L = b_U[1 + (1 - T)(D/E)]$$
$$= 1.02[1 + (1 - 0.40)(0.50/0.50)] = 1.02(1.6) = 1.63.$$

Finally, we use the Security Market Line to estimate Apex's postmerger cost of equity. If the risk-free rate is 10 percent and the market risk premium is 5 percent, then Apex's cost of equity, k_s, after the merger with Hightech, would be about 18.2 percent:[8]

$$k_s = k_{RF} + (RP_M)b = 10\% + (5\%)1.63 = 18.15\% \approx 18.2\%.$$

Valuing the Cash Flows. The current value of Apex to Hightech is the present value of the cash flows expected to accrue to Hightech, discounted at 18.2 percent (in millions of dollars):

$$V_{1993} = \frac{\$6.4}{(1.182)^1} + \frac{\$8.8}{(1.182)^2} + \frac{\$9.8}{(1.182)^3} + \frac{\$10.2}{(1.182)^4} + \frac{\$161.4}{(1.182)^5} \approx \$92.8.$$

---

[8]In this example, we used the Capital Asset Pricing Model to estimate Apex's cost of equity, and thus we assumed that investors require a premium for market risk only. We could have also conducted a within-firm, or corporate, risk analysis, in which the relevant risk would be the contribution of Apex's cash flows to the total risk of the postmerger firm.

In actual merger situations among large firms, companies almost always hire an investment banker to help develop valuation estimates. For example, when General Electric acquired Utah International, GE hired Morgan Stanley to determine Utah's value. We discussed the valuation process with the Morgan Stanley analyst in charge of the appraisal, and he confirmed that they applied all of the standard procedures discussed in this chapter. Note, though, that merger analysis, like the analysis of any other complex issue, requires judgment, and people's judgments differ as to how much weight to give to different methods in any given situation.

Thus, if Hightech could acquire Apex for $92.8 million or less, the merger would appear to be acceptable from Hightech's standpoint. Obviously, Hightech would try to buy at as low a price as possible, while Apex would hold out for the highest possible price. The final price is determined by negotiation, with the stronger negotiator capturing most of the incremental value. *The larger the synergistic benefits, the more room for bargaining, and the higher the probability that the merger will actually be consummated.*[9]

To consider the value on a per-share basis, assume that Apex has 10 million shares outstanding at a price of $6.25 per share, for a total market value of $62.5 million. Hightech could offer as much as $92.8/10 = $9.28 per share to Apex's stockholders, but at this price all of the merger gains would be captured by the target firm's shareholders. On the other hand, if Hightech tried to keep almost all of the value gain for its own shareholders and offered only $6.50 for each share of Apex, it is unlikely that the offer would be accepted. In theory, the synergistic gains could be split between the two firms' shareholders in virtually any proportions, but, as we will discuss in a later section, in practice most of the gains typically go to the target firm's shareholders.

POSTMERGER CONTROL

The employment/control situation is often of vital interest in a merger analysis. First, consider the situation in which a small, owner-managed firm sells out to a larger concern. The owner-manager may be anxious to retain a high-status position, and he or she may also have developed a camaraderie with the employees and thus be concerned about keeping operating control of the organization after the merger. Thus, these points are often stressed during the merger negotiations.[10] When a publicly owned firm not controlled by its managers is merged into another company, the acquired firm's management is also worried about its postmerger position. If the acquiring firm agrees to retain the old management, then manage-

---

[9]It has been estimated that of all merger negotiations seriously begun, fewer than one-third actually come to fruition. Also, note that in contested merger situations, the company that offers the most will usually make the acquisition, and the company that will gain the greatest synergistic benefits should bid the most.

[10]The acquiring firm may also be concerned about this point, especially if the target firm's management is quite good. Indeed, a condition of the merger may be that the management team agree to stay on for a period such as five years after the merger. Also, the price paid may be contingent on the acquired firm's performance subsequent to the merger. For example, when International Holdings acquired Walker Products, the price paid was an immediate 100,000 shares of International Holdings stock worth $63 per share plus an additional 30,000 shares each year for the next three years, provided Walker Products earned at least $1 million during each of these years. Since Walker's managers owned the stock and would receive the bonus, they had a strong incentive to stay on and help the firm meet its targets.

Finally, if the managers of the target company are highly competent but do not wish to remain on after the merger, the acquiring firm may build into the merger contract a noncompetitive agreement with the old management. Typically, the acquired firm's principal officers must agree not to affiliate with a new business which is competitive with the one they sold for a specified period, say, five years. Such agreements are especially important with service-oriented businesses.

ment may be willing to support the merger and to recommend its acceptance to the stockholders. If the old management is to be removed, then it will probably resist the merger.[11]

SELF-TEST QUESTIONS

What is the difference between an operating merger and a financial merger?

Describe the way that postmerger cash flows are estimated in a merger analysis.

What is the basis for the discount rate in a merger analysis? Describe how this rate might be estimated.

What impact does postmerger control have on a merger analysis?

STRUCTURING THE TAKEOVER BID

The acquiring firm's offer to the target's shareholders can be in the form of cash, stock of the acquiring firm, debt of the acquiring firm, or a combination of the three. The structure of the bid is extremely important, since it affects (1) the capital structure of the postmerger firm, (2) the tax treatment of both the acquiring firm and the target's stockholders, (3) the ability of the target firm's stockholders to reap the rewards of future merger-related gains, and (4) the types of federal and state regulations to which the acquiring firm will be subjected. In this section, we focus on how taxes and regulation influence the way in which acquiring firms structure their offers.

The form of payment offered to the target shareholders determines the personal tax treatment of the target's stockholders. Target shareholders do not have to pay taxes on the transaction if they maintain a substantial equity position in the combined firm, defined by the IRS to mean that at least 50 percent of the payment to target shareholders must be in shares (either common or preferred) of the acquiring firm. In such nontaxable offers, target shareholders do not realize any capital gains or losses until the equity securities they receive in the takeover are sold. However, capital gains must be taken and treated as income in the transaction year if an offer consists of over 50 percent cash and/or debt securities.

---

[11]Managements of firms that are thought to be attractive merger candidates often arrange *golden parachutes* for themselves. Golden parachutes are extremely lucrative retirement plans which take effect if a merger is consummated. Thus, when Bendix was acquired by Allied, Bill Agee, Bendix's chairman, "pulled the ripcord of his golden parachute" and walked away with $4 million. If a golden parachute is large enough, it can also function as a poison pill—for example, if the president of a firm worth $10 million would have to be paid $8 million if the firm is acquired. Congress has recently reduced the value of golden parachutes by increasing the tax consequences to the firm, but they seem to persist.

All other things being equal, stockholders prefer nontaxable offers, since they may then postpone the realization of capital gains and the payment of taxes. Furthermore, if the target firm's stockholders receive stock of the acquiring firm, they will benefit from any newly realized value after the merger takes place. Most target shareholders are thus willing to sell their stock for a lower price in a nontaxable offer than in a taxable offer. As a result, one might expect nontaxable bids to dominate. However, this is not the case—roughly half of all mergers have been taxable, and, as noted in Table 24-1, two of the top five mergers have been all-cash offers. Prior to 1986, if a firm paid more than book value for a target firm's assets in a taxable merger, it could write up those assets, depreciate the marked-up value for tax purposes, and thus lower the postmerger firm's taxes vis-à-vis the taxes of the two firms operating separately. At the same time, the target firm did not have to pay any taxes on the write-up at the time of the merger.

Under current law, if the acquiring company writes up the target company's assets for tax purposes, then the target company must pay capital gains taxes in the year the merger occurs. (These taxes can be avoided if the acquiring company elects not to write up acquired assets and depreciates them on their old basis.)

Note also that the maximum capital gains tax rate on personal income rose from 20 percent to 28 percent, a 40 percent increase, in 1986. This, of course, means that target companies' stockholders now net out less after a merger than they would have under the old law. When one considers the combined effects of the corporate and personal tax changes, it is clear that the tax treatment of mergers is significantly less favorable today than it was prior to 1987. This means that a lot less money will end up in the pockets of selling stockholders, so they will require larger premiums to sell.

Securities laws also have an effect on the construction of the offer. As we discussed in Chapter 19, the SEC has oversight over the issuance of new securities, including stock or debt issued in connection with a merger. Therefore, whenever a corporation bids for control of another firm through the exchange of equity or debt, the entire process must take place under the scrutiny of the Securities and Exchange Commission. The time required for such reviews allows target managements to implement defensive tactics and other firms to make competing offers, and, as a result, nearly all hostile tender offers are for cash rather than securities.

SELF-TEST QUESTIONS

What are some alternative ways of structuring takeover bids?

How do taxes influence the payment structure?

How do securities laws affect the payment structure?

THE ROLE OF INVESTMENT BANKERS

The investment banking community is involved with mergers in a number of ways: (1) they help arrange mergers, (2) they help target companies develop and implement defensive tactics, (3) they help value target companies, (4) they help finance

mergers, and (5) they speculate in the stocks of potential merger candidates. These merger-related activities have been quite profitable. For example, the investment bankers and lawyers who arranged the Campeau-Federated merger earned fees of about $83 million—First Boston and Wasserstein Perella earned about $29 million from Campeau, and Goldman Sachs, Hellman & Friedman, and Shearson Lehman Hutton received $54 million for representing Federated. No wonder investment banking houses were able to make top offers to finance graduates in the 1980s.

ARRANGING MERGERS

The major investment banking firms have merger and acquisition groups which operate within their corporate finance departments. (Corporate finance departments offer advice, as opposed to underwriting or brokerage services, to business firms.) Members of these groups strive to identify firms with excess cash that might want to buy other firms, companies that might be willing to be bought, and firms that might, for a number of reasons, be attractive to others. Also, if an oil company, for instance, decided to expand into coal mining, then it might enlist the aid of an investment banker to help it locate and then negotiate with a target coal company. Similarly, dissident stockholders of firms with poor track records might work with investment bankers to oust management by helping to arrange a merger. Investment bankers are reported to have offered packages of financing to corporate raiders, where the package includes both designing the securities to be used in the tender offer, and lining up people and firms who will buy the target firm's stock now, and then tender it once the final offer is made. The financing role is discussed in more detail in a later section.

Investment bankers have also taken some illegal actions in the merger arena. For one thing, they are reported to have *parked stock*—purchasing it for a raider under a guaranteed buy-back agreement—to help the raider avoid the disclosure rules. Some of this came out in connection with recent insider trading scandals.

DEVELOPING DEFENSIVE TACTICS

Target firms that do not want to be acquired generally enlist the help of an investment banking firm, along with a law firm that specializes in helping to block mergers. Defenses include such tactics as (1) changing the bylaws so that only one-third of the directors are elected each year and/or so that a 75 percent approval (a *supermajority*) versus a simple majority is required to approve a merger; (2) trying to convince the target firm's stockholders that the price being offered is too low; (3) raising antitrust issues in the hope that the Justice Department will intervene; (4) repurchasing stock in the open market in an effort to push the price above that being offered by the potential acquirer; (5) getting a white knight who is more acceptable to the target firm's management to compete with the potential acquirer; (6) getting a white squire who is friendly to current management to buy some of the target firm's shares, and (7) taking a poison pill, as described next.

Poison pills—which occasionally really do amount to virtually committing economic suicide to avoid a takeover—are such tactics as borrowing on terms

that require immediate repayment of all loans if the firm is acquired, selling off at bargain prices the assets that originally made the firm a desirable target, granting such lucrative golden parachutes to their executives that the cash drain from these payments would render the merger infeasible, and planning defensive mergers which would leave the firm with new assets of questionable value and a huge debt load to service. Currently, the most popular poison pill is for a company to give its stockholders *stock purchase rights* which allow them to buy at half-price the stock of an acquiring firm, should the firm be acquired. The blatant use of poison pills is constrained by directors' awareness that excessive use could trigger personal suits by stockholders against directors who voted for them, and, perhaps in the near future, by laws that would further limit management's use of pills. Still, investment bankers and antitakeover lawyers are busy thinking up new poison pill formulas, and others are just as actively trying to come up with antidotes.[12]

To illustrate a typical poison pill, consider Chrysler's poison pill share rights purchase plan. Chrysler's stockholders receive one full right in the poison pill plan for each share of common stock held. Each right entitles the holder to buy one-hundredth of a share of Chrysler junior participating cumulative preferred stock for $120. However, the primary purpose of the rights is to act as a poison pill. Certain events, as described next, will cause the rights either to "flip in" and hence entitle holders to buy Chrysler common stock at half its market value, or to "flip over" and hence entitle holders to buy common stock in an acquiring entity at half its market value.

A "flip in" will occur if a shareholder acquires 20 percent or more of the firm's common stock. Further, Chrylser's board could trigger the "flip in" if an owner of 10 percent or more of the firm's stock has "adverse" intentions, where "adverse" intentions are defined as any intentions to take actions that are detrimental to the long-term interests of Chrysler and its shareholders. A "flip over" will occur if a hostile takeover occurs, which is any takeover that is not supported by Chrysler's board of directors.

Another takeover defense that is being used frequently is the employee stock ownership plan (ESOP). ESOPs are designed to give lower-level employees an ownership stake in the firm, and current tax laws provide generous incentives for companies to establish such plans and fund them with the firm's common stock. As we discussed earlier, Polaroid used an ESOP to help fend off Shamrock Holdings' hostile takeover attempt. Also, Procter & Gamble recently set up an ESOP that, along with an existing profit-sharing plan, eventually will give employees a 20 percent ownership stake in the company. Since the trustees of ESOPs generally support current management in any takeover attempt, and since 85 percent of the votes is generally required to complete a merger, an ESOP can provide an effective defense against a hostile tender offer. Procter & Gamble stated that the ESOP was

---

[12]It has become extremely difficult and expensive for companies to buy "directors' insurance" which protects the board from losses from such contingencies as stockholders' suits, and even when insurance is available, it often does not pay for losses if the directors did not exercise due caution and judgment. This exposure is making directors extremely leery of actions that might trigger stockholder suits.

designed primarily to lower its costs by utilizing the plan's tax advantages and to improve employees' retirement security. However, the company also noted that the ESOP would strengthen its defenses against a takeover.

ESTABLISHING A FAIR VALUE

If a friendly merger is being worked out between two firms' managements, it is important to be able to document that the agreed-upon price is a fair one; otherwise, the stockholders of either company may sue to block the merger. Therefore, in many large mergers, each side will hire an investment banking firm to evaluate the target company and to help establish the fair price. For example, General Electric employed Morgan Stanley to determine a fair price for Utah International, as did Royal Dutch to help establish the price it paid for Shell Oil. Even if the merger is not friendly, investment bankers may still be asked to help establish a price. If a surprise tender offer is to be made, the acquiring firm will want to know the lowest price at which it might be able to acquire the stock, while the target firm may seek help in "proving" that the price being offered is too low.[13]

FINANCING MERGERS

Many mergers are financed with the acquiring company's excess cash. At other times, however, the acquiring company has no excess cash, hence it requires a source of funds to pay for the target company. Perhaps the single most important factor behind the 1980s merger wave was the widespread use of junk bonds, and the system that was developed to market these bonds.

As noted in Chapter 20, Drexel Burnham Lambert was the primary developer of junk bonds, defined as bonds rated below investment grade (BBB/Baa). Prior to Drexel's entry on the scene, it was almost impossible to sell low-grade bonds to raise new capital. Drexel then pioneered a procedure wherein a target firm's situation would be appraised very closely, and a cash flow projection similar to that in Table 24-2 (but much more detailed) would be developed. Part of the cash flow projection would generally include cash flows from major asset sales.

With the cash flows having been forecasted, Drexel's analysts would figure out a debt mix — amount of debt, maturity structure, and interest rate — that could be serviced by the cash flows. With this information, Drexel's junk bond people, operating out of Beverly Hills with a high degree of independence from the

---

[13]Such investigations must obviously be done in secret, for if someone knew that Company A was thinking of offering, say, $50 per share for Company T, which was currently selling at $35 per share, then huge profits could be made. One of the biggest scandals to hit Wall Street in the 1980s was the disclosure that Ivan Boesky was buying information from Dennis Levine, a senior member of the investment banking house of Drexel Burnham Lambert, about target companies that Drexel was analyzing for others. Purchases based on such insider information would, of course, raise the prices of the stocks and thus force Drexel's clients to pay more than they otherwise would have had to pay. Levine and Boesky, among others, went to jail for their improper use of inside information.

New York headquarters, would approach financial institutions (savings and loans, insurance companies, pension funds, and mutual funds) and wealthy individuals with a financing plan and an offer of a rate of return several percentage points above the rate on more conservative investments. Drexel's early deals worked out well, and the institutions that bought the bonds were quite pleased. These results enabled Drexel to expand its network of investors, and to commit to finance larger and larger mergers (and LBOs). T. Boone Pickens, who went after Phillips, Texaco, and several other oil giants, was an early Drexel customer.

At the present time, to be a successful investment banker in the mergers and acquisitions (M&A) business, a banker must be able to offer a financing package to clients, whether they are acquirers like Campeau who need capital to take over companies like Federated Department Stores or target companies like Union Carbide or CBS trying to finance stock repurchase plans or other defenses against takeovers. Drexel was the leading player in the merger financing game, but since Drexel's bankruptcy in early 1990 and subsequent demise, the role of chief takeover financier remains unfilled. However, Merrill Lynch, Morgan Stanley, Salomon Brothers, and others are all eager for the title.

Arbitrage Operations

Arbitrage generally means simultaneously buying and selling the same commodity or security in two different markets at different prices, and pocketing a risk-free return. However, the major brokerage houses, as well as some wealthy private investors, are engaged in a different type of arbitrage called *risk arbitrage*. The *arbitrageurs,* or "arbs" as they are called, speculate in the stocks of companies that are likely takeover targets. Vast amounts of capital are required to speculate in a large number of securities and thus reduce risk, and also to make money on narrow spreads, but the large investment bankers have the wherewithal to play the game. To be successful, arbs need to be able to sniff out likely targets, assess the probability of offers reaching fruition, and move in and out of the market quickly and with low transaction costs.

The risk arbitrage business has been rocked by insider trading scandals. Indeed, it was disclosed that the most famous arb of all, Ivan Boesky, had been buying inside information from executives of some leading investment banking houses to help make his millions. The Boesky affair slowed down risk arbitrage activity, but it will undoubtedly survive this setback.

Self-Test Questions

What are some defensive tactics that firms can use to resist hostile takeover attempts?

What is the difference between pure arbitrage and risk arbitrage?

What role did junk bonds play in the merger wave of the 1980s?

WHO WINS: THE EMPIRICAL EVIDENCE

The most recent merger wave has been notable not only for the great number of firms that have combined, but also for the high percentage of hostile takeovers. With all this activity, the following questions have emerged: Do corporate acquisitions create value, and, if so, how is the value shared between the parties involved?

Financial researchers have classified corporate acquisitions as part of "the market for corporate control." Under this concept, management teams are viewed as facing constant competition from other management teams. If the team that currently controls a firm is not maximizing the value of the firm's assets, then an acquisition will likely occur and increase the value of the firm by replacing its poor managers with good managers. Further, under this theory, intense competition will cause managers to combine or divest assets whenever such steps would increase the value of the firm.

Most researchers agree that takeovers increase the wealth of the shareholders of target firms, for otherwise they would not agree to the offer. However, there is a debate as to whether or not mergers benefit the acquiring firm's shareholders. In particular, managements of acquiring firms may be motivated by factors other than shareholder wealth maximization; for example, they may want to merge merely to increase the size of the corporations they manage, since increased size usually brings larger salaries and more job security, perquisites, power, and prestige.

The validity of the competing views on who gains from corporate acquisitions can be tested by examining the stock price changes that occur around a merger or takeover announcement. Such changes in the stock prices of the acquiring and target firms represent market participants' beliefs about the value created by the merger, and about how this value will be divided between the target and acquiring firms' shareholders. As long as the market participants are neither systematically wrong nor biased in their perceptions of the effects of mergers, examining a large sample of stock price movements will shed light on the issue of who gains from mergers.

One cannot simply examine stock prices around merger announcement dates, because other factors influence stock prices. For example, if a merger was announced on a day when the entire market advanced, the fact that the firm in question's price rose would not necessarily signify that the merger created value. Hence, studies examine *abnormal returns* associated with merger announcements, where abnormal returns are defined as that part of a stock price change caused by factors other than changes in the general stock market.

Many studies have examined both acquiring and target firms' stock price responses to mergers and tender offers.[14] Jointly, these studies have covered nearly every acquisition involving publicly traded firms from the early 1960s to the present, and they are remarkably consistent in their results: On average, the stock price

---

[14]For an excellent summary of the effects of mergers on value, see Michael C. Jensen and Richard S. Ruback, "The Market for Corporate Control: The Scientific Evidence," *Journal of Financial Economics*, April 1983, 5–50.

of target firms increases by about 30 percent in hostile tender offers, while in friendly mergers the average increase is about 20 percent. However, for both hostile and friendly deals, the stock prices of acquiring firms, on average, remain constant. Thus, the evidence strongly indicates (1) that acquisitions do create value, but (2) that shareholders of target firms reap virtually all of the benefits.

In hindsight, these results are not too surprising. First, target firms' shareholders can always say no, so they are in the driver's seat. Second, takeovers are a competitive game, so if one potential acquiring firm does not offer full value for a potential target, then another firm will generally jump in with a higher bid. Finally, managements of acquiring firms might well be willing to give up all the value created by the merger, because the merger would enhance the acquiring managers' personal positions with no explicit cost to their shareholders.

It has also been argued that acquisitions may increase shareholder wealth at the expense of bondholders—in particular, concern has been expressed that leveraged buyouts dilute the claims of bondholders. Specific instances can be cited where bonds were downgraded and bondholders did suffer losses as a direct result of an acquisition, but most of the studies find no evidence to support the contention that bondholders generally lose in corporate acquisitions.

SELF-TEST QUESTIONS

Explain how researchers can study the effects of mergers on shareholder wealth.

Do mergers create value? If so, who profits from this value?

Do the research results discussed in this section seem logical? Explain.

CORPORATE ALLIANCES

Mergers are one way for two companies to join forces, but many companies are striking cooperative deals, called *corporate alliances,* which fall far short of merging. Whereas mergers combine all of the assets of the firms involved, as well as managerial and technical expertise, alliances allow firms to create combinations that focus on specific business lines that have the most potential for synergies. These alliances take many forms, from straightforward marketing agreements to joint ownership of world-scale operations.

One form of corporate alliance is the *joint venture,* in which parts of companies are joined to achieve specific, limited objectives.[15] A joint venture is controlled by a management team consisting of representatives of the two (or more)

---

[15]Cross-licensing, consortia, joint bidding, and franchising are still other ways for firms to combine resources. For more information on joint ventures, see Sanford V. Berg, Jerome Duncan, and Phillip Friedman, *Joint Venture Strategies and Corporate Innovation* (Cambridge, Mass.: Oelgeschlager, Gunn and Hain, 1982).

parent companies. Joint ventures have been used often by U.S., Japanese, and European firms to share technology and/or marketing expertise. For example, General Electric recently announced a joint venture with Britain's unrelated General Electric Company to manufacture appliances, medical equipment, and electrical products. In the same month, Whirlpool announced a joint venture with the Dutch electronics giant Philips to produce appliances under Philips's brand names in five European countries. By joining with their foreign counterparts, U.S. firms were attempting to gain a strong foothold in Europe before the European community became one unified market. Although alliances are new to some firms, they are established practices to others. For example, Corning Glass now obtains over half its profits from 23 joint ventures, two-thirds of them with foreign companies representing almost all of Europe, as well as Japan, China, South Korea, and Australia.

In one of the most dramatic corporate alliances, IBM and Apple agreed in 1991 to cooperate in several important areas of hardware and software development. To begin, they planned to jointly develop software that will make it easier to link Apple and IBM computers on networks, which will help Apple place its hardware at large corporations. They also agreed to form a joint venture to develop new operating system software, which provides a PC's basic instructions. This joint venture is clearly targeted at unseating Microsoft, the developer of DOS, from its role as the prime provider of operating system software. The agreement also gave Apple access to IBM's reduced instruction set computing (RISC) chip—this will allow Apple to expand its product line into workstations, and potentially hurt Compaq's attempt to create a second standard for RISC chips. Finally, the alliance called for the two companies to jointly develop multimedia—the integration of video and sound with computer text. Multimedia is expected to be one of the hot items of the 1990s, and the collaboration between IBM and Apple will make it much harder for Japanese firms to compete in the market for multimedia computer systems.

SELF-TEST QUESTIONS

What is the difference between a merger and a corporate alliance?

What is a joint venture? Give some reasons why joint ventures may be advantageous to the parties involved.

LEVERAGED BUYOUTS

The pros and cons of *leveraged buyouts (LBOs)* were discussed in detail in Chapter 19. To briefly review the concept, in an LBO a small group of equity investors, usually including current management, acquires a firm in a transaction financed largely by borrowing. The debt is serviced with funds generated by the acquired company's operations and, often, by the sale of some of its assets. Generally, the acquiring group plans to run the acquired company for a number of years, boost its sales and profits, and then take it public again as a stronger company. Naturally, the acquiring group expects to make a substantial profit from the LBO, but the

inherent risks are great due to the heavy use of financial leverage. To illustrate the profit potential, Kohlberg Kravis Roberts & Company (KKR), the leading LBO specialist firm, averaged a spectacular 50 percent annual return on its LBO investments during the 1980s. However, the weak economy and strong stock prices have dampened the returns on LBO investments, and hence, recent activity has been much less than in its heyday of the 1980s.

To illustrate an LBO, consider KKR's $25 billion buyout of RJR Nabisco. RJR, a leading producer of tobacco and food products with brands such as Winston, Camel, Planters, Ritz, Oreo, and Del Monte, was trading at about $55 a share in October 1988. Then, F. Ross Johnson, the company's president and CEO, announced a $75-a-share, or $17.6 billion, offer to outside stockholders in a plan to take the firm private. This deal, if completed, would have been the largest ever business transaction. After the announcement, RJR's stock price soared to $77.25, which indicated that investors thought the final price would be even higher than Johnson's opening bid. Then, a few days later, KKR offered $90 per share, or $20.6 billion, for the firm. The battle between the two bidders raged until late November, when RJR's board accepted KKR's revised bid of cash and securities worth about $106 a share, for a total value of about $25.1 billion. Of course, the investment bankers' fees reflected the record size of the deal—the bankers received almost $400 million, with Drexel Burnham Lambert alone getting over $200 million. Johnson lost his job, but he did walk away with a multimillion-dollar golden parachute.

KKR wasted no time in restructuring the newly private RJR. In June 1989, RJR sold its five European businesses to France's BSN for $2.5 million. Then, in September, the firm sold the tropical fruit portion of its Del Monte foods unit to Polly Peck, a London-based food company, for $875 million. In the same month, RJR sold the Del Monte canned foods business to an LBO group led by Citicorp Venture Capital for $1.48 billion. Then, in October 1990, RJR sold its Baby Ruth, Butterfinger, and Pearson candy businesses to Nestlé, a Swiss company, for $370 million. In total, RJR sold off over $5 billion worth of businesses in 1990 to help buy down the tremendous amount of debt needed for the LBO. In addition to asset sales, in 1991 RJR went public again by issuing over $1 billion in new common stock at $11.25 per share, which placed about 25 percent of the firm's common stock in public hands. Also, as the firm's credit rating improved due to retirement of some of the LBO debt, RJR issued about $1 billion of new debt at significantly lower rates and used the proceeds to retire even more of the LBO debt.

LBOs have tended to be disastrous for bondholders, and the RJR deal was no exception. Both Metropolitan Life Insurance Company and ITT Corporation have filed suits against RJR in New York State. RJR bonds lost about 20 percent of their value as a result of the LBO, and this translated into a $40 million loss for Met Life alone. Both suits claim that the value of bondholdings was reduced substantially by the LBO, and ITT's suit goes on to charge that RJR's management knew that the LBO was coming and failed to disclose the information, while Met Life's suit claims that the LBO constituted a breach of trust by RJR's management. Undoubtedly, the outcome of these suits will be some time in coming, but, as we discussed in Chapter 20, the short-term impact of the LBO was a near paralysis of the industrial bond markets and the appearance of "super poison put" restrictive covenants.

The RJR Nabisco story is the classic LBO tale—a company is taken private in a highly leveraged deal, the private firm's high-cost junk debt is reduced through asset sales, and finally the company again goes public, which gives the original LBO dealmakers the opportunity to "cash out." As we write this section (March 1993), RJR's stock is selling for under $10, and the verdict is still out whether the LBO was successful or not. However, there have been some spectacularly successful LBOs. For example, in the deal that fueled the LBO wave, William Simon and Raymond Chambers (Wesray) bought Gibson Greeting Cards in 1982 for $1 million in equity and $79 million in debt. Less than 18 months later, Simon's personal investment of $330,000 was worth $66 million in cash and stock. Yet for every spectacular success there has been a matching failure. For example, in 1988 Revco became the first large LBO to file for Chapter 11 bankruptcy. It turned out that sales were nearly $1 billion short of the $3.4 billion forecast made at the time of the drugstore chain's buyout.[16]

SELF-TEST QUESTIONS

What is an LBO?

Have LBOs been profitable in recent years?

What actions do companies typically take to meet the large debt burdens resulting from LBOs?

How do LBOs typically affect bondholders?

DIVESTITURES

Although corporations do more buying than selling of productive facilities, a good bit of selling does occur. In this section, we briefly discuss the major types of divestitures, after which we present some recent examples and rationales for divestitures.

TYPES OF DIVESTITURES

There are three primary types of divestitures: (1) sale of an operating unit to another firm, (2) setting up the business to be divested as a separate corporation and then giving (or "spinning off") its stock on a pro rata basis to the divesting firm's stockholders, and (3) outright liquidation of assets.

---

[16]For a more detailed discussion of the impact of the RJR LBO on the firm's different classes of investors, see Nancy Mohan and Carl R. Chen, "A Review of the RJR-Nabisco Buyout," *Journal of Applied Corporate Finance,* Summer 1990, 102–108. For interesting discussions of highly leveraged takeovers, see Martin S. Fridson, "What Went Wrong with the Highly Leveraged Deals? (Or, All Variety of Agency Costs)," *Journal of Applied Corporate Finance,* Fall 1991, 57–67; and "The Economic Consequences of High Leverage and Stock Market Pressures on Corporate Management: A Round Table Discussion," *Journal of Applied Corporate Finance,* Summer 1990, 6–57.

Sale to another firm generally involves the sale of an entire division or unit, usually for cash but sometimes for stock of the acquiring firm. In a *spin-off*, the firm's existing stockholders are given new stock representing separate ownership rights in the division which was divested. The division establishes its own board of directors and officers, and it becomes a separate company. The stockholders end up owning shares of two firms instead of one, but no cash has been transferred. Finally, in a *liquidation* the assets of a division are sold off piecemeal, rather than as an operating entity. To illustrate the different types of divestitures, we present some recent examples in the next section.

DIVESTITURE ILLUSTRATIONS

1. In 1987, United Airlines sold its Hilton International Hotels subsidiary to Ladbroke Group PLC of Britain for $1.1 billion. Later, the company divested its Hertz rental car unit and Westin hotel group. The sales culminated a disastrous strategic move by United to build a full-service travel empire. The failed strategy resulted in the firing of Richard J. Ferris, the company's chairman. The move by the airline into nonairline travel-related businesses was viewed by many analysts as a mistake, because there really were not many synergies to be gained. Further, analysts feared that United's managers, preoccupied by running hotels and rental car companies, would not be able to maintain the company's posture in the highly competitive airline industry. The funds raised by the divestitures were subsequently paid out to United's shareholders as a special dividend.

2. IU International, a multimillion-dollar conglomerate that was listed on the NYSE, spun off three major subsidiaries — Gotaas-Larson, an ocean shipping company involved in petroleum transportation; Canadian Utilities, an electric utility; and Echo Bay Mining, a gold mining company. IU kept its distribution and manufacturing operations. IU's management originally acquired and combined several highly cyclical businesses such as ocean shipping and gold mining with stable ones such as utilities in order to gain overall corporate stability through diversification. The strategy worked reasonably well from an operating standpoint, but it failed in the financial markets. According to its management, IU's very diversity kept it from being classified in any particular industrial group, so security analysts tended not to follow the company and therefore did not understand it or recommend it to investors. (Analysts tend to concentrate on an industry, and they do not like to recommend — and investors do not like to invest in — a company they do not understand.) As a result, IU had a low P/E ratio and a low market price. After the spin-offs, the package of securities rose in market value from $10 to $75, which greatly exceeded general stock market gains.

3. AT&T was broken up in 1984 to settle a Justice Department antitrust suit filed in the 1970s.[17] For almost 100 years AT&T had operated as a holding company

---

[17]Another forced divestiture involved Du Pont and General Motors. In 1921, GM was in serious financial trouble, and Du Pont supplied capital in exchange for 23 percent of the stock. In the 1950s, the Justice Department won an antitrust suit which required Du Pont to spin off (to Du Pont's stockholders) its GM stock.

which owned Western Electric (its manufacturing subsidiary), Bell Labs (its research arm), a huge long-distance network system which was operated as a division of the parent company, and 22 Bell operating companies, such as Pacific Telephone, New York Telephone, Southern Bell, and Southwestern Bell. AT&T was reorganized into eight separate companies—a slimmed-down AT&T which kept Western Electric, Bell Labs, and the long-distance operations, plus seven new regional telephone holding companies that were created from the 22 old operating telephone companies. The stock of the seven new telephone companies was then spun off to the old AT&T's stockholders. A person who held 100 shares of old AT&T stock owned, after the divestiture, 100 shares of the "new" AT&T plus 10 shares of each of the seven new operating companies. These 170 shares were backed by the same assets that had previously backed 100 shares of old AT&T common.

The AT&T divestiture resulted from a suit by the Justice Department, which wanted to divide the Bell System into a regulated monopoly segment (the seven regional telephone companies) and a manufacturing/long-distance segment which would be subjected to competition. The breakup was expected to strengthen competition and thus speed up technological change in those parts of the telecommunications industry that are not natural monopolies.

4. Some years ago, Woolworth liquidated every one of its 336 Woolco discount stores. This made the company, which had had sales of $7.2 billion before the liquidation, 30 percent smaller. Woolco had posted operating losses of $19 million in the year before the liquidation, and its losses in the six months preceding it had climbed to an alarming $21 million. Woolworth's CEO, Edward F. Gibbons, was quoted as saying: "How many losses can you take?" Woolco's demise necessitated an after-tax write-off of $325 million, but management believed that it was better to go ahead and "bite the bullet" than to let the losing stores bleed the company to death.

5. As a result of some imprudent loans to oil companies and to developing nations, Continental Illinois, one of the largest U.S. bank holding companies, was recently threatened with bankruptcy. Continental then sold off several profitable divisions, such as its leasing and credit card operations, to raise funds to cover bad-loan losses and deposit withdrawals. In effect, Continental sold assets in order to stay alive. Ultimately, Continental was bailed out by the Federal Deposit Insurance Corporation and the Federal Reserve, which (1) arranged a $7.5 billion rescue package and (2) provided a blanket guarantee for all of Continental's $40 billion of deposits, which kept deposits in excess of $100,000 from fleeing the bank because of their uninsured status.

The preceding examples illustrate that the reasons for divestitures vary widely. Sometimes the market feels more comfortable when firms "stick to their knitting"; the United Airlines divestiture is an example. Similarly, if IU International's management is correct, there are cases in which a company has become so complex and diverse that analysts and investors just do not understand it and consequently ignore it. Other companies need cash either to finance expansion in their primary business lines or to reduce a large debt burden, and divestitures can be used to raise this cash; the RJR Nabisco example in the preceding section illustrates this

point. The actions listed also show that running a business is a dynamic process — conditions change, corporate strategies change in response, and as a result firms alter their asset portfolios by acquisitions and/or divestitures. Some divestitures, such as Woolworth's liquidation of its Woolco stores, occur in order to unload losing assets that would otherwise drag the company down, while the AT&T example is one of the many instances in which a divestiture is the result of an antitrust settlement. Finally, Continental Bank's actions represent a desperate effort to get the cash needed to stay alive.

SELF-TEST QUESTIONS

What are some reasons that companies divest assets?

What are the three primary types of divestitures?

HOLDING COMPANIES

Holding companies date from 1889, when New Jersey became the first state to pass a law permitting corporations to be formed for the sole purpose of owning the stocks of other companies. Many of the advantages and disadvantages of holding companies are identical to those large-scale operations already discussed in connection with mergers and consolidations. Whether a company is organized on a divisional basis or with subsidiaries kept as separate companies does not affect the basic reasons for conducting a large-scale, multiproduct, multiplant operation. However, as we show next, the use of holding companies to control large-scale operations has some distinct advantages and disadvantages over those of completely integrated divisionalized operations.

ADVANTAGES OF HOLDING COMPANIES

1. Control with fractional ownership. Through a holding company operation, a firm may buy 5, 10, or 50 percent of the stock of another corporation. Such fractional ownership may be sufficient to give the acquiring company effective working control or substantial influence over the operations of the company in which it has acquired stock ownership. Working control is often considered to entail more than 25 percent of the common stock, but it can be as low as 10 percent if the stock is widely distributed. One financier says that the attitude of management is more important than the number of shares owned: "If they think you can control the company, then you do." In addition, control on a very slim margin can be held through relationships with large stockholders outside the holding company group.

2. Isolation of risks. Because the various operating companies in a holding company system are separate legal entities, the obligations of any one unit are

separate from those of the other units. Therefore, catastrophic losses incurred by one unit of the holding company system are not translatable into claims on the assets of the other units. However, we should note that while this is a customary generalization, it is not always valid. First, the parent company may feel obligated to make good on the subsidiary's debts, even though it is not legally bound to do so, in order to keep its good name and to retain customers. Examples of this include American Express's payment of over $100 million in connection with a swindle that was the responsibility of one of its subsidiaries, and United California Bank's coverage of its Swiss affiliate's multimillion-dollar fraud loss. Second, a parent company may feel obligated to supply capital to an affiliate in order to protect its initial investment; General Public Utilities' continued support of its subsidiary's Three Mile Island nuclear plant is an example. And, third, when lending to one of the units of a holding company system, an astute loan officer may require a guarantee by the parent holding company. To some degree, therefore, the assets in the various elements of a holding company are not really separate. Still, a catastrophic loss, as could occur if a drug company's subsidiary distributed a batch of toxic medicine, may be avoided.[18]

DISADVANTAGES OF HOLDING COMPANIES

1. Partial multiple taxation.   Provided the holding company owns at least 80 percent of a subsidiary's voting stock, the IRS permits the filing of consolidated returns, in which case dividends received by the parent are not taxed. However, if less than 80 percent of the stock is owned, then tax returns cannot be consolidated. Firms that own over 20 percent but less than 80 percent of another corporation can deduct 80 percent of the dividends received, while firms that own less than 20 percent may deduct only 70 percent of the dividends received. This partial double taxation somewhat offsets the benefits of holding company control with limited ownership, but whether the tax penalty is sufficient to offset other possible advantages is a matter that must be decided in individual situations.

2. Ease of enforced dissolution.   It is relatively easy for the U.S. Department of Justice to require dissolution by disposal of stock ownership of a holding company operation it finds unacceptable. For instance, in the 1950s Du Pont was required to dispose of its 23 percent stock interest in General Motors Corporation, acquired in the early 1920s. Because there was no fusion between the corporations, there were no difficulties, from an operating standpoint, in requiring the separation of the two companies. However, if complete amalgamation had taken place, it would have been much more difficult to break up the company after so many years, and the likelihood of forced divestiture would have been reduced.

---

[18]Note, though, that the parent company would still be held accountable for such losses if it were deemed to exercise operating control over the subsidiary. Thus, Union Carbide was held responsible for its subsidiary's Bhopal disaster.

HOLDING COMPANIES AS A LEVERAGING DEVICE

The holding company vehicle has been used to obtain huge degrees of financial leverage. In the 1920s, several tiers of holding companies were established in the electric utility and other industries. In those days, an operating company at the bottom of the pyramid might have $100 million of assets, financed by $50 million of debt and $50 million of equity. Then, a first-tier holding company might own the stock of the operating firm as its only asset and be financed with $25 million of debt and $25 million of equity. A second-tier holding company, which owned the stock of the first-tier company, might be financed with $12.5 million of debt and $12.5 million of equity. Such systems were extended to five or six levels, but with only four holding companies, $100 million of operating assets could be controlled at the top by $3.125 million of equity, and the operating assets would have to provide enough cash income to support $96.875 million of debt. *Such a holding company system is highly leveraged—its consolidated debt ratio is 96.875 percent, even though the individual components only have 50 percent debt/assets ratios.* Because of this consolidated leverage, even a small decline in profits at the operating company level could bring the whole system down like a house of cards.

SELF-TEST QUESTIONS

What is a holding company?

What are some of the advantages of holding companies? What are some of the disadvantages?

SUMMARY

This chapter included discussions of mergers, divestitures, holding companies, and LBOs. The key concepts covered are listed below:

▶   A *merger* occurs when two firms combine to form a single company. The primary motives for mergers are (1) synergy, (2) tax considerations, (3) purchase of assets below their replacement costs, (4) diversification, and (5) gaining control over a larger enterprise.

▶   Mergers can provide economic benefits through *economies of scale* or through the *concentration of assets* in the hands of more efficient managers. However, mergers also have the potential for reducing competition, and for this reason they are carefully regulated by governmental agencies.

▶   In most mergers, one company (the *acquiring firm*) initiates action to take over another (the *target firm*).

▶ A *horizontal merger* occurs when two firms in the same line of business combine.

▶ A *vertical merger* is the combination of a firm with one of its customers or suppliers.

▶ A *congeneric merger* involves firms in related industries, but for which no customer-supplier relationship exists.

▶ A *conglomerate merger* occurs when firms in totally different industries combine.

▶ In a *friendly merger,* the managements of both firms approve the merger, whereas in a *hostile merger,* the target firm's management opposes the merger.

▶ An *operating merger* is one in which the operations of the two firms are combined. A *financial merger* is one in which the firms continue to operate separately, hence no operating economies are expected.

▶ In a *merger analysis,* the key issues to be resolved are (1) the price to be paid for the target firm and (2) the employment/control situation.

▶ To determine the *value of the target firm,* the acquiring firm must (1) forecast the cash flows that will result after the merger and (2) develop a discount rate to apply to the projected cash flows.

▶ A *joint venture* is a *corporate alliance* in which two or more companies combine some of their resources to achieve a specific, limited objective.

▶ A *divestiture* is the sale of some of a company's operating assets. A divestiture may involve (1) selling an operating unit to another firm, (2) *spinning off* a unit as a separate company, or (3) the outright *liquidation* of a unit's assets.

▶ The *reasons for divestitures* include to settle antitrust suits, to clarify what a company actually does, to enable management to concentrate on a particular type of activity, and to raise capital needed to strengthen the corporation's core business.

▶ A *holding company* is a corporation which owns sufficient stock in another firm to achieve working control of it. The holding company is also known as the *parent company,* and the companies which it controls are called *subsidiaries,* or *operating companies.*

▶ Advantages to holding company operations include the following: (1) control can often be obtained for a smaller cash outlay, (2) risks may be segregated, and (3) regulated companies can separate regulated from unregulated assets.

▶ Disadvantages to holding company operations include (1) tax penalties and (2) the fact that incomplete ownership, if it exists, can lead to control problems.

▶ A *leveraged buyout (LBO)* is a transaction in which a firm's publicly owned stock is acquired in a mostly debt-financed tender offer, and a privately owned, highly leveraged firm results. Often, the firm's own management initiates the LBO.

QUESTIONS

24-1 Define each of the following terms:

a. Synergy

b. Horizontal merger; vertical merger; congeneric merger; conglomerate merger

c. Friendly merger; hostile merger; defensive merger

d. Operating merger; financial merger

e. White knight; white squire; poison pill; golden parachute

f. Leveraged buyout

g. Joint venture

h. Divestiture; spin-off

i. Holding company; operating company; parent company

24-2 The four economic classifications of mergers are (1) horizontal, (2) vertical, (3) congeneric, and (4) conglomerate. Discuss how each type of merger differs in (a) the likelihood of governmental intervention and (b) the possibilities for operating synergy.

24-3 Firm A wants to acquire Firm B. Firm B's management agrees that the merger is a good idea. Might a tender offer be used?

24-4 Distinguish between operating mergers and financial mergers.

24-5 Suppose a holding company has subsidiaries which have issued preferred stock and bonds to public investors (all of the subsidiaries' common stock is owned by the holding company). The holding company's major asset is its stock in its subsidiaries, but the parent company does own in its own right certain operating assets. The holding company also issues its own bonds and preferred stock.

Given this information, discuss the relative riskiness of investments in the common, preferred, and bonds both of the holding company itself (the parent) and of the operating subsidiaries. Assume that all the operating assets are equally risky.

24-6 Two large, publicly owned firms are contemplating a merger. No operating synergy is expected. However, since returns on the two firms are not perfectly positively correlated, the standard deviation of earnings would be reduced for the combined corporation. One group of consultants argues that this risk reduction is sufficient grounds for the merger. Another group thinks this type of risk reduction is irrelevant because stockholders could themselves hold the stock of both companies and thus gain the risk reduction benefits without all the hassles and expenses of the merger. Whose position is correct?

PROBLEMS

24-1 (Simple merger analysis)   Mary's House of Beauty wishes to acquire Jane's Nail Emporium for $300,000. Mary expects the merger to provide incremental cash flows of about $55,000 a year for 10 years. She has also calculated her marginal cost of capital for this investment to be 12 percent. Conduct a capital budgeting analysis for Mary to determine whether she should purchase Jane's store.

24-2 (Merger analysis)   T. S. Hawkey Inc. a large building materials manufacturer, is evaluating the possible acquisition of the Marvin Laurence Company, a small aluminum siding manufacturer. Hawkey's analysts project the following postmerger cash flows for Laurence (in thousands of dollars):

	1994	1995	1996	1997
Net sales	$250	$288	$312	$338
Selling and administrative expenses	25	31	38	40
Interest	12	15	16	18

Cost of goods sold as a percentage of sales (including depreciation): 65%
Terminal growth rate of cash flows available to Hawkey: 8%

If the acquisition is made, it will occur on January 1, 1994. All cash flows are assumed to occur at year end. Laurence's current market-determined beta is 1.50, but its investment bankers think that its beta would rise to 1.68 if the merger takes place. Depreciation-generated funds would be used to replace worn-out equipment, so they would not be available to Hawkey's shareholders. The risk-free rate is 8 percent, and the market risk premium is 6 percent. The postmerger tax rate would be 40 percent.

a. What is the appropriate discount rate for valuing the acquisition?

b. What is Laurence's terminal value? What is the value of the Laurence Company to Hawkey?

(Do Parts c, d, and e only if you are using the computer problem diskette.)

c. If sales in each year were $100,000 higher than the base case amounts, and if the cost of goods sold/sales ratio were 60 percent, what would Laurence be worth to Hawkey?

d. With sales and the cost of goods sold ratio at the Part c levels, what would Laurence's value be if its beta were 1.8, k_{RF} rose to 10 percent, and RP_M rose to 7 percent?

e. Leaving all values at the Part d levels, what would the value of the acquisition be if the terminal growth rate rose to 20 percent or dropped to 3 percent?

24-3 (Merger analysis) Mehran Electric Corporation is considering a merger with the Rodriguez Lamp Company. Rodriguez is a publicly traded company, and its current beta is 1.40. Rodriguez has barely been profitable, so it has paid only 20 percent in taxes over the last several years. Additionally, Rodriguez uses little debt, having a market value debt ratio of just 25 percent.

If the acquisition is made, Mehran plans to operate Rodriguez as a separate, wholly owned subsidiary. Mehran would pay taxes on a consolidated basis, and thus the federal-plus-state tax rate would increase to 40 percent. Additionally, Mehran would increase the debt capitalization in the Rodriguez subsidiary to a market value of 40 percent of assets. Mehran's acquisition department estimates that Rodriguez, if acquired, would produce the following net cash flows to Mehran's shareholders (in millions of dollars):

Year	Net Cash Flow
1	$1.20
2	1.40
3	1.65
4	1.80
5 and beyond	Constant growth at 5%

These cash flows include all acquisition effects. Mehran's cost of equity is 16 percent, its beta is 1.0, and its cost of debt is 12 percent. The risk-free rate is 10 percent.

a. What discount rate should be used to discount the given cash flows?

b. What is the dollar value of Rodriguez to Mehran?

c. Rodriguez has 1.2 million common shares outstanding. What is the maximum price per share that Mehran should offer for Rodriguez? If the tender offer is accepted at this price, what would happen to Mehran's stock price?

MINI CASE

The CompuMax Company, a regional computer retailer, is cash rich due to several consecutive good years. One of the possible uses for the excess funds is an acquisition. Pam Olson, a recent B-school graduate, has been asked to place a value on Pacific Computer Products Inc., a small mail order hardware and software company that sells nationwide.

Listed next are the estimates of Pacific's earnings potential which Pam developed (in millions of dollars):

	1994	1995	1996	1997
Net sales	$10.0	$20.0	$25.0	$30.0
Cost of goods sold	80 percent of net sales			
Selling/administrative expenses	1.0	1.5	2.0	2.0
Interest expense	0.5	1.0	1.2	1.5
Retentions	0.5	0.5	0.1	0.1

The cost of goods sold includes depreciation expense, which would be used to replace worn-out assets. The interest expense listed here includes the interest (1) on Pacific's existing debt, (2) on new debt that CompuMax would issue to help finance the acquisition, and (3) on new debt expected to be issued over time to help finance expansion within the Pacific division. The retentions represent equity funds which are expected to be reinvested within the Pacific division to help finance growth.

Pacific currently uses 20 percent debt financing and pays taxes at a 30 percent rate. The beta coefficients of the large mail order houses average 1.5. If the acquisition takes place, CompuMax would increase Pacific's debt ratio to 50 percent. Further, since CompuMax is highly profitable, taxes on the consolidated firm would be 40 percent. Pam realizes that Pacific also generates depreciation cash flow, but she believes that these funds would have to be reinvested within the division to replace worn-out equipment.

Pam estimates the risk-free rate to be 10 percent, the market risk premium to be 5 percent, and the cash flow stream would grow at a constant 7 percent rate after 1997. CompuMax's management is new to the mergers game, so Pam asked you, her assistant, to answer some basic questions about mergers and perform the merger analysis. To structure the task, Pam developed the following questions:

a. Several reasons have been proposed to justify mergers. Among the more prominent are (1) tax considerations, (2) diversification, (3) control, (4) purchase of assets at below replacement cost, (5) breakup value, and (6) synergy. In general, which of the reasons are economically justifiable? Which are not? Explain.

b. Briefly describe the differences between a hostile merger and a friendly merger.

c. Use the data developed previously to construct Pacific's cash flow statements for 1994 through 1997. Why is interest expense deducted in merger cash flow statements whereas it is not normally deducted in capital budgeting cash flow analysis? Why are retentions deducted in the cash flow statement?

d. Conceptually, what is the appropriate discount rate to apply to the cash flows developed in Part c? What is the numerical estimate? How much faith can be placed in this estimate?

e. What is the estimated terminal value of the acquisition; that is, what is the estimated value of the Pacific Division's cash flows beyond 1997? What is the value of Pacific to CompuMax? Suppose another firm were evaluating Pacific as an acquisition candidate. Would they obtain the same value? Explain.

f. Assume that Pacific currently has 10 million shares outstanding. These shares are traded relatively infrequently, but the last trade, made several weeks ago, was at a price of $0.40 per share. Should CompuMax make an offer for Pacific? If so, how much should they offer per share?

g. There has been considerable research conducted to determine whether mergers really create value, and, if so, how this value is shared between the parties involved. What are the results of this research?

h. What merger-related activities are undertaken by investment bankers?

SELECTED ADDITIONAL REFERENCES AND CASES

Considerable empirical investigation has been conducted to determine whether stockholders of acquiring or acquired companies benefit most from corporate mergers. One of the classic works in this field is

Mandelker, Gershon, "Risk and Return: The Case of Merging Firms," *Journal of Financial Economics,* December 1974, 303–335.

Two of the more recent works are

Black, Bernard S., and Joseph A. Grundfest, "Shareholder Gains from Takeovers and Restructurings Between 1981 and 1986: $162 Billion Is a Lot of Money," *Journal of Applied Corporate Finance,* Spring 1988, 5–15.

Jarrell, Greg A., and Annette B. Poulsen, "The Returns to Acquiring Firms in Tender Offers: Evidence from Three Decades," *Financial Management,* Autumn 1989, 12–19.

For some additional insights into merger returns, see

Elgers, Pieter T., and John J. Clark, "Merger Types and Shareholder Returns: Additional Evidence," *Financial Management,* Summer 1980, 66–72.

Mueller, Dennis C., "The Effects of Conglomerate Mergers," *Journal of Banking and Finance,* December 1977, 315–347.

Wansley, James W., William R. Lane, and Ho C. Yang, "Abnormal Returns to Acquired Firms by Type of Acquisition and Method of Payment," *Financial Management,* Autumn 1983, 16–22.

For an interesting test of the existence of synergy in mergers, see

Haugen, Robert A., and Terence C. Langetieg, "An Empirical Test for Synergism in Merger," *Journal of Finance,* September 1975, 1003–1014.

For more insights into the likelihood of acceptance of a cash tender offer, see

Hoffmeister, J. Ronald, and Edward A. Dyl, "Predicting Outcomes of Cash Tender Offers," *Financial Management,* Winter 1981, 50–58.

Some additional works on tender offers include

Dodd, Peter, and Richard Ruback, "Tender Offers and Stockholder Returns," *Journal of Financial Economics,* November 1977, 351–373.

Kummer, Donald R., and J. Ronald Hoffmeister, "Valuation Consequences of Cash Tender Offers," *Journal of Finance,* May 1978, 505–516.

The following article examines the effect of merger accounting on stock price:

Hong, Hai, Gershon Mandelker, and R. S. Kaplan, "Pooling versus Purchase: The Effects of Accounting for Mergers on Stock Prices," *Accounting Review,* January 1978, 31–47.

For a selection of articles on LBOs, see the Spring 1989 issue of the Journal of Applied Corporate Finance *and the Spring 1992 issue of* Financial Management.

The Summer 1989 issue of the Journal of Applied Corporate Finance *also focuses on mergers and acquisitions.*

For a selection of articles on LBOs, see the Spring 1989 issue of the Journal of Applied Corporate Finance.

For a very interesting discussion of many of the important merger issues, see

"A Discussion of Mergers and Acquisitions," *Midland Corporate Finance Journal,* Summer 1983, 21–47.

Other recent articles that pertain to this chapter include the following:

Baker, George P., "Beatrice: A Study in the Creation and Destruction of Value," *Journal of Finance,* July 1992, 1081–1119.

Baker, George P., and Karen H. Wruck, "Lessons from a Middle Market LBO: The Case of O. M. Scott," *Journal of Applied Corporate Finance,* Spring 1991, 46–58.

Eckbo, B. Espen, "Mergers and the Value of Antitrust Deterrence," *Journal of Finance,* July 1992, 1005–1029.

Ezzell, John R., H. Christine Hsu, and James A. Miles, "An Analysis of Regulated Rates of Return for Wholly Owned Subsidiaries," *Journal of Financial Research,* Summer 1991, 167–180.

Kaplan, Steven, and Michael S. Weisbach, "The Success of Acquisitions: Evidence from Divestitures," *Journal of Finance,* March 1992, 107–138.

Mitchell, Mark L., and Kenneth Lehn, "Do Bad Bidders Become Good Targets?" *Journal of Applied Corporate Finance,* Summer 1990, 60–69.

Mohan, Nancy, M. Fall Ainina, Daniel Kaufman, and Bernard J. Winger, "Acquisition/Divestiture Valuation Practices in Major U.S. Firms," *Financial Practice and Education,* Spring 1991, 73–81.

Morck, Randall, Andrei Shleifer, and Robert W. Vishny, "Do Managerial Objectives Drive Bad Acquisitions?" *Journal of Finance,* March 1990, 31–48.

Romano, Roberta, "Rethinking Takeover Regulations," *Journal of Applied Corporate Finance,* Fall 1992, 47–57.

Weaver, Samuel C., Robert S. Harris, Daniel W. Bielinski, and Kenneth F. MacKenzie, "Merger and Acquisition Valuation," *Financial Management,* Summer 1991, 85–96.

Wruck, Karen H., "What Really Went Wrong at Revco?" *Journal of Applied Corporate Finance,* Summer 1991, 79–92.

The following case in the Brigham-Gapenski casebook illustrates merger analysis:

Case 40, "Nina's Fashions, Inc.," which focuses on merger valuation.

MULTINATIONAL FINANCIAL MANAGEMENT

oday, the United States no longer dominates the world economy, and innovation, new technologies, and capital flow across national boundaries. The most sophisticated companies are making breakthroughs in foreign labs, obtaining capital from foreign investors, and putting foreign employees on the fast track to the top. Now, dozens of America's top manufacturers, including Dow Chemical, Colgate-Palmolive, Gillette, Hewlett-Packard, and Xerox sell more of their products outside the United States than they do at home. Service firms are not far behind, as Citicorp, Disney, McDonald's, and Time Warner all receive over 20 percent of their revenues from foreign sales.

The trend is even more pronounced in profits. In the past three years, Coca-Cola made more money in both the Pacific and Western Europe than it did in the United States. As companies begin to reap half or more of their sales and profits from abroad, they are blending into the foreign landscape to win acceptance and to avoid political hassles.

At the same time, foreign-based multinationals are arriving on American shores in greater numbers than ever before. Sweden's ABB, the Netherlands' Philips, France's Thomson, and Japan's Fujitsu are all waging campaigns to be identified as American companies that employ Americans, transfer technology to America, and help the U.S. trade balance and overall economic health. Few Americans know, or likely care, that Thomson owns the RCA and General Electric names in consumer electronics and that Philips owns Magnavox.

This chapter was coauthored by Professor Roy Crum of the University of Florida.

These new "world companies" raise a host of questions for governments seeking to shape their nations' economic destinies. For example, does it make any difference what a company's nationality is as long as it provides jobs? What nation controls the technology developed by multinational corporations? What obligations do these companies have to adhere to rules imposed by Washington, Paris, or Tokyo on their foreign operations? And if a U.S. firm makes copiers in Japan and exports them to the United States, should they be counted in the trade deficit in the same way as Toyotas imported from Japan?

Managers of multinational companies face a wide range of issues that are not present when a company operates in a single country. In this chapter, we highlight the key differences between multinational and domestic corporations, and we discuss the impact of these differences on the financial management of U.S. businesses.

The term *multinational corporation* is used to describe a firm that operates in two or more countries. During the period since World War II, a new and fundamentally different form of international commercial activity has developed, and it has greatly increased worldwide economic and political interdependence. Rather than merely buying resources from foreign concerns, multinational firms now make direct investments in fully integrated operations, from extraction of raw materials, through the manufacturing process, to distribution to consumers throughout the world. Today, multinational corporate networks control a large and growing share of the world's technological, marketing, and productive resources.

THE RATIONALE FOR MULTINATIONAL CORPORATIONS

Companies, both U.S. and foreign, go "international" for six primary reasons.

1. To seek new markets. After a company has saturated its home market, growth opportunities are often better in foreign markets. Thus, such homegrown firms as Coca-Cola and McDonald's have aggressively expanded into overseas markets, and foreign firms such as Sony and Toshiba now dominate the U.S. consumer electronics market.

2. To seek raw materials. It is not surprising that many U.S. oil companies, such as Exxon, have major subsidiaries around the world to ensure access to the basic resources needed to sustain the company's primary business line.

3. To seek new technology. No single nation holds a commanding advantage in all technologies, so companies are scouring the globe for leading scientific and design ideas. For example, Xerox has introduced over 80 different office copiers

in the United States that were engineered and built by its Japanese joint venture, Fuji Xerox. Similarly, versions of the superconcentrated detergent that Procter & Gamble first formulated in Japan in response to a rival's product are now being marketed under the Ariel name in Europe and under the Cheer and Tide labels in the United States.

4. To seek production efficiency. Companies in high-production-cost countries are shifting production to low-cost countries. For example, GE has production and assembly plants in Mexico, South Korea, and Singapore, and Japanese manufacturers are shifting some of their production to lower-cost countries in the Pacific Rim. Even BMW and Mercedes-Benz, in response to high production costs in Germany, have announced that they will build production plants in the United States. The ability to shift production from country to country has important implications for labor costs in all countries. For example, when Xerox threatened to move its copier rebuilding work to Mexico, its union in Rochester, New York, agreed to work rule and productivity improvements that kept the operation in the United States. Some multinational companies make decisions almost daily on where to shift production. When Dow Chemical saw European demand for a certain solvent declining, the company scaled back production at a German plant and shifted the plant to another chemical which had previously been imported from the United States. Relying on complex computer models for making such decisions, Dow runs its plants at higher capacity and thus keeps capital costs down.

5. To avoid political and regulatory hurdles. The primary motivation for Japanese auto companies to produce in the United States was to circumvent U.S. import quotas. Now, Honda, Nissan, Toyota, Mazda, and Mitsubishi are all assembling automobiles or trucks in the United States. One of the factors that prompted U.S. pharmaceutical maker SmithKline and Britain's Beecham to merge was that they wanted to avoid licensing and regulatory delays in their largest markets, Western Europe and the United States. Now, SmithKline Beecham can identify itself as an inside player in both Europe and the United States. Finally, when Germany's BASF launched biotechnology research at home, it confronted legal and political challenges from the environmentally conscious Green movement. To counter these challenges, BASF shifted its cancer and immune system research to two laboratories in Boston suburbs. This location is attractive not only because of its large number of engineers and scientists but also because the Boston area has better resolved controversies involving safety, animal rights, and the environment. "We decided it would be better to have the laboratories located where we have fewer insecurities about what will happen in the future," said Rolf-Dieter Acker, BASF's director of biotechnology research.

6. To diversify. By establishing worldwide production facilities and markets, firms can cushion the impact of adverse economic trends in any single country. For example, General Motors softened the blow of poor sales in the United States during the 1990–91 recession with strong sales by its European subsidiaries. In general, geographic diversification works for companies because the economic ups and downs of different countries are not perfectly positively correlated, in spite of the strong links in the global economy.

The past decade has seen an increasing amount of investment in the United States by foreign corporations. This "reverse" investment, which is of increasing concern to U.S. government officials, has actually been growing at a higher rate in the past few years than has U.S. investment abroad. These trends are important because of their implications for eroding the traditional doctrine of independence and self-reliance that has always been a hallmark of U.S. policy. Just as U.S. corporations with extensive overseas operations are said to use their economic power to exert substantial economic and political influence over host governments in many parts of the world, it is feared that foreign corporations are gaining similar sway over U.S. policy. However, these developments suggest an increasing degree of mutual influence and interdependence among business enterprises and nations, to which the United States is not immune. Furthermore increasing foreign investment in the United States is a sign of the attractiveness of our economy.

Some recent events have occurred which have dramatically changed the international financial environment. Here are just a few.

1. The disintegration of the former Soviet Union and the movement toward market economies in the newly formed countries have created a vast new market for international commerce.

2. The reunification of Germany, coupled with the collapse of comm unsim in Eastern Europe, has created significant new opportunities for foreign investment.

3. The European Community and the European Free Trade Association have created a "borderless" region where people, capital, goods, and services move freely among the 19 nations without the burden of tariffs. Negotiations are also under way to create a single "Eurocurrency," which would greatly simplify economic exchange among the participating countries.

4. During the 1980s, U.S. bank regulations were loosened dramatically. One key deregulatory feature was the removal of interest rate ceilings, which allowed banks to attract more foreign deposits by raising rates. Another key feature was the removal of barriers to entry by foreign banks, which resulted in more cross-border banking transactions. Still, U.S. commercial and investment banks do not have as much freedom of action as foreign banks, which has led many U.S. banks to establish subsidiaries in Europe that can offer a wider range of services and, hence, increase global competition in the financial services industry.

SELF-TEST QUESTIONS

What is a multinational corporation?

Why do companies "go international"?

MULTINATIONAL VERSUS DOMESTIC FINANCIAL MANAGEMENT

In theory, the concepts and procedures discussed in the first 24 chapters of the text are valid for both domestic and multinational operations. However, several problems associated with the international environment increase the complexity

of the manager's task in a multinational corporation, and they often force the manager to modify the way alternative courses of action are evaluated and compared. Six major factors distinguish financial management as practiced by firms operating entirely within a single country from management by firms that operate in several different countries:

1. Different currency denominations. Cash flows in various parts of a multinational corporate system will be denominated in different currencies. Hence, an analysis of exchange rates, and the effects of fluctuating currency values, must be included in all financial analyses. Note that exchange rates affect not only the values of funds transferred between countries, but also the pricing—and hence competitiveness—of products shipped between countries.

2. Economic and legal ramifications. Each country in which the firm operates will have its own unique political and economic institutions, and institutional differences among countries can cause significant problems when the corporation tries to coordinate and control the worldwide operations of its subsidiaries. For example, differences in tax laws among countries can cause a given economic transaction to have strikingly dissimilar after-tax consequences, depending on where the transaction occurred. Similarly, differences in legal systems of host nations, such as the Common Law of Great Britain versus the French Civil Law, complicate many matters, from the simple recording of a business transaction to the role played by the judiciary in resolving conflicts. Such differences can restrict multinational corporations' flexibility to deploy resources as they wish, and can even make procedures illegal in one part of the company that are required in another part. These differences also make it difficult for executives trained in one country to operate effectively in another.

3. Language differences. The ability to communicate is critical in all business transactions, and here U.S. citizens are often at a disadvantage because we are generally fluent only in English, while European and Japanese businesspeople are usually fluent in several languages, including English. Although we can communicate easily with foreign top managers because English is the international language of business, we often cannot converse with lower-level managers, workers, and consumers. Thus, they can invade our markets more easily than we can penetrate theirs.

4. Cultural differences. Even within geographic regions that have long been considered relatively homogeneous, different countries have unique cultural heritages that shape values and influence the role of business in the society. Multinational corporations find that matters such as defining the appropriate goals of the firm, attitudes toward risk taking, dealings with employees, the ability to curtail unprofitable operations, and so on, can vary dramatically from one country to the next.

5. Role of governments. Most traditional models in finance assume the existence of a competitive marketplace in which the terms of trade are determined by the participants. The government, through its power to establish basic ground rules, is involved in this process, but its participation is minimal. Thus, the market provides both the primary barometer of success and the indicator of the actions

that must be taken to remain competitive. This view of the process is reasonably correct for the United States and a few other major Western industrialized nations, but it does not accurately describe the situation in most of the world. Frequently, the terms under which companies compete, the actions that must be taken or avoided, and the terms of trade on various transactions are determined not in the marketplace but by direct negotiation between the host government and the multinational corporation. This is essentially a political process, and it must be treated as such. Thus, our traditional financial models have to be recast to include political and other noneconomic facets of the decision.

6. Political risk.   The distinguishing characteristic of a nation that differentiates it from a multinational corporation is that the nation exercises sovereignty over the people and property in its territory. Hence, a nation is free to place constraints on the transfer of corporate resources and even to expropriate without compensation the assets of a firm. This is *political risk*, and it tends to be largely a given rather than a variable that can be changed by negotiation. Political risk varies from country to country, and it must be addressed explicitly in any financial analysis. Another aspect of political risk is terrorism against U.S. firms or executives abroad. For example, U.S. executives have been kidnapped and held for ransom in several South American countries.

These six factors complicate financial management within multinational firms, and they increase the risks faced by the firms involved. However, prospects for high profits often make it worthwhile for firms to accept these risks, and to learn how to minimize or at least live with them.

Self-Test Question

Identify and briefly explain six major factors that complicate financial management in multinational firms.

Exchange Rates

An *exchange rate* specifies the number of units of a given currency that can be purchased for one unit of another currency. Exchange rates appear in the financial sections of newspapers each day. Selected rates from the April 30, 1992, issue of *The Wall Street Journal* are given in Table 25-1. The values shown in Column 1 are the number of U.S. dollars required to purchase one unit of foreign currency on April 29, 1992; this is called a *direct quotation*. Thus, the direct U.S. dollar quotation on April 29, 1992, for the German mark was $0.6031, because one German mark could be bought for 60.31 cents. The exchange rates given in Column 2 represent the number of units of foreign currency that could be purchased for one U.S. dollar; these are called *indirect quotations*. The indirect quotation for the German mark is DM1.6580. (The "DM" stands for *Deutsche mark*; it is equivalent to the symbol "$.") Normal practice in the United States is to use indirect quota-

TABLE 25-1 ILLUSTRATIVE EXCHANGE RATES, APRIL 29, 1992	Direct Quotation: U.S. Dollars Required to Buy One Unit of Foreign Currency (1)	Indirect Quotation: Number of Units of Foreign Currency per U.S. Dollar (2)
British pound	$1.7725	0.5642
Canadian dollar	0.8370	1.1947
Dutch guilder	0.5360	1.8657
French franc	0.17892	5.5890
German mark	0.6031	1.6580
Greek drachma	0.005152	194.10
Indian rupee	0.03529	28.34
Italian lira	0.0008023	1,246.49
Japanese yen	0.007491	133.50
Mexican peso	0.0003252	3,075.50
Norwegian krone	0.1544	6.4755
Saudi Arabian riyal	0.26738	3.7400
Singaporean dollar	0.6046	1.6540
Spanish peseta	0.009612	104.04
Swedish krona	0.1670	5.9865
Swiss franc	0.6570	1.5220

Note: Column 2 equals 1.0 divided by Column 1. However, rounding differences do occur.

Source: *The Wall Street Journal,* April 30, 1992.

tions (Column 2) for all currencies other than British pounds, for which direct quotations are given. Thus, we speak of the pound as "selling at $1.77" but of the German mark as "being at 1.65."

It is also a universal convention on the world's foreign currency exchanges to state all exchange rates except British pounds on a "dollar basis"—that is, as the foreign currency price of one U.S. dollar as reported in Table 25-1, Column 2. Thus, in all currency trading centers, whether in New York, Frankfurt, London, Tokyo, or anywhere else, the exchange rate for the German mark on April 29, 1992, would be displayed as DM1.6580. This convention eliminates confusion when comparing quotations from one trading center with those from another.

We can use the rates in Table 25-1 to show how one works with exchange rates.[1] Suppose a U.S. tourist on holiday flies from New York to London, then to Paris, then on to Munich, and finally back to New York. When she arrives at London's Heathrow Airport on April 29, 1992, she goes to the bank to check the foreign exchange listing. The rate she observes for U.S. dollars is $1.7725; this

---

[1]The exchange rates listed in Table 25-1 actually apply only to wholesale ($1 million or more) trades between banks. The rates that banks offer retail customers on smaller amounts are usually more expensive; that is, customers pay more when they buy currencies and get less when they sell currencies. Furthermore, banks and other currency exchanges often add fixed charges to each retail exchange transaction. We abstract from these details in our illustration.

means that £1 will cost her $1.7725. Assume that she exchanges $2,000 for $2,000/$1.7725 = £1,128.35 and enjoys a week's vacation in London, spending £628.35 while there.

At the end of the week she travels to Dover to catch the Hovercraft to Calais on the coast of France and realizes that she needs to exchange her 500 remaining British pounds for French francs. However, what she sees on the board is the direct quotation between pounds and dollars ($1.7725) and the indirect quotation between francs and dollars (FF5.5890). (For our purposes, we assume that the exchange rates in effect on April 29 remain in effect throughout our example. This is very unrealistic for reasons explained later in this chapter.) The exchange rate between pounds and francs is called a *cross rate,* and it is computed as follows:

$$\text{Cross rate} = \frac{\text{Dollars}}{\text{Pound}} \times \frac{\text{Francs}}{\text{Dollar}} = \frac{\text{Francs}}{\text{Pound}}$$

$$= 1.7725 \text{ dollars per pound} \times 5.5890 \text{ francs per dollar}$$

$$= 9.9065 \text{ francs per pound}.$$

Therefore, for every British pound she would receive 9.9065 French francs, so she would receive $9.9065 \times 500 = 4,953.25 \approx 4,953$ francs.

When she finishes touring in France and arrives in Germany, the American tourist again needs to determine a cross rate, this time between French francs and German marks. The dollar-basis quotes she sees, as shown in Table 25-1, are FF5.5890 per dollar and DM1.6580 per dollar. To find the cross rate, she must divide the two dollar-basis rates:

$$\text{Cross rate} = \frac{\dfrac{\text{Marks}}{\text{Dollar}}}{\dfrac{\text{Francs}}{\text{Dollar}}} = \frac{\text{Marks}}{\text{Franc}}$$

$$= \frac{\text{DM1.6580 per \$}}{\text{FF5.5890 per \$}} = 0.2967 \text{ marks per franc.}$$

Then, if she had FF3,000 remaining, she could exchange them for $0.2967 \times 3,000$ = DM890.10, or about 890 marks.

Finally, when her vacation ends and she returns to New York, the quotation she sees is DM1.6580, which tells her that she can buy 1.6580 marks for a dollar. She now holds 50 marks, so she wants to know how many U.S. dollars she will receive for her marks. First, she must find the reciprocal of the quoted indirect rate,

$$\frac{1}{\text{DM1.6580}} = \$0.6031,$$

which is the direct quote shown in Table 25-1, Column 1. Then she will end up with

$$\$0.6031 \times 50 = \$30.15.$$

In this example, we made two very strong and generally incorrect assumptions. First, we assumed that our traveler had to calculate the appropriate cross rates. For retail transactions, it is customary to display the cross rates directly instead of a series of dollar rates. Second, we assumed that exchange rates remain constant over time. Actually, exchange rates vary every day, often dramatically. We will have more to say about exchange rate fluctuations in the next section.

SELF-TEST QUESTIONS

What is an exchange rate?

Explain the difference between direct and indirect quotations.

What is a cross rate?

THE INTERNATIONAL MONETARY SYSTEM

From the end of World War II until August 1971, the world was on a *fixed exchange rate system* administered by the International Monetary Fund (IMF). Under this system the U.S. dollar was linked to gold ($35 per ounce), and other currencies were then tied to the dollar. Exchange rates between other currencies and the dollar were controlled within narrow limits but then adjusted periodically. For example, in 1964 the British pound was fixed at $2.80 for £1, with a 1 percent permissible fluctuation about this rate. In effect, the United States was the world's central banker, because it was willing to trade gold at the prevailing fixed rates of exchange.

The problem with the fixed exchange rate system is that exchange rates tend to naturally fluctuate because of changes in the supply of and demand for dollars, pounds, and other currencies. These supply and demand changes have two primary sources. First, changes in the demand for currencies depend on changes in imports and exports of goods and services. For example, U.S. importers must buy British pounds to pay for British goods, whereas British importers must buy U.S. dollars to pay for U.S. goods. If U.S. imports from Great Britain exceeded U.S. exports to Great Britain, there would be a greater demand for pounds than for dollars; this would drive up the price of the pound relative to that of the dollar. In terms of Table 25-1, the dollar cost of a pound might rise from $1.7725 to $2.0000. The U.S. dollar would be said to be *depreciating,* whereas the pound would be *appreciating.* In this example, the root cause of the change would be the U.S. *trade deficit* with Great Britain. Of course, if U.S. exports to Great Britain were greater

than U.S. imports from Great Britain, Great Britain would have a trade deficit with the United States.[2]

Second, changes in the demand for a currency, and hence exchange rate fluctuations, depend on capital movements. For example, suppose interest rates in Great Britain were higher than those in the United States. To take advantage of the high British interest rates, U.S. banks, corporations, and even sophisticated individuals would buy pounds with dollars and then use those pounds to purchase high-yielding British securities. These purchases would tend to drive up the price of pounds.[3]

Before August 1971, dollar-pound exchange rate fluctuations were kept within the narrow one percent limit by regular intervention of the British government in the market. When the value of the pound was falling, the Bank of England would step in and buy pounds, offering gold or foreign currencies in exchange. These government purchases would push up the pound rate. Conversely, when the pound rate was too high, the Bank of England would sell pounds. The central banks of other countries operated similarly.

Of course, a central bank's ability to control its exchange rate was limited by its supply of gold and foreign currencies. With the approval of the IMF, a country could *devalue* its currency — which means to officially lower its value relative to other currencies — if it experienced persistent difficulty over a long period in preventing its exchange rate from falling below the lower limit, and if its central bank was running out of the gold and other currencies that could be used to buy its own currency and thus prop up its price. For just these reasons the British pound was devalued from $2.80 per pound to $2.50 per pound in 1967. This lowered the price of British goods in the United States and elsewhere and raised the prices of foreign goods in Britain, thus stopping the British trade deficit that had been

---

[2]If the dollar value of the pound moved up from $1.77 to $2.00, this increase in the value of the pound would mean that British goods would now be more expensive in the U.S. market. For example, a box of candy costing £1 in England would rise in price in the United States from about $1.77 to $2.00. Conversely, U.S. goods would become cheaper in England. For example, the British could now buy goods worth $2.00 for £1, whereas before the exchange rate change, £1 would buy merchandise worth only $1.77. These price changes would, of course, tend to *reduce* British exports and *increase* imports, and this, in turn, would lower the exchange rate, because people in the United States and other nations would be buying fewer pounds to pay for English goods. However, before 1971 the one percent limit severely constrained the market's ability to reach an equilibrium between trade balances and exchange rates.

[3]Such capital inflows would also tend to drive down British interest rates. If rates were high in the first place because of efforts by the British monetary authorities to curb inflation, the international currency flows would tend to thwart that effort. This is one of the reasons why domestic and international economics are so closely linked.

A good example of this occurred during the summer of 1981. In an effort to curb inflation, the Federal Reserve Board helped push U.S. interest rates to record levels. This, in turn, caused an outflow of capital from European nations to the United States. The Europeans were suffering from a severe recession and wanted to keep interest rates down in order to stimulate investment, but U.S. policy made this difficult because of international capital flows. Just the opposite occurred in 1992, when the Fed drove short-term rates down to record lows in the United States to promote growth while Germany, and most other European countries, pushed their rates higher to combat the inflationary pressures of reunification. Thus, investment in the United States was dampened as investors moved their money overseas to capture higher interest rates.

putting pressure on the pound in the first place. Conversely, a nation with an export surplus and a strong currency might *revalue* its currency upward, as West Germany did twice in the 1960s.

Devaluations and revaluations occurred only rarely before 1971. They were usually accompanied by severe international financial repercussions, partly because nations tended to postpone these needed measures until economic pressures had built up to explosive proportions. For this and other reasons the old international monetary system came to a dramatic end in the early 1970s, when the U.S. dollar, the foundation upon which all other currencies were anchored, was cut loose from the gold standard and, in effect, allowed to "float."

The United States and the other major nations currently operate under a system of *floating exchange rates,* whereby currency prices are allowed to seek their own levels without much governmental intervention. The central bank of each country does still intervene in the foreign exchange market, buying and selling its currency to smooth out exchange rate fluctuations to some extent, and there have been agreements by groups of countries to keep the relative values of their currencies within a predetermined range. Such an agreement by the Group of Seven at the Seoul Economic Summit in October 1985 caused the U.S. dollar to fall substantially against most major currencies. This action was endorsed as appropriate at the Washington Economic Summit in September 1987. The Group of Seven was also responsible for helping to stabilize the falling dollar in early 1988.

Each central bank also tries to keep its average exchange rate at a level deemed desirable by its government's economic policy. This is important, because exchange rates have a profound effect on the levels of imports and exports, which in turn influence the level of domestic employment. For example, if a country is having a problem with unemployment, its central bank might encourage a *decline* in the value of its currency. This would cause its goods to be cheaper in world markets and thus stimulate exports, production, and domestic employment. Thus in early 1993, the Clinton administration supposedly embarked on a campaign to "talk down" the dollar versus the yen in an attempt to cut the U.S. trade deficit by making Japanese goods more expensive in the United States and U.S. exports less expensive in Japan. Conversely, the central bank of a country that is operating at full capacity and experiencing inflation might try to raise the value of its currency to reduce exports and increase imports. Under the current floating rate system, however, such intervention can affect the situation only temporarily, if at all, because central bank interventions are quickly swamped by market forces.

Figure 25-1 shows how the values of German marks and Japanese yen moved in comparison with the dollar from 1981 to 1992. The dollar strengthened, or appreciated, against the mark from 1981 to 1985 but then generally weakened, or depreciated, from 1985 to 1992, with slight reversals in 1989 and 1991. The Japanese yen was relatively stable against the dollar in the first half of the decade, but then it appreciated from 1985 to 1988 (fewer yen to buy a dollar), depreciated during the last two years of the decade, and finally appreciated again from 1990 to 1992.

Exchange rate fluctuations can have a profound impact on international monetary transactions. For example, in 1985 it cost Honda Motors 2,380,000 yen to

FIGURE 25-1   YEN AND MARK EXCHANGE RATES

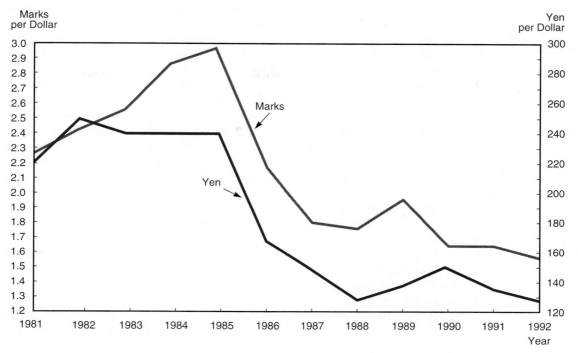

	Yen per Dollar	Marks per Dollar
1981	221	2.26
1982	249	2.43
1983	238	2.55
1984	237	2.85
1985	238	2.94
1986	168	2.17
1987	145	1.80
1988	128	1.76
1989	138	1.88
1990	145	1.62
1991	135	1.66
1992	127	1.56

Note: The exchange rates listed above are annual averages.

build a particular model in Japan and ship it to the United States. The model carried a U.S. sticker price of $12,000. Since the $12,000 sales price was the equivalent of (238 yen per dollar)($12,000) = 2,856,000 yen, the automaker had built a 20 percent markup into the U.S. sales price. However, three years later, the dollar had depreciated to 128 yen. Now, if the model still sold for $12,000, the yen

return to Honda would be only (128 yen per dollar)($12,000) = 1,536,000 yen, and the automaker would be losing about 35 percent on each auto sold. Even though U.S. prices held firm, the 46 percent depreciation of the dollar against the yen turned a healthy profit into a loss. In fact, for Honda to maintain its 20 percent markup, the model would have to sell in the United States for 2,856,000 yen/128 yen per dollar = $22,312.50. No wonder Honda now builds its most popular model, the Accord, in Marysville, Ohio!

You might be thinking that it takes years for major fluctuations in exchange rates to occur. However, major changes can occur in much shorter periods. Suppose, on January 1, 1986, a German investor wanted to take advantage of the comparatively high interest rates on U.S. Treasury securities, so he bought a 6-month T-bill for $9,700 that would be worth $10,000 at the end of June. This works out to about a 6 percent annual return. In January, the exchange rate was 2.44 marks per dollar, so the T-bill cost the investor 2.44($9,700) = 23,668 marks. At the end of June, the exchange rate was only 2.23 marks per dollar, so the investor's mark return was 2.23($10,000) = 22,300 marks. Thus, exchange rate fluctuations turned the 6 percent expected return into a 12 percent loss.

The inherent volatility of exchange rates under a floating system increases the uncertainty of the cash flows for a multinational corporation. Because these cash flows are generated in many parts of the world, they are denominated in many different currencies. Since exchange rates change, the dollar-equivalent value of the consolidated cash flows can also fluctuate. This is known as *exchange rate risk,* and it is a major factor differentiating the multinational corporation from a purely domestic one. However, there are numerous ways for a multinational corporation to manage and limit its exchange rate risk, and several of them are discussed in the next section.

Before closing our discussion of the international monetary system, we should note that not all currencies are *convertible.* A currency is convertible when the issuing nation allows it to be traded in the currency markets and is willing to redeem the currency at market rates. This means that, except for very limited central bank influence, the issuing government loses control over the value of its currency. Lack of convertibility creates major problems for international trade. For example, consider the situation faced by Pepsico when it wanted to open a chain of Pizza Hut restaurants in the Soviet Union. The Russian ruble is not convertible, so Pepsico could not take the profits from its restaurants out of the Soviet Union in the form of rubles. If it took rubles out, there would be no mechanism to exchange the rubles for dollars, so the investment in the Soviet Union would be worthless to a U.S. company. Instead, Pepsico arranged to use the ruble profit from the restaurants to buy Russian vodka, which it then shipped to the United States and sold. The profit on the vodka sales, which is in dollars, contains the profit from the Russian restaurants, as well as any added profits made on the vodka import business.

SELF-TEST QUESTIONS

What is the difference between a fixed exchange rate system and a floating rate system? Which system is better? Explain.

What does it mean to say that the dollar is depreciating with respect to the British pound? For a U.S. consumer of British goods, would this be good or bad? How could consumption changes arrest the decline of the dollar? What is a convertible currency?

TRADING IN FOREIGN EXCHANGE

Importers, exporters, and tourists, as well as governments, buy and sell currencies in the foreign exchange market. For example, when a U.S. trader imports automobiles from Germany, payment will probably be made in German marks. The importer buys marks (through its bank) in the foreign exchange market, much as one buys common stocks on the New York Stock Exchange or pork bellies on the Chicago Mercantile Exchange. However, whereas stock and commodity exchanges have organized trading floors, the foreign exchange market consists of a network of brokers and banks based in New York, London, Tokyo, and other financial centers. Most buy-and-sell orders are conducted by computer and telephone.[4]

SPOT RATES AND FORWARD RATES

The exchange rates shown earlier in Table 25-1 are known as *spot rates,* which means the rate paid for delivery of the currency "on the spot" or, in reality, no more than one day after the day of the trade. For most of the world's major currencies, it is also possible to buy (or sell) currencies for delivery at some agreed-upon future date, usually 30, 90, or 180 days from the day the transaction is negotiated. This rate is known as the *forward exchange rate.* For example, if a U.S. firm must make payment to a Swiss firm in 90 days, the U.S. firm's treasurer can buy Swiss francs today for delivery in 90 days, paying the 90-day forward rate of $0.6491 per Swiss franc (which equals 1.5405 SF per dollar). Forward rates are exactly analogous to futures prices on commodity exchanges, where contracts are drawn up for wheat or corn to be delivered at agreed-upon prices at some future date. The contract is signed today, and the future dollar cost of the Swiss francs is then known with certainty. Purchase of a forward contract is one technique for eliminating the volatility of future cash flows caused by fluctuations in exchange rates. This technique, which is called "hedging," will be discussed in more detail shortly.

Forward rates for 30-, 90-, and 180-day delivery, along with the spot rates for April 29, 1992, for the more commonly traded currencies are given in Table 25-2. If one can obtain *more* of the foreign currency for a dollar in the forward than in the spot market, the forward currency is less valuable than the spot currency, and the forward currency is said to be selling at a *discount.* Thus, because 1 dollar

---

[4]For a more detailed explanation of exchange rate determination and operations of the foreign exchange market, see Steven Bell and Bryan Kettell, *Foreign Exchange Handbook* (Westport, Conn.: Quorum Books, 1983).

INFLATION, INTEREST RATES, AND EXCHANGE RATES

Relative inflation rates, or the rates of inflation in foreign countries compared with that in the home country, have many implications for multinational financial decisions. Obviously, relative inflation rates will greatly influence future production costs at home and abroad. Equally important, they have a dominant influence on relative interest rates as well as exchange rates. Both of these factors influence the methods chosen by multinational corporations for financing their foreign investments, and both have a notable effect on the profitability of foreign investments.

The currencies of countries with higher inflation rates than that of the United States tend to depreciate over time against the dollar. Some countries for which this has been the case include France, Italy, Mexico, and all the South American nations. On the other hand, the currencies of Germany, Switzerland, and Japan, which in general have had less inflation than the United States, have appreciated relative to the dollar. *In fact, a foreign currency will, on average, depreciate (or appreciate) at a percentage rate approximately equal to the amount by which its inflation rate exceeds (or is less than) our own.*

Relative inflation rates are also reflected in interest rates. The interest rate in any country is largely determined by its inflation rate. Therefore, countries currently experiencing higher rates of inflation than the United States also tend to have higher interest rates, whereas the reverse is true for countries with lower inflation rates.

It is tempting for the treasurer of a multinational corporation to borrow in the countries with the lowest interest rates. However, this is not always the best strategy. Suppose, for example, that interest rates in Germany have generally been lower than those in the United States because of Germany's lower inflation rate. A U.S. multinational firm often could save interest by borrowing in Germany. However, because of relative inflation rates, the mark can be expected to appreciate in the future, causing the dollar cost of annual interest and principal payments on this debt to rise over time. Thus, *the lower interest rate could be more than offset by losses from currency appreciation.* Similarly, one should not expect multinational corporations to avoid borrowing in a country like Brazil, where interest rates have been very high, because future depreciation of the Brazilian cruzeiro could make such borrowing relatively inexpensive.

SELF-TEST QUESTIONS

What effects do relative inflation rates have on relative interest rates?

What happens over time to the currencies of countries with higher inflation rates than that of the United States? To those with lower inflation rates?

Why might a multinational corporation decide to borrow in a country like Brazil, where interest rates are high, rather than in a country like Germany, where interest rates are low?

INTERNATIONAL MONEY AND CAPITAL MARKETS

Stock ownership of U.S. multinational corporations that invest directly in foreign countries is one way for U.S. citizens to invest in world markets. A better way is to purchase stocks, bonds, or various money market instruments issued in foreign countries. U.S. citizens actually do invest substantial amounts in the stocks and bonds of large corporations headquartered in Europe, and to a lesser extent in firms headquartered in the Far East and South America. They also buy securities issued by foreign governments. Such investments in foreign corporations are known as *portfolio investments,* and they are distinguished from *direct investments* in physical assets by U.S. corporations.

EURODOLLAR MARKET

A *Eurodollar* is a U.S. dollar deposited in a bank outside the United States. (Although they are called Eurodollars because they originated in Europe, Eurodollars are really any dollars deposited in any part of the world, other than the United States.) The bank in which the deposit is made may be a host country institution, such as Barclay's Bank in London; the foreign branch of a U.S. bank, such as Citibank's Paris branch; or even a foreign branch of a third-country bank, such as Barclay's Munich branch. Most Eurodollar deposits are for $500,000 or more, and they have maturities ranging from overnight to about five years.

The major difference between Eurodollar deposits and regular U.S. time deposits is their geographic locations. The two types of deposits do not involve different currencies—in both cases, dollars are on deposit. However, Eurodollars are outside the direct control of the U.S. monetary authorities, so U.S. banking regulations, such as fractional reserves and FDIC insurance premiums, do not apply. Because of the lower cost structure to banks, the interest rate paid on Eurodollar deposits tends to be higher than domestic U.S. rates on equivalent instruments.

Although the dollar is the leading international currency, German marks, Swiss francs, Japanese yen, and other currencies are also deposited outside their home countries; these *Eurocurrencies* are handled in exactly the same way as Eurodollars.

Eurodollars are borrowed by U.S. and foreign corporations and governments which need dollars for various purposes, especially to pay for goods exported from the United States and to invest in the U.S. stock market. Also, U.S. dollars are used as an international currency, or international medium of exchange, and many Eurodollars are used for this purpose. It is interesting to note that Eurodollars were actually "invented" by the Soviets in 1946. International merchants did not trust the Soviets or their rubles, so the Soviets bought some dollars (for gold), deposited them in a Paris bank, and then used these dollars to buy goods in the world markets. Others found it convenient to use dollars this same way, and soon the Eurodollar market was in full swing.

Eurodollars are usually held in interest-bearing accounts. The interest rate paid on these deposits depends (1) on the bank's lending rate, as the interest a bank earns on loans determines its willingness and ability to pay interest on deposits,

and (2) on rates of return available on U.S. money market instruments. If rates in the United States were above Eurodollar deposit rates, these funds would be sent back and invested in the United States, whereas if Eurodollar deposit rates were significantly above U.S. rates, which is more often the case, more dollars would be sent out of the United States to become Eurodollars. Given the existence of the Eurodollar market, and the easy flow of dollars to and from the United States, it is easy to see why interest rates in the United States cannot be insulated from those in other parts of the world.

Interest rates on Eurodollar deposits (and loans) are tied to a standard rate known by the acronym *LIBOR,* which stands for *London InterBank Offered Rate.* LIBOR is the rate of interest offered by the largest and strongest London banks on dollar deposits of significant size. In April 1993, LIBOR rates were about half a percentage point above domestic U.S. bank rates on time deposits of the same maturity — for example, 2.7 percent for 3-month U.S. CDs versus 3.2 percent for LIBOR CDs. The Eurodollar market is essentially a short-term market; most loans and deposits are for less than one year.

In addition to dollar-denominated bank loans, corporations can borrow or lend short term by issuing or buying dollar-denominated commercial paper abroad. Such issues are called *Eurocommercial paper,* or just *Euro-CP.* Dealers who place Eurocommercial paper are willing to purchase outstanding paper prior to maturity, and hence, they have created a secondary market for these securities. Although the cost to U.S. issuers is often higher than the cost of domestic commercial paper, some multinational companies maintain a presence in the Eurocommercial paper market in case future large-scale borrowings might be required.

INTERNATIONAL BOND MARKETS

Any bond sold outside the country of the borrower is called an international bond. However, there are two important types of international bonds: foreign bonds and Eurobonds. *Foreign bonds* are bonds sold by a foreign borrower but denominated in the currency of the country in which the issue is sold. For instance, Bell Canada may need U.S. dollars to finance the operations of its subsidiaries in the United States. If it decides to raise the needed capital in the domestic U.S. bond market, the bond will be underwritten by a syndicate of U.S. investment bankers, denominated in U.S. dollars, and sold to U.S. investors in accordance with SEC and applicable state regulations. Except for the foreign origin of the borrower (Canada), this bond will be indistinguishable from those issued by equivalent U.S. corporations. Since Bell Canada is a foreign corporation, however, the bond will be called a foreign bond.

The term *Eurobond* is used to designate any bond sold in some country *other than* the one in whose currency the bond is denominated. Examples include a British firm's issue of pound bonds sold in France, a Ford Motor Company issue denominated in dollars and sold in Germany, and a German firm's sale of mark-denominated bonds in Switzerland. The institutional arrangements by which Eurobonds are marketed are different than those for most other bond issues, with the

most important distinction being a far lower level of required disclosure than is usually found for bonds issued in domestic markets, particularly in the United States. Governments tend to be less strict when regulating securities denominated in foreign currencies than they are on home-currency securities because the bonds' purchasers are generally more "sophisticated." The lower disclosure requirements result in lower total transaction costs for Eurobonds.

Eurobonds appeal to investors for several reasons. Generally, they are issued in bearer form rather than as registered bonds, so the names and nationalities of investors are not recorded. Individuals who desire anonymity, whether for privacy reasons or for tax avoidance, find Eurobonds to their liking. Similarly, most governments do not withhold taxes on interest payments associated with Eurobonds. If the investor requires an effective yield of 10 percent, a Eurobond that is exempt from tax withholding would need a coupon rate of 10 percent. Another type of bond—for instance, a domestic issue subject to a 30 percent withholding tax on interest paid to foreigners—would need a coupon rate of 14.3 percent to yield an after-withholding rate of 10 percent. Investors who desire secrecy would not want to file for a refund of the tax, so they would prefer to hold the Eurobond.

More than half of all Eurobonds are denominated in dollars; bonds in other currencies, including the Japanese yen, German marks, and Dutch guilders, account for most of the rest. Although centered in Europe, Eurobonds are truly international. Their underwriting syndicates include investment bankers from all parts of the world, and the bonds are sold to investors not only in Europe but also in such faraway places as Bahrain and Singapore. Up to a few years ago, Eurobonds were issued solely by multinational firms, by international financial institutions, or by national governments. Today, however, the Eurobond market is also being tapped by purely domestic U.S. firms such as electric utilities, which find that by borrowing overseas they can lower their debt costs.

In closing, we should note that more and more European financial transactions are being made, not in the currency of one country, but rather in *European currency units (ECUs)*. The ECU, which is simply a unit of account, is made up of the currencies of the 12 countries that belong to the European monetary system. For example, at one point in time, the ECU might consist of 1.332 French francs, 0.6242 German marks, 0.2198 Dutch guilders, 6.885 Spanish pesetas, and so on, where the weights represent the relative sizes of each country's economy. The ECU is recognized as a means of payment among European governments and private businesses. It is also used in international money and capital markets and as a foreign currency reserve by Europe's central banks. Although no ECU paper bills or coins exist, it is treated as any other currency—companies can make ECU deposits at banks, obtain ECU loans, and engage in ECU foreign exchange spot and forward transactions. Depending on exchange rate fluctuations of the individual currencies, which, at least in theory, are kept within narrow limits by governmental actions, one ECU might translate into, say, 10 German marks, or 33 French francs, or 12 Dutch guilders. Thus, companies can deposit an amount in a single currency, have it converted into ECUs as the unit of account, earn interest in ECUs at some stated rate, and then, at maturity, receive the ECU proceeds, with actual payment made in some currency that may or may not be the currency originally

deposited. The purpose of the ECU is to create a "currency" that is less volatile relative to its component currencies than any two currencies are to each other.

INTERNATIONAL STOCK MARKETS

New issues of stock are sold in international markets for a variety of reasons. For example, a non-U.S. firm might sell an entire issue in the United States because it can tap a much larger source of capital than in its home country. Also, a U.S. firm may tap a foreign market because it wants to create an equity market presence to accompany its operations in that country. Large multinational companies also occasionally issue new stock simultaneously in multiple countries. For example, Alcan Aluminum, a Canadian company, recently issued new stock in Canada, Europe, and the United States simultaneously, using different underwriting syndicates in each market.

In addition to new issues, outstanding stocks of large multinational companies are increasingly being listed on multiple international exchanges. For example, Coca-Cola's stock is traded on six stock exchanges in the United States, including the NYSE, four stock exchanges in Switzerland, and the Frankfurt stock exchange in Germany. Some foreign stocks are listed in the United States—an example here is Royal Dutch Petroleum, which is listed on the NYSE. In addition to direct listing, U.S. investors can invest in foreign companies through *American depository receipts (ADRs)*, which are certificates representing ownership of foreign stock held in trust. More than 800 ADRs are now available in the United States, with most of them traded on the over-the-counter (OTC) market. However, more and more ADRs are being listed on the New York Stock Exchange, with the latest being Germany's Daimler-Benz, which was listed in 1993.

INTERNATIONAL PORTFOLIO DIVERSIFICATION

One reason for individuals to invest in foreign securities is to obtain global diversification. To see what is involved, consider Figure 25-2, which shows the Capital Market Line (CML) as we developed it back in Chapter 5. The green shaded area represents the feasible set of portfolios of domestic risky assets; the grey shaded area represents the addition to the feasible set when international assets are included; k_{RF} represents the rate of return on domestic riskless assets; M_D is the domestic market portfolio; and M_G is the *global market portfolio,* which contains foreign as well as domestic risky securities. Note that there are no riskless foreign assets—even foreign Treasury bills are risky because of exchange risk. Since returns on foreign securities are not perfectly correlated with those on domestic securities, the inclusion of foreign assets in the portfolio shifts the boundary (or feasible) set of portfolios upward and to the left. This has the effect of rotating the CML upward, from CML_D to CML_G. This, in turn, permits an investor to move from portfolio P_1, on indifference curve I_1, to portfolio P_2, on the higher indifference curve I_2. P_2 contains a combination of domestic and foreign stocks, plus riskless domestic government securities, and it is better than P_1 in that it provides a higher expected return for a lower level of risk.

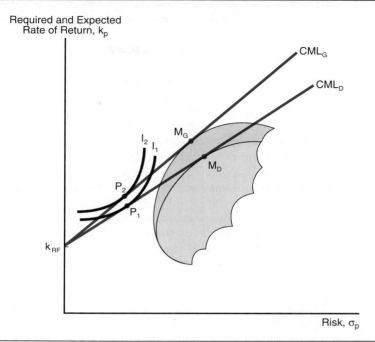

FIGURE 25-2

PORTFOLIO ANALYSIS
WITH GLOBAL
DIVERSIFICATION

SELF-TEST QUESTIONS

Differentiate between foreign portfolio investments and direct foreign investments.

What are Eurodollars?

Has the development of the Eurodollar market made it easier or more difficult for the Federal Reserve to control U.S. interest rates?

Differentiate between foreign bonds and Eurobonds.

Why do Eurobonds appeal to investors?

What is an ECU?

Within a CAPM framework, what is the rationale for U.S. investors to hold foreign securities?

MULTINATIONAL CAPITAL BUDGETING

Up to now, we have discussed the general environment in which multinational firms operate. In the remainder of the chapter we will see how international factors affect key corporate decisions, beginning in this section with capital budgeting.

Although the same basic principles of capital budgeting analysis apply to both foreign and domestic operations, there are some key differences. First, cash flow estimation is generally much more complex for overseas investments. Most multinational firms set up a separate subsidiary in each foreign country in which they operate, and the relevant cash flows for the parent company are the dividends and royalties repatriated from the subsidiaries. Second, these cash flows must be converted to the currency of the parent company and thus are subject to future exchange rate changes. For example, General Motors' German subsidiary may make a profit of 100 million marks in 1996, but the value of these profits to GM will depend on the dollar/mark exchange rate. How many *dollars* is 100 million marks worth? This is the relevant issue for GM's managers and stockholders.

Third, dividends and royalties are normally taxed by both foreign and home-country governments. Furthermore, a foreign government may restrict the amount of the cash flows that may be *repatriated* to the parent company. For example, some governments place a ceiling, stated as a percentage of the company's net worth, on the amount of cash dividends that may be paid by a subsidiary to its parent company. Such restrictions are normally intended to force multinational firms to reinvest earnings in the foreign country, although restrictions are sometimes imposed to prevent large currency outflows, which might affect the exchange rate.

Whatever the host country's motivation, the result is that the parent corporation cannot use cash flows blocked in the foreign country to pay current dividends to its shareholders, nor does it have the flexibility to reinvest these cash flows elsewhere in the world, where expected returns may be higher. Hence, from the perspective of the parent organization, *the cash flows relevant for the analysis of a foreign investment are the cash flows that the subsidiary can legally send back to the parent.* The present value of these cash flows is found by applying an appropriate discount rate, and this present value is then compared with the parent's required investment in the project to determine the project's NPV.

In addition to the complexities of the cash flow analysis, *the cost of capital may be different for a foreign project than for an equivalent domestic project, because foreign projects may be more or less risky.* A higher risk could arise from two primary sources—(1) exchange rate risk and (2) political risk—while a lower risk might result from international diversification.

Exchange rate risk reflects the inherent uncertainty about the home currency value of cash flows sent back to the parent. In other words, foreign projects have an added risk element that relates to what the basic cash flows will be worth in the parent company's home currency. The foreign currency cash flows to be turned over to the parent must be converted into U.S. dollars by translating them at expected future exchange rates. An analysis should be conducted to ascertain the effects of exchange rate variations, and, on the basis of this analysis, an exchange rate risk premium should be added to the domestic cost of capital to reflect the *exchange rate risk* inherent in the investment. As we have seen, it is sometimes possible to hedge against exchange rate fluctuations, but it may not be possible to hedge completely, especially on long-term projects, and, in addition, the costs of hedging must be subtracted from the project's cash flows.

Rank	Country	Political Risk	Financial Risk	Economic Risk	Composite Risk
1	Switzerland	93.0	50.0	39.5	91.5
9	United States	78.0	49.0	39.5	83.5
10	Canada	81.0	48.0	37.0	83.0
25	Venezuela	75.0	40.0	36.0	75.5
50	Israel	58.0	33.0	34.5	63.0
75	Panama	47.0	24.0	38.0	54.5
100	Peru	45.0	28.0	21.5	47.5
125	Burma	27.0	9.0	22.5	28.5
129	Liberia	10.0	8.0	12.0	15.0

Source: *International Country Risk Guide,* August 1991.

Political risk refers to any action (or the probability of such action) by a host government which reduces the value of a company's investment. It includes at one extreme the expropriation without compensation of the subsidiary's assets, but it also includes less drastic actions that reduce the value of the parent firm's investment in the foreign subsidiary such as higher taxes, tighter repatriation or currency controls, and restrictions on prices charged. The risk of expropriation of U.S. assets abroad is small in traditionally friendly and stable countries such as Great Britain or Switzerland. However, in Latin America, Africa, the Far East, and Eastern Europe, the risk may be substantial. Past expropriations include those of ITT and Anaconda Copper in Chile, Gulf Oil in Bolivia, Occidental Petroleum in Libya, Enron Corporation in Peru, and the assets of many companies in Iraq, Iran, and Cuba.

Several companies rate the political risk of countries, an admittedly tough task. For example, International Business Communications, a London company, publishes the *International Country Risk Guide,* which contains individual ratings for political, financial, and economic risk, along with a composite rating for each country. Table 25-3 contains selected portions of the August 1991 report. The political variable—which makes up 50 percent of the composite rating—includes factors such as government corruption and the gap between economic expectations and reality. The financial rating looks at such things as the likelihood of losses from exchange controls and loan defaults. The economic rating takes into account such factors as inflation and debt-service costs.

The maximum, or least risky, score is 100 for the political factors and 50 each for the financial and economic factors. Note that the United States is ranked ninth on the list, below Switzerland, Luxembourg, Norway, Austria, Germany, Netherlands, Brunei, and Japan. Liberia, as shown in Table 25-3, is ranked last.

Generally, political risk premiums are not added to the cost of capital to adjust for this risk. If a company's management has a serious concern that a given country might expropriate foreign assets, it simply will not make significant investments in that country. Expropriation is viewed as a catastrophic or ruinous event, and managers are extraordinarily risk averse when faced with ruinous loss possibilities.

However, companies can take steps to reduce the potential loss from expropriation in three major ways: (1) by financing the subsidiary with local capital, (2) by structuring operations so that the subsidiary has value only as a part of the integrated corporate system, and (3) by obtaining insurance against economic losses from expropriation from a source such as the Overseas Private Investment Corporation (OPIC). In the latter case, insurance premiums would have to be added to the project's cost.

The principles of capital budgeting in a multinational setting can be illustrated with data from International Electronics Corporation (IEC), which is analyzing a proposal to build a plant in Caribia to assemble electronic monitoring and testing equipment for sale worldwide through the company's marketing and distribution facility in Curaçao. If the project is accepted, a new subsidiary, IEC Caribia, will be incorporated in Caribia. It will be financed solely with common stock, all of which will be owned by the parent firm.

While the corporate income tax in Caribia is a low 20 percent compared with the 50 percent federal-plus-state rate that IEC pays in the United States, the government of Caribia places several restrictions on multinational corporations that will have an impact on the analysis. To preserve investment capital in Caribia, the government prohibits the removal of contributed equity until the investment is sold or otherwise liquidated. Thus, depreciation cash flows may not be repatriated until the end of the project's life. Dividends are not subjected to a withholding tax, but they must come only from net income, and they are restricted to a maximum of 20 percent of the contributed equity in any year. At the end of the project's life, any reinvested earnings can be repatriated by the parent. The investment, to be made in January 1994, consists almost entirely of plant and equipment, and the cost will be $10 million or 50 million Caribian pesos (P50 million). Because of the nature of technological change in the electronics industry, IEC bases its analysis on a time horizon of five years. At the end of the five years (in December 1998), the company estimates that the book value of the facility, 25 million Caribian pesos, is the best estimate of its market value.

The Caribian government recognizes the IEC has developed and patented much of the technology employed in the operations, and is willing to compensate the company for its use. IEC and the Minister of Commerce have reached an agreement that establishes a royalty rate of 10 percent of gross revenues to be paid directly to the parent. Management fees, however, are prohibited by law in Caribia. Table 25-4 summarizes the projected income statements for the Caribian subsidiary.

The data in Table 25-4 are straightforward down to "Dividend repatriated." In the 1994 column, we see that net income, 8 million pesos, is less than 20 percent of the 50 million pesos of original equity (0.2×50 million = 10 million pesos, which is the maximum dividend in any year), so the entire 8 million pesos can be returned to the parent as a dividend. Dividends in subsequent years are limited to 10 million pesos. IEC reports its worldwide net income to the U.S. Internal Revenue Service, but it receives *tax credits* for taxes paid overseas, including a credit for taxes paid by its subsidiary to the Caribian tax authorities. The amount of the

	1994	1995	1996	1997	1998
Revenues	50.00	55.00	60.00	65.00	70.00
Operating costs	30.00	30.00	35.00	35.00	40.00
Depreciation	5.00	5.00	5.00	5.00	5.00
Royalties (10% of revenue)	5.00	5.50	6.00	6.50	7.00
Income before tax	10.00	14.50	14.00	18.50	18.00
Caribian tax (20%)	2.00	2.90	2.80	3.70	3.60
Net income	8.00	11.60	11.20	14.80	14.40
Dividend repatriated (10.0 maximum)	8.00	10.00	10.00	10.00	10.00
U.S. tax on dividend	3.00	3.75	3.75	3.75	3.75
After-tax dividend	5.00	6.25	6.25	6.25	6.25
Royalty (10% of gross revenues)	5.00	5.50	6.00	6.50	7.00
U.S. tax on royalty (50%)	2.50	2.75	3.00	3.25	3.50
After-tax royalty	2.50	2.75	3.00	3.25	3.50
Net cash flow	7.50	9.00	9.25	9.50	9.75

credit depends on the dividend payout ratio of the subsidiary. With a 100 percent payout, the parent would pay the difference between the U.S. tax rate of 50 percent and the Caribian tax rate of 20 percent. For example, in 1994, when the payout was 100 percent, the subsidiary earned 10 million pesos before Caribian tax and paid 2 million in tax (20 percent) to the Caribian government, so an additional 30 percent tax, or 3 million pesos, must be paid to the U.S. government. The total tax paid on the dividend is limited to 5 million pesos, or 50 percent of taxable income; this is the same rate as would be paid if the subsidiary had been located in the United States, in which case it would have paid a 50 percent tax on 10 million pesos of net income.[5]

In 1995 through 1998, net income exceeds 10 millions pesos, the maximum dividend payment allowed under Caribian law, so dividends are set at 10 million. To see what is involved, consider 1995. Theoretically, the United States could tax the 14.5 million peso pre-tax income, getting 14.5(0.5) = 7.25 million pesos, less a credit of 2.9 million pesos, for a net tax bill of 4.35 million pesos, but this is not done. Alternatively, the United States could treat as taxable income only the dividends repatriated, which would produce a net tax bill of 10(0.5) − 2.9 = 2.1 million pesos, but this is not done either. Under U.S. law, taxes are collected on the portion of income that is actually repatriated. In the years 1995–1998, we proceed as follows: (1) We "gross up" the dividend payment to determine the before-tax net income which would be required to produce the actual dividend payment. This is equal to the dividend repatriated divided by (1.0 − Caribian tax

---

[5]If the foreign tax rate had been higher than the U.S. tax rate, the tax credit would be greater than the taxes owed to the U.S. government on equivalent before-tax earnings by a U.S. firm. This deficit could be used to offset U.S. taxes on income from other foreign subsidiaries in any part of the world.

TABLE 25-5	Year of Depreciation	Amount of Depreciation		Compounding Factor at 8 Percent		Terminal Value in 1998
DEPRECIATION CASH FLOWS REPATRIATED (MILLIONS OF CARIBIAN PESOS)	1994	5.0	×	$(1.08)^4$	=	6.802
	1995	5.0	×	$(1.08)^3$	=	6.299
	1996	5.0	×	$(1.08)^2$	=	5.832
	1997	5.0	×	$(1.08)^1$	=	5.400
	1998	5.0	×	$(1.08)^0$	=	5.000
		25.0		Total		29.333
				Less depreciation		25.000
				Taxable income		4.333
				Caribian tax (20%)		0.867
				After Caribian tax		28.466
				U.S. tax		1.300
				After U.S. tax		27.166

rate), or 10/0.8 = 12.5 million pesos. Had IEC Caribia had 12.5 million pesos of income, it would have paid 20 percent, or 2.5 million pesos, in taxes and has 10 million left for the dividend which it actually paid. (2) We now multiply this 12.5 million before-tax equivalent amount by the difference between the tax rate in the United States and the Caribian rate, or 30 percent, getting 0.30(12.5) = 3.75 million pesos. This is the additional tax liability in the United States on the income repatriated.[6]

However, 3.75 million pesos is not the total U.S. tax liability. An additional source of taxable income to the parent is the royalties paid by IEC Caribia. Royalties are an operating expense to the subsidiary, so they are not subject to Caribian tax. To the parent, however, they are income, and the royalties are taxed at the full 50 percent tax rate. Total operating cash flow to the U.S. parent, then, is the sum of the after-tax dividend and the after-tax royalty. This is shown in the last line of Table 25-4.

Since cash flows from depreciation cannot be repatriated until the company is liquidated at the end of 1998, they must be reinvested locally. Assume that there are no other attractive real asset investments available, so the depreciation cash flows will be invested in Caribian government bonds which earn 8 percent annual interest, with interest not subject to tax until it is repatriated. The accumulated and interest-compounded depreciation cash flow at the termination of the project is shown in Table 25-5 to be 27.166 million pesos after adjusting for Caribian and U.S. taxes.

---

[6]Notice that the foreign subsidiary's payout ratio has a major effect on total corporate taxes paid—if no dividends are repatriated, no U.S. taxes are paid. This works as an incentive for multinational corporations to reinvest earnings overseas. It also explains why U.S. oil companies and other multinationals often have very low U.S. taxes in relation to their reported income.

	Year Earned	Amount of Blocked Profits		Compounding Factor at 8 Percent		Terminal Value in 1998
TABLE 25-6	1994	0.0	×	$(1.08)^4$	=	0.000
BLOCKED OPERATING	1995	1.6	×	$(1.08)^3$	=	2.015
PROFITS (MILLIONS	1996	1.2	×	$(1.08)^2$	=	1.399
OF CARIBIAN PESOS)	1997	4.8	×	$(1.08)^1$	=	5.184
	1998	4.4	×	$(1.08)^0$	=	4.400
		12.0		Total		12.998
				Less investment		12.000
				Taxable income		0.998
				Caribian tax (20%)		0.200
				After Caribian tax		12.798
				U.S. tax[a]		4.799
				After U.S. tax		7.999

[a]Caribian taxes have already been paid on the blocked profits. The pre-tax income that gave rise to the 12.0 million pesos of blocked profits was 12.0/0.8 = 15.0. U.S. taxes at a rate of 30 percent must be paid on this income: 15.0(0.3) = 4.50. In addition, a 30 percent U.S. tax must be paid on the 0.998 million pesos of interest income: 0.998(0.3) = 0.299. Therefore, the total U.S. taxes payable upon repatriation of the interest-accumulated blocked profits are 4.50 + 0.299 = 4.799 million pesos.

Operating profits that exceed the dividend repatriation restrictions are also assumed to be invested in 8 percent Caribian government bonds. As shown in Table 25-6, the U.S. tax adjustment is more complex than it was for the depreciation cash flows because Caribian tax is only due on the interest income, but U.S. tax is due on both interest and "grossed up" operating profits. The total after-tax cash flow from blocked operating profits, approximately 8 million pesos, will be added to the 1998 end-of-project cash flow.

The next steps in the analysis are (1) to convert the annual cash flows as developed in Tables 25-4, 25-5, and 25-6, plus the terminal value (assumed to be equal to the ending book value), from pesos to dollars, and (2) to find the net present value of the project. We will assume that a 12 percent cost of capital is appropriate for this investment.[7] These steps are shown in Figure 25-3. Row 6 gives the annual net cash flows in pesos; the component parts of these cash flows are shown in Rows 1 through 5. The estimated exchange rates are shown in Row 7. The current rate, 5 pesos to the dollar, is expected to hold during 1993, but the peso is expected to depreciate thereafter at a rate of 5 percent per year.

Dividing the peso cash flows in Row 6 by the exchange rates in Row 7 gives the expected net cash flows in dollars shown in Row 8. Finally, the NPV of the dollar cash flows, $1.468 million, is shown in Row 9. Since its NPV is positive, the project should be accepted.

---

[7]This hurdle rate is based on the cost of capital employed in the project, adjusted as appropriate for risks associated with the foreign environment and any diversification or other benefits that are applicable.

FIGURE 25-3   PROJECT CASH FLOWS (IN MILLIONS)

	1993	1994	1995	1996	1997	1998
1. Initial investment (pesos)	(50.000)					
2. Cash flow from operations (pesos)		7.500	9.000	9.250	9.500	9.750
3. Depreciation cash flow (pesos)						27.166
4. Blocked profits (pesos)						7.999
5. Terminal value (pesos)						25.000
6. Net cash flow (pesos)	(50.000)	7.500	9.000	9.250	9.500	69.915
7. Forecasted exchange rate	5.00	5.00	5.25	5.51	5.79	6.08
8. Dollar cash flow	($10.000)	$1.500	$1.714	$1.679	$1.641	$11.499
9. NPV at 12% = $1.468						

SELF-TEST QUESTIONS

List some key differences in capital budgeting as applied to foreign versus domestic operations.

What are the relevant cash flows for an international investment?

Why might the cost of capital for a foreign project differ from that of an equivalent domestic project? Could it be lower?

What adjustments might be made to the domestic cost of capital for a foreign investment due to exchange rate risk and political risk?

INTERNATIONAL CAPITAL STRUCTURES

Significant differences have been observed in the capital structures of U.S. corporations in comparison with their German and Japanese counterparts. For example, the Organization for Economic Cooperation and Development (OECD) recently reported that, on average, Japanese firms use 85 percent debt to total assets (in book value terms), German firms use 64 percent, and U.S. firms use 55 percent. Of course, different countries use somewhat different accounting conventions with regard to (1) reporting assets on a historical versus a replacement cost basis, (2) the treatment of leased assets, (3) pension plan funding, and (4) capitalizing versus expensing R&D costs, and these differences make comparisons difficult. Still, even after adjusting for accounting differences, researchers find that Japanese and German firms use considerably more financial leverage than U.S. companies.

Why do international differences in financial leverage exist? Since taxes are thought to be a major reason for using debt, the effects of differential tax structures in the three countries have been examined. The interest on corporate debt is

deductible in each country, and individuals must pay taxes on dividends and interest received. However, capital gains are not taxed in either Germany or Japan. The conclusions from this analysis are as follows: (1) From a tax standpoint, corporations should be equally inclined to use debt in all three countries. (2) Since capital gains are not taxed in Germany or Japan, but are taxed in the United States, and since capital gains are associated more with stocks than with bonds, investors in Germany and Japan should show a preference for stocks as compared with U.S. investors. (3) Investor preferences should lead to relatively low equity capital costs in Germany and Japan, and this, in turn, should cause German and Japanese firms to use more equity capital than their U.S. counterparts. Of course, this is exactly the opposite of the actual capital structures, so differential tax laws cannot explain the observed capital structure differences.

If tax rates cannot explain the different capital structures, what else might explain the observed differences? Another possibility relates to financial distress costs. Actual bankruptcy, and even the threat of potential bankruptcy, imposes a costly burden on firms with large amounts of debt. Note, though, that the threat of bankruptcy is dependent on the *probability* of bankruptcy. In the United States, equity-monitoring costs are comparatively low — corporations produce quarterly reports, pay quarterly dividends, and must comply with relatively stringent audit requirements. These conditions are less prevalent in the other countries. Conversely, debt-monitoring costs are probably lower in Germany and Japan than in the United States. In Germany and Japan, the bulk of corporate debt consists of bank loans as opposed to publicly issued bonds, but, more important, the banks are closely linked to the corporations which borrow from them. German and Japanese banks often (1) hold major equity positions in their debtor corporations, (2) vote the shares of individual shareholders for whom banks hold shares in trust, and (3) have bank officers sit on the boards of debtor corporations. Given these close relationships, the banks are much more directly involved with the debtor firms' affairs, and as a result they are also more accommodating in the event of financial distress than U.S. bondholders would be. This, in turn, suggests that any given amount of debt gives rise to a lower threat of bankruptcy for a German or a Japanese firm than for a U.S. firm with the same amount of business risk. Thus, an analysis of both bankruptcy costs and equity-monitoring costs leads to the conclusion that U.S. firms ought to have more equity and less debt than firms in Japan and Germany.

We cannot state that one financial system is better or worse than another in the sense of making the firms in one country more efficient than those in another. However, as U.S. firms become increasingly involved in worldwide operations, they must become increasingly aware of worldwide conditions, and they must be prepared to adapt to conditions in the various countries in which they do business.

SELF-TEST QUESTION

Why do international differences in financial leverage exist?

MULTINATIONAL WORKING CAPITAL MANAGEMENT

CASH MANAGEMENT

The objectives of cash management in a multinational corporation are similar to those in a purely domestic corporation: (1) to speed up collections and to slow down disbursements as much as is feasible, and hence to maximize net float; (2) to shift cash as rapidly as possible from those parts of the business where it is not needed to those parts where it is needed; and (3) to obtain the highest possible risk-adjusted, after-tax rate of return on temporary cash balances. Multinational companies use the same general procedures for achieving these goals as domestic firms, but because of longer distances and more serious mail delays, lockbox systems and electronic funds transfers are even more important.

Although multinational and domestic corporations have the same objectives and use similar procedures, the multinational corporation faces a far more complex task. As was mentioned earlier in our discussion of political risk, foreign governments often place restrictions on transfers of funds out of the country, so although IBM can transfer money from its Salt Lake City office to its New York concentration bank just by pressing a few buttons, a similar transfer from its Buenos Aires office is far more complex. Buenos Aires funds are denominated in australs (Argentina's equivalent of the dollar), so the australs must be converted to dollars before the transfer. If there is a shortage of dollars in Argentina, or if the Argentinean government wants to conserve the dollars in the country to use for the purchase of strategic materials, then conversion, and hence the transfer, may be blocked. Even if no dollar shortage exists in Argentina, the government may still restrict funds outflows if those funds represent profits or depreciation rather than payments for purchased materials or equipment, because many countries, especially those that are less developed, want profits reinvested in the country in order to stimulate economic growth.

Once it has been determined what funds can be transferred out of the various nations in which a multinational corporation operates, it is important to get those funds to locations where they will earn the highest risk-adjusted returns. Whereas domestic corporations tend to think in terms of domestic securities, multinationals are more likely to be aware of investment opportunities all around the world. Most multinational corporations use one or more global concentration banks, located in money centers such as London, New York, Tokyo, Zurich, or Singapore, and their staffs in those cities, working with international bankers, know of and are able to take advantage of the best rates available anywhere in the world.

CREDIT MANAGEMENT

Like most other aspects of finance, credit management in the multinational corporation is similar to but more complex than that in a purely domestic business. First, granting credit is more risky in an international context because, in addition to the

normal risks of default, the multinational corporation must also worry about exchange rate fluctuations between the time a sale is made and the time a receivable is collected. For example, if IBM sold a computer to a Japanese customer for 120 million yen when the exchange rate was 120 yen per one dollar, IBM would obtain $1,000,000 for the computer. However, if it sold the computer on terms of net/6 months, and if the yen fell against the dollar so that one dollar would now buy 150 yen, IBM would end up realizing only 120,000,000/150 = $800,000 when it collected the receivable. As we discussed earlier, hedging can reduce this type of risk, but at a cost.

Credit policy is generally more important for a multinational corporation than for a purely domestic firm for two reasons. First, much U.S. trade is with poorer, less-developed nations, and in such situations granting credit is generally a necessary condition for doing business. Second, and in large part as a result of the first point, developed nations whose economic health depends upon exports often help their manufacturing firms compete internationally by granting credit to foreign countries. In Japan, for example, the major manufacturing firms have direct ownership ties with large "trading companies" engaged in international trade, as well as with giant commercial banks. In addition, a government agency, the Ministry of International Trade and Industry (MITI), helps Japanese firms identify potential export markets and also helps potential customers arrange credit for purchases from Japanese firms. In effect, the huge Japanese trade surpluses are used to finance Japanese exports, thus helping to perpetuate their favorable trade balance. The United States has attempted to counter with the Export-Import Bank, which is funded by Congress, but the fact that the United States has a large balance of payments deficit is clear evidence that we have been less successful than others in world markets in recent years.

The huge debt which countries such as Brazil, Mexico, and Argentina owe the international banks, including many U.S. banks, is well known, and this situation illustrates how credit policy (by banks in this case) can go astray. The banks face a particularly sticky problem with these loans, because if a sovereign nation defaults, the banks cannot lay claim to the assets of the country as they could if a corporate customer defaulted. Note too that although the banks' loans to foreign governments have gotten most of the headlines, many U.S. multinational corporations are also in trouble as a result of granting credit to business customers in the same countries in which the banks' loans to the government are on shaky ground.

By pointing out the risks in granting credit internationally, we are not suggesting that such credit is bad. Quite the contrary, for the potential gains from international operations far outweigh the risks, at least for companies (and banks) that have the necessary expertise.

INVENTORY MANAGEMENT

As in most other aspects of finance, inventory management in a multinational setting is similar to but more complex than that in a purely domestic one. First, there is the matter of the physical location of inventories. For example, where should

Exxon keep its stockpiles of crude oil and refined products? It has refineries and marketing centers located worldwide, and one alternative is to keep items concentrated in a few strategic spots, from which they can then be shipped to the locations where they will be used as needs arise. Such a strategy may minimize the total amount of inventories needed to operate the global business and thus may minimize the firm's total investment in inventories. Note, though, that consideration will have to be given to potential delays in getting goods from central storage locations to user locations all around the world. Both working stocks and safety stocks will have to be maintained at each user location, as well as at the strategic storage centers. Problems like the Iraqi occupation of Kuwait and the subsequent trade embargo, which brought with it the potential for a shutdown of production of about 25 percent of the world's oil supply, complicate matters even more.

Exchange rates also influence inventory policy. If a local currency, say, the Danish krone, were expected to rise in value against the dollar, a U.S. company operating in Denmark would want to increase stocks of local products before the rise in the krone, and vice versa if the krone were expected to fall.

Another factor that must be considered is the possibility of import or export quotas or tariffs. For example, Apple Computer Company recently obtained 256K memory chips from Japanese suppliers at bargain prices, but U.S. chipmakers had just charged the Japanese with dumping chips in the U.S. market at prices below cost and were seeking to force the Japanese to raise prices, so Apple decided to increase its chip inventory.[8] Then computer sales slacked off, and Apple ended up having an oversupply of expensive computer chips. As a result, Apple's profits were hurt, and its stock price fell, demonstrating once more the importance of careful inventory management.

As mentioned earlier, another danger in certain countries is the threat of expropriation. If that threat is large, inventory holdings will be minimized, and goods will be brought in only as needed. Similarly, if the operation involves extraction of raw material such as oil or bauxite, processing plants may be moved offshore rather than located close to the production site.

Taxes must also be considered, and they have two effects on multinational inventory management. First, countries often impose property taxes on assets, including inventories, and when this is done, the tax is based on holdings as of a specific date, say, January 1 or March 1. Such rules make it advantageous for a multinational firm (1) to schedule production so that inventories are low on the

---

[8]The term "dumping" warrants explanation, because the practice is so potentially important in international markets. Suppose Japanese chipmakers have excess capacity. A particular chip has a variable cost of $25, and its "fully allocated cost," which is the $25 plus total fixed cost per unit of output, is $40. Now suppose the Japanese firm can sell chips in the United States at $35 per unit, but if it charges $40 it will not make any sales because U.S. chipmakers sell for $35.50. If the Japanese firm sells at $35, it will cover variable cost plus make a contribution to fixed overhead, so selling at $35 makes sense. Continuing, if the Japanese firm can sell in Japan at $40, but U.S. firms are excluded from Japanese markets by import duties or other barriers, the Japanese will have a huge advantage over U.S. manufacturers. This practice of selling goods at lower prices in foreign markets than at home is called "dumping." U.S. firms are required by antitrust laws to offer the same price to all customers and, therefore, cannot engage in dumping.

assessment date and (2) if assessment dates vary among countries in a region, to hold safety stocks in different countries at different times during the year.

Finally, multinational firms may consider the possibility of at-sea storage. Oil, chemical, grain, and other companies that deal in a bulk commodity that must be stored in some type of tank can often buy tankers at a cost not much greater—or perhaps even less, considering land cost—than land-based facilities. Loaded tankers can then be kept at sea or at anchor in some strategic location. This eliminates the danger of expropriation, minimizes the property tax problem, and maximizes flexibility with regard to shipping to areas where needs are greatest or prices highest.

This discussion has only scratched the surface of inventory management in the multinational corporation—the task is much more complex than for a purely domestic firm. However, the greater the degree of complexity, the greater the rewards from superior performance, so if you want challenge along with potentially high rewards, look to the international arena.

SELF-TEST QUESTIONS

What are some factors that make cash management especially complicated in a multinational corporation?

Why is granting credit especially risky in an international context?

Why is credit policy especially important for a multinational firm?

What are some factors that increase the complexity of inventory management in multinational corporations?

SUMMARY

This chapter discussed the most important differences between multinational and domestic financial management. Some of the key concepts are listed below:

▶ *International operations* are becoming increasingly important to individual firms and to the national economy. A *multinational corporation* is a firm that operates in two or more nations.

▶ Companies go "international" for six primary reasons: (1) *to seek new markets,* (2) *to seek raw materials,* (3) *to seek new technology,* (4) *to seek production efficiency,* (5) *to avoid trade barriers,* and (6) *to diversify.*

▶ Six major factors distinguish financial management as practiced by domestic firms from that practiced by multinational corporations: (1) *different currency denominations,* (2) *economic and legal ramifications,* (3) *languages,* (4) *cultural differences,* (5) *role of governments,* and (6) *political risk.*

▶ The number of U.S. dollars required to purchase one unit of foreign currency is called a *direct quotation,* while the number of units of foreign currency that can be purchased for one U.S. dollar is an *indirect quotation.*

▶ Financial forecasting is more difficult for multinational firms, because *exchange rate fluctuations* make it difficult to estimate the dollars that overseas operations will produce.

▶ Prior to August 1971, the world was on a *fixed exchange rate system* whereby the U.S. dollar was linked to gold and other currencies were then tied to the dollar. After August 1971, the world monetary system changed to a *floating system* whereby major world currency rates float with market forces, largely unrestricted by any internationally agreed-upon limits. The central bank of each country does intervene in the foreign exchange market, buying and selling its currency to smooth out exchange rate fluctuations, but only to a limited extent.

▶ *Spot rates* are the rates paid for delivery of currency "on the spot," while the *forward exchange rate* is the rate paid for delivery of currency at some agreed-upon future date, usually 30, 90, or 180 days from the day the transaction is negotiated. The forward rate can be at either a *premium* or a *discount* to the spot rate.

▶ Granting credit is more risky in an international context because, in addition to the normal risks of default, the multinational firm must worry about *exchange rate changes* between the time a sale is made and the time a receivable is collected.

▶ Credit policy is especially important for a multinational firm for two reasons: (1) Much of the U.S. trade is with less-developed nations, and in such situations granting credit is a necessary condition for doing business. (2) The governments of nations such as Japan whose economic health depends upon exports often help their manufacturing firms compete internationally by granting credit to foreign customers.

▶ Foreign investments are similar to domestic investments, but political risk and exchange rate risk must be considered. *Political risk* is the risk that the foreign government will take some action which will decrease the value of the investment, while *exchange rate risk* is the risk of losses due to fluctuations in the value of the dollar relative to the values of foreign currencies.

▶ Investments in *international capital projects* expose the investing firm to exchange rate risk and political risk. The relevant cash flows in international capital budgeting are the dollar cash flows which can be turned over to the parent company.

▶ *Eurodollars* are U.S. dollars deposited in banks outside the United States. Interest rates on Eurodollars are tied to *LIBOR*, the London interbank offered rate.

▶ U.S. firms often find that they can raise long-term capital at a lower cost outside the United States by selling bonds in the *international capital markets.* International bonds may be either *foreign bonds,* which are exactly like regular domestic bonds except that the issuer is a foreign company, or *Eurobonds,* which are bonds sold in a foreign country but denominated in the currency of the issuing company's home country.

QUESTIONS

25-1 Define each of the following terms:
   a. Multinational corporation
   b. Exchange rate
   c. Fixed exchange rate system; floating exchange rates
   d. Deficit trade balance
   e. Devaluation; revaluation
   f. Exchange rate risk; convertible currency
   g. Spot rate; forward exchange rate
   h. Discount on forward rate; premium on forward rate
   i. Hedging exchange rate exposure
   j. Repatriation of earnings; political risk
   k. Eurodollar; Eurobond; international bond; foreign bond

25-2 Under the fixed exchange rate system, what was the currency against which all other currency values were defined?

25-3 Exchange rates fluctuate under both the fixed exchange rate and floating exchange rate systems. What, then, is the difference between the two systems?

25-4 If the French franc depreciates against the U.S. dollar, can a dollar buy more or fewer French francs as a result?

25-5 If the United States imports more goods from abroad than it exports, foreigners will tend to have a surplus of U.S. dollars. What will this do to the value of the dollar with respect to foreign currencies? What is the corresponding effect on foreign investments in the United States?

25-6 Why do U.S. corporations build manufacturing plants abroad when they could build them at home?

25-7 Should firms require higher rates of return on foreign projects than on identical projects located at home? Explain.

25-8 What is a Eurodollar? If a French citizen deposits $10,000 in Chase Manhattan Bank in New York, have Eurodollars been created? What if the deposit is made in Barclay's Bank in London? Chase Manhattan's Paris branch? Does the existence of the Eurodollar market make the Federal Reserve's job of controlling U.S. interest rates easier or more difficult? Explain.

PROBLEMS

25-1 (Exchange rates)   If British pounds sell for $1.79 (U.S.) per pound, what should dollars sell for in pounds per dollar?

25-2 (Currency appreciation)   Suppose that 1 French franc could be purchased in the foreign exchange market for 15 U.S. cents today. If the franc appreciated 10 percent tomorrow against the dollar, how many francs would a dollar buy tomorrow?

25-3 (Cross exchange rates)   Recently the exchange rate between U.S. dollars and the French franc was FF5.6 = $1, and the exchange rate between the dollar and the British pound was £1 = $1.79. What was the exchange rate between francs and pounds?

25-4 **(Cross exchange rates)** Look up the three currencies in Problem 25-3 in the foreign exchange section of a current issue of *The Wall Street Journal.* What is the current exchange rate between francs and pounds?

25-5 **(Exchange rates)** Table 25-1 lists foreign exchange rates for April 29, 1992. On that day how many dollars would be required to purchase 1,000 units of each of the following: Indian rupees, Italian lira, Japanese yen, and Saudi Arabian riyals?

25-6 **(Exchange rates)** Look up the four currencies in Problem 25-5 in the foreign exchange section of a current issue of *The Wall Street Journal.*

    a. What is the current exchange rate for changing dollars into 1,000 units of rupees, lira, yen, and riyals?

    b. What is the percentage gain or loss between the April 29, 1992, exchange rate and the current exchange rate for each of the currencies in Part a?

25-7 **(Results of exchange rate changes)** Early in September 1983, it took 245 Japanese yen to equal $1. Almost 10 years later, in June 1993, that exchange rate had fallen to 106 yen to $1. Assume the price of a Japanese-manufactured automobile was $8,000 in September 1983 and that any price change resulted solely from exchange rate fluctuations.

    a. Has the price, in dollars, of the automobile increased or decreased during the 10-year period because of changes in the exchange rate?

    b. What would the dollar price of the automobile be in June 1993, again assuming that the car's price was affected only by exchange rates?

25-8 **(Hedging)** Celec French Imports has agreed to purchase 15,000 cases of French wine for 16 million francs at today's spot rate. The firm's financial manager, Dennis O'Connor, has noted the following current spot and forward rates:

	U.S. Dollar/Franc	Franc/U.S. Dollar
Spot	0.17748	5.6344
30-day forward	0.17699	5.6499
90-day forward	0.17612	5.6781
180-day forward	0.17487	5.7186

On the same day, Mr. O'Connor agrees to purchase 15,000 more cases of wine in 3 months at the same price of 16 million francs.

    a. What is the price of the wine, in U.S. dollars, if it is purchased at today's spot rate?

    b. What is the cost, in dollars, of the second 15,000 cases if payment is made in 90 days and the spot rate at that time equals today's 90-day forward rate?

    c. If Mr. O'Connor is concerned about the dollar losing value relative to the franc in the next 90 days, what can he do to reduce his exposure to exchange rate risk?

    d. If he does not hedge his exposure to exchange rate risk, and the exchange rate for the French franc is 5.00 to $1 in 90 days, how much will he have to pay for the wine (in dollars)?

25-9 **(Foreign investment analysis)** After all foreign and U.S. taxes, a U.S. corporation expects to receive 3 pounds of dividends per share from a British subsidiary this year. The exchange rate at the end of the year is expected to be $1.76 per pound, and the pound is expected to depreciate 5 percent against the dollar each year for an indefinite period. The dividend (in pounds) is expected to grow at 10 percent a year indefinitely. The parent U.S. corporation owns 10 million shares of the subsidiary. What is the present value of its equity ownership of the subsidiary? Assume a cost of equity capital of 14 percent for the subsidiary.

25-10 **(Exchange gains and losses)**   You are the vice-president of International InfoXchange, headquartered in Chicago, Illinois. All shareholders of the firm live in the United States. Earlier this month you obtained a loan of 5 million Canadian dollars from a bank in Toronto to finance the construction of a new plant in Montreal. At the time the loan was received, the exchange rate was 87 U.S. cents to the Canadian dollar. By the end of the month it has unexpectedly dropped to 80 cents. Has your company made a gain or loss as a result, and by how much?

25-11 **(Capital budgeting analysis)**   The Smith-Capone Corporation of Chicago manufactures typewriters for the world market. In early 1994, the company's board of directors requests the international planning department of the company to evaluate a proposal for setting up a wholly owned subsidiary in Paralivia, a country of 50 million people in South America. The subsidiary will make typewriters for the Paralivian market. Paralivia is a rapidly developing country which has effectively invested its rich oil revenues to support a growing industrial economy. Currently, it imports all of its typewriters from abroad, and Smith-Capone is expected to capture a large portion of this market.

Political sentiment in Paralivia regarding foreign investments has been somewhat lukewarm because such investments have overtones of foreign economic control. Not long ago, the government passed a law requiring all foreign investments to pass to local ownership after 6 years or less. Paralivia recently adopted a parliamentary system of government after 20 years of military dictatorship under General Francisco, but the transition of power was peaceful. Gordon Lidder, chairman of the board of Smith-Capone, has expressed concern about the stability of the new government, but "usually reliable" sources indicate that the government has popular support and is unlikely to be toppled for at least 5 to 10 years.

The following financial information on the proposed project is available:

Paralivian currency: Because the inflation rate in Paralivia is about 5 percent higher than that in the United States, the Paralivian ringo is expected to depreciate relative to the dollar by about 5 percent a year. When the investment will be made, the exchange rate is expected to be 2 ringos per dollar.

Investment: The estimated investment is $30 million in 1995 for inventory, plant, and equipment. The parent corporation, Smith-Capone, will provide all the capital in the form of equity in the subsidiary. The project will begin to generate earnings in 1996. At the end of 6 years, in 2001, all plant and equipment will be sold to the Paralivian government for 20 million ringos. This amount of money, plus all accumulated cash, will be repatriated as a liquidating dividend.

Repatriation: Only dividends may be repatriated by the subsidiary to the parent company. Cash flows from depreciation may not be repatriated except as part of the liquidating dividend in 2001. However, these cash flows can, in the meantime, be invested in local money market instruments to yield a 15 percent tax-free return.

Taxes: The Paralivian corporate income tax rate is 25 percent. There is also a 10 percent withholding tax on dividends. The U.S. federal-plus-state tax rate is 50 percent on the gross earnings of the foreign subsidiary. However, the parent company gets a tax credit for taxes already paid to foreign governments. In the case of the liquidating dividend, the tax treatment is quite different. The Paralivian government will not tax this dividend. Smith-Capone has obtained a ruling from the U.S. Internal Revenue Service that the liquidating dividend also will not be taxed by the U.S. government.

Cost of capital: Based on the sovereign and exchange risk characteristics of Paralivia, Smith-Capone gives Paralivia a BB rating and requires a rate of return of 20 percent on equity.

Projected demand, costs, and exchange rates:

Year	Demand for Typewriters (Thousands)	Price (Ringos)	Unit Variable Operating Cost (Ringos)	Exchange Rate (Ringos per Dollar)
1996	50	1,000	400	2.1
1997	55	1,000	420	2.2
1998	60	1,100	440	2.3
1999	70	1,100	460	2.4
2000	80	1,200	490	2.5
2001	90	1,200	540	2.6

Fixed cost: Depreciation expense is 10 million ringos per year. Consider this to be the only fixed cost of the project.

Use the information above to answer the following questions.

a. Excluding the liquidating dividend, estimate the after-tax dividend received by the parent company each year.

b. Estimate the liquidating dividend, remembering that blocked depreciation flows are reinvested at 15 percent.

c. What is your recommendation for the project? (Consider its NPV, and specify any other relevant considerations.)

. . . .

**M I N I
C A S E**

Citrus Products Inc. is a medium-sized producer of citrus juice drinks with groves in Indian River County, Florida. Until now, the company has confined its operations and sales to the United States, but its CEO, George Gaynor, wants to expand into Europe. The first step would be to set up sales subsidiaries in Spain and Portugal, then set up a production plant in Spain, and, finally, distribute the product throughout the European Common Market. The firm's financial manager, Ruth Schmidt, is enthusiastic about the plan, but she is worried about the implications of the foreign expansion on the firm's financial management process. She has asked you, the firm's most recently hired financial analyst, to develop a 1-hour tutorial package that explains the basics of multinational financial management. The tutorial will be presented at the next board of directors' meeting. To get you started, Ms. Schmidt has supplied you with the following list of questions.

a. What is a multinational corporation? Why do firms expand into other countries?

b. What are the six major factors which distinguish multinational financial management from financial management as practiced by a purely domestic firm?

c. Consider the following illustrative exchange rates.

	U.S. Dollars Required to Buy One Unit of Foreign Currency
Spanish peseta	0.0093
Portuguese escudo	0.0067

(1) Are these currency prices direct quotations or indirect quotations?

(2) Calculate the indirect quotations for pesetas and escudos.

(3) What is a cross rate? Calculate the two cross rates between pesetas and escudos.

(4) Assume Citrus Products can produce a liter of orange juice and ship it to Spain for $1.75. If the firm wants a 50 percent markup on the product, what should the orange juice sell for in Spain?

(5) Now assume Citrus Products begins producing the same liter of orange juice in Spain. The product costs 200 pesetas to produce and ship to Portugal, where it can be sold for 400 escudos. What is the dollar profit on the sale?

(6) What is exchange rate risk?

d. Briefly describe the current international monetary system. How does the current system differ from the system that was in place prior to August 1971?

e. What is a convertible currency? What problems arise when a multinational company operates in a country whose currency is not convertible?

f. What is the difference between spot rates and forward rates? When is the forward rate at a premium to the spot rate? At a discount? How can a firm use the forward markets to hedge a future currency transaction?

g. What impact does relative inflation have on interest rates and exchange rates?

h. Briefly discuss the international capital markets.

i. What is the impact of multinational operations on each of the following financial management topics?

(1) Cash management

(2) Capital budgeting decisions

(3) Credit management

(4) Inventory management

SELECTED ADDITIONAL REFERENCES AND CASES

Perhaps the best way to obtain more information on multinational financial management is to consult one of the many excellent textbooks on the subject. For example, see

Levi, Maurice, *International Finance* (New York: McGraw-Hill, 1983).

Madura, Jeff, *International Financial Management* (St. Paul: West, 1992).

Rodriguez, Rita, and Eugene Carter, *International Financial Management* (Englewood Cliffs, N.J.: Prentice-Hall, 1984).

Shapiro, Alan C., *Multinational Financial Management* (Boston: Allyn and Bacon, 1989).

For some recent articles on multinational financial managment, see

Black, Fischer, "Equilibrium Exchange Rate Hedging," *Journal of Finance,* July 1990, 899–907.

Carre, Herve, and Karen H. Johnson, "Progress Toward a European Monetary Union," *Federal Reserve Bulletin,* October 1991, 769–783.

Frankel, Jeffry A., "The Japanese Cost of Finance," *Financial Management,* Spring 1991, 95–127.

Hammer, Jerry A., "Hedging Performance and Hedging Objectives: Tests of New Performance Measures in the Foreign Currency Market," *Journal of Financial Research,* Winter 1990, 307–323.

Hunter, William C., and Stephen G. Timme, "A Stochastic Dominance Approach to Evaluating Foreign Exchange Hedging Strategies," *Financial Management,* Autumn 1992, 104–112.

Lee, Insup, and Steve B. Wyatt, "The Effects of International Joint Ventures on Shareholder Wealth," *Financial Review,* November 1990.

Mahajan, Arvind, "Pricing Expropriation Risk," *Financial Management,* Winter 1990, 77–86.

Pauls, B. Dianne, "U.S. Exchange Rate Policy: Bretton Woods to Present," *Federal Reserve Bulletin,* November 1990, 891–908.

Two finance journals recently devoted entire issues to multinational financial management. See
Financial Management, Winter 1991.

Journal of Applied Corporate Finance, Winter 1991.

The following case from the Brigham-Gapenski casebook focuses on multinational capital budgeting:

Case 18, "Alaska Oil Corporation."

MATHEMATICAL TABLES

TABLE A-1   PRESENT VALUE OF $1 DUE AT THE END OF N PERIODS:

Equation:

$$PVIF_{i,n} = \frac{1}{(1 + i)^n}$$

Financial Calculator Keys:

	n	i		0	1.0
	N	I	PV	PMT	FV

TABLE
VALUE

Period	1%	2%	3%	4%	5%	6%	7%	8%	9%	10%
1	.9901	.9804	.9709	.9615	.9524	.9434	.9346	.9259	.9174	.9091
2	.9803	.9612	.9426	.9246	.9070	.8900	.8734	.8573	.8417	.8264
3	.9706	.9423	.9151	.8890	.8638	.8396	.8163	.7938	.7722	.7513
4	.9610	.9238	.8885	.8548	.8227	.7921	.7629	.7350	.7084	.6830
5	.9515	.9057	.8626	.8219	.7835	.7473	.7130	.6806	.6499	.6209
6	.9420	.8880	.8375	.7903	.7462	.7050	.6663	.6302	.5963	.5645
7	.9327	.8706	.8131	.7599	.7107	.6651	.6227	.5835	.5470	.5132
8	.9235	.8535	.7894	.7307	.6768	.6274	.5820	.5403	.5019	.4665
9	.9143	.8368	.7664	.7026	.6446	.5919	.5439	.5002	.4604	.4241
10	.9053	.8203	.7441	.6756	.6139	.5584	.5083	.4632	.4224	.3855
11	.8963	.8043	.7224	.6496	.5847	.5268	.4751	.4289	.3875	.3505
12	.8874	.7885	.7014	.6246	.5568	.4970	.4440	.3971	.3555	.3186
13	.8787	.7730	.6810	.6006	.5303	.4688	.4150	.3677	.3262	.2897
14	.8700	.7579	.6611	.5775	.5051	.4423	.3878	.3405	.2992	.2633
15	.8613	.7430	.6419	.5553	.4810	.4173	.3624	.3152	.2745	.2394
16	.8528	.7284	.6232	.5339	.4581	.3936	.3387	.2919	.2519	.2176
17	.8444	.7142	.6050	.5134	.4363	.3714	.3166	.2703	.2311	.1978
18	.8360	.7002	.5874	.4936	.4155	.3503	.2959	.2502	.2120	.1799
19	.8277	.6864	.5703	.4746	.3957	.3305	.2765	.2317	.1945	.1635
20	.8195	.6730	.5537	.4564	.3769	.3118	.2584	.2145	.1784	.1486
21	.8114	.6598	.5375	.4388	.3589	.2942	.2415	.1987	.1637	.1351
22	.8034	.6468	.5219	.4220	.3418	.2775	.2257	.1839	.1502	.1228
23	.7954	.6342	.5067	.4057	.3256	.2618	.2109	.1703	.1378	.1117
24	.7876	.6217	.4919	.3901	.3101	.2470	.1971	.1577	.1264	.1015
25	.7798	.6095	.4776	.3751	.2953	.2330	.1842	.1460	.1160	.0923
26	.7720	.5976	.4637	.3607	.2812	.2198	.1722	.1352	.1064	.0839
27	.7644	.5859	.4502	.3468	.2678	.2074	.1609	.1252	.0976	.0763
28	.7568	.5744	.4371	.3335	.2551	.1956	.1504	.1159	.0895	.0693
29	.7493	.5631	.4243	.3207	.2429	.1846	.1406	.1073	.0822	.0630
30	.7419	.5521	.4120	.3083	.2314	.1741	.1314	.0994	.0754	.0573
35	.7059	.5000	.3554	.2534	.1813	.1301	.0937	.0676	.0490	.0356
40	.6717	.4529	.3066	.2083	.1420	.0972	.0668	.0460	.0318	.0221
45	.6391	.4102	.2644	.1712	.1113	.0727	.0476	.0313	.0207	.0137
50	.6080	.3715	.2281	.1407	.0872	.0543	.0339	.0213	.0134	.0085
55	.5785	.3365	.1968	.1157	.0683	.0406	.0242	.0145	.0087	.0053

TABLE A-1   *continued*

Period	12%	14%	15%	16%	18%	20%	24%	28%	32%	36%
1	.8929	.8772	.8696	.8621	.8475	.8333	.8065	.7813	.7576	.7353
2	.7972	.7695	.7561	.7432	.7182	.6944	.6504	.6104	.5739	.5407
3	.7118	.6750	.6575	.6407	.6086	.5787	.5245	.4768	.4348	.3975
4	.6355	.5921	.5718	.5523	.5158	.4823	.4230	.3725	.3294	.2923
5	.5674	.5194	.4972	.4761	.4371	.4019	.3411	.2910	.2495	.2149
6	.5066	.4556	.4323	.4104	.3704	.3349	.2751	.2274	.1890	.1580
7	.4523	.3996	.3759	.3538	.3139	.2791	.2218	.1776	.1432	.1162
8	.4039	.3506	.3269	.3050	.2660	.2326	.1789	.1388	.1085	.0854
9	.3606	.3075	.2843	.2630	.2255	.1938	.1443	.1084	.0822	.0628
10	.3220	.2697	.2472	.2267	.1911	.1615	.1164	.0847	.0623	.0462
11	.2875	.2366	.2149	.1954	.1619	.1346	.0938	.0662	.0472	.0340
12	.2567	.2076	.1869	.1685	.1372	.1122	.0757	.0517	.0357	.0250
13	.2292	.1821	.1625	.1452	.1163	.0935	.0610	.0404	.0271	.0184
14	.2046	.1597	.1413	.1252	.0985	.0779	.0492	.0316	.0205	.0135
15	.1827	.1401	.1229	.1079	.0835	.0649	.0397	.0247	.0155	.0099
16	.1631	.1229	.1069	.0930	.0708	.0541	.0320	.0193	.0118	.0073
17	.1456	.1078	.0929	.0802	.0600	.0451	.0258	.0150	.0089	.0054
18	.1300	.0946	.0808	.0691	.0508	.0376	.0208	.0118	.0068	.0039
19	.1161	.0829	.0703	.0596	.0431	.0313	.0168	.0092	.0051	.0029
20	.1037	.0728	.0611	.0514	.0365	.0261	.0135	.0072	.0039	.0021
21	.0926	.0638	.0531	.0443	.0309	.0217	.0109	.0056	.0029	.0016
22	.0826	.0560	.0462	.0382	.0262	.0181	.0088	.0044	.0022	.0012
23	.0738	.0491	.0402	.0329	.0222	.0151	.0071	.0034	.0017	.0008
24	.0659	.0431	.0349	.0284	.0188	.0126	.0057	.0027	.0013	.0006
25	.0588	.0378	.0304	.0245	.0160	.0105	.0046	.0021	.0010	.0005
26	.0525	.0331	.0264	.0211	.0135	.0087	.0037	.0016	.0007	.0003
27	.0469	.0291	.0230	.0182	.0115	.0073	.0030	.0013	.0006	.0002
28	.0419	.0255	.0200	.0157	.0097	.0061	.0024	.0010	.0004	.0002
29	.0374	.0224	.0174	.0135	.0082	.0051	.0020	.0008	.0003	.0001
30	.0334	.0196	.0151	.0116	.0070	.0042	.0016	.0006	.0002	.0001
35	.0189	.0102	.0075	.0055	.0030	.0017	.0005	.0002	.0001	*
40	.0107	.0053	.0037	.0026	.0013	.0007	.0002	.0001	*	*
45	.0061	.0027	.0019	.0013	.0006	.0003	.0001	*	*	*
50	.0035	.0014	.0009	.0006	.0003	.0001	*	*	*	*
55	.0020	.0007	.0005	.0003	.0001	*	*	*	*	*

*The factor is zero to four decimal places.

TABLE A-2   PRESENT VALUE OF AN ANNUITY OF $1 PER PERIOD FOR n PERIODS:

Equation:

$$PVIFA_{i,n} = \sum_{t=1}^{n}\frac{1}{(1+i)^t} = \frac{1 - \dfrac{1}{(1+i)^n}}{i} = \frac{1}{i} - \frac{1}{i(1+i)^n}$$

Financial Calculator Keys:

n	i	1.0	0
N	I	PV	PMT	FV

TABLE VALUE

Number of Periods	1%	2%	3%	4%	5%	6%	7%	8%	9%
1	0.9901	0.9804	0.9709	0.9615	0.9524	0.9434	0.9346	0.9259	0.9174
2	1.9704	1.9416	1.9135	1.8861	1.8594	1.8334	1.8080	1.7833	1.7591
3	2.9410	2.8839	2.8286	2.7751	2.7232	2.6730	2.6243	2.5771	2.5313
4	3.9020	3.8077	3.7171	3.6299	3.5460	3.4651	3.3872	3.3121	3.2397
5	4.8534	4.7135	4.5797	4.4518	4.3295	4.2124	4.1002	3.9927	3.8897
6	5.7955	5.6014	5.4172	5.2421	5.0757	4.9173	4.7665	4.6229	4.4859
7	6.7282	6.4720	6.2303	6.0021	5.7864	5.5824	5.3893	5.2064	5.0330
8	7.6517	7.3255	7.0197	6.7327	6.4632	6.2098	5.9713	5.7466	5.5348
9	8.5660	8.1622	7.7861	7.4353	7.1078	6.8017	6.5152	6.2469	5.9952
10	9.4713	8.9826	8.5302	8.1109	7.7217	7.3601	7.0236	6.7101	6.4177
11	10.3676	9.7868	9.2526	8.7605	8.3064	7.8869	7.4987	7.1390	6.8052
12	11.2551	10.5753	9.9540	9.3851	8.8633	8.3838	7.9427	7.5361	7.1607
13	12.1337	11.3484	10.6350	9.9856	9.3936	8.8527	8.3577	7.9038	7.4869
14	13.0037	12.1062	11.2961	10.5631	9.8986	9.2950	8.7455	8.2442	7.7862
15	13.8651	12.8493	11.9379	11.1184	10.3797	9.7122	9.1079	8.5595	8.0607
16	14.7179	13.5777	12.5611	11.6523	10.8378	10.1059	9.4466	8.8514	8.3126
17	15.5623	14.2919	13.1661	12.1657	11.2741	10.4773	9.7632	9.1216	8.5436
18	16.3983	14.9920	13.7535	12.6593	11.6896	10.8276	10.0591	9.3719	8.7556
19	17.2260	15.6785	14.3238	13.1339	12.0853	11.1581	10.3356	9.6036	8.9501
20	18.0456	16.3514	14.8775	13.5903	12.4622	11.4699	10.5940	9.8181	9.1285
21	18.8570	17.0112	15.4150	14.0292	12.8212	11.7641	10.8355	10.0168	9.2922
22	19.6604	17.6580	15.9369	14.4511	13.1630	12.0416	11.0612	10.2007	9.4424
23	20.4558	18.2922	16.4436	14.8568	13.4886	12.3034	11.2722	10.3711	9.5802
24	21.2434	18.9139	16.9355	15.2470	13.7986	12.5504	11.4693	10.5288	9.7066
25	22.0232	19.5235	17.4131	15.6221	14.0939	12.7834	11.6536	10.6748	9.8226
26	22.7952	20.1210	17.8768	15.9828	14.3752	13.0032	11.8258	10.8100	9.9290
27	23.5596	20.7069	18.3270	16.3296	14.6430	13.2105	11.9867	10.9352	10.0266
28	24.3164	21.2813	18.7641	16.6631	14.8981	13.4062	12.1371	11.0511	10.1161
29	25.0658	21.8444	19.1885	16.9837	15.1411	13.5907	12.2777	11.1584	10.1983
30	25.8077	22.3965	19.6004	17.2920	15.3725	13.7648	12.4090	11.2578	10.2737
35	29.4086	24.9986	21.4872	18.6646	16.3742	14.4982	12.9477	11.6546	10.5668
40	32.8347	27.3555	23.1148	19.7928	17.1591	15.0463	13.3317	11.9246	10.7574
45	36.0945	29.4902	24.5187	20.7200	17.7741	15.4558	13.6055	12.1084	10.8812
50	39.1961	31.4236	25.7298	21.4822	18.2559	15.7619	13.8007	12.2335	10.9617
55	42.1472	33.1748	26.7744	22.1086	18.6335	15.9905	13.9399	12.3186	11.0140

TABLE A-2   *continued*

Number of Periods	10%	12%	14%	15%	16%	18%	20%	24%	28%	32%
1	0.9091	0.8929	0.8772	0.8696	0.8621	0.8475	0.8333	0.8065	0.7813	0.7576
2	1.7355	1.6901	1.6467	1.6257	1.6052	1.5656	1.5278	1.4568	1.3916	1.3315
3	2.4869	2.4018	2.3216	2.2832	2.2459	2.1743	2.1065	1.9813	1.8684	1.7663
4	3.1699	3.0373	2.9137	2.8550	2.7982	2.6901	2.5887	2.4043	2.2410	2.0957
5	3.7908	3.6048	3.4331	3.3522	3.2743	3.1272	2.9906	2.7454	2.5320	2.3452
6	4.3553	4.1114	3.8887	3.7845	3.6847	3.4976	3.3255	3.0205	2.7594	2.5342
7	4.8684	4.5638	4.2883	4.1604	4.0386	3.8115	3.6046	3.2423	2.9370	2.6775
8	5.3349	4.9676	4.6389	4.4873	4.3436	4.0776	3.8372	3.4212	3.0758	2.7860
9	5.7590	5.3282	4.9464	4.7716	4.6065	4.3030	4.0310	3.5655	3.1842	2.8681
10	6.1446	5.6502	5.2161	5.0188	4.8332	4.4941	4.1925	3.6819	3.2689	2.9304
11	6.4951	5.9377	5.4527	5.2337	5.0286	4.6560	4.3271	3.7757	3.3351	2.9776
12	6.8137	6.1944	5.6603	5.4206	5.1971	4.7932	4.4392	3.8514	3.3868	3.0133
13	7.1034	6.4235	5.8424	5.5831	5.3423	4.9095	4.5327	3.9124	3.4272	3.0404
14	7.3667	6.6282	6.0021	5.7245	5.4675	5.0081	4.6106	3.9616	3.4587	3.0609
15	7.6061	6.8109	6.1422	5.8474	5.5755	5.0916	4.6755	4.0013	3.4834	3.0764
16	7.8237	6.9740	6.2651	5.9542	5.6685	5.1624	4.7296	4.0333	3.5026	3.0882
17	8.0216	7.1196	6.3729	6.0472	5.7487	5.2223	4.7746	4.0591	3.5177	3.0971
18	8.2014	7.2497	6.4674	6.1280	5.8178	5.2732	4.8122	4.0799	3.5294	3.1039
19	8.3649	7.3658	6.5504	6.1982	5.8775	5.3162	4.8435	4.0967	3.5386	3.1090
20	8.5136	7.4694	6.6231	6.2593	5.9288	5.3527	4.8696	4.1103	3.5458	3.1129
21	8.6487	7.5620	6.6870	6.3125	5.9731	5.3837	4.8913	4.1212	3.5514	3.1158
22	8.7715	7.6446	6.7429	6.3587	6.0113	5.4099	4.9094	4.1300	3.5558	3.1180
23	8.8832	7.7184	6.7921	6.3988	6.0442	5.4321	4.9245	4.1371	3.5592	3.1197
24	8.9847	7.7843	6.8351	6.4338	6.0726	5.4509	4.9371	4.1428	3.5619	3.1210
25	9.0770	7.8431	6.8729	6.4641	6.0971	5.4669	4.9476	4.1474	3.5640	3.1220
26	9.1609	7.8957	6.9061	6.4906	6.1182	5.4804	4.9563	4.1511	3.5656	3.1227
27	9.2372	7.9426	6.9352	6.5135	6.1364	5.4919	4.9636	4.1542	3.5669	3.1233
28	9.3066	7.9844	6.9607	6.5335	6.1520	5.5016	4.9697	4.1566	3.5679	3.1237
29	9.3696	8.0218	6.9830	6.5509	6.1656	5.5098	4.9747	4.1585	3.5687	3.1240
30	9.4269	8.0552	7.0027	6.5660	6.1772	5.5168	4.9789	4.1601	3.5693	3.1242
35	9.6442	8.1755	7.0700	6.6166	6.2153	5.5386	4.9915	4.1644	3.5708	3.1248
40	9.7791	8.2438	7.1050	6.6418	6.2335	5.5482	4.9966	4.1659	3.5712	3.1250
45	9.8628	8.2825	7.1232	6.6543	6.2421	5.5523	4.9986	4.1664	3.5714	3.1250
50	9.9148	8.3045	7.1327	6.6605	6.2463	5.5541	4.9995	4.1666	3.5714	3.1250
55	9.9471	8.3170	7.1376	6.6636	6.2482	5.5549	4.9998	4.1666	3.5714	3.1250

TABLE A-3   FUTURE VALUE OF $1 AT THE END OF n PERIODS:

Equation: Financial Calculator Keys:

$FVIF_{i,n} = (1 + i)^n$

	n	i	1.0	0	
	N	**I**	**PV**	**PMT**	**FV**
					TABLE VALUE

Period	1%	2%	3%	4%	5%	6%	7%	8%	9%	10%
1	1.0100	1.0200	1.0300	1.0400	1.0500	1.0600	1.0700	1.0800	1.0900	1.1000
2	1.0201	1.0404	1.0609	1.0816	1.1025	1.1236	1.1449	1.1664	1.1881	1.2100
3	1.0303	1.0612	1.0927	1.1249	1.1576	1.1910	1.2250	1.2597	1.2950	1.3310
4	1.0406	1.0824	1.1255	1.1699	1.2155	1.2625	1.3108	1.3605	1.4116	1.4641
5	1.0510	1.1041	1.1593	1.2167	1.2763	1.3382	1.4026	1.4693	1.5386	1.6105
6	1.0615	1.1262	1.1941	1.2653	1.3401	1.4185	1.5007	1.5869	1.6771	1.7716
7	1.0721	1.1487	1.2299	1.3159	1.4071	1.5036	1.6058	1.7138	1.8280	1.9487
8	1.0829	1.1717	1.2668	1.3686	1.4775	1.5938	1.7182	1.8509	1.9926	2.1436
9	1.0937	1.1951	1.3048	1.4233	1.5513	1.6895	1.8385	1.9990	2.1719	2.3579
10	1.1046	1.2190	1.3439	1.4802	1.6289	1.7908	1.9672	2.1589	2.3674	2.5937
11	1.1157	1.2434	1.3842	1.5395	1.7103	1.8983	2.1049	2.3316	2.5804	2.8531
12	1.1268	1.2682	1.4258	1.6010	1.7959	2.0122	2.2522	2.5182	2.8127	3.1384
13	1.1381	1.2936	1.4685	1.6651	1.8856	2.1329	2.4098	2.7196	3.0658	3.4523
14	1.1495	1.3195	1.5126	1.7317	1.9799	2.2609	2.5785	2.9372	3.3417	3.7975
15	1.1610	1.3459	1.5580	1.8009	2.0789	2.3966	2.7590	3.1722	3.6425	4.1772
16	1.1726	1.3728	1.6047	1.8730	2.1829	2.5404	2.9522	3.4259	3.9703	4.5950
17	1.1843	1.4002	1.6528	1.9479	2.2920	2.6928	3.1588	3.7000	4.3276	5.0545
18	1.1961	1.4282	1.7024	2.0258	2.4066	2.8543	3.3799	3.9960	4.7171	5.5599
19	1.2081	1.4568	1.7535	2.1068	2.5270	3.0256	3.6165	4.3157	5.1417	6.1159
20	1.2202	1.4859	1.8061	2.1911	2.6533	3.2071	3.8697	4.6610	5.6044	6.7275
21	1.2324	1.5157	1.8603	2.2788	2.7860	3.3996	4.1406	5.0338	6.1088	7.4002
22	1.2447	1.5460	1.9161	2.3699	2.9253	3.6035	4.4304	5.4365	6.6586	8.1403
23	1.2572	1.5769	1.9736	2.4647	3.0715	3.8197	4.7405	5.8715	7.2579	8.9543
24	1.2697	1.6084	2.0328	2.5633	3.2251	4.0489	5.0724	6.3412	7.9111	9.8497
25	1.2824	1.6406	2.0938	2.6658	3.3864	4.2919	5.4274	6.8485	8.6231	10.835
26	1.2953	1.6734	2.1566	2.7725	3.5557	4.5494	5.8074	7.3964	9.3992	11.918
27	1.3082	1.7069	2.2213	2.8834	3.7335	4.8223	6.2139	7.9881	10.245	13.110
28	1.3213	1.7410	2.2879	2.9987	3.9201	5.1117	6.6488	8.6271	11.167	14.421
29	1.3345	1.7758	2.3566	3.1187	4.1161	5.4184	7.1143	9.3173	12.172	15.863
30	1.3478	1.8114	2.4273	3.2434	4.3219	5.7435	7.6123	10.063	13.268	17.449
40	1.4889	2.2080	3.2620	4.8010	7.0400	10.286	14.974	21.725	31.409	45.259
50	1.6446	2.6916	4.3839	7.1067	11.467	18.420	29.457	46.902	74.358	117.39
60	1.8167	3.2810	5.8916	10.520	18.679	32.988	57.946	101.26	176.03	304.48

TABLE A-3   *continued*

Period	12%	14%	15%	16%	18%	20%	24%	28%	32%	36%
1	1.1200	1.1400	1.1500	1.1600	1.1800	1.2000	1.2400	1.2800	1.3200	1.3600
2	1.2544	1.2996	1.3225	1.3456	1.3924	1.4400	1.5376	1.6384	1.7424	1.8496
3	1.4049	1.4815	1.5209	1.5609	1.6430	1.7280	1.9066	2.0972	2.3000	2.5155
4	1.5735	1.6890	1.7490	1.8106	1.9388	2.0736	2.3642	2.6844	3.0360	3.4210
5	1.7623	1.9254	2.0114	2.1003	2.2878	2.4883	2.9316	3.4360	4.0075	4.6526
6	1.9738	2.1950	2.3131	2.4364	2.6996	2.9860	3.6352	4.3980	5.2899	6.3275
7	2.2107	2.5023	2.6600	2.8262	3.1855	3.5832	4.5077	5.6295	6.9826	8.6054
8	2.4760	2.8526	3.0590	3.2784	3.7589	4.2998	5.5895	7.2058	9.2170	11.703
9	2.7731	3.2519	3.5179	3.8030	4.4355	5.1598	6.9310	9.2234	12.166	15.917
10	3.1058	3.7072	4.0456	4.4114	5.2338	6.1917	8.5944	11.806	16.060	21.647
11	3.4785	4.2262	4.6524	5.1173	6.1759	7.4301	10.657	15.112	21.199	29.439
12	3.8960	4.8179	5.3503	5.9360	7.2876	8.9161	13.215	19.343	27.983	40.037
13	4.3635	5.4924	6.1528	6.8858	8.5994	10.699	16.386	24.759	36.937	54.451
14	4.8871	6.2613	7.0757	7.9875	10.147	12.839	20.319	31.691	48.757	74.053
15	5.4736	7.1379	8.1371	9.2655	11.974	15.407	25.196	40.565	64.359	100.71
16	6.1304	8.1372	9.3576	10.748	14.129	18.488	31.243	51.923	84.954	136.97
17	6.8660	9.2765	10.761	12.468	16.672	22.186	38.741	66.461	112.14	186.28
18	7.6900	10.575	12.375	14.463	19.673	26.623	48.039	85.071	148.02	253.34
19	8.6128	12.056	14.232	16.777	23.214	31.948	59.568	108.89	195.39	344.54
20	9.6463	13.743	16.367	19.461	27.393	38.338	73.864	139.38	257.92	468.57
21	10.804	15.668	18.822	22.574	32.324	46.005	91.592	178.41	340.45	637.26
22	12.100	17.861	21.645	26.186	38.142	55.206	113.57	228.36	449.39	866.67
23	13.552	20.362	24.891	30.376	45.008	66.247	140.83	292.30	593.20	1178.7
24	15.179	23.212	28.625	35.236	53.109	79.497	174.63	374.14	783.02	1603.0
25	17.000	26.462	32.919	40.874	62.669	95.396	216.54	478.90	1033.6	2180.1
26	19.040	30.167	37.857	47.414	73.949	114.48	268.51	613.00	1364.3	2964.9
27	21.325	34.390	43.535	55.000	87.260	137.37	332.95	784.64	1800.9	4032.3
28	23.884	39.204	50.066	63.800	102.97	164.84	412.86	1004.3	2377.2	5483.9
29	26.750	44.693	57.575	74.009	121.50	197.81	511.95	1285.6	3137.9	7458.1
30	29.960	50.950	66.212	85.850	143.37	237.38	634.82	1645.5	4142.1	10143.
40	93.051	188.88	267.86	378.72	750.38	1469.8	5455.9	19427.	66521.	*
50	289.00	700.23	1083.7	1670.7	3927.4	9100.4	46890.	*	*	*
60	897.60	2595.9	4384.0	7370.2	20555.	56348.	*	*	*	*

*FVIF > 99,999.

TABLE A-4   FUTURE VALUE OF AN ANNUITY OF $1 PER PERIOD FOR n PERIODS:

Equation:

$$FVIFA_{i,n} = \sum_{t=1}^{n} (1 + i)^{n-t} = \frac{(1 + i)^n - 1}{i}$$

Financial Calculator Keys:

n	i	0	1.0	
N	**I**	**PV**	**PMT**	**FV**
				TABLE VALUE

Number of Periods	1%	2%	3%	4%	5%	6%	7%	8%	9%	10%
1	1.0000	1.0000	1.0000	1.0000	1.0000	1.0000	1.0000	1.0000	1.0000	1.0000
2	2.0100	2.0200	2.0300	2.0400	2.0500	2.0600	2.0700	2.0800	2.0900	2.1000
3	3.0301	3.0604	3.0909	3.1216	3.1525	3.1836	3.2149	3.2464	3.2781	3.3100
4	4.0604	4.1216	4.1836	4.2465	4.3101	4.3746	4.4399	4.5061	4.5731	4.6410
5	5.1010	5.2040	5.3091	5.4163	5.5256	5.6371	5.7507	5.8666	5.9847	6.1051
6	6.1520	6.3081	6.4684	6.6330	6.8019	6.9753	7.1533	7.3359	7.5233	7.7156
7	7.2135	7.4343	7.6625	7.8983	8.1420	8.3938	8.6540	8.9228	9.2004	9.4872
8	8.2857	8.5830	8.8923	9.2142	9.5491	9.8975	10.260	10.637	11.028	11.436
9	9.3685	9.7546	10.159	10.583	11.027	11.491	11.978	12.488	13.021	13.579
10	10.462	10.950	11.464	12.006	12.578	13.181	13.816	14.487	15.193	15.937
11	11.567	12.169	12.808	13.486	14.207	14.972	15.784	16.645	17.560	18.531
12	12.683	13.412	14.192	15.026	15.917	16.870	17.888	18.977	20.141	21.384
13	13.809	14.680	15.618	16.627	17.713	18.882	20.141	21.495	22.953	24.523
14	14.947	15.974	17.086	18.292	19.599	21.015	22.550	24.215	26.019	27.975
15	16.097	17.293	18.599	20.024	21.579	23.276	25.129	27.152	29.361	31.772
16	17.258	18.639	20.157	21.825	23.657	25.673	27.888	30.324	33.003	35.950
17	18.430	20.012	21.762	23.698	25.840	28.213	30.840	33.750	36.974	40.545
18	19.615	21.412	23.414	25.645	28.132	30.906	33.999	37.450	41.301	45.599
19	20.811	22.841	25.117	27.671	30.539	33.760	37.379	41.446	46.018	51.159
20	22.019	24.297	26.870	29.778	33.066	36.786	40.995	45.762	51.160	57.275
21	23.239	25.783	28.676	31.969	35.719	39.993	44.865	50.423	56.765	64.002
22	24.472	27.299	30.537	34.248	38.505	43.392	49.006	55.457	62.873	71.403
23	25.716	28.845	32.453	36.618	41.430	46.996	53.436	60.893	69.532	79.543
24	26.973	30.422	34.426	39.083	44.502	50.816	58.177	66.765	76.790	88.497
25	28.243	32.030	36.459	41.646	47.727	54.865	63.249	73.106	84.701	98.347
26	29.526	33.671	38.553	44.312	51.113	59.156	68.676	79.954	93.324	109.18
27	30.821	35.344	40.710	47.084	54.669	63.706	74.484	87.351	102.72	121.10
28	32.129	37.051	42.931	49.968	58.403	68.528	80.698	95.339	112.97	134.21
29	33.450	38.792	45.219	52.966	62.323	73.640	87.347	103.97	124.14	148.63
30	34.785	40.568	47.575	56.085	66.439	79.058	94.461	113.28	136.31	164.49
40	48.886	60.402	75.401	95.026	120.80	154.76	199.64	259.06	337.88	442.59
50	64.463	84.579	112.80	152.67	209.35	290.34	406.53	573.77	815.08	1163.9
60	81.670	114.05	163.05	237.99	353.58	533.13	813.52	1253.2	1944.8	3034.8

TABLE A-4   *continued*

Number of Periods	12%	14%	15%	16%	18%	20%	24%	28%	32%	36%
1	1.0000	1.0000	1.0000	1.0000	1.0000	1.0000	1.0000	1.0000	1.0000	1.0000
2	2.1200	2.1400	2.1500	2.1600	2.1800	2.2000	2.2400	2.2800	2.3200	2.3600
3	3.3744	3.4396	3.4725	3.5056	3.5724	3.6400	3.7776	3.9184	4.0624	4.2096
4	4.7793	4.9211	4.9934	5.0665	5.2154	5.3680	5.6842	6.0156	6.3624	6.7251
5	6.3528	6.6101	6.7424	6.8771	7.1542	7.4416	8.0484	8.6999	9.3983	10.146
6	8.1152	8.5355	8.7537	8.9775	9.4420	9.9299	10.980	12.136	13.406	14.799
7	10.089	10.730	11.067	11.414	12.142	12.916	14.615	16.534	18.696	21.126
8	12.300	13.233	13.727	14.240	15.327	16.499	19.123	22.163	25.678	29.732
9	14.776	16.085	16.786	17.519	19.086	20.799	24.712	29.369	34.895	41.435
10	17.549	19.337	20.304	21.321	23.521	25.959	31.643	38.593	47.062	57.352
11	20.655	23.045	24.349	25.733	28.755	32.150	40.238	50.398	63.122	78.998
12	24.133	27.271	29.002	30.850	34.931	39.581	50.895	65.510	84.320	108.44
13	28.029	32.089	34.352	36.786	42.219	48.497	64.110	84.853	112.30	148.47
14	32.393	37.581	40.505	43.672	50.818	59.196	80.496	109.61	149.24	202.93
15	37.280	43.842	47.580	51.660	60.965	72.035	100.82	141.30	198.00	276.98
16	42.753	50.980	55.717	60.925	72.939	87.442	126.01	181.87	262.36	377.69
17	48.884	59.118	65.075	71.673	87.068	105.93	157.25	233.79	347.31	514.66
18	55.750	68.394	75.836	84.141	103.74	128.12	195.99	300.25	459.45	700.94
19	63.440	78.969	88.212	98.603	123.41	154.74	244.03	385.32	607.47	954.28
20	72.052	91.025	102.44	115.38	146.63	186.69	303.60	494.21	802.86	1298.8
21	81.699	104.77	118.81	134.84	174.02	225.03	377.46	633.59	1060.8	1767.4
22	92.503	120.44	137.63	157.41	206.34	271.03	469.06	812.00	1401.2	2404.7
23	104.60	138.30	159.28	183.60	244.49	326.24	582.63	1040.4	1850.6	3271.3
24	118.16	158.66	184.17	213.98	289.49	392.48	723.46	1332.7	2443.8	4450.0
25	133.33	181.87	212.79	249.21	342.60	471.98	898.09	1706.8	3226.8	6053.0
26	150.33	208.33	245.71	290.09	405.27	567.38	1114.6	2185.7	4260.4	8233.1
27	169.37	238.50	283.57	337.50	479.22	681.85	1383.1	2798.7	5624.8	11198.0
28	190.70	272.89	327.10	392.50	566.48	819.22	1716.1	3583.3	7425.7	15230.3
29	214.58	312.09	377.17	456.30	669.45	984.07	2129.0	4587.7	9802.9	20714.2
30	241.33	356.79	434.75	530.31	790.95	1181.9	2640.9	5873.2	12941.	28172.3
40	767.09	1342.0	1779.1	2360.8	4163.2	7343.9	22729.	69377.	*	*
50	2400.0	4994.5	7217.7	10436.	21813.	45497.	*	*	*	*
60	7471.6	18535.	29220.	46058.	*	*	*	*	*	*

*FVIFA > 99,999.

TABLE A-5   VALUES OF THE AREAS UNDER THE STANDARD NORMAL DISTRIBUTION FUNCTION

z	0.00	0.01	0.02	0.03	0.04	0.05	0.06	0.07	0.08	0.09
0.0	.0000	.0040	.0080	.0120	.0160	.0199	.0239	.0279	.0319	.0359
0.1	.0398	.0438	.0478	.0517	.0557	.0596	.0636	.0675	.0714	.0753
0.2	.0793	.0832	.0871	.0910	.0948	.0987	.1026	.1064	.1103	.1141
0.3	.1179	.1217	.1255	.1293	.1331	.1368	.1406	.1443	.1480	.1517
0.4	.1554	.1591	.1628	.1664	.1700	.1736	.1772	.1808	.1844	.1879
0.5	.1915	.1950	.1985	.2019	.2054	.2088	.2123	.2157	.2190	.2224
0.6	.2257	.2291	.2324	.2357	.2389	.2422	.2454	.2486	.2517	.2549
0.7	.2580	.2611	.2642	.2673	.2704	.2734	.2764	.2794	.2823	.2852
0.8	.2881	.2910	.2939	.2967	.2995	.3023	.3051	.3078	.3106	.3133
0.9	.3159	.3186	.3212	.3238	.3264	.3289	.3315	.3340	.3365	.3389
1.0	.3413	.3438	.3461	.3485	.3508	.3531	.3554	.3577	.3599	.3621
1.1	.3643	.3665	.3686	.3708	.3729	.3749	.3770	.3790	.3810	.3830
1.2	.3849	.3869	.3888	.3907	.3925	.3944	.3962	.3980	.3997	.4015
1.3	.4032	.4049	.4066	.4082	.4099	.4115	.4131	.4147	.4162	.4177
1.4	.4192	.4207	.4222	.4236	.4251	.4265	.4279	.4292	.4306	.4319
1.5	.4332	.4345	.4357	.4370	.4382	.4394	.4406	.4418	.4429	.4441
1.6	.4452	.4463	.4474	.4484	.4495	.4505	.4515	.4525	.4535	.4545
1.7	.4554	.4564	.4573	.4582	.4591	.4599	.4608	.4616	.4625	.4633
1.8	.4641	.4649	.4656	.4664	.4671	.4678	.4686	.4693	.4699	.4706
1.9	.4713	.4719	.4726	.4732	.4738	.4744	.4750	.4756	.4761	.4767
2.0	.4773	.4778	.4783	.4788	.4793	.4798	.4803	.4808	.4812	.4817
2.1	.4821	.4826	.4830	.4834	.4838	.4842	.4846	.4850	.4854	.4857
2.2	.4861	.4864	.4868	.4871	.4875	.4878	.4881	.4884	.4887	.4890
2.3	.4893	.4896	.4898	.4901	.4904	.4906	.4909	.4911	.4913	.4916
2.4	.4918	4920	.4922	.4925	.4927	.4929	.4931	.4932	.4934	.4936
2.5	.4938	.4940	.4941	.4943	.4945	.4946	.4948	.4949	.4951	.4952
2.6	.4953	.4955	.4956	.4957	.4959	.4960	.4961	.4962	.4963	.4964
2.7	.4965	.4966	.4967	.4968	.4969	.4970	.4971	.4972	.4973	.4974
2.8	.4974	.4975	.4976	.4977	.4977	.4978	.4979	.4979	.4980	.4981
2.9	.4981	.4982	.4982	.4982	.4984	.4984	.4985	.4985	.4986	.4986
3.0	.4987	.4987	.4987	.4988	.4988	.4989	.4989	.4989	.4990	.4990

ANSWERS TO SELECTED END-OF-CHAPTER PROBLEMS

W e present here some intermediate steps and final answers to selected end-of-chapter problems. Please note that your answer may differ slightly from ours due to rounding differences. Also, although we hope not, some of the problems may have more than one correct solution, depending upon what assumptions are made in working the problem. Finally, many of the problems involve some verbal discussion as well as numerical calculations; this verbal material is not presented here.

2-1 **a.** Current ratio $= 1.98\times$; DSO $= 75$ days; Total assets turnover $= 1.7\times$; Debt ratio $= 61.9\%$.

2-2 A/P $= \$90,000$; Inv $= \$90,000$; FA $= \$138,000$.

2-4 **a.** Quick ratio $= 0.85\times$; DSO $= 37$ days; ROE $= 13.1\%$; Debt ratio $= 54.8\%$.

2-5 $\dfrac{NI}{S} = 2\%$; $\dfrac{D}{A} = 40\%$.

2-6 $\$262,500$; $1.19\times$.

2-7 Sales $= \$2,592,000$; DSO $= 36$ days.

2-8 TIE $= 3.5\times$.

2-9 ROE $= 24.5\%$.

2-10 7.2%.

2-12 **a.** $+5.54\%$.
b(2). $+3.21\%$.
(3). $+2.50\%$.

3-1 **a.** $k_1 = 9.20\%$; $k_5 = 7.20\%$.

3-3 **a.** 8.20%.
b. 10.20%.
c. $k_5 = 10.70\%$.

3-5 $Tax_{1993} = \$0$; $Tax_{1995} = \$4,500$; $Tax_{1996} = \$15,450$; $Refund_{1997} = \$19,950$.

3-6   **a.**   1993 advantage as a corporation = $1,651; 1994 advantage = $4,251; 1995 advantage = $5,551.

3-7   **a.**   Personal tax = $20,444.
       c.   MD yield = 7.59%; choose FL bonds.
       d.   18.18%.

3-8   **a.** k_1 in Year 2 = 13%.

3-9 k_1 in Year 2 = 15%; Year 2 inflation = 11%.

3-10   Tax = $107,855; NI = $222,145; Marginal tax rate = 39%; Average tax rate = 33.8%.

3-11   **a.**   Tax = $61,250.
       b.   Tax = $15,600.
       c.   Tax = $4,680.

3-12   1.5%.

3-13   AT&T bonds = 8.8%.

3-14   6.0%.

4-1   **a.**   17.0%.
       b.   17.75%; 1.18.

4-2   **a.** $1 million.

4-3   **a.**   A: 13.5%; 4.75; 2.2%; 0.16.
           B: 13.25%; 10.19; 3.2%; 0.24.
           C: 12.0%; 2.0; 1.4%; 0.12.

4-4   **a.**   12.92%.
       b.   1.69; 1.3%.
       c.   AB: 6.63; 0.94.
           AC: −3.00; −0.97.

4-5   **a.**   Average $\bar{k}$ A: 11.41%; B: 11.40%; AB: 11.41%.
       b.   A: 21.9%; B: 21.9%; AB: 21.3%.

5-1   **a.**   14.5%; 16.25%.
       b.   1.0; 1.43.
       c.   17.3%.

5-3   **a.**   15.6%.
       b.   (1) 16.6%.
           (2) 14.6%.
       c.   (1) 17.0%.
           (2) 12.8%.
       d.   (1) 16.4%.
           (2) 13.0%.

5-4   **b.**   15.75%.

5-5   **b.**   X: 10.6%; 13.1%.
           M: 12.1%; 22.6%.
       c.   8.6%.

5-6   **a.**   0.62.

6-1   **a.** $530.
       d. $445.

6-2   **a.** $895.40.
       b. $1,552.90.
       c. $279.20.
       d. $500.03; $867.14.

6-3   **a.**   ≈ 10 years.
       c.   ≈ 4 years.

6-4   **a.** $6,374.96.
       d(1). $7,012.46.

6-5   **a.** $2,457.84.
       c. $2,000.
       d(1). $2,703.62.

6-6   **a.**   Stream A: $1,251.21.

6-7   **b.**   7%.
       c.   9%.
       d.   15%.

6-8   **a.** $881.15.
       b. $895.40.
       c. $903.05.
       d. $908.35.

6-9   **a.** $279.20.
       b. $276.85.
       c. $443.70.

6-10   **a.** $5,272.40.
       b. $5,374.00.

6-11 **a.** Universal = 7%; Regional = 6.14%.

6-12 **a.** PMT = $6,594.94.

6-13 **a.** Z = 9%; B= 8%.
b. Z = $558.39; $135.98; 32.2%; B = $1,147.20; $147.20; 14.72%.

6-14 **a.** $61,203.
b. $11,020.
c. $6,841.

6-15 $1,000 today is worth more.

6-16 **a.** 15% (or 14.87%).

6-17 7.18%.

6-18 12%.

6-19 9%.

6-20 **a.** $33,872.
b. $26,243.04 and $0.

6-21 ≈ 15 years.

6-22 6 years; $1,106.01.

6-23 $PV_{7\%}$ = $1,428.57; $PV_{14\%}$ = $714.29.

6-24 $893.26.

6-25 $984.88 ≈ $985.

6-26 57.18%.

6-27 **a.** FV = $1,432.02.
b. PMT = $93.07.

6-28 i_{Nom} = 15.19%.

6-29 PMT = $36,948.95 or $36,949.61.

7-1 **a.** $1,251.26.
b. $898.90.

7-2 **a.** $1,250.
b. $833.33.
d. At 8%, V = $1,196.31.

7-3 **b.** PV = $5.29.
d. $30.01.

7-4 **a.** 7%.
b. 5%.
c. 12%.

7-5 **a(1).** $9.50.
(2). $13.33.
b(1). Undefined.

7-7 **a.** YTM = 3.4%.
b. YTM ≈ 7%.
c. $878.06.

7-8 **a.** Dividend 1996 = $2.66.
b. P_0 = $39.42.
c. Dividend yield 1994 = 5.10%; 1998 = 7.00%.

7-9 **a.** P_0 = $54.11.

7-10 **a.** YTM = 8%; YTC = 6.1%.

7-11 **a.** P_0 = $21.43.
b. P_0 = $26.47.
d. P_0 = $40.54.

7-12 **a.** New price = $31.34.
b. Beta = 0.49865.

7-13 **a.** V_L at 5 percent = $1,518.97; V_L at 8 percent = $1,171.15; V_L at 12 percent = $863.79.

7-14 **a.** YTM at $829 ≈ 15%.

7-15 **a.** 13.3%.
b. 10%.
c. 8%.
d. 5.7%.

7-16 $23.75.

7-17 **a.** k_C = 10.6%; k_D = 7%.

7-18 $25.03.

7-19 Bond = 9.33%.

7-20 YTC = 6.47%.

7-21 P_0 = $19.89.

8-1
  a. 10.0%.
  b. 8.0%.
  c. 6.0%.

8-2 10.25%.

8-3
  a. $15,000,000.
  b. $3,000,000; $12,000,000.
  c. k_s = 12.0%; k_e = 12.4%.
  d. $6,000,000.
  e. (1) 8.4%.
      (2) 8.6%.

8-4
  a. 4.8%; 12.3%.
  b. 10.05%.
  c. $432,000.
  d. 10.40%.

8-5 CL = $10,000,000 (11.14%);
    LTD = $19,782,600 (22.03%);
    CE = $60,000,000 (66.83%).

8-6
  a. 8.0%.
  b. $0.864.
  c. 12.0%.
  d. $6 million.
  e. $15 million.
  f. 15%; 12.71%.

9-1 NPV_S = $814.33; NPV_L = $1,675.34.
    IRR_S = 15.24%; IRR_L = 14.67%.
    $MIRR_S$ = 13.77%; $MIRR_L$ = 13.46%.
    PI_S = 1.081; PI_L = 1.067.

9-2
  b. IRR_A = 18.1%; IRR_B = 24.0%.
  d. At k = 10%: $MIRR_A$ = 14.1%; $MIRR_B$ = 15.9%.
     At k = 17%: $MIRR_A$ = 17.6%; $MIRR_B$ = 19.9%.
  e. 14.53%; 456.22%.

9-3
  a. $0; $-$10,250,000; $1,750,000.
  b. 16.07%.

9-4
  a. NPV_A = $18,108,510; NPV_B = $13,946,117.
    IRR_A = 15.03%; IRR_B = 22.26%.
  b. NPV_Δ = $4,162,393; IRR_Δ = 11.71%.

9-5
  d. 7.61%; 15.58%.

9-7
  a. Undefined.
  b. PV_C = $-$911,067; PV_F = $-$838,834.

10-2
  a. $89,000.
  b. $26,220; $30,300; $20,100.
  c. $24,380.

10-3
  a. $212,500.
  b. $72,501; $80,865; $59,955.
  c. $65,179.
  e. $5,766; $23,295.
  f. $-$620; $19,214; $51,000.
  g. $5,256.
  h. $-$52; $199,900.

10-4
  a. $88,400.
  b. $46,770; $52,890; $37,590; $33,510; $29,940.
  c. $-$10,000.
  d. $46,051.

10-5
  a. $880,000.
  c. $221,000; $278,600; $216,200; $182,600; $177,800.
  d. $133,800.
  e. NPV = $31,789.
  g. NPV = $15,296.
  h. NPV = $-$3,331.
  i. NPV = $37,034.

10-7
  a. 3 years.
  b. No.

10-8
  a. NPV = $106,537.

10-9
  a. 11.6%; 5.28%.
  c. $1,392.
  d. NPV = $768.
  e. NPV = $-$214.

11-1   Oil plant; PV_{costs} = $4,645,188.

11-2   **a.** $117,779.
      b. $445,060; 3.78; High.

11-3   **a.**   16.5%.

11-4   **a.**   5-year NPV = $1,843.
           4-year NPV = − $1,734.
           8-year NPV = $11,107.
      b.   8% NPV = $3,539.
           12% NPV = $280.

11-5   **a.**   15.3%.
      b. $38,589.

11-6 $10 million.

11-7 $42,000.

11-8 $62,000.

12-1   **a.**   ROI = 21.25% > WACC = 15%.
      b. $Q_{BE_{OLD}}$ = 40; $Q_{BE_{NEW}}$ = 45.45.

12-2   **a.** ROE_C = 15%; σ_C = 11%.

12-3   **a.** b_U = 1.13.
      b. k_{sU} = 15.65%; 5.65%.
      c.   1%; 2.42%; 4.62%.
      d.   4.62%.

12-4   **a.** V_U = V_L = $20 million.
      b. k_{sU} = 10%; k_{sL} = 15%.
      c. S_L = $10 million.
      d. $WACC_U$ = $WACC_L$ = 10%.

12-5   **a.** V_U = $12 million; V_L = $16 million.
      b. k_{sU} = 10%; k_{sL} = 15%.
      c. S_L = $6 million.
      d. $WACC_U$ = 10%; $WACC_L$ = 7.5%.

12-6   **a.** V_U = 9.6 million.
      b. V_L = $12.93 million.
      c. $3.33 million versus $4 million.

12-6 (cont.)
      d. V_L = $20 million; $0.
      e. V_L = $16 million; $4 million.
      f. V_L = $12.64 million; $4 million.

12-7   **a.** V_U = V_L = $14,545,455.
      b.   At D = $6 million: k_{sL} = 14.51%; WACC = 11.0%.
      c. V_U = $8,727,273; V_L = $11,127,273.
      d.   At D = $6 million: k_{sL} = 14.51%; WACC = 8.63%.
      e.   D = V = $14,545,455.

12-8   **a.**   A: $32.5 million; B: $30.0 million.
      b.   Project B.

12-9   **a.**   Harris: $10.0 million; Broske: $10.0 million.

12-10 **a.** $15 million.
      b.   D = $7.5 million; D/V = 52.8%.
      d.   D = $7.5 million; D/V = 43.6%.
      e.   D = $10.0 million; D/V = 83.3%.
      f.   D = $10.0 million; D/V = 67.8%.

13-1   **c.** $20.28; $17.96.

13-2   **a.**   V = $3,283,636.
      b. $16.42.
      c. $1.81.

13-3   **a.**   14.0%.
      c. $38.85.

13-4   **a.** $2.25; $2.70.

14-4   **a.** $6.00.
      b.   60%.
      c. $66.67 versus $100.00.

14-5   **a.**   62.22%; $15.45 million; 11.21%; 10.97%.
      b. $24 million.

15-1 **a.** $13.44 million.
  b. Notes payable = $31.44 million.
  c. Current ratio = 2.00×; ROE = 14.2%.
  d(1). − $14.28 million.
  (2). Total assets = $147 million; Notes payable = $3.72 million.
  (3). Current ratio = 4.25×; ROE = 10.84%.

15-2 **a.** Total assets = $33,534; AFN = $2,128.
  b. Notes payable = $4,228; AFN = $70; ΔInterest = $213.

15-3 **a.** AFN = $128,783.
  b. Notes payable = $220,392; ΔInterest = $8,371; AFN = $8,028.
  c. 3.45%.

15-4 **a.** AFN = $667.
  b. Increase in notes payable = $51; Increase in C/S = $368.

15-5 **a.** $480,000.
  b. $18,750.

15-6 AFN = $360.

16-1 **a(1).** 67.
  (2). 101.
  d(1). 95.
  (2). 142.

16-2 **a.** 32.
  b. $288,000.
  c. $45,000.
  d(1). 30.
  (2). $378,000.

16-3 **a.** ROE_T = 11.75%; ROE_M = 10.80%; ROE_R = 9.16%.

16-4 **a.** 83.
  b. $356,250.
  c. 4.8.

16-5 **a.** 56.
  b(1). 1.875.
  (2). 11.25%.
  c(1). 41.
  (2). 2.03.
  (3). 12.2%.

16-7 **a.** Feb. surplus = $2,000.

16-8 **a.** Oct. loan = $22,800.

17-1 **a.** $1,600,000.
  c. Bank = $1,200,000; Books = − $5,200,000.

17-2 **b.** $420,000.
  c. $35,000.

17-3 **a.** Wire transfer.
  b. $7,250.

17-4 **a.** C^* = $45,000.
  b. $22,500.
  c. 100.

17-5 **a.** $103,350.
  b. $97,500.

17-6 **a.** $100,000.
  c(1). $300,000.
  (2). Approximate cost = 36.73%; Effective cost = 43.86%.

17-8 **a.** $300,000.

17-9 **a.** 11.73%.
  b. 12.09%.
  c. 18%.

17-10 **b.** $384,615.
  c. Cash = $126.9; NP = $434.6.

17-11 **a(1).** $27,500.
  (3). $25,833.

17-12 b. Total dollar cost
= $160,800; 15.12%.

18-1 a. 28 days.
b. $46,667.
c. $36,667.

18-2 a. $DSO_0 = 23$ days; $DSO_N = 17.5$ days.
b. $11,760; $24,696.
c. $5,750; $5,250.
d. $20,000; $24,000.
e. +$20,138.

18-3 C3: +$46,811; C4: +$15,467; C5: +$8,538.

18-4 $\Delta NI = +$28,115.

18-5 a. March: $146,000; June: $198,000.
b. Q1: ADS = $3,000; DSO = 48.7 days; Q2: ADS = $4,500; DSO = 44.0 days; Cumulative: ADS = $3,750; DSO = 52.8 days.
c. 0–30 days: 65%; 31–60 days: 35%.
d. Receivables/Sales = 130%.

18-6 $\Delta NI = -$3,450.

18-7 a. 3,000 bags.
b. 4,000 bags.
c. 2,500 bags.
d. Every 12 days.

18-8 a. 5,200 units.
b. 65 orders.
c. Reorder point = 16,600 units.
d. (1) $11,628.
(2) $11,530.
(3) $11,552. At EOQ: $11,520.
e. (1) 6,300 units.
(2) 5,800 units.
(3) 4,500 units.

19-1 a. $24.75.
b. $24.00.

19-2 a. $700,000.
b. $3,700,000.
c. −$2,300,000.

19-3 964,115.

19-4 a. 1993: $12,000; $6,000; $90,000.
b. Edelman: $g_{EPS} = 8.0\%$; $g_{DPS} = 7.4\%$.
e. 1993: $3.00; $1.50; $22.50.
f. Kennedy: 15.00%; Strasburg: 13.64%.
g. 1993: Kennedy: 50%; Strasburg: 50%.
h. Kennedy: 43%; Strasburg: 37%.
i. Kennedy: $8\times$; Strasburg: $8.67\times$.

20-1 a. $2,570,925.
b. $1,558,201.
c. $2,774,097.
d. $1,769,842.

20-2 PMT = $402,115.

20-3 18.4%.

20-4 c. YTM ≈ 39%.
d. V = $41.96; $150.00.

20-5 a. Zero: 1,242,236; Annual coupon: 400,000.
b. Zero: 12%; 5.69%; Annual coupon: 14%; 7%.
c. Zero: 7.63%; Annual coupon: 9.24%.

21-1 a. Energen: 50%; Hastings: 33%.
b. D/A = 50%.

21-2 a. NAL = $44,204.
c. $346,572.
d. NAL = $122,083.

21-3   **a.** $2,638.
      c.   − $353.
      d. $11,668.
      e.   Best case: $5,069; Worst case: $207.

21-4   **a.**   NAL = − $1,461.
      c.   NAL = − $698.
      e.   NAL = − $190.

22-1   **a.** $1.41.
      b. $1.14.
      c. $5.65.
      d. $0.18.

22-2   **a.**   (1) − $5, or $0.
           (2) $0.
           (3) $5.
           (4) $75.
      d.   10%; $100.

22-4   **a.**   14.1%.
      b. $12 million before tax.

22-5   **b.**   Plan 1: 49%; Plan 2: 53%; Plan 3: 53%.
      c.   Plan 1: $0.59; Plan 2: $0.64; Plan 3: $0.88.
      d.   Plan 1: 19%; Plan 2: 19%; Plan 3: 50%.

22-6   **b.**   11.65%.

22-7   **b.**   Net gain = $9,531.
      d.   Net loss = $14,628.

23-1   **a.**   Total assets: $327 million.
      b.   Income: $7 million.
      c.   Before: $15.6 million. After: $13.0 million.
      d.   Before: 35.7%. After: 64.2%.

23-2   **a.** $0.
      b.   First mortgage holders: $300,000. Second mortgage holders: $100,000.
      c.   Trustee's expenses: $50,000. Wages due: $30,000. Taxes due: $40,000.

23-4   **a.** $3,200,000; $7,000,000; No.

24-1   NPV = $10,761.

24-2   **a.**   18.1%.
      b. $386,875; $286,806.
      c. $563,439.
      d. $391,444.
      e. $1,597,764; $324,768.

24-3   **a.**   19.3%.
      b. $10.37 million.
      c. $8.64; Nothing.

25-1   0.5587 pounds per dollar.

25-2   6.0606 francs per dollar.

25-3   10.0200 francs per pound.

25-5   Rupees: $35.29.
      Lira: $0.80.
      Yen: $7.49.
      Riyals: $267.38.

25-7   **b.** $18,490.57.

25-8   **a.** $2,839,698.99.
      b. $2,817,844.00.
      d. $3,200,000.00.

25-9 $58.67/share.

25-10 $350,000 gain.

SOLUTIONS TO SELF-TEST PROBLEMS

CHAPTER 2

ST-1 Billingsworth paid $2 in dividends and retained $2 per share. Since total retained earnings rose by $12 million, there must be 6 million shares outstanding. With a book value of $40 per share, total common equity must be $40(6 million) = $240 million. Since Billingsworth has $120 million of debt, its debt ratio must be 33.3 percent:

$$\frac{\text{Debt}}{\text{Assets}} = \frac{\text{Debt}}{\text{Debt + Equity}} = \frac{\$120 \text{ million}}{\$120 \text{ million} + \$240 \text{ million}}$$

$$= 0.333 = 33.3\%.$$

ST-2 a. In answering questions such as this, always begin by writing down the relevant definitional equations, then start filling in numbers. Note that the extra zeros indicating millions have been deleted in the calculations below.

(1)
$$\text{DSO} = \frac{\text{Accounts receivable}}{\text{Sales}/360}$$

$$40 = \frac{\text{A/R}}{\$1,000/360}$$

$$\text{A/R} = 40(\$2.778) = \$111.1 \text{ million}.$$

(2) $\text{Quick ratio} = \dfrac{\text{Current assets} - \text{Inventories}}{\text{Current liabilities}} = 2.0$

$$= \dfrac{\text{Cash and marketable securities} + \text{A/R}}{\text{Current liabilities}} = 2.0$$

$$2.0 = \dfrac{\$100 + \$111.1}{\text{Current liabilities}}$$

Current liabilities = ($100 + $111.1)/2 = $105.5 million.

(3) $\text{Current ratio} = \dfrac{\text{Current assets}}{\text{Current liabilities}} = 3.0$

$$= \dfrac{\text{Current assets}}{\$105.5} = 3.0$$

Current assets = 3.0($105.5) = $316.50 million.

(4)   Total assets = Current assets + Fixed assets

$$= \$316.5 + \$283.5 = \$600 \text{ million.}$$

(5)   ROA = Profit margin $\times$ Total assets turnover

$$= \dfrac{\text{Net income}}{\text{Sales}} \times \dfrac{\text{Sales}}{\text{Total assets}}$$

$$= \dfrac{\$50}{\$1,000} \times \dfrac{\$1,000}{\$600}$$

$$= 0.05 \times 1.667 = 0.0833 = 8.33\%.$$

(6) $\text{ROE} = \text{ROA} \times \dfrac{\text{Assets}}{\text{Equity}}$

$$12.0\% = 8.33\% \times \dfrac{\$600}{\text{Equity}}$$

$$\text{Equity} = \dfrac{(8.33\%)(\$600)}{12.0\%}$$

$$= \$416.50 \text{ million.}$$

(7)   Total assets = Total claims = $600 million

Current liabilities + Long-term debt + Equity = $600 million

$105.5 + Long-term debt + $416.5 = $600 million

Long-term debt = $600 − $105.5 − $416.5 = $78 million.

Note: We could have found equity as follows:

$$\text{ROE} = \frac{\text{Net income}}{\text{Equity}}$$

$$12.0\% = \frac{\$50}{\text{Equity}}$$

$$\text{Equity} = \$50/0.12$$

$$= \$416.67 \text{ million (rounding difference).}$$

Then we could have gone on to find current liabilities and long-term debt.

b. Kaiser's average sales per day were $1,000/360 = $2.8 million. Its DSO was 40, so A/R = 40($2.8) = $111.1 million. Its new DSO of 30 would cause A/R = 30($2.8) = $83.3 million. The reduction in receivables would be $111.1 − $83.3 = $27.8 million, which would equal the amount of cash generated.

(1)
$$\text{New equity} = \text{Old equity} - \text{Stock bought back}$$

$$= \$416.5 - \$27.8$$

$$= \$388.7 \text{ million.}$$

Thus,

$$\text{New ROE} = \frac{\text{Net income}}{\text{New equity}}$$

$$= \frac{\$50}{\$388.7}$$

$$= 12.86\% \text{ (versus old ROE of 12.0\%).}$$

(2)
$$\text{New ROA} = \frac{\text{Net income}}{\text{Total assets} - \text{Reduction in A/R}}$$

$$= \frac{\$50}{\$600 - \$27.8}$$

$$= 8.74\% \text{ (versus old ROA of 8.33\%).}$$

(3) The old debt is the same as the new debt:

$$\text{Debt} = \text{Total claims} - \text{Equity}$$

$$= \$600 - \$416.5 = \$183.5 \text{ million.}$$

$$\text{Old total assets} = \$600 \text{ million.}$$

$$\text{New total assets} = \text{Old total assets} - \text{Reduction in A/R}$$

$$= \$600 - \$27.8$$

$$= \$572.2 \text{ million.}$$

Therefore,

$$\frac{\text{Debt}}{\text{Old total assets}} = \frac{\$183.5}{\$600} = 30.6\%,$$

while

$$\frac{\text{New debt}}{\text{New total assets}} = \frac{\$183.5}{\$572.2} = 32.1\%.$$

CHAPTER 3

ST-1 a. Average $= (6\% + 7\% + 8\% + 9\%)/4 = 30\%/4 = 7.5\%$.

  b. $k_{\text{T-bond}} = k^* + IP = 3.0\% + 7.5\% = 10.5\%$.

  c. If the 5-year T-bond rate is 11 percent, the inflation rate is expected to average approximately $11\% - 3\% = 8\%$ during the next 5 years. Thus, the implied Year 5 inflation rate is 10 percent:

$$8\% = (6\% + 7\% + 8\% + 9\% + I_5)/5$$
$$40\% = 30\% + I_5$$
$$I_5 = 10\%.$$

ST-2

	1994	1995	1996
Thompson's Taxes as a Corporation			
Income before salary and taxes	$60,000	$90,000	$110,000
Less: salary	(40,000)	(40,000)	(40,000)
Taxable income, corporate	$20,000	$50,000	$ 70,000
Total corporate tax	$ 3,000[a]	$ 7,500	$ 12,500
Salary	$40,000	$40,000	$ 40,000
Less exemptions and deductions	(15,800)	(15,800)	(15,800)
Taxable personal income	$24,200	$24,200	$ 24,200
Total personal tax	$ 3,630[b]	$ 3,630	$ 3,630
Combined corporate and personal tax:	$ 6,630	$11,130	$ 16,130
Thompson's Taxes as a Proprietorship			
Total income	$60,000	$90,000	$110,000
Less: exemptions and deductions	(15,800)	(15,800)	(15,800)
Taxable personal income	$44,200	$74,200	$ 94,200
Tax liability of proprietorship	$ 7,579[c]	$15,979	$ 21,731
Advantage to being a corporation:	$ 949	$ 4,849	$ 5,601

[a]Corporate tax in 1994 $= (0.15)(\$20,000) = \$3,000$.

[b]Personal tax (if Thompson incorporates) in 1994 $= (0.15)(\$24,200) = \$3,630$.

[c]Proprietorship tax in 1994 $= \$5,535 + (0.28)(\$44,200 - \$36,900)$
$$= \$5,535 + \$2,044$$
$$= \$7,579.$$

The corporate form of organization allows Thompson to pay the lowest taxes in each year; therefore, on the basis of taxes over the 3-year period, Thompson should incorporate his business. However, note that to get money out of the corporation so he can spend it, Thompson will have to have the corporation pay dividends, which will be taxed to Thompson, and thus he will, sometime in the future, have to pay additional taxes.

CHAPTER 4

ST-1 a.   The realized return in each Period t is estimated as follows:

$$\bar{k}_t = \frac{D_t + P_t - P_{t-1}}{P_{t-1}}.$$

For example, the realized return for Stock A in 1989 was -12.24 percent:

$$\begin{aligned}\bar{k}_{1989} &= \frac{D_{1989} + P_{1989} - P_{1988}}{P_{1988}} \\ &= \frac{\$1.00 + \$9.75 - \$12.25}{\$12.25} \\ &= -0.1224 = -12.24\%.\end{aligned}$$

The table that follows shows the realized returns for each stock in each year, the averages for the 5 years, and the same data for the portfolio:

Year	Stock A's Return, $\bar{k}_A$	Stock B's Return, $\bar{k}_B$	Portfolio AB's Return, $\bar{k}_{AB}$
1989	-12.24%	-5.00%	-8.62%
1990	23.59	19.46	21.52
1991	35.45	44.10	39.78
1992	5.82	1.19	3.50
1993	28.30	21.11	24.71
$\bar{k}_{Avg}$	16.2%	16.2%	16.2%

b.   The standard deviation of returns is estimated as follows:

$$\sigma = \sqrt{\frac{\sum_{t=1}^{n}(\bar{k}_t - \bar{k}_{Avg})^2}{n - 1}}.$$

For Stock A, the estimated standard deviation is 19.3 percent:

$$\sigma_A = \sqrt{\frac{(-12.24 - 16.2)^2 + (23.59 - 16.2)^2 + \ldots + (28.30 - 16.2)^2}{5 - 1}}$$

$$= \sqrt{\frac{1,488.15}{4}} = 19.3\%.$$

The standard deviation of returns for Stock B and for the portfolio are similarly determined, and they are shown here:

	Stock A	Stock B	Portfolio AB
Standard deviation	19.3%	19.3%	18.9%

c. Since the risk reduction from diversification is small (σ_{AB} falls only from 19.3 to 18.9 percent), the most likely value of the correlation coefficient is 0.9. If the correlation coefficient were -0.9, the risk reduction would be much larger. In fact, the correlation coefficient between Stocks A and B is 0.93.

d. If more randomly selected stocks were added to the portfolio; σ_p would decline to somewhere in the vicinity of 15 percent. σ_p would remain constant only if the correlation coefficient were $+1.0$, which is most unlikely. σ_p would decline to zero only if the correlation coefficient, r, were equal to zero and a large number of stocks were added to the portfolio, or if the proper proportions were held in a two-stock portfolio with r $= -1.0$.

CHAPTER 5

ST-1 a. The market risk premium, which is the premium above the risk-free rate required on an average stock, is 5 percentage points:

$$RP_M = (k_M - k_{RF}) = 13.0\% - 8.0\% = 5.0\%.$$

b. Bigbee's required rate of return is 12.0 percent:

$$k_i = k_{RF} + (k_M - k_{RF})b_i$$

$$= 8.0\% + (13.0\% - 8.0\%)0.8$$

$$= 8.0\% + (5\%)0.8 = 8.0\% + 4.0\% = 12.0\%.$$

c. See the graph on the next page:

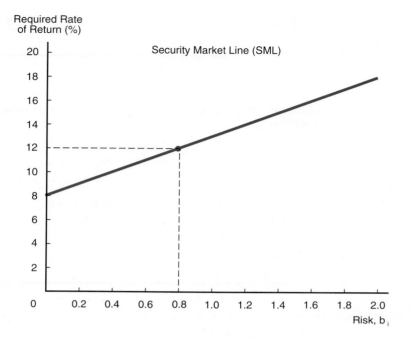

Required Rate of Return (%) vs Risk, b_i — Security Market Line (SML)

d. If inflation expectations increased by 2 percentage points, then the risk-free rate would increase to 8.0% + 2.0% = 10.0%. However, assuming that there is no change in investors' risk aversion, the required rate of return on the market would also increase by 2 percentage points, to 15.0 percent. Thus, the market risk premium would remain at 15.0% − 10.0% = 5.0%. The effect on Bigbee's stock would be to increase its required rate of return by 2 percentage points:

$$k_i = k_{RF} + (k_M - k_{RF})b_i$$

$$= 10.0\% + (15.0\% - 10.0\%)0.8$$

$$= 10.0\% + (5\%)0.8 = 10.0\% + 4.0\% = 14.0\%.$$

e. In this situation, Bigbee's required rate of return would be 13.6 percent:

$$k_i = k_{RF} + (k_M - k_{RF})b_i$$

$$= 8.0\% + (7\%)0.8 = 8.0\% + 5.6\% = 13.6\%.$$

f. If Bigbee's market risk increased to b = 1.2, its required rate of return would rise to 14.0 percent:

$$k_i = k_{RF} + (k_M - k_{RF})b_i$$

$$= 8.0\% + (5\%)1.2 = 8.0\% + 6.0\% = 14.0\%.$$

CHAPTER 6

ST-1 a.

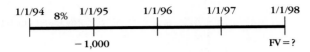

$1,000 is being compounded for 3 years, so your balance on January 1, 1998, is $1,259.71:

$$FV_n = PV(1 + i)^n = \$1,000(1 + 0.08)^3 = \$1,259.71.$$

Alternatively, using a financial calculator, input N = 3, I = 8, PV = −1000, PMT = 0, and solve for FV = $1,259.71.

b.

The effective annual rate for 8 percent, compounded quarterly, is

$$\begin{array}{c}\text{Effective}\\\text{annual}\\\text{rate}\end{array} = \left(1 + \frac{0.08}{4}\right)^4 - 1.0$$

$$= (1.02)^4 - 1.0 = 0.0824 = 8.24\%.$$

Therefore, FV = $1,000(1.0824)^3 = $1,000(1.2681) = $1,268.10. Alternatively, use FVIF for 2%, 3 × 4 = 12 periods:

$$FV_{12} = \$1,000(FVIF_{2\%,12}) = \$1,000(1.2682) = \$1,268.20.$$

Alternatively, using a financial calculator, input N = 12, I = 2, PV = −1000, PMT = 0, and solve for FV = $1,268.24.

Note that since the interest factors are carried to only four decimal places, rounding differences occur. Rounding differences also occur between calculator and tabular solutions.

c.

As you work this problem, keep in mind that the tables assume that payments are made at the end of each period. Therefore, you may solve this problem by finding the future value of an annuity of $250 for 4 years at 8 percent:

$$FVA_4 = PMT(FVIFA_{i,n}) = \$250(4.5061) = \$1,126.53.$$

Alternatively, using a financial calculator, input N = 4, I = 8, PV = 0, PMT = −250, and solve for FV = $1,126.53.

d.

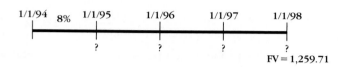

N = 4; I = 8; PV = 0; FV = 1259.71; solve for PMT = $279.56.

$$PMT(FVIFA_{8\%,4}) = FVA_4$$

$$PMT(4.5061) = \$1,259.71$$

$$PMT = \$1,259.71/4.5061 = \$279.56.$$

Therefore, you would have to make 4 payments of $279.56 each to have a balance of $1,259.71 on January 1, 1998.

ST-2 a. Set up a time line like the one in the preceding problem:

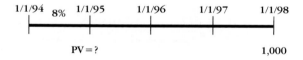

Note that your deposit will grow for 3 years at 8 percent. The fact that it is now January 1, 1994, is irrelevant. The deposit on January 1, 1995, is the PV, and the FV is $1,000. Here is the solution:

N = 3; I = 8; PMT = 0; FV = 1000; solve for PV = $793.83.

$$FV_3(PVIF_{8\%,3}) = PV$$

$$PV = \$1,000(0.7938) = \$793.80 = \text{Initial deposit to accumulate }\$1,000.$$

(Difference due to rounding.)

b.

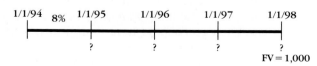

Here we are dealing with a 4-year annuity whose first payment occurs one year from today, on 1/1/95, and whose future value must equal $1,000. You should modify the time line to help visualize the situation. Here is the solution:

N = 4; I = 8; PV = 0; FV = 1000; solve for PMT = $221.92.

$$PMT(FVIFA_{8\%,4}) = FVA_4$$
$$PMT = \frac{FVA_4}{(FVIFA_{8\%,4})}$$
$$= \frac{\$1,000}{4.5061} = \$221.92 = \text{Payment necessary to accumulate } \$1,000.$$

c. This problem can be approached in several ways. Perhaps the simplest is to ask this question: "If I received $750 on 1/1/95 and deposited it to earn 8 percent, would I have the required $1,000 on 1/1/98?" The answer is no:

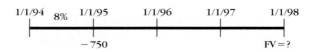

$$FV_3 = \$750(1.08)(1.08)(1.08) = \$944.78.$$

This indicates that you should let your father make the payments rather than accept the lump sum of $750.

You could also compare the $750 with the PV of the payments:

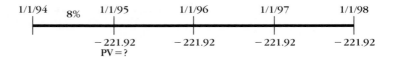

N = 4; I = 8; PMT = −221.92; FV = 0; solve for PV = $735.03.

$$PMT(PVIFA_{8\%,4}) = PVA_4$$
$$\$221.92(3.3121) = \$735.02 = \text{Present value of the required payments.}$$

(Difference due to rounding.)

This is less than the $750 lump sum offer, so your initial reaction might be to accept the lump sum of $750. However, this would be a mistake. The problem is that when you found the $735.02 PV of the annuity, you were finding the value of the annuity *today*, on January 1, 1994. You were comparing $735.02 today with the lump sum of $750 one year from now. This is, of course, invalid. What you should have done was take the $735.02, recognize that this is the PV of an annuity as of January 1, 1994, multiply $735.02 by 1.08 to get $793.82, and compare $793.82 with the lump sum of $750. You would then

take your father's offer to make the payments rather than take the lump sum on January 1, 1995.

d.

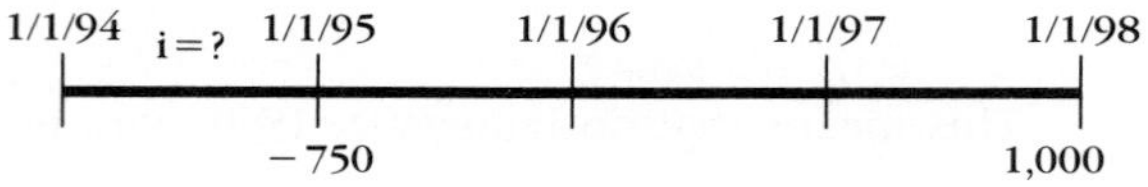

N = 3; PV = −750; PMT = 0; FV = 1000; solve for I = 10.0642%.

$$PV(FVIF_{i,3}) = FV$$

$$FVIF_{i,3} = \frac{FV}{PV}$$

$$= \frac{\$1,000}{\$750} = 1.3333.$$

Use the Future Value of $1 table (Table A-3 in Appendix A) for 3 periods to find the interest rate corresponding to an FVIF of 1.3333. Look across the Period 3 row of the table until you come to 1.3333. The closest value is 1.3310, in the 10 percent column. Therefore, you would require an interest rate of approximately 10 percent to achieve your $1,000 goal. The exact rate required, found with a financial calculator, is 10.0642 percent.

e.

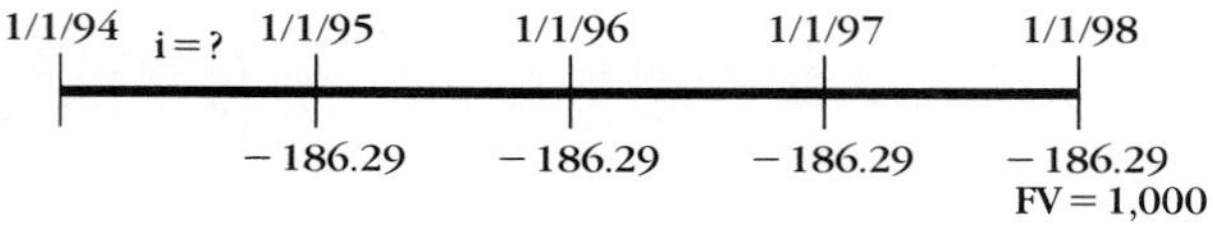

N = 4; PV = 0; PMT = −186.29; FV = 1000; solve for I = 19.9997%.

$$PMT(FVIFA_{i,4}) = FVA_4$$

$$\$186.29(FVIFA_{i,4}) = \$1,000$$

$$FVIFA_{i,4} = \frac{\$1,000}{\$186.29} = 5.3680.$$

Using Table A-4 at the end of the book, we find that 5.3680 corresponds to a 20 percent interest rate. You might be able to find a borrower willing to offer you a 20 percent interest rate, but there would be some risk involved—he or she might not actually pay you your $1,000!

f.

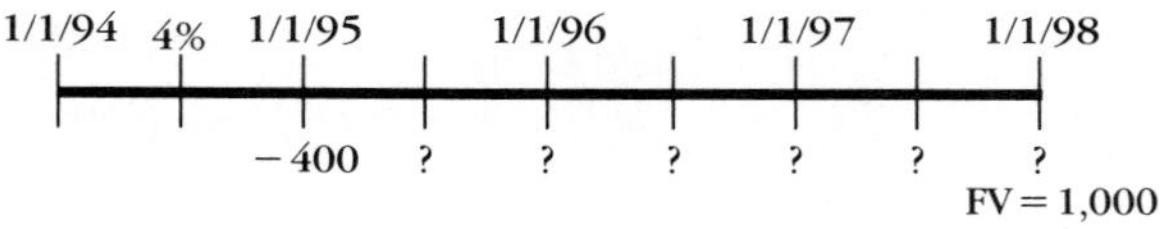

Find the future value of the original $400 deposit:

$$FV_6 = PV(FVIF_{4\%,6}) = \$400(1.2653) = \$506.12.$$

This means that on January 1, 1998, you need an additional sum of $493.88:

$$\$1,000.00 - \$506.12 = \$493.88.$$

This will be accumulated by making 6 equal payments which earn 8 percent compounded semiannually, or 4 percent each 6 months:

N = 6; I = 4; PV = 0; FV = 493.88; solve for PMT = $74.46.

$$PMT(FVIFA_{4\%,6}) = FVA_6$$

$$PMT = \frac{FVA_6}{(FVIFA_{4\%,6})}$$

$$= \frac{\$493.88}{6.6330} = \$74.46.$$

g.
$$\text{Effective annual rate} = \left(1 + \frac{i_{Nom}}{m}\right)^m - 1.0$$

$$= \left(1 + \frac{0.08}{2}\right)^2 - 1 = (1.04)^2 - 1$$

$$= 1.0816 - 1 = 0.0816 = 8.16\%.$$

h. There is a reinvestment rate risk here because we assumed that funds will earn an 8 percent return in the bank. In fact, if interest rates in the economy fall, the bank will lower its deposit rate because it will be earning less when it lends out the funds you deposited with it. If you buy certificates of deposit (CDs) that mature on the date you need the money (1/1/98), you will avoid the reinvestment risk, but that would work only if you were making the deposit today. Other ways of reducing reinvestment rate risk will be discussed later in the text.

ST-3 Bank A's effective annual rate is 8.24 percent:

$$\text{Effective annual rate} = \left(1 + \frac{0.08}{4}\right)^4 - 1.0$$

$$= (1.02)^4 - 1 = 1.0824 - 1$$

$$= 0.0824 = 8.24\%.$$

Now Bank B must have the same effective annual rate:

$$\left(1 + \frac{i}{12}\right)^{12} - 1.0 = 0.0824$$

$$\left(1 + \frac{i}{12}\right)^{12} = 1.0824$$

$$1 + \frac{i}{12} = (1.0824)^{1/12}$$

$$1 + \frac{i}{12} = 1.00662$$

$$\frac{i}{12} = 0.00662$$

$$i = 0.07944 = 7.94\%.$$

Thus, the two banks have different quoted rates—Bank A's quoted rate is 8 percent, while Bank B's quoted rate is 7.94 percent; however, both banks have the same effective annual rate of 8.24 percent. The difference in their quoted rates is due to the difference in compounding frequency.

CHAPTER 7

ST-1 a. This is not necessarily true. Because G plows back two-thirds of its earnings, its growth rate should exceed that of D, but D pays higher dividends ($6 versus $2). We cannot say which stock should have the higher price.

  b. Again, we just do not know which price would be higher.

  c. This is false. The changes in k_d and k_s would have a greater effect on G—its price would decline more.

  d. The total expected return for D is $\hat{k}_D = D_1/P_0 + g = 15\% + 0\% = 15\%$. The total expected return for G will have D_1/P_0 less than 15 percent and g greater than 0 percent, but $\hat{k}_G$ should be neither greater nor smaller than D's total expected return, 15 percent, because the two stocks are stated to be equally risky.

  e. We have eliminated a, b, c, and d, so e should be correct. On the basis of the available information, D and G should sell at about the same price, $40; thus, $\hat{k}_s = 15\%$ for both D and G. G's current dividend yield is $2/$40 = 5\%$. Therefore, g = 15\% − 5\% = 10\%.

ST-2 a. Pennington's bonds were sold at par; therefore, the original YTM equaled the coupon rate of 12%.

b.
$$V_B = \sum_{t=1}^{50} \frac{\$120/2}{\left(1 + \dfrac{0.10}{2}\right)^t} + \frac{\$1,000}{\left(1 + \dfrac{0.10}{2}\right)^{50}}$$

$$= \$60(\text{PVIFA}_{5\%,50}) + \$1,000(\text{PVIF}_{5\%,50})$$

$$= \$60(18.2559) + \$1,000(0.0872)$$

$$= \$1,095.35 + \$87.20 = \$1,182.55.$$

Alternatively, with a financial calculator, input the following: N = 50, I = 5, PMT = 60, FV = 1000, and solve for PV = $1,182.56.

c.
$$\text{Current yield} = \text{Annual coupon payment/Price}$$

$$= \$120/\$1,182.55$$

$$= 0.1015 = 10.15\%.$$

$$\text{Capital gains yield} = \text{Total yield} - \text{Current yield}$$

$$= 10\% - 10.15\% = -0.15\%.$$

d.
$$\$916.42 = \sum_{t=1}^{13} \frac{\$60}{(1 + k_d/2)^t} + \frac{\$1,000}{(1 + k_d/2)^{13}}.$$

Try $k_d = 14\%$:

$$V_B = \text{INT}(\text{PVIFA}_{7\%,13}) + M(\text{PVIF}_{7\%,13})$$
$$\$916.42 = \$60(8.3577) + \$1,000(0.4150)$$
$$= \$501.46 + \$415.00 = \$916.46.$$

Therefore, the YTM on July 1, 1994, was 14 percent.

Alternatively, with a financial calculator, input the following: N = 13, PV = −916.42, PMT = 60, FV = 1000, and $k_{d/2}$ = I = ? Calculator solution = $k_{d/2}$ = 7.00%; therefore, k_d = 14.00%.

e.
$$\text{Current yield} = \$120/\$916.42 = 13.09\%.$$

$$\text{Capital gains yield} = 14\% - 13.09\% = 0.91\%.$$

f. The following time line illustrates the years to maturity of the bond:

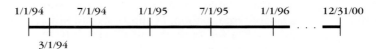

Thus, on March 1, 1994, there were 13⅔ periods left before the bond matures. Bond traders actually use the following procedure to determine the price of the bond:

(1) Find the price of the bond on the next coupon date, July 1, 1994.

$$V_{B\ 7/1/94} = \$60(PVIFA_{7.75\%,13}) + \$1,000(PVIF_{7.75\%,13})$$
$$= \$60(8.0136) + \$1,000(0.3789)$$
$$= \$859.72.$$

Note that we could use a calculator to solve for $V_{B\ 7/1/94}$ or we could substitute $i = 7.75\%$ and $n = 13$ periods into the equations for PVIFA and PVIF:

$$PVIFA = \frac{1 - \dfrac{1}{(1 + i)^n}}{i} = \frac{1 - \dfrac{1}{(1 + 0.0775)^{13}}}{0.0775} = 8.0136.$$

$$PVIF = \frac{1}{(1 + k)^n} = \frac{1}{(1 + 0.0775)^{13}} = 0.3789.$$

(2) Add the coupon, $60, to the bond price to get the total value, TV, of the bond on the next interest payment date: TV = $859.72 + $60.00 = $919.72.

(3) Discount this total value back to the purchase date:

$$\text{Value at purchase date (March 1, 1994)} = \$919.72(PVIF_{7.75\%,4/6})$$
$$= \$919.72(0.9515)$$
$$= \$875.11.$$

Here

$$PVIF_{7.75\%,2/3} = \frac{1}{(1 + 0.0775)^{2/3}} = \frac{1}{1.0510} = 0.9515.$$

(4) Therefore, you would have written a check for $875.11 to complete the transaction. Of this amount, $20 = (⅓)($60) would represent accrued interest and $855.11 would represent the bond's basic value. This breakdown would affect both your taxes and those of the seller.

(5) This problem could be solved *very* easily using a financial calculator with a bond valuation function, such as the HP-12C or the HP-17B. This is explained in the calculator manual under the heading, "Bond Calculations."

ST-3 The first step is to solve for g, the unknown variable, in the constant growth equation. Since D_1 is unknown but D_0 is known, substitute $D_0(1 + g)$ as follows:

$$\hat{P}_0 = P_0 = \frac{D_1}{k_s - g} = \frac{D_0(1 + g)}{k_s - g}$$

$$\$36 = \frac{\$2.40(1 + g)}{0.12 - g}.$$

Solving for g, we find the growth rate to be 5 percent:

$$\$4.32 - \$36g = \$2.40 + \$2.40g$$

$$\$38.4g = \$1.92$$

$$g = 0.05 = 5\%.$$

The next step is to use the growth rate to project the stock price 5 years hence:

$$\hat{P}_5 = \frac{D_0(1 + g)^6}{k_s - g}$$

$$= \frac{\$2.40(1.05)^6}{0.12 - 0.05}$$

$$= \$45.95.$$

[Alternatively, $\hat{P}_5 = \$36(1.05)^5 = \$45.95$.]

Therefore, Ewald Company's expected stock price 5 years from now, $\hat{P}_5$, is $45.95.

ST-4 a. (1) Calculate the PV of the dividends paid during the supernormal growth period:

$$D_1 = \$1.1500(1.15) = \$1.3225.$$

$$D_2 = \$1.3225(1.15) = \$1.5209.$$

$$D_3 = \$1.5209(1.13) = \$1.7186.$$

$$PV \ D = \$1.3225(0.8929) + \$1.5209(0.7972) + \$1.7186(0.7118)$$

$$= \$1.1809 + \$1.2125 + \$1.2233$$

$$= \$3.6167 \approx \$3.62.$$

(2) Find the PV of Snyder's stock price at the end of Year 3:

$$\hat{P}_3 = \frac{D_4}{k_s - g} = \frac{D_3(1 + g)}{k_s - g}$$

$$= \frac{\$1.7186(1.06)}{0.12 - 0.06}$$

$$= \$30.36.$$

$$PV \ \hat{P}_3 = \$30.36(0.7118) = \$21.61.$$

(3) Sum the two components to find the value of the stock today:

$$\hat{P}_0 = \$3.62 + \$21.61 = \$25.23.$$

Alternatively, the cash flows can be placed on a time line as follows:

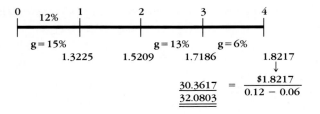

Enter the cash flows into the cash flow register, I = 12, and press the NPV key to obtain $P_0 = \$25.23$.

b.
$$\hat{P}_1 = \$1.5209(0.8929) + \$1.7186(0.7972) + \$30.36(0.7972)$$

$$= \$1.3580 + \$1.3701 + \$24.2030$$

$$= \$26.9311 \approx \$26.93.$$

(Calculator solution: $26.93.)

$$\hat{P}_2 = \$1.7186(0.8929) + \$30.36(0.8929)$$

$$= \$1.5345 + \$27.1084$$

$$= \$28.6429 \approx \$28.64.$$

(Calculator solution: $28.64.)

c.

Year	Dividend Yield	+	Capital Gains Yield	=	Total Return
1	$\dfrac{\$1.3225}{\$25.23} \approx 5.24\%$		$\dfrac{\$26.93 - \$25.23}{\$25.23} \approx 6.74\%$		$\approx 12\%$
2	$\dfrac{\$1.5209}{\$26.93} \approx 5.65\%$		$\dfrac{\$28.64 - \$26.93}{\$26.93} \approx 6.35\%$		$\approx 12\%$
3	$\dfrac{\$1.7186}{\$28.64} \approx 6.00\%$		$\dfrac{\$30.36 - \$28.64}{\$28.64} \approx 6.00\%$		$\approx 12\%$

CHAPTER 8

ST-1 a. *After-tax cost of debt:*

$$k_d(1 - T) = 12\%(1 - 0.40) = 12\%(0.60) = 7.20\%.$$

Cost of preferred stock:

$$k_{ps} = \frac{D_{ps}}{P_n} = \frac{\$11}{\$100 - \$5} = \frac{\$11}{\$95} \approx 11.6\%.$$

Cost of retained earnings (using DCF method):

$$k_s = \hat{k}_s = \frac{D_1}{P_0} + g = \frac{D_0(1 + g)}{P_0} + g$$

$$= \frac{\$3.60(1.09)}{\$60} + 9\% \approx 15.5\%.$$

Cost of retained earnings (using CAPM method):

$$k_s = k_{RF} + (k_M - k_{RF})b_i$$

$$= 11\% + (14\% - 11\%)1.51 \approx 15.5\%.$$

Cost of new common stock:

$$k_c = \frac{D_1}{P_0(1.0 - F)} + g = \frac{\$3.924}{\$60(0.9)} + 9\% \approx 16.3\%.$$

Since we are using the DCF k_s estimate as our final estimate for k_s, we can use the DCF k_c estimate as our final estimate for k_c. If this condition did not hold, we would apply the $16.3\% - 15.5\% = 0.8\%$ flotation cost adjustment to the final k_s estimate.

b. LCI's forecasted retained earnings are $\$17,142.86(1 - 0.30) = \$12,000$. Thus, the retained earnings break point, BP_{RE}, is $\$20,000$:

$$BP_{RE} = \frac{RE}{\text{Equity fraction}} = \frac{\$12,000}{0.60} = \$20,000.$$

c. *WACC using retained earnings:*

$$WACC_1 = w_d k_d(1 - T) + w_{ps}k_{ps} + w_{cc}k_s$$

$$= 0.25(7.20\%) + 0.15(11.6\%) + 0.60(15.5\%) \approx 12.9\%.$$

WACC using new common stock:

$$WACC_2 = 1.80\% + 1.74\% + 0.60(16.3\%) \approx 13.3\%.$$

d. See the graph at the top of page C-19.

e. Depreciation-generated cash flow pushes the retained earnings break point to the right by the amount of depreciation expense. Thus, the break point would shift to $\$20,000 + \$10,000 = \$30,000$.

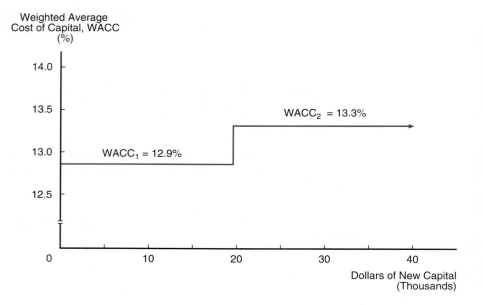

CHAPTER 9

ST-1 a. *Payback:*

To determine the payback, construct the cumulative cash flows for each project:

	Cumulative Cash Flow	
Year	Project X	Project Y
0	($10,000)	($10,000)
1	(3,500)	(6,500)
2	(500)	(3,000)
3	2,500	500
4	3,500	4,000

$$\text{Payback}_X = 2 + \frac{\$500}{\$3,000} = 2.17 \text{ years.}$$

$$\text{Payback}_Y = 2 + \frac{\$3,000}{\$3,500} = 2.86 \text{ years.}$$

Net Present Value (NPV):

$$NPV_X = -\$10,000 + \frac{\$6,500}{(1.12)^1} + \frac{\$3,000}{(1.12)^2} + \frac{\$3,000}{(1.12)^3} + \frac{\$1,000}{(1.12)^4}$$

$$= \$966.01.$$

With a financial calculator, input the following: $CF_0 = -10000$, $CF_1 = 6500$, $CF_2 = 3000$, $CF_3 = 3000$, $CF_4 = 1000$, $I = 12$, and solve for $NPV_X = \$966.01$.

$$NPV_Y = -\$10,000 + \frac{\$3,500}{(1.12)^1} + \frac{\$3,500}{(1.12)^2} + \frac{\$3,500}{(1.12)^3} + \frac{\$3,500}{(1.12)^4}$$

$$= \$630.72.$$

With a financial calculator, input the following: $CF_0 = -10000$, $CF_1 = 3500$, $CF_2 = 3500$, $CF_3 = 3500$, $CF_4 = 3500$, $I = 12$, and solve for $NPV_Y = \$630.72$.

Internal Rate of Return (IRR):
To solve for each project's IRR, find the discount rates which equate each NPV to zero:

$$IRR_X = 18.0\%.$$

$$IRR_Y = 15.0\%.$$

With a financial calculator, input the cash flows and interest rate as done in the NPV calculation, but, rather than using the NPV key, press the IRR key to arrive at the IRR.

Modified Internal Rate of Return (MIRR):
To obtain each project's MIRR, begin by finding each project's terminal value (TV) of cash inflows:

$$TV_X = \$6,500(1.12)^3 + \$3,000(1.12)^2$$
$$+ \ 3,000(1.12)^1 + \$1,000 = \$17,255.23.$$
$$TV_Y = \$3,500(1.12)^3 + \$3,500(1.12)^2$$
$$+ \ \$3,500(1.12)^1 + \$3,500 = \$16,727.65.$$

Now, each project's MIRR is that discount rate which equates the PV of the TV to each project's cost, $10,000:

$$MIRR_X = 14.6\%.$$

$$MIRR_Y = 13.7\%.$$

With a financial calculator, input the following: $N = 4$, $PV = -10000$, $PMT = 0$, $FV = 17255.23$, and solve for $I = MIRR_X = 14.6\%$. For Project Y input the following: $N = 4$, $PV = -10000$, $PMT = 0$, $FV = 16727.65$, and solve for $I = MIRR_Y = 13.7\%$.

Profitability Index (PI):

$$PI_X = \frac{PV \text{ benefits}}{PV \text{ costs}} = \frac{\$10,966.01}{\$10,000} = 1.10.$$

$$PI_Y = \frac{\$10,630.72}{\$10,000} = 1.06.$$

b. The following table summarizes the project rankings by each method:

	Project That Ranks Higher
Payback	X
NPV	X
IRR	X
MIRR	X
PI	X

Note that all methods rank Project X over Project Y. Additionally, both projects are acceptable under the NPV, IRR, MIRR, and PI criteria. Thus, both projects should be accepted if they are independent.

c. Choose the project with the higher NPV at k = 12%, or Project X. Note that both projects have 4-year lives—if Project X and Project Y had different lives and were repeatable, a different procedure would be required. This point is discussed in Chapter 10.

d. To determine the effects of changing the cost of capital, plot the NPV profiles of each project.

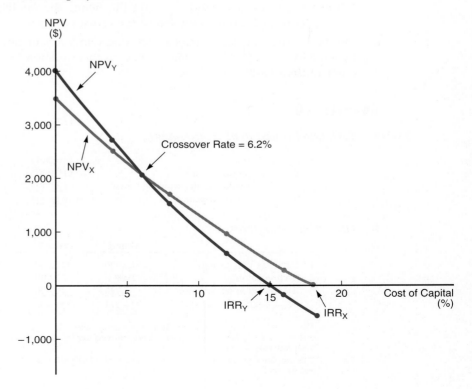

Discount Rate	NPV$_X$	NPV$_Y$
0%	$3,500	$4,000
4	2,545	2,705
8	1,707	1,592
12	966	631
16	307	(206)

The crossover rate occurs at about 6–7 percent. To find this rate exactly, create a Project Δ, which is the difference in cash flows between Projects X and Y:

Year	Project X − Project Y = Project Δ Net Cash Flow
0	$ 0
1	3,000
2	(500)
3	(500)
4	(2,500)

Then find the IRR of Project Δ:

$$\text{IRR}_\Delta = \text{Crossover rate} = 6.2\%.$$

Thus, if the firm's cost of capital is less than 6.2 percent, a conflict exists since NPV$_Y$ > NPV$_X$, but IRR$_X$ > IRR$_Y$. Note, however, that when k = 5.0%, MIRR$_X$ = 10.64% and MIRR$_Y$ = 10.83%, hence the modified IRR ranks the projects correctly, even to the left of the crossover point.

e. The basic cause of the conflict is differing reinvestment rate assumptions between NPV and IRR. The conflict occurs in this situation because the projects differ in their cash flow timing.

CHAPTER 10

ST-1 a. *Estimated investment requirements:*

Price	($50,000)
Modification	(10,000)
Change in net working capital	(2,000)
Total investment	($62,000)

b. *Operating cash flows:*

		Year 1	Year 2	Year 3
1.	After-tax cost savings	$12,000	$12,000	$12,000
2.	Depreciation*	19,800	27,000	9,000
3.	Depreciation tax savings**	7,920	10,800	3,600
	Net cash flow (1 + 3)	$19,920	$22,800	$15,600

*Depreciable basis = $60,000; the MACRS percentage allowances are 0.33, 0.45, and 0.15 in Years 1, 2, and 3, respectively; hence depreciation in Year 1 = 0.33($60,000) = $19,800, and so on.

**Depreciation tax savings = T(Depreciation) = 0.4($19,800) = $7,920 in Year 1, and so on.

c. *End-of-project cash flows:*

Salvage value	$20,000
Tax on salvage value*	(6,320)
Net working capital recovery	2,000
	$15,680

*Sale price	$20,000
Less book value	4,200
Taxable income	$15,800
Tax at 40%	$ 6,320

Note that Book value = Depreciable basis − Accumulated depreciation
= $60,000 − $55,800 = $4,200.

d. *Project NPV:*

$$NPV = -\$62,000 + \frac{\$19,920}{(1.10)^1} + \frac{\$22,800}{(1.10)^2} + \frac{\$31,280}{(1.10)^3}$$

$$= -\$1,547.$$

Using a financial calculator, input $CF_0 = -62000$, $CF_1 = 19920$, $CF_2 = 22800$, $CF_3 = 31280$, and $I = 10$; then solve for NPV $= -\$1,546.81$.

Since the earth mover has a negative NPV, it should not be purchased.

ST-2 *First determine the net cash flow at $t = 0$:*

Purchase price	($8,000)
Sale of old machine	3,000
Tax on sale of old machine	(160)*
Change in net working capital	(1,500)**
Total investment	($6,660)

*The market value is $3,000 − $2,600 = $400 above the book value. Thus, there is a $400 recapture of depreciation, and the firm would have to pay 0.40($400) = $160 in taxes.

**The change in net working capital is a $2,000 increase in current assets less a $500 increase in current liabilities, which totals a $1,500 increase in net working capital.

Now, examine the operating cash inflows:

Sales increase	$1,000
Cost decrease	1,500
Pre-tax operating revenue increase	$2,500

After-tax operating revenue increase:

$2,500(1 − T) = $2,500(0.60) = $1,500.

Depreciation:

Year	1	2	3	4	5	6
New*	$1,600	$2,560	$1,520	$960	$880	$480
Old	350	350	350	350	350	350
Change	$1,250	$2,210	$1,170	$610	$530	$130
Depreciation tax savings**	$ 500	$ 884	$ 468	$244	$212	$ 52

*Depreciable basis = $8,000. Depreciation expense in each year equals depreciable basis times the MACRS percentage allowance of 0.20, 0.32, 0.19, 0.12, 0.11, and 0.06 in Years 1–6, respectively.
**Depreciation tax savings = T(Δ Depreciation) = 0.4(Δ Depreciation).

Now recognize that at the end of Year 6 the firm would recover its net working capital investment of $1,500, and it would also receive $800 from the sale of the replacement machine. However, since the machine is fully depreciated, the firm must pay 0.40($800) = $320 in taxes on the sale. Note also that by undertaking the replacement now, the firm foregoes the right to sell the old machine for $500 in Year 6; thus, this $500 in Year 6 must be considered as an opportunity cost in that year. There is no tax effect here since the $500 salvage value would equal the old machine's Year 6 book value.

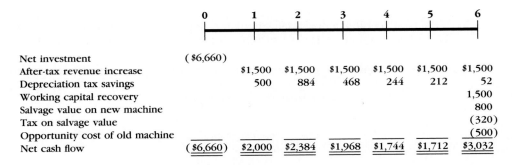

	0	1	2	3	4	5	6
Net investment	($6,660)						
After-tax revenue increase		$1,500	$1,500	$1,500	$1,500	$1,500	$1,500
Depreciation tax savings		500	884	468	244	212	52
Working capital recovery							1,500
Salvage value on new machine							800
Tax on salvage value							(320)
Opportunity cost of old machine							(500)
Net cash flow	($6,660)	$2,000	$2,384	$1,968	$1,744	$1,712	$3,032

With a financial calculator, input the following: $CF_0 = -6660$, $CF_1 = 2000$, $CF_2 = 2384$, $CF_3 = 1968$, $CF_4 = 1744$, $CF_5 = 1712$, $CF_6 = 3032$, and $I = 15$ to solve for NPV = $1,334.89.

The net present value of this incremetal cash flow stream, when discounted at 15 percent, is $1,335. Thus, the replacement should be made.

CHAPTER 11

ST-1 a.   First, find the expected cash flows:

Year	Expected Cash Flow			
0	0.2(− $100,000) + 0.6(− $100,000) + 0.2(− $100,000) =			($100,000)
1	0.2($20,000)	+ 0.6($30,000)	+ 0.2($40,000) =	30,000
2				30,000
3				30,000
4				30,000
5				30,000
5*	0.2($0)	+ 0.6($20,000)	+ 0.2($30,000) =	18,000

Next, determine the NPV based on the expected cash flows:

$$NPV = -\$100,000 + \frac{\$30,000}{(1.10)^1} + \frac{\$30,000}{(1.10)^2} + \frac{\$30,000}{(1.10)^3} + \frac{\$30,000}{(1.10)^4}$$

$$+ \frac{\$30,000 + \$18,000}{(1.10)^5} = \$24,900.$$

Using a financial calculator, input the following: $CF_0 = -100000$, $CF_1 = 30000$, $N_j = 4$, $CF_5 = 48000$, and $I = 10$ to solve for NPV $= \$24,900.19 \approx \$24,900$.

b. For the worst case, the cash flow values from the left-most cash flow column are used to calculate NPV:

$$NPV = -\$100,000 + \frac{\$20,000}{(1.10)^1} + \frac{\$20,000}{(1.10)^2} + \frac{\$20,000}{(1.10)^3} + \frac{\$20,000}{(1.10)^4} + \frac{\$20,000 + \$0}{(1.10)^5}$$

$$= -\$24,184.$$

Using a financial calculator, input the following: $CF_0 = -100000$, $CF_1 = 20000$, $N_j = 5$, and $I = 10$ to solve for NPV $= -\$24,184.26 \approx -\$24,184$.

Similarly, for the best case, use the values from the right-most column. Here the NPV is $70,259.

If the cash flows are perfectly dependent, then the low cash flow in the first year would mean a low cash flow in every year. Thus, the probability of the worst case occurring is the probability of getting the $20,000 net cash flow in Year 1, or 20 percent. If the cash flows are independent, then the cash flow in each year could be low, high, or average, and the probability of getting all low cash flows would be $0.2(0.2)(0.2)(0.2)(0.2) = 0.2^5 = 0.00032$.

c. Under these conditions, the NPV distribution is

P	NPV
0.2	($24,184)
0.6	26,142
0.2	70,259

Thus, the expected NPV is $0.2(-\$24,184) + 0.6(\$26,142) + 0.2(\$70,259) = \$24,900$. Note that, as is generally the case, the expected NPV is the same as the base case NPV found in Part a. The standard deviation is $29,904:

$$\sigma^2_{NPV} = 0.2(-\$24,184 - \$24,900)^2 + 0.6(\$26,142 - \$24,900)^2$$

$$+ 0.2(\$70,259 - \$24,900)^2$$

$$= \$894,261,126.$$

$$\sigma_{NPV} = \sqrt{\$894,261,126} = \$29,904.$$

The coefficient of variation, CV, is $\$29,904/\$24,900 = 1.20$.

d. Since the project's coefficient of variation is 1.20, the project is riskier than average, hence the project's risk-adjusted cost of capital is 10% + 2% = 12%. Now the project should be evaluated by finding the NPV of the base case as in Part a, but using a 12 percent discount rate. The risk-adjusted NPV is $18,357, and thus the project should be accepted.

ST-2 a. *Cost using retained earnings:*

$$k_s = \hat{k}_s = \frac{D_1}{P_0} + g = \frac{(\$1.85)(1.08)}{(\$50)} + 0.08 = 12.0\%.$$

$$WACC_1 = 0.3(8\%)(0.6) + 0.7(12.0\%) = 9.84\%.$$

Cost using new common stock:

$$k_e = \hat{k}_e = \frac{D_1}{P_0(1 - F)} + g = \frac{(\$1.85)(1.08)}{(\$50)(0.85)} + 0.08 = 12.7\%.$$

$$WACC_2 = 0.3(8\%)(0.6) + 0.7(12.7\%) = 10.33\%.$$

Break point:

$$\text{Break point} = \frac{\$56,000(0.5)}{0.7} + \$35,000$$

$$= \$40,000 + \$35,000 = \$75,000.$$

b. The MCC and IOS schedules are shown next:

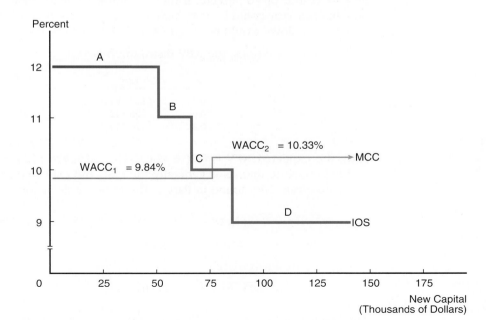

c. From this graph, we conclude that the firm should definitely undertake Projects A and B, assuming that these projects have about "average risk" in relation to the rest of the firm. Now, to evaluate Project C, recognize that one-half of its capital would cost 9.84 percent, while the other half would cost 10.33 percent. Thus, the cost of the capital required for Project C is 10.09 percent:

$$0.5(9.84\%) + 0.5(10.33\%) = 10.09\%.$$

Since the cost is greater than Project C's return of 10 percent, the firm should not accept Project C.

d. The solution implicitly assumes (1) that all of the projects are equally risky and (2) that these projects are as risky as the firm's existing assets. If the accepted projects (A and B) were of above-average risk, this could raise the company's overall risk, and hence its cost of capital. Taking on these projects could result in a decline in the company's value.

e. If the payout ratio were lowered to zero, this would shift the break point to the right, from $75,000 to $115,000:

$$\text{Break point} = \frac{\$56,000(1.0)}{0.7} + \$35,000$$

$$= \$80,000 + \$35,000 = \$115,000.$$

As the problem is set up, this would make Project C acceptable. If the payout were changed to 100 percent, the break point would shift to the left, from $75,000 to $35,000:

$$\text{Break point} = \frac{\$56,000(0.0)}{0.7} + \$35,000$$

$$= \$0 + \$35,000 = \$35,000.$$

The optimal capital budget would still consist of Projects A and B. This assumes that the change in payout would not affect k_s or k_d; as we shall see in Chapter 14, this assumption may not be correct.

CHAPTER 12

ST-1 a. Value of unleveraged firm, $V_U = EBIT(1 - T)/k_{sU}$:

$$\$12 = \$2(1 - 0.4)/k_{sU}$$

$$\$12 = \$1.2/k_{sU}$$

$$k_{sU} = \$1.2/\$12 = 10.0\%.$$

Therefore, $k_{sU} = \text{WACC} = 10.0\%$.

b. Value of leveraged firm according to MM model with taxes:

$$V_L = V_U + TD.$$

As shown in the following table, value increases continuously with debt, and the optimal capital structure consists of 100 percent debt. Note: The table is not necessary to answer this question, but the data (in millions of dollars) are necessary for Part c of this problem.

Debt, D	V_U	TD	$V_L = V_U + TD$
$ 0	$12.0	$ 0	$12.0
2.5	12.0	1.0	13.0
5.0	12.0	2.0	14.0
7.5	12.0	3.0	15.0
10.0	12.0	4.0	16.0
12.5	12.0	5.0	17.0
15.0	12.0	6.0	18.0
20.0	12.0	8.0	20.0

c. With financial distress costs included in the analysis, the value of the leveraged firm now is

$$V_L = V_U + TD - PC,$$

where

$$V_U + TD = \text{value according to MM after-tax model.}$$

$$P = \text{probability of financial distress.}$$

$$C = \text{present value of distress costs.}$$

D	$V_U + TD$	P	PC = (P)$8	$V_L = V_U + TD - PC$
$ 0	$12.0	0	$ 0	$12.0
2.5	13.0	0	0	13.0
5.0	14.0	0.0125	0.10	13.9
7.5	15.0	0.0250	0.20	14.8
10.0	16.0	0.0625	0.50	15.5
12.5	17.0	0.1250	1.00	16.0
15.0	18.0	0.3125	2.50	15.5
20.0	20.0	0.7500	6.00	14.0

Note: All dollar amounts in table are in millions.

Optimal debt level: D = $12.5 million.

Maximum value of firm: V = $16.0 million.

Optimal debt/value ratio: D/V = $12.5/$16 = 78%.

d. The value of the firm versus debt value with and without financial distress costs is plotted next (millions of dollars):

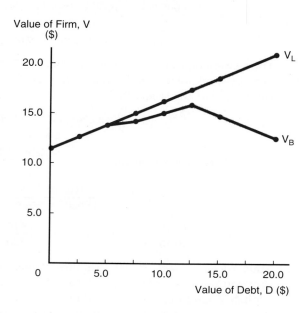

V_L = Value without financial distress costs.

V_B = Value with financial distress costs.

CHAPTER 13

ST-1 a.

$$S = \frac{(EBIT - k_dD)(1 - T)}{k_s}$$

$$= \frac{[\$4,000,000 - 0.10(\$2,000,000)](0.65)}{0.15} = \$16,466,667.$$

$$P_0 = S/n = \frac{\$16,466,667}{600,000} = \$27.44.$$

$$V = D + S = \$2,000,000 + \$16,466,667 = \$18,466,667.$$

b.

$$WACC = (D/V)(k_d)(1 - T) + (S/V)(k_s)$$

$$= \left(\frac{\$2,000,000}{\$18,466,667}\right)(10\%)(0.65) + \left(\frac{\$16,466,667}{\$18,466,667}\right)(15\%)$$

$$= 14.08\%.$$

c. Under the new capital structure,

$$S = \frac{[\$4,000,000 - 0.12(\$10,000,000)](0.65)}{0.17} = \$10,705,882.$$

$$V = \$10,000,000 + \$10,705,882 = \$20,705,882.$$

The new value of the firm will thus be $20,705,882. This value belongs to the *present* stockholders and bondholders, so we may calculate the new equilibrium price of the stock, P_1:

$$P_1 = \frac{V_1 - D_0}{n_0} = \frac{\$20,705,882 - \$2,000,000}{600,000} = \$31.18.$$

$$\text{Check: Shares repurchased} = \frac{\text{New debt}}{P_1} = \frac{\$8,000,000}{\$31.18} = 256,575.$$

$$P_1 = \frac{S_1}{n_1} = \frac{\$10,705,882}{600,000 - 256,575} \approx \$31.18.$$

$$\text{WACC} = \left(\frac{\$10,000,000}{\$20,705,882}\right)(12\%)(0.65) + \left(\frac{\$10,705,882}{\$20,705,882}\right)(17\%) = 12.56\%.$$

Thus, the proposed capital structure change would increase the value of the firm and the price of its stock (from $27.44 to $31.18), and lower its cost of capital. Therefore, the firm should increase its use of financial leverage. Of course, it is possible that some amount of debt other than $10 million would result in an even higher value, but we do not have enough information to make this determination.

d. Offhand, we would expect the value of the equity and the price of the stock to rise. We would also expect the value of the old debt to decline. Here is the situation:

$$S = \frac{(\text{EBIT} - I_{\text{Old}} - I_{\text{New}})(1 - T)}{k_s}$$

$$= \frac{[\$4,000,000 - 0.10(\$2,000,000) - 0.12(\$8,000,000)](0.65)}{0.17}$$

$$= \$10,858,824.$$

$$\text{Value of debt} = \text{Old debt} + \text{New debt}$$

$$= \$200,000/0.12 + \$8,000,000 = \$9,666,667.$$

$$V = D + S$$

$$= \$9,666,667 + \$10,858,824$$

$$= \$20,525,491.$$

$$P_1 = \frac{\text{New total value} - \text{New value of old debt}}{\text{Old shares outstanding}}$$

$$= \frac{\$20,525,491 - (\$200,000/0.12)}{600,000} = \$31.43.$$

In this case, the old stockholders gain from the use of increased leverage, and they also extract a further gain from the old bondholders. This illustrates why bond indentures place restrictions on the sale of future debt issues.

e.
$$\text{TIE} = \frac{\text{EBIT}}{\text{I}}.$$

$$\text{Original TIE} = \frac{\$4,000,000}{\$200,000} = 20 \text{ times.}$$

$$\text{New TIE} = \frac{\$4,000,000}{\$1,200,000} = 3.33 \text{ times.}$$

CHAPTER 15

ST-1 To solve this problem, we will define ΔS as the change in sales and g as the growth rate in sales, and then we use the three following equations:

$$\Delta S = S_0 g.$$

$$S_1 = S_0(1 + g).$$

$$\text{AFN} = (A^*/S)(\Delta S) - (L^*/S)(\Delta S) - MS_1(1 - d).$$

Set AFN = 0, substitute in known values for A^*/S, L^*/S, M, d, and S, and then solve for g:

$$0 = 1.6(\$100g) - 0.4(\$100g) - 0.10[\$100(1 + g)](0.55)$$

$$= \$160g - \$40g - 0.055(\$100 + \$100g)$$

$$= \$160g - \$40g - \$5.5 - \$5.5g$$

$$\$114.5g = \$5.5$$

$$g = \$5.5/\$114.5 = 0.048 = 4.8\%$$

$$= \text{Maximum growth rate without external financing.}$$

ST-2 Assets consist of cash, marketable securities, receivables, inventories, and fixed assets. Therefore, we can break the A^*/S ratio into its components—cash/sales, inventories/sales, and so forth. Then,

$$\frac{A^*}{S} = \frac{A^* - \text{Inventories}}{S} + \frac{\text{Inventories}}{S} = 1.6.$$

We know that the inventory turnover ratio is sales/inventories = 3 times, so inventories/sales = 1/3 = 0.3333. Further, if the inventory turnover ratio can be increased to 4 times, then the inventory/sales ratio will fall to 1/4 = 0.25, a difference of 0.3333 − 0.2500 = 0.0833. This, in turn, causes the A^*/S ratio to fall from A^*/S = 1.6 to A^*/S = 1.6 − 0.0833 = 1.5167.

This change has two effects: First, it changes the AFN equation, and second, it means that Weatherford currently has excessive inventories. Because it is costly to hold excess inventories, Weatherford will want to reduce its inventory holdings by not replacing inventories until the excess amounts have been used. We can account for this by setting up the revised AFN equation (using the new A*/S ratio), estimating the funds that will be needed next year if no excess inventories are currently on hand, and then subtracting out the excess inventories which are currently on hand:

Present conditions:

$$\frac{\text{Sales}}{\text{Inventories}} = \frac{\$100}{\text{Inventories}} = 3,$$

so

$$\text{Inventories} = \$100/3 = \$33.3 \text{ million at present.}$$

New conditions:

$$\frac{\text{Sales}}{\text{Inventories}} = \frac{\$100}{\text{Inventories}} = 4,$$

so

$$\text{New level of inventories} = \$100/4 = \$25 \text{ million.}$$

Therefore,

$$\text{Excess inventories} = \$33.3 - \$25 = \$8.3 \text{ million.}$$

Forecast of funds needed, first year:

$$\Delta S \text{ in first year} = 0.2(\$100 \text{ million}) = \$20 \text{ million.}$$
$$\text{AFN} = 1.5167(\$20) - 0.4(\$20) - 0.1(0.55)(\$120) - \$8.3$$
$$= \$30.3 - \$8 - \$6.6 - \$8.3$$
$$= \$7.4 \text{ million.}$$

Forecast of funds needed, second year:

$$\Delta S \text{ in second year} = gS_1 = 0.2(\$120 \text{ million}) = \$24 \text{ million.}$$
$$\text{AFN} = 1.5167(\$24) - 0.4(\$24) - 0.1(0.55)(\$144)$$
$$= \$36.4 - \$9.6 - \$7.9$$
$$= \$18.9 \text{ million.}$$

ST-3 a.
$$\text{Full capacity sales} = \frac{\text{Current sales}}{\text{Percentage of capacity at which FA were operated}} = \frac{\$36,000}{0.75} = \$48,000.$$

$$\text{Percentage increase} = \frac{\text{New sales} - \text{Old sales}}{\text{Old sales}} = \frac{\$48,000 - \$36,000}{\$36,000} = 0.33$$

$$= 33\%.$$

Therefore, sales could expand by 33 percent before Van Auken Lumber would need to add fixed assets.

b.

Van Auken Lumber: Pro Forma Income Statement for December 31, 1994 (Thousands of Dollars)

	1993	(1 + g)	Pro Forma 1994
Sales	$36,000	(1.25)	$45,000
Operating costs	30,783	(1.25)	38,479
EBIT	$ 5,217		$ 6,521
Interest	1,017		1,017
EBT	$ 4,200		$ 5,504
Taxes (40%)	1,680		2,202
Net income	$ 2,520		$ 3,302
Dividends (60%)	$ 1,512		$ 1,981
Addition to RE	$ 1,008		$ 1,321

Van Auken Lumber: Pro Forma Balance Sheet for December 31, 1994 (Thousands of Dollars)

	1993	(1 + g)	Additions	1994	AFN	1994 after AFN
Cash	$ 1,800	(1.25)		$ 2,250		$ 2,250
Receivables	10,800	(1.25)		13,500		13,500
Inventories	12,600	(1.25)		15,750		15,750
Total current assets	$25,200			$31,500		$31,500
Net fixed assets	21,600			21,600*		21,600
Total assets	$46,800			$53,100		$53,100
Accounts payable	$ 7,200	(1.25)		$ 9,000		$ 9,000
Notes payable	3,472			3,472	+2,549	6,021
Accruals	2,520	(1.25)		3,150		3,150
Total current liabilities	$13,192			$15,622		$18,171
Mortgage bonds	5,000			5,000		5,000
Common stock	2,000			2,000		2,000
Retained earnings	26,608		1,321**	27,929		27,929
Total liabilities and equity	$46,800			$50,551		$53,100
AFN =				$ 2,549		

*From Part a we know that sales can increase by 33% before additions to fixed assets are needed.

**See income statement.

c.

Van Auken Lumber: Pro Forma Income Statement for December 31, 1994 (Thousands of Dollars)

	1st Pass 1994	Financing Feedback	2nd Pass 1994
Sales	$45,000		$45,000
Operating costs	38,479		38,479
EBIT	$ 6,521		$ 6,521
Interest	1,017	+ 306*	1,323
EBT	$ 5,504		$ 5,198
Taxes (40%)	2,202		2,079
Net income	$ 3,302		$ 3,119
Dividends (60%)	$ 1,981		$ 1,871
Addition to RE	$ 1,321		$ 1,248

*Δ in interest = $2,549 $\times$ (0.12) = $306.

Van Auken Lumber: Pro Forma Balance Sheet for December 31, 1994 (Thousands of Dollars)

	1st Pass 1994	Financing Feedback	2nd Pass 1994
Total assets	$53,100		$53,100
Accounts payable	$ 9,000		$ 9,000
Notes payable	6,021		6,021
Accruals	3,150		3,150
Total current liabilities	$18,171		$18,171
Mortgage bonds	5,000		5,000
Common stock	2,000		2,000
Retained earnings	27,929	− 73*	27,856
Total liabilities and equity	$53,100		$53,027
AFN =			73

*Δ in RE addition = $1,248 − $1,321 = − $73.
Note: The cumulative AFN for the first 2 passes = $2,549 + $73 = $2,622.

d. The rate of return projected for 1994 under the conditions in Part c is (calculations in thousands):

$$\text{ROE} = \frac{\$3,119}{\$29,856} = 10.45\%.$$

If Van Auken Lumber attained the industry average DSO and inventory turnover ratio, this would mean a reduction in financial requirements of:

$$\text{Receivables:} \frac{\text{New A/R}}{\$45,000/360} = 90$$

New A/R $=$ $11,250.

Δ in A/R $=$ \$13,500 $-$ \$11,250 $=$ \$2,250.

$$\text{Inventory:} \frac{\$45,000}{I} = 3.33; I = \$13,500.$$

Δ in Inventory $=$ \$15,750 $-$ \$13,500 $=$ \$2,250.

Total Δ $=$ \$2,250 $+$ \$2,250 $=$ \$4,500.

If this freed capital was used to reduce equity, the new figures for common equity would be \$29,856 $-$ \$4,500 $=$ \$25,356. Assuming no change in net income, the new ROE would be:

$$\text{ROE} = \frac{\$3,119}{\$25,356} = 12.3\%.$$

One would, in a real analysis, want to consider both the feasibility of maintaining sales if receivables and inventories were reduced and also other possible effects on the profit margin. Also, note that the current ratio was \$25,200/ \$13,192 $=$ 1.91 in 1993. It is projected to decline in Part c to \$31,500/ \$18,244 $=$ 1.73, and the latest change would cause a further reduction to (\$31,500 $-$ \$4,500)/\$18,244 $=$ 1.48. Creditors might not tolerate such a reduction in liquidity and might insist that at least some of the freed capital be used to reduce notes payable. Still, this would reduce interest charges, which would increase the profit margin, which would in turn raise the ROE. Management should always consider the possibility of changing ratios as part of financial projections.

CHAPTER 16

ST-1 a. and **b.**

Income Statements for Year Ended December 31, 1993
(Thousands of Dollars)

	Vanderheiden Press		Herrenhouse Publishing	
	a	b	a	b
EBIT	$ 30,000	$ 30,000	$ 30,000	$ 30,000
Interest	12,400	14,400	10,600	18,600
Taxable income	$ 17,600	$ 15,600	$ 19,400	$ 11,400
Taxes (40%)	7,040	6,240	7,760	4,560
Net income	$ 10,560	$ 9,360	$ 11,640	$ 6,840
Equity	$100,000	$100,000	$100,000	$100,000
Return on equity	10.56%	9.36%	11.64%	6.84%

The Vanderheiden Press has a higher ROE when short-term interest rates are high, whereas Herrenhouse Publishing does better when rates are lower.

c. Herrenhouse's position is riskier. First, its profits and return on equity are much more volatile than Vanderheiden's. Second, Herrenhouse must renew its large short-term loan every year, and if the renewal comes up at a time when money is very tight, when its business is depressed, or both, then Herrenhouse could be denied credit, which could put it out of business.

ST-2   The Calgary Company: Alternative Balance Sheets

	Restricted (40%)	Moderate (50%)	Relaxed (60%)
Current assets	$1,200,000	$1,500,000	$1,800,000
Fixed assets	600,000	600,000	600,000
Total assets	$1,800,000	$2,100,000	$2,400,000
Debt	$ 900,000	$1,050,000	$1,200,000
Equity	900,000	1,050,000	1,200,000
Total liabilities and equity	$1,800,000	$2,100,000	$2,400,000

The Calgary Company: Alternative Income Statements

	Restricted	Moderate	Relaxed
Sales	$3,000,000	$3,000,000	$3,000,000
EBIT	450,000	450,000	450,000
Interest (10%)	90,000	105,000	120,000
Earnings before taxes (EBT)	$ 360,000	$ 345,000	$ 330,000
Taxes (40%)	144,000	138,000	132,000
Net income	$ 216,000	$ 207,000	$ 198,000
ROE	24.0%	19.7%	16.5%

CHAPTER 17

ST-1 a. First determine the balance on the firm's checkbook and the bank's records as follows:

	Firm's Checkbook	Bank's Records
Day 1: Deposit $500,000; write check for $1,000,000	($500,000)	$500,000
Day 2: Write check for $1,000,000	($1,500,000)	$500,000
Day 3: Write check for $1,000,000	($2,500,000)	$500,000
Day 4: Write check for $1,000,000; deposit $1,000,000	($2,500,000)	$500,000

After Upton has reached a steady state, it must deposit $1,000,000 each day to cover the checks written three days earlier.

b. The firm has 3 days of float; not until Day 4 does the firm have to make any additional deposits.

c. As shown above, Upton should try to maintain a balance on the bank's records of $500,000. On its own books it will have a balance of *minus* $2,500,000.

ST-2 First, determine the annual benefit to Kroncke from the reduction in cash balances under each plan:

$$\text{Average daily collections} = (30)(\$30,000) = \$900,000.$$

DTC:

Current collection float: $900,000 per day × 5 days = $4,500,000

New collection float: $900,000 per day × 3 days = 2,700,000

Float reduction: $1,800,000

Kroncke can reduce its average cash balances by $1,800,000 by using DTCs, and it can earn 11 percent, which will provide $198,000 of additional income:

$$\text{Additional income} = (\$1,800,000)(0.11) = \$198,000.$$

Wire transfer:

Current collection float: $900,000 per day × 5 days = $4,500,000

New collection float: $900,000 per day × 1 day = 900,000

Float reduction: $3,600,000

Kroncke can reduce its cash balances by $3,600,000 by using wire transfers, which will increase income by $396,000:

$$\text{Additional income} = (\$3,600,000)(0.11) = \$396,000.$$

Next, compute the annual cost of each transfer method:

$$\text{Number of transfers} = 30 \times 260 = 7,800 \text{ per year.}$$

$$\text{Fixed lockbox cost} = \$14,000 \times 12 = \$168,000 \text{ per year.}$$

DTC:

$$\text{Total costs} = (7,800)(\$0.75) + \$168,000 = \$173,850.$$

Wire transfer:

$$\text{Total costs} = (7,800)(\$11) + \$168,000 = \$253,800.$$

Finally, calculate the net additional income resulting from each transfer method:
DTC:

$$\$198,000 - \$173,850 = \$24,150.$$

Wire transfer:

$$\$396,000 - \$253,800 = \$142,200.$$

Therefore, Kroncke should adopt the lockbox system and transfer funds from the lockbox operators to the regional concentration banks using wire transfers.

ST-3 a.

Commercial bank loan

Amount loaned	$= (0.75)(\$250,000)$	$= \$187,500$
Discount	$= (0.09/12)(\$187,500)$	$= (1,406)$
Compensating balance	$= (0.20)(\$187,500)$	$= \underline{(37,500)}$
Amount received		$= \underline{\$148,594}$
Interest expense	$= (0.09)(\$187,500)$	$= \$16,875$
Credit department*	$= (\$4,000)(12)$	$= 48,000$
Bad debts*	$= (0.02)(\$250,000)(12) =$	$\underline{60,000}$
Total annual costs		$= \underline{\$124,875}$

*The costs of the credit department and bad debts are expenses that will be incurred if a bank loan is used, but these costs will be avoided if the firm accepts the factoring arrangement.

Factoring

Amount loaned	$= (0.85)(\$250,000)$	$= \$212,500$
Commission for period	$= (0.035)(\$250,000)$	$= (8,750)$
Prepaid interest	$= (0.09/12)(\$203,750) =$	$\underline{(1,528)}$
Amount received		$= \underline{\$202,222}$
Annual commission	$= (\$8,750)(12)$	$= \$105,000$
Annual interest	$= (0.09)(\$203,750)$	$= \underline{18,338}$
Total annual costs		$= \underline{\$123,338}$

b. The factoring costs are slightly lower than the cost of the bank loan, and the factor is willing to advance a significantly greater amount. On the other hand, the elimination of the credit department could reduce the firm's options in the future.

CHAPTER 18

ST-1 Under the current credit policy, the firm has no discounts, collection expenses of $50,000, bad debt losses of $(0.02)(\$10,000,000) = \$200,000$, and average accounts receivable of $(DSO)(Average sales per day) = (30)(\$10,000,000/360) = \$833,333$. The firm's cost of carrying these receivables is (Variable cost ratio)(A/R)(Cost of capital) = $(0.80)(\$833,333)(0.16) = \$106,667$. It is necessary to multiply by the variable cost ratio because the actual *investment* in receivables is less than the dollar amount of the receivables.

Proposal 1: Lengthen the credit period such that

1. Sales increase by $1 million.
2. Discounts = $0.
3. Bad debt losses = $(0.02)(\$10,000,000) + (0.04)(\$1,000,000)$

$$= \$200,000 + \$40,000$$

$$= \$240,000.$$

4. DSO = 45 days on all sales.
5. New average receivables = $(45)(\$11,000,000/360)$

$$= \$1,375,000.$$

6. Cost of carrying receivables = $(v)(k)(Average accounts receivable)$

$$= (0.80)(0.16)(\$1,375,000)$$

$$= \$176,000.$$

7. Change in cost of carrying receivables = $\$176,000 - \$106,667$

$$= \$69,333.$$

8. Collection expenses = $50,000.

Analysis of proposed change:

	Income Statement under Current Policy	Effect of Change	Income Statement under New Policy
Gross sales	$10,000,000	+ $1,000,000	$11,000,000
Less discounts	0	+ 0	0
Net sales	$10,000,000	+ $1,000,000	$11,000,000
Variable costs (80%)	8,000,000	+ 800,000	8,800,000
Profit before credit costs and taxes	$ 2,000,000	+ $ 200,000	$ 2,200,000
Credit-related costs:			
Cost of carrying receivables	106,667	+ 69,333	176,000
Collection expenses	50,000	+ 0	50,000
Bad debt losses	200,000	+ 40,000	240,000
Profit before taxes	$ 1,643,333	+ $ 90,667	$ 1,734,000
Taxes (50%)	821,666	+ 45,333	867,000
Net income	$ 821,667	+ 45,334	$ 867,000

The proposed change appears to be a good one, assuming the assumptions are correct.

Proposal 2: Shorten the credit period to net 20 such that

1. Sales decrease by $1 million.
2. Discount = $0.
3. Bad debt losses = $(0.01)(\$9,000,000)$

    $= \$90,000.$
4. DSO = 22 days.
5. New average receivables = $(22)(\$9,000,000/360)$

    $= \$550,000.$
6. Cost of carrying receivables = $(v)(k)(\text{Average accounts receivable})$

    $= (0.80)(0.16)(\$550,000)$

    $= \$70,400.$
7. Collection expenses = $50,000.

Analysis of proposed change:

	Income Statement under Current Policy	Effect of Change	Income Statement under New Policy
Gross sales	$10,000,000	− $1,000,000	$9,000,000
Less discounts	0	0	0
Net sales	$10,000,000	− $1,000,000	$9,000,000
Variable costs (80%)	8,000,000	− 800,000	7,200,000
Profit before credit costs and taxes	$ 2,000,000	− $ 200,000	$1,800,000
Credit-related costs:			
Cost of carrying receivables	106,667	− 36,267	70,400
Collection expenses	50,000	0	50,000
Bad debt losses	200,000	− 110,000	90,000
Profit before taxes	$ 1,643,333	− $ 53,733	$1,589,600
Taxes (50%)	821,666	− 26,866	794,800
Net income	$ 821,667	− $ 26,867	$ 794,800

This change reduces net income, so it should be rejected. The firm will increase profits by accepting Proposal 1 to lengthen the credit period from 25 days to 30 days, assuming all assumptions are correct. This may or may not be the *optimal,* or profit-maximizing, credit policy, but it does appear to be a movement in the right direction. However, before a final decision is made, the riskiness of the change must be considered.

ST-2 a.

$$\text{EOQ} = \sqrt{\frac{2(F)(S)}{(C)(P)}}$$

$$= \sqrt{\frac{(2)(\$5,000)(2,600,000)}{(0.02)(\$5.00)}}$$

$$= 509,902 \text{ bushels.}$$

Since the firm must order in multiples of 2,000 bushels, it should order in quantities of 510,000 bushels.

b.

$$\text{Average weekly sales} = 2,600,000/52$$

$$= 50,000 \text{ bushels.}$$

$$\text{Reorder point} = 6 \text{ weeks' sales} + \text{Safety stock}$$

$$= 6(50,000) + 200,000$$

$$= 300,000 + 200,000$$

$$= 500,000 \text{ bushels.}$$

c. Total inventory costs:

$$\text{TIC} = \text{CP}\left(\frac{Q}{2}\right) + \text{F}\left(\frac{S}{Q}\right) + \text{CP(Safety stock)}$$

$$= (0.02)(\$5)\left(\frac{510,000}{2}\right) + (\$5,000)\left(\frac{2,600,000}{510,000}\right) + (0.02)(\$5)(200,000)$$

$$= \$25,500 + \$25,490.20 + \$20,000$$

$$= \$70,990.20.$$

d. By ordering 650,000 bushels at a time, ordering costs would be reduced to $1,500, so total inventory costs would be:

$$\text{TIC} = (0.02)(\$5)\left(\frac{650,000}{2}\right) + (\$1,500)\left(\frac{2,600,000}{650,000}\right) + (0.02)(\$5)(200,000)$$

$$= \$32,500 + \$6,000 + \$20,000$$

$$= \$58,500.$$

Since the firm can reduce its total inventory costs by ordering 650,000 bushels at a time, it should accept the offer and place larger orders. (Incidentally, this same type of analysis is used to consider any quantity discount offer.)

CHAPTER 20

ST-1 a. $100,000,000/10 = $10,000,000 per year, or $5 million each 6 months. Since the $5 million placed into the sinking fund will be used to retire bonds immediately, no interest will be earned on it.

b. The debt service requirements will decline as follows (in millions of dollars):

Semiannual Payment Period (1)	Sinking Fund Payment (2)	Outstanding Bonds on Which Interest Is Paid (3)	Interest Payment[a] (4)	Total Bond Service (2) + (4) = (5)
1	$5	$100	$6.0	$11.0
2	5	95	5.7	10.7
3	5	90	5.4	10.4
.	.	.	.	.
.	.	.	.	.
.	.	.	.	.
20	5	5	0.3	5.3

[a]Interest is calculated as $(0.5)(0.12)($Column 3$)$; for example: interest in Period 2 $= (0.5)(0.12)($95$) = $5.7.

The company's total annual cash bond service requirement will be $21.7 million for the first year (semiannual payments 1 and 2). The requirement will decline by $0.12($10,000,000) = $1,200,000 per year for the remaining years.

c. Here we have a 10-year, 9 percent annuity whose future value is $100 million, and we are seeking the annual payment, PMT, in this equation:

$$\$100,000,000 = \sum_{t=1}^{10} PMT(1 + k)^t$$

$$= PMT(FVIFA_{9\%,10})$$

$$= PMT(15.193)$$

$$PMT = \$6,581,979 = \text{Sinking fund payment.}$$

The solution could also be obtained with a financial calculator: Input N = 10, I = 9, PV = 0, and FV = 100000000, and press the PMT key to obtain $6,582,009. The difference is due to rounding.

d. Annual debt service costs will be $100,000,000(0.12) + $6,582,009 = $18,582,009.

e. If interest rates rose, causing the bonds' price to fall, the company would use open market purchases. This would reduce its debt service requirements.

CHAPTER 21

ST-1 a. Cost of leasing:

	Year 0	Year 1	Year 2	Year 3	Year 4
Lease payment	($10,000)	($10,000)	($10,000)	($10,000)	$0
Payment tax savings	4,000	4,000	4,000	4,000	0
Net cash flow	($ 6,000)	($ 6,000)	($ 6,000)	($ 6,000)	$0
PV cost of leasing @ 6% = ($22,038)					

b. Cost of owning:

In our solution, we will consider the $40,000 cost as a Year 0 outflow rather than including all the financing cash flows. The net effect is the same since the PV of the financing flows, when discounted at the after-tax cost of debt, is the cost of the asset.

	Year 0	Year 1	Year 2	Year 3	Year 4
Net purchase price	($40,000)				
Maintenance cost		($1,000)	($1,000)	($1,000)	($1,000)
Maintenance tax savings		400	400	400	400
Depreciation tax savings		5,280	7,200	2,400	1,120
Residual value					10,000
Residual value tax					(4,000)
Net cash flow	($40,000)	$4,680	$6,600	$1,800	$6,520

PV cost of owning @ 6% = (<u>$23,035</u>)

Since the present value of the cost of leasing is less than the present value of the cost of owning, the truck should be leased. Specifically, the NAL is $23,035 − $22,038 = $997.

c. Use the cost of debt because most cash flows are fixed by contract and consequently are relatively certain; thus lease cash flows have about the same risk as the firm's debt. Also, leasing is considered as a substitute for debt. Use an after-tax cost rate because the cash flows are stated net of taxes.

d. The firm could increase the discount rate on the residual value cash flow. Note that since the firm plans to replace the truck after 4 years, the residual value is treated as an inflow in the cost of owning analysis. This makes it reasonable to raise the discount rate for analysis purposes. However, had the firm planned to continue using the truck, then we would have had to place the estimated residual value as an additional Year 4 outflow in the leasing section, but without a tax adjustment. Then, higher risk would have been reflected in a *lower* discount rate. This is all very ad hoc, which is why analysts often prefer to use one discount rate throughout the analysis.

SELECTED EQUATIONS

CHAPTER 2

$$\text{Current ratio} = \frac{\text{Current assets}}{\text{Current liabilities}}.$$

$$\text{Quick, or acid test, ratio} = \frac{\text{Current assets} - \text{Inventories}}{\text{Current liabilities}}.$$

$$\text{Inventory turnover ratio} = \frac{\text{Sales}}{\text{Inventories}}.$$

$$\text{DSO} = \begin{array}{c}\text{Days}\\\text{sales}\\\text{outstanding}\end{array} = \frac{\text{Receivables}}{\text{Average sales per day}} = \frac{\text{Receivables}}{\text{Annual sales}/360}.$$

$$\text{Fixed assets turnover ratio} = \frac{\text{Sales}}{\text{Net fixed assets}}.$$

$$\text{Total assets turnover ratio} = \frac{\text{Sales}}{\text{Total assets}}.$$

$$\text{Debt ratio} = \frac{\text{Total debt}}{\text{Total assets}}.$$

$$\text{D/E} = \frac{\text{D/A}}{1 - \text{D/A}}, \text{ and D/A} = \frac{\text{D/E}}{1 + \text{D/E}}.$$

$$\text{Times-interest-earned (TIE) ratio} = \frac{\text{EBIT}}{\text{Interest charges}}.$$

$$\text{Fixed charge coverage ratio} = \frac{\text{EBIT} + \text{Lease payments}}{\text{Interest charges} + \text{Lease payments} + \dfrac{\text{Sinking fund payments}}{(1 - \text{Tax rate})}}.$$

$$\text{Profit margin on sales} = \frac{\text{Net income available to common stockholders}}{\text{Sales}}.$$

$$\text{Basic earning power ratio} = \frac{\text{EBIT}}{\text{Total assets}}.$$

$$\text{Return on total assets (ROA)} = \frac{\text{Net income available to common stockholders}}{\text{Total assets}}.$$

$$\text{ROA} = \left(\frac{\text{Profit}}{\text{margin}}\right)(\text{Total assets turnover}).$$

$$\text{Return on common equity (ROE)} = \frac{\text{Net income available to common stockholders}}{\text{Common equity}}.$$

$$\text{Price/earnings (P/E) ratio} = \frac{\text{Price per share}}{\text{Earnings per share}}.$$

$$\text{Book value per share} = \frac{\text{Common equity}}{\text{Shares outstanding}}.$$

$$\text{Market/book (M/B) ratio} = \frac{\text{Market price per share}}{\text{Book value per share}}.$$

$$\text{ROE} = \left(\frac{\text{Profit}}{\text{margin}}\right)\left(\frac{\text{Total assets}}{\text{turnover}}\right)\left(\frac{\text{Equity}}{\text{multiplier}}\right)$$

$$= \left(\frac{\text{Net income}}{\text{Sales}}\right)\left(\frac{\text{Sales}}{\text{Total assets}}\right)\left(\frac{\text{Total assets}}{\text{Common equity}}\right)$$

$$= \frac{\text{Net income}}{\text{Common equity}}.$$

$$\text{Rate of return on investors' capital} = \frac{\text{Net income} + \text{Interest}}{\text{Debt} + \text{Equity}}.$$

CHAPTER 3

$$k = k^* + IP + DRP + LP + MRP.$$

$$k_{RF} = k^* + IP.$$

$$IP_n = \frac{I_1 + I_2 + \ldots I_n}{n}.$$

$$\text{Equivalent pre-tax yield on taxable bond} = \frac{\text{Muni yield}}{1 - T}.$$

CHAPTER 4

$$\hat{k} = \sum_{i=1}^{n} k_i P_i.$$

$$\sigma^2 = \sum_{i=1}^{n} (k_i - \hat{k})^2 P_i.$$

$$\sigma = \sqrt{\sigma^2} = \sqrt{\sum_{i=1}^{n} (k_i - \hat{k})^2 P_i}.$$

$$\text{Semivariance} = SV = \sum_{i=1}^{m} (k_i - \hat{k})^2 P_i.$$

$$CV = \frac{\sigma}{\hat{k}}.$$

$$\hat{k}_p = \sum_{i=1}^{n} x_i \hat{k}_i.$$

$$\sigma_p = \sqrt{\sum_{i=1}^{n} (k_{pi} - \hat{k}_p)^2 P_i}.$$

$$Cov(AB) = \sum_{i=1}^{n} (k_{Ai} - \hat{k}_A)(k_{Bi} - \hat{k}_B)P_i.$$

$$r_{AB} = \frac{Cov(AB)}{\sigma_A \sigma_B}.$$

$$\sigma_p = \sqrt{x^2 \sigma_A^2 + (1 - x)^2 \sigma_B^2 + 2x(1 - x)r_{AB}\sigma_A\sigma_B}.$$

Minimum risk portfolio: $x = \dfrac{\sigma_B(\sigma_B - r_{AB}\sigma_A)}{\sigma_A^2 + \sigma_B^2 - 2r_{AB}\sigma_A\sigma_B}.$

CHAPTER 5

Capital Market Line (CML): $\hat{k}_p = k_{RF} + \left(\dfrac{\hat{k}_M - k_{RF}}{\sigma_M}\right)\sigma_p.$

Security Market Line (SML): $k_i = k_{RF} + (k_M - k_{RF})b_i.$

$$b_p = \sum_{i=1}^{n} x_i b_i.$$

$$b_i = \frac{Cov(\bar{k}_i, \bar{k}_M)}{\sigma_M^2} = \frac{r_{iM}\sigma_i\sigma_M}{\sigma_M^2} = r_{iM}\left(\frac{\sigma_i}{\sigma_M}\right).$$

$$\sigma_i^2 = b_i^2 \sigma_M^2 + \sigma_{e_i}^2.$$

$$k_i = k_{RF} + (\lambda_1 - k_{RF})b_{i1} + \ldots + (\lambda_j - k_{RF})b_{ij}.$$

CHAPTER 6

$$FV_n = PV(1 + i)^n = PV(FVIF_{i,n}).$$

$$PV = FV_n\left(\frac{1}{1 + i}\right)^n = FV_n(1 + i)^{-n} = FV_n(PVIF_{i,n}).$$

$$PVIF_{i,n} = \frac{1}{FVIF_{i,n}}.$$

$$FVIFA_{i,n} = [(1 + i)^n - 1]/i.$$

$$PVIFA_{i,n} = [1 - (1/(1 + i)^n)]/i.$$

$$FVA_n = PMT\sum_{t=1}^{n} (1 + i)^{n-t} = PMT(FVIFA_{i,n}).$$

$$FVA_n \text{ (Annuity due)} = PMT(FVIFA_{i,n})(1 + i).$$

$$PVA_n = PMT\sum_{t=1}^{n} \left(\frac{1}{1 + i}\right)^t = PMT(PVIFA_{i,n}).$$

$$PVA_n \text{ (Annuity due)} = PMT(PVIFA_{i,n})(1 + i).$$

$$PV \text{ (Perpetuity)} = \frac{Payment}{Interest\ rate} = \frac{PMT}{i}.$$

$$PV_{Uneven\ stream} = \sum_{t=1}^{n} CF_t\left(\frac{1}{1 + i}\right)^t = \sum_{t=1}^{n} CF_t(PVIF_{i,t}).$$

$$FV_{Uneven\ stream} = \sum_{t=1}^{n} CF_t(1 + i)^{n-t} = \sum_{t=1}^{n} CF_t(FVIF_{i,n-t}).$$

$$FV_n = PV\left(1 + \frac{i_{Nom}}{m}\right)^{mn}.$$

$$\text{Effective annual rate} = \left(1 + \frac{i_{Nom}}{m}\right)^m - 1.0.$$

$$\text{Periodic rate} = i_{Nom}/m.$$

$$i_{Nom} = APR = (Periodic\ rate)(m).$$

$$FV_n = PVe^{in}.$$

$$PV = FV_n e^{-in}.$$

CHAPTER 7

$$V = \sum_{t=1}^{N} \frac{CF_t}{(1 + k_t)^t}.$$

$$V_B = \sum_{t=1}^{N} \frac{INT}{(1 + k_d)^t} + \frac{M}{(1 + k_d)^N} = INT(PVIFA_{k_d,N}) + M(PVIF_{k_d,N}).$$

$$V_B = \sum_{t=1}^{2N} \frac{INT/2}{(1 + k_{d/2})^t} + \frac{M}{(1 + k_{d/2})^{2N}} = \frac{INT}{2}(PVIFA_{k_{d/2},2N}) + M(PVIF_{k_{d/2},2N}).$$

$$\text{Price of callable bond} = \sum_{t=1}^{N} \frac{INT}{(1 + k_d)^t} + \frac{\text{Call price}}{(1 + k_d)^N}.$$

$$\text{Duration} = \sum_{t=1}^{N} \frac{t(PVCF_t)}{\sum_{t=1}^{N} PVCF_t} = \sum_{t=1}^{N} \frac{t(PVCF_t)}{\text{Value}}.$$

$$V_{ps} = \frac{D_{ps}}{k_{ps}}.$$

$$\hat{P}_0 = \text{PV of expected future dividends} = \sum_{t=1}^{\infty} \frac{D_t}{(1 + k_s)^t}.$$

$$\hat{P}_0 = \frac{D_0(1 + g)}{k_s - g} = \frac{D_1}{k_s - g}.$$

$$\hat{k}_s = \frac{D_1}{P_0} + g.$$

CHAPTER 8

Component cost of debt $= k_d(1 - T)$.

$$\text{Component cost of preferred stock} = k_{ps} = \frac{D_{ps}}{P_n}.$$

$$\hat{k}_M = \frac{D_1}{P_0} + g = k_{RF} + RP_M = k_M.$$

k_s = Company's own bond yield + Risk premium.

$$\hat{k}_e = \frac{D_1}{P_0(1 - F)} + g.$$

$$g = b(r).$$

$$WACC = w_d k_d(1 - T) + w_{ps} k_{ps} + w_{ce}(k_s \text{ or } k_e).$$

$$BP = \frac{\text{Total amount of lower cost of capital of a given type}}{\text{Fraction of this type of capital in the capital structure}}.$$

CHAPTER 9

$$ARR = \frac{\text{Average annual income}}{\text{Average investment}}.$$

$$NPV = \sum_{t=0}^{n} \frac{CF_t}{(1 + k)^t}.$$

$$\text{IRR: } \sum_{t=0}^{n} \frac{CF_t}{(1 + IRR)^t} = 0.$$

$$PI = \frac{\sum_{t=0}^{n} \dfrac{CIF_t}{(1 + k)^t}}{\sum_{t=0}^{n} \dfrac{COF_t}{(1 + k)^t}}.$$

$$\text{MIRR: } \sum_{t=0}^{n} \frac{COF_t}{(1 + k)^t} = \frac{\sum_{t=0}^{n} CIF_t(1 + k)^{n-t}}{(1 + MIRR)^n}.$$

CHAPTER 10

$$\text{Project } CF_t = \frac{CF_t \text{ for corporation}}{\text{with project}} - \frac{CF_t \text{ for corporation}}{\text{without project}}.$$

$$CF_t = [(R_{1t} - R_{0t}) - (C_{1t} - C_{0t}) - (D_{1t} - D_{0t})](1 - T) + (D_{1t} - D_{0t}).$$

$$CF_t = (R_t - C_t)(1 - T) + TD_t.$$

Ownership	Class of Investment			
Year	3-Year	5-Year	7-Year	10-Year
1	33%	20%	14%	10%
2	45	32	25	18
3	15	19	17	14
4	7	12	13	12
5		11	9	9
6		6	9	7
7			9	7
8			4	7
9				7
10				6
11				3
	100%	100%	100%	100%

$$\text{NPV(no inflation)} = \sum_{t=0}^{N} \frac{RCF_t}{(1 + k_r)^t} = \sum_{t=0}^{N} \frac{NCF_t}{(1 + k_n)^{t'}}$$

$$\text{NPV(with inflation)} = \sum_{t=0}^{N} \frac{NCF_t}{(1 + k_n)^t} = \sum_{t=0}^{N} \frac{RCF_t(1 + i)^t}{(1 + k_r)^t(1 + i)^{t'}}$$

CHAPTER 12

$$EBIT = PQ - VQ - F.$$

$$Q_{BE} = \frac{F}{P - V}.$$

Total risk $= \sigma_{ROE}$.

Business risk $= \sigma_{ROE(U)}$.

Financial risk $= \sigma_{ROE} - \sigma_{ROE(U)}.$

$$S = \frac{(EBIT - k_dD)(1 - T)}{k_s}.$$

$$V = D + S.$$

$$k_{sL} = k_{RF} + (k_M - k_{RF})b_U + (k_M - k_{RF})b_U(1 - T)(D/S).$$

$$b = b_U[1 + (1 - T)(D/S)].$$

$$b = b_U + b_U(P/S) + b_U(1 - T)(D/S).$$

$$V = \frac{EBIT(1 - T)}{WACC}.$$

$$V_L = V_U = \frac{EBIT}{WACC} = \frac{EBIT}{k_{sU}}.$$

$$k_{sL} = k_{sU} + (k_{sU} - k_d)(D/S).$$

$$V_L = V_U + TD.$$

$$V_U = \frac{EBIT(1 - T)}{k_{sU}}.$$

$$k_{sL} = k_{sU} + (k_{sU} - k_d)(1 - T)(D/S).$$

$$V_L = V_U + TD - \left(\begin{array}{c} PV\ of \\ expected \\ financial\ distress \\ costs \end{array}\right) - \left(\begin{array}{c} PV\ of \\ agency \\ costs \end{array}\right)$$

$$CF_L = (EBIT - I)(1 - T_c)(1 - T_s) + I(1 - T_d).$$

$$V_L = V_U + \left[1 - \frac{(1 - T_c)(1 - T_s)}{(1 - T_d)}\right]D.$$

$$V_U = \frac{EBIT(1 - T_c)(1 - T_s)}{k_{sU}}.$$

C<small>HAPTER</small> 13

$$EPS = \frac{(EBIT - k_dD)(1 - T)}{Original\ shares - Debt/Price}.$$

$$WACC = \left(\frac{D}{V}\right)k_d(1 - T) + \left(\frac{S}{V}\right)k_s.$$

$$P_1 = \frac{V_1 - D_0}{n_0}.$$

$$n_1 = n_0 - Shares\ repurchased.$$

$$= n_0 - \frac{Incremental\ debt}{Price\ per\ share}.$$

CHAPTER 14

$$k_i = k_{RF} + (k_M - k_{RF})b_i + (D_i - D_M)\lambda_i.$$

CHAPTER 15

$$AFN = (A^*/S)\Delta S - (L^*/S)\Delta S - MS_1(1 - d).$$

$$\text{Full capacity sales} = \frac{\text{Actual sales}}{\begin{array}{c}\text{Percentage of capacity at}\\ \text{which fixed assets were operated}\end{array}}.$$

$$\text{Target FA/Sales ratio} = \frac{\text{Actual fixed assets}}{\text{Full capacity sales}}.$$

$$\text{Required level of FA} = \text{Target FA/Sales ratio (Projected sales)}.$$

CHAPTER 16

$$\begin{array}{c}\text{Inventory conversion}\\ \text{period}\end{array} = \frac{\text{Inventory}}{\text{Sales}/360}.$$

$$\begin{array}{c}\text{Receivables collection}\\ \text{period}\end{array} = DSO = \frac{\text{Receivables}}{\text{Sales}/360}.$$

$$\text{Payables deferral period} = \text{Payables/Credit purchases per day}.$$

$$\begin{array}{c}\text{Inventory}\\ \text{conversion}\\ \text{period}\end{array} + \begin{array}{c}\text{Receivables}\\ \text{collection}\\ \text{period}\end{array} - \begin{array}{c}\text{Payables}\\ \text{deferral}\\ \text{period}\end{array} = \begin{array}{c}\text{Cash}\\ \text{conversion}\\ \text{cycle}\end{array}.$$

CHAPTER 17

$$\text{Total costs} = \text{Holding costs} + \text{Transactions costs}$$
$$= \frac{C}{2}(k) + \frac{T}{C}(F).$$

$$C^* = \sqrt{\frac{2(F)(T)}{k}}.$$

$$\begin{array}{c}\text{Approximate}\\ \text{trade credit}\\ \text{percentage}\\ \text{cost}\end{array} = \frac{\text{Discount percent}}{100 - \text{Discount percent}} \times \frac{360}{\begin{array}{c}\text{Days credit is}\\ \text{outstanding}\end{array} - \begin{array}{c}\text{Discount}\\ \text{period}\end{array}}.$$

$$EAR_{Simple} = \frac{\text{Interest}}{\text{Amount received}}.$$

$$EAR_{Simple} = \left(1 + \frac{k_{Nom}}{m}\right)^m - 1.0.$$

$$EAR_{Discount} = \frac{\text{Interest}}{\text{Amount received}} = \frac{\text{Nominal rate (\%)}}{1.0 - \text{Nominal rate (fraction)}}.$$

$$\text{Face value}_{\text{Discount}} = \frac{\text{Funds received}}{1.0 - \text{Nominal rate (fraction)}}.$$

$$\text{EAR}_{\text{Simple/CB}} = \frac{\text{Interest}}{\text{Amount received}} = \frac{\text{Nominal rate (\%)}}{1.0 - \text{CB (fraction)}}.$$

$$\text{Face value}_{\text{Simple/CB}} = \frac{\text{Funds required}}{1.0 - \text{CB (fraction)}}.$$

$$\text{EAR}_{\text{Discount/CB}} = \frac{\text{Nominal rate (\%)}}{1 - \text{Nominal rate(fraction)} - \text{CB(fraction)}}.$$

$$\text{Face value}_{\text{Discount/CB}} = \frac{\text{Funds required}}{1.0 - \text{Nominal rate(fraction)} - \text{CB(fraction)}}.$$

$$\text{Approximate rate}_{\text{Add-on}} = \frac{\text{Interest}}{\text{Amount received}/2}.$$

$$\begin{matrix}\text{Additional funds needed}\\\text{to meet CB requirement}\end{matrix} = \left(\text{CB\%} \times \text{Loan}\right) - \begin{matrix}\text{Cash available}\\\text{for CB}\end{matrix}.$$

$$\text{Loan} = \text{Funds needed} + (\text{CB\%} \times \text{Loan}) - \text{Available cash}.$$

$$\text{EAR}_{\text{With cash balances}} = \frac{\text{Nominal rate (\%)} \times \text{Loan}}{\text{Funds needed}}.$$

CHAPTER 18

$$\text{ADS} = \frac{\text{Annual sales}}{360}.$$

$$\text{Receivables} = \text{ADS} \times \text{DSO}.$$

$$\text{Cost of carrying receivables} = (\text{DSO})\left(\begin{matrix}\text{Sales}\\\text{per}\\\text{day}\end{matrix}\right)\left(\begin{matrix}\text{Variable}\\\text{cost}\\\text{ratio}\end{matrix}\right)\left(\begin{matrix}\text{Cost}\\\text{of}\\\text{funds}\end{matrix}\right).$$

$$\text{Opportunity cost} = \left(\frac{\text{Old sales}}{360}\right)(\Delta\text{DSO})(1 - v)(k).$$

$$A = \frac{\text{Units per order}}{2} = \frac{\text{S/N}}{2}.$$

$$\text{TCC} = (\text{C})(\text{P})(\text{A}).$$

$$\text{TOC} = (\text{F})(\text{N}) = \text{F (S/2A)}.$$

$$\begin{aligned}\text{TIC} &= \text{TCC} + \text{TOC}\\ &= (\text{C})(\text{P})(\text{A}) + \text{F(S/2A)}\\ &= (\text{C})(\text{P})(\text{Q/2}) + (\text{F})(\text{S/Q}).\end{aligned}$$

$$\text{EOQ} = \sqrt{\frac{2(\text{F})(\text{S})}{(\text{C})(\text{P})}}.$$

CHAPTER 20

Accrued value at end of Year n = Issue price $\times (1 + k_d)^n$.

Interest in Year n = Accrued value$_n$ − Accrued value$_{n-1}$.

Tax savings = (Interest deduction)(T).

CHAPTER 21

NAL = PV cost of owning − PV cost of leasing.

CHAPTER 22

Expiration value = $\dfrac{\text{Current price}}{\text{of stock}}$ − Striking price.

$V = P[N(d_1)] - Xe^{-k_{RF}t}[N(d_2)]$.

$d_1 = \dfrac{\ln(P/X) + [k_{RF} + (\sigma^2/2)]t}{\sigma\sqrt{t}}$.

$d_2 = d_1 - \sigma\sqrt{t}$.

$\dfrac{\text{Price paid for}}{\text{bond with warrants}} = \dfrac{\text{Straight-debt}}{\text{value of bond}} + \dfrac{\text{Value of}}{\text{warrants}}$.

Conversion price = $P_c = \dfrac{\text{Par value of bond given up}}{\text{Shares received}}$.

Conversion ratio = $CR = \dfrac{\$1,000}{P_c}$.

INDEX

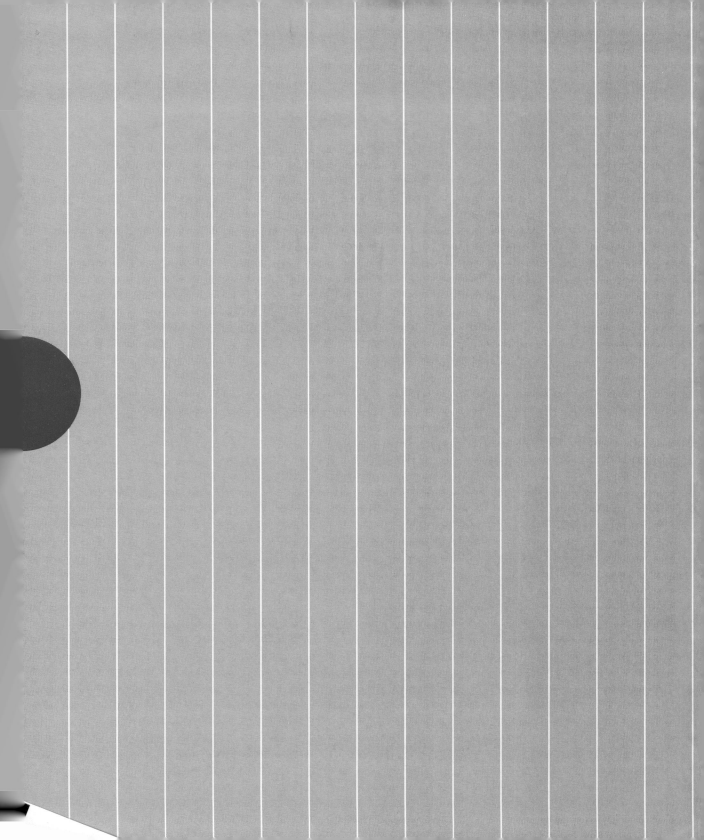

FINANCIAL MANAGEMENT

THEORY AND PRACTICE

k_{sL} Cost of equity of a levered firm

k_{sU} Cost of equity of an unlevered firm

M/B   Market to book ratio

MCC   Marginal cost of capital

MIRR   Modified internal rate of return

N   Calculator key denoting number of periods

n   (1) Life of a project (periods or years)
      (2) Number of shares outstanding

NPV   Net present value

NWC   Net working capital

P   (1) Price of a share of stock
      (2) Price per unit of output
      (3) Probability of occurrence

P/E   Price/earnings ratio

PI   Profitability index

PMT   (1) Annuity payment
      (2) Payment key on calculators

PV   Present value

Q   Unit sales

r   Correlation coefficient

ROA   Return on assets

ROE   Return on equity

RP   Risk premium

RP_M Market risk premium

S   (1) Dollar sales
      (2) Total market value of equity

SML   Security Market Line

Σ Summation sign (capital sigma)

σ Standard deviation (lowercase sigma)

T   Tax rate

t   Time

TIE   Times-interest-earned ratio

V   (1) Value
      (2) Variable cost per unit

V_L Total market value of a levered firm

V_U Total market value of an unlevered firm

w   Proportion or weight

w_d Weight of debt

w_{ps} Weight of preferred stock

w_{ce} Weight of common equity

WACC   Weighted average cost of capital

YTC   Yield to call

YTM   Yield to maturity